A SOCIAL HISTORY OF THE WELSH LANGUAGE

General Editor: Geraint H. Jenkins

A SOCIAL HISTORY OF THE WELSH LANGUAGE

Other volumes already published in the series:

The Welsh Language before the Industrial Revolution, edited by Geraint H. Jenkins (University of Wales Press, 1997)

Statistical Evidence relating to the Welsh Language 1801–1911, by Dot Jones (University of Wales Press, 1998)

Language and Community in the Nineteenth Century, edited by Geraint H. Jenkins (University of Wales Press, 1998)

The Welsh Language and the 1891 Census, by Gwenfair Parry and Mari A. Williams (University of Wales Press, 1999)

The Welsh Language and its Social Domains 1801–1911

Editor

GERAINT H. JENKINS

CARDIFF
UNIVERSITY OF WALES PRESS
2000

© University of Wales, 2000

All rights reserved. No part of this book may be reproduced, stored in a retrieval system, or transmitted, in any form or by any means, electronic, mechanical, photocopying, recording or otherwise, without clearance from the University of Wales Press, 6 Gwennyth Street, Cardiff, CF24 4YD.
www.wales.ac.uk/press

British Library Cataloguing-in-Publication Data
A catalogue record for this book is available from the British Library.

ISBN 0–7083–1604–2

The financial assistance of the Board of Celtic Studies towards the publication of this book is gratefully acknowledged.

Cover design by Elgan Davies, Welsh Books Council.
Typeset at the University of Wales Press, Cardiff.
Printed by Cambrian Printers, Aberystwyth

It is, perhaps, little known to what an extent this unknown tongue still keeps its hold upon the Welsh population.

The Times, 8 September 1866

Contents

List of Maps and Figures	ix
List of Contributors	xi
Preface	xiii
Abbreviations	xv
'Wales, the Welsh and the Welsh Language': Introduction *Geraint H. Jenkins*	1
1. Language Zones, Demographic Changes, and the Welsh Culture Area 1800–1911 *W. T. R. Pryce*	37
2. A Cauldron of Rebirth: Population and the Welsh Language in the Nineteenth Century *Brinley Thomas*	81
3. Landowners, Farmers and Language in the Nineteenth Century *R. J. Moore-Colyer*	101
4. The Coming of the Railways and Language Change in North Wales 1850–1900 *Dot Jones*	131
5. Tourism and the Welsh Language in the Nineteenth Century *David Llewelyn Jones and Robert Smith*	151
6. 'Separate Spheres'?: Women, Language and Respectability in Victorian Wales *Rosemary Jones*	177
7. The Church and the Welsh Language in the Nineteenth Century *R. Tudur Jones*	215
8. Nonconformity and the Welsh Language in the Nineteenth Century *R. Tudur Jones*	239
9. Welsh Literature in the Nineteenth Century *Robert Rhys*	265

10.	The Welsh Language in the Eisteddfod *Hywel Teifi Edwards*	293
11.	Printing and Publishing in the Welsh Language 1800–1914 *Philip Henry Jones*	317
12.	The Welsh Language and the Periodical Press *Huw Walters*	349
13.	The Welsh Language and Journalism *Aled Jones*	379
14.	The Welsh Language in Technology and Science 1800–1914 *R. Elwyn Hughes*	405
15.	The Welsh Language in the Blue Books of 1847 *Gareth Elwyn Jones*	431
16.	The British State and Welsh-language Education 1850–1914 *W. Gareth Evans*	459
17.	Elementary Education and the Welsh Language 1870–1902 *Robert Smith*	483
18.	The Welsh Language and Politics 1800–1880 *Ieuan Gwynedd Jones*	505
19.	The Languages of Patriotism in Wales 1840–1880 *Paul O'Leary*	533
20.	'Yn Llawn o Dân Cymreig' (Full of Welsh Fire): The Language of Politics in Wales 1880–1914 *Neil Evans and Kate Sullivan*	561
21.	'The Confusion of Babel'?: The Welsh Language, Law Courts and Legislation in the Nineteenth Century *Mark Ellis Jones*	587
Index		615

Maps and Figures

Language zones in the early 1800s	40
Long-term population changes: 1801–1831, 1831–1861, 1861–1891 and 1891–1911, based on the summation of intercensal decadal changes within each period	48
Net migration changes, 1841–1860, 1861–1890 and 1891–1910, based on the summation of net migration decadal changes within each period	50
Lifetime migration in general, 1861–1911	53
Lifetime migration from specific origins, 1861, 1891 and 1911	56–7
Language zones, c.1850	60
Language zones in the early 1900s and long-term trends at specific locations c.1750–1906	64
Persons able to speak Welsh (monoglots and bilinguals) in the population aged 3 years and over, 1911	68
Welsh speakers: percentage changes between 1901 and 1911	71
Language majorities, 1911, and language majority changes between 1901 and 1911	73
Territorial units for statistical and cartographic purposes (demographic data)	76
Number of Welsh-language newspapers launched, by decade, 1800–1909	381
Welsh-language titles launched as a percentage of the total number of newspapers established by decade, 1800–1909	381
Principal production centres of Welsh-language newspapers, 1800–1899	382
Number of Welsh-language newspapers launched before and after 1855	383

Contributors

Professor Hywel Teifi Edwards, Research Professor, Department of Welsh Language and Literature, University of Wales Swansea

Mr Neil Evans, Tutor in History and Co-ordinator of the Centre of Welsh Studies at Coleg Harlech and Honorary Lecturer in the School of History and Welsh History, University of Wales Bangor

Dr W. Gareth Evans, Reader, Department of Education, University of Wales Aberystwyth

Dr R. Elwyn Hughes, Former Reader in Nutritional Biochemistry, University of Wales Cardiff

Professor Geraint H. Jenkins, Director, University of Wales Centre for Advanced Welsh and Celtic Studies

Professor Aled Jones, Sir John Williams Professor and Head of Department of History and Welsh History, University of Wales Aberystwyth

Dr David Llewelyn Jones, Former Research Fellow, University of Wales Centre for Advanced Welsh and Celtic Studies

Mrs Dot Jones, Honorary Fellow, University of Wales Centre for Advanced Welsh and Celtic Studies

Professor Gareth Elwyn Jones, Research Professor, Department of Education, University of Wales Swansea

Emeritus Professor Ieuan Gwynedd Jones, formerly Professor of Welsh History, University of Wales Aberystwyth

Dr Mark Ellis Jones, Former Postgraduate Student, Department of History and Welsh History, University of Wales Aberystwyth

Mr Philip Henry Jones, Lecturer, Department of Information and Library Studies, University of Wales Aberystwyth

Ms Rosemary Jones, Former Research Fellow, University of Wales Centre for Advanced Welsh and Celtic Studies and member of staff of the Royal Commission on the Ancient and Historical Monuments of Wales

The late Professor R. Tudur Jones, formerly Honorary Professor, School of Theology and Religious Studies, University of Wales Bangor

Professor R. J. Moore-Colyer, Welsh Institute of Rural Studies, University of Wales Aberystwyth

Dr Paul O'Leary, Lecturer, Department of History and Welsh History, University of Wales Aberystwyth

Dr W. T. R. Pryce, Senior Lecturer in Geography and Staff Tutor, Faculty of Social Sciences, The Open University in Wales, Cardiff, and Honorary Fellow, University of Wales Centre for Advanced Welsh and Celtic Studies

Mr Robert Rhys, Senior Lecturer, Department of Welsh Language and Literature, University of Wales Swansea

Dr Robert Smith, Research Fellow, University of Wales Centre for Advanced Welsh and Celtic Studies

Ms Kate Sullivan, Postgraduate Student, Department of Theatre, Film and Television Studies, University of Wales Aberystwyth and Cataloguer, The Sound and Moving Image Collection, National Library of Wales

The late Professor Emeritus Brinley Thomas, formerly Professor of Economics, University of Wales Cardiff

Dr Huw Walters, Assistant Librarian, Department of Printed Books, National Library of Wales

Preface

Earlier volumes in this series have clearly shown that massive socio-economic change, which included demographic growth, industrialization and urbanization, marked a decisive turning point in the fortunes of the Welsh language in the nineteenth century. This study, the fifth volume in the series 'A Social History of the Welsh Language', seeks to shed new light on the distinctive place which Welsh occupied in a variety of social domains, the factors which promoted its welfare and the obstacles which stunted its growth. It is a well-known fact that English was reckoned to be the language of progress in this period, and robust groups of utilitarians, Darwinians, Celtophobes and upwardly-mobile Welsh speakers believed that Welsh and its sister Celtic languages were a grave, even absurd, social handicap. Those who were convinced that Welsh had no place in a swiftly modernizing society used their best endeavours to cordon it off into homespun, benign and 'unpolitical' domains such as the home, the rural workplace, the chapel and the local eisteddfod. However, the content of this volume presents a different picture. It reveals that Welsh not only prospered in its traditional domains but also fared well in contested spheres like politics, law, education and science. With the wisdom of hindsight, there clearly existed enormous potential for Welsh to become, both numerically and socially, a powerful influence in the life of the nation. That this did not fully materialize is partly addressed here and will figure prominently in our forthcoming volume on the fate of the language in the twentieth century.

Part of the charm of the nineteenth century lies in the fact that so much more Welsh-language material – in manuscript and print – is available to the social historian, and contributors to this volume have been encouraged to plunder it ruthlessly. I am grateful to all of them for their co-operation and forbearance in responding to my determination to set the highest standards of scholarship and accuracy. Sadly, two scholars of genuine distinction – Professor Emeritus Brinley Thomas and Professor R. Tudur Jones – passed away before the completion of this volume. In their respective fields they greatly enriched our understanding of our cultural heritage and earned the profound respect of their peers. The recent death of Professor Emeritus J. E.

Caerwyn Williams, doyen of Welsh and Celtic scholarship, was also a grievous blow to the Centre for Advanced Welsh and Celtic Studies and to this project in particular. By sharing his knowledge and experience with sweetness, charm and wit, he inspired great personal loyalty and close working relationships among young and senior research fellows at the Centre. His vast erudition and rich humanity will not soon be forgotten.

It is both a duty and a pleasure to record my debt to others. I am profoundly grateful to the research team at the Centre, with whom it has been both a privilege and a joy to work. I am extremely fortunate, too, in my support staff, without whom the task of commissioning, editing and publishing a multi-volume series in two languages would be considerably more taxing and probably impossible. The admirably scrupulous editorial standards of Mrs Glenys Howells have added lustre to this enterprise and, prior to the cruel illness from which she is now happily recovering, Miss Siân L. Evans processed the final draft of this volume with exemplary speed and accuracy. Mrs Aeres Bowen Davies provided unfailing secretarial support and Mr William H. Howells kindly undertook the labours of preparing the index. The maps were prepared by Mr John Hunt, Project Officer (Cartography) of the Faculty of Social Sciences at the Open University. As always, the staff of the National Library of Wales offered cheerful assistance and warm thanks are also extended to the staff of the University of Wales Dictionary project for providing a regular flow of valuable references. I am obliged to our publishers for gently guiding another bulky tome through the press.

November 1999 *Geraint H. Jenkins*

Abbreviations

BBCS	Bulletin of the Board of Celtic Studies
AC	Archaeologia Cambrensis
AHR	Agricultural History Review
BAC	Baner ac Amserau Cymru
BBCS	Bulletin of the Board of Celtic Studies
CA	The Carmarthen[shire] Antiquary
CCHMC	Cylchgrawn Cymdeithas Hanes y Methodistiaid Calfinaidd
DNB	Dictionary of National Biography
DWB	The Dictionary of Welsh Biography down to 1940 (London, 1959)
EA	Efrydiau Athronyddol
FHSJ	Flintshire Historical Society Journal
GH	Glamorgan Historian
JHSCW	Journal of the Historical Society of the Church in Wales
JMHRS	Journal of the Merioneth Historical and Record Society
JRASE	Journal of the Royal Agricultural Society of England
JWBS	Journal of the Welsh Bibliographical Society
LlC	Llên Cymru
MC	Montgomeryshire Collections
NLW	Manuscript at National Library of Wales
NLWJ	National Library of Wales Journal
P&P	Past and Present
PBA	Proceedings of the British Academy
PH	Pembrokeshire Historian
TAAS	Transactions of the Anglesey Antiquarian Society and Field Club
TCHS	Transactions of the Caernarvonshire Historical Society
TDHS	Transactions of the Denbighshire Historical Society
THSC	Transactions of the Honourable Society of Cymmrodorion
TIBG	Transactions of the Institute of British Geographers
TRHS	Transactions of the Royal Historical Society
TRS	Transactions of the Radnorshire Society
WHR	Welsh History Review
WPA	Welsh Political Archive (at the National Library of Wales)

'Wales, the Welsh and the Welsh Language': Introduction

GERAINT H. JENKINS

AT THE BEGINNING of the nineteenth century the bulk of the population of Wales habitually spoke Welsh. More than half a million were probably monoglot Welsh and, although their identity was closely associated with a specific and common territory and a shared historical memory based on myths and symbols as well as sober fact, the most powerful unifying bond was their native tongue. Champions of the Welsh language had every reason to look to the future with reasonable confidence even though Wales lacked institutions of statehood. Welsh was overwhelmingly predominant in the home, the workplace and in places of worship, all of which were nourished by a distinctive communal vernacular culture. Although Welsh was excluded from official life, there were no fears that it might perish as the principal medium of daily communication. Local dialects, rich in peasant lore, continued to thrive and the encroachment of English speech was so heavily confined to the urban towns and border counties that it seldom provoked comment. Welsh monoglottism was the norm and bilingualism was the exception.[1] All this changed with extraordinary speed within little more than a century. The Welsh found themselves obliged to adapt swiftly to the demanding rhythms of massive demographic growth and socio-economic change, as well as to the intrusiveness of a centralized bureaucracy. As Ceiriog, Wales's favourite poet in mid-Victorian times, wrote: 'Passing with the passing years / Ancient customs change and flow' ('Ar arferion Cymru gynt / Newid ddaeth o rod i rod').[2] Indeed, it could be argued that between 1801 and 1911 Wales changed more fundamentally than it had ever done before. By 1911, although Wales could boast the best part of a million Welsh speakers, English was widely reckoned to be the language of 'modernity'. The air was thick with talk of the merits of bilingualism and the traditional monoglot Welsh-speaking society was fast becoming a thing of the past. Only 190,292 (8.7 per cent) monoglot Welsh

---

[1] Geraint H. Jenkins (ed.), *The Welsh Language before the Industrial Revolution* (Cardiff, 1997).
[2] See John Ceiriog Hughes, *Aros Mae'r Mynyddoedd Mawr (Stand the Mighty Mountains Still)*. English translation by H. Idris Bell. Music by W. S. Gwynn Williams (Port Talbot, 1933).

speakers were recorded in the 1911 census and it had become abundantly clear that few parts of Wales could remain insulated from the English language.[3] In short, English, as well as Welsh, was an accepted fact of life by the eve of the Great War.

The fortunes of the Welsh language within specific domains in the long nineteenth century can therefore only be understood against this background of profound socio-economic change. At times it seemed as if a host of factors were conspiring to undermine the well-being of the Welsh language, for even those initiatives which appeared likely to enhance its future prospects contained the seeds of its long-term decline. There were deep sociolinguistic cross-currents at work in nineteenth-century Wales and, as we shall see, perceptions of and attitudes towards the Welsh language were coloured by tensions, ironies and ambiguities.

The massive expansion and redistribution of population clearly had profound linguistic and cultural implications. Between 1801 and 1851 the population nearly doubled, increasing from 601,767 to 1,188,914 before proceeding to more than double again, increasing to 2,442,041 by 1911. As the nineteenth century unfolded, the sociocultural disparity between rural and industrial Wales became starker than ever before. The demographic profile of Wales was heavily skewed in favour of the industrial counties of south Wales and by 1911 nearly two-thirds of the total population lived in Glamorgan and Monmouthshire. Rural Wales lost its people, especially its young people, in large numbers, for, as Dudley Baines has shown, they were not averse to venturing beyond Offa's Dyke. By 1901, 180,000 people from rural parts of Wales were living in the towns and cities of England, mostly on Merseyside, in the Welsh Midlands and London.[4] Even more significant, however, was the manner in which the rural counties of north, mid- and west Wales, traditionally the bastions of Welsh-speaking communities, lost thousands of their inhabitants through migration to the South Wales Coalfield, and, to a much lesser degree, to the North-east Wales Coalfield and the slate-quarrying districts. Glad to escape from the wretched poverty of rural life, unskilled labourers exchanged the scythe for the mandrel in the remarkable agglomeration of industrial settlements. This entailed a major redeployment of labour. The proportion of males involved in agriculture and fishing plummeted from 35.3 per cent in 1851 to 12 per cent in 1911, while the proportion employed in mines and quarries increased from 16.9 per cent to 31.7 per cent.[5] The drift from the land meant that agriculture lost its primary role and, as previous volumes in this series

---

[3] Dot Jones, *Statistical Evidence relating to the Welsh Language 1801–1911 / Tystiolaeth Ystadegol yn ymwneud â'r Iaith Gymraeg 1801–1911* (Cardiff, 1998).

[4] Dudley Baines, *Migration in a Mature Economy: Emigration and Internal Migration in England and Wales 1861–1900* (Cambridge, 1985), pp. 277–8.

[5] Jones, *Statistical Evidence relating to the Welsh Language*, p. 165. See also D. W. Howell and C. Baber, 'Wales' in F. M. L. Thompson (ed.), *The Cambridge Social History of Britain 1750–1950. Vol. 1. Regions and Communities* (Cambridge, 1990), pp. 281–354.

have convincingly shown, by the twilight of the Victorian age, paradoxically the high intensity of Welsh speakers in *Y Fro Gymraeg* (broadly the counties of north and west Wales) corresponded with a low population density.[6] Anglicizing influences might have been less apparent in the rural heartlands, but more people spoke Welsh in the South Wales Coalfield.

If rural counties were characterized by high levels of out-migration, the converse was true of what were often called the 'mining and manufactory districts'. People flocked to the industrializing counties in such unprecedented numbers that, according to Brinley Thomas, Wales was 'absorbing population at a rate not much less than the United States'.[7] Although by mid-century iron-smelting and copper-smelting had turned Wales into one of the major workshops of the world, by the end of our period its international reputation unquestionably rested on its role as a coal-exporting nation. There were 688 collieries in south Wales by 1910 and colossal coal-producing companies like Ocean, Powell Duffryn and Cory Brothers were thriving.[8] Attracted by high wages, greater job security and a more exciting lifestyle, skilled and unskilled manual workers migrated to the South Wales Coalfield from contiguous Welsh counties and from English border counties and the West Country in order to meet the insatiable demands of the coal industry. The population of Glamorgan, whose economy was completely dominated by coal mining, increased by 253 per cent between 1861 and 1911.[9] By a considerable margin, it was the most heavily populated and modernized county in Wales. These substantial net gains by migration (as well as by natural increase) had profound implications for the future well-being of the Welsh language. As will be explained in greater detail later, the short-term effect of internal migration was that the counties of Glamorgan and Monmouth drew an enormous transfusion of Welshness from the veins of rural society. By colonizing their own land, Welsh-speaking migrants ensured that the Welsh experience was radically different from that of the Irish, whose demographic and linguistic nemesis followed the cruel Famine years of 1845–9. Even so, there was a sting in the tail. In 1851, 88 per cent of those enumerated in Wales were Welsh born and 9.8 per cent English born. By 1911 the respective proportions were 80.7 per cent and 16 per cent. The greatest numbers of non-Welsh-born inhabitants were located in Glamorgan by 1911, and there is no doubt that the inward flow of non-

---

[6] Geraint H. Jenkins (ed.), *Language and Community in the Nineteenth Century* (Cardiff, 1998); Gwenfair Parry and Mari A. Williams, *The 1891 Census and the Welsh Language* (Cardiff, 1999).

[7] Brinley Thomas (ed.), *The Welsh Economy: Studies in Expansion* (Cardiff, 1962), p. 8.

[8] Trevor Boyns, 'Growth in the Coal Industry: The Cases of Powell Duffryn and the Ocean Coal Company, 1864–1913' in Colin Baber and L. J. Williams (eds.), *Modern South Wales: Essays in Economic History* (Cardiff, 1986), p. 153. See also L. J. Williams, *Was Wales Industrialised? Essays in Modern Welsh History* (Llandysul, 1995).

[9] John Davies and G. E. Mingay, 'Agriculture in an Industrial Environment' in A. H. John and Glanmor Williams (eds.), *Glamorgan County History. Volume V. Industrial Glamorgan* (Cardiff, 1980), p. 292.

Welsh speakers from c.1870 onwards and more particularly during the first decade of the twentieth century had adverse effects on the Welsh language. The 'new lease of life' for the language which Brinley Thomas refers to in this volume did not persist for more than two generations.[10]

The urban geography of Wales also changed markedly in this period. Nearly 60 per cent of the population of Wales lived in towns in 1911, three times more than the total numbers in 1851.[11] By 1911 five major urban centres – Cardiff (182,259), Rhondda (152,781), Swansea (114,663), Newport (83,691) and Merthyr (80,990) – dwarfed all others. For the first time in its history, Wales had produced thriving urban populations whose prosperity was principally based on the exploitation of metal and coal and on their capacity to process and export those resources. Like industrialization, urbanization was a driving force of sociolinguistic change. Industrial conurbations, market towns and ports comprised middle-class people, including shopkeepers, merchants, doctors, solicitors, bankers and clergymen, who were much more likely to be Anglicized than their country cousins. Cardiff, in particular, had become an internationally recognized centre of commerce and the self-styled 'Metropolis of Wales'.[12] Proud of their cosmopolitanism, its citizens took robust pride in their English speech and, according to the *Western Mail*, it was 'a town where the monoglot Welshman is practically unknown'.[13] In smaller urban communities, however, bilingualism was more common, though the linguistic balance was tilting ever more heavily towards English.

Although the mountain core remained a powerful barrier to rapid Anglicization, the demands of the booming economy meant that adequate transport facilities in the form of roads, canals and especially railways were required to support the expansion. Hailed by the *nouveaux riches* as the economic saviour of Wales, railways acted as a safety valve, releasing agricultural workers from a life of grinding poverty and offering them prospects of a better future elsewhere. In D. Tecwyn Lloyd's arresting metaphor, the railway was 'the Charon of the industrial century; the mediator of two worlds, the existentialist steed between This Poor Place and That Better Place' ('Charon y ganrif ddiwydiannol; cyfryngwr deufyd, y march dirfodol rhwng y Fan Dlawd Hyn a'r Fan Well Draw').[14] Railways not only penetrated deeply into the countryside, running mainly along an east–west axis, but also established densely-developed networks

[10] Philip N. Jones, 'Population Migration into Glamorgan 1861–1911' in Prys Morgan (ed.), *Glamorgan County History. Volume VI. Glamorgan Society 1780–1980* (Cardiff, 1988), pp. 173–202.
[11] Jones, *Statistical Evidence relating to the Welsh Language*, pp. 85–9; Harold Carter and C. Roy Lewis, *An Urban Geography of England and Wales in the Nineteenth Century* (London, 1990).
[12] Martin J. Daunton, *Coal Metropolis: Cardiff 1870–1914* (Leicester, 1977); Neil Evans, 'The Welsh Victorian City: The Middle Class and Civic and National Consciousness in Cardiff, 1850–1914', *WHR*, 12, no. 3 (1985), 350–87.
[13] *Western Mail*, 14 April 1891, p. 4.
[14] D. Tecwyn Lloyd, *Safle'r Gerbydres ac Ysgrifau Eraill* (Llandysul, 1970), p. 120.

in the South Wales Coalfield. By the end of the century, only the most remote and inaccessible parts of Wales remained untouched by the railway network. The cacophonous noise and unprecedented speed associated with 'the iron horse' ('yr haiarnfarch') or 'the steam horse' ('yr agerfarch') inevitably called forth a substantial body of writing in Welsh. At once admired and feared (they caused some horrifying accidents), railways and trains inspired many Welsh poets to put pen to paper. Indeed, the period from 1840 to 1875 has been called the golden age of 'railway verse' in Welsh[15] and cultural aspects of Wales's 'railway question' are considered in this volume by Dot Jones. Spokesmen of very different backgrounds were convinced that railways symbolized Progress, but it was also feared that heavy investment in railways was motivated by a desire to reinforce territorial and linguistic unification. By breaking down age-old habits of isolationism, railways inevitably diffused and popularized English lifestyles, ideals and speech patterns. As people travelled further and more swiftly, they encountered greater numbers of English speakers. To some degree, of course, the sociability and competitive spirit of Welsh eisteddfodau were strengthened by the railways and the fierce rivalries which characterized choral festivals were made possible by the swift access provided by special trains which carried music-makers to destinations far and near.[16] This helped to heighten the awareness of linguistic and dialectical differences, but the net result was to hasten Anglicizing processes. The major railway companies deliberately ensured that English predominated in this new domain by appointing bilingual or English speakers to 'responsible' posts and by ignoring the fact that substantial numbers of people spoke and understood Welsh only.

Railways, too, were a vital factor in the creation of the modern Welsh tourist industry. By building viaducts, bridges, stations, goods warehouses, railway hotels and guest houses, railway companies stimulated the growth of major holiday resorts in Wales. The case studies of Abergele (including Pen-sarn) and Aberystwyth included in this volume indicate the considerable economic benefits ushered in by the railways. Family holidays, excursions, weekend outings and Sunday school trips were all made possible by locomotives, and helped to invigorate the economy of coastal towns like Barry, Penarth, Tenby, the Mumbles, Llandudno and Rhyl, as well as spa centres like Llanwrtyd and Llandrindod. Tourism affected growing numbers of people and bred a growing familiarity with the English tongue. English-language entertainment catered for the well-to-do middle classes and the better-paid working classes, and rural-born domestic servants employed in hotels and lodging houses were required to master English swiftly. The growth of bilingualism and Anglicization in the later Victorian period was at least partly attributable to tourism and successive censuses

---

[15] Ibid., p. 107. See also Jack Simmons, *The Victorian Railway* (London, 1991), chapter 7.
[16] Gareth Williams, *Valleys of Song: Music and Society in Wales 1840–1914* (Cardiff, 1998), p. 119.

show that towns in lowland seaboard areas invariably included sizeable English-speaking populations. In many ways, therefore, 'King Rail' brought England and Wales closer together and encouraged the dissemination of English speech.

The fortunes of the Welsh language were also inextricably tied up with the powerful centralizing tendencies at work in Victorian Britain. Up to the nineteenth century successive governments had treated Wales as a principality, a subordinate colony inhabited by primitive peasants whose absurd language or 'patois' was an embarrassment. The general attitude was one of benign neglect and barely concealed contempt. Thus, the often quoted phrase 'Poor little Wales' was made half in jest, half in earnest.[17] The nineteenth-century state, however, was a much more intrusive animal, and its centralized institutions increasingly interfered in matters relating to social management and welfare. Following the Merthyr Rising and massive Chartist demonstrations, Wales came to be seen as something more than a quaint appendage to England. Government reports claimed to detect subversive trends, lawlessness and incivility in the South Wales Coalfield, as a result of which it was resolved to tame the Welsh, make them respectable and, most of all, Anglicize them. As the writings of Edward Said have revealed,[18] the colonization of 'others' was an integral part of the English national identity in the nineteenth century and we should not underestimate the 'emotional, intellectual and political dominance of the concept of England' in this period.[19] In government reports as well as encyclopaedias, Wales was subsumed under England.

Closely linked with these developments were the powerful arguments marshalled in favour of English as the language of 'modernity'.[20] The Welsh could not have been unaware of the sheer weight of numbers across Offa's Dyke. The population of England increased from 8.5 million in 1801 to 33.5 million in 1911, virtually all of whom spoke English.[21] Moreover, by the turn of the nineteenth century the far-flung British Empire spanned more than eleven million miles and included 345 million people, to many of whom English was not unfamiliar. English came to be viewed as the language of the powerful and the affluent, of war, conquest and empire, and as each year passed it threatened to pervade virtually every domain in Welsh life. The notion of Progress lay at the heart of Victorianism[22] and even the historian in a hurry cannot fail to be immediately

---

[17] T. R. Roberts, *Self-Made Welshmen* (Cardiff and Merthyr, 1907), p. 9.
[18] Edward W. Said, *Orientalism: Western Conceptions of the Orient* (Harmondsworth, 1985); idem, *Culture and Imperialism* (London, 1993).
[19] Adrian Hastings, *The Construction of Nationhood: Ethnicity, Religion and Nationalism* (Cambridge, 1997), p. 61. But see Linda Colley, 'Britishness and Otherness: An Argument', *Journal of British Studies*, 31, no. 4 (1992), 309–29.
[20] E. Glyn Lewis, 'Modernization and Language Maintenance' in Glyn Williams (ed.), *Crisis of Economy and Ideology: Essays on Welsh Society, 1840–1980* (B.S.A. Sociology of Wales Study Group, 1983), pp. 147–79; R. D. Grillo, *Dominant Languages: Language and Hierarchy in Britain and France* (Cambridge, 1989).
[21] Keith Robbins, *Nineteenth-Century Britain: Integration and Diversity* (Oxford, 1995), p. 6.
[22] See Peter J. Bowler, *The Invention of Progress: The Victorians and the Past* (Oxford, 1989).

impressed by the frequency with which the words 'buddiol' (beneficial), 'llesol' (profitable) and 'defnyddiol' (useful) occur in Welsh literature. It was believed that any language which could not compete effectively in the 'battle of life' was doomed to stagnate and perish. Laissez-faire individualism, economic determinism and the theory of evolution all emphasized the competitive spirit, and since Celtic languages on the peripheries of the Atlantic archipelago were deemed to be 'mean', 'undeveloped' and 'barbaric' they were clearly hindrances to Progress. 'There is a lurking conviction at the bottom of most Englishmen's hearts', wrote Henry Richard, 'that no people can be really civilised who don't talk English.'[23] It was implicit within the cultural imperialism of the day that the government had a responsibility to free the Welsh from the monoglottism which threatened to strangle them. In his volume on *Celtic Britain*, John Rhŷs simply took it for granted that the English were engaged 'linguistically speaking, in drowning the voice of [Goidel and Brython] in our own day'.[24] When Havelock Ellis completed a survey of the relative productiveness in genius in Britain, he attributed the dismal Welsh total of 28 (3.1 per cent), as opposed to 659 (74.2 per cent) for England, to 'the difficulty of a language not recognised as a medium of civilisation'.[25]

The forces which made for linguistic unity were often publicly aired in official governmental and non-governmental publications, the most celebrated of which was the Report of the Commissioners of Inquiry into the State of Education in Wales (1847), a report which entered the annals of Welsh folklore as 'The Treachery of the Blue Books'. A recurrent theme in this volume is the unquestioned influence of the Blue Books on the psychology of the Welsh, and its significance as a defining moment in the history of Wales cannot be exaggerated.[26] With breathtaking arrogance, the three young, English-speaking Anglican barristers who prepared the bulky report went far beyond their brief by painting a portrait of the Welsh as a squalid, immoral, degraded people whose 'peculiar language' was a hindrance to Progress. Never had the Welsh been so publicly and humiliatingly dishonoured, and there ensued much anguished breast-beating, shame and self-loathing as well as a deep sense of moral outrage. For the first time in its history, the Welsh language became a political issue; the Welsh and their language had been measured from the 'civilized' English viewpoint and found sadly wanting. By skilfully juxtaposing key words (barbarism/civilization; darkness/light; higher/lower), the three commissioners emphasized the superiority of English and the inferiority of Welsh. Pejorative epithets – 'evil',

[23] Henry Richard, *Letters on the Social and Political Condition of the Principality of Wales* (London, n.d.), p. 1.
[24] John Rhŷs, *Celtic Britain* (2nd ed., London, 1884), p. 276.
[25] Havelock Ellis, *A Study of British Genius* (London, 1904), pp. 23–4.
[26] The fullest and most recent analysis of the language of the Blue Books is Gwyneth Tyson Roberts, *The Language of the Blue Books: The Perfect Instrument of Empire* (Cardiff, 1998). See also Prys Morgan (ed.), *Brad y Llyfrau Gleision: Ysgrifau ar Hanes Cymru* (Llandysul, 1991).

'barrier', 'drawback', 'impediment' – were deployed to depict the native tongue and to strengthen arguments for expediting the progress of the English language throughout Wales.[27] Although such negative images of Wales and its language were already familiar, no previous government report had offered such a 'gross and hideous caricature'[28] and for many years afterwards Welsh publications were replete with detailed and indignant rebuttals and apologiae. Clearly the Report ushered in a profound identity crisis which forced the Welsh to embark on a prolonged and painful process of self-appraisal. From 1847 onwards they lived in dread of further mockery and humiliation at the hands of the English. Acutely conscious, as John Griffiths, rector of Neath, confessed, 'that there is an annual judgement passed upon us',[29] Welsh speakers made frantic attempts to redress the balance by presenting a sanitized image of themselves as a law-abiding, peace-loving, pious and moral people, but their self-respect had been severely damaged.

In general, however, the commissioners' animadversions on the Welsh language provoked less comment than the allegations of rampant immorality. Apart from Henry Richard, the only influential voice in the campaign to remove the linguistic stigma in the Report was that of Evan Jones (Ieuan Gwynedd), whose untimely death in 1852 robbed Welsh Nonconformity of one of its doughtiest champions.[30] Jones believed that the notion that Welsh was an obstacle to the dissemination of knowledge was 'preposterous nonsense' and he mocked the government's alleged goal of 'annihilating' the native tongue by setting up English-medium schools: 'As well you may hope to stay the foaming cataract in its descent.'[31] But Jones's protestations were drowned by the pro-English clamour of those who believed that Welsh was socially bankrupt. From the 1850s onwards there emerged a relatively small, but highly influential and successful petite bour-geoisie (some of whom were based in London), who unashamedly proclaimed the virtues of the English language and its crucial importance in the social, commercial and political world. This upwardly mobile middle class believed, as did John Jenkins, assistant commissioner to the Newcastle Report of 1861, that Welsh was 'the language of the past and not of the present'.[32]

Some of those who affected a lofty disdain for their native tongue and put on airs in the company of cultured English people were deeply affected by the view of Matthew Arnold, whose oft-quoted *On the Study of Celtic Literature* (1867) is

---

[27] Roberts, *The Language of the Blue Books*, pp. 186–8.
[28] Richard, *Letters on the Social and Political Condition of Wales*, pp. 2–3.
[29] Hywel Teifi Edwards, *Gŵyl Gwalia: Yr Eisteddfod Genedlaethol yn Oes Aur Victoria 1858–1868* (Llandysul, 1980), p. 54. For the way in which a sense of collective humiliation can nourish national identity, see Hagen Schulze, *States, Nations and Nationalism: From the Middle Ages to the Present* (Oxford, 1996), p. 175.
[30] Geraint H. Jenkins, 'Ieuan Gwynedd: Eilun y Genedl' in Morgan (ed.), *Brad y Llyfrau Gleision*, pp. 101–24.
[31] Evan Jones, *A Vindication of the Educational and Moral Condition of Wales* (Llandovery, 1848), p. 15.
[32] *Reports of the Assistant Commissioners on the State of Popular Education in England with Appendices*, XXI, Part 2 (1861).

the *locus classicus* of the pro-English zealot. Arnold believed that the inexorable march of Progress rendered redundant the Celtic peripheries and their languages. The 'lively nature' of the Celts meant that they lacked 'steadiness, patience, and sanity', which clearly ruled out any possibility of achieving a measure of self-government.[33] Since they were still living in the past, theirs would always be a subordinate, marginal existence. Arnold's contempt for 'barbaric cultures' was echoed by Dr Thomas Nicholas, one of the founders of the University movement in Wales. Captivated by 'the greatness of the English race' and the 'imperial tongue', Nicholas reminded his monoglot countrymen of the grave social handicap under which they laboured:

> . . . it is better they should share in the honour and dignity, the intelligence and enterprise of England, than rest contented with the obscurity which blind adherence to antiquated customs, and to a speech which can never become the vehicle of science or commerce, must entail upon them . . . Let the earnest *life* of England – its strong steady aim at the high and excellent, pulsate through all Wales, and the highest models in thought, art, character, be emulated; let the *English language*, which is destined soon to 'make the whole word kin', and which is the only medium for the introduction into Wales of all the life and civilization of England – be diffused far and wide among the people.[34]

His great ally, Hugh Owen, who believed that Welsh was certain to fall victim to the laws of Progress, sought to hasten its inevitable demise by converting the National Eisteddfod into a vehicle for free-enterprise commercialism. Determined that the Eisteddfod should appeal to the 'best people', he ensured that proceedings in the 'Social Science Section' were conducted in English. In a free market, he argued, Welsh should be left to fight its own corner. Both utilitarians and Darwinians warned Welsh speakers of the folly of seeking to stave off the inevitable and urged them to reconcile themselves to the demise of their native language. One of the arch-exponents of the notion of 'the survival of the fittest' was J. R. Kilsby Jones, a Nonconformist minister who had been raised in a community where English was as rare as gold sovereigns. In several challenging speeches and articles, he urged his countrymen to ponder whether the death of the Welsh language would prove advantageous or disadvantageous to Wales ('Pa un ai mantais ai anfantais i Gymru fyddai tranc yr iaith Gymraeg').[35] No one could convince him that the survival of Welsh was part of a divine plan or that it could suddenly be transformed into an effective competitor in the Darwinian linguistic

---

[33] Matthew Arnold, *On the Study of Celtic Literature* (London, 1867), pp. 97–116.
[34] Thomas Nicholas, *The Pedigree of the English People* (London, 1868), pp. 552–3.
[35] J. R. Kilsby Jones, 'Yr Anghenrheidrwydd o Ddysgu Seisoneg i'r Cymry', *Y Traethodydd*, V (1849), 118–26; idem, 'Pa un ai Mantais ai Anfantais i Gymru fyddai Tranc yr Iaith Gymraeg?', *Y Geninen*, I, no. 1 (1883), 18–23.

stakes. Indeed, as far as he was concerned, the sooner his native tongue vanished into the Celtic mists forever the more Wales would benefit.

Only the harshest historian would chastise Welsh-speaking progressives in the Victorian period for recognizing the necessity that their countrymen needed to learn to speak English fluently. There were strong, perhaps overwhelming, incentives to acquire English and it is an illusion to believe that, in a period when the economy of Wales was being altered beyond recognition, it would have been possible to sustain Welsh monoglottism on a large scale. The culpability of middle-class Welshmen lies rather in their willingness to connive at the deception which the commissioners had perpetrated upon the Welsh in 1847, namely that the English language was intrinsically superior to Welsh, that 'Welsh does not pay', that it should be withdrawn from the world of industry, technology, science and commerce, and that the widespread acquisition of English would, in the fullness of time, lead to the casting of Welsh to the winds. At a time when Wales was becoming a modern, industrialized nation and when the best part of a million people spoke Welsh, the Welsh élite chose to identify their native tongue with obscurantism, poverty and degradation.[36] By locking up Welsh in modest and unintimidating domains like the hearth, the chapel and the eisteddfod, they believed that the native tongue would become associated with an unprestigious way of life. As this message was dinned into the heads of people, especially the young and the mobile, English increasingly came to be viewed as the passport to success and Welsh as a worthless impediment to their advancement. While English was the language of getting on in the world, Welsh was the language of potato soup, straw beds, arid sermons and sol-fa. Small wonder that the Welsh were so ambivalent about their identity and language. In his evidence to the Royal Commission on Education in 1886–7, T. Marchant Williams observed that Welsh people were remarkably shy and embarrassed in the company of the English because they had been conditioned to believe that being Welsh was 'a disadvantage and a reproach to them'.[37] According to H. Isambard Owen, writing in *Y Cymmrodor* in 1887, the perception of Welsh as a subordinate language circumscribed by the needs of the past had led to 'a depressing sense of helplessness and inferiority in the people'.[38] In many ways, the mid-Victorian period were years of wasted opportunities and by the time champions of bilingualism took up the torch in the 1880s the psychological damage had been done.

We turn now to those domains which Welsh claimed as its own and those to which – with mixed fortunes – it aspired. In spite of the depredations wrought by depopulation (a malaise which afflicted every rural county in Wales from 1871

---

[36] Geraint H. Jenkins, *The Welsh and their Language in a British Context* (St. Petersburg, 1997), pp. 17–20.
[37] J. E. Southall (ed.), *Bi-lingual Teaching in Welsh Elementary Schools* (Newport, 1888), pp. 80–1.
[38] Isambard Owen, 'Race and Nationality', *Y Cymmrodor*, VIII (1887), 22.

onwards) and the remorseless encroachment of what Rees Pryce characterizes as the bilingual zone, the core of 'Inner Wales' remained, in sociolinguistic terms, remarkably robust. In the rural community domain (outside the long-established Englishries and Anglicized lowland vales), the Welsh language was predominant. Even as late as 1901, though less so by 1911, in a solid and continuous block of counties in north and west Wales (Anglesey, Caernarfonshire, Merioneth, Cardiganshire and Carmarthenshire) around 90 per cent of the population spoke Welsh. In the above-mentioned counties in 1911, the percentage of monoglot Welsh speakers was 37.3, 36.4, 37.5, 34.8 and 20.8 respectively.[39] When Henry Sweet conducted a pilot study of 'spoken North Welsh' in the Gwynant valley, Caernarfonshire, in the early 1880s, he discovered that the proportion of English words used in daily discourse was remarkably small 'considering the long and intimate intercourse between the speakers of the two languages'.[40] The colour and robustness of rural Welsh is best conveyed in 'Llythurau 'Rhen Ffarmwr' (Letters of the Old Farmer) published by William Rees (Gwilym Hiraethog) in *Yr Amserau* and in the 'joyful, shameless' ('llawen, digywilydd') poetry of lyricists and ballad-mongers.[41] Welsh was overwhelmingly the daily language in rural communities and it undoubtedly imbued the inhabitants with a strong sense of belonging, a measure of continuity, and recognized codes of behaviour. In field, mart and fair, Welsh predominated and in the organization of farm work, especially hay harvests, potato-lifting and threshing, Welsh-speaking rural inhabitants were bound together by shared endeavour, jovial companionship, and mutual pride in both skill and attainment.[42] Social and occupational classifications, as well as the values of the community, were expressed in distinctive local speech patterns, and it is significant that many rich idioms and metaphors were replete with ethnic and local connotations, e.g. 'gwŷr y cawl erfin' (the men of Carmarthenshire), 'gwin yr hen Gymro' (spring water) and 'mwyalch Seisnig' (a jackass).[43] Welsh names were bestowed on crops, livestock, implements and foodstuff.

---

[39] Jones, *Statistical Evidence relating to the Welsh Language*, pp. 228–37.
[40] Henry Sweet, 'Spoken North Welsh', *Trans. Philological Society* (1882–4), 484. See also David Thorne, 'Map Tafodieithol John Rhŷs: Y Cefndir Ieithyddol', *NLWJ*, XXIV, no. 4 (1986), 448–62.
[41] Thomas Parry, *A History of Welsh Literature*, translated by H. Idris Bell (Oxford, 1955), p. 327; E. G. Millward, *Cenedl o Bobl Ddewrion: Agweddau ar Lenyddiaeth Oes Victoria* (Llandysul, 1991), p. 9.
[42] David Jenkins, *The Agricultural Community in South-West Wales at the turn of the Twentieth Century* (Cardiff, 1971), pp. 10–13. See also the essays in Elwyn Davies and A. D. Rees (eds.), *Welsh Rural Communities* (Cardiff, 1960).
[43] 'Yr Hen Gyrus', 'Brawddegau y Werin', *Taliesin*, II, no. 8 (1861), 286–7; Morris Davies, 'Amrywieithoedd y Gymraeg', *Y Traethodydd*, III (1847), 1–16. Fearful that 'many dialectal words and idioms which have important bearings upon the history of the Welsh language are now being disused', Welsh philologists established in 1889 the short-lived 'Cymdeithas Llafar Gwlad' (Welsh Dialect Society). Robert Owen Jones, 'Datblygiad Gwyddor Tafodietheg yng Nghymru', *BBCS*, XXXIII (1986), 28.

Yet, all was not well in the countryside. Rural Wales was littered with famines, blights, riots and disturbances, in most of which linguistic differences were of some significance. Property and wealth were heavily concentrated in the hands of a small number of landed families who, as a governing élite, were able to dominate the lives of the plebeian majority. Farmers, cottagers and labourers eked out a precarious living on tiny farms, and as the years rolled by they came to believe that they had been poorly served by their masters. This is not the place to discuss the myriad factors which divided landowner and tenant, but we should not overlook the fact that a powerful radical Nonconformist lobby was determined to depict landlords as cruel, oppressive and neglectful during the heyday of the anti-tithe and disestablishment campaigns. As Richard Moore-Colyer reveals, the brittle relationship between landlord and tenant was exacerbated by the division of language. Although some landowners pretended to take an intelligent interest in the Welsh language, few of them were at ease, let alone fluent, in speaking Welsh. For them, English was unquestionably the language of social status and prestige, whereas Welsh was an outmoded tongue and a barrier to economic advancement. Few Welsh gentlemen, however well-disposed towards the ancient language of Wales, would have taken issue with Sir Llewelyn Turner, a Caernarfonshire landowner, who publicly declared: 'Wales . . . has ignorned [sic] herself by the isolation of so large a number of those who speak *only* Welsh . . . Providence and Parliament help those who honestly help themselves . . . *the only* road *by* which [Welshmen] can obtain the full advantages of that connection [with Greater Britain] is by the broad highway of the language of the majority.'[44] Such attitudes, shared by monoglot English-speaking stewards and agents as well, alienated them from the rest of society and deeply influenced existing class divisions and tensions. The common man, Beriah Gwynfe Evans argued, 'could see that Welsh was the language of the hewers of wood and the drawers of water, the language of labour and burdens, the language of hardship and want, while English was the language of those who seldom laboured but who earned fat salaries and enjoyed worldly comforts' ('gwelai mai Cymraeg oedd iaith y cymynwyr coed a'r gwehynwyr dwfr, iaith llafur a lludded, iaith caledi ac angen, tra mai Saesneg oedd iaith pawb oeddent esmwyth eu byd, bychan eu llafur, a mawr eu cyflogau').[45] Hostility to feudal landlordism was invariably expressed in Welsh and no rallying cry was more potent than 'Trech gwlad nag arglwydd' (A country is mightier than a lord). Yet, we must not exaggerate. The language barrier which separated landlord and steward from common people was not

---

[44] *North Wales Observer and Express*, 30 December 1887.
[45] Beriah Gwynfe Evans, '"Cymro, Cymru a Chymraeg", yn eu cysylltiad ag Addysg', *Trans. Liverpool Welsh National Society* (1889), 67–8. See also T. J. Hughes (Adfyfr), *Neglected Wales* (London, 1887), p. 7.

paralleled by other linguistic divisions within the Welsh-speaking community in the heartlands. Welsh remained a powerful unifying force within Inner Wales.[46]

Although cultural patriots were prone to associate the alleged 'Welsh way of life' with the rural countryside, the substantial influx of rural migrants into the industrial valleys of south Wales meant that the South Wales Coalfield, especially communities located in Glamorgan, contained a much higher proportion of Welsh speakers. By 1911 the total number of Welsh speakers in Glamorgan (393,692) was greater than the total of Welsh speakers in the six counties of Anglesey, Caernarfon, Denbigh, Flint, Merioneth and Cardigan. Clearly, therefore, there existed a Welsh-speaking industrial domain. Industrialization and urbanization precipitated extraordinary internal migration, and within the teeming and heavily peopled new industrial villages and towns there emerged intricate and subtle linguistic patterns. As previous volumes in this series have revealed, two languages were in competition in these communities, and the general pattern until at least the 1890s was for the Welsh language to retain the upper hand, except in those valleys where substantial numbers of English, Irish and Scottish incomers clustered together and resisted processes of acculturation.[47] Rhondda – the most populous part of the South Wales Coalfield – was identified by the Welsh Land Commissioners in 1896 as an urban area which made 'habitual use' of Welsh and even as late as 1911 it could boast 76,796 (55.9 per cent) Welsh speakers.[48] During the first phase of industrialization, incomers were expected, indeed required, to acquire a grasp of Welsh, however imperfect, to enable them to work alongside monoglot Welsh colliers. Working in confined and dangerous spaces for long hours meant that language contact was vital both for social and safety reasons. According to J. E. Southall, the Welsh collier believed that the coalface was a 'sacred place . . . he thinks that he is master there'.[49] Quoting the evidence of the Merthyr-born historian, David Watkin Jones (Dafydd Morganwg), D. Isaac Davies maintained in 1885 that eighteen of every twenty miners in south Wales spoke Welsh at work: 'Hyhi ydyw iaith y glofeydd' (She is

---

[46] E. G. Bowen, 'The Geography of Wales as a Background to its History' in Ian Hume and W. T. R. Pryce (eds.), *The Welsh and their Country* (Llandysul, 1986), pp. 64–87; David Howell, 'A "Less Obtrusive and Exacting" Nationality: Welsh Ethnic Mobilisation in Rural Communities, 1850–1920' in idem (ed.) in collaboration with Gert von Pistohlkors and Ellen Wiegandt, *Roots of Rural Ethnic Mobilisation* (Aldershot and New York, 1993), pp. 51–98.

[47] Jenkins (ed.), *Language and Community in the Nineteenth Century*, passim; Parry and Williams, *The 1891 Census and the Welsh Language*, pp. 31–216.

[48] K. S. Hopkins (ed.), *Rhondda Past and Future* (Rhondda Borough Council, n.d.), p. 121; Jones, *Statistical Evidence relating to the Welsh Language*, p. 230.

[49] Southall, *Bi-lingual Teaching in Welsh Elementary Schools*, p. 61. For further examples of the use of Welsh, see *Tarian y Gweithiwr*, 4 January 1878, 21 February 1879. See also Sian Rhiannon Williams, *Oes y Byd i'r Iaith Gymraeg: Y Gymraeg yn Ardal Ddiwydiannol Sir Fynwy yn y Bedwaredd Ganrif ar Bymtheg* (Caerdydd, 1992), chapter 4.

the language of the coal mines).[50] There is also evidence that in the 1880s non-Welsh-speaking incomers were assimilable and amenable to acculturation. At a coal mine in Treherbert which employed around five hundred miners, 147 of whom were not Welsh born, eighty of these could speak Welsh fluently, forty moderately well, twenty could understand it, and only seven remained monoglot English speakers.[51] When John Griffiths, archdeacon of Llandaff, enquired of a Glamorgan collier – 'Do the English colliers dovetail pretty well with the Welsh people; how do they do underground?' – he replied: 'We seldom have such a being as an English collier; before he has been underground for six months he comes out a Welshman.'[52]

If the evidence of William Thomas (Glanffrwd) is to be believed, the dialect heard within the coal mines of Glamorgan – a hybrid of the dialects brought in by in-migrants from Cardiganshire, Pembrokeshire and Breconshire – was the most corrupt in the whole of Wales ('[y] mwyaf llygredig o dafodieithoedd yr holl siroedd Cymreig').[53] Twentieth-century dialectologists, on the other hand, have discovered that a rich fund of Welsh nomenclature existed in mining communities, including sixty-two terms for different types of coal.[54] Coal which was worked easily at Llangennech was described as 'gwitho fel blawd' (works like flour), at Pontyberem as 'gwitho fel dŵr' (works like water) and in many pits in Glamorgan and Carmarthenshire as 'gwitho fel menyn' (works like butter). In the North-east Coalfield, too, miners at Rhosllannerchrugog were renowned for their distinctive vocabulary, idioms and gift of repartee at the coalface, while in the north-west slate-quarrying was universally acknowledged to be a Welsh-speaking industry.[55] Although quarrymen absorbed some English words like rubble ('rwbel'), journeyman ('jermon') and scraper ('sgrapar') into their vocabulary and likewise dubbed slates, according to their size and quality, Queens ('Cwîns'), Princesses ('Princus') and Duchesses ('Dytchis'), they fervently believed that no English speaker could ever master their intricate craft unless he resolved to become fluent in Welsh and fully master the appropriate technical glossary.[56] Essays on 'slate-splitting' figured prominently in competitions at local eisteddfodau and during oral literary jousts held in lunchtime breaks the authority

---

[50] D. Isaac Davies, *1785, 1885, 1985! Neu, Tair Miliwn o Gymry Dwy-Ieithawg mewn Can Mlynedd* (Dinbych, 1885), p. 43.
[51] J. E. Southall, *Wales and her Language* (Newport, 1892), p. 150.
[52] Idem, *Bi-lingual Teaching in Welsh Elementary Schools*, p. 61.
[53] Glanffrwd, 'Gwlad, Pobl, Iaith, a Defion Morganwg', *Y Geninen*, III, no. 1 (1885), 18. See also Peter Wynn Thomas, 'Dimensions of Dialect Variation: A Dialectological and Sociological Analysis of Aspects of Spoken Welsh in Glamorgan' (unpubl. University of Wales PhD thesis, 1990).
[54] Lynn Davies, *Geirfa'r Glöwr* (Amgueddfa Werin Cymru, 1976), pp. 47–8. See also *Ffraethebion y Glowr Cymreig* (Caerdydd, [1928]).
[55] J. Rhosydd Williams, *Hanes Rhosllannerchrugog* (Rhosllannerchrugog, 1945), p. 36; R. Merfyn Jones, *The North Wales Quarrymen 1874–1922* (Cardiff, 1981), p. 60.
[56] Emyr Jones, *Canrif y Chwarelwr* (Dinbych, n.d.), pp. 123–63.

of the finest craftsmen was seldom questioned.[57] Quarrymen like to think of their workplace as a Welsh fortress, and their resentment towards English-speaking owners, managers and agents deeply soured industrial relations. A clash of cultures lay at the root of 'Y Streic Fawr' (The Great Strike) at the Penrhyn Quarry, Bethesda, between 1900 and 1903, and the vigour with which the legitimate grievances of the quarrymen were aired provides incontestable evidence of the overwhelming Welshness of this industry.

By the turn of the century, however, the prospects of the Welsh language as a daily medium of discourse in the steam coal industry were not so bright. From the 1890s onwards there occurred a decisive shift in the number of non-Welsh-born in-migrants in the South Wales Coalfield. In 1917 the *Commission of Enquiry into Industrial Unrest* concluded:

> Until some 15 to 20 years ago, the native inhabitants had, in many respects, shown a marked capacity for stamping their own impress on all newcomers, and communicating to them a large measure of their own characteristics; of more recent years the process of assimilation has been unable to keep pace with the continuing influx of inmigrants.[58]

Our previous studies, especially of the 1891 census, have revealed that the surging tide of English, Irish and Scottish in-migrants into the steam coal districts meant that linguistic boundaries were in flux. Large numbers of incomers sought to preserve their own identity and cultural values by dwelling in tightly-knit residential quarters which insulated them from Welsh speakers. The shared experience of working underground, however, inevitably involved adjustment and accommodation which ultimately eroded linguistic and ethnic differences. Unless they were disadvantaged both socially and economically by their lack of Welsh, incomers were more than happy to remain monoglot English speakers and to resist assimilative processes. Within industrial communities, especially in towns in the eastern half of the coalfield, the number of Welsh-born people familiar with English was growing appreciably. A correspondent in *The Pontypridd Chronicle* feared that an 'English invasion' was underway: 'The invader is more subtle, more tangible; advancing silently, secretly and invisibly. He is not corporeal but lingual.'[59] English was attractive because it opened new windows of economic opportunity and provided working people with a wider range of enjoyable cultural and recreational activity, including rugby and soccer, theatres, cinemas and music halls. The long-term trend in industrial south Wales was clear: the

---

[57] R. Merfyn Jones, 'Y Chwarelwr a'i Gymdeithas yn y Bedwaredd Ganrif ar Bymtheg' in Geraint H. Jenkins (ed.), *Cof Cenedl: Ysgrifau ar Hanes Cymru* (Llandysul, 1986), pp. 139–40.

[58] *Commission of Enquiry into Industrial Unrest, No. 7 Division. Report of the Commissioners for Wales, including Monmouthshire* (London, 1917) (PP 1917–18 (Cd. 8668) XV), t. 15.

[59] T. I. Williams, 'Patriots and Citizens: Language, Identity and Education in a Liberal State: The Anglicisation of Pontypridd 1818–1920' (unpubl. University of Wales PhD thesis, 1989), p. 754.

numbers of non-Welsh speakers were becoming so sizeable that the traditional processes of acculturation could no longer operate.[60] Welsh might still be the predominant language at the coal face in anthracite communities, but in the more substantial steam coal districts its usage was more limited. Bilingualism, and possibly complete Anglicization, was increasingly reckoned to be a gain rather than a loss.

In both rural and industrial communities the role of the mother in language preservation was believed to be of paramount importance, especially since around a third of the population was composed of children under the age of fifteen.[61] Our study of the 1891 census has revealed that, outside the heavily industrialized districts where far more people were familiar with English and where there were fewer incentives to preserve Welsh, there were few signs of intergenerational linguistic slippage within Welsh-speaking families. During the Victorian period powerful ideological forces, designed to stiffen the role of the family unit, were at work,[62] and in an illuminating chapter Rosemary Jones explores the dynamics of female speech within the context of the notion of separate masculine and feminine spheres. In this development, too, the 1847 Blue Books played a seminal part. A swift and decisive rebuttal to the damning depiction of Welsh women as being 'universally unchaste' was required and was provided by a regular flow of didactic works and 'advice' books (written mostly but not exclusively by males) which sought to impose specific codes of behaviour on women. The true 'Cymraes' was expected to be pure, pious, respectable, discreet, submissive and thoroughly domesticated. As Jane Aaron has recently stressed: 'From the slanderous purgatory of the English there emerged a new heroine, pure, steel-like, and self-consciously Welsh' ('O burdan enllib y Sais ymrithiodd yr arwres newydd, yn bur, yn dduraidd, ac yn hunan-ymwybodol Gymreig').[63] The special destiny of 'The Angel at the Hearth' was to preserve the native tongue by instilling into her offspring a deep and abiding love of their language and culture. Implicit in this, too, was a responsibility to insulate her children from malign external influences, for in the eyes of Nonconformists there could be nothing more Welsh than the virtues of piety, honesty, chastity, thrift and temperance. It is doubtful, however, whether Welsh women fully accepted the rhetoric of

---

[60] Philip N. Jones, 'The Welsh Language in the Valleys of Glamorgan c.1800–1914' in Jenkins (ed.), *Language and Community in the Nineteenth Century*, pp. 147–80.

[61] Jones, *Statistical Evidence relating to the Welsh Language*, p. 11.

[62] Russell Davies, *Secret Sins: Sex, Violence and Society in Carmarthenshire 1870–1920* (Cardiff, 1996), pp. 156–61.

[63] Jane Aaron, *Pur fel y Dur: Y Gymraes yn Llên Menywod y Bedwaredd Ganrif ar Bymtheg* (Caerdydd, 1998), p. 10.

domesticity and private spheres or conformed to these prescribed models.[64] Women were clearly not mute or passive victims in Victorian Wales. The traditional components of their verbal armoury – cursing, scolding, nagging and gossiping – certainly did not vanish overnight. Indeed, the most feisty and sharp-tongued women consciously used their sex and their verbal powers to rail against their daily constraints and the idealized and narrowly conceived view (foisted upon them by males) of how they should behave. In both forceful and subtle ways, women deployed a range of verbal sanctions in pursuit of their goals, and in practice their attitudes towards the language and its preservation were rather more diverse than any historians have traditionally believed. This chapter, therefore, provides a fuller and more instructive understanding of the notion of the ideal Welsh woman and the degree to which female language and behaviour ran counter to precepts found in Welsh-language printed literature.

We must next consider religion. Although around half the population of Wales never darkened a place of worship on Census Sunday in 1851, throughout Britain it was generally believed to be the case that the Welsh were a peculiarly religious people. Only in retrospect can we see that organized religion did not necessarily shape or govern the beliefs of large numbers of people and that throughout the nineteenth century much evangelical grain fell on stony ground. Even so, religion stood in the mainstream of Welsh-language culture and its influence cannot be overemphasized.[65] As R. Tudur Jones explains, the Welshness of Nonconformity was beyond question. Indeed, by emphasizing the long, uninterrupted and inexorable evolution of an authentic 'Welsh-speaking Nonconformist nation', Nonconformist writers constructed their own version of the 'Whig interpretation of history'.[66] Even as Nonconformity expressed its confidence by building scores of enormous and expensive chapels, its apologists argued that the Nonconformist religion and 'the language of Cambria' were 'twin sisters of truth'.[67] Whereas the established Church was associated with 'Saxon bishops' who believed that Welsh

---

[64] For the background, see Catherine Hall, 'The Early Formation of Victorian Domestic Ideology' in eadem (ed.), *White, Male and Middle Class* (Cambridge, 1992), pp. 75–93. A recent critique has been offered by Amanda Vickery, 'Golden Age to Separate Spheres? A Review of the Categories and Chronology of English Women's History' in Pamela Sharpe (ed.), *Women's Work: The English Experience 1650–1914* (London, 1998), pp. 294–332. See also R. Tudur Jones, 'Daearu'r Angylion: Sylwadau ar Ferched mewn Llenyddiaeth, 1860–1900' in J. E. Caerwyn Williams (ed.), *Ysgrifau Beirniadol XI* (Dinbych, 1979), pp. 194–212.

[65] Glanmor Williams, *Religion, Language and Nationality in Wales* (Cardiff, 1979), pp. 25, 227–8; Ieuan Gwynedd Jones, *Mid-Victorian Wales: The Observers and the Observed* (Cardiff, 1992), pp. 59–66.

[66] Thomas Rees believed that Wales had been changed from 'a wilderness of irreligion and superstition into a well-cultivated garden of Evangelical Protestant Nonconformity'. Thomas Rees, *History of Protestant Nonconformity in Wales* (2nd ed., London, 1883), p. 466. See also R. Tudur Jones, *Grym y Gair a Fflam y Ffydd: Ysgrifau ar Hanes Crefydd yng Nghymru*, ed. D. Densil Morgan (Bangor, 1998).

[67] 'Mancunian', 'On the Advantages accruing to Englishmen from a Knowledge of the Welsh Language', *The Cambrian Journal*, III (1859), 248.

was 'barren nonsense'[68] and whose clergy, by dint of their Anglicized ways, were singularly ill-equipped to provide leadership for their flocks, Nonconformity claimed to be able to win the hearts and minds of both middle-class and working-class people by providing worshippers with powerful Welsh sermons and a 'chapel-vestry culture' composed of prayer and society meetings, the Band of Hope, penny readings, eisteddfodau, temperance festivals, hymn-singing festivals ('cymanfaoedd canu') and singing practices ('ysgolion cân'). Above all, few domains outside the family were as robustly Welsh-speaking as the Sunday school. In 1883 Dr Thomas Rees estimated that 461,468 pupils (around 30 per cent of the total population) were attending Nonconformist Sunday schools,[69] and, according to the socialist David Thomas, they were as effectively organized as the American Standard Oil Company.[70] Sunday schools not only strengthened Welsh by encouraging oral participation by children and adults alike, but also by developing the reading habit and a taste for doctrinal disputation. Throughout Wales it was clear that Nonconformity prospered best in those areas where the incidence of Welsh speaking was highest. Small wonder that its most avid supporters believed that the native tongue was a God-given gift and that it was uniquely fitted to convey religious truths. 'Nonconformity has won the common people. Why? It's language is Welsh; Welsh speakers are its flocks' ('Ymneillduaeth wedi ennill y werin. Paham? Y Gymraeg yw ei hiaith; y Cymry ydynt ei dëadelloedd'): so wrote T. E. Watkins (Eiddil Ifor) in 1853.[71]

But as they loudly trumpeted their successes and convinced themselves that they were the authentic representatives of Welshness at its best, Nonconformists became complacent and, by the twilight of the Victorian age, a little weary. In several ways, their very success led them to adopt misguided policies which undermined both their Welshness and self-esteem. Robin Okey has justifiably taken them to task for neglecting to lobby powerfully for the inclusion of Welsh in the curriculum of elementary schools, a course of action vigorously pursued by language groups in Europe.[72] Indeed, as the number of chapels and members, nourished and replenished by powerful religious revivals, proliferated, middle-class Nonconformists under the influence of Benthamite utilitarianism and Darwinism[73] embarked on Anglicizing policies in order to meet the needs of English-speaking incomers. Their predecessors – princely preachers like John Elias and Christmas

---

[68] E. T. Davies, *Religion in the Industrial Revolution in South Wales* (Cardiff, 1965), p. 118. For a more sympathetic view of the established Church, see Matthew Cragoe, 'A Question of Culture: The Welsh Church and the Bishopric of St Asaph, 1870', *WHR*, 18, no. 2 (1996), 228–54.
[69] Rees, *History of Protestant Nonconformity in Wales*, p. 464.
[70] Deian Hopkin, '"Y Werin a'i Theyrnas": Ymateb Sosialaeth i Genedlaetholdeb, 1880–1920' in Geraint H. Jenkins (ed.), *Cof Cenedl VI: Ysgrifau ar Hanes Cymru* (Llandysul, 1991), p. 176.
[71] *Seren Gomer*, XXXVI, no. 452 (1853), 205–6.
[72] Robin Okey, *Cymru a'r Byd Modern* (Aberystwyth, 1986), p. 10.
[73] John Wolffe, *God and Greater Britain: Religion and National Life in Britain and Ireland 1843–1945* (London, 1994).

Evans (farm servants), William Rees (a shepherd), Owen Thomas (a stonemason) and John Jones, Tal-y-sarn (a quarryman) – had always taken pride in the fact that theirs was a Welsh-speaking ministry. But by the 1860s the likes of J. R. Kilsby Jones, Lewis Edwards and Thomas Rees were increasingly enquiring 'Does the Welsh language have any practical use?' and 'Is it a language which will help our children get on in the world?' The provision of English-language chapels and services – dubbed the 'Inglis Côs' (English cause) by Robert Ambrose Jones (Emrys ap Iwan) – for the benefit of incomers precipitated furious controversy because it undermined Nonconformity's self-image as the national religion of Wales and also because, by encouraging Welsh speakers to join the 'English causes' in order to make them financially viable, the original Welsh-speaking congregations were depleted. Supporters of the 'English cause', however, were convinced that their policy would bring far greater dividends than the futile attempt to shore up an ailing tongue which Providence had already consigned to the dustbin of history. As Nonconformists began to believe their own propaganda, embattled Anglicans embarked on a remarkable recovery. Jolted into belated action by its unflattering image and by the threat of disestablishment, the established Church revived its fortunes with such conspicuous success that by 1910 it had recovered its former primacy as the largest religious body in Wales.[74] In numerical terms as well as its influence, Nonconformity was considerably less dominant and robust by the Edwardian period, and it must have been particularly galling to lose ground to an institution within which English services were twice as prevalent as Welsh services. The fortunes of Nonconformity and the Welsh language had traditionally been closely linked, and as one began to decline, so did the other.

Just as crucial for the maintenance and development of the Welsh language was the Welsh press, which became a motor of change of considerable importance.[75] Many contemporaries recognized that it was an essential enabling factor in sociolinguistic development as well as being a vital domain in its own right. Dafydd Llwyd Isaac of Pontypool referred to it as the *'propellum power'*,[76] while a speaker at the Church Congress held in Swansea in 1879 went so far as to describe it as 'the most powerful engine under God'.[77] In terms of sheer productivity, the Welsh press cannot be faulted in this period. The nineteenth century was an extraordinarily prolific period for Welsh publishing and, by investing in the printed word, writers, printers and publishers not only created and sustained a thriving book-market but also an articulate public opinion. Philip Henry Jones estimates that some 10,000 Welsh-language items were published within Wales,

[74] Matthew Cragoe, *An Anglican Aristocracy: The Moral Economy of the Landed Estate in Carmarthenshire, 1832–1895* (Oxford, 1996), pp. 243–4, 246.
[75] Philip Henry Jones and Eiluned Rees (eds.), *A Nation and its Books: A History of the Book in Wales* (Aberystwyth, 1998).
[76] Bethan Hopkins Williams, 'Hanes Cymdeithasol yr Iaith Gymraeg ar Sail Tystiolaeth y Cylchgronau rhwng 1840 a 1860' (unpubl. University of Wales MPhil thesis, 1998), p. 3.
[77] Cragoe, *An Anglican Aristocracy*, p. 242.

and to these must be added, according to Huw Walters's calculation, around 400 Welsh periodicals. This was of crucial significance in shaping and projecting a new identity for, as Adrian Hastings has observed, 'once an ethnicity's vernacular becomes a language with an extensive living literature of its own, the Rubicon on the road to nationhood appears to have been crossed'.[78] For the first time in its history, Wales had large and influential Welsh-language publishers who were capable of disseminating information and ideas to a mass reading public which was clearly thirsting for material. Among the growing number of editors and correspondents, Thomas Gee, William Rees, John Griffiths ('Y Gohebydd'), Lewis William Lewis (Llew Llwyfo), Beriah Gwynfe Evans and R. D. Rowlands (Anthropos) were extraordinarily accomplished men. Some major publications were landmarks in the construction of a national identity: among them were Thomas Charles's mammoth Scriptural dictionary, *Geiriadur Ysgrythyrawl* (4 vols., 1805–11) and the colossal ten-volume dictionary, *Y Gwyddoniadur Cymreig*, which took twenty-four years to complete and which was reprinted in 1891. Although it began to diversify its products from the mid-nineteenth century – and we should not discount heroic efforts to publish material of a scientific nature in Welsh – the Welsh press was generally considered to be the handmaiden of religion. It is true that the Welsh were hungry for knowledge about the fantasies and forgeries regarding Gomer, son of Japhet, Trojan forbears, and Druidic myths which Iolo Morganwg had popularized, but there was also a huge demand for the scriptures, denominational and chapel histories, autobiographies and biographies, commentaries and didactic writing. Much of this, no doubt, was sponsored by the Nonconformist intelligentsia who believed that reading predisposed men and women to respond more favourably to intense spiritual experiences and to satisfy their aspirations of self-improvement. It has been argued that farmers, farm labourers, quarrymen, craftsmen and miners were less interested in 'acrimonious theological squabbling' than in debating the fortunes of politics, peace and war in Europe and beyond,[79] and presumably not all colliers devoted their time to discussing niceties like 'How to reconcile the sovereignty of God with the responsibility of man'.[80] Miscellaneous material, especially ballads (of which *c*.8,000 were published),[81] almanacs and squibs also appealed to the literate labour force, but not until the end of this period were the Welsh working class urged to 'read, read, read' in order to contribute to the class struggle.[82]

[78] Hastings, *The Construction of Nationhood*, p. 12.
[79] D. Tecwyn Lloyd, 'The Welsh Language in Journalism' in Meic Stephens (ed.), *The Welsh Language Today* (Llandysul, 1973), pp. 152–3.
[80] Christopher Turner, 'The Nonconformist Response' in Trevor Herbert and Gareth E. Jones (eds.), *People and Protest: Wales 1815–1880* (Cardiff, 1988), p. 99.
[81] This figure is based on a database of ballad material in NLW.
[82] C. M. Baggs, 'The Miners' Institute Libraries of South Wales 1875–1939' in Jones and Rees (eds.), *A Nation and its Books*, p. 297.

Yet, the quality of Welsh literature scarcely matched the quantity. In a bid to rescue the poetry and prose of the nineteenth century from the harsh condescension of posterity, Robert Rhys offers a critical survey of the works of less well-known, as well as celebrated, purveyors of poetry and prose. The Welsh literary tradition was hamstrung by its nostalgia for the past, its association with Nonconformity, and its links with an education system which prized memorization and rote-learning. Under the baneful influence of the 1847 Report, many leading poets expended considerable energy in composing national epics worthy of Homer, Virgil and Milton which, so they fondly (but wrongly) believed, would rehabilitate the Welsh in the eyes of the world.[83] Lyric poets like Ceiriog, who churned out cloying, tear-jerking material, saw no incongruity in prizing, on the one hand, national sentiment and the Welsh tongue, and on the other the imperialist ambitions of the English-speaking state. As Rhys freely admits, with the signal exception of Daniel Owen, Emrys ap Iwan and O. M. Edwards, few writers possessed 'the critical faculties or the developed taste to produce a literature which was worthy of their ambitious aims'. Tastes varied, standards were palpably uneven and sometimes distressingly low, and the dearth of popular fiction was so lamentable that it made Daniel Owen a towering presence in the literary landscape. As Thomas Rees observed, 'the great bulk of our books are confined to divinity, history, poetry, and Welsh philology',[84] and by the twilight of the Victorian age it had become apparent that rather more nourishing fare was required to satisfy a public which had developed a taste for short stories and novels in English as well as what J. E. Southall dismissively referred to as 'unmitigated rubbish'.[85] Although considerable reserves of energy were devoted to the production of Welsh-language books and in cultivating the image of Wales as 'Gwalia dlos' (pretty Wales), 'hen Gymru wen' (pure old Wales) and 'Hen wlad y menig gwynion' (the land of the white gloves), the literary output was less creative and enlightened than one might have hoped. Not until the late nineteenth century did the initiative pass to new and more creative hands.

Although periodicals and magazines offered a diverse range of reading matter – on issues such as education, temperance, disestablishment, and land reform – the potential for extending the boundaries of the Welsh language was greater in the ever-growing number of newspapers. Even though the rate at which new Welsh-language newspapers were published gradually declined as the decades rolled by, following the abolition (by 1855) of tax on advertisements and the stamp duty on newspapers, the newspaper trade flourished mightily.[86] Within thirty-three years (1860–93), the number of newspapers published in Wales had increased from twenty-five to ninety-five (only five of which were in Welsh), an increase which

---

[83] E. G. Millward, *Yr Arwrgerdd Gymraeg: Ei Thwf a'i Thranc* (Caerdydd, 1998).
[84] Thomas Rees, *Miscellaneous Papers on Subjects Relating to Wales* (London, 1867), p. 45.
[85] Southall, *Wales and her Language*, p. 307.
[86] Aled Gruffydd Jones, *Press, Politics and Society: A History of Journalism in Wales* (Cardiff, 1993).

J. E. Vincent believed to be 'little short of phenomenal'.[87] *Baner ac Amserau Cymru*, founded by Thomas Gee in 1857 and the nearest thing to a truly national newspaper, was selling a minimum of 13,000 copies by the 1880s.[88] Although Welsh-language newspapers like *Tarian y Gweithiwr* and *Llais Llafur* found it hard to hold their own against powerful English-language and Cardiff-based papers like the *Western Mail* (from 1869) and the *South Wales Daily News* (from 1872), in general Welsh newspapers succeeded in developing their own vocabulary, rhetoric and goals. Indeed, Aled Jones believes that in a variety of novel and intriguing ways the newspaper press 'projected Welsh into the public domain in an unmistakably dynamic and modern form'.

It has often been assumed that the National Eisteddfod of Wales has traditionally lain at the heart of Welsh-speaking culture and language maintenance. As far as the nineteenth century is concerned, nothing could be further from the truth. It is a regrettable fact that the nineteenth-century Eisteddfod is neither remembered for its cultural achievements nor its promotion of the native tongue. Indeed, it served, at least in the public perception, as one of the most effective institutional vehicles for the dissemination of the English language. Even in the early decades of the century, when the Provincial and Cymreigyddion eisteddfodau were sustained by clerical bards, antiquarians and enthusiasts of aristocratic or gentry stock, attitudes towards Welsh were at best ambivalent, and when the Blue Books of 1847 ushered in a major crisis of national self-confidence it was only to be expected that the National Eisteddfod, which was held annually from 1861 onwards, would be appropriated by middle-class Anglophiles. While the chattering classes in England disparaged the pompous impostors and credulous fools ('those men with the queer names')[89] who were always so keen to gain eisteddfod honours or flaunt themselves in *gorsedd* ceremonies, avowed utilitarians like Hugh Owen and Thomas Nicholas resolved to restrict severely the use of Welsh in Wales's literary 'Olympiad'.[90] 'Three unusual things in an eisteddfod', claimed a waspish triad in 1864, 'every competitor satisfied, the Welsh speaking Welsh, and poets returning home without sampling something stronger than pop and ginger beer' ('Tri pheth anfynych mewn eisteddfod: Pob ymgeisydd yn foddlawn, y Cymry yn siarad Cymraeg, a'r beirdd yn dychwelyd adref heb brofi rhywbeth cryfach na phop a sinsir bîr').[91] This national focus and annual showpiece became increasingly vulnerable to what R. J. Derfel mockingly

---

[87] Beti Jones, *Newsplan: Report of the Newsplan project in Wales. Adroddiad ar gynllun Newsplan yng Nghymru* (London / Aberystwyth, 1994), p. 40.
[88] Philip Henry Jones, 'Cylchrediad *Y Faner*, Ffeithiau a Chwedlau', *Y Casglwr*, 28 (1986), 10–11.
[89] J. E. Southall, *The Future of Welsh Education* (Newport, 1900), p. 49.
[90] Emyr Humphreys, *The Taliesin Tradition: A Quest for the Welsh Identity* (Bridgend, 1989), pp. 177–8; Hywel Teifi Edwards, *The Eisteddfod* (Cardiff, 1990), pp. 22–7.
[91] *Y Punch Cymraeg*, 12 March 1864, p. 6.

dubbed 'the English madness' ('y gwallgofrwydd Seisnig').[92] Amid the stirring eloquence on the platform of the National Eisteddfod at Wrexham in 1876, for instance, one could easily detect the simmering tensions which divided Celtophobes and the common people. Joshua Hughes, bishop of St Asaph, declared that Wales could no longer hope to insulate itself from English influences and looked forward to the day when the Welsh were no longer 'hedged round by our language'. In response, the Revd D. Howell, vicar of Wrexham, doubted whether any other country in the world could muster thousands of working-class people to listen to 2,270 competitors, and rounded off his speech, to loud applause, with the rallying cry 'Oes y Byd i'r Iaith Gymraeg' (May the Welsh language live forever). Irked by a command to restrict his speech to five minutes, Henry T. Edwards, dean of Bangor, took for granted the impending demise of Welsh and urged the silent assembled throng to observe the pious civilities on its expiry: 'Treat the Welsh language, even if doomed to die, as you would treat an old man who has lived an honourable life.' In a vigorous rejoinder, Morgan Lloyd, MP for the Boroughs of Anglesey, provoked tumultuous applause by assuring his pessimistic 'friend' that 'neither the Welsh language nor the Welsh people are going to die . . . the Welsh language is gaining ground'.[93] Nevertheless, the Anglocentric preoccupations of the patrons of the National Eisteddfod held sway. In a sense, however, it is possible to overstate the importance of the National Eisteddfod. Local eisteddfodau were much more effective champions of the Welsh language and since the native tongue lay at the core of their activities they naturally enjoyed a much greater affinity with the common people. According to one fairly broad estimate, the number of places where local eisteddfodau were held increased from seven in 1847 to sixty-eight by 1898.[94] At grass roots level, the local eisteddfod was a fundamental factor in shaping the cultural sensibilities of Welsh speakers.

Of late education has been at the forefront of scholarly interest, and three chapters in this volume are devoted to it. No domain was more heavily predisposed towards the English language than education. This was a vital field, especially in the aftermath of the infamous Blue Books in 1847 when the state increasingly assumed responsibility for the context, content and funding of education. From a very early stage the arena of education was overwhelmingly English. The Blue Books clearly reveal the predominance of the English language in schools throughout Wales, presumably with the approval or at least the tacit acceptance of parents. Since social mobility and Anglicization were reckoned to be complementary processes, it was natural for the upwardly mobile middling sorts to view the acquisition of English as highly desirable. English was a

---

[92] R. J. Derfel, 'Cadwraeth yr Iaith Gymraeg', 'Yr Eisteddfod', 'Gwladgarwch y Cymry' in idem, *Traethodau ac Areithiau* (Bangor, 1864), pp. 151–68, 217–27.
[93] 'The National Eisteddfod for 1876, at Wrexham', *Y Cymmrodor*, I (1877), 48, 52, 63–7.
[94] David Morgan Richards, *Rhestr Eisteddfodau hyd y flwyddyn 1901* (Llandysul, 1914).

modernizing force, and only rustic fools would deny themselves the opportunity to ally themselves with progress and change. Although the common people do not seem to have displayed great enthusiasm for the Anglicizing trend in this domain, they were in no position to doubt or challenge the wisdom of their superiors. It was hard enough to scratch a living let alone mount a campaign on behalf of a language whose deficiencies were public knowledge. And since Welsh was safely ensconced in chapel and Sunday school, how could it be argued that English-medium schools would spell disaster for the Welsh language? The rights and wrongs of utilizing English as the sole medium of education were rarely rehearsed until the 1880s, by which time the notion that 'Welsh does not pay' was deeply rooted. *Y Punch Cymraeg* might identify education as 'the silent machinery to Anglicize the Welsh' ('y *machinery* dystaw i Seisnigeiddio y Cymry'),[95] but enthusiasm for Welsh as a classroom subject was very much a minority affair.

At both primary and intermediate level, therefore, the teaching of Welsh was either prohibited or discouraged. Indeed, for a pupil to speak Welsh in the classroom was judged a heinous crime. Although unconvincing efforts have been made of late to ignore or discount evidence of the use of what were variously described in different parts of Wales as the 'Welsh Not', the 'Welsh Mark' and the 'Welsh Ticket',[96] abundant testimony exists of brutal attempts by schoolmasters to rid pupils of their infuriating habit of using their native tongue in the classroom.[97] O. M. Edwards, whose depiction of 'The Devilish Old System' ('Yr Hen Gyfundrefn Felldigedig') was the most memorable indictment of the physical and psychological effects of the Welsh Not, remembered his headmistress as one who could only smile when speaking English.[98] Some of the more tyrannical headmasters caned Welsh-speaking pupils with sadistic glee and reminded them daily how disadvantaged Welsh monoglots would be in 'the race of life', thereby deepening the sense of inferiority felt by those whose first language was Welsh. The use and talismanic importance of the Welsh Not continued, especially in Welsh-speaking rural Wales, long after the Forster Act of 1870. At Trefdraeth school in Anglesey children were taught to sing 'Gwadu'r Iaith Gymraeg' (Betraying the Welsh Language), while pupils at Llangynfelyn school in

---

[95] *Y Punch Cymraeg*, 16 April 1864, p. 6; Departmental Committee on Welsh in the Educational System of Wales, *Welsh in Education and Life* (London, 1927), p. 47.

[96] See, for instance, Dai Smith, *Wales! Wales?* (London, 1984), p. 161 and Tim Williams, 'Language, Religion, Culture' in Trevor Herbert and Gareth E. Jones (eds.), *Wales 1880–1914* (Cardiff, 1988), pp. 74–7.

[97] O. M. Edwards, *Clych Atgof* (Wrecsam, 1921), chapter 1; J. Gwili Jenkins (ed.), *Adgofion Watcyn Wyn* (Merthyr Tydfil and Caerdydd, 1907), pp. 15–16; Henry Jones, *Old Memories* (London, 1922), pp. 30–2; John Jenkyn Morgan, 'Richard William: Yr Hen Ysgolfeistr Ungoes (1790–1875)', *Y Tyst*, 23 February 1956, p. 14; W. C. Elvet Thomas, *Tyfu'n Gymro* (Llandysul, 1972), pp. 101, 107–8; E. G. Millward, 'Yr Hen Gyfundrefn Felltigedig', *Barn*, 207–8 (1980), 93–5; D. Tecwyn Lloyd, *Drych o Genedl* (Abertawe, 1987), p. 48.

[98] W. J. Gruffydd, *Owen Morgan Edwards. Cofiant, Cyfrol 1, 1858–1883* (Aberystwyth, 1937), p. 69.

Cardiganshire were obliged to incant 'Hurrah for England'.[99] In order to inculcate the imperial spirit of the age, pupils were encouraged to drape themselves in the Union Jack on Empire Day and to pray for the Crown of Great Britain. Heroes of English history were held up for admiration in the classroom. When the celebrated bibliophile Bob Owen (b. 1885) left Llanfrothen school in Merioneth, he was much more familiar with the geography of the Lake District than that of Snowdonia, and although he had been raised within a stone's throw of the birthplace of unusually gifted poets like Rhys Goch Eryri and Dafydd Nanmor, the poetry thrust down his gullet in the classroom was that of 'brutal, third-rate English poets' ('beirdd cigyddlyd trydydd dosbarth Lloegr').[100] Boorish HMIs bemoaned the 'bilingual difficulty' and derided the clumsy attempts of pupils to repeat knowledge which had been tediously rehearsed in the classroom.

Welsh educationists did not begin to think seriously in terms of a 'bilingual opportunity' until the mid-1880s when the pressure group the Society for Utilizing the Welsh Language began to exercise decisive influence in high circles and to achieve modest success in developing Welsh as a specific subject in the curriculum.[101] Its chief spokesman, Dan Isaac Davies, voiced his ambition of setting on course a scheme of bilingual education which would ensure that by 1985 three million people in Wales would be proficient in English and Welsh.[102] The cynic might argue that the concessions made to Welsh in the late Victorian years were made in the light of the knowledge that English had already established itself as the High Prestige language of the majority, but, as William Edwards HMI made plain in 1887, the current educational policy was evidently riddled with deficiencies:

> When his [the pupil] school career ends, at the early age of 12 or 13, the environment is wholly Welsh, and it is not merely antecedently probable but a matter of experience that in parts of Cardiganshire, Merionethshire, and even of Glamorganshire, away from the town, the child frequently in a few months loses almost all his hold of English ... The people who are sanguine of the speedy success of the present system do not realise the difficulty of killing a language, which at the present moment is very far from moribund, and may live as long as Dutch or Danish.[103]

It is significant that some of the most positive responses to the inclusion of Welsh as an optional subject in elementary schools came from the Rhondda and county

---

[99] David A. Pretty, *Two Centuries of Anglesey Schools 1700–1902* (Llangefni, 1977), pp. 149–50, 212, 214–15; Cardiganshire Record Office, Llangynfelyn Board, Infants School, no. 46b (Logbook 1883–1902). See also Alexandra Road Board School, Aberystwyth, Logbook (Boys) 2Ca.
[100] Dyfed Evans, *Bywyd Bob Owen* (Caernarfon, 1977), p. 13.
[101] E. Glyn Lewis, *Bilingualism and Bilingual Education* (Oxford, 1981).
[102] Davies, *1785, 1885, 1985!*
[103] *The Future Development of the Welsh Educational System. Being the Proceedings of the Cymmrodorion Section of the National Eisteddfod of 1887* (London, 1887), p. 8.

boroughs in south Wales.[104] Our study of the 1891 census confirms that educational policies had by no means eradicated Welsh monoglottism among the 3–14 age group. On the other hand, the Intermediate Education Act of 1889 created schools which were happier to teach French than Welsh and which produced a new, educated, mobile middle class of teachers, doctors and ministers who were susceptible to Anglicization and to be 'exported' to England.[105] Although the humanist, anti-utilitarian, pro-Welsh language programme advocated by O. M. Edwards in his capacity as the first Chief Inspector of the Welsh Department of the Board of Education differed sharply from the ideals which had fired Hugh Owen, it had little immediate effect on Welsh education. Not until after 1945 was the role of the Welsh language in primary and secondary education seriously addressed.

In academia, too, Welsh was conspicuous by its absence. English was the sole medium employed for educational and administrative purposes within the national, federal university established in 1893. John Roberts of Llanbryn-mair justifiably feared that the first University College at Aberystwyth would do little to sustain the native tongue: 'What child in school knows not that a Welsh Stick exists for speaking Welsh? And it is certain there will be some kind of Welsh Stick in the Aberystwyth School' ('Pa blentyn fu mewn ysgol heb ddeall fod "Welsh Stick" am siarad Cymraeg? A diau y bydd "Welsh Stick" o ryw fath yn Ysgol Aberystwyth').[106] The personification of the 'Welsh Stick' proved to be its first principal, Thomas Charles Edwards who, having been discouraged from using Welsh by his father Lewis, set himself the goal of ensuring that Welsh students who sat at his feet learnt to speak like English gentlemen.[107] His staff rallied to his cause by striving to eliminate the slightest hint of a Welsh accent in their classrooms. Disapproving HMI reports were littered with comments like 'Emrys Jones [from Mold] has the Welsh accent rather strong when speaking English' and 'James Hedley Jacob's accent would be noticeable out of Wales'.[108] When thriving urban centres in north Wales staked their claim for a university college, a representative from Wrexham claimed that students who 'run the race of life' were judged by their English, and their 'Welsh stands them in no good stead at all'.[109] In the pre-war period, at Aberystwyth, Bangor and Cardiff, even Welsh was taught through the medium of English and examined in English. In schools,

---

[104] Roger Webster, 'Education in Wales and the Rebirth of a Nation', *History of Education*, 19, no. 3 (1990), 187.

[105] See Gareth Elwyn Jones, *Controls and Conflicts in Welsh Secondary Education 1889–1944* (Cardiff, 1982).

[106] Jones, *Grym y Gair a Fflam y Ffydd*, p. 220.

[107] T. I. Ellis (ed.), *Thomas Charles Edwards Letters*, NLWJ Supplement, III, no. 3 (1952), p. 110; Geraint H. Jenkins, *The University of Wales: An Illustrated History* (Cardiff, 1993), pp. 3, 53.

[108] W. Gareth Evans (ed.), *Fit to Educate: A Century of Teacher Education and Training 1892–1992* (Aberystwyth, 1992), p. 65.

[109] J. Gwynn Williams, *The University College of North Wales: Foundations 1884–1927* (Cardiff, 1985), p. 43.

colleges and universities, the low status of the Welsh language was unquestionable. By a combination of the 'stick' and the 'carrot', Welsh had been successfully marginalized in this particular domain.

One of the most important and perhaps surprising features of this period is the manner in which Welsh entered the political domain and exercised an influence which even the doughtiest eighteenth-century Welsh radical could scarcely have imagined possible. This development owed nothing to the benevolence of successive governments, for they remained wedded to the principle, enacted in legislation, that Wales was united and annexed to England and that its native language did not require or deserve public recognition. For the bulk of the nineteenth century, as J. E. Southall observed, governments regarded the Welsh language as 'a vexatious obstacle to the unification of the country'.[110] Whitehall mandarins believed in rolling forward the frontiers of the state in order to create within Britain a centralized 'national society',[111] and as the administrative framework developed – in public health, finance and education – the presence of the English language, spoken by government officials, inspectors and their servants, became far more noticeable. Indeed, it became a commonplace that public officials were seeking to extend the use of the English language 'as a form of compulsory social welfare'.[112] Parallel developments – the railways, postal services, the telegraph, and advanced means of mass production and retailing – all helped to make the state a more intrusive and visible presence. The message rang out clearly: England and Wales were one, and the 'Queen's English' was the language of officialdom.

But a different interpretation of the potential uses of language as a political instrument existed outside Westminster and Whitehall. One of the most striking features of the period from Chartism onwards was the development of a vibrant political discourse sustained in the Welsh language. In the old-style, corrupt and manipulative world of Eatanswill politics, Welsh had counted for nothing, but the demise of deference and the emergence of democratic politics offered an unprecedented opportunity for the native tongue to enter the political theatre and to generate its own distinctive, critical voice. Even though Welsh politicians operated within *British* politics,[113] paradoxically their very involvement served to invigorate and extend the use of the Welsh language. The key to this development was the radicalization of the Welsh middle and working class. The extension of the franchise (though confined to manhood suffrage) between 1867 and 1884–5, the removal of civic and religious disabilities, and the growth of education all meant that the Welsh were able to participate in the practice of

---

[110] Southall (ed.), *Bi-lingual Teaching in Welsh Elementary Schools*, p. i.
[111] See Keith Robbins, *Great Britain: Identities, Institutions and the Idea of Britishness* (London, 1998).
[112] Jose Harris, *Private Lives, Public Spirit: A Social History of Britain 1870–1914* (Oxford, 1993), pp. 19–23.
[113] Kenneth O. Morgan, *Wales in British Politics 1868–1922* (3rd ed., Cardiff, 1981).

politics, thereby enhancing their self-esteem and confidence. It became *de rigueur* for Liberals to speak Welsh at political meetings and for election addresses and songs to be delivered and printed in both languages. Even Conservative candidates, so often abused and vilified in the radical press, could no longer blithely disregard the need to communicate in Welsh with newly enfranchised voters, though how far their ritual declarations of support for the native tongue were either understood or believed is hard to judge. As Neil Evans and Kate Sullivan point out, in the Edwardian period Welsh became 'a versatile and durable political weapon'. This development proved an important catalyst in the language of politics. Paul O'Leary detects three principal keywords – liberty, virtue and loyalty – in Welsh-language patriotic discourse in mid-Victorian Wales and since this was a contested arena the language of patriotism was appropriated for different purposes by different groups. Although the image of Wales cultivated by Liberal Nonconformists like Henry Richard celebrated the Welsh *gwerin* as the most pious, sober, industrious, peace-loving people in Britain,[114] Henry T. Edwards, dean of Bangor, was able to steal Richard's thunder by reminding readers in his provocatively entitled work *The Church of the Cymry* (1870) of the debt Wales owed to Welsh-speaking reformers within the established Church since Elizabethan times.[115]

It also became a matter of considerable pride for language campaigners that Welsh speakers like Henry Richard, William Abraham (Mabon), David Lloyd George and Tom Ellis were much more genuine representatives of voting interests in Wales than their predecessors had been. According to R. W. Morgan, Tregynon, Conservative MPs were a bunch of 'old women' ('hen wrageddos') as far as the interests of the Welsh language were concerned: 'they can't between them summon up even the spirit of a gosling or a clucking hen' ('nis gallant godi cyd-rhyngddynt gymaint o ysbryd a chyw gŵydd neu hen iâr yn clowcian').[116] Although issues such as land reform, temperance, disestablishment and education were vigorously debated outside Welsh political circles, they touched a special nerve within Wales because they impinged on cherished linguistic and religious principles. Implicit, and sometimes explicit, in the campaign for separate legislation for Wales and for national institutions was a call for greater respect of the native language. Since they possessed a greater number of Welsh-speaking MPs, Liberal politicians had more room to manoeuvre and to claim to speak for the 'nation' by campaigning for Welsh translations for parliamentary legislation and

---

[114] Prys Morgan, 'The *Gwerin* of Wales: Myth and Reality' in Hume and Price (eds.), *The Welsh and their Country*, pp. 134–52; Christopher Harvie, 'The Folk and the *Gwerin*: The Myth and the Reality of Popular Culture in 19th-Century Scotland and Wales', *PBA*, 80 (1991 Lectures and Memoirs), 19–48; R. Merfyn Jones, 'Beyond Identity? The Reconstruction of the Welsh', *Journal of British Studies*, 31, no. 4 (1992), 330–57.

[115] Henry T. Edwards, *The Church of the Cymry: A Letter to the Right Hon. W. E. Gladstone, M.P.* (London, 1870). See also Cragoe, 'A Question of Culture', 243–4.

[116] R. W. Morgan, *Amddiffyniad yr Iaith Gymraeg* (Caernarfon, 1858), p. iv.

on behalf of the appointment of Welsh speakers to positions of influence, such as those occupied by bishops and judges.

Another major propellant was the notion that language could give expression to national sentiment. Mazzini, Kossuth and Garibaldi were familiar names in Welsh-language periodicals and newspapers, and in the post-1848 period debates about the 'principle of nationality' and the criteria of nationhood increasingly preoccupied the intelligentsia.[117] Among the small nations of Europe there was a growing belief that vernacular languages were entitled to become official languages in order to develop socially, culturally and politically. Welsh words like *cenedlgarwch* (patriotism), *cenedlaetholdeb* (nationalism), *cenedlgarwr* (patriot) and *cenedlaetholwr* (nationalist) entered the vocabulary in 1821, 1858, 1864 and 1898 respectively,[118] and were widely employed and articulated by members of Cymru Fydd, the Young Wales movement (1886–96), who were ardent champions of the Welsh language. However, national identity came to be chiefly associated with radical Nonconformist Liberalism, thereby excluding Anglicans, Roman Catholics, Conservative landowners and industrialists, and English-speaking incomers. The result was that the crusaders of the Cymru Fydd movement were publicly excoriated by commercial and urban interests in south Wales. When the movement dissolved in acrimony in 1896, the campaign to politicize the language and enhance its public status was gravely weakened.[119] Minor concessions to the native tongue, such as the provision of Welsh translations of parliamentary papers and legislation, were gained largely because they hardly posed a serious threat to the primacy of English.

As Kenneth O. Morgan has revealed, it is difficult to escape the conclusion that the Welsh were primarily interested in acquiring political parity and public recognition within late Victorian and Edwardian Britain.[120] Following the collapse of Cymru Fydd, the quest for separatism or 'Home Rule all Round' appeared less attractive and urgent. Yet, there were still nation-builders who believed that language and culture could lie at the heart of the swiftly modernizing Wales. Well versed in the aspirations of the smaller ethnic groups within Europe and heartened by the success of his Patagonian venture, Michael D. Jones believed that the Welsh had a moral responsibility to promote the native tongue as a political tool, especially since the annihilation of Welsh was, in his view, an integral part of the imperial ambitions of the English. His pungent

---

[117] Alun Davies, 'Cenedlaetholdeb yn Ewrop a Chymru yn y Bedwaredd Ganrif ar Bymtheg', *EA*, XXVII (1964), 14–23; Graham Day and Richard Suggett, 'Conceptions of Wales and Welshness: Aspects of Nationalism in Nineteenth-Century Wales' in Gareth Rees, Janet Bujra, Paul Littlewood, Howard Newby and Teresa L. Rees (eds.), *Political Action and Social Identity: Class, Locality and Ideology* (Basingstoke, 1985), pp. 91–116.

[118] *Geiriadur Prifysgol Cymru. A Dictionary of the Welsh Language. Cyfrol 1* (Caerdydd, 1950–67).

[119] Emyr Price, *Lloyd George y Cenedlaetholwr Cymreig: Arwr ynteu Bradwr?* (Llandysul, 1999), chapter 10.

[120] Kenneth O. Morgan, *Rebirth of a Nation: Wales 1880–1980* (Oxford, 1981), chapter 4.

denunciations of so-called British 'greatness' and his satires on 'Britannia', 'John Bull', roast beef and plum pudding were designed to eradicate 'the servile worship of the Englishman' ('Sais-addoliaeth gwasaidd').[121] Evan Pan Jones, too, was a master of invective and satire, and his campaign on behalf of 'Freedom, Patriotism, and Equality' ('Rhyddid, Cenedlgarwch, a Chydraddoldeb') struck chill into the hearts of the landowning élite.[122] Jones loathed the 'evil and conquering spirit' ('eu hyspryd trahaus a goresgynol') of the English, and delighted in tweaking the ear of John Bull in the periodicals *Y Celt* and *Cwrs y Byd*.[123] Conversely, Emrys ap Iwan reserved his sharpest barbs for Welshmen on the make, especially those who worshipped 'the English calf' ('y llo Seisnig'). An avowed Francophile, steeped in the classics and in European literature, Emrys ap Iwan was a brilliant polemicist. Nothing gave him greater satisfaction than 'plucking the hair of the half Welsh' ('Plicio Gwallt yr Hanner Cymry') and he often claimed that there were no more servile and self-abasing people in Europe than the Welsh.[124] He once memorably discomfited J. R. Kilsby Jones by informing him that if everyone shared his views all languages would perish ('Darfyddai am bob iaith ar wyneb y ddaear pe bai pawb fel chwi').[125] Having coined the word *ymreolaeth* (self-rule), he used it as a rallying cry in a series of forthright essays and articles designed to persuade the Welsh that all aspiring nations cherished their native tongue. To spurn Welsh, he argued, was a blasphemous deed for which there could be no forgiveness. Most important of all, Emrys ap Iwan was the first to insist that if Wales were to lose its language, all political activity would become redundant. In 1892, a year after critical data relating to the Welsh language had been gathered by the census, he declared: 'keeping Welsh alive is the most important subject in Wales at this time' ('cadw'r Gymraeg yn fyw ydyw y pwnc pwysicaf yng Nghymru ar hyn o bryd').[126] Outside the readership of *Y Geninen* and *Cymru*, however, it is hard to judge how much popular support existed for the coupling of language rights with the language of separatism or self-rule. Emrys ap Iwan had little knowledge, for instance, of the perceptions of the amorphous working class for the bulk of whom the future of the Welsh language as a political force was scarcely of overriding importance.

---

[121] Michael D. Jones, 'Gwaseidd-dra y Cymry', *Y Geninen*, XII, no. 4 (1894), 267–70; R. Tudur Jones, 'Michael D. Jones a Thynged y Genedl' in Geraint H. Jenkins (ed.), *Cof Cenedl: Ysgrifau ar Hanes Cymru* (Llandysul, 1986), pp. 95–124.
[122] Evan Pan Jones, *Oes a Gwaith y Prif Athraw y Parch. Michael Daniel Jones, Bala* (Bala, 1903), p. 319.
[123] Peris Jones-Evans, 'Evan Pan Jones – Land Reformer', *WHR*, 4, no. 2 (1968), 143–60; E. G. Millward, 'Beirdd Ceredigion yn Oes Victoria', *Ceredigion*, XI, no. 2 (1990), 183–8.
[124] Emrys ap Iwan, 'Cymru i'r Cymry!', *Y Geninen*, IV, no. 3 (1886), 155–62; idem, 'Breuddwyd Pabydd wrth ei Ewyllys', ibid., X, no. 1 (1892), 15–19; ibid., X, no. 2 (1892), 23–7; D. Myrddin Lloyd (ed.), *Detholiad o Erthyglau a Llythyrau Emrys ap Iwan. II. Llenyddol Ieithyddol* (Clwb Llyfrau Cymreig, 1939), pp. 103–25.
[125] Millward, *Cenedl o Bobl Ddewrion*, pp. 164–5.
[126] Emrys ap Iwan, 'At y Cymry o'r Cymry', *Y Geninen*, X, no. 2 (1892), 53.

Yet it would be highly misleading to believe that the Welsh language played no part in the growth of the Labour movement. Some of the prickliest essays on the links between patriotism and socialism were penned by R. J. Derfel, while Welsh was the language of socialism in newspapers like *Y Dinesydd* and in most of the dealings of the North Wales Quarrymen's Union. *Y Werin a'i Theyrnas* (1910) by David Thomas, Tal-y-sarn, became a *vade mecum* for Welsh-speaking socialists throughout north Wales.[127] Nor would it be true to say that only monoglot English speakers in south Wales were attracted to the 'new religion' of socialism. Welsh speakers like Mabon, William Lewis (Lewys Afan) and Tom Richards were perfectly capable of expressing the language of Labour and class in their own tongue, and in 1898, the year in which the South Wales Miners' Federation was established, the Welsh-language newspaper *Llais Llafur* (The Voice of Labour) was launched by Ebenezer Rees at Ystalyfera. By the eve of the Great War, however, the use of Welsh in Labour politics was in serious jeopardy. 'Bread and cheese we want, not language', cried hecklers at Aberfan in 1911 as Clem Edwards MP addressed them in Welsh.[128] Likewise, T. E. Nicholas, apostle of the Welsh working-class and an avowed Marxist who delivered over a thousand lectures on the Soviet Union in the inter-war years, was understandably moved more by poverty and inequality than by the diminishing role of Welsh in political life: 'If I have to carry someone on my back, it's not much difference to me whether he can speak Welsh or not.'[129] In the swiftly developing bilingual communities of the South Wales Coalfield, large numbers of electors could only be reached and influenced through the English language.

In no domain were the people of Wales more acutely aware of the sheer weight and pressure of the English language than in the administrative and legal sphere.[130] Although the Welsh language was used and heard frequently in the courts, it possessed no legal or official status. English was the official medium of the judiciary and its omnipotence was 'deeply ingrained in the mentality of those who administered law'.[131] John Thomas (Eifionydd), editor of *Y Geninen*, neatly summed up the impotence of Welsh in this domain in an *englyn*:

---

[127] Hopkin, '"Y Werin a'i Theyrnas"', pp. 176–88.
[128] Dylan Morris, 'Sosialaeth i'r Cymry – Trafodaeth yr ILP', *Llafur*, IV, no. 2 (1985), 53.
[129] Glyn Jones, 'The Making of a Poet', *Planet*, 113 (1995), 76.
[130] Harold Carter, 'Local Government and Administration in Wales, 1536–1939' in J. A. Andrews (ed.), *Welsh Studies in Public Law* (Cardiff, 1970), p. 47; Janet Davies, *The Welsh Language* (Cardiff, 1993), p. 52. For languages in Europe which gained official status, see Glanville Price (ed.), *Encyclopaedia of the Languages of Europe* (Oxford, 1998).
[131] Mark Ellis Jones, 'Law, Legislation and the Welsh Language in the Nineteenth Century' (unpubl. University of Wales PhD thesis, 1998), p. 295.

> Y Saesonaeg mewn bri sessiynol – sy'
> Ar sedd ein llys barnol, –
> Hi yw yr iaith gyfreithiol;
> A'r *Gymraeg* – mae hi ar ôl.[132]

(English enjoys fame in the sessions and on the seat of our law courts; She is the language of law, and the Welsh lags behind.)

In Wales the law was not simply viewed as an expression of privilege and class: it also represented Anglicization. Monoglot Welsh speakers and those who were barely bilingual had little confidence in the impartiality of the law for three reasons. Firstly, many of them spoke in righteous indignation of the arrogant disdain displayed by judges, magistrates and lawyers towards the Welsh. The bitter hatred which the Rebecca rioters nursed towards landowning families was partly attributable to the fact that magistrates treated tenant farmers 'like dogs', and the well-regarded reporter of *The Times*, Thomas Campbell Foster, fully recognized that their behaviour 'as a class' was oppressive, insulting, haughty and offensive.[133] Secondly, the anti-Welsh lobby was given much valuable grist to its mill by the education commissioners of 1847 who claimed that the native language 'distorts the truth, favours fraud, and abets perjury'.[134] This unwarranted slur on the character of the Welsh recurred often. Lord Penrhyn referred to the Welsh as 'a nation of liars'[135] and Homersham Cox once exclaimed: 'The infamous perjury committed all over Wales makes one's blood boil.'[136] The Registrar General, Brydges P. Henniker, publicly declared in the official census report of 1891 (published in 1893) that the Welsh were mendacious.[137] Thirdly, in a court of law the Welsh speaker was seriously disadvantaged. Confronted by bewigged monoglot English judges, slippery lawyers and incompetent interpreters, he or she swiftly discovered that the proceedings for the most part were incomprehensible. In the eyes of the law, therefore, those who spoke no English were second-class citizens, and officialdom believed that the only appropriate remedy for such country bumpkins was a rigorous dose of English-language education. Towards the end of the nineteenth century, D. Lleufer Thomas, the Carmarthenshire-born barrister, could barely contemplate the adverse effects of such a reprehensible judicial system on the mindset of monoglot Welsh people since the Acts of Union ('Anhawdd synied yr effaith niweidiol y mae y drefn wrthun o weinyddu

---

[132] D. Lleufer Thomas, '"Y Sessiwn yng Nghymru"', *Y Geninen*, X, no. 2 (1892), 19.
[133] David Jones, *Rebecca's Children: A Study of Rural Society, Crime, and Protest* (Oxford, 1989), pp. 96–8.
[134] *Reports of the Commissioners of Inquiry into the State of Education in Wales . . . in three parts. Part II. Brecknock, Cardigan, Radnor, and Monmouth* (London, 1847) (PP 1847 (871) XXVII), p. 66.
[135] 'Political Notes', *Cymru Fydd*, III, no. 11 (1890), 691.
[136] Jones, 'Law, Legislation and the Welsh Language', p. 230.
[137] Census of England and Wales, 1891, *Vol. IV. General Report, with Summary Tables and Appendices* (HMSO, 1893), 'Languages in Wales and Monmouthshire', pp. 81–3.

cyfiawnder drwy farnwyr na fedrant Gymraeg wedi gael ar feddyliau cenedl o Gymry uniaith am dros dri chant o flynyddau').[138]

In a chapter based on his pioneering doctoral thesis, Mark Ellis Jones examines how successive pressure groups exposed sores which had rankled over a long period. Following the deeply unpopular decision to abolish the Court of Great Sessions in 1830,[139] strenuous efforts were made by London-Welsh societies, the 'Llanover Circle' which coalesced around the redoubtable Lady Augusta Hall, and expatriate Welsh clergy in the West Riding to promote the case for making Welsh the medium of law. But although the appointment of Welsh-speaking judges and magistrates was clearly both necessary and equitable, those who had read the Blue Books of 1847 were not disposed to agree. Despite much huffing and puffing in Parliament by earnest, middle-class Welsh Liberals (who were extremely sensitive to accusations of seeking a 'Wales for the Welsh'), grievances remained unredressed. Indeed, insult was often added to injury, as the appointment of the egregious Homersham Cox and Cecil Beresford – to howls of disapproval – made plain. Small wonder that an anonymous writer in *Cymru Fydd* wrung his hands in despair: 'We have . . . alien judges, alien barristers, alien land agents, alien magistrates . . . These Canaanites do not understand us, do not care a fig about us, except as we are the occasion of their being plentifully provided with bread and cheese.'[140] Such a state of affairs made a mockery of justice and rankled deeply among the Welsh. Yet, little was done. The outspoken criticisms of Michael D. Jones and Emrys ap Iwan, and the unorthodox stratagems they deployed in order to exploit legal loopholes, were not replicated by others, and all demands for the repeal of the 'language clause' of the Act of Union of 1536 were either ignored or brushed aside. In this domain, what Tom Ellis referred to as 'contemptuous neglect'[141] was all too obvious, and the right of the Welsh speaker to use his native tongue in a court of law remained unrecognized until the Welsh Language Act of 1967.

★   ★   ★

In seeking to assess the status of the Welsh language and the roles it assumed in different domains, we should try to divest ourselves as far as possible of the perceptions which colour our understanding of the fate of the language in the twentieth century. Treating the past in the light of future developments is both unhistorical and unhelpful, for people living in the pre-1914 period would not have been aware that Welsh was in decline or that a calamitous collapse in the

---

[138] Thomas, ' "Y Sessiwn yng Nghymru" ', 19.
[139] Mark Ellis Jones, ' "An invidious attempt to accelerate the extinction of our language": The Abolition of the Court of Great Sessions and the Welsh language', *WHR*, 19, no. 2 (1998), 226–64.
[140] Anon, 'Cymru Fydd', *Cymru Fydd*, II, no. 5 (1889), 146.
[141] *Carnarvon and Denbigh Herald*, 28 October 1892.

number of Welsh speakers was just around the corner. It is certainly true, however, that by the first decade of the twentieth century major linguistic shifts had occurred and that bilingualism was deeply entrenched. By 1911 the proportion of the total population able to speak English was 91.3 per cent, and in many ways the development of bilingualism encouraged full-blown Anglicization. But it is easy to overlook the fact that the number of Welsh speakers (977,366 or 44.6 per cent in 1911) was still rising at the end of the long nineteenth century and that over the period as a whole it was the predominant language in Wales. That this should have been so, in a period marked by dramatic and unprecedented social and economic change, was remarkable. J. E. Southall, one of the most perceptive late nineteenth-century commentators on linguistic matters, was greatly impressed by 'the extraordinary vitality of the language, in the face of such adverse circumstances'.[142] Champions of the native tongue had every right to echo seventeenth-century parliamentarians in celebrating their own version of 'The Good Old Cause' ('Yr Hen Achos Da'), namely 'Cymry, Cymry, a Chymraeg' (Wales, the Welsh, and the Welsh language).[143]

The conventional view is that the role and influence of Welsh in this period was negligible and that by marginalizing it to the hearth, chapel and eisteddfod its status became 'subaltern and subject'.[144] It is certainly true that Welsh was outlawed from law and administration, that it was judged to be a language of no real consequence in the educational curriculum, that, with some exceptions, its commercial significance was low, and that it barely counted in domains such as science, technology and engineering. English had much working in its favour and no one could deny that (in sociolinguistic terms) it was a High Prestige language. But, as the evidence of this volume reveals, the complex and bewildering social processes at work in the nineteenth century did far more to sustain the Welsh language in a variety of domains than historians have been prepared to admit. The population explosion, the industrial revolution, improvements in transport and communication, religious revivals and the dissemination of printed information and knowledge were all essential building blocks which sustained the edifice of language and culture. Although the Welsh middle class believed, in the wake of the 1847 Blue Books, that the best way of averting further collective humiliation was to transform a predominantly Welsh-speaking population into English speakers, there was no evidence that Welsh was in terminal decline by 1911. Welsh was much more than a hermetically sealed treasure or handicap (depending on one's viewpoint at the time). In spite of the external pressures upon it, it prevailed and counted in a surprising number of domains. For the bulk of the century Welsh was the language of the hearth, the workplace (both rural and industrial), the chapel and, to a lesser extent, the church. The Welsh press not

---

[142] Southall, *Wales and her Language*, p. 361.
[143] Morgan, *Amddiffyniad yr Iaith Gymraeg*, p. iv.
[144] Gwyn A. Williams, *When was Wales? A History of the Welsh* (London, 1985), p. 210.

only sustained the native language but was also a powerful shaper of cultural identity. The 'new democracy' in the second half of the century paved the way for Welsh speakers to be drawn into political activity at grass-roots level and to associate themselves with the national movement which created a modern Welsh identity. As most of the following chapters indicate, these were years when Welsh was placed under the microscope and subjected to intense examination. Mistakes were made, opportunities spurned, and bitter lessons learnt, but it is easier for the historian to discern these more clearly and perhaps regretfully than was the case at the time. Although bilingualism and creeping Anglicization had become an enduring reality by 1911, it would be a mistake to believe that the well-being of the native language was a matter about which most people did not feel strongly. People *did* care, and the fact that so many writers leapt to the defence of Welsh is proof of growing self-confidence in the language as well as unease and anger over hostility towards it and its treatment in official circles. Moreover, no one can deny that it was an integral part of the 'increasingly passionate national awareness'[145] which characterized Edwardian Wales.

---

[145] Morgan, *Rebirth of a Nation*, p. 131.

1

Language Zones, Demographic Changes, and the Welsh Culture Area 1800–1911

W. T. R. PRYCE

NOTIONS OF regional location, clear affiliation with place, an endowed affinity with locality and a strong sense of community have always been integral to the idea of Wales and Welshness. Indeed, in the late twentieth century the question '*O ble 'chi'n dod*' (Where do you come from?) continues to be one of the first things that Welsh people still ask of each other – explicitly or implicitly – when they meet for the first time! Clearly, the country of Wales, by its very existence, constitutes a geographical phenomenon of very considerable long standing. For the modern Welsh man or woman to ask such questions on location and community implies that a generalized set of ideas as to the spatial and regional structures, into which individual communities can be fitted, is present in their minds. In other words, an explanatory model exists concerning the nature and make-up of their country, their nation, regional variations and the language used in different locations.

Language Areas in the Early Nineteenth Century

Until recently the known evidence on linguistic situations in the past was somewhat fragmentary and sketchy. The first population census in Britain was not taken until 1801 and, although the 1851 census recorded information on religious affiliations within Wales, details relating to the language or languages spoken by individuals were not recorded until 1891.[1] It is necessary, therefore, to turn to other sources that reflect local linguistic conditions throughout the country.

Despite the vigorous growth of Nonconformity, it is now clear that the specific language or the mix of Welsh and English used in parish churches throughout Wales closely reflected contemporary local circumstances.[2] The Act of

---

[1] W. T. R. Pryce, 'The British Census and the Welsh Language', *Cambria*, 13, no. 1 (1986), 79–100; Edward Higgs, *Making Sense of the Census: The Manuscript Returns for England and Wales, 1801–1901* (London, 1989), p. 29; B. Collins and W. T. R. Pryce, 'Census Returns in England, Ireland, Scotland and Wales' in P. Braham (ed.), *Using the Past: Audio Cassettes on Sources and Methods for Family and Community Historians* (Milton Keynes, 1995), pp. 46, 53; Gwenfair Parry and Mari A. Williams, *The Welsh Language and the 1891 Census* (Cardiff, 1999).

[2] W. T. R. Pryce, 'Welsh and English in Wales, 1750–1971: A Spatial Analysis based on the Linguistic Affiliation of Parochial Communities', *BBCS*, XXVIII, pt. 1 (1978), 1–36.

Uniformity of 1662 had obliged the bishops of the diocese of St David's, St Asaph, Bangor and Llandaff, as well as the Bishop of Hereford (whose diocese historically included several Welsh-speaking parishes in the borderland) to ensure that not only should both the Bible and the Prayer Book be translated into Welsh 'for the soul's health of the flock committed to their charge within Wales', but also that 'the whole of the Divine Service shall be said throughout Wales, within the dioceses where the Welsh tongue is commonly used, in the British or Welsh language'.[3] These requirements were taken seriously and, in consequence, Church administrators consistently monitored actual local practices by including a question on the language and/or languages used in specific parishes throughout the length and breadth of Wales in the 'notes and queries' issued prior to episcopal visitations.[4] Although centrally organized, the particular value of these visitation returns is that they were specific and purely local in nature. For this very reason we can be reasonably confident that the returns on language of worship would have been made by men with a close personal working knowledge of the communities they served. Although from time to time the documentary records themselves reveal that some livings were held by absentee vicars and rectors living in more comfortable circumstances in England, it is equally clear that on those occasions the returns had been completed by humble Welsh-speaking curates who, with a good working knowledge of local conditions, clearly acted as surrogates for absentee incumbents. In some dioceses the bishop's visitations occurred on a regular cycle, every three years or so. But although a large number of returns have survived, those that are available for analysis cannot be regarded as constituting a complete record of every visitation that took place in each diocese. On the other hand, there are sufficient data that can be co-ordinated around specific key dates. In this way, it is possible for us to explore in detail the relative regional and territorial significance of Welsh and/or English usage throughout the whole of Wales.

Minor differences occur in the way in which the actual visitation question on language of worship was drafted in each diocese, but the information submitted by local clergy is easily standardized so that each parish can be identified as falling into one of the following language status categories: Welsh is the sole language of worship; Welsh is the main language of worship; bilingual status: that is, Welsh and English are used on a roughly equal basis, catering by various means for both language groups; some Welsh is used in the services but English is the main language of worship; English is the sole language of worship.[5] In presenting the

---

[3] *Statutes at Large*, 14 Car. II, c. 27 (1662) (Act of Uniformity).

[4] Pryce, 'Welsh and English in Wales, 1750–1971', passim; Council for Wales and Monmouthshire, *The Report on the Welsh Language Today* (London, 1963), p. 13.

[5] For further details, see Pryce, 'Welsh and English in Wales, 1750–1971'; W. T. R. Pryce and Colin H. Williams, 'Sources and Methods in the Study of Language Areas: A Case Study of Wales' in C. H. Williams (ed.), *Language in Geographic Context* (Clevedon, 1988), pp. 213–22.

results of the analysis in cartographic form we need to remember that we are dealing with a somewhat generalized statement regarding the nature of regional conditions within a specific time period – a sort of 'period picture' or language 'stadial'[6] – rather than a sharp cross-section of actual conditions at a specific date, as, for example, is provided when modern census data are mapped. The four representative dates 1750, 1800, 1850 and 1900 constitute the chief points in time over which language changes are measured in each parish.[7] This, therefore, is the basis on which Figure 1 has been prepared. The point symbols representing each of the ancient parish churches reveal the linguistic status of local communities in the early 1800s as recorded in the church visitation records. However, as the map key indicates, each of these symbols also records the nature of the linguistic milieu in each locality, indicating which language continued to be used consistently between *c*.1750 and the early 1800s or whether changes occurred between these dates. It is important to remember that the three major language zones shown in Figure 1 constitute information of an *inferred* nature as to the linguistic status of whole areas and zones throughout the country. Through the adoption of these approaches, data which referred originally to specific local circumstances have been made to yield information that is of much wider regional significance.

Figure 1 provides us with a number of valuable insights regarding linguistic conditions within Wales at the beginning of the nineteenth century.[8] Clearly, virtually the whole of Wales was a Welsh-speaking country. Comparisons with conditions a generation earlier indicate that, with the exception of a few towns in the north and in the west, in the early 1800s the bilingual zone was restricted in location primarily to the borderland and also to a narrow territorial coverage. In south Wales it was confined to the coastal parishes of Glamorgan and to Gower. Further west, this same bilingual zone skirted the southern coastal parishes of Carmarthenshire before continuing westward to echo the famous *Landsker* line which for generations had marked off south Pembrokeshire from the rest of Wales.[9]

From many different locations throughout mainland Wales, bishops received reports that testified to the deep, intense and all-pervading Welshness of the people. At Llanbedrycennin (in the Conwy valley) in 1811, the Bishop of Bangor was informed that services in church were 'always in the language of the Country'.[10] Similarly, in 1809 the reply to the Bishop of St Asaph from Cerrigydrudion (Denbs.) was that 'The Welsh language is always used in this

---
[6] The term 'stadial' has been borrowed from Pleistocene geomorphology where the 'stadial moraine' marks temporary halts in the retreat of an ice sheet.
[7] Pryce, 'Welsh and English in Wales, 1750–1971', 7–8, 21.
[8] For conditions *c*.1750, see Pryce, 'Welsh and English in Wales, 1750–1971', 11; idem, 'The Welsh language 1750–1961' in H. Carter (ed.), *The National Atlas of Wales* (Cardiff, 1981–9), Section 3.1 (Map 3.1b). Figure 1 is published here for the first time.
[9] Brian S. John, 'The Linguistic Significance of the Pembrokeshire Landsker', *PH*, IV (1972), 7–29.
[10] NLW, Church in Wales Records, B/QA/19, 1811.

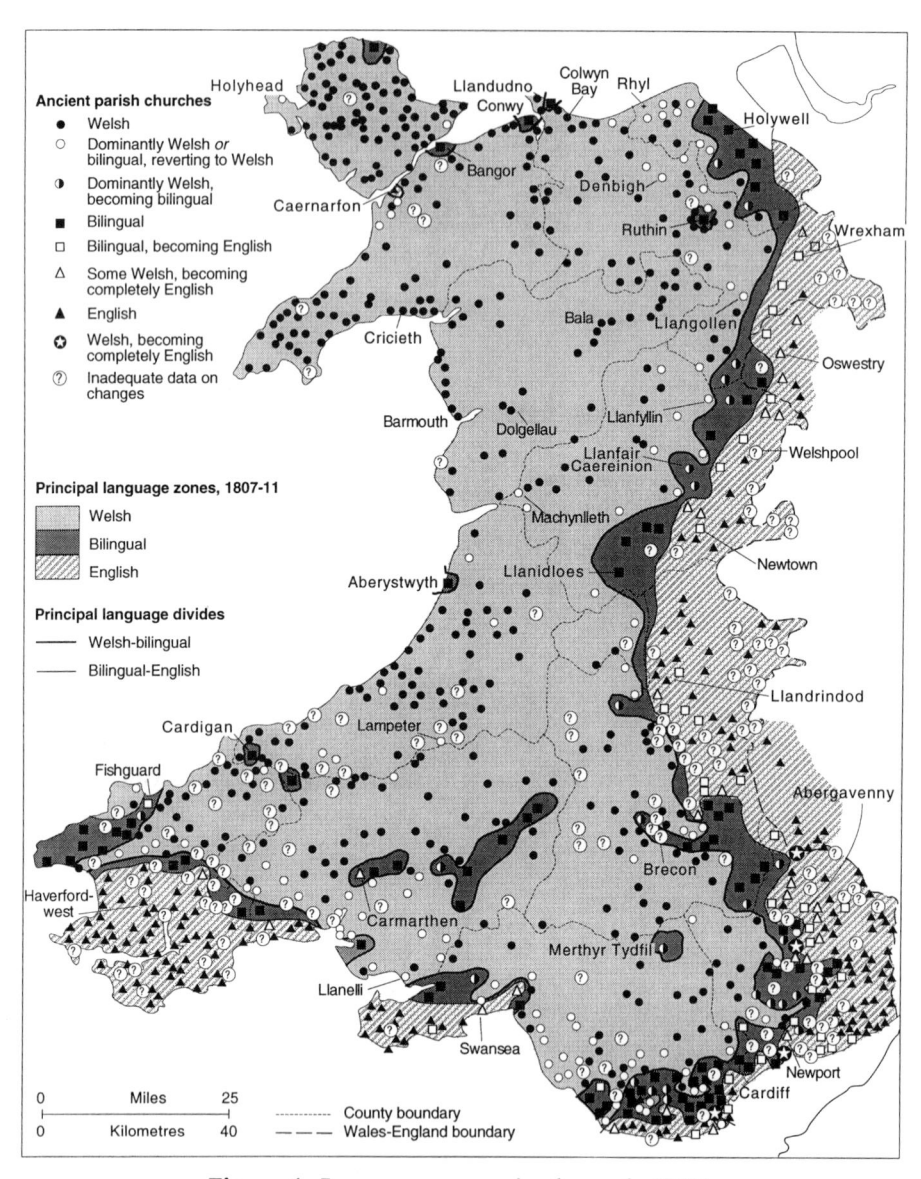

Figure 1. Language zones in the early 1800s

Church', but at Trelawnyd in Flintshire, where an English language service had been introduced, lack of provision in Welsh had prompted a drift towards Nonconformity:

> There are only two persons in the parish who do not understand Welsh, but there are many who, because they do not understand English sufficiently, change the Church for the Dissenters' meeting every other Sunday![11]

Occasionally, the clergy went to some pains to emphasize the appropriateness of their decision to conduct all their public services in Welsh. In 1811, for example, the Revd A. Williams wrote from Llandudno church, which, before the building of the resort town, was at an isolated location at the northern tip of the Great Orme:

> Divine Service [is] performed as antiently once a [Sun]Day only on account of the Situation of the Church – in Welsh most assuredly, as in Wales it is a Mockery to read the Service in English where the Congregation dont understand it, or indeed don't wish to have the Language of their Forefathers abolished.[12]

A few churches had introduced the occasional use of English either to meet the needs of holiday visitors or to satisfy the whims of Anglicized local gentry. In general, however, services in English were not well attended.[13] From Figure 1 it is clear that in south Wales much of upland Glamorgan still retained its inherent Welshness in the opening decade of the nineteenth century.[14] This is confirmed independently in the writings of Benjamin Malkin who, while touring in central Glamorgan, observed: 'it is very remarkable, that though it lies within little more than a mile of the great road from England to Milford and Ireland, there is perhaps scarcely a village . . . where less English is spoken'.[15]

Observations on the deep Welshness of the remote and relatively inaccessible uplands of Blaenau Morgannwg continued to be made in the reports of other English topographers writing at that time. In 1813, after describing the upper Rhondda as one of the 'wildest' of localities, Wood commented: 'the English language is scarce ever heard, and a person ignorant of the dialect of the natives would find it very difficult to make his wants known to them, however readily

---

[11] NLW, SA/QA/15, 1809.
[12] NLW, B/QA/19, 1811.
[13] NLW, B/QA/19, 1811, Llanbeblig and Caernarfon town returns.
[14] W. T. R. Pryce, 'Language Areas and Changes, c.1750–1981' in Prys Morgan (ed.), *Glamorgan County History. Volume VI. Glamorgan Society 1780–1980* (Cardiff, 1988), pp. 265–303.
[15] Benjamin H. Malkin, *The Scenery, Antiquities, and Biography, of South Wales* (London, 1804), pp. 72–3.

they might be attended to'.[16] Such linguistic conditions are fully attested in the visitation returns. On the other hand, several contiguous parishes between Llantrisant, Merthyr Mawr, Maesteg and Margam had introduced English for minor parts of the church service. These were the first signs of what were to develop into a series of linguistic shifts towards a full bilingual status in these parishes by the mid-nineteenth century (Figure 2). Only in north Glamorgan, at Merthyr Tydfil, already recognized as a vitally important centre for iron and coal working, and increasingly attracting in-migration from outside Wales, was it reported that the English language enjoyed the same status as did Welsh locally. But, with these exceptions, Welsh was the only language used by most people virtually everywhere. In 1809 this was so even in the valleys of western Monmouthshire, a part of Wales that was to experience a rapid and profound Anglicization in the second half of the century.[17] Thus it was reported to the Bishop of Llandaff that services were held once every Sunday 'in British' at Llanhilleth; at Capel Newydd all services were in Welsh; and at Aberystruth, Welsh was the language of worship as it had been 'for many ages past'.[18]

Nevertheless, as Figure 1 reveals, changes were beginning to occur. Compared with local conditions in the mid-eighteenth century, by the early 1800s a broad band of parishes within Welsh-speaking Wales had now begun to use English. All these churches in north-east Wales, east Montgomeryshire and Radnorshire served communities in direct contact with the bilingual zone itself. Together they constituted a broad band of territory that, by the mid-nineteenth century, was to become much more strongly bilingual. By this date, of course, north-east Wales was already in the throes of small-scale industrialization.[19] The progressive nature of these changes is clearly revealed in the visitation returns and also in the detailed reports by rural deans on individual parishes within the bilingual zone.[20] In industrializing east Flintshire a large number of Welsh-speaking churches in the mid-eighteenth century had become bilingual churches by the early 1800s, and within the new industrial townships in the east Denbighshire coalfield, churches such as those at Ruabon and Wrexham, which had recorded a bilingual status in 1749, had, by 1809, made drastic reductions in the use of Welsh and had become dominantly English parishes. Similar trends can be noted throughout the bilingual

---

[16] J. G. Wood, *The Principal Rivers of Wales Illustrated* (London, 1813), Part 1, p. 62.

[17] W. T. R. Pryce, 'Language Shift in Gwent, c.1770–1981' in N. Coupland (ed.), *English in Wales: Diversity, Conflict and Change* (Clevedon, 1990), pp. 48–83.

[18] NLW, LL/QA/23, 1809.

[19] W. T. R. Pryce, 'Migration and the Evolution of Culture Areas: Cultural and Linguistic Frontiers in North-east Wales, 1750 and 1851', *TIBG*, no. 65 (1975), 79–107. See also idem, 'Language Areas in North-east Wales c.1800–1911' in Geraint H. Jenkins (ed.), *Language and Community in the Nineteenth Century* (Cardiff, 1998), pp. 21–61.

[20] NLW, SA/RD/1–43 (1709–91, 1832, 1844). The rural deans' reports exist only for parishes within St Asaph diocese. See W. T. R. Pryce, 'Approaches to the Linguistic Geography of Northeast Wales, 1750–1846', *NLWJ*, XVII, no. 4 (1971–2), 344–5.

zone in other parts of Wales, notably in the counties of Montgomery, Brecon, Monmouth, Pembroke, in the Vale of Glamorgan, and in Gower.

All these reports indicate that the bilingual zone was now beginning to encroach into Welsh-speaking Wales. Even in the far west, well beyond the bilingual zone itself, where the great majority of parishes returned themselves as overwhelmingly Welsh in language, there is evidence that, despite their small size, some urban communities had started to function as diffusion points for Englishness. In part, this reflected the beginnings of the commercial seaside resort town. Although in 1809 the two Sunday services at Abergele were still conducted in Welsh, it was reported that 'part of morning service [is] in English for the Visitors & English Sermon on 1st. Sunday in Month'.[21] By this date, too, but still well before the building of the new town at Llandudno,[22] Llan-rhos church had adopted bilingual services. This marked the beginning of trends that, following the development of the new resort town, were to usher in profound changes. At Bangor, too, English enjoyed the same status in church services as did the Welsh language, although it seems clear that Welsh remained popular for evening worship and for the purpose of religious instruction.[23] In addition to the town of Caernarfon, the small port and copper mining centre of Amlwch was the only other place in north-west Wales to record a significant use of English.

Further south, small communities of English speakers, requiring services in their own language, evidently existed at Aberystwyth, Cardigan, Newcastle Emlyn and in Cenarth parish. English seems to have enjoyed considerable status in in the town of Carmarthen and nearby at Abergwili (where the palace of the bishop of St David's was situated). For unrecorded reasons, English had been introduced into the previously dominant Welsh services in a cluster of churches in the Tywi valley at Llandybïe, Llandeilo Fawr, Llandingad, Llangadog and Llangathen in east Carmarthenshire. English, alongside Welsh, continued to be the language of worship in these parishes throughout the nineteenth century.

As noted earlier, English-speaking communities were restricted to the eastern borderland, to a few coastal parishes in Glamorgan and to south Pembrokeshire. Throughout these areas, the great majority of parish churches recorded the sole and consistent use of the English language in all public services, thereby reflecting long-established local custom. But elsewhere, too, similar patterns had emerged. The incumbent of Llanmerewig in east Montgomeryshire informed the bishop that the one Sunday service was 'always in the English language – here is no

---

[21] NLW, SA/QA/15, 1809.
[22] Harold Carter, *The Towns of Wales* (Cardiff, 1965), pp. 301–7; idem, 'A Decision-making Approach to Town Plan Analysis: A Case Study of Llandudno' in Harold Carter and W. K. D. Davies (eds.), *Urban Essays: Studies in the Geography of Wales* (London, 1970), pp. 66–78.
[23] In 1811 it was reported from Bangor that 'the Welsh Lecture was lately instituted'. See NLW, B/QA/19, 1811.

Welsh duty'. But even in some parts of this long-standing Englishry,[24] there were signs that Welsh had not been entirely forgotten. At Tregynon, in the same county, all services in 1809 were in English, but 'a few occasional Welsh sermons are preached', while at Guilsfield, close to the Anglicized market town of Welshpool, the local clergy had finally decided to abandon the use of Welsh in all their services.[25] As Figure 1 shows, in the early nineteenth century the bilingual zone passed from the communities of north-east Montgomeryshire into western Shropshire and, thus, into England. In the mid-eighteenth century several of these parishes, including Oswestry town itself, still used Welsh in public worship even though they were located in England.[26] Bearing in mind the affiliation such communities had traditionally retained with Wales, this was not surprising.[27] However, by the early nineteenth century, although a few Welsh services were still held in the parish church at Oswestry, no such services were reported from most of the surrounding village communities. Llanyblodwel was the only church left in the Oswestry district where the Welsh language still enjoyed equal status with English.[28] Clearly, by the early 1800s the bilingual zone had shifted further west into Welsh-speaking Wales, leaving behind it only memories of a time when the national language of Wales was widely spoken in those parts of England.

Culture Areas and the Culture Region Idea

Close examination of the distributions shown in Figure 1 indicate that the most significant changes had occurred in the English-speaking zones of east Flintshire, Denbighshire and north-west Shropshire. All these were beginning to feel the social and cultural shock-waves of early industrialization. Elsewhere only occasional parishes switched from a bilingual status in the mid-eighteenth century to one that was overwhelmingly English by the early 1800s. These territorial relationships between Welsh and English are of very considerable interest, particularly because progressive changes can be linked to regional economic developments. By the early nineteenth century the former subsistence economy of the eighteenth century came to be transformed by large-scale industrialization and urbanization.

---

[24] E. Estyn Evans, 'An Essay on the Historical Geography of the Shropshire-Montgomeryshire Borderland', *MC*, XL, pt. 3 (1928), 242–71.
[25] NLW, SA/QA/15, 1809.
[26] Pryce, 'Welsh and English in Wales, 1750–1971', 10–12.
[27] B. G. Charles, 'The Welsh, their Language and Place-names in Archenfield and Oswestry' in Henry Lewis (ed.), *Angles and Britons* (Cardiff, 1963), pp. 85–110. See also J. E. Ambrose, 'A Geographic Study of Language Boundaries in Wales and Brittany' (unpubl. University of Glasgow PhD thesis, 1979).
[28] NLW, SA/QA/15, 1809.

It has long been accepted that language is the key indicator of the cultural distinctiveness of the Welsh people. This has always been the working assumption and, even in our own times, it has continued to be unchallenged:

> Language mapping is more than an academic exercise. It is an enquiry into the identity of a people and how that identity survives in the late twentieth century.[29]

The roots of these ideas may be discovered in the important report *Welsh in Education and Life* issued by the Board of Education in 1927, in the writings of H. J. Fleure and, in particular, the work of his successors in the Aberystwyth school of human geographers. Two different approaches continue to be widely used as an interpretative framework for explaining changes over time and the underlying dynamics which have continued to shape the regional geography and the cultural history of Wales. The first of these is E. G. Bowen's regionalization of the country into two major culture areas, which he termed 'Inner Wales' and 'Outer Wales'. Bowen's original intention was to provide a broad conceptual framework for the long-term interpretation of major events in Welsh history. He believed that Inner Wales was to be found in the northern and western parts of the country. These areas, he argued, had always drawn on their own resources, fostering and enriching Welsh culture to such an extent that innovations from outside were adapted and then fully absorbed into the Welsh way of life. Until recently, therefore, Inner Wales has been able to maintain its cultural distinctiveness. In contrast, Outer Wales, his second major culture province, was peripheral in nature and encompassed the eastern and southern parts of the country. Because of their regional location and vulnerability to external influences, the communities of Outer Wales had evolved to become much less homogeneous in language and culture than those of Inner Wales. Bowen emphasized that while these constituted the two great polarities that, for fundamental geographical reasons, had always existed, it was the growth of industry from the 1780s onwards which reinforced and heightened territorial differences.[30]

The second approach, first introduced into Welsh geographical research by Harold Carter and J. Gareth Thomas,[31] interprets regional differences within Wales in terms of the culture region model of D. W. Meinig. This heuristic device was

---

[29] John Aitchison and Harold Carter, *A Geography of the Welsh Language 1961–1991* (Cardiff, 1994), p. 7.

[30] E. G. Bowen, *Daearyddiaeth Cymru fel Cefndir i'w Hanes* (London, 1964). 'The Geography of Wales as a Background to its History', the English version of this radio lecture (translated by E. G. Bowen himself), appeared in Harold Carter and Wayne K. D. Davies (eds.), *Geography, Culture and Habitat: Selected Essays (1925–1975) of E. G. Bowen* (Llandysul, 1976), pp. 11–30. It has been reprinted also in I. Hume and W. T. R. Pryce (eds.), *The Welsh and Their Country: Selected Readings in the Social Sciences* (Llandysul, 1986), pp. 64–87.

[31] H. Carter and J. G. Thomas, 'The Referendum on the Sunday Opening of Licensed Premises in Wales as a Criterion of a Culture Region', *Regional Studies*, 3, no. 1 (1969), 61–71.

Table 1. The principal features of Meinig's culture region model, 1967, and its application to Wales

Meinig's regional components[1]	Essential characteristic features[1]	Bowen's terminology	Carter's terminology	Language zones, c.1750–1906 (Pryce)[6]
1. The CORE area	The zone of inner concentration. Areas that display greatest densities of occupance, intensity of organisation, strength, homogeneity, and all the principal features of the distinctive culture under study.	The Heartland[2] or 'Cymru Fewnol' (Inner Wales)[3]	'Y Fro Gymraeg'[4] or, alternatively, known as 'Cymru Gymraeg'[5]	Welsh/mainly Welsh
2. The DOMAIN territories	Areas and zones where the same cultural traits are everywhere dominant but with less intensity and complexity than in the Core. Regional peculiarities are more evident. In effect, the Domain is a transitional zone, where the culture of the Core is in active engagement with external influences.	'Cymru Allanol' (Outer Wales)[3]	'Cymru Gymraeg'[5]	Bilingual (Welsh and English)
3. The SPHERE	The outer zone of influence of the distinctive culture of the Core. Often, this is a zone of peripheral acculturation where the distinctive culture of the Core is represented only by certain elements; and where its people reside as outlying communities or as minorities within a different cultural milieu from outside.	'Cymru Allanol' (Outer Wales)[3]	'Cymru ddi-Gymraeg'[5] (Anglicized Wales)	Dominantly English/English monoglot areas

[1] Based on D. W. Meinig, 'Cultural geography' in idem, *Introductory Geography: viewpoints and themes* (Washington D.C., 1967), pp. 99–100.
[2] E. G. Bowen, 'The Heartland' in idem (ed.), *Wales, A Physical, Historical and Regional Geography* (London, 1957), pp. 270–81.
[3] E. G. Bowen, *Daearyddiaeth Cymru fel Cefndir i'w Hanes* (London, 1964), p. 25.
[4] H. Carter, 'Y Fro Gymraeg and the 1975 referendum on Sunday closing of public houses in Wales', *Cambria*, 3, no. 2 (1976), 89–101.
[5] H. and M. Carter, 'Cyfrifad 1971: Adroddiad ar yr Iaith Gymraeg yng Nghymru', *Barn*, 137 (1974), 206–11.
[6] W. T. R. Pryce, 'Welsh and English in Wales, 1750–1971: a spatial analysis based on the linguistic affiliation of parochial communities', *BBCS*, XXXVIII (1978), 1–36.

conceived originally for analysing the profile of the Mormon culture region and its development in Utah. Meinig's approach was based on the recognition of an inner 'core' area which had long been dominated by a distinctive culture group. This inner zone of concentration was envisaged as existing within a series of concentric outer zones which he termed the 'domain' and the 'sphere'. The territories of the *domain* encompass all the essential features to be found within the inner core area but, in reality, this is a transitional zone where regional differences and peculiarities are evident. The *sphere* is the outer peripheral zone of acculturation where representatives of the core culture area find themselves living as minorities in a setting that is increasingly alien. The continued existence of this regional complex, involving the three major zonal elements of core, domain and sphere, relies essentially on a strong measure of interdependency. Therefore, the changes which occur over time are brought about either by the expansion or the regression of one or other of the individual component elements. Clearly, Meinig's culture region model is a powerful conceptual and interpretative tool and its various components fully embrace and accommodate all the different areal and regional types that have been used in explaining the cultural geography of Wales (Table 1).[32]

Aspects of Demographic Change, 1801–1911

The growth of urban communities on the English side of the political divide was to impact upon Wales itself. To different degrees, the borderland towns and the larger regional cities of Liverpool, Manchester and Bristol were to become migration magnets for successive generations of Welsh people.[33] For such reasons, the changing population geography of Wales needs to be considered in a wider context. Despite the vast amount of demographic data published in census reports, researchers have to wrestle with considerable difficulties stemming from data inconsistency. The main problems arise from the fact that population numbers (published for individual parishes and townships), birth and death statistics (registration districts and subdistricts) and data on birthplace origins (tabulated only for administrative counties and, on occasion, some registration areas) are provided for different types of territorial unit.[34] In consequence, the researcher is obliged to sift, marshal and co-ordinate statistical information at a number of different spatial scales. From this considerable array of administrative areas, the

---

[32] D. W. Meinig, 'The Mormon Culture Region: Strategies and Patterns in the Geography of the American West, 1847–1964', *Annals of the Association of American Geographers*, 55, no. 2 (1965), 213–17.

[33] C. G. Pooley, 'Welsh Migration to England in the Mid-Nineteenth Century', *Journal of Historical Geography*, 9, no. 3 (1983), 287–305; W. T. R. Pryce, 'Migration: Concepts, Patterns and Processes' in J. and S. Rowlands (eds.), *Welsh Family History: A Guide to Research* (2nd ed., Birmingham, 1998), pp. 230–59.

[34] Pryce, 'The British Census and the Welsh Language'; Office of Population Censuses and Surveys, *Guide to Census Reports, Great Britain, 1801–1966* (London, 1977).

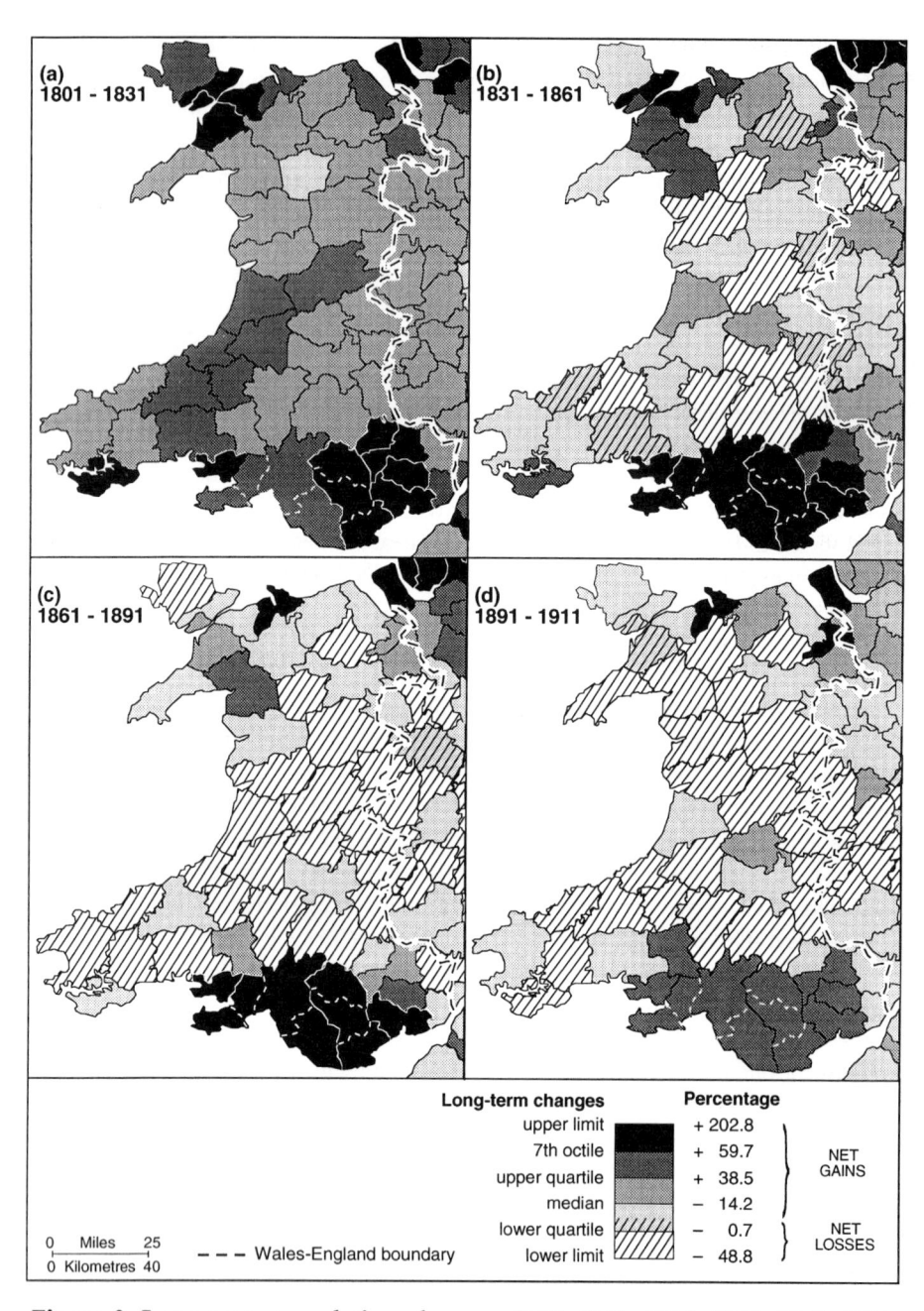

Figure 2. Long-term population changes: 1801–1831, 1831–1861, 1861–1891 and 1891–1911, based on the summation of intercensal decadal changes within each period

registration district emerges as the smallest territorial unit that is appropriate for statistical and cartographical purposes.

Because of successive boundary changes, further complications arise whenever investigation of changes over time is attempted. Several borderland registration districts overstepped the national boundary between Wales and England and in both Flintshire and Radnorshire a series of boundary changes mean that whole registration districts, or parts of a district, were switched to and fro between the two countries, sometimes successively! To arrive at territorial units which are comparable over time, several contiguous districts in industrial south Wales have been amalgamated, one to cover east Glamorgan, the other west Glamorgan. The disadvantage of this approach is that amalgamation leads to the loss of finer territorial detail. However, in the circumstances, this is unavoidable. In addition, it has been necessary to reconstitute some of the registration districts by reallocating birth data and population increases according to the proportions of the original parish populations involved. Given all these adjustments, we arrive at a total of 76 territorial units for the purpose of analysis, consisting of 40 located wholly within Wales, 25 in England, and 11 registration districts which overlapped into both countries (Appendix).

The progressive evolution of what emerges in spatial terms as a core and periphery pattern is evident from the detailed maps shown in Figure 2. It is clear that every registration district recorded sustained population growth from 1801 to 1831. In all likelihood, this was the tail-end of the strong population growth trends which had begun in the last quarter of the eighteenth century.[35] Soon, however, much of upland Wales began recording absolute population falls in the 1840s and 1850s. These decreases became further entrenched between 1861 and 1891 and continued into the early 1900s. In reality, all these signs reflected the final collapse of the old pre-industrial traditional society. In consequence, large numbers of 'surplus' country people were now released to work as labourers in the new industries. It is significant that these same demographic losses were also being recorded in rural communities on the English side of the border. In the second half of the nineteenth century, a few apparently anomalous areas managed to retain or actually increase their populations because of new economic initiatives created by industrialization elsewhere – for example, slate-quarrying or the construction of water reservoirs and dams to meet the needs of cities in England.

By the period 1861–91 three main areas of demographic growth dominated the population geography of the country. These centred on the old-established industrial region of north-east Wales, the quarrying districts of Merioneth and Caernarfon, and, most important of all, the coalfield valleys of west Monmouth and Glamorgan. By 1911 south Wales had undisputably emerged as the area of

---

[35] See David Williams, 'A Note on the Population of Wales, 1536–1801', *BBCS*, VIII, pt. 4 (1936), 359–63; W. T. R. Pryce, 'Parish Registers and Visitation Returns as Primary Sources for the Population Geography of the Eighteenth Century', *THSC* (1971), 271–93.

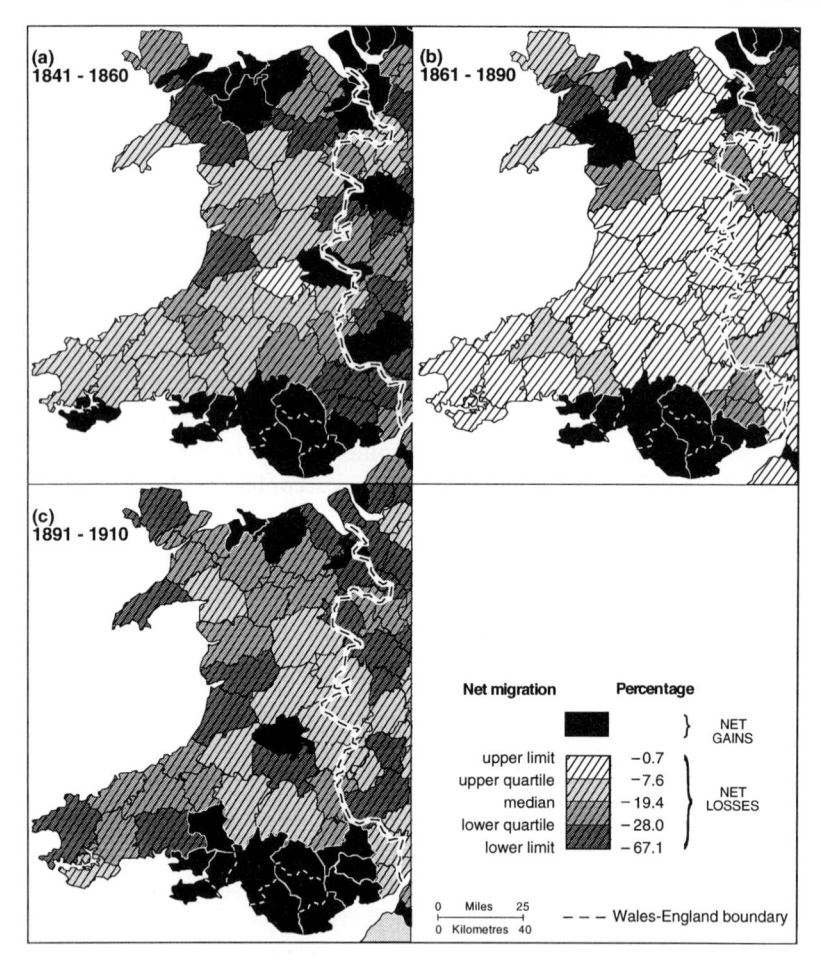

Figure 3. Net migration changes, 1841–1860, 1861–1890 and 1891–1910, based on the summation of net migration decadal changes within each period

strongest demographic growth. In marked contrast, the demographic growth formerly recorded in the quarrying districts of Caernarfon and Merioneth had now been eclipsed by the new holiday resort townships sprouting along the coastline between Bangor and Prestatyn. In north-east Wales, strong demographic growth was restricted to the more inland registration districts of the coalfield. By now, however, much of this growth was primarily regional in nature and, in fact, was a spillover of growth from north Cheshire, Merseyside and south Lancashire.[36] These, then were the broad overall patterns of change, but the

[36] R. Lawton, 'Genesis of Population' in Wilfred Smith (ed.), *A Scientific Survey of Merseyside* (Liverpool, 1953), pp. 120–3.

underlying demographic mechanisms involved shifts in the relative importance of natural growth (excess births over deaths) and the roles played by net migration into or from specific communities. Because of the lack of reliable data on births and deaths (essential for the calculation of migration balances), it is only from 1841 that such net migration trends can be examined.

The maps reproduced in Figure 3 confirm, in migration terms, the demographic decline of much of rural Wales. During the period 1841–60, with the exception of the north Wales coastal seaside resort zones, the southern coalfield, Gower and south Pembrokeshire, every locality experienced a decline as a result of sustained net out-migration, a trend which persisted from 1861 to 1910. Apart from north Merioneth (where, in the 1860s, the slate industry attracted increased numbers of workers) and the Rhaeadr district in central Wales (due to the building of the Elan valley dams for Birmingham Corporation in the 1890s),[37] population decline by out-migration occurred everywhere. Moreover, as the map for the period 1891–1910 reveals, this decline was to become more intensified towards the end of the century. Although the Welsh slate industry attracted appreciable numbers of migrants from all parts of north-west Wales and beyond up to the 1860s, as the demand for slates fell sharply this most linguistically Welsh of all industries in Wales contracted rapidly. As a result, the quarrying districts all recorded strong out-migration by the end of the century.[38] In contrast, the coal valleys and the port towns of south Wales became the major focus points for migrants from virtually every part of Wales and, increasingly from the 1890s, from outside.[39] Moreover, the rural exodus was widespread and, as the maps show, rural communities across the border in Cheshire, Shropshire and Herefordshire were affected in much the same way as those in central and west Wales. All these demographic shifts and changes are of considerable relevance in understanding the different regional contexts of linguistic changes. Were rural Welsh-speaking communities preserved simply because they lost so many of their people through out-migration or because they never became attractive destinations for replacement incomers? Clearly, net migration flows and balances are important considerations. The character of the changes may have been determined, at least in part, by the volume inflow of migrants in relation to the size of the receiving

---

[37] Census of England and Wales 1901, *Radnor: County Report* (London 1903), pp. 8–9; Census of England and Wales 1911, *Radnor: County Report* (London, 1914), pp. 30, 32.

[38] J. G. Jones, 'The Ffestiniog Slate Industry: The Industrial Pattern to 1831', *JMHRS*, VI, pt. 1 (1969), 50–65; idem, 'The Ffestiniog Slate Industry: The Industrial Pattern 1831–1913', ibid., VI, pt. 2 (1970), 191–213; P. E. Jones, 'Migration and the Slate Belt of Caernarfonshire in the Nineteenth Century', *WHR*, 14, no. 4 (1989), 610–29.

[39] Philip N. Jones, 'Population Migration into Glamorgan 1861–1911: A Reassessment' in Morgan (ed.), *Glamorgan County History, Vol. VI*, pp. 173–202; A. Poulin, 'La Famille Ouvrière dans une Communauté Minière du Sud du Pays de Galles: Treherbert, 1861–91' (unpubl. University of Montreal PhD thesis, 1996).

'host' community.[40] Could the new people be easily absorbed? Could the new people be integrated and assimilated into the long-established culture of the recipient community? The balance of numbers on one side or the other must have been crucial in the promotion of change or, alternatively, for the continuance of the cultural status quo.

It is evident that, even when the overall patterns of change have been established, the identification of cause and effect remains a most difficult challenge. In nineteenth-century Wales ordinary people regarded English as the direct challenger to the native tongue. The desire to acquire English had probably been conditioned by the sense of inferiority engendered by officialdom ever since the Act of Union in 1536. Moreover, changes in attitude by the indigenous Welsh seem to have been initiated, at least in part, through direct regular personal contact with English speakers. This applied particularly to the situation in borderland parishes but also in towns and market centres within the Welsh-speaking heartland, where the opportunities for personal contact and communication were greater. The arrival of new people in a community may have resulted in language status changes through 'relocation type' diffusion, whereas in the borderland the percolation of the English language into Welsh-speaking Wales constituted a form of 'expansion diffusion'.[41] Beyond recognizing these broad circumstances, it is difficult to disentangle all the complexities of the processes involved.

On the other hand, information on place of birth is not only a key indicator to the origins but also, by implication, to the ethnic identity and cultural distinctiveness of the people involved. From where did the new arrivals come? Town or countryside? Were they English in origin? Scottish? Irish or Welsh? If they were Welsh by birthplace, had they originated in a dominantly Welsh-speaking part of the country, from within E. G. Bowen's Inner Wales or from somewhere in Anglicized Wales, from within the territories included in his Outer Wales? During the course of his or her life, an individual probably would have moved several times, and this can be revealed, in part, by the recorded birthplaces of co-residing children. Indeed, some may have returned to their original place of birth but, if no children were listed in the census return, no evidence exists on

---

[40] A migrant is defined in this context as any person not born in the county of enumeration. In the analysis on which this chapter is based, migrants were divided into (i) those coming from adjacent counties, and (ii) those from further afield. However, because of the large area covered by individual counties and the need to use only broad categories of birthplace origin (as described in the text) these two categories have been amalgamated for this presentation of the principal movements. A considerable literature exists on the role of migration in promoting cultural change. For a recent discussion of these themes, see Ruth Finnegan and Brenda Collins, 'Staying and Moving: Links between Migration and Community' in W. T. R. Pryce (ed.), *From Family History to Community History* (Cambridge, 1994), pp. 162–80.

[41] W. T. R. Pryce, 'North-east Wales, 1750 and 1851', 75, 103–4. For a review of the diffusionist paradigm and a typology, see R. Morrill, G. L. Gaile and G. I. Thrall, *Spatial Diffusion* (London, 1988), pp. 10–13, 34–57.

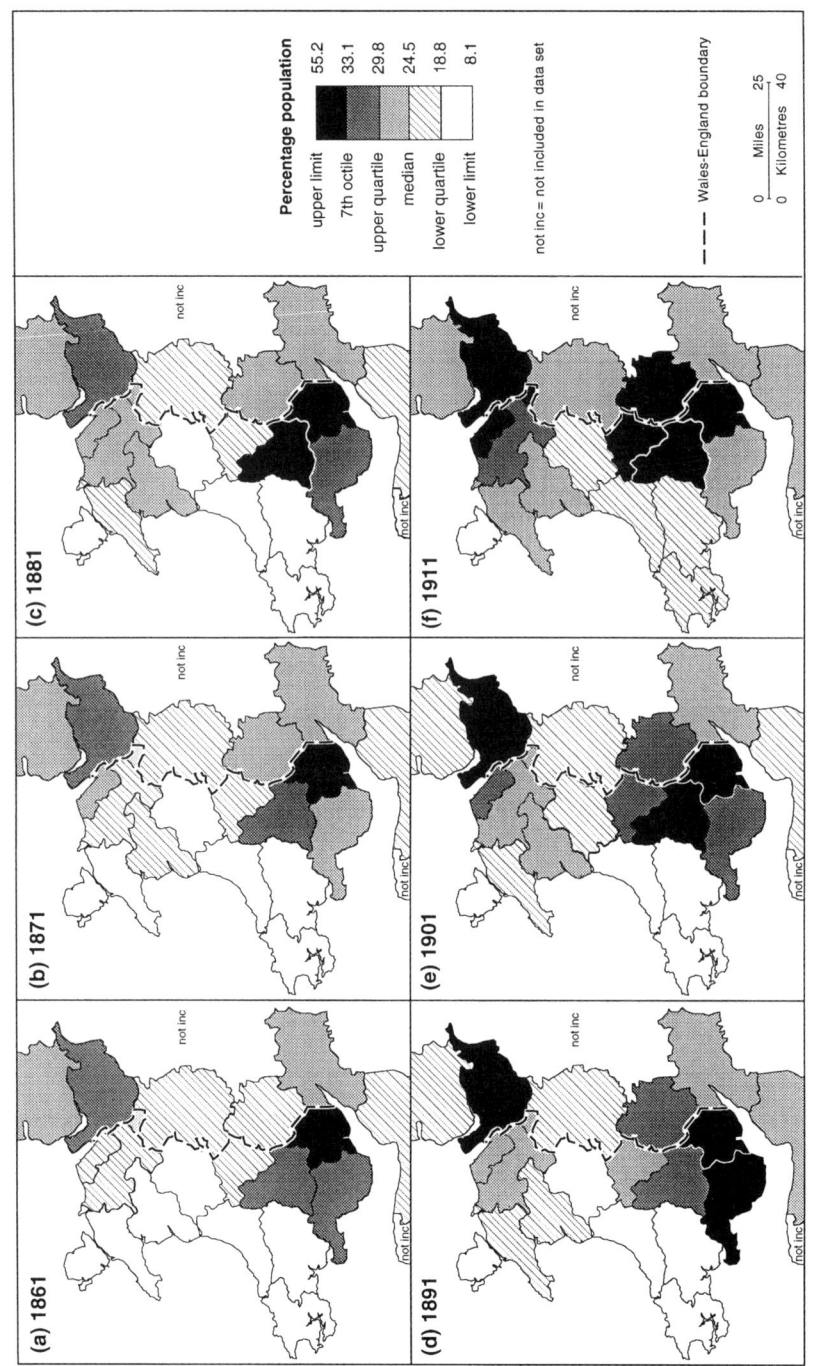

LANGUAGE ZONES, DEMOGRAPHIC CHANGES, AND THE WELSH CULTURE AREA   53

Figure 4. Lifetime migration in general, 1861–1911

intermediate moves. For these reasons, the birthplace evidence is widely regarded as a useful but incomplete measure of 'lifetime' migration. Nevertheless, information on birthplaces carries important messages for researchers in geolinguistics.[42]

Our analysis of these returns reveals that south-east Wales and Cheshire were the main destinations in 1861 and that in general these remained so up to 1911 (Figure 4). By the 1880s (Figure 4 (c)), north-east Wales recorded virtually a quarter of its population as in-migrants. In marked contrast, the number of migrants recorded in the rural counties of central Wales and south-west Wales were considerably lower, primarily because, in terms of net migration, these were sending areas. It is of the utmost significance in understanding the cultural geography of Wales that the lowest rates of in-migration were recorded repeatedly in the far west, especially in Cardiganshire (8.05 per cent in 1861; 9.28 per cent in 1871; 10.18 per cent in 1881; 12.44 per cent in 1891) and in Anglesey (12.5 per cent in 1861; 10.93 per cent in 1871).

When E. G. Bowen first introduced his ideas of Inner Wales and Outer Wales in 1964, he stated:

> The irony of the location of the Welsh coalfields is that they occur in Outer Wales, with the result that they have made this outer zone, after the Industrial Revolution, more populous than Inner Wales, and at the same time more English and cosmopolitan in character than the quieter valleys of Inner Wales that face the western seas.[43]

The validity of this interpretation is fully supported by the distributions shown in Figure 4. By 1911 every county recorded many more in-migrants, including Anglesey, where 17.26 per cent of the island's people had been born elsewhere, followed closely by Cardiganshire (19.51 per cent) and Montgomeryshire (20.69 per cent). Nevertheless, despite the increased admixture of population, Anglesey still recorded the lowest number of incomers. As the maps show, the main regional contrasts were between the western half of the country and the counties of the east and south, including the borderland areas (Figure 4 (f)).

In addition, the *specific* regional origins of migrants is of considerable significance. We know that the arrival of significant numbers of Welsh speakers reinforced the Welshness of industrial communities in Glamorgan and western Monmouthshire as, indeed, they had done a generation or so earlier in north-east Wales. On the other hand, large volume in-flows of English monoglots could

---

[42] Birthplace data were first collected in 1841 but only in a very generalized way; these recorded whether individuals had been born in the county of enumeration or elsewhere. The 1851 census reports listed birthplaces by county for persons enumerated in registration counties, districts and subdistrict. It was not until 1861 that the administrative county was adopted as the standard territorial unit for recording both the place of birth and the place of enumeration.

[43] Bowen, 'The Geography of Wales as a Background to its History', p. 27.

Table 2. Mean migration ratios, 1861, 1891, and 1911

This table shows the mean ratio across all counties for each of the migrant origins, listed in 1891 rank order.

MIGRANT ORIGINS	1861	MIGRANTS % INHABITANTS 1891	1911
(a) Wales as a whole			
England	5.08	7.19	9.08
Outer Wales[1]	4.49	5.14	5.84
Inner Wales[2]	2.89	2.91	2.74
Ireland	0.90	0.47	0.39
Scotland	0.16	0.36	0.22
Overseas[3]	0.17	0.29	0.35
(b) Border counties in England			
England	5.35	6.56	8.42
Outer Wales[1]	0.89	1.03	1.05
Scotland	0.20	0.42	0.21
Ireland	0.89	0.41	0.32
Overseas[3]	0.16	0.22	0.24
Inner Wales[2]	0.07	0.10	0.11

[1] Counties recording less than 80 per cent of the population able to speak Welsh in 1901: Brecon, Denbigh, Flint, Glamorgan, Monmouth, Montgomery, Pembroke, and Radnor.
[2] Counties with 80 per cent and over of the population able to speak Welsh in 1901: Anglesey, Caernarfon, Cardigan, Carmarthen and Merioneth (see W. T. R. Pryce, 'Wales as a culture region: patterns of change 1750–1971' in I. Hume and W. T. R. Pryce (eds.), *The Welsh and their Country* (Llandysul, 1986), p. 59).
[3] Listed in the published census reports under 'British Colonies and East Indies' and 'Foreign Parts (1861–71)' or as 'British Colonies or Dependencies' and 'Foreign Countries' (1881–1911).

easily bring about a complete language shift, with alarming speed in some colliery areas.[44] To explore these aspects, birthplaces have been regrouped on a regional basis to reflect major migrant source origins. Migrants born within Wales have been grouped either as having originated from within Inner Wales (counties with 80 per cent or more Welsh speakers in the population in 1901) or from Outer Wales (less than 80 per cent Welsh speakers).

The summary information presented in Table 2 enables us to compare migrant origins within Wales as a whole with those of migrants to the English borderland counties. In both areas English-born in-migrants formed large sections of local populations, their numbers increasing everywhere between 1861 and 1911. Since England had a much larger population than Wales, and therefore a more substantial reservoir of potential migrants, that is to be expected. Migrants born within Outer Wales are the next most important group, accounting for

[44] Sian Rhiannon Williams, 'Welsh in the Valleys of Gwent', *Planet*, 51 (1985), 116; eadem, *Oes y Byd i'r Iaith Gymraeg: Y Gymraeg yn Ardal Ddiwydiannol Sir Fynwy yn y Bedwaredd Ganrif ar Bymtheg* (Caerdydd, 1992), pp. 28–33, 103–24.

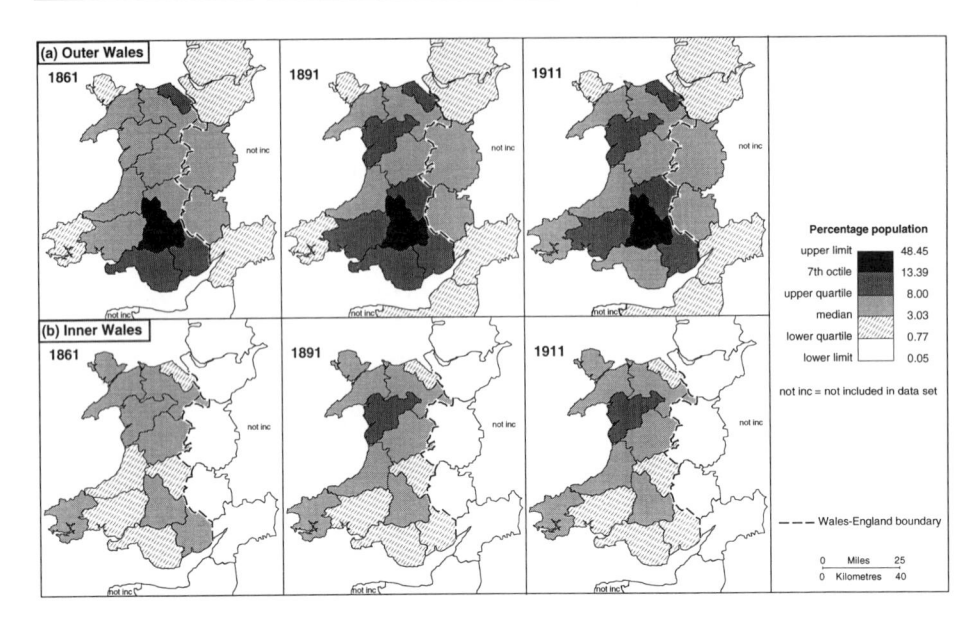

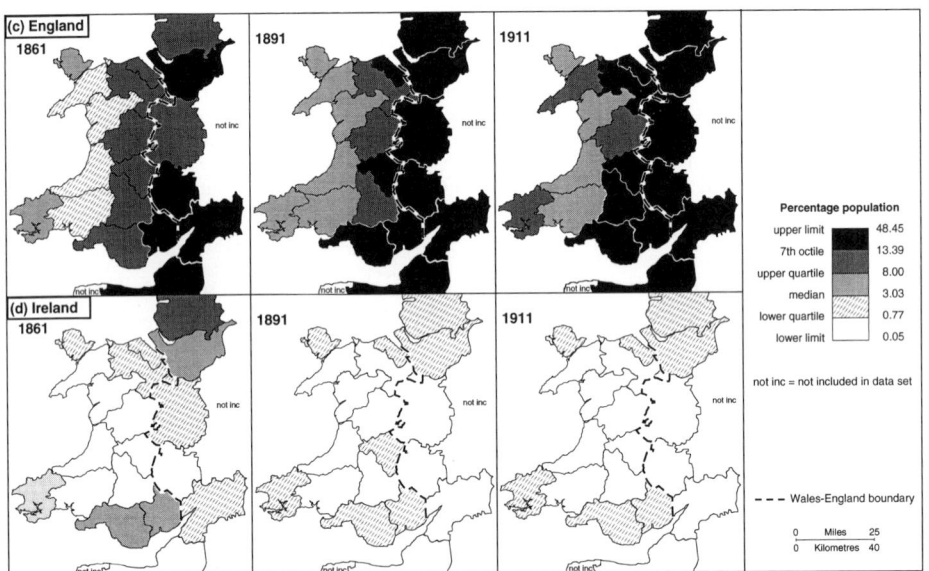

Figure 5. Lifetime migration from specific origins, 1861, 1891 and 1911

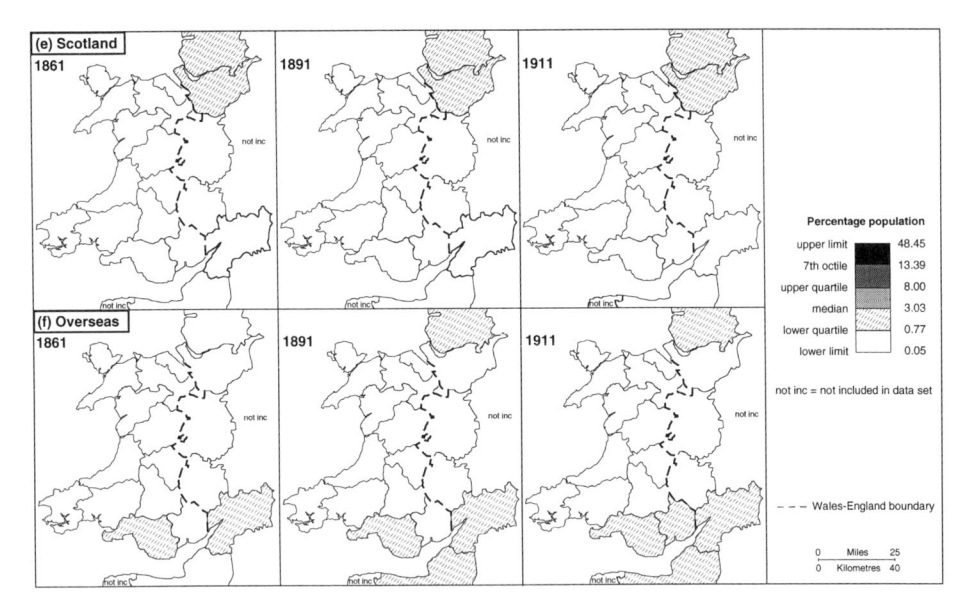

LANGUAGE ZONES, DEMOGRAPHIC CHANGES, AND THE WELSH CULTURE AREA 57

Figure 5 (continued)

5.8 per cent of the population in Wales in 1911. Those originating from within Inner Wales, however, constituted small proportions in Wales generally in 1861, 1891 and 1911, accounting for less than 3 per cent of the population (Table 2, section (a)).

As Figure 3 reveals, from the 1860s onwards much of Inner Wales was to become an area of demographic decline, characterized by sustained out-migration which deepened over time. The numbers coming from Inner Wales and settling in the borderland counties of England constituted a mere 0.1 per cent or so of the local population (Table 2(b)). In part, this reflected the ways in which the out-migration flows from Welsh-speaking Wales had become much more directed towards the new industrial communities within Outer Wales, rather than to destinations across the border with England which might have been much nearer, especially for migrants from parts of north and central Wales. These trends suggest the ways in which population transfers in late nineteenth-century Wales reflected the specific Welsh cultural milieu and, in all likelihood, the operation of long-distance chain migration stimulated by information feedback flows.[45] In this

---

[45] For a discussion on the nature of chain migration, see W. T. R. Pryce and Michael Drake, 'Studying Migration' in Pryce (ed.), *From Family History to Community History*, pp. 15–16.

particular context it is of considerable significance that, in contrast, migrants who had been born in Ireland or in Scotland (except for 1891), or in countries overseas, constituted marginally *larger* proportions of the local population in the English border counties than did out-migrants from Inner Wales (Table 2 (b)). As Brinley Thomas commented so tellingly, the nineteenth century was a century of considerable population redistribution in Wales. Unlike the situation in Ireland, the Welsh were in the process of re-colonizing their own land.[46]

That this must have been so has been demonstrated by detailed investigations in north-east Wales (with special reference to conditions in 1851) and in the Ogmore and Garw valleys of Glamorgan (1881). At local level, these research studies reveal that migrant origins and destinations seem to have been closely linked.[47] These same redistributional aspects are evident also from the maps of migrant source regions displayed in Figure 5. But now, however, further new dimensions begin to emerge.

Migrants from England gradually spread westwards into Wales in 1861, 1891 and 1911. The greatest concentrations were recorded in 1911, as might be expected on grounds of proximity, in north-east Wales and in the south-east quadrant where Glamorgan was the major destination (Figure 5 (c)). Migrants born in Outer Wales also arrived at these destinations but subsequently, in 1891 and 1911, they also flowed in large numbers into Merioneth (despite the decline in the slate industry there) and into south central Wales where they constituted a more significant presence than across the border in England (Figure 5 (b)).[48]

In some respects the regional distribution of migrants from Inner Wales appears to have been complementary to the migration flows from Outer Wales. Inner Wales people tended to seek out destinations primarily in the north and west. Merioneth again emerges as a sort of 'Klondyke', attracting people from all the surrounding Welsh-speaking areas as well as from locations further afield within Outer Wales (Figure 5(b)). These regional contrasts can be explained in terms of the nature of the migration processes themselves. Internal movements such as these were of a short-distance kind, involving step by step shifts from the countryside to the nearest emerging industrial centre. As E. G. Ravenstein pointed out, the underlying mechanisms were related primarily to economic motives.[49]

---

[46] Brinley Thomas, 'Wales and the Atlantic Economy', *Scottish Journal of Political Economy*, VI, no. 3 (1959), 169–92.

[47] Pryce, 'North-east Wales, 1750 and 1851'; Philip N. Jones, *Mines, Migrants and Residence in the South Wales Steamcoal Valleys: The Ogmore and Garw Valleys in 1881* (Hull, 1987).

[48] This chapter explores maintenance and change in culture areas over time. For this reason the individual maps of Figure 5 show the proportions of the resident population born at specific locations – *not* the proportion of all migrants from a specific origin in the county of enumeration.

[49] E. G. Ravenstein, 'The Laws of Migration', *Journal of the Statistical Society*, XLIII (1885), 167–235; Pryce and Drake, 'Studying Migration' in Pryce (ed.), *From Family History to Community History*, pp. 10–18.

Both Anglesey and Pembrokeshire, with their maritime connections with Ireland, recorded higher proportions of Irish-born people than elsewhere in rural Wales. But, except for Glamorgan in 1861, lifetime migration from Ireland seems to have been relatively unimportant throughout much of Wales. For the Irish, migration loci remained unambiguously in Lancashire and Cheshire. These locations, rather than places in Wales, had been the primary settlement areas following the tragic famine conditions of the 1840s, reflecting the key role of Liverpool as the major entry port (Figure 5 (d)). After the Irish-born, the numbers from Scotland, or from overseas, were few, with foreigners accounting for less than 3 per cent of the population in Glamorgan, where they were concentrated in the ports and in industrial districts like Merthyr Tydfil (Figures 5e and 5f).

From this analysis it appears that selective internal migration streams played a part in maintaining the cultural differences between Inner Wales and Outer Wales during the period from 1861 to 1911, and between the traditional Welsh-speaking communities of *Cymru Gymraeg* and the Anglicized communities of *Cymru ddi-Gymraeg*.

Language Areas in the Mid-Nineteenth Century

Although by the mid-nineteenth century much of the country remained dominantly Welsh in language, the most significant changes continued to arise as the bilingual zone advanced everywhere into Welsh-speaking Wales (Figure 6).[50] In north-east Wales, it had shifted as far west as Rhyl in Flintshire by the 1840s. In east Denbighshire, borderland parishes such as Chirk, which previously had made provisions for bilingual services, had abandoned Welsh completely.[51] Further south in Montgomeryshire, as the bilingual zone nudged its way westwards, hitherto strongly Welsh communities – such as Llanfechain and Llanfair Caereinion – had adopted a full bilingual status. At the same time, rural parishes such as Guilsfield, Llanllwchaearn (where the visitation returns mention the existence of a 'flannel manufacty' in 1842), and Mochdre (where bilingual services had been the norm in the early 1800s) now switched to the sole use of English.[52] In upland Radnorshire and north-west Breconshire, as well as in a large number of churches in the immediate vicinity of the town of Brecon, most parish churches had adopted bilingual services. The returns from Llan-ddew and Llan-y-wern in 1848 can be

---

[50] Figure 6 is based on returns from 913 out of an estimated total of some 1,086 parishes throughout Wales. For more details on these data sources and the method of map compilation, see Pryce, 'Welsh and English in Wales, 1750–1971', 9.

[51] Many of these changes are also interpreted, drawing on a variety of different sources, in A. H. Dodd, 'Welsh and English in East Denbighshire: A Historical Retrospect', *THSC* (1940), 34–65, and J. G. Edwards, 'Flintshire One Hundred Years Ago', *FHSJ*, 17 (1957), 67–81.

[52] NLW, SA/RD/52. Returns from parishes in the Deanery of Pool and Caereinion (1844) and the Deanery of Cedewain (1842).

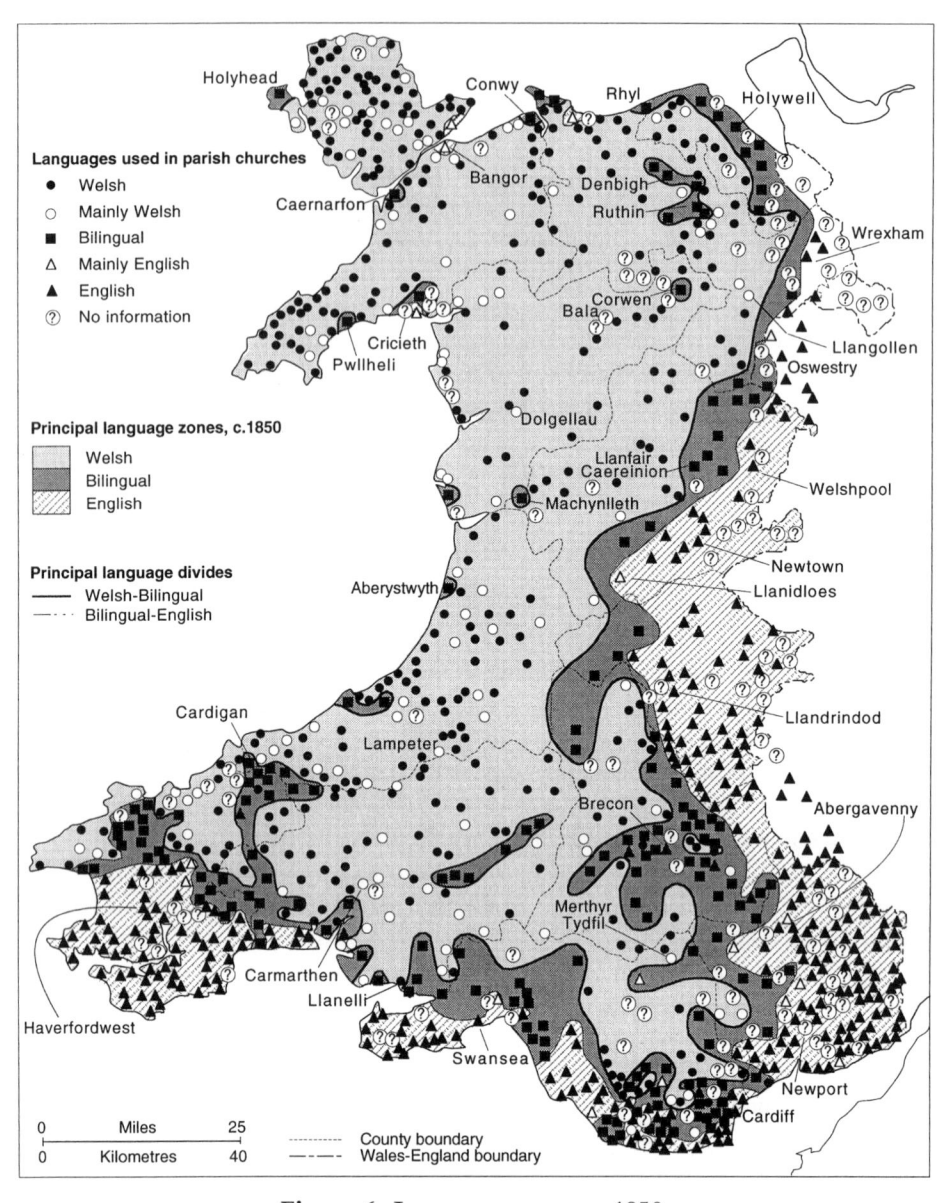

Figure 6. Language zones, *c*.1850

regarded as typical of the time. In these churches, the rector reported that the two Sunday services were conducted 'partly [in] Welsh', but, he added, 'of late owing to an influx of English to the Parish, I preach both languages'.[53]

Changes of much greater significance occurred throughout the new industrial townships in south Wales, where the bilingual zone now occupied virtually all the valleys of west Monmouthshire. From Llandenni and Llangwm, in the expanding Englishry east of the Usk river, came reports that 'very few speak or understand any other language than the English now'. Even at Llanelen (near Abergavenny) and at Trevethin (near Pontypool), where Welsh had been widely used for church services in the last quarter of the eighteenth century,[54] all worship was now in English. Nevertheless, although Welsh had disappeared from the public services, the local clergy still had to resort to the use of the language when visiting parishioners.[55] As the English zone encroached further inland from the coast of Glamorgan, it seems clear that, in turn, the bilingual zone itself was displaced so that it came to penetrate the hitherto dominantly Welsh-speaking valleys of the coalfield which by now had reached the early stages of commercial exploitation.

The ecclesiastical records contain important information which indicates that anti-Welsh attitudes, strongly favouring English for most things, were gaining ground. At St Hilary 'no Welsh was allowed to be spoken' by children in their catechism classes.[56] On the other hand, the sudden arrival of Welsh-speaking labourers meant that Welsh had to be re-introduced at St Martin's church, Eglwysilan, where it had been abandoned three years previously.[57] The decision of the churches to adopt a bilingual policy seems to have been a precondition for complete Anglicization. English was needed for communication with nearby areas already Anglicized. Indeed, this seems to have been the primary dynamic which had led to the expanding bilingual zone in the first place. In other words, the bilingual zone continued to evolve progressively through direct contact diffusion which may, or may not, have involved movements of people.

Figure 6 reveals that a considerable expansion had occurred in the western half of Glamorgan, beyond the Llwchwr valley in Carmarthenshire and around the Tywi estuary. In Pembrokeshire, although its southern limits still coincided roughly with the historic *Landsker*, by the 1850s there were undoubted signs of penetration further north towards Fishguard and into the Lower Teifi valley. The Anglican clergy, despite their own Welshness, seem to have been eager to introduce English, even in the most Welsh of places. For example, the rector of Llanstinan and Llanfair Nant-y-gof (five miles or so inland from Fishguard), who was evidently unfamiliar with writing in English, reported to his bishop that in

---

[53] NLW, SD/QA/206, 1848.
[54] NLW, LL/QA/5, 1771 (Deanery of Abergavenny).
[55] NLW, LL/QA/37 (Deaneries of Abergavenny and Monmouth; Deanery of Usk).
[56] For more details, see Pryce, 'Language Areas and Changes, c.1750–1981', 271–81.
[57] NLW, LL/QA/35, 1848.

each of his churches there was only one service on a Sunday 'at 10am and 2½pm on alternate Sabbaths [sic] and [I] place the English & Welsh promisceously [sic]'![58]

Compared with the situation at the beginning of the century, English had gained a strong foothold in many more parishes in the rural heartland. In part, these changes accompanied the development of service occupations, the railway system, holiday centres, and the settlement in rural Wales of upper-class retired English people. As a result, the churches at Beddgelert and Capel Curig introduced English services in the summer months.[59] At Llangorwen, north of Aberystwyth, the two Sunday services were always in Welsh but 'with a post epitome of the Sermon in English'. Similarly, the 1845 visitation return from Llangrannog stated: 'An English sermon is delivered every Sunday . . . for the benefit of half a dozen people – the other services are in Welsh.' Interesting evidence comes from the lower Teifi valley. Here, although public worship at Llechryd was 'in the Welsh language principally', at nearby Troed-yr-aur the two Sunday services were described in 1845 as 'partly English and partly Welsh'. In uncertain written English, the rector commented:

> I had at first here one whole English the other wholly Welch but the Rebecca riots drove away most of the English. Since, I have regularly Welch two services where I have no English attendants . . . [60]

To the east, across the mountains in north Breconshire, the bilingual zone continued to exert pressure on Welsh-speaking Wales, and in its vicinity sudden and sharp contrasts existed over short distances. A good number of parishes reported that, while Welsh was still used, at least part of the service was in English and that 'all the children speak English'.[61]

Sharp local changes in the linguistic milieu also occurred in the parishes of north Pembrokeshire within easy walking distance of the main bilingual zone. For example, a few miles east of the Fishguard town, services at Llanychlwydog in 1845 were conducted 'chiefly in the Welsh language', but nearby it was observed 'the coastguard being now stationed at Dinas and there being 2 or 3 other English residents parts of the Service and Sermon are given in English'.[62] Similar place-to-place variations were to be found in a number of coastal parishes elsewhere, especially within inland parts of the Vale of Glamorgan.[63]

Nevertheless, despite all these signs of incipient Anglicization, Welsh-speaking Wales still accounted for the greater part of the country in territorial terms.

[58] NLW, SD/QA/140, 1848 (Archdeaconry of St David's).
[59] NLW, B/QA/27, c.1850.
[60] NLW, SD/QA/17 Llangorwen (Archdeaconry of Cardigan).
[61] NLW, SD/QA/206, 1848 Llanwrthwl (Archdeaconry of Brecon and Radnor).
[62] NLW, SD/QA/17, 1845 (Archdeaconry of Cardigan).
[63] NLW, SD/QA/77, 1848 (Llansamlet return, Archdeaconry of Carmarthen); LL/QA/35, 1848 (Llanmihangel with Flemingston, Pendoylan, Michaelston-super-Ely, Deanery of Glamorgan).

Moreover, it appears that Welsh was still the preferred language of the majority of the people. This situation is reflected in the specific way in which the Bangor Bishop phrased his visitation query in c.1850: 'Qu. 10: Is English Service ever performed in your Church?'[64] In the light of contemporary trends this question is of considerable significance. The ancient diocese of Bangor served some of the most intensely Welsh parishes anywhere. Outside the holiday resorts and ports, the English language would still have been relatively unknown, especially in remote upland communities, even in the mid-nineteenth century.[65] In Bangor, where the choral services and sermons in the cathedral were in English, the Welsh language was still retained for those parts of the service closest to the people, namely the reading of the psalms and the singing of hymns.[66] Moreover, even in localities classified as fully bilingual in Figure 6, many more attended services conducted solely or primarily in Welsh than those conducted in English.[67]

Even so, the returns clearly reveal growing use of English. Occasionally, however, evidence of a local counter-trend may be found as, for example, when the bishop of Bangor was surprisingly informed that English worship had been abandoned at Aberffro and Llanfaelog 'since the completion of the railway'.[68] But in general the trend was towards an increased use of English. Initially introduced for the benefit of summer visitors, English-language worship eventually became the sole or dominant language throughout the year. In addition, as the cartographic analysis shows, the evolution of the urban hierarchy[69] meant that towns became centres from which the English language was diffused via their hinterlands into the dominantly Welsh-speaking core area, especially in the north-west and around Cardigan Bay.

The Welsh Core Area and Regional Patterns of Change

Compared with conditions in the 1850s, by the early 1900s many more communities had evolved towards full bilingual status. Nevertheless, the inner core areas of Welshness – E. G. Bowen's Inner Wales – still dominated much of the north and the west (Figure 7). By this date the clergy were required only to provide statistical returns on church attendances and the languages used for worship, but often they added their own unsolicited comments which provide interesting insights into local conditions. Thus, from the new ecclesiastical district

---

[64] NLW, B/QA/27 Abstract of Returns, c.1850.
[65] For a map showing the territorial coverage of the ancient dioceses, see Pryce, 'Welsh and English in Wales, 1750–1971', 4.
[66] NLW, B/QA/27, c.1850 (Bangor Cathedral return).
[67] NLW, B/QA/27, c.1848 (Holyhead return).
[68] NLW, B/QA/27, c.1850 (Anglesey Deanery).
[69] Harold Carter, *The Growth of the Welsh City System* (Cardiff, 1969); also Harold Carter and C. R. Lewis, *An Urban Geography of England and Wales in the Nineteenth Century* (London, 1990), pp. 54–92.

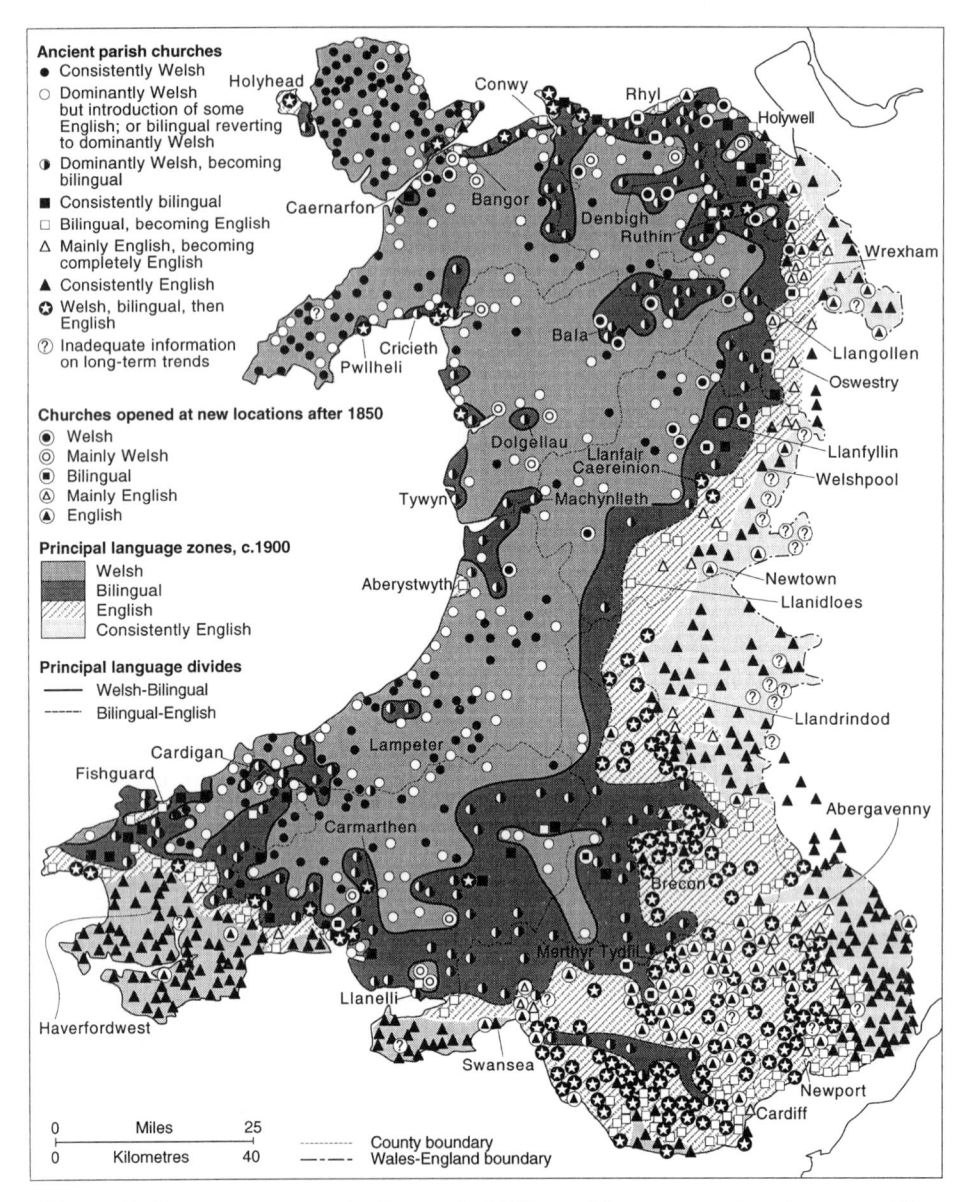

Figure 7. Language zones in the early 1900s and long-term trends at specific locations *c.*1750–1906

of Rhos-y-bol in Anglesey (formed out of Amlwch parish in 1874), the two Sunday services were always in Welsh, but in 'English rarely'. At Llanfair Pwllgwyngyll and Llandysilio (also in Anglesey), where there were five services in English and four in Welsh, and, also, at Llanbedrog in Llŷn, the Welsh services were 'much better attended' than those held in English, while at Llanddeiniolen English had been relegated to the chapel of ease so that all the services in the parish church could now be held solely in the Welsh language. A large number of churches reported, as on previous occasions, that English was used only in the summer months or, as at Tal-y-llyn, 'when English parties are present'.[70]

Further south in the central borderland, by 1902 the bilingual zone had continued to nudge westwards into Montgomeryshire. In consequence, appreciable differences occurred within the language geography of the central parts of the county. The linguistic transition between Welsh in the west and English in the east, between a small town and its rural hinterland, is amply demonstrated in a cluster of churches in the Banw valley. In the upland parish of Garthbeibio all services were in Welsh, with only two English services a year. A little further down the valley at Llanerfyl, and also at Pontrobert (established in 1854), the services were mainly in Welsh but English services had been increased to one a month or, as at Dolanog (established in 1856), 'occasionally'. In contrast, at Llanfair Caereinion, with its markets, craftsmen, flannel manufacturing activities, retail shops, banks and service professionals, and its more numerous connections with the outside world, Welsh and English alternated weekly in the Sunday services held in the town's substantial parish church.[71]

The numerous outliers and penetrations from the bilingual zone into Welsh-speaking Wales are significant because they confirm that the cultural invasion of the Welsh-speaking core areas had become much more intensified (compare Figure 7 with Figure 6). In the north, English speech had filtered along the length of the coastline as far as Caernarfon, linking Bangor, Menai Bridge and Beaumaris to the main resort towns. Moreover, by this date it is clear that the vales of Conwy and Clwyd had become corridors along which the processes of Anglicization flowed inland, thereby diluting the Welshness of the main core area. Services in many more churches in the maritime parishes around Cardigan Bay also had become bilingual. Evidently, the diffusion of English into rural Wales was linked to processes of urbanization. Indeed, all the findings presented in Figure 7 confirm the important point made by S. W. Williams that diffusion processes had been in operation long before 1901.[72] The towns involved were still very small and

[70] NLW, B/QA/33, 1900 Llanenddwyn with Llanddwywe returns; Tal-y-llyn return (Merioneth); SA/QA/28, 1902, Llanuwchllyn, Corwen and Rug (chapel of ease) returns (Merioneth); Bryneglwys return (Denbs.).
[71] NLW, SA/QA/28, 1902. Dolanog parish was created out of Llanfihangel-yng-Ngwynfa.
[72] S. W. Williams, 'The Urban Hierarchy, Diffusion, and the Welsh Language: A Preliminary Analysis, 1901–71', *Cambria*, 8, no. 1 (1981), 37.

embryonic in nature, and outside them the linguistic milieu rapidly graded into the traditional Welshness of the countryside. In a very real sense, therefore, it was rural Wales, the countryside that had lost so many of its people from the 1830s onwards, which conserved Welshness and the distinctive cultural identity of the nation.

The unsolicited comments submitted with the visitation forms provide much valuable information on local conditions and changes which had occurred within English-speaking areas. All churches in the Gower peninsula had conducted their services in English since at least 1755. Nevertheless, in 1900 the sermon text in Llanrhidian parish (which included Pen-clawdd) and the occasional sermon were delivered in Welsh.[73] But, as the rector observed, of the children 'who can converse [in Welsh], certainly none can read W.' and 'All the intelligent W. folk are Nonconformists – practically without exception'![74] Further west, in south Pembrokeshire, while some Welsh was still being used at Tenby (presumably for Welsh visitors on holiday), at Uzmaston it was reported 'Parish absolutely English, except a few [who] have migrated into it and perhaps use Welsh in private.'[75]

By the early 1900s, too, the great majority of parishes within the Radnorshire and Breconshire section of the middle borderland were returned as using the English language only. From Cefn-llys (close to the spa town of Llandrindod Wells), where there had been bilingual services at least up to 1762,[76] the bishop was told, somewhat emphatically but quite erroneously, 'Welsh died out 200 years ago'. Although the resident population had been English in speech for generations, Welsh services had been introduced on Sunday afternoons in Builth parish church during the 'visitors' season', but the rector reported that 'too few came to encourage me to continue'. From several Breconshire parishes came comments that confirm the existence of attitudes that, in general, were now openly antagonistic towards the continued use of Welsh. Thus, at Llanfihangel Abergwesyn, it was emphasized 'the children's parents *want* English'. Although Welsh was the language of the Sunday school at Llanwrtyd, a little further south at Boughrood (Bochrwyd) it was claimed (again erroneously) that 'No Welsh is spoken in the county', while at Crickhowell it was stated, much more realistically, that the 'Sunday school children here do not speak or understand Welsh', implying, of course, that the language was still used by the older people.[77]

In effect, therefore, and particularly in a context where some local dignitaries might have been actively hostile to Welsh, it seems that bilingualism was a

---

[73] NLW, SD/QA/61, 1755 (Archdeaconry of Carmarthen).
[74] NLW, SD/QA/114, 1900 (Archdeaconry of Carmarthen).
[75] NLW, SD/QA/175, 1900 (Archdeaconry of St David's).
[76] NLW, SD/QA/181, 1762 (Archdeaconry of Brecknock).
[77] NLW, SD/QA/248, 1900 (Archdeaconry of Brecknock and Radnor).

transitional stage in the one-way process towards complete Anglicization.[78] Given the conditions and attitudes which prevailed throughout the nineteenth century, once a community had became bilingual, the next generation failed to retain Welsh as a spoken language. The inliers of Welsh speech within the main bilingual zone, as in Glamorgan (Figure 7), were, in reality, residual features in the cultural geography of industrial south Wales, left behind after the advancing tide of industrialization and Anglicization had passed further into the Welsh heartland. Indeed, the industrial valleys of Monmouthshire and Glamorgan recorded the greatest territorial advances of Englishness anywhere in the whole of Wales. These two counties, above all others, experienced the most profound cultural changes through industrialization, urbanization and the arrival of large numbers of migrants between c.1850 and the early 1900s. The 'progressive rolling back' of Inner Wales in this way has been confirmed independently by P. N. Jones in his important analysis of the linguistic changes which occurred in some 500 or so Baptist chapels in these very same communities.[79]

The Culture Region Complex in the Early 1900s

Meinig's culture region model offers an important and appropriate framework in which to interpret all the changes discussed in this chapter. By the end of the century, not only had the bilingual domain zone penetrated further into the Welsh core area but it had also expanded to occupy a much broader territory than a century earlier. Also of considerable significance is the way in which virtually every small town or holiday resort within Welsh-speaking Wales has become a local centre for the diffusion of English. In some parts of Wales, as on the northern littoral, towns gained an increased vitality which continued to erode the inner core areas of Welshness.

Inconsistencies of geographical scale between the demographic and linguistic data mean that we are not able to identify direct cause and effect links between culture area changes and demographic movements. Nevertheless, it appears that the Welshness of the core areas was maintained because, paradoxically, these communities were simultaneously both sending and receiving areas in the migration process. The census evidence suggests that at least some of the out-migrants from the inner core areas were replaced by the selective in-migration of people who themselves had been born in other parts of Wales, especially Inner Wales.

---

[78] Until recently some informed commentators seem to have assumed that bilingualism was inevitably a one-way change process that ended in full Anglicization. See, for example, Iorwerth C. Peate, *Syniadau* (Llandysul, 1969), pp. 77–88; idem, *Tradition and Folk Life: A Welsh View* (London, 1972), p. 137. In the early twenty-first century, the success of the Welsh-medium schools' movement is a direct challenge to the validity of that viewpoint.

[79] Philip N. Jones, 'Baptist Chapels as an Index of Cultural Transition in the South Wales Coalfield before 1914', *Journal of Historical Geography*, 2, no. 4 (1976), 346–60.

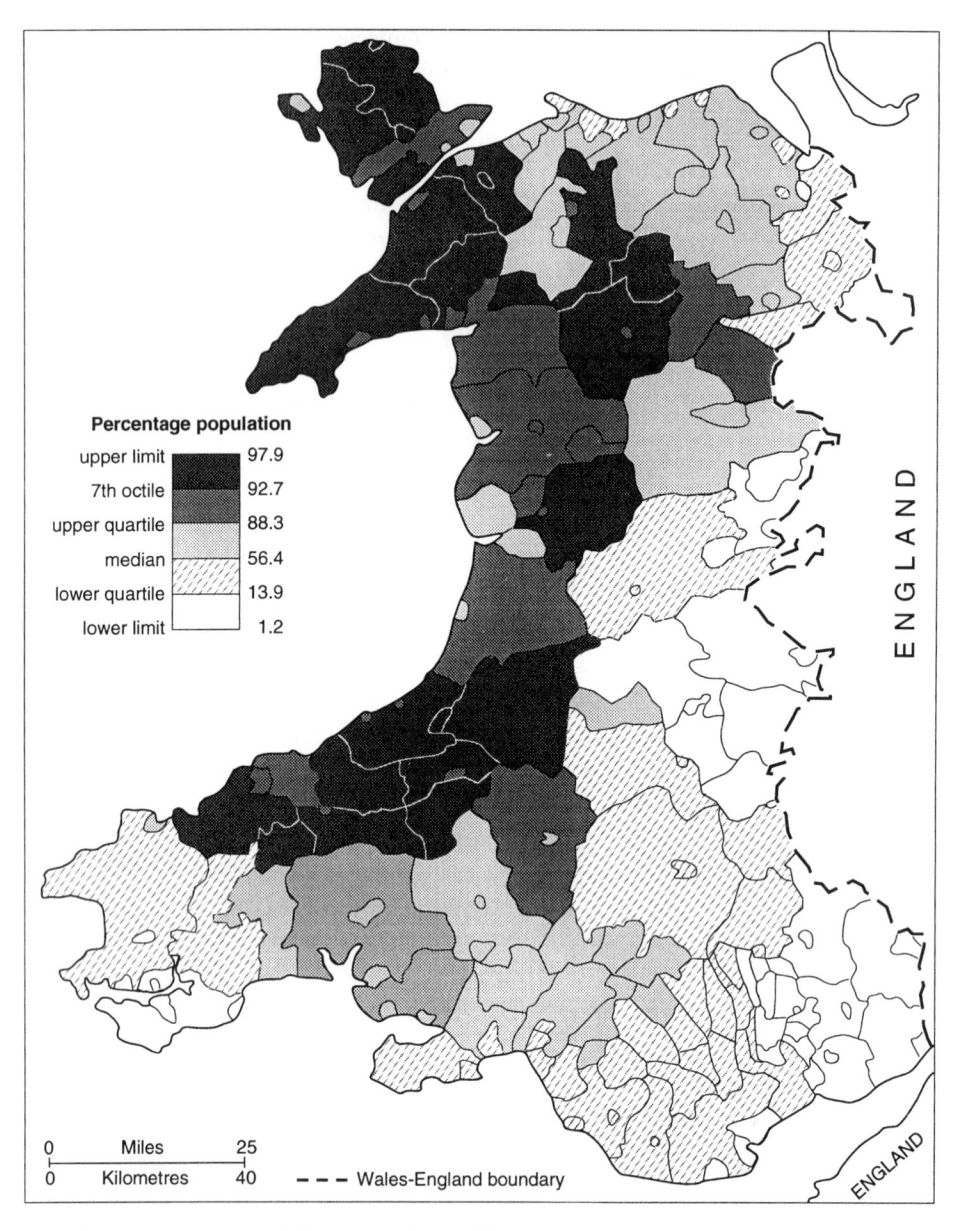

Figure 8. Persons able to speak Welsh (monoglots and bilinguals) in the population aged 3 years and over, 1911

In his original formulation of the culture region idea, Meinig maintained that the contact points between different peoples would probably be marked by signs of conflict rather than co-operation. In landscape terms these might take the form of territorial challenges and the construction of defence lines, fortifications and other signs indicating that the lands of a distinctive people had been entered. In the case of Wales, it is the bilingual zone between Inner Wales and Outer Wales, the transitional zone between *Cymru Gymraeg* and *Cymru ddi-Gymraeg* which is of the utmost significance in this context. On the basis of the geographic evidence discussed in this chapter, the bilingual zone appears to have functioned as the territory of active engagement with external forces and become, therefore, the equivalent in functional terms of Meinig's 'domain' territories. In the light of the nineteenth-century attitudes which strongly favoured the introduction of English for all the people, the bilingual zone can also be regarded, using Meinig's parlance, as the 'strategic front'. In short, the bilingual zone, whether seen from an English or a Welsh point of view, was the Anglicizing zone where, from 1800 onwards, the greatest threats to the long-term survival of the core Welsh areas further inland were being mustered.

Language Geography in 1911

Although covering only urban and rural administrative areas (but still not parishes), the 1901 census data on Welsh speakers constituted a significant improvement on the first enumeration in 1891.[80] Starting in 1901, we can draw on these data to explore the detailed changes, decade by decade. Figure 8 reveals the distribution of the Welsh-speaking population (Welsh monoglots and bilingual Welsh-English speakers, aged 3 years and over) in 1911. The census information confirms the detailed areal distributions based on the analysis of the language of worship in churches. The continued dominance of the Welsh-speaking core (areas with 88 per cent or more Welsh speakers) is immediately striking, but towns, in general, recorded lower proportions than their immediate hinterlands. Of considerable interest is the fact that in 1911 the Welsh-speaking core extended across north Wales, reaching the English border in the Llansilin area, immediately west of Oswestry. Also of much interest is the manner in which the communities of east Carmarthenshire (within the hinterland of Llanelli, and especially the Gwendraeth and Aman valleys), recorded very high proportions of Welsh speakers in the population. In these localities, traditional farming was combined with the seasonal working of anthracite coals. As a result, in-migration

---

[80] The numbers of Welsh speakers in civil parishes were first published in 1921, see Pryce, 'The British Census and the Welsh Language'. See also J. E. Southall, *The Welsh Language Census of 1891* (Newport, 1895); idem, *The Welsh Language Census of 1901* (Newport, 1904).

rates were lower here than in Glamorgan and whole communities continued to live their everyday lives through the medium of Welsh.[81]

In marked contrast, Outer Wales is represented in those eastern areas where less than 14 per cent of the local population were returned as speakers of the Welsh language in 1911. These included virtually all the local government areas of the borderland: the detached Maelor district of east Flintshire, Welshpool and Newtown in the Severn valley, the whole of Radnorshire and virtually the whole of Monmouthshire. In a very large number of these localities Welsh speakers accounted for under 3 per cent of the population. Monmouth borough, with just 1.2 per cent of its population returned as Welsh speakers, recorded the lowest proportion in the whole of Wales.

Taken in association with neighbouring areas, all these borderland areas can be regarded as representing the very outer zones of Welshness. While still an integral part of administrative Wales, for historical and for economic reasons these communities were tied to 'county towns' across the border in England, and they continued to exist within that particular social and cultural ambience. Seen from a purely Welsh perspective, such localities would not have been especially attractive as places of permanent settlement for Welsh people, either for economic or cultural reasons. In short, all these areas can be regarded as displaying features inherent to the *sphere* territories of Meinig's culture region model.

Local government areas, because of size variations, do not afford a statistical mesh that is fine enough to reflect local differences, especially over much of central Wales. The areas that seem to approximate to Meinig's *domain* zone are those extensive districts shown in Figure 8, where the proportion of Welsh speakers fell within the inter-quartile range (that is, between 88.3 and 13.94 per cent). These constitute the transitional areas that, in 1911, were in the throes of significant demographic and linguistic change, especially those falling below the median of 56.4 per cent Welsh speakers (Figure 8). The holiday and retirement resort towns of the north coast were among them. So, too, were the industrialized townships of the north-east coalfield, much of south Montgomeryshire and the Severn valley, and the whole of the county of Brecon. In south Wales, the coal valleys of Monmouthshire, parts of east and central Glamorgan, the town of Swansea (but not its industrial hinterland), Gower and much of Pembrokeshire qualified for inclusion. It should be noted, however, that because local details are masked by the large size of local authority areas, the linguistic situation shown on this map for Pembrokeshire is very much overgeneralized.

We can explore some of the underlying dynamics further by identifying localities where the most significant language changes occurred between 1901 and 1911. Since even minor changes in small base populations can yield misleadingly

---

[81] H. Carter and J. G. Thomas, 'Population and Language' and G. M. Howe, 'The South Wales Coalfield' in E. G. Bowen (ed.), *Wales: A Physical, Historical and Regional Geography* (London, 1957), pp. 254, 387.

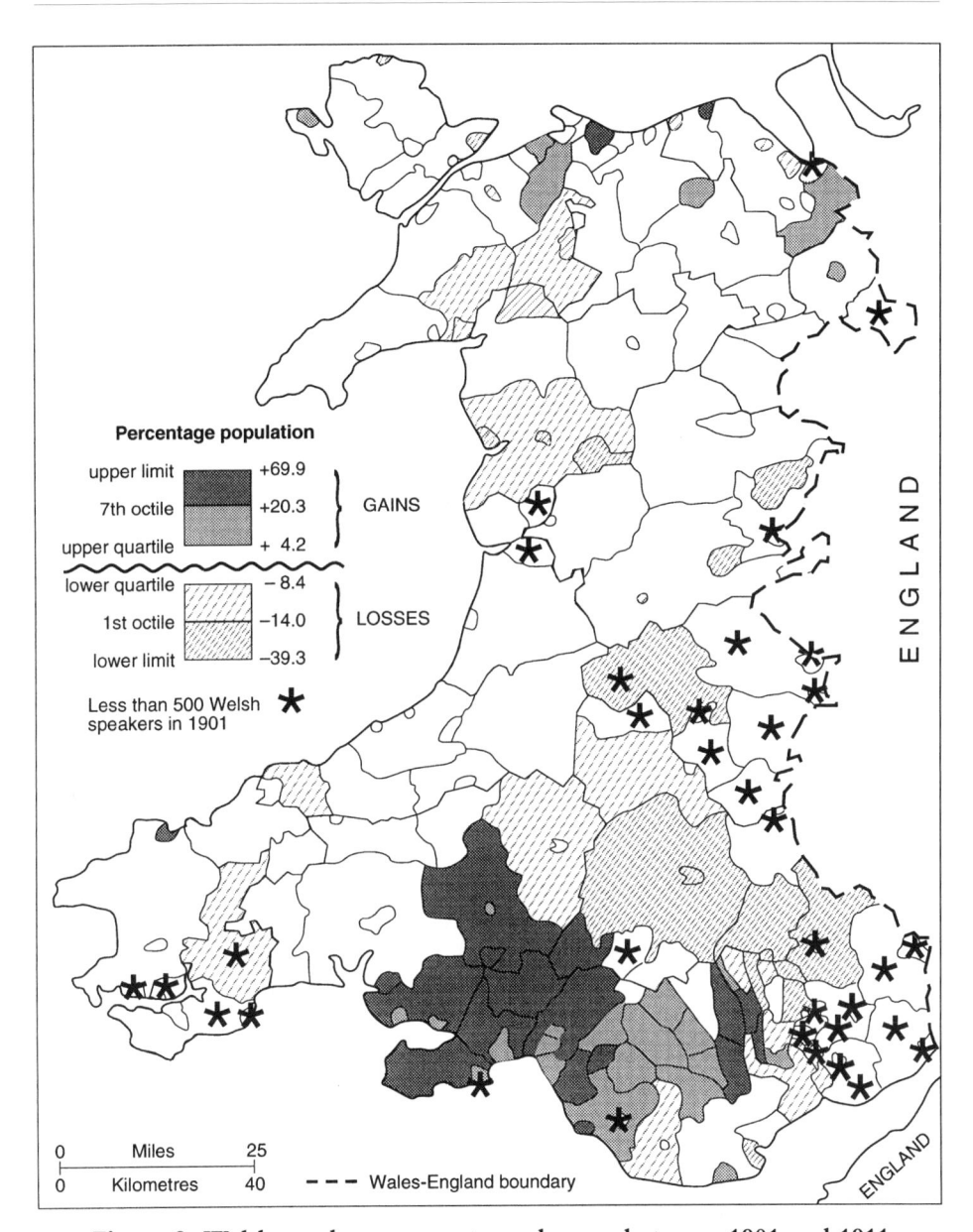

LANGUAGE ZONES, DEMOGRAPHIC CHANGES, AND THE WELSH CULTURE AREA 71

Figure 9. Welsh speakers: percentage changes between 1901 and 1911
(This map shows only areas of maximum gains (above the upper quartile of all changes) and greatest losses (below the lower quartile) in local government areas. Localities with fewer than 500 speakers of Welsh in 1901 have been excluded from the analysis of change.)

high rates of percentage change, areas enumerating fewer than 500 Welsh speakers in 1901 have been excluded from this analysis (Figure 9). It is significant that the great majority of the high growth rates of Welsh speakers in the early twentieth century occurred within the industrial communities of west Glamorgan and east Carmarthen – that is, in an arc of industrial communities sweeping around from Margam, in the east, to include, in the west, the Aman and Gwendraeth valleys. The Rhymni valley, marking the boundary between the counties of Glamorgan and Monmouth, was another locality where the number of Welsh speakers increased significantly. These were the most buoyant of localities for Welshness, but the increases also spilled over into the central valleys of the steam coalfield.

All this evidence reveals that in the opening decades of the twentieth century the Welsh were still actively colonizing their own country. A constant flow of Welsh speakers reinforced not only the Welshness of the colliery communities but also industrial centres such as Llanelli, which witnessed a 16.49 per cent increase of Welsh speakers in 1901–11. Beyond the coalfield, growth further south was smaller at Aberafan (9.80 per cent increase 1901–11) and in the new industrial port townships on the coast such as Burry Port (13.87 per cent increase) and Barry (7.03 per cent increase). To a considerable extent, these increases were caused primarily by inward labour migration from rural communities which lay within the migration field of industrial south Wales. Thus we find significant complementary decreases of Welsh speakers in upland Radnorshire, north Carmarthenshire, Breconshire, north Monmouthshire and also within the rural coastal plains of south-east Wales and Pembrokeshire. By 1911 all these areas had been sending migrants to the new industrial communities for more than two generations.[82]

In north Wales, holiday resort townships like Prestatyn (24.59 per cent increase in Welsh speakers 1901–11), Colwyn Bay (23.11 per cent increase) and Penmaenmawr (10.52 per cent increase) recorded more Welsh speakers in 1911 than a decade earlier. Other growth points were Denbigh Borough (4.81 per cent increase), Hawarden Rural District on Deeside in Flintshire (11.6 per cent increase), and Wrexham (15.82 per cent increase). By this date Wrexham, which possessed all the distinctive features of a true urban community,[83] had grown into a locally important service centre and had emerged as the regional capital of industrial north-east Wales.

These increases confirm that the Welsh were now responding in droves to the profound socio-economic changes which had occurred within less than a century in their own country. Increasingly they sought new opportunities, not simply in labouring occupations, but also in the provision of services and the professions.

---

[82] Jones, 'Population Migration into Glamorgan, 1861–1911', pp. 173–202.
[83] S. Irish, 'Spatial Patterns in the Small Town in the Nineteenth Century – a Case Study of Wrexham' (unpubl. University of Wales PhD thesis, 1987).

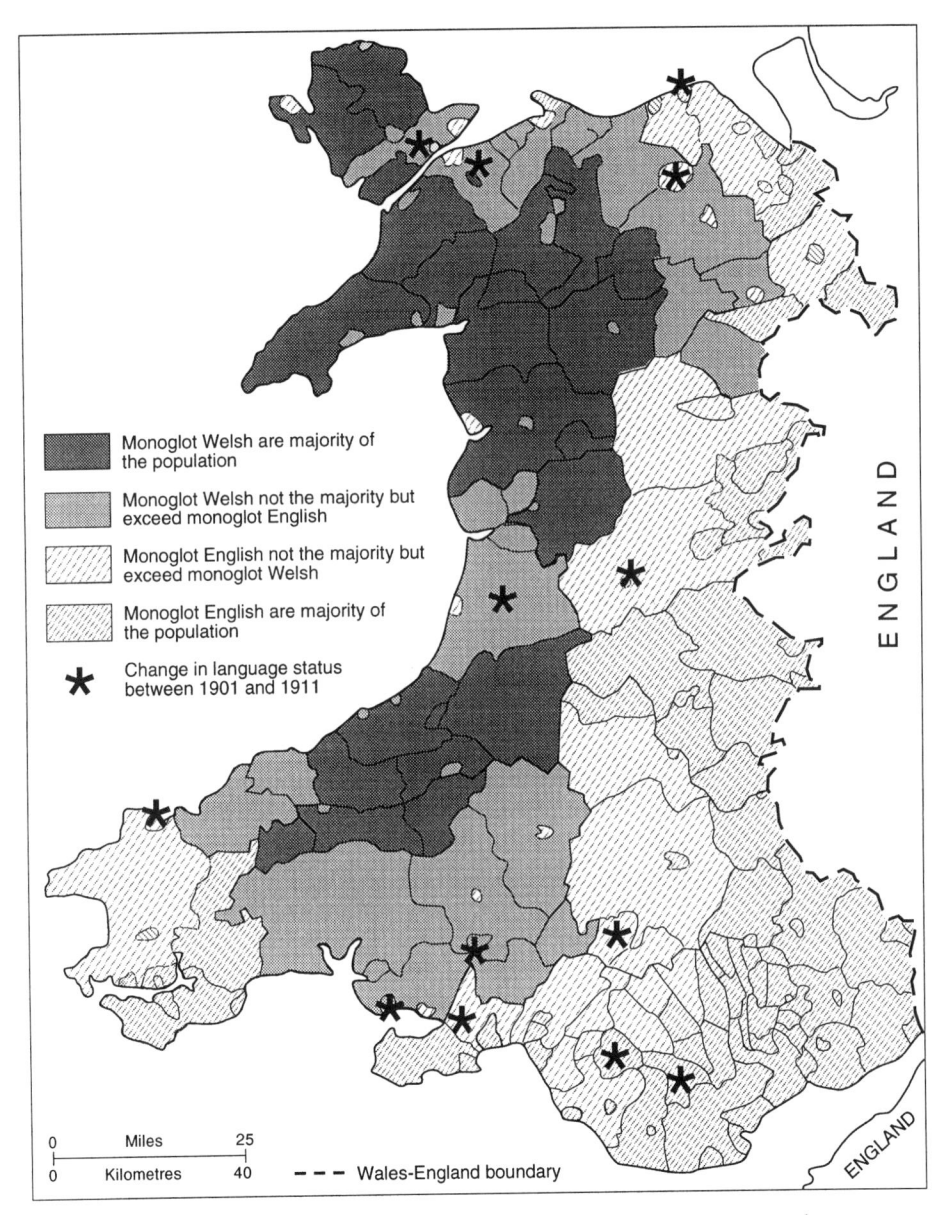

LANGUAGE ZONES, DEMOGRAPHIC CHANGES, AND THE WELSH CULTURE AREA 73

Figure 10. Language majorities, 1911, and language majority changes between 1901 and 1911

Ports such as Holyhead (4.66 per cent increase in Welsh speakers 1901–11) and Fishguard (34.76 per cent increase) were among other centres where the Welsh language was gaining strength. Conversely, the reduction in demand for building materials in the formerly booming industrial areas had brought decline to the slate-quarrying communities. Bethesda, Dolwyddelan, Blaenau Ffestiniog and Corris all recorded significant population losses. Since people in these communities had lived and worked primarily through the medium of the Welsh language, such losses would eventually have serious repercussions for the future maintenance of the central Welsh core region.

Language Area Majorities in 1911

Differences in perceptions of self and community, language and territory are inherent to many of the great national controversies which have punctuated Welsh life throughout the nineteenth century, whether in education, landownership or religion.[84] In exploring the issues surrounding the long-running skirmishes between Nonconformists and the established Church, the Royal Commissioners adopted a stance which derived primarily from cultural considerations. Their investigations involved the preparation of maps which classified each local authority area into one of four different language status categories, depending on the majority language spoken by the people in 1901. Where no clear majorities existed, comparisons were made as to dominant language usage among monoglots. In effect, the commission constructed a map depicting all the essential features of the Welsh culture area as it had evolved by the end of the nineteenth century.[85] Figure 10, which depicts the linguistic situation in 1911, is based on that same approach. This new type of map provides a synoptic view of territorial relationships between the two languages. It constitutes another form of data presentation that is different but nevertheless complementary to Figures 8 and 9 based on relative values and percentage changes. Once again, the extensive core areas of Inner Wales, where the monoglot Welsh were in the majority, is clearly evident in north-west and west central Wales, especially in Cardiganshire and north Pembrokeshire. At the other end of the linguistic spectrum, Outer Wales is represented in the eastern borderland communities where the monoglot English population had attained a clear majority. Clearly, in the morphological context of Meinig's culture region, these communities constitute the 'sphere' territories.

[84] *Reports of the Commissioners of Inquiry into the State of Education in Wales . . . in three parts* (London, 1847); Royal Commission on Land in Wales and Monmouthshire, *Report* (London, 1896) (PP 1896 XXXIV); Royal Commission on the Church of England and Other Religious Bodies in Wales and Monmouthshire, *Report* (5 vols., London, 1910–11).

[85] Royal Commission on the Church of England and Other Religious Bodies, *Report*, I, part 2 (1911), Appendix, 'Language Map of Wales and Monmouthshire (based on the census of 1901)' (London, 1911). The method of compilation is evaluated in Pryce and Williams, 'Sources and Methods in the Study of Language Areas: A Case Study of Wales', pp. 189–90.

Between the two major culture provinces the important transitional domain territories can be identified. In these localities processes of language change and ascendancy were in operation, and neither of the monoglot groups constituted a majority.

But, in addition, Figure 10 also reveals evidence of the progressive changes which would continue throughout the later decades of the twentieth century. The territorial retreat of the core Welsh-speaking area is evident in a number of key localities whose regional locations are significant: Prestatyn and Denbigh town in north-east Wales; local authority areas on either side of the Menai Straits in north-west Wales; the Glamorgan coalfield and the anthracite coalfield extending into east Carmarthenshire; and also Fishguard. Most significant of all were the status changes in central Wales in the Aberystwyth Rural District Council area, where the number of monoglot Welsh ceased to constitute a majority of the population in 1911. These latter changes need to be considered in the context of the links that this area was evidently developing with the Anglicized communities of south Montgomeryshire, across the mountains in the upper Severn valley. Here we see the first signs which heralded the eventual break-up of the heartland core area into separate northern and southern components, a development which attracted some concern after the 1971 census.[86]

Less intensely Welsh than was the case in the early 1800s, the inner core area still existed in 1911. By then, however, it had contracted to occupy less of the national territory than previously, but its very existence was still bound up, symbiotically, with the outer series of concentric regional structures. These structures were essential to the continued survival of the whole culture region complex.

The situation charted in Figure 10 is that of a country which, in the words of Kenneth O. Morgan, had reached its 'Edwardian high noon'.[87] Henceforth, although the public sense of national awareness and confidence would grow, the everyday use of the Welsh language would be less and less community-based. This certainly occurred within the Meinig-type transitional 'domain' areas which fringed the cultural core areas in the north and west of the country. Within these intermediate communities, the Welsh language remained alive, continued to be widely used and enjoyed good standing. Nevertheless, its use became increasingly confined to particular networks and social settings, especially to religious activities, traditional farming life, small community businesses and individual families.[88]

---

[86] E. G. Bowen and H. Carter, 'Preliminary Observations on the Distribution of the Welsh Language at the 1971 Census', *The Geographical Journal*, 140, pt. 3 (1974), 432–40.

[87] Kenneth O. Morgan, *Rebirth of a Nation: Wales 1880–1980* (Oxford, 1982), pp. 123–55.

[88] The ways in which Welsh became restricted to specific usage domains (as opposed to the territorial 'domain' of Meinig's culture region model) are discussed in the 'historical overview' provided in John Aitchison and Harold Carter, *A Geography of the Welsh Language 1961–1991* (Cardiff, 1994), p. 30 onwards.

Appendix

Wales and the border areas: territorial units for statistical and cartographic purposes 1801–1911

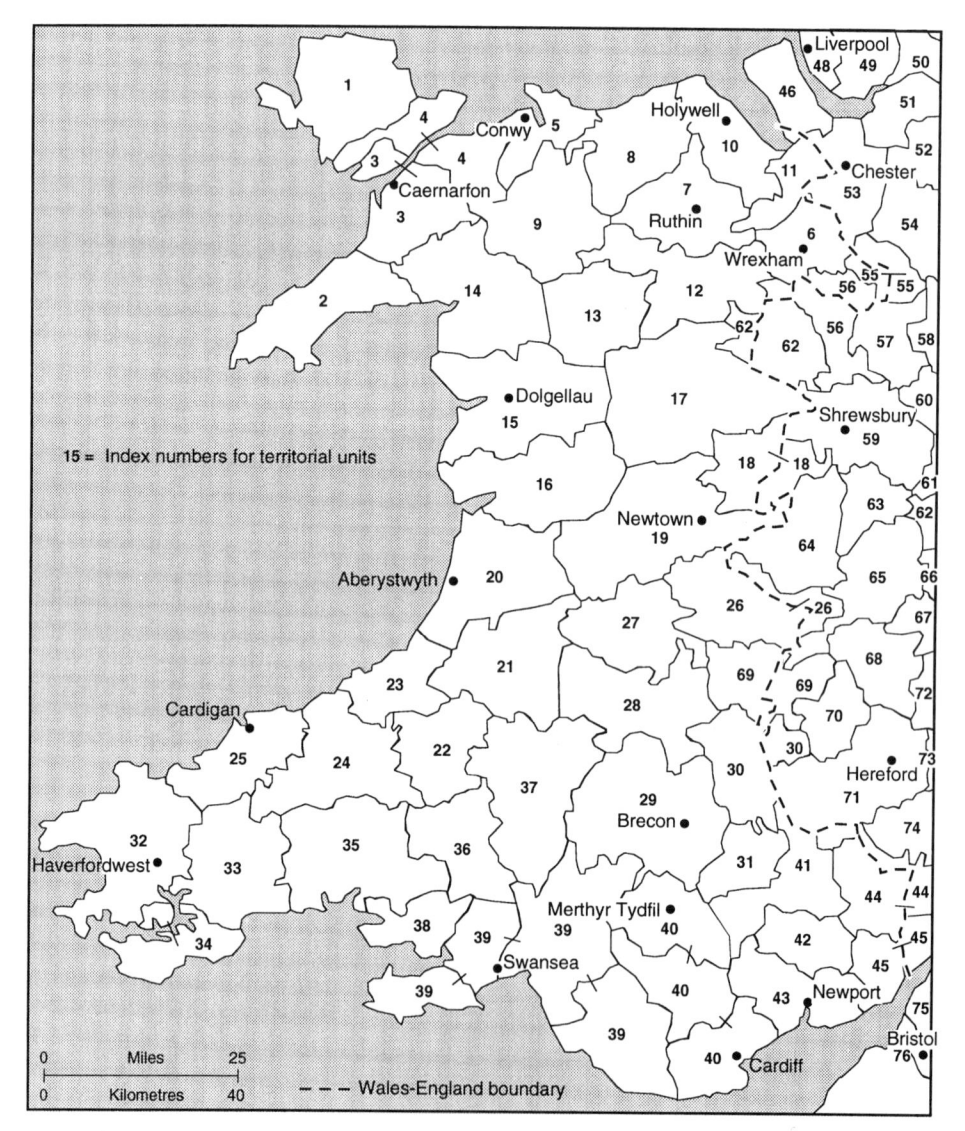

Figure 11. Territorial units for statistical and cartographic purposes (demographic data)

LANGUAGE ZONES, DEMOGRAPHIC CHANGES, AND THE WELSH CULTURE AREA

The areas listed below are based directly on the composition of registration districts as recorded in the 1871 census. Because of inconsistent boundaries, some territorial units have been adjusted to produce the standardized areas shown in Figure 11. Details of these adjustments are given in the notes below.

The official names of registration districts and registration counties appear below in the form recorded in the census reports.

Areas overstepping the Wales–England national boundary are marked below with an asterisk*.

Base map reference number	Areal Unit Name	Origin (Registration District: reference number and name)	Registration County
1	Anglesey	627 Anglesey	Anglesey
2	Pwllheli	623 Pwllheli	Carnarvonshire
3	Caernarfon	624 Carnarvon	Carnarvonshire
4	Bangor	625 Bangor	Carnarvonshire
5	Conwy	626 Conway	Carnarvonshire
6	Wrexham	615 Wrexham	Denbighshire
7	Ruthin	616 Ruthin	Denbighshire
8	St Asaph	617 St. Asaph	Denbighshire
9	Llanrwst	618 Llanrwst	Denbighshire
10	Holywell	614 Holywell	Flintshire
11	Hawarden[1]	452 Chester (part)	Cheshire
12	Corwen	619 Corwen	Merionethshire
13	Bala	620 Bala	Merionethshire
14	Ffestiniog	622 Festiniog	Merionethshire
15	Dolgellau	621 Dolgelley	Merionethshire
16	Machynlleth	610 Machynlleth	Montgomeryshire
17	Llanfyllin	613 Llanfyllin	Montgomeryshire
18	*Forden	612 Forden	Montgomeryshire
19	Newtown	611 Newtown	Montgomeryshire
20	Aberystwyth	601 Aberystwith	Cardiganshire
21	Tregaron	602 Tregaron	Cardiganshire
22	Lampeter	599 Lampeter	Cardiganshire
23	Aberaeron	600 Aberayron	Cardiganshire
24	Newcastle Emlyn	598 Newcastle in Emlyn	Cardiganshire
25	Cardigan	597 Cardigan	Cardiganshire
26	*Knighton[2]	607 Presteigne; 608 Knighton	Radnorshire
27	Rhaeadr	609 Rhayader	Radnorshire
28	Builth	603 Builth	Brecknockshire
29	Brecon	604 Brecknock	Brecknockshire
30	*Hay	606 Hay	Brecknockshire
31	Crickhowell	605 Crickhowell	Brecknockshire
32	Haverfordwest	596 Haverfordwest	Pembrokeshire
33	Narberth	594 Narberth	Pembrokeshire
34	Pembroke	595 Pembroke	Pembrokeshire
35	Carmarthen	593 Carmarthen	Carmarthenshire
36	Llandeilo Fawr	592 Llandilofawr	Carmarthenshire
37	Llandovery	591 Llandovery	Carmarthenshire
38	Llanelli	590 Llanelly	Carmarthenshire

Base map reference number	Areal Unit Name	Origin (Registration District: reference number and name)	Registration County
39	West Glamorgan[3]	586 Bridgend; 587 Neath; 588 Swansea; 589 Gower	Glamorganshire
40	East Glamorgan[3]	583 Cardiff; 584 Pontypridd; 585 Merthyr Tydfil	Glamorganshire
41	Abergavenny[4]	579 Abergavenny; 580 Bedwellty	Monmouthshire
42	Pontypool	581 Pontypool	Monmouthshire
43	Newport	582 Newport	Monmouthshire
44	*Monmouth	578 Monmouth	Monmouthshire
45	*Chepstow	577 Chepstow	Monmouthshire
46	Wirral and Birkenhead[5]	453 Wirral; 454 Birkenhead	Cheshire
47	Liverpool	455 Liverpool	Lancashire
48	West Derby	456 West Derby	Lancashire
49	Prescot	457 Prescot	Lancashire
50	Warrington	460 Warrington	Lancashire
51	Runcorn	448 Runcorn	Cheshire
52	Northwich	449 Northwich	Cheshire
53	Chester[1]	452 Chester (part)	Cheshire
54	Nantwich	451 Nantwich	Cheshire
55	*Whitchurch	356 Whitchurch	Shropshire
56	*Ellesmere	354 Ellesmere	Shropshire
57	Wem	355 Wem	Shropshire
58	Market Drayton	357 Market Drayton	Shropshire
59	*Shrewsbury	351 Atcham	Shropshire
60	Wellington	358 Wellington	Shropshire
61	Madeley	350 Madeley	Shropshire
62	Bridgnorth	348 Bridgnorth	Shropshire
62	Oswestry	353 Oswestry	Shropshire
63	Church Stretton	346 Church Stretton	Shropshire
64	Clun	345 Clun	Shropshire
66	Cleobury Mortimer	347 Cleobury Mortimer	Shropshire
65	*Ludlow	344 Ludlow	Shropshire
68	Leominster	342 Leominster	Herefordshire
69	*Kington	343 Kington	Herefordshire
70	Weobly	340 Weobly	Herefordshire
71	*Hereford	339 Hereford	Herefordshire
72	Bromyard	341 Bromyard	Herefordshire
73	Ledbury	337 Ledbury	Herefordshire
74	Ross	338 Ross	Herefordshire
75	Thornbury	323 Thornbury	Gloucestershire
76	Bristol	320 Bristol; 321 Clifton	Gloucestershire

NOTES

[1] Hawarden area (area no. 11) comprises Hawarden Registration Subdistrict (parishes of Higher Kinnerton, Hawarden, Saltney, Treyddyn, Hope, Marford and Hoseley) which in 1871 was part of no. 452 Chester Registration District. Data have been extracted from the latter according to local percentage shares of the population.

[2] On 1 July 1877 Presteigne Registration District was dissolved and its territory divided between Knighton (Radnorshire) and Kington (Herefordshire) Registration Districts. The Knighton area used for mapping purposes is based on the amalgamation of the former Presteigne, Knighton and

Llanbister Registration Districts for the period 1841–71. Data have been allocated to both the Knighton and Kington areas according to local percentage shares of the population.

[3] Because of successive boundary changes from 1871 onwards the registration districts of Cardiff, Pontypridd and Merthyr Tydfil have been merged to form the East Glamorgan area for mapping purposes. West Glamorgan comprises the registration districts of Bridgend, Neath, Pontardawe, Swansea and Gower.

[4] Bedwellty Registration District was created by regrouping parts of Abergavenny Registration District on 1 July 1861. Data for these two registration districts have been merged to produce a consistent territorial unit between 1801 and 1911.

[5] Because of successive boundary changes, the data for the registration districts of Liverpool and Toxteth Park (known as West Derby up to 1871) have been merged to create a consistent territorial unit for statistical and mapping purposes.

2

A Cauldron of Rebirth: Population and the Welsh Language in the Nineteenth Century

BRINLEY THOMAS

IN AN ARTICLE, 'Wales and the Atlantic Economy', published in 1959,[1] the present writer argued that the population explosion in Wales in the second half of the nineteenth century was a blessing to the Welsh language. Welsh people who had to leave the countryside did not have to emigrate to England or overseas: they were able to migrate to the rapidly expanding industrial areas of south and north Wales, where they raised large Welsh-speaking families. The 1891 census recorded 870,730 Welsh speakers in Wales (excluding Monmouthshire), 72 per cent of whom were living in the five counties most affected by industrialization, namely Glamorgan, Carmarthenshire, Denbighshire, Flintshire and Caernarfonshire. I ventured to conclude as follows:

> Instead of bemoaning the rural exodus, the Welsh patriot should sing the praises of industrial development. In that tremendous half-century before the First World War, economic growth in Wales was so vigorous that her net loss of people by emigration was a mere 4 per cent. of her bountiful natural increase over the period. Few countries in Europe came anywhere near to that. The unrighteous Mammon in opening up the coalfields at such a pace unwittingly gave the Welsh language a new lease of life and Welsh Nonconformity a glorious high noon.[2]

This doctrine did not go down very well; it departed too abruptly from the orthodox view enshrined in the Welsh history textbooks. Had we not all been brought up to believe that industrialization and capitalism were a powerful Anglicizing force which swept over most of Wales in the nineteenth century, leaving the rural counties of the north and west as the strongholds of the Welsh tradition? The countryside – *cefn gwlad* – was regarded as the heartland of all that is enduring in our national culture, and the flight from the land had been a

---

[1] Brinley Thomas, 'Wales and the Atlantic Economy', *Scottish Journal of Political Economy*, VI, no. 3 (1959), 169–92, reprinted in Brinley Thomas (ed.), *The Welsh Economy: Studies in Expansion* (Cardiff, 1962), pp. 1–29.
[2] Idem, 'Wales and the Atlantic Economy', *Scottish Journal of Political Economy*, 192.

paralysing disease. David Williams, a leading Welsh historian, in his authoritative *A History of Modern Wales*, published in 1950, put the matter as follows:

> In the course of the nineteenth century the industrialisation of Wales added a further division in so far as it brought in a large non-Welsh population which has never been assimilated . . . The building of roads and railways, and the enormous growth of Welsh industry as part of the economic development of Britain, profoundly affected Welsh life; so much so that there is a marked tendency to regard Welsh culture as being in essence the culture of rural Wales and not of the industrial areas.[3]

My studies had led me to the opposite proposition that, from the point of view of the Welsh language, industrialization in the nineteenth century was the hero, not the villain, of the piece. For some time there was scepticism about this notion, but then the intellectual climate began to change and the dissenting proposition became respectable enough to appear as a question in an A-level Welsh history examination paper. Several economic historians and geographers entered this field of research and a substantial body of new evidence accumulated. Indeed, it appears that the heresy of yesterday may now be admitted to the canon.

However controversy still persists. Dudley Baines, in his book on migration in England and Wales, 1861–1900,[4] criticizes what he calls '. . . the Brinley Thomas thesis that the pattern of Welsh migration was qualitatively different from the English'.[5] The essence of his case is as follows:

> Emigration (abroad, including Scotland and Ireland) from rural Wales was at its peak in the decade (1880s) when the South Wales coalfield was at its maximum rate of expansion in the century . . . The pattern of emigration from rural Wales was no different from the pattern from most of the English urban and rural counties. Consequently, the industrialization of Wales cannot have seriously affected either the rate or the timing of emigration from the Welsh rural counties.[6]

This argument, however, is based on misleading statistics. Baines's total of 40,600 Welsh rural-born emigrants in the 1880s represents persons born in rural Wales, wherever they were living in England and Wales.[7] The figure needs to be corrected for stage emigration, that is, persons born in rural Wales who had moved to Glamorgan, Monmouthshire or England, and had emigrated abroad

---

[3] David Williams, *A History of Modern Wales* (London, 1950), p. 269.
[4] Dudley Baines, *Migration in a Mature Economy: Emigration and Internal Migration in England and Wales, 1861–1900* (Cambridge, 1985). Chapter 10 is devoted to 'Wales and the Atlantic Economy, 1861–1910'.
[5] Ibid., p. 268.
[6] Ibid., p. 270. Rural Wales in Baines's analysis means the counties of Wales other than Glamorgan and Monmouthshire.
[7] Ibid., Tables 10.2 and 10.3, based on Appendix 1.

from their new places of residence. Baines's own estimate of average stage emigration from rural Wales for 1861–1900 is 43 per cent for males and 40.5 per cent for females.[8] This correction yields the following result:

Areas of departure of Welsh rural-born emigrants	1881–90
England	10,300
Glamorgan and Monmouthshire	6,800
Rural Wales	23,500

Thus, the volume of direct net emigration abroad from rural Wales in the 1880s is 23,500 not 40,600. This is 2.4 per cent of the native population instead of Baines's 4.2 per cent. In contrast, the rate of emigration from England in that decade is 3.5 per cent.[9] The inference drawn by Baines that the rate of emigration from rural Wales in the 1880s was 'exceptionally high',[10] in line with the English pattern, is unwarranted. The industrialization of Wales was the major factor determining the rate and timing of emigration from Welsh rural and industrial counties. Baines himself implicitly admits this when he finds that 'the migration pattern of industrial South Wales and London was quite different from that in the other urban counties',[11] and he adds that this distinctive pattern 'is consistent with the idea that the building cycle in London and South Wales was distinct from that in the country as a whole'.[12] This point confirms the present writer's analysis.[13]

Baines expressed strong judgements on Anglicization and Welsh culture, without any reference to the census sources on the Welsh-speaking population. Stressing that half the population of Glamorgan in 1901 was of English extraction, he declares that 'the migration of rural Welsh to Glamorgan and Monmouth cannot of *itself* disprove the view that industrial Wales was Anglicized in the late nineteenth and early twentieth centuries'.[14] There is no dispute about the powerful wave of Anglicization early in the twentieth century or that Monmouthshire had been thoroughly Anglicized by the late nineteenth century. The question at issue is the scale of Welshness achieved in Wales (excluding Monmouthshire) by the end of the nineteenth century, and the part played in its causation by migration and natural increase induced by industrialization.

[8] Ibid., p. 254. Baines points out that 'most of the lifetime migrants from the counties of Montgomery, Merioneth, Flint, Caernarfon and Anglesey were living in Lancashire and the West Midlands, where the natives were also more likely to emigrate in the 1880s' (p. 257). For a study of the Welsh communities in England, see Emrys Jones, 'The Welsh Language in England c.1800–1914' in Geraint H. Jenkins (ed.), *Language and Community in the Nineteenth Century* (Cardiff, 1998), pp. 231–59.
[9] Baines, *Migration in a Mature Economy*, Table 10.3.
[10] Ibid., p. 270.
[11] Ibid., p. 245.
[12] Ibid., p. 206.
[13] See Brinley Thomas, *Migration and Urban Development* (London, 1972), pp. 26–39.
[14] Baines, *Migration in a Mature Economy*, p. 277.

An important feature of Welsh migration was its bias in favour of the valley communities as against the coastal towns. In 1891, 197,283 (65 per cent) of the population of 301,957 in the registration districts of Merthyr Tydfil, Pontypridd and Neath were Welsh speakers, as against 22,515 (14 per cent) of the population of 164,134 in the Registration District of Cardiff.[15] As Philip Jones has pointed out, this clustering resulted in 'a massing of reserves',[16] so that Welshness in the valleys had intensity and depth instead of being spread thinly over a wide area.[17] In 1891 in Wales (excluding Monmouthshire) 870,730 out of a population of 1,425,581, or 61 per cent, were Welsh speakers. They were distributed as follows: 320,072, or 37 per cent, in Glamorgan; 306,980, or 35 per cent, in partly industrialized counties; and 243,678, or 28 per cent, in rural counties.[18] The main explanatory factors are the net migration of rural Welsh into industrial areas, and the natural increase of these in-migrants and of the indigenous Welsh in the industrial areas, allowing for those who left Wales. There is nothing in Baines's book which refutes this conclusion. Following a thorough appraisal of the evidence, Philip Jones reached the following verdict:

> Seen in the perspective of the economic history of the Celtic countries from the late eighteenth century forward, Professor Thomas's argument is a very valid one. During the eighty or so years after 1800 Welsh rural emigration was diverted to an industrial region within Wales, where it immensely strengthened the fabric of Welsh cultural life in the *nineteenth century*, rather than being dissipated in the alien culture realms of England, America, or Australasia.[19]

It is proposed here to examine broadly the whole of the nineteenth century. The title of this article, 'A Cauldron of Rebirth', suggested itself as the writer read Emyr Humphreys's brilliant book, *The Taliesin Tradition: A Quest for the Welsh Identity*. In this paragraph, the author is referring to *Pedair Cainc y Mabinogi* (The Four Branches of the Mabinogi):

> Great works of art are rarely put together by accident. These dramatic tales have a timeless element, but they were written for an audience well acquainted with the repertoire. There was, for example, a story about Pwyll and Pryderi leading an expedition to Annwn (the Underworld or the Otherworld) in order to capture its chief treasure, the cauldron of rebirth, or resuscitation. A poem of considerable antiquity known as *Preiddiau Annwfn* (The Spoils of Annwfn) deals with a similar raid, but led on

[15] Dot Jones, *Statistical Evidence relating to the Welsh Language 1801–1911/Tystiolaeth Ystadegol yn ymwneud â'r Iaith Gymraeg 1801–1911* (Cardiff, 1998), p. 226.
[16] Philip N. Jones, 'Some Aspects of Immigration into the Glamorgan Coalfield between 1881 and 1911', *THSC* (1969), 88.
[17] Ibid.
[18] Jones, *Statistical Evidence relating to the Welsh Language*, p. 226.
[19] Jones, 'Some Aspects of Immigration into the Glamorgan Coalfield between 1881 and 1911', 93.

that occasion by Arthur. This obscure poem has a refrain: '*Nam saith ni ddyriaith*' ('Only seven came back'), which would seem to be echoed in the ending of the tragic second story in the *Pedair Cainc, Branwen Ferch Llŷr* (Branwen, the Daughter of Lear), where only seven warriors returned from the ill-fated expedition to Ireland, which also involved a cauldron of rebirth. The contemporary audience must have been well aware of the symphonic correspondences both between incidents and between variant versions. In this case they would also have been alive to the military value of a utensil that could be used for recycling dead soldiers. A people at the wrong end of an historic sequence of demographic swings would know just how much value, ironic or otherwise, to attach to such a conception.[20]

That last sentence was music to the ears – 'an historic sequence of demographic swings'. In that phrase, Emyr Humphreys had an unerring instinct for the language of demographers. The theme of this chapter is that the Welsh in the nineteenth century were at the *right* end of an historic sequence of demographic swings; they captured the cauldron of demographic rebirth from industrial capitalism (which we can regard as either the Underworld or the Otherworld, according to taste). Between 1841 and 1901 the population of Wales doubled to just over two million, of whom nearly 50 per cent spoke Welsh. In sharp contrast, Ireland and the number speaking Irish Gaelic were at the *wrong* end of an historic sequence of demographic swings. Between 1841 and 1901 the population of Ireland was almost halved from 8,175,000 to 4,459,000, of whom only 19 per cent were Gaelic speakers. Dr Garret FitzGerald, ex-Prime Minister of Ireland, published a masterly analysis of the decline of Gaelic in the *Proceedings of the Royal Irish Academy* in 1984.[21] He revealed that a sharp decline in the speaking of Gaelic among the young began in the first half of the nineteenth century – before the Great Famine and before state-aided primary education was introduced.

The movements of population which affected the number of Welsh speakers arose out of the fact that Wales happened to be endowed with valuable resources of high-grade coal, iron, steel, non-ferrous metals and slate. Wales became the scene of major technological advances and dynamic capitalist investment. The argument here is not concerned with the period after 1900. A watershed was reached at the end of the nineteenth century. With the exception of Monmouthshire, the dominating increase in English in-migration into Wales (which David Williams located in the nineteenth century) did not occur until the first decade of the twentieth century. The question is: what was the effect of population growth and migration on the number of Welsh speakers in Wales at the end of the nineteenth century? To put it another way: what would have

---

[20] Emyr Humphreys, *The Taliesin Tradition: A Quest for the Welsh Identity* (Bridgend, 1989), pp. 25–6.
[21] Garret FitzGerald, 'Estimates for Baronies of Minimum Level of Irish-speaking amongst Successive Decennial Cohorts: 1771–81 to 1861–71', *Proceedings of the Royal Irish Academy*, 84, C, no. 3 (1984), 117–55.

happened to the Welsh-speaking population in the nineteenth century if Wales had not had an industrial revolution but had been, like Ireland, a predominantly agricultural society without coal, iron, steel, non-ferrous metals and slate?

The Industrial Revolution

The industrial revolution can best be understood as Britain's response to an energy crisis in the second half of the eighteenth century.[22] At the heart of the problem was a severe shortage of timber and timber products such as charcoal; Britain was dangerously dependent on foreign sources – particularly Norway, Sweden, and Russia – for supplies of timber and iron. This crisis could not be solved until coal or coke could be substituted for charcoal in refining pig iron into bar iron. It was necessary to switch the energy base of the economy from wool fuel to fossilized fuel, that is, from the *flow* of solar energy to the *stock* of solar energy underground. After many inventors had tried in vain to solve the technical problems, success came at last in 1784 when the great inventor, Henry Cort, patented his puddling and rolling process. This proved to be a landmark. Britain's plentiful supplies of coal could now be substituted for charcoal to produce a brand new type of bar iron. It was the quality of Henry Cort's new bar iron, together with James Watt's steam engine, which made possible the modern world of machine tools, railways and steamships. The industrialization of the world in the last two hundred years has been fuelled largely by the terrestrial dowry of coal, iron, oil, electricity and gas.

The industrial revolution was a drama in three acts. In Act I, between 1784 and 1800, the energy crisis was solved; in Act II, between 1800 and 1846, the foundations of a modern economy were laid through the creation of machine tools, railways and steamships; Act III, from 1846 to 1900, was the era of fulfilment when Britain became the workshop of the world and the centre of the Atlantic economy.[23] In each act of this great drama, south Wales played a directive role. It was in south Wales that the new puddling process and the steam locomotive were first used. Richard Crawshay introduced puddling in Cyfarthfa in November 1787, and Richard Trevithick ran a steam engine along a tramline in Merthyr Tydfil in 1804, the first in the world. By the mid-nineteenth century, south Wales was a leading producer of pig iron; after 1860 its unrivalled steam coal dominated world markets. The nineteenth century was the unique story of a dynamic Wales with a record rate of industrial growth. Between 1780 and 1901 the population of Wales increased fivefold from about 400,000 to over two million. The implication is unavoidable. Without the cauldron of economic and

---

[22] Brinley Thomas, 'Towards an Energy Interpretation of the Industrial Revolution', *Atlantic Economic Journal*, VIII (1980), 1–15.

[23] Idem, *Migration and Economic Growth: A Study of Great Britain and the Atlantic Economy* (2nd ed., Cambridge, 1973), chapter XV.

demographic rebirth and the creation of a large industrialized Welsh-speaking working class, what was hailed as the rebirth of a nation by the end of the nineteenth century would have been impossible.

The interplay between industrial change and the growth of the Welsh-speaking population during each of the three phases of the industrial revolution will now be examined.

The End of the Eighteenth Century

In the last two decades of the eighteenth century Wales was in the throes of a cultural as well as an industrial renaissance. Thanks to the Methodist Revival, Griffith Jones's circulating schools and the Sunday schools, the majority of people were literate in their mother tongue. Apart from its profound religious significance, this was one of the most remarkable literacy programmes in history. For example, in the Vale of Glamorgan there was a strong increase in the number of Welsh speakers in the second half of the eighteenth century. An illustration can be given through a translation of a letter written by Iolo Morganwg in the 1780s and the reply to him by Lewis Hopkin of Llandyfodwg. This is what Iolo wrote:

> The Welsh language in Glamorgan is greatly increasing as is clearly to be seen, and this in great part through the Welsh schools being more numerous in our county than in almost any county of Wales, and also very largely through the dissenters who are one and all Welsh readers. And in several of the parishes of Glamorgan where there was only a church service in English, it is now in Welsh or at least half of it is so.[24]

Here is Lewis Hopkin's reply:

> As to your opinion of the Welsh language in Glamorgan you are right that it is on the increase . . . I know of hardly any parishes where the whole church service is in English from the Usk to the Neath, apart from Cardiff, Newport, Cowbridge and Llantwit Major, [and there is] need enough of Welsh in these places since the ordinary people there use Welsh more than English.[25]

By the beginning of the nineteenth century, as Brian James's researches have demonstrated,[26] Welsh was the normal language used throughout the Vale of Glamorgan, except of course among the gentry. We dare not imagine the language Iolo Morganwg would use if he came back and saw his beloved Vale as it is now – almost entirely Anglicized, with only a few beautiful Welsh place names left as sorrowful reminders of a rich culture long departed.

---

[24] B. Ll. James, 'The Welsh Language in the Vale of Glamorgan', *Morgannwg*, XVI (1972), 34.
[25] Ibid.
[26] Ibid., 23–8.

That culture was at its richest at the end of the eighteenth century, as Prys Morgan has shown in his illuminating book, *The Eighteenth Century Renaissance*.[27] One of the greatest sons of the Vale was Richard Price, author of *Observations on the Nature of Civil Liberty* (1776), staunch supporter of the American and French Revolutions, whose views prompted Edmund Burke to write his *Reflections on the Revolution in France* (1790). The Atlantic connection had an outstanding representative in Morgan John Rhys. The Cymmrodorion and the Gwyneddigion also had a wide influence. The Atlantic connection has been vividly portrayed by Gwyn A. Williams in his 'Druids and Democrats', *The Search for Beulah Land* and *Madoc: The Making of a Myth*.[28]

At the end of the eighteenth century, Wales was in the vanguard of the industrial revolution and there was a rich legacy of Welshness, powered by religious Dissent, cultural renaissance and political radicalism. Wales entered the nineteenth century with a strong sense of nationhood, and much of its inspiration came from the remarkable group of Welshmen in London, the real capital of Wales at the time.

1800–1846

For the first fifteen years of the new century, Britain was at war. One of the great advantages of the new iron made possible by the industrial revolution was that lighter cannons with greater firepower could be produced, and this was a crucial factor in the victory over Napoleon. The Battle of Waterloo was won not on the playing fields of Eton but in the puddling furnaces of south Wales.

The output of pig-iron in south Wales increased tenfold between 1806 and 1847 (from 71,000 to 707,000 tons), and in north Wales the expansion was fivefold (from 3,000 to 16,000 tons). Coal output in south Wales went up sevenfold (from 1,200,000 tons to 8½ million tons), and in north Wales it rose fourfold to 1½ million tons. The areas that were being turned into hives of industry at this fantastic pace were drawing in thousands of young workers from the rural areas, particularly agricultural labourers from Pembrokeshire, Carmarthenshire, Breconshire and Cardiganshire. In the first half of the nineteenth century the population of south Wales grew from 315,000 to 726,000. Of this increase of 411,000, about two-thirds were in Glamorgan and Monmouthshire, and the vast majority of the in-migrants were Welsh speakers.

The cradle of the industrial revolution in Wales was Merthyr Tydfil, and what a Welsh cradle it was. Fortunately, a statistical survey of the town in 1841 was carried out by G. S. Kenrick, manager of the Varteg works; it was published in the

---

[27] Prys Morgan, *The Eighteenth Century Renaissance* (Llandybïe, 1981).
[28] Gwyn A. Williams, *The Welsh in their History* (London, 1982), pp. 31–64; idem, *The Search for Beulah Land* (London, 1980); idem, *Madoc: The Making of a Myth* (London, 1979).

Journal of the Statistical Society of London in 1846.[29] The population of Merthyr was 33,000, and 84 per cent of them were Welsh. There were twenty-six Nonconformist chapels with accommodation for over 13,000; they were entirely Welsh and the attendance was described as 'full' or 'tolerably full'. The two Church of England churches accommodated 1,500 and the attendance was estimated at 850. There were 6,800 children between 3 and 12 years of age, and seven out of every ten of these attended Welsh Sunday schools.

The Census of Religious Worship in 1851 registered the enormous triumph of Nonconformity. In 1851 there were 2,770 Welsh Nonconformist chapels in Wales, accommodating 611,000 people, or 70 per cent of all church accommodation.[30] There was a fascinating contrast between the worshipping habits of the church and chapel folk. In the whole of Wales in 1851, the number attending Church of England *evening* services was only 40,000, whereas in the Nonconformist chapels the attendance in the evening was 369,000, ten times that number.[31] The building of new churches in the industrialized areas could not keep pace with the extraordinary increase in population. In north-east Wales, according to the researches of W. T. R. Pryce, industrial growth caused the number of Welsh speakers to double, from 62,000 to 118,000, in the first half of the nineteenth century.[32] By 1851 the population of the whole of Wales was 1,188,914. It had almost doubled since 1801; it was overwhelmingly Nonconformist, and three of every five were living in industrial areas.

The history of the Welsh language in Monmouthshire in the 1820s and 1830s throws a flood of light on the impact of the industrial revolution. We need to distinguish between the old Dissenting denominations which originated in the seventeenth century and the new ones which came with the Welsh revival of the eighteenth century. The language of Old Dissent was English. In eastern and northern Monmouthshire at the end of the eighteenth century, the Dissenting churches which had been founded by Howel Harris and his followers were as English as those of John Wesley. All this was changed by the population movements brought about by the industrial revolution. Thousands of Welsh-speaking young people moved into the Monmouthshire valleys from the rural

---

[29] G. S. Kenrick, 'Statistics of Merthyr Tydvil', *Journal of the Statistical Society of London*, IX (1846), 14–21.

[30] Census of Great Britain 1851, *Religious Worship. England and Wales. Report and Tables* (London, 1853) (PP 1852–3 LXXXIX), Table B.

[31] Ibid. The intense devotion of Welsh Nonconformists to religious worship continued throughout the second half of the nineteenth century. Baines, in the book already cited, is not impressed by the evidence. The calibre of his argument may be judged by the following assertion: 'It does not follow from the fact that the Rhondda had 151 nonconformist chapels containing 85,105 seats which 'alone could accommodate three-quarters of the entire population of the Rhondda Urban District', that the seats were filled, or that they were filled by Welshmen.' Baines, *Migration in a Mature Economy*, p. 277.

[32] W. T. R. Pryce, 'Migration and the Evolution of Culture Areas: Cultural and Linguistic Frontiers in North-east Wales, 1750 and 1851', *TIBG*, 65 (1975), 92.

areas of Montgomeryshire, Breconshire, Carmarthenshire and Cardiganshire. This was a massive in-migration of Welsh Calvinistic Methodism which radically altered the linguistic balance in Monmouthshire in favour of Welsh. In Y Farteg and Nant-y-glo (1829), Ebbw Vale (1830), and Rhymni (1837) new Welsh churches were established, Old Dissent became a minority, and the Wesleyans became a Welsh denomination. Here the border county of Monmouthshire, so susceptible to English influences, was being reoccupied by a large Welsh-speaking population. This was the demographic basis for a Welsh cultural revival in Monmouthshire in which the eisteddfod was a prominent feature. It was also the basis for a militant Welsh-speaking working class in the Monmouthshire valleys, where iron-making was expanding rapidly. The researches of Sian Rhiannon Williams have stressed the vital role of migration in the rise and fall of the Welsh language in the county of Gwent.[33]

The congested townships in the iron and coal areas of Glamorgan and Monmouthshire had to come to terms with the industrial revolution. In the twenty-five years after 1815, south Wales was a volcano which erupted several times. In the agricultural districts of Carmarthenshire and north Pembrokeshire, the severe depression after the end of the Napoleonic Wars led to the Rebecca Riots. The countryside and the expanding industrial areas were closely interlinked through migration. A climax was reached in the armed uprising of the Chartists in 1839.

Recent research has argued that the response of Welsh workers to the injustices and degradation of the industrial revolution was heavily influenced by the ethnic barrier dividing them from the English. For centuries English rulers had sought to destroy the Welsh identity. The ironmasters who now controlled Welsh lives were mainly foreigners from England. The workers were conscious not only of being an oppressed class but also of being a different nation in their own right with a separate language and culture. The enemy was not just the capitalist but the hated English capitalist. Preparations for an armed rising in 1839 could be kept secret from the authorities because they were carried out in the Welsh language, and the majority of the population was on the side of the rebels. Despite the assurances given to the Chartist leader, John Frost, there was no support from workers in other parts of Britain. The armed assault on Newport in November 1839 was crushed by English troops. The significance of the rising was profound. Ivor Wilks, in his authoritative book on the subject, concludes that 'industrialisation produced the first serious challenge to the English dominion in Wales since, perhaps, the fifteenth century'.[34]

---

[33] Sian Rhiannon Williams, 'Welsh in the Valleys of Gwent', *Planet*, 51 (1985), 112–18; eadem, *Oes y Byd i'r Iaith Gymraeg: Y Gymraeg yn Ardal Ddiwydiannol Sir Fynwy yn y Bedwaredd Ganrif ar Bymtheg* (Caerdydd, 1992); eadem, 'The Welsh Language in Industrial Monmouthshire c.1800–1901' in Jenkins (ed.), *Language and Community in the Nineteenth Century*, pp. 203–29.

[34] Ivor Wilks, *South Wales and the Rising of 1839* (London, 1984), p. 251.

The fusion of Dissent, Welshness and political radicalism proved to be a powerful force in the grim setting of uncontrolled industrial exploitation. The government in London and the ruling authorities in south Wales had no illusion about the threat. What was the answer? How could this militant Welsh-speaking working class be made to mend its ways? In 1846 the House of Commons decided to set up a commission to inquire into the state of education in Wales, and in 1847 Wales was shocked by the infamous Blue Books. The strategy had been clearly stated by the mover of the motion, William Williams, MP for Coventry, a self-made, Welsh-speaking businessman. These were his words:

> It should be borne in mind that an ill-educated and undisciplined population, like that existing amongst mines in South Wales, is one that may be found most dangerous to the neighbourhood in which it dwells, and that a band of efficient schoolmasters is kept up at a much less expense than a body of police or soldiery.[35]

This brought loud cheers in the House of Commons. Seldom has the policy of social control been more explicitly spelt out – a band of efficient schoolmasters would be much more cost-effective than a body of police or soldiers.

Only one comment need be made on *Brad y Llyfrau Gleision* (The Treachery of the Blue Books). All the efforts made to force English education upon Wales were unable to prevent a spontaneous upsurge in the speaking of Welsh among the mass of the people from the 1850s to the 1890s. The cauldron of demographic rebirth was far more efficient than the Anglicizing Victorian schoolmasters. No one in 1847 ever dreamt that within fifty years over a million people would be speaking Welsh.

The impact of the industrial revolution on the lives of people brings to mind that great Welshman, Robert Owen, born in Newtown in 1771. He was an enigmatic personality – a mill-owner with his eye on the millennium, a successful capitalist who was the founding father of British socialism. He was far in advance of his time. He saw clearly that, to quote his words, 'the general diffusion of manufacture throughout a country generates a new character in its inhabitants . . . and will produce the most lamentable and permanent evils unless its tendency be counteracted by legislative interference and direction'.[36] His famous schools for workers' children at his New Lanark mills were among the wonders of the age. They attracted over 20,000 visitors between 1815 and 1825. In a book of extraordinary originality, *A New View of Society* (1814), Owen proposed a Ministry of Employment which would organize public investment to counter unemployment during slumps, together with a system of unemployment and wage statistics in every county. It was a century later before anything like it was

---

[35] *Parliamentary Debates* (Hansard), 3rd series, vol. 84, col. 848 (10 March 1846).
[36] Robert Owen, *Observations on the Effects of the Manufacturing System* (London, 1815), p. 5. See Brinley Thomas, 'Robert Owen of Newtown (1771–1858)', *THSC* (1960), 18–35.

achieved. At an early age Robert Owen went to London because he had a brother there. If the brother had been at Merthyr Tydfil, Owen might have become an ironmaster instead of a textile mill-owner. South Wales could have done with a capitalist with a social conscience.

1846–1900

The last phase in the industrial drama began in 1846, the year when Ireland was devastated by the disastrous failure of the potato crop and Britain repealed the Corn Laws, thereby inaugurating the era of free trade.

In 1851 the parish of Ystradyfodwg (which later became a large part of the Rhondda) had a population of only 950. It was a well-wooded valley of incredible beauty. At that time, an able-bodied squirrel could go all the way from Tonypandy to Maerdy without touching the ground. By 1871, with the opening of twenty steam-coal pits and the Taff Vale Railway, the population of the parish had increased from 950 to 17,000. Between 1871 and 1911 the population of the Rhondda Valleys grew from 24,000 to 153,000 as a result of the insatiable demand for Welsh steam coal throughout the world. At the end of this amazing expansion there were 24,000 persons per square mile built upon. Describing the Rhondda in 1896, the Report of the Welsh Land Commission declared:

> Speaking broadly, the characteristics of Welsh life, its Nonconformist development, the habitual use of the Welsh language, and the prevalence of a Welsh type of character, are as marked as in the rural districts of Wales.[37]

The growth of the Welsh-speaking population was due not only to in-migration from the Welsh countryside but also to the natural increase (the excess of births over deaths) in the industrial areas. The majority of the migrants were men of between 15 and 30 years of age and they married young. Each wave of in-migrants was a rejuvenating stimulus; the marriage rate was exceptionally high, and the birth rate in the colliery districts was the highest in Britain. In the forty years between 1861 and 1901, the population of Glamorgan increased by more than half a million; less than a third of this (167,000) was due to net inward migration, and over two-thirds (367,000) was due to excess of births over deaths.[38] The bountiful number of children raised in the Welsh coal-mining valleys was a major factor.

---

[37] Royal Commission on Land in Wales and Monmouthshire, *Report* (London, 1896) (PP 1896 XXXIV), p. 176.
[38] Brinley Thomas, 'The Migration of Labour into the Glamorganshire Coalfield, 1861–1911', *Economica* (1930), reprinted in W. E. Minchinton (ed.), *Industrial South Wales, 1750–1914* (London, 1969), pp. 37–55.

The Welsh Nonconformist Culture

From the mid-century onwards the new industrial communities developed a remarkable cultural life which was heavily influenced by Nonconformity. The railway age had arrived and this greatly increased travel and means of communication. The democratic culture expressed itself in an extraordinary range of publications in the Welsh language. By the late 1890s there were 28 monthlies, 25 newspapers, two quarterly journals, two bi-monthlies, making a total of 32 magazines and 25 newspapers. The total circulation of Welsh weekly periodicals exceeded 120,000 and that of Welsh magazines 150,000. Nor were children neglected; for example, *Trysorfa y Plant* had a huge circulation. The main publishing centres were in Glamorgan and Carmarthenshire in the south, and in Caernarfonshire and Denbighshire in the north. One of the leading Welsh firms put the annual value of all Welsh literature published at £200,000.[39]

It was a deeply religious culture and it had a robust self-assurance. It is easy to exaggerate its solemnity, as some historians such as A. L. Rowse are apt to do. The stern element in the Puritan view of life could not extinguish what John Cowper Powys called 'that peculiar vein of Rabelaisian humour which appears not only in a genius like Twm o'r Nant but is forever cropping up out of the hidden recesses of the Welsh nature'.[40] By their very nature, the Nonconformist chapels shunned the state and relied entirely on their own resources. This democratic culture was particularly rich and creative in the slate-quarrying districts of north Wales. The contrast between the 1870s and 1830s may be seen in the strength of the temperance movement which began as a religious issue and became a major political goal. As Kenneth O. Morgan has pointed out, 'the 1881 Welsh Sunday Closing Act was a landmark in British constitutional history, the first legislative statement of the nationhood of Wales'.[41] On the industrial front there was relative quiescence; the heroes of the past, Dic Penderyn and Lewsyn yr Heliwr, were held in honour, but the charismatic leader of the south Wales miners in the Victorian age was William Abraham (Mabon), the peace-loving Nonconformist.

The 'media' in Victorian Wales did not confine themselves to religious topics. Ieuan Gwynedd Jones has thrown new light on the wide range of cultural issues discussed in the newspapers and journals, and in the numerous local eisteddfodau.[42] A rich variety of topics, from heavy philosophy to light entertainment, are to be found in publications such as *Taliesin, Seren Cymru, Y Gwron, Y Gweithiwr*, and dozens of others. A favourite theme was the importance of the Welsh language in the working man's struggle for justice.

---

[39] D. Lleufer Thomas, 'Bibliographical, Statistical and other Miscellaneous Memoranda', Royal Commission on Land, *Report* (1896), appendix C, pp. 195–7.
[40] John Cowper Powys, *Obstinate Cymric: Essays 1935–47* (London, 1973), p. 40.
[41] Kenneth O. Morgan, *Rebirth of a Nation: Wales, 1880–1980* (Oxford, 1981), pp. 36–7.
[42] Ieuan Gwynedd Jones, *Communities: The Observers and the Observed* (Cardiff, 1985), pp. 13–20.

As a result the long-term programme of cultural control devised by the English establishment in 1847 had been a total failure as far as the Welsh working class was concerned. The infamous Blue Books were no match for the cauldron of rebirth. In 1886, D. Isaac Davies published a book of essays under the title, *Yr Iaith Gymraeg, 1785, 1885, 1985! neu Tair Miliwn o Gymry Dwy-ieithawg mewn Can Mlynedd* (The Welsh Language, 1785, 1885, 1985! or, Three Million Bilingual Welsh People in a Hundred Years).[43] The new society looked to the future with sturdy optimism. Indeed, the demographic tide was flowing so strongly in favour of the Welsh language in the 1880s that Isaac Davies and his followers failed to recognize the flaws in their long-term bilingual policy.[44]

The Welsh language was safe in communities where the growth of the Welsh-speaking population was substantially greater than the in-migration from England. Up to the 1890s, in the words of a commission of inquiry in 1917, 'the native inhabitants had, in many respects, shown a marked capacity for stamping their own impress on all newcomers, and communicating to them a large measure of their own characteristics'.[45] There were numerous examples of non-Welsh in-migrants learning Welsh in order to be able to do their jobs. An inspector of mines in 1885 declared that nine of every ten miners in the steam-coal pits of south Wales carried out their duties in Welsh.[46] For several years after 1900 the Rhondda District of the South Wales Miners Federation continued to print its rules in Welsh and English, and summarized every report in Welsh.[47]

Nevertheless, even before the Welsh language reached its peak, there were some disturbing signs of change. The middle class was increasingly opting for English as the passport to material gain. If Sir Hugh Owen had had his way, the National Eisteddfod would have become a bilingual 'Social Science Association', with out-houses for poetry and music. Fortunately, that did not happen; the National Eisteddfod became a major force in Welsh life. In the religious sphere, Welsh denominations were zealous in looking after the spiritual needs of the English in-migrants by providing English services and separate chapels for them. This did far more to Anglicize the Welsh than to evangelize the English, as a Congregational minister in Monmouthshire pointed out as early as 1867.[48] In many areas of public life the Welsh were always decent enough to turn to English if there were one or two present who did not understand Welsh. The road to Anglicization was paved with many acts of Welsh good intentions.

[43] D. Isaac Davies, *Yr Iaith Gymraeg 1785, 1885, 1985! Neu, Tair Miliwn o Gymry Dwy-Ieithawg mewn Can Mlynedd* (Dinbych, 1885); see also J. Elwyn Hughes, *Arloeswr Dwyieithedd: Dan Isaac Davies 1839–1887* (Caerdydd, 1984).
[44] Robin Okey, 'The First Welsh Language Society', *Planet*, 58 (1986), 90–6.
[45] *Commission of Enquiry into Industrial Unrest, No. 7 Division. Report of the Commissioners for Wales, including Monmouthshire* (London, 1917) (PP 1917–18 (Cd. 8668) XV), p. 15.
[46] Davies, *Yr Iaith Gymraeg*, p. 43.
[47] David Smith, 'Introduction' in idem (ed.), *A People and a Proletariat* (London, 1980), p. 12.
[48] Williams, 'Welsh in the Valleys of Gwent', 116.

In certain areas, the retreat of Welsh began early, for example, in the Vale of Glamorgan where, at the beginning of the century, Welsh had been the language of everyday life, literature and religion. In 1884 Thomas Powel, professor of Celtic at the newly created College in Cardiff, persuaded the Cymmrodorion to survey the 'use of the Welsh language in elementary schools in Welsh-speaking districts'.[49] They found that, of the 123 schools questioned in Glamorgan, 77 were in favour of the introduction of Welsh but 48 were firmly against. The opponents argued that the exclusion of Welsh was the surest means of promoting facility in English, and one of the reasons put forward by those who wanted Welsh in the schools was significant – it would help to eradicate the sense of shame felt by many Welsh children. There can be no doubt that many who had been brought up in Welsh homes became indifferent and even opposed to their children speaking the mother tongue. This attitude was deplored and denounced by Welsh leaders such as D. Isaac Davies. He was saddened by the fact that many Welsh people, particularly women and teenage girls, were ashamed to acknowledge that they could understand Welsh, and he was convinced that any census count would be misleading unless those who did not care for the language could be persuaded to be proud of being bilingual.[50] The Anglicization of Monmouthshire was mainly due to substantial English in-migration accompanied by the out-migration of many thousands of Welsh people from the declining iron districts of the expanding coal communities in the Rhondda and Aberdare valleys.

The watershed in the fortunes of the language came in the 1890s. Up until then, the assimilation forces were stronger over most of Wales than was the English in-migration. Over a million people spoke Welsh. Then suddenly, in the first ten years of the twentieth century, there was a flood of 100,000 in-migrants from outside Wales. Even in the Rhondda, the status of Welsh was now threatened, so much so that David James (Defynnog), secretary of the Welsh Language Society for twenty-five years, published a book, *The Rhondda Scheme for Teaching Welsh*, in 1910, to try to maintain a knowledge of Welsh among the young. The proportion of Welsh speakers in the population of Wales fell from 49.9 per cent in 1901 to 43.5 per cent in 1911. Thus began a long-period decline until the Welsh-speaking proportion reached 20.8 per cent in 1971, 18.9 per cent in 1981 and 18.7 per cent in 1991.[51]

The French Language in Canada

An instructive comparison can be drawn between the rise and fall of the Welsh language and the fortunes of the French language in Canada. Wales was not

---

[49] J. Parry Lewis, 'The Anglicisation of Glamorgan', *Morgannwg*, IV (1960), 28–40.
[50] Davies, *Yr Iaith Gymraeg*, pp. 22–3.
[51] For an up-to-date analysis of the census results, see John Aitchison and Harold Carter, *A Geography of the Welsh Language 1961–1991* (Cardiff, 1994).

unique in experiencing a cauldron of rebirth. In a similar manner industrialization was a blessing to the French language in the province of Quebec. The Scottish capitalists who developed a large industrial and financial sector based on Montreal enabled French-speaking migrants from the rural areas of Quebec to be employed in Canada. They were able to remain in their own culture. Like the Welsh miners in the valleys of south Wales, the French Canadians had a very high birth rate and the French-speaking population increased rapidly. In 1871 there were 930,000 French speakers in Quebec, most of them in rural areas; by 1961 there were 4½ million French speakers, with over 3 million living in the industrial areas.[52] But for the enterprise of those mainly Scottish capitalists, most of the French Canadians leaving the rural areas of Quebec would have had to emigrate to the United States and they would have become English speakers.

It is ironic that, both in Wales and Quebec, the nationalist parties have fiercely attacked past industrialization as a destructive influence on their language. For a Welshman, it is also bitterly ironic that the supportive attitude of nineteenth-century English governments to the French language in Canada is a glaring contrast to their attempts to destroy the Welsh language. The 1847 commission declared that 'the Welsh language is a vast drawback to Wales and a manifold barrier to the moral progress and the commercial prosperity of the people. It is not easy to overestimate its evil effects'.[53] Conversely, the Constitution of Canada, based on the Durham Report (1867) contained strong guarantees for the language and culture of the French Canadians. René Levesque, leader of the Quebec nationalists, appealed to this constitution in his fight against Pierre Trudeau's policy for the future of federalism in Canada. Here, however, successive British governments in the nineteenth century based their policy towards the Welsh language on the arrogant doctrines of the 1847 Blue Books. There was a perverse quirk in the attitude of the English. They had a soft spot for minority languages in faraway countries, but they had nothing but contempt for the Celtic language next door to them in these islands. If British governments in the nineteenth century had applied to the Welsh language the same civilized policy which they adopted towards French in Canada, the status and destiny of Welsh would have been very different.

Some Speculations

What would have happened if Wales had been wholly agricultural and had not been industrialized? Her population of 400,000 in the mid-eighteenth century might have grown to about 700,000 by the middle of the nineteenth century, on

---

[52] *Canada Population Census* (Ottawa, 1971).
[53] *Reports of the Commissioners of Inquiry into the State of Education in Wales . . . in three parts* (London, 1847) (PP 1847 XXVII).

two conditions: if the Welsh had taken to the potato as the Irish did, and if Welsh agriculture had been able to compete with the Irish in exporting dairy products and grain to the industrial areas of England. However, in 1845 Wales might have been attacked by the same potato fungus that ruined Ireland and such a disaster would have meant mass emigration to England and overseas. The population would then have probably fallen to about 400,000. But even if Wales had escaped such a tragedy, Welsh farmers would not have been able to avoid the disastrous consequences of the great agricultural depression which began in the 1880s, when cheap food from overseas flooded the market. Welsh agriculture did not have any special comparative advantage; even when it had the huge purchasing power of the coalfields at its doorstep, the number of men employed in farming fell by 50 per cent between 1881 and 1901. Without that industrial market, things would have been much worse. In all probability, the population of Wales would have fallen to below half a million by 1901. Even if the Welsh-speaking proportion was as high as 70 per cent, the number speaking Welsh at the beginning of the twentieth century would have been only about 300,000, instead of over a million as it actually was. A small agrarian society would not have had the resources to create institutions such as the National Library, the National Museum, and the University.

Nevertheless, the patriot will reply, would not quality be better than quantity? This tiny Welsh nation of about half a million, rooted in its traditional heartland, would have brought forth a great renaissance of Welsh literature, even if it were a nation of R. S. Thomas's hill farmers struggling to exact a bare living from a cruel earth. That is certainly possible. However, Wales would have had to face not only the great agricultural depression of the 1880s but also the relentless avalanche of English and American influences in the twentieth century. During the course of the twentieth century Welsh children could not have stayed on the farm; they would have had to emigrate to England and overseas, as the Irish did. The likelihood is that the Welsh nation would be an aged society surviving in a small rural bunker, a *casa geriatrica*, instead of a large youthful urban society which can afford cultural institutions to express and strengthen the national identity.

That is not how the poets see it. Here is R. S. Thomas, writing in 1974:

> The
> industrialists came, burrowing
>   in the corpse of a nation
> for its congealed blood. I was
>   born into the squalor of
> their feeding and sucked their speech
>   in with my mother's
> infected milk, so that whatever
>   I throw up now is still theirs.[54]

---

[54] R. S. Thomas, *What is a Welshman?* (Llandybïe, 1974), p. 12.

And here is a translation of some lines by Saunders Lewis in 1939:

> The tramway climbs from Merthyr to Dowlais,
> Slime of a snail on a heap of slag;
> Here once was Wales, and now
> Derelict cinemas and rain on the barren tips; . . .
> We have neither language nor dialect, we feel no insult,
> And the masterpiece that we gave to history is our country's M.P.s.[55]

Where does the truth lie – in the poetic or the prosaic view? As a biological species, the Welsh were fortunate; in the nineteenth century, they found themselves in a very favourable niche and they multiplied fast. Their number increased fivefold, and the Welsh language was given a new lease of life by a unique sequence of demographic swings. It was a windfall and in the nature of things it could not last. At the height of Victorian optimism, there was a dream of three million bilingual Welsh people by 1985; that dream turned into a nightmare in the twentieth century. The hectic capitalist growth, the population explosion, and the Nonconformist golden age went into reverse. The economic environment became very unfavourable, and the population of Wales hardly increased at all. According to the 1991 census, the number of Welsh speakers was 508,098 out of a population of 2,723,623 aged 3 and over.

In conclusion, a word must be said about the so-called Welsh identity crisis. Emyr Humphreys declares eloquently that the essential basis of Welshness is the continuity of the Welsh language and its literature, traceable as far back as the sixth century. It is this continuity that has enabled the Welsh to survive many a threat of extinction. On the other hand, there is the opposite point of view exemplified by Gwyn A. Williams:

> The existence of a historic British nation, dominated by but qualitatively distinct from the English polity, is a central fact in the modern history of these islands . . . The history of Welsh is totally incomprehensible without it. The Welsh, the original British, have survived by finding a distinctive place for themselves within a British nation.[56]

This is the Taliesin tradition versus the Gramsci effect!

To resolve this conflict, it is necessary to recognize that a major cause of the decline of the Welsh language was the collapse of the Welsh economy after the First World War. Between 1860 and 1913, south Wales was the most dynamic part of Britain's capitalist economy; far from being an exploited colony, Wales had a faster rate of economic development than any part of England or Scotland.

---

[55] Saunders Lewis, 'The Deluge 1939'; translation taken from Alun R. Jones and Gwyn Thomas (eds.), *Presenting Saunders Lewis* (Cardiff, 1973), p. 177.

[56] Williams, *The Welsh in their History*, p. 195.

Because of the dazzling heights reached just before the Great War, the subsequent fall was all the more disastrous. The class war in the coalfields intensified, and the clarion call was Marxist not Methodist. What the potato famine did to the Irish economy, the great depression did to the Welsh economy. In the twentieth century, economic and demographic contraction, the decline of Nonconformity, severe unemployment and emigration, together with several other important factors, have been a curse to the language.

This does not mean that the future of the Welsh lies in a second-hand British identity. Cultural and linguistic continuity is a necessary condition of being a separate nation. When Welsh literature has ceased to renew itself and has become a mere memory, we shall have lost a vital part of our identity. If Wales is to survive, everything possible must continue to be done to reverse the long decline in the fortunes of the Welsh language. The striking levelling-off in the rate of decline between 1971 and 1991 is a great tribute to the wholehearted labours of thousands of Welsh patriots who have made the language the centrepiece of the national effort. *Cenedl heb iaith, cenedl heb galon.* A nation without language is a nation without heart.

3

Landowners, Farmers and Language in the Nineteenth Century

R. J. MOORE-COLYER

TO ATTEMPT to seek an unequivocal and definitive role for language in the context of social and economic relationships in nineteenth-century rural Wales is akin to chasing shadows. Given the absence of reliable statistical data on both the social and geographical distribution of the Welsh language for much of the century, and the extent to which the language issue was manipulated and distorted by various groups for political advantage, the edges of reality are profoundly blurred. We know, or at least we *think* we know, that since language is a vital vehicle of culture, a language barrier between social classes would inevitably colour their mutual perception, and perpetuate nascent alienation. But is this merely illusion, a kind of self-fulfilling prophecy which neatly confirms an established system of prejudice? After all, as far as relations between the landed gentry and their farming tenants was concerned and, for that matter, the relationship between those tenants and their labourers, the situation in mid-Victorian Wales was probably not markedly different from that in England. As class consciousness deepened and the dividing lines between social groupings became clearly etched into the social fabric of the nineteenth-century countryside, barriers to association and mutual understanding soon followed. The education system and the Church, of course, perpetuated class notions which ran like a woven skein through rural literature and became almost engrained in landscape and genre painting.[1] Against this sort of background the fact that many a Welsh gentleman, unable to speak the tongue of his ancestors, had difficulty in communicating with his tenants, was probably of minor importance. Put simply, alienation was already institutionalized by a class system whose nature inhibited communication, irrespective of language considerations. Even a man like the Welsh-speaking Thomas Colby of Pantyderi, scion of the Colbys of Ffynhonnau, Pembrokeshire, who lived in a simple and modest manner, was careful to maintain the distinction between himself and the servants with whom he sat at his table.[2]

---

[1] John Barrell, *The Dark Side of the Landscape: The Rural Poor in English Painting, 1730–1840* (Cambridge, 1980), passim.
[2] David Jenkins, *The Agricultural Community in South-West Wales at the Turn of the Twentieth Century* (Cardiff, 1971), pp. 18–19.

Again, as this chapter will show, the niceties of class distinction were also observed between the farming and labouring population who shared not only the same language but, in some cases, a similar economic background.

Essentially, the bulk of this chapter will be concerned with exploring these social relationships and the extent to which they mediated the management of the estate and the farming economy. In the process an attempt will be made to discuss the importance (or otherwise) of the Welsh language as a vehicle of estate and agricultural business. As a point of departure, reference will be made to the rather limited array of nineteenth-century language statistics, an exercise which reveals two basic, and seemingly insuperable problems. In the parish of Llanidloes in 1872, according to the local historian Edward Hamer, some three-quarters of the population knew Welsh, while half of the total could be described as bilingual.[3] By 1891, the year for which official language statistics first become available, the population of the Llanidloes registration district had become overwhelmingly English or English/Welsh speakers; only 187 people were returned as monoglot Welsh. Among these were listed a number of professionals, including Samuel Jones (bank manager), David Lewis (solicitor's clerk) and Mary, Elizabeth and Louise Jones, spinster ladies working as schoolteachers. To accept that these individuals could function effectively in their professions as monoglot Welsh speakers in a community like Llanidloes requires total suspension of disbelief! That the accuracy of the census left much to be desired is also exemplified by the case of Elizabeth Davies, a farmer of Glanaman, Carmarthenshire. Mrs Davies was returned as a monoglot Welsh speaker, and while her son Thomas was bilingual (as was her daughter Elizabeth), it was claimed that her two youngest daughters, Margaret and Sarah, spoke English only! Individuals no doubt had their own reasons for claiming or denying their facility in one or another language. Those returned as being bilingual underscore the second structural difficulty with the language census material, that of determining what actually constitutes bilingualism. In the context of the present chapter, was a bilingual farmer fully capable of speaking and reading both languages, thereby having access to the rapidly-growing technical agricultural literature in English? Was the landowner, alleged to be bilingual, capable of discussing the minutiae of tenancy agreements and land law with farmers in colloquial Welsh? Or did bilingualism imply a thorough command of one language and a halting and hesitating grasp of the second? Ultimately, definition must remain elusive unless detailed background information about a particular individual is available. Although farmers might have spoken English, and their workers a little of that language, observed an anonymous memorialist of the parish of Llanfechain on the English border in 1872, 'it is most certain that none of them can fully understand a protracted address made to them in the English tongue'.[4]

[3] Edward Hamer, 'A Parochial Account of Llanidloes', *MC*, V (1872), 17.
[4] 'A Slight Historical and Topographical Sketch of the Parish of Llanfechain', ibid., 273–4.

By 1901 approximately half the population of Wales continued to speak Welsh, an average which conceals wide variations between administrative counties. Thus, in the counties Cardigan, Caernarfon, Carmarthen, Merioneth and Anglesey, in excess of 90 per cent of inhabitants were Welsh speakers, a proportion not significantly different from that which prevailed a century earlier. Elsewhere, in the counties of Glamorgan, Brecon and Flint, for example, the percentage of Welsh speakers had dwindled from an estimated three-quarters in 1801 to between 40 and 50 per cent by the close of the nineteenth century, while in Radnorshire a mere 6 per cent retained the language by this time.[5]

One might reasonably assume that the farm, by its very nature, would remain the bastion and stronghold of the ancient tongue, yet a small-scale survey of three Montgomeryshire parishes tends to confirm the anecdotal evidence that even here the English language was coming into regular use by the middle of the century. In the winter of 1846, the Revd Robert Thomas (1817–88) supervised an educational survey of the parishes of Llanfair Caereinion, Castell Caereinion and Manafon, carefully noting the occupations and linguistic capabilities of his respondents. Table 1, drawn from Thomas's survey, indicates that whereas significant numbers of farm labourers and servants remained monoglot Welsh speakers, bilingualism appears to have been an increasingly important feature of these essentially agricultural communities.[6]

Some fifty years after Thomas's investigations, the returns of the census enumerators for Montgomeryshire reveal stark contrasts between language ability among farmers and their workers living in exclusively rural areas and those located close to the English-dominated urban centres of Welshpool and Newtown (Table 2).

It is significant that while numerous farmers in the Llanbryn-mair district were returned as monoglot Welsh their children claimed to be bilingual. Meanwhile, among the Welshpool/Newtown group, bilingual farmers and labourers were almost exclusively possessed of Welsh-sounding surnames in contrast to those of monoglot English speakers, thereby confirming the point that bilingualism normally implies the native speaker learning the outside language rather than vice versa. If farmers and their labourers in the eastern counties of Wales and those living in proximity to urban centres were becoming progressively acquainted with English, the Welsh language continued overwhelmingly to dominate farming communities in the counties of the north and south-west. In Glanaman (Carmarthenshire), for example, where farmers and their staff comprised 8 per cent of the population, there were no monoglot English speakers and a mere 10 per cent capable of using both Welsh and English. Again, in Llanymawddwy

---

[5] W. T. R. Pryce, 'Welsh and English in Wales, 1750–1971: A Spatial Analysis based on the Linguistic Affiliation of Parochial Communities', *BBCS*, XXVIII, pt. 1 (1978), 27.
[6] NLW, MS 23220E. I am grateful to Mrs Dot Jones for this reference.

Table 1. Language capability in three Montgomeryshire parishes, 1846

Occupation	Welsh only	Welsh/English	English only
Farmers (male)	41	243	16
Farmers (female)	3	7	2
Farmers' relatives (males)	26	109	14
Farm labourers/servants (male)	61	109	16
Farm labourers/servants (female)	62	54	10

Table 2. Language capability in the Census Registration Districts of Llanbryn-mair, Welshpool and Newtown, 1891

	Farmers Welsh only	Farmers English only	Farmers Welsh/English	Labourers/servants Welsh only	Labourers/servants English only	Labourers/servants Welsh/English
Llanbryn-mair	109	0	8	96	1	2
Welshpool/Newtown	0	46	21	0	103	30

(Merioneth), where more than one third of the community were either farmers or farm workers, only five of a total of 158 were registered as bilingual. These included the locally-born shepherd, cowhand and waggoner of a farmer, Robert Jones, himself bilingual at the age of seventy, and one Mathew Tye, whose name bespeaks an English origin and who may represent a rare example of an English labourer managing to come to grips with the Welsh tongue.

English was perceived by many as 'the language of infidelity and atheism, of secularism, of the higher criticism, of extreme liberality in theology', but it was nevertheless the vehicle of social and economic progress and however passionate Welshmen may have been about their mother tongue, a knowledge of English was one of the ways by which they could attain material prosperity.[7] Indeed, it was observed in 1844 that widespread ignorance of English was a 'great drawback upon the advancement of the community'.[8] In recognition of this the celebrated Denbighshire poet John Ceiriog Hughes insisted on speaking English both on the station platform and at home after his appointment as stationmaster at Llanidloes on the Cambrian Line in 1865.[9] So deeply-seated and widespread was this concern to learn English that parents whose knowledge of the language was little more than vestigial would struggle to speak it to their children, while others

---

[7] Ieuan Gwynedd Jones, *Mid-Victorian Wales: The Observers and the Observed* (Cardiff, 1992), p. 70.
[8] *Report of the Commissioners of Inquiry for South Wales* (PP 1844 XVI), p. 36.
[9] See Chapter 4, pp. 146–7.

would even allow them to learn the catechism provided it was taught in English.[10] A depressing catalogue of school inspectors from Matthew Arnold to the Revd Shadrach Pryce descanted on the theme of the regressive nature of the Welsh language (except, perhaps, as a vehicle for learning English) and, although there was some sympathy for bilingualism by the 1890s, it failed to become a cornerstone of the policy of the Board of Education before the appointment of O. M. Edwards as Chief Inspector in 1907.[11] As younger farmers in north Wales increasingly began to come to terms with the second language by the later nineteenth century, the opportunity to do so was denied to others by physical isolation.[12] Thus, in the exclusively Welsh area around Tregaron (Cardiganshire) non-farming youths travelled outside the locality to seek work and often to learn English, whereas farmers' sons were tied to the land and language by the nature of their occupation.[13]

Yet Welsh had always been, and would continue to be, the language of the barn, byre and kitchen fireside. As such it represented an expression of cultural continuity, conferred a sense of belonging and security, and offered a bulwark against an uncertain and dangerous world outside. The language provided a sort of psychic cohesion and social cement which proved invaluable at times when the community came under threat from external, if not alien, forces. Time and again, enclosure commissioners and Poor Law administrators were confronted by Welsh-speaking communities adamant to protect what they perceived as their ancient rights, while the egregious Augustus Brackenbury ('Y Sais Bach') had just cause to remember the effectiveness of group action when he finally abandoned his attempt to disturb the denizens of the Mynydd Bach region of Cardiganshire. As Rebecca, guardian of 'the people's law', stalked the countryside in the mid-1840s, her followers communicated in Welsh, arranging their covert activities and clandestine meetings in a tongue impenetrable to most soldiers, policemen and other representatives of authority. As dark oaths and promises were sworn over bayonets and bibles in field corners or obscure cottages, they were articulated in Welsh; this secret language was thus the verbal expression of frustration and resentment.[14] It was also a language of which its practitioners were inordinately proud, and if they showed some pragmatic interest in learning English they invariably turned to Welsh for their religious practices, reading and social intercourse. In his evidence to the Welsh Land Commission, whose purpose was to establish the underlying causes of depression in Welsh agriculture, David Owen

---

[10] Jones, *Mid-Victorian Wales*, p. 121.
[11] W. Gareth Evans, 'The "Bilingual Difficulty": HMI and the Welsh Language in the Victorian Age', *WHR*, 16, no. 4 (1993), 494–507.
[12] Royal Commission on Land in Wales and Monmouthshire, *Minutes of Evidence*, vol. I (1894), Q. 4687.
[13] Ibid., vol. III (1895), Q. 46670.
[14] David Williams, *The Rebecca Riots* (Cardiff, 1955), p. 56; David J. V. Jones, *Rebecca's Children: A Study of Rural Society, Crime and Protest* (Oxford, 1989), p. 313.

Edwards of Glandyfi, Cardiganshire, encapsulated the Welshman's view of his tongue in a simple, but eloquent sentence, replete with all manner of undertones. Replying through an interpreter to the suggestion that he might well be able to speak English, he observed: 'No, I am not an Englishman at all; I do not pretend to be one; I am more loyal to my language and to my country.'[15]

In common with his fellows throughout the country, David Owen Edwards was obliged to master the growing number of technical terms associated with nineteenth-century agriculture and its cognate rural crafts. If the new equipment originating in England required appropriate Welsh terminology, indigenous hand-tools, be they seed-lips, billhooks, peat spades or hay forks, exhibited a bewildering variety of local types, all of which were dignified by dialect nomenclature.[16] There were, moreover, specific Welsh terms applied to the separate components of cultivation equipment, while no self-respecting farmer would admit to ignorance of the difference between the knee-made field rick ('tas ben-glin') and its hand-made counterpart ('tas law').[17] Where it was important to appreciate that oats required to be harvested when the colour of a woodpigeon ('lliw'r ysguthan'), and that sheaves might only properly be counted by way of the *drefa* (24 sheaf unit), it is not difficult to appreciate that Welsh would long remain the language of day-to-day farming activities.

Landholding, Farming and Education

By 1872 the whole of the agricultural land of Wales was owned by some 16,000 people with, for example, over half the acreage of the former administrative county of Gwynedd being in the possession of thirty-seven families.[18] Landed estates, however, by no means dominated the whole country and in some districts freehold occupation was common, if not the norm. In late eighteenth-century Montgomeryshire, up to 40 per cent of the land was in the hands of freeholders or small owners, with yeoman occupiers farming one third of the acreage in the south-western counties.[19] Similarly, in the Cardiganshire parishes of Blaenpennal, Nancwnlle, Lledrod, Llanbadarn Fawr, Llangeitho and Llanrhystud, where no single large owner held sway, between 22 and 48 per cent of the land remained freehold by the 1890s.[20] Many of these freeholds (often carved out from common, waste or mountain land with the connivance of large landowners) were of

---

[15] Royal Commission on Land, *Minutes of Evidence*, vol. III (1895), Q. 49599.
[16] J. Geraint Jenkins, *Agricultural Transport in Wales* (Cardiff, 1962), passim.
[17] Ffransis G. Payne, *Yr Aradr Gymreig* (Caerdydd, 1975), passim.
[18] John Davies, 'The End of the Great Estates and the Rise of Freehold Farming in Wales', *WHR*, 7, no. 2 (1974), 187.
[19] Melvin Humphreys, *The Crisis of Community: Montgomeryshire, 1680–1815* (Cardiff, 1996), p. 98.
[20] Royal Commission on Land, *Minutes of Evidence*, vol. III (1895), pp. 580–97; R. J. Moore-Colyer, 'Farmers and Fields in Nineteenth-century Wales: The Case of Llanrhystud, Cardiganshire', *NLWJ*, XXVI, no. 1 (1989), 32–57.

relatively recent origin, some having been purchased as the landed estates began to dispose of off-lying properties in the 1870s and 1880s.[21] Elsewhere, ancient yeoman families, resisting the blandishments of more affluent neighbours, continued to cling to their hereditary property, their fierce attachment to the land fortifying them against hard times and financial stress.[22]

To many radical ruralists in nineteenth-century Britain, the rise of freehold farming offered a panacea for some of the social problems of the countryside. It was viewed not only as a bulwark against social discontent, but also as a means of creating a 'morally healthy' class of sturdy independent small landholders. But while the ownership of a few acres might confer status within the community, the combined effects of the need to raise a deposit on purchase and the inevitable mortgage payments (often higher on an annual basis than the rent for an equivalent acreage) might well mean that the economic position of the new freeholder was little better, or even worse, than would have been the case had he remained a tenant. Where his capital reserves were limited, the freeholder had little choice but to direct resources from the business of farming to the business of landownership, so that in times of economic depression he could only survive by the exploitation of unpaid family labour or the time-honoured process of progressive belt-tightening. The eighty-four freeholders in Tre-lech a'r Betws in Carmarthenshire, two-thirds of whom occupied holdings of less than a hundred acres, enjoyed a certain social status, but they paid for it with unremitting hard labour.[23] Where the freehold embraced less than fifty acres, a living was virtually impossible in the depressed years of the late nineteenth century, and owners would be forced either into by-employments or into renting additional acres from adjacent landlords from whose very control freeholding had released them.

But, of course, freeholding above all promoted freedom, freedom to farm as one wished, freedom of political and religious expression, and freedom of language. Freeholding earned respect, both from one's fellow farmers and, perhaps more importantly, from the local gentry, who could not ignore the fact that freeholders enjoyed voting rights. However much some landowners might disapprove of Dissenting theology and its concomitant social attitudes, they fully realized that in a predominantly Nonconformist community freeholders could act in concert to influence the outcome of an election contest. It was, therefore, politic to handle them with care, so that when a group of Nonconformists sought leave to build a meeting house on land belonging to the Gogerddan estate, the proprietor was advised by his local agent: 'I am of opinion it is of your interest to

---

[21] For the enthusiasm of tenants to purchase what they regarded as their birthright see, inter alia, Roger Phillips, *Tredegar: The History of an Agricultural Estate, 1300–1956* (Newport, 1990), p. 222; William R. Morgan, *A Pembrokeshire Countryman Looks Back* (Tenby, 1988), p. 80; Philip Riden and Keith Edwards, *Families and Farms in Lisvane, 1850–1950* (Cardiff, 1993), pp. 56–8.
[22] Royal Commission on Land, *Report* (1896), pp. 557–71.
[23] Jones, *Rebecca's Children*, p. 49.

grant them a lease as there are many freeholders belonging to that congregation and will be affronted if you will refuse it.'[24]

Whether he farmed as a freeholder or the tenant of a landed estate, the average farmer in nineteenth-century Wales was regarded by most outsiders with a blend of pity and contempt. English travellers, Scottish land agents, Anglicized landlords and the more substantial Welsh farmers vied with each other in condemning the general run of husbandmen as being backward, inward-looking, obscurantist, idle and lacking in ambition. 'My English ways', observed Thomas Herbert Cooke, who spent a stormy period as agent of the Middleton Hall estate in Carmarthenshire during the Rebecca Riots, 'do not suit Welsh notions and my opinion of the Welsh farmers is that they know less than their own horses. They are too ignorant to be taught. They are 100 years behind the worst managed English districts.'[25] Twenty years later E. C. L. Fitzwilliams of Cilgwyn wrote of two farms on his property which had recently changed hands: 'The state in which these farms have been left is deplorable. Neither of them laid out a single penny in repairs in the twenty years they have had the premises. I am afraid that this is only a type of most of the Welsh farmers of the neighbourhood who speak nothing but the blessed "iaeth [sic] Gymraeg" '.[26] Such uncharitable and rather misleading quotations could be cited *ad nauseam*. Even T. J. Jenkin, who would eventually rise to become Director of the Welsh Plant Breeding Station, complained of the slovenly appearance of farms and the 'torpid' nature of farmers in the 1920s. Welsh farmers, he wrote, lacked self-motivation and 'pride in farming as a vocation with the love of good farming for its own sake'.[27] Comments of this sort (in Jenkin's case offered by a man from a farming background in receipt of a generous salary) are more a reflection of muddled thinking than an insight into the Welsh agricultural economy. Leaving aside any considerations of soil conditions, poor quality farm buildings and so on, it must be appreciated that the approach of the mid-nineteenth-century Welsh farmer towards his vocation was fundamentally different from that of most of his English colleagues. Farming gave the Welshman a stake in the soil and, provided he could pay the rent and support his household

---

[24] For other examples, see Richard Colyer, 'The Pryse Family of Gogerddan and the Decline of a Great Estate, 1800–1960', *WHR*, 9, no. 4 (1979), 407–31.

[25] NLW, MS 21209C.

[26] NLW, Cilgwyn MS 36. For details of practical farming in nineteenth-century Wales, see R. J. Colyer, 'Aspects of the Pastoral Economy in pre-Industrial Wales', *JRASE*, 144 (1983), 30–56; idem, 'Crop Husbandry in Wales before the Onset of Mechanisation', *Folk Life*, 21(1982–3), 49–70; idem, 'Horses and Equine Improvement in the Economy of Modern Wales', *AHR*, 39, pt. 2 (1991), 126–42; idem, 'The Size of Farms in Late Eighteenth and Early Nineteenth Century Cardiganshire', *BBCS*, XXVII, pt. 1 (1976), 119–26. Apart from their persistent adherence to traditional practices, farmers generally failed also to grasp the marketing opportunities offered by the expanding railway system. D. W. Howell, 'The Impact of Railways on Agricultural Development in Nineteenth-century Wales', *WHR*, 7, no. 1 (1974), 62.

[27] T. J. Jenkin, 'The Expression of Welsh Agriculture', *Journal of the Agricultural Society. UCW*, XXIV (1935), 11.

at an appropriate level from the produce of the land, the pursuit of high levels of profit was not his only consideration. To him, religious observance, bonds of kinship and standing in the community were of paramount significance and, as Alwyn D. Rees so convincingly demonstrated, the completion of a poem or essay for the local eisteddfod was every bit as important as producing abundant surpluses of wealth. Few men would dream of bringing in the hay on a Sunday, regardless of the weather, since 'loss of crops is preferable to the loss of status which would result from unfaithfulness, not only to one's God, but to the standards cherished by one's forbears'.[28]

Such an attitude, combined with an intense sense of belonging to the land, a pride in self-reliance, localism of tradition and nuance of language, provided cohesion to the fabric of rural society. Individual and group security arose from a world view that '. . . the old ways were always the best: the old order, the old customs, the old methods', and this would only begin to disintegrate as technological developments in the following century delivered profound psychological blows.[29] The persistence of tradition, embodied in the long continuance of mutual dependence at focal points in the farming year, offered a means of survival, but at the same time a disincentive to innovation and initiative. In this situation, an individual breaking ranks and suggesting change was seen to be challenging the security of the group and avoiding his traditional obligations towards society. Cognate with this outlook was a deep suspicion of outsiders and external influences.[30] Thus would T. H. Cooke's 'English ways' be seen as an imposition, a threat to security and an insidious erosion of confidence. His English language, too, was probably perceived as a malignant and disruptive influence; the language of progress perhaps, but equally the language of the pursuit of Mammon and of questionable moral standpoints which would ultimately threaten the carefully nurtured continuity of generations.

To the average farmer reared in this tradition, the well-intentioned efforts of the paternalistic and highly-Anglicized gentry classes to promote novel agricultural methods by way of the county agricultural societies probably had little effect. Whatever gloss the gentry patrons may have put on their motives, others could not avoid the suspicion that the activities of the local agricultural society were as much a means of offering a palliative to compensate the smaller tenant or

---

[28] Alwyn D. Rees, *Life in a Welsh Countryside: A Social Study of Llanfihangel yng Ngwynfa* (Cardiff, 1950), p. 144. My own grandfather, a Tory churchman from Northamptonshire, held the same views in the 1930s.

[29] David Parry-Jones, *My Own Folk* (Llandysul, 1972), pp. 91–2. For English parallels, see Richard Jefferies, *The Toilers of the Field* (London, 1892), p. 246, and for technological change see, inter alia, J. Geraint Jenkins, *Agricultural Transport in Wales* (Cardiff, 1962), pp. 11–27; idem, 'Rural Industry in Brecknock', *Brycheiniog*, XIV (1970), 1; Elfyn Scourfield, 'Rural Society in the Vale of Glamorgan' in Prys Morgan (ed.), *Glamorgan County History. Volume VI. Glamorgan Society 1780–1980* (Cardiff, 1988), pp. 225–32.

[30] A. H. Bunting (ed.), *Change in Agriculture* (London, 1970), passim.

labouring man for being on the lower rungs of the economic ladder as a positive contribution to agrarian prosperity.[31] While the business of the county societies was conducted exclusively in English, the Welsh language became increasingly the medium of the more democratic, farmer-run societies established in the 1840s and 1850s. Yet even these, whose purpose was to provide an educational forum for those who could not afford to attend the shows and other activities sponsored by the old county societies, were patronized in the main by the more affluent who had the time and leisure to be away from their holdings.[32]

Besides the patronage of the county agricultural societies, the gentry, whether resident or absentee, sought to promote new methods of farming on their estate home farms. Hence the Alderney, Guernsey and Ayrshire cattle, the Southdown sheep, the neatly hoed rows of turnips and other manifestations of what was widely referred to as 'the spirit of improvement'.[33] These farms yielded provisions for the house and stables and a surplus for sale in the local community, and were seen by many landowners as vehicles for agricultural advance, offering tenants an opportunity to view the practical application of novel techniques.[34] Their effectiveness would have entirely depended upon the local relevance of the systems being demonstrated and how clearly the landowner or his agent was able to transmit information to the tenants in a form which they could readily comprehend. The logic of crop rotations might be there for all to see, but the arcane skills and advanced planning required for their success demanded careful and detailed explanation, not merely a bland statement in a tenancy agreement. Above all, unfamiliar systems and technologies had to be seen to be practicable, if they were to stand any chance of being emulated by tenants. Unfortunately, many of the new farming methods put into practice by the gentry were neither profitable nor of the remotest relevance to the realities of farming in Wales. The extraordinary, and sometimes bizarre, farming activities of Thomas Johnes (d.1816) of Hafod, Cardiganshire, provide a somewhat extreme example of the combination of lofty motives and admirable intentions with a want of common sense. Guided by his friend and mentor, the agriculturalist and political economist

---

[31] For details, see Richard Colyer, 'Early Agricultural Societies in South Wales', *WHR*, 12, no. 4 (1985), 567–81; D. W. Howell, 'Merioneth Agriculture and the Farming Community a Century Ago', *JMHRS*, VIII, pt. 1 (1977), 71–8; H. Edmunds, 'History of the Brecknockshire Agricultural Society, 1755–1955', *Brycheiniog*, II (1956), 32–6; W. H. Howse, 'Radnorshire Agriculture Societies', *TRS*, XV (1945), 28; J. D. K. Lloyd, 'Montgomery in the Nineteenth Century', *MC*, LVIII (1963–4), 94; I. Rees, *Rings and Rosettes: The History of the Pembrokeshire Agricultural Society, 1784–1977* (Llandysul, 1977), passim.

[32] Thomas J. Hopkins, 'Two Hundred Years of Agriculture in Glamorgan', *GH*, 8 (1974), 70–4.

[33] Benjamin H. Malkin, *The Scenery, Antiquities, and Biography, of South Wales* (2 vols., London, 1807), I, p. 416.

[34] Francis Jones, 'The Vaughans of Golden Grove', *THSC* (1966), 188; idem, 'Some Farmers of Bygone Pembrokeshire', ibid. (1943–4), 133–51; D. W. Howell, 'The Economy of the Landed Estates of Pembrokeshire c. 1680–1830', *WHR*, 3, no. 3 (1967), 267; R. J. Colyer, 'The Gogerddan Demesne Farm 1818–22', *Ceredigion*, 7, no. 2 (1973), 170–88.

James Anderson (whose experience was drawn from the rich farmlands of East Lothian), Johnes attempted to persuade his tenants to grow turnips and wheat, to introduce poorly-adapted non-local cattle breeds and, oblivious of the impossibility of marketing them in a locality of traditional tastes, to make Stilton, Gloucester and Parmesan cheeses. The tenants had the good sense to ignore most of his recommendations and were especially sceptical of his enthusiasm for improving local wool quality by introducing Merino sheep to the wet, acidic hills of Cardiganshire. Sheep seem to delight in dying at any time, but to anticipate success in west Wales with a breed originating on the desiccated plains of central Spain is to exhibit a naive, if touching, faith in the miraculous![35] It is hardly surprising that such outlandish and alien notions were rejected wholesale by the allegedly 'backward' tenantry, who continued to adopt a cautious and conservative approach to their farming throughout much of the century. Moreover, it is probably fair to conclude that *where* tenants were prepared to emulate systems adopted by their landlords, they would have been more likely to take notice of a Welsh-speaking resident squire whose interests were closer to their own than of an absentee proprietor whose instructions were executed by an English or Scottish agent.

Notwithstanding the comment by those early luminaries of agricultural education, William Fream and William Somerville of Newcastle, that science was not for labouring folk who should be satisfied with labouring, local farmers' groups met regularly to discuss agricultural matters in the Welsh language in the late nineteenth century.[36] While some of these meetings were held at the instigation of local enthusiasts or opinion leaders, others were run as extramural classes by rural schools. Typically, in 1893, Thomas Jones, head of Penmorfa Board School, Penbryn (Cards.), worked closely with his pupil-teacher Tom Elias to organize an agricultural class for farmers of all ages in the Rhydlewis area of the county.[37] But the primary thrust in this direction came from the Departments of Agriculture established at the University Colleges of Aberystwyth and Bangor in the early 1890s. Some twenty years previously, during the 1877–8 session of the new College at Aberystwyth, Professor Henry Tanner of the Royal Agricultural College, Cirencester, had delivered a widely-appreciated series of twenty lectures on scientific agriculture. This enterprise had been funded by a gift of £200 from Henry Parnall, a London businessman and Vice-President of the College, the residue of this money being used to cover the cost of a translation into Welsh, by Cadwaladr Davies of Bangor, of Tanner's 'First Principles of Agriculture', copies of

---

[35] R. J. Moore-Colyer, *A Land of Pure Delight: Selections from the Correspondence of Thomas Johnes of Hafod, Cardiganshire (1748–1816)* (Llandysul, 1992), pp. 32–4.
[36] Cyril Tyler, 'The History of the Agricultural Education Association, 1894–1914', *Agricultural Progress*, 48 (1973), 3.
[37] W. S. Jones, 'A Brief Survey of Agricultural Education in Wales during the past twenty-five years', *Journal of the Agricultural Society. UCW*, XXVII (1938), 14–15.

which were distributed gratis to farmers. In June 1891, as a means of building on Tanner's foundations, Principal T. Francis Roberts appointed Thomas Parry, the first of three lecturers in agriculture. With his colleagues James Wilson and Alan Murray, both of whom were Scotsmen, Parry was charged with the task of lecturing in agriculture at extramural locations and establishing field demonstrations of a wide range of improved farming activities. Given that these stalwarts had little alternative but to travel by rail, on foot, on horseback and by bicycle in the generally inclement climatic conditions of west Wales, their work took on something of an epic character as they stalked the countryside with proselytizing zeal. But for all their enthusiasm, of the three men only Parry could speak Welsh, the importance of which at this time is reflected in details of the attendance at classes. At the six lectures given by Wilson at St Clears in the winter of 1892, for example, attendance declined from an initial fifty to eight, while Murray drew 120 people to his first lecture at Cynwil Gaeo, Carmarthenshire, but, no doubt to his embarrassment, no one appeared at the last lecture of the series. In contrast, Parry regularly attracted audiences in excess of two hundred, a tribute to his linguistic and pedagogical skills.[38] That he was clearly an effective and persuasive communicator is apparent from the evidence of J. Morgan Davies of Ffrwd-fâl who told the Welsh Land Commissioners that Parry 'manages to use the Welsh language for scientific purposes better than anyone I ever heard'.[39] In pursuit of its quest to further the interests of local farming, the University College at Aberystwyth had established a number of agricultural scholarships by the mid-1890s. Expressing his disappointment, in a speech in 1904, that so few farmers had put forward their sons for scholarships compared to those who had tendered for theology studentships, Alan Murray failed to realize the kudos associated with preferment in church and chapel, besides which the bleak prospects for the agricultural industry at the time were hardly conducive to the furtherance of its academic study.[40] It is just possible, moreover, that farmers were inclined towards the view of the writer of the Book of Ecclesiasticus that a man can rarely become wise whose hand is to the plough and whose talk is of bullocks.[41]

In early nineteenth-century England, the complex web of agricultural information linkages was supported by the burgeoning farming press, and by 1810 some 20,000 copies of weekly journals dealing with dairying, stockbreeding, poultry and general agricultural matters were being sold.[42] Complemented by a number of

---

[38] But his estimable career came to an abrupt halt in 1900 when he was dismissed from the College following allegations of assault on two women at the Farmers' Arms Hotel, Brynaman. For this, and much of the foregoing paragraph, see Richard Colyer, *Man's Proper Study: A History of Agricultural Science Education in Aberystwyth, 1878–1978* (Llandysul, 1982), pp. 30–6.

[39] Royal Commission on Land, *Minutes of Evidence*, vol. III (1895), Qs. 37560–1.

[40] Colyer, *Man's Proper Study*, p. 36.

[41] Ecclesiasticus 38: 25.

[42] Nicholas Goddard, 'The Development and Influence of Agricultural Periodicals and Newspapers, 1780–1880', *AHR*, 31, no. 2 (1983), 123.

long-standing periodical works like the *Journal of the Royal Agricultural Society of England*, the *Transactions of the Highland and Agricultural Society*, and numerous specialist and general texts, these represented a formidable volume of agricultural information. In Wales the situation was rather different, and if a limited range of agricultural information, and pamphlets, booklets and essays appeared under the sponsorship of eisteddfodau, few tracts of any significance were available in the tongue spoken by the bulk of farmers.[43] Works like William Owen Pughe's translation of Thomas Johnes' nostrums, *Cynghorion priodor o Garedigion I ddeiliaid ei dyddynod* (1800), whose eccentricities of spelling and dialect made it incomprehensible to most farmers, were of little practical value and, although the agricultural writer William Youatt claimed in 1837 that the recent improvement in Welsh mountain sheep could be attributed in part to the translation into Welsh of 'some tracts of plain instruction', texts of genuine utility were few and far between.[44] Despite the good intentions of Nonconformist divines like the Revd John Owen of Tyn-llwyn (1808–76), whose *Detholiad Magwraeth a Rheolaeth y Da Byw mwyaf priodol I Dywysogaeth Cymru* (1860) was widely sought after, the Welsh Land Commissioners admitted that the lack of well-informed agricultural literature in Welsh was a barrier to progress.[45] The year following the publication of the final report of the Commission, the academic and civil servant Cadwaladr Bryner Jones (1872–1954) produced *Egwyddorion Gwrteithio*, in which he attempted to set out the scientific principles of manuring. In his foreword, Bryner Jones explained that the book had been written in response to the complaints of farmers throughout Wales that no accessible source of information on this subject was available in Welsh.[46] Several years previously, the Board of Agriculture had begun to print Welsh versions of some of its advisory pamphlets, although production of bilingual forms of the official June Agricultural Returns did not occur until 1907.[47] But this provided little more than lip service. As the Welsh Land Commission Report was at pains to point out, few, if any, of the Board of Agriculture's inspectors travelling in Wales understood Welsh, while none of the various pieces of ameliorative legislation, including the Ground Game Act, the Allotments Act and the Fertilizers and Feeding Stuffs Act, had been translated. It

---

[43] Appendix B of the Report of the Welsh Land Commission lists a number of eisteddfod prize essays and kindred works. Of the sixty-four reports on agricultural matters emanating from the Colleges at Aberystwyth and Bangor, only seven were issued in Welsh.

[44] It was claimed in the early 1930s that only four Welsh-language volumes dealing with agriculture were available. A. O. Evans, 'Some Welsh Agricultural Writers', *Welsh Journal of Agriculture*, VIII (1932), 71–84.

[45] Royal Commission on Land, *Report* (1896), p. 288.

[46] For details of the career of this remarkable man, who was involved in virtually all aspects of the development of Welsh agriculture for half a century, see Llewelyn Phillips, 'Prominent Welsh Agriculturists: Cadwaladr Bryner Jones, 1872–1954', *Journal of the Agricultural Society. UCW*, LX (1979), 143–9.

[47] In its 'Notes on Ox Warble Fly', the Board recognized the linguistic differences between north and south. Thus *Nodiadau ar Gleren yr Ych* and *Nodiadau ar Wybedyn y Gweryd*.

had been alleged that a translation of the Agricultural Holdings Act (1883) had arisen from the pen of 'a Welsh barrister', but this was not available for general inspection, so that many farmers were ignorant of the fact that the permissive Act of 1875 had been amended by the tighter 1883 legislation.[48]

The above, however, is not to claim a complete absence of relevant periodical literature in Welsh, and if monthlies like *Yr Amaethydd* and *Yr Amaethwr* folded within a short time after their foundation, other journals offered comment on agricultural and rural matters. *Seren Gomer* gave details of market conditions together with comment on a wide vista of countryside issues, including rents, common lands, tithes and the game laws, while the radical monthly *Y Diwygiwr* provided regular editorial notes on the prevailing state of Welsh farming. Together with other shorter-lived journals between 1830 and 1850, *Seren Gomer* and *Y Diwygiwr* were read by upwards of ten thousand people each month and, according to Thomas Williams, the Lampeter magistrate's clerk, comprised 'the staple means of information'.[49] Again, Samuel Roberts's *Y Cronicl* and Thomas Gee's *Y Traethodydd* focused on the widespread grievances of the agricultural community after the mid-1840s. In like manner, William Rees (Gwilym Hiraethog) attracted many readers with his 'Llythurau 'Rhen Ffarmwr' (Letters of the Old Farmer), published in the fortnightly *Yr Amserau*, which he edited for the first decade of its life. Subsequent to the amalgamation of Thomas Gee's *Baner Cymru* and *Yr Amserau*, the offspring, *Baner ac Amserau Cymru* joined *Y Genedl Gymreig* as the most widely-read newspaper among the farming population. However, although these journals and newspapers devoted a limited amount of space to practical farming matters, their agrarian content was essentially political, with a strong commitment to promoting the interests of farmers in the land question debate and, in particular, giving maximum publicity to their cause over the vexed issue of tithes.[50] As Ieuan Gwynedd Jones has noted with respect to political comment in the circulating Welsh-language publications, the tortuous use of language and circumlocution of argument tended to militate against clarity and to blur the edges of reality.[51] In any event, the lack of widely available and authoritative scientific and technical texts on farming in the tongue of the overwhelming majority of farmers must inevitably have remained a stumbling block to agricultural progress.

The Farmer and his Men

Even the most cursory study of the graphic art of the eighteenth and nineteenth centuries highlights profound temporal changes in the perception of the rural

---

[48] Royal Commission on Land, *Report* (1896), pp. 91–2.
[49] Jones, *Rebecca's Children*, p. 81.
[50] Royal Commission on Land, *Report* (1896), Appendix B.
[51] Ieuan Gwynedd Jones, *Explorations and Explanations: Essays in the Social History of Victorian Wales* (Llandysul, 1981), p. 110.

labourer in British society. By the late eighteenth century the wistful and artificial pastoral imagery had given way to a cheerful (and, to the modern eye, rather distasteful) portrayal of the 'industrious poor' which yielded, within a few decades, to a romantic image of natural harmony wherein the labouring man merged as far as possible into his surroundings, his cottage sunk deep in shade, and his chief virtue being to be seen but not heard. As they peer from the gloom towards the highly-lit mansions of the rich or the ample stockyards of the farmer, labourers are revealed as shadowy figures; visible certainly, but sufficiently far away to save the viewer from confronting awkward questions as to why they are so ragged and why their expressions bear a look of mingled defiance and hopelessness. Their farmer employers, meanwhile, grew steadily in status and affluence, more especially after the Napoleonic Wars, which brought unprecedented prosperity to the agricultural interest. English writers, from Clare, Eliot and Cobbett through Flora Thompson and M. R. Mitford to Hardy and Richard Jefferies, testified to the farmer's growing craving for status, reflected in his display of pecuniary strength through conspicuous consumption.[52] As the farmer's sense of *amour propre* intensified, there developed a widening gulf between himself and his workers so that in 1844 a leader-writer in *The Times* could observe that, compared to the past, ' . . . the closeness of the tie between master and man is broken; the term of servitude is now a more uncertain and changeable one'.[53]

In his deposition before the Welsh Land Commission, Tom Ellis attempted to minimize the existence of social differences between the Welsh farmer and labourer by emphasizing a basis of equality fostered by the common bond of Nonconformity.[54] Some modern historians, impressed by the long continuance of the tradition in Wales of the 'living-in' labourer working closely alongside his employer, also perceive a lack of social distinction.[55] Others, however, have argued that the degree of democracy implied by mutual religious observance and a shared language is grossly overestimated and that the farmer strove, by a variety of means, to maintain a distinctive social distance from his workers. Nineteenth-century propagandists for the farmer also thought along these lines. Samuel Roberts and Gwilym Hiraethog, who espoused the cause of the small farmer in his resistance to tithes, rates and other contentious issues, saw little political advantage to be gained 'by stirring the agricultural workers; they counted for

---

[52] Paul Johnson, 'Conspicuous Consumption and Working-Class Culture in late Victorian and Edwardian Britain', *TRHS*, 38 (1988), 27–42; for typical examples, see Select Committee on Agriculture, *Minutes of Evidence*, BPP 2, 1833, p. 527 and Flora Thompson, *Lark Rise to Candleford* (London, 1944), pp. 52–4; R. J. Moore-Colyer, 'Farmer and Labour Force in the Nineteenth Century', *JRASE*, 148 (1987), 120–9.
[53] *The Times*, 10 June 1844.
[54] Royal Commission on Land, *Minutes of Evidence*, vol. I (1894), Qs. 1700–09.
[55] D. W. Howell, 'The Agricultural Labourer in Nineteenth-Century Wales', *WHR*, 6, no. 3 (1973), 284–5; idem, 'Labour Organization among Agricultural Workers in Wales, 1872–1921', *WHR*, 16, no. 1 (1992), 63–92.

nothing and could be virtually disregarded'.[56] That a clear and unequivocal distinction existed is further emphasized by the evidence of written agreements between the two parties in which only the farmer is accorded the dignity of the prefix 'Mr', while the written accounts of the more substantial farmers, setting out details of perquisites and part-payment of wages in kind, underline the carefully-orchestrated class differences. A distinction, of course, needs to be made between the relative positions of the *gwas* (living-in servant) and the *gweithiwr* (day labourer) vis-à-vis the farmer, but current evidence suggests that to argue the case for a single, unstratified class of farming/labouring folk is to overstretch credibility.[57] Yet the Welsh Land Commission did precisely this: their argument for the absence of social cleavage was based substantially on the fact that farmers were readily prepared to send their sons to labour on other holdings.[58] They failed to note, however, that these sons were dispatched from home primarily to gain experience, and in recognition of their status as farmers' sons on the recipient farm they were invited to eat with master and mistress in the 'best kitchen', as opposed to the 'back kitchen', the province of labourers and servants.[59] Again, like the travelling stallion man or the farmer, a farmer's son visiting another farm would stay overnight in the best bedroom and would not be expected to clamber into the loft with the servants.[60] The latter were generally confined to the chill and gloom of the outhouses, and if some were allowed to spend a few precious hours of a winter evening in the back kitchen, they were normally expected to go 'to their stables and to their loft'.[61] John Hughes of Aberffraw, Anglesey, echoing the statement of his close neighbour Richard Rowland that farmers did not consider their servants and labourers 'as made of the same flesh as they', was firmly of the view that the class gulf arose from differences in education. Admitting, with other witnesses before the Welsh Land Commission, that the *smaller* farmers had their offspring educated at the same schools as their workers, Hughes observed that it was increasingly common practice for the more prosperous to pack off their children to boarding schools.[62] By this means the common bond of a shared language would be eroded by the social attitudes inculcated by an educational background steeped in privilege and class consciousness.

---

[56] David A. Pretty, *The Rural Revolt that Failed: Farm Workers' Trade Unions in Wales, 1889–1950* (Cardiff, 1989), pp. 2–5. The labourer was not entirely ignored by the periodical press. *Y Celt*, established in 1878 and a consistent advocate of land nationalization, espoused the labourer's cause, while *Y Werin*, under the editorship of John Jones (Ap Ffarmwr) lent support to the short-lived labourer's union which had its roots in Anglesey and Caernarfonshire.

[57] Richard Colyer, 'Conditions of Employment amongst the Farm Labour Force in Nineteenth Century Wales', *Llafur*, 3, no. 3 (1982), 33–41.

[58] Royal Commission on Land, *Report* (1896), p. 598.

[59] Jenkins, *Agricultural Community*, pp. 55–7.

[60] Ibid., p. 266.

[61] Royal Commission on Land, *Report* (1896), pp. 640–1.

[62] Royal Commission on Land, *Minutes of Evidence*, vol. II (1894), Qs. 20937–42, 21975–6, 22542–4.

To the extent that successful farmers served as minor administrators as well as employers, they enjoyed considerable local power, and whether or not this was used as a means of exploitation would presumably vary with the personal qualities and upbringing of the individual. Of Welsh farmers in the early 1920s, only 10 per cent had risen from labouring backgrounds, while three-quarters were themselves the sons of farmers. Among these the great majority had known no other occupation than that of residents or workers on the parental farm, a fact which, it might be argued, would serve to perpetuate entrenched views and social outlooks.[63]

The traditional link between the farm and the community, fostered and strengthened by a long-established pattern of mutual obligations, was steadily breaking down by the closing decades of the nineteenth century.[64] This was accelerated, in the arable areas of Wales, by the widespread adoption of the reaper-binder by 1900, an innovation which drastically reduced the need for part-time labour.[65] Elsewhere, the need for part-time workers declined less as a result of mechanization than as a consequence of the extensive abandonment of residual labour-intensive arable systems in favour of livestock grazing in response to the depressed agricultural conditions of the eighties and nineties.[66] As the demand for seasonal labour declined in the livestock-rearing areas (which, of course, pre-dominated in Wales), it was still necessary to retain a permanent and committed labour force to serve the livestock economy. This was made all the more difficult as emigration to the rapidly-developing industrial areas of the south, aided by the railways, so siphoned off labour that numbers of farm workers declined by 45.7 per cent between 1851 and 1911.[67] This movement of young agricultural workers into the southern valleys substantially strengthened the Welsh-speaking population therein, so that by 1885 some 90 per cent of miners in south Wales spoke Welsh as they went about their daily tasks.[68] Apart from a simple quantitative effect, emigration from rural districts maintained the local level of agricultural wages at increasing levels in real terms, and as his financial position improved the labourer had less need for perquisites so that the subservience embodied in a system where payment of wages were partly in kind began to evaporate. To his recently-gained political independence, then, the labourer added a sense of

---

[63] A. W. Ashby and J. M. Jones, 'The Social Origin of Welsh Farmers', *Welsh Journal of Agriculture*, II (1926), 19.
[64] For co-operation in farm tasks, see Jenkins, *Agricultural Community*, passim.
[65] David H. Morgan, *Harvesters and Harvesting, 1840–1900: A Study of the Rural Proletariat* (London, 1981), pp. 17–21.
[66] Royal Commission on Labour, *Agricultural Labour in Wales* (1893), Report of D. Lleufer Thomas, p. 7.
[67] Howell, 'The Impact of Railways', 59.
[68] See Chapter 2, p. 94.

freedom from the need for a 'cap-in-hand' approach to his master, from which followed an inevitable change in their relationship.[69]

In the south, where grain production remained a significant component of the agricultural economy, the diminishing harvest labour force was supplemented, where required, by annual drafts of farm workers from the agriculturally-depressed areas of Wiltshire, Gloucestershire, Devon and Somerset. While the transient nature of most of these people would have left little impression upon the Welsh language where it remained in general use, their presence each year must have influenced the outlook, attitudes and aspirations of the indigenous population.[70] In other parts of Wales, in particular the central and western districts, labour shortfalls were often overcome by the employment of children from English reformatory schools, these being frequently the only English speakers in monoglot Welsh communities. Some children, of course, only remained on farms for brief spells, although anecdotal evidence suggests that a continual supply of this source of cheap labour was sustained over a considerable period. Many viewed their presence as having a malign and corrupting influence, whereby innocent locals were introduced to such dangerous and pernicious habits as smoking, yet others were keen to secure the services of reformatory children to instruct their own offspring in English. The quality of English so imparted probably left much to be desired! In the meantime, concerned for the spiritual welfare of the outsiders, chapels introduced the English language to some of their services and in this respect the presence of the children may have had a potentially powerful Anglicizing effect. Thus, as Brinley Thomas memorably observed, was the road to Anglicization paved with many acts of good Welsh intentions.[71] But there was little new in this matter of language change by contagion. For generations the peregrinations of drovers and other trans-border migrants had been instrumental in introducing English elements into everyday speech, while in those areas contiguous to the Bristol Channel English followed patterns of trade.[72]

The Gentry and the Welsh Language

For all his impeccable Welsh ancestry (and he set much store by his Welshness), Thomas Johnes of Hafod could neither speak nor read Welsh, a fact which he confessed with much shame to Walter Davies (Gwallter Mechain).[73] It would, however, be strictly inaccurate to maintain that the gentry *as a class* were totally ignorant of Welsh by the nineteenth century. The largely anecdotal evidence

---

[69] L. J. Williams and Dot Jones, 'The Wages of Agricultural Labourers in the Nineteenth Century: The Evidence from Glamorgan', *BBCS*, XXIX, pt. 4 (1982), 752.
[70] Royal Commission on Land, *Report* (1896), p. 602.
[71] See Chapter 2, p. 94.
[72] M. I. Williams, 'Some Aspects of the Economic and Social Life of the Southern Regions of Glamorgan 1600–1800', *Morgannwg*, 3 (1959), 36–7.
[73] NLW, MS 1805, f. 517.

which exists probably obscures the extent of at least a degree of bilingualism within that social group. In the early part of the century, for example, families in the south-west like the Lloyds of Coedmor, the Colbys of Ffynhonnau and the Bowens of Llwyn-gwair were fluent Welsh speakers, with George Bowen of Llwyn-gwair regularly dispatching his children to Welsh-language Sunday schools. Even in south Pembrokeshire, the young Hugh Owen of Orielton was obliged to learn Welsh during his school holidays, although the depths of his enthusiasm for the task remain unrecorded![74] Welsh may even have been the everyday norm for minor gentry families like the Davieses of Ffrwd-fâl, Carmarthenshire, or homely figures like Thomas Colby, Pantyderi, Tregaron, who lived in a style little different from that of his more substantial tenants.[75] Among the great landed magnates at the close of the century, like W. R. M. Wynne of Peniarth and Hugh Ellis Nanney of Gwynfryn, Cricieth, Welsh was by no means a dead letter, for both men believed that knowledge of the tongue facilitated dealings with their tenants.[76] Their kinsman, Sir Watkin Williams Wynn (1772–1840), fifth baronet of Wynnstay, had married the daughter of a prime minister and turned down the Viceregalty of India, yet he retained his Welsh and was well-respected as a decent, understanding and humane landlord.[77] Far to the south, Sir Watkin's contemporaries at Aberpergwm, Llwynmadog and Dolau Cothi, respectively in the Vale of Neath, Breconshire and Carmarthenshire, also considered it right and proper to have some grasp of Welsh.[78]

How *well* these people spoke Welsh, and how assiduously they encouraged their children to do so, remains a matter for conjecture. Perhaps the testimony of John Aeron Thomas to the Welsh Land Commission, applauding the growing interest in Welsh among the gentry and their children, should not be taken too seriously since there are numerous examples to the contrary.[79] John Jones of Ystrad, MP (d. 1842), a civilized and cultivated Welsh speaker, was implacably opposed to the sustenance of the language, while the radical Edward Crompton Lloyd Hall, who played so equivocal a role in the Rebecca Riots, condemned the Welsh tongue since he believed that it distorted the truth and was 'the language of slavery'.[80] Around the same time, Jane Evans of Highmead, Carmarthenshire, the descendant of a Welsh family of great antiquity, who both spoke and wrote Welsh with fluency, vehemently forbade her children from so doing on the grounds, as H. M. Vaughan put it with extraordinary indelicacy, 'that bilingualism in early

---

[74] D. W. Howell, *Patriarchs and Parasites: The Gentry of South-West Wales in the Eighteenth Century* (Cardiff, 1986), pp. 199–200.
[75] NLW, Castle Hill MSS, 2536–7; Jenkins, *Agricultural Community*, p. 19.
[76] Royal Commission on Land, *Minutes of Evidence*, vol. I (1894), Qs. 9564, 11318.
[77] T. W. Pritchard, *The Wynns at Wynnstay* (Caerwys, 1982), pp. 150–2.
[78] Herbert M. Vaughan, *The South Wales Squires* (London, 1926), p. 201.
[79] Royal Commission on Land, *Minutes of Evidence*, vol. III (1895), Q. 51862.
[80] Williams, *The Rebecca Riots*, pp. 14–24.

youth tends to stunt rather than to enlarge the juvenile mind and talents'.[81] The claims of the staunchly Unionist Sir Pryse Pryse of Gogerddan, Cardiganshire (1838–1906) and his son Pryse Loveden Pryse (1862–1900) to be fluent in Welsh were queried by the Aberaeron postmaster, Thomas Davies, in the 1890s. In his evidence to the Welsh Land Commission he admitted that Sir Pryse could speak a little Welsh, but like many gentlemen with a smattering of the language, 'you cannot call him a Welshman'. In fact, he remarked, warming to his theme, with the exception of Major Hughes of Allt-lwyd and Mr Lloyd of Waunifor, there were few Cardiganshire gentlemen who could be accorded the title of 'a thorough Welshman'.[82]

One might conclude from this brief review that on balance, although there were exceptions, the ability of the overwhelming majority of the landed gentry to speak Welsh probably extended little further than the barest essentials by the close of the nineteenth century. While they may have been able to give the simplest everyday instructions to tenants and estate workers, their capacity to sustain a conversation might be likened to that of the late twentieth-century Englishman, equipped with schoolboy French, attempting to explain the laws of cricket to a Parisian. Yet, be they resident or absentee, Anglicized Welsh or English *advenae*, the gentry as a whole remained alive to their duties as patrons of the indigenous culture. They subscribed to Welsh books and periodicals, promoted eisteddfodau and supported antiquarian organizations like the Cymmrodorion Society and the Society of Ancient British Bowmen, the latter established in 1818 under the auspices of the Wynnstay family.[83] Similarly, many were prepared to lend material support to the building and restoration of schools, the funding of local dispensaries to the poor, the underwriting of local Friendly Societies and other charitable enterprises.[84] A complex blend of motives, including an awareness of Christian obligations, the importance of self-preservation, a sense of *noblesse oblige* and straightforward political expediency coloured their approach towards charity and towards Nonconformity. There were, of course, extremists of the ilk of Edward Corbet of Ynysymaengwyn and John Pugh Pryse of Mathafarn, two fiercely anti-Methodist landowners who viewed alienation from the established Church as tantamount to treason. Nevertheless, the landed classes as a whole were tolerant of religious Nonconformity in its various manifestations.[85] Few cared for theological

---

[81] Vaughan, *South Wales Squires*, p. 202.
[82] Royal Commission on Land, *Minutes of Evidence*, vol. III (1895), Qs. 47844–51.
[83] See, in particular, Prys Morgan, 'The Hunt for the Welsh Past in the Romantic Period' in E. J. Hobsbawm and T. Ranger (eds.), *The Invention of Tradition* (Cambridge, 1983), pp. 43–100.
[84] See, for example, R. J. Colyer, 'The Gentry and the County in Nineteenth-Century Cardiganshire', *WHR*, 10, no. 4 (1981), passim; A. M. E. Davies, 'Wages, Prices, and Social Improvements in Cardiganshire, 1750–1850', *Ceredigion*, X, no. 1 (1984), 46–9.
[85] H. Thomas, 'Edward Corbet, Ynysymaengwyn: An Eccentric Country Squire', *JMHRS*, IV, pt. 2 (1962), 143–5; Peter R. Roberts, 'The Social History of the Merioneth Gentry c. 1680–1840', ibid., IV, pt. 3 (1963), 219.

niceties and nuances, and if the liberal ideals embodied in Nonconformity were anathema to a class holding firm patrician convictions as to the nature of society, their attitudes were usually tempered by common sense. They realized that honours in the battle for the hearts and minds of the people were moving away from the church towards the chapel, but were still careful to accede to the requests of Nonconformists for land to build meeting houses, themselves donating funds to dissenting groups engaged in building projects.[86]

As was the case in the rest of Britain, many nineteenth-century Welsh landowners were, for a variety of reasons, either wholly or partially absent from their estates. This is not to argue that they showed no interest in their properties, since their voluminous books of correspondence with agents, bailiffs and stewards indicate quite the opposite. Inherently, there was nothing wrong with absenteeism, provided that the affairs of the estate were left in the hands of a capable and trustworthy agent. However, the combination of absentee landlord and incompetent and unenlightened agent was a sure means of promoting discontent among tenants, estate workers, and the many members of the community who depended upon the estate for their livelihood.[87] With the increasingly complex legal aspects of estate management in the nineteenth century, even resident owners came to employ agents in the hope that a degree of professionalism would be brought to bear on such matters as collecting rents, settling leases, and the whole gamut of interrelationships between an estate and its tenants.[88] The concern for developing a professional approach towards management meant that the older system of drawing estate stewards from among the ranks of the Welsh-speaking lesser gentry gave way to the recruitment of men purposely trained in estate offices. When the feckless 2nd Earl of Powis took on John Probert as his agent, he acquired a trained professional of similar calibre to the highly competent and efficient Hall W. Keary, agent to the Duke of Newcastle at Hafod in the 1830s.[89] These men, 'professed land-stewards, well versed in several departments of rural economy', as Walter Davies (Gwallter Mechain) observed, were in marked contrast to others who 'aspire no higher than receiving of rents and fees, and drawing of cumbersome leases and contracts, little calculated to benefit either landlord or tenant'.[90] The latter, many of them lawyers or clergymen, were frequently ignorant of the mores of the tenant farmer and were roundly

---

[86] For church and chapel building, see Ieuan Gwynedd Jones, 'The Rebuilding of Llanrhystud Church', *Ceredigion*, VII, no. 2 (1973), 99–116; NLW, Rogers Lewis Deposit, 1971: NLW, Minor Deposits 1088A; NLW, Aberglasney MSS 28.
[87] C. S. Read, 'On the Agriculture of South Wales', *JRASE*, Ser. I, X (1849), 148.
[88] Richard Colyer, 'The Land Agent in Nineteenth-Century Wales', *WHR*, 8, no. 2 (1977), 401–25.
[89] Humphreys, *Crisis of Community*, pp. 136–7; R. J. Moore-Colyer, 'The Hafod Estate under Thomas Johnes and Henry Pelham, Fourth Duke of Newcastle', *WHR*, 8, no. 4 (1977), 282–4.
[90] Walter Davies, *General View of the Agriculture and Domestic Economy of South Wales* (2 vols., London, 1815), I, p. 120.

condemned from chapel pulpit and by radical press as avaricious and overbearing, if not downright malicious, in their treatment of those less fortunate than themselves.[91] The Welsh Land Commission was not entirely impressed by these all-embracing anti-agent polemics, yet only the highly charitable would have spared the egregious Herbert Lloyd of Carmarthen from opprobrium. This corrupt lawyer-agent, of whom it was said 'a reckless streak had blurred the distinction between the pursuit of reputation and notoriety', fished happily in the murky waters of local political intrigue and, by exploiting the gentry's penchant for litigation, acquired substantial wealth.[92] Ironically, Lloyd was a Welsh speaker and might perhaps have been expected to take a tolerant and understanding view of the allegedly anachronistic farming methods practised by tenants on the estates under his management. To those English or Scottish agents involved with many of the larger estates, however, the apparent inefficiency and obscurantism of the tenantry was a source of constant irritation and their letter-books echo with frustration and annoyance. Any attempt at mutual understanding was inevitably hampered by the inability of these people to speak Welsh and, in some cases, their unashamed contempt for the language and all it represented.

Thomas Johnes of Hafod, though supportive of the Welsh tongue and the scholarship associated with it, nevertheless had little respect for the moral or physical qualities of his fellow countrymen. Indeed, he was wedded to the conventional view that Welsh working men were indolent, reactionary, untrustworthy and inclined to drink, all qualities in diametric contrast to those of the thrifty and industrious Scots with whom he had come into contact as a student at the University of Edinburgh. So great was his faith in the sterling character of the northern people that he enlisted the help of his friends, the diplomat Sir Robert Liston, and the surgeon and editor of the *Edinburgh Review*, Robert Anderson, in attracting capital-rich Scottish tenants to Hafod. By their example, he fondly hoped, such gifted individuals would encourage the recalcitrant locals to adopt 'improved' farming techniques. Concurrently, James Todd and John Greenshields, respectively his Scottish gardener and bailiff, together with the curmudgeonly Edinburgh printer, James Henderson, descended on Cardiganshire to help realize the Hafod dream.[93] Very soon others followed in their wake, and by 1812 a McFarlane was managing the Falcondale estate in Cardiganshire and George Robson and Adam Murray were working at nearby Trawsgoed. Robson's brother Thomas oversaw the Nanteos property, William Pitt Currie the far-flung acres of Slebech, while McLarens, Flutters and Mackies occupied a

---

[91] Henry Richard, *Letters and Essays on Wales* (2nd ed., London, 1883), p. 122.
[92] R. G. Thomas, 'Herbert Lloyd of Carmarthen', *THSC* (1971), 109–19.
[93] Moore-Colyer, *Land of Pure Delight*, pp. 3–4. Henderson, who printed a number of Johnes' translations of the French chronicles of the Hundred Years War, was one of the few Scotsmen to master Welsh.

variety of estate posts elsewhere.[94] In selecting Scottish agents and bailiffs, Welsh landed gentlemen were concerned less with personal qualities than professional abilities. Sir Stephen Glynne of Hawarden, although an indefatigable antiquary, was an ineffectual landlord who leaned heavily upon his agent, George Robertson of Kincardineshire. Robertson had been recommended by Sir John Gladstone as 'a first rate agriculturist and excellent man of business', in view of which Glynne chose to ignore the fact that he was not only a Presbyterian but also the father of two illegitimate children by two different women.[95]

There can be little doubt that the appointment of such people over the heads of local Welshmen was both a source of resentment and a means of heightening the language barrier running across many estates.[96] On properties adjacent to the English border, where English had long been common currency, there were few language difficulties by the late nineteenth century and men like J. H. Warburton Lee, agent to the Hanmer property in Flintshire, could claim that his dealings with tenants could be effected as readily in the English as in the Welsh tongue.[97] On the other hand, when Robert Gardiner of Trawsgoed argued somewhat arrogantly that he could 'sense' the needs of tenants, so that language was no impediment to his daily work, this probably struck a hollow note with his interlocutors.[98] This sort of evidence ran counter to that offered in the bulk of submissions to the Land Commission, and tenant farmers throughout Wales lined up to testify to the problems of trust and confidence stemming from the inability of agents to comprehend the tongue of the people. Colonel Wynne-Finch of Voelas may have admitted the desirability of employing Welsh-speaking agents, yet his own agent, in many respects an agreeable man, was a monoglot English speaker whom tenants were reluctant to approach.[99] At Rhiwlas, not far from Wynne-Finch's borders, tenants had been overseen by three non-Welsh-speaking agents in the previous thirty years, while of the seven agents employed on Sir Arthur Stepney's estate at Llandybïe in the past generation, only two understood Welsh.[100] Language apart, many of those agents, it was averred, were inadequately trained and lacked the requisite skills in both estate management and agriculture.[101] In the Bala area, agency was sometimes undertaken by small tradesmen who were both ignorant of their profession and not above abusing their position by setting farmer against farmer and using their influence with landlords to settle

---

[94] S.C. Agriculture, 1833, B.P.P., 2, 13; Hilary M. Thomas, 'Margam Estate Management, 1765–1860', *GH*, VI (1968), 14; NLW, Falcondale 26, 128; NLW, Misc. Deeds, 1921.
[95] A. G. Veysey, 'Sir Stephen Glynne, 1807–74', *FHSJ*, 30 (1982), 151–70.
[96] Jones, *Rebecca's Children*, p. 57.
[97] Royal Commission on Land, *Minutes of Evidence*, vol. IV (1895), Qs. 56438, 57652.
[98] Ibid., *Minutes of Evidence*, vol. III (1894), Q. 49130.
[99] Ibid., *Minutes of Evidence*, vol. I (1894), Q. 15091.
[100] Ibid., *Minutes of Evidence*, vol. III (1894), Q. 38354.
[101] Ibid., *Minutes of Evidence*, vol. I (1894), Q. 12721.

old family scores.[102] Inevitably, however, the level of management competence varied between agents and depended in large measure on the determination of owners to ensure a high standard of professionalism. In appointing Henry Currie as his principal agent, the proprietor of the Gwydir estate near Llanrwst secured the services of a highly-qualified professional who dispatched local sub-agents to his offices in Scotland for training across the broad spectrum of agency duties.[103] But such training did not embrace the learning of Welsh, so that most of the Gwydir management team, as on many other estates, depended on the services of translators. This led to severe difficulties in terms of the explanation of legal complexities and technical language and, more importantly, in terms of loss of confidentiality. The situation on the Nanteos estate in Cardiganshire offers a typical example. Under the life tenancy of the Welsh-speaking W. E. Powell (1788–1854), cordial relations prevailed between tenants and estate office, despite Powell's frequent absences from Wales when the property was supervised by the Aberystwyth solicitor, James Hughes of Glanrheidol. Powell's heir, W. T. R. Powell (1815–78), was the very antithesis of his father: he was a boorish figure who earned much local opprobrium by attempting to coerce his tenants during the election of 1868. Neither he nor his agent, W. E. Phelp, were able to speak Welsh, and in their dealings with farmers relied on the interpretative skills of one Davy Edwards, a somewhat shady character given to imparting his own gloss to a conversation.[104] James Jones, tenant of Tyllwyd, Llanfarian, had been present in the estate office at an interview between Phelp and a monoglot tenant, during the course of which Edwards's translations had totally failed to convey the respective views of the participants.[105] Confusion was thereby heaped upon confusion in an atmosphere wherein confidentiality was quite impossible.

As they assembled the voluminous evidence before them, the Welsh Land Commissioners concluded that whatever may have formerly been the case, the blanket argument that the agents of the 1890s were 'harsh, unscrupulous, arbitrary and cruel' could not be sustained. Yet they could not put aside the language question, often the root of misunderstanding, and were unequivocally of the view that the ability to speak Welsh should be a *sine qua non* of employment for agents in areas where that tongue was in daily use. Besides, they felt, such men should acquire, together with the requisite technical training, 'the average degree of culture and knowledge of a University man'.[106] In so doing they would absorb those qualities of humanity, judgement and toleration so lamentably lacking in previous generations of agents.

---

[102] Ibid., *Minutes of Evidence*, vol. I (1894), Q. 16623 (a).
[103] Ibid., *Minutes of Evidence*, vol. I (1894), Q. 14114.
[104] R. J. Colyer, 'Nanteos: A Landed Estate in Decline, 1800–1930', *Ceredigion*, 9, no. 1 (1980), 58–77.
[105] Royal Commission on Land, *Minutes of Evidence*, vol. III (1895), Q. 48645.
[106] Ibid., *Report* (1896), pp. 249–76.

Estate Management and Estate Relations

Recent studies of the economy and management of the Welsh landed estates in the nineteenth century have raised serious questions regarding the reliability of some of the more extreme anti-landlord tirades of an earlier period. Leaving aside the vexed question of the Game Laws — as problematic in England as in Wales — and of the political issues beyond the scope of this chapter, it is necessary to address the matter of whether or not the institutional aspects of estate management materially influenced landlord/tenant relations.[107] It is, moreover, important to consider the widespread contemporary criticism of the Welsh landed classes — criticism embracing such technical matters as tenurial systems, farm amalgamation and tenant right — against the background of the severe economic plight facing many estates by the later decades of the century.

The simple fact was that for an array of reasons, some self-imposed and others externally determined, many estates found themselves in severe economic doldrums by the 1880s. Thus, while they recognized the duties they bore towards their tenants, and the trust they held for future generations, the need for financial stringency precluded them from discharging their obligations. Forced to adopt such measures as farm amalgamation, distasteful to themselves and anathema to the tenants, they came increasingly to take a severely businesslike view of estate management in the interest of ensuring that at least part of the property passed intact to their heirs.[108]

By the mid-nineteenth century the pre-existing system of leases for lives had almost entirely been replaced by either leases for a fixed term of years or by the annual tenancy. Nevertheless, family succession to farms tended to remain the rule rather than the exception, with sons succeeding their fathers and widows their sons with a regularity that all but amounted to custom.[109] In the main, tenants were issued with printed agreements encapsulating a whole range of restrictive covenants and proscriptions on rotational practice, their function being to encourage good husbandry and to enhance the value of the farm and the prosperity of its tenant. While these agreements implied a laudable concern on the part of a landlord to improve the standard of farming on his estate, many, having been freely adapted from English models, were of questionable relevance to

---

[107] For field sports and the Game Laws, see, inter alia, R. J. Moore-Colyer, 'Gentlemen, Horses and the Turf in Nineteenth Century Wales', *WHR*, 16, no. 1 (1992), 47–62; idem, 'Field Sports, Conservation and the Countryside in Georgian and Victorian Wales', *WHR*, 16, no. 3 (1993), 308–25; C. P. Chenevix Trench, *The Poacher and the Squire* (London, 1967); P. B. Munsche, *Gentlemen and Poachers: The English Game Laws, 1671–1831* (Cambridge, 1981); Royal Commission on Land, *Report* (1896), pp. 499–505.

[108] For details, see Colyer, 'The Gentry and the County', passim; Royal Commission on Land, *Report* (1896), Appendix.

[109] Lewis W. Lloyd, 'Corsygedol, Ardudwy's Principal Estate', *JMHRS*, VIII, pt. 1 (1977), 36; Colyer, 'Farmers and Fields in Nineteenth-century Wales', 32–57.

conditions in Wales. Critics, who believed that agreements should be simplified in order to facilitate the 'free play of intelligence' of the tenant, and to allow him the flexibility to adjust to changing market conditions, condemned the existing documents on the grounds of obsolescence and excessive complexity.[110] In reality, though, vigorous enforcement of agreements was rare, since, in times of agricultural depression in particular, insistence upon conformity to the letter of the covenant could promote genuine hardship. But it is equally clear that whereas some estate offices viewed the covenant as a means of advancing the cause of good husbandry, others saw it as a way of tightening the estate's hold over the tenants – a stick with which to threaten those who might be tempted to poach or, perhaps, cast their votes in an unacceptable manner.

Tenancy agreements with restrictive clauses were the norm both in England and Wales, although, in the case of the former, ancient food and service rents which had been a condition of earlier tenancies had long been forgotten. But on many Welsh estates, such stipulations remained in force into the late nineteenth and even the early twentieth centuries. In 1900 the tenants of the Cilgwyn estate were each expected to provide two turkeys or two geese for their landlord at Michaelmas, while between 1876 and 1878 those at Gogerddan delivered no fewer than 12 turkeys, 56 geese, 12 ducks, 628 fowls, 2,570 eggs and two tongues to the kitchens of the mansion.[111] This none-too-subtle acknowledgement of the subservient role of the tenant must surely have been viewed as an imposition, an overt symbol of deference demanded of a tenant by a landlord who was probably ignorant of his language and hard put even to remember his name.

Of equal concern to the tenants as its contents or context was the language in which the agreement was framed, since it was patently absurd to expect a man slavishly to adhere to the terms of a document in a tongue incomprehensible to him. On some properties where owners and agents were sensitive to the interests of tenants, bilingual agreements had been available for some years, but on others they were issued in English only, and tenants were justifiably aggrieved.[112] Although a tenant could request a translation (normally carried out by a Welsh-speaking clerk in the agent's office), the complexities of legal language and the problems inherent in translating subtle nuances could lead to difficulties, and it was widely believed by the close of the century that *printed* Welsh agreements were essential.[113] But there were dissenting views. Sir John Russell Bailey, whose lands were located in an English-speaking area, saw little purpose in providing Welsh-language leases, while Thomas Prichard, a Welsh-speaking farmer and county councillor from Anglesey, voiced his objection to Welsh translations on the grounds that they would lead to confusion. In support of his view he cited the

[110] Royal Commission on Land, *Report* (1896), pp. 488–99.
[111] Colyer, 'The Pryse Family of Gogerddan', 407–31.
[112] Royal Commission on Land, *Minutes of Evidence*, vol. II (1894), Qs. 19693–6.
[113] Ibid., Qs. 19198–200.

example of a legal case concerning a Welsh-language will, 'in which there was a great dispute about the meaning of certain words in the Welsh language and it cost more than the property was worth'.[114] Making the further point that tenants often contrived to lose their leases and agreements, he suggested that if translations or printed forms were made available, then the English version should be considered the legally binding version.

Whereas landlords normally permitted natural succession to tenancies, the lack of security implicit in the annual tenancy arrangement was a cause of some concern among farming tenants. This was intensified by the fear that the purchase of estates, or outlying estate land, by unsympathetic outsiders might give rise to a new generation of landlords who would be keen to realize some return on their capital investment by exacting higher rents. Thus, it was argued, the perceived lack of security would act as a disincentive to tenants' capital investment and general improvement in farming practice. The absence of legal tenant right was another major bone of contention. The steep increase in off-farm inputs characteristic of much of mid-nineteenth-century farming – fertilisers, artificial feeds, drainage and so on – represented, in Britain as a whole, a major investment of tenant-generated funds. Under the carefully codified framework of landlord-tenant relations, there were no legal means whereby tenants were compensated for unexhausted improvements of this sort if they chose to quit their farms, and a powerful and vociferous lobby agitated throughout the 1850s and 1860s for recognition in law of the principle of compensation.[115] For technical, economic and attitudinal reasons, Welsh tenants' capital investment on a per acre basis remained substantially below that prevailing in England. Nevertheless, Welsh tenants joined in the chorus for *legal* tenant right and were not satisfied by the informal compensatory arrangements long practised by their landlords. The latter, however, strove to retain these arrangements and even after the passing of the permissive Agricultural Holdings Act of 1875 and the statute of 1883, which legally compelled compensation, they frequently failed to apply the letter of the law. By so doing they reinforced what they regarded as their seigneurial right to play the primary role in the relationship with their tenants, concurrently lending further ammunition to their detractors and those bent on forcing a wedge between gentry and farmer.

At the very least, the evidence before the Welsh Land Commission is equivocal in the light which it casts on the landlord/tenant association, particularly with respect to the language question. In areas of the country which had been predominantly English speaking for several generations, neither landowners and their agents nor their tenants felt that language or religious barriers tempered their

[114] Ibid., Q. 19395.
[115] J. R. Fisher, 'Landowners and English Tenant Right, 1845–1852', *AHR*, 31, pt. 1 (1983), 15–25; J. R. McQuiston, 'Tenant Right: Farmer against Landlord in Victorian England, 1847–1883', *Agricultural History*, XLVII (1973), 95–113.

mutual relations.[116] Sir John Russell Bailey of Glanusk, who could see little purpose in the Welsh language, revealed that of the 19,515 people in the neighbourhood of Crickhowell, a mere 1,585 claimed to be monoglot Welsh, 'and where they are I am sure I do not know; I never find them'.[117] Perhaps, he implied, they were able to speak English, but were not prepared to admit the fact. How far the language divide created difficulties in Welsh-speaking areas probably depended on the tact and consideration shown by landowners and their local agents. The popular and able John Morgan Davies of Ffrwd-fâl, agent to the Bronwydd, Tre-gib, Dolau Cothi and Glansefin estates, reckoned that although owners may not have spoken Welsh, some had a sketchy understanding of the language and, in any case, convivial relations with the tenantry were maintained by his intermediacy.[118] Other witnesses proffered a contrary view and outlined a cool, if not downright frosty scenario. Landowners, stormed Thomas Williams of Cydweli, 'are alien in race, language, religion and politics', and besides, were more than willing 'to lend their ears to low and unprincipled persons who try to wriggle into their favour by telling them tales about their tenants'.[119] A broadly similar viewpoint was echoed by the Llandysul surgeon Enoch Davies, who testified to the eroding of 'homely' relations, and went on to suggest that the agents' best interests were served when their employer knew no Welsh, since their power was thereby enhanced.[120] So was the monoglot English landlord firmly wedged between the proverbial rock and hard place.

But irrespective of the language divide, relations between the landed gentry and their tenants were probably less inimical than the well-meaning polemicists of the time would have us believe. After all, farming tenants continued willingly to beat for shooting parties, to support the local foxhunt, to contribute to presents for the coming of age of heirs, and generally to participate in the various rites of passage associated with the *plas*. In 1890, for example, the tenants of Castell Gorfod and Glanbrydan in Carmarthenshire held meetings to consider ways of celebrating the majority of the heirs to their respective estates, and their colleagues at Dinefwr presented their landlord with an album of photographs and addresses in commemoration of the recent death of his wife.[121] Farmers, moreover, in their uncoordinated and rather spasmodic agitation, showed little enthusiasm for a variety of causes calculated to influence adversely their relationships with their landlords, to which the limited progress in Wales of the Anti-Corn Law League

---

[116] Royal Commission on Land, *Minutes of Evidence*, vol. III (1895), Qs. 52445, 53239, 53838.
[117] Ibid., Qs. 49786–948.
[118] Ibid., Q. 37525.
[119] Ibid., Q. 37076. For such Machiavellian machinations, see Moore-Colyer, *Hafod Estate*, passim.
[120] Royal Commission on Land, *Minutes of Evidence*, vol. III (1895), Qs. 44303–4.
[121] Matthew Cragoe, *An Anglican Aristocracy: The Moral Economy of the Landed Estate in Carmarthenshire, 1832–1895* (Oxford, 1996), p. 254.

bears witness.[122] Equally, when Thomas Gee, proprietor of the fervently anti-gentry *Baner*, attempted to set up the Land League in the 1880s, his money-raising efforts among the farmers yielded a derisory £62. Gee's efforts to continue to fan the flames of the Tithe War began to wane in the late eighties in the face of farmer indifference. Anti-tithe agitation was seen as a means to greater ends – of Church disestablishment, secularization of education and the establishment of a Welsh university – matters which, like the notions of cultural and political nationalism articulated by the *Cymru Fydd* societies, were of little import to most practical men.[123] Resentment against the depredations of both lay tithe impropriators and a church for which they felt little sympathy or affection, would have certainly struck deep into the souls of Welsh farmers.[124] But, above all, they were realists. Confronted by severe agricultural depression, they appreciated that their financial survival on the land necessitated grim determination by themselves and their landlords, and that despite the catalytic efforts of Nonconformist divines, cultural, religious and political differences took second place.[125] If many of them accepted the case of the radical critics that landlords had reneged upon some of their traditional duties and had rejected their linguistic birthright, farmers were none the less aware of the constructive contribution to agriculture and land management of numerous members of the landed classes. As the critics stormed the bastion of privilege and bludgeoned away at the issues of alleged political oppression and cultural alienation, they failed to effect a wholesale breakdown in relations between the owners and tillers of the soil, although, it must be said, those relations were no longer based on sentiment, but upon economic realities. Farmers, meanwhile, struggled to maintain both their social status and their economic well-being in the depressed decade of the nineties, and while tenants enjoyed some relief by way of rent abatements, the new freeholders squared up to the inexorable haemorrhage of mortgage repayments. Henceforth the pursuit of a surplus would be the touchstone of survival, and as Welsh remained the language of the hearthside and the daily medium of communication with the workforce in 'Welsh Wales', there was a growing imperative to learn English, widely perceived as the language of material prosperity. That justly celebrated scientist, philosopher

---

[122] Ryland Wallace, 'The Anti-Corn Law League in Wales', *WHR*, 13, no. 1 (1987), 22; J. Graham Jones, 'Select Committee or Royal Commission?: Wales and the "Land Question", 1892', ibid., 17, no. 2 (1994), 208.

[123] R. M. Morris, 'The Tithe War', *TDHS*, 32 (1983), 51–97; D. Richter, 'The Welsh Police, the Home Office and the Welsh Tithe War of 1886–1891', *WHR*, 12, no. 1 (1984), 50–75. For men like Evan Pan Jones, heavily influenced by Alfred Russel Wallace's land nationalization movement, such matters as language, religion and home rule were of low priority compared to the need to wrestle the land of Wales from private hands of whatever race. See Peris Jones-Evans, 'Evan Pan Jones: Land Reformer', *WHR*, 4, no. 2 (1968), 143–59.

[124] Jill Barber, '"A Fair and Just Demand?": Tithe Unrest in Cardiganshire, 1796–1823', ibid., 16, no. 2 (1992), 183.

[125] J. E. Vincent, *The Land Question in South Wales* (London, 1897), pp. 18–24; J. P. D. Dunbabin, *Rural Discontent in Nineteenth-Century Britain* (London, 1974), Chapters 10–13.

and man-of-action Sir R. G. Stapledon, whose contribution to the development of Welsh agriculture has yet to be exceeded, was wont to harangue his students at Aberystwyth along these lines in the 1920s. Emphasizing the vital importance to the farmer and agricultural scientist of mastering English, he observed: 'Wales is not nearly big enough for you Welshmen – you all want to get reputations outside Wales and a very great number of you want to get jobs outside Wales – and you Welshmen as a whole cannot talk or write English for nuts. Also I have a grave suspicion that your language is not a good one in which to think accurately and progressively.'[126] We have no record of the response of his students, but in articulating these views Stapledon was reflecting both the attitudes of Englishmen and those of a growing number of Welsh people towards their mother tongue. To outsiders at the close of the nineteenth century, the Welsh language was a quaint survival, raising fierce passions among its practitioners but having little relevance to the new age of scientific agriculture. Stapledon and others would have regarded the notion of conducting Welsh-medium tutorials on the theory and practice of manuring with the same level of enthusiasm as the suggestion that they be held in Serbo-Croat. Revival and renaissance was to come much later.

---

[126] R. G. Stapledon, unpubl. lecture notes, currently in the archive of the Welsh Institute of Rural Studies, Aberystwyth.

4

The Coming of the Railways and Language Change in North Wales 1850–1900[1]

DOT JONES

> Ac unir pob mynydd, pob moel a phob dyffryn,
>   Bydd cyflym a difyr, a dedwydd pob taith;
> Pryd hyn bydd y Reilffordd yn ddrych ac arwyddlun
>   O undeb ysbrydol pob llwyth a phob iaith.[2]
>
> (Every mountain, every hill, and every vale will unite,
>   Every journey will be swift, entertaining and delightful;
> Then the railway will be a mirror and symbol
>   Of the spiritual unity of every tribe and every language.)

In mid-nineteenth-century Wales the coming of the railways promised sight of a golden future, an economic and social revolution which would unite all and enable Wales to exploit fully its rich natural resources and gain recognition in the wider world. At that time few Welsh people believed that railway communications were a threat to their native language. Indeed why should they? Except in peripheral, long-established, Anglicized areas, Welsh was the dominant, everyday language of the mass of the population. In the counties of Anglesey, Caernarfon, Merioneth and Cardigan less than one per cent of the population lived in parishes where English was the only language of church services.[3] Even in Glamorgan and Monmouthshire, non-Welsh-speaking in-migrants in the growing industrial communities were generally obliged to learn Welsh if they wished to settle and

---

[1] I am grateful to John Williams for comments on an early draft of this chapter, and to Neil Evans, William P. Griffith, Paul O'Leary, Ernest Sandberg and Mari A. Williams for valuable references. Particular thanks are due to Huw Walters of the National Library of Wales, who generously helped with Welsh-language sources.

[2] The last four lines of the prize-winning poem 'Dyfodiad y Reilffyrdd i Gymru' entered by 'Gwilym Teilo' (William Davies, Llandeilo) in the 1856 Eisteddfod at Llanelli, published in *Detholiad o'r Cyfansoddiadau Buddugol yn Eisteddfod Llanelli* (Llanelli, 1857), pp. 155–8.

[3] See W. T. R. Pryce, 'Welsh and English in Wales, 1750–1971: A Spatial Analysis Based on the Linguistic Affiliation of Parochial Communities', *BBCS*, XXVIII, pt. 1 (1978), 1–36.

work in places where there was either a strong Welsh-speaking base or where other newcomers were from Welsh-speaking areas.[4]

Yet fifty years later, within two generations, the situation regarding the Welsh language was very different. The proportion of those entered in the 1901 census as being able to speak 'Welsh only' in the four most Welsh counties had fallen to about 50 per cent and in Wales as a whole to just 15 per cent. The forces responsible for the proportional decline were a complex amalgam of factors, including migration, economic change, education policy, and social attitudes. The increased opportunities for communication provided by the rapid growth of railways in the second half of the nineteenth century also contributed significantly to this process.

As John Davies claims: 'It is difficult to discover any aspect of the life of Wales which was not transformed by locomotion.'[5] Many books have been written on the development of railways in Wales, mostly, it must be admitted, for the railway enthusiast rather than the social historian.[6] An exception is Jack Simmons's excellent volume, *The Victorian Railway*, which gives fair coverage of Welsh matters within a British context and, in a chapter on 'Language and Literacy', includes a short section on the Welsh language which mentions the introduction of English railway terms, the failure of railway companies to recognize that many of their customers in Wales spoke Welsh only, and allegations of discrimination against Welsh-speaking workmen which flared up during the period 1890–5.[7]

None were more directly concerned with the spread of the railway networks than those involved with their construction and operation. This chapter focuses on the language ability of railway workers as a force for language change, using mainly information contained in census enumerators' books but also supplemented by contemporary comment. The issue of alleged discrimination by the London and North Western Railway Company in the dismissal and intended prohibition of the employment of monoglot Welsh workmen, including the practicality of such a policy in Welsh-speaking areas, is examined in some detail.

---

[4] For evidence from Gwent, see Sian Rhiannon Williams, 'Welsh in the Valleys of Gwent', *Planet*, 51 (1985), 112–18. See also John Brunton, *John Brunton's Book: Being the Memoirs of John Brunton, Engineer* (Cambridge, 1939), pp. 17–18. Brunton was obliged to learn Welsh for his first job, as resident engineer on the construction of a tramway from the Ynyscedwyn Iron Works at the head of the Swansea Valley in 1830.

[5] John Davies, *A History of Wales* (London, 1993), p. 409.

[6] From the series *A Regional History of the Railways of Great Britain*: vol. 11, Peter E. Baughan, *North and Mid Wales* (2nd ed., Nairn, 1991); vol. 12, D. S. M. Barrie, *South Wales* (Newton Abbot, 1980). A useful chronological listing of railway incorporations, constructions and amalgamations may be found in R. Emrys Jones, *Rheilffyrdd Cymru: The Railways of Wales* (Caernarfon, 1979). See also Rex Christiansen, *Forgotten Railways: North and Mid Wales* (Newton Abbot, 1976); J. Page, *Forgotten Railways: South Wales* (Newton Abbot, 1979). More Welsh references can be found in George Ottley, *A Bibliography of British Railway History. Supplement* (London, 1988), pp. 166–77.

[7] Jack Simmons, *The Victorian Railway* (New York, 1991), pp. 193–4.

The emphasis in this chapter is on north Wales, but it could also be argued that the conclusions are applicable to the country as a whole.

Although Wales had been closely involved with early railway developments – the first steam locomotive specifically designed to run on rails had been tested at Penydarren in 1804, the Oystermouth Railway had become the first ever to carry fare-paying passengers in 1807, and the Ffestiniog Railway, built to carry slate from Blaenau Ffestiniog to Porthmadog, had become the first ever narrow gauge railway in 1836 – the English contagion of Railway Mania in the 1830s and 1840s had left the map of Wales comparatively untouched.[8] The pattern of industrial development, capital accumulation, population distribution and the added difficulties of topography in Wales led to a very different pattern of railway growth from that experienced in England. In 1850 there were only two major passenger lines, the Irish mail routes, whose primary purpose was to link England with Ireland. For goods, however, there were numerous local lines for the transport of iron, slate, and coal, including the famous Taff Vale Railway from Merthyr Tydfil to Cardiff. In Wales the major growth came in the 1860s and 1870s with a flurry of activity by small and large companies. These took the form of speculative plans which failed before they left the drawing board, new and ambitious constructions, and company amalgamations and takeovers. By 1922, 136 companies had operated railways in Wales, though no more than 54 at the same time in the late 1870s. Gradually, three big companies came to dominate: the London and North Western in the north and east, the Great Western in the south, and the Cambrian in mid-Wales. The headquarters of each was located in England.

In the 1850s this activity was all in the future and was eagerly awaited, for there was great enthusiasm in Wales for the progress which railways symbolized. Previously inconceivable civil engineering feats were involved in railway construction and one favourite pastime was to compare such feats with the great constructions of history. The line from London to Birmingham, for example, completed over a five year period by 20,000 men who moved 400 million cubic feet of earth, was celebrated as the greatest public work ever undertaken.[9] Even embellishments were designed on a grand scale. On the north Wales line the construction of the magnificent tubular Britannia Bridge, spanning the Menai Straits for the Chester and Holyhead Railway Company, included four huge crouched lions 35ft long and 12ft high, carved in limestone, two on either side of the approaches to the bridge. If the company had not encountered financial

---

[8] See F. Llewellyn-Jones, 'Wales and the Origins of the Railway Revolution', *THSC* (1983), 115–31. For 'The First Known Account of a Railway Journey' on the Oystermouth railway, see Elizabeth Isabella Spence, *Summer Excursions through parts of Oxfordshire . . . and South Wales* (2nd ed., 1809), ii, 98, as quoted in Jack Simmons, *Railways: An Anthology* (London, 1991), pp. 8–9.

[9] Frederick S. Williams, *Our Iron Roads: Their History, Construction, and Social Influences* (London, 1852), pp. 128–9.

difficulties, there would also have been a huge figure of Britannia[10] on the central tower.[11]

Railway navvies, allegedly 'that despicable race of men', traditionally enjoyed a bad reputation; stories of lawlessness, drunkenness and immorality were often spread prior to their arrival.[12] At Allt-wen in Glamorgan in January 1847 heads of household already concerned about the reprehensible behaviour of their young people on the Sabbath – 'fairs, markets (drinks and liquor and such things), feasts, games, debauchery and drinking, lovemaking, wakes, riots, fights, etc.' ('ffair, marchnad (diodydd a gwirodydd, a phethau felly), gwleddoedd, chwareuyddiaethau, cyfeddach a diota, carwriaeth, mabsantau, terfysgoedd, ymladdau, etc.') – held a meeting to discuss how 'to save the youngsters of the area from the grip of such corruptions; those which will, by all accounts, greatly increase when all the *Navigators* from other areas come to work on the new railways' ('achub ieuenctyd ein hardal o afael y llygredigaethau hyn; y rhai, wrth bob tebyg, a gynhydda yn ddirfawr, pan ddel yr holl *Navigators* o leoedd ereill i weithio ar yr reilffyrdd newyddion').[13]

Apparently, time did not improve the image of the navvies. Twenty-five years later, the Welsh-language newspaper, *Y Tyst a'r Dydd*, warned its readers of the dishonesty of navvies soon to arrive in great numbers in the Maesteg district:

> Yr oeddwn wedi arfer meddwl nad oedd y lle hwn yn cael ei flino rhyw lawer gan y bachau pum bys. Modd bynag y mae y rheilffyrdd wedi dwyn lluaws ohonynt yn mherson y *navvies*. Y maent eisoes wedi dangos eu hystranciau anonest. Yspeiliwyd £14 a rhyw sylltau oddi wrth rhyw weithiwr tlawd o'r enw David Emanuel, ac nid yw wedi clywed sôn amdanynt. Heblaw hynyna, y mae rhai masnachwyr wedi cael y *smooth side* ganddynt. Hyderaf y bydd hyn yn rhybudd i bobl y lle hwn rhag llaw. Dysgwylir rhyw ruthr ofnadwy o honynt pan y bydd y rheilffyrdd hyn yn eu llawn gwaith. Nid yw *navvy* yn ddyn i'w *drustio*. Purion yw codi y doll wrth fod y creadur hwn yn pasio y dollfa. Pobl ddefnyddiol ydynt i rwygo y ddaear, a phethau felly; ond pan elont i rwygo llogellau a meddianau pobl wirion, gwareder ni rhagddynt.[14]

---

[10] Ibid., p. 181, where the figure is wrongly claimed to have been 'Science'.

[11] *Illustrated London News*, 23 March 1850. See also Peter E. Baughan, 'Open Throughout – the Britannia Tubular Bridge', *The Chester and Holyhead Railway*, vol. I (Newton Abbot, 1972), pp. 120–42; Wilfred L. Steel, *The History of the London and North-Western Railway* (London, 1914), pp. 213–24. A fascinating account of the conception, preliminary experiments, and construction of both the Britannia and Conway bridges, by the resident engineer, is found in Edwin Clark, *The Britannia and Conway Tubular Bridges with General Inquiries on Beams and on the Properties of Materials used in Construction* (2 vols., London, 1850). See also N. Rosenberg and W. G. Vincenti, *The Britannia Bridge: The Generation and Diffusion of Technical Knowledge* (Cambridge, Mass. and London, 1978).

[12] See David Brooke, *The Railway Navvy: 'That Despicable Race of Men'* (Newton Abbot, 1983); Terry Coleman, *The Railway Navvies* (London, 1965); James E. Handley, *The Navvy in Scotland* (Cork, 1970).

[13] 'Pen-Teulu' (Philip Griffiths), 'Cyfarfod Neillduol yn yr Alltwen', *Y Diwygiwr*, XII, no. 139 (1847), 50–1.

[14] *Y Tyst a'r Dydd*, 5 September 1873, p. 6.

(I had thought this area was not much troubled by the light-fingered. However, the railway has brought many of them in the form of navvies. They have already shown their dishonest tricks. £14 and a few shillings were stolen from a poor worker by the name of David Emanuel, and he has not seen them since. Apart from that some businessmen have experienced their smooth side. I very much hope this will be a timely warning to the people of this place. We expect a large rush when this railway is fully worked. The navvy is not a man to be trusted. It would be a good idea to charge a toll on this creature as he passes the tollgate. They are useful people for tearing up the earth and such things, but when they go to tear up the pockets and possessions of innocent people, may we be spared.)

More serious were the charges of disorder. Scripture readers from the Town Missionary Society were employed on the north Wales line, but this did not prevent riot on occasions.[15] In May 1846 magistrates at Bangor sent for troops during anti-Irish disturbances after Welsh, English and Scottish workers had threatened to expel by force the Irish from the district.[16] While many of the stories of dreadful deeds committed by navvies were undoubtedly true, it is sometimes forgotten that the hard core of experienced 'career' navvies was augmented by local men, usually unemployed or underemployed agricultural labourers who were themselves not unblemished. David Brooke has recently come to their defence by highlighting their skill and achievements in what were often atrocious living and working conditions.[17]

The 1851 census enumerators' books for north Wales contain few entries for 'navvy' under occupation. The usual entry for the equivalent work is 'railway labourer', often reclassified as 'platelayer' though, strictly speaking, platelayers comprised the more permanent gangs of men responsible for the maintenance of a section of railway line, the track side, fences and any culverts or bridges. In foggy weather they were also responsible for safety by holding signal lamps to warn drivers.[18]

The enumerators' books for Anglesey reveal that there were more than 300 railway labourers working on the Llanfair–Holyhead section of the north Wales line in April 1851. The section had already been operating for almost three years, but work on extensions to the line at the Holyhead end continued. Table 1 shows the place of birth of those enumerated as railway labourers or platelayers in Anglesey in the 1851 census. As there was no language question in the census

---

[15] Q. 1765, Evidence of Capt. C. R. Moorsom, Director of the Chester and Holyhead Railway, before the Select Committee on Railway Labourers (BPP 1846 (530) XIII).
[16] Brooke, *The Railway Navvy*, pp. 117–18; Coleman, *The Railway Navvies*, p. 24.
[17] Brooke, *The Railway Navvy*, pp. 168–9, quoted as 'A Just Appraisal' in Jack Simmons, *Railways: An Anthology* (London, 1991), pp. 172–3.
[18] For a contemporary classification and description of the various railway occupations, see (author not given) *Railways and Railway Men* (London and Edinburgh, 1892).

Table 1. Railway Labourers/Platelayers, birthplace by status within household. Anglesey 1851

Birthplace	Head	Relative	Visitor	Lodger	TOTAL	*Percentage*
Anglesey	74	52	8	41	175	*54.5*
Caernarfonshire	13	4	4	8	29	*9.0*
Denbighshire	13	1	1	29	44	*13.7*
Flintshire	4	–	1	11	16	*5.0*
Other Wales★	3	–	3	2	8	*2.5*
Ireland	2	–	–	11	13	*4.0*
England	14	5	–	14	33	*10.3*
Scotland	–	1	–	1	2	*0.6*
Sweden	–	–	–	1	1	*0.3*
TOTAL	123	63	17	118	321	**100.0**
Percentage	*38.3*	*19.6*	*5.3*	*36.8*	*100.0*	

★ Cardiganshire 1, Carmarthenshire 2, Glamorgan 1, Merioneth 1, Monmouthshire 1, Pembrokeshire 2.
Source: Census enumerators' books for Anglesey, 1851.

until 1891, birthplace has to be used as an indicator of language ability, and clearly those from the counties of Anglesey, Caernarfon and Denbigh were more likely to be Welsh-speaking than the remainder. The relation of a workman to the head of the household in which he was enumerated gives an indication of permanence; lodgers and visitors were generally transient workers. What the figures show quite clearly is the extent of Welsh involvement in the construction work, with over 50 per cent from Anglesey and 80 per cent from north Wales. Of the 40 per cent temporary visitors or lodgers, the majority were from north Wales. The few railway engineers and inspectors identified in the census trawl were nearly all of English origin.

The 1861 census identifies a similar pattern of employment at the height of work on the famous Talerddig cutting on the Newtown and Machynlleth Railway, for which David Davies, Llandinam, was the contractor. This 115 ft rock cutting was the deepest in the world at that time, a remarkable feat of organization and effort using only gunpowder and manpower.[19] Only a relatively small number of outside navvies were employed, the vast majority from adjacent parishes, and those who were not resident usually lodged with fellow workmen or their neighbours. The impression is one of integration with the local community. It does, however, suggest a high labour turnover; as the line proceeded some men

---

[19] For a full account of work on this famous cutting, see Herbert Williams, *Davies the Ocean: Railway King and Coal Tycoon* (Cardiff, 1991), pp. 59–63, and Gwyn Briwnant-Jones, *Railway through Talerddig* (Llandysul, 1990).

returned home, and others joined. Similar evidence is presented by David Brooke, in a more extensive examination of census material for 1851–71, in which he gives figures for the number of railway labourers in Wales, according to railway company and place of birth.[20] Although Brooke's wider study also provides evidence of a different employment pattern on other lines – in particular the use of Irish labour on the Taff Vale Railway in 1851 and the Merthyr, Tredegar and Abergavenny Railway in 1861 – it could be argued that in the construction of the railways in north and mid-Wales, even though engineers and railway inspectors were invariably English, the increased demand for local labour held back the tide of rural exodus in so far as the increased Welsh presence served as a buffer against non-Welsh-speaking, transient workmen.

Despite fears of the corrupting moral influence of the navvy army, railways represented progress and were generally welcomed with enthusiasm in mid-nineteenth-century Wales.[21] Numerous eisteddfod essays and poems were written and recited in praise of railways either for serious and sound economic reasons or simply to celebrate the sheer romance and drama of rail travel.[22] The period 1840–75 has been described as the golden age of railway poetry in Welsh; railways were variously described as 'Haiarnfarch' or 'March Haearn' (Ironhorse), and 'Agerfarch' (Steamhorse).[23] Voices of doubt concerning the benefits of railways and progress were drowned by the flood of enthusiasm. When the bard John Jones (Talhaiarn) warned: 'The birth of the steam engine heralded the death of the Welsh language' ('Pan anwyd y *steam engine*, ganwyd angau y Gymraeg'),[24] *Y Punch Cymraeg*, the Welsh Punch periodical, published a cartoon mocking his fears. It shows Wales welcoming Dic Siôn Dafydd, the archetypal Welshman who since Tudor times had aped English ways and who was now bringing progress and wealth to Wales with the development of railway communication.[25] The

---

[20] Brooke, *The Railway Navvy*, Appendix, pp. 171–4, discusses the enumeration of railway construction workers. Figures for Wales are contained in Tables IV and V, pp. 181–2, 190 and are analysed on pp. 30–2.

[21] For example, John Lloyd James (Clwydwenfro) in 'Teithio gyda'r Trên', *Y Byd Cymreig*, 1 March 1866, p. 1, encouraged readers to travel by train and offered useful advice such as avoiding drinking alcohol and being patient when queuing for a ticket.

[22] 'Masnach yn Nghymru a'i Rhagolygon mewn cyssylltiad a Ffyrdd Haiarn' (Trade prospects for Wales in connection with Railways), *Seren Cymru*, 10 October 1862, 405–6, reports on a paper presented by L. Hartley at the Caernarfon Eisteddfod. In the 1865 National Eisteddfod at Aberystwyth, a prize was offered for the six best *englynion* (a concise, four line, thirty syllable, strictly metred Welsh poem) on the subject of 'The Aberystwyth Railway'.

[23] D. Tecwyn Lloyd, *Safle'r Gerbydres ac Ysgrifau Eraill* (Llandysul, 1970), pp. 101–25.

[24] As quoted in Dewi M. Lloyd, *Talhaiarn* (Caernarfon, 1993), p. 54. Some English writers also deplored the effect of the railways in Wales. See John Kimberley Roberts, 'A Note on English Writers and Welsh Railways', *The Anglo-Welsh Review*, 17, no. 39 (1968), 136–8.

[25] The cartoon is open to an alternative interpretation. See Hywel Teifi Edwards, 'Y Gymraeg yn y Bedwaredd Ganrif ar Bymtheg' in Geraint H. Jenkins (ed.), *Cof Cenedl II: Ysgrifau ar Hanes Cymru* (Llandysul, 1987), p. 131. However, *Y Punch Cymraeg* was known for its modernist stance and for taking every opportunity to deride the churchman Talhaiarn.

vigorous Welsh press and the strength of Welsh Nonconformity was surely sufficiently strong to withstand any threat to the well-being of the language. English might become the language of business and finance, but it would not affect the strength of Welsh in other crucial domains. Bilingualism, so it was argued, should be embraced not feared. A Denbigh clergyman wrote as follows of Snowdon:

> All-conquering English rushes on apace,
> Railways already drive it to thy base:
> Soon shall 'Dim Saesneg' be a sound gone by,
> And, like the echoes of the breezes, die.
> 'Tis well 'twere so! the people now are one,
> Need but one tongue to work in unison.[26]

Even those who forecast the decline of the language believed that the Anglicization of Wales was a matter for rejoicing rather than regret.

However, as the railway network spread, locally-based companies were gradually taken over by large companies whose headquarters were located outside Wales. In north Wales the Chester and Holyhead Railway was amalgamated with the Bangor and Caernarfon in 1854. When the line was finally swallowed up by the London and North Western Railway Company in 1867, LNWR had already been operating it on lease for eight years.[27] The takeover had direct consequences for the pace of language change in the localities through which the line passed. The recruitment policy of the LNWR regarding the language of their employees was one of increasing pressure on local officers to appoint English-speaking staff. At a routine meeting of the Traffic Committee at Euston in 1868, the year following the takeover by LNWR, the Holyhead District Engineer, Hedworth Lee, who had formerly been the Engineering Manager for the Holyhead and Chester line, asked whether the LNWR Rule Book could be printed in Welsh for the benefit of the men in his district who could not read English. At the very least, he might have expected a sympathetic hearing. In the early days of the Chester and Holyhead Railway a decision had been made to appoint Welsh-speaking staff where possible for the ease of doing business with local producers of mineral and agricultural goods. Following the takeover and the shift of the decision-making base to London, however, attitudes changed appreciably. The response of the Traffic Committee at Euston was minuted as follows:

---

[26] T. Hughes, cited by Raymond Garlick, *An Introduction to Anglo-Welsh Literature* (Cardiff, 1970), p. 56, as quoted in Keith Robbins, *Nineteenth-Century Britain* (Oxford, 1988), p. 28.

[27] For histories of the Chester and Holyhead Railway and the LNWR, see Baughan, *The Chester and Holyhead Railway*, vol. I; Steel, *The History of the London and North-Western Railway*; George P. Neele, *Railway Reminiscences* (first published 1904, reprinted Wakefield, 1974).

In future no Welshmen to be appointed to a responsible post who cannot read and write English, and the men now employed for whom the rule book is proposed to be translated to be informed that they must learn to speak and read English, to entitle them to remain in the service.[28]

Hedworth Lee returned to Bangor a disappointed man. The new ruling seems neither to have been made public nor to have been widely implemented, but the matter resurfaced in 1890 when the newly-appointed Divisional Engineer, William Dawson, undertook the task of reading all the minutes recorded since 1850. He stumbled across the ruling made twenty years previously. Unsure how to proceed, he sent a copy of the ruling to Harry Footner, the Company's chief engineer at Euston, requesting further instructions. This straightforward request precipitated a revealing exchange of correspondence which portrays a diligent manager uneasily attempting to carry out impracticable directives passed down by an ignorant or insensitive company official located in a head office remote from events in north Wales.

In January 1891, two months after the request had been made, instructions arrived from Footner:

obtain from your Foreman when any man is engaged, a certificate that he can speak English, or make some arrangement which will ensure our having only men who can well understand instructions given to them and who can express themselves clearly on any question that forms part of their duty.[29]

Dawson obediently forwarded the instructions to the Permanent Way Inspectors. He was also obliged to provide Footner with a list of monoglot Welsh workmen. When asked why men who could not speak English had been taken on during the previous year, Dawson was stung to defence. He replied:

I understand the Directors instructions that no Welshman must be appointed to a *responsible position* who cannot speak English and this instruction has been observed since I first became aware of it. As a matter of fact the total number of men taken on since 1889 who cannot speak English is 20, all of whom are *labourers* . . . I do not think we could carry out our work if the order applied to all men.

Alas, Footner was unsympathetic: 'If you cannot get the requisite number of labourers, let me know and I will endeavour to send you some.' According to Dawson's recollection, when the two met at Euston in June 1894, Footner 'censured' him for allowing non-English-speaking labourers and lengthmen to be

---

[28] PRO Rail 410/2053.
[29] Ibid.

taken on and told him to 'get rid of them'. Like Hedworth Lee before him, a chastened William Dawson returned to Bangor. This time, however, he acted swiftly. He immediately issued to inspectors what later became known as 'THE CIRCULAR':

Permanent Way Dept., Bangor   To Inspectors
June 19, 1894
Circular

Men Unable to Speak English

Notwithstanding any instructions upon the subject I find that a number of men have been taken on who cannot speak English, or can only speak English a little.

The service of all such men are to be dispensed with, as it is contrary to the company's rules, to have them in their employ. Let me know which of the men you can dispense with first.

I do not wish you to serve all the men with a week's notice at once, but they must be paid off gradually, unless they learn to speak English in the meantime. Let me have your report upon the subject before the end of the month.

Signed: W. Dawson[30]

A second circular was sent out at the beginning of July. It was only then, in Dawson's words, that the public 'got wind' of what was happening. 'Cymro Fedr Siarad "Saesneg"' (A Welshman Who Speaks English) sent a letter to *Baner ac Amserau Cymru*:

Pa 'gebyst' sydd ar y Saeson yma? A raid i ni fod dan eu traed dros byth?

Mae'n cael ei chwedleua yn y cornelau, tua Bangor yma, na chaiff neb weithio ar y ffordd haiarn toc, os nad all efe siarad Saesneg. Maent wedi rhoi Saeson yn *gangers* yn mhob man, bron. Saeson sydd yn cael y swyddi goreu ar hyd y llinell, er fod Cymry sydd yn medru Saesneg yn dda yn deall y gwaith lawn cystal, a gwell na llawer o honynt.

A chlywais sibrwd fod tua deugain o Saeson yn Crewe, wedi eu dethol yn barod i gymmeryd lle y Cymry nad allant siarad Saesneg, er y gallant ei deall.

Os ydyw hyn yn bod, y mae'n gywilyddus i'r cwmni eu bod yn bwriadu gwneyd y fath beth, ac yn ddiraddiad ar ein genedl na ddylid ei oddef.[31]

(What 'on earth' is wrong with these English? Do we have to be trodden by them forever?

It is whispered on street-corners, around Bangor here, that soon no one will be allowed to work on the railway unless he can speak English. They have placed English gangers nearly everywhere. The English get the best jobs along the line, despite the fact that Welshmen who can speak English well understand the work just as well, and even better than some of them.

---

[30] Ibid.
[31] *BAC*, 18 July 1894, p. 9.

I have heard a rumour that around forty Englishmen in Crewe have already been chosen to take the place of the Welsh who cannot speak English, although they are able to understand it.

If this is the case, it is a disgrace that the company intends to act in such a way, and it is a slur on our nation which we should not suffer.)

The letter was printed with the comment that, although the rumour was difficult to believe, it raised an issue that deserved to be widely discussed. Before publishing the letter Thomas Gee, editor of *Y Faner*, had written to Dawson asking if it was true that monoglot Welshmen were about to be paid off. This letter had been forwarded to Footner for instructions how to respond but since no advice was forthcoming no response was made. After several weeks without an explanation from the Company, a leading article appeared in *Y Faner* repeating the request for an explanation.[32] Again, there was no response. Over the next few weeks eleven platelayers in Anglesey were paid off, following instructions issued by Dawson. News of the dismissals spread rapidly throughout north Wales and the issue was publicized both as an injustice to the dismissed men and an insult to the Welsh nation. Dawson panicked and initially claimed that the men had been paid off as part of the usual autumn reduction of workmen for the winter. Unsurprisingly, no one believed him. Local government bodies discussed the matter at regular meetings, special public meetings were held, more letters of protest were written, and ideas were canvassed as how best to effect an explanation from the Company. Resolutions passed by the Blaenau Ffestiniog Urban District Council in January 1895 were typical of those ratified by many Councils, Boards of Guardians and other bodies. The attack was three-pronged: a letter of protest was sent to the Directors of the Company, local businesses were requested not to support the LNWR Company, and Welsh MPs were asked to block every parliamentary act relating to the Company until the injustice was rectified.[33] Others hinted at retaliation in the form of a revaluation of the rateable value of the Company's property. The Chairman of the Conwy Board of Guardians claimed that writing letters was useless and that they would have to 'go and bullyrag the lion in his den' by sending a deputation to London.[34] But the Company refused to meet any deputations or give any explanation. Interference in their recruitment policy was judged an impertinence and they clearly expected that the storm would shortly die away.

However, when the condemnation of the Company by the Flint Town Council was reported in *The Times*, the issue had reached London and could no

---

[32] Ibid., 5 September 1894, p. 9.
[33] Ernest Jones, *Senedd Stiniog: Hanes Dinesig Ffestiniog, 1895–1974* (Blaenau Ffestiniog, 1975), pp. 21–2.
[34] *Carnarvon and Denbigh Herald*, 18 January 1895, p. 3.

longer be ignored.[35] It could, however, be ridiculed. *Punch* seized the opportunity to publish a short satirical piece entitled 'Travels in Taffy-land; or, Wales Blowing'. It began as follows: 'Would you tell me Porter, if the next train is the one for Aberystwyth? I am really much obliged for your reply, but as I have not a Cymric dictionary at hand, I am totally unable even to guess at your meaning.' It continued in similar vein, chronicling a series of misunderstandings and disasters on a journey which, of course, never reached Aberystwyth: 'Thank Heaven! I am back at Chester, where the hotel people do talk English; and in future I shall vote steadily at elections against any party that does not make the total suppression of all so-called "national tongues" within the British Isles a part of its recognised programme.'[36]

But the matter could not be so easily laughed away. In February 1895 the LNWR Board held its half-yearly meeting at Euston. When the issue was raised by J. Bryn Roberts, a Welsh-speaking shareholder and MP for Caernarfon, the Chairman, Lord Stalbridge, began in conciliatory mood by admitting that the old rule had been ignored and gave assurances that the Company bore no hostility towards Welsh-speaking workmen but that safety considerations meant that there should not be more than one man in a gang who could speak only Welsh. But Bryn Roberts was not easily placated. Claiming support from 'Conservative and Liberal, churchmen and dissenters, rich and poor, aye and Englishmen as well as Welshmen', he dismissed the safety argument and launched a counter-argument that station staff should be required to know Welsh. This was greeted with laughter at the meeting. The Chairman then lost patience and scoffed:

> If the nationality of Wales was imperilled in consequence of eight men out of a thousand being discharged in the autumn he did not think the London & North Western Company could be blamed . . . it must be remembered that before very long there would be nobody in Wales who could not speak English as well as Welsh . . . in a few years this case would not arise.[37]

The Board seemingly approved of this response; little sympathy with the grievance was expressed and no concessions were made.

The Chairman and his Board, however, underestimated the growing depth and strength of the opposition. Welsh Members of Parliament now took up the cause. Not only were Welsh MPs particularly active at this time, but Welsh matters were also highly visible on the parliamentary agenda in the form of Disestablishment, Education, and the Agricultural Land Commission. Following an unsuccessful attempt to raise the matter during the third reading of the London and North Western Railway Bill, on the grounds that the Company was using powers given

---

[35] *The Times*, 2 January 1895, p. 9.
[36] *Punch*, 12 January 1895, p. 21.
[37] *Carnarvon and Denbigh Herald*, 22 February 1895, p. 2.

by Parliament to the prejudice of Welsh workmen, the matter was eventually discussed under a separate motion of censure. The motion criticized the action of the Company in declining to employ monoglot Welshmen as labourers in the most Welsh-speaking areas while at the same time employing in the same districts officials who were completely ignorant of the language of the people with whom they came into contact and had business relations. An amendment called for the setting up of a select committee to consider the matter in depth.

MPs and Directors had already received from David Lloyd George a long, carefully reasoned letter setting out the grievances. He condemned the Company for operating 'a definite and deliberate policy, the object of which is getting rid of all the Welsh monoglot Workmen on the Company's line'. He pointed out that 'if the language rule was enforced it would exclude the bulk of the labouring community in North Wales' and that 'in India, knowledge of English is not essential to employment as platelaying on the railway. On the contrary, knowledge of the native language is demanded as a qualification for the chief officers on the various lines'. He further emphasized that 'there is no practical difficulty in the way of translating the regulations' and that 'no accident has ever occurred on this line through linguistic misunderstanding'.[38]

During the debate Lloyd George, Bryn Roberts, Sir George Osborne Morgan, and Abel Thomas all spoke in protest of the Company's actions, but still the Company claimed injured innocence. Their skilful spokesman, David Plunket, MP for Dublin University and a LNWR director, considered the charges absurd: 'the Company', he insisted, 'had the most friendly feelings, not only for the Welsh nationality, but for the Welsh language.' In exasperation, Abel Thomas pointed out that:

> This particular line went through a district in many parts of which more than 70 per cent of the population spoke Welsh only, and it might happen that the guard, through not being able to communicate with a man who lived in a cottage by the side of the line and spoke Welsh only, might not be able to signal to stop a train, and so avert an accident. If the London and North Western Railway Company were not going to employ guards who spoke both English and Welsh then the company ought to buy up all the cottages along the line and fill them with people who spoke English. That was the ridiculous argument followed to its ridiculous conclusion.

Yet, at the end of a heated debate, with the motion withdrawn, the Company merely agreed to examine the matter further. Future policy remained unchanged. Men who spoke the Welsh language only would not be employed in any responsible capacity where their employment might supposedly endanger the

---

[38] PRO Rail 410/2053.

Table 2. Language spoken by railway workers in North Wales[1]

Type of worker	Number				Percentage			
	Welsh only	Welsh and English	English only	Total	Welsh only	Welsh and English	English only	Total
Inspectors/ senior officials	3	9	41	52	5.8	17.3	78.8	100.0
Stationmasters	8	56	35	99	8.1	56.6	35.4	100.0
Rail clerks	16	93	34	143	11.2	65.0	23.8	100.0
Porters, guards, signalmen	196	338	99	633	31.0	53.4	15.6	100.0
Engine drivers, firemen, etc.	130	157	56	343	37.9	45.8	16.3	100.0
Platelayers/ rail labourers	399	192	45	636	62.3	30.2	7.1	100.0
Refreshment/ bookstall staff	3	4	23	30	10.0	13.3	76.7	100.0
Total (including miscellaneous)	**755**	**851**	**342**	**1948**	**38.8**	**43.7**	**17.6**	**100.0**
Population over 2 years of age[2]					65.5	24.8	9.7	100.0

[1] Counties of Denbigh (excluding Wrexham), Merioneth, Caernarfon and Anglesey.
[2] Excludes a small number who made no language statement or who indicated other languages.

safety of traffic and the lives of the passengers.[39] Even in deepest Welsh Wales the language of safety was assumed to be English.

The Company had employed a variety of tactics to ignore the complaint: silence, lies, flippancy, excuses, and indignation that others should presume to question its employment policy. Its intransigence and arrogant imperialism won the day, for Welsh MPs turned to other matters. A month later, at a conference of North Wales County Councils, the Chairman, Alexander McKillop, considered the grievances to have been remedied and urged the meeting to invite the three railway companies to extend their railways as far as possible into north Wales.[40] All was seemingly forgiven and forgotten.

Countless words had been spoken and written about the issue. But what actually happened in practice? Was the hapless William Dawson, castigated by both sides, able to 'get rid of them', i.e. any railway employee who could not speak English? The official recruitment policy of the LNWR might have been to insist on English-speaking staff, but could this be strictly implemented in areas where 90 per cent of the population were entered in the census as monoglot Welsh speakers?

[39] *Parliamentary Debates* (Hansard), 4th series, vol. 32, cols. 1023–4 (5 April 1895), cols. 1605–10 (25 April 1895); ibid., vol. 33, cols. 780–5 (9 May 1895), cols. 961–96 (10 May 1895).
[40] *Carnarvon and Denbigh Herald*, 14 July 1895, p. 3.

Table 2 shows the number of railway workers in the four north Wales counties of Anglesey, Caernarfon, Merioneth, and west Denbigh, classified according to occupation and language ability as entered in the 1891 census.[41] Most, but not all, were LNWR employees; it includes the Cambrian line, along the coast from Dolgellau and Barmouth to Pwllheli, the Great Western from Corwen through Bala Junction to Dolgellau and Blaenau Ffestiniog, and the Ffestiniog line from Porthmadog to Blaenau Ffestiniog. The census trawl identified about 2,000 railway workers, one third of whom were platelayers or railway labourers. It thus becomes abundantly clear why William Dawson panicked when ordered to 'get rid of them'; there were about 300 labourers and platelayers alone and probably another 250 other staff employed by the LNWR who, according to census enumeration, could not speak English. Indeed, the lists he had sent to Euston had evidently underestimated the problem. It was obvious that the scale of monoglot Welsh employment was just too great to admit publicly. On the other hand, the numbers as reflected in terms of percentages reveal that only in the case of platelayers and labourers did the language percentages roughly correspond to the language ability of the population as a whole. For employment in all other railway occupations, there was a clear advantage in being able to speak English.

The appointment of Englishmen with no understanding of Welsh as stationmasters had been a long-standing grievance. In 1872 'Sylwedydd' complained:

Gofynwch rywbeth yn Gymraeg i Lordiaid y Railway, cymerant arnynt nad ydynt yn eich deall. Os gofynwch iddynt yn Saesneg, nid yw yn bosibl eu deall hwythau. Edrychant ar y Cymro fel *clown*, ac edrych y Cymro arnynt hwythau fel bonglerwyr diegwyddor.[42]

(If you ask the Railway Lords something in Welsh, they pretend they don't understand you. If you ask them in English, it is not possible to understand them. They regard the Welshman as a clown, and the Welshman regards them as unscrupulous bunglers.)

The complaint was still being made in 1895:

In many a Welsh locality the doctor and lawyer must know Welsh, the shopkeeper could not turn a penny without it, the clergyman must know it by law, but the station master remains throughout the years ignorant of the language of the customers of the Company he serves.[43]

---

[41] Wrexham subdistrict is excluded from this study because, according to the 1891 Census, linguistically it had already become more English than Welsh.
[42] 'Y Rheilffyrdd', *Y Tyst a'r Dydd*, 27 September 1872.
[43] Author not given (probably the editor, O. M. Edwards), 'An Expensive Misconception', *Wales*, II (1895), 213–14.

Census evidence tends to corroborate this impression. A third of the stationmasters located in north Wales were entered as unable to speak Welsh in the 1891 census. On the LNWR lines, only the stationmaster at Dolwyddelan was entered as monoglot Welsh. His role is dubious as he is also entered as a lodger, so he may well have been there only as a stopgap. The only passenger line in north Wales in 1891 to employ monoglot-Welsh station staff to any extent was the Ffestiniog Railway, where all stationmasters could speak Welsh.[44] The Cambrian line, with its headquarters in Oswestry, was the most Welsh of the big three (LNWR, GW, Cambrian) in planning, finance, construction and operation, but, when retired engine driver Edwin Evans wrote his reminiscences of the Cambrian line in the 1880s, he repeated familiar allegations and recalled the practical difficulties:

> The first stationmasters of whom I have a recollection were men drafted from other lines, on the same principle as the engineers, without a knowledge of the language and custom of the Principality. The appointments without a doubt frequently caused inconvenience and controversy, especially at outlying stations from a business point of view, owing to the inability of the official to converse in the vernacular. The writer of these lines when a mere youth recollects being called on to act as interpreter in many cases between traders and stationmasters when transacting business.[45]

Moreover, when David Davies, Llandinam, the driving force behind the construction of the Cambrian lines, was invited to give a speech at the 1865 National Eisteddfod of Wales in Aberystwyth, the *Aberystwyth Observer* reported:

> He claimed himself a great admirer of the old Welsh language, and he had no sympathy with those who reviled their country and language (applause). Still he had seen enough of the world to know that the best medium to make money by was English; and he would advise every one of his countrymen to master it perfectly (applause). If they were content with brown bread, let them of course remain where they were; but if they wished to enjoy the luxuries of life, with white bread to boot, the way to do so would be by the acquisition of English. He knew what it was to eat both (cheers).[46]

In the case of both stationmaster and platelayer, English was considered the preferred language of the railway domain.

It was not only English-born incomers who revelled in the use of English in thoroughly Welsh communities. The Denbighshire-born John Ceiriog Hughes, 'the greatest of Welsh lyric poets', insisted on speaking English both at home and

---

[44] Much has been written about the Ffestiniog line. See, for example, J. I. C. Boyd, *The Festiniog Railway. Vol. 1. History and Route, 1800–1953* (Blandford, 1975).
[45] *Cambrian News*, 22 July 1932, p. 2.
[46] *Aberystwyth Observer*, 30 September 1865, as quoted in Williams, *Davies the Ocean*, pp. 97–8.

at the station when he became a Cambrian line stationmaster at Llanidloes in 1865 and later manager of the Van line which linked Caersŵs to the lead mines at Van. While engaged as a railway clerk at Manchester, he had been urged to return to Wales by his friend and fellow poet William Williams (Creuddynfab) because 'ordinary people will look up to you and grand people will become your acquaintants. A Stationmaster in Wales "ranks" much higher than a Stationmaster in England' ('bydd pobl gyffredin yn edrych i fyny atoch a phobl fawr yn ymgyfeillachu. Y mae Station Master yng Nghymru yn "rankio" yn uwch o lawer na Station Master yn Lloegr').[47] Ceiriog was an interesting and eccentric character in dress and manner. David Jones, the grocer at Van, describes his first meeting with Ceiriog in 1875: 'He wore a top hat of the best material, a frock-coat and a light-coloured waistcoat. And his walk was as though he had had military training' ('Gwisgai "top-hat", o'r defnydd goreu, "frock-coat", a gwasgod oleu. A'i gerddediad fel pe wedi cael triniaeth filwrol').[48] His military-style strut and English speech were part of the outward display which indicated that he expected due respect and deference.

In the more rural communities, a stationmaster and his family might have greater influence on local attitudes to language change than the vicar or the schoolmaster. At Groeslon, Caernarfon, for example, the stationmaster, Samuel Walton of Frodsham, Cheshire, apparently could speak English only and was the only head of household not to fill in a Welsh version of the household schedule in an enumeration district containing 182 households. In mid-Wales, at Ystradmeurig, Cardiganshire, the stationmaster, Henry Young from Haverfordwest, his wife and eighteen year-old daughter were the only people in the parish entered as monoglot English. The Young family was included in a total of only thirteen people entered as unable to speak Welsh out of a total population of 2,475 in the Gwnnws subdistrict of Tregaron. Census entries regarding language ability, however, need to be considered with caution. As Ernest Sandberg has pointed out, the railway employee was likely to be entered as unable to speak Welsh not only because of his or her migratory character but also because of a 'kind of work elitism that emphasised an English language orientation and work culture'.[49] Of all railway employees, the stationmaster would be the most likely to stress his competence in English.

Although many stationmasters were, indeed, Englishmen, and were entered in the census as monoglot English speakers, there was at least an opportunity for a

---

[47] As quoted in Hywel Teifi Edwards, *Ceiriog* (Caernarfon, 1987), p. 7. See also Williams, *Davies the Ocean*, pp. 144–7.
[48] Edwards, *Ceiriog*, p. 9.
[49] Ernest Sandberg, 'Bala and Penllyn: The Demographic and Socio-economic Structures of an Embryonic Welsh Town in the Second Half of the Nineteenth Century' (unpubl. Open University MPhil thesis, 1994), pp. 357–8. This work also contains an interesting section on 'The Railway Navvies in Arenig, 1881', pp. 279–82.

bilingual Welshman to rise to that post. The appointments to which the monoglot Welshman had no access were ancillary staff in refreshment rooms and bookstalls. Almost without exception these occupations were filled by monoglot English incomers. Travellers were ill-advised to ask for a 'paned o de' instead of 'a cup of tea' at any of the refreshment rooms attached to the main line stations on the LNWR lines in north Wales. At Bangor, Jane Sutherland, the manageress from Dudley Port in Staffordshire, and both her resident assistants, Clara Jones from London and Ada Head from Nottingham, were entered in the census as able to speak English only. Similarly, at Betws-y-coed, the manageress, bar assistant, and cellarman, from Congleton, Birmingham, and Walsall respectively, were all entered as able to speak English only. The linguistic pattern found among other railway staff is more complex, but it is clear that the Welsh-born were much more likely to be bilingual than those born in England, many of whom came from 'railway rich' regions such as Cheshire and the Midlands.

English railway words which entered the Welshman's vocabulary in north Wales include 'trên' (train), 'steshon' (station, although the literary 'gorsaf' was also used), 'portar' (porter), 'sliper' (sleeper) and 'bocs signals' (signal box). Jack Simmons claims that 'Welsh seems to be the only western European language that never assimilated the word *locomotive* from English. In North Wales the machine was represented by "injan drên" (train engine), in the South by "endjin"'.[50] In a Welsh poem, 'Tri Tro Trên', about train journeys, Ceiriog used English words like 'a number', 'lumber', 'waiting-room', 'lumber train', which were introduced by the railways and widely used by stationmasters.[51] Letters and articles in Welsh newspapers and periodicals concerning the railways invariably included a sprinkling of English terms. Attempts at translation were not always successful in either direction. A station in north Wales in 1875 displayed the notice:

> List of booking. You passengers must be careful. For have them level money for ticket and to apply at once for asking tickets when will booking window open. No tickets to have after departure of the train.[52]

Another, in Welsh, near Swansea is misspelt, with incorrect syntax, and a strange vocabulary:

> Cadwch y glwyd hon yng ngaued Dderwi am gadail yn agored Dau gen swllt – wyrth orchymyn.[53]

---

[50] Jack Simmons, 'The Welsh Language' in idem, *The Victorian Railway* (New York, 1991), pp. 193–4. For interesting comment about railway language in general, see ibid., pp. 174–94, and Frank McKenna, *The Railway Workers, 1840–1970* (London, 1980), pp. 230–54.
[51] John Ceiriog Hughes, *Yr Oriau Olaf* (Liverpool, 1888), pp. 97–8.
[52] Quoted in Simmons, *The Victorian Railway*, p. 185.
[53] 'Y Rheilffyrdd', *Y Tyst a'r Dydd*, 27 September 1872.

(Probable meaning: Keep the gate shut. Fine for keeping it open Forty shillings – By Order.)

By the end of the nineteenth century English tourists could be forgiven for thinking that few people in Wales actually spoke Welsh. Unlike the Welsh, they could travel the railway system without the inconvenience of language difficulties.[54] Railway companies remained impervious to local claims of discrimination against Welsh-speaking workmen even when those protests entered parliamentary debate. The coming of the railways introduced a new and powerful arterial system which was responsible not only for planting monoglot English-speaking staff in otherwise Welsh-speaking strongholds but also for revolutionizing communications within Wales. David Howell has shown how the coming of the railways affected agricultural markets.[55] Social habits were also affected. D. Lleufer Thomas commented upon the parishes through which the London and North-Western's Central Anglesey line passed:

> I do not know of any district which, while still remaining purely agricultural, has been so greatly influenced by the introduction of railways as this portion of Anglesey. It has enabled the poorer classes to make large sums of money out of commodities which, in other districts, are generally neglected, and it has also enabled them to spend such money freely upon excursions and other forms of pleasure previously unknown to them.[56]

As protective barriers of rural isolation were broken down by the railways, the idea that English was the language of commercial prosperity and of the future took a firm hold. The railway revolution was as much about culture and society as about economics, and, in the final analysis, it stands alongside migration and education as a principal agent of language change in nineteenth-century Wales.

---

[54] See Henry T. Edwards, *Wales and the Welsh Church* (London, 1889), p. 196. For an account of the contribution of the railways in the development of Llandudno, Colwyn Bay and Rhyl, see Allan Fletcher, 'The Role of Landowners, Entrepreneurs and Railways in the Urban Development of the North Wales Coast during the Nineteenth Century', *WHR*, 16, no. 4 (1993), 514–41.

[55] David Howell, 'The Impact of Railways on Agricultural Development in Nineteenth-century Wales', *WHR*, 7, no. 1 (1974), 40–62, and idem, *Land and People in Nineteenth-Century Wales* (London, 1977), pp. 121–7.

[56] Royal Commission on Labour, *The Agricultural Labourer. Wales*. Reports by D. Lleufer Thomas. BPP 1893–4 [c6894 – xiv] XXXVI, p. 128. For a contemporary view denying the Anglicizing effect of railways in rural areas, see Editorial 'Y Gymraeg', *Y Gwladgarwr*, 30 May 1868.

5

Tourism and the Welsh Language in the Nineteenth Century

DAVID LLEWELYN JONES and ROBERT SMITH

If the Welsh people want English tourists to visit their coasts they must provide the features that will attract English tourists, they must spend money on sanitation and public works, they must provide places of amusement and recreation, and they must try to look at those matters from the tourist, not from their own point of view.[1]

These observations by F. E. Hamer, published in an article in 1900, are indicative of the extent to which contemporary commentators viewed tourism as a vital ingredient of the Welsh economy at the beginning of the twentieth century. Observers like Hamer were convinced that the ability to attract English visitors, combined with a willingness on the part of the Welsh to adapt to meet the needs of tourists, was crucial to the nation's future prosperity. Their judgement was based in part on an acknowledgement of the benefits which visitors had brought to countless resorts in both England and Wales during the final decades of the nineteenth century. The expansion of tourism was based firmly on the growth of the industrial bourgeoisie which drew its wealth from the industrial and commercial expansion witnessed in Britain during the reign of Victoria. The numbers employed in administrative or secretarial posts in England and Wales had increased from around 100,000 in 1861 to more than 750,000 in 1911, thereby creating a class of worker who was not tied to farm nor workshop and who, unlike the working class, enjoyed a considerable degree of financial security.[2] The annual holiday was an essential ingredient in the lives of such people and their patronage was a considerable influence on the expansion of tourism in resorts in Wales such as Llandudno, Colwyn Bay, Rhyl and Abergele, which rapidly developed into major attractions catering largely for the needs of affluent visitors from industrial areas around Manchester and Liverpool. Improvement in railway communications provided a further impetus to the tourist industry. The early

---

[1] F. E. Hamer, 'The Undeveloped Resources of Wales', *Young Wales*, VI (1900), 222–30.
[2] Jose Harris, *Private Lives, Public Spirit: A Social History of Britain 1870–1914* (Oxford, 1993), pp. 129–34.

success of resorts on the north Wales coast owed much to the completion of the railway to Holyhead in 1848 and the railway was equally important for the prosperity of resorts in south Wales such as Barry, Porth-cawl and Tenby. Tourism in mid-Wales also benefited from the completion of the Cambrian railway in 1864, which brought resorts such as Aberystwyth, Aberdyfi, Barmouth and Tywyn into direct contact with the commercial centres of the Midlands and north-west England.[3] This chapter will consider the experience of Aberystwyth and Abergele, two towns which witnessed the sociolinguistic consequences of growing numbers of tourists in the late Victorian period.

Abergele

Nineteenth-century Abergele was one of the oldest and most flourishing market towns on the coast of north Wales.[4] Since the later middle ages the town had benefited from its proximity to the rich agricultural region of the Vale of Clwyd[5] both because of its role in the commercial life of the area and because inhabitants of rural areas sought entertainment there. During the early nineteenth century several iron and lead mines had been developed and the area boasted numerous limestone quarries. The regular influx of visitors, however, contributed most to the town's prosperity during the early Victorian period. The impression gained by early visitors, however, was less than complimentary.[6] The diarist Richard Fenton complained about the condition of the town during his visit in 1808,[7] and other travellers were equally critical of this 'small shabby town'.[8] Nevertheless, visitors arrived in growing numbers, and Abergele became a particularly popular destination for the sick and the aged. Castell Gwrych, described as 'the lion of Abergele'[9] and compared by Henry Irwin Jenkinson to one of the castles of the Far East, was one important attraction.[10] Yet it was the beach and the striking beauty of the rural area towards Llanfair Talhaearn and Llangernyw which were largely responsible for the growth of tourism. In 1808 a traveller from Conwy to Abergele described the panorama which opened before his eyes:

> . . . the principal object of attraction is a fine expanse of the main ocean, which now owing to the fineness of the morning, bore a very placid and beautiful appearance.

---

[3] See the series *A Regional History of the Railways of Great Britain*: vol. 11, Peter E. Baughan, *North and Mid Wales* (2nd ed., Nairn, 1991); vol. 12, D. S. M. Barrie, *South Wales* (Newton Abbot, 1980).

[4] Ellis Wynne Williams, *Hanes Eglwys Mynydd Seion Abergele* (Dinbych, 1968), p. 8.

[5] Frank Price Jones, *Crwydro Gorllewin Dinbych* (Llandybïe, 1969), pp. 129–30; Ellis Wynne Williams, *Abergele: The Story of a Parish* (Abergele, 1968), pp. 44–5.

[6] Lucy Toulmin Smith, *The Itinerary in Wales of John Leland* (London, 1906), p. 95.

[7] Richard Fenton, *Tours in Wales (1804–1813)* (London, 1917), p. 4.

[8] Clwyd Record Office, Ruthin, DD/DM/228/78.

[9] *Abel Heywood's Guide Book: Illustrated Guide to Abergele*, p. 7.

[10] Henry Irwin Jenkinson, *Smaller Jenkinson's Practical Guide to North Wales* (London, 1878), p. 42.

Green, blue, yellow, purple and pink, some of these colours pure, others indiscriminately blended together, decked its bosom in gay confusion, whilst a variety of vessels, each pursuing its destined tracks, and gradually diminishing from the broad whiteness of a sail, to a speck, fairly discernible on the level line of the horizon diversified the wide flat-surface of the sea, and added to the whole scene an air of cheerfulness and of active life.[11]

Tourism became an increasingly important part of the town's economy during the first half of the nineteenth century and it was one of the factors which ensured that Abergele witnessed a steady increase in its population at a time when the population of the surrounding rural villages was in decline (Table 1):

Table 1. Population of Abergele according to sex, 1801–1911

Year	Males	Females	Total	Number +/-	Percentage +/-
1801	848	900	1748		
1811	926	1018	1944	196+	11.2+
1821	1161	1156	2317	373+	19.2+
1831	1250	1256	2506	189+	8.2+
1841	1369	1292	2661	155+	6.2+
1851	1397	1458	2855	194+	7.3+
1861	1594	1714	3308	453+	15.9+
1871	1518	1676	3194	114–	3.4–
1881	1496	1676	3172	22–	0.7–
1891	1505	1681	3186	14+	0.4+
1901	1479	1671	3150	36–	1.1–
1911	1469	1709	3178	28+	0.8+

The population of Abergele increased in every decade, reaching a high point of 3,308 in 1861. Thereafter, there was a slight decline in the population, partly because of the growth and popularity of neighbouring resorts such as Rhyl, Llandudno and Colwyn Bay. In 1820 Rhyl contained little more than 'a few scattered sod cabins', but during the following decade it was transformed into a bustling town.[12] It soon boasted a promenade and pier, whereas plans to develop similar attractions in Abergele and Pen-sarn were not realized and the resort's popularity declined.[13] The population of Abergele remained comparatively stable

---

[11] Clwyd Record Office Ruthin, DD/DM/228/78, *Journal of an excursion made in the autumn of 1808 through several counties of north Wales – Romantic Cambria, Hail! (1808).*

[12] A. H. Dodd, 'The Rise of the North Wales Coastal Resorts', *Llandudno Conference Souvenir of the National Union of Teachers* (London, 1939), p. 78; *Black's Picturesque Guide through North and South Wales and Monmouthshire* (Edinburgh, 1858), p. 30.

[13] Clwyd Record Office, Ruthin QSD/DP/1–2, 9, Plans of Pen-sarn (Abergele) Pier; Williams, *Abergele: The Story of a Parish*, p. 51; idem, *Plastai'r Fro* (Abergele, 1994), p. 9; Allan Fletcher, 'The Role of Landowners, Entrepreneurs and Railways in the Urban Development of the North Wales Coast during the Nineteenth Century', *WHR*, 16, no. 4 (1993), 514–41.

between 1871 and 1911 at a time when it might have been expected to increase appreciably. The principal explanation for this is the reluctance of the owners of the three major estates, Kinmel, Gwrych and Pentre, to sell property for the development of housing estates.

Despite the fact that there was no spectacular increase in Abergele's population during the nineteenth century, the period from 1861 and 1911 were years of rapid civic development.[14] The town hall was built in 1867 and several chapels were extended. Growing numbers of visitors were drawn by the combination of natural beauty and the seaside. The majority of visitors were increasingly attracted to the bathing facilities at Pen-sarn rather than to the town of Abergele itself. A railway station was opened at Pen-sarn in 1845 and houses were built specifically to accommodate visitors during the holiday season.[15] In 1878 Henry Irwin Jenkinson confirmed earlier reports that Pen-sarn rather than Abergele was the main destination for tourists.[16] His impression was echoed in a handbook for travellers in north Wales, published in 1885, in which it was noted that Abergele had been 'somewhat eclipsed as a watering-place by Pen-sarn . . . a modern rival, near the station, which extends its terrace and villas, many of them lodging-houses, along the sea, and close to the smooth sands'. Pen-sarn's attractions were also promoted in *Abel Heywood's Guide Books: Illustrated Guide to Abergele*, published in 1893, which made special reference to facilities available for children and opportunities to play cricket, tennis and bowls. Indeed, it would appear that Pen-sarn's development was not impeded by the fact that lodging houses were located some way from the coast and did not afford a view of the sea.

As a result of Pen-sarn's development, changes occurred in the linguistic character of Abergele and its neighbourhood.[17] The celebrated Dr Samuel Johnson, who passed through Abergele in 1774, observed that the majority of the people spoke Welsh and that English was rarely used, even in services held by the Anglican church.[18] The number of English speakers increased substantially during the second half of the nineteenth century, however, as increasing numbers of summer tourists, some of whom later settled as permanent residents, arrived from Lancashire. Handsome houses were built, often in order to accommodate English in-migrants. Although Welsh songs were occasionally heard in concerts held in the town hall, English was the principal language of entertainment. For instance, on 1 September 1883 the *Abergele Visitor* announced the arrival of Sam Hague's Minstrels to amuse the crowds with songs and Anglo-American entertainment.[19]

[14] Williams, *Abergele: The Story of a Parish*, p. 84.
[15] Mark Luke Louis, *Gleanings in North Wales with Historical Sketches* (Liverpool, 1854), p. 27.
[16] *Smaller Jenkinson's Practical Guide to North Wales*, p. 7.
[17] Jones, *Cnwydro Gorllewin Dinbych*, pp. 129–30.
[18] J. O. Halliwell-Phillips, *Notes of Family Excursions in North Wales* (London, 1860), p. 447; Adrian Bristow, *Dr Johnson & Mrs Thrale's Tour in North Wales 1774 – with an introduction and notes* (Wrexham, 1995), p. 45.
[19] *The Abergele and Pensarn Visitor*, 1 September 1883.

However, it would be wrong to assume that the Anglicization of cultural activity in Abergele was entirely a reflection of the influence of summer visitors. Penny-readings held during the autumn and winter months were conducted in English,[20] and few inhabitants supported Welsh activities such as the literary meetings, led by the archdruid Clwydfardd, held in St Paul's schoolroom at the end of May 1882.[21]

Another example of the Anglicization of Abergele were efforts made to provide for the spiritual needs of English-speaking visitors and in-migrants. Although Welsh was clearly the language of Anglican worship until the 1820s, there was a growing tendency to provide English-medium services for monoglot English visitors during the summer months.[22] Increasingly, too, Nonconformists sought to make provision for English worshippers. In 1858 members of Mynydd Seion, the Calvinistic Methodist chapel in Abergele, decided to conduct services in English at Pen-sarn during the summer months for the benefit of visitors and in 1876 it was decided to establish an English chapel there. This was warmly welcomed by preachers such as Dr Owen Thomas, the celebrated leader of Welsh Calvinistic Methodism in Liverpool. Addressing the assembled throng during the ceremony held to lay the foundation stone, Thomas declared that it would be impossible to resist the Anglicization of the north Wales coast:

> I consider it wisdom and sound policy on the part of Welshmen to encourage as far as necessary the movement on foot for providing religious accommodation for the English-speaking portion of the community in the Principality, as well as those who in perpetually increasing numbers visit it. I yield to no man in patriotism; I am ready to cry with the most vehement 'Oes y byd i'r iaith Gymraeg'. I do not see that the Welsh language is dying as rapidly as some would have us think; it won't die while I live, and I do not expect it will die soon. Nevertheless, the growth of English is apparent; even the lads in the streets at their play speak it, which to me is incontestable a proof as any that the language is gaining ground. When the late Dr Arnold heard the sound of the first railway whistle, he exclaimed, 'Here is an end of despotism in England!' I think I may similarly say in reference to the incursions of the steam highway into our country, 'Here is an end of Welsh for Wales'. In the natural course of things the language cannot exist more than a century or two, and it is our duty to provide against the future.[23]

These sentiments were echoed by several other speakers. David Roberts, Tan'rallt, a prominent figure in Nonconformist circles in Abergele, claimed that Welsh would soon be displaced as the language of daily life in Abergele because of the influence of tourism and the manner in which education promoted a knowledge of English. Scathing remarks were made about those who refused to accept that linguistic shifts were inevitable. Particular scorn was reserved for

---

[20] John R. Ellis, *A History of Abergele and District* (Abergele, 1948), p. 77.
[21] *The Abergele and Pensarn Visitor*, 27 May 1882.
[22] NLW, Church in Wales Records, SA/QA/6.
[23] *The Abergele and Pensarn Visitor*, 28 July 1877.

Robert Ambrose Jones (Emrys ap Iwan), a tireless campaigner for the preservation of Welsh.[24] He was barely eighteen when he penned a short essay in French describing Abergele:

Nid yw'r dref ei hun yn hardd iawn nag yn fawr, ond y mae ei safle yn un tra dymunol, a'i chwmpasoedd yn dra hardd, llawer o dai newyddion a helaeth wedi eu cyfodi ar gyfer yr ymwelwyr a ddenir bob haf gan y golygfeydd amrywiol, ac yn enwedig gan ei thraethau enwog.[25]

(The town itself is not very pretty nor big, but its situation is quite pleasant, and its hinterland quite pretty, numerous new and extensive houses have been built for the visitors who are drawn each summer by the various views, especially by its famous beaches.)

During his childhood the language heard on the streets was 'a delicate Welsh, the rich Welsh of the Vale of Clwyd and the Hiraethog mountain' ('Cymraeg rhywiog, Cymraeg cyfoethog Dyffryn Clwyd a Mynydd Hiraethog'),[26] but he was acutely conscious that English was rapidly gaining ground in the locality. Emrys ap Iwan was a doughty opponent of the principle of establishing English chapels in Welsh-speaking areas, and he argued that an English chapel in Pen-sarn would contribute to the decline of Welsh in the locality since visitors would live their lives through the medium of English rather than seek to integrate themselves

Table 2. Language spoken in Abergele and Denbighshire (population aged 2 years and over)

	Abergele		Denbighshire	
	Number	*Percentage*	Number	*Percentage*
Welsh	1171	*38.6*	37195	*33.6*
Bilingual	1444	*47.7*	35030	*31.7*
English	416	*13.7*	38310	*34.7*
Total	**3031**	***100.0***	**110535**	***100.0***

within the local Welsh community.[27] His views went unheeded, however, and the 'English cause' flourished in Pen-sarn. Table 2 reveals that almost half the population of Abergele (47.7 per cent) was bilingual in 1891 but that the town also included a relatively high proportion of monoglot Welsh speakers (38.6 per cent); this meant that 86.3 per cent of the town's inhabitants were able to speak

---

[24] Ellis Wynne Williams, 'Emrys ap Iwan', *Y Ddarlith Flynyddol, Cymdeithas Emrys ap Iwan Abergele* (Clwyd, 1983), p. 7.
[25] Thomas Gwynn Jones, *Emrys ap Iwan – Cofiant* (Caernarfon, 1912), p. 7.
[26] Gwynfor Evans, *Seiri Cenedl y Cymry* (2nd ed., Llandysul, 1987), p. 237.
[27] Williams, '*Emrys ap Iwan*', p. 6.

Table 3. Language according to age (population aged 2 years and over)

	Number				Percentage			
	Welsh	Both	English	Total	Welsh	Both	English	Total
2–4	114	60	28	202	56.4	29.7	13.9	100.0
5–14	296	346	94	736	40.2	47.0	12.8	100.0
15–29	202	413	104	719	28.1	57.4	14.5	100.0
30–44	187	279	79	545	34.3	51.2	14.5	100.0
45–59	162	212	59	433	37.4	49.0	13.6	100.0
60–74	164	109	47	320	51.2	34.1	14.7	100.0
75+	46	25	5	76	60.5	32.9	6.6	100.0
Total	**1171**	**1444**	**416**	**3031**	**38.6**	**47.7**	**13.7**	**100.0**

Welsh and that 61.4 per cent could speak English. A striking feature of the evidence contained in Table 2 is the difference between the percentage figures for Abergele and those for Denbighshire as a whole. The percentage of monoglot Welsh speakers was similar, but whereas there was a higher percentage of monoglot English speakers in Denbighshire than in Abergele a much higher percentage of bilingual people lived in the town than in the county.

Table 3 reveals that language ability varied according to age. With the exception of those over 75, the percentage of English monoglots remained comparatively constant, but there are striking variations in terms of the percentage of monoglot Welsh speakers and those who spoke both languages. Although 56.4 per cent of children between 2 and 4 were monoglot Welsh speakers, the proportion of the population who had no knowledge of English declined in each group below 60 years of age. The fact that the highest proportions of monoglot Welsh speakers were to be found among the oldest and youngest members of society strongly suggests that Welsh was the language of the hearth and that the

Table 4. Language according to birthplace (population aged 2 years and over)

	Number				Percentage			
	Welsh	Both	English	Total	Welsh	Both	English	Total
Abergele	629	735	54	1418	44.4	51.8	3.8	100.0
Rest of Denbighshire	333	337	9	679	49.0	49.7	1.3	100.0
Rest of Wales	196	290	27	513	38.2	56.5	5.3	100.0
England	12	76	281	369	3.2	20.6	76.2	100.0
Scotland	–	1	20	21	–	4.8	95.2	100.0
Ireland	–	3	17	20	–	15.0	85.0	100.0
Others	1	2	8	11	9.1	18.2	72.7	100.0
Total	**1171**	**1444**	**416**	**3031**	**38.6**	**47.7**	**13.7**	**100.0**

local economy and schooling were factors which promoted knowledge of English.

Table 4 reveals that the majority of the inhabitants of Abergele hailed from the locality. As many as 1,418 (46.8 per cent) had been born in the town itself and 679 (22.4 per cent) came from other parts of Denbighshire. A total of 513 (16.9 per cent) had been born in other parts of Wales, and 369 (12.2 per cent) were born in England. Only 44 per cent of those born in Abergele were monoglot Welsh speakers. Even so, some caution is required in interpreting this evidence. For instance, the fact that five (8.9 per cent) of the 56 born in Liverpool were monoglot Welsh speakers and 23 (41.1 per cent) were bilingual indicates that robust pockets of Welshness existed in Liverpool in the late nineteenth century.

Table 5. Language according to enumeration districts
(population aged 2 years and over)

District	Number				Percentage			
	Welsh	Both	English	Total	Welsh	Both	English	Total
3	320	482	58	860	37.2	56.0	6.8	100.0
4	263	534	227	1024	25.7	52.1	22.2	100.0
5	167	225	78	470	35.5	47.9	16.6	100.0
6	98	140	32	270	36.3	51.8	11.9	100.0
7	139	27	1	167	83.2	16.2	0.6	100.0
8	184	36	20	240	76.7	15.0	8.3	100.0
Total	**1171**	**1444**	**416**	**3031**	**38.6**	**47.7**	**13.7**	**100.0**

Abergele was divided into six enumeration districts, each of which boasted different linguistic characteristics (Table 5). The highest proportion of monoglot English speakers (22.2 per cent) was recorded in district 4, the coastal area which included Pen-sarn and the railway station. This was also the area with the lowest proportion of monoglot Welsh speakers (25.7 per cent). District 5, which included the village of Tywyn on the outskirts of Rhyl, included 16.6 per cent who were monoglot English speakers, and the coastal areas favoured by tourists were evidently the most Anglicized parts of Abergele. The highest proportion of monoglot Welsh speakers (83.2 per cent) lived in district 7, towards the south of the town in the direction of thoroughly rural communities such as Llanfair Talhaearn. Only 0.6 per cent of the inhabitants of this district were recorded as monoglot English speakers, the lowest of any of the enumeration districts surveyed in this study. The highest proportion of those who spoke both languages (56.0 per cent) lived in the west of the parish in district 3, situated close to Gwrych Castle and Llanddulas. The largest number of English-born residents lived in the holiday centres of Pen-sarn (19.3 per cent) and Tywyn (13.0 per cent), while 94 per cent of those enumerated in the southern district were natives of Denbighshire. Table 6 confirms that the most popular tourist areas also contained the highest proportion of people born outside Wales:

Table 6. Place of birth according to enumeration districts

District	Number					Percentage				
	Denbigh	Rest of Wales	England	Other	Total	Denbigh	Rest of Wales	England	Other	Total
3	640	144	68	8	860	74.4	16.7	8.0	0.9	100.0
4	634	174	198	18	1024	61.9	17.0	19.3	1.8	100.0
5	286	112	61	11	470	60.9	23.8	13.0	2.3	100.0
6	203	36	18	13	270	75.2	13.3	6.7	4.8	100.0
7	157	7	2	1	167	94.0	4.2	1.2	0.6	100.0
8	177	40	22	1	240	73.7	16.7	9.2	0.4	100.0
Total	2097	513	369	52	3031	69.2	16.9	12.2	1.7	100.0

The census records that 57 (1.9 per cent) of those enumerated in Abergele and Pen-sarn derived their livelihood from tourism; of these, 50 (87.7 per cent) were women (Table 7). Only 15 (26.3 per cent) were monoglot Welsh speakers, 34 (59.7 per cent) were bilingual, and 8 (14.0 per cent) were monoglot English. 60 per cent of those recorded as monoglot Welsh speakers were over sixty years old, while 44.1 per cent of those aged 45–60 were bilingual. A total of 44 individuals were recorded as lodging-house keepers, of whom 31 lived in Pen-sarn. Some combined two occupations: Catherine Davies, a 51-year-old widow from Llannefydd, kept a dairy as well as providing accommodation for visitors at Bowdon House. Only one English-born bilingual lodging-house keeper was recorded: Anne Williams, a 73-year-old widow who kept a lodging house at 2 Castle Terrace, had been born in Liverpool. Others born in England included natives of the counties of Cheshire, Lincoln, Stafford and Warwick. As many as 250 female domestic servants were recorded in the town, of whom 27 (10.8 per cent) were employed in lodging houses or hotels. Of these, 23 (85.2 per cent) were bilingual, two were monoglot Welsh speakers and two were monoglot English.

Table 7. Language spoken by hoteliers, lodging-house keepers and boarding-house keepers, according to place of birth

	Number				Percentage			
	Welsh	Both	English	Total	Welsh	Both	English	Total
Abergele	6	10	–	16	37.5	62.5	–	100.0
Rest of Denbighshire	5	8	–	13	38.5	61.5	–	100.0
Rest of Wales	4	15	1	20	20.0	75.0	5.0	100.0
England	–	1	7	8	–	12.5	87.5	100.0
Total	15	34	8	57	26.3	59.7	14.0	100.0

The census was conducted on the evening of Sunday, 5 April 1891, before the holiday season had begun in earnest.[28] As a result, only 34 visitors were recorded in Abergele, of whom 19 were female and 15 were male. Not surprisingly, 18 (52.0 per cent) of these visitors were enumerated in Pen-sarn. Although Abergele and Pen-sarn were advertised as desirable locations for family holidays, the census indicates that 26 of those staying there in April were single, while 5 were married and 3 were widows. Although Abergele was attractive to people of all ages, especially during the summer, people aged between 15 and 59 were a particularly important age group during the spring months. There is no information concerning the occupation of twelve visitors; six were recorded as living on their own means and the remainder pursued a variety of occupations. Thomas Birchall, a 56-year-old unmarried farmer from Rainford in Lancashire stayed with Robert and Elizabeth Hughes at the Old Chandler in Market Street; W. Blake Marsh, a 41-year-old doctor from Monmouthshire, lodged at Plas Ucha on the outskirts of the town. In both cases, English was noted as their only language. Two monoglot Welsh-speaking hawkers resided with Catherine Jones at 12 Water Street, Abergele, one a native of Caernarfon and the other a local man. In total, 14 (41.1 per cent) of visitors hailed from England, and all except one were monoglot English speakers. Six came from Lancashire and three from Hampshire. The only Welsh-speaking visitor from England was John Mellor, a 28-year-old single man born in Yorkshire.

The census is therefore clearly an incomplete source of information about visitors. The large number of visitors who arrived each summer were not present in April and evidence from other areas suggests that the term 'visitor' was applied loosely by those who recorded the information. More valuable evidence is contained in the lists of visitors which were published in the local newspaper each week during the summer months. These included an entry for every hotel and lodging house and noted the names of the visitors and the town in which they lived. Although this is an immensely important source, some caution is required in considering the evidence. For instance, it is difficult to estimate the total number of visitors present at any given time because the lists noted families rather than individuals. Thus the lists might indicate that a 'Mr and Mrs Jones and family' were in residence in one particular lodging house, but that 'Messrs Davies' and 'Misses Harris' were staying in another. These lists also made no reference to the language spoken by visitors, a major disadvantage in view of the fact that visitors from Wales were not all Welsh speakers and that visitors from England included many who were familiar with the native tongue. However, despite these limitations, the evidence contained in these lists cannot be discounted and for this study the lists for August 1873, 1878, 1883, 1888, 1893 and 1898 have been considered.

---

[28] Edward Higgs, *Making a Clearer Sense of the Census* (London, 1996), p. 173.

Table 8. Total number of entries of visitors to
Abergele and Pen-sarn 1873–1903

Year	July	August	September
1873	578	861	491
1883	393	720	592
1893	247	842	783
1903	229	646	595

In 1873, 14.3 per cent of all visitors came from Lancashire and their importance to the tourist trade in Abergele increased sharply in the final decades of the nineteenth century; in August 1898 no fewer than 43.5 per cent of visitors present in the town came from Lancashire. The importance of Liverpool is also evident. In 1873 only five visitors to Abergele or Pen-sarn lived in Liverpool, but within fifteen years this figure had increased to fifty-eight. A similar increase was witnessed in the number arriving from Manchester; only eighteen had travelled to Abergele and Pen-sarn in 1873, but by 1898 the figure had increased to fifty-two. Only four came from Chester in 1873, but by 1893 the figure had reached twenty. During these years Cheshire and Lancashire rapidly became the most vigorous 'exporters' of visitors to Abergele and Pen-sarn and since large numbers of Welsh speakers lived in Manchester and Liverpool it is likely that at least some visitors were Welsh speakers.[29] However, the majority were clearly monoglot English speakers whose presence both directly and indirectly influenced language change in Abergele and Pen-sarn. The centre of the town remained 'definitely Welsh', according to W. T. Palmer,[30] but this was largely because visitors dwelt in Pen-sarn, which, as we have seen, was far more Anglicized. The decline in the power and influence of the Kinmel, Gwrych and Pentre Mawr estates meant there was nothing to prevent the further expansion of the tourist industry in Abergele in the years after the First World War and this contributed to further language shifts within the locality.[31] Writing in 1932, H. V. Morton noted the extent to which the coast of north Wales had become the playground of visitors from north-west England and the Midlands:

> Along the forty-odd miles of this road between Rhyl and Carnarvon are dotted some of the best-known and best-liked towns in the whole of Wales. This stretch of lovely coast is the playground of the individual cities of the Midlands and the North. No true Midlander and no true son of Lancashire is entirely ignorant of it. It is a part of Wales designed by nature and Man to capture the leisure moments of crowds.[32]

---

[29] R. Merfyn Jones and D. Ben Rees, *The Liverpool Welsh and their Religion: Two Centuries of Welsh Calvinistic Methodism* (Liverpool, 1984), p. 24.
[30] W. T. Palmer, *Things Seen in North Wales* (London, 1928), p. 26.
[31] Williams, *Abergele: The Story of a Parish*, p. 51.
[32] H. V. Morton, *In Search of Wales* (London, 1932), p. 60.

To sum up. During the nineteenth century Abergele was both a market town and an increasingly busy holiday resort catering mostly for visitors from north-west England. Although Anglicizing tendencies were becoming increasingly evident, on balance Welsh remained the stronger of the two languages at the end of the nineteenth century. Only one in eight of the population were unable to speak Welsh in 1891, and almost 40 per cent were monoglot Welsh speakers. However, the percentage of monoglot Welsh speakers was in sharp decline among young adults. The annual pilgrimage of scores of visitors, predominantly from north-west England, clearly encouraged the process of Anglicization in Abergele. It is significant that the tourist centres of Tywyn and Pen-sarn contained the highest percentage of monoglot English speakers and that few monoglot Welsh speakers were recorded in those registration districts in 1891. The Anglicization of areas such as Tywyn and Pen-sarn was closely associated with the fact that English was the language of recreation and entertainment and that the native language and culture were largely disregarded by those who provided for the needs of tourists in the area. Moreover, the evidence regarding Abergele disproves F. E. Hamer's contention concerning the reluctance of the Welsh to meet the needs of their English guests, for Abergele's civic leaders made a determined effort to adopt English customs and the English tongue during the closing decades of the nineteenth century. Even the town's Nonconformist chapels, traditional citadels of the Welsh language, increasingly demonstrated their willingness to meet the needs of summer visitors. Support among the town's Welsh-speaking leaders for the English tongue derived in part from an awareness of the impoverished nature of monoglot Welsh-speaking communities in the town's rural hinterland, which contrasted with the affluence enjoyed by Anglicized coastal resorts such as Rhyl and Colwyn Bay. Those who objected to the process of Anglicization were therefore largely ignored, primarily because of the vital importance of the tourist trade to the local economy.

Aberystwyth

Y mae Aberystwyth yn dref o hen adgofion i mi, ac yn rhan o'm breuddwydion. Ond y mae ei gwedd yn newid ym mis Awst, a phrin y gwn ple'r wyf. Acen Birmingham, papurau Birmingham, chwaeth Birmingham, – o'r dau cant oedd yn aros yn yr un ty a mi, nid oedd un yn gwybod mwy am Gymru na fod yr awyr yn iach a'r bwyd yn dda.[33]

(Aberystwyth is a town that has old memories for me, and is part of my dreams. But its appearance changes during the month of August, and I hardly know where I am. The Birmingham accent, Birmingham newspapers, Birmingham tastes, – of the two hundred who stayed in the same house as me, there was not one who knew more about Wales other than that the air was fresh and that the food was good.)

[33] Mawddwy, 'Gwibdaith Haf', *Cymru*, XXIX, no. 168 (1905), 263–4.

Table 9. Population according to sex 1801–1901

Year	Males	Females	Total	Number +/−	*Percentage +/−*
1801	733	1025	1758		
1811	939	1325	2264	506+	*28.8+*
1821	1498	2050	3556	1292+	*57.1+*
1831	1820	2308	4128	572+	*16.1+*
1841	2128	2788	4916	788+	*19.1+*
1851	2284	2905	5189	273+	*5.5+*
1861	2400	3162	5562	373+	*7.2+*
1871	2943	3777	6720	1158+	*20.8+*
1881	3119	3969	7088	368+	*5.5+*
1891	2894	4006	6900	188−	*2.7−*
1901	3434	4580	8014	1114+	*16.1+*

So wrote Mawddwy in an article published in *Cymru* in 1905. By that time Aberystwyth had become a popular destination for hundreds of visitors each summer and one of the most important holiday resorts in Wales. Since the closing years of the eighteenth century a steady stream of visitors had been attracted to the town by picturesque attractions such as the iron-age fort of Pen-dinas, the natural beauty of the Rheidol estuary, and the Pumlumon mountains.[34] The bracing climate also attracted sick or debilitated visitors. Sir Charles Clarke, a prominent physician, noted 'that in certain cases a fortnight spent at Aberystwyth will do more good than a month at any other watering place', and although most visitors arrived in the town in search of entertainment it was also a resting place for the old and the sick.[35] Although tourism contributed immensely to the economic life of the town, Aberystwyth was also firmly established as a lively commercial centre serving the needs of a large rural hinterland. Trade and commerce benefited from the arrival of the Cambrian Railway in 1864 and from railway links with south Wales after 1867, and the town was also the centre of a thriving fishing industry.[36]

Table 9 reveals that the population of Aberystwyth increased steadily throughout the nineteenth century, with the exception of the period between 1881 and 1891. Although the district's boundaries were extended in 1883 to include 559 additional inhabitants, the population fell from 7,088 in 1881 to

---

[34] These aspects are emphasized in works like T. O. Morgan, *Morgan's New Guide to Aberystwyth and Neighbourhood* (Aberystwyth, 1874), pp. 70–88; *Slater's Commercial Directory* (Manchester, 1868); *Kelly's Commercial Directory* (London, 1891); Askew Roberts and Edward Woodall, *Gossiping Guide to Aberystwyth and District* (Wrexham, n.d.), p. 16. See also R. C. B. Oliver, 'Holidays at Aberystwyth: 1798–1823 (From the Diary of Captain Frederick Jones)', *Ceredigion*, X, no. 3 (1986), 269–86.

[35] Cited in *Slater's Commercial Directory* (1868), p. 23. Sir Charles Mansfield Clarke (1782–1857) was a surgeon interested in the health of women and children. It is not known how long he stayed in Aberystwyth.

[36] William Troughton, 'The Barque *Hope* of Aberystwyth', *Ceredigion*, XII, no. 3 (1995), 85–101.

6,900 in 1891. No single reason can be cited to explain this phenomenon, although the decline of the Cardiganshire lead mines and a reduction in the numbers employed as sailors throughout the county probably contributed to the decline in the town's population.[37]

The arrival of the Cambrian Railway brought renewed vigour to efforts to exploit the town's potential as a tourist resort.[38] The Hafod Hotel Company erected the Queen's Hotel, an impressive building on the sea front with commanding views of the sea, which opened in 1866. An equally impressive edifice was planned by Thomas Savin, a prominent figure in the expansion of the railways in Wales. He commissioned the renowned architect, J. P. Seddon, to design the Castle Hotel on the south side of the promenade. The venture was a commercial failure, however, and thereafter no large hotel was built which could compete with the Queen's Hotel.[39] Hotels such as the Belle Vue on the promenade, the Gogerddan Arms in Great Darkgate Street, the Commercial Hotel opposite the station and the Talbot Hotel in Market Street catered mainly for the needs of commercial travellers rather than tourists and it appears that Aberystwyth never became a destination for the upper classes who patronized large hotels in towns such as Llandudno and Tenby.[40] The efforts of public bodies were also important to the success of the tourist industry in Aberystwyth. Careful attention was paid to the design of the attractive and substantial residences built in Queen's Road, Marine Terrace, Portland Street and North Parade.[41] Most of these houses had three or four floors and could easily accommodate visitors.[42]

In the early decades of the nineteenth century tourist attractions were mostly country walks along Constitution Hill, Cwm Woods, Elysian Grove and Pen-dinas or occasional concerts by travelling musicians from Germany.[43] From the end of the 1860s onwards, however, a determined effort was made to expand the provision made for visitors. A pier, six hundred feet in length and situated on the south side of the promenade, was opened on Good Friday 1865; public baths were opened in Newfoundland Street in 1877, and a camera obscura was placed in the castle

---

[37] W. J. Lewis, *Born on a Perilous Rock* (Aberystwyth, 1980), pp. 11–16, 200–12; Ieuan Gwynedd Jones (ed.), *Aberystwyth, 1277–1977* (Llandysul, 1977); E. L. Ellis, *The University College of Wales Aberystwyth* (Cardiff, 1972), pp. 33–65; Iwan Morgan (ed.), *University College of Wales Aberystwyth. The College by the Sea (A Record and a Review)* (Aberystwyth, 1928), especially W. R. Evans, 'The First Student's Reminiscences', pp. 53–6; J. M. Angus, 'Reminiscences of the Early Years', pp. 57–60; C. H. Herford, 'Impressions of Aberystwyth (1887–1901)', pp. 96–100; Waldo Williams, 'Digs', pp. 233–6.
[38] Herbert Williams, *Davies the Ocean: Railway King and Coal Tycoon* (Cardiff, 1991), pp. 95–112.
[39] Iwan Morgan, 'The Story of the Buildings' in idem, *The College by the Sea*, pp. 29–46.
[40] Ivor Wynne Jones, *Llandudno, Queen of the Welsh Resorts* (Cardiff, 1975), pp. 16–19.
[41] Harold Carter and Sandra Wheatley, 'Residential Patterns in Mid-Victorian Aberystwyth' in Jones, *Aberystwyth*, pp. 46–84.
[42] Douglas Hague, 'The Architecture of the Town' in ibid., pp. 88–95; H. M. Colvin, 'An Architectural Sideshow – Aberystwyth in the Eighteenth and Nineteenth Centuries', *Wales*, IV, no. 6 (1945), 68–72.
[43] Lewis, *Born on a Perilous Rock*, pp. 201–2.

grounds.[44] The Bijou Theatre offered opportunities to enjoy concerts and plays, and during the 1880s boxing booths and shooting galleries appeared in the town.[45] Even more spectacular progress was witnessed following the establishment of the Aberystwyth Improvement Company as a means of promoting tourist facilities and the standard of living in the town. The company was responsible for improvements to the existing promenade and played a key role in establishing, in 1896, the pier pavilion and the electric railway which carried visitors to the top of Constitution Hill.[46] Each evening during the summer season the hill was illuminated by hundreds of small lamps, and firework displays and confetti shows became a regular feature. The pier pavilion and the Coliseum in Terrace Road became popular venues for evening concerts and a skating rink was built on land opposite the Town Hall.[47] The success of these attractions contributed to the town's standing and, as Aberystwyth began to enjoy a reputation as one of the liveliest resorts on Cardigan Bay, it habitually advertised itself as 'the Biarritz of Wales'.[48]

With few exceptions, English was the language of entertainment in Aberystwyth. The columns of the *Cardigan Bay Visitor* are laden with references to entertainment provided by the Harry Collins Minstrels, a group of coloured dancers who made annual visits to the town in the 1890s.[49] Some of the stars of the London stage, including Arthur Robertson and Harold Wardroper, also performed in the pier during this period and the pavilion also hosted regular visits by the Arthur Sturgess Pantomime during the summer months.[50] The Coliseum was the venue for renditions by the Gigantic Vaudeville Company, concerts by Ella Hills and Ethel Dyon, and contributions by the Royal Strolling Players, who provided entertaining conversations in Old English.[51] As was the case in other tourist centres in Victorian Wales, the language and culture of Wales never featured in such entertainments. Indeed, there is hardly any reference to Wales in programmes, except on rare occasions such as when Clara Novello Davies brought a Welsh women's choir to Aberystwyth in 1905. When the Rheidol United Juvenile Choir performed the cantata *The Prince of Wales* by Owain Alaw, the cast wore traditional Welsh costume but performed in English.[52] English, too, was the language of the more boisterous entertainment found in the skating rink, which also served as a boxing ring in the evenings.[53]

[44] Ibid., pp. 11–16.
[45] Ibid.
[46] *Cardigan Bay Visitor*, 30 June 1896.
[47] Ibid.
[48] Among the descriptions used at the end of the nineteenth century and the beginning of the twentieth century were 'The Brighton of Wales', 'The Naples of Wales' and 'The Queen of Welsh Watering Places'.
[49] *Cambrian News*, 11 August 1893, 19 June 1897.
[50] Ibid., 13 July 1905.
[51] Ibid., 3 August 1905.
[52] Ibid., 17 August 1905.
[53] Ibid., 5 August 1910.

The boxing ring and, possibly, the Bijou Theatre did not chime well with the town's image as a bastion of Nonconformist piety.[54] Commentators such as Mawddwy warned that the town's development as a tourist resort was a threat to the moral character of the rising generation, who were increasingly rejecting the language as well as the religious faith of their parents:

Y mae Aberystwyth yn mynd yn dlysach ac yn gyfoethocach o hyd. Ond y mae elfennau goreu ei bywyd mewn perygl. Gwneir camwri dybryd a'i phlant. Ni welant hwy ond ymbleseru a chwarae, a thybiant mai hynny yw prif amcan bywyd. Ni fedrant sylweddoli mai ar eu gwyliau y mae'r Saeson hyn, ni wyddant mor galed ac egniol y gweithiant ym mwg Birmingham trwy gydol y flwyddyn i ennill eu hwythnos wyliau. Nid oes dim a'm gwna mor brudd yn Aberystwyth a chydmaru'r hen a'r ieuanc, – y naill yn ddiddan, yn weithgar, ac yn feddylgar; y llall yn ddiddim, Seisnigaidd a llac.[55]

(Aberystwyth is getting prettier and richer all the time. But the best aspects of its life are in danger. A grave injustice is done to the children. They see nothing but pleasure and play, and they believe that those are the primary things in life. They cannot understand that the English people are on holiday, they do not know how hard and energetic they work in the smoke of Birmingham throughout the year to earn their week's holiday. Nothing makes me more sad in Aberystwyth than to compare the old and the young, – the former contented and busy and thoughtful; the other purposeless, Anglicized and slack.)

In his reminiscences of student life in the town, however, R. T. Jenkins claimed that immoral or coarse entertainment was not a feature of life in Aberystwyth during the summer season, and that alcohol was abhorrent to many leading figures in the town.[56] Machines revealing *What the Butler Saw* and the *Peep Show* were clearly not part of the life of Victorian and Edwardian Aberystwyth.[57]

This aura of respectability is reflected in the efforts of religious leaders to provide for the spiritual needs of visitors.[58] The care for souls led to the building or extension of several English places of worship. St Michael's church was rebuilt in 1833 and Nonconformists were equally active in building impressive English-language chapels in Newfoundland Street, Portland Street and Alfred Place.[59] Leading Nonconformists also appear to have recognized the importance of tourism

[54] Gwyn A. Williams, *The Making of a Unitarian: David Ivon Jones 1883–1924* (London, 1995), pp. 14–20.
[55] Mawddwy, 'Gwibdaith Haf', 263–4.
[56] R. T. Jenkins, *Edrych yn Ôl* (Dinbych, 1968), pp. 102–35.
[57] Goronwy Rees, *A Bundle of Sensations* (London, 1960), pp. 19–32.
[58] Hague, 'The Architecture of the Town' in Jones, *Aberystwyth*, pp. 88–95; Ieuan Gwynedd Jones, 'Religion and Politics: The Rebuilding of St Michael's Church Aberystwyth and its Political Consequences', *Ceredigion*, VII, no. 2 (1973), 117–30.
[59] Mary Brown, *English Methodism in Aberystwyth* (Aberystwyth, 1969), pp. 30–5, 42–66; W. J. Lewis, *The English Congregational Church, Portland Street, Aberystwyth, 1866–1966* (Aberystwyth, n.d.), pp. 20–5; T. I. Ellis, *Thomas Edward Ellis: Cofiant* (Lerpwl, 1944), p. 48.

and the need to provide spiritual succour for Welsh speakers who spent their vacations in Aberystwyth. Chapels such as Seilo, Tabernacl, Bethel and Seion sought to attract the most prominent preachers to the town during the summer season.[60] For instance, renowned ministers such as the Revds Owen Jones, Ffestiniog, and Robert Davies, Shrewsbury, preached at Seilo in early August 1869. The Revd D. C. Davies of London preached at the same venue in the summer of 1873, William Jones, Penrhyndeudraeth, in August 1878, and Lewis Edwards of Bala in the summer of 1883.[61] The tradition continued in the twentieth century when the town received regular summer visits by ministers such T. J. Edwards of Merthyr, W. E. Prydderch of Swansea and Philip Jones of Porth-cawl, all of whom were powerful orators who attracted large congregations.[62] It was no accident that chapels sought to attract major preachers in July and August and all the evidence suggests that religious leaders made a conscious effort to attract visitors to the town's churches and chapels during the summer months.

A total of 6,680 inhabitants over the age of two were enumerated in Aberystwyth in the 1891 census. There is no record of the language spoken by forty individuals, and five individuals spoke foreign languages, three French speakers and two Italian. A total of 1,751 were enumerated as monoglot Welsh speakers, 3,482 as speaking both English and Welsh, and 1,402 as monoglot English speakers (Table 10). More than three-quarters of the town's inhabitants, 5,233 (78.9 per cent), were recorded as being able to speak Welsh and only slightly fewer, 4,884 (73.6 per cent), were able to speak English.

Table 10. Language spoken by population (aged 2 years and over) of Aberystwyth and Cardiganshire

	Aberystwyth[1]		Cardiganshire[2]	
	Number	*Percentage*	Number	*Percentage*
Welsh	1751	*26.4*	61624	*74.5*
Bilingual	3482	*52.5*	17111	*20.7*
English	1402	*21.1*	3979	*4.8*
Total	**6635**	*100.0*	**82714**	*100.0*

[1] Excluding 40 individuals whose language was not given, 3 French speakers and 2 Italian speakers.
[2] Excluding 255 individuals whose language was not given and 10 who spoke other languages.

---

[60] E. D. Jones, *Trem ar Ganrif yn Hanes Eglwys Gynulleidfaol Baker Street, Aberystwyth* (Aberystwyth, 1978), pp. 3–11; Moelwyn I. Williams, *Y Tabernacl Aberystwyth, 1785–1985* (Aberystwyth, 1986), pp. 32–47; F. W. Jones, *Canmlwydd Seilo Aberystwyth* (Aberystwyth, 1963), pp. 15–31; Llewelyn Morgan, *Hanes Wesleyaeth yn Aberystwyth* (Aberystwyth, 1911), pp. 25–43.
[61] NLW, Welsh CM Archives 18197. Ministry Account Book, Seilo Chapel, Aberystwyth.
[62] Ibid.

The linguistic pattern of the town was in sharp contrast to that in the Registration District, where 89.3 per cent were recorded as Welsh speakers and only 10.7 per cent were monoglot English speakers. At the same time, the census indicates that Aberystwyth was the most Anglicized part of Cardiganshire, for within the county nearly three-quarters of the population were monoglot Welsh speakers and only 4.8 per cent were monoglot English speakers. Monoglot English speakers recorded in Aberystwyth accounted for 64.6 per cent of the total for the Aberystwyth Registration District and 35.2 per cent of the total recorded in Cardiganshire.

Table 11. Language spoken by age (population aged 2 years and over)

Age	Number				Percentage			
	Welsh	Both	English	Total	Welsh	Both	English	Total
2–5	167	167	119	453	36.8	36.9	26.3	100.0
6–14	311	638	283	1232	25.2	51.8	23.0	100.0
15–24	299	922	326	1547	19.3	59.6	21.1	100.0
25–44	400	939	362	1701	23.5	55.2	21.1	100.0
45–64	376	627	238	1241	30.3	50.5	19.2	100.0
65+	198	189	74	461	43.0	41.0	16.0	100.0
Total	**1751**	**3482**	**1402**	**6635**	**26.4**	**52.5**	**21.1**	**100.0**

Nearly three-quarters of people in all age groups spoke Welsh in 1891. A generational decline in the proportion who spoke Welsh does not appear to have occurred, although fewer monoglot Welsh speakers were present in the younger age groups. Monoglot Welsh speakers were few within the 15–24 age group. It is also significant that nearly a quarter of the population of Aberystwyth belonged to this group. This was therefore a relatively young community, very different from some of the rural villages of Cardiganshire. The influence of schooling following the 1870 Education Act was clearly a factor influencing the growth of a knowledge of English within this age group.[63] Yet the nature of the local economy, not least the tourist trade, also had a profound impact on the language spoken by young people in the town. A high proportion of those in the 15–24 age group were employed as servants and a significant number of others were employed in seasonal work associated with the tourist trade. As a result, they came into regular contact with the English language and were provided with opportunities to make use of what they had learnt in school.

Most of those enumerated in Aberystwyth in 1891 had been born in the town or in the surrounding countryside (Table 12). No fewer than 3,440 (51.8 per

---

[63] Griffith G. Davies, 'Addysg Elfennol yn Sir Aberteifi 1790–1902', *Ceredigion*, IV, no. 4 (1963), 359; A. L. Trott, 'Aberystwyth School Board and Board School 1870–1902', ibid., II, no. 1 (1952), 3–17; idem, 'The Implementation of the 1870 Forster Education Act in Cardiganshire', ibid., III, no. 3 (1959), 207–30.

Table 12. Language spoken by place of birth (population aged 2 years and over)

Place of birth	Number				Percentage			
	Welsh	Both	English	Total	Welsh	Both	English	Total
Aberystwyth	972	2148	320	3440	28.3	62.4	9.3	100.0
Rest of Cardiganshire	630	700	24	1354	46.5	51.7	1.8	100.0
Rest of Wales	128	485	254	867	14.7	55.9	29.4	100.0
England	15	138	722	875	1.7	15.8	82.5	100.0
Other	–	11	57	68	–	16.1	83.9	100.0
Not stated	6	–	25	31	19.4	–	80.6	100.0
Total	**1751**	**3482**	**1402**	**6635**	**26.4**	**52.7**	**20.9**	**100.0**

cent) hailed from the town itself, the vast majority of whom, 3,120 (90.7 per cent), were Welsh speakers; of these 972 (31.2 per cent) were Welsh monoglots. Less than half the 1,354 in-migrants from other parts of Cardiganshire were recorded as monoglot Welsh speakers. This suggests that in-migrants to Aberystwyth soon became familiar with English. Some 867 (13.1 per cent) of the town's population were in-migrants from other parts of Wales, a high proportion of whom came from Montgomeryshire and Merioneth. 875 (13.2 per cent) of those enumerated in Aberystwyth were in-migrants from England. Nearly a fifth of those born in England were able to speak Welsh. Most were from London, Liverpool and the border counties, where there were sizeable Welsh-speaking communities. It does not appear, however, that any appreciable number of in-migrants from England had learnt Welsh in Aberystwyth.

Table 13. Language spoken by hoteliers, lodging-house keepers and boarding-house keepers by place of birth

Place of birth	Number				Percentage			
	Welsh	Both	English	Total	Welsh	Both	English	Total
Aberystwyth	9	61	3	73	12.3	83.6	4.1	100.0
Rest of Cardiganshire	13	20	–	33	39.4	60.6	–	100.0
Rest of Wales	–	10	5	15	–	66.7	33.3	100.0
England	–	3	9	12	–	25.0	75.0	100.0
Other	–	1	2	3	–	33.3	66.7	100.0
Total	**22**	**95**	**19**	**136**	**16.2**	**69.9**	**13.9**	**100.0**

136 people were recorded as lodging-house keepers in Aberystwyth (Table 13), the vast majority of whom maintained comparatively large three-storey houses. It was common for two or three lodgers to be recorded and lists of visitors suggest that such houses accommodated two or three families during the holiday season.

Only 22 (16.2 per cent) of the town's lodging-house keepers were recorded as monoglot Welsh speakers and only 19 (13.9 per cent) were monoglot English speakers. Women accounted for 125 (91.9 per cent) of the town's lodging-house keepers, of whom 46 (33.8 per cent) were heads of household. It is also significant that many of those who were recorded as married women were the wives of sailors, porters or other low-paid workers. This suggests that the holiday trade provided an important source of income for women who were the heads of their households and that tourism provided a necessary supplement for the income of many families.[64] In-migrants from England were not prominent in the tourist industry in Aberystwyth, but the majority of those who offered accommodation to visitors hailed from the town or the surrounding area. As many as 106 (77.9 per cent) had been born in Cardiganshire, and 73 of them had been born in Aberystwyth. The effects of tourism on language change is again evident in the fact that few monoglot Welsh speakers were recorded among those who hailed from rural Cardiganshire.

A total of 515 individuals were employed in domestic service in Aberystwyth. Of these, 53 were employed in lodging houses: 31 (58.5 per cent) of them were bilingual, seventeen (32.1 per cent) were monoglot English speakers, and five (9.4 per cent) were monoglot Welsh speakers. Clearly, some knowledge of English was required by the vast majority of domestic servants who served tourists in Aberystwyth. The majority of these servants came from the locality; 32 (60.4 per cent) were born in Cardiganshire, eight were born in other parts of Wales, and only thirteen were born in England or abroad. This again suggests that tourism was not only a source of employment for natives of Cardiganshire but that it also promoted the spread of bilingualism among servants as well as lodging-house keepers. Those who were employed in public houses, however, were slightly more Anglicized. A total of 49 were recorded as hoteliers and innkeepers, of whom 19 (38.8 per cent) were monoglot English speakers, while 19 (51.4 per cent) of those recorded as bar staff were unable to converse in Welsh.

A total of 1,558 households were enumerated in Aberystwyth on 5 April 1891. Nuclear households accounted for only 588 (37.7 per cent) of the total, a reflection, in part, of the nature of the housing stock in the town and the fact that many houses could accommodate extended families, lodgers and boarders or visitors. No fewer than 391 lodgers or boarders were enumerated and 164 visitors were also recorded, representing a total of 555 or 8.4 per cent of the population over 2 years of age. In 53 (40.0 per cent) cases, lodgers were enumerated in houses listed in trade directories as offering accommodation to visitors during the holiday season. This suggests that in many lodging houses it was common practice to let a limited number of rooms to lodgers or boarders throughout the year and to accommodate visitors in other rooms during the summer season. A significant

---

[64] John K. Walton, *The Blackpool Landlady: A Social History* (Manchester, 1978), p. 9.

number of Welsh speakers were recorded as visitors in Aberystwyth in April 1891. Of the total of 164, 30 were recorded as monoglot Welsh speakers, 63 as bilingual, and 71 monolingual English. No fewer than 56 (34.1 per cent) visitors had been born in Cardiganshire, which suggests that some exiles from the county took the opportunity to return to their roots during the quiet month of April. Visitors recorded in the census included fifteen coal miners, seven dressmakers and two lead miners, but the largest number of visitors were drawn from the middle or lower middle class. 71 (43.0 per cent) visitors were aged between 15 and 29 and a further 35 (21.6 per cent) between 30 and 44.[65] This suggests that the pleasures of Aberystwyth were also appreciated by younger people and that the town's appeal was by no means confined to the retired or the elderly.

Lists of visitors published in the weekly press reveal that Aberystwyth witnessed a steady expansion of the tourist industry throughout the last quarter of the nineteenth century. The total number of entries for the first week in August rose from 525 in 1873 to 660 in 1883 and peaked at 801 in 1893, although the decline to 644 by 1898 suggests that 1893 was an unusually successful year for the tourist industry in Aberystwyth (Table 14).

Table 14. Total entries, by home address, for visitors, 1873–93

	Number			Percentage		
	1873	1883	1893	1873	1883	1893
Cardiganshire	3	9	11	0.5	1.4	1.4
Rest of Wales	135	132	213	25.7	20.0	26.6
Shropshire	31	40	5	5.9	6.1	0.6
Lancashire	27	70	78	5.1	10.6	9.7
Gloucestershire	36	21	23	6.8	3.2	2.9
Worcestershire	8	15	10	1.5	2.3	1.2
Herefordshire	20	19	26	3.8	2.9	3.2
London	78	84	47	14.8	12.7	5.9
Staffordshire	30	46	95	5.7	7.0	11.9
Warwickshire	48	83	171	9.1	12.6	21.3
Rest of England	76	103	78	14.5	15.6	9.7
Other	12	13	8	2.2	2.0	1.0
Not stated	21	25	36	4.3	3.7	4.5
Total	**525**	**660**	**801**	*100.0*	*100.0*	*100.0*

Visitors from England made up nearly three-quarters of all entries noted in Aberystwyth in each of these lists. In the first week of August 1873 there were 354 entries for visitors from England, representing 67.4 per cent of the total for that week. Of these, 77 came from London, 48 from Warwickshire, 35 from Gloucestershire, 31 from Shropshire and 30 from Staffordshire. Since 21 of the 30 from Staffordshire lived either in Wolverhampton or West Bromwich and 40 of the 48

[65] *Welsh Gazette*, 24 August 1905.

who came from Warwickshire had addresses in Birmingham, 61 (11.6 per cent) of the visitors recorded that week came from industrial areas in the West Midlands. The influence of visitors from the West Midlands was also evident in 1883, although there was also a noticeable increase in the numbers who came from Lancashire, nearly half of whom lived in the industrial areas around Manchester. By the Edwardian period Aberystwyth was also attracting growing numbers of Welsh-speaking visitors from south Wales, especially from the anthracite coalfield. These figured among the most loyal customers of some of the cheaper lodging houses; many of them brought their own food and gave their provisions to the landlady to cook on their behalf. They were also frequent and devout worshippers in Welsh chapels.

The tourist industry was an important element in the local economy in Aberystwyth and a valuable source of income for families in a town which suffered from the absence of highly-paid, skilled employment. Tourism provided an array of opportunities for light work which could be undertaken by children, especially in the summer months, and which generated a valuable source of income at a time when the rural economy was in decline. The development of tourism in the town owed much to the efforts of entrepreneurs from outside the area, notably Thomas Savin, and to the vigorous promotion of Cardigan Bay by the Cambrian Railway Company. The efforts of those born in Aberystwyth were equally important to the town's development. Public investment by the Aberystwyth Improvement Company coincided with improvements to the standard of provision made by hoteliers and lodging-house keepers. The vast majority of those whose livelihood was connected to tourism were Welsh speakers, although few were unable to speak English. The arrival of visitors from England encouraged fluency in English, particularly among female lodging-house keepers and domestic servants. A large number of housewives acquired a knowledge of English through the tourist trade and it is clear that their ability to speak both languages was an important factor in the decline of the numbers of monoglot Welsh speakers in the town. Mawddwy suggested that English was the language of public entertainment in Aberystwyth, while Welsh was increasingly associated with the sombre and pious world of the Nonconformist chapel. English was the language of communication on the railways, in public business and education and this reinforced the impression that it was the language of social progress. By the end of the nineteenth century Aberystwyth was by far the most Anglicized part of Cardiganshire.

Conclusion

During the second half of the nineteenth century tourism became an increasingly important element of the economic life of seaside towns along the Welsh coast.[66]

---

[66] W. J. Thomas, 'The Economics of the Welsh Tourist Industry' (unpubl. University of Wales MA thesis, 1951); C. Baber and D. W. Howell, 'Wales' in F. M. L. Thompson (ed.), *The Cambridge Social History of Britain 1750–1950* (3 vols., Cambridge, 1990), I, pp. 281–354.

By the end of the Victorian period a combination of civic and private endeavour had established Aberystwyth as one of the largest and most popular holiday resorts in Wales. By contrast, Abergele did not experience the expansion seen in neighbouring resorts, and within a reasonably short period of time the town would attract fewer visitors than smaller tourist centres such as Pwllheli and Llanfairfechan.[67] The initial success of both Aberystwyth and Abergele owed much to sea-bathing and the picturesque views, which could be enjoyed by visitors to both resorts, and their ease of access by railway.[68] By the 1890s, however, Aberystwyth offered livelier holidays as civic and business leaders developed entertainments akin to those available in Rhyl and the larger English towns.[69] The culture of the music hall, replete with cabaret, dancing minstrels and the popular songs of the London stage, became an integral part of summer life in both towns. However, neither town encouraged the prurient pursuits associated with the peep show; nude bathing was prohibited and men and women were actively discouraged from occupying the same beach.[70] At the same time, those who managed boarding houses in Aberystwyth and Abergele insisted on strict rules of behaviour which disapproved of alcohol and forbade licentiousness.

The tourist industry formed a vital part of the economic prosperity of both towns. In particular, tourism provided women with a respectable living at a time of limited opportunities for females in the labour market. Widows and single women were particularly prominent as hotel and lodging-house keepers in both towns and it is also clear that appreciable numbers of married women who earned a living through tourism supplemented the meagre earnings of the head of household.[71] A large number of hoteliers and domestic servants in both Abergele and Aberystwyth had been born in the surrounding rural areas. Evidence relating to the coastal towns suggests that a small number of young people secured employment in the tourist trade, indicating that tourism constituted one means of overcoming structural deficiencies in the economy of the towns themselves and the surrounding area.[72] The arrival of visitors also provided an impetus to efforts to improve public amenities in both Abergele and Aberystwyth. Municipal endeavour was particularly noticeable in Aberystwyth, where efforts to attract visitors resulted in considerable improvements to public health and civic facilities available to the town's permanent residents.[73]

[67] Walton, *The Blackpool Landlady*, p. 27.
[68] Allan Williams and Gareth Shaw, 'Riding the Big Dipper: The Rise and Decline of the British Seaside Resort in the Twentieth Century' in Shaw and Williams (eds.), *The Rise and Fall of British Coastal Resorts: Cultural and Economic Perspectives* (London, 1997), pp. 1–18.
[69] H. Cunningham, 'Leisure and Culture' in Thompson (ed.), *The Cambridge Social History of Britain 1750–1950*, II, pp. 310–13.
[70] Walton, *The Blackpool Landlady*, p. 140.
[71] Ibid., pp. 87–9.
[72] Baber and Howell, 'Wales', pp. 281–354.
[73] Allan Williams and Gareth Shaw (eds.), *Tourism and Economic Development: Western European Experiences* (London, 1988), pp. 1–3.

The disadvantages of an economy dependent on tourism were also apparent. Both Abergele and Aberystwyth regularly suffered in the wake of periodic economic problems in the manufacturing areas of England.[74] Given the labour-intensive nature of the tourist industry, these economic fluctuations had a disproportionate effect on the prosperity of both towns and were a source of further financial instability. It is also clear that employment generated by tourism was seasonal, often unskilled and poorly paid. Children and young adults formed a substantial part of the workforce and some were employed illegally to undertake menial work.[75]

Abergele (especially Pen-sarn) developed as Liverpool and Manchester emerged as important commercial centres during the nineteenth century, and Aberystwyth likewise benefited from the economic prosperity of Birmingham. The industrial areas which surrounded those cities became equally important to both resorts. Aberystwyth attracted a continuous flow of visitors from Wolverhampton, West Bromwich and Wednesbury, towns which were rapidly emerging as centres of English engineering. The success of the engineering industry was based on small factory units, some of which were barely more than workshops and were managed by a family or a small partnership. As a result, there emerged a large class of small industrialists who had the financial means to take a holiday and who were captivated by the seaside and the countryside of Wales.[76] For its part, Abergele, in common with other resorts on the north Wales coast, attracted a large number of working-class visitors from the industrial areas of Lancashire. An appreciable number of visitors came from the centres of the textile industry, especially after factory hours were reduced in the 1870s and as employers began to recognize certain days of the year as holidays. The comparative prosperity of the working class of Lancashire, which was partly caused by the fact that women's earnings supplemented men's wages, was another important ingredient in the success of resorts in north Wales. At the same time, Lancashire's textile districts rapidly developed an array of saving schemes through friendly societies and the co-operative movement, which became an integral part of the culture of the more respectable members of the working class. Saving for an annual holiday became a feature of the lives of many of those who participated in these schemes and their patronage was crucial to the success of the tourist industry in north Wales.[77]

Seaside resorts and some inland spa towns enjoyed a degree of affluence which was the envy of the penurious agricultural districts which surrounded them. Resort towns were vibrant communities, bustling with the vigour of the young

---

[74] *Aberystwyth Observer*, 1 September 1898.
[75] Shaw and Williams, *The Rise and Fall of British Coastal Resorts*, pp. 1–18; Gwynedd Record Office, Dolgellau, Dolgellau School Attendance Committee Records, A/11/26.
[76] Asa Briggs, *The History of Birmingham Borough and City, 1865–1938* (2 vols., London, 1952), II, pp. 28–66; Richard Dennis, *English Industrial Cities of the Nineteenth Century: A Social Study* (Cambridge, 1984), pp. 186–99.
[77] Cunningham, 'Leisure and Culture', p. 285.

people who formed a significant part of their population and characterized by the joyous effervescence of the promenade and the music hall. The prosperity of these towns largely derived from improvements in railway connections and the steady flow of middle-class and some working-class English visitors. By the end of the nineteenth century, both were established and successful tourist centres, although Abergele's popularity had waned somewhat because of competition from neighbouring resorts and the failure of the town's municipal leaders to exploit its full potential. Both towns were also distinctive communities where the devout world of Welsh Nonconformity met the robust culture of the English music hall. The Welsh language was stronger in Aberystwyth and Abergele than in most resorts; most of those who maintained hotels and lodging houses in both towns had been born close to the locality and were able to speak Welsh. However, few hoteliers or their servants were monoglot Welsh speakers, although a significant portion of domestic servants hailed from villages where Welsh was the only language spoken by the majority of the inhabitants.

A clear language shift occurred both in Abergele and Aberystwyth during the nineteenth century, and this was reflected in the generational decline of the percentage of the population who were monoglot Welsh speakers. This change occurred in part because of factors such as the education system and the way in which English became acknowledged as the natural language of commerce and business in Abergele and Aberystwyth, as elsewhere. But tourism also undoubtedly contributed to the process of Anglicization. The need to converse with visitors from England encouraged a familiarity with the English language among the inhabitants of both towns. Although Welsh continued to be the spoken language of a significant portion of the inhabitants of both towns, its use was confined to an increasingly narrow range of domains and it certainly had no place in commercial activity, official business or tourism. By the turn of the nineteenth century, the vigorous middle class which sought to develop the economic potential of both Aberystwyth and Abergele was increasingly convinced of the need to acquire a thorough knowledge of English. These attitudes permeated the wider community and were powerful agents of linguistic change in both resorts.

6

'Separate Spheres'?: Women, Language and Respectability in Victorian Wales

ROSEMARY JONES

LANGUAGE, as several sociolinguists have so cogently argued, is not a 'natural', static aspect of human interaction or a purely utilitarian method of communicating information. Instead, language – like gender or class – is essentially a *cultural* phenomenon and, as such, is closely interwoven with the social structures and value systems of particular communities at particular points in time. This chapter seeks to examine the complex relationship between language, gender and the wider social values of Victorian Wales, primarily by discussing contemporary notions of respectable womanhood. It must be remembered that language – and the perceived parameters of respectable feminine discourse – played a central role in the structuring of gender values during the nineteenth century and was of pivotal importance to the various, and sometimes conflicting, models of womanhood which gained currency in the popular literature of the period.

Language, of course, was an important marker of social status for women, more so than for their male contemporaries. The main elements of a woman's conversation – her tone of voice, the vocabulary she deployed, the area or context within which the conversation took place – were all factors which helped to determine her respectability and standing within the wider community. Unlike men, who had other means at their disposal for securing status and respect within the community at large – for example, through their professional careers – women who wished to consolidate their position within society were obliged at least to pay lip service to agreed social norms. Moreover, while language – and verbal constraints – were central to the images of respectable womanhood which pervaded the popular literature of the Victorian period, language was also central to the ways in which alternative, less acceptable models of womanhood were constructed and, in turn, marginalized. This may be discerned, for example, in the images of the female 'gossip' which pervade the Welsh-language literature of the period. To illustrate these themes, the following discussion will focus on the so-called concept of 'separate spheres' for men and women – and the related cult of female domesticity – an ideology which was of central importance to contemporary notions of respectable womanhood and manhood.[1] As will be shown, the concept of 'separate spheres' not only played a defining role in the structuring and remodelling of gender values during the middle decades of the nineteenth century but also placed strict limitations on the language and demeanour of 'respectable' women, particularly on their freedom of expression within the 'public' arena or in the presence of the opposite sex.

The prevailing images of Welsh womanhood and of marriage, which dominate popular literature prior to the Victorian period, highlight the verbal aggressiveness and inherent 'disorderliness' of women, particularly in relation to their husbands. The 'female tongue' – a woman's primary weapon of attack – was presented as a perennial source of martial discord and gender conflict.[2] Unlike the Victorian patriarch, whose social, political and economic role in relation to his wife was more clearly defined, husbands in previous generations felt threatened by the power of the female tongue and made concerted efforts to curb its licence. Scolding women were subjected to a barrage of highly-ritualized and sometimes brutal popular punishments, such as being ducked in a local pond or river or paraded through the neighbourhood, where they were exposed to the ridicule of the community at large.[3] Since at that time gender relations within marriage were

---

[1] On the concept of 'separate spheres' see, for example, Leonore Davidoff and Catherine Hall, *Family Fortunes: Men and Women of the English Middle Class, 1780–1850* (London, 1987), esp. chapters 3 and 8; Catherine Hall, *White, Male and Middle-Class: Explorations in Feminism and History* (Cambridge, 1992), esp. chapters 3 and 4; Anna Clark, 'The Rhetoric of Chartist Domesticity: Gender, Language, and Class in the 1830s and 1840s', *Journal of British Studies*, 31, no. 1 (1992), 62–88; Wally Seccombe, 'Patriarchy Stabilized: The Construction of the Male Breadwinner Wage Norm in Nineteenth-century Britain', *Social History*, 11, no. 1 (1986), 53–76; Sonya O. Rose, 'Gender and Labor History: The Nineteenth-century Legacy', *International Review of Social History*, 38 (1993), 145–62. For the domestic ideal in nineteenth-century Wales, see Sian Rhiannon Williams, 'The True "Cymraes": Images of Women in Women's Nineteenth-Century Welsh Periodicals' in Angela V. John (ed.), *Our Mothers' Land: Chapters in Welsh Women's History, 1830–1939* (Cardiff, 1991), pp. 69–91.

[2] For gender relations prior to the Victorian period see, for example, Anna Clark, *The Struggle for the Breeches: Gender and the Making of the British Working Class* (London, 1995); Susan D. Amussen, *An Ordered Society: Gender and Class in Early Modern England* (Oxford, 1988); eadem, 'The Gendering of Popular Culture in Early Modern England' in Tim Harris (ed.), *Popular Culture in England, c.1500–1850* (Basingstoke, 1995), pp. 48–68. For images of the scolding or 'disorderly' woman in Wales see, for example, *Dyddan-Gerdd; Sef, Casgliad o Ganiadau Difyr. O Waith Ioan Siencyn, y Bardd Bach o Aberteifi* (Carmarthen, 1823), pp. 3–21, and Charles Redwood, *The Vale of Glamorgan: Scenes and Tales among the Welsh* (London, 1839), pp. 271–95.

[3] On the punishment of scolds during the early modern period see, in particular, David Underdown, 'The Taming of the Scold: The Enforcement of Patriarchal Authority in Early Modern England' in Anthony Fletcher and John Stevenson (eds.), *Order and Disorder in Early Modern England* (Cambridge, 1985), pp. 116–36 and Martin Ingram, '"Scolding women cucked or washed": A Crisis in Gender Relations in Early Modern England?' in Jenny Kermode and Garthine Walker (eds.), *Women, Crime and the Courts in Early Modern England* (London, 1994), pp. 48–80. The punishment of scolds in Wales prior to the Victorian period is discussed briefly in Rosemary A. N. Jones, 'Women, Community and Collective Action: The *Ceffyl Pren* Tradition' in John (ed.), *Our Mothers' Land*, pp. 26–8. See also Redwood, *The Vale of Glamorgan*; 'Brecknockshire traditions', *AC* (1858), 159; Marie Trevelyan, *Glimpses of Welsh Life and Character* (London, 1893), p. 81.

viewed as a model for wider social and political stability, such sanctions were designed to limit the 'disorderly' woman's powers of expression, while simultaneously reminding other female spectators of their subordinate role within the wider patriarchal establishment.

Images of the scolding wife, the embodiment of female power and 'disorder', were in marked contrast to idealized stereotypes of Welsh womanhood which prevailed during the Victorian era and this shift in emphasis – coupled with the virtual disappearance of popular sanctions against the scolding wife – indicates that a deep-seated change in gender relations and values had taken place by the middle decades of the nineteenth century. By that time, many of the gender-related tensions which characterized earlier periods had been effectively dissipated and it was clear that men had become increasingly less sensitive about the power of the female tongue. At least women's 'disorderly speech', when deployed against the male head of household, was no longer perceived as a realistic threat to the wider social and political establishment.

The reasons for this apparent shift in gender relations are multifarious and beyond the immediate scope of this chapter; but of central importance was the increasing polarization of gender roles from around the 1830s, brought about, to a large extent, by a widespread acceptance of the new ideology of 'separate spheres' for men and women. Central to this ideology was the underlying precept that each sphere of activity and responsibility within society should be endowed with distinct gender connotations and obligations. Men were increasingly associated with the 'public' world of workplace and formal political action, and were expected to be good breadwinners as well as chivalrous defenders of the 'weaker sex', while women, for their part, presided over the 'private' domestic sphere of home and family, and were expected to provide high standards of domestic comfort as well as offer their husbands a much-needed haven from the economic and political pressures of the outside world. Wives were still expected to be submissive and defer to the will of the husband, but they were also now given sole control of a distinct domain – that of home and family – and, within the confines of that domain, were accorded a greater degree of respect, status and autonomy.

The concept of 'separate spheres', and the related cult of domesticity, was not an entirely new ideology – its roots lay in the religious changes of the eighteenth century,[4] but it gathered momentum during the Victorian period when the definition of womanhood as being primarily related to home and family became firmly entrenched and the concept of 'separate spheres' for men and women came to be viewed as a cornerstone of wider social and political stability. These ideals,

---

[4] For earlier discourses on marriage which are reminiscent of the domestic ideal see, for example, William Williams (Pantycelyn), *Ductor Nuptiarum: neu Gyfarwyddwr Priodas, Mewn Dull o Ymddiddan rhwng Martha Pseudogam, a Mary Eugamus* (Aberhonddu, 1777) and Roger Owen, *Traethawd ar y Cyflwr Priodasol . . .* (Aberystwyth, 1813).

underpinned by religious Nonconformity, were reiterated in the Welsh-language periodicals of the period, and were disseminated with particular vigour and conviction in journals such as *Y Gymraes* and *Y Frythones*, which were aimed at a specifically female audience and whose stated purpose was therefore to elevate the character of Welsh womanhood by ensuring their usefulness within the domestic sphere as dutiful wives, mothers and domestic servants.[5] Moreover, although these ideals have often been associated with middle-class society, it needs to be stressed that the concept of 'separate spheres' was by no means a class-specific ideology and that it appears to have been embraced and supported by a wide cross-section of Welsh society, from working-class as well as middle-class backgrounds.

To what extent the concept of 'separate spheres' ever reflected the reality of gender-related experience in nineteenth-century Wales is a matter for further debate. In rural Wales, for instance, the notion of the breadwinning husband and domesticated wife was not a practical option for many working-class families or those engaged in agricultural production, and female manual labour continued to be of crucial importance to the agricultural economy throughout the nineteenth century. On the other hand, official census data suggest that Wales had a relatively low percentage of women who participated in the formal economy – fewer, in fact, than was the case in England – and that the employment structure in Wales reinforced rigid gender divisions, with men being associated increasingly with heavy industry and those women who sought paid employment outside the home increasingly resorting to domestic service, an area of work which, in a sense, reinforced links between women and the domestic sphere. In the industrialized areas of south Wales, for example, the concept of 'separate spheres' was an economic reality for most working-class families, with the formal workplace being restricted to men, and women being offered very few employment opportunities outside the home.[6]

Nevertheless, whatever the economic reality of the situation, the concept of 'separate spheres' seems to have been a well-rooted and all-pervasive ideal, which penetrated and influenced all aspects of the social, cultural, religious and political life of Victorian Wales. It undoubtedly succeeded at a rhetorical, ideological level, if not always on a practical level of day-to-day interaction, and influenced the standards of behaviour expected of respectable married couples. It did much to dissipate the gender antagonism associated with earlier periods, and helped to generate new models of womanhood which supplanted earlier images of the scolding virago. In particular, it encouraged an increasing romanticization of the domestic role of the Christian wife and mother. Wives were no longer portrayed

---

[5] See, for example, the editor's introductory address in the first volume of *Y Gymraes*, published in 1850.

[6] On the employment of women in nineteenth-century Wales, see L. J. Williams and Dot Jones, 'Women at Work in Nineteenth Century Wales', *Llafur*, 3, no. 3 (1982), 20–32 and Angela V. John, 'Introduction' in John (ed.), *Our Mothers' Land*, pp. 1–2.

as scheming, scolding viragos, bent on wresting power from the male head of household. On the contrary, the prevailing images stressed the woman's vulnerability and fragility; wives were increasingly portrayed as meek, submissive, inferior creatures in need of chivalrous compassion and protection. Above all, it exerted a profound influence over the language and demeanour of women – at least over the ideal standards of language and demeanour which respectable women sought to emulate. Whereas in previous centuries the power of the 'female tongue' had been constrained through public punishment and ridicule, from the middle decades of the nineteenth century 'women's words', in so far as they were still perceived as being a threat to social stability, increasingly came to be proscribed by the force of ideological constraints and, in particular, social pressure to conform to prevailing notions of respectable femininity. This, in turn, exerted a profound effect not only on the language and demeanour of individual women but also on the shared oral culture which had long been the mainstay of neighbourhood networks in the closely-knit communities of both rural and industrial Wales. By attacking women's 'gossip', for instance, exponents of the domestic ideal were, in a very fundamental sense, conspiring to fragment and devalue the various informal mechanisms which played a key role in cementing social and economic links between female neighbours.[7] Moreover, by consistently undermining and discrediting women's gossip in this manner, exponents of the ideal presented a direct threat to one of the few mechanisms which women had at their disposal to influence public opinion and behaviour. Gossip was a valuable method of social regulation; it could make or break reputations and its importance in the hands of women, who often became self-appointed custodians of community morality, should not be underestimated. By participating in networks such as the *Clwb Te* (Tea Club), a female gossip circle which was particularly popular in south Wales until the early part of the nineteenth century, women were able to exert a limited degree of informal, quasi-public power over their immediate neighbourhoods.[8]

This chapter will therefore seek to examine the impact of 'separate spheres' and the cult of domesticity not only on the language and demeanour of individual women who sought to elevate their position within society but also on the shared

---

[7] The literature on women's 'gossip' is now extensive but see, in particular, Melanie Tebbutt, *Women's Talk? A Social History of 'Gossip' in Working-class Neighbourhoods, 1880–1960* (Aldershot, 1995); eadem, 'Women's talk? Gossip and "women's words" in working-class communities, 1880–1939' in Andrew Davies and Steven Fielding (eds.), *Workers' Worlds: Cultures and Communities in Manchester and Salford, 1880–1939* (Manchester, 1992), pp. 49–73; Ellen Ross, '"Not the sort that would sit on the doorstep": respectability in pre-World War I London neighbourhoods', *International Labor and Working Class History*, no. 27 (1985), esp. 51–2.

[8] For the *Clwb Te* see, for example, Isaac Foulkes, *'Cymru Fu': yn Cynwys Hanesion, Traddodiadau, yn nghyda Chwedlau a Dammegion Cymreig* (Wrexham, [1862]), pp. 90–1 and Edward Matthews, *Hanes Bywyd Siencyn Penhydd* (Gwrecsam, 1867), pp. 43–4. In some parts of south Wales, meetings of the *Clwb Te* provided a means of formally welcoming newly-married women to the exclusive gossip circle of their married female neighbours.

neighbourhood culture of women during the Victorian period. In addition, some attempt will be made to assess the precise impact which these ideals exerted, in practice, on the everyday lives of the majority of Welsh women during the nineteenth century. To what extent, for example, did women embrace these ideals and use them as a means of elevating their own social position *vis-à-vis* their less respectable female neighbours? To what extent, if at all, did women seek to subvert or renegotiate the boundaries of 'separate spheres' as delineated in the Welsh-language periodicals of the period? Before discussing such issues, however, attention must firstly be focused on the main tenets of the domestic ideal, as expounded by the popular literature of the day, and the precise constraints which these ideals sought to place on women's freedom of expression and movement.

The prevailing view of Welsh womanhood during the Victorian era emphasized the silent, submissive role of the woman within the 'private' world of home and family. In contrast to what was believed in previous centuries, a woman's power and influence was now reckoned to emanate from her silent, all-pervasive, matriarchal influence within the home. The respectable Victorian wife and mother, revered and idolized as a self-sacrificing 'angel in the house', was expected to attend dutifully to the needs of the male head of household, as well as to those of her children, and refrain from active participation in any unseemly 'public' activities which might compromise her morality, modesty or privacy. In essence, the ideal mode of feminine discourse, illustrated by the well-known Welsh proverb 'Hardd ar ferch, bod yn ddistaw' (Silence is the best ornament of a woman), was deemed to be silence, and respectable women were encouraged to converse in low, restrained tones.[9] In 1881, for example, *Y Frythones* urged its readers to avoid conversing in a loud, aggressive manner:

> Siaradwch yn esmwyth. Y mae llais uchel, ystormus, yn profi diffyg dygiad i fyny. Egwyddor gyntaf a dyfnaf moesgarwch ydyw, gwneuthur i'r rhai o'n cwmpas deimlo yn hyfryd a mwynhaol; ac y mae dull a thôn arw ac eofn o siarad yn annymunol i'r rhan amlaf o bobl.[10]

> (Converse softly. A noisy, strident voice is evidence of a flawed upbringing. The first and most fundamental principle of good manners is to make those around us feel pleasant and at ease; and a brusque and brazen manner and tone of voice is displeasing to the majority of people.)

Whereas modesty and humility were among the foremost virtues of the respectable Victorian woman, she was also educated and well-informed, and this

---

[9] J. J. Evans, *Diarhebion Cymraeg (Detholiad, gyda Chyfieithiad i'r Saesneg). Welsh Proverbs (A Selection, with English Translations)* (Llandysul, 1965), p. 34.
[10] 'Hyn a'r Llall', *Y Frythones*, III, no. 7 (1881), 225; see also *Y Gymraes*, VIII, no. 94 (1904), 101.

was reflected in the edifying subject matter which dominated her conversations.[11] In 1860, for example, *Y Brython* contrasted the wise and perceptive outpourings of the virtuous woman – 'Y Ferch Rinweddol' (The Virtuous Female) – with the feckless and inconsequential conversations of her less well-educated sisters:

> Mae yn *ferch synwyrol yn ei hymddiddanion*. 'Hi a egyr ei genau yn ddoeth' . . . Mae ei chalon wedi ei llenwi â gwybodaeth, ac o helaethrwydd y galon hono y llefara hi. Mae llawer o ferched yng Nghymru na chlywir byth mo honynt yn llefaru yn gall. Rhyw goeg-ddigrifwch, ac ymadroddion ffôl a ddeuant yn wastad dros eu gwefusau. Rhyw bethau gwrthun a dibwys hefyd, y rhan amlaf ydynt destynau eu hymddyddanion. Yn ofer y ceisir ymddiddan â hwy am ddim buddiol a gwerthfawr.[12]

> (She is a *woman of sensible conversation*. 'She openeth her mouth with wisdom' . . . Her heart is filled with knowledge, and it is from the magnanimity of this heart that she speaks. Many women in Wales are never heard to utter anything sensible. Only empty pleasantries and foolish phrases pass their lips. The subjects of their discourse are mostly objectionable and trivial. All attempts at worthwhile and constructive conversation are fruitless.)

Yet, despite being able to express an opinion on a variety of subjects, the virtuous Victorian woman was not self-opinionated; she knew when to speak and when to remain silent in the company of others, and she deferred to those who 'knew better'. As women's magazines were quick to emphasize, a necessary component of the 'art of conversation' was an instinctive sense of which social settings demanded restraint. Women, they claimed, had a tendency to speak too freely, and exercising control was the first lesson of conversation. Practising silence was a greater sign of strength than the most eloquent discourse and nothing undermined their influence so much as excessive chatter.[13] In addition, they should refrain from using 'bad' or indecent language, which was deemed to be a moral blemish which detracted from a woman's natural beauty.[14] Purity of language was a necessary prerequisite of moral purity. A woman must not only demonstrate chastity by her outward behaviour, for genuine humility required that her heart, thoughts and conversations were also pure.[15] Unseemly language sapped confidence and blighted love, blunted feelings and endangered relations.[16] Bad language was deemed to be even more reprehensible when deployed by a woman, and many contemporaries would have agreed with the assertion that

---

[11] 'Diwylliad y Rhyw Fenywaidd', *Y Beirniad*, V (October, 1864), 156.
[12] 'Y Ferch Rinweddol', *Y Brython*, III, no. 24 (1860), 381.
[13] Ellen Hughes, 'Ymgom a'r Genethod', *Y Gymraes*, VII, no. 82 (1903), 99–100. For a similar viewpoint, see also ibid., VI, no. 66 (1902), 34–6.
[14] *Y Frythones*, III, no. 9 (1881), 274: comments by 'Hen Lanc'.
[15] 'Diwylliad y Rhyw Fenywaidd', 155.
[16] 'Geiriau Anweddus Merched a Gwragedd', *Y Frythones*, V, no. 4 (1883), 129.

uncouth and unbecoming language from a woman was far worse than from a man.[17]

In her dealings with her husband, the respectable Victorian wife was expected to behave in a meek and compliant manner, and to address him in respectful, restrained and deferential tones.[18] In 1861, for example, *Cyfaill y Werin* extolled the attributes of 'Y Wraig Rinweddol' in the following terms:

> Nid yw yn feistrolgar ar ei phriod – ymresyma ac ymgynghora ag ef ar bob achos da a phwysig, a chydsynia ag ef mewn pob peth rhesymol. Mynega rinweddau ei phriod, a chuddio ei golliadau. Diwygia ef gyda sirioldeb, pwyll, a hynawsedd. Defnyddia bob moddion i feithrin cariad a thangnefedd. Ceidw yn glir oddiwrth ymrysonau, ac ymrafaelion. Ymddyga yn mhob peth yn ddoeth – cymhedrol ei hymadroddion – serchus a chyfeillgar – teimladwy a hoffus o'i phriod.[19]

(She does not dominate her husband – she discusses and consults with him on all important matters, and agrees with him in all reasonable things. She extols the virtues of her spouse and conceals his failings. Her manner towards him is cheerful, tactful and genial. She takes every opportunity to nurture love and tranquillity. She avoids arguments and disputes. Her behaviour in all respects is prudent – her remarks moderate – she is loving and friendly – sensitive and fond of her husband.)

In contrast to earlier images of marriage, which highlighted the contentious and competitive elements of the husband–wife relationship, greater emphasis was now placed on marital harmony and the overriding need to foster a sense of mutual respect and co-operation.[20] In particular, this new model of marital harmony entailed addressing one another in a kind and respectful manner.[21] The main responsibility for securing domestic harmony was placed firmly on the wife, who was expected to do her utmost to avoid or defuse confrontational situations within the home. In contrast to the scolding and contentious virago of previous generations, who regarded the home as the main arena within which to state and defend her claim to supremacy over her husband, the dutiful Victorian wife provided her spouse with a peaceful and tranquil sanctuary, where he could escape from the pressure of the outside world. Indeed, marriage to a woman who possessed a peaceable and affectionate disposition was seen as being a necessary prerequisite of domestic harmony.[22] As *Y Dysgedydd* declared in 1859, a good-tempered wife produced a good-tempered husband, thus ensuring a dispute-free

---

[17] Ibid. See also ibid., IV, no. 4 (1882), 127 for a similar viewpoint.
[18] E.g. *Y Gymraes*, I, no. 3 (1850), 95.
[19] 'Y Wraig Rinweddol', *Cyfaill y Werin*, 20 December 1861, p. 14.
[20] This vision of marriage was enshrined in the Rules of Discipline endorsed by Welsh Calvinistic Methodists. See *Hanes, Cyfansoddiad, Rheolau Dysgybliaethol, ynghyd a Chyffes Ffydd y Corff o Fethodistiaid Calfinaidd yn Nghymru* (Salford, 1876), p. 30.
[21] *Y Gwladgarwr*, 7 February 1863, p. 3.
[22] 'Gair at Miriam o Benllyn', *Y Geiniogwerth*, IV (September, 1850), 248.

home.[23] In return, husbands would view these home comforts as a counter-attraction to the tavern and resolve to spend more time at home with their wives and families, or participate in 'rational', family-orientated leisure pursuits.

The relationship between husband and wife was deemed to be a private matter, and the dutiful wife refrained from broadcasting her husband's shortcomings in the hearing of others, particularly in the company of female neighbours, since this was certain to undermine the respectability of both parties:

> Gofaler rhag ymddiried i chwedleuwyr unrhyw goll neu anmherffeithrwydd a ganfydda yn ei gwr, nac un o'r mân ymrafaelion a gymerant le yn achlysurol yn y sefyllfa briodasol . . . Os gwneir y fath ymddiriedaeth, pa mor gryf bynag fyddo'r archiad ar un llaw, a'r ymrwymiad ar y llaw arall, o berthynas i ddirgelrwydd y pethau, gellir bod yn sicr y byddant yn fuan yn sylwedd ymddyddanion y gymmydogaeth.[24]

> (Avoid entrusting to gossips any failing or imperfection in your husband, or any of the minor squabbles which occasionally occur in the marital state . . . If such information is revealed, no matter how strong the charge by one party, and the commitment of the other, to keep these matters secret, it is certain they will soon be the subject of conversation throughout the neighbourhood.)

The respectable Victorian woman also refrained from ridiculing or criticizing her husband in the presence of children, and taught them to address the male head of household with similar respect and deference.[25]

It was widely recognized, too, that mothers exerted an immense influence over the moral, cultural and spiritual development of their children. As *Y Frythones* observed in 1879:

> Mynych y clywir plant yn dweyd, 'Fel hyn a'r fel y gwelsom ein tad a'n mam yn gwneyd, ac yr ydym ninau am wneyd yr un modd.' Os bydd y rhieni gan hyny yn anfoesgar, yn gelwyddog, yn rhodiana o dŷ i dŷ, felly fel rheol y bydd eu plant. Oddiar wefus y fam, ac oddiwrth ei hesiampl hi, y rhaid cael y dylanwad i adfer y byd. Yr hon oedd gyntaf yn y camwedd, ac a barodd y dinystr, a ddylai hefyd fod yn gyntaf yn y rhinweddau a weithiant tuag at ei adferiad. Dylanwad mam, dan fendith y Goruchaf, yw'r oruchwyliaeth ddynol benaf er dychweliad yr hil ddynol at eu dyledswyddau, ac i ystad o ddedwyddwch.[26]

> (Children are frequently heard saying, 'This is what we saw our mother and father doing, so we will do exactly the same.' Therefore if the parents are ill-mannered,

---

[23] 'Aelwyd Lan, Prydau Parod, a Thymer Dda', *Y Dysgedydd*, XXXVIII (September, 1859), 343.

[24] 'Dyledswyddau a Chyfrifoldebau Mam', *Y Brython*, II, no. 1 (1858), 5.

[25] See, for example, *Y Dysgedydd*, XXXVIII (September, 1859), 344 and *Y Brython*, II, no. 1 (1858), 5.

[26] 'Gwarchod Cartref', *Y Frythones*, I, no. 12 (1879), 372. See also *Y Cronicl*, VII, no. 79 (1849), 335; *Y Brython*, V, no. 41 (1863), 320; *Y Beirniad*, X (July, 1869), 17; and *Y Frythones*, V, no. 4 (1883), 129, for the moral and cultural influence of Welsh mothers.

untruthful, and wander from house to house, their children will act likewise. It is by the mother's lips, and her example, that the world can be restored. She who first transgressed, and caused the downfall, should also be first to exercise those virtues which will lead to its restoration. The mother's influence, with the blessing of the Almighty, is the main human medium for returning the human race to its duties and to a state of happiness.)

The main responsibility for the religious instruction of the children lay firmly with the mother, who exerted a strong influence over the spiritual as well as moral development of her offspring during their formative years.[27] But, as Evan Jones (Ieuan Gwynedd), editor of *Y Gymraes*, stated in 1850, it was the mother, rather than the father, who also left the deepest imprint on the language and demeanour of her children: 'The "Mother's Language" will be the child's language, – the mother's habits will be the child's; as she thinks so will he, because it is she who teaches him everything' ('"Iaith y Fam" fydd iaith y plentyn, – arferion y fam fydd ei arferion yntau; fel y meddylia hi y meddylia yntau, oblegid hi ydyw pob peth yn ei addysg').[28] Mothers were encouraged to set a good example by using restrained, polite language in the presence of their offspring, and to instil in them a sense of how to converse and behave in the company of others:

> Arferer hwynt i ymddwyn a siarad yn weddaidd, ac i ymwrthod ag ofersain, ac arfer geiriau ac enwau anaddas . . . Dylent arferyd rhoddi parch dyladwy i'r rhai uwch-radd, cyd-radd, ac îs-radd iddynt, ac i ochel hyfdra a chynefindod tuag at y personau mwyaf adnabyddus iddynt . . . Gofaler rhag rhoddi annogaeth iddynt i fod yn rhy siaradus, yn enwedig mewn cwmpeini . . . Gocheler haeriadau a gwrth-ddywedyd, a phob taeru ac ymgecru . . . Bod yn ofalus rhag siarad ar draws ereill a fyddo yn ymddyddan . . . Gocheler gwneyd ystumiau neu ymddangos yn chwithig wrth eistedd neu siarad mewn cwmpeini; . . . Peidio adrodd chwedlau hirfaith a diflas mewn cwmpeini . . .[29]

(Accustom them to seemly behaviour and speech, and to reject empty chatter and the use of unsuitable words and names . . . They should be taught respect for those of higher, equal and lower rank than they, and to avoid forwardness and familiarity with those best known to them . . . Take care not to encourage them to talk too much, especially in company . . . Avoid assertive and contradictory remarks, and all arguments and disagreements. Take care not to intrude in the conversations of others . . . Avoid making gestures or appearing awkward when sitting or conversing in company; . . . Do not relate rambling and tedious stories in company . . .)

---

[27] For two interesting articles on this theme, see Revd W. Jones (Fourcrosses), 'Y Fam ac Addysg Grefyddol y Plant', *Y Gymraes*, XIII, no. 151 (1909), 54–5 and 'Gwragedd Cymru a'r Ddyledswydd Deuluaidd', ibid., IV, no. 48 (1900), 131–2 and ibid., no. 49, 157.

[28] *Y Gymraes*, I, no. 1 (1850), 6; editor's introductory address.

[29] *Y Brython*, I, no. 1 (1858), 6.

It was also a primary duty of Welsh mothers to ensure that the language of the home was pure and to protect their children from exposure to lewd, indecent or intemperate language, since this was believed to represent the first stage in a wider process of moral and eventually sexual degeneration.[30] The use of pure language on the hearth was deemed to be one of the main moral bulwarks of the nation:

> I fagu cenedl lân ei moes, a dyrchafol ei hysbryd, rhaid cael aelwyd bur ei hiaith a'i harferion . . . Ar aelwydydd isel o ran iaith ac arferion y megir rhegwyr, meddwon, troseddwyr, a phuteiniaid. Prin y mae rhieni yn ystyried fod eu geiriau a'u hymddygiadau beunyddiol, yn ymwthio i mewn rhwng plygion dirgelaf natur y plant, ac yn dylanwadu ar eu bywyd. Druan o lawer plentyn bach! Ni chafodd gynorthwy gan ei fam i dyfu yn gymeriad prydferth![31]

> (Purity of language and habit at home are essential in the development of a nation of moral integrity and elevated spirit . . . It is in homes of coarse language and habit that blasphemers, drunkards, criminals, and prostitutes are raised. Parents scarcely consider the effect of their daily speech and behaviour on the deepest recesses of their children's minds, and how it influences their lives. Pity many a small child! Their mothers give them no assistance in nurturing a beautiful character!)

The respectable woman was encouraged to police the language of all members of her household, including lodgers and servants, and to chastize those who deployed foul or intemperate language in her presence.[32]

Outside the immediate confines of the home, too, the respectable Victorian woman was expected to avoid the company of those who used bad language and, when this proved unavoidable, she was enjoined to upbraid culprits in no uncertain terms.[33] In particular, respectable young women were expected to avoid the company of young men who used bad language in the presence of the opposite sex, since this not only implied a lack of respect on their part but also flouted an important component of masculine respectability during the Victorian period – the protection of the 'weaker sex' from such exposure to vulgar or indecent language.[34] It was a common complaint, too, that respectable women often felt unable to venture into those public thoroughfares which were deemed to have become the preserve of men, mainly as a result of the bad language to which they were often exposed. As an 'Unprotected Female' confided to the editor of the *Cambrian News* in 1878: 'I am afraid to venture out after dark . . . Heaps of young sailors keep possession of the corners of the streets, and their language is so horrible, cursing,

---

[30] E.g. *Y Gymraes*, I, no. 4 (1850), 134–5.
[31] 'Mamau y Genedl', *Y Gymraes*, XV, no. 173 (1911), 26.
[32] See, for example, Bert L. Coombes, *These Poor Hands: The Autobiography of a Miner working in South Wales* (London, 1939), p. 24.
[33] E.g. *Y Frythones*, VI, no. 2 (1884), 62.
[34] E.g. *Y Gymraes*, IV, no. 48 (1900), 133.

swearing, and using such shocking words that no female can pass near them.'[35] Respectable women were repeatedly enjoined to boycott those venues – such as the workplace, the public house, fairs and markets – associated with the 'public' world of men and which were usually perceived as promoting uncouth language and degenerate behaviour. Philanthropic observers frequently voiced concern about the vulnerability of those women who worked in a predominantly male environment and were supposedly 'unsexed' and morally degraded in the process. Considerable concern was often expressed, for example, about the fate of those women who were employed as barmaids in public houses, where they were confronted with lewd songs, lying tales and swearing.[36] As the temperance reformer, Daniel Dafydd Amos, lamented in his brief 'Word to Barmaids and Others' ('Gair at Forwynion Tafarnwyr ac Ereill'), published in *Y Diwygiwr* in 1849, the public house was a den of iniquity seething with buffoonery, indecency and blasphemy.[37]

Similar concerns were voiced about the detrimental effect which the bad language commonly heard at fairs and markets was believed to exert on the language and morality of younger Welsh women. In 1881, for instance, *Y Frythones* condemned the indecent language which was invariably deployed by the gangs of youth who attended these fairs:

> y mae yn waradwydd i grefydd a gwareiddiad ein gwlad, y fath eiriau isel, anweddus, anniwair, a ffiaidd, a ddefnyddia y llanciau hyn mewn ymddyddan â merched ieuainc hyd y ffair. Bydd y rhai hyny, ysywaeth, yn gallu gwrando arnynt heb gymaint a gwrido, ac hyd yn nod ar brydiau gan ddangos boddhad, a'u hateb yn yr un iaith, a thrwy yr un geiriau anweddus ac anghymeradwy.[38]

> (the crude, unseemly, obscene and repugnant language used by these youths in conversations with young girls at the fair is a disgrace to the religion and civilization of our country. They in their turn, regrettably, are capable of listening without so much as a blush, and sometimes even show satisfaction, and reply in similar vein, using the same indecent and distasteful words.)

Furthermore, it was argued that these same young men tempted young women to frequent public houses while they attended the fair, and that early exposure to the indecent language which characterized public house culture could lead to moral and sexual degradation:

> Teimlem dosturi wrth weled merched ieuainc gwridog a phrydweddol wedi syrthio mor isel yn ngraddfa moesoldeb, fel ag i gymeryd eu tynu a'u llusgo gan hogiau ffol a haner meddw, i dafarndai! . . . Pa fodd y mae merched ieuainc . . . yn hoffi aros yn swn

---

[35] *Cambrian News*, 22 March 1878.
[36] 'Gair at Forwynion Tafarnwyr ac Ereill', *Y Diwygiwr*, XIV, no. 172 (1849), 331.
[37] Ibid.
[38] 'Ffeiriau Cymru', *Y Frythones*, III, no. 9 (1881), 287.

rhegfeydd a dadwrdd bloesg y rhai sydd wedi yfed yn ehelaeth o'u damnedigaeth eu hunain; pa fodd yr ymddangosant megys yn gysurus yn nghanol ymladdfeydd, ymgecraeth, ac annuwioldeb, nid ydym yn abl dyfalu. Ofnwn fod llawer merch ieuanc brydweddol, benderfynol hefyd hwyrach o fyw bywyd rhinweddol a phur, wedi crwydro ymaith i lwybrau'r ysbeilydd, heb ddychwelyd yn hir os byth, a hyny fel canlyniad dechreu yn y fan hon – yn y ffair, ac yn y dafarn.[39]

(It was a shame to see young girls, rosy-cheeked and handsome, having fallen so low into the depths of immorality as to allow foolish and inebriated youths to entice and drag them to taverns! . . . Why young girls . . . enjoy the loud swearing and incoherent uproar of those who have drunk deeply of their own damnation; why they appear comfortable in the midst of brawls, quarrels and ungodliness, we are at a loss to guess. We fear that many a fair and determined young woman, having previously led a virtuous and unblemished life, has strayed onto the path of the despoiler, without returning for long if ever, as a result of attending fairs and taverns.)

Exposure to the lewd language and gestures of male colleagues was also cited by many contemporaries as adequate justification for denying women access to the male-dominated workplace. In 1853, for example, *Y Cronicl* published an article on 'The propriety, or impropriety of women working out' ('Y priodoldeb, neu ynte yr anmhriodoldeb i fenywod weithio allan'), which highlighted the corrupting influence which exposure to the indecent language of male colleagues was believed to exert on the morality and modesty of working women:

nid oes genyf un ammheuaeth nad yw yr arferiad yn achosi ymddyddanion anweddaidd, ymddygiadau afreolus, drychfeddyliau llygredig, a moesau drwg; ac nid wyf yn petruso dweyd ei fod yn eu hanaddasu i gyflawni y dyledswyddau priodasol fel y dylent, . . . ac i fod yn famau addas a ran cyrff a meddyliau i ddwyn, i feithrin, ac addysgu y genedl ddilynol.[40]

(I have no doubt that this practice results in lewd conversations, unruly behaviour, corrupt thoughts, and bad morals; and I do not hesitate to state that it prevents them from carrying out their marital duties as they should, . . . and from being fit mothers, both physically and mentally, to raise, nurture, and teach the future generation.)

In her dealings with female neighbours, the respectable Victorian woman was expected to display a peaceable and affable disposition and to refrain from spreading discord and strife in the wider community. She was instead urged to foster a spirit of reconciliation and harmony consistent with notions of good neighbourliness and to deploy considerable tact when mediating in petty disputes between neighbours:

[39] Ibid.
[40] 'Y Priodoldeb, neu ynte yr Anmhriodoldeb i Fenywod Weithio allan', *Y Cronicl*, XI, no. 120 (1853), 111.

Y mae yn caru personau ei chymydogion; edrych yn siriol arnynt, ac ymddyddana yn gyfeillgar â hwynt . . . Y mae y wraig dda yn caru bod mewn heddwch â'i chymydogion. Nid â i anghydfod â hwynt ei hun; ac os gwel hwy yn myned, yn lle bod yn danwydd i chwanegu y tân, ceisia ei ddiffodd . . . nid yw yn 'myned o dŷ i dŷ' i daenu chwedlau ofer, ac i farnu pwy sydd uniawn, a phwy sydd heb fod.[41]

(She loves her neighbours; she regards them cheerfully and converses with them amicably . . . The good woman wishes to live in peace with her neighbours. She does not engage in disputes with them herself; and if she encounters a dispute, instead of adding fuel to the fire she seeks to extinguish it . . . she does not 'wander from house to house' spreading rumours, judging who is right, and who is wrong.)

For example, the obituary of Mrs Mary Davies, a Borth woman who died in 1881, extolled the virtues of her neighbourly disposition:

Un o egwyddorion rhagorol ei hysbryd ydoedd, na fyddai byth yn siarad yn isel am ereill yn eu habsenoldeb. Byddai hefyd yn wyliadwrus iawn wrth siarad am wendidau a diffygion dynion, ac yn hynod o ochelgar yn ei chondemniad o bawb. Gwerthfawr iawn ydoedd yn mysg ei ffryndiau a'i chydnabod ar gyfrif ei thymer a'i thalent i wneuthur heddwch, ac i ddwyn tangnefedd i mewn. Os, yn anffodus, y cymerai rhyw annealldwriaeth neu anghydfod le rhwng rhywrai a'u gilydd, byddai hi bob amser, gyda'i geiriau synwyrol, a'i rhesymau cryfion, yn llwyddo i dawelu llawer ar yr ystorm gynhyrfus . . .[42]

(One of her abiding principles was that she would never talk ill of others in their absence. She would also be very circumspect when conversation turned to the weaknesses and shortcomings of men, or to the condemnation of anyone. She was greatly valued by her friends and acquaintances on account of her disposition and talent for mediation. If there should be some unfortunate misunderstanding or disagreement between certain individuals, she would always succeed, by her sensible words and firm reasoning, in going a long way to quieten the storm . . .)

The respectable Victorian woman was expected to avoid aggressive verbal outbursts with female neighbours and consciously distance herself from the 'vulgar' street culture which sustained women's gossip networks. As *Y Frythones* proclaimed in 1879, prudent and respectable Christian women should remain within the confines of their own homes, keeping their own counsel, dutifully attending to their duties and, above all, respecting their neighbour's right to privacy:

[41] 'Rhinweddau Gwraig Dda', *Y Dysgedydd*, XXXVIII (December, 1859), 461–2.
[42] *Y Frythones*, III, no. 7 (1881), 214–15. For a similar obituary, in which the peaceful disposition of the deceased is favourably contrasted with the contentious disposition of gossips and other breeders of discord, see ibid., II, no. 6 (1880), 178 (obituary of Anne Owens of Llangrannog).

Y mae yr Ysgrythur yn gorchymyn yn bendant, fod i wragedd 'warchod gartref yn dda', a gofalu yn ddigoll am achosion y teulu. Gartref, gan hyny, y dylent hwy fod; nid yn rhodiana o dŷ i dŷ, gan fod yn wag-siaradus, yn ymyraeth â materion rhai ereill, yn hel a thraethu chwedlau, ac heb ofalu fawr pa un a fyddont ai gwir ai gau. Nid oes nemawr drefn ar gartrefi y gwragedd sy'n hoff o grwydro oddiamgylch.[43]

(The Scriptures specifically command that women should 'look after the home well' and dedicate themselves to family matters. They should therefore stay at home; not wander from house to house, indulging in empty chatter, interfering in other people's business, acquiring and spreading gossip, not caring whether it is true or false. Disorder abounds in the houses of women who enjoy roaming.)

Home, family and the provision of domestic comforts were very much the 'proper' sphere of respectable Victorian womanhood, and any time spent outside the home which was not directly related to a woman's role as housekeeper was to be devoted to useful or charitable pursuits, such as visiting the sick and infirm, rather than sowing the seeds of discord among neighbours.[44]

Furthermore, gossip and the defamation of others were judged to be contrary to the teachings of the Scriptures and therefore deserved widespread condemnation.[45] Gossip, it was argued, was incompatible with a Christian lifestyle and was considered particularly reprehensible in a minister's wife.[46] As numerous obituaries reveal, ministers' wives often felt compelled to distance themselves from the wider communal networks of female neighbours. For example, it was reported that the wife of the Revd Cadwalader Jones, Dolgellau, was especially careful not to interfere in the affairs of others and that by avoiding gossip she succeeded in earning the respect of the whole community, both rich and poor.[47] Similarly, Anne Jones, wife of the Revd David Jones of Beaumaris and Bangor, shunned the local gossip networks patronized by her female neighbours:

Yr oedd ynddi gasineb a gwrthwynebrwydd calon at yr arferiad cyffredin, ond iselwael hwnw, sef cerdded tai i glywed ac adrodd ystoriau; a byddai rhai o'r rhywogaeth grwydrol hyn yn cwyno weithiau, y byddai bob amser yn absenoli ei hun o'u cyfarfodydd. Ei hatebiad iddynt fyddai, 'Nid yw yn fy natur; y mae gan bob gwraig ddigon o waith yn ei thŷ ei hun'.[48]

---

[43] 'Gwarchod Cartref', *Y Frythones*, I, no. 12 (1879), 372. See also *Cyfaill y Werin*, 20 December 1861 and *Y Gymraes*, XIII, no. 156 (1909), 136, for similar comments.

[44] *Y Beirniad*, V (October, 1864), 159.

[45] E.g. *Y Frythones*, VI, no. 4 (1884), 113–14 and *Y Gymraes*, VII, no. 78 (1903), 35–6.

[46] See, for example, William Williams (Pantycelyn), *Drws y Society Profiad* (Caernarfon, 1906 edn.), pp. 51–2, in which ministers' wives were enjoined to set a good example in this respect. *Drws y Society Profiad*, first published in 1777, was reprinted in 1839 and would have been widely read by a mid-nineteenth century audience. I am grateful to Dr Eryn Mant White for this reference.

[47] 'Llais o'r Bedd', *Y Dysgedydd*, XXX (April, 1851), 109.

[48] *Seren Cymru*, 11 October 1872, p. 2.

(She thoroughly loathed and opposed that common but base practice of walking from house to house to hear and relate gossip; and some members of this itinerant species would sometimes complain that she always absented herself from their gatherings. Her reply to them would be, 'It is not in my nature; every woman has enough to do in her own home'.)

The recreational interests of the respectable minister's wife revolved, instead, around chapel-based activities and the pursuit of other Christian 'good works'. When the spirit of 'good neighbourliness' demanded that she spent time in the homes of female neighbours, she was at pains to exonerate herself from any accusations of gossip, diverting the conversation, wherever possible, to matters of religious import:

> Pan y byddai yn achlysurol yn galw yn nhai ei chyfeillion, a phan y byddai ei chymydogesau yn ymweled â hithau, byddai yn ddigon gwyliadwrus a chrefyddol i beidio athrodi nac enllibio neb; ac yn gyffredin, os nid bob amser, cymerai ryw ddull i droi yr ymddyddan am bethau crefyddol . . . Agorai ei genau yn ddoeth bob amser, a chyfraith trugaredd oedd ar ei thafod.[49]

(When she occasionally paid her friends a visit, and when her neighbours visited her, she would be sufficiently vigilant and religious to avoid maligning or slandering anyone; and generally, if not always, would seek to turn the conversation to things religious . . . She would choose her words carefully, her remarks typifying her generous spirit.)

Gossips, on the other hand, were invariably portrayed as ignorant, idle and slovenly housewives, who lived in squalor and were a continual source of neighbourhood discord and strife. As well as squandering their husbands' hard-earned wages on tea and other luxury items, gossips were rarely to be found at home attending to their domestic chores and were notorious for their disorderly homes.[50] As a correspondent to *Y Gwladgarwr* wrote in 1865: 'In the morning, almost before the sun has arisen . . . she can be seen, one or two children in her arms, her hair uncombed, like that of a goat, and her children bearing the marks of the Wolverhampton sweeps' ('Yn y boreu, braidd cyn codi yr haul . . . ceir ei gweled, ac un neu ddau o'r plant ar ei breichiau, ei gwyneb heb weled lliw'r dwfr am yr wythnos flaenorol, ei gwallt heb ei gribo, mal blew yr afr, a'r plant yn dwyn nodau sweeps Wolverhampton').[51] This stereotype of the female gossip as a feckless and slovenly housewife was encapsulated, too, in the following description of 'Sianw Gorsddu', the fictitious village gossip who appeared in the *Efail y Gof* series in *Seren Cymru*:

---

[49] *Y Dysgedydd*, XXXVII (August, 1858), 297; obituary of Mrs Elizabeth Griffiths (wife of the Revd Evan Griffiths), a native of Barmouth, who later emigrated to Wisconsin.
[50] 'Y Drwg o Chwedleua', *Y Brython*, II, no. 5 (1859), 69.
[51] *Y Gwladgarwr*, 22 July 1865, p. 2.

'does dim yn gasach genyf nâ gweled benyw front, hagr, yn sefyll fel post glwyd ar ben trothwy ei drws, gan wylied symudiadau pawb a phob peth; neu ynte yn myned o dŷ i dŷ, gan siglo ei chynffon fel *spaniel*, a chasglu yn nghyd holl glecs a budreddi y gymmydogaeth. Edrychwch ar ei thŷ! Caiff y lludw aros o dan y tân nes dyfod i gyssylltiad â'r barau; bydd y cloc heb ei *windo* oddiar y noswaith o'r blaen; y gïeir ar y bwrdd yn bwyta'r toes; ci y tŷ nesaf a'i drwyn yn y crochan a'r cawl; y plant yn rhedeg ar hyd y llawr yn nhroed eu hosanau; y gath yn cysgu ar ei *shawl* oreu; y *tea kettle* wedi berwi yn sych ar y tân; hen het wellt yn stopio'r gwynt drwy'r ffenestr; a'r mochyn wedi talu ymweliad â'r parlwr. Buasai gystal genyf gael fy nghlymu wrth gorn tarw a gorfod cydfyw a menyw o'r nodwedd hyn: dyna beth fuasai *transportation for life* . . . buasai gryn getyn ddoethach i Sianw Gorsddu aros gartref i grafu tatws, i gyweirio hosanau, a golchi crys Twm ei gwr, nâ myned ar hyd y wlad i hau clecs, a gwasgaru celwyddau.[52]

(there is nothing worse than seeing a dirty, ugly woman standing like a gatepost on her door-step, watching everyone and everything's movements; or going from house to house, wagging her tail like a spaniel, and collecting all the gossip and filth of the neighbourhood. Look at her house! The ashes can stay under the fire until they touch the bars; the clock remains unwound from the night before; the hens on the table are eating the dough; next door's dog has its snout in the cauldron and the soup; the children are running about in their socks; the cat is sleeping on the best shawl; the tea kettle has boiled dry on the fire; an old straw hat blocks the draught through the window; and the sow has paid a visit to the parlour. I would rather be tied to a bull's horns than have to live with such a woman: that's what I would call transportation for life . . . it would be far better for Sianw Gorsddu to stay at home to peel the potatoes, darn the socks, and wash her husband Twm's shirt, than to roam far and wide gossiping and spreading lies.)

Derogatory images such as these helped to cement popular male perceptions of female gossip as an essentially subversive pastime which distracted women from their traditional domestic duties. As a result, men were actively discouraged from marrying women with a propensity for gossip, since they were believed to make poor and inattentive wives. In 1860, for example, *Y Gwladgarwr* advised its male readers to avoid marrying giggling, gossipy, footloose women.[53] Young women were similarly encouraged to believe that inveterate gossips would have difficulty in attracting husbands.[54]

It was argued, too, that the moral and financial impoverishment of many Welsh families, particularly working-class families, was as inextricably linked to the evils of women's gossip as it was to the persistent drunkenness of many male heads of

---

[52] *Seren Cymru*, 24 December 1880, p. 3. The *Efail y Gof* column comprised a series of humorous conversations between several fictitious characters.
[53] *Y Gwladgarwr*, 6 October 1860, p. 2; see also *Pembrokeshire Herald*, 13 September 1850.
[54] See, for example, the fictitious dialogue between two bachelors intent on marriage which appeared in *Y Gymraes*, V, no. 62 (1901), 166.

household.[55] Indeed, in some respects, drunkenness on the part of husbands was deemed to be a direct consequence and penalty of women's gossip, since those women who spent their days in dogged pursuit of gossip and scandal had insufficient time at their disposal to provide the domestic comforts which husbands had come to expect and which acted as a counter-attraction to the public house.[56] In much the same way as nagging scolds were said to have driven their husbands to the public house during the previous century, so compulsive gossips who neglected their household duties conspired to undermine the moral as well as economic fabric of their households by forcing their husbands to seek solace, as well as sundry domestic comforts – such as a warm fire and hot meal – in the local tavern.[57] By attending to their household duties in a diligent and dutiful manner, especially by providing their husbands with good food, clean clothes and other domestic comforts, wives, it was argued, could play a key role in saving them from the evils of alcohol, thereby securing a happier home environment and higher standard of living for the family as a whole.

As well as being reckoned slovenly housewives, gossips were also presented as feckless and irresponsible mothers who paid scant attention to the physical, cultural and spiritual well-being of their children.[58] Not only was the persistent gossip impeding her own moral and educational development, but she was also neglecting that of the next generation by failing to set a good example to her children.[59] Gossip, it was argued, was the product of ignorance and, as such, was a root cause of the cultural and intellectual poverty which was allegedly rife among so many Welsh children:

> Diffyg dysg yw yr achos o'u ffaeleddau. Hyny sydd wedi crebachu eu meddwl, a llygru eu chwaeth, – nes ydyw yn fwy dewisol gan lawer o honynt wrando chwedlau Bessi'r Glap, na darllen y GYMRAES. Hyny sydd yn peri eu bod yn fudr ac anfedrus yn eu trefnidedd deuluaidd. A hyny hefyd sydd yn eu hanghymwyso i addysgu a dysgyblu eu plant. Magant dueddfryd at glap a chleber ffol yn eu merched, yn lle at wybodaeth fuddiol. Dywedant wrthynt yn eu siamplau, fod hustyngiaeth Nani'r Wyau yn werthfawrocach nâ diliau Elen Egryn.[60]

> (The reason for their failings is lack of education. It is this which has shrivelled their minds and corrupted their taste, – to such a degree that many of them prefer listening to Bess the Gossip than reading the GYMRAES. The consequence is that they are dirty

---

[55] E.g. *Yr Annibynwr*, VII, no. 78 (1863), 137.
[56] For an example of an essay which makes this point, see *Y Dysgedydd*, XXXVIII (September, 1859), 341–4.
[57] For an example of an earlier ballad which satirizes the scolding wife who drives her husband to the public house, see Hugh Jones, *Cerdd o Ymddiddan rhwng yr Oferddyn a'r Dafarn-wraig*. NLW Ballad Collection ('Baledi a Cherddi', vol. 15, no. 5).
[58] E.g. *Y Brython*, II, no. 5 (1859), 69.
[59] E.g. *Y Frythones*, VI, no. 9 (1884), 274.
[60] 'Merched Cymru', *Y Gymraes*, I, no. 4 (1850), 362–3.

and unskilled in family management. It also means that they lack the competence to teach and discipline their children. They nurture a propensity for gossip and mindless chatter in their daughters, instead of useful knowledge. They tell them that Nanni Eggs' tittle-tattle is more worthwhile than the best of Elen Egryn.)

Rather than engage in malicious gossip and idle storytelling, mothers were repeatedly encouraged to educate themselves and cultivate more refined tastes and manners, since this would have a beneficial effect on the moral, spiritual and intellectual development of their children and the Welsh nation as a whole.[61]

Condemnation of the female gossip during the Victorian period was therefore inextricably linked to a reaffirmation of the values associated with the domestic ideal and popular notions of feminine respectability. In order to emphasize the prudence and piety of respectable womanhood, images of the virtuous Victorian woman – 'y wraig rinweddol' – were directly contrasted with those of the inveterate female gossip – 'y wraig chwedleugar'.[62] Attacks on gossip were expressed in ways which elevated and reinforced these gender ideals and values while simultaneously undermining the gregarious women's culture which had been its mainstay during earlier periods. In short, the female gossip was presented as the antithesis of all that was considered noble and virtuous in respectable Victorian womanhood. She represented a direct challenge to the images of womanhood, marriage and gender co-operation which pulpit and press were attempting to inculcate and, to a large extent, superseded the 'scolding' wife as the main cultural and symbolic manifestation of female 'disorder' in Victorian Wales.

Despite being largely associated with English middle-class society, the domestic ideal and the notion of separate spheres for men and women appear to have struck a particularly resonant chord in Victorian Wales. Indeed, it could be argued that the domestic ideal – and the romanticized images of Welsh womanhood which domesticity promoted – were central to the development of a sense of national consciousness and cultural pride during the nineteenth century. It must be remembered that the domestic ideal had a strong religious basis, a factor which may help to account for its popularity in Wales, where Nonconformist denominations exerted a powerful influence over the social, cultural, religious and political life of the nation throughout the nineteenth century. But the popularity of the domestic ideal was also reinforced by the Blue Books controversy of 1846–7, which was central to the articulation and reinforcement of popular

[61] 'At Ferched Ieuainc Cymru', ibid., I, no. 5 (1850), 143.
[62] The contrast between these two models of Victorian womanhood is reflected, for example, in an imaginary dialogue on gossip, entitled 'Y Ddwy Gyfeillach', published in Y Frythones, III, no. 10 (1881), 318–21; ibid., no. 12, 377–9.

notions of feminine respectability during the Victorian period.[63] The 1847 Report vilified the character of the Welsh people, denouncing them as backward, impoverished and degenerate, both morally and culturally. It heaped particular odium on Welsh-speaking mothers, whose alleged moral laxity and sexual licentiousness were cited as a root cause of the ignorance and deprivation of the nation as a whole. Not surprisingly, the main responsibility for refuting these allegations was placed on the shoulders of Welsh women and, as the century progressed, the Welsh home or *aelwyd* – and the mothers who presided over that domain – came to be viewed as the nation's main bulwark against moral and cultural degeneration. As *Y Frythones* declared in 1889:

> Y cartref ydyw y sefydliad pwysicaf yn yr holl fyd. Yno y derbynia y meddwl dynol yr argraffiadau cyntaf a dyfnaf, ac y dodir sylfaen y cymeriad i lawr. Cartrefi Cymru, i raddau helaeth, sydd yn gyfrifol am gymeriad cenedl y Cymry; os cartrefi digysur a llygredig, gostyngir safon purdeb yn meddwl y genedl, cynefinir ei chwaeth a'r hyn sydd annheilwng a diraddiol, gwneir hi yn egwan a llwfr i wynebu temtasiynau ac anhawsderau, ac yn ddiegni i gymeryd gafael ar yr hyn sydd fawr a da mewn bywyd. O'r ochr arall, os cartrefi dedwydd a da, lle y plenir ac y meithrinir egwyddorion rhinwedd a moes, bydd y dynion a'r merched sydd yn troi allan o honynt i lenwi y gwahanol sefyllfaoedd mewn cymdeithas, yn ddynion a merched cywir a da, teilwng o ymddiried a pharch, yn eofn dros y gwir a'r sylweddol, yn llafurus a diwyd i ragori yn yr hyn sydd wir dda a gwir fawr, a'u bywydau yn lles a bendith i'r byd.[64]

(The home is the most important institution in the whole world. It is there that the human mind is exposed to the first and deepest impressions, and that the foundations of character are laid. It is Welsh homes, to a great degree, which are responsible for the character of the Welsh nation; if comfortless and corrupt, the standard of purity of the nation's mind is debased, its tastes become accustomed to the unworthy and the degrading, it becomes feeble and cowardly in the face of temptation and hardship, and is unable to take hold of what is great and good in life. Conversely, if its homes are happy and good, and within them are planted and nurtured the principles of virtue and morality, the men and women they produce to fill the various situations in society will be good, upright men and women, worthy of trust and respect, fearless in pursuit of truth and substance, hard-working and determined to excel in that which is truly good and truly great, and their lives will be a boon and blessing to the world.)

The domestic sphere was central to the process of moral and social reform, and the morality of future generations was believed to depend on the benign influence

---

[63] For the background to the Blue Books controversy, see Prys Morgan (ed.), *Brad y Llyfrau Gleision: Ysgrifau ar Hanes Cymru* (Llandysul, 1991); idem, 'From Long Knives to Blue Books' in R. R. Davies, Ralph A. Griffiths, Ieuan Gwynedd Jones and Kenneth O. Morgan (eds.), *Welsh Society and Nationhood: Historical Essays Presented to Glanmor Williams* (Cardiff, 1984), pp. 199–215.

[64] A paper read by Anna Ionawr to 'Cymdeithas Ryddfrydol Merched Penllyn, Meirionydd', entitled 'Cyfran y Merched yn Ffurfiad Cymeriad Cenedl y Cymry', *Y Frythones*, XI, no. 10 (1889), 302–3.

of Welsh mothers within the home. In an article on the importance of 'Yr Aelwyd' (The Hearth), which appeared in *Y Gymraes* in 1896, it was claimed:

> Ar famau ieuainc Cymru, y tuhwnt i bawb eraill, yr ymddibyna 'Cymru Fydd'. Nid ar y Senedd, na'r Brifysgol, na'r Colegau, na'r Ysgolion, ond yn benaf ar athrofa yr aelwyd. Y fam yw brenhines yr aelwyd, a thra urddasol yw ei swydd a'i theyrnas . . . Oddiwrthi hi y daw elfenau uchaf, puraf, a mwyaf cysegredig bywyd cymdeithasol dyn, ac ar ei chymeriad a'i dylanwad hi yn benaf y gorphwys dyfodol y byd.[65]

> ('Future Wales' depends on the young mothers of Wales more than anyone else. Not on Parliament, nor the University, nor the Colleges, nor the Schools, but primarily on the institute of the hearth. The mother is queen of the hearth, and her role and domain are very noble . . . She is the source of the highest, purest, most sacred elements of man's social life, and it is on her character and influence that the future of the world mainly rests.)

Indeed, by participating in this process of moral regeneration, Welsh women were thought to have discovered their 'true' vocation.[66]

Widespread endorsement of the domestic ideal inevitably exerted a strong influence over the images of Welshness and of Welsh nationhood which pervaded the Victorian era. These values became so deeply ingrained in the Welsh psyche that a sentimental attachment to the *aelwyd* was often regarded as being an inherently Welsh characteristic.[67] The romanticization of the domestic role of the mother, and of the Welsh-speaking *aelwyd* generally, was a notable feature of the Welsh-language literature of the Victorian period, and, in a sense, the respectability of the entire nation was believed to depend upon the character of its womenfolk. Indeed, it often became a matter of national as well as local pride to defend the honour of Welsh womanhood against the accusations of outside critics. Moreover, the ideal Welsh woman, as portrayed in the popular literature of the period, was seen to espouse the values and tenets associated with the cult of domesticity. Many of the virtues and moral attributes associated with respectable Victorian womanhood came in time to be viewed as the 'natural', inherent characteristics of the 'true *Cymraes*' (Welsh woman) and those women who openly refuted these ideals were no longer considered to be true Welsh women or *Cymruesau*.[68]

The deep-seated relationship between the domestic ideal and concepts of Welshness was further reinforced by the emphasis commonly placed in the literature of the period on the need to sustain and promote a widespread use of the Welsh language within the domestic sphere. Once again, it was considered a

---

[65] *Y Gymraes*, I, no. 2 (1896), 19. For a similar comment, see also ibid., II, no. 21 (1898), 84.
[66] E.g. *Y Frythones*, XI, no. 10 (1889), 305.
[67] E.g. *Y Gymraes*, I, no. 1 (1896), 1; comments by Archdeacon Howell of Gresford.
[68] Williams, 'The True "Cymraes"', p. 187.

primary duty of respectable and patriotic Welsh mothers to uphold the moral character of the nation by ensuring that the Welsh language, which was believed to be more conducive than English to the pursuit of a sober and righteous lifestyle, was transmitted to successive generations of Welsh children. As 'Gwenllian Gwent' stated in the first volume of *Y Gymraes*, published in 1850:

> Famau Cymru! siaradwch Gymraeg wrth eich plant. Eich esgeulusdod beius *chwi*, a brâd eich calon fydd yr achos, os na bydd i'ch hiliogaeth floesg swnio eu geiriau cyntaf yn yr iaith a roddodd Duw i'n henafiaid yn moreu y byd. Oddiwrthych chwi (ac nid eu tadau) y dysgant garu Duw yn eu hiaith eu hunain . . . bydded iaith yr aelwyd, ac iaith crefydd, yr hon a osododd Duw yn rhan i'r Cymry, a chyhyd ag y cadwont hi, ni raid iddynt ofni na bydd iddynt darian ac astalch yn erbyn Satan a'i gynllwynion. Ffurfiwch yn meddyliau eich plant, a chefnogwch yn eich gwyr, benderfyniad i amddiffyn iaith Cymru. Nac arweinier chwi ar gyfeiliorn gan wag-falchder, ac na chymhellwch hwy i ddynwared eu bod yn Saison. Gwerthfawrogwch eich cymydogion Seisonig am yr hyn sy dda ynddynt, a gochelwch y drwg. Ond cedwch eich hawl ddiymwad i fod yr hyn y gwnaeth Duw chwi – i siarad yr iaith a ddysgwyd i chwi gan Dduw – ac uwchlaw y cyfan i'w addoli Ef yn eich iaith eich hunain; yr hon, yn nesaf at hyny, sydd i chwi ac i'ch plant yn rhagfur o gadernid yn erbyn ymosodiad arferion drwg a llygredigaethau.[69]

> (Mothers of Wales! speak Welsh to your children. It is *your* careless neglect, and your heart's betrayal that will be the cause if your inarticulate progeny do not utter their first words in the language which God gave our forefathers when the world was young. It is from you (and not their fathers) that they will learn to love God in their own language . . . let the language of the hearth, and the language of religion, be that which God granted to the Welsh, and as long as they preserve it, they need not fear that they lack a shield against Satan and his schemes. Instil in the minds of your children, and support in your husbands, a determination to defend the language of Wales. Do not be led astray by false pride, and do not urge them to imitate the English. Value your English neighbours for that which is good in them, and shun that which is bad. But retain your indisputable right to be what God made you – to speak the language taught to you by God – and above all to worship Him in your own tongue; that which is a bulwark of strength for you and your children against the assault of evil practices and corruption.)

In the opinion of Gwenllian Gwent, and other like-minded patriots, the creation of a sense of Welsh national pride was inextricably linked to the creation of a wider sense of moral purpose and rectitude, and the 'true *Cymraes*' had failed in her moral as well as her patriotic duty if she neglected to instil in her children a love of their native language and culture.

Sentiments such as these retained their currency throughout the Victorian period, but were expressed with particular rigour during the late nineteenth and

---

[69] *Y Gymraes*, I, no. 1 (1850), 10. 'Gwenllian Gwent' was probably a pseudonym used by Lady Llanover (see Williams, 'The True "Cymraes"', p. 73).

early twentieth centuries, when they played a key role in the resurgence of Welsh national consciousness. This was a period which experienced a renewed emphasis on the links between the Welsh language and the character of the nation, and Welsh mothers, who were repeatedly urged to converse with their children in Welsh, were again held responsible for transmitting to successive generations all that was considered good and noble in Welsh society and culture. As *Y Gymraes* stated in 1910:

> Y mae cartrefi gwlad, un ai yn amddiffynfa i'r genedl, neu yn fedd iddi. Adeiladwyr y cartrefi yw gwir adeiladwyr y genedl . . . Rhaid i bob gwraig gofio fod athrylith cenedl yn gudd yn yr iaith. Pan gyll cenedl ei hiaith, cyll ei nodweddion gwahaniaethol. Mam wan o feddwl yw hono a adawa i'w phlentyn golli iaith ei wlad a'i genedl ei hun, tra yn medru ieithoedd cenhedloedd eraill – na alwer hi yn fam![70]

(The homes of a nation are either its bastion or its grave. Home builders are the true nation builders . . . Every wife must remember that a nation's genius lies in its language. When a nation loses its language, it loses its distinctive features. Weak-minded is the mother who allows her child to lose the language of his own country and nation, while being able to speak the languages of other nations – let her not be called a mother!)

The cult of domesticity – and romanticized images of Welsh-speaking mothers who presided over the domestic sphere – remained central to the preservation of the unique characteristics of the Welsh people, and to the creation of a sense of national consciousness and pride, until at least the early decades of the twentieth century. As *Y Gymraes* again proclaimed in 1912:

> a cholli tir wna Cymru hyd nes yr el yn ol at hen arferion aelwydydd y dyddiau gynt. Cartrefi Cymru sydd wedi ei gwneyd yn wahanol i bob gwlad arall. Ynddynt y dysgai y plant adnodau, ac emynau, alawon ein gwlad, a chanu'r delyn . . . Mae'n hen bryd i ni, os am gadw ein cenedlaetholdeb i edrych ati fod nodweddion cartrefi Cymreig yn cael eu cadw. Pa raid i ni oddef i'n nodweddion gael eu llyncu i fyny gan arferion yr estroniaid sydd yn dyfod i fyw yn ein plith?[71]

(and Wales will lose ground until she returns to the old customs of the hearths of days gone by. It is the homes of Wales which distinguish it from every other country. Within them children learn the verses, hymns and tunes of our country, and play the harp . . . The time has come for us, if we wish to retain our nationality, to see to it that the characteristics of Welsh homes are preserved. Why must we allow our characteristics to be absorbed by the customs of foreigners who come to live in our midst?)

---

[70] 'Geiriau un o Ferched yr Iwerddon', *Y Gymraes*, XIV, no. 164 (1910), 66.
[71] 'Dadl: Cartrefi Cymru', *Y Gymraes*, XVI, no. 187 (1912), 51–2.

It needs to be emphasized, however, that the model of Welsh womanhood which pervaded the Welsh-language literature of the period was by no means the only model which gained currency in Victorian Wales. While many women no doubt aspired to the model of respectable womanhood espoused by pulpit and press, others undoubtedly turned their back on their cultural and national roots, viewing them as an impediment to social and economic advancement, and aspiring instead to the models of respectable, refined femininity embraced by their English or more Anglicized sisters.[72] Although most verbal exchanges would have been conducted for the greater part of the nineteenth century through the medium of Welsh, an increasing number of Welsh women preferred to converse in English, especially in 'polite' company. As one woman writer declared in 1901 in the columns of *Young Wales*: 'it must be confessed that in the past the Welshwoman of culture and refinement systematically tabooed her *hên iaith* – [and] that in the present day she is still following the same unpatriotic line'.[73] In many social circles, particularly among the professional classes and in the more 'cosmopolitan' urban areas, there was an increasing tendency to venerate all things English – a social phenomenon which was often sneeringly termed *Saisaddoliaeth* in the Welsh-language press – and the ability to converse in English was viewed as a particularly valuable social asset by fashion-conscious and upwardly-mobile women.

In Victorian Wales, when language seems to have been an important marker of social status for many women (more so than for men) and when considerable social prestige was attached to the acquisition of English, women often led the way in the process of Anglicization. The ability to converse in English – the language of social advancement and 'getting on in the world' – appears to have been an important hallmark of respectability for working-class as well as middle-class women and, from an early date, there is evidence to suggest that many Welsh-speaking mothers made deliberate attempts to converse with their offspring in English, believing it to be in their children's best interests. The Revd Evan Evans, Nant-y-glo, recalls an incident from the 1820s when he heard a mother from Pontypool addressing her children in a strange mixture of Welsh and English:

> Un o'r pethau cyntaf dynodd fy sylw at iaith fratiog y werin yno oedd clywed gwraig nas medrai nemawr Saesneg yn ceisio siarad Saesneg â'r plant, ac un diwrnod yn dweyd wrth ei merch fechan, 'Go to shop yn glou, glou, to fetch a pound o fenyn i fi. Make haste yn ol.' Yr oedd llawer o blant y Cymry yn y dref a'i chwmpasoedd y pryd hwnw nas medrent siarad na Chymraeg na Saesneg yn briodol . . .[74]

---

[72] Some of the tensions and contradictions implicit in these two conflicting models of respectable womanhood may be discerned in a fictitious dialogue on the Welsh language in *Y Gymraes*, VIII, no. 96 (1904), 140–2.

[73] 'The Women of Wales Circle', *Young Wales*, no. 78 (1901), 137.

[74] *Cyfaill yr Aelwyd*, VI, no. 10 (1886), 275.

(One of the things which drew my attention to the fragmented language of the people there was hearing a woman who knew hardly any English attempting to speak English to her children, and one day telling her small daughter, 'Go to shop yn glou, glou, to fetch a pound o fenyn i fi. Make haste yn ol.' Many Welsh children in the town and surrounding area at that time were unable to speak either Welsh or English properly . . .)

The preference for English was not simply linked to a purely utilitarian desire for economic advancement. From an early date there was a tendency to regard English as the language of gentility and 'good taste'. In 1841, for example, the Revd William Jones, curate of Llanbeulan, noted how the 'higher classes' in Wales 'speak in a broken manner, and mix abundance of English words with their Welsh. The more this is done the more elegant the speaker considers himself to be'.[75] This tendency to interlace Welsh-medium conversations with an abundance of English or to attempt to speak the native tongue with a markedly English accent seems to have been emulated by a broad spectrum of Welsh society, including those women from the middling and working classes who harboured social aspirations.[76] English was very much *de rigueur* in certain polite circles, even among those whose command of the language was partial and imperfect. As the poet Ebenezer Thomas (Eben Fardd) observed in 1839, when he was forced to exchange social niceties with a group of pretentious local women at Caernarfon:

> The females were disgusting companions on accnt. of their foppishness & affection . . . though they could speak English but imperfectly, much less write it, and one of them could neither speak nor write, yet they talked Welsh so affectedly and englishly that you might almost fancy them native English women having learnt a little Welsh . . . They were, therefore, puerile and despicable in my sight.[77]

As the nineteenth century wore on, it appears that the images of respectable Welsh-speaking womanhood depicted in journals such as *Y Frythones* and *Y Gymraes* were increasingly at odds with the reality of everyday experience, and that many Welsh women would have empathized with the sentiments expressed in 1904 by a female character in a fictitious dialogue on the subject in *Y Gymraes*: 'I feel that there is something vulgar in speaking Welsh' ('Byddaf yn teimlo fod rhywbeth yn vulgar mewn siarad Cymraeg').[78]

---

[75] William Jones, *A Prize Essay, in English and Welsh, on the Character of the Welsh as a Nation, in the Present Age* (London and Carnarvon, 1841), p. 22.

[76] See, for example, the article written by a Welsh-speaking woman from Birmingham, which condemned the practice among Welsh-speaking women of using an abundance of English words when conversing with each other in Welsh. *Y Gymraes*, I, no. 3 (1850), 81.

[77] E. G. Millward (ed.), *Detholion o Ddyddiadur Eben Fardd* (Caerdydd, 1968), p. 116. I am grateful to Mr Trefor M. Owen for this reference.

[78] 'Ymgom dwy am yr Iaith Gymraeg', *Y Gymraes*, VIII, no. 96 (1904), 140–2.

It appears, therefore, that many Welsh women who subscribed to the domestic ideal did so within a largely English or Anglocentric framework and rejected those aspects – such as the venerated position of the Welsh-speaking *aelwyd* as the main moral bulwark of the nation – which were expounded in a uniquely Welsh manner and were considered unpalatable or irrelevant to their own circumstances and tastes. This, of course, leads us to question the extent to which other values and constraints associated with 'separate spheres' and the cult of domesticity were embraced and endorsed by the majority of Welsh women during the Victorian period. To what extent did the notions of feminine respectability expounded by the leading Welsh-language periodicals of the day reflect and inform the everyday lives of 'ordinary' Welsh women? To what extent, if at all, were these values circumvented, adapted, refashioned or even flagrantly rejected by the women concerned?

Despite the all-pervasive influence of 'separate spheres', historians should beware of casting the Victorian woman as the passive and perpetual victim of patriarchal domination. The images of respectable womanhood presented in the periodicals of the period represent only the views and aspirations of women who embraced those ideals. It is beyond the scope of this chapter to discuss the extensive verbal repertoire which women continued to deploy in defence of their own and their families' interests, but there is ample evidence that many women blatantly rejected, or at least temporarily circumvented, such ideals by, for example, engaging in verbal slanging matches, scolding and nagging their husbands, and cursing or gossiping about their immediate neighbours. Verbal slanging matches between female neighbours, which sometimes degenerated into extremely animated affairs involving the womenfolk of an entire street or community, remained an integral feature of women's neighbourhood culture in most parts of Wales until at least the early decades of the twentieth century. In 1863, for instance, *Y Gwladgarwr* reported in the following terms a particularly volatile dispute between the female residents of two streets in Aberdare:

> Drwg genym hysbysu fod cymydogaethau rhanau uchaf Monk ac Ynyslwyd Streets . . . wedi cael eu haflonyddu yn fawr ddiwedd yr wythnos ddiweddaf, trwy fod menywod (a'r rhai hyny yn rhai Cymreig) yn trafod eu gilydd a'u tafodau. Yr oedd eu llefferydd yn warthus, ac yn iselhad i ddynoliaeth.[79]

> (We regret to report that the neighbourhoods at the top of Monk and Ynyslwyd Streets . . . were greatly disturbed at the end of last week, due to women (and Welsh women at that) engaging in a slanging match. Their language was disgraceful and an insult to humanity.)

---

[79] *Y Gwladgarwr*, 28 February 1863, p. 5.

Similarly, women often played a central role in the informal, community-based disturbances which were witnessed in both rural and industrial areas throughout the nineteenth century.[80] Although most women exercised no formal political power, female protesters frequently spearheaded attacks upon the community's perceived 'enemies' and subjected unpopular individuals – such as bailiffs, land surveyors, blacklegs and informers – to a barrage of verbal invective. For example, during a strike at Aberdare in 1857, the air was said to be 'rent with mingled ironical cheers, groans and hisses' as crowds of women and children harangued and intimidated blacklegs on their way to and from work.[81] Again, during the so-called Tithe War of the late 1880s and early 1890s, when the verbal harassment of bailiffs, auctioneers and other tithe officials was an almost daily occurrence, a correspondent to the *Western Mail* decried the sight of 'women and girls acting indecently, filling the air with filthy expressions that would shame the strumpets of . . . anywhere'.[82] By engaging in such acts of verbal insubordination, thereby subverting the prevailing images of respectable womanhood already described, the supposedly 'weaker' members of society were able to convey a sense of symbolic resistance to their allotted position within the wider scheme of gender as well as class relations. In a sense, too, it may be argued that those women who featured at the forefront of community protest were seeking to capitalize upon the licence of their sex – in particular upon the long-established licence of the female tongue to 'tell the truth' about unjust rulers – and, as a result of these deep-seated notions of female privilege, may on occasions have felt empowered to behave in an even more 'disorderly' and licentious manner than their menfolk.[83]

None the less, it must be conceded that the Victorian cult of domesticity and the concept of 'separate spheres' had a profound impact on the status and influence of women within the 'public' arena, particularly within the context of formal political or religious activity. The increasing emphasis on the home as a woman's proper sphere, coupled with the development of more institutionalized and male-dominated methods of political protest, such as trade unionism and formal political pressure groups, helped to ensure that relatively few women were afforded an official voice in the affairs of the wider community. The world of institutionalized politics was increasingly viewed as the preserve of men and, as Sally Alexander, Dorothy Thompson and other social historians have argued, the

---

[80] For the role of women in popular protest, see David J. V. Jones, *Before Rebecca: Popular Protest in Wales 1793–1835* (London, 1973), esp. chapters 1 and 2; idem, *Rebecca's Children: A Study of Rural Society, Crime and Protest* (Oxford, 1989), esp. chapter 4; Jones, 'Women, Community and Collective Action', esp. 31–7; Angela V. John, 'A Miner Struggle? Women's Protests in Welsh Mining History', *Llafur*, 4, no. 1 (1984), 72–90.
[81] *The Cambrian*, 25 December 1857.
[82] *Western Mail*, 30 June 1891; letter from '"Student 69–70", Carmarthenshire'.
[83] On notions of female privilege in popular protest see, for example, E. P. Thompson, *Customs in Common* (London, 1991), pp. 325–31 and Natalie Zemon Davis, *Society and Culture in Early Modern France* (Oxford, 1987), chapter 5.

gradual replacement of traditional, community-based forms of protest by more institutionalized methods of political agitation led to an effective marginalization or 'withdrawal' of women in formal political terms.[84] Admittedly, women continued to deploy verbal sanctions such as the haranguing of bailiffs or blacklegs in support of wider political movements, but these types of community-based, direct-action tactics were becoming increasingly more marginalized and obsolete by the end of the nineteenth century, and were usually regarded as supplementary to the formal or institutionalized political tactics devised by their more 'respectable' menfolk. The 'public' world of formal political oratory increasingly belonged to men, while those women who wished to participate in political demonstrations often had no choice but to adopt a stereotypically 'disorderly' role, as they had done during previous generations. During the Tithe War, for instance, formal political rhetoric like that witnessed at a meeting of farmers held in the parish of Llanddewi Aber-arth in 1888, at which 'each member endeavoured to outdo the previous speaker in emphatic protests',[85] was seen as predominantly the preserve of men, with the 'oratorical' skills of women being confined to the heckling and haranguing of tithe agents and bailiffs.

Whereas the middle decades of the nineteenth century witnessed the confirmation of men as responsible political citizens, with a strong voice in the political decision-making process, most women were effectively condemned to domestic isolation and public silence. Female public oratory was viewed as a strange aberration not to be encouraged. As Alice Gray Jones (Ceridwen Peris), an early female temperance reformer, later observed, contemporary public opinion was opposed to women ascending the stage to address an audience. Woman's proper place was at home and silence was her virtue.[86] Those women who succeeded in acquiring a limited amount of influence within the 'public' arena did so within strictly-delineated parameters, which tended to focus attention on chapel-related activities such as lay preaching and temperance reform. Yet even within the respectable domain of Nonconformity, their position was still regarded as subordinate and marginal, with women being refused permission to become chapel elders or ministers. The first generation of female temperance reformers were often debarred from preaching in pulpits – a predominantly male domain – and

---

[84] For further information on the marginalization of women within formal working-class politics in England during the early and mid-nineteenth century, see Dorothy Thompson, 'Women and Nineteenth-century Radical Politics: A Lost Dimension' in Juliet Mitchell and Ann Oakley (eds.), *The Rights and Wrongs of Women* (Harmondsworth, 1976), pp. 112–38; Sally Alexander, 'Women, Class and Sexual Differences in the 1830s and 1840s: Some Reflections on the Writing of a Feminist History', *History Workshop Journal*, no. 17 (1984), 125–49; Hall, *White, Male and Middle Class*, esp. chapters 6, 7; and Clark, *Struggle for the Breeches*.

[85] *Cambrian News*, 23 March 1888.

[86] Alice Gray Jones (Ceridwen Peris), *Er Cof a Gwerthfawrogiad o Lafur Mrs Mathews* (Lerpwl, 1931), p.14, quoted in Ceridwen Lloyd-Morgan, 'From Temperance to Suffrage?' in John (ed.), *Our Mothers' Land*, p. 148.

on some occasions were even denied access to the chapel itself, with meetings being relegated instead to the adjacent schoolroom.[87]

Moreover, those women who demanded a political voice and gained a limited amount of public influence through, for example, the temperance movement were usually viewed with suspicion and disdain by their male contemporaries. For example, Cranogwen's biographer notes that when she first made an appearance as a lay preacher many male members of the congregations found her presence extremely disconcerting, if not actually threatening: 'When they saw Cranogwen in the pulpit addressing a crowd of men, they thought the end of the world had come. They delighted in suggesting that she was a man in the form of woman, or vice versa; and we heard some insinuating that she belonged to neither sex' ('Pan welsant Cranogwen yn y pulpud yn annerch torf o ddynion, credasant fod diwedd y byd wedi dod. Bu'n wych ganddynt awgrymu mai gwryw ar wedd benyw, neu fenyw ar wedd gwryw, ydoedd; a chlywsom rai yn awgrymu nad oedd yn perthyn i'r naill ryw neu'r llall').[88] In the view of most Nonconformist elders, women should remain on the hearth, silent and submissive, and those who defied convention by addressing public assemblies, to the detriment of their traditional wifely duties, were often deemed to have 'unsexed' themselves in the process.

Even so, despite the seemingly oppressive and certainly exclusive nature of 'separate spheres', there is evidence to suggest that many women, from working-class as well as middle-class backgrounds, wholeheartedly and voluntarily embraced these values, viewing them as a necessary and integral component of outward respectability. It needs to be stressed that the cult of domesticity was not simply a dominant patriarchal ideology imposed by men on women in a heavy-handed and arbitrary manner. As Joanna Bourke has revealed, the 'relegation' of women to the domestic sphere was not necessarily viewed as oppressive or demeaning.[89] Many women took great pride in their new role as housewives, viewing it as a valuable vehicle of self-expression as well as a useful means of consolidating their power within the home. In the novels of Kate Roberts, for example, works which have been described as 'a celebration of domesticity and female solidarity', the female protagonists define and express themselves and their relationships with others through the values and social obligations associated with the domestic ideal.[90] Moreover, as has already been shown, many women

---

[87] Sarah Jane Rees (Cranogwen), one of the few female lay preachers, was refused permission to preach from the pulpit. See Williams, 'The True "Cymraes"', p. 88.

[88] D. G. Jones, *Cofiant Cranogwen* (Caernarfon, 1933), pp. 88–9, quoted in Lloyd-Morgan, 'From Temperance to Suffrage?', p. 149.

[89] Joanna Bourke, 'Housewifery in Working-Class England 1860–1914', *P&P*, no. 143 (1994), 167–97.

[90] See Noragh Jones, 'The Comforts and Discomforts of Home: Feminism and Kate Roberts' Domestic Themes', *Planet*, 107 (1994), 75–82. Kate Roberts herself took great pride in the merits of domestic labour and was scornful of 'liberated' women who derided and downgraded the values associated with domesticity.

undoubtedly shared a conviction that the moral, spiritual, cultural and even political influence which they exerted within society emanated from this all-pervasive, matriarchal role within the home. In particular, by presiding over the Welsh-speaking *aelwyd*, and ensuring that the cultural values associated with Welshness were transmitted to successive generations, patriotic Welsh mothers were able to express great pride in their largely domestic role and harness it in the furtherance of a wider political and national cause.

In addition, as Catherine Hall and other social historians have pointed out, women often played a key role in defining and articulating the precise boundaries of this new ideology of domesticity. Attacks on 'gossipy' women, for example, were not simply an attempt on the part of men to marginalize and emaciate the power of women's words. Women frequently internalized and endorsed these values, using them as a means of delineating the social boundaries between themselves and their less respectable sisters, and often initiating attacks on other women – such as gossips – who failed to conform to accepted norms. Many of the scathing attacks on women's gossip which appeared in Welsh-language journals such as *Y Frythones* and *Y Gymraes* were, in fact, penned by women. Similarly, the obituaries which frequently appeared in the Welsh-language press imply that many women of a religious disposition who sought respectable status were at pains to distance themselves from the gossip networks of their female neighbours. For example, Mrs Tibbott, who died at Llanfyllin in 1852, was clearly averse to gossip, never visiting neighbours except on legitimate business.[91] This same virtue was attributed to Mrs Evans of Llanengan, whose obituary appeared in *Y Gymraes* in 1908, and who was said to be as scrupulous in her choice of words as in her use of time.[92] Respectable women such as these displayed considerable discretion and restraint in their verbal exchanges with neighbours, and refused to listen to the gossip of others. According to the obituary of Mrs Jones of Llandygwydd, for instance, published in *Seren Cymru* in 1880, she was a woman who never spoke ill of anyone, and if she had nothing good to say, would remain silent.[93] Mrs Sarah Evans of Llanedi, who died in 1880, was said to have given short shrift to those who gossiped or defamed the character of others in her presence: 'Having once poured out their bile in her presence, they never felt the desire to do so again.'[94] Similarly, Miss Rachel James, who was for several years placed in charge of the 'Branch shop' at Abermeurig, disliked the gossiping tendencies of most of the other young female shop assistants of a similar age to herself, and only participated if the topic was of sufficient merit. She always spoke kindly and respectfully of others, and refused to succumb to considerable public pressure from customers to gossip when working in the shop, never criticizing anyone and electing for silence

[91] 'Pregeth Anghladdol', *Y Dysgedydd*, XXXI (April, 1852), 103.
[92] *Y Gymraes*, XII, no. 143 (1908), 123.
[93] *Seren Cymru*, 20 February 1880, p. 5.
[94] Ibid., 10 December 1880, p. 7.

rather than discourse with the gossips.[95] Women such as these preferred to socialize with spiritually-minded women who, like Mrs Jones of Gwernymynydd (who died in 1855), discussed the teachings of the Scriptures when conversing with female neighbours: 'This was the subject of conversation at home, when out walking, and when she met her friends.'[96]

The extent to which these values were embraced and endorsed by a large section of the female population is also confirmed by the characteristically defensive attitude of many women who were accused of being fond of gossip. For example, when such accusations were directed against the womenfolk of a specific neighbourhood, the women in question often made a concerted effort to register their disapprobation and defend their collective reputation. In 1865, when a correspondent using the pseudonym 'Carw Coch' submitted a letter to *Y Gwladgarwr* on the evils of gossip, which perpetuated the popular stereotype of the female gossip as a slovenly, slatternly housewife who neglected her domestic duties, his female neighbours in Trecynon were enraged and threatened to hold a meeting in protest.[97] The sensitivity and defensiveness of women, when impugned in this way, also helps to explain why newspaper correspondents who singled out the gossipy slatterns of a particular community for ridicule were often at pains to stress that their disparaging comments were not intended as an insult to the other, more respectable women who resided in the same neighbourhood or, by implication, as an affront to the 'good name' of the community as a whole.[98]

There can be no doubt that widespread acceptance of the values associated with the domestic ideal, and the cult of respectability generally, had important implications for the collective neighbourhood ties and gossip networks of women. For example, the declining fortune of the *Clwb Te* was a direct result of the Victorian cult of respectability. As Isaac Foulkes observed in 1862, the 'Cymdeithas De', as he termed it, was ebbing rapidly due to the country's obsession with morality, education and religion.[99] Gossip was perceived to be at odds with the notions of privatized domestic behaviour which respectability implied, and widespread acceptance and assimilation of the values commonly associated with the domestic ideal – and of the negative stereotypes and preconceptions surrounding 'women's talk' already described – must therefore have exerted an adverse effect on women's neighbourhood networks and on their collective oral culture in particular. After all, criticism of gossip not only denigrated and devalued the language and behaviour of individual female participants, but also denigrated a woman's relationship with her immediate

---

[95] *Y Frythones*, I, no. 4 (1879), 113–14. She was twenty years old when she died.
[96] *Y Dysgedydd*, XXXIV (June, 1855), 220.
[97] *Y Gwladgarwr*, 5 August 1865, p. 6: letter from 'G. Medi' re. 'Helynt Trecynon'. For the original letter from 'Carw Coch', entitled 'Cwd y Glap', see *Y Gwladgarwr*, 22 July 1865, pp. 2–3.
[98] See, for example, the disparaging remarks about the gossips of Porthmadog which were published in *Y Gymraes*, II, no. 12 (1851), 372.
[99] Foulkes, '*Cymru Fu*', pp. 90–1.

neighbours and helped to undermine and downgrade the spirit of neighbourliness, co-operation and mutual dependency which characterized women's culture generally. In this respect, those women who voluntarily distanced themselves from the gossip circles of their peers must, on occasions, have experienced a deep sense of alienation, isolation and displacement. Mrs Mary Jones of Tanygrisiau, for example, whose obituary appeared in the *Methodist* for 1856, stood aloof from the gossip networks of her neighbours, her thoughts being 'rhy goethedig' (too refined) to enable her to take pleasure in small talk, and she was actively criticized by her female neighbours for not visiting them.[100] As Ellen Ross has revealed, women who set themselves apart from the gossip circles of their female neighbours were also effectively rejecting the mutual support networks and value systems of the wider neighbourhood and, as such, were often forced to pay a high social price for the privilege of privacy.[101]

It also needs to be stressed, however, that even those women who outwardly conformed to popular notions of respectable femininity were by no means as constrained or as subdued as has sometimes been assumed. Despite the pervasiveness of the domestic ideal, and the apparent willingness of Victorian wives to defer to the wishes and opinions of the male head of household, individual women still found considerable scope for manoeuvre and negotiation. Although the Victorian era witnessed a marked change in the ideal standards of behaviour which governed marital relationships, in reality gender conflict between husband and wife remained prevalent, even among couples who outwardly subscribed to the patriarchal ideal.[102] In the opinion of one Llangrannog resident, for instance, male and female were not equal, for either the wife was master of the husband or the husband master of the wife, and oppression was rife in almost every home.[103] Moreover, the possession of a caustic tongue was still cited by many contemporaries as being a wife's main defence mechanism *vis-à-vis* her husband, and many wives continued to deploy an array of disruptive and confrontational verbal strategies as a means of negotiating a degree of power and autonomy within marriage.[104] Although the 'nagging' or scolding wife was no longer the butt of popular literature, as in earlier periods, there is evidence to

---

[100] 'Adgofion am Mrs Jones, Tanygrisiau', *Methodist*, III (June, 1856), 181.
[101] Ross, 'Not the sort that would sit on the doorstep', 52.
[102] Anna Clark argues that the concept of 'separate spheres' for men and women resolved gender conflict at an ideological level only: 'it succeeded only on the level of rhetoric, not everyday experience'. See Anna Clark, 'Womanhood and manhood in the transition from plebeian to working-class culture: London, 1780–1845' (unpubl. Rutgers, New Jersey, PhD thesis, 1987), p. iii.
[103] NLW, David Thomas MS B62, p. 25 (evidence from an unidentified Llangrannog informant).
[104] Joanna Bourke, *Working-Class Cultures in Britain 1890–1960: Gender, Class and Ethnicity* (London and New York, 1994), pp. 74–81; eadem, 'Housewifery in Working-class England', 191–4. For similar observations on the use of defiant language by wives, see Sheila Rowbotham, 'The Trouble with Patriarchy' in Raphael Samuel (ed.), *People's History and Socialist Theory* (London, 1981), p. 365.

suggest that a wife's nagging tongue continued to be a source of friction, as well as an effective means of gaining the proverbial upper hand, within many households.[105] As one Rhondda magistrate observed when a woman who 'was always nagging her husband' summoned him before the bench for desertion: 'The tongue is a very cruel weapon, and many . . . are driven out of their senses by the nagging of someone else.'[106] Indeed, in many households, the use of particularly defiant, insubordinate or aggressive language on the part of the wife was often cited by her spouse as legitimate grounds for wife-beating. For example, a study of domestic violence in the coalmining districts of Wales and Scotland during the 1920s observed that wife-beaters often pleaded 'provocation', in word or manner, when explaining the motive or justification for their ill-treatment of their wives.[107] Wives, for their part, were encouraged to blame themselves for domestic strife and to feel they had invited physical abuse by 'nagging' or otherwise 'provoking' their husbands.

In addition to the various forms of open defiance and insubordination already described, the seemingly submissive wife, who resented her husband's patriarchal authority, could also resort to a variety of covert, non-confrontational verbal strategies such as subtle manipulation, deliberate prevarication, disdainful silence or ridiculing her husband's personal behaviour in the presence of neighbours. By resorting to these subtle verbal strategies, wives were able to gain the upper hand in many households; in particular, strategies of this type could prove particularly effective in households where the husband was quick to lose his temper. Moreover, a disgruntled wife could also effectively humiliate her husband or undermine his reputation and credibility within the community at large by making insulting or slanderous allusions to his personal behaviour in the presence of neighbours. As a correspondent to *Y Cylchgrawn* observed in 1854, private quarrels between husband and wife could spill over into the public arena, with wives often publicly berating their husbands for extreme cruelty when they might in fact be as good as any in the neighbourhood.[108] One Llanelli woman who suspected her husband of having an adulterous affair with a younger woman went so far as to spread a rumour to this effect about the town, the ultimate outcome of which was that both the husband and his alleged mistress were burnt in effigy by

---

[105] For an interesting mid-nineteenth century representation of the 'nagging' wife, see the ballad entitled 'Tychangerdd Newydd i'r Glep-wraig' (the term *clepwraig* being used in this context to describe a nagging rather than a 'gossipy' wife). NLW, 'Baledi a Cherddi', vol. 25, no. 125.
[106] *Rhondda Leader*, 22 June 1918, p. 4.
[107] Stuart Macintyre, *Little Moscows: Communism and Working-class Militancy in Inter-war Britain* (London, 1980), p. 142. Other studies have also observed that a wife's verbal insubordination towards her husband was often considered to be sufficient justification for domestic violence. See, for example, Nancy Tomes, 'A "Torrent of Abuse": Crimes of Violence Between Working-class Men and Women in London, 1840–1875', *Journal of Social History*, 11, no. 3 (1978), 328–45.
[108] 'Gair at wragedd Cymru', *Y Cylchgrawn*, IV, no. 34 (1854), 20. Nonetheless, the writer was quick to point out that wives often leapt to their husbands' defence if they became the object of other people's criticism.

disaffected neighbours.[109] Gossip, slander and the deliberate spreading of malicious accusations continued to be popular weapons in the aggrieved wife's arsenal of defence.

Similarly, many women who outwardly conformed to the basic tenets of domesticity did not necessarily pursue a life of domestic isolation and privacy. For instance, many who sought to distance themselves from the gregarious street culture of their less respectable female neighbours undoubtedly remained sensitive to the power and emotional comfort which communal pastimes such as gossip could confer. Although middle-class women, notably the wives of wealthy farmers and professional men, could afford to remain aloof from the mutual aid networks of their poorer female neighbours, social and recreational links with like-minded women remained important and, in particular, gossip networks retained their popularity as a means of maintaining such links. Respectability, it would seem, did not demand a complete disjunction from women's gossip networks; 'respectable' women simply became more circumspect about such matters, and sought other, more socially-acceptable outlets for policing and passing judgement on the indiscretions of their neighbours. Gossip now took place in more secluded settings, such as the local sewing circle or formal tea-drinking sessions within private homes, rather than within the public arena of doorstep and street. Unlike their working-class sisters, respectable middle-class women were not expected to maintain an open house for female neighbours and social visits to one another's homes were often by formal invitation as well as being restricted to a prearranged 'calling day' ('diwrnod galw'). In marked contrast to the boisterous tea-drinking sessions which had characterized women's culture during earlier periods, by the latter part of the nineteenth century the 'tea parties' which respectable women frequented were decidedly formal, sombre affairs, in which the rules and refinements which governed Victorian etiquette were rigidly adhered to and the family's best china was temporarily displayed in all its grandeur for the benefit of female neighbours. Nonetheless, beneath the façade of sobriety, gentility and outward respectability, these highly-formalized social gatherings were an important means of maintaining social links with female neighbours and of disseminating the latest gossip and scandal. In the words of T. Gwynn Jones (b. 1871) who, as a young boy, had been present at several such gatherings:

> 'Diwrnod galw' fyddai'r dydd y dôi cymdogesau neu hen gyfoedion i edrych am fy mam, neu yr âi hi i edrych amdanynt hwy. Byddai te mewn hen 'lestri c'heni', a gedwid yn ofalus mewn cwpwrdd cornel, ar y diwrnod hwnnw . . . rhai wedi bod yn y teulu er amser Nain . . . Byddai'n rhaid i hogyn bach fod yn boenus o lonydd ac yn annaturiol o dda. Er bod fy mam yn un lawen wrth natur a braidd yn ffraeth ei gair, go gwynfannus fyddai'r ymddiddan bron bob amser ar achlysur felly, sôn am drwbl ac afiechyd hon a'r

---

[109] *South Wales Press*, 18 April, 13 June 1895.

llall, neu am ferch rhyw hen gydnabod wedi priodi yn is na'i stad, felly beth oedd i'w ddisgwyl ond trwbl? Ar dro byddai sôn fod merch un arall wedi 'priodi'n dda' dros ben, hynny yw, yn uwch na'i stad, efallai. Trwbl fyddai weithiau ar ôl y fargen honno hefyd. Dywedid yn aml yn ystod yr ymddiddan mai 'dyna fel y mae hi yn yr hen fyd yma'.[110]

('Calling day' was the day when neighbours or old friends would come to visit mother, or she would go to visit them. On that day they would have tea in old 'china crockery', which was kept carefully in a corner cupboard . . . some of it having been in the family since Grandmother's time . . . Small boys would have to be painfully still, and unnaturally good. Although mother had a cheerful disposition and ready wit, the conversation on these occasions was almost invariably about people's misfortunes, their troubles and illnesses, how some girl had married beneath her station, and so what was to be expected but disaster? Sometimes there was mention of a girl who had 'made a very good marriage', that is, above her station perhaps. This arrangement also was likely to lead to disaster. It would often be said during the conversation 'that's how it is in this old world'.)

Chapel networks, too, could provide a respectable outlet for the dissemination of gossip and, in some respects, actively encouraged such activity, since the code of discipline associated with chapel membership often created a social ethos which endorsed collective public scrutiny of the private behaviour of others.[111]

Even so, it needs to be pointed out that many women who wholeheartedly endorsed certain aspects of the domestic ideal simultaneously embraced, with equal enthusiasm, other 'public' or communal pastimes which were seemingly at odds with the basic tenets of that ideal. Large sections of the female population, especially those who lived in working-class communities in the South Wales Coalfield, did not embrace largely middle-class standards of behaviour, which emphasized the merits of excessive privacy. Instead, they adapted and tempered the domestic ideal to suit the specific needs and values of closely-knit working-class communities. They may have embraced certain aspects of the domestic ideal, such as a rigid adherence to high standards of domestic cleanliness and an emphasis on the duty of the Welsh matriarch to police the language and behaviour of male members of the household, but they also retained the collective and gregarious features of women's neighbourhood culture which emphasized the benefits and obligations of mutual dependency and communal solidarity. In particular, gossip remained an integral component of the mutual support networks sustained by women throughout the nineteenth century. Lacking alternative recreational facilities, poorer women who resided in working-class neighbourhoods continued to occupy the public space which had been their traditional domain; they continued to gossip in the street, on doorsteps, at the communal bakehouse or

---

[110] T. Gwynn Jones, *Brithgofion* (Llandybïe, 1944), pp. 58–9.

[111] One of the main purposes of the Calvinistic Methodist society, for example, was to mediate and intervene in disputes between chapel members. See *Hanes, Cyfansoddiad, Rheolau Dysgybliaethol, ynghyd a Chyffes Ffydd y Corff o Fethodistiaid Calfinaidd yn Nghymru*.

wash-house, and in local shops and street markets. Front doors were kept open all day and female neighbours felt at liberty to 'pop' in and out of each other's houses for an unheralded cup of tea and a chat.[112] Moreover, those women who demanded excessive privacy or set themselves apart from these networks by refusing to keep an open house or participate in local gossip were shunned by the wider 'speech community' of women. Unlike middle-class women, whose financial situation was less precarious, working-class women could not afford to distance themselves from the various mutual aid mechanisms devised by their female neighbours. They felt compelled to remain part of the wider community of women for practical economic as well as social reasons; and participation in local gossip was a necessary part of this process of integration.[113]

Furthermore, although the female gossip was invariably portrayed as a slovenly or poverty-stricken housewife who neglected her home and family, in reality most working-class women did not regard the pursuit of gossip and a rigorous devotion to domestic labour as being two mutually exclusive and incompatible pastimes. On the contrary, a disciplined approach to housework and a sense of pride in domestic labour seem to have been characteristic of women's culture in most working-class neighbourhoods throughout the Victorian era. From an early date, for example, the women of the South Wales Coalfield developed a reputation for household cleanliness and numerous contemporary observers commented on their collective obsession with domestic labour.[114] Indeed, high standards of domestic cleanliness and general household management (along with chastity, the ability to manage money and to instil respectable manners in their children) provided an important yardstick by which to measure a woman's respectability and status in relation to her neighbours, and those women who failed to live up to these standards often found themselves the object of neighbourhood gossip and ridicule.[115] Under such circumstances, keeping up appearances was of paramount importance, and gossip networks and other verbal sanctions could, ironically, provide the means whereby women imposed the cult of domesticity and the sexual division of labour upon each other.

It may be concluded, therefore, that most women, particularly those who resided in working-class neighbourhoods, displayed a great deal of resourcefulness in adapting the domestic ideal to suit their own individual needs and circumstances. They set their own standards of behaviour, based to a certain extent on

[112] E.g. Philip Massey, 'Portrait of a Mining Town', *Fact*, no. 8 (1937), 49; James Hanley, *Grey Children: A Study in Humbug and Misery* (London, 1937), pp. 51, 54–5; Coombes, *These Poor Hands*, pp. 22–3.

[113] Cf. Ross, 'Not the sort that would sit on the doorstep'.

[114] For references to obsessive attention to housework in the industrialized areas of south Wales see, for example, Rosemary Crook, '"Tidy Women": Women in the Rhondda between the Wars', *Oral History*, 10, no. 2 (1982), 40–6; S. Minwel Tibbott and Beth Thomas, *O'r Gwaith i'r Gwely: Cadw Tŷ 1890–1960 / A Woman's Work: Housework 1890–1960* (Cardiff, 1994).

[115] Cf. Crook, 'Tidy Women'.

the cult of domesticity but at the same time retaining those aspects of women's culture which emphasized communal solidarity, mutual dependency and complex ties of kinship and neighbourhood. As a number of social historians have recently observed, to discuss the behaviour of women within simple paradigms such as 'active agents' versus 'passive victims', or within the exclusive context of the public/private dichotomy, is both simplistic and misleading.[116] In practice, the experiences of individual women, and interpretations of agreed standards of respectable behaviour, were extremely fluid, with many women moving quite easily between two seemingly contradictory and conflicting models of womanhood and of female discourse. Furthermore, by engaging in 'public' gossip about the 'private' lives of neighbours – thereby influencing, albeit indirectly, the 'public' fortunes of moral transgressors – women were able to circumvent the sometimes arbitrary distinctions between the 'public' and the 'private'.[117] Far from being passive, downtrodden or voiceless victims, many Victorian women, including those who outwardly conformed to the images of feminine respectability already described, were extremely resilient and resourceful. They may have endorsed the domestic ideal, but they often did so largely on their own terms and continued to deploy a wide range of verbal sanctions as a means of gaining the proverbial 'last word' and of negotiating for themselves a marked degree of status and autonomy, both within marriage and the wider patriarchal establishment.

---

[116] See, for example, Kermode and Walker (eds.), *Women, Crime and the Courts*, pp. 7–8.

[117] The power of gossip to influence the 'public' or economic fortunes of its victims should not be underestimated. In 1857, for example, a Rhyl policeman was forced to resign his post when his adulterous affair with a married woman became common knowledge. See Clwyd Record Office, Flintshire Constabulary Papers, FP/2/7, Chief Constable's Order Book, 1857–75, p. 31; FP/2/1, Letter Book, 1857–8, p. 195.

7

The Church and the Welsh Language in the Nineteenth Century

R. TUDUR JONES

ACCORDING to Walter T. Morgan, 'the need to supply the means of grace to all parishioners in the language of their choice was the most baffling problem which the Church in Wales had to face in the nineteenth century'.[1] It will become obvious in due course why this was so difficult, but the general background is significant. Throughout the nineteenth century the Church in Wales was still part of the Church of England. This meant, of course, that in the view of ecclesiastical leaders the Church in Wales was represented by only four dioceses in the province of Canterbury, to be treated in the same way as all the others. As a result it was natural that Church dignitaries refused to countenance any linguistic differences on the grounds that they caused inconvenience and interfered with the movement of non-Welsh-speaking clerics to various parts of the Church in Wales.

Inconvenience was not the only relevant factor. The fact that the Church was linked to the state meant that it was heavily influenced by the prejudices and assumptions of English political and ecclesiastical leaders. By the nineteenth century England's aggressive nationalism was nearing the heyday of empire. This coincided with the proclamation of Queen Victoria as Empress of India in 1876. In administering a great empire, of mixed population, it was an advantage to have one official language. An essential feature of the imperial mind was the promotion of English at the expense of other languages, which were held in scorn. While it is true to say that among the empire's administrators there were many individuals who insisted on learning the languages of the people whom they governed, English people on the whole showed their loyalty to the British Empire by poking fun at other languages. R. R. W. Lingen made this point in his report on the schools of Carmarthenshire, Pembrokeshire and Glamorgan in the Blue Books of 1847:

---

[1] Walter T. Morgan, 'The Diocese of St. David's in the Nineteenth Century. C. The Unreformed Church (iii)', *JHSCW*, XXIII, no. 28 (1973), 28.

> I have no hesitation in saying that a child might pass through the generality of these schools without learning either the limits, capabilities, general history, or language of that empire in which he is born a citizen . . .[2]

In this statement Lingen sees education as the handmaiden of imperialism. But English imperialism comprised strong religious elements. Prayers for the royal family had been included in the order of service of the Book of Common Prayer since the days of Thomas Cranmer, but by Victorian times this had developed into a kind of imperial theology which considered conquering other nations and taking control of countries overseas to be part of the stewardship of Providence. This devotion reached its emotional peak in Rudyard Kipling's 'Recessional', which was published on Victoria's Diamond Jubilee on 22 June 1897, but has often been sung as an Armistice Day hymn, even in Wales. In the song God is He 'Beneath whose awful Hand we hold Dominion over palm and pine', and He is asked to save those who love the empire from 'Such boasting as the Gentiles use / Or lesser breeds without the Law'. It was not uncommon for the Welsh people to be listed among the 'lesser breeds'. In a legal case brought before the Court of Arches in 1773, when the churchwardens of the parish of Trefdraeth and Llangwyfan in Anglesey, with the support of the Society of Cymmrodorion, challenged the appointment of a monoglot Englishman as parish priest, the notion that England had a divinely-appointed mission to save the souls of inferior peoples was expressed. Among other things, the solicitor defending the appointment maintained that:

> Wales is a conquered country; it is proper to introduce the English language, and it is the duty of the bishops to promote the English, in order to introduce the language . . . It has always been the policy of the legislature to introduce the English language into Wales.[3]

In other words, there was a religious motive behind the desire to suppress the language, despite the fact that the law made it clear that Welsh-speaking clerics were to be appointed to Welsh-speaking parishes. A law passed at the beginning of Victoria's reign was quite specific on this matter:

> Whereas in many benefices in Wales . . . many of the inhabitants are imperfectly, or not at all, instructed in the English language, it is expedient that persons to be hereafter

---

[2] *Reports of the Commissioners of Inquiry into the State of Education in Wales . . . in three parts. Part I. Carmarthen, Glamorgan, and Pembroke* (London, 1847) (PP 1847 (870) XXVII), p. 28.
[3] *The Depositions, Arguments and Judgment in the Cause of the Church-Wardens of Trefdraeth, in the County of Anglesea, against Dr Bowles* (London, 1773), p. 59.

instituted or licensed to such benefices should possess an adequate knowledge of the Welsh language.[4]

This clause was not particularly strong since it stipulated that the appointment of Welsh-speaking clerics was 'expedient' rather than 'obligatory'. However, it is easier to pass laws than to change the powerful prejudices of influential people. Overall, those in favour of using Welsh within the Church in Wales were faced with formidable difficulties.

We must begin with the bishops. In a long letter to W. E. Gladstone on 22 January 1870, Henry T. Edwards expressed his views unequivocally:

> The regeneration of the Church of the Cymry, by the restoration of the masses into her fold, can assuredly be effected by none other than native Bishops and native clergy . . . It requires no arguments to prove that the presence in Wales during a hundred and fifty years of Bishops incapable of performing Episcopal functions in the language of the people, has been an indecent violation of the principle of the twenty-fourth Article, and an undeserved outrage upon the national sensibilities of the Cymric people.[5]

The burden of the twenty-fourth article of the Articles of Faith of the Church of England was simple and unambiguous: 'It is contrary to the Word of God, and to the practice of the Early Church, to pray publicly in Church, or to administer the Sacraments, in an idiom which the people may not understand.' Little use, however, was made of this in attempts to ensure enhanced status for the Welsh language within the Church.

To what extent could the severe words of Henry T. Edwards about the nineteenth-century Church be justified? During the century the four dioceses of Wales were served by twenty-five bishops; William Cleaver was bishop of Bangor from 1800 to 1806 and subsequently bishop of St Asaph until 1815.[6] With the exception of five Welshmen and one Scot (namely James Colquhoun Campbell,

---

[4] 1 and 2 Victoria, c.106, section 103. See D. R. Thomas, *The History of the Diocese of St. Asaph* (3 vols., Oswestry, 1908), I, p. 181.

[5] Henry T. Edwards, *Wales and the Welsh Church* (London, 1889), p. 162. There is a biography of Edwards (1837–84) at the beginning of the book. He was vicar of Caernarfon at the time. He was promoted dean of Bangor in 1876.

[6] Perhaps it would be helpful to name the bishops and the date of their election: William Cleaver (1800), John Randolph (1807), Henry William Majendie (1809), Christopher Bethell (1830), James Colquhoun Campbell (1859), Daniel Lewis Lloyd (1890). St Asaph: Lewis Bagot (1790), Samuel Horsley (1802), William Cleaver (1806), John Luxmore (1815), William Carey (1830), Thomas Vowler Short (1846), Joshua Hughes (1870), Alfred George Edwards (1889). Llandaff: Richard Watson (1782), Herbert Marsh (1816), William van Mildert (1819), Charles Richard Sumner (1826), Edward Copleston (1827), Alfred Ollivant (1849), Richard Lewis (1883). St David's: Lord George Murray (1800), Thomas Burgess (1803), John Banks Jenkinson (1825), Connop Thirlwall (1840), William Basil Tickell Jones (1874). These are all included in *DNB*, except for Campbell and Lewis Lloyd.

who was bishop of Bangor from 1859 to 1890), all these prelates were Englishmen, and all except Joshua Hughes, who graduated BD from St David's College, Lampeter, were graduates of Oxford or Cambridge. Some of these, namely Thomas Burgess, Connop Thirlwall and Thomas Vowler Short, were celebrated scholars. Charles Richard Sumner – a friend of King George IV until he voted in favour of Catholic emancipation in 1829 – was consecrated bishop of Llandaff on 21 May 1826 but was at the same time dean of St Paul's in London. He made one visitation to his diocese but on 12 December 1827, some sixteen months after his appointment as bishop of Llandaff and before anyone had made his acquaintance, he had been preferred to the bishopric of Winchester, following in the footsteps of his predecessor, Richard Watson. The latter had been appointed Professor of Chemistry at Cambridge in 1764, although he had no knowledge of chemistry, then Regius Professor of Divinity, although he had no theological knowledge, and then bishop of Llandaff in October 1782, although he knew nothing about Wales. It is true that in due course he would make something of a name for himself as a chemist and theologian, but he took not the slightest interest in the running of his diocese. His time was spent on his estate in Westmorland, experimenting on ways to improve the soil.[7] As for John Banks Jenkinson, bishop of St David's from 1825 to 1840, he was 'entirely ignorant of the Welsh language and [had] not the most distant intention of ever learning it'; in fact, he disliked Wales, except for Montgomeryshire.[8] Between 1800 and 1806, while he was bishop of Bangor, William Cleaver was also principal of Brasenose College, Oxford, and he spent most of his time there. Lord George Murray, bishop of St David's between 1801 and 1803, chose to spend his time seeking to perfect a telegraph system for the navy rather than familiarizing himself with the culture of his diocese. To sum up, the majority of these alien bishops had no understanding of the special needs of the Church in Wales, they had no interest in the Welsh language, and knew nothing of its literature nor of its cultural traditions. One regular complaint made against them was that they were eager to appoint non-Welsh speakers to positions and livings in Wales. It was said of the diocese of Llandaff around 1816: 'nearly all the dignitaries in connection with the diocese were English, and this had a prejudicial effect upon the work and progress of the Church in South Wales'.[9] A. J. Johnes argued that bishops ignorant of the language and feelings of the Welsh people 'will necessarily tend to fill the Welsh Church with men but little versed in that language and those feelings',[10] or, as

[7] There is a scathing article by 'Morfa', 'Richard Watson, Esgob Llandaf' in *Yr Haul*, VII, no. 82 (1905), 433–9.
[8] D. T. W. Price, *A History of Saint David's University College Lampeter. Volume I: to 1898* (Cardiff, 1977), p. 28, n. 22, p. 32, n. 42.
[9] E. C. M. Willmott, *The Cathedral Church of Llandaff: A Description of the Building and a Short History of the See* (London, 1907), p. 89.
[10] A. J. Johnes, *On the Causes which have produced Dissent from the Established Church in the Principality of Wales* (London and Llanidloes, 1870), p. 56.

Henry T. Edwards put it, 'an alien Episcopate productive of a clergy in its own likeness'.[11]

Not all these bishops were indifferent towards the Welsh language. Alfred Ollivant, a native of Manchester, was Vice-Principal of St David's College, Lampeter, from 1827 until 1843 when he returned to Cambridge as Regius Professor of Divinity. While at St David's College he held the living of Llangeler, where he preached regularly in Welsh.[12] It was said that his knowledge of Welsh exercised 'considerable weight' in his appointment as bishop of Llandaff in 1849,[13] but there is some evidence that his Welsh was somewhat lame.[14] Although it has been claimed that Christopher Bethell knew not a word of Welsh, this was not entirely true. He caused a stir among worshippers at Bangor cathedral by refusing to wear a periwig, which was part of a bishop's traditional garb, but another attraction was his peculiar Welsh. The pronunciation of *ch* and *ll* was quite beyond him. During one of his sermons he attacked the '*ffliw-ffleidr*' – rather than the *chwiw-leidr* (chance-thief) – who had broken into his palace! In short, his command of the language left much to be desired.[15] Bishop James Colquhoun Campbell was a Scotsman from Argyll. When it was understood that Bangor was seeking a Welsh-speaking bishop, a large congregation attended the cathedral to hear his first sermon in 1859 only to discover that it was almost incomprehensible.[16]

Connop Thirlwall was a Londoner, born in the parish of Stepney. He worked as a barrister for a short period after completing his course at Cambridge, during which time he won considerable renown for his edition of Schleiermacher's commentary on the gospel of St Luke. Following his ordination in 1827 he increasingly devoted himself to scholarship. His most mature work was his eight-volume history of Greece.[17] Thirlwall's reputation as one of the kingdom's most distinguished scholars was such that he was assured of a grave in Westminster Abbey at the end of his days. He was steeped in French, Italian and German, as well as the classical languages, but his knowledge of Wales was scant and there was much public criticism when he was offered the diocese of St David's. David James (Dewi o Ddyfed) felt so strongly on the matter that he wrote him a forceful letter on 3 August 1840 urging him to refuse the invitation:

---

[11] Edwards, *Wales and the Welsh Church*, p. 162. He also uses strong words to describe the influence of appointing outsiders on Welsh clerics, ibid., p. 164.

[12] Price, *A History of Saint David's University College Lampeter*, p. 35. See also J. Morgan, *Four Biographical Sketches* (London, 1892), pp. 1–60, *DNB* and *DWB*.

[13] J. Vyrnwy Morgan (ed.), *Welsh Political and Educational Leaders in the Victorian Era* (London, 1908), p. 125.

[14] Wilton D. Wills, 'The Clergy in Society in Mid-Victorian South Wales', *JHSCW*, XXIV, no. 29 (1974), 28.

[15] William Hughes, *Recollections of Bangor Cathedral* (Bala, 1904), pp. 23–4. Dean Cotton said of Bethell, 'he was like a teapot that drew well, but was defective in the spout', ibid., p. 22.

[16] Ibid., p. 56.

[17] Connop Thirlwall, *A Critical Essay on the Gospel of Luke* (London, 1825); idem, *History of Greece* (8 vols., London, 1835–44).

Efallai eich bod yn wybodus mai yr iaith Gymraeg a arferir yn Esgobaeth Tŷ-ddewi . . . a bod yn angenrheidiol i'r Esgob, tu ag at weinyddu amrywiol ddyledswyddau pwysig ei swydd uchel gydag effeithioldeb, ac er boddlonrwydd, fod yn feddiannol ar wybodaeth drwyadl o'r iaith Gymraeg . . . Bydd yn eithafnod anghyssondeb os cymerwch yr Esgobaeth; ond gweddiaf ar Dduw, ar fod yn wiw ganddo gadw y niwed o'm gwlad.[18]

(Perhaps you are aware that the Welsh language is used in the Diocese of St David's . . . and that it is necessary for the Bishop, in order to carry out the various important duties of his high office effectively, and satisfactorily, to have a thorough knowledge of the Welsh language . . . It will be the most extreme inconsistency if you accept the Diocese, but I shall pray to God that He will not allow my country to be thus harmed.)

Thirlwall accepted the appointment, however, and on his first Sunday he pronounced the blessing in Welsh; in a letter to his friend, R. M. Miles, dated 26 September 1840, he wrote: 'I am learning Welsh much faster than I expected and can now read any common Welsh book with tolerable ease.'[19] No one doubted Thirlwall's ability as a linguist and, as far as his new flock was concerned, his interest in the Welsh language boded well. But these expectations remained unfulfilled. The bishop was a man of aristocratic bent, who disliked the common clergy and could be cruelly discourteous in his dealings with them.[20] Such behaviour, moreover, was quite common and regular complaints were made about it. W. J. Rees of Cascob referred to Church dignitaries treating the parish clergy as an 'inferior "caste"'.[21] Since he kept his clergymen at arm's length, it was more difficult for Thirlwall to perfect his Welsh. As it was, his congregations had difficulty in following his sermons. Yet he was not unappreciative of those who sought to give Welsh its proper place, as when he offered the office of archdeacon to Dewi o Ddyfed. An example of his desire to appoint Welsh-speaking clergy in Welsh-speaking parishes may be seen in the case of the parish of Lampeter Velfrey in Pembrokeshire. When Richard Lewis, a native of Henllan who later became bishop of Llandaff, was appointed to that benefice in 1851, a question was raised regarding his command of the Welsh language. Thirlwall decided that Lewis should sit an examination, which he duly failed. He appealed to the Archbishop of Canterbury and it was ruled that he should take a service and preach before a critical congregation in Caernarfon. He did so to the congregation's satisfaction, and the appointment was confirmed.[22]

---

[18] *Yr Haul*, V, no. 63 (1840), 281–3; ibid., no. 64 (1840), 315. On David James (Dewi o Ddyfed, 1803–71), see *DWB*.
[19] John Connop Thirlwall, *Connop Thirlwall: Historian and Theologian* (London, 1936), p. 122.
[20] For examples, see ibid., pp. 125–8.
[21] Johnes, *An Essay on the Causes*, p. 66.
[22] *Y Geninen*, XXIV, no. 1 (1906), 1–2.

What of Welshmen on the episcopal bench? Joshua Hughes of Nevern in Pembrokeshire was a naturally fluent Welsh speaker and one of the most eloquent preachers of his generation. It was said of him: 'he loved the old language of his countrymen . . . He pointed out the cruel wrong that had been done in countless instances by ignoring the fact that the Welsh language was the only language properly understood by a very large number of his countrymen.'[23] Alfred George Edwards, who became bishop of St Asaph in 1889 and the first archbishop of Wales in 1920, was also a Welshman, but he did not share the keen concern of his brother, Dean Henry T. Edwards, for the Welsh language. As for W. Basil Jones, he had much in common with the 'Anglo Bishops'. He was able to speak Welsh, but not fluently. It is somewhat misleading to speak of his 'patriotic instincts'[24] because, in a letter to Joshua Hughes, dated 14 October 1869, he wrote: 'Welsh nationality is little more than an exaggerated provincialism.'[25] There were differing views concerning the Welshness of Richard Lewis who was elected to Llandaff in 1883 and whose command of Welsh had been put to the test at the beginning of his career. In his obituary the dean of Bangor wrote:

> Fel gwladgarwr Cymreig dangosai ofal neillduol am fod hawliau Cymry unieithog yn cael eu cydnabod . . . Os byddai angen am offeiriad yn gwybod Cymraeg mewn plwyf, ni chai un anwybodus o'r iaith byth ei bennodi.[26]

(As a Welsh patriot he took particular care that the rights of monoglot Welsh people were acknowledged . . . If a parish needed a priest with a knowledge of Welsh, one who was ignorant of the language would never be appointed.)

A different note was struck in the obituary in *Yr Haul*. Evidently, not everyone appreciated Richard Lewis's 'patriotism':

> gallasai yr Esgob Lewis wneyd mwy o'r Gymraeg yn ei esgobaeth, a chydnabod yn well lafur y clerigwyr Cymreig . . . nid oes Eglwysi gwir gryfion o Gymry yn addoli yn iaith eu mham, ond mewn rhyw ddwsin o fanau yn yr holl Esgobaeth![27]

(Bishop Lewis could have made more of Welsh in his diocese, and acknowledged better the work of the Welsh clergy . . . in only about a dozen places in the whole diocese are there truly strong congregations who worship in their mother tongue.)

---

[23] J. Vyrnwy Morgan (ed.), *Welsh Religious Leaders in the Victorian Era* (London, 1905), p. 56.
[24] Idem (ed.), *Welsh Political and Educational Leaders in the Victorian Era*, p. 150.
[25] Quoted by Price in *A History of Saint David's University College Lampeter*, p. 116. According to T. I. Ellis in his article in *DWB*, 'he had little regard for the separate nationhood of Wales'. See also *Y Geninen* (Gŵyl Ddewi, 1897), 39–41.
[26] Griffith Roberts, 'Diweddar Esgob Llandaf', *Y Geninen*, XXIV, no. 1 (1906), 5.
[27] *Yr Haul*, VII, no. 74 (1905), 55.

Daniel Lewis Lloyd was another Welshman preferred to the diocese of Bangor in 1890, the first to hold that office in two hundred years. A specialist in hymnology, he was responsible for preparing the hymn book *Emyniadur yr Eglwys*.

The bishop who was most supportive of the Welsh language during the nineteenth century was Thomas Burgess,[28] a native of Odiham in Hampshire. He became bishop of St David's in 1803 and was preferred to the diocese of Salisbury in 1823. Burgess endeavoured to learn Welsh but, although he was a distinguished scholar and master of the classical languages, he found it difficult and his pronunciation caused problems for his congregation.[29] In October 1804 he established the Society for Promoting Christian Knowledge and Church Union in the Diocese of St David's. One of its aims was to publish religious tracts in Welsh and English, but Burgess was at the time opposed to Welsh schools.[30] He later changed his mind, not least under the influence of the Revd Eliezer Williams,[31] vicar of Lampeter, who had come to the town at Burgess's request and opened a school where many ordinands were trained. The school attached considerable importance to acquiring competence in both spoken and written Welsh.[32]

Burgess began to take a warm interest in the culture of Wales. Like many others, he believed that the neglect of the language by the Church was one reason for the growth of Methodism in his diocese. He lent his support to the 'literary clerics' ('personiaid llengar'), and it was he who ensured the appointment of John Jenkins (Ifor Ceri) to the parish of Kerry in Montgomeryshire in 1807[33] and W. J. Rees to the living of Cascob in Radnorshire in 1806.[34] David Rowland (Dewi Brefi), who was appointed curate of St Peter's Church in Carmarthen in January 1818,[35] suggested that a society be established to safeguard and foster the bardic tradition in south Wales. Burgess became interested in the idea and chose 'Cymdeithas Cambria' (Cambrian Society) as an appropriate name for the society – indeed, Dewi Brefi allowed him to take the credit for its genesis. The bishop hoped that it would improve the educational standards of the clergy and encourage wider use of the Welsh language in Church services.[36] He called a

---

[28] On his career, see D. W. T. Price, *Bishop Burgess and Lampeter College* (Cardiff, 1987).
[29] Ibid., p. 37.
[30] Ibid., p. 33.
[31] J. W. James, *A Church History of Wales* (Ilfracombe, 1945), p. 171. Eliezer Williams (1754–1820) was the son of Peter Williams the elucidator (1723–96), see *DWB*.
[32] For a full description of the school and its curriculum, see Price, *A History of Saint David's University College Lampeter*, pp. 9–11, and Owain W. Jones and David Walker (eds.), *Links with the Past: Swansea and Brecon Historical Essays* (Llandybïe, 1974), p. 179.
[33] For Jenkins (1770–1829), see *DWB*.
[34] For William Jenkins Rees (1772–1855), see *DWB* and Mary Ellis, 'W. J. Rees, 1772–1855: A Portrait', *TRS*, XXXIX (1969), 24–35; ibid., XL (1970), 21–8; ibid., XLI (1971), 76–85; ibid., XLII (1972), 55–63.
[35] For David Rowland (Dewi Brefi, 1782–1820), see *DWB*. For a study of the activities of these clerics, see Bedwyr Lewis Jones, 'Yr Hen Bersoniaid Llengar' (Penarth, 1963).
[36] Price, *Bishop Burgess and Lampeter College*, p. 45.

meeting in Carmarthen on 28 October 1818, where it was decided to form the Dyfed Cambrian Society, and the following day, in the Bishop's Palace at Abergwili, the ambitious aims of the society were framed. Among other things, a comprehensive catalogue of all Welsh manuscripts in private and public libraries in Wales and England and on the Continent would be compiled, under the supervision of Iolo Morganwg. Another of the society's aims was 'to collect every printed Welsh book and keep them in the old library of the Cymmrodorion in the school in Gray's Inn Lane in London'. Before long there were Cambrian Societies in Gwynedd, Powys and Gwent. 'Cymdeithas Gymroaidd Gwynedd' was founded in September 1819, the Cymmrodorion of Powys in June 1819, and the Gwent Society in December 1821. The Cambrian societies were responsible for the revival of the eisteddfod at this time. Dyfed Cambrian Society held its first eisteddfod at Carmarthen between 8 and 10 July 1819.[37]

The 'old literary clerics' maintained a Church tradition dating back to the days of scholars like William Salesbury, Richard Davies, William Morgan, Edmwnd Prys and John Davies, Mallwyd. They combined love for their Church with pride in the literary and scholarly past of Wales. The leaders in the nineteenth century were Walter Davies (Gwallter Mechain),[38] Ifor Ceri and W. J. Rees, the last of whom shouldered the heaviest administrative burdens. They had corresponded with one another since 1810. Gwallter formed a link with eighteenth-century writers such as Owen Jones (Owain Myfyr), William Owen Pughe and Evan Evans (Ieuan Fardd). Others associated with the Kerry circle were Dewi Brefi, Rowland Williams, vicar of Meifod between 1819 and 1830,[39] and David Richards (Dewi Silin) and his brother Thomas, who kept a school at Berriew from 1813 until 1826 when he became vicar of Llangynyw. These two brothers hailed from Darowen, and were the sons of Thomas Richards.[40] Both John Blackwell (Alun) and Evan Evans (Ieuan Glan Geirionydd) were pupils of Thomas Richards the younger.[41] No one made a greater contribution to the movement than Thomas Price (Carnhuanawc). He was ordained on 12 September 1812 and, after serving as curate in various parishes, he became vicar of Llanfihangel Cwm-du in 1825. Carnhuanawc was an ardent supporter of the eisteddfod and a successful competitor. He made a name for himself by publishing *Hanes Cymru a Chenedl y Cymry* (1836–42, in parts) and became sufficiently

---

[37] For details, see ibid., pp. 45–9.
[38] For Walter Davies (Gwallter Mechain, 1761–1849), see D. Silvan Evans (ed.), *Gwaith y Parch. Walter Davies* (3 vols., Caerfyrddin, 1866–8) and *DWB*.
[39] For Rowland Williams (1779–1854), see *DWB*.
[40] For David Richards (Dewi Silin, 1783–1854) and Thomas Richards (1785–1855) see *DWB* s.n. their father Thomas Richards (1754–1837). For letters from Gwallter Mechain to the father and the son, Thomas, see Myrddin Fardd, '*Adgof uwch Anghof*: *Llythyrau Lluaws o Brif Enwogion Cymru, Hen a Diweddar* (Pen y Groes, 1883), pp. 53–69.
[41] For John Blackwell (Alun, 1797–1840), rector of Maenordeifi, see *Ceinion Alun* (Llundain, 1851) and *DWB*.

proficient in the Breton language to correct Le Gonidec's translation. He opened a school at Gellifelen in the parish of Llanelli in Breconshire, where tuition was given through the medium of Welsh. As rural dean, he used his authority to encourage clergymen to use the Welsh language in the instruction of children and adults. In many ways, Carnhuanawc was a pioneer as far as the use of Welsh was concerned.[42]

These men were champions of the Welsh language, but strong opposition to their activities existed within the Church. Some Pembrokeshire clerics deplored the work of Bishop Burgess in launching the Cambrian Society because they believed it would 'transmute a Christian praying, preaching Priesthood into a Parcel of minstrels, Harpers and God knows what unsanctified articles'.[43] Some, like David Williams of Romsey, ranted in English newspapers against any activity which might extend the life of the Welsh language. His ambition, shared by others like him, was to eliminate the language in order to make Wales part of the English nation.

The 'literary clerics' were also responsible for launching a church periodical entitled *Y Gwyliedydd*. Edited by Rowland Williams and published between 1822 and 1837, it promoted the interests and convictions of these clergymen. Despite the assiduity of W. J. Rees in seeking to persuade people to support eisteddfodau in various parts of Wales between 1819 and 1824, his efforts were only partly successful. An attempt was made to win the support and patronage of the Anglicized gentry, but to no avail. They also showed little interest in the literary schemes of Ifor Ceri and Bishop Burgess and their circle. Furthermore, there was an antiquarian flavour to the clerics' intentions. As far as scholarship was concerned, that was perfectly creditable, but if Welsh was to flourish in the Church in Wales it needed to win the hearts and minds of the people.

This was uppermost in Burgess's mind in drawing up the programme of his Church Union Society, which he established on 10 October 1804. Among its aims was 'to distribute Bibles and Common-Prayer Books' at reduced prices among the poor and free copies of small religious tracts in Welsh and English. The society was remarkably active. In 1805 it secured 20,126 books for distribution as well as 9,000 publications which it printed at its own expense.[44] In addition, the Church of England Treatise Society, established in Bristol in 1811, distributed some Welsh treatises such as *Paratoad erbyn marw, neu'r Eglwyswr ar ei glaf wely* and *Bywyd William Tindal* and *Sylwadau ar Addoliad Cyhoeddus*, in about 1818. In these

---

[42] For Thomas Price (Carnhuanawc, 1787–1848), see Jane Williams (Ysgafell), *The Literary Remains of the Rev. Thomas Price Carnhuanawc with a Memoir of his Life* (Llandovery, 1854–5) and Mary Ellis's portrait in *Yr Haul a'r Gangell* (Winter, 1974), 32–40.

[43] In a letter to David Rowland, September 1818. It is quoted in Jones, 'Yr Hen Bersoniaid Llengar', p. 23.

[44] The society's report was printed annually from 1804 to 1823. See also Price, *Bishop Burgess and Lampeter College*, p. 31.

various ways Thomas Burgess contributed to improving the lot of the Welsh language in his diocese. His most lasting contribution, however, was the establishment of St David's College, although he had left the diocese of St David's before the college opened. The topic of education will be discussed in due course.

The preparation of Welsh reading matter was also of interest to people in other dioceses. In 1830 a society for the distribution of treatises was formed in St Asaph, with Richard Richards of Caerwys as secretary and John Blackwell as treasurer.[45] The diocese of Bangor could boast a group of clergymen comparable with Ifor Ceri's circle in so far as their enthusiasm regarding the wider use of the Welsh language was concerned, but their literary interests were more restricted. On 3 December 1804, at a meeting in the cathedral Chapter House Room under the chairmanship of Dean John Warren, it was decided to form a society for 'the publication of short treatises on religious topics in Welsh'.[46] John Jones, vicar of Bangor from 1802 until 1819, was secretary for the first year and the dean was elected treasurer. At the end of the year Rowland Williams became secretary and remained in the post thereafter, and Hugh Owen was elected treasurer, though he was succeeded by John Williams of Treffos, Anglesey, at the end of the second year. John Warren, John Jones, Rowland Williams, Hugh Owen and John Williams had all been educated at Jesus College, Oxford, a college well known for nurturing an interest in the Welsh language among its students.

John Warren was appointed dean of Bangor in November 1793 and is commemorated by a tablet in the cathedral. Richard Davies was installed as rector of Llantrisant in Anglesey in October 1802, where he maintained the hospitable tradition of the literary clerics by his patronage of poets and writers.[47] John Jones (who died on 13 May 1834 at the age of fifty-eight) was vicar of Bangor from 1802 until 1819 and Archdeacon of Merioneth between 1809 and 1834. It was he who composed the words on Goronwy Owen's memorial in the cathedral. John Williams of Treffos, who died on 5 September 1826 at the age of eighty-six, was installed as rector of Llansadwrn in September 1782 and Canonicus Primus of the cathedral in 1821. At the time when the Treatise Society was formed, Rowland Williams was a teacher at Friars School, Bangor, and curate of Llandygái. He held several livings thereafter, including that of Meifod from 1819 to 1836, where he came into contact with Ifor Ceri and his circle. Thomas Ellis Owen, the scourge of Methodists, was rector of Llandyfrydog from 1794 to 1812, and Hugh Owen – who died on 15 March 1810 at the age of sixty-two – was Canonicus Tertius at

---

[45] *Y Gwyliedydd*, VII (1830), 293. Richard Richards (1780–1860), curate, and later rector of Caerwys from 1816 to 1849, was the eldest son of Thomas Richards, Darowen. See Mary Ellis's delightful portrait of him in *Yr Haul a'r Gangell* (Spring, 1976), 15–20, and also *DWB*.

[46] The minutes were published by A. Owen Evans in *The Minutes and Proceedings of an old Tract Society of Bangor Diocese (1804–1812)* (Bangor, 1918).

[47] See Dafydd Thomas and Griffith Williams, *Awdlau Newyddion, sef Dwy Farwnad er coffadwriaeth am y Parch. Richard Dafies, A.M. o Fangor* (Bangor, 1820). Dafydd Ddu Eryri and Gutyn Arfon were the two poets who composed the odes.

the cathedral between 1793 and 1805. Evan Rees, rector of Rhiw in Llŷn from 1776 onwards, died on 19 November 1811 at the age of seventy-five. Richard Jones was installed as rector of Llanhychan in Denbighshire in July 1806 and died on 23 April 1814.[48]

Between January 1805 and April 1809 more than fifteen Welsh treatises and leaflets were distributed and the total number of copies exceeded 15,000. Those responsible went to some trouble to devise an efficient system of distribution. Special emphasis was laid on the importance of Sunday schools, and on 1 October, for instance, it was decided to donate twelve copies of three treatises to every clergyman who agreed to establish a Sunday school in his parish. Bishop John Randolph (who was in Bangor from 1806 until 1809) was encouragingly supportive of the intention to publish 'short treatises in the Welsh language'.[49] But the society proved short-lived and for reasons not entirely clear its activities came to an end in 1811. There was no direct connection between this society and the treatise society established in Bangor twenty years later.

These were respectable, moderate men. Except for Carnhuanawc and Dewi Brefi, none of them were likely to set the world alight. But soon more strident views were expressed by clergymen who were prepared to challenge a system which, in their opinion, was harming the Welsh language and the Church in Wales. These men were far enough away from the blandishments of the bishops of Wales. In 1821 several Welsh-speaking clergymen serving parishes in Yorkshire began to celebrate St David's day, but in 1835 it was decided to formalize the society and, on St David's day of that year, the group met in the vicarage at Almondbury, where Dewi o Ddyfed was curate and it was he who chaired the meeting. Thus was formed the Association of Welsh Clergy in the West Riding of the County of York. They met once a year in one another's homes to celebrate the national festival, but they also had something akin to an executive committee which met in advance to decide which topics might be useful to discuss. The secretary was Joseph Hughes (Carn Ingli), a native of Newport in Pembrokeshire, who had been educated at Ystradmeurig School and St David's College, Lampeter. Although he had been ordained by Bishop Jenkinson in the diocese of St David's in 1829, his ministry in Wales had been brief, and after serving as a curate in Llanfihangel Penbedw in Pembrokeshire he moved to England. He served in Almondbury, then Liverpool, before returning to Yorkshire to take the living of Meltham. He was a keen supporter of the eisteddfod and

---

[48] Short biographies of these clerics are included in A. O. Evans's edition of the society's minutes and also in his book, *A Chapter in the History of the Welsh Book of Common Prayer* (3 vols., Bangor, 1922), III, pp. 237–324.

[49] His letter to the society's secretary, dated 18 January 1807, is to be found in Evans, *Minutes and Proceedings*, pp. 52–3.

would often return to Wales to take a prominent part as leader and competitor.[50] The group's most dynamic member was Lewis Jones, a native of Llanfihangel Genau'r-glyn in Cardiganshire, who had also been educated at Ystradmeurig. He was presented to the living of Almondbury in 1822 and was exceptionally active there. He established eighteen new churches and installed Welshmen in each of them. He was elected president of the Society.[51] Another prominent member was Thomas Jones (Llallawg), a native of Manordeifi in Pembrokeshire, who came to Yorkshire at Lewis Jones's invitation and from 1846 was the incumbent of All Saints at Netherthong. He was the biographer of Joseph Hughes and Lewis Jones, and one of the founders of the Cambrian Archaeological Association.[52]

These clerics were interested in all aspects of Welsh life and petitioned the authorities on educational matters as well as administration of the law. But what exercised them most were the shortcomings of the Church in Wales and the treatment it meted out to the Welsh language. Unlike their predecessors, they insisted on exposing the iniquities of the system and did so by petitioning Parliament or by directly attacking non-Welsh-speaking bishops. In 1835 they 'adopted an elaborate memorial to Sir Robert Peel, the then Prime Minister of England, on the necessity of appointing in accordance with the spirit of the Reformation, Welsh bishops to the four Welsh Sees'. This, they recorded in their minutes, 'had been their starting point, and from that day to this they had never once lost sight of it'.[53] Not a year passed without the government's attention being drawn to the matter. Whenever a bishop was, in their opinion, guilty of disregarding the Welsh language, they would write to him in protest. For example, with regard to the appointment of monolingual bishops, they argued 'that the Principality of Wales is entitled, both on national and Scriptural grounds, to the appointment of bishops who are acquainted with the Welsh language in its colloquial and literary use'.[54] At a meeting in 1853 they expressed astonishment that the four bishops had authorized the use of a revised edition of the Welsh Common Prayer Book, even though they had no knowledge of the language in which it was written. And in 1853 a petition was sent to the bishops in Wales declaring, among other things:

> the systematic appointment of Englishmen, utterly ignorant of the language, to fill that important office [i.e. the office of bishop] in Wales, is a ruthless violation of the first principles of common sense, of common justice, and of the Gospel of our Lord Jesus

---

[50] For Joseph Hughes (1803–63), see *Yr Haul*, 10, no. 116 (1866), 230–3 and *DWB*. According to Carn Ingli in the Society's Report, 1 March 1853, they were meeting on 'the thirty-second anniversary of this society', *Report of the Proceedings of the Association of Welsh Clergy . . . March 1st 1853*, p. 4.
[51] For Lewis Jones (1793–1866), see *DWB*.
[52] For Thomas James (1817–79), see *DWB*.
[53] *Report of the Proceedings . . . March 1st 1855*, p. 26.
[54] Ibid. (1853), p. 16.

Christ – leading to the practical exhibition of that barbarous anomaly in the Welsh Church, which St. Paul deprecated and put down in the church at Corinth – that a minister should speak in the church in a language not understood of the people . . .[55]

These men nursed definite ideas about the place of language in worship, as is now evident, and they also upheld the theory about the nature of the Church in Wales as set out in Bishop Richard Davies's 'Epistol at y Cembru' (1567). 'The Church in Wales', wrote Carn Ingli in 1853, 'is the sole representative of the old Celtic Church in this kingdom' ('Yr Eglwys yng Nghymru yw unig gynrychiolydd yr hen Eglwys Geltaidd yn y deyrnas hon'), and he set about tracing its origins to Brân, son of Caradog, who had first brought Christianity to Britain from Rome. Hughes then proceeded to attack the monk Augustine for his vanity and impudence in excommunicating the British bishops because they conformed to the customs and superstitions of Rome. This is, of course, pseudo-history, but it should not be disregarded, for such ideas were contributing to the growth of confidence in the national tradition of the Church in Wales. This, in turn, nurtured a conviction that the language was essential to the life of the nation. Incidentally, one of the concerns of these clergymen (and of Thomas Burgess too) was that the Catholic Church was teaching its priests Welsh.[56] In many ways, there was some significance to the Yorkshire clergymen's protests in their efforts to persuade the Church in Wales to afford the Welsh language an honourable place in its life and administration.

Were these men justified in airing such grievances? Walter T. Morgan has placed historians in his debt by analysing in detail the fortunes of the language in the diocese of St David's during the first half of the century on the basis of the Ecclesiastical Revenues Commission Report and the bishop's visitation of 1828. His conclusions are remarkable.[57] In any consideration of the number of benefices which were in the gift of the bishops, it is evident that there was a marked difference between the two dioceses of north Wales and their two counterparts in the south. Of the 144 livings in the diocese of St Asaph, 120 were in the gift of the bishop. Similarly in Bangor, 78 of the 124 benefices were under the bishop's patronage. But in Llandaff only six out of 192 were in the bishop's gift and in St David's 102 out of 413. Some sixty-six livings in the diocese of St David's were in districts where the ability to speak Welsh was essential. Few of these, according to Walter T. Morgan, were in the possession of clergy not conversant with at least some Welsh.[58] The 'Anglo' bishops can be most criticized in their appointments

---

[55] Ibid., p. 17.
[56] Ibid., pp. 27–30.
[57] Morgan, 'The Diocese of St. David's in the Nineteenth Century', 18–55. In 1835 the Commission to examine the state of the Church was formed and its resolution was made on the basis of the *Ecclesiastical Revenues Commission Report*, Appendix, p. 46.
[58] Morgan, 'The Diocese of St. David's in the Nineteenth Century', 24.

to offices and prebends in the Cathedral Church of St David's and Christ College, Brecon. This is where the service of good Welshmen might have been acknowledged. But, on the whole, this did not occur. Of the twenty prebends at Brecon in 1833, only four were held by Welshmen, although W. J. Rees of Cascob and Archdeacon Thomas Beynon were among them. In the parishes, those who were guilty of appointing alien clergymen were private patrons, alien bishops and corporations such as universities and colleges. The bishops who knew no Welsh were especially at fault for failing to promote able preachers such as David Griffiths of Nevern, David Parry, 'Y Gloch Arian' (The Silver Bell), and David Herbert of Llansanffraid in Cardiganshire,[59] men who would have been able to communicate particularly well with the Welsh speakers. What of the parishes? In the diocese of St David's the provision of Welsh-language services was substantial. In only sixteen of the 103 churches in the archdeaconry of Cardigan were English services held. In the archdeaconry of Carmarthen Welsh services were held in all except twenty-three churches. In the archdeaconry of St David's Welsh was used in thirty-one of the 108 churches and in Breconshire Welsh was used in all but nine of its seventy-four parishes. The provision varied according to demand. There were, however, some exceptions. The town of Swansea can be used as an example to illustrate how it was possible to avoid providing services in Welsh. Chancellor Hewson (who knew no Welsh) claimed that there had been no Welsh services there for fifty years, and yet the perpetual curate of nearby Llangyfelach preached to congregations of a thousand and more, most of whom had moved there from the town of Swansea. The conclusion which must be drawn on the basis of Walter T. Morgan's analysis is that the criticism of non-Welsh-speaking bishops voiced by the Yorkshire clergymen and Dean Henry T. Edwards were not without substance, but that the provision in the parishes was much better than one might have expected in the light of some outspoken comments made about the Englishness of the Church in the heated campaign for Disestablishment.

The most conscious effort to ensure a proper place for Welsh in higher education for clergymen was made by some of the leaders of the Church in Wales. When he came to St David's in 1803 Bishop Thomas Burgess's aim was to establish a worthy seminary within his diocese. He immediately set about raising funds and by 1809 he and his assistants were planning how the college – which was to be called St David's College – would be administered. There would be a staff of six, including a principal and two lecturers who would be Welsh speakers.[60] Many thought of it, therefore, as 'a Welsh college'. Although fund-raising proved a huge task, the plans were completed and on 12 August 1822, on

[59] For David Griffiths (1756–1834), David Parry (1794–1877) and his father-in-law David Herbert (1762–1835), see *DWB*.
[60] For the story in full, including a detailed account of the place of the Welsh language in the college, see Price, *A History of Saint David's University College Lampeter*.

an exceptionally warm day, Bishop Burgess laid the foundation stone after failing to complete his speech because tears were streaming down his cheeks. In 1825, while the college was in the course of construction, the bishop moved to Salisbury. Two years later, on St David's day 1827, St David's College opened its doors to students.

The guardian angel of the Welsh language in the college was Archdeacon Thomas Beynon,[61] who was anxious from the outset that Welsh should have its proper place in the life and work of the college. Beynon was not a man to be taken lightly. He was exceptionally generous in his financial support for the college and took it for granted that his views would be respected. He was to be disappointed and it was a substantial financial loss to the college when he decided not to bequeath anything in his will to 'an English college'.[62] Beynon did not have a high opinion of Rice Rees's command of Welsh,[63] even though the latter was Professor of Welsh at the college from 1827 to 1839. The chair remained empty from 1843 until 1854 and, despite the fact that the work was undertaken by the lecturers, there was concern that the intentions of the founders were not being carried out.[64] A bitter dispute ensued in pamphlets and articles in the press, and wounding remarks were made about the college, including some regarding its attitude towards the Welsh language. Archdeacon John Williams and Sir Benjamin Hall added fuel to the fire.[65] There was clearly cause for complaint. D. T. Jones was completely unsuited to be Professor of Welsh and D. Silvan Evans had not had the opportunity to earn his academic spurs since he had only spent two years in college.[66] Nor was David Williams, who succeeded him as lecturer and professor, equipped for the post and he gave only one hour's instruction in Welsh a week. The truth is that there was little order to the teaching of the subject until John Owen took charge in 1879. He was a fluent Welsh speaker from Llanengan in Llŷn and an accomplished scholar who ensured that Welsh became part of the degree course. Owen had an opportunity to bring about an improvement in the language's status when he became principal in 1892.[67] Yet, the senior officers of the college were lukewarm in their attitude towards the Welsh language. Neither Principal Llewelyn Lewellin nor Francis

---

[61] For Thomas Beynon (1744–1833), patron of poets and eisteddfodau, see *DWB*.

[62] Price, *A History of Saint David's University College Lampeter*, p. 38.

[63] For Rice Rees (1804–39), see *DWB*.

[64] The succession is as follows: Professors: Rice Rees, 1827–39; David Thomas Jones, 1839–43; David Williams, 1854–67; Joseph Hughes, 1868–79; John Owen (later to become the bishop), 1879–85; Owen Evans, 1886–9 and Robert Williams, 1889–1903. Lecturers: Daniel Silvan Evans, 1848; David Williams, 1849–54.

[65] For details of the debate and those who contributed to it, see Price, *A History of Saint David's University College Lampeter*, pp. 78–85.

[66] For Daniel Silvan Evans (1818–1903), appointed Professor of Welsh at the University College of Wales, Aberystwyth, in 1875, see *DWB*.

[67] For John Owen (1854–1926), see the two volumes by Eluned E. Owen, *The Early Life of Bishop Owen: A Son of Lleyn* (Llandysul, 1958) and *The Later Life of Bishop Owen* (Llandysul, 1961).

John Jayne showed the slightest enthusiasm for the native tongue and the vice-principal, J. J. S. Perowne, was stoutly opposed to the teaching of Welsh and believed that it should be removed from the syllabus. For these reasons St David's College did not succeed in realizing the wishes of those who supported the language; nor did it fully conform to the aims and objectives of its founders.

The story was different in the case of some of the church schools. At his school in Lampeter, Eliezer Williams strove to give Welsh an honourable place in the secondary course which he offered his pupils. Even more famous was Ystradmeurig School, which kept its character as a patron of Welsh under John Williams 'Yr Hen Syr' (The Old Sir), who succeeded its founder, Edward Richard, as headmaster. Welsh was the language of the school under Richard and he had succeeded in fostering in his pupils a zeal for the language and its literature.[68] John Williams, the son of 'Yr Hen Syr' and one of the ablest schoolmasters of his generation, became the first warden of Llandovery College, which was established in 1847 and which became an institution that held Welsh in high esteem.

Before leaving the world of scholarship, reference must be made to another matter which caused considerable controversy, particularly among the clergy. At a time when the teaching of Welsh grammar, syntax and literature was limited, many people regarded the Bible as the standard. The writing of Welsh was not taught in Sunday schools and therefore some guidance was required on spelling and sentence construction. As a result, the orthography of the Welsh Bible was important both socially and educationally.

The British and Foreign Bible Society was founded on 7 March 1804 and, since Thomas Charles of Bala had played a prominent part in its establishment, it was decided that its first publication should be a Welsh Bible, under Charles's editorship. Charles took the Bible of 1799, which had been published by the SPCK, as his model and set about revising it. On 21 June 1804 the Society asked him whether 'Mr Owen, Penton Street' would be a suitable proof-reader. Charles agreed. The 'Mr Owen' was William Owen Pughe.[69] When John Roberts, curate of Tremeirchion and editor of the 1799 Bible, got wind of these developments, he decided to protest. He wrote to George Gaskin, Secretary of the SPCK, on 31 December 1804, drawing his attention to the Bible Society's intentions.[70] He had

---

[68] For Edward Richard (1714–77) and John Williams (1745/6–1818), see *DWB*. For the school and the famous people educated there, see D. G. Osborne-Jones, *Edward Richard of Ystradmeurig* (Carmarthen, 1934).

[69] The standard study on Charles (1755–1814) is D. E. Jenkins, *The Life of the Rev. Thomas Charles, B.A., of Bala* (3 vols., Denbigh, 1908). An account of the quarrel regarding orthography, together with details of the correspondence between the different sides, is to be found in the second volume. For Pughe, see Glenda Carr, *William Owen Pughe* (Caerdydd, 1983). He adopted the surname Pughe following the death of Rice Pughe, vicar of Nantglyn and a distant relative. He died on 8 October 1806, leaving him a considerable bequest.

[70] For John Roberts (1775–1829), see *DWB*. He was made vicar of Tremeirchion in 1807.

not seen Charles's revisions but was aware that William Owen Pughe's theories had influenced the orthography of Thomas Charles's *Trysorfa Ysprydol* (1799) and feared that the same principles would be applied to the Bible Society's new Bible. The matter soon came to the attention of Church leaders. On 9 January 1805 Gaskin wrote to Beilby Porteus, bishop of London and one of the vice-presidents of the Bible Society,[71] who then wrote to Lord Teignmouth, the Society's president.[72] On the same day, 9 January 1805, at the request of the SPCK, William Agutter wrote to Teignmouth confirming John Roberts's misgivings as facts. John Roberts's letter had been read to the society, and it was evident that:

> in the new edition of the Bible in Welsh very unwarrantable liberties are taken in altering the translation. For this there can be no authority; and it has already excited a prejudice against the designs of the Society. Perhaps some alterations might be desirable, yet without an adequate authority it could establish a dangerous precedent.[73]

In fairness, John Roberts's allegation was not that Charles had altered the translation but that he had tampered with the orthography, but such matters were no doubt something of a closed book to the English. Gradually more and more important people – bishops, clergymen and scholars – were drawn into the whirlpool. And to make matters worse, there was disagreement between the Bible Society and the SPCK concerning which edition of the Welsh Bible to choose as a model – the 1799, 1752 or 1746 edition. The Bible Society nominated Gwallter Mechain as mediator between the two parties – a curious choice, in view of the fact that he was a close friend of John Roberts. By 22 February Charles had completed his revision of the Bible and had sent it to Gwallter Mechain. But John Roberts was still uneasy and expressed his concern once again in a letter to Thomas Smith, secretary of the Sunday School Association: 'Like the British Constitution, our Welsh orthography is already fixed and established; any attempt to overthrow the one as well as the other, I think equally improper.'[74] In his opinion, the standard orthography was that of Dr John Davies, Mallwyd, found in the Bible of 1620. The quarrel became even more public with the publication of *An Address to Lord Teignmouth . . . By a Country Clergyman* (1805). The anonymous author was Thomas Sikes, incumbent of Guilsborough in Northamptonshire.[75] His pamphlet was a stinging attack on the Bible Society and reference to the Welsh Bible was confined to a short appendix. In that Bible, he

---

[71] This is the present name of the society and is less clumsy than the original!
[72] For Beilby Porteus (1731–1808), see *DNB*. The letter may be found in William Dealtry, *A Vindication of the British and Foreign Bible Society* (2nd ed., London, 1811), Appendix C, pp. viii–ix.
[73] Ibid., p. viii. John Shore (1751–1834) was first Baron of Teignmouth. He was president of the society from 1804 until his death, see *DNB*.
[74] Dealtry, *A Vindication*, Appendix C, pp. x–xi. Agutter was chaplain of the 'Asylum for Female Orphans' in London.
[75] Jenkins, *Life of the Rev. Thomas Charles*, II, pp. 569–70.

wrote, 'such liberties are taken in its translation as are by no means warrantable'. He admitted that he did not know a word of Welsh and was thus unable to express an opinion on the veracity of the rumour.[76] A reply was published immediately in the form of a pamphlet entitled *A Letter to a Country Clergyman, occasioned by his Address to Lord Teignmouth . . . By a Sub-urban Clergyman*, written by John Owen, Secretary of the Bible Society.[77] When he came to discuss the insinuations made by Sikes about the Welsh Bible, he explained that Charles had not changed the orthography but had only rendered it more consistent and that he had done so on the basis of the various authorized editions.[78] In short, Sikes's guns were very effectively spiked. The sharp edge to the attack on his work perplexed Charles, but in a letter to Robert Jones of Rhos-lan he claimed he had received an assurance that 'J. Humphreys' was at the root of it. The aggrieved Humphreys had helped him with the *Geiriadur Ysgrythyrawl* and had been cast out when the partnership was brought to an end in August 1804.[79] Despite the furore, on 13 May 1805 the Bible Society appointed William Owen Pughe to read the proofs of the new Bible. The Bible Society's work had prompted the SPCK to prepare a new edition, and the following day, 14 May, the arrangements were made. And who were the editors? John Roberts and Gwallter Mechain. For weeks Gwallter had been busy playing a double game and keeping a firm grasp on the revised Bible which Charles had sent him.

Thomas Charles completed the task of revision and the Bible was sent to the Cambridge Press for printing. William Owen Pughe made such a hash of reading the proofs that the Bible Society rejected him and his orthography. As a result the Bible Society's New Testament was published in 1806 and the complete Bible the following year – shorn of William Owen Pughe's orthography. The dispute continued to smoulder and emitted one more flame in 1810 when Christopher Wordsworth published his *Reasons for declining to become a Subscriber to the British and Foreign Bible Society*. Wordsworth, the poet's younger brother, was a distinguished scholar who, in 1820, became Master of Trinity College, Cambridge.[80] The work, an attack on the Bible Society as an institution hostile to the Church of England, revived the old insinuations about the Welsh Bible which, it claimed, had caused such 'great dismay' among the clergy of Wales that

---

[76] He died on 14 December 1834 at the age of sixty-eight. See J. Owen, *The History of the Origin and First Ten Years of the British and Foreign Bible Society* (London, 1816), pp. 32, 155–9, 222–5.

[77] Thomas Sikes, *An Address to Lord Teignmouth . . . By a Country Clergyman* (London, 1805), pp. 35–6.

[78] John Owen (1766–1822) was curate of Fulham, Middlesex, and rector of Pegelsham, Essex, from 1808 onwards. See *Gentleman's Magazine*, LXXXIII (1813), 226–8 and *DNB*.

[79] John Owen, *A Letter to a Country Clergyman* (London, 1805), p. 57.

[80] An English translation of the letter to Robert Jones is to be found in Jenkins, *Life of the Rev. Thomas Charles*, II, pp. 578–9. John Humphreys (1767–1829) was a native of Caerwys and was ordained by the Calvinistic Methodists in 1816. He and Charles were later reconciled.

they were turning to the SPCK for a supply of correct Bibles.[81] William Dealtry replied in *A Vindication of the British and Foreign Bible Society* (1810). He bungled the Welsh references so badly that when Charles saw the pamphlet he sent Dealtry his corrections,[82] which were incorporated in a second edition published in 1811.[83] Dealtry's *Vindication* is a lively and entertaining work which includes an able defence of the Bible Society as well as valuable information about the way in which the Society's Bible had been prepared. A further exchange of pamphlets between Wordsworth and Dealtry followed.

No sooner had the Bible Society decided to publish a new edition than John Roberts – a keen supporter of the Society – began to ask yet more questions.[84] He now suggested that the approval of the bishops of Wales should be sought for the new edition. Charles was disheartened to learn of the fresh misgivings but, with the generosity which never deserted him, he added: 'I shall do nothing to revile him but will seek to follow the example of He who "when he was reviled, reviled not again"' ('ni wnaf ddim i'w dilorni ond ceisio dilyn esiampl yr Un "pan ddifenwyd na ddifenwodd drachefn"').[85] When the Committee of the Bible Society met on 30 October 1813 it decided to adopt John Roberts's suggestion: proofs of the Bible were sent to the bishops and they gave their approval. According to the minutes of the Bible Society's meeting held on 3 October 1814, a copy of the new Welsh Bible, modelled on the SPCK's Bible of 1810, was given to each member. Two days later, Thomas Charles died. Wales is substantially indebted to John Roberts for safeguarding the Welsh Bible from the follies of William Owen Pughe, and to Thomas Charles for his geniality in the face of bitter criticism and for his flexibility in accepting John Roberts's suggestions.

Another small storm concerning orthography is worth placing on record. On 11 November 1825 Joseph Tarn, Secretary of the Bible Society, wrote to John Jones (Tegid),[86] Precentor of Christ Church, Oxford, suggesting that a bilingual New Testament should be published. Although it was to be a joint project with the Bible Society, this would appear under the patronage of the SPCK. John Jones immediately wrote to his friend, Gwallter Mechain, to enquire which

---

[81] According to the article about him in *DNB*, he was a man 'with sympathy for whatever was good and noble in others, and tolerance for dissenters'. The pamphlet does not substantiate this description.

[82] Christopher Wordsworth, *Reasons for declining to become a Subscriber to the British and Foreign Bible Society* (London, 1810), p. 13.

[83] William Dealtry (1775–1847) graduated from Trinity College, Cambridge, in the same year as Wordsworth. They knew each other although as Churchmen they were poles apart in their beliefs.

[84] D. E. Jenkins's criticism of John Roberts and his friends in *Life of the Rev. Thomas Charles*, III, p. 495, and in other places, is too harsh. He and Charles shared the same evangelical convictions and Roberts's letters indicate that he was inspired by a genuine zeal to protect the accuracy of the text of the Welsh Bible.

[85] Jenkins, *Life of the Rev. Thomas Charles*, III, p. 498.

[86] For John Jones (1792–1852), see *DNB* and *DWB*.

orthography was best suited to the task. He had also consulted Dr Charles Lloyd about the matter and the latter's advice was to 'do things in a quiet way without consulting the "Blind leader of the Blind", the Polyphemus of the flock, the Rev. J. Roberts, of Tremeirchion'.[87] This unsound piece of advice was duly followed and the work appeared under the title *The New Testament in Welsh and English. Testament Newydd . . .* (1826). A rumpus ensued. John Jones was one of the supporters of William Owen Pughe's orthography, but William Bruce Knight, vicar of Margam and chancellor of the diocese of Llandaff from 1825, now entered the fray as his adversary.[88] Knight was an excellent Hebrew scholar with a good command of Welsh. Indeed, Sir John Morris-Jones claimed that to him belonged 'the chief credit' for rescuing the Welsh Bible 'from the vandalism of Pughe's followers'[89] – a verdict not entirely fair to John Roberts of Tremeirchion. At the Carmarthen Eisteddfod of 1823 John Roberts had won a prize for a treatise which was subsequently published under the title *Reasons for rejecting the Welsh Orthography that is proposed and attempted to be introduced, with a view to superseding the system that has been established since the publication of Dr Davies's Grammar and Dictionary, and Bishop Parry's Edition of the Welsh Bible* (1825). The title reveals Roberts's point of view and William Bruce Knight was in complete agreement with him. Naturally, Gwallter Mechain was ill pleased with both of them. Of Roberts he wrote: 'a pious man, and a good divine according to the Geneva creed; but bigoted in his system of orthography', and Knight, he maintained, 'stands on the shoulders of Mr Roberts'.[90]

In the spring of 1828 the Welsh text of the New Testament was published separately under the editorship of John Jones.[91] Knight immediately expressed his opposition to the orthography, and petitioning against the Testament began. In the diocese of Bangor a petition to the bishop was signed by seventy-two clergymen[92] and at Llandaff Knight and eighty of his supporters signed another.[93] John Jones believed that Henry Majendie[94] was behind this flurry of activity and that John Roberts was egging him on. The upshot was that the SPCK and the Bible Society rejected John Jones's Testament and the printing was halted,

---

[87] Letter dated 12 November 1825, in D. Silvan Evans (ed.), *Gwaith Gwallter Mechain. Volume III. The English Works of the Rev. Walter Davies, M.A. (Gwallter Mechain)* (Carmarthen and London, 1868), pp. 220–1.

[88] For Knight (1785–1845), see Evans, *A Chapter in the History of the Welsh Book of Common Prayer*, III, pp. 237–50 and *DWB*.

[89] John Morris-Jones, *A Welsh Grammar, historical and comparative* (Oxford, 1913), p. xviii.

[90] Evans (ed.), *The English Works of . . . Walter Davies*, p. 248.

[91] Ibid., pp. 232, 239.

[92] The number, according to John Jones, was seventy-five. Ibid., p. 238.

[93] For the petitions, see William Bruce Knight, *Remarks, Historical and Philological, on the Welsh Language* (Cardiff, 1830).

[94] Henry Majendie, Prebendary of Penmynydd in the diocese of Bangor and son of Bishop William Majendie, was vicar of Speen in Berkshire. For Jones's doubt, see Evans (ed.), *The English Works of . . . Walter Davies*, pp. 238–9.

although an appreciable number of copies had already been sold. John Jones was unrepentant. He defended his position in his pamphlet, *A Defence of the Reformed System of Welsh Orthography* (1829) and the following year he published a treatise which had won him the gold medal at an eisteddfod in Carmarthen, namely *Traethawd ar Iawn-lythreniad neu Lythyraeth yr iaith Gymraeg*. The adjudicators were none other than Gwallter Mechain and William Owen Pughe.[95] This was more than William Bruce Knight could bear and he replied with his *Remarks, Historical and Philological, on the Welsh Language* (1830). He presented his learned arguments in favour of the classical orthography ably and convincingly. And, except for the publication of two more pamphlets, one by Jones and the other by Knight, that was the end of the attempt by William Owen Pughe and his followers to interfere with the orthography of the Welsh Bible.[96]

To sum up. A detailed examination reveals that considerable tension existed between two parties throughout the nineteenth century. On the one hand, the bishops and Church dignitaries cared little for the Welsh language and knew next to nothing about the literature and history of Wales. Some of them believed that it would be a service if its demise were to be hastened. It is true that there were some exceptions, such as Thomas Burgess and Connop Thirlwall, but it was inevitable that alien bishops would appoint clergy who were either themselves alien or who shared their prejudices with regard to Welsh. On the other hand, throughout the century a succession of clergymen looked upon the Church as an essentially Welsh institution. They took delight in its past contribution to the cultural and spiritual life of Wales. But it was not easy to campaign against the deep prejudices of their opponents because the power to decide who was to be honoured with preferment within the Church lay in their hands.

Towards the end of the century the tension was given eloquent expression by Canon David Jones who, having been brought up as a Calvinistic Methodist in Llangeitho, had become an excellent Welsh scholar and one of the most powerful preachers in the Church. He had also lectured in Welsh at St Mary's College, Bangor, from 1889 to 1895. In his book, *The Welsh Church and Welsh Nationality* (1893), he argued powerfully in favour of giving Welsh its proper place in the Church in Wales. He believed it was the Church of Wales, even though it was called the Church of England. He took delight in the work of those luminaries who had defended the dignity of Welsh from Bishop Richard Davies to Dean Henry T. Edwards and did not refrain from berating those church dignitaries who scorned the language. This is how he viewed the battle at the end of the century:

---

[95] Letter from Jones to Charles Lloyd, 31 March 1829. Ibid., pp. 237–9.
[96] For the quarrel regarding the amendment of the Book of Prayer following Victoria's ascent to the throne, see Evans, *A Chapter in the History of the Welsh Book of Common Prayer*, passim.

The body of the clergy are becoming more and more sympathetic with the genius, the national temperament, and characteristics of the people. Authority and power are from above; popular influence and reform have hitherto come from below. The inferior clergy, as they are called, are winning their way among the Welsh-speaking masses, in the face of formidable difficulties; but the dignitaries, as such, are still content, for the most part, to confine their attention to the English-speaking section . . . it can be proved that . . . [the Church] was saved from actual extinction in Welsh centres, not by well-paid incumbents, but by Welsh-speaking curates, who kept alive the fire on her altars for a miserable pittance, while the alien and alienised pluralists who hired them, were accumulating or dissipating fortunes in luxury and lethargy.[97]

Strong words, but not without justification. The picture was confused and if Welsh had its enemies it also had its fervent allies throughout the century. But people like David Jones were in a difficult position. He argued wholeheartedly in favour of cultural nationalism, but set his face against any kind of political nationalism. By 1893 the disestablishment of the Church had become a heated subject. Would disestablishment mean hastening the end of the Church or would it bring about a fairer deal for the language? On the other hand, the fact that it had been an inextricable part of the Established Church of England for so long had cost the Welsh language dearly. Only time would tell in whose favour this complicated battle would turn.

---

[97] David Jones, *The Welsh Church and Welsh Nationality* (Bangor, 1893), pp. 113–14; for David Jones (d. 2 June 1909 at the age of sixty-two), see R. R. Hughes, *Biographical Epitomes of the Bishops and Clergy of the Diocese of Bangor* (1932), Part IV, 462–3. He was rector of Llanfair-pwll, 1888–95.

8

Nonconformity and the Welsh Language in the Nineteenth Century

R. TUDUR JONES

ALTHOUGH it will be necessary to qualify the statement as the following analysis develops, on the whole it can be said that Welsh was the language of the Nonconformist churches in the nineteenth century. Their worship, administration and dealings with one another in conference, assembly and association were carried out in Welsh. There were, of course, exceptions to the rule prior to 1800 and thereafter. The records of Eglwys Mynydd-bach in Llangyfelach, like many others, were kept in English, and it was common for English inscriptions such as 'Baptist Chapel' and 'Salem Independent Chapel' to be placed on the façade of chapel buildings.[1] By 1800 these denominations were becoming increasingly successful in winning the affections of common people who had no knowledge of English. A growing number of the leaders, moreover, came from the same social class. One of the characteristics of these churches was that members were granted a prominent place in their administration, and in the running not only of individual churches but also of inter-church meetings such as Methodist Associations. It was therefore inevitable that Welsh was the language of these meetings.

As in all Protestant churches, a central place was given to the Bible, and in this case it was the Welsh Bible. Every church member was expected to have his or her own copy of the Bible and to master its contents. But since members were also expected to assimilate its contents within a doctrinal framework, it was essential that theological guidelines were prepared for that purpose. Among the 'Old Dissenters' – the Congregationalists and Baptists – the learning of catechisms was a regular discipline. There was widespread use of 'Catecism Byrraf y Gymanfa' (The Shortest Catechism of the Assembly) – the catechism presented to Parliament by the Westminster Assembly of April 1648. There was, for example, *Catechism o'r Scrythur, Yn Nhrefn Gwyr y Gymanfa*, published in 1717 with the approval of eleven Dissenting ministers. Indeed, one of the first books to be

---

[1] Photographs of some of these plaques are included in Anthony Jones, *Capeli Cymru* (Caerdydd, 1984), illustrations 59–70.

printed in Wales was *Eglurhaad o Gatechism Byrraf y Gymanfa* (1719), a translation by John Pugh, the Congregational minister of Henllan, of the original English version by Thomas Vincent. Matthew Henry's *Catecism byr i Blant*, translated by Jenkin Evans, an Oswestry minister, had been available since 1708. The catechism of the Church of England was widely used both outside and within that church, as was the catechism of Griffith Jones, Llanddowror. With the dawn of the nineteenth century came *Yr Hyfforddwr* by Thomas Charles of Bala, the first edition of which was published in 1807. By the end of the century it had appeared in eighty editions. During the century, moreover, a substantial number of catechisms were published, some with very limited circulation.

In order to appreciate their significance, it should be borne in mind that adults and especially children were steeped in these catechisms. In some churches, mastery of the catechism was a condition of full membership. There must have been tens of thousands of children brought up in Calvinistic Methodist churches who carried the contents of *Yr Hyfforddwr* in their heads for the rest of their lives. As far as the language was concerned, this meant that they were well used to treating quite abstruse subjects through the medium of Welsh. Indeed, learning by heart was considered very important in Nonconformist churches. Not everyone had the powers of Margaret Jones of Ganllwyd, Merioneth, who learnt the whole of the New Testament in the year 1821, nor of Dr Owen Thomas who, as a child, could recite the New Testament from beginning to end,[2] but there were very many people who were familiar with this discipline.

The discipline of the churches combined the printed and spoken word. There can hardly have been a time in the history of Wales when so many people were exposed to so much public speaking, of which the sermon was the most common form. Preachers travelled from place to place in order to spread the Gospel. In the eighteenth century the Old Dissenters did not approve of Methodists who roamed the country on preaching tours, but by the end of the century they, too, had adopted the practice. In 1790, for example, Christmas Evans set out – not at the invitation of any church or committee, but of his own accord – on a journey that would take him from Llŷn to south Wales. Since the Baptists of Llŷn could not afford to buy him a horse, he travelled on foot as far as Penrhyn-coch, then on to Aberystwyth, Newcastle Emlyn, Cardigan, Blaen-waun and Newport, Pembrokeshire. His preaching was not confined to chapels. By his own testimony: 'The cemeteries and meeting-houses would be full of people thronging to hear me in mid-harvest. I would often preach in the open air at evening – and the singing and praising would continue for as long as the light lasted' ('Byddai llon'd y mynwentydd a'r tai cyrddau o wrandawyr yn ymdyru i'm gwrando yn nghanol y cynhauaf medi. Byddwn yn pregethu allan yn fynych yn yr hwyr – a'r canu a'r

---

[2] *Y Dysgedydd*, I, no. 11 (1822), 344; D. Ben Rees, *Pregethwr y Bobl: Bywyd a Gwaith Dr Owen Thomas* (Lerpwl, 1979), p. 19.

molianu yn parhau dan ddydd goleu').[3] His most recent biographer has claimed that it is quite probable that no nineteenth-century preacher, of whatever denomination, travelled the length and breadth of Wales, and beyond, more often than Christmas Evans.[4] During his lifetime he travelled between north and south Wales 43 times and delivered 164 sermons.[5] Then there was John Jones of Tal-y-sarn, whose last preaching tour of south Wales began in Cardiff on 14 October 1855 and took him through the Vale of Glamorgan to Carmarthen, Llechryd, Blaenannerch, Cardigan, Tŵr-gwyn, Newcastle Emlyn and Swansea and back to north Wales, to Llangollen and Wrexham, finishing on 27 November. He set off again on 3 December, when he travelled through Merioneth and Caernarfonshire and completed his journey on the last day of the year.[6] By then the era of itinerant preaching in the old style was drawing to a close and, as the railways spread like a web through Wales, the practice of wandering from place to place on foot or on horseback was losing its appeal. An enormous network of meetings and assemblies was formed and itinerant preachers travelled around in trains without getting their feet wet. The purpose of all this activity was to spread the Gospel among the Welsh-speaking people. As regards the language, since the preachers attracted thousands of listeners, thousands were given the opportunity of hearing robust Welsh. Their vocabulary was enriched and they received excellent training in public speaking. Preachers provided a fine example of how Welsh should be used in public life.

What did the preachers make of the language as a medium? One of the difficulties in any discussion on this matter is that we have to depend so heavily on printed sermons; several generations were to pass before it became possible to record the speaking voice. Before they were printed, sermons were heavily edited according to the fashionable canons of the day. Only a few examples exist of sermons taken down verbatim in short-hand, as in the case of a sermon delivered by Evan Harries of Merthyr Tydfil in Bala in 1836,[7] or the twenty-eight sermons of John Jones, Tal-y-sarn, taken down by his son, Thomas Lloyd Jones.[8] A clearer idea of the quality of preaching is to be obtained in the remarkable chapter in Owen Thomas's history of Welsh preaching, and in particular his descriptions of preachers whom he had actually heard.[9]

[3] William Morgan, *Cofiant, neu hanes bywyd, y diweddar Christmas Evans* (Caerdydd, 1839), p. 25.
[4] D. Densil Morgan, *Christmas Evans a'r Ymneilltuaeth Newydd* (Llandysul, 1991), p. 82.
[5] J. T. Jones, *Christmas Evans* (Llandysul, 1938), p. 47.
[6] Owen Thomas, *Cofiant y Parchedig John Jones, Talsarn* (Wrexham, [1874]), pp. 711–13, 717.
[7] Roger Edwards, *Y Gofadail Fethodistaidd* (Dinbych, 1880), pp. 144–8. According to this book, Harries was born in 1784; according to *DWB* he was born in 1786. He died on 20 November 1861. See also Thomas Levi, *Cofiant a phregethau y Parch. Evan Harries, Merthyr* (Abertawy, [1869]).
[8] Thomas, *Cofiant John Jones*, p. 1032.
[9] Ibid., pp. 792–970. Owen Thomas had a remarkable memory. When he was a child he learnt the Epistle according to St James while his parents were attending a service. He made notes of the sermons he heard. It appears that he could read both English and Welsh when he was between four and five years old. John J. Roberts, *Cofiant y Parch. Owen Thomas, Liverpool* (Caernarfon, 1912), p. 24, and Rees, *Pregethwr y Bobl*, p. 17.

Since the century had raised so many preachers, there was considerable variety in the way they deployed the language. There was, on the one hand, the dignified, well-ordered style of preachers such as Henry Rees and Edward Morgan of Dyffryn Ardudwy, and, on the other, the *hwyl* of the likes of Dafydd Rolant.[10] Even more extreme were Dafydd Evans of Ffynnonhenri, whose colourful exegesis of biblical stories bordered on the indecent, and the 'Jack' preachers whom David Owen (Brutus) pilloried and satirized.[11] The sermons were heavily influenced by various literary styles – that of the Puritans, Hugh Blair and Dr Edward Williams, as well as the contemporary English style, and that of spoken Welsh. Henry Rees admitted that his discovery of Puritan literature had made a deep impression on him and that the literature of Dr John Owen had changed the course of his life.[12] The works of Dr John Owen (1616–83) were extremely popular during the first half of the nineteenth century, owing to the fact that he was a great-grandson of Baron Lewis Owen and that Hugh Owen of Bronclydwr was his mother's first cousin. He influenced men as different from one another as William Rees (Gwilym Hiraethog), John Davies of Nerquis, Edward Morgan of Dyffryn Ardudwy, Owen Thomas and many more. Imitation of Puritan preachers and their preoccupation with dividing their sermons into sections and subsections had a detrimental effect on Henry Rees's sermons, but he soon abandoned this style. He refused to abandon the detailed way in which he prepared his sermons, however, and they were often rewritten three or four times.[13] Hugh Blair was appointed Regius Professor of Rhetoric and Belles Lettres at the University of Edinburgh in 1762. He published his lectures on Rhetoric in 1783 and became extremely popular. His sermons, which he began publishing in 1777, were also highly regarded. In the public's view, they were the finest examples of the polished style of the eighteenth century,[14] 'though it was said he took so long to dress his sermons that they caught cold'.[15] Considerable attention was paid to Blair's ideas in connection with Welsh

---

[10] For Henry Rees (1798–1869), see Owen Thomas, *Cofiant y Parchedig Henry Rees* (2 vols., Wrexham, 1891) and *DWB*; for Edward Morgan (1817–71), see Griffith Ellis, *Cofiant y Parchedig Edward Morgan, Dyffryn* (1906) and *DWB*. For Dafydd Rolant (1795–1862), see Owen Jones, *Cofiant y diweddar Dafydd Rolant y Bala* (Wrexham, [1863]) and *DWB.*, s.n. Rowland, David.

[11] For Dafydd Evans (1778–1866), Baptist minister, see *DWB* and Benjamin Thomas (Myfyr Emlyn), *Dafydd Evans, Ffynonhenry, Castellnewydd-Emlyn* (Llanelli, 1870), of which thousands of copies were sold. For David Owen (Brutus, 1795–1866), see *DWB*. For his attacks against the 'Jacks', see David Owen (Brutus), *Wil Brydydd y Coed*, ed. Thomas Jones (Caerdydd, 1949) and idem, *Bugeiliaid Epynt*, ed. Thomas Jones (Caerdydd, 1950).

[12] Thomas, *Cofiant y Parchedig Henry Rees*, I, pp. 116–17.

[13] Ibid., I, p. 121.

[14] For Hugh Blair (1718–1800), see Nigel M. de S. Cameron (ed.), *Dictionary of Scottish Church History and Theology* (Edinburgh, 1993) and the introduction to his *Lectures on Rhetoric and Belles Lettres* (London, 1823), I.

[15] John W. Oman, *Concerning the Ministry* (London, 1936), p. 124.

poetry,[16] but the ideas which are of interest to students of poetry had little or no influence on preaching styles. Other parts of his work are more relevant to that subject. He had much to say in his three volumes of lectures about language, syntax and grammar. More importantly, he had chapters on preaching style as well as a detailed description of the best way to prepare an address or sermon. When someone accused Christmas Evans of failing to write his sermons according to Blair's rules, he replied that he was 'his own Blair'.[17] He was referring to these parts of Blair's lectures. He adapted his general principles to preaching – his emphasis on the 'sublime' – and held that large parts of the Bible's style were a suitable pattern because its pages are replete with sublime subjects. The preacher must reject the trivial and the ordinary, as well as the moribund, and care must be taken that the language of preaching is pure and simple, so that the sublime is not insulted with inappropriate words and the insignificant is not inflated and treated as if it were sublime.[18]

The foremost of Blair's disciples in Wales was William Williams (Caledfryn), although he did not accept every one of Blair's shibboleths. In 1861 he wrote an article entitled 'Arddull y Pulpud' (Pulpit Style),[19] in which he claimed that the purpose of preaching was 'to teach, to satisfy, and to influence', a definition he had derived from Dr Edward Williams. He was no doubt referring to Williams's book, *The Christian Preacher* (1800),[20] wherein he found the quotation from an essay by John Claude, a French Protestant minister. But the original definition derives from Cicero and was adapted to Christian preaching by Augustine,[21] and is therefore a wholly classical definition. Caledfryn insisted that sermons should contain noble thoughts, but that since these were already found in the Bible, a preacher should not seek to add to the power of Scripture by using a noble style and grandiloquent turns of phrase. Simple, unassuming language was best suited to the great themes of the preacher, and in this he echoed Blair almost word for word. A preacher should employ a variety of styles and avoid 'bombast on the one hand and low, impoverished speech on the other'('chwyddiaith ar un llaw, ac iaith isel salw, ar y llaw arall').[22] He then turned to the importance of language. Grammar must be properly understood and dialect avoided. Obscurity of thought

---

[16] This was done by Gwenallt in his study of Islwyn, by Huw Llywelyn Williams in *Safonau Beirniadu Barddoniaeth yng Nghymru yn y Bedwaredd Ganrif ar Bymtheg* (Llundain, 1941) and by E. G. Millward, 'Eben Fardd fel Beirniad', *LlC*, III, no. 3 (1955), 162–87.

[17] John Thomas, *Traethodau, Pregethau, yn nghyd a hanes ei daith yn America* (Utica, N.Y., 1865), p. 128.

[18] Blair, *Lectures*, I, pp. 69, 75, 87, 89.

[19] William Williams, *Cofiant Caledfryn* (Bala, 1877), pp. 107–34. For William Williams (Caledfryn, 1801–69), see also *DWB*.

[20] See W. T. Owen's interesting remarks in *Edward Williams D.D. 1750–1813: His Life, Thought and Influence* (Cardiff, 1963), pp. 72–5.

[21] See Charles Rollin, *The Method of Teaching and Studying the Belles Lettres* (London, 1734), II, pp. 51, 304–5.

[22] Williams, *Cofiant Caledfryn*, p. 114; cf. Blair, *Lectures*, II, p. 293.

and expression must be avoided by eschewing made-up words such as *'cythreuledigion'* (devilishnesses) and *'tragwyddoldebau'* (eternities). He mounted a scathing attack on the use of coarse and inappropriate expressions, such as *'braich o gnawd'* (an arm of flesh), in the pulpit. 'An arm of flesh!', he exclaimed, 'An arm of flesh is not worth anything; it supports no weight; there is no bone in an arm of flesh' ('Braich o gnawd! nid ydyw braich o gnawd werth dim; ni ddeil ddim pwysau; nid oes dim asgwrn mewn braich o gnawd'). Metaphors and inappropriate turns of phrase came under his lash in the same way, reaching a climax in a ferocious attack on preachers who told stories and anecdotes in the pulpit.[23] He disapproved of preachers who mispronounced the language, used English words and displayed scholarship. In short, he followed Blair fairly closely. Indeed, striking similarities are revealed when two sermons on the same subject are compared: 'the way of this world that passeth away' in Blair's *Sermons* and *Cofiant Caledfryn*. Although the Scot excels in his construction of sentences, comparison of the texts in their entirety is most revealing. The truth is that Caledfryn's protest suggests that it was necessary to advise preachers to improve their style, although there was an obvious danger that his classical emphasis would produce preaching by rote.

Some preachers were prone to go to extremes. Brutus was not far from the truth in his attacks on the 'Jacks'. One reason for this was that some preachers had seized upon Blair's declarations about sublimity without reading in detail his lengthy explanation of his ideas. This had created the 'poetic preaching' which aroused the fury of Dr John Thomas, Liverpool:

Y mae gennym ddosbarth o bregethwyr barddonol. Mae yr hyn a elwir yn grebwyll a darfelydd yn gryf iawn ynddynt. Rhoddant dafod ac iaith i bob peth trwy y greadigaeth; personolant y cwbl mewn natur, crwydrant trwy y cyfan-fyd yn ol ac yn mlaen, ffrwynant y gwynt, a marchogant y cwmwl . . . A phan y byddo dychymyg barddonol cryf yn cael ei ffrwyno gan farn gywir . . . y mae yn brydferth dros ben. Ond pan y clywom ddynion yn mwrddro meddyliau, yn cymysgu ffugyrau, ac yn galw yr epäod disynwyr yr esgorodd eu heneidiau bwhwmanllyd arnynt, yn 'syniadau barddonol', ac yn disgwyl i ni gydnabod dychmygion eu hymenyddiau meddalion yn 'farddoniaeth ysgrythyrol', y mae yr haerllugrwydd yn fwy nag a all ein natur ddyoddef.[24]

(We have a class of poetic preachers. What is called fancy and imagination is very strong in them. They give tongue and expression to everything in creation; they personalize everything in nature, they wander through the universe, to and fro, they rein in the

---

[23] Williams, *Cofiant Caledfryn*, pp. 122–3. He maintained that the practice began some forty years earlier (i.e. *c.*1820). He listed preachers who never used anecdotes in their sermons: David Charles, John Elias, Ebeneser Morris, Ebenezer Richards, Thomas Richards, George Lewis, Thomas Phillips, Griffith Hughes (Y Groes-wen), William Jones (Bridgend), Williams o'r Wern, David Morgan (Machynlleth), John Breese, Joseph Harris, John Herring and Christmas Evans.
[24] Thomas, *Traethodau, Pregethau*, pp. 118–19.

wind, and they ride the clouds . . . And when a strong poetic imagination is reined in by correct judgement . . . it is exceedingly beautiful. But when we hear men murdering their thoughts, mixing up figures of speech, and calling the senseless apes to which their wavering souls have given birth 'poetic ideas', and expecting us to recognize the imaginings of their soft minds as 'scriptural poetry', their effrontery is more than our nature can bear.)

One wonders who these preachers were, with their 'fancy' and 'imagination'. We can venture a guess. In *Y Dysgedydd* (February 1850), there appeared an article by 'Siôn Gymro' attacking 'imaginative preaching' ('pregethu dychmygion'). For John Davies (Siôn Gymro), 'imaginative' could be applied to statements such as: 'God raises a mortgage on the sun before he sells a sinner' ('Bod Duw yn codi *mortgage* ar yr haul cyn gwerthu pechadur'), or a description of hell 'as a place with a clock whose pendulum has stopped at midnight' ('fel man y byddai cloc ynddo, a'r *pendulum* wedi sefyll ar hanner nos'), or 'take a dragon's feathers to adorn and strengthen the wings of an angel' ('Cymeryd plu draig i addurno a chryfhau adenydd angel'), or 'put a soul in the best sitting room in heaven in which to play the pianoforte' ('rhoi enaid yn y *best sitting room* yn y nef i chwarae y *pianoforte*').[25]

It is significant that the man who entered the fray in order to criticize the classicism of Siôn Gymro was John Roberts (J.R.). His argument was that there were similar metaphors and similes in the Bible and that those which concerned Siôn Gymro were as poetic as the biblical examples. The debate dragged on until 1852, but Siôn Gymro was unable to hold the fort of classicism against the arguments of J.R. and his colleagues. 'Poetic preaching' had arrived.[26] There is no doubt that J.R. was the apostle of this kind of preaching by virtue of his simple, chatty and interesting style. Later on he was to mix the chatting with excessive shouting.[27] He was a seminal influence on young preachers. When Edward Humphreys, at the beginning of his career, used short, alliterative sentences in the style of J.R., Dr Hugh Jones feared that Samuel Davies would not support him since Davies's denominational zeal extended even to preaching style and he believed that poetic preaching was characteristic of the Congregationalists.[28] Whether this was true or not, Humphreys succeeded in transferring the style into the Wesleyan camp. We must go one step further. According to H. Elvet Lewis

---

[25] For John Davies (Siôn Gymro, 1804–84), see *DWB* and the biography by Ben Davies, *Siôn Gymro, sef buchedd a gwaith John Davies, Glandŵr a Moreia, Penfro* (Llandysul, 1938).

[26] A synopsis of the argument is to be found in E. Pan Jones, *Cofiant y Tri Brawd o Lanbrynmair a Conwy* (Bala, 1892), pp. 254–8. For John Roberts (J.R., 1804–84), see *DWB* and R. Tudur Jones, 'J.R., Conwy', *TCHS*, 21 (1960), 149–71. J.R. was S.R.'s brother.

[27] See J. Thomas, *Hanes Eglwysi Annibynol Cymru. Cyfrol V* (Dolgellau, 1891), p. 309.

[28] Edward Davies, *Cofiant y Parch. Edward Humphreys* (Bangor, 1915), p. 37. Edward Humphreys (1846–1913) was a Wesleyan minister. Dr Hugh Jones (1837–1919) was secretary of the Circuit of Llanrhaeadr at the time and Samuel Davies ('Yr Ail', 1818–91) was superintendent of the circuit. See *DWB* for Jones and Davies.

(Elfed), J.R. was the greatest influence on his preaching,[29] and following the publication of Elfed's volume of sermons, *Planu Coed a Phregethau Eraill*, in 1898, he too had a great many imitators.

It is noticeable that the language of preachers grew simpler as the century unfolded. For as long as the influence of Blair and the English style were interwoven with the theories of William Owen Pughe,[30] there were many atrocious examples of Welsh writing, particularly in the periodicals published during the first quarter of the century. The same weakness is apparent in printed sermons, although common sense and the practical requirements of communication safeguarded the spoken language of the pulpit against this deterioration. David Jones of Gwynfe expressed it in an interesting way, during a conversation with Evan Lewis of Brynberian:

> Dywedai wrthyf ryw dro wedi iddo ddechreu pregethu ei fod am ddysgu siarad ac areithio, ac iddo brynu *Blair's Rhetoric* . . . ond iddo ef ddysgu mwy yn Nghaerfyrddin un tro pan yn pasio y *conduit*. Yr oedd yno dyrfa o wragedd a phlant yn edrych ac mewn cyffro; fe drodd i wrando beth oedd yn bod, ac fe ddeallodd yn fuan fod yno ddwy wraig yn dyfrio eu gilydd, ac fe sylwodd arnynt. Yr oeddent yn troi eu lleisiau ac yn cymhwyso eu geiriau, ac yn gofalu gosod y pwys lle byddai yn debyg o bigo y llall. 'Ac mi ddysgais fwy wrth wrando y gwragedd yn tafodi eu gilydd na ddysgais yn *Blair's Rhetoric*, sef bod yn naturiol – dyna yr *art* oll.'[31]

(He once told me that, after he had begun preaching, he wanted to learn how to speak in public, and that he had bought *Blair's Rhetoric* . . . but that he had learnt more while passing a conduit in Carmarthen. There had been a crowd of women and children looking on in excitement; he stopped to listen to what was going on, and soon found that two women were calling each other names, and he watched them. They were raising their voices and choosing their words, and taking care to place the emphasis where it was likely to prick the other. 'And I learnt more from listening to those women abusing each other than I had learnt from *Blair's Rhetoric*, namely to be natural – that's all the art there is to it.')

It is interesting to observe that when David Jones began preaching in 1818 the authority on rhetoric was Blair. But having heard the Carmarthen women quarrelling, it became easier to deny his authority! Furthermore, other books on rhetoric were supplanting Blair. In 1817 the students of Carmarthen were

---

[29] Emlyn G. Jenkins, *Cofiant Elfed, 1860–1953* (Aberystwyth, 1957), p. 52. For Howell Elvet Lewis (1860–1953), see also Dafydd Owen, *Elfed a'i Waith* (Abertawe, 1963).

[30] For these, see Glenda Carr, *William Owen Pughe* (Caerdydd, 1983).

[31] D. M. Lewis, *Cofiant Evan Lewis, Brynberian* (Aberystwyth, 1903), pp. 9–10. The author of the biography was David Morgan Lewis (1851–1937), Professor of Physics at the University College of Wales, Aberystwyth from 1891 to 1919, and son of Evan Lewis (1813–96). See *DWB*. David Jones died on 25 April 1859 at 71 years of age. See T. Rees and J. Thomas, *Hanes Eglwysi Annibynol Cymru* (4 vols., Liverpool, 1871–5), III, pp. 571–2.

examined (in English) in grammar and Belles Lettres, among other subjects,[32] and by 1832 Rhetoric had become an examination subject.[33] Rhetoric was an examination subject at the Gwynedd Academy in 1823.[34] The committee of the Baptists' academy at Abergavenny gave permission for Blair's lectures on Rhetoric to be purchased as early as 23 June 1814, and by 1828 Rhetoric was an established part of the academy's syllabus.[35]

By the latter half of the century new textbooks had become popular. In 1866 Alexander Bain, Professor of Logic at the University of Aberdeen, published *A Manual of English Composition and Rhetoric*, which was later used as a textbook at the colleges of Trefeca,[36] Haverfordwest,[37] and Pontypool.[38] At Carmarthen, however, Ebenezer Porter's *Lectures on Homiletics*[39] was in use. Most significant of all is that English was the medium of instruction. The 'preaching class', at which students preached in the presence of their lecturers and fellow-students, was part of the training given at theological colleges until the end of the century, but because of the dearth of evidence it is difficult to know how many students preached in Welsh in these classes.

How much Welsh was studied by ministers and priests in the training academies? At Llanfyllin Academy in 1821 a Welsh examination was conducted, namely 'Analyse Isaiah 53 according to the rules of grammar',[40] and similarly, in 1823, students were required to analyse chapter I of the Book of Proverbs.[41] By 1825 Welsh had disappeared, although in 1833 a deputation from London stressed the value of teaching the native language: 'No less attention to the cultivation of the Welsh, the philology of which is extremely interesting and its capabilities, especially for sacred oratory, very great.'[42] The policy of the Baptists' Academy in Abergavenny was avowedly anti-Welsh. In 1822 it was emphasized that the aim of the institution was to train young men in the mysteries of the English language, its grammar and pronunciation.[43] But was it not the responsibility of the colleges of the denomination in Bristol, Bradford and Stepney to teach English to Welsh students? Not at all! The Welsh language was the dividing line between the Welsh and the English; it was the responsibility of the academy to overcome this by

---

[32] H. McLachlan, *English Education under the Test Acts* (Manchester, 1931), p. 59.
[33] G. Dyfnallt Owen, *Ysgolion a Cholegau yr Annibynwyr* (Abertawe, 1939), p. 64.
[34] *Y Dysgedydd*, II, no. 8 (1823), 240.
[35] *An Account* (annual report) (1815), p. 10; ibid., (1828), p. 8.
[36] *Y Drysorfa*, XLIII, no. 515 (1873), 344–6.
[37] *Report* (annual report) (1881), p. 11.
[38] *Report* (annual report) (1875), p. 12.
[39] *Y Diwygiwr*, XXXVI (August, 1871), 254.
[40] *Seren Gomer*, IV, no. 70 (1821), 220–1.
[41] *Y Dysgedydd*, II, no. 8 (1823), 240.
[42] Cited in Owen, *Ysgolion a Cholegau'r Annibynwyr*, p. 118.
[43] *An Account of the Baptist Educational Society* (London, 1822), p. 7.

ensuring that the Welsh were qualified to receive their education in England rather than by providing a Welsh-medium education.[44]

Welsh was the Achilles heel of these colleges throughout the century. Even in 1865 Dr John Kennedy, one of Brecon College's examiners, complained that the students' ignorance of English was arresting their development and interfering with the examination, and this possibly explains why Welsh disappeared from the syllabus.[45] Things took a turn for the better during the 1870s when it was decided that the examination would be based on the grammar of David Rowlands (Dewi Môn).[46] Welsh was not taught at the Presbyterian College at Carmarthen, although in 1834 representatives of the Presbyterian Board insisted that students 'should retain their knowledge and ease of their mother tongue, and be able to employ it with all the force, the pathos, and the sublimity which are its characteristics'.[47] No change occurred until 1894 when it was decided to include Welsh in the syllabus and provide six lectures on the language and literature of Wales.[48] The Baptists' College in Pontypool followed the policy of the Academy at Abergavenny by abolishing Welsh from the syllabus. In 1877 Robert Jones of Llanllyfni voiced his disapproval:

Fel rheol gyffredin, y mae yn rhaid i bregethwr, cyn y gallo wneyd yn dda, fod yn gyfarwydd âg iaith y bobl y byddo yn llafurio yn eu mysg . . . y mae yma filoedd heb wybod dim Saesonaeg, a dylai pregethwyr wybod hyny, a gofalu am eiriau Cymraeg . . . Dylai, ar bob cyfrif, fod mwy o ymgeledd nag sydd i'r iaith Gymraeg yng Ngholegau Cymru. Y mae yn anhawdd i lawer o fechgyn a fagwyd lle y mae Cymraeg gwael, i fod yn Gymreigwyr da.[49]

(As a general rule, a preacher must, before he can do well, be familiar with the language of the people among whom he labours . . . there are thousands here who know no English, and preachers should know that, and take care to use Welsh . . . There should certainly be concern for the Welsh language in the Colleges of Wales. It is not easy for many lads brought up where Welsh is weak to become good Welsh speakers.)

Welsh had only a marginal role at Lewis Edwards's Calvinistic Methodist College in Bala. It took its place in the syllabus next to Mathematics and Greek, but the

---

[44] Ibid., p. 4.
[45] *Report* (annual report) (1864–5), p. vii. For John Kennedy (1813–1900), Chairman of the Congregational Union of England and Wales, 1872, see *Congregational Year Book* (London, 1901), pp. 192–4.
[46] *Report* (annual report) (1874), p. 6. For David Rowlands (Dewi Môn, 1836–97), Professor and Principal of Brecon College, 1871–97, see *DWB*, where it states that his grammar was published in 1897. His lectures probably contained information from the grammar before that date.
[47] Cited in Owen, *Ysgolion a Cholegau'r Annibynwyr*, p. 71.
[48] Ibid., p. 92.
[49] In a letter to the Revd Thomas Phillips Davies, Bethesda, Caernarfonshire, dated 26 May 1877, and printed in Owen Davies, *Cofiant a Llythyrau y Parch. Robert Jones, Llanllyfni* (Llangollen, 1903), pp. 347–8. For Robert Jones (1806–96), see also *DWB*.

examinations were not in Welsh. When Roger Edwards was the examiner in 1867, all except one of the students wrote their papers in English.[50] Indeed, in his study of Lewis Edwards's career, Trebor Lloyd Evans came to the conclusion that English was the official language of the College, despite the fact that nine of every ten students entering the Welsh-speaking ministry were drawn from among the common people, the considerable majority of whom were Welsh speakers.[51] Yet, David Elias, brother of John Elias and a man well known for his pessimism and prejudices, claimed sarcastically that either the college lecturers in 1852 were incapable of teaching English, or the scholars lacked the ability to learn English, or the College was too Welsh.[52] At Trefeca College, students were expected to write no more than one essay in Welsh.[53] Officially, however, Welsh was one of the subjects taught by Dr J. Harris Jones after 1866,[54] and in 1874 Edward Matthews began to assemble a worthy collection of Welsh books for the college.[55]

Opposite Lewis Edwards's college in Bala stood the Congregational College, the head of which was Michael D. Jones. If Lewis Edwards's college was an English institution where little Welsh was taught, it could be said that Michael D. Jones's college was a Welsh establishment which taught a little English. According to the college committee's annual report for 1855–6: 'A good deal of attention is given to the Welsh language . . . as well as to the subjects that Students are taught in other Academies' ('Yr ydys yn rhoi gryn sylw i'r Gymraeg . . . yn gystal ag i'r pynciau yr addysgir Myfyrwyr ynddynt mewn Athrofâu eraill'),[56] and Welsh remained an examination subject and a medium of instruction until the retirement of Michael D. Jones. Even so, he lectured in English and students were expected to be able to speak in public in English. The students worried about having to pray in English in college services.[57] Among the Baptists, Welsh was one of the examination subjects in 1865 but it disappeared soon afterwards.[58] They began to teach Welsh grammar at Haverfordwest College in 1869 but it was not an examination subject.[59] Following T. Witton Davies's appointment in 1881, more

---

[50] *Y Drysorfa*, XXI, no. 248 (1867), 294.
[51] Trebor Lloyd Evans, *Lewis Edwards, ei fywyd a'i waith* (Abertawe, 1967), p. 123. For Lewis Edwards (1809–87), see T. C. Edwards, *Bywyd a Llythyrau y diweddar Lewis Edwards* (Liverpool, 1901); G. Tecwyn Parry, *Y diweddar Barch. Lewis Edwards, M.A., D.D., Bala, a'i Weithiau* (Llanberis, 1896) and *DWB*.
[52] Letter from John Hughes (1827–95), Liverpool and Caernarfon, to Lewis Jones, Bala, dated 29 November 1852, in John Williams, *Cofiant a phregethau . . . gan John Hughes* (Liverpool, 1899), p. lxi. For David Elias (1790–1856), see *DWB*.
[53] *Y Drysorfa*, XLIII, no. 515 (1873), 344–6.
[54] W. P. Jones, *Coleg Trefeca 1842–1942* (Llandysul, 1942), p. 37. For John Harris Jones, see Edward Matthews and J. Cynddylan Jones, *Cofiant y Parchedig J. Harris Jones* (Llanelly, 1886).
[55] Jones, *Coleg Trefeca*, p. 42.
[56] *Adroddiad Pwyllgor Athrofa Ogleddol yr Annibynwyr am 1855–6*.
[57] Silyn Evans, *Cofiant Robert Rowlands, Aberaman*, p. 24. For the college syllabus, see W. J. Parry, *Cofiant Tanymarian* (Dolgellau, 1886), pp. 26–7.
[58] *Y Greal* (1865), 210–11.
[59] *Report* (1869), p. 12.

prominence was given to the native language. In 1888–9 he held classes on Welsh grammar,[60] and in 1890 his classes on *Gweledigaetheu y Bardd Cwsc* were conducted through the medium of Welsh.[61]

Overall, Welsh was the weak spot of these institutions. There were several reasons why this should have been so. The belief that English was the language of higher education was extremely powerful and it persisted until the middle of the twentieth century. The influence of England grew even stronger throughout the nineteenth century and with the world-wide spread of the Empire, which also meant the spread of the English language, the notion that there was no future for Welsh was soon reinforced. Being a monoglot Welshman, however, was no bar to a young man becoming a shining light in the religious firmament in Wales. The most striking example was John Jones of Tal-y-sarn, who allegedly went to his grave without knowing a word of English.[62] Nevertheless, if a student wished to become acquainted with scholarly books, he had to master the English language; there was a deeply rooted belief that Welsh speakers had sufficient knowledge of the language for everyday purposes and that there was no need to give the language any scholarly attention in a college syllabus. Similarly, if students were intent on ministering in predominantly English-speaking areas, colleges should concentrate their efforts on preparing them to achieve their goal. Dr William Davies of Ffrwd-fâl informed John Williams of Newcastle Emlyn that he should go to college if he wanted to become a minister in a town such as Llanelli, whereas this was not necessary were he to become a minister in a rural area,[63] whereupon Williams left school and entered the ministry. It was also widely believed that a knowledge of English provided the means to escape from a life of poverty in Wales and embark upon a more comfortable life in England or the colonies. As J. R. Kilsby Jones maintained in a particularly crude address on 'The Advantage that accrues to the Welshman from having a practical knowledge of the English language' ('Y Fantais a ddeillia i'r Cymro o feddu gwybodaeth ymarferol o'r iaith Saesneg'): 'The ignorance among the Welsh of the language of their enterprising and wealthy neighbours, the English, has been a great obstacle to improving their circumstances. Nothing has cost, or is costing, the Welshman more dearly than his mother tongue' ('Mae anwybodaeth y Cymry o iaith eu

---

[60] *Report* (1889). For Thomas Witton Davies (1851–1923), Professor at Haverfordwest College, 1881–91, Principal of the Baptist College, Nottingham, 1891–8, Professor of Hebrew at the Baptist College, Bangor, 1898–1905, and Professor of Hebrew at the University College of North Wales, Bangor, 1905–21, see *DWB*. For Hugh Hughes (Tegai, 1805–64), Congregational minister, see *DWB*.

[61] *Report* (1890), p. 13.

[62] Thomas, *Cofiant John Jones*, p. 229.

[63] B. Williams (ed.), *Cofiant y diweddar Barchedig John Williams* (Abertawy, 1874), p. 24. For John Williams (1819–69), see Rees and Thomas, *Hanes Eglwysi Annibynol*, III, pp. 421–2. For William Davies (1805–59), Congregational minister, see *DWB*. He kept a grammar school at Ffrwd-fâl, Llansawel, from 1835 to 1854 and taught Hebrew at Carmarthen College from 1856 to 1859.

cymydogion anturiaethus a goludog y Saeson wedi bod yn rhwystr mawr iddynt i wella eu hamgylchiadau. Nid oes dim wedi costio, na dim yn costio yn bresenol, mor ddrud i'r Cymro â iaith ei fam').[64] The anxiety over mastering English was mirrored in the personal lives of many religious leaders. John Hughes (1796–1860), author of *Methodistiaeth Cymru* (3 vols., 1851–6), corresponded with his daughter Catherine in English.[65] Similarly, Robert Jones of Llanllyfni wrote in (rather broken) English to Abel J. Parry,[66] while Henry Rees corresponded with his daughter and grandchildren in English.[67] His brother, Gwilym Hiraethog, composed an English elegy in memory of Henry; he also corresponded with his daughters in English and composed English prayers to be used at their school in Porthmadog.[68] The English spoken by William Williams of Wern was pretty lame and yet he insisted on conducting family worship in English since this was the language most familiar to his wife and children.[69] A. J. Parry once claimed that reading *Drych y Prif Oesoedd* had made him a keen patriot and Anglophobe, and yet English was the language of his home and study, and he always maintained that he thought in English.[70] Most curious of all is the fact that all Michael D. Jones's love letters were written in English.[71] It would be idle to list more examples since there are so many of them. A kind of fickleness with regard to the language, and doubts about its future, prevailed among very many religious leaders during the period under study. Despite all this, it was surprising that the theological colleges neglected the Welsh language to such an extent, considering that a high proportion of their students would spend their lives serving Welsh-speaking congregations.

The Sunday school was one of the most influential institutions to be created by the churches.[72] Despite a certain amount of opposition towards the end of the eighteenth century, once established Sunday schools became extremely popular. Because Welsh was the language of the Sunday schools, they appealed to

[64] J. Vyrnwy Morgan, *Kilsby Jones* (Wrexham, 1898), pp. 208–9. James Rhys Kilsby Jones (1813–89) was a Congregational minister.
[65] R. Edwards and J. Hughes (eds.), *Buchdraeth y diweddar Barch. John Hughes Liverpool* (Wrexham, [1864]), p. 192.
[66] Owen Davies, *Cofiant a Llythyrau y Parch. Robert Jones, Llanllyfni* (Caernarfon, 1903), pp. 398–9.
[67] Thomas, *Cofiant Henry Rees*, p. 723.
[68] T. Roberts and D. Roberts, *Cofiant y Parch. W. Rees, D.D. (Gwilym Hiraethog)* (Dolgellau, 1893), pp. 385–90, 409–12. For William Rees (Gwilym Hiraethog, 1802–83), see also *DWB*.
[69] D. S. Jones, *Cofiant Darluniadol y Parchedig William Williams, o'r Wern* (Dolgellau, 1894), pp. 381, 202. For William Williams (1781–1840), see also W. Rees (Gwilym Hiraethog), *Cofiant y Diweddar Barch. W. Williams o'r Wern* (Dinbych, 1842) and *DWB*. For an obituary of his wife, see *Y Dysgedydd*, XV, no. 176 (1836), 201–3.
[70] T. Frimston (ed.), *Cyfrol Goffa: Hanner Canrif o Lafur Gweinidogaethol y Parch. Abel J. Parry* (Colwyn Bay, 1906), pp. 63, 208. For A. J. Parry (1833–1911), a Baptist minister, see *DWB*.
[71] In the manuscript collection of the University of Wales, Bangor.
[72] For a valuable synopsis of one stratum in the history of Sunday schools, see G. Wynne Griffith, *Yr Ysgol Sul: Penodau ar Hanes yr Ysgol Sul yn bennaf ymhlith y Methodistiaid Calfinaidd* (Caernarfon, 1936).

monoglot Welsh speakers and it was never conceived that they would be used to teach English. Furthermore, the dearth of educational resources meant that many learnt to read in Sunday school. The fact that they were held on a Sunday was advantageous at a time when ordinary workers laboured all week and had little leisure. In Wales, unlike other countries, both adults and children attended Sunday school. Handbooks such as Thomas Charles's *Rheolau i ffurfiaw a threfnu yr Ysgolion Sabbothawl* (Rules on the formation and organization of Sunday schools) (1813) were readily available. Whether the pupils were children or adults, the first task was to teach them to read. Teaching aids such as *Arweinydd i'r Anllythrenog i ddysgu darllain Cymraeg* (A Guide for the Illiterate to learn to read Welsh), published in 1798 by Robert Davies of Nantglyn,[73] a layman of the Church in Wales, or *Drych i'r Anllythrennog* (A Mirror for the Illiterate), published in 1788 by Robert Jones of Rhos-lan, were used. The latter proved immensely popular and by 1820 eleven editions had been published.[74] These, together with Thomas Charles's *Yr Hyffordduur* (The Instructor), were the first of a mass of books written for Sunday schools during the nineteenth century. Older pupils needed commentaries, books such as *Esponiad ar y Testament Newydd* (Commentary on the New Testament) by Dr George Lewis,[75] or his substantial theological manual *Drych Ysgrythyrol* (Scriptural Mirror) (1796). The *Geiriadur Ysgrythyrawl* was also extremely popular and ran to seven editions during the century. Several editions of the Bible were published with explanatory notes on its contents.[76] But it was during the last quarter of the century that the practice of publishing commentaries on the individual books of the Bible began. Each denomination published its own annual commentary, to be used as a Sunday school textbook. These were widely circulated and adult Sunday school classes would spend the year reading and digesting them. By this time, especially after the centenary of the Sunday school movement in 1885, written examinations had been introduced. Hitherto, the Sunday schools had confined themselves to oral work, but now they began to teach writing skills, following the example of the day schools.

Reference has already been made to the importance of the catechism and the emphasis placed on learning from memory. In 1885 the Arfon Presbytery produced a detailed report on its Sunday schools which gives a clear picture of the

[73] For Robert Davies (Bardd Nantglyn, 1769–1835), bard and grammarian, see *DWB*.
[74] The content of his book has changed somewhat over the years. For Robert Jones (1745–1829), see *DWB* and the introduction to G. M. Ashton (ed.), *Drych yr Amseroedd [gan] Robert Jones Rhos-lan* (Caerdydd, 1958).
[75] Volume I, 1802; Volume II, 1807; Volume III, 1810; Volume IV, 1815. His son-in-law, Edward Davies (1796–1857), edited Volume V, 1825; Volume VI, 1828; Volume VII, 1829. For George Lewis (1763–1822), see *DWB* and T. Lewis, 'George Lewis, 1763–1822', *Y Cofiadur*, 10–11 (1934), 1–32.
[76] R. Tudur Jones, 'Esbonio'r Testament Newydd yng Nghymru, 1860–1890' in Owen E. Evans (ed.), *Efrydiau Beiblaidd Bangor III* (Abertawe, 1978), pp. 161–99; idem, 'Astudio'r Hen Destament yng Nghymru, 1860–1890' in Gwilym H. Jones (ed.), *Efrydiau Beiblaidd Bangor II* (Abertawe, 1977), pp. 150–78.

enormous work they had achieved. The Sunday school at Beddgelert, for example, had 670 members, although the average attendance over the year was 480. The 'memory work' achieved in 1885 was as follows: verses from the Bible, 195,774; chapters from *Yr Hyfforddwr*, 216; chapters from *Rhodd Mam*, 115; chapters from *Rhodd Tad*, 102; verses, 5,580; recitation of the Ten Commandments, 19. The report's statistics for the whole Presbytery are astonishing: verses from the Bible, 2,228,775; chapters from *Yr Hyfforddwr*, 3,921; chapters from *Rhodd Mam*, 11,878; chapters from *Rhodd Tad*, 3,592; verses 58,991; recitation of the Ten Commandments, 1,338.[77] A later generation of educationists would refer disparagingly to placing inordinate emphasis on learning so much by heart, but, at a time when Welsh was not taught in day schools, Sunday schools gave thousands of children the opportunity of using the language, of acquiring biblical vocabulary and idioms, and of learning some of the nation's classical hymns. William Roberts (Nefydd) was no doubt exaggerating when he asked:

paham mae cymaint o ysgrifenwyr galluog yn Nghymru, yn ysgrifio traethodau campus; ac hefyd yn llanw y cyhoeddiadau misol â gweithiau talentog (heb gael na Choleg, nac Athrofa, nac hyd yn oed ddiwrnod o Ysgol) mwy nâ'n cymydogion yn Lloegr, a'r Iwerddon, a gwledydd eraill?

(why do so many able writers in Wales write splendid essays; and also fill the monthly periodicals with talented work (without having been to College, nor Academy, nor even having had a day's schooling) more than our neighbours in England, Ireland, and other countries?)

His reply was 'The Sunday School'.[78] Despite the exaggeration, his point was perfectly valid. At least, it can be said that Sunday school training was a starting point for many who, in due course, would become celebrated writers and poets.

Sunday schools formed an extraordinarily large organization. By 1891 there were 73,802 Sunday school teachers in Wales, compared with 10,839 day school teachers. By 1905, when the Disestablishment Commission made its detailed inquiries, four-tenths of the population of Wales were Sunday school members. In Cardiganshire 67 per cent of the population attended Sunday school. In the Rhondda in 1905 nearly 43 per cent of the population were Sunday school members and in Penllyn the percentage was 67 per cent.[79] The same source reveals that the percentage of Sunday school members in other places was high: 57 per cent in Bangor, 60 per cent in Bethesda, 55 per cent in Caernarfon and 76 per

---

[77] The Report is at Gwynedd Archives in Caernarfon.
[78] William Roberts, *Crefydd yr Oesoedd Tywyll* (Caerfyrddin, 1852), p. 35. For William Roberts (Nefydd, 1813–72), Baptist minister, see *DWB*.
[79] Royal Commission on the Church of England and other Religious Bodies in Wales and Monmouthshire, *Report, Volume V, Appendices to Minutes of Evidence. Church of England* (1910), p. 100 (PP 1910 (Cd. 5436) XVIII); ibid., *Volume VI, Appendices to Minutes of Evidence. Nonconformist County Statistics*, pp. 278–92, 298 (PP 1910 (Cd. 5437) XVIII).

cent in Ffestiniog. Naturally, some of the individual schools were very large. There were 940 members at Salem Chapel, Caernarfon, 701 at Hyfrydle, Holyhead, and 467 at Jerwsalem, Ffestiniog. However, the leaders failed to recognize the need for legislation to safeguard the valuable work of the churches and the Sunday schools and to protect the public status of the language, especially in the day schools. Within their own field, however, they made a very rich contribution.

In the previous chapter the difficulties encountered by the Church in Wales in seeking to provide the means of grace for a bilingual society were discussed. The same difficulties troubled the Nonconformist churches, though not in the same way. Generally, the system adopted was to establish separate Welsh and English churches. On the whole, this method proved to be satisfactory, although difficulties arose from time to time.

Let us begin with the Wesleyan Methodists. By the Deed of Declaration of 9 March 1784, John Wesley ensured that his personal authority over his movement would be ratified in a conference which included a hundred preachers. This was to be the high court of the new denomination. Laymen were not included among the 'Legal Hundred'. Indeed, Wesley's intention was to ensure that authority in every part of the denomination lay in the hands of ministers. This meant that the system was an oligarcy governed from the centre.[80] It is true, as Dr Hugh Jones, the historian of the denomination pointed out, that 'the Welsh Provinces had wider degrees of self-government than any other section of the Connexion',[81] but he was writing in 1911 and over the previous hundred years the Welsh Wesleyans more than once had cause to complain about a lack of sympathy for the Welsh language on the part of the denomination's leadership. During the years immediately following the establishment of the 'Welsh Mission' in 1800, the growth of Wesleyanism was remarkably rapid. But in 1814 several administrative changes were made, and the Wesleyan circuits of Swansea, Brecon, Cardiff, Merthyr Tydfil and Carmarthen were combined. As a result, there were heated exchanges between those who wished to preach in Welsh only and those who were in favour of preaching in English. In 1815 the local leaders recommended that the circuits should be treated according to language, thereby restoring the system as it had existed prior to 1814. The Conference of 1815 adopted the suggestion, but this only lasted a year since the Conference changed its mind again and once more confirmed the combining of the circuits and a reduction in the number of Welsh-speaking preachers. According to A. H. Williams: 'In 1816 Welsh Wesleyan Methodism undoubtedly received the greatest blow in all its history.'[82]

---

[80] With Wesley's arrangements in 1784, 'Autocracy was to give way to hierarchy, but a hierarchy none the less autocratic', A. H. Williams, *Welsh Wesleyan Methodism 1800–1858: Its Origins, Growth and Secessions* (Bangor, 1935), p. 196.

[81] Hugh Jones, *Hanes Wesleyaeth Cymreig* (4 vols., Bangor, 1911–14), I, p. 7.

[82] Williams, *Welsh Wesleyan Methodism*, p. 139.

During the course of the century Wesleyanism suffered a number of schisms, the common cause of which was dissatisfaction with the extreme authority of the Conference of ministers.[83] It does not appear that the Welsh-speaking protesters gave a prominent place to complaints concerning the language, but it is certain that the subject formed part of the background. Another skirmish which echoed the new national spirit occurred later in the century. The South Wales Provincial Meeting in 1880 had established a commission to draw up a scheme for uniting the circuits. Its report, presented at the provincial Meeting on 23 May 1881, recommended that all the causes in south Wales, both Welsh and English (except for some in the north of the area, such as those at Aberystwyth, Llanidloes and Ystumtuen), should form a single province. Samuel Davies ('The Second'), a member of the Commission, suggested – in the face of considerable opposition – that it should proceed with caution, but the scheme was rejected by thirty-four votes to eighteen. An amendment was moved to the effect that 'Wesleyanism in South Wales, North Wales and Monmouthshire, both Welsh and English, should be formed in one Conference'. Samuel Davies objected to this because he was not in favour of uniting north and south.[84] He was anxious to defend the Welsh-speaking circuits from falling under the jurisdiction of their English-speaking counterparts. From first to last, the Conference in England showed scant sympathy for the point of view of the Welsh-speaking Welsh. For instance, what would they have made of events at the Whitsun preaching meeting in Penmachno in 1884? The Venerable Richard Roberts of London was present as a visitor, but he was recognized and was obliged, much against his will, to 'say a few words'. He was bundled into the pulpit and began to speak in English. The congregation responded by shouting 'Cymraeg, Cymraeg!' (Welsh, Welsh!) and continued to do so until he complied with their wishes.[85] The Welsh-speaking Wesleyans were unwilling to be taken lightly, but there were also other voices to be heard. One correspondent stated: 'I am first of all a Methodist, and dearer to me than even my mother's language is the Connexion in whose principles I have been instructed' ('yr wyf gyntaf oll yn Fethodist, ac anwylach i mi nag hyd yn nod iaith fy mam yw y Cyfundeb yr addysgwyd fi yn ei egwyddorion ganddi hi'), and so he rejoiced in the success of the English-speaking causes.[86]

Because both the Congregationalists and the Baptists had a congregational system, the tension between the languages did not affect them in the same way. For them each congregation was a sovereign unit and therefore entitled to use the language of its choice. As the spread of the industrial revolution in mid-century brought non-Welsh speakers into Wales in large numbers, and as the development of the railways attracted tourists, the issue of how Congregationalists could

[83] A. H. Williams reviews the schisms relating to Wales in ibid., Section III.
[84] Hugh Jones, *Cofiant y Diweddar Barch. Samuel Davies* (Bangor, 1904), pp. 141–2.
[85] Ibid., p. 173.
[86] *Y Gwyliedydd*, XVII, no. 894 (1893), 1.

provide these people with the means of grace was raised. The answer was to establish English-language causes and to build new chapels. The chief exponent of this viewpoint was the historian Thomas Rees of Swansea.[87] He established an English cause while he was minister of Ebeneser, Aberdare (1840–2), and again during his time at Carmel, Beaufort (1849–61), where he opened a chapel in April 1859 and called it Capel Barham, in honour of Lady Barham, the patroness of preachers.[88] In 1853 he called a conference in Beaufort to consider the setting up of English causes in Wales, with Thomas Thompson, Lady Barham's son-in-law, presiding.[89] No formal arrangements were made on this occasion. In October 1858 Thomas Rees read a paper at the annual meetings of the Congregational Union of England and Wales in Halifax. It was in broad outline a history of the Congregationalists in Wales, but he took the opportunity to declare that the increase in the English-speaking population of Wales called for 'effective preaching in English'.[90] At a conference held in Cardiff in November 1860, which was presided over by W. D. Wills of Bristol and attended by people like Samuel Morley and Henry Richard,[91] it was agreed to establish the Association of English Causes in South Wales and Monmouthshire. The prime movers, with Thomas Rees, were John Davies of Cardiff and Thomas Williams of Merthyr Tydfil,[92] the society's secretary and treasurer respectively.[93] The Association of English Causes in North Wales was formed in 1876, and by 1879 John Thomas of Liverpool had become its principal leader and a powerful advocate on its behalf.[94] It cannot be said that this development caused much consternation,

[87] For Thomas Rees (1815–85), see John Thomas, *Cofiant y Parchedig T. Rees, D.D., Abertawy* (Dolgellau, 1888) and *DWB*.

[88] For Diana (1762–1823), daughter of Charles Middleton (Baron Barham after 1805) and wife of Gerard Noel Edwardes, who changed his surname to Noel in 1798, see Donald M. Lewis (ed.), *The Blackwell Dictionary of Evangelical Biography 1730–1860* (Oxford, 1995), pp. 58–9. She gave birth to thirteen children. In 1813, when she inherited her father's title, she moved to Fairy Hill, Gower. For the cause in Cendl (Beaufort), see *The Evangelical Magazine*, XXXIII (1855), 274–5.

[89] According to John Thomas in *Cofiant . . . T. Rees*, p. 193, he was living in Bath, but according to Rees and Thomas, *Hanes Eglwysi Annibynol*, II, p. 333, his address was Piercefield Park, Chepstow.

[90] The paper is published in Thomas Rees, *Miscellaneous Papers on Subjects relating to Wales* (London, 1867), pp. 70–83.

[91] For William Day Wills (1798–1879), see B. L. Manning, *The Protestant Dissenting Deputies* (Cambridge, 1952), p. 485. Thomas Rees, a heavy smoker, was a good customer of the tobacco factory. For Samuel Morley (1809–86), see *The Congregationalist* (1886), 711–19 and *DNB*. For Henry Richard (1812–88), see *DNB* and *DWB*.

[92] For John Davies (1824–74), see Rees and Thomas, *Hanes Eglwysi Annibynol*, IV, 286–300 and John Thomas, *Cofiant y Parch. J. Davies, Caerdydd* (Merthyr Tydfil, 1883), pp. 139–40.

[93] For Thomas Williams (1823–1903) (with illustration), see *Y Dysgedydd*, LXXXI (June, 1902), 213–16; ibid., LXXXII (August, 1903), 308–10; *Y Diwygiwr*, LXVIII (September, 1903), 261–5. According to Pedrog, the first person to draw the attention of the Congregational Union (in 1854) to the need for English chapels was Richard Parry (Gwalchmai). For the establishment of the Association, see John Thomas, *Cofiant . . . T. Rees*, pp. 191–4.

[94] Owen Thomas and J. Machreth Rees, *Cofiant y Parchedig John Thomas, D.D. Liverpool* (Llundain, 1898), pp. 358–9.

though it aroused the scorn of Michael D. Jones and his supporters. In 1878 he wrote that Disraeli had made English the official language of Cyprus in the hope that in time the English would be able 'to ram the English language down the throats of the Cypriots with British bayonets', adding, 'This is a splendid chance for the Association of English Chapels to broaden its activities by helping the English to build English chapels for the Cypriots in order to stamp out their language' ('Dyma faes ardderchog i Gymdeithas y Capeli Seisnig i eangu ei gweithrediadau drwy helpu Saeson i godi capeli Seisnig i'r Cypriaid er mwyn difodi eu hiaith').[95] He wrote a remarkably incisive article attacking the society but, with the exception of the Welsh-speaking churches, some of whose members were invited to form a nucleus in order to establish English causes, the work of the society caused little stir.[96]

What little tension that existed among Baptists regarding the language issue occurred in the relationship between the assemblies. The assembly was the institution in which representatives of the individual congregations could discuss matters which were of general interest or where they could co-operate in pursuing their public or inter-church aims. The denomination's historian, T. M. Bassett, writes: 'The one Association had been divided in 1790 and as the number of churches increased during the nineteenth century and indeed, to some extent as the number of English churches increased, the three Associations then formed were further subdivided.'[97] From time to time the boundaries of the assemblies were changed,[98] but the difference in language had to be taken into consideration in the development of these arrangements. This is how it was achieved:

> The Monmouthshire English Association was formed in 1857 and in 1860 another English Association was formed from among some of the English churches in Glamorgan and Carmarthenshire. This Association in turn was subdivided in 1913 into the East Glamorgan English Association and the West Glamorgan and Carmarthenshire English Association . . . The English Baptist Union of North Wales was formed in 1879 . . .[99]

In this way the Baptists avoided linguistic difficulties in assembly meetings by grouping churches according to their language. The Baptist Union of Wales was established on 21 August 1866. Not all the Welsh-speaking assemblies were keen to join and the English Assembly of Monmouthshire and the English Assembly of Glamorgan and Carmarthenshire decided against it. As far as the English churches which belonged to the Union were concerned, by 1900 none of their representatives were making a distinguished contribution to the Union's work

[95] *Y Celt*, 23 August 1878, 8.
[96] Ibid., 2 May 1890, 1–2.
[97] T. M. Bassett, *The Welsh Baptists* (Swansea, 1977), p. 337.
[98] See ibid. for the details.
[99] Ibid.

and the Union was not holding meetings in their areas. As a result, an English section of the Union was established and in 1902 began to work alongside the Welsh section.[100]

It was among the Calvinistic Methodists that the debate over the 'English cause', as it came to be known, attracted most public attention. In September 1802 the Bangor Association received a deputation from the Lancashire Presbytery which declared 'it is known that the English language . . . has gained considerable ground in several of the main towns and most populous districts of Wales, and everything suggests that it will continue thus in the years ahead', and that therefore the denomination should make an orderly start in building English-language places of worship. A committee was formed to consider the matter and its suggestion that preachers should be willing to hold services in English wherever there was a demand for them was adopted at the Abergele Association, held in December 1862.[101] In his address to the General Assembly at Llanidloes in 1867 Lewis Edwards argued:

> Y mae yn fwy na phryd i ni godi addoldai i bregethu yn yr iaith Saesoneg yn holl brif drefydd y Dywysogaeth . . . Nid y gofyniad ydyw, A ddylem ni wneuthur a allom i gadw a choledd yr iaith Gymraeg? Gobeithiaf nad oes neb o honom yn gwadu hyn. Ond y gofyniad syml ydyw, Os byddwn yn gweled, er ein holl ymdrechion, fod yr iaith Gymraeg yn darfod yn rhai o drefydd Cymru, pa beth yw ein dyletswydd yn y cyfryw amgylchiad?[102]

> (It is high time that we built places of worship in which to preach in the English language in all the main towns of the Principality . . . The question is not, Should we do what we can to retain and foster the Welsh language? I hope there is no one who would deny that. But the simple question is, If we should see, despite all our efforts, that the Welsh language is dying out in some towns in Wales, what would be our duty in such circumstances?)

He believed that the English tide was part of the Almighty's plan and thus 'our wisdom as well as our duty is to bow before Providence'. By 1869 he was extremely enthusiastic about the plans to build English chapels. In a letter to Richard Davies of Treborth, dated 9 April, he claimed that if people expressed a wish to establish an English cause in places like Rhyl or Llandudno, the first step would be to deploy one of the ministers to work there and arrange for prominent preachers, Congregational or Presbyterian, to draw attention to the cause. The

---

[100] Ibid., p. 356.
[101] Edward Jones, *Y Gymdeithasfa: yn cynwys gweithrediadau Cymdeithasfa Chwarterol y Methodistiaid Calfinaidd yn Ngogledd Cymru, a'r Gymanfa Gyffredinol . . . hyd y flwyddyn 1890* (Caernarfon, 1891), p. 394.
[102] ' "Ein Gwaith fel Cyfundeb, a'r Cymhwysderau angenrheidiol": Anerchiad y Parch. Dr Edwards, Bala, yn Nghymanfa Gyffredinol Llanidloes', *Y Drysorfa*, XXI (September, 1867), 322.

next step would be to encourage members from the Welsh cause to form a nucleus of an English congregation, 'and before they can be of any use they must not only extend their patronage to the English cause by an occasional visit but pass over bodily to the English'.[103] This suggestion raised the hackles of many in the churches. It was therefore no wonder that Dr Owen Thomas, at the General Assembly in Liverpool in May 1869, presented a diplomatic motion in an attempt to calm the waters:

> Wedi cymeryd i sylw gynydd lledaeniad yr iaith Saesoneg yn Nghymru, a'r posibilrwydd y gallai yn gynt fe ddichon nag yr ydym ni yn tybied, ddyfod, o leiaf yn ein prif drefi, yn iaith y werin . . . penderfynwyd:– Ein bod, tra yn anog ein cydwladwyr er mwyn gwladgarwch, ac yn neillduol er mwyn crefydd, i ymlynu yn ffyddlawn wrth, ac i ddwyn eu plant i fyny i ddysgu yr iaith Gymraeg, eto yn dymuno ar i'r amrywiol Gyfarfodydd Misol trwy yr holl Siroedd gymeryd yr achos hwn i'w hystyriaeth fwyaf difrifol . . .[104]

(Having taken notice of the increasing spread of the English language in Wales, and the possibility that it may more rapidly than we think become, at least in our main towns, the language of the common people . . . it was decided that, while urging our compatriots, for the sake of love of country, and particularly of religion, to remain faithfully attached to the Welsh language, and to bring up their children to learn it, it was also desirable that Monthly Meetings throughout Wales should give this matter their most serious consideration . . .)

The real aim of the motion was to urge the entire Assembly to set to work with enthusiasm in supporting the movement for English chapels. At the Assembly in Dolgellau in June 1870 it was decided to establish a Fund for the English Causes, and Caernarfon, Bangor, Machynlleth, Llanidloes and Bala were named as suitable places where such causes could be launched, by 'sending from among them a number of serious and industrious men to form English Causes' – an echo of Lewis Edwards's suggestion in his letter to Richard Davies, who was a member of one of the committees supervising the work.[105] In 1876 Robert Ambrose Jones (Emrys ap Iwan) launched his campaign against the movement with his article, 'Y Dwymyn Seisnig yng Nghymru' (The English Fever in Wales), which was published on 27 December in *Y Faner*, the newspaper of Thomas Gee, who gave enthusiastic support to Emrys ap Iwan's stand. In 1881 the Conference of English Churches was established with the aim of providing its delegates with an opportunity of

---

[103] Edwards, *Bywyd a llythyrau . . . Lewis Edwards*, p. 417. For Richard Davies (1818–96), merchant and Member of Parliament, see *DWB*. He was married to Anne, daughter of Henry Rees. For a critical account of the commercial side of the Davies family, see Aled Eames, *Ships and Seamen of Anglesey 1558–1918: Studies in Maritime and Local History* (Denbigh, 1973), pp. 214–70.

[104] Jones, *Y Gymdeithasfa*, pp. 357–8.

[105] Ibid., p. 395.

meeting one another. By 1887 there were forty English churches in north Wales and their chapels had been built at a cost of £40,000.

Public attention to the quarrel over the English causes, however, was largely attracted by the skirmish between Lewis Edwards and his former pupil, Emrys ap Iwan. As on several previous occasions, Lewis Edwards spoke warmly in favour of the movement for English causes at the Assembly held in Dolgellau in June 1880: 'As the kingdom is going English, we must follow suit', he maintained, 'and there is a danger for us in battling against the English language that we lose sight of people's souls, and battle instead against the progress and survival of the Connexion' ('Gan fod y deyrnas yn mynd yn Saeson, y mae yn rhaid i ninnau fyned ar ei hôl, ac y mae perygl i ni wrth ymladd yn erbyn y Saesneg golli golwg ar eneidiau y bobl, ac ymladd yn erbyn cynnydd a pharhad y Cyfundeb'). But before completing his speech, he urged preachers to be loyal to their denomination and expressed a wish that deacons would bar the disloyal ones from preaching. He wanted them 'to mark that man who would not work with the causes with which the Assembly has decided to continue. Put a mark on him, mark him out – not in public but to show disapproval of his work in some negative way' ('roddi marc ar y gwr hwnnw na byddo yn gweithio gyda'r achosion ag y mae y Gymdeithasfa wedi penderfynu myned ymlaen gyda hwy. Rhoddi marc arno – ei farcio allan, nid yn gyhoeddus ond dangos eu hangymeradwyaeth o'i waith mewn rhyw ddull nacaol').[106] That is to say, do not engage him to preach. Emrys ap Iwan was incensed by these remarks, believing that he was one of those who had come under the lash of 'the bull from Bala', as he called him. In his letter replying to Lewis Edwards's address, Emrys ap Iwan went to some lengths to undermine his adversary's reasoning before coming to the crux of the dispute between them. This is the key passage in his letter:

> Nid wyf fi, fel un o'r ffyddloniaid Cymreig, yn erbyn i rai ddysgu yr iaith Saesneg . . . Ond dywedyd yr ydwyf na ddylent wneud dim i ddisodli eu hiaith eu hunain. Hyn yw y gwahaniaeth rhyngof fi a Dr Edwards: sef, ei fod ef yn pleidio y trefniant goreu a ddychmygwyd erioed i droi y Cymry yn Saeson uniaith; a minnau yn pleidio trefniant a bair iddynt gadw eu Cymraeg wrth ddysgu Saesneg . . . Pe bae y Doctor a'i blaid, yn siarad ac yn gwario hanner cymaint i Gymreigio y Cymry ag y maent yn ei siarad a'i wario i'w Seisnigo; a phe bae ein haelodau seneddol, yn hytrach na gwastraffu eu hamser i helpu y Saeson i wneud deddfau Seisnig, yn ymuno â'u gilydd i fynnu deddfau cyfaddas i'r Cymry, byddai gwybodaeth, a moes, a chrefydd yn llawer uwch yng Nghymru nag ydynt yn awr . . . [107]

---

[106] The original report is published in *Y Goleuad*, 3 July 1880, and in T. Gwynn Jones, *Emrys ap Iwan. Dysgawdr, Llenor, Cenedlgarwr: Cofiant* (Caernarfon, 1912), pp. 86–7.

[107] Jones, *Emrys ap Iwan*, p. 92. The letter is also published in D. Myrddin Lloyd (ed.), *Detholiad o Erthyglau a Llythyrau Emrys ap Iwan* (3 vols., Aberystwyth, 1937, 1939, 1940), III, pp. 81–8.

(I am not, like those loyal to Welsh, opposed to those who wish to learn English . . . But I maintain that they should do nothing to supplant their own language. Herein lies the difference between Dr Edwards and me: namely, that he argues in favour of the best means ever imagined of turning the Welsh into monoglot English people; while I am in favour of an arrangement which allows them to keep their Welsh while learning English . . . If the Doctor and his party were to speak and spend half as much on making the Welsh more Welsh as they do on Anglicizing them; and if our members of parliament, rather than wasting their time in helping the English make English laws, came together to insist on laws appropriate to the Welsh, then knowledge, and morals, and religion would be much higher in Wales than they are now . . .)

Of course, Lewis Edwards's suggestion that his opponents should be disciplined had nothing to do with the essence of the argument about the English causes and Emrys ap Iwan was exaggerating when he suggested that 'large prizes given by wealthy people had persuaded [Lewis Edwards] to plead according to their whims' ('fod gwobrwyon mawr y cyfoethogion wedi denu [Lewis Edwards] i bleidio eu mympwyon'). Like many of his kind, Lewis Edwards could be fickle in his attitude towards Welsh, at times warmly zealous on its behalf and, at other times, as in his support for English causes, heavily under the influence of the belief that there was no holding back 'the English tide'.[108] What is significant in the dispute is that Emrys ap Iwan, like Michael D. Jones, was proposing a broader philosophy regarding the relationship between language and society, and between language and religion, than the one offered by Lewis Edwards and his colleagues.

To sum up. What is the social significance of the evidence? Through their evangelizing, their preaching, their Sunday schools and the enormous corpus of literature they published, the Nonconformist churches during the century under discussion reared tens of thousands of Welsh readers and people who were able to express their thoughts effectively through the medium of the language. The skills thus developed within a religious context could easily be adapted to work outside that context, and since many people's most profound experiences were closely associated with Welsh, they felt a strong commitment to the language within the religious context.

On the whole, the pattern which was increasingly adopted as the number of English speakers increased was to separate the Welsh and English services. The Church in Wales had discovered that bilingual services were unacceptable and that it was better to provide Welsh and English services at different times, but, with some exceptions towards the end of the century, in the same building. The arrangement favoured by the other denominations was to incorporate churches according to their language within different buildings. Behind this separation there was a deeper duality. Many of the leaders, as well as their followers, had been mesmerized by the belief that the Welsh language would not survive for

---

[108] A balanced view of his attitude is given by Trebor Lloyd Evans, *Lewis Edwards*, pp. 162–7.

much longer and that to make provision for it was only a temporary measure. Reference was often made to 'the English tide'. In Michael D. Jones's view, the use of such a metaphor was foolish. He maintained: 'By this could be meant that the English flood is akin to the deluge which drowned the world . . . when in fact it is only the Welsh themselves who have destroyed their language by casting it out from their family, from their place of worship, from business, and from the day schools' ('Gellid meddwl wrth hyn mai rhywbeth fel y dilyw a foddodd y cynfyd . . . yw y dilyw Seisnig, pan mewn gwirionedd mai y Cymry eu hunain yn unig a ddifodant y Gymraeg trwy ei thaflu allan o'r teulu, o'r addoldy, o fasnach, ac o'r ysgolion dyddiol').[109] This observation underlines the duality which characterized the thinking of many religious leaders who had created a division between the religious and the secular context, the one in Welsh and the other in English. One consequence was uncertainty about where exactly lay the line between them, and that is why fluent Welsh speakers corresponded with one another in English and even raised their children as monoglot English speakers.

The Nonconformists at the beginning of the century were sects (in the sociological sense of the word). One of the most obvious characteristics of a sect is that it protects the peculiarity of its creed by erecting a solid wall between it and the hostile world around it.[110] The language of these sects was Welsh and very often the language was considered to be a bulwark against the atheism of England and America. But changes occurred in mid-century. With the great increase in their membership, improvement in educational facilities, the extension of the franchise, and the spread of radical ideas, the Nonconformist sects grew into denominations with an eye to bringing an influence to bear on the world about them and to becoming successful players on the wider stage. In order to make such a mark, English was necessary. But there were powerful factors at work in that world which militated against conferring status and honour upon the Welsh language. One of them was that so many leaders had swallowed whole the economic philosophy of *laissez-faire* and transplanted it to the world of culture. John Roberts of Conwy rather crudely expressed this belief when he declared: 'Free market and competition make the world go round' ('Rhydd fasnach a chydymgeisio yw yr hyn a geidw y byd yn ei le'); indeed, he believed that competition was 'the heavenly order' ('trefn y nef').[111] In adapting the market gospel to language (as did J.R.), it was of necessity impossible for Welsh to hold its own against a language which had the support of all the media in the service of a powerful state. The 'competition' was basically unfair. Furthermore, there were psychological and sociological influences at work, in so far as the snobbery and

[109] *Y Celt*, 24 April 1891, 1.
[110] For a detailed analysis of the development, see Alun Tudur's thesis, 'O'r Sect i'r Enwad: Datblygiad Enwadau Ymneilltuol Cymru 1840–1870' (unpubl. University of Wales PhD thesis, 1993).
[111] *Y Cronicl* (1873), 105; ibid. (1874), 224–6.

middle-class ethos of England, with its strong prejudices against other languages, were seducing those Welsh people who were anxious to make a favourable impression.

Nevertheless, some stood up to challenge the duality between the holy Welsh context and its secular English counterpart. Therein lies the significance of protests by people like the Yorkshire clerics, Thomas Price (Carnhuanawc), Evan Jones (Ieuan Gwynedd), Michael D. Jones and Emrys ap Iwan. Their philosophy of language was broader and deeper than that of people such as Bishop Basil Jones, Kilsby Jones, Lewis Edwards, and the *nouveaux riches* like Richard Davies of Treborth, because they sought to adapt the same Christian principles in a critical way to the cultural policies of the English government. Emrys ap Iwan powerfully expressed this conviction:

> Cofiwch . . . eich bod yn genedl, trwy ordeiniad Duw; am hynny, gwnewch yr hyn a alloch i gadw'r genedl yn genedl, trwy gadw'i hiaith, a phob peth arall a berthyno iddi . . . Gan i Dduw eich gwneuthur yn genedl, ymgedwch yn genedl; gan iddo gymmeryd miloedd o flynyddoedd i ffurfio iaith gyfaddas ichwi, cedwch yr iaith honno . . . [112]

> (Remember . . . that you are a nation, by the ordinance of God; therefore do what you can to keep the nation a nation, by retaining its language, and everything else that belongs to it . . . In as much as God has made you a nation, keep yourself a nation; since he took thousands of years to make a fitting language for you, keep that language . . .)

---

[112] Robert Ambrose Jones (Emrys ap Iwan), *Homiliau* (Dinbych, 1906), p. 53. See also R. Tudur Jones, 'Yr Eglwysi a'r Iaith yn Oes Victoria', *LlC*, 19 (1996), 146–67.

9

Welsh Literature in the Nineteenth Century

ROBERT RHYS

OTHER CHAPTERS in this volume provide the background against which the century's literature must be read, together with the context without which a proper understanding of the work of poets and prose writers cannot be acquired. Any attempt to assess the century's poetry must acknowledge the enormous influence of the eisteddfodau, whether for better, or, by common assent, for worse, as well as the demand from religious quarters, and increasingly during the latter half of the century from the concert hall, for material suitable for public performance, both solo and congregational. What would the course of the century's prose have been, certainly during its latter half, without that cultural explosion associated with the press? The growth of fiction is inextricably bound up with the flourishing of that journalistic culture which gave William Rees (Gwilym Hiraethog) and Robert Ambrose Jones (Emrys ap Iwan) their opportunity in the pages of *Y Faner*, David Owen (Brutus) in *Yr Haul*, and Daniel Owen in *Y Drysorfa* and *Y Cymro*. Another context which demands examination is the nature of the critical response to the century's literature made during the twentieth century. More often than not, the phrase 'the last century' has carried negative and disparaging connotations. Saunders Lewis began his *Introduction to Contemporary Welsh Literature* in 1926 with the sweeping statement that Welsh literature had reached its lowest point in 1870, and that it had been plunged into the depths by the philistine expectations of Nonconformist society.[1] In the previous year W. J. Gruffydd in *Y Llenor* had severely criticized David Owen (Dewi Wyn o Eifion), a poet highly respected by his contemporaries.[2] These are only two examples of the confident surge of a generation of writers and critics who believed that, in drawing water again from the wells of the old native tradition, they were providing their nation's literature with a life-giving force. By and large, the critical responses remained in the same key throughout the twentieth century. The voice of John Morris-Jones and W. J. Gruffydd is

---

[1] Saunders Lewis, *An Introduction to Contemporary Welsh Literature* (Wrexham, 1926), pp. 1–16.
[2] W. J. Gruffydd, 'Dewi Wyn o Eifion', *Y Llenor*, IV (1925), 9–24.

constantly to be heard in Thomas Parry's treatment of the nineteenth century in his *Hanes Llenyddiaeth Gymraeg* (1944), and one of Parry's students, Bedwyr Lewis Jones, was most apologetic in his introduction to his *Blodeugerdd o'r Bedwaredd Ganrif ar Bymtheg* in 1965.[3] A reaction against the constant disparagement of the century's poetry was reflected in the introduction to an anthology compiled by R. M. Jones, published in 1988, which served as a stimulus for literary debate in the Welsh periodical press for several months thereafter.[4] Only time will tell whether R. M. Jones's introduction will be considered the first fruit of a more favourable attitude to the literature of the century, but it needs to be noted that none of the other critics mentioned were exclusively condemnatory.

Bearing in mind the enormous bulk of what was produced during the nineteenth century, this chapter has of necessity a limited aim, namely to provide a balanced and representative picture by making a selective critical survey of its literature, both poetry and prose.

Poetry

The Welsh poetic culture of the nineteenth century sprang from many sources. The minds and words of the poets were being moulded by spiritual forces, by socio-political trends and by various literary conventions; some forms, such as the *awdl* written for eisteddfodau, and the evangelical hymn, had their roots firmly in the eighteenth century, while others like the 'secular' lyric owed more to the old 'free' metres and imitated to some extent the conventions of contemporary English verse.

Our survey begins with a collection from the first decade of the century, a volume edited by David Thomas (Dafydd Ddu Eryri), *Corph y Gaingc* (1810). It consists mainly of his own work, but he also included poems by his hero, Goronwy Owen, and by other contemporary poets, including Robert Williams (Robert ap Gwilym Ddu), Dewi Wyn o Eifion and John Roberts (Siôn Lleyn). Dafydd Ddu Eryri was fifty years old in 1810 and his volume, a celebration of his work as a poet and teacher of poets, seeks to give the impression of a fertile and unbroken tradition linking three generations of poets, namely the chief poet of the previous century in the strict metres, Goronwy Owen, who had died in exile in 1769 when Dafydd Ddu was ten years old, Dafydd Ddu himself as a bridge at

---

[3] Bedwyr Lewis Jones, *Blodeugerdd o'r Bedwaredd Ganrif ar Bymtheg* (Aberystwyth, 1965), pp. xi–xl.
[4] R. M. Jones (ed.), *Blodeugerdd Barddas o'r Bedwaredd Ganrif ar Bymtheg* (Cyhoeddiadau Barddas, 1988), pp. 11–29. See review by Hywel Teifi Edwards, 'Blodeugerdd y Cyfle a Gollwyd', *Barn*, 312 (1989), 38–40. Bobi Jones responded in three articles, 'Barddoniaeth y 19eg Ganrif, 1', *Barn*, 316 (1989), 35–7; 'Barddoniaeth y 19eg Ganrif, II', ibid., 317 (1989), 33–5; 'Barddoniaeth y 19eg Ganrif, III', ibid., 318/19 (1989), 33–6. For Hywel Teifi Edwards's response, see 'R. M. Jones a'i Flodeugerdd', *Barn*, 321 (1989), 9–10, and Bobi Jones again in 'Cerddi a'r Ysbryd', *Barn*, 325 (1990), 6–9 and lastly by Hywel Teifi Edwards, 'R. M. Jones a'i Flodeugerdd', *Barn*, 326 (1990), 35–6.

the centre, and those of his pupils who had attended his poetry classes in Caernarfonshire from their inception in 1783. Dafydd's work is usually skilful and polished, whether in the traditional strict metres (Bedwyr Lewis Jones was right in detecting obvious echoes of Goronwy Owen in his verse),[5] or in the winter and summer carols which he composed on the pattern popular at least since the days of Huw Morys in the seventeenth century, or else in the religious poems 'in the sense of Isaac Watts' and in the metrical psalms which are associated mainly with Edmwnd Prys. The occasional poem in the free metres, such as 'Fy anwyl Fam fy hunan' (My own dear mother), looks back in its metre to the old 'free' poetry and forward in its tone to the lyric of a later period, but the nearest his work comes to 'innovation' is in the *awdlau* which he wrote for the eisteddfodau of the Gwyneddigion towards the end of the eighteenth century; the critical view of the literary quality of these poems is unanimously unfavourable. This writing is imitative and lacking in vitality, reproducing conventions faithfully enough but without the authoritative mastery of Goronwy Owen or the rough vitality of Thomas Edwards (Twm o'r Nant), the poet and writer of interludes who died in the year in which *Corph y Gaingc* was published.

The most renowned of Dafydd Ddu's contemporaries whose work was included in *Corph y Gaingc* were two farmers from Eifionydd, namely Robert Williams (Robert ap Gwilym Ddu) of Betws Fawr and David Owen (Dewi Wyn o Eifion) of Gaerwen. Dafydd Ddu Eryri corresponded with both, and enjoyed their company during his period as a schoolmaster at Llanystumdwy. There has been a tendency during the twentieth century to regard Dewi Wyn as the embodiment of everything which was wrong with Welsh poetry in the nineteenth century – the long, uninspired, expository *awdlau*, and the inflated, verbose, unnatural style. The undoubted popularity of Dewi Wyn during his lifetime was later used as a scourge to whip the abysmal lack of taste among the century's readers and critics. It is true that he made something of a name for himself as an eisteddfod poet with *awdlau* like 'Amaethyddiaeth' (Agriculture), which he composed for the Tremadog Eisteddfod of 1811, and especially with his most famous poem, the unsuccessful *awdl* written for the Denbigh Eisteddfod of 1819 on the subject 'Elusengarwch' (Charity). However, it is difficult to find satisfactory extracts from his work, let alone inspiring ones. Nevertheless, his work was perceptively discussed, for example, by another Eifionydd poet, Ebenezer Thomas (Eben Fardd),[6] and it is quite likely that his neighbour at Betws Fawr was one of those who understood the defects of Dewi Wyn's work, for Robert ap Gwilym Ddu succeeded in practising the discipline and economy not found in the work of Dewi Wyn. An obvious feature of his sure literary instincts was his decision never to compose an eisteddfodic *awdl*. He was the most versatile and

---

[5] Jones, *Blodeugerdd o'r Bedwaredd Ganrif ar Bymtheg*, p. 86.
[6] Eben Fardd, 'Athrylith ac Ysgrifeniadau Dewi Wyn', *Y Traethodydd*, I (1845), 356–64.

competent of the young poets writing at the turn of the century and his numerous *englynion, cywyddau*, carols and hymns have, over two centuries, satisfied the tastes of readers. There is more substance to the literary career of the poet of Betws Fawr, and he is a literary personality in a manner unlike that of his contemporaries. Although he wrote in the same traditional metres as Dafydd Ddu Eryri, he had his own voice, best expressed, perhaps, in the moving *cywydd* written in memory of his only daughter who died at the age of fifteen. In his religious verse he did more than reproduce the fine but familiar patterns of the carol – his best hymns, of which 'Mae'r gwaed a redodd ar y groes' (The blood which ran on the Cross) is the most famous, combine directness of expression and a controlled use of the more conscious literary devices which became part of the repertoire of the hymn writers of north Wales.[7]

The skilful traditionalism fostered by Dafydd Ddu Eryri and his circle was only one aspect of Welsh poetic culture. Dafydd Ddu was, after all, a poet of his community and district, and most of the hundreds of subscribers to *Corph y Gaingc* were from north Wales, and the majority from Caernarfonshire. The popular literary medium for mass consumption was undoubtedly the evangelical hymn, and by the beginning of the nineteenth century the gap which had characterized the relationship between the pioneering poet in the free metres from Llanfair-ar-y-bryn (William Williams) and the conservative classicist of Llanfair Mathafarn (Goronwy Owen) had closed considerably, thanks mainly perhaps to the splendid contribution of Thomas Jones of Denbigh, a fine hymn writer and an accomplished poet in the strict metres, as his 'Cywydd i'r aderyn bronfraith' (*Cywydd* to the thrush) of 1793 demonstrates.[8] As the century proceeded, some of the best poets of north Wales, such as Eben Fardd, Peter Jones (Pedr Fardd) and Evan Evans (Ieuan Glan Geirionydd), penned hymns which would prove to be of permanent value to Welsh congregations.

During the first decade of the century two significant collections of hymns appeared, namely *Grawnsyppiau Canaan* (1805) by Robert Jones of Rhos-lan, and *Hymnau o fawl i Dduw a'r Oen*, published by Thomas Charles a year later. It was in these collections that the work of Ann Griffiths of Llanfihangel-yng-Ngwynfa, Montgomeryshire, first appeared. Ann Griffiths (née Thomas) lived most of her short life during the eighteenth century, and its fiery evangelical zeal is apparent in her work. But her verses were composed in the first years of the nineteenth century, and only later were they arranged and recorded by the Revd John Hughes of Pontrobert from the memory of his wife Ruth, who had been a maidservant in Ann's home. The renown of Ann Griffiths, and the popularity of

---

[7] *Gardd Eifion*, the poetry of Robert ap Gwilym Ddu, edited by the Revd William Williams (Gwilym Caledfryn), was published in 1841. For a selection of Robert ap Gwilym Ddu's work, see Stephen J. Williams, *Robert ap Gwilym Ddu: Detholion o'i Weithiau* (Caerdydd, 1948).

[8] The *cywydd* was discussed by Saunders Lewis, 'Cywydd gan Thomas Jones, Dinbych', *Y Llenor*, XII (1933), 133–43.

her hymns was such that in the fifth volume of *Y Gwyddoniadur Cymreig* in 1866 it was said of her: 'the charm and divine quality of her hymns are almost incomparable, and they commemorate her splendidly in the heart of every Christian who has read them and tasted their sweetness' ('y mae swyn a nefoleidd-dra ei hymnau bron yn anghymarol, ac wedi gwneyd ei choffadwriaeth yn fendigedig yn nghalon pob Cristion sydd wedi eu darllen ac wedi profi eu melusder').[9] By the time O. M. Edwards published his enchanting account of his visit to Dolwar Fach in *Cymru* in the early 1890s,[10] commemoration had begun to yield to mythological and cult-like elements, a tendency which has increased during the twentieth century, and which, significantly, has coincided with the attempt to drive a wedge between 'the fiery, blessed Ann' ('y danbaid fendigaid Ann'), as Cynan described her, and the Calvinistic religion of her time. Some of her verses were written in the heat of the effects of inspired Calvinistic preaching on her mind and heart, including the famous hymn 'Wele'n sefyll rhwng y myrtwydd' (See, standing between the myrtles), which is typical of the way in which intensely subjective experiences are expressed through a framework of scriptural allusion.

The popularity of the evangelical hymn as a literary medium was still strong at the beginning of the century, as is revealed by the volumes of Titus Lewis, *Mawl i'r Oen a laddwyd; sef Pigion o Hymnau perthynol i addoliad cyhoeddus*, and Edward Jones of Maes-y-plwm, *Hymnau &c. Ar Amryw Destunau ac Achosion*, published in 1810. These did not possess the sheer excitement of Ann Griffiths's work nor the craftsmanship of Pedr Fardd, a native of Eifionydd who spent most of his life in Liverpool and who published collections of hymns in 1825 and 1830. Pedr Fardd is perhaps the best example of one who bridged the gap between Llanfair Mathafarn and Llanfair-ar-y-bryn. He published his first book, *Mêl Awen*, in 1823; couched in the strict metres, its debt to Goronwy Owen is evident. For example, in his 'Anerchiad i Dewi Wyn a Robert ap Gwilym Ddu, dau o brif-feirdd Eifionydd yn Swydd Caernarfon' (Address to Dewi Wyn and Robert ap Gwilym Ddu, two chief poets from Eifionydd in Caernarfonshire), there is an echo of Goronwy's longing for his homeland.[11] But strong though the conventions were which drew him to Goronwy Owen, the social contacts with the Nonconformist culture of Liverpool were stronger. He was a deacon in the Calvinistic Methodist chapel, Pall Mall, and it was for his denomination's Sunday school festivals in the city that he wrote many of his hymns. For that substantial congregation he wrote mellifluous hymns such as 'Daeth ffrydiau melys iawn' (Very sweet streams came) and 'Cyn llunio'r byd'

---

[9] *Y Gwyddoniadur Cymreig*, edited by the Revd John Parry, Vol. V (Dinbych, 1866), p. 149. For the works of Ann Griffiths, see E. Wyn James (ed.), *Rhyfeddaf Fyth . . . Emynau a Llythyrau Ann Griffiths, ynghyd â'r byrgofiant iddi gan John Hughes, Pontrobert, a rhai llythyrau gan gyfeillion* (Gregynog, 1998).

[10] 'Dolwar Fechan', *Cymru*, I (1891), 8–13.

[11] *Mêl Awen – sef Gwaith Awenyddawl Peter Jones o Lynlleifad neu Pedr Fardd, yn cynnwys Awdlau, englynion a chywyddau ar amrywiol destunau* (Llynlleifiad, 1823), pp. 77–82.

(Before creating the world), taking advantage of his technical skill to create clusters of *cynghanedd sain* in the hymn metre. Thomas Parry has claimed of hymn writers such as Pedr Fardd that 'some of their best hymns are as beautiful as the modern lyric',[12] an observation which again reflects the assumption of the twentieth century that other periods must be judged according to its own standards; in fact, of course, it was the hymn writers who gave the lyricists many of their formal patterns.

Eben Fardd belonged to a younger generation, and his literary career neatly illustrates the way in which the poets of his generation chose their subjects according to various conventions. According to E. G. Millward, Eben Fardd began his career with his roots in the classicism of the eighteenth century and the poetic tradition of Eifionydd. But he swiftly adopted the mannerisms of the pre-Romantic poets of England, and by the end of his life it is no exaggeration to say that he was one of the most important pioneers of Welsh romanticism.[13] It is generally agreed that his *awdl* 'Dinistr Jerusalem gan y Rhufeiniaid' (The Sack of Jerusalem by the Romans),[14] with which he won the chair at the Powys Eisteddfod in 1824, is one of the pinnacles of eisteddfodic poetry in the strict metres, despite the influence of the synthetic vocabulary of William Owen Pughe, who had published *Coll Gwynfa*, his strange translation of *Paradise Lost*, five years previously.[15] He was bitterly disappointed by the failure of his Christian epic on the subject of 'Yr Adgyfodiad' (The Resurrection) to win the chair at Rhuddlan Eisteddfod in 1850, but it received enormous, indeed extravagant, praise from Lewis Edwards in the pages of *Y Traethodydd*, where he referred to the poem as 'the noblest composition ever to have appeared in the Welsh language'.[16] Although it is easy to list the artistic shortcomings of the poem, and correct to bemoan the fact that it prompted so many other poets to make even more bungled efforts in the same vein, Eben Fardd's attempt, together with the uncritical judgement of Lewis Edwards, at least underlines the desire to broaden the horizons of the Welsh language, to make it the medium of a more ambitious and more sublime literature. But it is in his less ambitious work that Eben Fardd's gifts can be seen to have respite from the ambitions of his time: in 'Cywydd Ymweliad â Llangybi, Eifionydd' (*Cywydd* on a Visit to Llangybi, Eifionydd) (1854), in the charming *tribannau*, 'Molawd Clynnog' (In Praise of Clynnog), in the poem on the *tri-thrawiad* metre to his native district, 'Eifionydd', and above all in the moving hymn 'Crist yn Graig Ddisigl' (Christ the Steadfast Rock) which was published in his collection, *Hymnau* (1861). Needless to say, it was that simple statement of faith which, of all his poems, became a part of the cultural inheritance of the Welsh people.[17]

---

[12] Thomas Parry, *A History of Welsh Literature*, translated by H. Idris Bell (Oxford, 1955), p. 319.
[13] E. G. Millward, *Eben Fardd* (Caernarfon, 1988), p. 49.
[14] The *awdl* was published in the poet's first volume, *Caniadau* (Caernarfon, 1841).
[15] *Coll Gwynfa*, translated by Idrison [William Owen Pughe] (Llundain, 1819).
[16] Eben Fardd, 'Yr Adgyfodiad : Pryddest', *Y Traethodydd*, VII (1851), 24–77.
[17] For these poems, see Jones, *Blodeugerdd Barddas o'r Bedwaredd Ganrif ar Bymtheg*, pp. 160–8, 187.

Eben Fardd's first book, *Caniadau* (1841), contained a poem of thirty lines, 'Myfyrdod ar Lan Afon' (Contemplation on the Bank of a River), in which can be heard the essence of the lyrical, meditative poetry which was to become increasingly popular. This tendency can be seen even more clearly during the 1840s in the work of a young poet from Cardiganshire, namely Daniel Silvan Evans, author of *Blodau Ieuainc* (1843) and *Telynegion* (1846). The poem in the free metres, 'Llinellau i'r Gog' (Lines to the Cuckoo), from his first book, is a clumsy example of the new 'poetic' language which took the fancy of so many poets, but which seldom compared favourably with the elegant craftsmanship of the hymn. D. Silvan Evans proceeded to make a substantial contribution as a lexicographer and editor, and he is sometimes cited as one of the most brilliant examples of 'the old literary clerics', a term coined by R. T. Jenkins and used by Bedwyr Lewis Jones as the title of his study of the contribution made by churchmen to Welsh scholarship and culture during the first half of the nineteenth century.[18] We are not concerned here with tracing their efforts in the fields of the eisteddfod and scholarship, but the poetry of D. Silvan Evans refers us to the fertile relationship between the growth of Welsh lyrical poetry and the church movement which was centred around the tireless activity of such men as John Jenkins (Ifor Ceri) and W. J. Rees. Silvan Evans was a Congregationalist who became a churchman, and it was not uncommon for someone of Nonconformist background to find himself under the wing of the literary clerics. The transfer often followed in the wake of success at the eisteddfod; that is what happened to two of the most notable poets of the second quarter of the century, namely John Blackwell (Alun) and Ieuan Glan Geirionydd.[19] Although both wrote well in various metres – Alun's *awdlau* are among the best of his time and compare favourably with prize-winning *awdlau* of the twentieth century, while the hymns of Ieuan Glan Geirionydd, 'Ar lan Iorddonen ddofn' (By Jordan's deep bank) and 'Fy Nhad sydd wrth y llyw' (My Father is at the helm), are justly familiar – they are both mainly associated with the lyric and, bearing in mind the central place of that form in the literary-cultural revival of the twentieth century, the early antecedents should not be ignored. Even so, the mantle of progressive pioneer does not lie easily on the shoulders of either poet; indeed, the antiquarian motive in Alun's involvement with the free metres is a strong one, and sometimes the poems are disappointingly rehashed and imitative, as in the case of 'Cerdd Hela' (A Hunting Poem), located in Glamorgan and based on a similar poem by Lewis Hopcyn.[20] Alun probably discovered the Glamorgan poem in Ifor Ceri's

---

[18] Bedwyr Lewis Jones, *'Yr Hen Bersoniaid Llengar'* (Penarth, 1963).
[19] A short biography of John Blackwell is included in Griffith Edwards (Gutyn Padarn) (ed.), *Ceinion Alun* (Llundain, 1850), pp. 1–59, and of Evan Evans in Richard Parry (Gwalchmai) (ed.), *Geirionydd* (Rhuthyn, 1862), pp. 9–50.
[20] See Bedwyr Lewis Jones, 'Rhamantiaeth "Yr Ysgol Ramantaidd a Thelynegol"' in J. E. Caerwyn Williams (ed.), *Ysgrifau Beirniadol VII* (Dinbych, 1971), pp. 104–14.

manuscript collection in his rectory at Kerry in Montgomeryshire, a convenient meeting place for those literary-minded clerics who came to spend a term at Thomas Richards's school in Berriew.[21] The fever of collecting old books, folk tales and verses had gripped Alun before he settled in Montgomeryshire, as is evident from his letter to R. Llwyd of Chester early in 1824: 'I have derived considerable pleasure and profit in the perusal of these curiosities, and a few pieces which I thought excelled, I have taken the liberty to copy . . . I am determined to bestow my exertions to collect, and my mind to study such remains of our forefathers.'[22] Nor did he merely blow the dust from the relics; the folk tradition was still vibrant enough during the formative years of the poets under consideration. The study of contemporary harpists undertaken by Robert Griffith reveals that several were active in the Conwy valley, where Ieuan Glan Geirionydd lived, and Ieuan himself was trained in the craft.[23] Gwen Guest and Bedwyr Lewis Jones have shown that Welsh poets also came under the influence of their popular English contemporaries whose work appeared in the literary periodicals, comparatively inferior verse which was recycled in such newspapers as the *Chester Chronicle*.[24] It has also been argued that Ieuan and Alun prepared the ground for the later sweeping success of John Ceiriog Hughes, John Jones (Talhaiarn) and Richard Davies (Mynyddog) by making the old free metres respectable, disinfecting them from the stench of the tavern, and giving them a veneer of that primness which audiences in the second half of the nineteenth century were to insist upon.

During the 1850s a new generation of poets began publishing their first books. Although the literary cleric Owen Wyn Jones (Glasynys) was not the most talented among them, it is clear that his books *Fy Oriau Hamddenol* (1854) and *Lleucu Llwyd ynghyda Chaneuon eraill* (1858) met the demand for natural, unassuming verse which was free from obtrusive literary devices, as is shown by the revealing words of an anonymous reviewer of *Lleucu Llwyd* in *Y Brython* in 1858:

> Bardd o'r iawn ryw yw Glasynys, ac y mae mwy o wir farddoniaeth yn fynych mewn un ganig o'r eiddo, nag a geir mewn cryn lyfryn o waith ambell un a gymmer arno ei fod yn fardd pwysig dros ben, ac a'ch gosodai chwi i lawr ym mhlith anwybodusion penaf y greadigaeth, pe methai genych ganfod barddoniaeth o'r fath ardderchocaf yn ei waith. Os caiff ambell un o'n rhigymwyr ddigon o glec yn y llinell, a digon o gydseiniaid geirwon i ymfrwydro â'u gilydd, a digon o dywyllwch i ordoi'r cwbl, dyna

---

[21] See Stephen J. Williams, 'Ifor Ceri – Noddwr Cerdd' in Brynley F. Roberts (ed.), *Beirdd ac Eisteddfodwyr: Erthyglau gan Stephen J. Williams* (Abertawe, 1981), pp. 18–46.
[22] Gutyn Padarn, *Ceinion Alun*, p. 86.
[23] Robert Griffith, *Llyfr Cerdd Dannau* (Caernarfon, 1913).
[24] Jones, 'Rhamantiaeth "Yr Ysgol Ramantaidd a Thelynegol"', pp. 104–14; Gwendoline Guest, 'Bywyd a Gwaith John Blackwell (Alun) 1797–1840' (unpubl. University of Wales MA thesis, 1971).

farddoniaeth, yn ei dyb ef . . . Y mae yn iechyd calon i un gyfarfod ag ambell lyfryn fel llyfryn Glasynys, wedi i un gael hanner ei ddieneidio wrth geisio ymlwybran trwy gyfansoddiadau llyffetheiriog beirdd y glec, y sothach, a'r ansynwyr.[25]

(Glasynys is a true poet, and there is often more real poetry in one of his verses than is to be found in a whole booklet of work by some who claim to be exceedingly important poets, and who put you down among the chief ignoramuses of creation if you fail to discover poetry of the finest quality in their work. If some of our rhymesters write an occasional good line, and get enough rough consonants to struggle with one another, and enough obscurity to crown the whole, that is poetry in their estimation . . . It does one a world of good to encounter a booklet like that of Glasynys, after one has been daunted by trying to work one's way through the shackled compositions of the poets who rely on the *clec*, on rubbish, and on the nonsensical.)

This is a *cri de cœur* against the false mutilation of the literary language and the poseurs who hid behind pretentious pseudonyms. The protest against poetic follies was a sign of how ready the ground was to receive the sweetest poets of the third quarter of the century, namely Talhaiarn, who published his first book in 1855, and Ceiriog, whose *Oriau'r Hwyr* appeared in 1860. By listening to Ceiriog discuss the details of his craft and the audience's expectations in the opening part of *Y Bardd a'r Cerddor* (1863), we can sense the temperament and aesthetics of the period. We see him popularizing still more the kind of poetry in the free metres which was written by Alun and others, often literally 'lyrical' poetry since it was meant to be sung to the accompaniment of the harp, and written as a response to the urgent demand of the new cultural market which was centred on the eisteddfod and the concert hall. The title of the opening part of his book, which is a combination of literary manifesto and sound technical advice, is 'Awgrymiadau ynghylch ysgrifennu caneuon a geiriau i gerddoriaeth' (Suggestions about the writing of songs and words for music). The author had no doubt but that he was speaking at a time of revolution in the history of Welsh culture: 'There is greater demand nowadays than ever before for words suitable for singing, and the occasions on which these songs can be used, in concerts and other entertainments, are more than twice or thrice as much as they were years ago. Society has also risen a step higher, so that many of the old poems have become unsuitable for present popular taste. Indeed, a new phase has begun in the songs of the people' ('Y mae mwy o alwad nag erioed y dyddiau hyn am eiriau i'w canu, ac achlysuron i wneud defnydd o'r cyfryw ganeuon, mewn cyngherddau a chyrddau adlonawl, wedi dyblu a threblu rhagor yr hyn oeddynt flynyddoedd yn ol. Y mae cymdeithas hefyd wedi esgyn ris yn uwch, nes mae lluaws o'r hen gerddi wedi myned yn anaddas i chwaeth bresenol y bobl. Yn wir y mae cyfnod newydd wedi

---

[25] *Y Brython*, 9 July 1858, 37. For the best introduction to the life and work of Glasynys, see Saunders Lewis, *Straeon Glasynys* (Aberystwyth, 1943).

dechreu ar ganiadau y genedl').[26] And in announcing the new phase he argued that it had to go hand-in-hand with a rejection of the old: 'The time of tavern poetry, like druidic theology, has come to the end of its existence . . . What was formerly popular has become an unacceptable burden on present taste. No subject is now tolerated unless it tends to the uplifting or moral' ('Y mae adeg prydyddiaeth y dafarn, fel duwinyddiaeth dderwyddol, wedi cyrhaedd pen pellaf ei bodolaeth . . . y mae yr hyn oedd boblogaidd gynt wedi dyfod yn fwrn gwrthwynebus i'r chwaeth bresenol. Ni oddefir un testyn yn awr os na bydd o duedd ddyrchafedig neu foesol').[27] But there was a price to pay for Ceiriog's readiness to serve the musician, as well as the taste and expectations of the masses. Gwenallt believed that Ceiriog was a piano poet[28] who proclaimed that 'when a well-known tune needs words, then the poet must go the whole way to meeting the musician' ('pan ddigwyddo fod tôn adnabyddus mewn angen am eiriau, yna rhaid i'r bardd fyned yr holl ffordd at y cerddor');[29] it is he who tells the poet to adopt a wholly practical attitude towards his work. Ceiriog was too uncritically obedient to his audience to hope to please more stringent later readers, although critics as various as R. Williams Parry and R. M. Jones have acknowledged the remarkable achievement of his best lyrics, one describing 'Nant y Mynydd' (Mountain stream) as the most perfect lyric in Welsh poetry, and the other stating that he was capable sometimes of striking a note of astonishing purity.[30] But the gaps left by Ceiriog's sentimentality are easy enough to perceive, despite the fact that he indicated that he would have liked to loosen the Victorian collar a little, sometimes in his songs, but especially in his comic and satirical prose. Nevertheless, his role as a writer of popular literature cannot be denied and it was as the maker of images of Welsh life that readers found him attractive, for better or for worse, for a century and more.[31]

The harp which he had heard in the Harp inn in the days of his childhood at Llanfair Talhaiarn was close to Talhaiarn's heart, and he composed a number of humorous and singable songs, among which were 'Mae Robin yn swil' (Robin is shy). His natural muse was not sufficiently modest to please contemporary taste, but he bowed to what was expected of him as a poet by writing words for tunes and arrangements by John Owen (Owain Alaw) and John Thomas (Pencerdd Gwalia).[32] According to Saunders Lewis, in a review of *Hanes Llenyddiaeth*

---

[26] John Ceiriog Hughes, *Y Bardd a'r Cerddor: gyda Hen Ystraeon am danynt* (Gwrecsam, 1863), p. 5.
[27] Ibid., p. 32.
[28] D. Gwenallt Jones, 'Ceiriog' in Dyfnallt Morgan (ed.), *Gwŷr Llên y Bedwaredd Ganrif ar Bymtheg a'u Cefndir* (Llandybïe, 1968), p. 212.
[29] Hughes, *Y Bardd a'r Cerddor*, p. 36.
[30] R. Williams Parry, 'Ceiriog – Bardd heb ei debyg' in Bedwyr Lewis Jones (ed.), *Rhyddiaith R. Williams Parry* (Dinbych, 1974), pp. 108–17; Jones, *Blodeugerdd Barddas o'r Bedwaredd Ganrif ar Bymtheg*, p. 24.
[31] See Hywel Teifi Edwards, *Ceiriog* (Caernarfon, 1987).
[32] See Dewi M. Lloyd, *Talhaiarn* (Caernarfon, 1993).

Gymraeg in 1946, Talhaiarn was 'the only poet of his time who was intensely conscious of the tragedy of man's life'.[33] This claim was made on the basis of the long poem, or collection of poems, 'Tal ar Ben Bodran'. A poem of twenty cantos, it was composed on the pattern of similar poems by Byron, Talhaiarn's literary hero, and it makes use of *ottava rima*, which is to be found in the English poet's work. The cohesive device is the conversation between the poet and his Muse, but the reader should not expect a symmetrical, linked poem. The device is a stratagem, according to Dewi M. Lloyd, to bring together imitations, satire, the practice of various metres, critical comments and original poems,[34] but as the work progresses it includes the more serious, contemplative elements which attracted the attention of Saunders Lewis.

We need to mention another important poet who published his first book during the 1850s, namely William Thomas (Islwyn), a native of the Sirhywi valley in Monmouthshire. He published a slim volume of verse, *Barddoniaeth*, in 1854, but his muse had been fired by the death of his fiancée, Ann Bowen, in November 1853, and although he did not publish his second collection, *Caniadau*, until 1867, it is clear that the period 1854–6 was a remarkably productive one for him.[35] This was when he composed several well-known poems like the hymn 'Gwêl uwchlaw cymylau amser' (See, above the clouds of time) and the first epic poem on the subject of 'Y Storm' (The Storm), which was kept in manuscript and of which the full version was not printed until 1980, although O. M. Edwards had printed parts in *Gwaith Islwyn* in 1897.[36] Although he wrote uninspired *awdlau*, Islwyn was one of those who favoured the liberty of the free metres. 'When the poetic genius soars to its highest realms', he wrote in an essay on the Scottish poet and critic Alexander Smith, 'nearest to the heavenly and the unconquerable, he cannot afford, in the splendour of his vision, to fall back down to earth to turn the pages of the dictionary for a rhyme' ('Pan fyddo yr athrylith barddonol yn esgyn i'w gylchoedd uchelaf, agosaf i'r nefol a'r didranc, nis gall fforddio, gan ysblander y weledigaeth, i ddisgyn i lawr i'r daearol i droi tudalennau geirlyfr am gyfodlair').[37] Despite all his shortcomings, it is Islwyn who takes the Welsh muse into the world of complex imagery and intellectual aspiration. Yet, the number of satisfactory poems written in that register by Islwyn or any of his ilk is small. Islwyn's best poems, nevertheless, managed to satisfy the intelligence and imagination of readers in more than one generation, and the selection made by R. M. Jones succeeds in conveying the poetic energy of the poet at his best.[38]

The search for a generation of similar stature arising between 1870 and 1890 is a vain one, and it would be easy to have fun at the expense of poets who gained

---

[33] Saunders Lewis, *Meistri a'u Crefft* (Caerdydd, 1981), pp. 271–2.
[34] Lloyd, *Talhaiarn*, p. 70.
[35] See D. Gwenallt Jones, *Bywyd a Gwaith Islwyn* (Lerpwl, 1948).
[36] Meurig Walters (ed.), *'Y Storm' gyntaf gan Islwyn* (Caerdydd, 1980).
[37] Islwyn, 'Alexander Smith', *Y Llenor*, XI (1897), 33.
[38] Jones, *Blodeugerdd Barddas o'r Bedwaredd Ganrif ar Bymtheg*, pp. 299–340.

critical acclaim at eisteddfodau, such as Thomas Tudno Jones (Tudno), whose work was published posthumously in the volume *Telyn Tudno* (1897), J. J. Roberts (Iolo Carnarvon), the winner of three national crowns in succession between 1890 and 1892, and John Owen Williams (Pedrog), the collector of much eisteddfodic furniture. These poets were known collectively as 'Y Bardd Newydd'; they were, for the most part, preacher-poets whose compositions were long and expository in style, and their work became ideal aunt sallies for later critics. Of these Alun Llywelyn-Williams wrote: 'The plain truth is that the *Bardd Newydd* was not really a poet, that he had no inkling of what poetry was' ('Y gwir plaen yw nad oedd y Bardd Newydd ddim yn fardd, nad oedd ganddo glem ar farddoniaeth').[39] There is a lighter touch, here and there, in the work of Watkin Hezekiah Williams (Watcyn Wyn), for example, the author of *Caneuon* (1871), *Odlau'r Efengyl* (1882) and *Hwyr Ddifyrion* (1883),[40] but the most interesting poet to emerge during these years was undoubtedly the young preacher from Blaen-y-coed in Carmarthenshire, Howell Elvet Lewis (Elfed). He was born in 1860 and lived until 1953, during which period he became an extremely popular national figure. He composed some of the most popular hymns of his time, but by the end of the twentieth century the response to his work had become more critical; *The New Companion to the Literature of Wales* (1998) states plainly: 'With the exception of his hymns, his subsequent poetry is unremarkable.' By and large, his work is rather dull, but it pleased his contemporaries greatly, to a large extent because it appealed to the admirers of Ceiriog and Islwyn by combining the prettiness of the former and some measure of the philosophical meditation of the latter.[41] He is also considered to be a morning star heralding the reawakening which was to occur in Welsh poetry after his day, because his work demonstrated the purity of modest craftsmanship as well as a readiness to draw upon native folk tales for its material and images. It is not difficult to discover an emphasis and idiom which the younger poets who came of age in the new century grasped so resolutely. During the 1880s and 1890s Elfed wrote several poems which were partly successful, among them the popular *pryddest* 'Gorsedd Gras' (The Throne of Grace), in which Daniel Owen found solace during his last illness, the love poem 'Llyn y Morynion' (The Lake of the Maidens), 'Gwyn ap Nudd', and 'Rhagorfraint y Gweithiwr' (The Worker's Privilege), the poem which includes one of his most famous lines, 'Nid cardod i ddyn ond gwaith' (Not charity for a man but work).[42] The evidence of these years suggests that Elfed, despite his shortcomings, was

---

[39] Alun Llywelyn-Williams, 'Y Bardd Newydd' in Morgan, *Gwŷr Llên y Bedwaredd Ganrif ar Bymtheg*, p. 277.

[40] See Bryan Martin Davies, *'Ruy'n gweld o bell . . .' Bywyd a Gwaith Watcyn Wyn* (Gwasanaeth Diwylliant Llyfrgell Dyfed, 1980), and Huw Walters, *Canu'r Pwll a'r Pulpud* (Cyhoeddiadau Barddas, 1987).

[41] See, for example, Branwen Jarvis, '"Garedig Ysbryd": Golwg ar Ganu Elfed', *LlC*, XVIII, no. 1 and 2 (1994), 114–26.

[42] His work is published in *Caniadau Elfed* (Caerdydd, 1909).

laying the foundations of a significant career as a poet, but it was not to be, and he has no real place in the poetry of the twentieth century.

If Elfed in several respects is the most interesting poet of the period, John Morris-Jones was probably the most influential. His only book of poetry was published in 1907, but his translations of Heine, together with his *awdl* 'Cymru Fu: Cymru Fydd' (The Wales of the Past: the Wales of the Future), a poem classical in style and radical in its message, appeared in O. M. Edwards's periodical *Cymru* in the early 1890s.[43] The following lines from a *pryddest* by Iolo Carnarvon, 'Ardderchog Lu y Merthyri' (The Splendid Legion of Martyrs) reveal that which Morris-Jones reacted against:

> Tystion i a thros wirionedd oeddynt hwy yn mhlith eu rhyw;
> *Tystion* – cynddrychiolent Iesu Grist yn marw ac yn byw.
> Credent wironeddau sanctaidd nes y deuent drwy eu ffydd
> Gref yn wironeddau dysglaer dröent nos ein byd yn ddydd.[44]

(They were witnesses to and for truth among their people; *witnesses* – they represented Jesus Christ dead and alive. They believed in holy truths until they became by their faith strong in the shining truths which turned the night of our world into day.)

The poem contains more than nine hundred lines in this vein. The contrasting appeal of the succinct, the pretty and the unpreacherly charming was clear. What strikes the reader most forcibly about some of Morris-Jones's early exercises is the way in which he takes pleasure in the phonology of Welsh and the sound of poetry for its own sake, deliberately unphilosophical and with no message, but with a confidence and academic authority not possessed by his predecessors earlier in the century. The 'Llythyrau' ('At O. M. E.'), which he wrote between 1886 and 1889, are perfect examples, as the first verse of the second in the series demonstrates:

> I Fynwy fawr o'r Fona fau,
> O lannau Menai lonydd
> I lannau Hafren lydan lon,
> At union bert awenydd,
> Cyfeirio cerdd am gerdd a wnaf,
> Os medraf, megis mydrydd.[45]

(To great Monmouthshire from my Anglesey, from the banks of quiet Menai to the banks of broad and contented Severn, I shall address poem after poem to a sweet poet, if I can, like a rhymester.)

---

[43] John Morris Jones, *Caniadau* (Rhydychen, 1907).
[44] J. J. Roberts (Iolo Carnarvon), *Ymsonau* (Caernarfon, 1895), p. 13.
[45] Morris Jones, *Caniadau*, p. 34.

Morris-Jones did not always write in such a carefree way, and Alun Llywelyn-Williams has revealed the significance of the *awdlau* composed during the 1890s – 'Cymru Fu: Cymru Fydd' and 'Salm i Famon' (Psalm to Mammon) – as the poet expressed his anger at the philistine and materialistic aspects of contemporary society in a style which suggested a debt to William Morris and John Ruskin, and which struck a note of protest similar to that heard in the work of a young poet from Betws-yn-rhos, T. Gwynn Jones.[46] During the latter years of the century Morris-Jones wrote his most polished verse, namely his magisterial translation of the *Ruba'iyat* of Omar Khayyám.[47] Like that of Elfed, Morris-Jones's career as a poet did not develop during the new century, and perhaps he should be considered mainly as a poet who pointed the way for poets of richer imagination and expression such as T. Gwynn Jones.

Prose

In the introduction to his great novel *Enoc Huws* (1891), Daniel Owen was able to look back at major changes he had witnessed in Welsh literary culture during his lifetime. It could hardly be denied, he wrote, that the Welsh people now possessed a literature. But it was a literature of a special kind, one which was restricted in its styles and registers. It was natural that the novelist should note the obvious lacunae in a field in which he had been a pioneer; the greater part of Welsh life was still fallow land unturned by the nation's authors. Daniel Owen was referring to exterior social life. The landscape of the inner spiritual life had received the attention of some of the nation's weightiest writers, and the nation had performed miracles in the field of educational literature, with the publication of Thomas Charles's *Geiriadur Ysgrythyrawl* and *Y Gwyddoniadur Cymreig* as its most outstanding achievements. The greyness of the century's literature has been attributed to the educational, utilitarian motive, but it would be a serious mistake to draw the curtain too abruptly on what it has to offer. It is generally agreed that Thomas Jones (of Caerwys, Mold and Denbigh) was the ablest of the Methodist writers at the beginning of the century. He made his most important and most popular contribution as the translator of Gurnal and with his adaptations of Fox and others, but in 1820, the year of his death, he published a

---

[46] Alun Llywelyn-Williams, *Y Nos, y Niwl a'r Ynys: Agweddau ar y Profiad Rhamantaidd yng Nghymru, 1890–1914* (Caerdydd, 1960), pp. 58–62, 110–11.
[47] Morris Jones, *Caniadau*, pp. 161–82.

classic autobiography.[48] In view of the criticisms made of the pseudo-respectability and false modesty of the century's later literature, it is surely significant that Thomas Jones was willing to explore the innermost crannies of the soul, to study the unpleasant and painful weariness of the flesh, and to record it accurately and honestly.

Thomas Jones set about writing his memoirs in response to Thomas Charles's encouragement. They had been co-editors of *Y Drysorfa Ysbrydol* (1799) and were staunch co-workers. Although Charles did not consider that he had as good a mastery of Welsh as his colleague, the *Geiriadur Ysgrythyrawl* (1805–11) contains a wealth of notable essays characterized by thoroughness of learning, detail of argument, and lively, spirited conviction of expression.[49] It was Charles, too, who urged Robert Jones of Rhos-lan to record aspects of the history of Methodism. He did so in his *Drych yr Amseroedd* (1820), a volume which set the tone for considerable autobiographical, exhortatory writing by Methodists during the nineteenth century, and one which twentieth-century critics have been more than ready to include within the canon of the Welsh literary tradition.[50] Among other writers of the period, one of the most industrious was Azariah Shadrach (1774–1844), who spent his most productive phase as a Congregational minister in Aberystwyth. He published more than twenty booklets between 1800 and 1840 and on his tombstone he was described as 'the Bunyan of Wales'.[51] It is not difficult to understand Shadrach's popularity. He understood the value of dividing educational and doctrinal material into short, incisive sections, and he often used his own poems to underline the moral. The 36-page booklet *Allwedd Myfyrdod neu Arweinydd i'r Meddwl Segur* (Carmarthen, 1809) consists of sixteen short chapters with titles such as 'Allwedd Myfyrdod wrth rodio ar Lan y Môr' (The Key to Contemplation while walking the Seashore) and 'Allwedd Myfyrdod wrth ddal yr Aradr' (The Key to Contemplation while holding the Plough).

---

[48] For a list of the publications of Thomas Jones, see Jonathan Jones, *Cofiant y Parch. Thomas Jones o Ddinbych* (Dinbych, 1897), pp. 396–406. *Y Cristion mewn Cyflawn Arfogaeth*, his translation of sections of the classic by the English Puritan, William Gurnal, *The Christian in Compleat Armour*, was published in two parts in Mold in 1796 and in Ruthin in 1809. It was printed in one volume by Gwasg Gee in Denbigh, in 1862, for example, and as late as 1883. His 1,165 page volume, *Hanes y Merthyron yn Mhrydain Fawr*, was published in Denbigh in 1813. It was in great demand throughout the century: a 'cheap edition' was published in two volumes by Gee in Denbigh in 1893. His autobiography was published under the title, *Cofiant, neu Hanes Bywyd a Marwolaeth y Parch. Thomas Jones* (Dinbych, 1829); see also Idwal Jones (ed.), *Hunangofiant y Parch Thomas Jones o Ddinbych* (Aberystwyth, 1937).

[49] The *Geiriadur* was published in four parts between 1805 and 1811. For the life and work of Thomas Charles, see D. E. Jenkins, *The Life of the Rev. Thomas Charles of Bala . . . in three volumes* (Denbigh, 1908). The seventh edition of the *Geiriadur* was published in one volume (xvi + 944 pages) by Hughes and Son, Wrexham, in 1893.

[50] Robert Jones, *Drych yr Amseroedd*, ed. Glyn M. Ashton (Caerdydd, 1958).

[51] See Charles Ashton, *Hanes Llenyddiaeth Gymreig, o 1651 O.C. hyd 1850* (Liverpool, 1893), pp. 506–12.

It has already been suggested that the significance of the newspaper in the development of the century's prose cannot be overemphasized, and in this respect the establishment of *Yr Amserau* under the editorship of Gwilym Hiraethog in 1843 was an important milestone. The editor's own contributions were particularly influential. 'Llythurau 'Rhen Ffarmwr' (Letters of the Old Farmer), which were published as a series in *Yr Amserau* between 1846 and 1851 (and then in book form in 1878), dealt with current affairs, and their significance lies in the manner in which they used the author's native dialect (he came from Llansannan in Denbighshire) as an alternative literary medium and one which was well suited to expressing radical convictions and to challenging the system. Gwilym Hiraethog realized that the Welsh language needed the freedom of unofficial, unrespectable registers if it was to be a medium for bold and lively writing. But, of course, as editor he had to rebuke his alter ego, 'the Old Farmer', on account of his vulgar language!: 'The expressions "myn diaist", "cynddeiriog", "bogs arnynt", "i'w crogi" etc . . . are so unseemly. I shouldn't allow them to appear in the pages of *Yr Amserau* except to take an opportunity of showing how odious they are' ('Mor anweddaidd ac erchyll yw yr ymadroddion – "myn diaist", – "cynddeiriog", – "bogs arnynt" – "i'w crogi" &c . . . Ni buasem yn gadael iddynt ymddangos ar wyneb yr *Amserau*, ond yn unig er cael y fantais i ddangos eu gwrthuni').[52] In this respect, as E. G. Millward has argued, Gwilym Hiraethog was echoing Twm o'r Nant and John Jones (Jac Glan-y-gors) from the end of the previous century, but it was a highly influential echo in so far as one aspect of the century's prose-style was concerned. As for literary forms, his next major venture was even more influential. In 1853 he published *Aelwyd F'Ewythr Robert: neu, Hanes Caban F'Ewythr Tomos*, an adaptation of Harriet Beecher Stowe's extremely popular novel, *Uncle Tom's Cabin*. According to E. G. Millward, *Aelwyd F'Ewythr Robert* gave a powerful boost to the growth of fiction in Welsh and it was often deployed as proof that the 'novel' could be as beneficial as the Welsh translation of *The Pilgrim's Progress*.[53] From 1853 fiction became a common element in what was published in Welsh newspapers and periodicals. When Gwilym Hiraethog's adaptation was published in book form in 1853, Daniel Owen was an apprentice tailor, and it is likely that he first heard the story being read in the workshop of Angell Jones in Mold. By the end of the decade he was turning his own hand to translating a popular moral tale. His adaptation of the novel by Timothy Shay Arthur, *Ten Nights in a bar-room and what I saw there*, appeared in the pages of *Charles o'r Bala* in 1859.[54] Needless to say, it was not by the tellers of moral tales

[52] *Yr Amserau*, 25 February 1847, p. 3.
[53] E. G. Millward, 'Gwilym Hiraethog: Llenor y Trawsnewid' in idem, *Cenedl o Bobl Ddewrion: Agweddau ar Lenyddiaeth Oes Victoria* (Llandysul, 1991), p. 91; see also Ioan Williams, *Capel a Chomin: Astudiaeth o Ffugchwedlau Pedwar Llenor Fictoraidd* (Caerdydd, 1989), pp. 31–54.
[54] See Bedwyr Lewis Jones, 'Deng Noswaith yn y "Black Lion" Daniel Owen', *LlC*, VIII, no. 1 and 2 (1964), 84–6.

that the most entertaining writing of the third quarter of the century was produced. We must turn, rather, to authors whose literary motives were more complex and whose spirit was more free, those who diverged from the standard and the predictable. That is especially true of biography, the origins of which can be traced to the same historical exhortatory motivation as gave birth to Thomas Jones's *Hunangofiant* and *Drych yr Amseroedd*. The development of the form has been traced by Saunders Lewis, who deservedly praised John Owen, the biographer of Daniel Rowland, and Owen Thomas, the biographer of John Jones of Tal-y-sarn, among others.[55] But it was almost inevitable that the form would deteriorate into platitude and obsequiousness. As Emyr Gwynne Jones has said: 'Having had a surfeit of the praise and endless idealization of so many quite uninteresting and colourless lives, it is a delight to come upon a biography which is in some way *different*' ('Wedi llwyr ddiflasu ar y canmol a'r delfrydu diddiwedd ar lu o fucheddau digon anniddorol a di-liw, hyfrydwch pur yw taro ar ambell gofiant sydd mewn rhyw ffordd neu'i gilydd yn *wahanol*').[56] This specific reaction arises not only from the instinct of every competent writer and poet to insist on expressing himself in an idiom which is free of platitudes but also from a desire to speak the truth plainly and without flattery.

Telling the truth, of course, can cause offence, as Edward Matthews, the popular preacher and editor from the Vale of Glamorgan, discovered on publishing his striking 'biography', *Hanes Bywyd Siencyn Penhydd*, in 1849. The subject of this work was Jenkin Thomas (1746–1807), an unlettered Methodist preacher, a 'character' on account of his attire, behaviour and sayings. In celebrating by dint of his imagination, and on the basis of stories he had heard in the Vale, the life of a man who had died six years before the author was born, Matthews in around 1850 was deliberately injecting a dose of the rough, working-class, but lively Methodism of eighteenth-century Glamorgan into the respectable body of his denomination. In his discussion of 'the colourful, working-class, grotesque characters' who are to be found in the works of Matthews, Ioan Williams has argued that the influence of Sir Walter Scott was to be clearly discerned.[57] Edward Matthews was seeking, therefore, to diverge amusingly and imaginatively from the path of the official biography. In turning to the work of Brutus, we encounter an author who believed that the biography was only one example of the conceited prejudice of the worst class of Nonconformist, the 'Jacks' as he referred to them disparagingly. Like so many malicious satirists, Owen was an angry man with an axe to grind. He had brought ignominy and shame upon himself by seeking to obtain money by fraud from a religious fund; he had been expelled by the Baptists and disappointed by the Congregationalists before turning to the Anglican Church, for which he began editing a new

---

[55] Saunders Lewis, 'Y Cofiant Cymraeg', *THSC* (1935), 157–73.
[56] Emyr Gwynne Jones, 'Cofiannau' in Morgan, *Gwŷr Llên y Bedwaredd Ganrif ar Bymtheg*, p. 181.
[57] Williams, *Capel a Chomin*, pp. 8–9.

magazine, *Yr Haul*, in 1835. In fact, because of his personal circumstances, Owen became an outlaw, an iconoclast who stood outside the respectable society of his day and who sought to challenge religious and literary shibboleths with a measure of freedom denied to others. He set about satirizing the Nonconformist biography with uncommon zeal (although he also wrote conventional ones), as the titles of his pseudo-biographies suggest: *Cofiant Wil Bach o'r Pwll-dwr, Cofiant Siencyn Bach y Llwywr* and *Cofiant Dai Hunan-dyb*. His most famous work, and the one which has attracted particular attention from twentieth-century critics, was *Wil Brydydd y Coed*, which was serialized in *Yr Haul* between 1863 and the author's death in 1866.[58] It is not difficult to accept Thomas Jones's description of the work as 'a crudely satirical, loosely constructed novel',[59] so slack indeed that the fact that it is unfinished does not affect its strengths. The aim of the story is to excoriate Nonconformity, especially Congregationalism, for its sectarianism and schismatic chapels and its unlettered, gibbering preachers, and it does so by means of a truly memorable comic creation, namely the chief character William Morgans, a young hypocrite who is gluttonous, cunning and carnal. As well as poking fun at some of the degenerate platitudes of contemporary preachers, Owen used the full resources of his native dialect to paint splendidly Hogarthian pictures of a group of people whose stomach was their god. Although he was often an unfair and clumsy satirist, the idiom employed by Brutus has a significant place in the development of the imaginative prose of the century.

If Welsh is often seen at its most mischievous when it leaves the paths of platitude, care must be taken not to underestimate the dignity bestowed upon the written language by some of the splendidly ambitious publishing ventures of the third quarter of the century. The most ambitious was *Y Gwyddoniadur Cymreig*, an encyclopaedia published in parts, mainly under the editorship of John Parry, between 1854 and 1879.[60] On a smaller scale, but typical of the energy and confidence of the period, were *Hanes y Brytaniaid a'r Cymry* (1872–4), edited by R. J. Pryse (Gweirydd ap Rhys), the popular selection made by Robert Jones of Llanllyfni, *Gemau Diwynyddol* (1865), the useful biographical dictionary of Isaac Foulkes, *Enwogion Cymru* (1870), and the volume edited by Owen Jones, *Cymru, yn Hanesyddol, Parthedegol a Bywgraphyddol* (1875). The finest piece of biographical writing in the period was *Cofiant John Jones, Talsarn*, published by Owen Thomas in 1874.

We left fiction in the laboriously moralistic pit of temperance stories in the 1850s. During the years which followed, stout efforts were made to establish the new form by Gwilym Hiraethog, Lewis William Lewis (Llew Llwyfo) and Isaac

---

[58] David Owen (Brutus), *Wil Brydydd y Coed*, ed. Thomas Jones (Caerdydd, 1949).
[59] Ibid., p. xxviii.
[60] See Roger Jones Williams, 'Hanes Cyhoeddi *Y Gwyddoniadur Cymreig*', *LlC*, IX, no. 3 and 4 (1967), 135–65; idem, 'Rhai sylwadau ar gynnwys *Y Gwyddoniadur Cymreig*', *LlC*, XII, no. 1 and 2 (1972), 92–116.

Foulkes.[61] One of the most indefatigable storytellers was Roger Edwards of Mold, editor of *Y Drysorfa*, the Calvinistic Methodist monthly, who published five novels in the pages of the magazine between 1866 and 1872. His aim was to meet the obvious need for interesting but improving literature capable of providing its readers with spiritual succour. He did not, however, possess the literary gifts to achieve this aim, and it was a younger Methodist from Mold who was to tackle the realist novel of the Victorian Age and make it a medium for the rich expression of the contemporary world. Daniel Owen was a student at Bala Theological College when Edwards's first story, 'Y Tri Brawd a'u Teuluoedd' (The Three Brothers and their Families), appeared in *Y Drysorfa*, and by the time he had written his own first piece of fiction in 1878 all real hostility to the new form had virtually disappeared among the Methodists.[62] It is worth noting that it was in 1870, the year of Welsh literature's greatest shame, according to Saunders Lewis, that Daniel Owen published his first original prose work, a sincere and controversial portrait of one of the leaders of Methodism. The journalistic sketch was one of the most influential conventions in the growth of fiction at this time, as exemplified in the early works of Dickens and Thackeray, and the pen-portrait was the basis of Daniel Owen's first story, 'Cymeriadau ymhlith ein Cynulleidfaodd' (Characters among our Congregations), published in *Y Drysorfa*, at the urgent prompting of Roger Edwards, in 1878.[63]

Daniel Owen had for years been one of Edwards's foot soldiers in Mold, a loyal fighter in the campaigns of militant Nonconformity against godlessness, injustice and Anglicanism. He was wholly sincere in lending his support to his teacher with regard to the moral function of culture. But he did not place his literary gifts at the service of the movement.[64] Although his career as a writer coincided with the years when membership and buildings and influence were on the increase (R. Tudur Jones, after all, has claimed that 'Wales was a Christian country in 1890. The nation had its face towards the dawn' ('Gwlad Gristionogol oedd Cymru ym 1890. Yr oedd y genedl â'i hwyneb tua'r wawr')),[65] the worm was already in the spiritual wood, according to the testimony of some contributors to *Y Drysorfa*. They spoke not of a dawn but of a sunset, and the complaint was heard that the tide was ebbing in so far as spiritual quality and authenticity were concerned as against the high tide of numbers, respectability and moral influence, and perhaps as a result of it. Owen did not indulge in high-blown rhetoric about the light of

---

[61] For a list of fictional works published in the nineteenth century, see E. G. Millward, 'Ffugchwedlau'r Bedwaredd Ganrif ar Bymtheg', *LlC*, XII, no. 3 and 4 (1973), 244–64.
[62] Roger Edwards's story appeared in *Y Drysorfa* between February 1866 and April 1867.
[63] See D. Gwenallt Jones, 'Nofelau Cylchgronol Daniel Owen', *LlC*, IV, no. 1 (1956), 1–14. The novelist's early development is discussed in Williams, *Capel a Chomin*; see also Robert Rhys, 'Neilltuaeth Cystudd 1876–1881: Pregethau, Cymeriadau, Nofel', *Taliesin*, 92 (1995), 49–78.
[64] See Robert Rhys, 'Cristnogaeth a Llenyddiaeth: Partneriaid Anghymarus? Golwg ar Yrfa Daniel Owen', *Diwinyddiaeth*, XLVI (1995), 3–23.
[65] R. Tudur Jones, *Ffydd ac Argyfwng Cenedl, Cyfrol 1 Prysurdeb a Phryder* (Abertawe, 1981), p. 15.

the liberal-Nonconformist dawn, but with telling meticulousness he set about painting the colours of the sunset. And because he did so from within the fold, and combined real concern for the state of things with a readiness to record the more comic aspects of the decline, he produced much more richly significant texts than those of the Nonconformist propagandists and the anti-propagandist Brutus. Nor was this honesty restricted to church matters, for he refused to join the ranks of those who responded to the climate after 1847 by producing unchangingly exalting and defensive images of Welsh life. He made fun of this tendency in the striking opening paragraph of his novel *Enoc Huws*, where the narrator insists that closing one's eyes is no sign of holiness, and that only a fool believes that the whole history of Wales is to be found in the popular songs 'Cymru Lân, Gwlad y Gân' (Pure Wales, Land of Song) and 'Hen Wlad y Menig Gwynion' (The Old Land of the White Gloves).[66] The great principle of the English realist novelists, truth-to-life, was embraced because, like them, he detested hypocrisy, but also because he had inherited the emphasis laid by the great preachers on serious and accurate self-questioning.

Although he followed the confessional mode of the Methodists more often than is sometimes thought, the view of those critics who have insisted that Daniel Owen was mainly a social novelist, one who was at his best when discussing people in their relationships with others, must be accepted.[67] He seized the opportunity of using the realist novel to produce a keenly intelligent commentary on contemporary society. He had difficulty in finding a convincing storyline but, as Dafydd Glyn Jones and Ioan Williams have observed,[68] that is not a centrally significant consideration, since it is through characters, or rather through conflict between characters, that the novels express their values and vision. And the most revealing thing about the characters, more often than not, is their way of speaking. We have here the key to an understanding of Daniel Owen's genius and to his greatness as a writer of Welsh in the nineteenth century. Although neither his orthography nor syntax pleased the most pedantic purists of the new century, there is no doubting the novelist's mastery of contemporary registers, nor his ability to satirize the falsest style of his time. His characters reveal themselves by the way they speak, and the author was aware that the great social division of the Victorian age, between respectable people and those who were not, was reflected in the contrasting languages they employed. This device is to be seen in his earliest works, for example in the conflict between the devout and plain-speaking old woman, Gwen Rolant, and the foolish, ambitious deacon, George Rhodric, in *Offrymau Neillduaeth*.[69] One of the most amusing and obvious examples occurs in

[66] Daniel Owen, *Profedigaethau Enoc Huws* (Wrecsam, 1891), p. 14.
[67] See, for example, John Rowlands, *Ysgrifau ar y Nofel* (Caerdydd, 1992), p. 29.
[68] Dafydd Glyn Jones, '*Enoc Huws* a Hunan-dwyll' in J. E. Caerwyn Williams (ed.), *Ysgrifau Beirniadol III* (Dinbych, 1967), pp. 289–314; Williams, *Capel a Chomin*.
[69] Daniel Owen, *Offrymau Neillduaeth; sef Cymeriadau Biblaidd a Methodistaidd* (Wyddgrug, 1879), pp. 121–4.

Y Dreflan when Mr Smart, who places inordinate emphasis on 'appearance' and being 'respectable', encounters the unaffected Peter Pugh.[70] A more subtle and ambiguous use of the device is made in *Rhys Lewis* (1885), in the splendid verbal contentions between Bob and Mari Lewis which convey the tension between two generations as a more radical form of politics challenges the world-view of the older generation of Calvinistic Methodists who look back more to the balmy breezes of yesteryear rather than forward to the new Socialist dawn. In the view of many readers, Bob Lewis is Owen's most attractive hero, but one of the conditions of the novelist's support for him is that he makes him speak disconcertingly like some of the sanctimonious dogmatists who are roundly condemned in his other novels, particularly in comparison with his mother, a woman whose speech is a rich combination of scriptural language and the dialect of the vale of Alun. Daniel Owen also proved in this novel his genius for converting his own life into an exciting literary experience which came closer than the historian to catching the spirit of his time and which impressed on the imagination of his readers lively pictures of mid-century education, college education in Bala and industrial unrest, among other things.

The pinnacle of Daniel Owen's career, and of the century's imaginative writing, was *Profedigaethau Enoc Huws*, a novel which first appeared during 1890–1 in *Y Cymro*, a new weekly newspaper published and edited by Isaac Foulkes in Liverpool. Foulkes knew that a new novel by Daniel Owen could put the new infant of the Welsh press on its feet, and so it proved. This novel presents the author's most mature and intense contemplation of a matter first raised in the essay 'Hunan-dwyll' (Self-deception), namely the way in which certain aspects of hypocrisy and fraud are part of the fabric of society at every level. In *Enoc Huws* he used one of the greatest scandals of his time and place, namely fraud by speculators in the lead industry, as a powerful image, emphasizing that the main perpetrator, Captain Trefor, is a religious hypocrite. In everything he wrote up to *Enoc Huws*, Daniel Owen looked upon the life of his denomination and country with open eyes and recorded it, on the whole, with an accuracy which is both ironic and intelligent. He was still composing, at the urgent request of editors such as Foulkes and O. M. Edwards, during the last five years of his life at a time when his powers were in decline, but his writing no longer bore the same intensity, and in *Gwen Tomos* and *Straeon y Pentan* he was content to tell a tale about the old days, albeit fluently and entertainingly.[71]

Daniel Owen's career was not the only one to begin in earnest in 1876: 'Soon after coming home from the Continent, Emrys began writing for the papers, work which he was to continue to undertake energetically and well for years

---

[70] Idem, *Y Dreflan: Ei Phobl a'i Phethau* (Wrexham, 1881), pp. 87–96.
[71] The major novels of Daniel Owen are discussed in detail in Rowlands, *Ysgrifau ar y Nofel*, and Williams, *Capel a Chomin*. Earlier studies include Saunders Lewis, *Daniel Owen* (Aberystwyth, 1936) and John Gwilym Jones, *Daniel Owen: Astudiaeth* (Dinbych, 1970).

thereafter' ('Yn fuan wedi dyfod adref o'r Cyfandir, dechreuodd Emrys ysgrifennu i'r papurau, gwaith a wnaeth yn fedrus ac egnïol am flynyddoedd'). These are the words of T. Gwynn Jones in his highly influential biography of Emrys ap Iwan, which was published in 1912.[72] Emrys ap Iwan was an essayist, or more correctly perhaps, a pamphleteer, and his principal medium was the polemical letter to the press. Between 1876 and 1903 he published a plethora of essays, mainly in *Y Faner* and *Y Geninen*, thundering against the subservience of the Welsh people in their attitude to the English and the English language (reserving some of his sharpest barbs for his own denomination, the Calvinistic Methodists, and their efforts to establish English causes), criticizing the abysmal stylistic poverty of much written Welsh of the time, recommending a dose of the classics as medicine, and also commenting on religious matters. In his day Emrys ap Iwan was a controversial figure on account of his opinions and readiness to challenge men like Lewis Edwards who tended to be idolized. He was considered by his contemporaries an able and honest man, but somewhat inflexible and perhaps rather arrogant. There is a hint of the same criticism in the words of Saunders Lewis when he reproaches him for being an individual who did not seek to found a movement or fight for his principles.[73] He published no volume of literature during his lifetime, but following his death he was elevated by twentieth-century critics to a position above almost any other writer of the nineteenth century. He is considered to be the father of Welsh political nationalism and received much of the credit for reconnecting Welsh prose with the classical wealth of the past, thereby preparing the ground for the renaissance of the twentieth century. He was claimed by twentieth-century writers, the very people who were so ready to condemn the shortcomings of his predecessors, as one of them. Although there is a danger of losing sight of the century's wealth by praising Emrys ap Iwan, John Morris-Jones and O. M. Edwards, we cannot doubt the considerable influence of Emrys ap Iwan, his attitudes as well as his style, on the mind of the Welshman in the twentieth century. Saunders Lewis noted the revolutionary effect of the biography by T. Gwynn Jones on the life of Welsh-speaking soldiers during the First World War,[74] and he took Emrys ap Iwan as an ideal model for the Welsh writer because he rejected English influences and drew on European culture, especially that of France, and on the best of his own country's tradition. Three volumes of his articles were published under the editorship of D. Myrddin Lloyd in 1937–40,[75] the years of the reaction to Penyberth and its consequences, thereby winning for the writer from Abergele a new group of admirers as well as an important place in the growth of the modern Welsh mind.

[72] T. Gwynn Jones, *Emrys ap Iwan. Dysgawdr, Llenor, Cenedlgarwr: Cofiant* (Caernarfon, 1912), p. 55.
[73] Saunders Lewis, 'Emrys ap Iwan' in idem, *Ysgrifau Dydd Mercher* (Aberystwyth, 1945), p. 75.
[74] Ibid., p. 74.
[75] D. Myrddin Lloyd (ed.), *Detholiad o Erthyglau a Llythyrau Emrys ap Iwan* (3 vols., Aberystwyth, 1937, 1939, 1940).

According to Thomas Parry, the two prose writers who provided the 'stepping stones' which would lead the literature of Wales out of the morass of the nineteenth century were Emrys ap Iwan and O. M. Edwards.[76] As in the case of Emrys ap Iwan and Daniel Owen, Owen Edwards went from Llanuwchllyn to the Theological College at Bala, but then went on to Aberystwyth and Oxford. He is often contrasted with Emrys ap Iwan on account of his more elevating and idealistic interpretation of the common people, and his political-literary motives are voiced clearly enough in his introduction to the first volume of one of the many periodicals he founded, namely *Cymru*, in 1891:

> Amcan CYMRU ydyw gwneyd yr ychydig allaf fi a'm cydweithwyr . . . i adrodd hanes Cymru, i adrodd ei thraddodiadau, i roddi llafar eto i'w beirdd a'i llenorion, i godi arwyr ein hen wlad yn eu hol. A gwnawn hyn oherwydd mai cyfnod addysg Cymru ydyw'r cyfnod hwn. Yng nghyfnod ei haddysg, ni ddylid anghofio beth fu Cymru, trwy 'godi'r hen wlad yn ei hol' y rhoddir cryfder i gymeriad Cymro, purdeb i'w enaid, dysg i'w athrylith, a dedwyddwch i'w fywyd . . . Ni cheisiaf gelu f'ymdrech i wneyd CYMRU'N ddyddorol. Hoffwn i'w holl erthyglau fod, nid yn unig yn glir a sylweddol, ond hefyd yn fyw ac yn ddifyr . . . yr wyf yn credu hefyd fod tuedd yng Nghymru i feddwl mai dysg ydyw tywyllwch ymadrodd, ac na fedrir gosod meddwl dwfn allan ond yn glogyrnaidd a thrwy eiriau celfyddyd. Ni waeth gennyf os dywedir fod erthyglau CYMRU'N 'ysgeifn ac yn boblogaidd', os llwydda eu hysgrifenwyr i osod y gwir allan ym mhurdeb tryloew ei dlysni.[77]

> (The aim of CYMRU is to do what little I and my colleagues are able . . . to recount the history of Wales, to tell of its traditions, to allow its poets and writers to find their voice again, to raise up the heroes of our old country once more. And we shall accomplish all this because we live in a time when Wales is to receive education. We should not forget what Wales has been; by 'restoring the old country to what it was' we shall give strength to the character of the Welshman, purity to his soul, learning to his genius, and joy to his life . . . I shall not try to conceal my effort to make CYMRU interesting. I should like all its articles to be not only clear and substantial but lively and entertaining . . . I believe, too, that there is in Wales a tendency to think that learning clouds expression, and that deep thought cannot be set out except clumsily and in highfalutin words. I shan't care if it is said that the articles in CYMRU are 'light and popular', if their writers succeed in setting out the truth in all the shining purity of its comeliness.)

This was not, of course, an agenda for others, since Edwards had already published travel essays and the first of the essays of *Cartrefi Cymru*, namely 'Dolwar Fechan'. Saunders Lewis argued that his strength was in the writing of journalism or reportage, and that he was a combination of the historian, the writer and the

---

[76] Parry, *A History of Welsh Literature*, p. 373.
[77] Introduction to *Cymru*, I (1891).

visionary.[78] The charming, concrete writing of Owen Edwards typified precisely the principles which the young scholar John Morris-Jones had been writing about in the Welsh press since 1887. There was, of course, a close relationship between the two, for they had both belonged to the group which had founded Cymdeithas Dafydd ap Gwilym at Oxford in 1886. Reference has already been made to the central place held by Morris-Jones in the development of Welsh poetry towards the close of the century; his influence was no less on Welsh prose. He achieved this not as an author, but as a scholar and editor, in a series of articles and then in his substantial introduction to his new edition of Ellis Wynne's classic work, *Gweledigaetheu y Bardd Cwsc*, in 1898.[79] The following paragraph praising Ellis Wynne's style clearly reveals the nature of Morris-Jones's agenda for the Welsh writers of his day; they were to resist English influences and rediscover the secret of the genius of Welsh prose by studying the classics. And the editor's own style, of course, was an essential part of his argument:

> Nis gallodd neb ar ol Elis Wyn, oddigerth fe allai Oronwy Owen, ysgrifennu cryfed a chyfoethoced Cymraeg rhydd. Y mae ei arddull yn lân oddiwrth y priod-ddulliau Seisnig a'r ymadroddion llac, eiddil sy weithian, ysywaeth, mor gyffredin. Ni ddywed efe 'oeddynt wedi gweled' am 'welsent', neu 'oedd wedi myned' am 'aethai'; ac nid yw'n tra-mynychu'n ddiachos eiriau gwan fel *cael*, – ni ddywed 'wedi cael eu claddu' am 'wedi eu claddu', neu 'gwelwn y lleill yn cael eu taflu', am 'gwelwn daflu'r lleill', nac 'y mae hi yn cael ei galw' am 'hi a elwir'. Y dull cryf cryno sydd gan Elis Wyn; ond yr awron rhy fynych y gwelir y dulliau gwan gwasgarog a ollyngwyd i'n Cymraeg ysgrifenedig o iaith dlodaidd mân siaradach.[80]

> (No one who came after Elis Wyn, except Goronwy Owen, was able to write Welsh prose as vigorously and as richly. His style is free from English idiom and the slack, weak expressions which are, too, sometimes so common. He does not write '*oeddynt wedi gweled*' for '*welsant*' or '*oedd wedi mynd*' for '*aethai*'; and he does not needlessly over-use weak words like *cael*, – he does not write '*wedi cael eu claddu*' for '*wedi eu claddu*', nor '*gwelwn y lleill yn cael eu taflu*' for '*gwelwn daflu'r lleill*', nor '*y mae hi yn cael ei galw*' for '*hi a elwir*'. Elis Wyn's style is vigorous and succinct; but nowadays we see too often the weak, circumlocutory styles which have been allowed to enter written Welsh from the impoverished colloquial language.)

He is highly critical of those who polluted the pure fountain of the native language; although William Morgan does not escape rebuke, it is William Owen

---

[78] Saunders Lewis, 'Owen M. Edwards' in Gwynedd Pierce (ed.), *Triwyr Penllyn* (Caerdydd, 1956), p. 35.
[79] See Geraint Bowen, 'John Morris-Jones' in idem, *Y Traddodiad Rhyddiaith yn yr Ugeinfed Ganrif* (Llandysul, 1976), pp. 55–76. For examples of work by Morris-Jones, see 'Gomer ap Iapheth', *Y Geninen*, VIII, no. 1 (1890), 1–7; idem, 'Cymraeg Rhydychen', ibid., 214–23.
[80] Ellis Wynne, *Gweledigaetheu y Bardd Cwsc*, edited by J. Morris Jones (Bangor, 1898), pp. xxxiii–iv.

Pughe who is blamed for leading writers astray in such matters as orthography, vocabulary and syntax. Morris-Jones took it as his responsibility and historic opportunity to undo Pugheism and English influence by recommending the 'vigorous, succinct style' as a model for the writers of the new century. He used his power as a university professor, regular eisteddfod critic and editor to promote the model, which was eagerly adopted, although not slavishly, by writers of genius. Neither the style of Parry-Williams's essays, nor the stories of Kate Roberts, nor Saunders Lewis's novel *Monica*, can be fully appreciated without acknowledging the work of Morris-Jones.

★ ★ ★

In 1902 there appeared, under the editorship of the Revd J. Morgan Jones, a volume entitled *Trem ar y Ganrif, sef Arolwg ar y Bedwaredd Ganrif ar Bymtheg, Parthed Crefydd, Gwleidyddiaeth, Addysg, Barddoniaeth, Caniadaeth Gynulleidfaol, a Llenyddiaeth*. Half the 320 pages of this volume are devoted to a discussion of religion, with a chapter for each denomination. The shortest chapter by far is the editor's, which is entitled 'Llenyddiaeth Gyffredinol y Ganrif' (General Literature of the Century), that is to say, prose. Evan Rees (Dyfed) was the author of the chapter on the century's poetry, and it is worth considering which aspects these contributors emphasized. The editor's essay completely ignores fictional or 'imaginative' literature. It is possible that he had been let down by a contributor who had failed to submit his essay, but the whole tenor of his contribution suggests that he did not consider some of the writers discussed in the present chapter – Matthews, Brutus, Daniel Owen and O. M. Edwards – as being worthy of attention, and certainly not at the expense of the best of the religious writing of the century. Therefore, in chronicling the pinnacles of the second half of the century, only works on history, commentaries, philosophical and instructional writing are mentioned, among which are Owen Thomas's biographies of John Jones and Henry Rees, *Testament yr Ysgol Sabbothol*, *Y Tadau Methodistaidd*, and of course *Y Gwyddoniadur*, which was reckoned to be, in many ways, the most important book in the Welsh language. Although later critics would wonder at the narrowness of the survey made by John Morgan Jones, his prejudice was often in favour of works which were the fruit of unremitting labour and unfaltering seriousness of purpose. And the cultural gains of that seriousness of purpose, which was based on a clear and confident Christian world-view, were certainly and inexpressibly greater than any perceived losses. The observations of other contributors to the book remind us, however, that not many men of letters in the nineteenth century had the critical faculties or the developed taste to produce a literature which was worthy of their ambitious aims.

More than one contributor to *Trem ar y Ganrif* boasted of the astonishing industry of the period. In his essay on the established Church, J. Myfenydd

Morgan is prompted to ask, 'What did those who were alive in previous centuries do?' ('Pa beth fu y rhai oeddynt yn byw yn y canrifoedd blaenorol yn wneyd?')[81] Dyfed, too, takes pride in statistics – 'perhaps the number of our poets was never so great' ('efallai na fu nifer ein prydyddion yn lluosocach mewn un cyfnod')[82] – and in the quality of the poetry produced during the century – 'In thus taking a wide view of the century's poetry in Welsh, and comparing the products of various centuries, in the light of fair criticism, we believe that it is inexpressibly more excellent than ever before' ('Wrth gymeryd golwg eang fel hyn ar farddoniaeth Gymreig y ganrif, a chydmaru cynyrchion gwahanol oesoedd, yn ngoleuni beirniadaeth deg, credwn ei bod yn anhraethol ragorach nag y bu erioed o'r blaen').[83] It is easy to understand this false confidence when it is borne in mind how many real feats were achieved during the century, but such a lack of critical judgement could only harm the literary standards of the time. Dyfed was not by any means entirely lacking in discernment, and he was ready enough to acknowledge that there were plenty of inferior poets in the ranks, and yet the narrowness of his reading or the shackles of moral prejudice led him to declare that the *cywyddau* of David Richards (Dafydd Ionawr) were superior to anything in that metre in the Welsh language, and that the love poems of Dafydd ap Gwilym 'in comparison with those of Dafydd Ionawr . . . are merely the crackling of thorns under a cauldron' ('o'u cydmaru ag eiddo Dafydd Ionawr . . . ond clindarddach drain dan grochan').[84] Alun was doubtless one of the most accomplished poets of the century, but he hardly merits being greeted as one who 'taught Welsh poets how to write an Elegy' ('ddysgodd i'r bardd Cymreig sut i ganu Marwnad').[85] The common prejudices against everything which was not consciously 'useful' are reflected in the cavalier treatment meted out to Twm o'r Nant ('am ei deilyngdod llenyddol, nid oedd yn ddim amgen na baledwr pen ffair' ('as for his literary worth, he was no better than a fairground balladeer'))[86] and Talhaiarn ('bardd ydoedd heb ei ddifrifoli' ('he was not a serious poet')).[87]

A reaction occurred against the kind of critical blindness exemplified in Dyfed's observations among a generation of literary men whose understanding and senses had been awakened to the classics of other times and other languages and to the importance of purity of expression and consistent orthography. It would be an exaggeration to claim that the emphasis on restoring native syntax and standardizing orthography led to a new kind of critical blindness, but this explains the treatment received by the novels of Daniel Owen – undoubted masterpieces – by editors in the first half of the twentieth century, as well as some of the

---

[81] J. Morgan Jones (ed.), *Trem ar y Ganrif* (Dolgellau, 1902), p. 79.
[82] Ibid., p. 49.
[83] Ibid., p. 74.
[84] Ibid., pp. 54–5.
[85] Ibid., p. 60.
[86] Ibid., p. 54.
[87] Ibid., p. 71.

sweeping pejorative comments made about the century's prose.[88] The exaltation of the concise in the field of poetry and prose was a wholly understandable reaction by the 'renaissance' generation of the twentieth century against the worst excesses of their predecessors, but it had its unfortunate effects, among which were the arrested development of the Welsh novel for fifty years and the curtailment of poetic ambitions. A prodigious century, of uneven standard and uncertain taste — it is unlikely that this typical assessment of nineteenth-century literature will be much altered. But there has been too much of the spirit of arrogant youth in the behaviour of the twentieth century towards its predecessors and it is possible that only in the twenty-first century, when the nineteenth century ceases to be 'the last century', will its contribution to the literary heritage of the Welsh people come to be properly assessed.

---

[88] For example, Thomas Parry's harsh edition of *Gwen Tomos* (Wrecsam, 1937).

10

The Welsh Language in the Eisteddfod

HYWEL TEIFI EDWARDS

ON THE EVIDENCE of the census returns for 1891 when for the first time the number of Welsh speakers was officially reckoned, J. E. Southall concluded that, of the 2,012,876 inhabitants of Wales, around a million of them spoke Welsh.[1] Turning a blind eye to the fact that the number of Welsh speakers, seen as a percentage of the total population, had been declining throughout the century, it was trumpeted that the number speaking 'the language of heaven' had never been so large. If statistics favoured it, what need was there to worry about its future in an age which put its faith in quantifiable progress? The plain truth, however, is that responsible Welsh people in 1891 had every reason to fear for the future of their language because there were so many negative attitudes, like maggots in an apple, gnawing at its core, and it was particularly reprehensible that those attitudes could be seen at work in the National Eisteddfod – supposedly a fortress of Welshness. Anticipating its visit to Swansea in 1891, the *Cambria Daily Leader* argued for further reducing the mother tongue's role:

> The Gorsedd is the only seat from which Cymraeg has not been ousted, and its tenure of even that sacred spot is shaky. On the platform Welsh is a barbarous tongue and at the Cymmrodorion gatherings it tumbles at the sound of its own voice.[2]

Such a comment should not be thought exceptional. The Welsh language had been a target for dissidents in the Victorian National Eisteddfod from the moment the first was held in Aberdare in 1861. The first series came to an end in 1868, and when the current series started in Merthyr Tydfil in 1881 the language again found itself at the mercy of the nation's promoters. In the wake of the National Eisteddfod at Caernarfon in 1886 – Caernarfon represented the heart of a county in which 89.5 per cent of the population spoke Welsh, according to the 1891

---

[1] J. E. Southall, *Wales and her Language* (Newport, 1892).
[2] Hywel Teifi Edwards, 'Eisteddfod Genedlaethol Abertawe, 1891' in Ieuan M. Williams (ed.), *Abertawe a'r Cylch* (Llandybïe, 1982), p. 26.

census – *Baner ac Amserau Cymru* protested that 'the only respect accorded the language was its almost total dismissal from the proceedings short of proclaiming its demise' (' "yr unig barch" a gawsai "oedd ei chadw allan mor llwyr ag oedd yn bosibl bron, heb gydnabod ei marwolaeth" '). Instead of slogans hypocritically wishing it eternal life, it would be more honest to 'to put up "Beware of the Welsh" ' ('gosod i fyny "Beware of the Welsh" '). That would be 'unutterably a more consistent and honourable way for the committees to act' ('yn annhraethol fwy cysson ac anrhydeddus yn y pwyllgorau'). When the nationalist, Michael D. Jones, contributed to a symposium on the National Eisteddfod in *Y Traethodydd* in 1890, he spoke of it as 'a big toffy "stall" selling sweets to aristocrats, squires and linguistic quislings' (' "stondin" daffy fawr i werthu melusion i bendefigion, ysweiniaid a Dic Shon Dafyddion'), and it is significant that Robert Ambrose Jones (Emrys ap Iwan), the arch-opponent of 'John Bull' and his lackeys in Wales, would not frequent it. In 1902, the year before his chairing in the National Eisteddfod at Llanelli, 1903, for his *awdl*, 'Y Celt' (The Celt), the Revd J. T. Job's view of that year's lamentably Anglicized affair was that 'It is our own servile and un-Welsh spirit which accounts for our overloading the table so often with English titbits' ('Ein hyspryd gwasaidd ac anghymreigaidd ni ein hunain sydd yn cyfrif am y danteithion Seisnig sydd gennym ar ein bwrdd mor aml'). The point is clear enough without summoning further witnesses. If we persist in thinking of the Victorian National Eisteddfod as a fortress, we should think of the Welsh language as another Branwen sullied in Matholwch's kitchen.[3]

The National Eisteddfod was born in the 1860s, in the shadow of 'The Treachery of the Blue Books', and it is well known that the three commissioners – R. R. W. Lingen, J. C. Symons and H. Vaughan Johnson – who published their offensive report, following 'an inquiry into the state of education in Wales, especially into the means afforded to the labouring classes of acquiring a knowledge of the English language', were unanimous in their view that their language kept the Welsh 'under the hatches'. It was the root cause of their backwardness and turpitude and, according to Symons, the Welsh in the districts he had visited testified that their ignorance of English was 'a constant and almost an insurmountable obstacle to their advancement in life'. Although a number of Anglicans and Nonconformists effectively rebutted many of the report's conclusions, it opened a confused, hurtful and extremely damaging chapter in the long on-going story of the language's travail. In 1849 E. R. G. Salisbury, who established the famous library in Cardiff and boasted of his descent from William Salesbury, the translator of part of the New Testament into Welsh in 1567, claimed that he was 'pretty well convinced that the extermination of the Welsh language (as a *living* one) would be the greatest possible blessing to Wales'; in 1851

---

[3] *BAC*, 10 November 1886, p. 6; Michael D. Jones, 'Yr Eisteddfod', *Y Traethodydd*, XLV (1890), 439; J. T. Job, 'Awgrymiadau Y'nglyn a'r Eisteddfod Genedlaethol', *Y Geninen*, XX, no. 4 (1902), 255.

H. A. Bruce MP (later Lord Aberdare) did not mince his words when stating that its survival was 'a serious evil, a great obstruction to the moral and intellectual progress of my countrymen'; and in 1860, when John Jenkins published his *Report on the State of Popular Education in the 'Welsh Specimen Districts'*, he rejected bilingualism and endorsed the commissioners' view in 1847 that Welsh was useless as a medium for providing a practical and scientific education: 'The Welsh language . . . contains no materials to supply, nor is its literature adequate to meet the requirements of knowledge in modern times; it is the language of the past and not of the present.' As E. G. Millward and R. Elwyn Hughes have clearly shown, such a conclusion was hopelessly skewed, but it was the 'progressive' viewpoint, as well as the viewpoint of Lingen, Symons and Vaughan Johnson, who declared that the Welsh had no literature to speak of. In the Victorian National Eisteddfod, unfortunately, neither the commissioners, nor Salisbury, nor Bruce, nor Jenkins, would be without support.[4]

Eisteddfod literature will not be discussed in this chapter. Rather, the aim is to outline the cultural context which to a great extent accounts for the general mediocrity of what was written – mainly by poets who lost heart in an age dismissive alike of their lineage and their language. Of the numerous competitors, John Ceiriog Hughes alone composed prize-worthy poems that evoked a national response, namely his love poem, 'Myfanwy Fychan o Gastell Dinas Bran' in 1858, and his pastoral, 'Alun Mabon', in 1861 – two poems which idealized the sweethearts of Wales and gave the lie to the Blue Books' charge of widespread licentiousness. Ceiriog sweetly versified his countrymen's reaction to the commissioners' slanders and became their laureate despite winning neither Chair nor Crown. It is a fact that eisteddfod poetry by and large attracted few readers, and regrettably the Victorian National Eisteddfod did very little to promote Welsh fiction. It cannot lay claim to a single noteworthy novel. In a century whose voluminous products in a vast array of fields testify to its confident vigour, it is striking that the great bulk of eisteddfod literature is crippled by want of confidence. Faced with the deprecation of his language, his metrics – should he aspire to be a *cynganeddwr* who wrote in the traditional strict metres – indeed his very calling in a utilitarian age, the Welsh poet was easily beset by an awareness of futility.[5]

It should be realized that the fate of the language in the National Eisteddfod was decided by what befell it in the provincial eisteddfodau – ten in all – which

---

[4] Gareth Elwyn Jones, 'Llyfrau Gleision 1847' in Prys Morgan (ed.), *Brad y Llyfrau Gleision: Ysgrifau ar Hanes Cymru* (Llandysul, 1991), pp. 35, 42–3; J. Gwynn Williams, *The University Movement in Wales* (Cardiff, 1993), p. 196; H. A. Bruce, *The Present Position and Future Prospects of the Working Classes in the Manufacturing Districts of South Wales* (Cardiff, 1851), p. 12; E. G. Millward, 'Pob Gwybodaeth Fuddiol' in Morgan (ed.), *Brad y Llyfrau Gleision*, pp. 146–65; R. Elwyn Hughes, *Nid Am Un Harddwch Iaith: Rhyddiaith Gwyddoniaeth y Bedwaredd Ganrif ar Bymtheg* (Caerdydd, 1990).
[5] Hywel Teifi Edwards, *Codi'r Hen Wlad yn ei Hôl 1850–1914* (Llandysul, 1989), pp. 27–58.

were held between 1819 and 1834, and in the Cymreigyddion eisteddfodau – another ten – held in Abergavenny between 1835 and 1853. In short, despite the fact that the chief supporters of both series were activated by a strong initial desire to enhance the status of the language, they found themselves providing a platform for the 'superior' English language at the expense of the mother tongue. To accept that it was wise, as John Jones (Talhaiarn) put it, to act in agreement with 'the broad principle of considering what will be most attractive to the aristocracy, the gentry, the middle classes and the people generally', meant being ready to speak the language of 'our best people' and being pleased to hear the homespun Welsh language praised time and again in crinoline English. And from the outset, its value as the mother tongue of a virtuous, orderly people – a people content with their lot – was loudly proclaimed. Proof of its usefulness was that it merited the stamp of English approval in an eisteddfod.

The provincial eisteddfod was an Anglican venture, but it should not be assumed that it was therefore an English venture. On the contrary, its prime mover, the Revd John Jenkins (Ifor Ceri), vicar of Kerry, near Newtown, and the clerics who supported him, were enthusiastically intent on realizing the aims of the famous Edward Lhuyd, and those of the Cymmrodorion and the Gwyneddigion, the two influential expatriate societies in London. It is true that they were not as militant as the Association of Welsh Clergy in the West Riding of the County of York, which was established on St David's day, 1835, at the prompting of the Revd David James (Dewi o Ddyfed) and the Revd Joseph Hughes (Carn Ingli), but they were in earnest. They aspired to undertake pioneering work in the fields of literature, music, history and antiquarianism which would exhibit the riches of Welsh culture, and they were encouraged in their aims by Thomas Burgess, Bishop of St David's, and Archdeacon Thomas Beynon.[6]

Four societies were established to achieve their ends, namely the Cambrian Society in Dyfed, presided over by Lord Dynevor in 1818; the Cambrian Society in Gwynedd, presided over by Sir Robert Vaughan and the Cymmrodorion Society in Powys, presided over by Sir Watkin Williams Wynn, in 1819; and the Cambrian Society in Gwent and Morgannwg, presided over by Sir Charles Morgan in 1821. Support was also given to efforts in London to revive the Honourable Society of Cymmrodorion, and subsequently 'The Cymmrodorion Society, or the Metropolitan Cambrian Institute' was relaunched in 1820. The contact with London, together with the attraction of four aristocratic presidents, meant that from the outset there would be an open door in the provincial

---

[6] Bedwyr Lewis Jones, 'Yr Hen Bersoniaid Llengar' (Penarth, 1963); Mari Ellis, 'Rhai o Hen Bersoniaid Llengar Maldwyn' in Gwynn ap Gwilym and Richard H. Lewis (eds.), Bro'r Eisteddfod: Cyflwyniad i Faldwyn a'i Chyffiniau (Llandybïe, 1981), pp. 85–116; Hywel Teifi Edwards, Yr Eisteddfod: Cyfrol Ddathlu Wythganmlwyddiant yr Eisteddfod 1176–1976 (Llandysul, 1976), pp. 34–49.

eisteddfodau for the fashionable metropolitan culture, and before Ifor Ceri died in 1829 he had long since been disillusioned by the futility of the 'Cambrian Olympiads' which were held in Carmarthen (1819 and 1823), Wrexham (1820), Caernarfon (1821), Brecon (1822 and 1826), Welshpool (1824), Denbigh (1828), Beaumaris (1832) and Cardiff (1834).

Inevitably, the provincial eisteddfodau slipped away from the enthusiasts in the Kerry circle and lost their proper purpose when the urge to respond to the expectations of a 'higher culture', to display the British loyalty of the Welsh, proved stronger than the desire to nourish the native culture. Hungering for the patronage of aristocrats with little more to offer – apart from their prizes – than English commendations in exchange for flattery, a committed promotion of Welsh-language culture would soon cease to be the *sine qua non* of the eisteddfod. Following the visits of Viscount Clive of India to the Welshpool Eisteddfod in 1824, the Duke of Sussex, George IV's brother, to the Denbigh Royal Eisteddfod in 1828, and the Duchess of Kent and her daughter, Princess Victoria, to the Beaumaris Eisteddfod in 1832, it was apparent that London's splendour had blinded the Welsh to what the Kerry circle had intended, and the provincial venture petered out in Cardiff in 1834 to the accompaniment of the aristocracy's horse-drawn carriages bound for the ball in the castle.

In retrospect it becomes clear how the process of yielding to the charms of Anglicization began from the moment the Revd John Bowen brought a section of the Bath Harmonic Society to give two concerts at the Carmarthen Eisteddfod in 1819 which drew 'an assemblage of rank, fashion, and respectability' to applaud them. Coinciding with that new development, Iolo Morganwg grasped the opportunity to wed the Gorsedd of Bards and the eisteddfod on the lawn of the Ivy Bush, ordaining, among others, the Bishop of St David's, a somewhat reluctant druid. The concert would usurp the National Eisteddfod from 1863 onwards, and the *gorsedd* would be a continuous source of unease for the progressives on whom the derision of the English press weighed heavier than Doomsday. In the essentially English concert, the Welsh identified with the metropolitan culture. Between the *gorsedd* stones they stood apart as risible fantasists who would not accept that the age of superstition, like that of the Welsh language, was over. In 1819, in the first important eisteddfod of the nineteenth century, the Welsh language was stamped with the imprint of yesteryear, and it would bear that imprint throughout the century.[7]

Following the appointment of John Parry (Bardd Alaw), the Cymmrodorion Society's 'Registrar of Music', to organize the concerts in the provincial eisteddfodau after 1820, Ifor Ceri's aims were to remain unfulfilled. He had good reason to curse Parry's 'Anglo-Italian farce', and Angharad Llwyd also protested at

---

[7] Meredydd Evans, 'Cyngherddau'r Ganrif Ddiwethaf' in Gwynn ap Gwilym (ed.), *Eisteddfota 2* (Abertawe, 1979), pp. 80–98.

the way poets were made mere 'catspaws of the musicians'. Ifor Ceri remarked bitterly on the declining Welshness of 'our great people', and foresaw a short life for the concert; but it proved otherwise. As a result of the nation's increasing pride in 'The Land of Song' in the second half of the century, the appeal of concert and *cymanfa* were to prove equally intoxicating, and the bards lamented the loss of their former glory. In 1832 Sir Robert Bulkeley regretted their demotion, stating that although he was 'totally ignorant' of their language he believed them to be as talented as ever. It was one thing, however, to plead their worth in an eisteddfod; it was another to strive to extend the influence of the Welsh language in the real world. It was one thing, for example, to give prizes for *englynion* in praise of the train; it was quite another to insist that running a railway should be any concern of the Welsh language.[8]

But if its druidic defenders gave the language a negative image, and if it was hardly possible to argue convincingly for its commercial utility, it did nevertheless have a thoroughly relevant contemporary role in moulding the fitting conduct and loyalty of a folk without peer within the bounds of Empire. In the 'Cambrian Olympiads' a purposeful propaganda campaign was begun that extolled Welsh as one of 'the languages of containment' which, according to Rod Mengham, were to withstand the ills of 'the language of conflict, disruption and renewal' which shaped the general awareness of how nations and societies were created and sustained during the explosive period between the 1790s and the 1840s. For the English, naturally, and for many Victorian Welsh people, there could only be one 'language of containment' in Britain, but for those who did not will the death of their language, the rock-solid argument in its favour was that it, and it alone, spoke for Welsh tractability. In scorning it, the English showed that they were blind to their own advantage. Immediately after the publication of the Blue Books, 'Pure Wales, docile Wales' ('Cymru lân, Cymru lonydd') was enshrined as an emblematic 'fact' in the *englyn* – 'A Welshman and his Language, and his Country' ('Cymro a'i Iaith, a'i Wlad') – which was composed by the Revd William Williams (Caledfryn) in 1848 in answer to the calumnies. It was the Welsh language which kept Wales pure and docile – the Revd Evan Evans (Ieuan Glan Geirionydd) had so testified in his 'Awdl ar Hiraeth Cymro am ei wlad mewn Bro Estronawl' (An *awdl* on a Welshman's longing for his country in a foreign land) which won him the Chair in the eisteddfod at Wrexham in 1820 – and it would be adduced by eisteddfod rhetoricians in defence of the language for the remainder of the century.[9]

[8] William Jones (ed.), *The Gwyneddion for 1832: Containing the Prize Poems, etc., of the Beaumaris Eisteddfod and North Wales Literary Society* (London, 1839), p. iii.
[9] Rod Mengham, *The Descent of Language, writings in praise of Babel* (London, 1993), pp. 123–40; Caledfryn, 'Cymro, a'i Iaith, a'i Wlad', *Y Dysgedydd*, XXVII (August, 1848), 247; Ieuan Glan Geirionydd, 'Awdl ar Hiraeth Cymro am ei Wlad mewn Bro Estronawl', *Powysion: sef odlau ac Ynglynion a ddanfonwyd i Eisteddfod Gwrecsam, Medi 13, 1820* (Denbigh, 1821), pp. 105–6.

In 1820 the Englishman, Reginald Heber, Bishop of Calcutta from 1823 until he died in 1826, came to Wrexham to declare that the persecution of a nation's mother tongue was tantamount to an assault on its innate genius, and as such was nothing short of barbarous behaviour. He was ashamed to contemplate 'the systematic and persevering hostility, of which, on the part of your English Rulers, the Welsh Language was for many years the object'. He hoped that such wretched times had passed and urged his audience to strengthen 'their patriotic exertions till they have compensated for ages of past depression, or indifference'. Without speaking as plainly as Heber, the Revd Thomas Price (Carnhuanawc), the charismatic vicar of Cwm-du, the Revd John Blackwell (Alun), the Revd Edward Hughes (Y Dryw) and Ieuan Glan Geirionydd all spoke passionately on occasions in praise of that equable Welsh Wales which England should give thanks for in troubled times. Carnhuanawc was its most winning advocate, and for him the right of the language to survive was beyond question. Since it was a means to create 'as happy, as peacable, and as loyal a people, as any in the British dominions, surely it has every claim to be encouraged as an instrument of invaluable service'. In 1832, when the Merthyr rising was still fresh in the memory, the young Victoria could return to London undisturbed, assured by Alun that 'in the days of sedition and threatened anarchy, the Principality has always been tranquil and happy as Goshen'. The common people were making sure progress, 'they are growing in intelligence, and are growing in moral worth', as was proved by their willingness to leave the government of the country to their betters. Far more important than their want of political understanding was that they were 'learned and exemplary in all the duties of their stations: they fear their God; they honour their king'.[10]

By 1834 the eisteddfod had played its part in establishing the wholesomeness of the native language as an irrefutable argument for its right to survive. There was no denying its antiseptic efficacy. If the Welsh needed the English language to fill their pockets, they required their mother tongue to succour heart and soul. And if it could not be denied that the mother tongue had to yield daily to the English language in the secular world, there was comfort in believing that the Welsh could not live virtuously without it, and that consequently it was a national necessity. At the Welshpool Eisteddfod in 1824, a prize was given for *englynion* to be inscribed on the gravestone of Dic Siôn Dafydd – the proverbial degenerate Welshman who aspired to be an Englishman – who was believed to have perished at the Carmarthen Eisteddfod in 1823 after going into decline in 1819. Another prize was offered for *englynion* on 'Gwarth y Cymro a gywilyddio arddel Iaith ei Wlad' (The disgrace of the Welshman who is ashamed to speak his native tongue). Dic, of course, was to survive his burial and tramp into the twentieth

---

[10] *The Gwyneddion for 1832*, pp. xxv–vi, xxxvii–ix; Jane Williams (Ysgafell), *The Literary Remains of the Rev. Thomas Price, Carnhuanawc* (2 vols., Llandovery, 1855), II, p. 136.

century, but competitions of this kind provided an opportunity to deny the fact of his malodorous existence by versifying a wish:

> Boed gan Gymro, 'mhob broydd, – o'i brifiaith
> Bur fost, yn lle c'wilydd;
> Fel na ddel, tra y del dydd,
> Lediaith ar ein haelwydydd.

(May Welshmen everywhere express pride, not shame, in their mother tongue, so that till the end of time our homes may be free of mongrel speech).[11]

On examining the series of eisteddfodau held by the Cymreigyddion of Abergavenny between 1834 and 1853, it can be seen that, as with the Kerry circle's venture, the founders' aims were frustrated by the inability of the majority of their supporters to speak Welsh – particularly those of the highest rank whose presence, much sought after, necessitated the constant use of English. The society was established in 1833 'er coleddiad yr Iaith Gymmraeg' (to cherish the Welsh language), and one of the rules required 'that every conversation or extended address is to be in the Welsh Language only' ('fod i bob ymddiddan neu lafariad parhaus gael eu dwyn ymlaen yn yr Iaith Gymmraeg yn unig'). For a decade, while Thomas Bevan (Caradawc) and John Evans (Ieuan ap Gruffydd) acted as secretaries, the minutes were kept in Welsh, but the goodwill the language enjoyed proved inadequate as a breakwater to prevent the English tide from swamping it. In Abergavenny, as in the provincial eisteddfodau, the more aware the Welsh were of English eyes upon them, the greater the danger of their being content with praising their mother tongue 'fel jwg ar seld' (as a mere jug on a dresser). The last of these eisteddfodau closed in 1853 on a very pro-British note.[12]

The Abergavenny Cymreigyddion was the offspring of the parent society established in London in 1792, and its prominent siblings in south Wales were located in Merthyr Tydfil, Aberdare and Pontypridd. Lively eisteddfodau were held in these three centres – the Merthyr Cymreigyddion gave a boost to temperance and the Welsh novel in a noteworthy eisteddfod held in 1854 – and in Pontypridd, Iolo Morganwg's druidic myth was celebrated by 'Cymdeithas y Maen Chwyf' who held *gorseddau* (bardic moots) on the common overlooking the town. But of all these societies, the Abergavenny Cymreigyddion undoubtedly exercised the most wide-ranging appeal and influence, primarily because it had as

---

[11] *Powysion, sef Awdlau, Cywyddau, ac Ynglynion, a ddanfonwyd i Eisteddfod Trallwng, Medi, 1824* (Bala, 1826), p. 242.

[12] Mair Elvet Thomas, *Afiaith yng Ngwent: Hanes Cymdeithas Cymreigyddion y Fenni, 1833–1854* (Caerdydd, 1978), pp. 4, 38; idem, *The Welsh Spirit of Gwent* (Cardiff, 1988), pp. 10–11; Edwards, *Yr Eisteddfod*, pp. 49–57.

its patron a woman remarkable both for her wealth and her commitment to Welsh culture.

The wife of Sir Benjamin Hall, who was William Crawshay's grandson, Augusta Waddington, Lady Llanover, was an autocratic woman who had entry to the highest social circles in the land. It appears that under the influence of Lady Coffin Greenly, Titley Court, Herefordshire – a lady who spoke Welsh fluently and competed in the provincial eisteddfodau as 'Llwydlas' (her *nom de plume*) – Augusta also came to treasure the Welsh language without mastering it to the same degree, and her desire to promote it was intensified after hearing an oration by Carnhuanawc at the Brecon Eisteddfod in 1826. It is certain that 'the Welsh cause' appealed greatly to the romantic in Lady Llanover, but she was no mere dreamer. Until her death in 1896 she turned Llanover Court into a forcing-house for the kind of Welshness she prized, and she worked for the benefit of the language in the fields of religion, education and folk culture. It is no exaggeration to say that she saved the triple harp from extinction by means of competitions in the Abergavenny eisteddfodau, that she secured life-giving prominence for folk songs and dances, and – to some dismay – that she devised a national costume for the 'authentic' Welsh woman. She was a tireless missionary for the kind of Welshness she considered a credit to the nation and an adornment to Britain, and the series of eisteddfodau which she, together with Carnhuanawc until his death in 1848, were mainly responsible for directing, should be seen as an advertisers' promotion. She was essentially a matriarchal advertising agent intent on creating an image of Welshness whose authenticity would be beyond doubt in England as in Wales.[13]

In the Cardiff Eisteddfod of 1834 she won a prize for an essay 'On the advantages of preserving the language and dress of Wales'. Soon afterwards she was admitted as an ovate in a *gorsedd* at Pontypridd, and was subsequently known, most fittingly, as 'Gwenynen Gwent' (The Bee of Gwent). In her prizewinning composition she maintained that the Welsh would be 'a dejected and degenerate race' ('hiliogaeth ddigalon a dirywiedig') without their language. With their tongue intact they would be far worthier subjects of the queen, even as the womenfolk in their national flannel and clogs would bear superior witness to the virtue and inherent good sense of the Welsh woman, than would the butterflies of the towns in their cotton and fancy shoes. The same prescriptive truths were aimed at readers of *Y Gymraes* (1850–1), the first Welsh periodical for women edited by the arch-defender of their morals, the Revd Evan Jones (Ieuan Gwynedd), and published with the financial assistance of Lady Llanover – to no avail. It did not sell. Despite the slanders of the Blue Books of 1847, it appears that

---

[13] Thomas, *Afiaith yng Ngwent*, pp. 119–26; Prys Morgan, *Gwenynen Gwent* (Eisteddfod Genedlaethol Casnewydd, 1988).

Welsh womenfolk had no wish to be pressed between the hard covers of male entreaties and castigations.[14]

Thanks to the status and connections of the Llanover Court family, the wealthy families of south Wales and the borderlands supported the Abergavenny eisteddfodau which were held annually from 1834 to 1838, and thereafter in 1840, 1842, 1845, 1848 and 1853. A Member of Parliament since 1831, and appointed Director of Public Works in 1855, Sir Benjamin Hall, as well as being supportive of his wife and the Cymreigyddion, was an all-important link with London's grandest circles, and that link would be strengthened by the marriage of Frances, Augusta's sister, to Chevalier Charles Bunsen, a Prussian who was appointed 'Envoi Extraordinary and Minister Plenipotentiary to the Court of St James' in 1842. Although families like the Morgans of Tredegar, the Guests of Dowlais, the Williamses of Aberpergwm and the Rolls of Hendre had an instinctive sympathy with the aims of the Cymreigyddion, they were also clearly reaffirming their position by supporting eisteddfodau which the Prince of Wales and Connop Thirlwall, Bishop of St David's, were prepared to recognize, eisteddfodau which attracted Celtic scholars from the Continent to compete in them, and which welcomed princes from India to grace the proceedings, namely Chundermohun Chatterjee in 1842, and in 1845 his uncle, Dwarkanauth Tagore, grandfather of the poet, Rabindranath Tagore. The Abergavenny eisteddfodau blossomed into somewhat exotic occasions. In the ever lengthening processions which preceded the competitions – processions which gave the local woollen industry a prominent place – the 'best people' in their resplendent coaches strove to make the most lasting impression, and by 1845 the show had become so popular that a purpose-built hall was provided for the eisteddfod-goers.[15]

It was the Welsh language which paid the price of Abergavenny's display. In 1834 Carnhuanawc had expressed the hope that he would live to see the English language elegized in Welsh, adding 'but it is not likely' ('ond nid tebygol'). Indeed, he was obliged to turn to English before concluding even then, because so few understood him. In accepting that attracting the attention of 'the best people' would serve Wales best, the fate of the Welsh language was settled. It is significant that the noteworthy compositions to emerge from Abergavenny were meant for 'the best people', in particular Maria Jane Williams's pioneering collection of folk songs which, after winning the prize in 1837, was published with Lady Llanover's assistance in 1844 as *Ancient National Airs of Gwent and Morganwg*, and Thomas Stephens's seminal critical essay on 'The Literature of Wales during the Twelfth and Succeeding Centuries', which won the Prince of Wales prize of 25 guineas in 1848 and was published in 1849 at Sir Josiah John

---

[14] Gwenynen Gwent, 'Y Buddioldeb a Ddeillia oddiwrth Gadwedigaeth y Iaith Gymraeg, a Dullwisgoedd Cymru', *Y Geninen Eisteddfodol*, VIII (1890), 68–71.
[15] Thomas, *Afiaith yng Ngwent*, pp. 1–52, 119–26.

Guest's expense as *The Literature of the Kymry*. As Daniel Huws has observed, *Ancient National Airs* was privately printed, there were 368 subscribers, it was dedicated to Queen Victoria, and it was from the outset a rare book. Thomas Stephens also explained that he wrote the nineteenth century's most important eisteddfod essay in English because that was the best way to serve his country, 'as the preponderance of England is so great, that the only hope of obtaining attention to the just claims of the Principality is by appealing to the convictions and sympathies of the reading part of the English population. It is full time for some of us to do this . . .'[16]

The Welsh were to exult in Stephens's achievement, as they were to rejoice in the fact that two German scholars, Albert Schulz and Carl Meyer, won two substantial prizes, 80 guineas in 1840 and 70 guineas in 1842, for essays on the influence of Welsh literature on the literatures of Europe. The value of the prizes says more than enough about the importance attached to the subject by the Welsh, and when Chevalier Bunsen awarded the prize to Schulz's German essay in 1840, an essay translated by Mrs Berrington, Sir Benjamin Hall's sister, and published in 1841 as 'An Essay on the Influence of Welsh Tradition upon the Literature of Germany, France and Scandinavia', Carnhuanawc, who had long since proclaimed the European importance of the Welsh language, could scarcely contain himself: 'a foreigner, a profound scholar, says we are right, and traces the progress of the traditions of Wales through foreign lands'. There was equal satisfaction in 1842 when Meyer's French essay was awarded the prize by James Cowles Prichard, the renowned author of *The Eastern Origin of the Celtic Nations* (1831), and Meyer's subsequent appointment as librarian of Windsor Castle simply doubled the satisfaction. His essay was translated into English by Jane Williams (Ysgafell), Carnhuanawc's biographer, and it appeared in *The Cambrian Journal* in 1854 entitled, 'An Essay on the Celtic Languages, in which they are compared with each other, and considered in connection with the Sanscrit, and the other Caucasian Languages.'[17]

It should be noted that the striking compositions to emerge from the Abergavenny eisteddfodau were not written in Welsh. No Welsh poetry or prose of any literary distinction was produced. It was the use of English to bring to light the earlier riches of Welsh culture which mattered, and the establishment of the Welsh MSS Society in 1836 and the subsequent publication of Charlotte Guest's translation of the *Mabinogion* in 1839, with Lady Llanover's financial assistance, chimed with the aims of the Cymreigyddion. In 1842, as he displayed an edition of *Liber Landavensis* (The Book of Llandaff) as an example of the MSS Society's usefulness, Carnhuanawc boasted that it was 'not only valuable as an antiquarian

---

[16] *Ancient National Airs of Gwent and Morganwg. Collected and arranged by Maria Jane Williams. A Facsimile of the 1844 Edition. With Introduction and notes on the songs by Daniel Huws* (The Welsh Folk-Song Society, 1988), p. vii; Thomas, *Afiaith yng Ngwent*, p. 101.

[17] Thomas, *Afiaith yng Ngwent*, pp. 85–91.

document, but evidence that the banks of the Towy are not less fertile in the works of art than those of the Thames or Seine . . .'[18]

In 1845 Carnhuanawc was adjudged by James Cowles Prichard the winner of the prize for an essay on 'The Comparative Merits of the Remains of Ancient Literature in the Welsh, Irish and Gaelic Languages, and their value in elucidating the Ancient History, and the Mental Cultivation of the Inhabitants of Britain, Ireland and Gaul'. There was much talk of the Celtic connection in Abergavenny, and in 1838, when the Comte de Villemarqué and François Rïo led a Breton deputation to the eisteddfod, many passionate vows were made to strengthen the ties and work together so that past Celtic glories should be revealed and future triumphs secured. Nothing came of it. It was not until 1899 that a platform for a celebration of Pan-Celticism was provided at the Cardiff National Eisteddfod, an event which proved unsuccessful. For the sober Welsh, the kilted exuberance of the Scots and the political intensity of the Irish was embarrassing, if not dangerous. Their chief concern, as Patrick Pearse observed scornfully, was to keep in harmony with England.[19]

In 1848, the year in which Carnhuanawc died, the imperious historian, Henry Hallam, visited the eisteddfod held under the patronage of the Prince of Wales. He had refused to attend in 1838 when he awarded John Dorney Harding the prize for 'An Essay on the Influence of Welsh Tradition upon European Literature' because he was deeply suspicious of Welsh patriotism, but by 1848 he could declare, much to the pleasure of his audience, that their loyalty to the Crown was beyond doubt. He was assured by Archdeacon John Williams, who had rewarded Thomas Stephens's essay, that the Welsh did not seek to live apart from England; their only wish was to live 'on equal terms with their friends beyond the Severn'. Despite expressions of anger against the Blue Books of 1847 by Carnhuanawc and Lady Llanover, the eisteddfod in 1848 was not turned into a protest meeting. On the contrary, the emphasis as ever was on reconciliation and securing recognition.[20]

The Abergavenny venture ended in 1853 in a gush of British patriotism. Foremost among the appreciative visitors was Lord Wellesley, nephew of the Duke of Wellington, who proposed a toast to the Cymreigyddion committee in gratitude for their loyal sentiments. He, too, had been thrilled by Talhaiarn, poet and architect in the employ of Sir Joseph Paxton, who had helped to oversee the building of the Crystal Palace which housed the Great Exhibition in 1851. Still in a state of euphoria after attending the first imperial 'Cymanfa' of Victoria's reign, Talhaiarn read his 'Address to the Queen', which he had composed to celebrate her fleeting visit to Wales in 1852, and concluded his sycophantic recital by

---

[18] Williams, *Literary Remains*, II, p. 295.
[19] Thomas, *Afiaith yng Ngwent*, pp. 127–37; Clive Betts, *A oedd Heddwch?* (Cardiff, 1978), pp. 67–92.
[20] Thomas, *Afiaith yng Ngwent*, p. 45.

exhorting his audience to remember that they were privileged to be united with an unutterably greater nation whose pre-eminence was visible the world over. Despite his pride in his ancestors, 'nothing shall tempt me to utter one word in disparagement of England and the English'. In January 1854 the Abergavenny Cymreigyddion folded, but Talhaiarn in 1853 had sounded the *raison d'être* of the national eisteddfodau, which would be held from 1861 onwards. The great desire to create a National Eisteddfod which would erase the memory of the condemnatory Blue Books of 1847 and provide an annual opportunity to extol Wales as an imperial asset would open the door to progressives who were more than ready to set aside the obstructive Welsh language. In the words of R. J. Derfel, the eisteddfod movement faced the years of 'the English madness' ('y gwallgofrwydd Saesneg').[21]

The Great Llangollen Eisteddfod was held in September 1858. It was organized by the Revd John Williams (Ab Ithel), the most zealous of Iolo Morganwg's followers, and it was sufficiently eventful to achieve in time folkloric fame. One particular event deserves attention. Ab Ithel and his supporters were intent on projecting the Gorsedd of Bards and on organizing competitions which would primarily reveal the past splendours of the nation, its share in Britain's glory and the worthiness of its current condition. It is clear from their programme that the aims of Ifor Ceri had not been forgotten, and equally clear that the memory of the Blue Books of 1847 was very much alive. Ebenezer Thomas (Eben Fardd) was chaired for an *awdl* entitled 'Maes Bosworth' (Bosworth Field) – the field of deliverance for the Victorian Welsh, who boasted that their forefathers on that day in 1485 had laid the foundations of the Tudor dynasty and the British Empire. A prize of twenty pounds and a Silver Star was also to be won for an 'Essay on the discovery of America in the 12th century by Prince Madoc ap Owen Gwynedd'.

Ab Ithel expected an essay which would prove Britain's title to the New World – thanks to the Welshman – but the best work by far was written by the scrupulous Thomas Stephens, who comprehensively demolished the Madoc myth. Ab Ithel refused him the prize and when Stephens stood up to protest the band was ordered to drown him out. The audience insisted on his right to speak, warmly applauding him when he claimed that his ambition was to be an honest presenter of his nation's history and literature to the world. It was shameful that a nation should parade fantasies in its quest for fame: 'He, for one, would be content with simple truthfulness; he would never be a jackdaw decked out with borrowed feathers, but would be content with his own plumage, brilliant or plain as that might be.' This was the voice of a man who laboured constantly in the shadow of the Blue Books, and the insulting treatment meted out to him drove irate eisteddfod-goers to the Cambrian Tent to demand the reform of the

---

[21] Hywel Teifi Edwards, *Gŵyl Gwalia: Yr Eisteddfod Genedlaethol yn Oes Aur Victoria 1858–1868* (Llandysul, 1980), pp. 302–5.

eisteddfod. In the railway age which had made the Llangollen 'extravaganza' a practical proposition, a progressive, well-organized National Eisteddfod which would give no one cause to doubt either its honesty or its utility was long overdue.[22]

At the Denbigh Eisteddfod in 1860, it was decided to launch 'Yr Eisteddfod', a national institution governed by a number of 'directors' from among whom a working Council would be elected by a substantial General Committee. Months were to pass before a constitution for 'Yr Eisteddfod' was finalized, but in May 1861 a plan prepared by William Morris (Gwilym Tawe) was published and adopted by the Council 'with a few trivial alterations . . . as the basis on which the Eisteddfod should be conducted in future'. The most significant feature of Gwilym Tawe's scheme which needs to be underlined in this chapter is the emphasis placed upon the essential Welshness of the proposed national eisteddfodau:

> Eu hamcan ddylai fod cynnal i fyny yr iaith Gymraeg, llenyddiaeth, arferion, celfyddydau, etc., cadwraeth ei chofianau, hynafiaethau, iawnderau, breiniau, anrhydedd, a'i gogoniant; cefnogi ymchwiliadau i'w hanes, ei chelfau, defodau, cymdeithasau, ei hiaith, llenyddiaeth, a'i chyfreithiau, ei sefyllfa foesol, feddyliol, a gweithyddol, etc., ac yn gyffredinol llwydd Cymru a'i phobl, gyda thuedd a sel genhedlaethol.[23]

> (Their aim should be to maintain the Welsh language, literature, customs, arts etc., to conserve its records, antiquities, rights, privileges, honour and its glory; to support research into its history, crafts, rituals, societies, its language, literature and its laws, its moral, intellectual and industrial condition, etc., and in general to further the prosperity of Wales and its people with national zeal.)

Gwilym Tawe aspired to create a 'Sefydliad Gwladwriaethol Cymreig' (A Welsh National Institution), an institution which would promote patriotism which was 'the only way to save it from disregard, if not dissolution' ('yr unig lwybr i'w chadw rhag diystyrwch, os nid difodiant'). And since the bards had been traditionally the staunchest upholders of the Welsh language, they should be awarded a privileged position in the administration of 'Yr Eisteddfod'. Indeed, he believed that half the members of the Council should be bards. In the light of what occurred between 1861 and 1868, one thing is abundantly clear. Gwilym Tawe's scheme may have been accepted, but it was certainly not acted upon.

Before proceeding with an account of 'Yr Eisteddfod', it is necessary to outline briefly some cultural developments in England in the first half of the nineteenth

---

[22] G. J. Williams, 'Eisteddfod Llangollen, 1858', *TDHS*, 7 (1958), 139–61; J. Iorwerth Roberts, 'Eisteddfod Fawr Llangollen, 1858', ibid., 8 (1959), 133–56; Gwyn A. Williams, *Madoc: The Making of a Myth* (London, 1979), pp. 199–202.

[23] Edwards, *Gŵyl Gwalia*, pp. 9, 13.

century which conditioned the Welsh response to the Blue Books of 1847 and resulted in the possibilities of the National Eisteddfod being constrained by the likely English view of its usefulness. That view, which became 'the greatest and most highly civilized people that ever the world saw', to quote Macaulay's valuation of his nation, was a particularly lofty one.[24]

In his book, *Racial Myth in English History* (1982), Hugh A. MacDougal has revealed how the Anglo-Saxon myth reached its flood tide in the nineteenth century. The myth stressed that the pre-eminence of the English was attributable to their Teutonic descent. Teutonic strengths had made them superior to other peoples and had marked them out as natural leaders. Similarly, Nancy Stepan has shown in *The Idea of Race in Science: Great Britain 1800-1960* (1982), that the reappearance of a belief in the Great Chain of Being between 1800 and 1850 intensified the power which the Anglo-Saxon myth exercised. The nineteenth century – the imperial century in which scholars in Europe and America sought explanations for the physical, intellectual and moral differences between the races, and strained to discover why some excelled so much in civilization over others – was a great century for the science of race. Prompted by Darwinism and the new biological sciences, by new developments in ethnology and anthropology, philology and phrenology, imperialists sought 'proofs' which would justify believing in a 'law of race' which determined the existence of superior and inferior peoples. The traditional monogenist viewpoint was attacked by promoters of the polygenist viewpoint, who maintained that in view of the stark differences between the races there were more than one human species. None benefited more heavily from this climate than the Englishman, who found himself as the brightest star in the Teutonic firmament looking down on the 'lesser breeds', or the 'cheap races', to use Charles Dilke's slighting categorization.[25]

The National Eisteddfod had to confront this deprecation of the 'cheap races' which characterized England's imperial stance in the nineteenth century. It should be remembered that its authority had been challenged by the Indian Mutiny in 1857, by the rioting in Morant Bay in Jamaica in 1865, and by the Maori's fight for freedom in the New Zealand wars between 1864 and 1868. England's 'right' to rule others was being challenged, and as Edward Said has claimed, in the 1860s the English and French awareness of their respective might could hardly permit them to believe that the suppressed natives could ever force them to yield their colonies or say anything 'that might perhaps contradict, challenge or otherwise disrupt the prevailing discourse'. As for the Celts, who throughout the century were suspect creatures at best (as is testified by the observations of authors as authoritative as Macaulay, Carlyle, Mill, Freeman, Froude, Acton and Green), the

[24] Hugh A. MacDougal, *Racial Myth in English History: Trojans, Teutons and Anglo-Saxons* (Montreal, 1982), p. 91.
[25] Nancy Stepan, *The Idea of Race in Science: Great Britain 1800-1960* (London, 1982), chapters 1-4; MacDougal, *Racial Myth in English History*, p. 99.

Fenian bombing sorties between 1865 and 1867 made them particular objects of imperial anger. 'Celtophobia' was given its head and 'Paddy' was simianized at a time when 'the missing link' was a topic of general conversation. The Irishman's besetting sin, to quote Ronald Hyam, was his scorn for the 'Anglo-Saxonist "magic" sense of superiority', and it caused bitter offence.[26]

Like the Irish, the Welsh who frequently regretted the temerity of their Celtic cousins had to face the Englishman's readiest weapon – his contempt. And in Scotland, as Colin Kidd has so clearly shown, the Highlanders had to suffer the enmity of several Lowlanders who excelled in vituperation all others in the ranks of British Teuton-worshippers. David Masson, the Scotsman who edited *Macmillan's Magazine*, complained in 1861 that the disparagement of the Celt had made him unacceptable in some circles, 'and anyone who is in that unfortunate predicament has to go back in his pedigree for some Teutonic grandmother, or other female progenitor, through whom he may plead his blood as at least half-and-half'. From the inception of 'Yr Eisteddfod' in 1860 to its demise in 1868, the National Eisteddfod was annually scorned by some of the most prominent representatives of the English press lest it should attempt to promote a distinctive – if not recalcitrant – culture. The recurrent charge was that it could not fulfil any constructive purpose unless it were thoroughly Anglicized. The Council members concurred; the National Eisteddfod was Anglicized, union as a junior partner with England was celebrated, and the Welsh language was demoted – ostensibly without remorse.[27]

As he had done in the last of the Abergavenny eisteddfodau in 1853, Talhaiarn attended the last of the Council's national eisteddfodau in 1868 to make obeisance to Victoria's England: 'We are a quiet, law-loving people, and we never require to be dragooned into obedience. We are eminently loyal, and we willingly submit to the rule of our gracious Queen and her government.' And as if in repayment for such submission, that same year a prize of 150 guineas – the largest by far during the reign of 'Yr Eisteddfod' – was awarded to John Beddoe, president of Bristol Anthropological Society, for an essay 'On the origin of the English Nation, more especially with reference to the question how far they are descended from the Ancient Britons'. The subject had been set, to no avail, since 1862 when a prize of 50 guineas was first offered, and one of the unsuccessful competitors was Dr Thomas Nicholas, who published his book, *The Pedigree of the English People*, in 1867. He was accused of plagiarism by another would-be prizewinner, Luke Owen Pike, but George Osborne Morgan MP successfully defended his reputation. The essential purpose of Nicholas's book was to convince the world of

[26] Edwards, *Gŵyl Gwalia*, pp. 309–21; Edward W. Said, *Culture and Imperialism* (London, 1993), p. xxiv.
[27] David Masson, 'Gaelic and Norse Popular Tales: An Apology for the Celt', *Macmillan's Magazine*, 3 (1860–1), 213–24; Colin Kidd, 'Teutonist Ethnology and Scottish Nationalist Inhibition, 1780–1880', *Scottish Historical Review*, LXXIV (1995), 45–68.

the part the Welsh had played in bringing to the fore 'one of the most colossal creations of time – the English nation', and to assure the Welsh that that was more than sufficient recompense for losing their liberty – and probably their language.[28]

The reign of 'Yr Eisteddfod' decided the fate of the Welsh language in the National Eisteddfod for the remainder of the century. The emphasis would be on Britishness, on accommodating Welsh as the language of religiosity and tractable patriotism, and on thinking like utilitarians about the needs of Wales in the progress-laden, monoglot English meetings of Hugh Owen's 'Social Science Section' and the Cymmrodorion Section which succeeded it in 1880. Central to the undertaking was the need to merit England's approbation, to pass the test. Rector John Griffiths, President of the Eisteddfod Council, was in deadly earnest in 1867 when he declared that the Welsh were aware 'that we shall have many eyes upon us, that we shall be scanned narrowly . . . We are aware that there is an annual judgment passed upon us'. He was not the only one to voice the anxieties of a 'shame culture' during a decidedly neurotic decade in the history of the National Eisteddfod and the Welsh language.[29]

The year 1866 speaks volumes. Matthew Arnold was invited to preside at the Chester National Eisteddfod following the series of lectures on Celtic literature which he had delivered in Oxford between December 1865 and May 1866 and which were subsequently published as *On the Study of Celtic Literature* in 1867, the year in which his best-known book, *Culture and Anarchy*, was published. In his lectures he again castigated the 'Philistinism' of England's middle classes and the coarse over-emphasis on the Teutonic inheritance of the English. It was time to acknowledge their Celtic spiritual inheritance which he described as 'Celtic magic', that highly imaginative delight which the Celts took in the natural world and their rejection, as devotees of the muse, of the 'despotism of fact', and it was time, too, to give the Celtic strain in them an opportunity to counteract the excessive materialism which vulgarized English life. He was unable to preside at Chester, but he sent a letter to underline the points already made in his lectures, adding that it was time for the Celts to exert a beneficial influence on the English as the Greeks had done on the Romans. It is important to understand that Arnold spoke as the apostle of 'sweetness and light', an apostle sufficiently assured of English superiority that he did not fear giving offence to his countrymen by urging them to find good in some of the characteristics of less favoured people. But he was asking too much. *The Times* exploded.[30]

It chose to vent its anger in particular against the Welsh language, even though Arnold himself wished to see its rapid demise. When he had been a school inspector with responsibility, at one time, for parts of Wales, he had urged its

---

[28] Edwards, *Gŵyl Gwalia*, pp. 304–5, 380–1, 451–2.
[29] Ibid., p. 334.
[30] Ibid., pp. 326–31.

rejection. In his Oxford lectures he had wanted it dead in order to ensure the 'homogeneity' of Great Britain, and he had denied that it no longer served any purpose as a language of literature. His 'Celtic magic' was a wine long, long since bottled: 'For all serious purposes in modern literature . . . the language of a Welshman is and must be English . . . I repeat, let us all as soon as possible be one people; let the Welshman speak English, and, if he is an author, let him write English.' Arnold was a cultural imperialist who defended Governor Eyre's 'administrative massacre' in Jamaica and, according to Edward Said, it was thought that his concept of 'culture' should be specifically viewed as a check on disorder. It is a pity that Said did not deal with his attitude towards the Welsh language in *Culture and Imperialism* (1993), in which he expatiates on various attempts made by imperialists to turn successful battles into total cultural submission by preventing the vanquished from continuing to tell their story. It is quite evident that Arnold had in mind the termination of Welsh Wales's story when he lectured 'like an angel' in Oxford.[31]

Nevertheless, in the eyes of *The Times*, *The Daily Telegraph* and even the *Liverpool Daily Post* he was guilty of traducing his race. It was not possible for the 'lesser breeds' to improve their betters, to summarize the *Post*, and it was fruitless to seek leadership from the Celts: 'They are not the race to light or lead the way to progress.'[32] The undeniable proof of that in Wales was the continuing existence of the Welsh language. *The Daily Telegraph* repeated the old lie about a language without one word 'that will help in the smallest degree the spread of science',[33] but *The Times* was intent on stoning it to death:

> The Welsh language is the curse of Wales . . . Their antiquated and semibarbarous language, in short, shrouds them in darkness . . . If Wales and the Welsh are ever thoroughly to share in the material prosperity, and, in spite of Mr Arnold, we will add the culture and the morality of England, they must forget their isolated language, and learn to speak English, and nothing else . . . For all practical purposes Welsh is a dead language.[34]

Salvation would come to Wales from England, and England only, and it should be every sensible Welshman's duty to teach his compatriots to appreciate 'their neighbours' more than themselves. It was folly for the Welsh to set up an Industrial Exhibition, 'the sooner all Welsh specialities disappear from the face of the earth, the better', and it was mere vanity for so unprogressive a people to believe that they could speak two languages. One language would suffice for 'the mass'; bilingualism would simply cause confusion and create a 'bilingual difficulty' which would

---

[31] Said, *Culture and Imperialism*, pp. 157–8.
[32] Edwards, *Gŵyl Gwalia*, p. 329.
[33] Ibid.
[34] Ibid., pp. 327–8.

multiply problems and wasteful obstacles. In the editorials of *The Times* in September 1866, the mouthpiece of the most splendid of the 'dear races' talked down to one of the 'cheap races' as if the integrity of the Great Chain of Being was at stake.

The furore caused in 1866 is revealing. It shows how fiercely ready the English were to declare their superiority and how sadly eager the progressive Welsh were to welcome to their National Eisteddfod the propagator of an imperial culture who liked to romanticize about their otherworldliness while urging them in the same breath to reject their mother tongue. What more need be said about the care of 'Yr Eisteddfod' for the Welsh language in view of the urgency to provide a platform for an English critic intent on silencing its literature for ever? There is this to add. Immediately following the events at Chester, 'Eisteddfod y Cymry' (The Eisteddfod of the Welsh people) was held in Neath, an eisteddfod organized with the aid of Lady Llanover, Maria Jane Williams and the composers of 'Hen Wlad fy Nhadau' (The Land of my Fathers), among others, to put the alien National Eisteddfod to shame. It proved a financial disaster. The crowds stayed away, mainly because there was an outbreak of cholera in Neath, but the progressives welcomed the failure as proof of the folly of holding a 'Welsh' eisteddfod in the age of Progress. A skit in *Cronicl Cymru* describes David Livingstone, after a vain search in Africa, reaching Wales and finding 'the missing link' when observing the *gorsedd* ceremonies in 'Eisteddfod y Cymry'. Like the unruly 'Paddy', the traditional eisteddfod-goer was also to be simianized in the interests of progressivism.[35]

The Council of 'Yr Eisteddfod' discounted the protest at Neath. They would have no truck with it: 'We repudiate exclusiveness as incompatible with advance. Our great object is "SOCIAL PROGRESS", and we believe that the course of action that we advocate has a tendency to elevate and refine a thriving and a most orderly people.' John Griffiths had eloquently denied in 1863, 1865 and 1866 that the National Eisteddfod was bent on obstructing the spread of English, and in 1867 his denial was even more eloquent:

> We conduct our proceedings in English, our papers in the several departments of Art and Social Science are written in English. We offer prizes for essays showing the advantages to Wales of being in union with England. Oppose the spread of the English language! Nothing more preposterous.

'Yr Eisteddfod' could not afford to spend time on ensuring the continuation of the Welsh language; it would look after itself: 'I think our time might be better employed than in bolstering-up a language that may be of a questionable advantage.' Such was the opinion of John Griffiths who was regarded by his fellow-Welshmen as one of the staunchest devotees of their mother tongue.[36]

---

[35] Ibid., pp. 371–6; *Cronicl Cymru*, 29 Medi 1866.
[36] Edwards, *Gŵyl Gwalia*, p. 358.

In the Welsh press, especially in *Baner ac Amserau Cymru* and *Y Gwladgarwr*, the arrogant Englishman who expected the world to conform with him was set upon from time to time. Thomas Gee condemned *The Spectator* in 1863, *The Times* in 1866 and *The London Review* in 1867 for insisting that the Welsh should aspire to be English, but Gee himself, at a time when he was publishing *Y Gwyddoniadur Cymreig* (1854–79), was content in the 1860s to yield the material world to the English language, claiming that the Welsh language would live on the hearth and in chapel, and if not it would probably find new life, if not eternal life, on the banks of the Mississippi! On the National Eisteddfod platform, however, plain speaking in defence of the language was not encouraged, and castigation of the English in the manner of Reginald Heber in 1820 was ruled out. It is true that Dewi o Ddyfed, as was his wont, indulged himself at the Englishman's expense in the National Eisteddfod at Swansea in 1863, but that was the only opportunity afforded him to ruffle feathers. His imprudence offended 'Gohebydd', the doyen of Welsh correspondents, and Dewi o Ddyfed was allowed to sin no more.[37]

The proper way to speak up for the Welsh language was the old way, that espoused by the Revd Edward Hughes in 1828 when he thanked it for isolating the common people from 'the pestilent contamination of such writers as Paine, Hone [*sic*], Carlisle [*sic*] and I will even add Cobbett!', and that espoused by Caledfryn in 1865 when he praised, yet again, 'the language of containment': 'Tom Payne [*sic*] and Voltaire have never dared to show their faces in Welsh. The Welsh are a nation of docile, peaceable people and remarkably loyal to the government. When was it ever heard of us, as a nation, rising in rebellion? Never!' ('Ni feiddiodd Tom Payne [*sic*] a Voltaire ddangos eu gwynebau erioed yn Gymraeg. Cenedl o bobl lonydd a heddychol, a hynod o ffyddlawn i'r llywodraeth, ydyw'r Cymry. Pa bryd y clywyd am danom fel "cenedl" yn codi mewn gwrthryfel? Erioed!'). And having declared that serviceable truth he had only to read a poem prophesying that the language would live 'as long as the Welshman's blood/Beats in his breast' ('tra byddo gwaed y Cymro/Yn ergydio dan ei fron'). It would resist the train and the locust-like in-migrants and, as for the increasing number of defecting natives, there was no cause for concern. It was a simple matter to pretend that they did not exist, or at least that they did not count. William Thomas (Glanffrwd) was to take that stance when he composed his prizewinning *pryddest*, 'Y Gymraeg', for the London National Eisteddfod in 1887.[38]

The National Eisteddfod audiences were deafened annually by speeches in praise of the union with England and frequent exhortations to learn and speak English – the language of salvation. Weird and wonderful things were said to

---

[37] Ibid., pp. 324–5, 329, 333, 368–9.
[38] *The Gwyneddion or, An Account of the Royal Denbigh Eisteddfod, held in September, 1828* (Chester, 1830), p. 15; Edwards, *Gŵyl Gwalia*, pp. 362–3, 365–6; E. Vincent Evans (ed.), *Cofnodion a Chyfansoddiadau Eisteddfod Genedlaethol 1887 Caerludd* (Cardiff, n.d.), pp. 104–25.

justify jettisoning the Welsh language, including calling on God and his great providence on the one hand, and Darwin's theory of evolution on the other, as irrefutable arguments against any 'artificial' attempts to extend its life. As far as the Welsh language was concerned, it would be equally futile to interfere with the dispensations of both God and man. And not a whit less weird and wonderful was the way Hussey Vivian MP sought to persuade his listeners in 1863 that they had to be English men and women as well as Welsh men and women, and that they should strive to make Wales the best country in England; or the insistence of John Williams of Tre-ffos in Anglesey that the true benefactors of Wales did not want to 'resurrect' a mother tongue which had once been treasured by 'a highly refined' people: 'They did not want to have it back again: it was nonsense to think of such a thing'; or the way the mayor of Ruthin addressed the English in his audience in 1868 when calls for 'Cymraeg!' had become too insistent to ignore: 'The English ladies and gentlemen are proverbial for one good quality, that is, their patience and forbearance. I now beg of them to exercise this good quality for a few minutes, while I am addressing the Welsh audience as requested in their native tongue.' It is not recorded that any one of the 'English friends' demurred.[39]

In conclusion, the influence exerted by Hugh Owen's 'Social Science Section' on the prevailing ethos of the national eisteddfodau of the 1860s, and those which followed from 1880 onwards, must be underlined. As an earnest civil servant in London who had set his sights since the 1840s on erecting an 'educational edifice' in Wales, he had recognized the value of his friend, the Revd Henry Solly's 'Social Science Association', before he visited the first National Eisteddfod held at Aberdare in 1861. In 1862 he grafted his Section onto it, and from then until 1868 'the National' was permeated by the utilitarian mentality of Owen and his supporters, men such as Dr Thomas Nicholas from the Presbyterian College at Carmarthen, J. B. R. James from St John's Training College at Highbury, and Lewis Hartley, a Manchester businessman – three who made a point of scorning the Welsh bardic tradition as they stressed the profitable practicality of studying geology at the expense of the strict metres, and called for an English-medium system of education in Wales in order to enable middle-class children to compete with their peers throughout Britain. It was as a result of the special session of the Section held in 1863 to discuss the need for higher education in Wales that the campaign which led to the founding of the College at Aberystwyth in 1872 got underway, and it is not surprising that it made no provision for teaching Welsh when it first opened its doors to students. It is true that the University of London, which was to ratify the degrees of the first College of the University of Wales, would not recognize Welsh as a degree subject, but one has only to read Thomas Nicholas's paper, 'High Schools and a University for Wales', to find sufficient proof that securing a place for Welsh did not occupy his mind as he planned for

---

[39] Edwards, *Gŵyl Gwalia*, pp. 348, 357, 376.

the future in 1863. The same was true of Hugh Owen, the 'reformer' who invited Matthew Arnold to Chester in 1866. In both the National Eisteddfod and the College in Aberystwyth, English was the language that would light up Wales for the world to see.[40]

That was made abundantly clear by the Cardiganshire schoolmaster in Anglesey who came to the National Eisteddfod at Llandudno in 1864 to read a paper on 'Welsh Philology' in the 'Social Science Section'. He spoke with the authority of a scholar already conversant with the principles of comparative philology, and he sounded the death knell of fantasists such as John Edwards (Meiriadog) who, in an essay on 'Ardderchogrwydd yr Iaith Gymraeg' (The Excellence of the Welsh Language) in 1861, had traced the descent of the language back to Adam: 'Nid oes ond yr annysgedig a wada hyn'! (Only the uneducated will deny this!) John Rhŷs denied it.[41]

At Chancellor James Williams's prompting, Rhŷs went to Oxford – he listened to Matthew Arnold's lectures – and in 1868 he revisited the National Eisteddfod at Ruthin to speak on 'Cymro, Cymru a Chymraeg' (The Welshman, Wales and the Welsh language). He had recently delivered the lecture before the Société de Linguistique de Paris and he had good news to announce. Although he could see no hope of survival for the Welsh language, the Welsh *hwyl* could survive without it, and since it was doomed to yield to a 'noble antagonist' it would be best to undertake a close study of it without delay, 'and carefully registering all its idioms and vocables, they would do more to perpetuate it and advance Celtic philology, than by for ever rhyming and inflicting useless reading on their friends'. At the Liverpool Ordovices Eisteddfod in 1871, he again sounded the death knell of the language; it could not survive. Therefore: 'Seeing and recognizing, as we do, that our mother tongue is departing, let it depart in peace' ('Gan weled a chydnabod, fel yr ydym yn gwneyd, fod ein mam-iaith yn ymadael, gadawer iddi ymadael mewn heddwch'). That would be the wish of every true Welshman, and every Englishman should respect it, for there was a limit to a Welshman's forbearance: 'A Celt, perhaps, may excuse the picking of his pocket, if it is done politely, but he will never forgive the man who deliberately hurts his feelings' ('Gall Celtiad, hwyrach, esgusodi ysbeilio ei logell, os gwneir hyny mewn ffordd foneddigaidd, ond ni faddeua byth i'r dyn a archolla ei deimladau yn fwriadol'). At the Wrexham National Eisteddfod in 1876, he set about mocking the Gorsedd of Bards for peddling 'flapdoodle' to the people, and in 1877 he returned to Oxford as the first occupant of the Chair of Celtic Studies which had been established following the case Arnold had made out for it in 1866. The appointment could not fail to meet with his approval.[42]

[40] For a full discussion of Hugh Owen's 'Social Science Section', see Edwards, *Gŵyl Gwalia*, pp. 53–112.
[41] Ibid., pp. 360–1.
[42] Ibid., pp. 376–7.

When the reign of 'Yr Eisteddfod' came to an end, Hugh Owen appealed to the public to assist in clearing the debt, admitting as he did so that 'the National' truly needed the support of the common people. There was no response and he, together with John Griffiths, had to stump up a hundred pounds apiece to keep 'Yr Eisteddfod' from the clutches of the law. However, when the National Eisteddfod Association was established in 1880 at Owen's prompting, and the second series of national eisteddfodau got under way, the Welsh language suffered the same fate as before. In 1886, twenty years after 'Eisteddfod y Cymry' was held at Neath, Lady Llanover was prepared to support another such protest, this time at Caerwys. Thomas Gee also gave it his blessing, but the tide did not turn.[43]

The Cymmrodorion Section was to adopt the role of the 'Social Science Section', and the visit of the Prince of Wales and his family to the Jubilee Eisteddfod in London in 1887, and again to the National Eisteddfod at Caernarfon in 1894, occasioned severe bouts of 'the English madness'. Nor did the Welsh language profit from the nationalistic fervour which gave rise to the 'Cymru Fydd' movement between 1885 and 1896, and it was appropriate, since Matthew Arnold was received with the greatest respect on its platform, that 'The Society for Utilizing the Welsh Language for the Purpose of Serving a Better and More Intelligent Knowledge of English', should have been established in the National Eisteddfod at Aberdare in 1885. There is no reason to doubt the sincerity of the desire of Dan Isaac Davies and his supporters to secure a foothold for the Welsh language in the elementary schools. What is significant is that the English title of 'Cymdeithas yr Iaith Gymraeg' shows that its promoters believed the language was most likely to gain admittance to the 'educational edifice' as a handmaiden of English. It would have been unwise to argue the case for teaching Welsh on the basis of the inherent value of the language, and in the 'Memorial' which the Society submitted in 1886 to the Cross Commission on Elementary Education it did its best to be reasonable: 'The "maintenance" of the Welsh language is no part of this Society's objects . . .' Its survival was a matter for providence. When Dan Isaac Davies appeared before the Commission he expressed his hope that it would be ousted in the schools by one of the continental languages. The tactic worked, but the price paid for propitiating the Philistinism which 'Siluriad' excoriated in *Y Geninen* in 1885 was the demotion of the Welsh language in the education system for generations.[44]

In 1893 W. Llewelyn Williams pressed 'The Claims of the Welsh Language' before the Cymmrodorion in the National Eisteddfod held at Pontypridd, maintaining that the children of in-migrants, let alone the native child population, should learn it. For the majority of his listeners he simply did not make sense, and the National Eisteddfod approached the end of the century an obdurate

---

[43] Ibid., pp. 49–52, 394–6.
[44] J. Elwyn Hughes, *Arloeswr Dwyieithedd: Dan Isaac Davies 1839–1887* (Caerdydd, 1984), pp. 209–11; Siluriad, '"Philistiaeth" yn Nghymru', *Y Geninen*, III, no. 4 (1885), 276–83.

Anglophone. In two strict-metre poems, 'Cymru Fu: Cymru Fydd' (Past Wales: Future Wales) (1892–4) and 'Salm i Famon' (A Psalm for Mammon) (1893–4), John Morris-Jones scorned the institution before he was appointed to the Chair of Welsh at Bangor in 1894, where, fittingly since he was one of Sir John Rhŷs's former students, he continued to lecture in English to his students until his death in 1929. From 1902 onwards he was to star on the National Eisteddfod platform as the pre-eminent adjudicator of the Chair competition, without, it appears, showing the slightest desire to acknowledge that he would have been denied the opportunity to disport himself had it not been for the resolution of the Gorsedd of Bards who survived his contempt and that of the rout of progressives who had preceded him.[45]

It is not to the 'cognoscenti' of the 'Social Science Section' and the Cymmrodorion that thanks are due for securing a place, however marginal, for the Welsh language in the National Eisteddfod which betrayed it in the Victorian age. It was the 'outlandish "eisteddfodwyr"', who cherished the old traditions, who kept it alive, and enabled it to experience a revival in the twentieth century.

---

[45] John Morris Jones, *Caniadau* (Rhydychen, 1907), pp. 55–70, 71–92.

11

Printing and Publishing in the Welsh Language 1800–1914

PHILIP HENRY JONES

IN RECENT decades, perceptions of nineteenth-century Welsh publishing have been shaped by the claim made by Professor G. J. Williams that the second half of the century – more specifically the years between 1860 and 1890 – constituted the 'golden age' of Welsh-language publishing.[1] Williams maintained that the demand for Welsh books was so great that substantial works could be published 'without any difficulty' despite the poverty of Welsh readers. Indeed, the Welsh-language market was so profitable (a leading Welsh publisher, Charles Hughes, estimated that about £100,000 was spent in 1875 on 'Welsh literature of all kinds')[2] that several prominent English and Scottish firms successfully exploited it by issuing expensive books in parts.[3] According to this interpretation, the precipitous decline in Welsh-language book publishing during the early twentieth century was attributable primarily to the Anglicizing effects of the state educational system: as monoglot Welsh readers died out, their bilingual successors turned to English books. It does not, however, explain why bilingual readers should have developed such a strong preference for English books; nor does it examine the possibility that weaknesses in the Welsh book trade might have played some part in the process. In an attempt to answer these two inter-related questions, this chapter will examine the scale, nature, methods, and problems of the Welsh-language book trade during the nineteenth century.

The majority of the presses established in sixteen places in Wales between 1718 and 1780 were short-lived. Although Carmarthen became the major centre for

---

[1] G. J. Williams, *Y Wasg Gymraeg Ddoe a Heddiw* (Y Bala, 1970) and idem, 'Cyhoeddi Llyfrau Cymraeg yn y Bedwaredd Ganrif ar Bymtheg', *JWBS*, IX, no. 4 (1965), 152–61. But see Philip Henry Jones, 'A Golden Age Reappraised: Welsh-language publishing in the nineteenth century' in Peter C. G. Isaac and Barry McKay (eds.), *Images & Texts: Their Production and Distribution in the 18th and 19th Centuries* (Winchester, 1997), pp. 121–41.

[2] *Report of the Committee appointed to inquire into the Condition of Intermediate and Higher Education in Wales and Monmouthshire: Vol. II, Minutes of Evidence and Appendices* (PP 1881 (C. 3047) XXXIII) (Aberdare Evidence), Q. 6281.

[3] This development is reappraised in Philip Henry Jones, 'Scotland and the Welsh-language Book Trade during the Second Half of the Nineteenth Century' in Peter Isaac and Barry McKay (eds.), *The Human Face of the Book Trade* (Winchester, 1999), pp. 117–36.

Welsh-language printing from the early 1720s onwards, printing offices were not set up in other Anglicized centres of polite life until the latter decades of the century: Wrexham and Brecon (both in 1772), Haverfordwest (1779), and Swansea (1780). Significant expansion began in the late 1780s as a result of the growing demand for printed material of all kinds. Industrialization, urbanization, and the increasing complexity of economic and social relationships created a demand for jobbing printing, the mainstay of most presses. That growth continued unchecked despite high wartime prices is impressive testimony to the increasing demand for print, but developments in Wales cannot be attributed exclusively to indigenous factors since the book trade in England also grew rapidly during the same period. By the later 1820s virtually every town of any significance (outside Anglicized Radnorshire) contained at least one printing office that usually established a tradition of printing which has continued without a break to the present day.

The expansion of Welsh-language publishing was facilitated by developments external to the book trade, most notably the increase in the absolute number of Welsh speakers and the growth of vernacular literacy, which combined to create an extensive monoglot reading public. These potential readers were turned into actual readers by religious and cultural pressures which promoted a positive image of reading, and were enabled to buy books by a slow (if faltering) rise in disposable incomes. The book trade also benefited from the remarkable improvements from the 1840s onwards in transport, postal services, and facilities for transferring money. As printing in Wales itself expanded, Welsh printing in border towns declined, though Chester remained a significant centre until the 1840s. Of the towns in England favoured by Welsh emigrants, Liverpool alone developed a significant Welsh-language press and this retained its importance up to the mid-twentieth century. The expansion of the press attracted printers from outside Wales, mainly from nearby towns such as Chester, where Robert Saunderson and the elder Thomas Gee served their apprenticeship, but also a few from farther afield, such as Charles Heath of Monmouth, who had been apprenticed in Nottingham. These newcomers reinforced the trend towards higher standards of craftsmanship established in the later eighteenth century,[4] and passed their skills on to their apprentices.

In nineteenth-century England a close connection existed between libraries and the book trade; indeed, certain types of publication, such as the three-decker novel, were wholly dependent upon the library market. Since Welsh books were seldom purchased by libraries of any kind,[5] their publishers had to rely upon sales to readers. The number of potential purchasers of Welsh books cannot be

---

[4] Eiluned Rees, *The Welsh Book-trade before 1820* (Aberystwyth, 1988), pp. xxix–xxx.
[5] Philip Henry Jones, 'Welsh Public Libraries to 1914' in idem and Eiluned Rees (eds.), *A Nation and its Books: A History of the Book in Wales* (Aberystwyth, 1998), pp. 277–86.

ascertained. The claim made by Thomas Rees in 1867 that 'Welsh books and newspapers are chiefly circulated among not above half a million of people' is clearly far too generous; his figure of 120,000 for the aggregate circulation of periodicals and newspapers is probably a better indication of the potential market in the 1860s for Welsh-language material.[6] Since readers may well have purchased periodicals or newspapers rather than books, even this figure should probably be scaled down.

As well as being comparatively few in number, purchasers of Welsh books, as Rees emphasized, were to be found among the poorer classes of society, 'artizans, miners, small farmers, and agricultural labourers'. A few years later Charles Hughes also maintained that his firm's books were bought by 'working people, tradespeople, shopkeepers'.[7] Since their customers could afford to spend little on reading matter, Welsh publishers had to concentrate throughout the century on producing cheap books. The majority of the current Welsh books listed by John Evans of Carmarthen in his 1812 catalogue cost sixpence,[8] and as late as the mid-1890s sixpence or a shilling could be described as 'the two Welsh national prices'.[9] Even though a 3s. 6d. book was fairly cheap by English standards,[10] Welsh books costing 3s. 6d. or more were far less common than G. J. Williams suggested. Charles Hughes could pride himself on having published a dozen or more titles at that price,[11] and in 1885 Daniel Owen maintained that publishing a four-shilling Welsh book was a hazardous venture.[12]

A major problem was that the limited size of the market meant that Welsh books could not be produced as cheaply as those in English. The belief that Welsh books represented poor value for money probably lay behind persistent claims from the 1840s (if not earlier) that those readers who had the choice turned from 'expensive' Welsh books to 'the language in which they get so much more for their money' ('yr iaith y cânt gymaint yn ychwaneg am eu harian').[13] Other writers, notably Evan Jones (Ieuan Gwynedd), accused Welsh readers of being unwilling to pay a realistic price for their books since they were 'too eager for cheap books and for squeezing the last farthing out of the claws of author and publisher' ('yn rhy awyddus am lyfrau rhad, ac am wasgu allan y ffyrling eithaf o grafanc awdwr a chyhoeddwr').[14] Whether Welsh readers were miserly or whether they were shrewd judges of value, the result, as T. M. Jones pointed out, was the same:

[6] Thomas Rees, *Miscellaneous Papers on Subjects Relating to Wales* (London, 1867), p. 48.
[7] *Aberdare Evidence*, Qs. 6276, 6285.
[8] Rees, *Welsh Book-trade*, p. xli.
[9] W. Eilir Evans, 'Welsh Publishing and Bookselling', *The Library*, VII, no. 84 (1895), 395.
[10] Simon Eliot, *Some Patterns and Trends in British Publishing 1800–1919* (London, 1994), p. 60.
[11] *Aberdare Evidence*, Q. 6281.
[12] Daniel Owen, *Hunangofiant Rhys Lewis, Gweinidog Bethel* (Wrecsam, 1885), p. [5].
[13] 'Mentor', 'Sefyllfa Bresenol yr Iaith Gymraeg', *Y Diwygiwr*, XI, no. 129 (1846), 114.
[14] Evan Jones, 'Crybwyllion Llenyddol', *Y Gymraes*, II, no. 12 (1851), 380.

Os eir i swyddfeydd argraphu Cymru ac i'r masnachdai llyfrwerthol, ceir gweled rhai o'r llyfrau Cymreig goreu yn haenau trwchus heb neb yn eu ceisio! . . . Nid oes dim wedi bod mor ddamniol i lenyddiaeth buraf llyfrau Cymreig na thelerau llawer iawn rhy uchel i'r bobl allu cydymffurfio â hwy.[15]

(If one goes to Welsh printing offices and to booksellers' shops one sees some of the best Welsh books in thick layers, with no one seeking them! . . . Nothing has been so fatal to the purest literature of Welsh books than prices that were far too high for people to bear.)

Determining the precise scale of nineteenth-century Welsh-language publishing poses severe problems in the absence of a comprehensive bibliography of Welsh publications from the close of *Libri Walliae* in 1820 to the commencement of *Bibliotheca Celtica* in 1909. The best-known estimate, supplied by Charles Ashton to the Welsh Land Commission in 1896, is that 8,425 Welsh-language publications appeared between 1801 and 1895.[16] However, Ashton himself recognized that he had failed to record many books published in Wales,[17] and it is possible that some ten thousand Welsh-language items were published in Wales itself between 1801 and 1900 – perhaps many more, if individual printings of ballads and similar matter are included in the reckoning. Some titles, particularly the cheaper ones, were produced in large numbers: 70,000 copies of a 16-page penny almanac in 1877,[18] 27,700 copies of a 1s. 6d. English-Welsh letter writer between 1870 and 1898,[19] and 10,000 copies of most titles in Gee's cheap Sunday school series in the 1870s.[20] Several of the shilling volumes of popular verse published by Hughes of Wrexham from the 1860s onwards enjoyed extensive sales; no fewer than 17,500 copies of the third collection of verse by Richard Davies (Mynyddog) were printed between 1877 and 1899.[21]

Employment in printing and its ancillary trades in Wales increased from 1,238 in 1851 to 6,899 by 1911,[22] though much of this growth should be attributed to the English-language newspaper press of south Wales and to the expansion of a

---

[15] Thomas Morris Jones, 'Rhagoriaethau a Diffygion y Wasg Gymreig', *Transactions of the National Eisteddfod of Wales, Bangor, 1890* (Liverpool, 1892), p. 139.

[16] Conveniently reproduced in John Rhys and David Brynmor-Jones, *The Welsh People* (London, 1900), pp. 532–3.

[17] By 1897 he stated that he had 'discovered many more' (Charles Ashton, 'Welsh literature of the Victorian period', *Young Wales*, III (1897), 166).

[18] NLW, MS 15517C, p. 9.

[19] Ibid., p. 59; NLW, MS 15518C, f. 16r.

[20] NLW, Thomas Gee MSS J 1, Machine-room and piece book, 1868–77.

[21] As well as the Wrexham printings recorded in NLW, MS 15517C, p. 88 and MS 15518C, f. 28r, the first edition (of unknown size) was published in Utica, New York, during Mynyddog's visit to the USA in 1877.

[22] Based on Labour Tables 1 in John Williams, *Digest of Welsh Historical Statistics* (2 vols., The Welsh Office, 1985), I, pp. 95–102.

paper-making industry which catered for a British market. Even the largest printer-publishers to specialize in producing Welsh-language books, such as Gee of Denbigh or Hughes of Wrexham, employed no more than some fifty hands and much Welsh-language printing was undertaken by far smaller concerns such as John Jones of Llanidloes, who employed five men in 1851, or Adam Evans of Machynlleth who, in 1861, employed a man and a boy.[23] Most of the smaller firms remained content to earn a relatively secure living as printers who turned out the occasional book on behalf of its author. Thus, only thirteen of the 109 titles Adam Evans is known to have printed between 1849 and 1896 bear his name as publisher.[24] For small concerns such as these, book printing was essentially an adjunct to their normal activity of satisfying the local demand for jobbing printing and possibly producing a denominational periodical or weekly newspaper.[25] Very few Welsh printer-publishers attempted to achieve nation-wide sales for their products. Indeed, it could be argued that a truly national market for Welsh books did not exist. The assertion that 'North Wales cares little, and knows less, about books published in South Wales . . . on the other hand, South Walians are somewhat partial to books published in North Wales',[26] gains support from the fact that William Spurrell of Carmarthen could be described as 'the only important Welsh book firm in South Wales'.[27]

Many publications – typically the work of minor authors or the transactions of local *eisteddfodau* – were intended for a geographically circumscribed readership. In counties such as Anglesey and Cardigan, printing was largely confined to serving a local or at most regional market throughout the century.[28] The unfortunate consequences were pointed out by J. E. Southall in the early 1890s:

> By far the larger part of the 1,000 poetical works estimated to have been issued during this century have been put in the hands of small printers . . . who have trusted to their own immediate circle for the sale of their works. The result has been a low bill for inferior workmanship, poor paper, and poor ink, and a very limited circulation; they would like to get at all Wales, instead of half a county, but how to do it they know not, and perhaps after a few years the remainder of their stock is destroyed, or sold for waste paper.[29]

---

[23] J. Iorwerth Davies, 'A History of Commercial Printing and Printers in Montgomeryshire, 1789–1960' (unpubl. FLA thesis, 1975), pp. 511, 505.
[24] Based on list, ibid., pp. 55–80.
[25] A typical example is discussed in Philip Henry Jones, 'The Welsh Wesleyan Bookroom, 1824–8: A New Set of Printing Accounts' in Peter Isaac and Barry McKay (eds), *The Reach of Print: Making, Selling and Using Books* (Winchester, 1998), pp. 37–49.
[26] Evans, 'Welsh publishing and bookselling', 394–5.
[27] J. E. Southall, *Wales and her Language* (Newport, 1892), p. 305.
[28] For Anglesey, see Bedwyr Lewis Jones, *Argraffu a Chyhoeddi ym Môn* ([Llangefni], 1976), pp. 16–17; for Cardiganshire, David Jenkins, 'Braslun o Hanes Argraffu yn Sir Aberteifi', *JWBS*, VII, no. 4 (1953), 174–92 (with English summary).
[29] Southall, *Wales and her Language*, p. 308.

Even the largest printer-publishers found it necessary to supplement (or perhaps support) book publishing by other activities; Gee, for instance, published a profitable twice-weekly newspaper, and from the 1860s onwards Hughes rapidly became the most important publisher of Welsh music. No Welsh firm transformed itself into a publishing house. Indeed, Hughes, which had been compelled from the 1850s onwards to contract out much of its book production to firms in London and Edinburgh because of lack of space, invested heavily in new premises and plant in the mid-1890s in order to expand its printing operations.

The larger printer-publishers possessed sufficient financial resources to survive several unsuccessful publishing ventures. They were also well-placed to exploit the reverses which smaller, undercapitalized firms experienced from time to time. Hughes, for instance, acquired a number of titles of proven sales appeal at distress prices as a result of the financial difficulties of Griffith Jones of Bala in the 1860s,[30] and of Isaac Foulkes and Isaac Clarke in 1872.[31] Such growth at the expense of weaker competitors contributed to a widening of the gap between the leading printer-publishers and the smaller, local concerns during the second half of the century. Even so, the relatively small size of the largest Welsh firms compelled them to be cautious. As Charles Hughes told the Aberdare Committee: 'We only publish what we think will pay for publishing.'[32] He could not afford to risk his money on uncertain ventures:

> There is an increasing acquaintance with the English language, and as the providing of a supply of books in Welsh is a thing entirely dependent on private enterprise, it is difficult to get persons to risk the laying out of their capital on scientific and literary books in the Welsh language on the chance of whether they would take.[33]

A decade later, T. M. Jones similarly pointed out that limited sales made Welsh publishers overcautious:

> Gwelir fod cylch darllenwyr Cymreig yn gyfyng a bychan. Canlyniad naturiol hyn ydyw fod yn dra anhawdd cael cyhoeddwr yn Nghymru yn barod i ymgymeryd â chyhoeddi llyfr Cymraeg o werth. Dywedir yn ddystaw fod genym awdwyr galluog yn cael eu gwrthod gan gyhoeddwyr! Onid yw hyn yn tueddu a [sic] ddigaloni athrylith Gymreig?[34]

---

[30] NLW, Hughes and Son Donation 1958, Hughes letter-book 1, 1862–73, (28[b]), R. Hughes & Son to Griffith Jones, 23 July 1863.
[31] NLW, Hughes and Son Donation 1958, Hughes letter-book 1, 1862–73, (143–4), Hughes & Son to Ll. Adams, Ruthin, 2 August 1872.
[32] *Aberdare Evidence*, Q. 6428.
[33] Ibid., Q. 6324.
[34] Jones, 'Rhagoriaethau a Diffygion y Wasg Gymreig', p. 139.

(It will be seen that the circle of Welsh readers is limited and small. A natural consequence of this is that it is very difficult to get a Welsh publisher to undertake publishing a substantial Welsh book. It is said, quietly, that we have able authors who are rejected by publishers! Does this not tend to dishearten Welsh genius?)

His assertion was substantiated by a letter of rejection from Charles Tudor Hughes in 1887 to one of his firm's most popular authors, the Revd Owen Evans:

> We could not entertain any proposal to bring such a Volume out; the sale of Volumes of Sermons (be they ever so good) is at a minimum, we are sure that we have already involved ourselves in considerable loss by the publishing of such Volumes, and there seems no prospect now, of our being able to retrieve our loss.[35]

Throughout the century the output of the Welsh-language press was heavily biased towards religious works, collections of verse, biographies of preachers, grammars and dictionaries, and antiquarian studies. By mid-century this imbalance gave rise to considerable concern, possibly as a consequence of the post-1847 emphasis on 'useful knowledge'. In 1850 Ieuan Gwynedd complained that publishing 'thousands of sermons that are no more than jabbering and thousands of elegies less worthy than the brayings of an ass' ('miloedd o bregethau nad ydynt amgenach nâ bragawthan, a miloedd o farwnadau llai eu teilyngdod nâ nadau asyn') had retarded the growth of useful knowledge. 'Science and the arts are neglected for a shibboleth, the elements of general knowledge are put aside, and the study of useful knowledge is postponed until two days after the millennium' ('Esgeulusir y gwyddorion a'r celfau am shibboleth; cedwir elfenau gwybodaeth gyffredinol o'r neilldu, a gadewir heibio efrydiaeth o wybodaeth ymarferol, hyd yr ail dranoeth ar ol y milflwyddiant').[36] So little was done to broaden the subject coverage of Welsh books that forty years later T. M. Jones could still maintain: 'We are singularly unproductive in books on the popular sciences, and what we possess is little better than a translation of what is available in English. How poor we are in standard and lasting works on mental and moral philosophy!' ('Yr ydym yn hynod ddigynyrch mewn llyfrau ar y gwyddorau poblogaidd, ac nid yw yr hyn a feddwn fawr gwell na chyfieithiad o'r hyn geir yn yr iaith Saesneg. Mor dlawd ydym mewn llyfrau safonol a pharhaol ar athroniaeth feddyliol a moesol!').[37] The youth of Wales, he regretfully concluded, had to turn to English books which exposed them to dubious influences. Claims such as these are borne out by the biographies and autobiographies of Welshmen who grew up during the later nineteenth century. To R. T. Jenkins, English was the language

---

[35] NLW, Hughes and Son Donation 1958, Hughes letter-book 2, 1887 (32), Hughes & Son to Revd Owen Evans, 20 April 1887.
[36] Evan Jones, 'Llenyddiaeth Gymreig', *Y Gymraes*, I, no. 12 (1850), 371.
[37] Jones, 'Rhagoriaethau a Diffygion y Wasg Gymreig', p. 144.

in which exciting books were to be found.[38] W. J. Gruffydd said of the young O. M. Edwards: 'He read intensively a great deal of English literature; thus far [1880] he had not laid hands on any Welsh books of real value' ('Darllenai lawer ar draws ac ar hyd yn llenyddiaeth Lloegr; hyd yn hyn [1880] nid oedd wedi cael gafael ar ddim llyfrau Cymraeg o nemor gwerth').[39]

The preponderance of religious works reflected the intimate link between press and pulpit. Because of their education, relative leisure, and the financial problems caused by the disparity between their income and their status, Nonconformist ministers naturally turned to authorship.[40] Since many printer-publishers were also preachers or prominent denominational figures, the output of their presses reflected their values. Throughout the century discussions of the Welsh press praised its 'purity', a typical example being the claim made by David Rees in 1861:

> Hyd yma nid oes llyfr annuwiaidd, amheuaethol, ffugebol, aflwys, na brwnt, wedi cael cenad i ymwisgo yn ein hoff iaith ni; ac y mae y werin Gymreig wedi ei chadw gan ei hiaith i raddau mawr, a chan y llenyddiaeth bur yr ymarferent â hi i raddau mwy, rhag ysbwrial meddwol ffugebiaeth, annuwiaeth, a bryntni y wasg Seisnig.[41]

(Hitherto no atheistic, sceptical, fictional, distasteful, or filthy book has been allowed to appear in our own dear language, and the *gwerin* of Wales has been preserved by its language to a great extent and by the pure literature to which it is accustomed to a greater extent, from the intoxicating rubbish of fiction, atheism, and filth of the English press.)

During the opening decades of the century readers required solid theological fare (often of a violently controversial nature), but by its last quarter lighter material was in demand. In the late 1870s it was claimed that reading tastes in Ffestiniog had deteriorated since the mid-1860s; newspapers had supplanted theological tomes and threatened to produce a generation of light readers ('cenhedlaeth ysgafn o ddarllenwyr').[42] In the early 1890s Watkin Hezekiah Williams (Watcyn Wyn) maintained that the attention span of Welsh readers was now so limited that their reading was confined to '*Tit-Bits*' in both English and Welsh,[43] and in 1899 Evan Williams deplored the changing tastes of Welsh quarrymen; although they now read more, they preferred books that were interesting and easy to understand to the substantial works hitherto favoured.[44]

---

[38] R. T. Jenkins, *Edrych yn Ôl* (Llundain, 1968), pp. 31–2.

[39] W. J. Gruffydd, *Owen Morgan Edwards, Cofiant. Cyfrol I, 1858–1883* (Aberystwyth, 1937), p. 164.

[40] Gwilym Hiraethog claimed that he was compelled 'to make two and two into something more than four, by the labours of my pen'. T. Roberts and D. Roberts, *Cofiant y Parch. W. Rees, D.D. (Gwilym Hiraethog)* (Dolgellau, 1893), p. 220.

[41] *Y Diwygiwr*, XXVI, no. 315 (1861), 360.

[42] William Jones, *Hanes Plwyf Ffestiniog* (Blaenau Ffestiniog, 1879), pp. 84–6.

[43] Watcyn Wyn, 'Cymru ar Ddiwedd y Bedwaredd Ganrif ar Bymtheg', *Y Geninen*, XI, no. 3 (1893), 186.

[44] Evan Williams, 'Y Chwarelwyr', *Cymru*, XVI, no. 93 (1899), 216.

It has been persuasively argued that historians of the Welsh novel have paid too much attention to contemporary denunciations of fiction,[45] but despite the increasing respectability enjoyed by Welsh novels from the 1850s onwards following the appearance of propagandist works such as translations of *Uncle Tom's Cabin*, considerable suspicion of the genre persisted to the late 1880s.[46] Possibly for this reason, the widespread popular demand for Welsh fiction was primarily met by serials in periodicals or weekly newspapers rather than by novels published in book form.

As in previous centuries, many books were translated into Welsh since monoglot Welsh readers were eager to read English best-sellers. Around a tenth of the books published by Gee during the second half of the century were direct translations, and perhaps a further 5 to 10 per cent were free translations, adaptations, or imitations.[47] Publishers tended to favour translations since they were a cheap source of copy. Works published in the United States enjoyed no copyright protection in Britain until the 1890s, and the translation rights of works published in England could normally be acquired comparatively cheaply. The main concern of authors of English religious works was to ensure that their message reached the Welsh: thus its English publisher granted Gee the right to publish a translation of D. L. Moody's *Addresses* without charge, hoping that 'the circulation of them in Wales may be blessed of God to many souls'.[48] Authors of secular works often had no idea of the value of the Welsh translation rights; thus R. O. Pringle told Gee that he was the 'best judge' of what the right to translate *Animals of the Farm* was worth.[49]

By mid-century the heavy reliance on translations gave rise to considerable disquiet. Noah Stephens maintained that there were too many and that their Welsh was unidiomatic;[50] Thomas Stephens feared that excessive dependence on foreigners ('estroniaid') might lead to 'intellectual slavery' ('caethwasanaeth deallol');[51] Lewis Edwards considered that translations were 'ruinous to Welsh literature';[52] and R. J. Derfel denounced them as yet another symptom of the lack of national self-respect:

---

[45] Notably by E. G. Millward: see 'Tylwyth Llenyddol Daniel Owen' in idem, *Cenedl o Bobl Ddewrion: Agweddau ar Lenyddiaeth Oes Victoria* (Llandysul, 1991), pp. 120–36.
[46] An amusing example can be found towards the end of Dyfed's dreadful *awdl*, 'Cariad at ein Gwlad, ei Sefydliadau, a'i Llenyddiaeth' (1888), printed in *Y Geninen*, XI, no. 4 (1893), 242–6.
[47] The writer of *Ysbryd yw Duw*, a tract first published by Gee in 1860, disarmingly admitted that many of the sayings and comments as well as the style of the Revd John Todd of America had been borrowed in the composition of this booklet.
[48] NLW, Thomas Gee MSS P 63, James C. Hawkins to Thomas Gee, 12 August 1875.
[49] NLW, Thomas Gee MSS P 49, R. O. Pringle to Thomas Gee, 26 December 1874.
[50] Noah Stephens, 'Llenyddiaeth bresenol Cymru', *Y Diwygiwr*, XIV, no. 167 (1849), 167.
[51] Quoted in R. J. Owen, 'Agwedd bresennol llenyddiaeth Gymreig', *Y Llenor*, VI (1896), 64–5.
[52] NLW, Saunders Lewis Collection, Letters from Lewis Edwards to Owen Thomas, 1849–82, I (166–71), Lewis Edwards to Owen Thomas, 27 January 1860.

> Os gellir cyhoeddi cyfieithiadau o lyfrau Seisnig uchelbris yn Gymraeg, paham, yn enw gwladgarwch a synwyr cyffredin, nad ellir cyhoeddi llyfrau dysgedig a drudfawr o waith Cymry yn iaith y Cymry hefyd?[53]

(If it is possible to publish translations of expensive English books in Welsh, why, in the name of patriotism and common sense, is it not also possible to publish scholarly and expensive books by Welshmen in the language of the Welsh?)

However, no attempt was made in nineteenth-century Wales to challenge the hegemony of English publications by launching a campaign to translate works written in languages other than English. There was nothing, for instance, comparable to the spate of Czech translations from 1860 onwards of Slavonic and Romance titles which were specifically intended to emancipate Czech literature from the crushing influence of German.[54]

Welsh-language authorship, apart from a few full-time journalists employed by periodicals and, increasingly, by newspapers, was a part-time occupation. In 1848 John Thomas asked: 'Who in Wales would publish a book for *personal* gain? Very often our authors become debtors' ('Pwy yn Nghymru a gyhoeddai lyfr er mwyn elw *personol*? Yn aml iawn y mae ein hawdwyr yn syrthio yn golledwyr'),[55] and in 1850 Ieuan Gwynedd complained: 'In England, authors are paid; in Wales they are starved . . . There is no support for anyone to turn author, and because of that books are published accidentally or for passing gain' ('Yn Lloegr, mae yr awdwyr yn cael eu talu; yn Nghymru maent yn cael eu newynu . . . Nid oes gefnogaeth i neb droi yn awdwr, ac am hyny cyhoeddir llyfrau ar ddamwain neu er mwyn budd achlysurol').[56] J. R. Kilsby Jones doubted in 1863 whether three men gained a living from the pen in Wales,[57] and maintained twenty years later that it was futile to expect that a Welsh author could earn his bread, let alone cheese and butter.[58]

Throughout the century Welsh authors published and sold their own books on a large scale, a practice characterized in 1895 as being 'probably indigenous and peculiar to Wales'.[59] Its full extent cannot be established because Welsh imprints are often ambiguous.[60] Sometimes authors were compelled to publish their own work because the trade doubted its market appeal. Printer-publishers had little

---

[53] R. J. Derfel, *Traethodau ac Areithiau* (Bangor, 1864), p. 99.
[54] Eliska Ryznar and Murlin Croucher, *Books in Czechoslovakia. Past and Present* (Wiesbaden, 1989), p. 35.
[55] *Y Diwygiwr*, XIII, no. 155 (1848), 179.
[56] Jones, 'Llenyddiaeth Gymreig', 370–1.
[57] Vyrnwy Morgan, *Kilsby Jones* (Wrexham, [1897]), p. 212.
[58] J. R. Kilsby Jones, 'Pa un ai Mantais neu Anfantais i Gymru fyddai Tranc yr Iaith Gymraeg?', *Y Geninen*, I, no. 1 (1883), 21.
[59] Evans, 'Welsh Publishing and Bookselling', 395.
[60] Philip Henry Jones, 'A Nineteenth-century Welsh Printer: Some Aspects of the Career of Thomas Gee (1815–98)' (unpubl. FLA thesis, 1977), p. 31.

incentive to risk their own money on uncertain ventures since they knew they would be paid for printing executed on behalf of authors, whatever the fate of the book. Should it prove to be unexpectedly successful, they stood a fair chance of eventually acquiring the copyright.[61] Another incentive to self-publishing was the hope of greater profit by dealing directly with the public. As Ieuan Gwynedd put it: 'Mr So and So requires twenty pounds. How can he obtain them? He has to write a book, agree with the printer about its printing, and go on pilgrimage through the country to sell it' ('Mae ar Mr Hwn a Hwn eisiau ugain punt. Sut y gall eu cael? Rhaid iddo ysgrifenu llyfr, cytuno â'r argraphydd am ei argraphu, a myned ar bererindod drwy y wlad i'w werthu').[62] Self-publishing also reflected a widespread mistrust of publishers which was briskly dismissed by R. J. Derfel:

> Camgymeriad . . . ydyw i'r awdwr gyhoeddi ei waith ei hun: y cyhoeddwr yw yr un priodol at y gwaith. Gallai ef wneyd i lyfr dalu ag a fyddai yn golled i bawb arall. Ond y mae ar awduron rywfodd gymaint o ofn i'r cyhoeddwr fyned yn gyfoethog ar eu traul, fel y cyhoeddant eu gwaith eu hun . . . os ewch at yr awdwr gyda bwriad i'w gynorthwyo i gael ei lyfr allan, mae yn dechreu pryderu yn y fan yn nghylch y *copyright* . . . Faint tybed ydyw gwerth *copyright* llyfr nad ellir ei werthu?[63]

> (It is a mistake . . . for the author to publish his own work: the publisher is the appropriate one for that task. He could make a work pay that would be a loss to anyone else. But authors somehow are so frightened that publishers will grow rich at their expense, that they publish their own works . . . if you approach an author with the intention of helping him to get his book out he immediately begins to worry about the copyright . . . What, I wonder, is the value of the copyright of a book that cannot be sold?)

Self-publishing was normally financed by means of the subscription system. In 1895 subscription publishing was described as being 'still in occasional use',[64] but this underestimated its importance: Daniel Owen secured advance orders for 983 copies of *Rhys Lewis* in 1885 and E. Pan Jones no fewer than 1,779 for *Cofiant y Tri Brawd* in 1893. R. J. Derfel cogently summed up the most serious disadvantage of the subscription system: 'It is futile to expect to obtain sufficient names to make a profit for practically any book before it has been published' ('Oferedd yw dysgwyl cael digon o enwau at lyfr yn y byd braidd i sicrhau elw cyn i'r llyfr gael ei gyhoeddi').[65] Press advertisements and editorial comment indicate that

---

[61] Thus in 1853 Gee acquired the copyright of *Anrheg i'r Ieuenctyd*, a work first printed by his father for its author, John Foulkes, in 1839. Gee subsequently published several large editions of the work up to 1895. Jones, 'A Nineteenth-century Welsh Printer', p. 39.
[62] Jones, 'Llenyddiaeth Gymreig', 371.
[63] Derfel, *Traethodau ac Areithiau*, p. vi.
[64] Evans, 'Welsh Publishing and Bookselling', 396.
[65] Derfel, *Traethodau ac Areithiau*, p. v.

throughout the century authors frequently experienced great difficulty in obtaining sufficient subscribers to proceed with a proposed work.[66] Many books which were advertised as 'ready for publication' never appeared because of lack of support. Such problems provided the larger printer-publishers with opportunities for acquiring promising titles cheaply. In 1867, for example, Gee bought from Thomas Lloyd Jones, son of the immensely popular preacher John Jones of Tal-y-sarn, the copyright of twenty-two of his father's sermons, together with 'an introduction and all other matter which he intended to include in the volume which has already been advertised; and also . . . the whole of the subscribers' names which he has already received'.[67] For an outlay of sixty pounds, Gee had acquired one of his firm's best-selling titles which enjoyed an initial print order of some ten thousand copies.[68]

Publishers employed several methods of remunerating authors for their work. The oldest and simplest – outright purchase of copyright – was invariably used by Gee. From the author's point of view it had two serious disadvantages: he lost all control over his work, and would not receive any additional reward should it prove to be unexpectedly successful. The prevalence of the custom may thus have encouraged authors to publish their own work. Rather than disposing outright of the copyright, authors might lease it for a specified period or sell the right to publish a given number of copies. Jennette Morgan, for instance, sold the right to publish in twelve parts the first edition of between 3,000 and 5,000 copies of the sermons of her late husband, Edward Morgan, Dyffryn, for five pounds per thousand printed of each part.[69] Hughes gradually adopted the more modern royalty system during the second half of the nineteenth century.[70] Even so, the firm continued to purchase certain copyrights (such as those of the novels of Daniel Owen), and from time to time resorted to more elaborate arrangements, including the leasing of copyrights with provision for sale of the stereotype plates of the work to the author at cost price should the agreement not be renewed.[71]

Whatever system was adopted, the scales were always heavily weighted in the publisher's favour. Since copy was apparently always in plentiful supply, publishers enjoyed a buyer's market and could afford to drive a hard bargain.

---

[66] An excellent example of such problems is the dictionary by Thomas Edwards (Caerfallwch); publication was delayed for several years because no more than 350 of the 1,000 names required could be obtained in eight months. *Seren Gomer*, XIX, no. 250 (1836), 202.

[67] NLW, Thomas Gee MSS O 16, Articles of Agreement between Revd Thomas Lloyd Jones and Thomas Gee, 10 June 1867.

[68] NLW, Thomas Gee MSS J 1, Machine-room and piece book, 1868–77.

[69] NLW, E. Morgan Humphreys Collection, Morgan Dyffryn and Humphreys Correspondence, Agreement between Jennette Morgan and David Humphrey Jones, 1874.

[70] NLW, Hughes and Son Donation 1958, Hughes letter-book 2, 1887 (96), Charles Tudor Hughes to Mrs L. Edwards, 30 August 1887.

[71] NLW, Hughes and Son Donation 1958, Hughes letter-book 1, 1862–73 (48), R. Hughes & Son to Lewis Edwards, 30 January 1865.

Authors frequently had little or no idea of the cash value of their work, and few could deal with publishers as forcefully as did Lewis Edwards:

> There are several booksellers in Wales who would have given me £20 at least for one edition of a sixpenny book on any subject and in fact I had declined offers to that effect ... I shall write 24 pages for ... £10. But if you wish me to write 48 pages you must give me £15 ... and allow the copyright to remain with me.[72]

The arrangements for paying authors varied considerably. Some were supplied with copies of their book, a method particularly favoured by preachers who could sell their latest book while on preaching or lecturing tours. Thus Gee acquired the copyright of the two-volume religious epic *Emmanuel* from William Rees (Gwilym Hiraethog) in exchange for 500 copies of the second part.[73] When cash was disbursed, publishers might pay up to ten to fifteen pounds as a lump sum. Larger amounts would be paid in instalments; although a few authors of proven reliability were paid at regular intervals,[74] the normal practice was to link payment to the progress of work through the press.[75] Contemporaries believed that the lack of financial reward and, in particular, of recognition by a more extensive readership tended to discourage scholarly writing in Welsh. Scholars had the option of writing in English and many chose to do so. As early as the 1860s, John Hughes, Everton, claimed that he had experienced great difficulty in persuading the most able Welsh writers to contribute to 'Y Gyfres Gymraeg'.[76]

The nineteenth century witnessed a revolution in printing technology as metal replaced wood as the material of its productive plant, the unlimited power of steam replaced human muscle power, and its prime raw material, paper, became increasingly cheap and plentiful. At the beginning of the century all printing paper was made by hand from rags and was subject to heavy rates of duty. Because of its high price, paper accounted for a substantial proportion – half or more – of the total cost of producing a book.[77] There could often be shortages of the required kind of paper since the traditional method of paper making involved a delay of six weeks (or longer, if drought or frost intervened) between placing an order and the

---

[72] NLW, Thomas Charles Edwards Collection, 3264a, Lewis Edwards to R. Hughes & Son, 9 March 1861.
[73] NLW, Thomas Gee MSS O 12, Memorandum of agreement between William Rees and Thomas Gee, 29 November 1864.
[74] One of the rare examples is NLW, Thomas Gee MSS O 21, Articles of agreement between John Ogwen Jones and Thomas Gee, 10 November 1870, in which Gee agrees to pay £150 in six quarterly instalments of £25 from April 1871 to July 1872 for a commentary on the New Testament.
[75] NLW, Thomas Gee MSS O 20, Articles of agreement between Thomas Gee and Mary Morris, 17 March 1869.
[76] Owen, 'Agwedd Bresennol Llenyddiaeth Gymraeg', 62.
[77] Rees, *Welsh Book-trade*, p. li.

paper being ready.[78] Adverse weather conditions could further delay delivery of the paper to customers.[79] The Fourdrinier paper-making machine, introduced from 1804 onwards, so greatly increased productive capacity that as early as 1824 the total output of machine-made paper in the United Kingdom exceeded that of hand-made.[80] The rapid expansion of production exacerbated the problem of obtaining sufficient raw material, particularly since many foreign countries restricted exports of rags to protect their own paper industries. From 1857 onwards, esparto grass rapidly came to be employed as a substitute for rags.[81] Since esparto was not sufficient to satisfy demand, mechanical wood pulp (finely ground logs) began to be used in Britain for cheap paper (newsprint) in the early 1870s. The more stable chemical wood pulp, used on a commercial scale from 1883 onwards,[82] soon became the major constituent of book-printing papers. These technological advances, together with the final abolition of excise duties on paper in 1861, reduced the price per pound of a typical book printing paper from 1s. 6d. at the beginning of the nineteenth century to 2d. at its close. Paper as an element in the production costs of a book consequently declined from some two-thirds of the total in 1800 to less than a tenth by 1900.[83]

Although Welsh paper mills are known to have been in operation from 1706 onwards, much of their output consisted of coarse wrapping papers, and most printing paper had to be imported from England.[84] Locally made paper was routinely used by Wrexham printers in the late eighteenth and early nineteenth centuries,[85] but Welsh paper appears to have been little used elsewhere and then only because of local patriotism or for expensive English-language titles.[86] The introduction of paper-making machinery into Wales from 1821 onwards led to the increasing concentration of the industry.[87] Despite the expansion of Flintshire paper manufacturing during the second half of the century, notably at the

---

[78] Marjorie Plant, *The English Book Trade: An Economic History of the Making and Sale of Books* (3rd edn., London, 1974), p. 329.
[79] *Seren Gomer*, 25 March 1818, quoted in Rees, *Welsh Book-trade*, p. xxxvi.
[80] A. H. Shorter, *Paper Making in the British Isles: A Historical and Geographical Study* (Newton Abbot, 1971), p. 109.
[81] A. Dykes Spicer, *The Paper Trade: A Descriptive and Historical Survey of the Paper Trade from the Commencement of the Nineteenth Century* (London, 1907), p. 16.
[82] P. Gaskell, *A New Introduction to Bibliography* (Oxford, 1972), p. 222.
[83] Plant, *The English Book Trade*, p. 340.
[84] Shorter, *Paper Making in the British Isles*, p. 187.
[85] Eiluned Rees, 'The Welsh Printing House from 1718 to 1818' in Peter C. G. Isaac (ed.), *Six Centuries of the Provincial Book-trade in Britain* (Winchester, 1990), pp. 111–12.
[86] Expensive Llangenni paper was used for the first volume of Theophilus Jones's *History of the County of Brecknock* (Brecknock, 1805), and excellent Afonwen paper for John Jones, *An Address, wherein are considered, the relative Duties of the Rich and Poor* (Denbigh, 1829), an example of vanity publishing by a clergyman.
[87] Alun Eirug Davies, 'Paper-mills and Paper-makers in Wales 1700–1900', *NLWJ*, XV, no. 1 (1967), 4.

Oakenholt Mill set up by McCorquodale in 1871,[88] Hughes of Wrexham dealt almost exclusively with English paper makers. Little archival evidence has survived to identify the suppliers of other Welsh printer-publishers during this period, but watermarks indicate that Gee dealt with Lancashire firms such as James Wrigley of Bury during the later 1850s. The expansion of the railway system from mid-century onwards (which both Gee and Hughes enthusiastically promoted) undoubtedly facilitated the penetration of the Welsh market by English firms.

Since printing type remained expensive until the mechanization of typecasting from mid-century onwards virtually halved its price,[89] Welsh printers limited their stock to the necessary minimum. Shortages of type could therefore occur even in the largest offices; as late as 1858 Gee's office experienced difficulties because so much type was locked up in standing formes.[90] The eccentric printer, John Jones of Llanrwst, made his own type,[91] but this probably reflected his delight in handicraft rather than any rational assessment of costs. Other Welsh printers bought their type from English or Scottish typefounders. Since letter frequencies in Welsh are very different from those of English,[92] features such as the relative scarcity of lower-case 'd', 'l', 'w' and 'y' in English fonts caused problems to those who attempted to print Welsh using limited quantities of type. During the nineteenth century printers ordering type came to indicate that they required 'Welsh fonts' where the proportion of sorts reflected Welsh letter frequencies.[93]

Welsh books were set by hand throughout the century. Since compositors could be expected to set only about a thousand ens per hour, allowing for reading and correcting the first proof and distributing the type after printing,[94] the larger offices employed fairly large numbers of them. By 1860 Gee had ten or twelve engaged on bookwork and jobs, and a further eight or nine setting his newspaper.[95] Hughes at that time employed about a dozen men,[96] some of whom may have served both at case and press.

Normalizing the accidentals of the text required a good knowledge of Welsh and advertisements for compositors generally stressed the need for this. The absence until 1928 of a standardized orthography was a serious problem; each

---

[88] Shorter, *Paper Making in the British Isles*, pp. 188–9.
[89] Gaskell, *A New Introduction to Bibliography*, p. 208.
[90] NLW, MS 965E (Thomas Stephens 62) (i) (252), Gweirydd ap Rhys to Thomas Stephens, 14 December 1858.
[91] Gerald Morgan, *Y Dyn a Wnaeth Argraff: Bywyd a Gwaith yr Argraffydd Hynod, John Jones, Llanrwst* (Llanrwst, 1982), p. 17.
[92] Lucien Alphonse Legros and John Cameron Grant, *Typographical Printing-surfaces: The Technology and Mechanism of their Production* (London, 1916), pp. 126–7 and Table 14, pp. 132–3.
[93] NLW, Hughes and Son Donation 1958, Hughes letter-book 1, 1862–73 (113[b]), R. Hughes & Son to Miller & Richard, Edinburgh, 16 September 1869.
[94] Gaskell, *A New Introduction to Bibliography*, p. 54.
[95] NLW, MSS 10897D, 20151C.
[96] According to the 1861 Census Enumerator's book, Hughes employed twelve men, seven boys, and nine girls.

printing office had its own system of spelling, as had every author. Difficulties were particularly acute when producing periodicals or works of composite authorship. Gee attempted to overcome the problem by preparing for his office a list of the approved spellings of 489 difficult words by 1844,[97] and supported proposals for reforming the orthography in the later 1850s by printing *Orgraph yr Iaith Gymraeg* (1859) and adopting many of its recommendations.

The larger Welsh offices employed the widely used system of concurrent production, whereby the more urgent work such as jobs or periodicals was given priority, and book-work was used to keep the compositors occupied during relatively slack periods. Titles which were not immediately required could thus take a long time to set, and authors frequently complained of delays.[98] The flexibility provided by concurrent production, however, made it possible to produce books quickly, should the need arise, by concentrating the resources of the office upon them. Gee, for instance, assigned six compositors to the task of setting a 279-page biography of H. M. Stanley between 19 February and 27 May 1890 in order to take advantage of the public enthusiasm inspired by his wedding in July of that year.[99] Perhaps because of this method of working, even the largest, best-equipped, and most professionally organized offices were frequently censured for their inaccuracy; a review of the *Proceedings* of the 1861 Conwy National Eisteddfod criticized the excessive number of misprints perpetrated by Hughes,[100] and as late as 1890 T. M. Jones could claim:

> Ceir, mewn rhai amgylchiadau, y cyhoeddwyr mewn brys gormodol am ddwyn y llyfr allan, heb gymeryd y pwyll a'r gofal digonol i ddiwygio y prawf-leni, a'r canlyniad ydyw i gamgymeriadau anhapus iawn ddigwydd, ac ychydig o lyfrau gyhoeddir na bydd raid cael tudalen i'r 'Gwelliant Gwallau'.[101]

> (The publisher is sometimes in too much haste to bring out the book to take the requisite time and care to correct the proofs, and the result is that the most unfortunate errors occur, and few books are published that do not require a page of errata.)

Despite the additional cost (Welsh was charged for as a 'foreign language'),[102] Welsh books were set in London up to the late 1860s, both as reprint copy and

---

[97] NLW, MS 964E (Thomas Stephens 61) (i) (65), D. Silvan Evans to Thomas Stephens, 13 January 1859.
[98] Thus Lewis Edwards believed that Gee was excessively dilatory in setting *Athrawiaeth yr Iawn* (NLW, Saunders Lewis Collection, Letters from Lewis Edwards to Owen Thomas, 1849–82, I (166–71), Lewis Edwards to Owen Thomas, 27 January 1860).
[99] NLW, Thomas Gee MSS J2, Machine-room and piece book 1877–90.
[100] *Yr Herald Cymraeg*, 20 November 1863.
[101] Jones, 'Rhagoriaeth a Diffygion y Wasg Gymreig', pp. 143–4.
[102] Ellic Howe (ed.), *The London Compositor . . . 1785–1900* (London, 1947), p. 331.

from authors' manuscript.[103] Experienced Welsh compositors worked in London offices,[104] and a few (such as Gwenlyn Evans) were also employed by those Scottish firms which exploited the Welsh market from the 1860s onwards.[105]

Mechanized composition was first introduced into Welsh newspaper offices where some use was made of cold-metal machines during the 1870s.[106] Such machines were rendered obsolete by the first hot-metal machine, the Linotype, which could accomplish the work of eight to ten compositors. This was used in Wales from the early 1890s onwards; Gee acquired his first machine in 1895–6.[107] Although successfully used for bookwork in the United States, in Britain the Linotype was restricted to setting newspapers; books were not set by machine until the advent of the Monotype, first used in Wales in 1904.[108]

The high cost of type and the fragility of formes of type made it both expensive and inconvenient to keep much material in standing type. The alternative, resetting, was costly and could lead to errors. By enabling printers to produce relatively cheap metal replicas of pages of type that could be stored and reused as required, stereotyping made possible both the publication of extensive works in part form and the production of cheap reprints of books which had proved popular.[109] Stereotyping was therefore the technological innovation which, more than any other, made possible the 'golden age' of Welsh-language publishing.

Although the first viable method, the plaster-of-Paris process, was costly and complex, it was adopted by a few Welsh printers. Gee set up his foundry in 1853–4 and rapidly built up a large stock of plates,[110] and Hughes followed suit in the early 1860s. Stereotyping offered additional benefits to the latter since it could send plates of work composed at Wrexham to be printed elsewhere. The plaster of Paris process was superseded by the wet-flong (*papier mâché*) process. Hugh Humphreys of Caernarfon may have been one of the first in Wales to use the method in 1863.[111] Since it required little outlay on equipment (less than £20 by the 1880s),[112] the smaller offices could now undertake their own stereotyping. An

---

[103] NLW, Hughes and Son Donation 1958, Hughes letter-book 1, 1862–73 (11), R. Hughes & Son to [?Clay, Son and Taylor], 11 December 1862.
[104] Davies, 'A History of Commercial Printing', p. 326.
[105] *Caernarvonshire Record Office Bulletin*, 3 (1970), 14.
[106] Aled Gruffydd Jones, *Press, Politics and Society: A History of Journalism in Wales* (Cardiff, 1993), p. 74.
[107] D. Delta Evans, 'Y Faner 50 Mlynedd yn ol: Atgofion Hen Ysgriblwr', *BAC*, 21 July 1943.
[108] *Monotype Recorder*, 36 (3), (1937), 10.
[109] An advertisement printed on the wrappers of part 3 of Gee's reprint of Volume 1 of *Testament yr Ysgol Sabbathol* (1872) outlines an ambitious programme of reprints in part form which was to commence in July 1871.
[110] Philip Henry Jones, 'Ymweliad "Y Gohebydd" â Swyddfa Argraffu Thomas Gee, Awst 1860', *TDHS*, 40 (1991), 22–4.
[111] *Golud yr Oes*, December 1863, 514.
[112] John Southward, *Practical Printing: A Handbook of the Art of Typography* (London, 1882), p. 552.

additional advantage was that the cheapness of the new process made it practicable to prepare moulds of each book set as a matter of routine.

The wooden hand-press – essentially unchanged since Gutenberg's day – was theoretically capable of some 250 impressions an hour but in practice its productivity was considerably lower.[113] The iron hand-presses – first the Stanhope, subsequently the Columbian and the Albion – which became available from the first decade of the nineteenth century onwards did not improve productivity since their ability to work a larger type area at one pull was offset by the greatly increased time required for 'make ready', the process of preparing these more precise presses for printing.

Iron presses were first used in Wales during the second decade of the nineteenth century, initially in newspaper offices; in February 1819 John Daniel of Carmarthen advertised for sale a Stanhope press which had been used for printing the *Carmarthen Journal*.[114] They came to be widely used from the early 1830s onwards as their price fell and a second-hand market developed. Most printers were convinced that each type of press had its own virtues and some, like William Bird of Cardiff, who came to possess a demy Columbian, a double-royal Columbian, and a crown folio Albion, attempted to acquire a range of models.[115] Despite the increasing use of iron presses, wooden presses were still employed side by side with them in some offices to mid-century. John Jones, Llanrwst, was, as always, an exception, constructing a number of presses on the Ruthven pattern for his own use during the 1820s.[116]

Although steam-powered machinery was used to print *The Times* in November 1814, the earliest machines were not suitable for bookwork since they produced a poor impression and tended to wear type unacceptably quickly. It was not until 1823 that London book printers began to use machines specially developed for book printing.[117] English printers outside London (other than newspaper offices) were slow to mechanize: as important a firm as Clays of Bungay did not install machines until 1855.[118] The first Welsh printer to mechanize was Thomas Gee who, recognizing that the growing demand for Welsh material had made the hand press a serious production bottleneck, had two steam-powered machines in operation by March 1853,[119] several weeks before the generally accepted introduction of steam printing to Wales by the Swansea weekly, the *Cambrian*.[120] Hughes of Wrexham had acquired its first machine (supplementing three hand-

---

[113] Gaskell, *A New Introduction to Bibliography*, pp. 139–40.
[114] R. D. Rees, 'A History of the South Wales Newspapers to 1855' (unpubl. University of Reading MA thesis, 1955), p. 384.
[115] Ifano Jones, *A History of Printing and Printers in Wales to 1810* (Cardiff, 1925), p. 106.
[116] Morgan, *Y Dyn a Wnaeth Argraff*, pp. 9–11.
[117] W. B. Clowes, *Family Business 1803–1953* (London, [1953]), pp. 21–4.
[118] James Moran, *Clays of Bungay* (Bungay, 1978), p. 78.
[119] *Y Cronicl*, March 1853, p. 74.
[120] Jones, *A History of Printing*, p. 185.

presses) by 1857,[121] P. M. Evans, Holywell, had mechanized by 1858,[122] and Hugh Humphreys of Caernarfon, who described himself as a 'printer by steam' in 1862, possessed two machines by 1863.[123] Investment in expensive machinery required careful consideration: although they published a weekly newspaper, J. T. Jones and T. L. Jones of Aberdare concluded in 1856 that it was 'better to postpone having a Machine for some time again'.[124]

The first machines soon had to be supplemented or replaced. By August 1860 Gee's office contained four machines, including a double platen used for bookwork and a cylinder machine used for newspaper printing.[125] Hughes disposed of its original double demy machine in 1863 for £90,[126] probably replacing it with a cylinder machine, which was itself replaced in the spring of 1869 by a new double demy platen machine costing £280.[127] By then the volume of printing work was so great that Hughes was considering acquiring an additional cylinder machine from William Dawson of Otley.[128] As in England, the most popular machine from the 1860s to the end of the century and beyond was the Dawson-designed Wharfedale stop-cylinder machine and its many imitators. Smaller printers, who occasionally produced books or pamphlets for local authors as a supplement to their jobbing work, tended to acquire the treadle-driven jobbing platen machines, which became available from the 1860s onwards.[129] The availability of flexible, productive, but inexpensive machines, which could be operated by cheap boy-labour, led to a sharp fall in jobbing costs and may well have encouraged the founding of small printing offices.[130]

Powered printing machinery was steam driven until the advent of the more economical and flexible gas engines in the early 1870s.[131] By the first decade of the twentieth century, gas was beginning to be superseded in its turn by electricity.[132] The adoption of steam printing machines markedly increased productivity. As early as 1855 two of Gee's pressmen could print twenty-five or more tokens (over

[121] Philip Henry Jones, 'Richard Hughes a Hanes Cynnar Hughes a'i Fab', *Y Casglwr*, 54 (1994–5), 5.
[122] *Y Traethodydd*, XIV (1858), 240.
[123] *Golud yr Oes*, December 1863, 514.
[124] NLW, MS 3367E, Thomas L. Jones to J. T. Jones, 1 December 1856.
[125] Jones, 'Ymweliad "Y Gohebydd"', 21.
[126] NLW, Hughes and Son Donation 1958, Hughes letter-book 1, 1862–73 (23), R. Hughes & Son to an unidentified recipient, 5 May 1863.
[127] NLW, Hughes and Son Donation 1958, Hughes letter-book 1, 1862–73 (90), R. Hughes & Son to Messrs Davies & Primrose, Leith, 26 January 1869.
[128] NLW, Hughes and Son Donation 1958, Hughes letter-book 1, 1862–73 (93), R. Hughes & Son to William Dawson & Sons, 16 February 1869.
[129] James Moran, *Printing Presses: History and Development from the Fifteenth Century to Modern Times* (London, 1973), p. 149.
[130] Moran, *Printing Presses*, p. 153.
[131] Richard E. Huws, 'A History of the House of Spurrell, Carmarthen, 1840–1969' (unpubl. FLA thesis, 1981), p. 67. See also idem, 'Spurrell of Carmarthen' in Jones and Rees (eds.), *A Nation and its Books*, pp. 189–96.
[132] Reflected in the names of printing offices such as Y Wasg Drydan, Aberdare (*c.*1911).

6,000 impressions) per working day, and between 1 January and mid-February 1861 his machine room was averaging some 4,800 impressions per day.[133] Later machines such as the Wharfedale were capable of 800–1,200 impressions per hour but since they could (depending on their size and that of the forme to be printed) print on double or quad size sheets, the possible output ranged from either 1,600 to 2,400 or from 3,200 to 4,800 impressions per hour. In practice, such speeds were rarely, if ever, attained (or indeed required) by Welsh printers: by the later 1860s printing machines had become sufficiently productive to meet any likely demand for Welsh-language books.

In the hand-press period, the need to strike a balance between the costs of composition and presswork meant that the optimum print run normally lay between 500 and 2,000 copies.[134] However, when machinery was used, the unit cost per copy produced fell quite sharply for the first 10,000 copies and then continued to decrease more gradually.[135] In other words, once an office had mechanized its printing, it was the anticipated sales of a work rather than any technical limitations which governed the size of the print order. That the economies of scale deriving from mechanization would inevitably mean that Welsh books would be more expensive than those produced for the vast English market had been appreciated by certain Welsh printers as early as 1840:

> A chofied hefyd fod argraffu *cant* o lyfrau ymron mor gostus ag argraffu *mil*, ïe, *deng mil*, oddigerth gwerth y papur a'r gwasgiad. Felly bwrier fod argraffiad 500 o lyfrau Cymreig yn costio £50, ac argraffiad 10,000 o lyfrau Seisonig o'r un faintioli yn costio £200, pa un o'r ddau gyhoeddwyr a gaiff fwyaf o elw? Onid hawdd fydd i'r Sais roi mwy am arian?[136]

> (And remember also that printing a *hundred* books costs almost as much as printing a *thousand*, indeed, *ten thousand*, apart from the cost of paper and presswork. If an edition of 500 Welsh books costs £50, and an edition of 10,000 English books of the same size costs £200, which of the two publishers will make the greater profit? Will it not be easier for the Englishman to provide more for the money?)

Reliable evidence for nineteenth-century edition sizes has been preserved in publishers' archives, notably those of Gee and Hughes. Since Gee possessed ample storage space he could take full advantage of mechanization to print impressions of up to 10,000 copies, while Hughes normally printed no more than 1,500 to 3,000 copies at a time because of lack of warehouse space. On the other hand, from the 1860s onwards Gee was often seduced by the temptation of decreasing unit costs

---

[133] NLW, MS 20151C.
[134] Gaskell, *A New Introduction to Bibliography*, pp. 160–3.
[135] Ibid., p. 304.
[136] *Y Gwladgarwr*, VIII, no. LXXXIX (1840), wrapper, p. [2].

to print more copies than the market could absorb, so that thousands of remainders had accumulated by the end of the century.[137]

Setting aside such local considerations, there was normally a link between the cost of a book and its print run, cheaper works enjoying larger print orders and/or more frequent reprints than more expensive books. A few costly works, however, were produced on a large scale: the initial print order for the first edition of *Y Gwyddoniadur* (subsequently greatly increased) was for 6,000 copies,[138] and 5,000 copies were printed of the first impression of Lewis Edwards's *Traethodau Llenyddol*.[139] Since authors who published their own work were understandably reluctant to risk financial loss, they tended to have fewer copies printed than did printer-publishers. Evan Evans, for instance, regretted that no more than 2,000 copies of his *Esboniad ar Ddammegion Crist* had been printed for him in 1859, since he soon realized that he could soon have disposed of 3,000 copies had he entrusted the book to the trade.[140]

From the development of the codex to the 1820s, its binding formed an integral part of the finished book. Since each binding had to be individually constructed by hand, no economies of scale were possible and to avoid tying up capital unproductively, books were normally supplied in quires and bound by the bookseller or binder to the purchaser's own specifications. The only books normally sold ready bound were works such as prayer books which could be expected to sell quickly.

By the early nineteenth century a few Welsh books were offered for sale in paper boards as a temporary binding for a first reading. More decorative paper-covered boards were used by Welsh printer-publishers from the early 1820s onwards[141] but were superseded by the development of prefabricated cloth-covered cases into which books could be inserted. The various operations of forwarding (preparing the book to receive the case), case-making, and sticking the book into the case could then be broken down into steps, each one of which could be mechanized. This was a slow process in Britain, partly because many early machines were not wholly satisfactory, partly because of the expense of mechanization, but largely because most of the processes required little physical strength and could thus be carried out by cheap female labour; Gee's office, for instance, employed some fifteen women and girls in its bindery by 1860.[142]

---

[137] *BAC*, 16 September 1903.
[138] NLW, Thomas Gee MSS J 1, Machine-room and piece book, 1868–77.
[139] NLW, Hughes and Son Donation 1958, Hughes letter-book 1, 1862–73 (48), R. Hughes & Son to Lewis Edwards, 30 January 1865.
[140] Advertisement in Evan Evans, *Coleg y Darllenydd* (Wrexham, 1860).
[141] *Powysion*, published by Gee in 1821, is the earliest example I have seen.
[142] Jones, 'Ymweliad "Y Gohebydd"', 24.

An increasing number of Welsh printer-publishers entrusted their edition binding to specialist English firms.[143] As well as contracting much of its edition binding to trade binders in London (and later Edinburgh), Hughes made extensive use at its Wrexham bindery of prefabricated cases produced to its own specifications by London firms such as James Burn. From the 1850s onwards cases became increasingly ornate as the cost of gilt blocking and of blind or ink-stamped designs was progressively reduced. The more striking bindings reflect the fact that books could serve many purposes – they might be a fashionable article of furniture, an indication of status (like the parlour piano), a Sunday-school prize or reward, or a gift indicating respect: what more appropriate gift for a departing pastor than a set of *Y Gwyddoniadur* bound in extra morocco with gilt edges? At the lower end of the market, many Welsh books were offered for sale in paper wrappers as well as cloth bound, a practice which Ieuan Gwynedd characteristically attributed to Welsh miserliness: 'In England a book without a cover is despised, but in Wales sixpence is begrudged for a cloth case, as if it ate out the heart of creation' ('Yn Lloegr, dibrisir llyfr heb glawr iddo, ond yn Nghymru, grwgnechir chwe cheiniog am rwymiad lliain, fel pe byddai yn bwyta calon y greadigaeth').[144] In fact, Welsh readers realized that since its binding represented a high proportion – perhaps a third – of the price of a cheap book, it made economic sense for them to buy books in paper covers and then bind several together cheaply.

On balance, the leading Welsh printer-publishers adopted the appropriate technological advances at the right time. By the 1830s they had caught up with their English provincial counterparts, and by the later 1860s possessed printing machines capable of meeting any demand for Welsh books. Their restricted market, however, prevented them from taking full advantage of the potential economies of scale offered by mechanization. There is no evidence that technical advances improved the quality or the aesthetic appeal of Welsh books. Noah Stephens complained as follows in 1849:

Mae llawer llyfryn a'i bapyr mor wael, a'i gysodiad mor esgeulus, a'i argraffwaith mor arw, a'i rwymiad mor anghelfydd, a'i ymddangosiad allanol mor amddifad o chwaeth, modd y llenwir y meddwl o ragfarn ato cyn darllen un gair sydd ynddo.[145]

(Many a booklet has such poor paper, is so carelessly set, so crudely printed, so clumsily bound and looks so unattractive that one's mind is filled with prejudice against it before perusing a single word of its content.)

---

[143] Thus Spurrell initially executed his own binding but by the 1880s sent substantial orders to firms in London. Huws, 'A History of the House of Spurrell', p. 65.
[144] Jones, 'Llenyddiaeth Gymreig', 370.
[145] Stephens, 'Llenyddiaeth Bresenol Cymru', 167.

His criticisms were echoed forty years later by T. M. Jones:

> Nid yw y Wasg Gymreig bob amser yn ddigon gofalus fod y llyfrau gyhoeddir ganddi o'r *gwneuthuriad allanol goreu a phrydferthaf* . . . Weithiau ceir papyr teneu, brau, a darfodedig . . . Pryd arall ceir llythyren (*type*) fân iawn – llawer rhy fân, aneglur, a thywyll i fod yn ddarllenadwy iawn.[146]

> (The Welsh press does not always take sufficient care to ensure that the books it publishes are *well-made and attractive* . . . Sometimes the paper is thin, brittle, and impermanent . . . At other times the type is very small – far too small, unclear, and obscure to be very readable.)

The persistent image of the Welsh book as a downmarket product, made to a price but not offering very good value for money, may well have reinforced negative perceptions arising from its limited and often outdated subject coverage.

Charles Hughes informed the Aberdare Committee that 'one great difficulty' of the Welsh book trade was 'the machinery of circulation' and proceeded to claim that since there had been 'no machinery to bring the books within the reach of the people' until the early 1860s, he and his father had been compelled to 'create a class of people to sell our books'.[147] Although his experience of the London book trade may have induced Hughes to exaggerate, bookselling in Victorian Wales displayed several distinctive features.

Throughout the century would-be purchasers complained that Welsh books were difficult to obtain. In a series of letters published in 1886 in *Baner ac Amserau Cymru* (the second of which was so critical of Welsh publishers that Gee insisted it be toned down), Dan Isaac Davies identified the lack of a centralized wholesaling service for Welsh books as the key problem.[148] His view was developed by several writers during the 1890s:

> In Wales there is no central emporium where books and periodicals published in the vernacular can be procured. Every Welsh publisher plays for his own hand, and no more. No general Welsh catalogue is ever published, and . . . it is impossible to say what books are printed, or know where to seek for information. This selfish and short-sighted policy on the part of Welsh publishers recoils to their own disadvantage and does injustice to the author, for it limits the circulation and sets an unnecessary tariff on the sale, with the result that Welsh readers, failing to get what they want in Welsh, are often driven to the English market, where they buy things 'cheap and nasty'.[149]

---

[146] Jones, 'Rhagoriaeth a Diffygion y Wasg Gymreig', pp. 143–4.
[147] *Aberdare Evidence*, Q. 6299.
[148] J. Elwyn Hughes, *Arloeswr Dwyieithedd: Dan Isaac Davies 1839–1887* (Caerdydd, 1984), pp. 56, 127–8.
[149] Evans, 'Welsh Publishing and Bookselling', 396.

By 1908 O. M. Edwards could claim that booksellers (particularly those in south Wales) found it so expensive and inconvenient to deal directly with a multitude of publishers, and were so poorly informed about which titles were available, that many had concluded that Welsh books were more trouble than they were worth.[150] He, too, was convinced that the solution lay in a central wholesaling agency:

> Angen llenyddol pennaf Cymru yn y dyddiau hyn yw cael ystordy yn Llundain lle y cedwir cyflenwad o bob llyfr Cymraeg gyhoeddir . . . Oni fyddai'n werth i gyhoeddwyr Cymru ymgyfuno i gael siop gyfanwerthol mewn rhywle cyfleus yn Llundain, fel y geill pob *agent* Llundeinig anfon unrhyw lyfr Cymraeg mor ddidrafferth ag unrhyw lyfr Saesneg?[151]

> (The chief need of Welsh literature today is a storehouse in London stocked with a supply of every Welsh book that is published . . . Would it not be worthwhile for Welsh publishers to unite in order to have a wholesale shop at some convenient place in London, so that every London agent could supply any Welsh book as easily as any English book?)

Despite the consensus that such a facility was necessary, it was not until 1966 that the Welsh Books Centre was established.

Books were sold to the public by a wide variety of outlets, many of which dealt in books as a sideline. Although specialized booksellers' shops gradually became less uncommon, few carried a good stock of Welsh books. In the mid-1890s Richard Jones Owen (Glaslyn) maintained: 'A Welsh book is scarcely suffered to appear in the windows of our booksellers. I recently examined one of Smith's bookstalls, and the only Welsh book I found there was *Cymru* and two or three Welsh newspapers' ('prin y caiff llyfr Cymraeg le o gwbl yn ffenestri ein llyfrwerthwyr. Bum yn ddiweddar yn edrych dros un o ystol-lyfrau Smith, a'r unig lyfr Cymraeg a gefais yno oedd y *Cymru*, ynghyd â dau neu dri o newyddiaduron Cymreig'),[152] and in 1913 O. M. Edwards claimed that, apart from Swansea and Carmarthen, few books to tempt the multitude were displayed in the towns of south Wales.[153] By the mid-1920s it was said that:

> throughout the whole of Wales there are not more than ten booksellers' shops where a new Welsh book can be bought without inordinate trouble. The booksellers' windows are crowded with cheap English novels of the ephemeral kind, and when Welsh books are exhibited at all, they are too often mere 'old stock' for which there can be but little demand.[154]

---

[150] O. M. Edwards, 'Diwedd Blwyddyn', *Cymru*, XXXV, no. 209 (1908), 247.
[151] Idem, 'Llyfrau a Llenorion', *Cymru*, XLV, no. 266 (1913), 141.
[152] Owen, 'Agwedd Bresennol Llenyddiaeth Gymraeg', 57.
[153] Edwards, 'Llyfrau a Llenorion', 141.
[154] Departmental Committee on Welsh in the Educational System of Wales, *Welsh in Education and Life* (London, 1927), p. 179.

A disproportionate number of the few specialist Welsh bookshops were run by eccentrics like W. J. Roberts (Gwilym Cowlyd)[155] or by unworldly figures such as John Athanasius Jones (Athan Fardd).[156]

Older forms of distribution survived side by side with these commercial outlets. The long-established custom of selling books in Nonconformist chapels began to come under attack during the 1840s. In 1849 Noah Stephens believed it was necessary to restate the traditional defence: 'The purity of Welsh literature should, to some extent, be attributed to the means employed to publish and distribute books . . . until now the press has been patronized by the class possessing the purest and highest morals' ('Mae purdeb llenyddiaeth Gymreig, i raddau, i'w briodoli i'r dull a arferir i gyhoeddi a dosbarthu llyfrau . . . [mae'r] wasg hyd eto wedi bod dan nawdd y dosbarth puraf ac uwchaf eu moesau').[157] However, the practice fell into disuse, its decline possibly outpacing the development of other means of distribution.

Itinerant booksellers, who sold new books and disposed of otherwise unsaleable remainders,[158] were of great importance since they covered the remotest rural areas and took their wares to the homes of their customers. Although many – such as Richard Jones, Aberangell[159] – were honest and reliable, Charles Hughes found it necessary to warn John Curwen that there was 'very much greater risk with these itinerant Booksellers than those who keep a shop'.[160] A further problem was their reluctance to handle cheap books: 'They are not partial to any small Books, no Book of less value than 2d will be noticed by them',[161] a point which Hughes reiterated in his evidence to the Aberdare Committee: 'It is difficult to get the booksellers of Wales who, many of them, are colporteurs, to take a small publication like a tract; if they can get a sixpenny book they will take it rather than take a halfpenny tract.'[162]

Local *dosbarthwyr* (distributors), most of whom sold books and periodicals as an ancillary occupation, played a vital part in selling Welsh books:

> These men formed, in their day, an almost perfect channel for the publication of all kinds of literature, and the vast quantity of books published in Welsh in the 19th century was made possible only by their devotion and industry.[163]

---

[155] G. Gerallt Davies, *Gwilym Cowlyd 1828–1904* (Caernarfon, 1976).
[156] Watcyn Wyn, 'Athan Fardd', *Cymru*, III, no. 13 (1892), 83–4.
[157] Stephens, 'Llenyddiaeth bresenol Cymru', 166.
[158] Thus Hugh Jones, Llangollen, advertised 'old remainders [. . .] at very low prices' for 'itinerant booksellers and others' (*Yr Amserau*, 31 August 1853).
[159] A. Lloyd Hughes, 'Richard Jones, Aberangell (1848–1915): llyfrwerthwr teithiol', *JMHRS*, VIII, no. 4 (1980), 447–9.
[160] NLW, Hughes and Son Donation 1958, Hughes letter-book 1, 1862–73 (69[a] & 70), R. Hughes & Son to John Curwen, 2 December 1867.
[161] NLW, Hughes and Son Donation 1958, Hughes letter-book 1, 1862–73 (69 [a] & 70), R. Hughes & Son to John Curwen, 2 December 1867.
[162] *Aberdare Evidence*, Q. 6286.
[163] *Welsh in Education and Life*, p. 178.

Concessionary postal rates for printed matter and cheap clerical labour made it economic for publishers to maintain a multitude of small accounts with men such as Evan Lloyd, a smith who distributed some four or five pounds' worth a year of Gee's publications in the Corwen area during the 1860s.[164] *Dosbarthwyr* remained important until the end of the century; as late as 1887 Charles Tudor Hughes claimed that seven out of ten copies of an expensive biblical dictionary had been sold by *dosbarthwyr* rather than by booksellers.[165] Their numbers then declined so rapidly that by the mid-1920s it could be said that 'very few of them are left, and Welsh life is the poorer and the position of the language the more precarious for their disappearance'.[166] Charles Hughes frequently complained of the 'liberal allowance' his firm had to make to the trade in order to ensure that retailers kept a 'thorough interest' in the sale of its books.[167] Until the beginning of 1922, retailers who stocked the firm's publications expected to receive a one-third discount on every copy sold and one free copy for every twelve they handled as well as six months' credit, terms which in England applied to cheaper books.[168]

No matter how aesthetically pleasing or technically competent the product, success in publishing ultimately depends on balancing debt and credit. For much of the century this was far from easy to achieve since, as Charles Hughes complained, 'the greatest difficulty . . . is not so much to sell the stock as get the money'.[169] Retailers were very reluctant to clear their accounts with publishers: 'very rarely do we get our a/cs settled at the end of 6 months even when we get amongst old established people. There is so much hanging back when the time of payment comes'.[170] Indeed, according to Ieuan Gwynedd, some accounts were never settled:

Tystia un o gyhoeddwyr gorau y Dywysogaeth nad yw yn cael tâl am fawr fwy nâ haner ei lyfrau. Nid ydym yn meddwl fod neb yn dysgwyl tâl am fwy nâ thri o bob pedwar, a dedwydd fyddant os daw hyny i law yn gynt na'r amser a dreuliodd yr Hen Wr Llwyd o'r Cornel i wrando y gerddoriaeth a'i swynodd.[171]

(One of the best publishers in the Principality testifies that he is not paid for much more than half his books. We do not think that anyone expects to be paid for more than three

---

[164] University of Wales, Bangor MS 8468B.
[165] NLW, Hughes and Son Donation 1958, Hughes letter-book 2, 1887 (18), Charles Tudor Hughes to Thomas Thomas, 28 March 1887.
[166] *Welsh in Education and Life*, p. 178.
[167] NLW, Hughes and Son Donation 1958, Hughes letter-book 1, 1862–73 (48), R. Hughes & Son to Lewis Edwards, 30 January 1865.
[168] Plant, *The English Book Trade*, p. 408.
[169] NLW, Hughes and Son Donation 1958, Hughes letter-book 1, 1862–73 (46), R. Hughes & Son to John Roberts, 'Ieuan Gwyllt', 6 December 1864.
[170] NLW, Hughes and Son Donation 1958, Hughes letter-book 1, 1862–73 (13), Charles Hughes to an unidentified recipient, 5 January 1863.
[171] Jones, 'Llenyddiaeth Gymreig', 371.

in every four and they will be happy to receive that before a very lengthy period of time has elapsed.)

Bad debts could soon mount up to an alarming level: in July 1865 four south Wales booksellers owed Hughes over £94.[172] Other publishers experienced similar difficulties: in 1870, J. T. Jones & Son of Aberdare had to send a printed circular begging subscribers to their massive *Geiriadur Bywgraffyddol* to pay their debts since the firm had lost 'between three and four hundred pounds through unprincipled men who have emigrated to America and other places' ('rhwng tri a phedwar cant o bunau ar law dynion diegwyddor, y rhai ydynt wedi ymfudo i America a lleoedd eraill').[173] In 1886 Adam Evans was still receiving payment for a book, the last part of which had appeared in 1879.[174] The troubles of the enterprising but sadly undercapitalized Isaac Clarke illustrate how the smaller printer-publishers struggled along from hand to mouth; in 1861 he informed John Ceiriog Hughes that he could not pay him £12 'cash down' for the copyright of *Oriau'r Bore*: 'My money [for several publications] is all over the country from Cardiff to Holyhead, – and it is indeed a difficult task to collect it' ('Mae fy arian mewn cysylltiad â *Taliesin*, y *Gems*, a'r argraffiad 1af o'r *Oriau*, ar hyd y wlad o Gaerdydd i Gaergybi, – ac yn wir gwaith anhawdd iawn yw eu hela i mewn').[175] The larger printer-publishers attacked the problem of bad debts during the 1860s. Hughes systematically weeded out the worst risks: 'This year we have been very unfortunate, however we are very careful and gradually drawing the string tighter with customers who are not to be depended upon.'[176] Before the end of the century credit was extended only to traders who could provide satisfactory bank or trade references, and by the beginning of the twentieth century defaulters were pursued by a Liverpool-based trade protection society. For his part, Gee gained considerable notoriety for his readiness to bring County Court actions against debtors such as the unfortunate Gwilym Cowlyd.[177]

Publishers' links with retailers were strengthened during the 1860s as the major Welsh firms began to follow the example set by the English book trade a

---

[172] NLW, Hughes and Son Donation 1958, Hughes letter-book 1, 1862–73 (52[a] – 53[b]).
[173] Printed circular enclosed in NLW, MS 3370B.
[174] Davies, 'A History of Commercial Printing', p. 54.
[175] NLW, MS 10181D (Ceiriog 17) (48), Isaac Clarke, Ruthin, to John Ceiriog Hughes, 30 July 1861.
[176] NLW, Hughes and Son Donation 1958, Hughes letter-book 1, 1862–73 (46), R. Hughes & Son to John Roberts, 'Ieuan Gwyllt', 6 December 1864.
[177] Davies, *Gwilym Cowlyd*, pp. 39–40.

generation earlier[178] by employing travellers.[179] Joseph Roberts, for example, called twice a year on Hughes's behalf on every significant bookseller in Wales and in those English towns with large Welsh communities in order to publicize new books, receive orders, and attempt to collect money owed to the firm.[180] Since Welsh books were also purchased by Welsh settlers overseas, the larger printer-publishers such as Gee and Hughes apparently found it worth their while to appoint representatives in the United States during the 1860s and 1870s.[181]

The decentralized pattern of bookselling through a wide variety of outlets made the larger publishers keenly aware of the importance of publicity. As well as placing paid advertisements in periodicals, Gee could advertise twice weekly at no expense to himself in his *Baner*. Hughes made effective use of its music monthly, *Y Cerddor*, and of *Almanac y Miloedd*. Both firms also attempted to secure favourable press notices of new books. Gee regularly sent complimentary copies of major publications to leaders of Welsh opinion in order to solicit endorsements which could be selectively quoted in advertisements. From mid-century onwards both firms issued substantial catalogues of their publications in large impressions to supplement press advertisements and catalogues bound into books.[182] Individual titles, even fairly cheap books selling for a shilling or two shillings, were vigorously promoted by means of prospectuses, some of which were issued on a very large scale: Gee, for instance, printed 11,000 copies of a prospectus for *Y Gwyddoniadur* in 1871.[183] New titles and special offers were also publicized by handbills and posters. During the 1860s Hughes experimented, rather unsuccessfully, with exhibitions of books at the National Eisteddfod[184] as well as attempting to sell books directly to the public there, a method which had to be abandoned because of complaints by booksellers.[185]

From the late 1880s onwards Welsh book publishers encountered increasingly adverse conditions. Many failed to recognize that reading tastes were changing.

---

[178] Graham Pollard, 'The English Market for Printed Books: The Sandars Lectures, 1959', *Publishing History*, IV (1978), 40.

[179] Robert Williams, Gee's chief clerk, acted as traveller for that firm for over half a century (*BAC*, 25 August 1943); H. Humphreys, Caernarfon, advertised the post of traveller in 1867 (*Yr Herald Cymraeg*, 2 September 1867); P. M. Evans advertised for a traveller in north and south Wales in 1870 who had to be 'experienced, a careful book-keeper, energetic and of a good character' (*Y Goleuad*, 8 October 1870).

[180] NLW, Hughes and Son Donation 1958, Hughes letter-book 1, 1862–73 (69[a] & 70), R. Hughes & Son to John Curwen, 2 December 1867.

[181] D. Hywel E. Roberts, 'The Printing of Welsh Books in the United States – An Introductory Survey', *JWBS*, XII, no. 1 (1983–4), 22. See also idem, 'Welsh Publishing in the United States of America' in Jones and Rees (eds.), *A Nation and its Books*, pp. 253–64.

[182] For example, Hughes printed 5,000 copies of a catalogue of its books in June 1877 and 10,000 copies in July 1886 (NLW, MS 15517C, pp. 87, 147).

[183] NLW, Thomas Gee MSS J 1, Machine-room and piece book, 1868–77.

[184] A report in *Yr Herald Cymraeg*, 27 October 1866, states that Hughes had exhibited two hundred books at the Chester eisteddfod.

[185] NLW, MS 10183D (Ceiriog 19), Charles Hughes to John Ceiriog Hughes, 1 August 1871.

Several of Gee's later large-scale ventures, such as *Yr Allor Deuluaidd*, a collection of family devotions, were mentally rooted in the world of the fifties and sixties, and proved to be expensive failures.[186] Hughes was rather more aware of the changed climate; although Charles Hughes had believed in 1880 that there was no real market for Welsh novels,[187] his successor, Charles Tudor Hughes, enthusiastically set about publishing the works of Daniel Owen from the mid-1880s onwards. The Liverpool publisher, Isaac Foulkes, attempted to meet the grave challenge posed by cheap English reprint series by launching two series of Welsh classics, a shilling series, 'Cyfres y Ceinion' (The Series of Gems), followed in 1898 by a 3*d.* series, 'Y Clasuron Cymreig' (The Welsh Classics). At the end of the century Hughes also began to exploit the series concept by recycling popular titles from its backlist in 'Cyfres Boblogaidd yr Aelwyd' (The Popular Series of the Hearth), and launching new books in 'Cyfres yr Ugeinfed Ganrif' (The Twentieth-Century Series) and 'Cyfres Milwyr y Groes' (The Soldiers of the Cross Series).

In general, however, Welsh publishers reacted negatively to changing conditions by becoming increasingly reluctant to innovate or to broaden their lists. Worse still, O. M. Edwards claimed in 1899 that they had become reluctant to reprint successful works, and were beginning to dispose of remainders as waste paper:

Aeth *Gwaith Goronwy Owen*, er cystal ei bapur a'i lythyrau, i lapio siwgr. Gwelais gyfrolau gweddill *Llenyddiaeth y Cymry* yn myned ym Mangor am rôt yr un. Clywais y gallesid gweled cyfrolau *Cofiant Ieuan Gwynedd* yn yr un cyflwr yng Nghaerfyrddin dro yn ol. Onid oes rhyw gyhoeddwr gwladgarol ariangarol yn gweled fod gwerthiant parhaus i'r cyfrolau hyn?[188]

(*Gwaith Goronwy Owen*, despite its excellent paper and type, went to wrap sugar. I saw remainder copies of *Llenyddiaeth y Cymry* sold in Bangor for a groat apiece. I have heard that *Cofiant Ieuan Gwynedd* could have been seen in a similar condition in Carmarthen a little while ago. Does not some patriotic and money-loving publisher realize that these volumes have a continual sale?)

In an attempt to revive sales, Hughes embarked upon a campaign of price cutting in the early 1890s by running special offers such as cut-price coupon promotions, bargain parcels of remainders, and 'gifts' of free copies of older titles to those who bought new works.[189] Gee followed this example in 1903 when it held a sale to dispose of thousands of remainders, some dating back to the 1860s.[190]

---

[186] University of Wales, Bangor MS 3590 (83), Morris T. Williams to Thomas Richards, 11 September 1940.
[187] *Aberdare Evidence*, Q. 6299.
[188] *Cymru*, XVII, no. 98 (1899), 108.
[189] Several bargain offers were advertised on the wrappers of *Y Cerddor* in January 1892.
[190] *BAC*, 16 September 1903.

E. Morgan Humphreys summed up the pre-war malaise in a letter to T. Gwynn Jones:

> onid oes rhywbeth difrifol o'i le ar gyhoeddwyr Cymreig? Y mae rhyw ddiffyg anturiaeth, diffyg hysbysebu, neu ryw falldod felly arnynt. Nid wyf yn sicr prun ai ar y cyhoeddwyr yntau ar y llyfrwerthwyr y mae'r bai mwyaf, ond y mae cryn ddiffyg ar y naill fel y llall.[191]

> (is there not something seriously amiss with Welsh publishers? They are suffering from some lack of enterprise, lack of advertising, or some similar blight. I'm not sure whether the publishers or booksellers are most to blame, but each of them is considerably lacking.)

His strictures are borne out by the Hughes letter-books for 1912–14, which display a profoundly negative attitude. In August 1913 the firm refused to publish a volume of Welsh verse, claiming 'nid yw y wlad yn prynnu barddoniaeth ar hyn o bryd' (the country is not buying verse at present);[192] when rejecting another manuscript, it informed its author that 'We do not feel disposed to buy anything in the way of copyrights just at present, the market for Welsh publications being much too uncertain';[193] and in January 1914, when W. Llewelyn Williams was told it would take three years to clear the remaining 300 copies of *Gwilym a Benni Bach*, Hughes added:

> We may say that we are finding it increasingly difficult to get sufficient sales for Welsh books to make it profitable. The sale of Welsh books during the last 5 or 6 years has steadily diminished, but we are hoping each year to [?see] a revival in this respect, and 2 or 3 years hence we trust there will be a brighter outlook.[194]

The most imaginative response to new challenges came from outside the book trade. From the late 1880s onwards O. M. Edwards began to publish periodicals and books designed to appeal to his idealized vision of the Welsh *gwerin*. Although his monthly magazine, *Cymru*, was a major success, sales of several of his books were disappointing. That he failed to gain the desired number of subscribers for his series of Welsh classics, 'Cyfres y Fil' (The Thousand

---

[191] NLW, T. Gwynn Jones Collection, G 2187, E. Morgan Humphreys to T. Gwynn Jones, 17 March 1912.
[192] NLW, Hughes and Son Donation 1958, Hughes letter-book 4, 1913–14 (141), R. Hughes & Son to G. O. Parry, Bala, 27 August 1913.
[193] NLW, Hughes and Son Donation 1958, Hughes letter-book 4, 1913–14 (171[b]), R. Hughes & Son to D. L. Jones, Cardigan, 12 September 1913.
[194] NLW, Hughes and Son Donation 1958, Hughes letter-book 4, 1913–14 (409[b]), R. Hughes & Son to W. Llewelyn Williams, 7 January 1914.

Series),[195] is a further indication of the decline in demand for Welsh books by the beginning of the twentieth century. The battle had already been lost when publishers of the 'golden age' failed to produce and promote those innovative products which might have recruited a new generation of purchasers to replace a monoglot Welsh readership that was inexorably contracting.

---

[195] E. D. Jones, 'Cefndir Cyfres y Fil', *Y Casglwr*, 1 (1977), 12.

12

The Welsh Language and the Periodical Press

HUW WALTERS

THE ORIGINS of the nineteenth-century periodical press are to be found in the previous century when two kinds of periodical were founded by two quite different movements. The year 1735 has a special significance for both movements and the periodicals which they produced. In that year Lewis Morris of Anglesey founded *Tlysau yr Hen Oesoedd*, the first Welsh-language periodical to be published. Morris was aware of the decline in Welsh culture as the gentry had gradually become more Anglicized and turned their back on the bardic tradition, and – 'in order to induce the Anglicized Welsh to read Welsh, and to grasp what they had hardly ever heard of, – that in former times there had been education and knowledge in Wales' ('er mwyn denu'r Cymry Seisnigaidd i ddarllen Cymraeg, ac i graffu ar beth na chlywsant erioed braidd sôn amdano, – sef bod addysg a gwybodaeth gynt yng Nghymru')[1] – he introduced the readers of *Tlysau yr Hen Oesoedd* to the works of Dafydd ap Gwilym and Tomos Prys of Plas Iolyn, and the tales of Taliesin as they were related in the Welsh manuscripts.

This attempt failed, however, and no other Welsh periodical appeared until the close of the century when four radical, short-lived titles were launched.[2] Nevertheless, *Tlysau yr Hen Oesoedd* is the first kind of periodical which proved popular

---

[1] *Tlysau yr Hen Oesoedd* (Caergybi, 1735), p. 3.
[2] For detailed descriptions of the output of the Welsh periodical press from 1735 until 1850, see Huw Walters, *Llyfryddiaeth Cylchgronau Cymreig 1735–1850 / A Bibliography of Welsh Periodicals 1735–1850* (Aberystwyth, 1993). On the development of the periodical press in Wales, see idem, *Y Wasg Gyfnodol Gymreig, 1735–1900* (Aberystwyth, 1987); Brynley F. Roberts, 'Welsh Periodicals: A Survey' in Laurel Brake, Aled Jones, Lionel Madden (eds.), *Investigating Victorian Journalism* (London, 1990), pp. 71–84; Aled Gruffydd Jones, 'Y Wasg Gymreig yn y Bedwaredd Ganrif ar Bymtheg' in Geraint H. Jenkins (ed.), *Cof Cenedl III: Ysgrifau ar Hanes Cymru* (Llandysul, 1988), pp. 89–116; idem, *Press, Politics and Society: A History of Journalism in Wales* (Cardiff, 1993); E. Morgan Humphreys, *Y Wasg Gymraeg* (Lerpwl, 1945); T. H. Lewis, 'Y Wasg Gymraeg a Bywyd Cymru, 1850–1901', *THSC* (1964), 93–127, 222–36; G. J. Williams, *Y Wasg Gymraeg Ddoe a Heddiw* (Y Bala, 1970); E. G. Millward, 'Cymhellion Cyhoeddwyr yn y XIX Ganrif' in Thomas Jones (ed.), *Astudiaethau Amrywiol a Gyflwynir i Syr Thomas Parry-Williams* (Caerdydd, 1968), pp. 67–83. Much valuable information is to be found in T. M. Jones (Gwenallt), *Llenyddiaeth Fy Ngwlad* (Treffynnon, 1893), although the volume needs to be used with care. See also J. Ifano Jones, *A History of Printing and Printers in Wales to 1810* (Cardiff, 1926).

among a small section of Welsh people who lived in London. At that time London was an important centre for Welsh movements, and in many ways it was a surrogate capital. Thousands of Welsh people flocked to the English capital during the eighteenth century, among them men who cherished the Welsh language and championed its history and literature. They included the brothers Richard and Lewis Morris, Owen Jones (Owain Myfyr) and William Owen Pughe, who zealously set about forming societies such as the Honourable Society of Cymmrodorion in 1751 and the Gwyneddigion Society in 1770.[3] Under the editorship of William Owen Pughe and the aegis of the Gwyneddigion Society, *The Cambrian Register* was published in three volumes between 1795 and 1818. The Gwyneddigion and the Cymreigyddion Societies also sponsored *Y Greal: Sev Cynulliad o Orchestion ein Hynaviaid a Llofion o Vân Govion yr Oesoedd*, of which nine issues were published between 1805 and 1807, once again under the editorship of William Owen Pughe. The Cymreigyddion also supported *The Cambro-Briton*, another monthly published in London between 1819 and 1822 under the editorship of that strange and difficult man, John Humffreys Parry.

At the beginning of the nineteenth century, therefore, these expatriate societies led the way in the publishing of Welsh periodicals. But shortly thereafter the centre of Welsh literary life shifted back to Wales, and the place of the expatriate societies was taken by a number of literary clerics, including John Blackwell (Alun), Walter Davies (Gwallter Mechain), John Roberts of Tremeirchion, Evan Evans (Ieuan Glan Geirionydd), John Jenkins (Ifor Ceri), Thomas Price (Carnhuanawc), John Williams (Ab Ithel), and later Daniel Silvan Evans. These men were therefore heirs of a tradition begun in London, and it was they who were responsible for some of the principal Welsh periodicals of the nineteenth century, such as *Y Gwyliedydd, Y Gwladgarwr, Cylchgrawn y Gymdeithas er Taenu Gwybodaeth Fuddiol, The Cambrian Journal* and *Y Brython*.

But let us return to 1735. In the spring of that year, when Lewis Morris was preparing *Tlysau yr Hen Oesoedd* for the press, Howel Harris experienced a spiritual awakening during a communion service in Talgarth church. Daniel Rowland, the 22-year-old curate of Nancwnlle and Llangeitho, had a similar experience, again in 1735. These two men became the principal leaders of the Methodist movement, one of the most powerful and influential movements modern Wales has ever seen. By the end of the eighteenth century the leaders of this movement were acutely conscious of the fact that itinerant preachers and Sunday school teachers and pupils lacked suitable reading material. In 1799

---

[3] For the fortunes of the Welsh in London, see G. J. Williams, 'Bywyd Cymreig Llundain yng nghyfnod Owain Myfyr', *Y Llenor*, XVIII (1939), 73–82, 218–32; R. T. Jenkins and Helen M. Ramage, *A History of the Honourable Society of Cymmrodorion and of the Gwyneddigion and Cymreigyddion Societies* (London, 1951); Glenda Carr, 'William Owen Pughe yn Llundain', *THSC* (1982), 53–73; eadem, 'Bwrlwm Bywyd y Cymry yn Llundain yn y Ddeunawfed Ganrif' in Geraint H. Jenkins (ed.), *Cof Cenedl XI: Ysgrifau ar Hanes Cymru* (Llandysul, 1996), pp. 59–87.

Thomas Charles of Bala and Thomas Jones of Denbigh founded a periodical entitled *Trysorfa Ysprydol*, the first religious and denominational periodical. Published intermittently between 1799 and 1827, it provided a firm foundation for every denominational periodical published in its wake.

These denominational periodicals, of course, were legion, and the enormity of what was produced was remarkable, particularly in view of the dearth of educational opportunities and the prevailing economic circumstances. The Wales of David Rees of Llanelli and Lewis Edwards of Bala was markedly different from that of Lewis Morris a century earlier. A notable social revolution had occurred in the life of the nation during this period. Wales had experienced a series of extremely powerful religious revivals, its population had increased enormously, and its economy transformed as a consequence of new industrial developments. The growth and progress of the periodical press can therefore be regarded as a direct response to this social revolution, and it is evident from contemporary literature that the Welsh themselves were conscious of this growth. For instance, Lewis Edwards, in a review of *Gwaith Dafydd Ionawr* in *Y Traethodydd* in 1852, wrote thus:

> Yn y dyddiau hyn o gyffröad llênyddol, pan mae y wasg Gymreig yn fwy cynnyrchiol nag erioed . . . y mae yn rhaid i bawb addef nad oes y tebygolrwydd lleiaf fod yr iaith Gymraeg mewn perygl o farw yn fuan, nac ychwaith fod athrylith y Cymry wedi gwanhau . . . a'n barn ddiduedd ydyw, fod y cyfnod hwn yn rhagori ar bob un a fu o'i flaen yn hanes y genedl, ac yn rhagarwyddo oes euraid mewn llênyddiaeth Gymreig.[4]

(In these days of literary awakening, when the Welsh press is more productive than ever before . . . everyone must admit that there is not the slightest likelihood that the Welsh language is in immediate danger of dying, nor that the genius of the Welsh people has been weakened . . . and our impartial opinion is that this period excels in comparison with every previous one in the history of the nation, and heralds a golden age in Welsh literature.)

We ought at this point to remind ourselves of the most important titles of the denominational press. John Parry of Chester had already founded *Goleuad Cymru*, a periodical for Calvinistic Methodists, in 1818, and *Y Drysorfa*, the denomination's principal journal, appeared in 1830. The Wesleyans had founded *Yr Eurgrawn Wesleyaidd* as early as 1809, and this was to have the longest life of any denominational publication. *Seren Gomer*, the first Welsh newspaper, was relaunched as a fortnightly in 1818, and came to prominence as a periodical for Baptists even though it had no official connection with their denomination until 1880. *Seren Gomer* differed from most denominational periodicals in that it did not confine itself to religious matters. But the chief publications of the Baptists during

---

[4] [Lewis Edwards], 'Adolygiad: *Gwaith Dafydd Ionawr*', *Y Traethodydd*, VIII (1852), 94.

this period were *Cyfrinach y Bedyddwyr*, edited by John Jenkins of Hengoed, and *Greal y Bedyddwyr*, edited by John Herring of Cardigan. *Y Gwir Fedyddiwr*, which circulated in the south-east of Wales for a period of twenty years, belongs to the 1840s, and *Y Greal* was published from the denomination's office in Llangollen between 1858 and 1919.

Congregationalists were also prominent as publishers. Their main periodical was *Y Dysgedydd*, founded in 1821. David Owen (Brutus) was responsible for *Yr Efangylydd* during the early 1830s and *Y Diwygiwr* was founded by David Rees of Llanelli in 1835 to serve congregations in south Wales. Eight years later *Cronicl y Cymdeithasau Crefyddol* appeared for the first time: this was an influential, if somewhat fractious and prickly, monthly which was edited at various times by the brothers John and Samuel Roberts of Llanbryn-mair. *Yr Haul*, the periodical of the established Church, was launched at Llandovery in 1835 – again under the editorship of Brutus – and among other Church publications can be listed *Yr Eglwysydd*, *Baner y Groes*, an Oxford Movement monthly, and *Amddiffynydd yr Eglwys*. The only denominational periodical founded before 1850 and still in existence today is the Unitarian *Yr Ymofynydd*, which was established in 1846.

These, then, were the main denominational periodicals, although several smaller periodicals were published under the aegis of the religious denominations, very often as a consequence of denominational and church schisms. Among them were the periodicals of the Scottish Baptists and the Campbellite Baptists, or the minor periodicals of the reformed Wesleyans, known in Welsh as 'y Wesle bach'. Some periodicals, such as *Trysorfa Grefyddol Gwent a Morganwg*, *Yr Ystorfa Weinidogaethol* and *Trysorfa Efangylaidd*, served particular areas, or specific parishes, or individual churches and chapels. It should also be noted that smaller sects such as the Mormons and Swedenborgians were together responsible for some six titles between 1847 and the beginning of the twentieth century. During the latter half of the century, in the wake of the new developments which had occurred in congregational singing and the growing popularity of tonic sol-fa, an appreciable number of music periodicals, for example, *Y Cerddor Cymreig*, *Greal y Corau*, *Cerddor y Cymry* and *Y Solffaydd*, were published under the editorship of ministers such as John Roberts (Ieuan Gwyllt) and John Mills (Ieuan Glan Alarch). The religious denominations were also responsible for many temperance and missionary periodicals, and the children's periodicals of the day, including *Addysgydd*, *Pethau Newydd a Hen*, *Yr Athraw i Blentyn*, *Y Tywysydd*, *Y Cyfaill Eglwysig*, *Y Winllan*, *Perl y Plant* and *Trysorfa y Plant*. Most of these titles were short-lived, although some continued for a century or more. It is perhaps not surprising, bearing in mind contemporary taste, that the children's periodicals contained much the same kind of material as the adult periodicals. The aim of these publications, after all, was to be the handmaiden of morality and religion and the values glorified by Victorian society. It was reckoned that the best way of safeguarding children from the temptations of the world was to strike fear in their hearts and induce them to devote their lives to the service of God. As a consequence, these periodicals are replete with religious fables and stories about the death of virtuous children. Their editors, who were without exception ministers of religion, had no notion of what appealed to young readers.

Although more secular journals such as *Y Traethodydd, Yr Adolygydd, Golud yr Oes, Y Gwerinwr* and a host of similar periodicals did exist, they, too, were edited by ministers and preachers, several of whom edited more than one. William Williams (Caledfryn) edited eleven periodicals in all, and Owen Jones (Meudwy Môn) was responsible for half a dozen titles.[5] As well as being ministers, some editors were also printers and publishers, such as David Rees in Llanelli, John Jenkins in Hengoed, Josiah Thomas Jones in Caernarfon and later at Carmarthen and Aberdare, Evan Griffiths in Swansea, and Hugh Jones in Llangollen.[6] The nineteenth-century Welsh periodical press therefore comprised two main streams, both of which had their origins in the eighteenth century, namely the Welsh societies in London on the one hand and the Methodist and Nonconformist movement in Wales on the other.

One of the principal interests of the London Welsh, men such as Owain Myfyr, William Owen Pughe and John Humffreys Parry, was the antiquity of the Welsh language, and the science of the Celtic languages provided a fine opportunity for many pseudo-scholars. At this time scholars from the Celtic countries were seeking to prove that their own mother tongue was the primitive or original language from which all other languages were derived.[7] For William Owen Pughe, therefore, Welsh – or *Gomeraeg*, the language of Gomer, grandson of Noah – was the first language. He claimed that each syllable was significant, and that most other languages derived directly or indirectly from this primitive Welsh. As a result it became fashionable to consider Welsh as a divine gift from the earliest times. It was the language of the Garden of Eden and the language of heaven, and for this reason the periodicals of the London Welsh societies were full of lengthy treatises on subjects like 'The progress of the colonization of Europe from the dispersion of Babel to the commencement of history' and 'The Welsh language and its affinity to the oriental languages, and those of the south of Europe'.

---

[5] Gwilym Rees Hughes, 'Caledfryn fel Golygydd', *Y Cofiadur*, 35 (1966), 34–56; Huw Walters, 'Cyfnodolion Meudwy Môn', *TAAS* (1993), 69–81.

[6] On the activities of these men, see Iorwerth Jones, *David Rees: Y Cynhyrfwr* (Abertawe, 1971), pp. 69–131; John and Llewelyn Jenkins, *Hanes Buchedd a Gweithiau Awdurol y Diweddar John Jenkins D.D., Hengoed* (Caerdydd, 1859), pp. 99–107; Glyn M. Ashton, 'Josiah Thomas Jones 1799–1873', *Y Cofiadur*, 35 (1966), 3–22; R. Maldwyn Thomas, 'Josiah Thomas Jones yn Nhref Caernarfon', ibid., 37 (1972), 69–84; Owen Morris, 'Llyfryddiaeth Ieuan Ebblig. A Checklist of the Publications of Evan Griffiths, Swansea, between 1830 and 1867', *NLWJ*, XXVI, no. 2 (1989), 59–101, 165–221; Huw Walters, 'Cyfnodolion Hugh Jones, Llangollen', *TDHS*, 41 (1992), 93–104.

[7] See the chapter 'Anfeidrol Ynfydrwydd' in Glenda Carr, *William Owen-Pughe* (Caerdydd, 1983), pp. 70–95; G. J. Williams, 'William Owen [-Pughe]', *LlC*, VII, no. 1 and 2 (1962), 1–14.

Several of Pughe's theories were swallowed whole by John Humffreys Parry, editor of *The Cambro-Briton*, another publication which contained articles on topics such as 'The Language of Paradise', 'Affinity between Welsh and Hebrew' and a host of shorter pieces on Coelbren y Beirdd and other creations by Iolo Morganwg. The content of William Owen Pughe's *Greal* was similar, except that it was printed in the editor's own outlandish orthography, a fact which eventually led to the demise of the periodical. Iolo Morganwg claimed that the syntax and idioms of the *Greal* were 'nothing but rank Hottentotic'.[8] As a result the publication came to an end with its ninth issue, but not before William Owen Pughe had edited a new edition of Henri Perri's *Egluryn Phraethineb* as a supplement to the last number. *Egluryn Phraethineb*, first published in 1595, and the orthographical experiments undertaken by Henri Perri and other humanists, were of special interest to Pughe and it is more than likely that he regarded himself as the successor of such humanists since they all shared the same objectives.

The influence of William Owen Pughe's ideas was far-reaching. It was no coincidence that the fortnightly edited by Joseph Harris of Swansea was called *Seren Gomer*. Nor was it a coincidence that on the covers of the first issues the title was printed in the arcane letters of Coelbren y Beirdd. But the debate over orthography continued over a long period, notably among three groups of writers: supporters like Thomas Edwards (Caerfallwch) and John Jones (Tegid); those who steered a middle course like Gwallter Mechain; and opponents such as John Roberts of Tremeirchion, editor of *Cylchgrawn Cymru*, and later Daniel Silvan Evans. Beriah Gwynfe Evans devised his own orthography and used it for a while during the 1880s in his popular periodical *Cyfaill yr Aelwyd*. It was therefore no easy task to persuade the Welsh people that the theories of William Owen Pughe, Iolo Morganwg and their followers were foolish. Indeed, some of the more credulous Welshmen, such as Edward Foulkes, Owen Morgan (Morien) and Owen Eilian Owen, continued to uphold such ideas in the Welsh periodicals of the 1890s. This incensed John Morris-Jones to such an extent that he led a special campaign against them in the pages of the periodicals and later in his own periodical, *Y Beirniad*.

The heirs of the tradition begun by the Welsh societies in London were the literary-minded clerics, several of whom founded their own periodicals. The first and most important was *Y Gwyliedydd*, founded in 1822, with Rowland Williams, a scholar and clergyman from Ysgeifiog, as its main editor, and Gwallter Mechain, John Jones (Tegid), and Ifor Ceri among its most zealous contributors. Unlike Nonconformist periodicals, *Y Gwyliedydd* carried substantial articles on the history and antiquities of Wales, its literature and folk customs. *Y Gwladgarwr*, published under the editorship of Ieuan Glan Geirionydd between 1833 and 1841, was a similar publication. In the mid-1830s Alun launched *Cylchgrawn y Gymdeithas er*

[8] NLW, MS 13221E, f. 142.

Taenu Gwybodaeth Fuddiol.[9] D. Silvan Evans, the last of these literary-minded clerics, edited one of the most popular periodicals of the century, namely *Y Brython*, published in Porthmadog during the 1860s. *Y Brython* carried articles on the history and literature of Wales, *cywyddau* by the old poets, and selections of old harp-stanzas, material which few at the time held in high esteem. It also carried a regular column entitled 'Llên y Werin', a term coined by Silvan Evans himself as a translation of the English word 'folklore'.[10]

The purview of these periodicals was extremely wide. It is true that they carried a great deal of religious material – sermons, commentaries and church news – but attention was also given to general knowledge, with an emphasis on literature and antiquities as well. In his preface to the first number of *Y Gwladgarwr*, the editor claimed that he was anxious to provide the monoglot Welshman with the means of acquiring general knowledge, and to introduce him to subjects which other publications failed to provide.[11] This accounts for the fact that such a wide spectrum of articles on subjects like astronomy and science were published and that editors often referred to the need to provide succour for the native tongue and lent their generous support to every movement which strove to foster the language.

These periodicals also devoted much space to the activities of patriotic Welsh societies established throughout Wales, and the eisteddfodau and competitive gatherings held in almost every district by mid-century. Apart from *Seren Gomer*, however, denominational periodicals paid little attention to activities of this kind, at least during the first three decades of the century. Indeed, they could be quite hostile towards the literary societies and eisteddfodau, as the comments of 'Philus', a contributor to *Y Dysgedydd*, the Congregational monthly, in 1825 indicate:

Yn eich Cyhoeddiad clodwiw, yn nghyd ag amryw fanau ereill, yr wyf yn gweled ac yn clywed llawer iawn am Gymdeithasau ac Eisteddfodau, er cadw ac amddiffyn yr iaith Gymraeg; pa rai sydd yn cael mwy o le, na'r cyfarfodydd sydd er amddiffyn duwioldeb. Yr wyf yn credu fy mod mor awyddus, ac eiddigeddus dros yr hen iaith Gymraeg, ag un o'r rhai sydd yn aelodau yn y Cymdeithasau uchod: eto, yr wyf yn ystyried fod taro yn erbyn *pechod, ac amddiffyn duwioldeb*, yn fwy o bwys na chadw'r iaith yn ei phurdeb; ac

---

[9] For the activities of these clerics, see Bedwyr Lewis Jones, '*Yr Hen Bersoniaid Llengar*' (Penarth, 1963); idem, 'Yr Offeiriaid Llengar' in Dyfnallt Morgan (ed.), *Gwŷr Llên y Bedwaredd Ganrif ar Bymtheg a'u Cefndir* (Llandybïe, 1968), pp. 42–53. Some of these periodicals are discussed in Lizzie Mary Jones, 'Hanes Llenyddol *Y Gwyliedydd* (1822–1837)' (unpubl. University of Wales MA thesis, 1936); F. A. Cavenagh, 'Cylchgrawn y Gymdeithas er Taenu Gwybodaeth Fuddiol', *JWBS*, III, no. 4 (1927), 168–72, and ibid., no. 6 (1929), 253–6; Gwendoline Guest, 'Bywyd a Gwaith John Blackwell (Alun), 1797–1840' (unpubl. University of Wales MA thesis, 1971), pp. 193–219.

[10] On *Y Brython*, see O. Gaianydd Williams, '*Brython* Tremadog', *JWBS*, III, no. 4 (1927), 172–80; Thomas Parry, 'Daniel Silvan Evans, 1818–1903', *THSC* (1981), 112–13.

[11] *Y Gwladgarwr*, I (1833), iii.

mewn gair, yr wyf yn credu, Syr, fod y Cymdeithasau Cymreig yn *bechadurus*, ac o ganlyniad yn debyg o fod yn fwy o ddinystr i'n iaith, na'i chadwraeth . . .[12]

(In your praiseworthy Publication, as well as in various other places, I see and hear a very great deal about Societies and Eisteddfodau, for the preservation and defence of the Welsh language; these take up more space than meetings for the defence of godliness. I believe that I am as desirous and zealous in favour of the old Welsh language as any who are members of the said Societies: even so, I consider that to combat *sin and defend godliness* is more important than maintaining the purity of the language; and in short, I believe, Sir, that the Welsh Societies are *sinful*, and as a consequence are likely to do more for the destruction of our language than its conservation . . .)

These denominations were chiefly preoccupied with eternal life. For instance, Brutus outlined the policy of *Yr Efangylydd*, one of the Congregationalists' monthlies, of which he became editor in 1835:

Barnodd yr Ymddiriedolwyr nad ydoedd unrhyw ysgrifau i gael ymddangos yn yr *Efangylydd*, oni fyddent grefyddol a moesol, ac yn tueddu at ehangu gwybodaeth y darllenyddion mewn pethau a berthynant i iechydwriaeth dyn . . . Ystyriwyd mai teithwyr buain tua byd arall ydyw y rhai y mae a wnelom ni â hwynt, ac mai ein dyledswydd ydoedd gadael y pethau a berthynant i blantos heibio, ac mai yr ymgais oreu fyddai i adeiladu ein darllenyddion ar eu sancteiddiaf ffydd, fel y cynnyddont mewn gras a gwybodaeth, ar ddelw Duw eu Hachubwr.[13]

(The trustees took the view that no essays should appear in the *Efangylydd* which were not religious and moral, but which tended to promote readers' knowledge in matters pertaining to man's salvation . . . It was thought that those with whom we were concerned were speedy travellers on their way to another world, and that it was our duty to put aside childish things, and that the best endeavour would be to encourage our readers in their highest faith, so that they might grow in grace and knowledge, in the image of God their Saviour.)

By July 1835 Brutus, who had been a Baptist minister before joining the Congregationalists, had left 'the sectarians', as he liked to call them, and joined the established Church after his appointment as editor of *Yr Haul*, the Church monthly. Addressing his readers in its inaugural issue, he claimed that the aim of *Yr Haul* was 'to be the vehicle for rational religion'.[14] The editors and publishers of the other denominational periodicals shared this aim and followed a similar pattern as far as their content was concerned. Although mainly devoted to religious and theological subjects, they also carried home and foreign news,

---

[12] *Y Dysgedydd*, IV, no. 2 (1825), 53.
[13] *Yr Efangylydd*, I (1831), iii.
[14] *Yr Haul*, I (1836), 7.

synopses of parliamentary activities, riddles and puzzles, poetry columns, announcements of births, marriages and deaths, and, in the case of *Y Diwygiwr* under the editorship of David Rees, monthly articles on politics.

Since Welsh was the language, often the only language, of the majority of the readers of these periodicals, the material necessarily was in Welsh. It was widely believed that Welsh was the original language. 'It is the sweet language of old paradise', wrote Joseph Harris in the inaugural issue of *Seren Gomer*, 'in which Adam and Eve conversed about the ineffable wisdom of their blessed Creator' ('Iaith felusber yr hen Baradwys yw, yn yr hon yr ymddiddanai Adda ac Efa am anrhaethol rym ac anfeidrol ddoethder eu Creawdwr bendigedig').[15] Small wonder, then, that Wales was regarded as a nation elect of God and religious by nature. 'We almost tend to think', wrote Noah Stephens in *Y Diwygiwr* in 1849, 'that there is something in the turn of the Welsh mind which points it towards theology' ('Braidd na thueddir ni i dybied . . . fod rhywbeth yn nhröad y meddwl Cymreig yn ei bwyntio at dduwinyddiaeth').[16] As a result, it is not surprising that so many contemporary editors and men of letters were of the opinion that Welsh was a particularly suitable language in which to hold religious debates and discuss philosophical questions.[17] Proof positive of this was the nature of that produced by the Welsh press itself. 'Welsh literature is remarkable for its religious character and high moral tone', wrote the historian Thomas Rees of Swansea.[18]

Some of the periodical editors of the day believed that it was impossible to discuss anything but religious and theological matters in Welsh and that the language was wholly unsuited to discussion of science and the arts. David Rees of Llanelli deplored an article on a scientific subject which had been published in *Y Beirniad* in 1862: 'We do not much care for writing in Welsh on secular subjects because all who read it are likely to understand it better in English. Scientific, philosophical and artistic terms have not been used in Welsh' ('Nid ydym yn fawr dros ysgrifenu yn Gymraeg ar bynciau ofyddol oblegyd y mae'r neb a'u darlleno yn Gymraeg yn debyg o allu eu deall yn well yn Seisneg. Nid yw y termau gwyddorol, athronyddol, a chelfyddydol, wedi cael eu defnyddio yn y Gymraeg').[19] Even so, several of these periodicals, including the denominational periodicals, carried articles on scientific topics, and the discussion of science in Welsh was much more common than has hitherto been thought, as R. Elwyn Hughes has shown.[20] Some periodicals were wholly devoted to scientific subjects;

---

[15] *Seren Gomer*, I (1818), 1.
[16] Noah Stephens, 'Llenyddiaeth Bresenol Cymru', *Y Diwygiwr*, XIV, no. 167 (1849), 166.
[17] The nature and quality of this material is discussed by Meredydd Evans, 'Athronyddu yn Gymraeg: Braenaru'r Tir', *EA*, LVIII (1995), 68–89.
[18] Thomas Rees, 'Welsh Literature' in idem, *Miscellaneous Papers on Subjects Relating to Wales* (London, 1867*)*, p. 4.
[19] [David Rees], 'Adolygiad: *Y Beirniad*', *Y Diwygiwr*, XXVII, no. 325 (1862), 352.
[20] R. Elwyn Hughes, *Nid am un Harddwch Iaith: Rhyddiaith Gwyddoniaeth y Bedwaredd Ganrif ar Bymtheg* (Caerdydd, 1990).

among them were *Meddyg Teuluaidd* and *Y Cynghorydd Meddygol Dwyieithawg*, two medical journals published in the 1820s. Another notable example was *Y Brud a Sylwydd: The Chronicle and Observer*, the bilingual and short-lived periodical of Joseph Davies of Liverpool, of which eight issues appeared in 1828. The editor was greatly interested in science and in diffusing scientific knowledge among his compatriots, but he couched his material in unusually awkward language. He sought to coin new Welsh words for contemporary needs, and although the large majority of his neologisms have now fallen into desuetude he added to the vocabulary of the language by inventing words to meet all the requirements of philosophy, science and economics.[21] Other periodicals which carried a good deal of scientific information were *Y Cymmro, neu Drysorfa Celfyddyd a Gwybodaeth*, which managed to survive for two years (1830–2) even though it was published in London; *Yr Amaethydd* (1845–6); and *Y Wawr: Sef Cylchgrawn Llenyddol a Chelfyddydol*, the monthly edited by Robert Parry (Robyn Ddu Eryri) and published in Cardiff in 1850–1.

This period also saw the establishment of branches of philanthropic societies throughout Wales. Although most of these clubs, such as the Oddfellows, the Foresters and the Shepherds, were sections of English societies, some, particularly the Oddfellows, developed a specifically Welsh complexion. Like all other movements, these Friendly Societies published their own literature and periodicals. Four numbers of *Y Gwron Odyddol* were issued from Josiah Thomas Jones's press in Cowbridge between January and April 1840, and four issues of *Yr Odydd Cymreig* from the press of Llewelyn Jenkins in Cardiff between January and December 1842. But there was one truly Welsh philanthropic society which developed independently of those founded in England during the same period, and one of its chief aims was to support the Welsh language and its culture. It was named after Ifor ap Llywelyn or Ifor Hael of Basaleg in Monmouthshire, the patron of Dafydd ap Gwilym, and known in Welsh as Cymdeithas Ddyngarol y Gwir Iforiaid and in English as the Philanthropic Order of True Ivorites.

The principal characteristic of the Ivorites was their attachment to the Welsh language. From the outset Welsh was the official language of the society; all its officers were Welsh speakers and all business was carried out in Welsh. As part of their scheme to promote the language Ivorite literature was published in Welsh, and several periodicals were launched during the 1840s, among them *Yr Iforydd* (1841–2), *Y Gwir Iforydd* (1841–2), *Ifor Hael* (1850–1), and *Y Gwladgarwr* (1851). Although these periodicals were intended to serve the society by publishing news about its activities and informing the lodges of its resolutions from time to time, they also included a variety of material of a more general nature. Most carried

---

[21] For the history of the periodical, see O. E. Roberts, 'Y Brud a Sylwydd', *Y Faner*, 22 September 1978, 12–13.

home and foreign news, essays on various subjects such as science, botany, philosophy, history, geography, book reviews, poetry and puzzles.[22]

A new chapter in the history of the periodical press was opened with the founding of *Y Traethodydd* by Thomas Gee in 1845, with Lewis Edwards as its chief editor. The new periodical was modelled on English quarterlies such as *Blackwood's Magazine* and *The Edinburgh Review*, and its content reflected the editor's interest in theology, philosophy and education.[23] In the view of the editors, Welsh was the language of religion and morality. Indeed, it was often considered to be a weapon for the defence of the Welsh people against the sins of the age. While on a preaching tour in the valleys of Glamorgan and Monmouthshire during the summer of 1870 John Roberts of Conwy, editor of *Cronicl y Cymdeithasau Crefyddol*, observed that the Welsh language was in decline in these areas. He also deplored the low morals of some of the inhabitants:

> Ond pa beth bynag a ddywedir, myned i lawr y mae hi [y Gymraeg] yn Nghymru, yn enwedig yn y De, ac yn fwy neillduol yn Mynwy. Mae ei haul wedi cyrhaedd ei gaerau, a hanner fyned o'r golwg. Ni bydd yn yr oes nesaf nemawr i son am dani, nac i alaru ar ei hol; a drwg genym weled arwyddion mewn ambell fan y collir gyda hi hen arferiadau crefyddol y Cymry. Y mae gwehilion Saeson Iwerddon, Scotland, a Lloegr, yn dyfod i weithfaoedd y De, ac y mae plant y Cymry yn dysgu eu hiaith a'u harferiadau ffieiddiaf. Gwelsom olygfeydd gwir ofnadwy mewn ambell fan *nos Sadwrn y talu*, – yr holl feibion a'r merched yn feddwon, a'r plant yn ysmocio; ond nid yn Gymraeg, a buasai yn ddrwg genym glywed yr hen iaith yn dyfod allan o'r fath eneuau, ac yn arfer y fath eiriau . . . Yr oedd yn dda genym mai math o Saesonaeg oeddynt yn siarad. Gwell genym i'r hen Gymraeg fod yn y bedd nag yn y fath fudreddi.[24]

(But whatever may be said, it [the Welsh language] is in decline in Wales, especially in the South, and more particularly in Monmouthshire. Its sun is setting and has half-disappeared from view. In times to come there will be hardly any mention of it, nor any mourning for it; and we are sorry to see signs in some places that with it have been lost the old religious customs of the Welsh people. The dregs of Ireland, Scotland and England have come to the work-places of the South, and Welsh children are learning their language and their most loathsome ways. We saw truly horrible scenes in some places *on Saturday pay-night*, – all the men and women drunk, and the children smoking; but not in Welsh, and we should be sorry to hear the old language coming from such lips, and using such words . . . We were glad that they were speaking some kind of English. We should prefer the old Welsh language to be in its grave than amid such squalor.)

---

[22] On these titles, see Morgan Bassett, 'Iforiaeth', *Seren Gomer*, XXXII, no. 4 (1940), 121–8, and ibid., no. 6, 192–5.

[23] For the history of *Y Traethodydd*, see J. E. Caerwyn Williams, 'Hanes *Y Traethodydd*', *Y Traethodydd*, CXXXVI (1981), 34–49; idem, 'Hanes Cychwyn *Y Traethodydd*', *LlC*, XIV, no. 1 and 2 (1981–2), 111–42; idem, '*Y Traethodydd*, 1845–1995', *Y Traethodydd*, CL (1995), 5–45. For its attitude towards the native language during the last century, see Harri Williams, '*Y Traethodydd* a'r Gymraeg', *Taliesin*, 42 (1981), 54–62.

[24] [John Roberts], 'Gorlifiad y Saesonaeg', *Cronicl y Cymdeithasau Crefyddol*, XXVIII (1870), 220.

At this time new railways were being opened in Wales, and editors of Welsh periodicals dreaded the alien influences which they ushered in. The cartoon published in *Y Punch Cymraeg* in the 1860s is familiar enough. It depicts a woman in Welsh costume standing in the middle of a railway track in a bid to stop a train. The train, driven by Dic Siôn Dafydd, is representative of Mammon. David Rees, too, foresaw the railways spreading across Wales, 'conveniently transporting atheistic English people and foul books of all kinds to every corner of the land' ('yn gyfleus i drosglwyddo Seison anffyddol a llyfrau bryntion o bob math i bob cwr o'r wlad'). He went on: 'The youth of Wales were never in such danger as they are in now. We cannot be too diligent in spreading suitable literature' ('Ni bu ieuenctyd Cymru erioed mewn cymaint perygl ag ydynt ynddo yn awr. Nis gellir bod yn rhy lafurus i daenu llenyddiaeth briodol').[25] By this, of course, he meant religious literature. In his condemnation of the works of Emerson, Thackeray, Carlyle and Dickens in *Y Diwygiwr*, David Rees wrote: 'Until now Wales has been protected against such a terrible curse because the press has been bound to the pulpit, and one supports the other' ('Y mae Cymru hyd yma wedi ei dyogelu rhag y fath felldith ofnadwy, o herwydd fod y wasg wedi ei chydio a'r pwlpud, a bod y naill yn ategu y llall').[26]

Not every editor agreed with David Rees, however, because fiction had already become popular in Welsh by the middle of the nineteenth century. Most of the journals of the day, including the denominational periodicals, contained different kinds of 'fiction' and 'historical fiction' (although there was none in *Y Diwygiwr* during the editorship of David Rees). Several editors had realized that such literature could have a beneficial as well as a deleterious effect, as Roger Edwards of Mold, editor of the Methodist periodical *Y Drysorfa*, explained in his postscript to his serialized novel 'Y Tri Brawd a'u Teuluoedd' (The Three Brothers and their Families), which was published between February 1866 and April 1867:

> Gweled yr oeddem fod ein pobl ieuainc yn arbenig yn chwannog i ddarllen cyfansoddiadau o natur chwedl-adroddiadol, a bod llawer o bethau gwag ac ofer o'r natur hwn, a rhai o honynt o duedd llygredig a niweidiol, yn cael eu cynnyg iddynt, hyd yn nôd yn yr iaith Gymraeg; a chofiasom am Whitfield yn cymeryd rhai o'r tônau mwyaf poblogaidd a genid yn y chwareudai i'w defnyddio yn addoldai y Tabernacl a'r Tottenham Court Road; a phan aeth rhywun i ymliw âg ef o'r herwydd, efe a atebodd, 'Beth! a ydych yn meddwl y gadawaf i satan gael y tônau goreu iddo ei hun?' Nid oeddem ninnau yn foddlawn i satan gael iddo ei hun y dull hwn o ysgrifenu sydd mor ddeniadol i'r lliaws yn gyffredinol.[27]

---

[25] *Y Diwygiwr*, XXVI, no. 315 (1861), 361.
[26] Ibid., 360.
[27] [Roger Edwards], 'Y Tri Brawd a'u Teuluoedd', *Y Drysorfa*, XXI (1867), 140.

(We observed that our young people in particular were eager to read compositions of a fictional nature, and that many vacuous and frivolous things of this kind, and some of a corrupting and harmful tendency, were being offered to them, even in the Welsh language; and we recalled Whitfield taking some of the most popular tunes sung in the music halls for use in Tabernacl and the Tottenham Court Road; and when someone rebuked him for this, he replied, 'What! do you think I will let Satan have the best tunes for himself?' Nor were we willing for Satan to have this kind of writing, which is so enticing for the generality, to himself.)

By adopting the novel as a literary genre, the periodical press would be able to influence the morals of the Welsh people, and a host of serialized novels were published in Welsh periodicals up to the beginning of the twentieth century.[28] It is true that several of them were translations, such as 'Deng Noswaith yn y Black Lion', an early adaptation by Daniel Owen of *Ten Nights in a Bar Room*, a temperance novel by the American writer Timothy Shay Arthur, which appeared in the periodical *Charles o'r Bala*, probably the most unimaginative title for a periodical ever published in Welsh.[29] It is not surprising that several of these early novelists were ministers and preachers, among them Roger Edwards himself, Edward Matthews of Ewenny, and William Rees (Gwilym Hiraethog), and that the chapel and its society provided the main material for their novels. The same was true of the literary output of Daniel Owen, the greatest of these novelists, whose earliest writings were published in *Y Drysorfa*.[30] The growth and popularity of the novel in Welsh is also clearly attested by the fact that in 1861 William Aubrey of Llannerch-y-medd was able to launch a penny monthly entitled *Y Nofelydd, a Chydymaith y Teulu*, of which twelve issues appeared before it was wound up in December 1861. It might have met with greater success had it been sponsored by an enterprising and progressive publisher such as Thomas Gee.

Reference has already been made to *Cylchgrawn y Gymdeithas er Taenu Gwybodaeth Fuddiol*, which was edited by Alun. This publication was modelled on *The Penny Magazine*, one of the most popular periodicals in England, and it was Alun's declared policy to carry articles on general topics rather than religious articles. It is highly ironic, however, that a shortage of articles on religious subjects eventually led to the demise of the *Cylchgrawn* after eighteen numbers. Its first twelve issues were published by William Rees in Llandovery before it was moved to the office of John Evans in Carmarthen in January 1835, where it expired in June of the same year. William Rees sketched the reasons for its failure in the evidence he submitted to the commissioners appointed to examine the state of education in Wales in 1846:

[28] For a list of these serialized novels, see E. G. Millward, 'Ffugchwedlau'r Bedwaredd Ganrif ar Bymtheg', *LlC*, XII, no. 3 and 4 (1973), 244–64.
[29] Bedwyr Lewis Jones, 'Deng Noswaith yn y Black Lion', *LlC*, VIII, no. 1 and 2 (1964), 51–62.
[30] The serialized novels of these four authors are discussed in Ioan Williams, *Capel a Chomin: Astudiaeth o Ffugchwedlau Pedwar Llenor Fictoraidd* (Caerdydd, 1989).

In 1834 I started a Welsh monthly periodical called the *Cylchgrawn* (in connexion with the Society for the Diffusion of Useful Knowledge), on the same plan as *The Penny Magazine*, but published monthly at 6d. I continued it for twelve months, at a loss of £200. When I gave it up, it was continued by Mr Evans of Carmarthen for another six months; who also lost by it, and then it was abandoned. It wanted religious information, and consequently excited but little interest. The people have not been accustomed to think much upon any but religious topics. The great want is good secular education.[31]

Some years later Thomas Stephens, the literary-minded chemist and scholar from Merthyr Tydfil, referred to the over-dependence of the Welsh press on the religious denominations. 'It is not to the credit of the nation that it is unable or unwilling to maintain one publication without it being connected with religious denominations, but that is how it is' ('Nid yw yn glod mawr i'r genedl, ei bod yn analluog, neu yn anewyllysgar, i gynnal un cyhoeddiad heb ei fod mewn cyssylltiad ag enwadau crefyddol', meddai, 'ond felly y mae').[32] Inordinate dependence on institutional religion was one of the main characteristics of the Welsh periodical press during the nineteenth century, and the comments of Thomas Stephens echo those of the education commissioners about the quality of contemporary literature in the Welsh language: 'Their schools, literature and religious pursuits may have cultivated talents for preaching and poetry, but for every other calling they are incapacitated. For secular subjects they have neither literature or language.'[33]

Although it was as a consequence of 'The Treachery of the Blue Books' that the Welsh began to nurture a complex about their image in the eyes of the world, the alleged deficiencies of their language had troubled many Welsh people long before this. Indeed, twenty-three years before the publication of the education commissioners' report, a series of articles about the Welsh language had been published in *Seren Gomer* and these were hotly debated for many months thereafter. These articles, written by David Owen, editor of *Lleuad yr Oes*, *Yr Efangylydd* and later *Yr Haul*, and published under the pseudonym Brutus, brought the author to public attention for the first time, and thereafter he was known to all and sundry by the name of Brutus. His aim was to attack the parochiality of the monoglot Welshman and prompt him to widen his horizons by learning English:

Yn awr y mae yr Omeraeg yn rhwystr i ni gynnyddu mewn gwybodaeth, ac i ymgeisio at wybodaeth, am hyny ein dyledswydd ydyw gwneuthur aberth o honi a'i dilëu, fel trwy hyny y rhoddem le i iaith, trwy gyfrwng yr hon y gwnawn gynnyddu mewn pethau, ac y mae rhwystrau anorfod o'n blaen, cyhyd ag y coleddom yr iaith Gymraeg

---

[31] *Reports of the Commissioners of Inquiry into the State of Education in Wales . . . in three parts. Part I. Carmarthen, Glamorgan, and Pembroke* (London, 1847) (PP 1847 (870) XXVII), pp. 234–5.
[32] Thomas Stephens, 'Agwedd Bresennol Llëenyddiaeth yn Nghymru', *Y Wawr*, 2 (1851), 35.
[33] *Reports of the Commissioners into the State of Education in Wales, Part I*, p. 235.

... Yn awr yr wyf yn gofyn i bob meddwl diduedd ... pa un gwell ganddynt fod yn Saeson enwog, neu yn Gymry anenwog?[34]

(Now Welsh prevents us from increasing our knowledge, and from striving to attain knowledge, and for that reason our duty is to sacrifice it and exterminate it, that by doing so we can make room for a language through which we might make progress, and there are inevitable obstacles before us for as long as we cherish the Welsh language ... I now ask every impartial mind ... whether they prefer to be famous English people, or obscure Welsh?)

These sentiments were echoed by J. R. Kilsby Jones in *Y Traethodydd* twenty-five years later and, as we shall see presently, in *Y Geninen* shortly before his death in the 1880s.[35]

The Blue Books were a turning point in the history of education and literature in Wales, and the development of the periodical press must be considered in the light of the accusations made by the commissioners. There occurred a remarkable increase in the kind of literature considered useful and purposeful, and it became accepted that only by means of education and general knowledge could the ordinary Welshman climb the social ladder. Editors of periodicals believed in education as medicine for the ills of society, and the notion that ignorance was at the root of contemporary evils was common during this period. Henceforth the philosophy of Samuel Smiles would carry the day – education would be a means by which the humblest Welshman could rise in the world and improve his lot. These attitudes are reflected in the material produced by the periodical press during the second half of the century, and in the 1850s several titles which aimed at educating the Welsh were published. Reference has already been made to *Y Wawr*, the monthly edited by Robyn Ddu Eryri, which contained a great deal of scientific material.[36] Another example was *Y Gwerinwr*, edited by John Thomas of Liverpool in the 1850s. The long-winded subtitle of *Y Gwerinwr* was an accurate description of its content and aim: *Athraw Misol, er Dyrchafiad Cymdeithasol, Meddyliol a Moesol y Dosbarth Gweithiol* (The Monthly Teacher, for the Social, Intellectual and Moral Advancement of the Working Class).

During the same period *Yr Adolygydd* and *Y Beirniad* were founded by several Congregational ministers following the pattern set by *Y Traethodydd*, the better-known periodical associated with Lewis Edwards, which carried long articles on subjects such as geology, agriculture and mining.[37] Although his name does not

---

[34] *Seren Gomer*, VII, no. 102 (1824), 83–4.
[35] [J. R. Kilsby Jones], 'Yr Angenrheidrwydd o Ddysgu Seisoneg i'r Cymry', *Y Traethodydd*, V (1849), 118–26. On Kilsby Jones, see E. G. Millward, 'Pob Gwybodaeth Fuddiol' in Prys Morgan (ed.), *Brad y Llyfrau Gleision: Ysgrifau ar Hanes Cymru* (Llandysul, 1991), pp. 146–65.
[36] The main characteristics of *Y Wawr* are discussed in Huw Walters, 'Gwawr Robyn Ddu Eryri', *Y Casglwr*, 11 (August 1980), 3.
[37] These two forgotten but important titles are discussed in Huw Walters, '*Yr Adolygydd*' a'r '*Beirniad*': *Eu Cynnwys a'u Cyfranwyr* (Aberystwyth, 1996).

appear on *Yr Adolygydd*, it is known that its first editor was Evan Jones (Ieuan Gwynedd), and it was he, more than anyone else, who emerged as the principal champion of Welsh Nonconformity against the insinuations of the Blue Books, as well as the chief spokesman on behalf of voluntary education. Ieuan Gwynedd was also the founder and editor of *Y Gymraes*, the first periodical for the women of Wales, in which he seized the opportunity of defending the nation's womenfolk against the accusations of the education commissioners. Although Ieuan Gwynedd's loyalty to the Welsh language cannot be impugned, his religious and Nonconformist beliefs were much more important to him. 'Charming though the sound of our venerable language is to me,' he wrote, 'I should be much more content for it to perish than to lose the religious privileges of my country' ('Er mor swynol ydyw acenion ein hen iaith hybarch i mi, llawer boddlonach fyddwn iddi hi drengu na breintiau crefyddol fy ngwlad').[38] In *Y Diwygiwr* David Rees claimed that no one could prevent the demise of Welsh, for everything was in the hands of Providence,[39] a view shared by John Roberts in *Y Cronicl*. In the inaugural issue of *Y Geninen* in 1883, Kilsby Jones observed 'that the survival of a language is subject to the laws of Providence, and therefore nothing else can kill or preserve it' ('fod parhad iaith yn ddarostyngedig i ddeddfau Rhagluniaeth, ac felly ni fedr dim arall ei ladd neu ei chadw yn fyw').[40] This is why so many set about founding English causes within their denominations with such enthusiasm; they included David Rees, Lewis Edwards, Thomas Rees of Swansea, and John Davies of Cardiff, one of the editors of *Y Beirniad*, the Congregational quarterly.[41] John Roberts of Conwy also stressed the need for students in the denominational colleges to master English and for their teachers to ensure a worthy place for the language in the curriculum. He wrote in July 1866:

> *Saesoneg* yw iaith Prydain, iaith ein llysoedd, iaith ein masnach, iaith y genedl sydd yn codi yn ein hysgolion Cenedlaethol a Brutanaidd; ie, yr iaith sydd yn llifo dros ddyffrynoedd Cymru, a bron cyrhaedd penau ei mynyddau; ac os na wahoddir hi gan athrawon ein hathrofaau i bulpudau Ymneillduaeth, bydd crefydd ein hynafiaid wedi colli tir yn yr ugain mlynedd nesaf.[42]

> (*English* is the language of Britain, the language of our courts, the language of our commerce, the language of the nation which is growing up in our National and British

---

[38] Quoted in Geraint H. Jenkins, 'Ieuan Gwynedd: Eilun y Genedl' in Morgan (ed.), *Brad y Llyfrau Gleision*, p. 122.

[39] *Y Diwygiwr*, XVII, no. 207 (1852), 319.

[40] J. R. Kilsby Jones, 'Pa un mantais neu anfantais i Gymru fyddai tranc yr iaith Gymraeg?', *Y Geninen*, I, no. 1 (1883), 18.

[41] See Frank Price Jones, 'Yr Achosion Saesneg', *CCHMC*, LVII, no. 3 (1972), 66–80; ibid., LVIII, no. 1 (1973), 2–11; A. H. Williams, 'Thomas Rees a'r Achosion Saesneg', *Y Cofiadur*, 40 (1975), 3–34; R. Tudur Jones, 'Yr Eglwysi a'r Iaith yn Oes Victoria', *LlC*, 19 (1996), 146–67.

[42] *Cronicl y Cymdeithasau Crefyddol*, XXIV (1866), p. 176. For John Roberts's attitude towards the Welsh language, see R. Tudur Jones, 'J. R., Conwy', *TCHS*, 21 (1960), 168–70.

Schools; yea, the language which is flowing through the valleys of Wales, and almost reaching to the tops of our mountains; and if it is not invited by the teachers at our colleges into the pulpits of Nonconformity, the religion of our forefathers will have lost ground in the next twenty years.)

Even so, a much more positive attitude in favour of Welsh was also to be found in the periodical press. By the last quarter of the century the old radicalism represented by the generation of David Rees, Lewis Edwards and the brothers Samuel and John Roberts, with their consistent emphasis on the virtues of the free market and utilitarianism, was in decline. The likes of R. J. Derfel, Michael D. Jones and Robert Ambrose Jones (Emrys ap Iwan) regularly emphasized the fact that the Welsh language, more than anything else, was the cornerstone of their nationality. 'Our language, in the present circumstances, is the only bond which can maintain our nationhood' ('Mae ein hiaith, yn ol amgylchiadau presenol pethau, yr unig rwymyn a ddichon gynnal i fyny ein cenedloldeb'), wrote R. J. Derfel as early as 1853. 'When our language dies, our nation will die . . . Supposing, to be logical, our nation gains something by becoming absorbed among the English, I do not think it will gain enough to make up for our nationhood' ('Pan dderfydd am ein hiaith, fe dderfydd am ein cenedl . . . A chaniatâu, er mwyn ymresymu, yr ennillai ein cenedl rywbeth drwy ymgolli yn y Saeson, nid wyf yn meddwl yr ennillent ddigon i dalu am eu cenedloldeb').[43] It is relevant to note that Derfel was in favour of founding a daily Welsh newspaper as early as 1864.[44] He was also aware that many Welsh people cared little for their language. 'Nothing in the world can kill a language nor a nation except the nation itself', he wrote in 1893. 'If ever we were to die as a nation, it would be by suicide' ('Nis gall yn y byd a ddichon ladd iaith na chenedl ond y genedl ei hun. Os byth y byddwn ninau farw fel cenedl, byddwn farw fel hunan-leiddiaid').[45] In the same article he emphasized the need to foster a generation of new scholars who would set about editing and publishing texts of poetry and prose of the Middle period, and he called for the establishment of a National Library which would safeguard the literary treasures of the nation.

Michael D. Jones, too, took advantage of the opportunity to express his opinions frankly about Welsh politics and the status of the Welsh language in his monthly contributions to *Y Ddraig Goch*, a periodical serving the inhabitants of the Welsh Colony in Patagonia, of which twenty-four numbers were published in Bala between 1876 and 1877 under the editorship of Richard Mawddwy Jones.

[43] R. J. Derfel, 'Parhad yr Iaith Gymraeg: Papyr a Fwriadwyd i'w Ddarllen yn un o Gyfarfodydd y Cymreigyddion ym Manceinion', *Y Greal*, II (1853), 222. For his life and works see the two volumes edited by D. Gwenallt Jones, *Detholiad o Ryddiaith Gymraeg R. J. Derfel* (Llundain, 1945).

[44] R. J. Derfel, 'Papur newydd dyddiol Cymreig' in idem, *Traethodau ac Areithiau* (Bangor, 1864), pp. 189–92.

[45] Idem, 'Dyletswydd Cymru Sydd tuag at ddyrchafu Cymru Fydd', *Y Geninen*, XI, no. 2 (1893), 158.

He constantly attacked the imperialism of England and stressed time and again that the servility of the Welsh was one of the consequences of the English conquest. 'Conquest has made the Welsh terribly servile, to such an extent that in many parts of Wales they are calling for the demise of the Welsh language, and all Welsh customs, and are ready to bow down completely to the English' ('Mae goresgyniad wedi gwaseiddio'r Cymry yn ddirfawr, nes y maent mewn llawer o fanau yng Nghymru yn gwaeddi am ddifodi'r iaith Gymraeg, a phob arferion Cymreig, ac y maent am lwyr blygu i oresgyniad y Saeson'), he wrote in June 1877.[46] He was also incensed by the growing tendency among Nonconformist denominations to establish English causes in Welsh-speaking towns:

> Mae y duwinyddion sydd yn ein mysg yn apostolion capeli Seisnig yn mynych son am anuwioldeb beirdd a Chymreigyddion, a'u hergyd bob amser ar goryn Cymreigiaeth. Ni soniant am anuwioldeb y plant beilchion a godant, y merched pluog a diwaith a fagant, ond molant rhyw ddoctoryn bychan o Sais y dygwydd iddynt fod mewn ffafr gydag ef, a Saeson, Saeson, Saeson sydd yn eu geneuau o hyd. Plygu yw hyn oll i fod yn wasaidd ddarostyngedig i oresgyniad Seisnig, a gwneud yn orphenol, yn enw crefydd, yr hyn y mae'r cledd heb ei berffeithio eto. Yr oedd caethfeistri yr Unol Daleithiau yn galw am gymhorth crefydd i gadw caethion. Mae Dic Shon Dafyddiaid Cymru yr un fath yn galw am gymhorth crefydd Crist i orphen goresgyniad ein gwlad.[47]

> (The theologians among us who are the apostles of English chapels often speak of the ungodliness of poets and those who cherish things Welsh, and chastise them on account of their Welsh sympathies. They do not speak of the ungodliness of the vain children they raise, the feathered and idle women whom they bring up, but they praise some little English doctor with whom they happen to be in favour, and all they talk about are the English, the English, the English. All this bowing and scraping is being servile and subject to the English conquest, and completing, in the name of religion, what the sword has not yet accomplished. The slave-owners of the United States called for religious assistance in keeping slaves. The Dic Siôn Dafydds of Wales in the same way are calling for assistance from the Christian religion to complete the conquest of our country.)

He also condemned railway companies for employing monoglot Englishmen in Welsh-speaking areas: 'No one should have a job on the railways of Wales unless he learns the language of the inhabitants. A monoglot Englishman is of no use to commerce in Wales, any more than a monoglot Welshman in England' ('Ni ddylai un gael swydd ar gledrffordd yn Nghymru os na ddysg iaith y trigolion. Nid yw Sais uniaith o ddim gwerth i fasnachu yn Nghymru, mwy na Chymro uniaith yn Lloegr').[48]

---

[46] *Y Ddraig Goch*, II, no. 18 (1877), 67–8.
[47] Ibid., I, no. 10 (1876), 112–13.
[48] Ibid., 114.

The articles by Michael D. Jones in *Y Celt*, a Congregational weekly, and in *Y Geninen* in the 1890s attracted most attention and had the widest circulation. Once again his message was the same. The servility of the Welsh themselves was mainly responsible for the helplessness and debility of the Welsh language in the face of the English tide, and that servility was directly attributable to the conquest of the nation:

> Wedi goresgyn unrhyw genedl, dull y Seison yw gosod pobl oresgynedig o dan anfanteision, ond drwy ymdoddi i'r genelaeth fawr Seisnig; ac ni cheir dyrchafiad yn un ffordd arall. Ni cheir gweinyddu cyfraith ond yn Seisonaeg, a dyma'r unig gyfrwng y ceir addysg drwyddo, ond rhyw ganiatad bychan diweddar, megys arfer y Gymraeg i ddeall Seisonaeg . . . Mae yr yspryd yma wedi gwaseiddio ein cenedl fel na chariant fasnach ymlaen ond yn iaith y goresgynwr, a llwfrdra anesgusodol sydd yn peri i'r Cymry barhau hyny. Mae hyn yn ei gwneud yn analluadwy i Gymro lwyddo'n gymdeithasol fel bancwr neu fasnachwr heb ymollwng i fod yn Sais, am y rheswm na fyn y Cymry fasnachu ond yn iaith y gorthrymwr, a'r Cymry hyn a godir ganddynt yw'r rhai parotaf o bawb i boeri am ben ein cenedl ar ol eu dyrchafiad.[49]

(After the English conquer any nation, their policy is to place conquered people under disadvantages until they are absorbed into the powerful English nation; and they cannot be elevated in any other way. The law cannot be administered except in English, and that is the only medium for the acquisition of education, apart from some recent small concession such as the use of Welsh to explain the English . . . This spirit has made our nation servile so that commerce is only in the language of the conqueror, and it is inexcusable cowardice which makes the Welsh tolerate it. A Welshman cannot succeed socially as a banker or a tradesman without pretending to be an Englishman, because the Welsh trade only in the language of the conqueror, and these, having raised themselves up, are the most ready to spit on our nation.)

He maintained that the Welsh themselves were to blame for the deterioration of their language:

> Mawr yw sŵn y bobl yma yn aml am y gorlifiad Seisnig sydd yn dyfod ar draws ein gwlad, fel pe byddai gan Seison rhyw fôr anferth o Seisonaeg i'w ollwng ar ein traws, nad allem er pob ymdrech ei wrthwynebu. Y Cymry eu hunain sydd o'u gwirfodd yn gollwng y Seisonaeg i fewn, ac yn gwneud egni i droi y Gymraeg allan o'u teuluoedd, o'u capeli, o'u masnach, ac yn llwfr oddef i Seison i'w throi o'u llysoedd cyfreithiol.

---

[49] Michael D. Jones, 'Difodi y Gymraeg yn Barhad o Oresgyniad Cymru', *Y Geninen*, IX, no. 4 (1891), 244.

Mae at ewyllys y Cymry eu hunain i'r Gymraeg farw neu fyw; ac os lleddir hi, arnynt hwy eu hunain y bydd y bai.[50]

(There is often much talk about the English flood which is sweeping our country, as if the English had a vast sea of English to pour over us, which no effort on our part can withstand. It is the Welsh themselves, of their own volition, who let English in, and make efforts to turn Welsh out of their homes, their chapels, their commerce, and cravenly allow the English to exclude it from their courts of law. It is up to the Welsh themselves whether the language will live or die; and if it is killed, they themselves will be to blame.)

He also deplored the custom of turning original Welsh place names into English, and the growing tendency among Welsh people to give their homes English names. 'Having learnt a little English,' he wrote, 'many a coquette insists on not calling her house by its old name of Tygwyn, Tydu, or Tycoch, but translates it into Whitehouse, Blackhouse and Redhouse. Members of this empty-headed woman's family insisted on calling Penbontarogwy "Bridge End" and Melin Wen, near Carmarthen, "White Mill"' ('Ar ol dysgu tipyn o Seisonaeg, y mae aml i goegen gorniog na fyn alw ei chartref wrth ei hen enw Tygwyn, Tydu, neu Tycoch, wedi ei gyfieithu yn Whitehouse, Blackhouse, a Redhouse. Rhai o deulu yr hogen benwan yma a fynodd alw Penbontarogwy yn "Bridge End", a Melin Wen, ger Caerfyrddin, yn "White Mill" ').[51]

Michael D. Jones expected that the new Cymru Fydd movement would replace the Liberal Party in Wales and develop into an independent national party which would campaign for self-government. He believed that Welsh politicians were divided among opposition groups which ruled from London and, furthermore, that only self-government could ensure the well-being of the Welsh language. But he was disappointed by the decision of Cymru Fydd to campaign for disestablishment of the Church, education and the land question rather than for self-government. Like Michael D. Jones, Emrys ap Iwan also refused to accept that the Welsh language was destined to decline under the pressures of progress and commerce, or on account of some providential law, as David Rees, Lewis

---

[50] Ibid., 246. The only biography of Michael D. Jones is by E. Pan Jones, *Oes a Gwaith y Prif Athraw y Parch. Michael Daniel Jones, Bala* (Y Bala, 1903). See also D. Gwenallt Jones, 'Hanes Mudiadau Cymraeg a Chenedlaethol y Bedwaredd Ganrif ar Bymtheg' in D. Myrddin Lloyd (ed.), *Seiliau Hanesyddol Cenedlaetholdeb Cymru* (Caerdydd, 1950), pp. 118–26; idem, 'Michael D. Jones (1822–1898)' in Gwynedd Pierce (ed.), *Triwyr Penllyn* (Caerdydd, 1957), pp. 1–27. For a detailed discussion on Michael D. Jones's contributions to the *Celt*, see R. Tudur Jones, 'Cwmni'r *Celt* a Dyfodol Cymru', *THSC* (1987), 113–51. See also idem, 'Michael D. Jones a Nimrodiaeth Lloegr', *Y Genhinen*, 24, nos. 3 and 4 (1974), 161–4; idem, 'Michael D. Jones a Thynged y Genedl' in Geraint H. Jenkins (ed.), *Cof Cenedl: Ysgrifau ar Hanes Cymru* (Llandysul, 1986), pp. 95–124.

[51] Jones, 'Difodi y Gymraeg', 246. Michael D. Jones was incensed by the affectation of these Welsh people, as he reveals in his scathing article, 'Mrs Davey, Sunny Cottage, near Carmarthen', *Y Geninen*, X, no. 1 (1892), 13–14.

Edwards and Kilsby Jones believed. Welsh, he wrote, was the chief mainstay of the Welshman's nationality:

> Lle bynnag y bo gwlad fach ynglŷn â gwlad fawr, ac yn enwedig lle y bo pobl y wlad fach yn ddarostyngedig i bobl y wlad fawr, y mae hanes yn dangos mai ei phriod iaith yw anadl einioes y wlad fach. Pan ymadawo hon a'i hiaith, y mae hi yn rhoddi i fyny ei hyspryd; ac ar ôl colli ei hyspryd, y mae ei chorff yn fuan yn newid ei liw, yn llygru, ac yn ymgolli yn y llwch . . . Y Gymraeg sy wedi'n cadw ni yn genedl hyd yn hyn; a'r Gymraeg yn unig a'n ceidw yn genedl rhag llaw.[52]

> (Wherever a small country has to do with a large country, and particularly where the people of a small country are subject to the people of a large country, history shows that its own language is the lifeblood of the small country. When it abandons its language, it gives up the ghost; and having lost its spirit, its body soon afterwards loses its colour, is corrupted and lost in the dust . . . It is the Welsh language which has kept us a nation thus far; and it is only Welsh which will keep us a nation hereafter.)

For Emrys ap Iwan, the fate of the language was a political matter and, as in the case of Michael D. Jones, his nationalism arose directly from his Christian convictions. 'I do not count fidelity or infidelity to a language as an arguable matter. I cannot recommend anything which includes a tendency to Anglicize the Welsh people without going against my political convictions' ('Nid wyf fi yn cyfrif ffyddlondeb neu anffyddlondeb i iaith yn bwnc dadleuadwy. Nid allwn i bleidio dim a thuedd ynddo i Seisnigo'r Cymry heb fyned yn erbyn fy argyhoeddiadau politicaidd') was his bold declaration to the Association which met at Llanidloes in 1881 when he was refused ordination because he had opposed the growing tendency among Calvinistic Methodists to establish English causes in Welsh-speaking areas.[53] The debate was conducted mainly in the columns of *Y Goleuad* and *Baner ac Amserau Cymru*, but Emrys ap Iwan delivered the same message in a host of other articles which appeared in *Y Geninen* between 1883 and his death in 1906.

Emrys ap Iwan deplored the use of English idioms as well as the clumsy style of writers of the day in his famous essay 'Plicio Gwallt yr Hanner Cymry' (Plucking the Hair of the Semi-Welsh), which was published in *Y Geninen* in 1889 and in which he listed dozens of examples of English idioms in Welsh dress. He also claimed that sectarianism, and the theological arguments to which it gave rise, had a baneful effect on the quality of contemporary Welsh.[54] He vented a similar

---

[52] Emrys ap Iwan, 'Dysgu Cymraeg yn yr Ysgolion Beunyddiol', *Y Geninen*, XXI, no. 4 (1903), 217.

[53] T. Gwynn Jones, *Emrys ap Iwan: Dysgawdr, Llenor, Cenedlgarwr* (Caernarfon, 1912), p. 114. See also Saunders Lewis, 'Emrys ap Iwan yn 1881' in R. Geraint Gruffydd (ed.), *Meistri'r Canrifoedd: Ysgrifau ar Hanes Llenyddiaeth Gymraeg* (Caerdydd, 1974), pp. 371–6.

[54] 'Nehemiah o Ddyffryn Clwyd', i.e. Emrys ap Iwan, 'Plicio Gwallt yr Hanner Cymry', *Y Geninen*, VII, no. 2 (1889), 116.

message in a series of articles published under the title 'Breuddwyd Pabydd wrth ei Ewyllys' (A Papist's Dream at his Will) in *Y Geninen* between 1890 and 1892. This is a satire on the sectarianism and servility of the Welsh. The narrator, Father Morgan, dreams about the state of Wales in the year 2012. He sees Protestantism in ruins, and the country, at last, thanks to the 'Catholic Union', liberated from the Anglicizing Nonconformist sects. He dreams that he is listening to a series of lectures on the history of Wales and of the Catholic Church, and by means of these lectures we are given a picture of what Wales might become, with regard to life and customs and language, if only it were faithful to itself rather than to the English.[55] Emrys ap Iwan also wished to restore literary standards and, as part of his mission, he set about encouraging his readers to familiarize themselves with the works of the Welsh prose-masters, writers such as Morgan Llwyd, Charles Edwards, Ellis Wynne and Theophilus Evans. 'He who emulates the best work of the best authors is something more than an imitator,' he wrote, 'he is an apprentice who is on the way to becoming a master' ('Y mae y neb a efelycho yr awduron gora yn eu petha gora yn rhywbeth amgen na dynwaredwr, disgibl yw hwnnw sydd ar y ffordd i fynd yn feistr').[56] That was also the burden of his message in 'Llenyddiaeth Grefyddol y Cymry Gynt' (The Religious Literature of Wales in the Past), an essay which was published in *Y Geninen*. It is in this sense that Emrys ap Iwan can be considered a precursor of the Welsh literary renaissance at the beginning of the twentieth century.[57]

The overwhelming majority of articles by R. J. Derfel, Michael D. Jones and Emrys ap Iwan were published in *Y Geninen*, under the editorship of John Thomas (Eifionydd). In the same periodical, too, appeared some of Dan Isaac Davies's pioneering articles on bilingualism.[58] Launched in 1881, this quarterly devoted a good deal of space to some of the burning issues of the day, and there was considerable controversy in its pages during the 1880s and 1890s regarding the orthography of the Welsh language, when the likes of John Rhŷs, John Morris-Jones and John Puleston Jones – 'the Oxford boys', as they were known – led the attack on 'Pugheism'.[59] Eifionydd was himself an able and experienced editor, and he provided writers of various persuasions with an opportunity of expressing their views on current topics.

[55] 'Y Tad Morgan', i.e. Emrys ap Iwan, 'Breuddwyd Pabydd wrth ei Ewyllys', *Y Geninen*, VIII, no. 3 (1890), 160e–160h; ibid., IX, no. 2 (1891), 84–96, no. 3, 169–71; ibid., X, no. 1 (1892), 15–19, no. 2, 23–7.
[56] Emrys ap Iwan, 'Y Classuron Cymreig', *Y Geninen*, XII, no. 1 (1894), 1.
[57] On Emrys ap Iwan, see Bobi Jones, 'Emrys ap Iwan a'r Iaith Gymraeg' (Annual lecture of Emrys ap Iwan Society, Abergele, 1984) (Yr Wyddgrug, 1984), pp. 1–21; Hywel Teifi Edwards, 'Emrys ap Iwan a Saisaddoliaeth: Maes y Gad yng Nghymru'r 70au' (Annual lecture of Emrys ap Iwan Society, Abergele, 1986) (Yr Wyddgrug, 1986), pp. 1–20.
[58] Dan Isaac Davies, 'Cymru Ddwyieithog', *Y Geninen*, III, no. 3 (1885), 208–12; idem, 'Plant Cymru, a Phlant y Cymry', ibid., V, no. 1 (1887), 59–63.
[59] See, e.g., the following articles in *Y Geninen*: John Rhŷs, 'Cymraeg yr Oes Hon', VII, no. 3 (1889), 129–38; J. Puleston Jones, 'Cymraeg Cymreig', VIII, no. 2 (1890), 89–93, 249–53; IX, no. 4 (1891), 247–51.

The nature of the periodical press during the latter half of the nineteenth century was much more varied than it had been during the first half of the century, and some lightness of touch becomes evident. To this period belongs *Golud yr Oes*, a popular periodical published by Hugh Humphreys in Caernarfon in 1862–4. Among the most enterprising and inventive of contemporary printers, Humphreys had adopted new printing techniques such as engraving from steel and copper plates. Engravings and cartoons were also among the chief characteristics of *Y Punch Cymraeg* (1858–64). Although it was modelled on the English *Punch*, this publication was not intended for nobles and landowners who poked fun at one another in the world of fashion and politics. The readership of *Y Punch Cymraeg* consisted of ordinary men and women, and its editors targeted everyone and everything which deserved to be ridiculed. The content of *Cyfaill yr Aelwyd* (1881–94) was more serious; this was a popular monthly containing poetry, serialized novels, and articles on science and current affairs under the editorship of Beriah Gwynfe Evans. Nevertheless, the periodical press was mainly a religious and denominational press and, as Emrys ap Iwan observed, one of the inevitable consequences was that abstract philosophical subjects figured prominently. The periodicals published during the first half of the century are brim-full of theological debate: arguments between Calvinists and Arminians, between Baptists and Congregationalists, debates about the Atonement, infant baptism, and the concept of predestination. There were also debates on moral questions, notably between total abstainers and those who were temperate in their taking of strong drink, a theme which had strained the patience of readers of Welsh periodicals during the 1830s and 1840s.[60] It is therefore no wonder that readers frequently complained about these bitter feuds. 'It is not fitting that such a spirit should appear in the writings of religious people', wrote one contributor to *Y Drysorfa Gynnulleidfaol* as early as 1849. 'By arguing, they are trampling on one another and demeaning the publication to an extent' ('Nid yw yn weddus i ysbryd o'r fath i ymddangos mewn ysgrifau crefyddwyr . . . Y maent trwy ddadlu [a] sathru ar eu gilydd . . . yn iselhau y Cyhoeddiad i raddau').[61] Sectarianism remained in the ascendancy throughout the last quarter of the century and the denominations seized every opportunity to anathematize one another in the periodical press, including the more secular journals. Indeed, one anonymous contributor to *Y Geninen* in 1892 suggested that sectarianism was mainly responsible for the failure of the Welsh periodical press:

---

[60] For a discussion of the nature and content of the temperance periodicals, see Huw Walters, 'Y Wasg Gyfnodol Gymraeg a'r Mudiad Dirwest, 1835–1850', *NLWJ*, XXVIII, no. 2 (1993), 153–95.

[61] 'Dadleuaeth y Misolion', *Y Drysorfa Gynnulleidfaol*, VII, no. 73 (1849), 14. The same complaint was voiced by Benjamin Price ('Y Cymro Bach') in his article 'At Olygwyr y Misolion Cymreig', *Y Bedyddiwr*, IV (1845), 232–5. This was also published in Samuel Evans (ed.), *'Y Cymro Bach': Sef Casgliad o Weithiau Awdurol y Diweddar Barch. Benjamin Price* (Caerdydd, 1855), pp. 191–9.

Pa gylchgrawn neu bapyr newydd a allodd fyw yn Nghymru erioed heb iddo gael ei gylchio â rhagfarn enwadol, a'i lanw âg ymosodiadau ar enwadau eraill? Nid oes neb yn meddwl am dderbyn newyddiadur ar gyfrif ei deilyngdod llenyddol, ond am mai ei enwad ef, neu ei blaid ef yn yr enwad hwnw, sydd yn ei gyhoeddi. A'r canlyniad yw – ni allwyd cadw cyhoeddiad cenedlaethol erioed yn fyw yn Nghymru am gyhyd o amser ag y bu Nebuchodonosor yn pori glaswellt.[62]

(What periodical or newspaper has ever been able to survive in Wales without being surrounded by denominational prejudice and being given to attacks on other sects? No one thinks of taking a paper on account of its literary merit, but because it is published by his denomination, or his faction within that denomination. And the result is – no national publication has ever been able to survive in Wales for longer than the time Nebuchadnezzar chewed grass.)

What of the reader who could not be expected to enjoy theology, the philosophy of religion, and biographies of eminent, and not so eminent, preachers? What about the ordinary man who had not the slightest interest in endless denominational strife? It is pertinent to ask whether the Welsh periodical press had something light, interesting and entertaining to offer, something which did not require explanation by reference to a biblical dictionary or a theological commentary. After all, unless the Welsh press could offer something which was of interest to him, the ordinary Welshman would have no choice but to turn to English periodicals for an abundant supply of light, secular and popular reading. And once he began to enjoy that, and to believe that light reading matter was available only in English, he was less likely to return to reading Welsh.

O. M. Edwards realized this and, during the 1890s, he set about providing popular literature in Welsh, in the form of periodicals such as *Y Llenor*, *Heddyw*, *Cymru* and *Cymru'r Plant*. Edwards had already been deeply influenced by Michael D. Jones and his ideas.[63] He served his apprenticeship as co-editor of *Cymru Fydd*, the bilingual monthly published by the movement of the same name. Under the editorship of Edwards and his fellow-editor, Richard Humphreys Morgan, the nature of the periodical changed. It became less political, and reports of the activities of the Liberals and of the branches of Cymru Fydd were no longer included. The articles were lighter and were not confined to political topics. However, the Cymru Fydd movement did not live up to Owen Edwards's expectations. Nor did the periodical published under the aegis of the movement meet with success. Indeed, from the time of *Cylchgrawn Cymru*, edited by John Roberts of Tremeirchion (1814–15), to this day, no bilingual periodical has ever succeeded. As a

---

[62] *Y Geninen*, X, no. 4 (1892), 224.
[63] E. G. Millward, 'O. M. Edwards a Michael D. Jones' in J. E. Caerwyn Williams (ed.), *Ysgrifau Beirniadol V* (Dinbych, 1970), p. 163.

consequence, *Cymru Fydd* came to an end with the publication of the issue for April 1891, and in bidding his readers farewell Owen Edwards wrote:

> Y mae llawer o'r camddealltwriaeth rhwng y gwahanol bleidiau yng Nghymru yn codi o'r ffaith nad oes yr un blaid yn deall hanes Cymru. Hoffwn yn ol y gallu bychan a roddwyd imi, ddarlunio'r amser a fu fel yr oedd – ac nid fel Rhyddfrydwr neu Geidwadwr, Methodist neu Annibynwr . . . Wrth ystyried hyn oll, penderfynais droi fy llafur dros Gymru i gyfeiriad arall. Penderfynais gyhoeddi misolyn amhleidiol – misolyn a wnai rywbeth dros Hanes a Llenyddiaeth Cymru . . . Ei amcan fydd gwasanaethu efrydwyr hanes a llenyddiaeth Gymreig a chynorthwyo hyrwyddwyr addysg y wlad. Y mae llawer digwyddiad cyffrous yn hanes Cymru, y mae digon yn hanes ein gwlad i godi ein huchelgais, i gryfhau ein gobeithion, i ffurfio moddion addysg i'n plant. Felly – i godi'r hen wlad yn ei hôl yn ystyr eang a heddychlon y geiriau fydd arwyddair *Cymru*.[64]

> (Much of the misunderstanding between the various parties in Wales arises from the fact that not one of them understands the history of Wales. I should like, with the limited ability given to me, to depict times gone by as they were – and not as a Liberal or Conservative, Methodist or Independent . . . With regard to all this, I have decided to turn my labours on behalf of Wales in another direction. I have decided to publish a non-party monthly – one which would do something for the History and Literature of Wales . . . Its aim will be to serve students of Welsh history and literature and assist in promoting the education of the country. There are many exciting events in the history of Wales, there is enough in the history of our country to make us ambitious, to reinforce our hopes, to form the means of education for our children. So – to raise the old country to its former glory in the wide and peaceful sense of the words will be the motto of *Cymru*.)

Cymru, the new monthly founded by Owen Edwards in August 1891, is the most notable of the Welsh periodicals produced at the close of the nineteenth century, and the manifesto of its editor is remarkably similar to that of Lewis Morris in *Tlysau yr Hen Oesoedd* a century and a half earlier. In Morris's day, it was the gentry of Wales, the chief patrons of the Welsh language in former times, who had turned their back on the language, whereas at the end of the nineteenth century it was being rejected by the common people – *y werin* was the word used by Owen Edwards. His aim in *Cymru* was to provide popular and non-denominational literature. The Welsh literature of the nineteenth century had been 'useful', 'purposeful' and 'edifying', but Edwards proved that literature could also be entertaining and interesting. *Cymru* was not a political nor a denominational periodical, but a medium for showing why Wales was Wales, and why it was a nation with its own history, culture and literature. It was intended as a publication which would teach the nation that its unique character contained

---

[64] 'Au Revoir', *Cymru Fydd*, IV, no. 4 (1891), 233–4.

much more than the disestablishment of the established Church, the land question, education and similar topics which figured so prominently in the priorities of Cymru Fydd. Whatever may be said about the myth of the Welsh peasant which was created to a large extent by Owen Edwards in *Cymru*, he succeeded in providing a periodical which was attractive and popular and which included such a wealth of material on all kinds of subjects that it was completely different from every other periodical of the time. All this was done, in the editor's own words, in order 'to raise the old country to its former glory' ('codi'r hen wlad yn ei hôl'). Edwards was also the first to attempt to meet the needs of the English-speaking Welsh by providing them with English-language periodicals of a Welsh character.

It is now commonplace to speak of the nineteenth century as the golden age of Welsh publishing and the most productive period in the entire history of our literature. From the point of view of quantity, if not quality, it was undoubtedly 'the great century', and it is no coincidence that it was also the golden age of Welsh Nonconformity. Some 145 Welsh or bilingual periodicals were published under various titles between 1800 and 1850, and about 250 between 1851 and 1900, a total of approximately 400 periodicals throughout the whole century. During the first fifty years the main printing and publishing centres were located in comparatively small towns in largely rural areas, such as Caernarfon, Dolgellau, Llanidloes, Llandovery, Carmarthen and Aberystwyth. During the second half of the century this activity spread to Aberdare, Merthyr Tydfil, Cardiff, Llanelli, Blaenau Ffestiniog, Bethesda and Wrexham in the wake of industrial developments in those areas.[65] Indeed, by the end of the century all the main towns had their own printing press, very often producing small periodicals of a local character. The plurality of these periodicals was in itself a sure sign of literary activity, and it was fashionable until comparatively recently to disparage and revile them, forgetting, perhaps, that sociological conditions and literature are intertwined.[66] After all, the press was maintained throughout the century largely by common working people – labourers, quarrymen and miners. Moreover, it is important to understand the function of literature for writers of the day – a

[65] A large number of articles on local printers and publishers have appeared during recent years. See, e.g., R. Maldwyn Thomas, 'Y Wasg Gyfnodol yn Nhref Caernarfon hyd 1875, gyda Sylw Arbennig i Argraffwyr a Chyhoeddwyr' (unpubl. University of Wales MA thesis, 1979); Brynley F. Roberts, 'Argraffu yn Aberdâr', *JWBS*, XI, no. 1–2 (1973–4), 1–53; J. Iorwerth Davies, 'The History of Printing in Montgomeryshire, 1789–1960', *MC*, 65 (1977), 57–66; ibid., 66 (1978), 7–28; ibid., 68 (1980), 67–85; ibid., 70 (1982), 71–98; ibid., 71 (1983), 48–60; ibid., 72 (1984), 37–44; ibid., 73 (1985), 38–53; David Jenkins, 'Braslun o Hanes Argraffu yn Nhref Aberteifi', *JWBS*, VII, no. 4 (1953), 174–92; Bedwyr Lewis Jones, *Argraffu a Chyhoeddi ym Môn* (Llangefni, 1976); Huw Walters, 'Gwasg Gyfnodol Tref Llanymddyfri', *CA*, XXX (1994), 57–69; Stan I. Wicklen, 'The History of Printing in the Conwy Valley up to 1914' (unpubl. University of Wales MA thesis, 1984).

[66] See J. E. Caerwyn Williams, 'Amodau Cymdeithasegol Llenyddiaeth', *Lleufer*, V, no. 3 (1949), 111–16; T. J. Morgan, *Diwylliant Gwerin ac Ysgrifau Eraill* (Llandysul, 1972).

literature which saw life through the eyes of the common people, and which was a means of shedding light on their problems, their hopes and yearnings. A fair proportion of the editors of Welsh periodicals were of the same social background as their readers and the literature they produced was of necessity a true mirror of the contemporary mind. 'When we look at Welsh literature, it can be called the literature of the workers', wrote a contributor to *Yr Eurgrawn* in 1865. 'It is completely in the hands of workers, and ministers of the gospel, and those ministers, for the most part, were once themselves literary-minded workers' ('Pan edrychwn ar lenyddiaeth Gymraeg, gellir ei galw yn llenyddiaeth y gweithwyr. Y mae yn hollol yn nwylaw y gweithwyr, a gweinidogion yr efengyl, a'r gweinidogion hyny, gan mwyaf, wedi bod unwaith yn weithwyr llengar').[67]

There was also a ready market for these periodicals, the bulk of which was almost entirely in the hands of the religious denominations. Publications were mostly distributed in the churches, chapels and Sunday schools, much to the disapproval of the more puritanically minded members. In *Yr Haul* in 1847 Brutus protested against the growing tendency to sell books and periodicals in places of worship,[68] but this custom continued throughout the century.[69] It is difficult, however, to discover accurate statistics regarding the circulation of these periodicals, mainly because very few archives and account-books from the publishing houses and printing offices have survived. Thomas Stephens of Merthyr Tydfil carried out a survey of the Welsh periodical and newspaper press in the middle years of the century. He wrote to the main publishers and printers, seeking information about their publications and their circulation. This evidence must be used with caution, however, because some of Stephens's correspondents were more reluctant than others to reveal their secrets. In 1858 William Spurrell, the printer and publisher from Carmarthen, refused to provide any information about his publications, and Josiah Thomas Jones, again of Carmarthen, must have been less than serious when in 1846 he answered Stephens's enquiry about the circulation of *Y Drysorfa Gynnulleidfaol* thus: 'Sir, in answer to your enquiry, I have to inform you that the extent of the *Drysorfa* circulation for this year is 1,500, – but next year it will be nearly double the number.'[70] Stephens published the results of his earliest research in *Y Wawr* in 1851, giving circulation figures for twenty-three of the principal Welsh periodicals in mid-century. Since circulation

---

[67] *Yr Eurgrawn Wesleyaidd*, LVII (1865), 19.
[68] *Yr Haul*, XII (1847), iii–iv. See also the comments of 'Siôn yr Ochr Draw', 'Y Marchnadoedd Sanctaidd', ibid., XI (1846), 101–2.
[69] A dispute on this matter between John Thomas, Bwlchnewydd (and, subsequently, Liverpool) and Robert Jones, Trewen, appeared in *Y Diwygiwr* between February and December 1848. See also 'Llyfrwerthu yn Nghymru', *Y Cylchgrawn*, 2 (1852), 62–3; 'Tŷ Fy Nhad yn Dŷ Marchnad', a series of letters published in *Y Tyst a'r Dydd,* 26 October–14 December 1883.
[70] NLW, MS 965E, I, f. 285.

figures at this time are so scarce, Stephens's list is printed below.[71] Details of their denominational connections, whether official or unofficial, are noted in brackets:

Y Geiniogwerth (Calvinistic Methodists)	12,900
Cronicl y Cymdeithasau Crefyddol (Congregationalists)	7,320
Y Gymraes	3,500
Y Golygydd (Congregationalists)	3,000
Yr Athraw i Blentyn (Baptists)	3,000
Y Wawr-ddydd	2,580
Tywysydd yr Ieuainc (Congregationalists)	2,500
Y Diwygiwr (Congregationalists)	2,400
Y Drysorfa (Calvinistic Methodists)	2,300
Y Bedyddiwr (Baptists)	1,800
Y Wawr	1,700
Y Traethodydd (Calvinistic Methodists)	1,600
Seren Gomer (Baptists)	1,500
Y Dysgedydd (Congregationalists)	1,512
Y Drysorfa Gynnulleidfaol (Congregationalists)	1,500
Ifor Hael (Friendly Society)	1,050
Yr Athraw (Calvinistic Methodists)	1,025
Yr Haul (The Established Church)	1,000
Yr Adolygydd (Congregationalists)	900
Yr Eurgrawn Wesleyaidd (Wesleyans)	900
Y Tyst Apostolaidd (Baptists)	900
Yr Ymofynydd (Unitarians)	800

These statistics reveal considerable variation, and it is known that some periodicals founded after 1851, when Stephens carried out his survey, proved far more successful than any title found in this list. *Trysorfa y Plant*, the children's monthly edited by Thomas Levi and published by the Calvinistic Methodists, sold, on average, 19,000 copies in 1864, and by 1881 a total of 45,000 copies a month were being sold.[72]

The overwhelming majority of Welsh periodicals during the first third of the nineteenth century were denominational and this probably accounted for both their strength and their weakness. It was not until the last quarter of the century that the content of Welsh periodicals became lighter and more secularized, following the launch of more popular titles such as *Y Geninen*, *Cyfaill yr Aelwyd*, *Cwrs y Byd*, *Heddyw* and *Cymru'r Plant*. Editors of these periodicals were aware of the dangers facing the Welsh language towards the end of the nineteenth century.

---

[71] Stephens, 'Agwedd Bresennol Llëenyddiaeth yn Nghymru', 38.
[72] On Thomas Levi and his periodical, see Dafydd Arthur Jones, *Thomas Levi* (Caernarfon, 1996), pp. 39–58; idem, 'Hen Swynwr y 'Sorfa Fach': Thomas Levi (1825–1916)' in Jenkins (ed.), *Cof Cenedl XI*, pp. 89–116.

Therefore, for the great majority of nineteenth-century editors Welsh was, on the whole, the language of religion and theology, the eisteddfod and the singing festival. As John Roberts claimed in *Cronicl y Cymdeithasau Crefyddol* in 1877, it was of no use to those who wished to get on in the world:

> Nid yr ieithoedd goreu, cyfoethocaf eu hadnoddau, sydd yn byw ac ymeangu, onide, buasai gobaith am yr Hebraeg, Groeg, Lladin a'r Gymraeg; ond ieithoedd *masnach* sydd yn byw – ieithoedd cyfoeth ac anrhydedd. Y rhai hyn fynant fod yn ieithoedd swyddfau, cledrffyrdd, telegraph, stiwardiaid, a'u harglwyddi; banciau, senedd-dai, cyfreithwyr, meddygon, llysoedd barn, a llysoedd brenhinol; a rhaid iddynt ddyfod yn ieithoedd pulpudau ac argraffdai. Dyna paham y mae y Ffrancaeg, Germanaeg, a'r Saesoneg wedi llethu yr ieithoedd a enwyd.[73]

> (The best languages, those with the richest resources, are not the ones which live and flourish, otherwise there would have been hope for Hebrew, Greek, Latin and Welsh; it is the languages of *commerce* which live – the languages of wealth and honour. It is those which become the languages of the office, the railway, the telegraph, stewards, and their lords; of banks, parliaments, lawyers, doctors, courts of law, and the royal courts; and they must become the languages of the pulpit and the printing press. That is why French, German, and English have stifled the languages named.)

The spiritual and religious condition of Wales figured uppermost in the minds of these men, and the continuance of Nonconformity was of greater importance to them than the survival of the native tongue. David Rees and his fellow-editors believed that, since the Welsh language existed, it was their duty to use it as a medium for promoting their values.[74] This was the only way in which they could influence the mind of the nation, and since the future of the language was in the hands of Providence, nothing could be done to prevent its demise if that was the will of God.

The nineteenth-century Welsh periodical press reflects the ideas and complexes of contemporary Welsh people with regard to the Welsh language. Not until the last quarter of the century was a determined campaign on its behalf sustained in the periodicals, and this was mainly the result of the awakening stimulated by nationalists such as Michael D. Jones, Emrys ap Iwan and O. M. Edwards. The astonishing fact is that a minority language like Welsh was able to maintain so many periodicals throughout the century. Indeed, Thomas Watts, Keeper of the Department of Printed Books at the British Museum, commented on the plurality of Welsh periodicals as early as 1861 when he wrote: 'In almost every country the periodical portion of its literature has now assumed an importance unknown to previous stages of its history, but in no country is it so predominant as in Wales.'[75] It is a matter for celebration that all this publishing activity had occurred in Welsh

---
[73] *Y Cronicl*, XXXV, no. 407 (1877), 73.
[74] *Y Diwygiwr*, XX, no. 234 (1855), iv.
[75] Thomas Watts, *A Sketch of the History of the Welsh Language and Literature* (London, 1861), p. 68.

at all. At meetings of the General Assembly of the Calvinistic Methodists held in Aberystwyth in 1867, Roger Edwards of Mold, editor of *Y Drysorfa* at the time, declared that their ministers should not only increasingly apply themselves to preaching in English but that Welsh authors should also write in English.[76] Had editors and contributors to Welsh periodicals acted upon this advice, there is no doubt that the future of the Welsh language would have been placed in severe jeopardy.

---

[76] 'Gweithrediadau y Gymanfa Gyffredinol', *Y Drysorfa*, XX, no. 237 (1866), 388.

13

The Welsh Language and Journalism

ALED JONES

GEORGE BORROW'S account of a chance meeting with a waggoner at an inn in Llanarmon, Denbighshire, one October afternoon in 1854, inadvertently captured a moment of rare poignancy in the history of the Welsh language and its journalism. The waggoner, Borrow recalled, was 'intently staring' at a Welsh-language newspaper 'full of dismal accounts' of the Crimean war:

'What news?' said I in English.
'I wish I could tell you,' said he in very broken English; 'but I cannot read.'
'Then why are you looking at the paper?' said I.
'Because,' said he, 'by looking at the letters I hope in time to make them out.'[1]

By gazing, uncomprehendingly but with enormous concentration, at what he knew to be important, Borrow's waggoner stood on a frontier between a predominantly oral popular culture and one that was shortly to be saturated with cheap print. From the perspective of its social history, this involved a transformation of no small account for the Welsh language. For while the encounter clearly revealed an individual's aspiration to be fully literate, it signified also a number of deeper trends in the cultural history of nineteenth-century Wales. Although his English may have been 'very broken', the waggoner, none the less, understood and spoke two languages. Into this bilingual oral world, a relatively new form of printed communication had recently intruded. Throughout the United Kingdom, the mid-1850s had witnessed the sudden expansion of a cheap, weekly newspaper press which, for the first time, was unencumbered by the price rationing of taxation.[2]

---

[1] George Borrow, *Wild Wales* (London, 1955), p. 323. I am grateful to Dr Michael Roberts for drawing my attention to this reference.

[2] For further information on the repeal of the Stamp Duty, known as the 'Taxes on Knowledge', see C. D. Collet, *History of the Taxes on Knowledge: Their Origin and Repeal* (London, 1933); J. H. Wiener, *The War of the Unstamped: A History of the Movement to Repeal the British Newspaper Tax, 1830–1836* (Ithaca, New York, 1969). For a history of the newspaper press in England, see A. J. Lee, *The Origins of the Popular Press in England, 1855–1914* (London, 1976) and L. Brown, *Victorian News and Newspapers* (Oxford, 1985). For studies of Welsh-language journalism, see E. Morgan Humphreys, *Y Wasg Gymraeg* (Caernarfon, 1944), D. Tecwyn Lloyd, *Gysfenu i'r Wasg Gynt* (Caerdydd, 1980), and Aled Gruffydd Jones, *Press, Politics and Society: A History of Journalism in Wales* (Cardiff, 1993).

Also by this time, newspapers written in Welsh had radiated outwards from the towns where they were printed into the rural hinterlands, chiefly through the agency of such village inns as the one visited by George Borrow in Llanarmon. There, fresh news from the Russian front might be consumed along with beer, and become known to a wider circle through conversation, argument and even humour. Through the mediation of the literate, the diverse contents of newspapers thus became public knowledge.[3] This chapter will consider some of the broader implications for the Welsh language and its speakers of the expansion of this journalism, a process which resulted both in the greater public exposure of the language and the evolution of new forms of writing.

Journalism, as a relatively recent form of communication in Wales, was modelled mainly on an English-language precedent. Unlike the older almanacs and the political and religious magazines of seventeenth- and eighteenth-century Wales,[4] weekly newspapers were launched only after the turn of the nineteenth century, more than a hundred years after the first newspapers had appeared in England.[5] The first issue of the English-language weekly newspaper, the *Cambrian*, came off the press in Swansea in 1804, where, a decade later, Joseph Harris launched the first Welsh-language newspaper, *Seren Gomer*, in January 1814. The failure of the latter after only eighteen months unnerved other potential producers of Welsh-language news weeklies, and, while a second series of *Seren Gomer* was launched as a periodical in 1818, it took more than twenty years for a publisher to dare to repeat Harris's experiment in news journalism. Shortly before the Stamp Duty on newspapers was reduced from 4*d*. to 1*d*. in 1836, Roger Edwards launched *Cronicl yr Oes* in Mold, the eventual demise of which in December 1839 encouraged William Rees (Gwilym Hiraethog) to fill the niche in the Welsh-language market with *Yr Amserau*, which first appeared in Liverpool in 1843. Emboldened by the commercial success of this venture and further encouraged by the total repeal of the remaining penny Stamp Duty in 1855, Thomas Gee of Denbigh launched *Baner Cymru* in 1857 (which became known as *Baner ac Amserau Cymru* following its incorporation of *Yr Amserau* in 1859).[6] New Welsh-language titles also began to appear in other towns in Wales, the largest numbers being launched in the 1850s, the 1870s and the 1880s.

---

[3] Despite his illiteracy, the waggoner indicated in his conversation with Borrow that he already held strong and well-informed views on the relative merits of the Russian, French and British armies, Borrow, *Wild Wales*, p. 323.

[4] For a fuller account, see Geraint H. Jenkins, *Literature, Religion and Society in Wales, 1660–1730* (Cardiff, 1978) and idem, *Thomas Jones yr Almanaciwr 1648–1713* (Caerdydd, 1980).

[5] The first daily newspaper in Britain, the *Daily Courant*, was first published in 1702. For a chronology of newspaper history, see G. Boyce, J. Curran, and P. Wingate, *Newspaper History: From the 17th Century to the Present Day* (London, 1978), pp. 407–8.

[6] T. Gwynn Jones, *Cofiant Thomas Gee* (2 vols., Dinbych, 1913). See also Philip Henry Jones, '*Yr Amserau*: The First Decade 1843–52' in Laurel Brake, Aled Jones and Lionel Madden (eds.), *Investigating Victorian Journalism* (London, 1990), pp. 85–103.

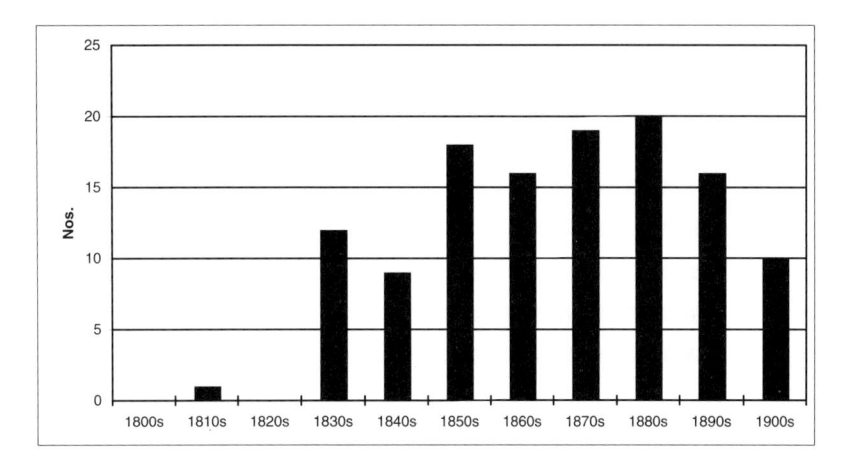

Figure 1. Number of Welsh-language newspapers launched, by decade, 1800–1909

Source: Beti Jones, *Report of the NEWSPLAN project in Wales* (1994)

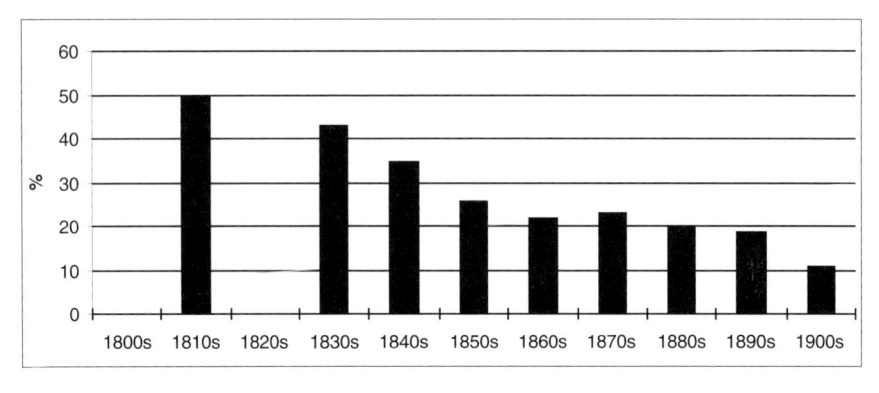

Figure 2. Welsh-language titles launched as a percentage of the total number of newspapers established by decade, 1800–1909

Source: Beti Jones, *Report of the NEWSPLAN project in Wales* (1994)

As a proportion of the total number of newspapers launched in Wales during this period, however, the rate at which new titles were established, with the sole exception of the 1870s, gradually declined. This reflected both the greater expansion of English-language journalism in Wales, and also the extent to which the established Welsh-language titles had saturated the Welsh-speaking newspaper market. Welsh-language newspapers were produced in centres where not only was there a concentration of adequate printing technology, and of skilled editorial and composing staff, but also of advertisers and readers. Caernarfon, where sixteen

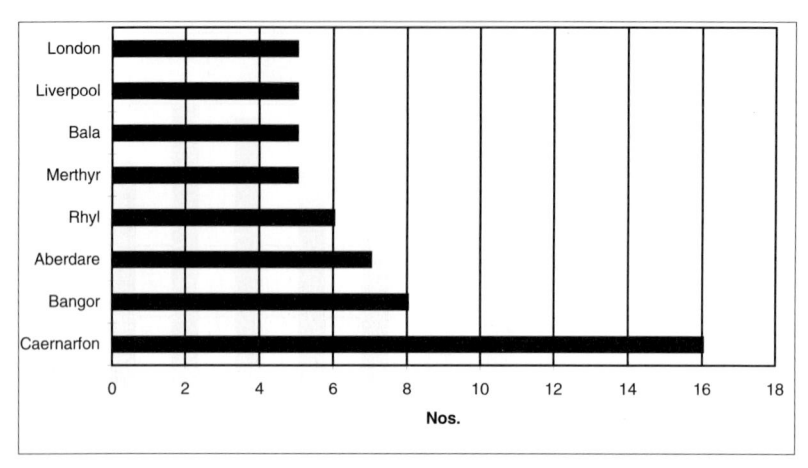

Figure 3. Principal production centres of Welsh-language newspapers, 1800–1899

Source: Beti Jones, *Report of the NEWSPLAN project in Wales* (1994)

titles were launched in this period, was by far the most important nineteenth-century production centre, followed by Bangor (eight), Aberdare (seven) and Rhyl (six). Significantly, three of the four major centres were located on the north Wales coast, all being either adjacent to, or within a short distance of, the new railway stations of the Chester to Holyhead line. The existence of the railway was an essential prerequisite for newspaper growth. While being the cheapest and most efficient means of distributing copies to retailers and subscribers, it was also an effective way of gathering local news and of acquiring, swiftly and regularly, mail and daily newspapers from other parts of the United Kingdom.[7] Merthyr and Bala, where as many Welsh titles were launched as in Liverpool or London, came close behind with five titles each.

However, the pattern of growth of the Welsh-language newspaper press, defined in this case by the numbers of fresh titles established in each decade, was determined as much by a combination of population and urban growth, industrial development, technological improvements in printing and legislative reform as by the coming of the railways. With one significant exception, that growth pattern in

---

[7] The railways also brought in English-language competitors from the other side of the border. Borrow recalled seeing a copy of the *Bolton Chronicle* near Llangollen in 1854 (Borrow, *Wild Wales*, p. 115). Sunday newspapers such as the *News of the World* and *Reynolds's News* made significant inroads into the Welsh newspaper market from the 1840s. The ability of larger numbers of Welsh people to read English further increased the share of English-language newspapers produced in Wales, as well as that of the national British press, in relation to Welsh-language titles. For the growth of a powerful 'national' British press, see L. Brown, *Victorian News and Newspapers*, passim.

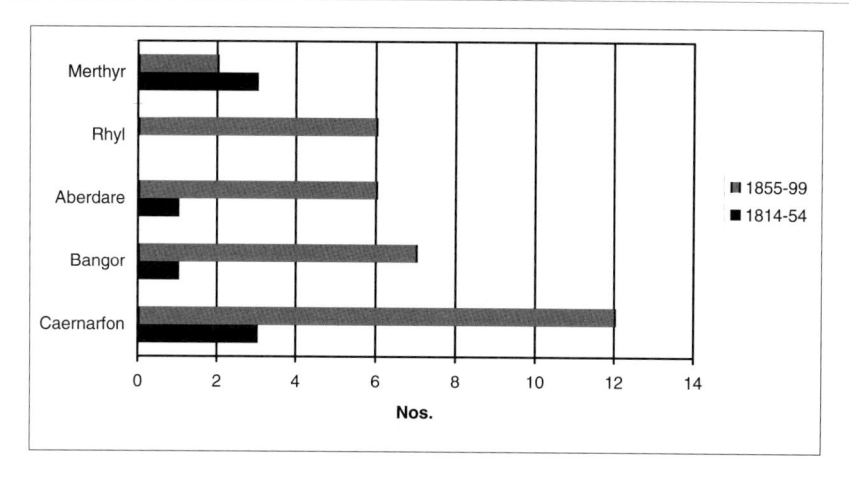

Figure 4. Number of Welsh-language newspapers launched before and after 1855

Source: Beti Jones, *Report of the NEWSPLAN project in Wales* (1994)

all the Welsh production centres corresponded closely to the general shape of the post-1855 expansion of the newspaper press in Britain as a whole. Of fifteen towns in Wales where only one Welsh-language title was produced in the nineteenth century, only in two (Holywell and Cowbridge) were these titles started before 1855, and of the eight most important centres of production listed in Figure 3, only in Merthyr Tydfil were more Welsh-language titles launched prior to 1855 than after.

But if Welsh-language newspapers were often indistinguishable in their formats, their sources of news and advertising, and their broader pattern of growth, from the flood of other English-language provincial weeklies that had emerged in the 1850s and 1860s, journalism in Welsh nevertheless embodied from the beginning a number of notable peculiarities. While editors were aware, often keenly so, of the contents, standards of journalism and political orientations of the English press, the response to their older and, in most cases, better-resourced, neighbour took a number of different forms. One was to affect a posture of ironic detachment, which contained elements of disdain and a sense of superiority. The title of William Rees's *Yr Amserau*, for example, was chosen not so much as a tribute to the London *Times*, but as a critique of it, a means of contrasting the nobility of the one against the corruption of the other:

> Efe a gymer rybydd oddiwrth y dynghedfen druenus a dynodd ei *namesake* (yn yr iaith arall, sef *Times* Llundain) arno ei hun, trwy droi oddiar lwybr gonestrwydd a gwirionedd, a thynu i lawr yr hyn gynt a adeiladasai; – cablu a dirmygu yr egwyddorion o ryddid a chyfiawnder y buasai unwaith yn eu proffesu a'u hamddiffyn; – a gwerthu ei

hunain i bob isel-fudr wasanaeth, hyd nes aeth ei ddryg-nodwedd yn ddiarebol drwy holl Ewrop . . .[8]

(It heeds the pitiful fate which befell its namesake (in the other language, namely the London *Times*), in turning from the path of honesty and truth and pulling down what it had formerly built up; abusing and deriding the principles of freedom and justice it had at one time advocated and defended; – and selling itself for every mean end, such that its evil reputation is known throughout the whole of Europe . . .)

A second feature of newspapers in Wales was the extent of the interpenetration between the journalism of the country's two languages. It is important to remember that in Wales, English as well as Welsh-language titles carried material in Welsh, and that most Welsh-speaking editors and writers, as well as many readers, could easily transfer from one language to the other. Lewis William Lewis (Llew Llwyfo) informed his regular readers in *Y Gwron* that he had voluntarily left the employ of the paper's publisher, the Revd Josiah Thomas Jones of Aberdare, in January 1858, 'being unable to maintain himself and his family; and that he [had] been engaged to carry out a new project BY A PARTY THAT WILL PAY him for his services'.[9] That party, which happily disregarded the charges of incompetence and absenteeism laid against Lewis by his previous employer, was the English-language title *Merthyr Telegraph*, published by Peter Williams in the neighbouring town of Merthyr Tydfil. Lewis was engaged by Williams primarily as the editor of the paper's poetry section, 'Y Gongl Gymreig', in which, in an otherwise English-language newspaper, virtually all the material printed was in Welsh. A third consideration for the great majority of Welsh-language titles was their poverty. Few could attract the advertising revenues or sustain the same readership levels as their English-language counterparts. In these straitened circumstances, the retention of such popular writers as Llew Llwyfo in the face of better remunerated jobs in the English sector was only one among many difficulties faced by publishers of Welsh-language newspapers. As William Rees of *Yr Amserau* bitterly observed, the work of the editor of a Welsh-language paper was both qualitatively different from that of an English newspaper, and substantially under-remunerated in relation to it:

beth yw llafur Golygydd Newyddiadur Seisnig mewn cymhariaeth i un Cymreig? Y mae y papurau Seisnig yn gallu helpio eu gilydd, pan y rhaid i'r Golygydd Cymreig, ysgrifenu, nid ei *leading article* yn unig, ond cyfieithu ac ysgrifenu yr holl newyddion gyda hyny . . . am lai na degwm y tâl a ga y Golygyddion Seisnig.[10]

---

[8] *Yr Amserau*, 23 August 1843.
[9] *Merthyr Telegraph*, 2 January 1858.
[10] *Yr Amserau*, 3 December 1846.

(what is the toil of an English Newspaper Editor in comparison with that of his Welsh counterpart? The English papers can assist each other whereas the Welsh Editor has to write not only the leading article but also translate and write all the news . . . for less than a tenth of the remuneration of English Editors.)

But the most remarkable peculiarity of Welsh journalism in the nineteenth century in relation to the history of the Welsh language was the phenomenon of the religious newspaper. Titles such as *Y Goleuad*, launched by Calvinistic Methodists in 1869, while conforming to the shape, size, format and mix of news, editorial and advertising of the commercial weeklies, nevertheless described the world in peculiarly Welsh religious and political terms. The religious denominations sponsored the titles which served as their mouthpieces by providing them with editors, writers, advertisers, publishers, distribution networks, and even with occasional subsidies to help them survive lean times.[11] It is no accident that the majority of Welsh-language newspaper editors in the nineteenth century were ordained ministers of one or other of the principal religious denominations. Nonconformists in particular saw the dissemination of news in Welsh as a religious act. The masthead of *Yr Amserau*, which in all probability was the paper being gazed at by George Borrow's waggoner in 1854, rhetorically challenged its readers with the question 'can ye not discern the signs of the times?' ('oni fedrwch arwyddion yr amserau?')[12] Drawn from a biblical source, Matthew 16:3, the implied reply was that readers could discern the signs of the times simply by examining the pages of *Yr Amserau*. In 1857 Samuel Evans of Carmarthen, editor of the Baptist-leaning *Seren Cymru*, explained in greater detail to his readers the nature of the ties that bound journalism to religion. He maintained that the regular purchase of godly news in Welsh ought to be regarded, in two quite distinct senses, as a religious duty:

> Dylem ni, fel crefyddwyr, ddeffroi o ddifrif; mae y wasg anffyddaidd yn y deyrnas hon yn troi allan fwy o lyfrau ddeg o weithiau bob blwyddyn nâ'r wasg sydd yn cefnogi crefydd! . . . Nid wyf yn golygu mai pethau crefyddol sydd, nac a ddylent fod, mewn pob newyddiadur; ond dylid cofio fod adnabyddiaeth âg amgylchiadau yr oes, ïe, pob gwybodaeth, yn talu treth i grefydd Crist.[13]

(We, as religious people, should arouse ourselves; the atheistic press in this kingdom turns out ten times as many books every year as the press which supports religion! . . . I do not mean that religious affairs are, or should be, in every newspaper; but it should be borne in mind that understanding of the circumstances of the times, yes, all knowledge, is like paying tax to the religion of Christ.)

---

[11] For a fuller history of *Y Goleuad*, see R. Buick-Knox, *Wales and 'Y Goleuad'* (Caernarfon, 1969).
[12] *Yr Amserau*, 23 August 1843.
[13] *Seren Cymru*, 3 October 1857.

The notion that news was a religious phenomenon, and that purchasing a newspaper was a form of religious taxation which kept at bay the flood of infidel publications, while enabling those who absorbed and acted on the knowledge which they contained to be better Christians, had powerful ideological implications. This was most evident in the language of political journalism. The Welsh-language press, though in numerous ways tied to British party politics, developed its own politico-religious vocabulary and rhetorical style, and the following fragment from a leading article, which appeared in *Y Goleuad* on the occasion of the defeat of France and the establishment of the Paris Commune in 1871 reveals the way in which a news story could be framed within a distinctively Christian and evangelical reading of the events:

Ffrainc a'i pheryglon

Wedi'r cwbl, y gelyn penaf a fedd Ffrainc i arswydo rhagddo ydyw hi ei hun. Mae ei pherygl y dyddiau hyn yn cyfodi, nid oddiar orthrwm a thrahausder y Germaniaid yn gymaint ag oddiar annoethineb, byrbwylldra, a balchder calon y genedl. Mae drwgnwydau cenedlaethol y Ffrancod yn amlwg o ddechreu y rhyfel hyd ei derfyniad . . . Mae gennym bob achos i ddiolch am drefn a manteision y sefydliadau yr ydym ni danynt yn y wlad hon; ac yn neillduol am y dylanwad mawr sydd gan y Bibl, ac egwyddorion y Bibl, ar feddwl a chalon helaeth o drigolion Prydain.[14]

(France and its dangers

After all, the greatest enemy France possesses is itself. The threat to it these days arises not so much from the oppression and arrogance of the Germans as from the imprudence, impetuousness and pride of the nation. The reckless national passions of the French have been evident from the commencement of the war to its conclusion . . . We have every cause to be grateful for the orderliness and benefits of the institutions under which we live in this country; and in particular for the great influence of the Bible, and the principles of the Bible, on the minds and hearts of the inhabitants of Britain.)

Religious bodies were not alone in encouraging and creating new forms of Welsh-language journalism. Readers will be familiar with the contribution made by Welsh Liberalism (often indistinguishable from Nonconformist involvement),[15] but far less is known about the activities of the Conservative Party.[16] In

---

[14] *Y Goleuad*, 11 March 1871.
[15] For studies of the inter-relationships between journalists, Nonconformist organizations and the Liberal Party in Wales, see, for example, K. O. Morgan, *Wales in British Politics 1868–1922* (rev. ed., Cardiff, 1970), and idem, *Rebirth of a Nation: Wales 1880–1980* (Oxford, 1981).
[16] This imbalance is gradually being redressed; see, for example, Felix Aubel, 'The Conservatives in Wales 1880–1935' in Martin Francis and Ina Zweiniger-Bargielowska (eds.), *The Conservatives and British Society, 1880–1990* (Cardiff, 1996), pp. 96–110.

1877 Tory pamphlets were translated into Welsh for circulation in Wales,[17] and a year later a grant was made to the North Wales Conservative Alliance 'to aid in the publication of pamphlets in the Welsh language'.[18] In 1890, shortly after the expansion of the Welsh electorate following the Reform Act of 1885, William Barton of Birmingham criticized the distribution of election propaganda in English in the Welsh-speaking districts, intimating that they may as well have been 'printed in Chinese'.[19] Two years later, F. McLure of East Glamorgan bluntly described how the vibrancy of the Welsh-language Liberal Nonconformist press stacked the odds against the Tory Party in south Wales:

> In addition to the other powers ranged against us, we have also the vernacular press, the Welsh press. It is not only exceedingly radical, but it is edited by nonconformist ministers, and the same conduct they carry on as political agents is carried on in the Welsh press from week to week, and we have no means, no power, of contending with that except by the distribution of literature and also by establishing some papers on our own behalf.[20]

Despite repeated calls by rank and file activists from Wales and England, the Conservative Party centrally did little to aid such fragile Conservative Welsh-language newspapers as *Y Dywysogaeth* in challenging the almost complete dominance of Liberal Nonconformity over mid-Victorian Welsh political culture. But political evangelization apart, the primary function of the newspaper was to sell news. Most newspapers carried a combination of local, national and foreign reports, the latter, with few exceptions, being derived from translations and summaries from English newspapers. This enabled journals such as *Yr Haul* in 1835 to carry an impressive range of foreign material (in one early issue, news reports were printed from twelve countries on three continents). Local reports, however, were written either by local correspondents, paid by the line, or by the editor himself. The emergence of a distinctive and readable Welsh reporting style, however, was slow and uncertain. A strong biblical influence infused many of the early local reports and is discernible in the following account of a horse-riding accident which appeared in *Y Gwron* in Carmarthen in 1852:

> W. G. H. Thomas, Yswain, o'r dref hon, a gyfarfu a dygwyddiad peryglus, yr hyn a allasai droi allan yn angeuol iddo. Yr oedd er ys tro wedi bod yn anhwylus, ac un diwrnod, aeth allan i farchogaeth, ac ar ei ffordd tuag adref, dychrynodd yr anifail a farchogai, ac yntau a syrthiodd i'r llawr oddiar ei gefn. Cafodd archoll ar ei ben, a briwiau ereill; anfonwyd am feddygon yn ddioed, a thrwy diriondeb rhagluniaeth y mae eto ar wellad.[21]

---

[17] *Archives of the British Conservative Party* (Harvester Microfilm) 1877, p. 4.
[18] Ibid., 1878, p. 4.
[19] Ibid., 1890, p. 49.
[20] Ibid., 1892, p. 32.
[21] *Y Gwron*, 22 April 1852.

(W. G. H. Thomas, Esquire, of this town, was involved in a dangerous incident which might have had fatal consequences for him. He had been unwell for some time, and one day, went out to ride, and on his way home his horse was startled, and he fell to the ground. He received a wound to his head, and other injuries; the doctors were called immediately, and through the compassion of providence he is once again on the mend.)

By 1880, however, a more sophisticated reporting style had emerged. Contrast the above with the following opening paragraph of an account of a colliery explosion in Risca which appeared in *Baner ac Amserau Cymru* in June 1880:

Yn gynnar boreu heddyw, yn Risca, digwyddodd un o'r trychinebau arswydus hyny sydd, fel y mae yn ofidus gorfod dyweyd, yn cymmeryd lle mor fynych yn maes glô Deheudir Cymru, a'r tebygolrwydd ydyw, nad oes dim llai na chwech ugain o fywydau wedi syrthio yn aberth iddo. Pan oedd yr ysgrifenydd yn myned yn nhyfeiriad mangre y trychineb, yr oedd gweithfeydd y Rhiwderyn a Rogerstone yn anfon colofnau anferth o ager a nwy i fyny i'r awyrgylch; a'r rhai hyny yn ymgymysgu gyda ac yn ymgolli yn fuan yn y cymmylau dyfrllyd oeddynt wedi eu taenu yn isel dros yr holl fro.[22]

(Early this morning, in Risca, there occurred one of those dreadful tragedies which, it grieves one to admit, happen all too frequently in the South Wales Coalfield, and it is likely that no fewer than one hundred and twenty lives have fallen sacrifice to it. As the writer travelled in the direction of the disaster, the works at Rhiwderyn and Rogerstone were throwing out massive columns of steam and gas to the atmosphere; these intermingled and were quickly lost in the watery clouds which were spread low over the whole district.)

The difference between the two news reports lies not only in the scale of the tragedy being described, but in the pungency of the writing. Crucially, in contrast to the former, the latter is an eyewitness account. The reporter was there, and so, in an imaginative sense, is the reader. The reporter, by locating himself so firmly in the vividly described landscape, leads the reader into the story and into the full horror of the disaster. Sharply observant and informative, the page-long account which follows sustains the strong visual sense of the opening, and not only tells an unfolding story but also effectively creates a mood of foreboding, desolation and tragedy. Industrial conditions had made new ways of writing necessary, and in reports such as these we find not only the origins of a distinctly Welsh form of journalism, but also a new way of writing in Welsh.

Notwithstanding such developments, the quality of language employed in newspapers was a cause for concern for some readers, many of whom found in the enhanced technology of the new press a powerful agency whose tendency was to erode literary standards. Necessarily hurried translations of news from English-

---

[22] *BAC*, 21 July 1880.

language sources, which included idiomatic passages, must surely have contributed to this sense of unease. One review of the press at the end of the nineteenth century complained of the 'shoddy Welsh' of the newspapers, while others berated their 'pompous Anglicized style'.[23] In retrospect, it may be argued that the criticism was not altogether justified. Some newspaper editors were clearly anxious that their publications should contribute actively to the process of improving the condition of written and spoken Welsh. In a declaration 'To the Welsh', printed in the first issue of the relaunched *Seren Gomer* on 28 January 1818, the editor disputed the inevitability of the decline of Welsh and sought to use the publication as part of a mission to breathe new life into the language:

> Yr ydym hyderus fod llawer eto yn ein gwlad yn hiraethlon am weled eu hiaith yn cael ei phuro fwy-fwy, a phob rheidiol nawdd yn cael ei weini iddi, modd y gellai yn ei henaint adnewyddu ei nerth, ac ymddangos fel dynes ieuanc ymlodau ei dyddiau, er bod estroniaid wedi bwyta ei chryfdwr, a phenwyni wedi ymdaenu ar hyd-ddi, a'i haml feibion yn anystyriol o hyny. – Cawsom achos i gredu fod ein *Seren* ddiweddar wedi gwneuthur ychwaneg o ddaioni nag a ragfeddyliasom, trwy dywys cànoedd i ddarllen a deall Cymraeg . . .[24]

(We are confident that many in our country long to see the language being increasingly purified, and provided with all necessary support, so that it might in its old age renew its vigour, and appear as a young woman in the flower of her youth, despite the erosion of its strength by foreigners, the hoariness which enshrouds it, and the heedlessness of its numerous sons. – We have reason to believe that our late *Seren* achieved more good than had been previously thought, by guiding hundreds to read and understand Welsh . . .)

Foremost among the powers of journalism, it was suggested, was its capacity to purify, standardize and strengthen the integrity of both written and spoken Welsh:

> Oni chynhelir rhyw gyfrwng cyffredin o'r fath hyn, buan iawn yr â yr hyn a elwir Cymraeg, mor aniben a chlytiog ag yw'r Saesneg a'r Ffrangaeg, ac yn anheilwng o arddeliad; yn awr y mae cryn wahaniaeth mewn siarad, nid yn unig rhwng y bobl yn gyffredin, ymhob sîr, ond rhwng athrawon ac ysgrifenwyr, a'r argraff-wasc wedi ei darostwng i fympwy dynion o wahanol feddyliau a thueddiadau; ac er fod y rhan fwyaf yn galw am iaith ysgrythurol, gan dybied y medrant ddeall eu Beiblau, ond hawdd profi fod llawer o eiriau yn cael eu harferyd mewn gwahanol barthau o'r Dywysogaeth mewn ystyr llwyr wahanol i'r hwn y defnyddir hwy yn y llyfr sanctaidd.[25]

---

[23] John Rhys and David Brynmor-Jones, *The Welsh People* (London, 1900), p. 510, and *DWB*, p. 500, s.v. Owen Jones (Meudwy Môn, 1806–89): 'His prosiness and proxility are typical of the pompous Anglicized style of the 19th cent. at its worst.' Sixty-five years earlier, Ieuan Gryg had criticized the poor standard of written Welsh in *Y Cenhadydd*, 15 August 1841.

[24] *Seren Gomer*, 28 January 1818.

[25] Ibid.

(Unless some common medium such as this is sustained, what is called the Welsh language will soon become as chaotic and inconsistent as English and French, and unworthy to be championed; there are now considerable variations in language not only between ordinary people, in all counties, but between teachers and writers, and the press is subject to the whim of men of diverse notions and tendencies; and although the majority call for a scriptural language, believing that they can understand their Bibles, it can be easily proven that many words used in various parts of the Principality are employed in a totally different sense from that in the holy book.)

By the same token, good newspaper journalism in Welsh was intended to improve the general level of education of the Welsh people as a whole, thereby ensuring that the Welsh would no longer be considered to be inferior in knowledge or ability to their English neighbours: 'Also, it is painful to think that the Welshman is deprived of the means of knowledge, thereby appearing to be a foolish creature besides the Englishman, who is in the same material circumstances as himself' ('Hefyd, tost yw meddwl fod Cymro yn amddifad o foddion gwybodaeth, a thrwy hyny yn ymddangos fel creadur wedi ei hurtio, yn ymyl Sais, a fyddo yn yr un sefyllfa fydol ag yntef').[26] This opening declaration of intent, which ushered in the second series of *Seren Gomer* in 1818, could in some respects be regarded as a manifesto for the Welsh press. From that formative point onwards it could be argued that all Welsh-language journalism professed a dual purpose. While all newspapers sought to inform, educate and entertain their readers, Welsh-language titles were also, implicitly or explicitly, engaged in a cultural mission to preserve, improve and extend the Welsh language.[27] This more specific linguistic and cultural dimension added urgency to their task, and gave them an importance (including, no doubt, a self-importance) far beyond that which may be suggested by their circulation figures or their profit margins. Of course, this is not to say that all newspapers were always able to live up to the exacting standards of *Seren Gomer*, but several of them deliberately sought to use their influence to help 'purify' the language. Samuel Evans, editor of *Seren Cymru*, for example, made a concerted effort to address the issues raised by the Revd Daniel Silvan Evans in a paper on improving the Welsh language read at the Porthmadog Eisteddfod of October 1851. Silvan Evans, an Anglican minister who, in 1875, became Professor of Welsh at the new University College at Aberystwyth, had advocated the urgent need to produce a more uniform orthography for the language, and called for extensive consultation with writers and critics throughout Wales to establish the agreed ground rules for such an enterprise. By devoting column space in *Seren Cymru*, Samuel Evans not only

[26] Ibid.
[27] I am indebted to Mr Dylan Iorwerth for persuading me of the longer-term significance of the matters raised by the opening address of *Seren Gomer* in 1818.

provided a forum where that nationwide discussion could easily and effectively take place, but he also took a leading role in defining the terms of the argument. He explained his mission in a leading article published in October 1851:

> Eisteddfod Porthmadog a'r Iaith Gymraeg
>
> Nid ydym ni . . . yn barnu fod yn analluadwy cael yr Iaith, o ran ei sillebiaeth, beth bynag, i ryw radd o unffurfiaeth . . . Er mwyn cyflawni hyn, yr ydym yn awr yn hysbysu y bydd i ni gyhoeddi rhes o Draethodau ar Iawn-lythreniaeth y Gymraeg . . . yn y rhai yr egluw ein barn yn gyflawn ar y pwnc, ac ymdrechwn beidio gosod dim gerbron heb ei fod yn sylfaenedig ar ansawdd a theithi yr Iaith; ac hefyd byddwn yn gwahodd pawb a ewyllysiont, i ddyfod yn mlaen i wneyd sylwadau ar y Traethodau hyny, os byddant yn anghytuno a'u hegwyddorion a'u cynnwysiad; ond gan y byddwn ni yn ysgrifenydd adnabyddus, byddwn yn dysgwyl i bawb ereill ysgrifenu yn eu henwau priodol, er mwyn cadw o fewn terfynau boneddigeiddrwydd a 'chymmydogaeth dda'. Trwy y mesur hwn, bydd i'r pwnc gael ei egluro yn drwyadl, a bydd holl Lenorion Cymru yn deall meddyliau eu gilydd . . .[28]
>
> (Porthmadog Eisteddfod and the Welsh Language
>
> We do not . . . judge it impossible to secure for the Language, with regard to its spelling at least, a certain level of uniformity . . . In order to achieve this, we are now advising that we will be publishing a series of Essays on the Correct Spelling of Welsh . . . in which we will express our opinion in full on the subject, and we will endeavour not to set forth anything which is not based on the quality and traits of the language; and we will also invite anyone who so wishes to make observations on these Essays, if they disagree with their principles and content; but since our identity is well-known, we will expect everyone else to write under their own names, to ensure we stay within the bounds of politeness and 'good neighbourliness'. In this way, the subject will be scrupulously clarified, and every Writer in Wales will understand each other's thoughts . . .)

The editor, however, took issue with Silvan Evans on one important matter. Where the Eisteddfod had called for a conference both of writers (of prose and poetry) and of critics to resolve the many difficulties involved in standardizing written Welsh, *Seren Cymru* insisted that a third, equally adept, if largely hidden, section of the Welsh literary world should also be actively involved in this process, namely the printers. While writers and critics contradicted each other on matters of literary style, Samuel Evans demurred, it was often the typesetters who had the clearest notions of how to spell and to punctuate:

> Gwyddom am rai Cyssodwyr yn Nghymru ag sydd yn deall y pwnc yn lled dda; a gwr Awdwyr hefyd, ei bod yn arferiad cyffredinol ganddynt i 'adael y sillebiaeth a'r

---

[28] *Seren Cymru*, 30 October 1851.

attalnodau i ofal y rhai hynny,' a chyfaddefa llawer, yn ddigon rhwydd a gonest, 'nad ydynt hwy yn deall dim ar y pynciau hyny'.[29]

(We know of some Compositors in Wales who understand the subject fairly well; and Authors know this too, it being common practice amongst them to 'leave the spelling and punctuation in their hands', and many admit, freely and honestly, that 'they understand nothing of these matters'.)

It was a nicely judged reminder to the literary lights of the time that much of the quality of their work, let alone its readability, was ensured as much by its means of transmission as by their creative talents, that is to say, by the indispensable but poorly appreciated efforts of the printers and editors of books, journals and newspapers. These columns on the standardization of Welsh ('Llythyriaeth yr Iaith Gymraeg') ran regularly in *Seren Cymru* until 13 May 1852. Most, if not all, were probably written by Daniel Silvan Evans himself, who, in 1856, brought out a book of the same title. Two years later, as editor of *Y Brython* in Tremadog, he printed a fresh series of articles on the grammar, history and culture of Welsh in regular columns like 'Llên y Werin', 'Ieithyddiaeth' and 'Yr Iaith Gymraeg'.[30] It is also worth noting at this point that many Welsh-language newspaper editors and publishers strongly advocated that their readers should learn to speak and to become literate in English. David Owen (Brutus), editor of *Yr Haul* between 1835 and his death in 1865, argued consistently in favour of the extension of a knowledge of English in Wales, while by the late 1870s Thomas Gee, publisher of *Baner ac Amserau Cymru*, had provided a number of practical means whereby this end might be achieved by producing five Welsh–English dictionaries and two popular guides to learning English.[31]

Educational articles and publications of this kind were intended to be widely read both by established writers and those who had little experience of writing for the press. It is difficult to say whether or not they stimulated readers to become writers, but there can be little doubt that the existence of locally-based cheap newspapers, whose editors positively encouraged reader participation, enabled some readers to venture into print. They did so mainly in two ways, by writing letters to the editor and by offering songs and poems for publication. In both respects, newspapers in particular generated a lively culture of popular writing in many parts of Wales. As one might expect, readers' letters covered a vast array of subject matter, parochial and foreign, political and literary. Some editors printed brief replies to unprinted letters, while others devoted entire pages to the musings of their readers. For editors, these columns may have been regarded at best as generators of sale-inducing

[29] Ibid.
[30] *Y Brython*, 25 June 1858, 2 July 1858.
[31] See *A Catalogue of Works, Printed and Published by Thomas Gee, Denbigh, Sept 1878*; John Ceiriog Hughes, *Oriau'r Bore: Llyfr II* (Wrexham, [1862]), p. 9.

controversy and, at worst, as cheap space-fillers, but for readers they were of interest principally for two reasons: they provided an indication of individual and, in certain circumstances, of collective opinion at particular times, and they contained, often inadvertently, valuable items of news which would otherwise not have been recorded. The following example from the Merthyr weekly, *Y Fellten*, for May 1874 amply illustrates the extent to which some letters met both of these criteria:

> Mr Gol., – Yr ydym ninau bellach fel Alcanwyr Ystalyfera, wedi ein taflu i ben ein ffyrdd, ac ni wyddom am ba achos; am hyny penodwyd tri o ddynion cymhwys i siarad â'r meistr ar y mater, a chafwyd yn hysbys mai yr achos oedd, 'am ein bod yn Undebwyr'; ond yr ydym eisoes wedi canfod gormod gwerth mewn Undeb i'w gollwng o'n gafael, a bydded i ni, frodyr anwyl, gadw ein Hundeb i fyny, nes cael holl drais a gormes Ystalyfera, yn gydwastad â chyfiawnder.[32]

> (Mr Editor, – We now, like the Alcam Workers of Ystalyfera, have been thrown out of work, and we do not know why; as a result we appointed three competent men to speak to the master concerning the matter, and we were informed that the reason was, 'because we are Union men'; but we have already discovered the Union to be too valuable to be given up, and let us, dear brothers, continue with the Union, until all the violence and oppression of Ystalyfera is replaced with justice.)

These powerful opening sentences were followed by a detailed account of a tinplate workers' march and rally, where speakers addressed the crowds in both languages against an employers' lockout. It simultaneously constitutes a news story, an advocacy of the rights of trade unionism, and an appeal for popular support based on the shared moral imperatives of fairness and justice. As a voluntary form of writing, the reader's letter reflects the writer's sensitivity to the importance of printed as well as oral communication. Thriving newspaper poetry columns also bear testimony to the voluntary ethos. In some, the newspaper became a subject of poetic writing as well as a convenient and relatively easily secured location for its publication. R. Ellis of Sirhywi, for example, welcomed the first issue of *Seren Cymru* with the following verse:

> Yn lle cawl heb ddim lliwcig,
> A maidd glas meddw-eglwysig,
> A glasdwr hen eglwysdai,
> Cawn drylwyr synwyr a sai',
> Cawn hoff rym ac yni ffraeth,
> I'n harwain mewn llenoriaeth.
> 'SEREN CYMRU' gy ei gwawr,
> A lona bob rhyw lenawr.[33]

---

[32] *Y Fellten*, 8 May 1874.
[33] *Seren Cymru*, 13 August 1851.

(Instead of meatless soup,
And servile church whey,
And the watery milk of the old churches,
We will have sound sense which stands,
We will have admirable strength and eloquent energy,
To lead us in learning.
'SEREN CYMRU' precious its dawn,
Will please scholars of all kinds.)

Ellis's manifest disapproval of a vapid Anglicanism may be no more than religious sectarianism conducted by other means, but as a composition it does not lack literary skill. Surprisingly, the appearance of new English-language titles was also on occasion effusively greeted in Welsh verse. An early issue of the *Merthyr Telegraph*, for example, included in its 'Gongl Gymreig' the following *englyn* by John Garnon (Ieuan Ferddig):

Englynion i'r *Telegraph*

E fyr noda ei feirniadaeth – hawliau,
    Ac helynt dynoliaeth;
Cawn yn ei gol, fuddiol faeth,
    Oludog adeiladaeth.[34]

(*Englynion* to the *Telegraph*

It concisely records its appraisal – of the rights,
    And affairs of mankind;
In its lap, beneficial nourishment, we have
    A prosperous edifice.)

What is striking here is not that the two newspapers are greeted in remarkably similar terms, but that the non-denominational and English-language *Merthyr Telegraph* is welcomed, in Welsh, with the same degree of enthusiasm as the strongly Nonconformist, Welsh-language *Seren Cymru*. In this bilingual culture,[35] where literate Welsh speakers could scan English-language newspapers as readily as ones in the Welsh language, poetry in newspapers of both languages contributed to what may be described as a weekly printed eisteddfod, the prize for the successful poet being publication and the ensuing recognition, whether in local circles or in a national competitive arena. But poetry columns may also be read in

---

[34] *Merthyr Telegraph*, 23 January 1858.
[35] During his short stay in Merthyr Tydfil in November 1854, George Borrow gained the impression that 'Welsh is the language generally spoken, though all have some knowledge of English', Borrow, *Wild Wales*, p. 505.

other ways as documents of social tension and individual aspiration. In 1873 a Birchgrove coal miner recalled in verse in the bilingual Merthyr weekly, *Amdiffynydd y Gweithiwr / The Workman's Advocate*, the oppressive conditions of his childhood in rural Glamorgan:

> Yr wy'n cofio Llansamlet, hen gartrau fy nhad,
> Y bechgyn yn wilo, a'u trade yn llawn gwad,
> A'r dramwyr yn dramo, gwaith ceffyl yn wir,
> A'r meistri yn marchog dros wyneb y tir.[36]

> (I recall Llansamlet, my father's old carts,
> The lads wheeling, their feet bleeding,
> The tramsmen loading the trams, really horses' work,
> And the masters riding over the land.)

There is little trace of pastoral romanticism in the image of rural Welsh life projected by this collier writing for an industrial readership in an urban newspaper. Less affected by the conventions of 'high' literature, this more direct vernacular writing articulated the pride and the anxieties of a newly industrialized class. Other verses printed in the same publication speak of the dilemmas of the migrant worker and of the ambivalence which industrial workers felt towards their own country folk, inhabitants of the same rural areas in the west where so many of them had originated. One, appropriately written to be sung to the tune of 'Y mochyn du' (The black pig), suggests something of the contempt which newly-unionized workers in Merthyr in 1874 felt towards those recent migrants from the west who were prepared to work longer hours for less pay, thereby undermining the craft solidarity of the Welsh-speaking industrial working class:

> Deffro f'awen, seinia ganiad
> 'Nawr yn beraidd i'r Tinceriad,
> Sydd yn ceisio galw'u hunain
> Yn Alcanwyr Ynys Prydain.

> Cytgan: Gwŷr gwaith mawr sydd yn awr
> Gwŷr gwaith mawr sydd yn awr
> Yn dystymio crefft Alcanwyr
> Trwy holl Gymru lan a lawr.

> Dic y Porthmon o Sir Benfro,
> A Wil Shibwns, sydd yn brago
> Gallant weithio am dair wythnos
> Heb gael hanner awr o orphwys.

[36] *Amddiffynydd y Gweithiwr*, 11 October 1873.

Cytgan: etc.

Gwelir Shoni Goch y Cardi
A'i holl nerth yn gollwng ati,
Yn llawn chwys a *snobs* yn aflan,
Fel hen hwch ym Mhwll y Domen.

Cytgan: etc.[37]

(Awake my muse, sing a song
Sweetly now to the Tinkers,
Who are trying to call themselves
The Alcam Workers of the British Isles.

> Chorus: The men of great labour are now
> The men of great labour are now
> Degrading the Alcam Workers' craft
> Throughout the whole of Wales.

Dic the Drover from Pembrokeshire,
And Wil Onions, are bragging
They can work for three weeks
Without half an hour's rest.

Chorus: etc.

Red Shoni from Cardiganshire is seen
Labouring with all his strength,
Sweating profusely and grimy,
Like an old sow in Pwll y Domen.

Chorus: etc.)

The force and immediacy of the values expressed here are noteworthy only in so far as they are directed not against the Irish or other immigrant groups, but against the Welsh themselves. Linked to an older tradition of the broadside and the ballad, they also provide modern readers with a glimpse into another, altogether more raucous and dangerous Wales, a mid-Victorian Welsh-speaking Wales of protest and the tavern eisteddfod, a world in which until relatively recently the horned bull had put in an occasional appearance in the theatre of industrial conflict.[38] Even in the age of Henry Richard, who won Merthyr for the Liberals

---

[37] Ibid., 28 November 1874.
[38] Report on threatening letters signed by 'Horned Bull' to strike-breakers, *Merthyr Telegraph*, 23 January 1858.

in 1868, this Merthyr newspaper continued to provide a platform for sentiments shunned by Liberal leaders and chapel society.[39]

Some sceptics believed that there was a trace of that other Wales in the growing popularity of the Welsh novel, which was encouraged by the monthly periodicals and thereafter by the weekly newspapers. Like news reporting, and unlike poetry, fiction did not have deep roots in the culture. In fact, fiction and news writing emerged at almost exactly the same time: the latter following the repeal in 1855 of the Stamp Duty on newsprint, the former as a consequence of the Merthyr Temperance Eisteddfod of Christmas 1854, which offered a prize for a novel in Welsh on 'the reformed drunk as hero'. Three of the six entries were published in book form during the following year. Another landmark, which whetted the Welsh appetite for fiction, was the publication in 1852 of Harriet Beecher Stowe's *Uncle Tom's Cabin*. Hugely popular, copiously illustrated and, thanks to the absence of a copyright agreement between Britain and the United States, relatively cheap (the first edition sold for three shillings and sixpence), Beecher Stowe's novel had led William Rees to write his own anti-slavery version of it, *Aelwyd F'Ewythr Robert*, which was completed, astonishingly, in 1853 and published by Thomas Gee in Denbigh in the same year. The popularity of the novel was further demonstrated by the decision by Rees to begin the serialization of his new novel, *Cyfrinach yr Aelwyd* in *Y Dysgedydd* in 1856. Brutus followed with the publication, again in serial form, of his own *Wil Brydydd y Coed* in *Yr Haul* between September 1863 and December 1865. Roger Edwards (*Y Tri Brawd a'u Teuluoedd* in *Y Drysorfa* in 1866–7) and William Rees (*Helyntion Bywyd Hen Deiliwr* in *Y Tyst* in 1867) continued to write fiction for their own journals before Daniel Owen began to serialize his dramatic novel, *Profedigaethau Enoc Huws*, in *Y Cymro* in 1890.[40] Daniel Owen's serials introduced a new raciness into Welsh fiction, which was much admired by readers but strongly suspected by sections of the Nonconformist establishment. In this sense, newspaper editors were transitional figures who helped to legitimate fiction and to integrate such new cultural forms as the novel into the mainstream of accepted literature. However, as Saunders Lewis pointed out, the nineteenth-century Welsh novel was in fact heavily indebted to the hagiographical tradition of Welsh Nonconformist biographical writing,[41] and the improving nature of so much nineteenth-century fiction in Welsh belies Nonconformist concern about its potential to undermine

---

[39] For a fuller discussion of labour, Liberalism and religion in Welsh society at this time, see Ieuan Gwynedd Jones, *Communities: Essays in the Social History of Victorian Wales* (Llandysul, 1987), and idem, *Explorations and Explanations: Essays in the Social History of Victorian Wales* (Llandysul, 1981).

[40] R. Hughes Williams, 'Y Nofel yng Nghymru', *Y Traethodydd*, LXIV (1909), 121; Dafydd Jenkins, 'Y Nofel Gymraeg Gynnar' in William Rees (Gwilym Hiraethog), *Helyntion Bywyd Hen Deiliwr* (Aberystwyth, 1940), pp. xi–xxxii.

[41] Saunders Lewis, 'Y Cofiant Cymraeg', *THSC* (1933–5), 157.

moral values. Indeed, Mrs Harris, a character in William Rees's *Aelwyd F'Ewythr Robert*, pleaded for more Welsh fiction precisely on these moral grounds:

> Mi fum i'n meddwl lawer gwaith . . . bod arno ni eisieu cael mwy o lyfre fel '*Caban F'Ewythr Tomos*' yn Gymraeg, i ddenu pobol i ddarllen llyfrau fyddo'n cymysgu difyrwch âg adeiladaeth, i loni a dysgu y meddwl ar yr un pryd. Y mae llyfrau o'r fath hono yn bethau lled ddyeithr i ni, yn ein iaith ein hunain. Gallent wneyd lles dirfawr i ddiddyfnu dynion ieuainc, a hen hefyd, oddiwrth yr hen arferion ffiaidd o fyn'd at eu gilydd i'r tafarnau i ymgyfedda a diota – pethau sy'n dinystrio iechyd, ac amgylchiadau, moesau, ac eneidiau dynion.[42]

> (I have often thought . . . that we need more books like '*Caban F'Ewythr Tomos*' in Welsh, to encourage people to read books which are both entertaining and instructive, to cheer and educate the mind at the same time. Such books are fairly unfamiliar to us, in our own language. They could be of great benefit in weaning young men, and old ones also, away from the loathsome habit of congregating together in taverns to feast and drink – a practice which undermines the health, and the circumstances, morals and souls of men.)

By providing new outlets for such story writers as Beriah Gwynfe Evans, in addition to printing translations of English-language serial novels supplied by such agencies as Tillotson's of Bolton,[43] Welsh newspapers helped both to create and to satisfy a public demand for popular fiction. It is less certain whether by so doing, as William Rees's Mrs Harris had so earnestly hoped, they also contributed to a deeper process of social stabilization.

A related genre, which acquired a degree of popularity in newspapers between the 1840s and the 1870s, involved writing in dialect. While dialect words and phrases may occasionally be found in readers' letters, editors themselves appear to have been its most adept producers. Often generated as a marketing tool to advertise and perhaps also to popularize the paper, dialect prose, however, raises difficult questions about the editor's motivation and the intended effects of the writing on the readership. The best known instance of dialect writing in newspapers is the 'Llythurau 'Rhen Ffarmwr' series written by William Rees in *Yr Amserau*. First appearing under the byline 'Yr Hen Roland' in December 1846, ''Rhen Ffarmwr' expressed forthright opinions in the language of north-east Wales. His first 'letter' described his attachment to the paper, and his belief that readers of little or no formal education might still have something of value to communicate to a wider public:

---

[42] William Rees, *Aelwyd F'Ewythr Robert* (Dinbych, 1853), p. 167.
[43] For syndicated fiction in newspapers, see A. G. Jones, 'Tillotson's Fiction Bureau: The Manchester Manuscripts', *Victorian Periodicals Review*, XVII, nos. 1–2 (1984), 43–8.

Syr, – Mi rydw i wedi derbyn a darllen yr *Amsere* er pan ddoeth o allan gynta hyd y rwan; ac wedi cael pleser garw iawn wrth i ddarllen o; mi rydw i o'r farn mai papur da o'i hwyl ydi o, ac y mae arna'i ofn direswm iddo beidio dwad allan.

Mi ddaru i mi feddwl ganweth am syfenu rhwbeth i'w roid ynddo fo; ond yr oedd arna'i ofn na 'naech chi mo'i roi o i fewn, am nad ydw i yn ddigon o slaig i syfenu yn ramadegol, fel y byddwch chi, y sleigion mawr yma, yn gneud: ond yr ydw i'n meddwl fod llawer hen wladwr plaen fel fi a fy ffasiwn yn meddu llawn cystal sens a chithe a'ch ffasiwn, ond bod chi hwrach yn medru deyd ych meddwl yn dipyn mwy taclus na mi.[44]

(Sir, – I have received and read *Yr Amserau* since it first came out till now; and have had much pleasure from reading it; I'm of the opinion that it's a paper of good spirit, and I have an unreasoning fear that it will stop coming out.

I have thought a hundred times about writing something to put in it; but I was afraid that you wouldn't put it in, because I'm not enough of a scholar to write grammatically, as you great scholars can: but I think that many plain old countrymen such as myself and my kind have just as much sense as you and your kind, except that you perhaps are able to express yourselves much more neatly than me.)

The use of dialect is problematic in the light of the efforts that were soon to be made by some newspaper editors to standardize the written language, but it is perhaps also a recognition of the possibility that newspaper text at this time was read aloud to family or friends, as well as contemplated in silence. In the hands of William Rees, it may also have been a point of contact between 'high' literary culture and a more popular taste, and evidence suggests that the circulation of *Yr Amserau* did increase following the serialization of the fictitious letters. While dialect may have been easier to read, particularly when vocalized, than what then passed for 'standard' text, it is hard to imagine that it was any easier to write. Requiring a ear finely-tuned not only to the rhythms and idioms of local speech, but also, on occasion, to other Welsh accents, it was a style that was ever in danger of slipping into the patronizing or the farcical. Effective dialect writing, like good comedy, had serious purposes. In 1858, before the great migrations from the north to the coalfields of the south had begun, Samuel Evans in Carmarthen nonetheless brought together the accents of north and south-west Wales in his weekly dialect column, 'Cynnadledd y Cryddion' (the Shoemakers' Conference) in *Seren Cymru*. Set in the workshop of the imaginary shoemaker Morgan Jones, 'a kind of *newsroom* and *lecture theatre* for the people of the village and the district',[45] where men and women congregated to read copies of *Seren Cymru*, *Y Gwron*, *Yr Amserau* 'and a few other English papers',[46] the fictitious reports sought to persuade their

---

[44] *Yr Amserau*, 3 December 1846. Rees was less successful in transliterating Beecher Stowe's representation of Afro-American dialect into Welsh: see, for example, *Aelwyd F'Ewythr Robert*, p. 34.

[45] *Seren Cymru*, 3 October 1857. The character of Morgan Jones may have been based on William Morgan Evans, printer, publisher and owner of *Seren Cymru*.

[46] Ibid., 13 June 1857. The first 'Cynnadledd y Cryddion' column appeared on this date.

readers to look out from their villages and, through the medium of the newspaper press, to embrace the world. In this fragment, Hugh Roberts, a young migrant from Merioneth, attempts to induce Catws, the sceptical wife of one of the workshop regulars, to buy and read *Seren Cymru*:

> *Hugh Roberts.* – Wel, Catws, beth yda chi yn feddwl o'r byd 'ma rwan? Yr ydach chi wedi darllen yn y *Times,* neu rw bapyr arall, 'ddyliwn, fod 'Mherawdwr Ffrainc a 'Mherawdwr Rwsia wedi cwrdd yn Germani, ac fod rhyw bwys politicaidd yn eu cyfarfyddiad; beth 'ddyliech chi, Catws, fydd y canlyniad?
> *Catws.* – Beth yw yr ots gen i am yr hen dacle 'ny? Ac w'i yn meddwl dof 'da tithe reitach gwaith i 'neyd nâ boddran 'da'r hen bapyre newy' 'ma o hyd . . .
>
> (*Hugh Roberts.* – Well, Catws, what do you think of the world then? You've read in the *Times*, or some other paper, I suppose, that the Emperor of France has met the Emperor of Russia in Germany, and that their meeting has some political importance; what do you think will come of it, Catws?
> *Catws.* – What do I care about those rascals? And I would have thought that you had better things to do than bother with those old newspapers . . .)

Notwithstanding the contrasting pronunciation, speech rhythms and vocabularies of north-west and south-west Welsh, the reader is led to believe that Hugh and Catws understand each other perfectly. Although Catws eventually relents under the force of argument and promises to allow her husband to buy the paper each week with housekeeping money, the shoemaker himself then expresses some misgivings about the low standards of some of the journalism he had read in the past:

> *Morgan Jones.* – Beth sy' gyda fi yn erbyn y cyhoeddiade a'r newspapyrs yma yw, 'u bod nw yn diffio'u gilydd yn shompol, ac yn hala dyn'on drwg i wherthin am ben crefyddwyrs; ond w'i yn meddwl 'u bod nw 'nawr yn well nâ buo nw . . .
>
> (*Morgan Jones.* – What I've got against these publications and newspapers is that they're always abusing each other, and giving evil men the chance to laugh at religious people; but I think they're better now than they were . . .)

In the midst of these Carmarthenshire accents, the north Walian returns and, though with a sharply different voice, underlines the same appeal for more readers to buy copies of *Seren Cymru*:

> *Hugh Roberts.* – Dyda ni yng Nghymru ran ddim gystal â'r 'Mericanied efo'r darllen 'ma; yr own i yn darllen 'stalwm fod gweithiwrs mewn rhai llefydd yn y 'Merica, yn agos bod y gun yn derbyn y *daily papers*. Ma' llawer o genedlo'dd o'n bla'n ni yn y peth hwn. 'Ddyliwn i y b'ase yn dda i wragedd Cymru ddysgu gwers efo gwragedd 'Merica,

a gwledydd er'ill. Ma' mwy o ddarllen yn y Gogledd nag yn y South. Dyna yr 'Herald Cymreig', ma' o ddeuddeg i bymtheg mil o hono fo yn ca'l 'u hargraffu bob wsnos; a pam na alle chi yn y South yma godi *circulation* SEREN CYMRU i bump neu chwech mil rwan?[47]

(*Hugh Roberts*. – We in Wales aren't as good as the Americans when it comes to reading; I read some time ago that workers in some places in America nearly all read the daily papers. Many nations are ahead of us in this respect. I reckon it would be a good thing for Welsh women to follow the example of women in America and other countries. There's more reading in the North than the South. Take the 'Herald Cymreig', about twelve to fifteen thousand copies of it are printed every week; so why can't you here in the South now raise the circulation of SEREN CYMRU to five or six thousand?)

It is difficult to judge the extent to which printed representations of everyday speech, including the use of borrowed words, familiarized readers with the regional varieties of Welsh or raised the status of the spoken language in relation to the literary form. What can be conjectured, however, is that by printing verses and prose in dialect regularly over extended periods of time, newspapers succeeded in expanding the possibilities of written Welsh.

Newspapers also extended the range of Welsh in one other important but hitherto largely neglected respect. By developing Welsh forms in its advertising, the weekly press enabled the language to enter, if not into the world of commerce, then certainly into the sphere of mass consumerism. Here, Welsh was imaginatively stretched and coerced into new and unfamiliar forms. In English-language newspapers, Welsh was intended to have a mystical appeal, and advertisements for 'Owain Glyndwr wines and spirits' and 'Cymro Wafers' (a 'safe and speedy cure for all affections connected with the Lungs or Breath') appeared in such weeklies as the *Merthyr Telegraph* in February 1858.[48] By 1880 *Baner ac Amserau Cymru* was advertising a wide range of domestic consumer goods and medicines in Welsh, including 'Coffi Dant y Llew Wm. Schweitzer', 'Y gwaedburydd Enwog. Pelennau Burdock Thompson', 'Swyn Belenau Peswch Beecham', 'Enaint Holloway' and 'Gwaed-gymmysgedd Bydenwog Clarke's, meddygyniaeth rhag y dropsi'. Its 'situations vacant' columns also advertised in Welsh ('Yn Eisieu, mewn Factory, Nyddwr, cyfarwydd â gwaith gwlad. Cyfle da i ddyn ieuangc sobr a pharchus . . .').[49] This was the language of an incipient Welsh commercial capitalism, reflecting the underlying reality that newspapers themselves were small businesses whose fortunes were heavily reliant on the abilities of other small businesses to establish a profitable consumer base among Welsh-speaking newspaper readers. Newspaper prospectuses, which sought to

---

[47] Ibid., 3 October 1857.
[48] *Merthyr Telegraph*, 20 February 1858.
[49] *BAC*, 21 July 1880.

attract financial support for new journalistic ventures, were also often printed in Welsh precisely in order to address potential investors in their own language.

These, and other related uses of Welsh in nineteenth-century journalism, challenge the view expressed in *The Times* in 1880 that Welsh was 'a language confined very much . . . to ordinary conversation, newspapers and periodical writing', and one which was 'not a mercantile language, and . . . deficient in all educational and technical terms'.[50] The point missed by *The Times* was that it was precisely in the popular press that these 'deficiencies' were chiefly being addressed, and where the public uses of the language were being extended into the new and 'modern' domains of news writing, fiction, education and commerce. Nevertheless, external perceptions of Welsh were important, and once again the newspaper press was among the most visible manifestations of its existence and its condition. The Revd William Binns, in an address to the Blackpool Literary and Scientific Society in November 1898, correctly noted that English was not the sole language of the British Isles and regretted that Welsh continued to be spoken as a 'mere survival' by 'what we may call aborigines . . . or partly undeveloped members of the complex national mechanism'. In time, or, in Binns' own social Darwinian phrase, 'in the process of evolution', he assured his audience that the Welsh would 'drop their peculiarities, and will be absorbed, to their own advantage, into the one body, with many members, of the English-speaking people who occupy Great Britain, Ireland, Canada, Australia, New Zealand, South Africa, islands in many seas, and settlements on many coasts [who] all . . . acknowledge in various degrees the supremacy of the Imperial Government'.[51] The extension of the English language, in Binns' view, was the only true indication of a people's loyalty to the British Empire. His was an argument, taken to an extreme if logical conclusion, against the modernization or, other than as an arcane academic specialism, even the continued existence of Welsh, a view which was widely shared by his contemporaries. Significantly, however, it was not a view shared by all. The editor and newspaper historian Alexander Andrews approached the question of the Welsh language in a radically different way, forming his judgement almost entirely on what he knew of the growth and social status of Welsh-language journalism. Alluding to *The Times*'s criticism of Welsh 'as the curse of Wales',[52] Andrews conceded that:

> the preservation and perpetuation of a native tongue may stand in the way of an entire amalgamation and thorough effacing of all distinctive features between the ruling and the dependent race; but it certainly elevates the latter, and puts it upon more equal, and therefore more contented, terms with the dominant and ruling race . . . The periodical

[50] Quoted in the *Cambrian News*, 23 January 1880.
[51] Lancashire Record Office, Preston, uncatalogued address by the Revd William Binns to the Blackpool Literary and Scientific Society, 17 November 1898.
[52] *The Times*, 8 September 1866.

press is a far more efficient engine in maintaining the last remnant of a people's pride and rights than any other; and, in the principality of Wales . . . we find it stoutly holding its ground; yet does it cause any trouble to us – does it nurture plots or foment disorder? In Ireland there is no vernacular press, and what does England gain by Ireland's loss in this respect?'[53]

Andrews's notion of the Empire as a union governed by an acknowledgement of cultural difference may posit an alternative model of dependence, one in which the press performs a functionalist role by ensuring political cohesion through social control, but at least it was one which recognized both the centrality and the legitimacy of the part played by the Welsh-language newspapers in maintaining and extending a people's 'pride and rights'. The newspaper press gave Welsh a public platform, one that could be seen within and outside Wales, by Welsh and non-Welsh speakers. It stimulated interest in the language and its forms, while encouraging its readers to become equally fluent and literate in English. Most importantly, newspapers enabled the language to be read, regularly and in large quantities, by an unquantifiable but undeniably sizeable number of people, thereby ensuring the continuation of Welsh as a popular literate language. For all its financial disadvantages and its sectarian divisions, the newspaper press projected Welsh into the public domain in an unmistakably dynamic and modern form. By staring at the unintelligible printed marks on a page of an open newspaper, Borrow's illiterate waggoner had shown that he had, after all, understood the signs of the times.

---

[53] *The Newspaper Press*, 1 August 1867, 163.

14

The Welsh Language in Technology and Science 1800–1914

R. ELWYN HUGHES

THE TITLE of this chapter is anachronistic since this categorization of knowledge belongs to the twentieth century. Two centuries ago and, indeed, down to the end of the nineteenth century, such classification was not important. In the Humphreys Catalogue published in Caernarfon in 1880, books which today would be classed as scientific and technical were listed as 'Educational and Miscellaneous'. This chapter will therefore examine the use of Welsh for the discussion of subjects which would fall today into the categories of 'science' or 'technology'. The most appropriate term would probably be 'applied Welsh'.

The beginning of the nineteenth century was characterized by a striking increase in the number of scientific and technological activities in the Welsh language – both orally, and perhaps even more importantly, through the written word. To a large extent these initiatives reflected the English pattern, although they had specifically Welsh features. This progress can be discussed from two perspectives – the motives which were responsible for it, and the way in which it manifested itself. It is possible to discuss the motives, in turn, under three heads: firstly, the material (mainly books) which were produced for didactic or training purposes; secondly, the endeavour to disseminate general information about scientific matters (mainly by means of articles in journals and lectures) but with no thought to their usefulness or practical benefit; and thirdly, discussion of scientific subjects through the medium of Welsh for ideological reasons, such as the corroboration of current religious beliefs or (most curiously) the conviction that to read more about science in Welsh would encourage the reader to become familiar with the English language.[1]

---

[1] In June 1850 Lord Powis, presiding over a meeting of the Society for the Diffusion of Useful Knowledge in Wales, described the kind of Welsh-language material the new society should provide, namely works dealing with farming, cookery, manufacturing techniques and machinery. The previous year, however, John Jones, one of the founders of the Society, had stated 'that to raise the intellectual character of the Welsh people by means of their own language . . . prepares them for the acquisition of English . . .' See A. L. Trott, 'The Society for the Diffusion of Useful Knowledge in Wales 1848–1851', *NLWJ*, XI, no. 1 (1959), 33–75.

Table 1. Classification of 'scientific' books in Welsh published between 1800 and 1920[1]

Subject	Number of books
Agriculture	44
Botany, Herbals	16
Chemistry, Physics	12
Cookery, Domestic Science	20
Geology, Geography	35
Gardening	18
Technical handbooks (e.g. mining)	11
Medicine	79
Veterinary Science	21
Mathematics	22
Natural Sciences	13
Astronomy	14
Others (History, General Science etc.)	25
Total	**330**

[1] The table is based on Owain Owain and Iolo Wyn Williams, 'Llyfrau Gwyddonol Cymraeg: Rhan II – Llyfrau cyn 1940', appendix to *Y Gwyddonydd*, XIII (1975), i–x, with additions by the author. See also R. Elwyn Hughes, *Llyfrau Ymarferol Echdoe. Llyfryddiaeth gydag Anodiadau* (Pen-tyrch, 1998).

Let us first consider the training manuals, which formed the most important category by far. During the period under review, agriculture, horticulture and veterinary medicine, taken together, accounted for more than a quarter of all the Welsh scientific books published, and medical and quasi-medical books made up a similar proportion.

The medical and quasi-medical books were probably the most interesting of the technical publications. One of the characteristics of the medical world was a strong element of professional jealousy and an unwillingness to reveal its 'secrets' to the lay mind. The distinction between qualified doctors and others (such as bone-setters) was more marked than among, say, veterinary surgeons. The result was that although a substantial number of medical and quasi-medical books appeared during the course of the century, most of them were of a popular nature and intended for use in the home. This was the field which corresponded to what was described in English as 'domestic medicine'; indeed, two of the most notable examples of this genre were translated into Welsh – William Buchan's *Domestic Medicine*, of which more than twenty editions were published in English between 1769 and 1846, and Richard Reece's *The Medical Guide*, which was first published in 1802;[2] both books were intended primarily for 'the intelligent layman'.

[2] [Hugh Jones, trans.], *Dr Buchan's . . . meddyginiaeth deuluaidd* (Caernarvon, [1823]), pp. xviii, 682; Richard Reece, *Yr Hyfforddwr Meddygol* (Merthyr, 1816), pp. [iii], 287. Buchan's book was extremely popular; it was translated into Italian (1781), French (1783), Spanish (1785), and Portuguese (1788), in addition to Welsh [1823].

Similar examples continued to be published in Welsh throughout the century, some of which were adaptations of popular English booklets of quite poor quality. An occasional original Welsh title was also published, such as D. G. Evans's popular book, *Cynghorion Meddygol a Meithriniad y Claf*, which was written because there was 'no book in the Welsh language to serve as a guide when one is physically indisposed' ('yr un llyfr yn yr iaith Gymraeg i'ch cyfarwyddo pan fo un o dan unrhyw anhwylder corphorol'). The author's intention was not 'to advise anyone to try to do without a doctor' ('cynghori neb i geisio gwneyd heb feddyg') but, rather, 'to draw their attention to the medicines which might be used before consulting a doctor' ('tynu eu sylw at y moddion a ellir eu defnyddio cyn ymgynghori â'r meddyg').[3]

It appears that the only doctor who attempted to address his colleagues in an original Welsh medical work was William Evan Hughes (d. 1884) of Trefriw and Llanrwst. Early in his medical career, Hughes published the first part of *Y Meddyg Teuluaidd* (1841), a book which would be 'as useful to the professional as to the layman' ('mor fuddiol i'r broffes ag i'r cyffredin') and which would be acceptable to 'those with more in their heads than the urinoscopists and the Ladies' Doctors' ('rhai sydd a mwy yn y Coryn, na darllenwyr y dŵr – y rhai cyfarwydd – a'r Doctoriaid Benywaidd').[4] This was the most ambitious of all the technical books published in Welsh during the nineteenth century. Hughes's intention was to combine basic information about physiology and anatomy with the most recent remedies, and to include numerous and detailed references to the chief authorities in the field. He also intended to write a Welsh book on Anatomy, which would include the physiology of the human body, and also a book on Chemistry,[5] but these ambitions were never realized. As far as we know, the books on Anatomy and Chemistry did not materialize and only two parts of *Y Meddyg Teuluaidd* were published. Another medical book designed mainly for professional practitioners was *Geni a Magu, sef, Llawlyfr y Fydwraig a'r Fag-wraig . . .* by D. W. Williams, which was published around 1870.[6] It appears that Williams discussed his book in Welsh with the surgeon John Pughe of Aberdyfi (the translator of the Physicians of Myddfai) – a rare example of Welsh nineteenth-century doctors corresponding with one another in Welsh.[7]

Those responsible for most of these orthodox publications and for some of the medical articles which appeared from time to time in Welsh periodicals were

---

[3] D. G. Evans, *Cynghorion Meddygol a Meithriniad y Claf* (Wrexham, [1898]), p. [iii].
[4] W. E. Hughes, *Y Meddyg Teuluaidd* (Llanrwst, 1841), a note on the back cover.
[5] Ibid., p. 75; see also John Roberts's almanac for 1841 in which there is an advertisement for *Y Meddyg Teuluaidd* by W. E. Hughes, and a note stating, 'Cyhoeddir hefyd, gan yr un awdur Lyfr ar Fferylltiaeth [*sic*]' (Also to be published by the same author is a Book on Chemistry).
[6] D. W. Williams, *Geni a Magu, sef, Llawlyfr y Fydwraig a'r Fag-wraig* (Caernarfon, n.d.).
[7] R. Elwyn Hughes, 'David William Williams – Arloeswr Meddygaeth Gymraeg', *Cennad*, 14 (1995), 31–9.

qualified doctors.[8] Very few people without medical qualifications ventured to discuss pure medicine in Welsh. An exception was John Davies of Llandeilo, whose *Y Cyfaill Meddygol* was published in 1861.[9] H. Ll. Williams, a registered doctor in New York, wrote his *Y Meddyg Teuluaidd* for Welsh immigrants to the United States and published it in Utica in 1851.[10] He was therefore obliged to adapt his material to the diseases and conditions of that country; his isolated situation was perhaps responsible for his unfamiliar vocabulary and choice of obsolete words like 'darymred' (diarrhoea), 'chwilbol' (urethra), 'rhodnell' (penis) and so on.

A number of Welsh books relating to 'quasi-medical' or peripheral subjects such as phrenology, mesmerism, hydrotherapy and 'somatology' were also published. (Surprisingly, however, no books on physiognomy – or 'wynebgoeledd', as Thomas Edwards (Caerfallwch) called it – were published in Welsh although it was an extremely popular field in England at the time.) Here the situation was completely different since they were written not by qualified doctors but by men like William Williams (Creuddynfab), a railway worker and literary critic who was keenly interested in phrenology. Indeed, the attention paid to phrenology in the Welsh press during the nineteenth century was one of the mysteries of the period. Phrenology was a wholly materialistic 'science'; it maintained that all human faculties were attributable to particular patterns in the brain and that it was possible to reveal the nature of these patterns by means of an examination of the external shape of the skull. This was strict predestination which would have defeated even the most Calvinistic of Methodists. Nevertheless, phrenology was welcomed with open arms by the Welsh press and there was no shortage of space devoted to it, even in some of the denominational periodicals, at a time when authors were reluctant to discuss other materialistic concepts, such as Darwinism, in Welsh.

Between 1839 and 1897 at least seven Welsh books on phrenology were published,[11] George Coombe's influential book, *The Constitution of Man*, was translated into Welsh by Jenkin Evans in 1883, and a host of relevant articles

---

[8] Among the registered doctors who contributed extensively to Welsh periodicals were John Williams of Llanrwst – articles on anatomy in *Y Gwyliedydd*, 1832, and on botany in *Y Protestant*, 1840. See R. Elwyn Hughes, '"Corvinius" a "Llywelyn Conwy"; *Juvenilia* Cymraeg Dau Naturiaethwr', *NLWJ*, XXIII, no. 4 (1984), 366–76; Jesse Conway Davies – articles on anatomy and physiology in *Y Tyst Apostolaidd*, 1847. See R. Elwyn Hughes, *Nid am Un Harddwch Iaith: Rhyddiaith Gwyddoniaeth y Bedwaredd Ganrif ar Bymtheg* (Caerdydd, 1990), pp. 16, 115–16; and Ellis Henry Ellis, whose forty articles published in *Y Genedl* during 1877–9 were described by Glyn Penrhyn Jones as 'brilliant expositions in Welsh on neurology'. Glyn Penrhyn Jones, 'Some Aspects of the Medical History of Caernarvonshire', *TCHS*, 23 (1962) 67–91.

[9] John Davies, *Y Cyfaill Meddygol: yn traethu ar achosion, natur, ac arwyddion y prif glefydau, damweiniau, etc., ynghyd a chynghorion meddygol er eu gwella. Wedi ei gasglu o weithiau yr awduron goreu . . .* (Llandilo, 1861).

[10] H. Ll. Williams, *Y Meddyg Teuluaidd: yn cynnwys fferylliaeth perthynol i'r corff dynol* (Utica, 1851).

[11] Huw Edwards, *Cylch Cyflawn* (Dinbych, 1994), pp. 111–17.

appeared, such as those by Morgan Philip on 'Practical Phrenology' and 'Dietetic Phrenology' (how to change the brain's constitution by careful eating) published in *Yr Haul* in 1848 and a comprehensive article by Creuddynfab in *Golud yr Oes* in 1863.[12] The discussion of phrenology was no easier than the discussion of other 'sciences'. Indeed, the names of the various faculties were a considerable stumbling block, so much so that Creuddynfab was prompted to prepare a vocabulary of them which was used by Jarvis in his *Pwyllwyddeg ac Mesmeriaeth* in 1854; it included terms such as 'hilgaredd' (philoprogenitiveness), 'maethedd' (alimentiveness), 'brïedd' (veneration) and so on.[13] Forty years later, 'hilgarwch', 'bwydgarwch' and 'mawrfrydedd' were the words suggested by J. Valant Williams in his list of Welsh phrenological terms.[14] A comparison of the two vocabularies underlines the change which had occurred in the way technical terms were coined and indicates how simpler, more concise terms had replaced the kind of terms devised in the tradition of William Owen Pughe and comprising archaic and grandiloquent elements.

These attempts to Cymricize 'official' medicine can be contrasted with the strong tradition of herbal literature which existed in Wales (and in every other European country, for that matter). Their common aim was to cure disease, but orthodox medicine was something 'external' which had been grafted on to Welsh from outside. Many of the herbals contained 'traditional' knowledge – or so it was believed, although a good deal of the material had been adapted from the body of medical treatises which had been imported from Europe over the centuries.

The 'official' medical books were obliged to come to terms with problems of vocabulary and presentation; the herbals, on the other hand, had only to combine two categories of data, the names of plants on the one hand and the names of diseases on the other. The herbals had no special significance in the general development of medicine during the nineteenth century. In Welsh, however, despite the fact that they were not numerous, they represented a specific aspect of technological communication. Some were translations or adaptations of an English book, such as John Wesley's *Primitive Physick*, first translated into Welsh by John Evans in 1759 and of which there would be several editions during the nineteenth century. The same was true of Culpepper's famous herbal, several Welsh adaptations of which were published during the century. Culpepper's influence was apparent not only on the translations which openly acknowledged their debt to him, but also on collections which claimed to be original Welsh works, such as the attractive little book *Y Llysieulyfr Teuluaidd*, published by

---

[12] Morgan Philip, 'Pwyllwyddoreg Ymarferol', *Yr Haul*, XIII (1848), 147–9; idem, 'Pwyllwyddoreg Ymborth', ibid., 189–90; William Williams (Creuddynfab), 'Pwyllwyddeg', *Golud yr Oes*, I (1863), 373–6.

[13] A. W. Jarvis, *Pwyllwyddeg (phrenology) a Mesmeriaeth* (Caernarfon, 1854), pp. 11–14.

[14] J. Valant Williams, 'Names of the Mental Faculties in English and Welsh', *The British Phrenological Year Book, 1898* (London, 1898), pp. 33–4.

R. Price and E. Griffith in Swansea in 1849. For more 'native' treatments, the collections based on local customs must be consulted, such as the relevant section of *Hanes Plwyf Llandyssul* (1896) or *Y Berllan* (1870), the nearest we have in Welsh to an early 'Flora'.[15] It is difficult to avoid associating the popularity of the herbals with another unique Welsh characteristic, namely the custom of ensuring that almost every dictionary contained an appendix of plant names. This can be traced to the *Dictionarium Duplex* of Dr John Davies in 1632.

The trinity of 'agriculture, horticulture and veterinary medicine' also belonged to the category of 'instructional books'. The veterinary books came closest to emulating their comprehensive English counterparts. This is understandable, for veterinary medicine did not become an acknowledged profession until 1844; farmers therefore required reliable books in their own language lest they (to quote from the introduction to one of the early veterinary books) 'were deprived of knowledge about these things' ('yn ol o foddion gwybodaeth ynghylch y pethau hyny').[16] These veterinary books became extremely popular during the first half of the century and a number of them ran to several editions.[17] Since they all relied heavily on their English counterparts no distinctive characteristics are discernible in them. The most professional and ambitious production in this category was doubtless *Meddyg y Fferm – Arweinydd i Drin a Gochel Clefydau mewn Anifeiliaid* (1881), a translation of a well-known English book by James Law.

At the beginning of the century Welsh farming methods were considered primitive in comparison with the more enlightened methods used in England. This was the constant refrain among travellers who ventured into Wales in increasing numbers at the time.[18] Some of the Welsh agricultural volumes aimed to compensate for this deficiency by introducing the Welsh people to the enlightened agricultural ideas of England. To this end Thomas Johnes of Hafod arranged for a Welsh translation of *A Cardiganshire Landlord's Advice to his Tenants* to be made available to his tenants; later in the century another 'humanitarian' work was published, namely *Garddwr i'r Amaethwr a'r Bwthynwr* (1860) by Charles Ewing. Although the author was a professional horticulturist, it is doubtful whether he understood the real needs of the 'Welsh cottager' – his treatment of 'bricyllwyd' (apricot) and 'ffigysbren' (fig tree), for example, is fuller than his treatment of 'cloron' (potatoes). The book was originally written in English and subsequently translated into Welsh, but only the Welsh version was published. It received the patronage of sixteen prominent 'friends of Wales', including the Earl

---

[15] Thomas [Christopher] Evans, 'Traethawd ar "Lysieuaeth Plwyf Llangynwyd"', *Y Berllan: sef Cyfansoddiadau Buddugol Eisteddfod Maesteg . . . 1869* (Cwmafon, 1870), pp. 61–83.

[16] 'Ewyllysiwr da i'r Cymry', [?C. Griffiths], *Meddyg Anifeiliaid* (Gwrecsam, 1814), p. [iii].

[17] Glyn M. Ashton, 'Llyfrau Cymraeg ar Feddyginiaethau Anifeiliaid, 1801–25', *LlC*, XII, no. 3 and 4 (1973) 216–43.

[18] See, for example, 'The Welsh Farmer' [*c.*1843] in A. R. Wallace, *My Life: A record of events and opinions* (2 vols., London, 1905), I, pp. 206–22; R. Elwyn Hughes, *Alfred Russel Wallace: Gwyddonydd Anwyddonol* (Caerdydd, 1997), pp. 162–82.

of Powis, Lord Llanover, Lord Palmerston, the Bishop of Bangor, and Owen Meyrick of Bodorgan.[19] Some of the patrons agreed to buy 500 copies each for distribution among their tenants, and it is therefore surprising that the book is now so rare.

Gardening books were simple and wholly didactic, and mostly 'borrowings' from English-language material.[20] In his volume *Y Garddwr Cymreig* (*c*.1870), R. M. Williamson acknowledged that he had collected his material from the work of the best-known authors. The content of *Garddwriaeth y Bwthyn . . . yr Ardd Lysiau* [1881] by John Davies, a storekeeper from Ystalyfera, was more original and largely drawn from personal experience. *En passant*, while discussing potatoes, he makes an interesting observation:

> Gan nas gwn ond am un llyfryn cymraeg ar y pwngc, rhoddaf i chwi ei hanes yn fyr . . . Gelwid ef 'Traethawd ar Wrteithiad Bytatws' . . . gan D. Thomas, Brookland, Garddwr Ymarferol, Caerfyrddin, argraffwyd gan W. M. Evans, Swyddfa 'Seren Cymru' 1859, pris 6ch. Gan fod yr awdur yn bregethwr, bu yma ar gefn yr *Hobby*, fel y dywedai Brutus, yn ei werthu. Prynais ef ganddo . . .[21]

(Since I know of only one welsh booklet on the subject, I shall tell you about it briefly . . . It was called 'Traethawd ar Wrteithiad Bytatws' . . . by D. Thomas, Brookland, Practical Gardener, Carmarthen, printed by W. M. Evans, *Seren Cymru* Office 1859, price 6*d*. Since the author was a preacher, he was here on his *Hobby*, as Brutus used to say, selling it. I bought it from him . . .)

Another field into which the Welsh language ventured at the beginning of the nineteenth century was cookery, and what was later called 'domestic science'. The earliest printed example of cookery material in Welsh were the fifteen recipes which were added as an appendix to the 1740 edition of *Llyfr Meddyginiaeth a Physygwriaeth* . . . (Thomas ab Robert Shiffery); fourteen of these were direct translations (although this was not acknowledged by the author) of recipes included in Mary Kittelby's book, *A Collection of above three hundred receipts* (1714).[22] About twenty Welsh cookery books (or books including a section on cookery) were published during the course of the nineteenth century, most of which were adaptations of English material, although this was not acknowledged except in a general way. For various reasons, copies of some of these cookery books are now extremely rare. One of the rarest is *Holl Gelfyddyd Cogyddiaeth* (*c*.1850), a translation of Elizabeth Price's *The New Book of Cookery; or every Woman a perfect Cook* (London, [*c*.1780]).

[19] Charles Ewing, *Garddwr i'r Amaethwr a'r Bwthynwr* (Caernarfon, 1860).
[20] Melfyn R. Williams, 'Amser i Balu – ac i Arddio yn Gymraeg', *Y Casglwr*, 1 (1977), 11.
[21] John Davies, *Garddwriaeth y Bwthyn* (Ystalyfera, [1881]), pp. 36–7. It appears that Davies did not know of an earlier book on potatoes, namely *Traethawd ar Drin Pytatws* (Caernarfon, 1846).
[22] R. Elwyn Hughes, 'Welsh Cookery Books', *Petits Propos Culinaires*, 50 (1995), 51–3.

Unlike some of the other technical books, cookery books, by and large, were comparatively easy to understand. The most common problem was how to describe the occasional new process in Welsh. The author of the earliest cookery material must be admired for the way in which he translated 'new' instructions into Welsh. 'Gadewch iddynt ferwi hyd onid elont yn gandrill . . .' is his translation of 'Let it boil until the Meat is all to Rags' and 'ai dewychu ef yn o dew gyda mwydion Bara gwynn a Pheilliaid Gwenith' is his attempt to convey 'and thicken it like thick butter with grated bread and fine flour'.[23]

Welsh nineteenth-century cookery books were somewhat less successful in this respect, and a good deal of borrowing from one to another can be detected. In the Welsh version of Elizabeth Price's book, recipes such as 'To ragoo cucumber', which were considered too difficult to translate, were omitted, and some of the terms, such as 'hufen llamdro' (whipped cream) and 'oerlydrwydd' (icing), were rather clumsy. When faced with difficult technical terms, the Wesleyan minister, the Revd Thomas Thomas, author ('compiler and adaptor' would have been a more appropriate description) of the comprehensive book *Llyfr coginio a chadw tŷ* (*c.*1880), evaded the problem by retaining the original English word. As a result, his book was riddled with expressions like 'Queen's sauce at blum pudding' and 'Forcemeat at pike pobedig'.

The most successful of the Welsh cookery books was probably *Coginiaeth a Threfniadaeth Deuluaidd cyfaddas i anghenion gwragedd gweithwyr Cymru* by Mrs S. A. Edwards of Corwen. It had been submitted to a competition at the London Eisteddfod of 1887, where one of the adjudicators was the wife of Sir John Rhŷs. In his preface, Sir Vincent Evans underlined the difference between this volume and those which were already available:

Ceidw deulu y gweithiwr mewn golwg trwy yr holl draethawd. Gŵyr pob gwraig sydd yn cadw tŷ natur y cynghorion a geir yn gyffredin mewn llyfrau ar goginiaeth. Eu bai mynychaf ydyw, mai ar gyfer y cyfoethog yr ysgrifenwyd y rhan fwyaf o honynt, a bod y dysgleidiau a ddisgrifir ynddynt yn ddrudion a gwastraffus. Cymmerant yn ganiataol fod 'y wlad yn llifeirio o laeth a mêl' i bawb – i'r tlawd, yn gystal ag i'r arianog. Ond y mae awdures y traethawd hwn wedi ymgadw yn lled dda rhag llithro gormod yn y cyfeiriad a nodwyd.[24]

(The worker's family is borne in mind throughout the whole essay. Every woman who keeps house is aware of the nature of the advice commonly given in books about cookery. Their most frequent fault is that most of them were written for the wealthy, and that the dishes they describe are expensive and wasteful. They take it for granted that 'the land is flowing with milk and honey' for everyone – for the poor, as well as for

---

[23] *Llyfr Meddyginiaeth a Physygwriaeth* (Amwythig, n.d.), pp. [45–6].
[24] S. A. Edwards, *Coginiaeth a Threfniadaeth Deuluaidd* (Dinbych, 1889), p. iii.

the rich. But the author of this work has managed quite well to avoid slipping too far in the direction noted.)

The section 'Cogyddiaeth Deuluaidd' (pp. 23–60) included simple instructions which reflect perfectly the title and aim of the book. No recipe was too grand, and several typically Welsh dishes, such as 'llymru' (flummery), 'shot llaeth enwyn' (oatbread and buttermilk), and 'shot posel' (posset), were included. Of all the Welsh cookery books published during the period under review, Edwards's book was best suited to the nature and potential of the community for which it was intended.

Books on mathematics, the handmaiden of the sciences, are best placed among the training books. This was certainly the view of John William Thomas (Arfonwyson), the most enthusiastic pioneer in this particular field. During his short and unhappy life he strove hard to introduce his Welsh-speaking compatriots to the rudiments of mathematics and astronomy.[25] He believed that knowledge of mathematics not only enriched the daily life of the ordinary Welshman but also opened the door to the other sciences. There is some evidence to suggest that his imperfect knowledge of English had militated against his career as a computer at Greenwich (in the 'Tremle Brenhinol', as he used to say), and it is therefore difficult to understand why he was so anxious for his compatriots to familiarize themselves with science in Welsh.[26] However, no one can doubt his enthusiasm for the cause. He edited the periodical *Tywysog Cymru* for the first six months of its existence in 1832, ensuring that a prominent place was given to articles on science and mathematical problems.

Arfonwyson's *Darlith ar Seryddiaeth* was published around 1840, but his most important work was *Elfenau Rhifyddiaeth*, published in parts in 1831–2 when he was only twenty-seven. As he himself acknowledged, at least five other Welsh books on mathematics had already been published, though, in his opinion, they all had their shortcomings: 'they are all too short and also some of them are so disorderly in the things they treat that one thing is often confused with another' ('y maent oll yn ry fyr a rhai o honynt hefyd mor annosbarthus ar y pethau a drinant, fel nas gwyddys yn gyffredin, bod un peth yn wahanol i beth arall ynddynt').[27] But the volume was a failure. The author was accused of pilfering the ideas of other writers and some found his style clumsy and his terms meaningless. One reviewer wrote: 'I fail to find some of your words in a dictionary and some of them are similar to one another – *deseb* very similar to *deiseb* &c' ('Ffaeliwyf a chael rhai o'ch geiriau mewn geiriadur, a mae rhai o naddunt yn debig i'w gilydd

---

[25] Hughes, *Nid am Un Harddwch Iaith*, pp. 85–8; see also Ll. G. Chambers, 'Elfennau Rhifyddiaeth: Tamaid Anorffenedig', *Y Gwyddonydd*, XI (1973), 128–31.
[26] See the correspondence between J. W. Thomas and G. B. Airey, Greenwich Papers, RGO 6/525.
[27] John William Thomas, 'At y Cymry', *Elfenau Rhifyddiaeth*, 2 (1831), note on the back cover.

– deseb yn debig iawn i deiseb, &c').[28] It cannot be denied that his treatment is much less concise and more difficult to understand than that of Evan Lewis in *Rhifyddiaeth yn rhwyddach* published four years previously; it is also obvious that he had 'borrowed' some of his material. But the *Elfenau* received considerable attention in the Welsh press and particularly enthusiastic support from one of Arfonwyson's friends, Thomas Edwards (Caerfallwch). Nevertheless, it is evident that a substantial number of subscribers had difficulty in comprehending his curiously phrased instructions and their support waned. Arfonwyson abandoned his proposed *magnum opus* after three issues only. The failure of *Elfenau* was the most bitter disappointment of his unhappy life.

Yet, mathematics was given an honourable place in the periodicals, including, curiously enough, the theological ones. It became one of the principal pastimes of the literary-minded Welsh to challenge their compatriots by setting them mathematical puzzles. Periodicals such as *Seren Gomer* carried many such puzzles throughout the century and it might almost be said that a knowledge of mathematics was a qualification for the editorship of some of the denominational journals in mid-century.

These categories excepted, instructional books were extremely rare. There was nothing to compare, for example, with the many volumes on the natural sciences, fishing and other various crafts which were so typical of the material published in England during the same period. It is true that four or five books on mining appeared, but, on the whole, these were confined to the coal-mining areas of south Wales; the most ambitious was *Ymddiddan ar fwngloddfeydd* (1892), a translation by the Revd W. Hughes of William Hopton's well-known book, 'A conversation on mines'. Some publications discussed specific subjects, such as *Y Gwenynydd* (The Beekeper) (1888) by H. P. Jones and Michael D. Jones, and the booklet *Awyriad Anneddau* (Ventilation of Buildings). This was published by Spurrell in Carmarthen in 1849, and reflected the belief which was prevalent at the beginning of the century that fresh air was almost as important as food. On the whole, however, nineteenth-century Welsh writers were reluctant to venture into unfamiliar territory.

With the occasional exception, very little instructional material appeared in periodicals. A technical article on the growing of flax was published in *Yr Adolygydd* in 1852[29] and a series of twelve articles on agriculture in the Anglican periodical *Yr Haul* in 1840.[30] From time to time an attempt was made to launch a specialist journal, such as *Yr Amaethydd* (1845–6) and *Y Meddyg Teuluaidd* (1827), but these were short-lived and comparatively undistinguished publications. As

---

[28] 'E. E.', 'Beirniadaeth', *Seren Gomer*, XV, no. 199 (1832), 109–10.
[29] Anon, 'Amaethiad Llin', *Yr Adolygydd*, 3 (1853), 318–35.
[30] 'Delta', 'Yr Amaethwr', *Yr Haul*, V (1840), 13–15, 55–7, 89–91, 122–3, 153–5, 185–6, 217–18, 249–50, 280–1, 313–14, 346–7, 378–9.

might be expected, the principal medium of instruction among the Welsh-speaking Welsh was the book.

We turn now to the second topic, namely technical material intended either to broaden the horizons of the Welsh reader or simply to entertain him. Throughout the century periodicals were suffused with material of this kind, which was of no practical benefit whatsoever. Indeed, the impression gained is that the demand for this type of material was stronger among the Welsh than among the English. As a result, an appreciable proportion of the scientific material which appeared in periodicals was written by 'laymen' (and sometimes by the editor himself). For example, Rowland Williams, editor of *Y Gwyliedydd*, was responsible for most of the seventy-five articles on the natural sciences published in his journal between 1822 and 1837,[31] and the young Thomas Jones (Glan Alun) wrote almost all the scientific material which appeared in his periodical, *Y Wenynen* (1835).[32]

One of the pioneers of 'periodical science' hid behind the initials 'T.E.' This was probably Thomas Edwards, editor of *Yr Eurgrawn Wesleyaidd* (1816–18), who published an article in virtually every issue of *Yr Eurgrawn* between 1814 and 1819.[33] He encompassed several branches of science, incorporating into his articles some of the chief characteristics of successful scientific prose. T.E. was certainly a master of his subject.[34] He ushered in a tradition which continued throughout the century, and there was hardly a general Welsh periodical thereafter which did not include 'educational' scientific articles from time to time. Geology and astronomy were the most popular subjects, mainly because they were considered to be compatible with the religious convictions of the period. For example, a series of six articles on astronomy was published by 'Didymus' in *Greal y Bedyddwyr* in 1827. James Morris of Merthyr published a series of 'letters' discussing geology in *Y Diwygiwr* in 1854 and a similar series by William Richard Jones (Goleufryn) appeared in *Y Cylchgrawn* in 1866.

Although astronomy and geology received most attention, the material was not confined to these subjects alone. The antiquarian Robert Williams published a long series of ornithological articles in *Y Gwyliedydd* between 1832 and 1834,[35] and there were several attempts to convey botany in Welsh, including articles by the surgeon John Williams (Corvinius) in *Y Gwladgarwr* in 1836 and in *Y Protestant* in 1840.[36] Other examples were D. L. Moses's ambitious series which began in *Yr Ymofynydd* in 1851, six articles by Rhys Pryse in *Y Drysorfa Gynnulleidfaol* in 1845–8, and a rather unsuccessful series (mainly on account of problems of vocabulary) by

[31] L. M. Jones, 'Hanes Llenyddol "Y Gwyliedydd" (1822–1837) gyda Mynegai i'w Gynnwys' (unpubl. University of Wales MA thesis, 1936).
[32] Glan Alun [Thomas Jones], 'Rhagymadrodd', *Y Wenynen* (Gwrecsam, 1836), p. [iii].
[33] R. Elwyn Hughes, '"T.E. . . . Llundain": Arloeswr Gwyddoniaeth Gymraeg', *Y Gwyddonydd*, XXII (1984), 44–6.
[34] Idem, *Nid am Un Harddwch Iaith*, pp. 51–66.
[35] Idem, '"Corvinius" a "Llywelyn Conwy"', 368–9.
[36] Ibid., 370–2.

David Gwalchmai James in *Yr Athraw* in 1839. Occasionally people ventured into less familiar fields; seven articles on 'Optics', written by an anonymous author, were published in *Y Gwladgarwr* during 1835 and 1836 and eight articles on physiology by R. Isaac Jones (Alltud Eifion), a Tremadog chemist, appeared in *Y Brython* in 1860.

Most of these 'educational' articles appeared in theological periodicals. However, from time to time an attempt was made to launch a periodical designed specifically to accommodate technical, or 'artistic' material, to use the language of the period. One example was *Y Greal*, founded in 1805 with the intention of publishing material on 'Biology . . . astronomy . . . agriculture, horticulture, tree husbandry, handicrafts and mining'.[37] However, its treatment of these subjects proved inadequate during its brief life. *Y Brud a Sylwydd* was launched in 1828 mainly for the discussion of 'scientific' topics in Welsh:

> Pe nas gallasai ein cydwladwyr, trwy ryw foddion neu gilydd, ymarfer â un gyfran arall o ddysg nag a ddeillient o'r cyhoeddiadau goreu yn y Gymraeg, nis gallent fod yn hyfedr i braidd un drin ag sydd er cynnaliaeth ac ymgeledd y bywyd hwn. Maes yw hwn ag sy'n agos yn hollol ddiwrtaith yn y Gymraeg, er nad yw ein hiaith yn lai hywedd nâg ieithoedd ereill i'w wneyd yn gynnyrchiol.[38]

> (If our fellow countrymen are not able, by some means or another, to practise a branch of learning other than what they can acquire from the best publications in Welsh, they can hardly be proficient in dealing with the maintenance and succouring of this life. This is a field which is almost wholly uncultivated in Welsh, although our language is not less adapted than others to making it productive.)

But *Y Brud*, too, was short-lived. It received some praise because it was the first periodical to make a serious attempt 'to draw the attention of the Welsh to these sciences' ('alw sylw y Cymry at y gwyddorion (*sciences*) hyn'),[39] but others complained about the inflexibility of its language, and, following a brief period of experimental bilingualism, it came to an end before the year was out. Two years later another periodical inclined to favour scientific subjects appeared, namely *Y Cymro* (1830) [*Y Cymmro* 1831]. Its proposed modernism was underlined by the well-known engraving by Hugh Hughes printed on its cover, namely a 'cut' portraying the new technological world which, in the editor's view, was about to dawn – 'the steamship, the commercial workplace, the smelting houses and the balloon' ('y cwch angerdd, y weithfa fasnachol, y mwyndai tawdd a'r awyr-ged'). *Y Cymro* survived for two years only.

In June 1850 appeared the first number of *Yr Adolygydd*, under the editorship of Evan Jones (Ieuan Gwynedd). Among its aims was 'to show what has been

---

[37] *Y Greal*, I (1805), the paper cover, p. [1].
[38] [Joseph Davies], 'Rhagymadrodd', *Y Brud a Sylwydd*, I (1828), 3.
[39] Idris o Gybi [Robert Roberts], 'Seryddiaeth a Daearyddiaeth', ibid., 120–1.

Table 2. Classification of scientific books by period

1800–29	51
1830–59	130
1860–89	106
1890–1919	43

accomplished by Science for the sake of mankind' ('dangos yr hyn a wneir gan Wyddoriaeth er mwyn dyn'),[40] but its commitment to its declaration of faith was hardly robust. Of the 120 articles published between 1851 and 1853, only three could claim to be 'scientific'. Another periodical which appeared in 1850 was *Y Wawr*, a 'Literary and Arts Magazine' which gave priority to 'Knowledge', especially scientific knowledge. It carried a large number of scientific articles mainly concerning astronomy and physics, and one would not disagree with the suggestion that it was the first Welsh scientific periodical.[41] In the wake of 'much slander, libel and scorn' ('llawer o enllib, athrod a dirmyg'), as the editor put it, *Y Wawr* folded in little more than a year.

It does not appear that these attempts to bring scientific culture to the Welsh-speaking Welshman left any lasting impression on most of their readers. In reviewing the state of the Welsh press in 1851, Thomas Stephens wrote:

> Pa beth am leenyddiaeth wyddorol y wlad? Nid oes gennym yr un! Y mae gennym draethawd neu ddau ar Seryddiaeth; cyfieithad o'r *Christian Philosopher*; cyfrol ar Amseryddiaeth gan Lloyd; ac un arall ar Ddaearyddiaeth (Geography) gan Mr J. T. Jones; a thyna'r cwbl . . . [nid] oes gwybodaeth o'r fath yw gael gan Gymro yn un lle arall ond yn y Wawr, ac yn y Chambers Cymraeg . . .[42]

> (What about the country's scientific literature? We do not have one! We have an essay or two on Astronomy; a translation from the *Christian Philosopher*; a book on Chronology by Lloyd; and another on Geography by Mr J. T. Jones; and that is all . . . knowledge of this kind is not available anywhere to the Welshman except in *Y Wawr*, and in the Welsh Chambers . . .)

Such comments, and by Stephens of all people, are rather unexpected. By 1850 (the year Stephens's essay was published), well over a hundred Welsh-language technical books had appeared (Table 2) and several hundred periodical articles, and it is strange that Stephens knew of only about half a dozen of them, given that he was a chemist and an able literary historian. However, others at this time

---

[40] Advertisement for 'Yr Adolygydd' on the back cover of *Y Gymraes*, I (1850).
[41] Iolo Wyn Williams, 'Nodiadau o'r Colegau', *Y Gwyddonydd*, IV (1966), 173.
[42] Thomas Stephens, 'Agwedd Bresennol Llëenyddiaeth yn Nghymru', *Y Wawr*, 2, no. 13 (1851), 62; Stephens himself had offered a prize of five guineas for the best Welsh translation of 'Mrs Marcett's [*sic*] "Dialogues on Opticks"' in Abergavenny Eisteddfod, 1848, see *Yr Haul*, XIII (1848), 99.

testified that the technical material failed to make any impression on Welsh readers. A contributor to *Y Diwygiwr* in 1846 was unambiguous in his opinion on this score: 'if we search the libraries for writings on nature and the attributes of the air, the power and effects of the elements, the size and movement of the planets, or the constitution of the vegetable and animal world – they have not yet come through the Welsh printing press' ('os chwiliwn y llyfrgelloedd am ysgrifeniadau ar natur a phriodoliaethau yr awyr, grym ac effaith yr elfenau, maintioli a symudiad y planedau, neu gyfansoddiad y byd llysieuog ac anifeilaidd – ni ddaethant etto trwy yr argraffwasg Gymreig!').[43] David Thomas of Llanelli aired a similar view at about the same time: 'We regret that the Welsh printing press has produced hardly any scientific works, except for the Geography of J. T. Jones, the Astronomy of Simon Lloyd, and the Christian Philosopher, which is a translation of the work of Dr Dick' ('Drwg genym nad yw yr argraffwasg Gymreig wedi cynyrchu nemawr o weithiau gwyddorol, heblaw Daearyddiaeth J. T. Jones, Amseryddiaeth Simon Llwyd, a'r Anianydd Cristionogol, yr hwn sydd gyfieithiad o waith Dr Dick').[44] It is therefore hard to judge to what extent efforts made in the first half of the century to broaden the knowledge of Welsh speakers on scientific matters by means of the written word achieved success. It might even be claimed that the Welsh had a blind spot regarding scientific knowledge in general.

The third motive for bringing scientific material to the attention of the Welsh were ideological reasons. Reference has already been made to the still-born belief that broadening the 'secular' knowledge of the Welsh was increasingly likely to encourage them to use the English language.[45] Comments to this effect were made by the Revd John Jenkins in an address at an eisteddfod in Swansea in 1841:

> it was an astounding fact, that there was not in the Welsh language a single work connected with the sciences . . . Mr Jenkins expressed an opinion that in the course of a century or two the Welsh language would altogether cease to be known as a living language. He stated that it was strictly necessary that the Welsh artizan should be furnished with scientific works in his own language; and it was on that principle the Committee offered . . . prizes for the best translation into Welsh, of the articles on the *General Properties of Matter* and on *Mechanics*, being the first six lectures in Mrs Marcet's *Conversations on Natural Philosophy* [prize £15] . . . [this] would have a tendency towards inspiring Welshmen with a desire for a knowledge of the [English] language.[46]

However, contemporary writers of scientific material would hardly have been aware of this motive. On the other hand, there was a good deal of scientific activity in Welsh for another ideological reason, namely the upholding of current

---

[43] 'Mentor' [R. Owen], 'Sefyllfa Bresennol yr Iaith Gymraeg', *Y Diwygiwr*, XI, no. 129 (1846), 113–15.
[44] David Thomas, 'Traethawd ar yr Argraffwasg', *Taliesin*, II (1860), 168–82.
[45] Trott, 'The Society for the Diffusion of Useful Knowledge', passim.
[46] 'Druidic Eisteddfod', *The Cambrian*, 28 August 1841, p. 3.

religious beliefs, and the realization of this aim within a framework of natural religion. This had been Dafydd Lewis's motive in publishing his *Golwg ar y Byd* in 1725. Similarly, over a century later, Glan Alun included a relatively high proportion of 'scientific' articles in *Y Wenynen*: 'On land and sea, in air and fire, by night and day, in the seasons of the year, in the constitution of man's mind and body . . . in all these things the greatness and wisdom, goodness and patience, foresight and providence of the Almighty are very clearly shown forth. With a wide knowledge of these things . . . I believe that it is impossible for anyone not to be a true Christian' ('Yn y môr a'r tir, yn yr awyr a'r tân, yn y nos a'r dydd, yn nhymorau'r flwyddyn, yn nghyfansoddiad corph a meddwl dyn . . . yn yr holl bethau hyn y mae mawredd a doethineb, daioni ac amynedd, rhagwybodaeth a rhagddarbodaeth y Goruwchaf yn ymddangos yn eglur iawn. Gyda gwybodaeth eang o'r pethau hyn . . . tybiaf mai anmhosibl i neb beidio bod yn wir Gristion').[47] The same opinion had already been expressed by Robert Roberts (Idris o Gybi, 1777–1836), author of *Daearyddiaeth* (1816): 'by astronomy and geography alone can we gain knowledge of the greatness of God' ('trwy seryddiaeth a daearyddiaeth yn unig y cawn un wybodaeth am fawredd Duw').[48]

To this end a number of well-known 'natural religion' books were translated, such as *Yr Anianydd Cristionogol* (1860) (a translation by Thomas Levi of Thomas Dick's *Christian Philosopher*) and *Duwinyddiaeth Naturiol neu Yr Amlygiadau o Dduw mewn Natur* (?1861) (a translation by Hugh Jones of William Paley's *Natural Theology*). As William Rees (Gwilym Hiraethog) emphasized in his editorial notes in *Y Faner* in 1857, the cornerstones of this natural religion were astronomy and geology;[49] Rees's own scientific interests, which were not insignificant, were confined to these two fields.[50] These attempts to make religion convey science were responsible for an appreciable proportion of Welsh scientific material during the second half of the nineteenth century. However, as will be indicated below, natural religion did not always have the effect of promoting a wider knowledge of science, nor for that matter did it reinforce religious convictions.

There were, therefore, two main methods of presenting science and technology through the medium of Welsh in the nineteenth century. On the whole, didactic material was presented in books, booklets and pamphlets. On the other hand, elevating or entertaining material was presented through the medium of thousands of articles in the various journals. But the material was not restricted to these two methods. Two other conduits were part of the effort to Cymricize science, namely the lecture and the eisteddfod.

---

[47] [Glan Alun], 'Arweiniad i Mewn', pp. 2–3.
[48] Idris o Gybi, 'Seryddiaeth a Daearyddiaeth', 121.
[49] 'Daiareg', *Y Faner*, 9 September 1857, p. 1.
[50] R. Elwyn Hughes '"Erw o Dir ym Middlesex"; Rhai Sylwadau ar Wyddoniaeth Gwilym Hiraethog', *Y Traethodydd*, CXLII (1987), 172–89.

Of necessity, those who chose to lecture on scientific subjects in Welsh-speaking areas were obliged to do so in the native tongue. Lecturers such as Robert Roberts of Holyhead, who lectured on astronomy, and Gwesyn Jones of Rhayader, who lectured on geological subjects, became quite famous.[51] John Peter (Ioan Pedr), too, enjoyed something of a reputation as a lecturer on scientific subjects; indeed, he gained his fellowship of the Geological Society partly on account of his lecturing in all parts of Wales.[52] However, no one did more to promote the idea of scientific lectures in Welsh than the mathematician Griffith Davies, the first FRS to write widely on scientific topics in Welsh. He suggested in 1829 that the Cymreigyddion Society of London should organize a series of lectures on 'useful knowledge'. His suggestion was accepted and Davies himself delivered four lectures, 'Navigation' ('Mordwyaeth'), 'Geography' ('Daearyddiaeth'), 'Pneumatics' ('Awyrolaeth') and 'Hydrostatics' ('Awsafiaeth'). Davies was not one to conceal his various talents and he arranged for his lectures to be published in periodicals for the edification of Welsh readers. It did not trouble him that exactly the same lecture might appear simultaneously in different periodicals, and his lectures can be found in *Seren Gomer*, *Y Gwyliedydd*, *Y Cymro* and *Lleuad yr Oes* between 1830 and 1832.[53] It is difficult to assess the appeal of Davies's material since his vocabulary, so heavily influenced by William Owen Pughe, was outlandish and his subject matter comparatively difficult.

On a smaller scale, the eisteddfod also provided an opportunity for promoting scientific discussion in Welsh. Little contribution was made by the National Eisteddfod, for its 'Social Science Section' was wholly committed to the principle that the sciences should be discussed through the medium of English.[54] But the smaller provincial eisteddfodau were more fruitful. It was not unusual for the prose sections of these eisteddfodau to include a 'scientific' competition. Occasionally competitors were required to write an original essay on a specific scientific subject and at other times a prize was offered for the best translation of a standard English work. At the Ivorite Eisteddfod held in Pontypridd in 1851 a prize of one guinea was offered for 'The best short essay on the Laws of Motion' and at St Dogmaels Eisteddfod in 1859 J. R. James of Cardigan was rewarded for

---

[51] See, for example, 'Seryddiaeth – Adroddiad am Ddwy Ddarlith gan Seryddwr Môn', *Y Gwyliedydd*, VIII (1831), 256; 'Amrywiaethau', *Seren Gomer*, XIII, no. 173 (1830), 64. For the lecturing of Gwesyn Jones, see *Yr Annibynwr*, I (1857), 251–3; Jones's lectures have been incorporated in his book, *Y Byd cyn Adda* (Penybont, 1858).

[52] Hughes, *Nid am Un Harddwch Iaith*, tt. 157–9; manuscript versions of Peter's scientific lectures (including some Welsh-language material) are to be found in NLW, MS 2618B.

[53] For details of the life and publications of Griffith Davies, see Ll. G. Chambers, 'Griffith Davies (1788–1855) FRS Actuary', *THSC* (1988), 59–77; Hughes, *Nid am Un Harddwch Iaith*, pp. 75–6. Hugh Hughes produced engravings of different scientific apparatus to be published with Davies's lectures. Peter Lord, *Hugh Hughes, Arlunydd Gwlad 1790–1863* (Llandysul, 1995), p. 198.

[54] Hywel Teifi Edwards, *'Gŵyl Gwalia': Yr Eisteddfod Genedlaethol yn Oes Aur Victoria 1858–1868* (Llandysul, 1980), pp. 53–112.

a highly technical essay on 'The usefulness of lime in agriculture'.[55] A prize of ten pounds was offered for '*Hyfforddwr i'r Gwyddorau . . .* similar to . . . "Joyce's Scientific Dialogues"' at the Dolgellau Eisteddfod of 1853 and J. E. Thomas of Rhayader won a similar prize at the Llandudno Eisteddfod in 1864 for an essay on 'The Geology of Wales'. A frequent winner on scientific and quasi-scientific subjects in local eisteddfodau was John Rhys of Penydarren in Merthyr Tydfil, a good example of a layman who, by dint of perseverance and practice, acquired considerable expertise in the discussion of technical subjects in Welsh.[56] Several prize-winning essays were published but medical subjects were omitted from eisteddfod programmes, and this again underlines the perceived intellectual difference between medicine and other branches of learning. By and large, however, the eisteddfodau made a considerable contribution to the fields of science and technology; the total number of scientific publications which saw the light of day during the century would have been substantially smaller had it not been for the material produced for eisteddfodau.

Three factors militated against the success of the 'science in Welsh' movement during the nineteenth century, namely the polarized or hierarchical nature of the population, the Bible-centric nature of Welsh society, and problems associated with vocabulary.

The division between English and Welsh activity in Wales during the nineteenth century was more apparent in the world of science and technology than in any other field of knowledge. In agriculture and mining, for example, Welsh was the daily language, but every attempt to promote or formalize activities in these areas was characterized by a tendency to turn to English. English was the language of the various agricultural societies, even in Welsh-speaking areas, and the same was true of the colleges. The Presbyterian College at Carmarthen boasted a strong scientific tradition and at the beginning of the century its library had one of the best collections of scientific books in Wales. But not a single Welsh book, let alone a Welsh scientific book, figured among the thousands of books housed there.[57] The same pattern prevailed in similar libraries throughout the length and breadth of Wales.

The 1840s saw an astonishing growth in the Mechanics' Institutes in Wales and an appreciable proportion of their 'cultural' activities were associated with scientific subjects. As far as can be ascertained, however, even in Welsh-speaking areas these activities were conducted in English.[58] Hugh Davies's attempt to

---

[55] J. R. James, 'Traethawd ar Ddefnyddioldeb Calch mewn Amaethyddiaeth', *Taliesin*, II (1860), 87–94. James's *nom de plume* was 'Gwyddonydd' (Scientist) – an early example of the word in print.
[56] See, for example, Philotheoros [John Rhys/Rees], 'Gwythienau Glo', *Yr Ymofynydd*, I (1848), 115–16; also, Hughes, *Nid am Un Harddwch Iaith*, pp. 93–8.
[57] R. Elwyn Hughes, 'Gwaddol Gwyddonol Coleg Caerfyrddin', *Y Gwyddonydd*, XXXI (1994), 4–8.
[58] Thomas Evans, *The Mechanics' Institutes of South Wales* (unpubl. University of Sheffield PhD thesis, 1966).

persuade the authorities to adopt his *Llysieuaeth Cymreig* as a textbook to be studied by ordinands for the priesthood met with failure.[59] Lewis Weston Dillwyn, doyen of South Wales naturalists in the first half of the century, responded in a similar manner when Davies invited him to sell a number of copies of his *Welsh Botanology* (the second part – 'Llysieuaeth Cymreig' – was in Welsh): 'there are very few of those who speak that can read Welsh and among those few I apprehend there would not at present . . . be found many purchasers'.[60] This occurred at a time when a high proportion of the inhabitants of south Wales were Welsh monoglots, but what Dillwyn had in mind was that very few members of his own select circle understood Welsh. The situation was summed up in an enlightened article in *The Athenaeum* in 1856, in which Welsh periodicals were referred to as 'The peasant literature of Wales': i.e. Welsh and its literature were regarded as something which belonged to the monoglot, 'uneducated' common people, while science, on the other hand, was considered to be an exalted activity which was of no interest to the general public. For this reason the language of science was English.

The situation regarding science in the Swansea area and the Vale of Neath (where Dillwyn lived) during the first half of the century illustrates perfectly the curious dichotomy which existed in Wales. This was the main centre of Welsh scientific activity, and when the British Association was invited to hold its annual meetings in Swansea in 1848 it was able to call on the support of five local Fellows of the Royal Society. But the local Welsh-speaking communities had no part in these scientific activities. Although the naturalist Alfred Russel Wallace, who worked in the Neath area during the 1840s, made an effort to learn the native language and later expressed his support for teaching science through the medium of Welsh, he nevertheless identified himself wholly with the English establishment in Neath.[61] All this, of course, was an aspect of the common assumption that English was the language of discourse in Wales and that science (like education) was an important part of it.

The belief that English was the proper language of intellectual activity had been grafted onto Wales by an external education system. But there was also an important internal element which militated against scientific study in Welsh. This was the Bible-centric nature of the Welsh-speaking society. The tension between a literal interpretation of the Bible and recent scientific discoveries was nowhere more marked than in Wales during the first half of the nineteenth century. There had always been a certain prejudice on the part of some Welshmen against science. 'Although science is good, literature is better' ('Er fod gwyddiant [gwyddoniaeth] yn dda, eto fod llenyddiaeth yn well'), claimed Lewis Edwards in

---

[59] NLW, MS 6664C (Rhuddgaer 1), p. 57. A letter from John Roberts of Oswestry.
[60] Ibid., p. 17. A letter from L. W. Dillwyn of Swansea.
[61] R. Elwyn Hughes, 'Alfred Russel Wallace; Some Notes on the Welsh Connection', *British Journal for the History of Science*, 22 (1989), 401–18.

discussing how to improve the intellectual condition of the Welsh.[62] Current scientific knowledge penetrated the pages of *Y Gwyddoniadur Cymreig*, causing some disquiet in the minds of several Nonconformist leaders in Wales. John Jones, Tal-y-sarn, fiercely criticized the scientific content of *Addysg Chambers i'r Bobl* (1851) because it demonstrated 'too great a desire to find no place for the Almighty in the world' ('gormod o awydd i droi yr Hollalluog allan o'r byd') and he referred sarcastically (this was before Darwin's theory of evolution) to 'the withered minds which boast that they have descended from the ape and orang-utan' ('y crebachod sydd yn ymffrostio eu bod wedi disgyn oddiwrth yr epa a'r orang-outang').[63]

As a result, the discussion of science in Welsh became a sensitive issue. Some subjects were 'acceptable to religion' while others were completely forbidden. As has already been mentioned, it was believed that astronomy and, to a lesser degree, geology were 'safe' fields of study because they revealed the wisdom and powers of God the Creator and because they presented no challenge to the literal truth of the Bible. These two fields therefore accounted for a high proportion of 'pure science' publications in Welsh.

But natural religion is a double-edged weapon and any aspect of science which cast a shadow on the religious orthodoxy of the day was unwelcome. This was a significant consideration in determining the nature of the scientific works which appeared in Welsh. The chaff of natural theologians such as Chalmers, Dick and Paley was translated into Welsh, but more standard works such as *Vestiges of the Natural History of the Creation* (1844) by Robert Chambers and *Origin of Species* (1859) by Charles Darwin remained untranslated.

The way in which evolution was ignored by the Welsh press underlined this tension. The period from 1840 to 1870 was characterized in Europe by considerable 'proto-evolutionary' interest in the question of man's origins and by arguments about monogenesis or polygenesis.[64] Somewhat unexpectedly, a weak echo of these arguments was published in an article in *Yr Adolygydd* in 1852.[65] The Revd Thomas Price (Carnhuanawc) also touched on the same problem in English in *An essay on the physiognomy and physiology of the present Inhabitants of Britain* (1829). There was no further discussion of evolutionary matters until Ioan Pedr published an article in *Y Traethodydd* in 1872, the first serious attempt to offer a complete treatment of evolution in Welsh. In essence this was an anti-Darwinian article which reflected the utter confusion in the Welsh Bible-centric mind when

---

[62] Lewis Edwards, 'Llenyddiaeth a Gwyddiant' in idem, *Traethodau Llenyddol* (Wrexham, n.d.), p. 597.
[63] Owen Thomas, *Cofiant y Parchedig John Jones, Talsarn* (Wrexham, [1874]), pp. 720–1.
[64] Nancy Stepan, *The Idea of Race in Science: Great Britain 1800–1960* (London, 1982); see also a report concerning a lecture by Dr Thomas Williams of Swansea in *The Cambrian*, 16 January 1846, p. 2.
[65] Anon, 'Disgyniad Dynolryw o'r un Rhieni', *Yr Adolygydd*, 2 (1852), 168–75.

faced with an unexpected external challenge to its most sacred creeds. R. D. Roberts responded to the situation in a similar way. Roberts was a lecturer at the University of Cambridge and a well-qualified scientist. Between 1883 and 1891 he published in *Y Traethodydd* nine authoritative articles on aspects of biology and managed to avoid discussing evolution and Darwinism in every one of them. T. H. Lewis has drawn our attention to another example of the limited capability of the Welsh Bible-centric mind during the nineteenth century, namely by explaining the dearth of references to Robert Owen and Owenism in the Welsh press: 'Owen was not "a religious man", and he emphasized, above all else, the need to improve man's environment. But to religious people in Wales in those days, the need for "grace from on high" was not unimportant' ('Nid oedd Robert Owen yn "grefyddwr", a phwysleisiai ef, yn anad dim, yr angen am wella amgylchfyd dyn. Eithr i grefyddwyr Cymru yn y blynyddoedd hynny, nid peth dibwys ydoedd yr angen am "ras oddi uchod"').[66]

The consequence of all this was a tendency to avoid important themes such as evolution, the origin of man, and the relationship between the brain and the mind. For this reason Welsh science in this period was defective and unrepresentative. Restrictions on the nature of the material for discussion was also partly responsible for the attention paid to technology and applied science in the Welsh press, at the expense of certain aspects of 'pure' science. Some Welshmen increasingly veered in the direction of this conceptually-neutral attitude towards technology, as did Gwilym Hiraethog in the pages of *Y Faner* and Samuel Roberts in *Y Cronicl*, in order to avoid those aspects of pure science which threatened the strength of Welsh Bible-centric society.[67]

There is no doubt, however, that the greatest problem was the dearth of suitable technical terms available to convey scientific concepts in Welsh. Almost everyone who sought to write in Welsh on scientific subjects was aware of this problem. Very often those who ventured into the field made preliminary remarks to the effect that the lack of suitable terms was the main stumbling block which militated against the growth of science through the medium of Welsh. 'It is impossible to write on any science in Welsh without debasing the essay with English words, or awkward, clumsy, inflexible, and unusual words' ('Annichonadwy ydyw ysgrifenu ar unrhyw wyddor yn y Gymraeg heb anurddo yr ysgrif â geiriau Seisnig, neu eiriau chwythig, clogyrnog, anystwyth, ac annghyffredin'), wrote the author of an article on human physiology in *Y Beirniad* in 1860.[68] This had always been a problem in Welsh, perhaps more so than in other languages, because Welsh had no tradition of a developing science. It is true that a number of 'technical' or quasi-technical terms had always existed in Welsh.

---

[66] T. H. Lewis, 'Y Wasg Gymraeg a Bywyd Cymru, 1850–1901', *THSC* (1964), 222–36.
[67] This theory is discussed in Hughes, '"Erw o dir yn Middlesex"', passim.
[68] Anon, 'Anianaeth Ddynol', *Y Beirniad*, I (1860), 23–9.

Specific areas of activity such as agriculture, quarrying and mining had given rise to their own unique vocabularies, but use of these terms was usually confined to people working in these particular sectors. An appreciable degree of variation existed in the terms devised, partly because of the lack of a governing authority but also because such terms were principally designed to meet local needs.

To the extent that a specific occupation was associated with a local community, some of these terms spilled into the surrounding society, sometimes surviving in English after the corresponding Welsh term had fallen into disuse. As late as the mid-nineteenth century, after the demise of Welsh as a living language in Cardiff, the old Welsh terms for the measures – 'llestrad' (bushel), 'cwer-llestrad' (peck), and 'pedwran' (ten-and-a-half pounds)[69] – were still in use in the town's Anglicized market. The tenacity of the 'native' terms in this respect may be contrasted with the short-lived nature of many 'synthetic' terms which had to be coined for discussion of the new sciences during the nineteenth century. This lay at the heart of the problem – the choice between native elements and those 'international' ones which had been imported in the creation of technical vocabulary. Whoever wishes to create a technical vocabulary in a minority language is faced by these two possibilities. On the one hand, it is possible to borrow or adapt 'international' terms (via English, usually, in the case of Welsh), and Cymricize them according to demand. On the other hand, the traditional resources of Welsh can be tapped either by reviving old terms no longer in use and giving them a new meaning or by coining or synthesizing new terms by drawing on the native resources of the language.[70]

By and large, Welsh speakers in the nineteenth century preferred not to borrow or adapt international terms. One exception was Robert Ambrose Jones (Emrys ap Iwan) who, in a discussion of 'The Way to Make Foreign Words Welsh' ('Y Ffordd i Gymreigio Geiriau Estronol') in 1881, recommended forms such as 'sinsur' (ginger), 'sianel' (channel), 'Tolemaig' (Ptolemaic), 'senith' (zenith), 'botaneg' (botany) and 'ffotograffiaeth' (photography).[71] Rather than accept his suggestion, however, most of those who were anxious to discuss science through the medium of Welsh chose to coin their own 'native' terms, many of which were totally uncharacteristic of the language. Whenever an acceptable native term was not forthcoming, these writers tended to use the original English term, in italics, without any attempt to Cymricize it. D. P. Davies's highly acclaimed

---

[69] John Winstone, 'Reminiscences of Old Cardiff', *Transactions of the Cardiff Naturalists' Society*, XV (1883), 60–75.
[70] See L. Hogben, *The Vocabulary of Science* (London, 1969); R. Elwyn Hughes, 'Llunio Geirfa Wyddonol Gymraeg', *Trafodion y Gymdeithas Wyddonol Genedlaethol*, 4 (1981), 49–52; Berian Williams, 'Termau ar Gyfer Dysgu Gwyddoniaeth trwy Gyfrwng y Gymraeg' in *Y Gymraeg mewn Addysg Uwchradd* (Aberystwyth, 1982), pp. 15–35.
[71] Robert Ambrose Jones (Emrys ap Iwan), *Camrau mewn Grammadeg Cymreig* (Dinbych, 1881).

articles on agricultural science were impaired by his unbridled tendency to italicize English technical terms.[72]

The national pride of the literary-minded Welsh was probably responsible for the fact that they chose not to borrow or adapt international terms. The first half of the nineteenth century could almost be described as a period of philological nationalism. Most of the 'native word-coiners' belonged to the school of thought mainly associated with Edward Williams (Iolo Morganwg) and William Owen Pughe and their unshakeable belief in the antiquity, purity and comprehensive nature of the Welsh language. In Iolo's opinion, the communicative span of a language reflected the breadth of the culture of the society which maintained it:

> a language possessing terms for science, and philosophical ideas of its own unborrowed from any other tongue proves that those nations that spoke it were self-civilized to a degree corresponding with the science or knowledge that such a set of terms and phrases express and indicate . . .[73]

It was therefore a matter of national pride to ensure that Welsh terms were made available to convey all the facts and concepts of science. The adapting of English or international terms would have reflected unfavourably on the purity and self-sufficiency of the Welsh language. Here is the advice of Rowland Williams of Ysgeifiog, the author of several dozen articles on the natural sciences in *Y Gwyliedydd*:

> works of science in this tongue [Welsh] are comparatively rare – its appropriate terms not well fixed, and as yet little understood. The inexhaustible resources of the Welsh language are able to supply these by self-evolutions without borrowing (like the English) from the Greek, or other tongue . . .[74]

However, the 'native terms' movement is mainly associated with the name of William Owen Pughe. When placed in the hands of the uninformed and ignorant, Pughe's dictionary was an extremely dangerous weapon. J. E. Caerwyn Williams claimed that, for a time, writers and public speakers displayed their 'knowledge' by using words which no one had ever heard before.[75] Pughe's influence on the scientific prose of the century was just as harmful. Some of his synthetic terms, such as 'alsoddeg' (algebra), survived for a number of years, but others of his neologisms – such as 'alwythen' (portal vein), 'afluchiasrwydd'

---

[72] D. P. Davies, 'Traethawd ar Fferylliaeth Amaethyddol', *Cyfansoddiadau Buddugol Eisteddfod Llanbedr, Alban Hefin 1859* (Aberystwyth, 1860), pp. 33–87.
[73] Edward Williams (Iolo Morganwg), 'Miscellanea', NLW, MS 13089, f. 305.
[74] *The Cambrian*, 26 July 1850, p. 3.
[75] J. E. Caerwyn Williams, 'Rhyddiaith Ysgolheigion a Haneswyr' in Geraint Bowen (ed.), *Y Traddodiad Rhyddiaith yn yr Ugeinfed Ganrif* (Llandysul, 1976), p. 311.

(electrode) and 'elltyflysaidd' (exogenic) – were utterly unacceptable and even scientifically misleading. One of Pughe's supporters was Thomas Edwards (Caerfallwch), a wholly uncritical admirer of his work and the principal propagandist for his ideas to the scientific world. Edwards clearly defined his own standpoint in the preface to his long-awaited dictionary in 1850:

> English terms in chemistry, geology, anatomy, and other sciences, have derived their nomenclatures from the Greek; but in the attempt to compose new words, to fill what I considered a chasm in Welsh literature, my source and authority were the roots of our own language, which were so simple, pure, and copious, as to render it perfectly unnecessary, to have recourse to any other.[76]

It appears that a number of writers were wholly uncritical in their adoption of some of the scientific terms suggested by the lexicographers. Nevertheless, the lack of consistency between various lists of terms continued to be a cause for concern. By the middle of the century there were at least seven different terms in use for the English word 'oxygen', namely 'ufelai', 'surbar', 'bywnwy', 'dwrbair', 'ufelnwy', 'oxygene' and 'oxygen'. In *Seren Gomer* in 1834 William Jones (Gwrgant) had already shown that there was considerable inconsistency between some of the words listed in Edwards's dictionary and the corresponding terms used by Arfonwyson, another self-appointed word-coiner of some distinction.[77]

The most scathing criticism of the lexicographers, however, came from authentic scientists. In *Y Gwyliedydd* in 1826 Thomas Edwards listed terms like 'ulai' (hydrogene) and 'uvelai' (oxygen), the exact words which Pughe had incorporated in his dictionary. Unfortunately, however, Pughe had betrayed his lack of scientific knowledge by using a similar term, 'ufelaidd', to represent 'sulphurous'; Edwards subsequently coined the word 'uvelair' to denote 'sulphur' in a list which he completed in 1826.[78] John Williams (Corvinius), a medical doctor, rejected this, arguing that it might convey the false impression that a close chemical relationship existed between oxygen and sulphur:

> Galwa *Caerfallwch* . . . *Sulphur* yn Ufelair; ac efe alwa *Oxygen* yn Ufelai: nid oes dim yn y naill yn tebygu yn ei natur i'r llall, gan hyny paham y tardda yr enwau oddiar yr un gwreiddyn?[79]
>
> (Caerfallwch calls . . . *Sulphur* Ufelair; and *Oxygen* he calls Ufelai; there is nothing in the one which resembles the other, so why do the names derive from the same root?)

---

[76] Thomas Edwards (Caerfallwch), *Geirlyfr Saesoneg a Chymraeg* (Holywell, 1850), p. xi.
[77] William Jones (Gwrgant), 'Unweddiad', *Seren Gomer*, XVII, no. 223 (1834), 108–9.
[78] Thomas Edwards (Caervallwch), 'Yr Iaith Gymraeg, Mabinogion, Geirlyvr, etc', *Y Gwyliedydd*, IV (1826), 272–5.
[79] John Williams (Corvinius), 'Gofyniad', *Y Gwyliedydd*, X (1833), 88.

Other scientists were extremely critical of what they believed to be the tendency of lexicographers to interfere in scientific matters. Conway Davies, another doctor from Clwyd, claimed in 1857: 'Caerfallwch and Sylvan Evans are splendid Welsh scholars, but it is obvious that they are not chemists from the words they propose' ('Y mae Caerfallwch a Sylvan Evans yn ysgolheigion Cymreig gwych, ond amlwg yw nad ydynt yn fferyllwyr, oddiwrth y geiriau a gynigant'),[80] and, according to Taliesin T. Jones, author of *Y Traethiadur Gwyddorawl* (1869) and a Fellow of the Chemical Society: 'The same imperfection belongs to neologisms in every branch of science, to a greater or lesser degree' ('Y mae yr un anmherffeithrwydd yn perthyn i'r celfeiriau yn mhob cangen o wyddoniaeth, i raddau mwy neu lai').[81]

In general, therefore, the attempt to create a satisfactory scientific vocabulary during the nineteenth century failed. The dead hand of the lexicographers had a detrimental effect on the growth of Welsh science not only because many of the terms coined were scientifically inappropriate but also because they promoted the belief that the creation of overblown and rhetorical Welsh was a desirable development even in science. In this connection we might bear in mind T. J. Morgan's comment that lexicographers tended to treat the language as though it were an organic device, attributing to it human virtues and cherishing it in a wholly anthropomorphic way – 'the Genius of Language', as the lexicographer John Walters put it.[82] All this, of course, was contrary to the scientist's belief that language was for communication only.

It is interesting to note that, in coining new terms, the tendency to rely on ancient Welsh elements and to reject international terms was quite different from that which occurred in England at that time. By the beginning of the century, the flow of new technical terms into English was derived 'from the springs of far-off Athens and Rome. The borrowings and misusings of ordinary English words had been checked'.[83] A lonely voice in the wilderness was that of William Barnes who, in mid-century, pleaded for the coining of composite Anglo-Saxon words such as 'twy-breat'd' (amphibious), 'matter-lore' (chemistry), 'wire-spell' (telegram), and 'pain-dunting' (anodyne).[84]

It cannot be denied that problems of vocabulary were a considerable hindrance to the development of science through the medium of Welsh. The situation was further confused by a sub-argument regarding the Welsh counting system. Iolo Morganwg, Arfonwyson, Hugh Hughes (Tegai), D. Griffiths of Holywell and T. W. Jenkyn (Siencyn ap Tydfil) all claimed that the system should be rationalized and the traditional method replaced by a decimal system.[85] The burden of

[80] J. C. Davies (Democritus), *Traethawd ar y Llosgnwy Tanddaearol* (Aberdâr, 1857), p. 5.
[81] Taliesin T. Jones, *Y Traethiadur Gwyddorawl* (Ffestiniog, 1869), p. 226.
[82] T. J. Morgan, 'Geiriadurwyr y Ddeunawfed Ganrif', *LlC*, IX, no. 1 and 2 (1966), 3–18.
[83] T. H. Savory, *The Language of Science* (London, 1967), p. 60.
[84] William Barnes, *An Outline of English Speech-Craft* (London, 1878), pp. 47–83.
[85] Details about the arguments regarding counting are to be found in Hughes, *Nid am Un Harddwch Iaith*, pp. 8–10.

their argument was that it would be easier and quicker to say 'nawdeg naw' (ninety-nine) than 'pedwar ar bymtheg a phedwar ugain'.[86] But, despite evidence that the decimal method had been a resounding success in Llanbryn-mair, arguments in favour of reforming the counting system – one of the few public discussions on an aspect of scientific communication in Welsh – fell on stony ground, and the natural conservatism of the Welsh carried the day.[87]

It was therefore no wonder that science through the medium of Welsh had such a dusty reception. One wonders how many readers of *Yr Athraw* understood David Gwalchmai's untranslatable articles on 'Botany'?: '... gelwir y blodeuyn yn uwchafol, pan bydd derbynsyl y blodeuyn uwch law y blaendardd (*germ*), a gelwir yn îsafol pan y bydd îs law y blaendardd ... gelwir y blodeu sydd â'r cwpansyl a'r gwychliwddail, yn flodau cyflawn ...'[88] This kind of writing proved too difficult for the ordinary people of Wales. It was as if the situation had not changed at all since the editor of *Y Brud a Sylwydd* had declared in 1828: 'We have not had the pleasure of reading hardly one book ... on any scientific or artistic subject in which the Welsh has not been horribly mangled, not to mention the writer's ignorance of the subject with which he was dealing' ('Ni chawsom y llawenydd o ddarllain braidd un llyfr ... àr [*sic*] un pwnc gwyddorol neu gelfyddol, na byddai y Gymräeg yn cael ei dirdynu yn echrydus ynddo, heb son am anwybodaeth ei ysgrifenydd am y pwnc y traethai yn ei gylch').[89] By the end of the nineteenth century the number of Welsh scientific publications – both books and periodical articles – had dwindled by half.

The fact that the most ambitious and substantial works – books such as *Elfenau Rhifyddiaeth* (1830) by J. W. Thomas, *Y Meddyg Teuluaidd* (1841) by W. E. Hughes, and *Allwedd Llysieuaeth* (?1840) by Ellis Jones – remained uncompleted suggests that even the most able and ambitious authors failed to communicate successfully with their readers. By the end of the century marked changes in linguistic patterns in Wales and the need to cater for the particular needs of monoglot Welsh speakers became much less acute. This was reflected in a further decrease in the number of Welsh scientific publications. Nevertheless, the turn of the century produced two books which, from the point of view of both content and structure, were more characteristic of the modern period than of the nineteenth century, namely *Egwyddorion Gwrteithio* by C. Bryner Jones in 1897 and *Gwersi mewn Llysieueg* by George Rees in 1896. Two other titles which should be mentioned are *Y Bydoedd Uwchben* by Caradoc Mills (1914) and *Adar ein Gwlad* by John Ashton (1906).

For a while thereafter no one perceived the need to provide scientific material in Welsh on a large scale. The renaissance which occurred in the second half of

[86] Llewelyn, Abertawe, 'Rhifyddiaeth Cymreig', *Seren Gomer*, III, no. 4 (1820) 111–13.
[87] J. R., Llanbrynmair, 'Rhifyddiaeth Cymreig', ibid., IV, no. 74 (1821), 334.
[88] D. G. James, 'Llysieuwriaeth: Am Ffrwythiant', *Yr Athraw*, IV (1839), 228.
[89] [Joseph Davies], *Y Brud a Sylwydd*, I (1828), 121–2.

the twentieth century, associated with the pioneer writing of O. E. Roberts and Eirwen Gwynn, and later with the launch of *Y Gwyddonydd* and the establishment of the Welsh scientific societies, was a movement completely *de novo* in the sense that it was free of the conditions and restrictions which had hampered the development of science through the medium of Welsh during the nineteenth century and also because it drew its strength from a new ideology. Since it is not part of any Welsh tradition, it therefore owes nothing to the nineteenth century. Science in Welsh during the period between 1800 and 1914 was an isolated and temporary phenomenon, and what is surprising is not necessarily what was accomplished but the tenacity of the attempt.

15

*The Welsh Language in the Blue Books of 1847**

GARETH ELWYN JONES

THE ATTITUDE of the authors of the 1847 Report into the state of education in Wales has become a byword for bias; within the so-called Blue Books, prejudice of class, religion and language emerges in virtually every judgement. The prejudices are indisputable, and echo those of a government and social hierarchy finding great difficulty in coming to terms with the new Wales of the nineteenth century. Under the impact of industrialization and population growth, former checks and balances had been undermined. Welsh society, from Tudor times, had been cemented by a landed class which had exercised untrammelled authority by virtue of property, office and personal influence.[1] By virtue of estate, birth and education, together with, ideally, personal qualities of grace, courage and justice, the heads of the landed families of Wales had exercised power and exacted deference as their due.

In practice, of course, such a model of society underwent constant modification, but it was not fundamentally undermined until the late eighteenth century when, in rural and urban Wales, old checks and balances seemed to be fatally flawed. Popular uprisings had been frequent in Wales since the 1790s. These in turn agitated the government and social commentators into an unprecedented concern with analysing the Welsh character and motives for action so as to propound remedies. It was axiomatic to governments which, despite the Reform Act of 1832, so overwhelmingly represented traditional interests that violent social protest in Wales was the product of disordered minds. This attitude is epitomized in the writings of the most intellectually incisive, yet harshest of the education commissioners of 1846–7, R. R. W. Lingen, notably in the first few pages of his analysis of the situation in the counties of Glamorgan, Carmarthen and Pembroke. The inhabitants were credited with 'the most unreasoning

---

* I am most grateful to Mrs Shan Davies for her assistance and to Professor Geraint H. Jenkins for his valuable comments. This chapter was completed before the publication of Gwyneth Tyson Roberts, *The Language of the Blue Books: The Perfect Instrument of Empire* (Cardiff, 1998).

[1] J. Gwynfor Jones, 'Concepts of Order and Gentility' in idem (ed.), *Class, Community and Culture in Tudor Wales* (Cardiff, 1989), pp. 121–58.

prejudices or impulses',[2] examples of which were participation in the Rebecca Riots and the Chartist movement. Implicit in his analysis of the reasons for these prejudices and impulses is the notion of a strange and inadequate language. Attitudes to language in the Report, therefore, must be set in their widest social context. But it was certainly not only the Welsh language which respectable opinion in Wales as well as England saw as the reason for a society in disarray. Here was an industrializing society, without the social cement of a respectable middle class, prone to riot, living in conditions of squalor, and without the means to stabilize the situation either in the long or short term.

The Welshman who was responsible in Parliament for prompting the Report, William Williams, MP for Coventry, believed that the Welsh language was inadequate for his fellow countrymen. It was a view shared by many influential Welshmen, particularly those who had succeeded in leaving Wales. London Welshmen of Williams's group saw in Wales a people gravely disadvantaged by a non-functional language and a romanticized history. Thomas Nicholas, born in Solva, German-educated and former tutor at the theological college in Carmarthen, was one of the prime movers in that London–Welsh group working for the foundation of a university for Wales. He condemned the Welsh language and the Welsh attachment to the past unequivocally:

> Shut in by the barriers of a different speech – a speech which can never be naturalised in the realms of experimental science and commerce – and held in check by an infatuated worship of the past, [Wales] is now sadly in the rear of her nearest neighbour.[3]

Although written in 1862, these comments encapsulated the ingrained prejudices of a mid-Victorian Welshman who had embraced the ethic of material progress and self-help.

The education commissioners and London Welshmen such as William Williams and Hugh Owen held similar views. The 'prejudices and impulses' which, according to the commissioners, had led the Welsh unsuspectingly to undermine the foundations of order by rioting were echoed in the 'bright, nimble and fugitive' mentalities of a Welsh people too like 'globules of Mercury'[4] for their own or their nation's good. What would transform the Welsh from being a threat to that wider society perceived by the commissioners, and from Nicholas's 'subjugated enervated race'[5] into participants in the unlimited opportunities of Victorian empire but education? This was a new religion among the putative

---

[2] *Reports of the Commissioners of Inquiry into the State of Education in Wales . . . in three parts. Part I. Carmarthen, Glamorgan, and Pembroke* (London, 1847) (PP 1847 (870) XXVII), p. 6.
[3] Quoted in J. Gwynn Williams, *The University Movement in Wales* (Cardiff, 1993), p. 24.
[4] Ibid.
[5] Ibid., p. 25.

social scientists within and outside Wales. And for some, a new religion was doubly necessary in Wales. The foundations of the old were increasingly subject to scientific questioning, and its consequent inapplicability to the rational, materialist, market-orientated new world of Victorian commerce was reflected in an equally inappropriate language, perceived, as we shall see, to be attuned to theology and little else.

Any consequent re-ordering of society in mid-century, to commissioners or London Welshmen, posed enormous problems. While the religious census of 1851 revealed that the Welsh, in terms of accommodation if nothing else, were the most religious of people, the 1847 Report showed that they were far from being the most educated. At every level the deficiencies in the educational hierarchy were all too apparent. In the 1850s and 1860s Nicholas was extraordinarily of the opinion that existing elementary education was adequate for the workers of Wales, and the grave lack was of middle school and university education. Hugh Owen, on the other hand, while sharing Nicholas's views on these deficiencies, realized the appalling inadequacies of elementary school education.

The Blue Books, then, paint a picture of educational underprivilege. Elementary education in the 1840s was provided by the religious denominations, often in collaboration with the voluntary societies, by private venture and by a few works' schools. The Anglican ideal of a school in every parish was far from being realized. In any case, it was an ideal which was increasingly anachronistic. Parishes varied enormously in size and the industrialization of Wales had resulted in concentrations of population in some of the least well-served areas. The only really successful experiment in mass education in modern Wales had been the circulating schools of Griffith Jones, with their limited aims and primitive organization. Anglican schools, whether supported by the National Society or not, were wholly inadequate to cope with new demographic and social configurations in Wales. Non-denominational schools, supported by the British Society, were a slower growth as a result of positive opposition from the Voluntaryists, especially in south Wales, and a lack of organization. A few works' schools, especially the Guest venture in Merthyr, were of high quality, but few industrialists had yet made substantial investment. Some were shamed into doing so in 1846–7. Private venture schools, as the Blue Books were to demonstrate, were at best expensive and inadequate, at worst appalling in the quality of both their accommodation and teaching. There were few trained teachers and there had been no provision in Wales for their training until colleges opened in Brecon in 1845 (transferring to Swansea five years later) and Carmarthen in 1848.[6]

The Welsh language was therefore one among many characteristics of a society in which large sections were both rebellious and disadvantaged, a society in

---

[6] W. Gareth Evans, 'The "Bilingual difficulty": The Inspectorate and the Failure of a Welsh Language Teacher-Training Experiment in Victorian Wales', *NLWJ*, XXVIII, no. 3 (1994), 325.

which, paradoxically, the leaven was provided by religion and Sunday school education in Welsh. However, as we have seen, these were not the means by which opinion-formers believed the Welsh might shake off the shackles of the past and enter into the new inheritance of Great Britain, with its wealth, its empire and its opportunities. There is no necessity to subscribe fully to the notion of internal colonialism to see parallels between the imperial mission to bring civilized Britain to the dark corners of the world and attitudes to seemingly alien parts of the United Kingdom. Policy-makers had a common view of native languages throughout the empire; they should be superseded by civilized English. There were equivalents in Africa to the Welsh Not. Much informed Welsh opinion believed that the interests of their fellow countrymen, entitled to their share of the spoils, were best served by similar policies. It is hardly surprising, then, that the commissioners came to Wales in 1846 with their judgement of the Welsh language pre-empted by their class, linguistic and religious prejudices.

The commissioners were given specific terms of reference by James Kay-Shuttleworth, Secretary to the Committee of Council on Education. Kay-Shuttleworth had been Secretary to the Board of Health in Manchester in the 1830s and an assistant Poor Law commissioner in East Anglia; both offices had revealed to him the appalling conditions of disease, dirt and ignorance in which the poor were condemned to live. As First Secretary to the Privy Council on Education, appointed in 1839, he worked tirelessly to implement the kind of reforms which, as a result of his experiences in urban and rural England, he regarded as central to ameliorating the horrors he had experienced.[7] His was a social, not a narrowly educational, mission.

The notorious terms of reference are, therefore, hardly surprising, although there is controversy as to who amended Kay-Shuttleworth's draft to include investigation into the moral condition of the Welsh people. Kay-Shuttleworth, the enlightened educator, shared current prejudices. This was to be 'an inquiry . . . into the state of education in . . . Wales, especially into the means afforded to the labouring classes of acquiring a knowledge of the English language'.[8] The matter of language was central to the commission, and uncontentious at that stage both to English educationalists and Welsh social theorists. It was axiomatic that acquisition of English was the key to adequate educational provision and any worldly preferment to which the Welsh might aspire. Other of the terms of reference were to prove far more contentious, as has been the identity of their

---

[7] R. Aldridge and P. Gordon, *Dictionary of British Educationists* (London, 1989), p. 138.

[8] *Reports of the Commissioners of Inquiry into the State of Education in Wales*, terms of reference. Among the most recent books to be published on the *Reports* is Prys Morgan (ed.), *Brad y Llyfrau Gleision: Ysgrifau ar Hanes Cymru* (Llandysul, 1991). A version of one of the most significant essays in that book, by Ieuan Gwynedd Jones, has been published in his *Mid-Victorian Wales: The Observers and the Observed* (Cardiff, 1992), under the title of '1848 and 1868: "Brad y Llyfrau Gleision" and Welsh Politics', pp. 103–65.

originator. The commissioners were also instructed to 'form some estimate of the general state of intelligence and information of the poorer classes in Wales, and of the influence which an improved education might be expected to produce, on the general condition of society, and its moral and religious progress'.[9] In these phrases lay the potential for the indictment of a nation and what it held most proud. Given that the language of religion was predominantly Welsh, as was the language of the Sunday schools which Kay-Shuttleworth regarded as 'the most remarkable, because the most general, spontaneous effort of the zeal of Christian congregations for education', the explosive reaction to moral indictments in the Report had linguistic overtones. In retrospect, this made it far easier for the terms of reference relating to the language to be conflated with the Welsh Not mentality of those seeking a scapegoat for the decline of Welsh. This is not how the terms of reference were seen at the time.

The pedigrees of the commissioners predetermined their views on the Welsh language. For example, R. R. W. Lingen was educated at Bridgnorth Grammar school and Trinity College, Oxford. He took a first class degree in classics and became a Fellow of Balliol in 1841. He was called to the bar in 1847. He was Kay-Shuttleworth's successor as Secretary to the Privy Council Committee on Education and later achieved the highest civil service office in the country as Permanent Secretary at the Treasury. He endeared himself neither to the Welsh in 1846–7 nor to any in the education service in his later career, and although his was an incisive intellect he had scarcely been prepared for that which he would encounter in Wales.[10] J. C. Symons and Henry Vaughan Johnson were not quite as formidable but they shared Lingen's middle-class and Anglican background.

To conform to their terms of reference, the commissioners were required to accumulate a vast amount of detail and they did so with notable thoroughness and speed. Kay-Shuttleworth's terms of reference were sent to the commissioners on 1 October 1846. Henry Vaughan Johnson was responsible for reporting on the counties of Anglesey, Caernarfon, Denbigh, Flint, Merioneth and Montgomery, Symons on the counties of Brecon, Cardigan, Radnor and Monmouth, and Lingen on the three counties of Glamorgan, Carmarthen and Pembroke. Each commissioner provided an analysis of conditions in his area in wide-ranging essays containing historical, sociological and linguistic analysis, and it is from these reports that attitudes to the Welsh language most clearly emerge. The reports themselves rested on masses of more detailed evidence. For example, the information relating to Lingen's area, hundred by hundred, parish by parish, occupies 266 pages, while the statistics and statistical reports occupy a further 226 pages. The 1847 Report comprises, in total, 1,256 pages of tightly packed

---

[9] *Reports of the Commissioners of Inquiry into the State of Education in Wales*, terms of reference.
[10] Aldrich and Gordon, *Dictionary of British Educationists*, p. 150.

information. The commissioners returned this formidable array of information to Kay-Shuttleworth between March and October 1847.

The link between social structure and the Welsh language was immediately and graphically highlighted. In Lingen's words: 'My district exhibits the phenomenon of a peculiar language isolating the mass from the upper portion of society . . . the Welsh element is never found at the top of the social scale, nor in its own body does it exhibit much variety of gradation . . . the farmers are very small holders . . . the Welsh workman never finds his way into the office . . .'[11] Such analysis came naturally to the commissioners. It was common ground that there was social dislocation on a grand scale across Wales. Between 1821 and 1841 the population of Wales had virtually doubled. There was massive and disruptive expansion in the industrial communities in Glamorgan and Monmouthshire as they sucked in the surplus population of poverty-stricken rural Wales. We have already seen that traditional forms of control had broken down under this and other pressures. The greater gentry had long since become divorced from their tenant communities, in religion and language as well as lifestyle. The gentry alone had the resources to provide some greater measure of schooling in rural parishes, but the gross inadequacy of their contribution, direct and indirect, drew condemnation from the commissioners. In the industrial areas owners were intent on maximizing profits, not educating workers. Symons was particularly condemnatory, reporting that the only group to be indifferent to his enquiries were ironmasters.

In this context, Lingen's comments on the lack of social mobility become crucial. With those in a position of social dominance not interested in promoting the education of their tenants or workers, the motivation which might have come from below was stunted by social immobility. To ascribe this to the language was, of course, grossly simplistic, but in the context of mid-century industry and empire, understandable.

★   ★   ★

Perhaps the most remarkable feature of the historiography of the Blue Books has been the readiness to indict the commissioners for a situation which they were simply recording. The chasm between the language of the people and the language of the day schools was already a fact of life in Wales. Vaughan Johnson reported that 80 per cent of the population of the counties he surveyed – Anglesey, Caernarfon, Denbigh, Flint, Merioneth and Montgomery – 'habitually speak Welsh'.[12] Only in one school in these counties was Welsh the language of instruction and there is some doubt about the accuracy of information obtained in respect of that school. In 46 schools both languages were employed. English was

---

[11] *Reports of the Commissioners of Inquiry into the State of Education in Wales, Part I*, pp. 2, 3.
[12] Ibid., *Part III. North Wales* (PP 1847 (872) XXVII), p. 5.

the language of instruction in 530 schools. Vaughan Johnson commented that 'the professed object for which day-schools have been established in North Wales is to teach the English language'.[13]

To the educationalist the mismatch had the worst of consequences. In the national and British schools, only rarely did Johnson find textbooks other than the English-language Bible. Even the clergy, he argued, were beginning to question the wisdom of teaching the rudiments of reading in this manner. Where other textbooks were used, he found it impossible to categorize them because pupils provided their own. Teachers therefore cultivated the habit of grouping pupils according to which texts they possessed. The resulting mismatch in ability was compounded by the unsuitability of the reading, writing and grammar texts which were most common – all, in Johnson's view, 'difficult and repulsive'.[14] Here was a recipe for confusion, under-achievement and retarded conceptual development. When these features were allied with the language problem, the mix was disastrous. Monoglot Welsh children had inappropriate teaching materials in English, mediated without the aid of English–Welsh dictionaries or grammars, often by teachers whose own grasp of English was rudimentary:

> Every book in the school is written in English; every word he speaks is to be spoken in English; every subject of instruction must be studied in English, and every addition to his stock of knowledge in grammar, geography, history, or arithmetic, must be communicated in English words; yet he is furnished with no single help for acquiring a knowledge of English.[15]

The state could not have hoped for a more compliant attitude on the part of its teachers; their whole object was to teach English. The attitudes of the commissioners and the teachers in this respect were wholly compatible. At issue were the means, not the end, and there were two crucial impediments to that end – the lack of suitable materials and the lack of adequate teacher training. Johnson's summing up was exemplary:

> it is difficult to conceive an employment more discouraging than that of the scholars, compelled as they are to employ six hours daily in reading and reciting chapters and formularies in a tongue which they cannot understand, and which neither their books nor their teachers can explain.[16]

Historians have stressed the gross deficiencies in the Welsh education system revealed by the Blue Books. Yet, it should be borne in mind that poor buildings,

---

[13] Ibid.
[14] Ibid., *Part III*, p. 11.
[15] Ibid.
[16] Ibid.

inadequate teaching materials and, above all, inefficient teaching were commonplace in England, too, especially in those areas which had been rapidly industrialized. Indeed, the inadequacies of the system in England and the inability of successive governments to mitigate them may be relevant both to the substance and tone of the 1847 Report. So it was that Johnson, when highlighting the gross deficiencies of teachers, mingled criticisms just as applicable in England with those specific to Wales. In the parish of Cilcain in Flintshire, Thomas Jones ran a private adventure school. He was a former miner, forced to retire by ill health. Such teachers were unexceptional throughout England. Additionally, though, 'his knowledge of English is so limited that I was frequently obliged to interpret my questions into Welsh in order to obtain an answer'.[17] In the church school at Llanfair-is-gaer the schoolmaster was a former shopkeeper who had become disabled and taken up teaching: 'He speaks very broken English, both in point of grammar and pronunciation; and his questions on Scripture were feeble.'[18] Johnson piles on example after example to drive home the point.[19] They do not identify disparity of purpose; they highlight the inadequacies of achieving an accepted goal. Criticisms of the educational method, however, carry a wider significance. Debate still rages as to the advisability of the total immersion method of language teaching; in the context of teacher ignorance of the English language on this scale, and the inadequacy of the textbooks, a method which wholly excluded the use of the Welsh language was almost completely counter-productive. It was most succinctly summed up in comments on Aberffro school in Anglesey:

> The master has the reputation of being a good scholar, but he has never been trained to teach, and his method of teaching is very antiquated. He has no books, except one or two Bibles, a Church Catechism, and a copy of Walkinghame's arithmetic. None of the children can read with ease. They understand nothing of what they read in English, and are unable to translate the simplest English words into Welsh. The master assured me that they knew nothing of the meaning of what they read; that it was impossible for them to do so, considering that at home they never heard a word spoken in English, and considering the utter worthlessness of his materials for translation. He does not attempt to assist them by any system of interpretation *viva voce*, or by any kind of explanation in Welsh of what is read or learned.[20]

In such a context, Johnson regarded the use of the infamous Welsh Not as positively harmful:

> The *Welsh stick*, or *Welsh*, as it is sometimes called, is given to any pupil who is overheard speaking Welsh, and may be transferred by him to any school-fellow whom

---

[17] Ibid., *Part III*, p. 15.
[18] Ibid.
[19] Ibid., *Part III*, pp. 16, 17.
[20] Ibid., p. 17.

he hears committing a similar offence. It is thus passed from one to another until the close of the week, when the pupil in whose possession the Welsh is found is punished by flogging. Among other injurious effects, this custom has been found to lead children to visit stealthily the houses of their school-fellows for the purpose of detecting those who speak Welsh to their parents, and transferring to them the punishment due to themselves.[21]

Over the years the Welsh Not became and, in much popular memory remains, the ultimate symbol of coercion of the Welsh people by an alien, colonial power intent on the subjugation of a nation's language and, by implication, its soul. This is not the message in 1847. Johnson, in so far as he was the mouthpiece of the establishment, condemned the practice not only as educational nonsense but also as promoting dishonesty. His comments were based on one example, that of Llandyrnog, Denbighshire, which mentioned the practice of suspending a piece of wood with the words 'Welsh stick' engraved on it around the neck of a boy found speaking Welsh.

Of course, Johnson's aim was to ensure that the Welsh could speak English. The method which he believed would be effective was the bilingual approach which, had it been adopted and become educationally respectable, might have changed both the history of the language in Wales and its politics. But such a change would have required a transformation in teacher training throughout Wales and England, reminding us that the fate of the language in the nineteenth century was linked inextricably with policies determined by English priorities. Even so, the juxtaposition of the poor quality of teachers with basic errors found in the teaching of English and the general inadequacy of teacher training provide a constant, harmonized refrain in Johnson's report. He used the evidence from Llanfynydd church school in Flintshire to make the point:

> the master does not understand Welsh, and no kind of interpretation or explanation is attempted. The master was formerly a labourer, and now keeps a toll-gate. He has never been trained to teach, and appears to have been little educated.[22]

To reinforce the point that the thrust of Johnson's report was critical of the quality of teachers generally, rather than Welsh teachers specifically, he highlighted the inadequate English of teachers from neighbouring English counties.[23] He was even-handedly critical of monoglot English teachers, irrespective of the standard of their grammar. He drew attention to the experience of children at Brymbo church school, near Wrexham, to generalize that 'in schools where English

---

[21] Ibid., p. 19.
[22] Ibid.
[23] Ibid., *Part III*, p. 17.

teachers are employed, the confusion and ambiguity is increased'.[24] It was pedagogy, rather than the language, which was at fault in the strictures against teachers whose inadequacies he highlighted graphically and unremittingly. Such pedagogic shortcomings were apparent even when teachers were competent in the subject matter. In Johnson's words, 'ignorance of Scripture . . . is less frequent among Welsh teachers than ignorance of the proper method of teaching Scripture to others'.[25] Since the Welsh Sunday schools traditionally attracted adults as well as children, many day school teachers attended and became particularly knowledgeable in the Scriptures. Once removed to the day schools, they were ineffectual: 'being accustomed to read and explain the Bible in Welsh, they are at a loss when confined, as in all day-schools, to the English version and the English language'.[26]

The general organization of teaching in the larger schools compounded the problem. The complexities of bilingualism apart, diatribes in the Report against ineffectual teaching methods and learning by rote were equally applicable to schools in England. The schools of both the umbrella societies, the British Society and the National Society, used teaching methods dictated by cheapness, and the monitorial system operated in more than a third of the schools in Johnson's area.[27] This system, whereby a master instructed older pupils who then 'taught' the younger pupils depended, if it were to be effective at all, on a routine of mechanical orders, drilled responses and rote learning. Johnson's strictures against the monitors in Welsh schools merely introduced one more criticism in a catalogue of ineffectuality. Concerning the British school at Llandderfel, Merioneth, he highlighted the inadequacy of the monitors: 'With one exception, the monitors were unequal to their duties. One of them read more incorrectly than his own pupils. They used Welsh to communicate their wishes to the scholars, and appeared to know very little English . . .'[28]

The inter-relationship of the language with general teaching inadequacy was constantly and even-handedly reiterated. National schools, affiliated to the Church of England, were no better than British schools. In the national school in Llangollen the master, until recently a bookseller, understood 'very little Welsh. The younger pupils in his school understand no English'.[29] The monitors there were unable to operate if the master's attention was taken elsewhere. In the church school at Penmachno, Caernarfonshire, pupils who were questioned spoke no English and the master's English was very poor.[30] Workhouse schools were similarly condemned. In that belonging to the Ruthin Union, some of the

[24] Ibid., *Part III*, p. 18.
[25] Ibid., *Part III*, p. 24.
[26] Ibid., *Part III*, p. 24.
[27] Ibid., *Part III*, p. 29.
[28] Ibid., *Part III*, p. 29.
[29] Ibid., *Part III*, p. 30.
[30] Ibid.

pupils could quite satisfactorily repeat parts of the catechism by rote, but their 'knowledge of English was very limited, and is not likely to increase, for no kind of interpretation is adopted; not a word is allowed to be spoken in Welsh, either by the master or scholars'.[31]

Even if the standard of teaching in general had been higher, Johnson was obviously of the opinion that the structure of the system was such that language teaching was made unnecessarily difficult. He believed, as do modern educationalists, that the younger a child learns a language the more effectively it does so. 'Infant schools', he argued, 'afford the most effectual means of imparting a knowledge of the English language to Welsh children, and the only means which can enable children, upon the present system of Welsh schools, to derive any practical benefit from their subsequent course of instruction.'[32] The problem was that very few pupils (4.5 per cent) under the age of five received any education.

Any close analysis of Johnson's comments reveals that he had no truck with traditional solutions, a fact which adds substance to speculation that the real agenda, as far as he was concerned, was to demonstrate that only a state-sponsored education would correct the shortcomings in the system. Scattered through his, and the other commissioners' judgements, is the notion that support from the traditional philanthropists of education, the gentry, reinforced by that of the clergy, was insufficient. They established schools which excluded 'the great majority of the poor' but above all they 'overlooked the defect which lies at the root of all other deficiencies, – the want of books expressly adapted, and of teachers properly qualified, to teach English to Welsh children. The majority appear unconscious that English may remain an unknown language to those who can read and recite it fluently . . .'[33] Most crucially, and having implications far beyond formal education, Johnson believed that even if teachers were fluent in both languages and had the necessary teaching materials, a further impediment was the prejudice of Welsh parents against the employment of their own language, even as a medium of explanation: 'Welsh parents . . . consider all time as wasted which is spent learning Welsh.'[34]

The picture painted of adult education in north Wales was different. Secular education, to use Johnson's phrase, occurred in a few night schools, forty-seven in all, with an average of just under fourteen scholars in each. Forty-one of these were conducted in English only, by day school teachers. There were no schools of industry or Mechanics' Institutes. In Bala and Porthmadog there had been attempts to establish reading rooms and/or lending libraries and in both of these periodicals and newspapers were provided in both Welsh and English. Johnson

---

[31] Ibid., *Part III*, p. 44.
[32] Ibid., *Part III*, p. 38.
[33] Ibid., *Part III*, p. 34.
[34] Ibid.

was impressed by 'the eagerness of the labouring classes to take advantage of these institutions . . .'[35]

It is significant that he discussed Sunday schools in the context of adult education. For children, he regarded them as 'the main instrument of civilization'.[36] They were certainly numerous – 1,161 in the six counties of north Wales. The linguistic contrast with the day schools was dramatic – 809 of these schools (70.8 per cent) were held in Welsh only. A further 237 (20.7 per cent) were conducted bilingually, with only 97 (8.5 per cent) in English only, very largely in the counties of Denbigh (25), Flint (18) and Montgomery (41).[37] Even if these numbers are not strictly accurate, it is obvious that the schools were held in the natural language of their people, both Welsh- and English-speaking.

Johnson's analysis of the resulting situation is illuminating. He noted especially the compartmentalization of life into religious and secular. It was not only the language of the schools which was distinct but also the matter: 'In the week-day schools all profess to learn English, in the Sunday-schools . . . all learn Welsh; the object which the poor desire from the former is secular knowledge; the end to which they devote their whole attention in the Sunday-school is religion, to the exclusion of every other study.'[38] There was no equivocation in his assessment of the impact of the Sunday schools – 'the main instrument of civilization in North Wales'.[39] He believed that they had moulded the language, literature and 'general intelligence of the inhabitants'.[40] The argument was that the use of Welsh as the language of religion had immensely reinforced its value for theological disputation. However, the imbalance between matters religious and secular was dramatic as a result of the influence of the Sunday schools: 'its [the Welsh language] resources in every other branch remain obsolete and meagre'.[41] Johnson supported the argument by analysing, in his words, 'all the works at present printed and read in North Wales . . .' in the Welsh language. According to his categorization, of the 405 titles available, 309 related to religion or poetry, '50 to scientific subjects, which are intelligible to the few who are Welsh scholars, but unknown in the cottages or even the schools of the poor', and the remainder were mainly trivia.[42] Periodical literature, substantially emanating from the religious denominations, was even more biased towards theological topics. *Y Cylchgrawn*, 'which originated in an attempt to diffuse useful knowledge as a separate subject, survived only a few months . . .'[43] One of his informants had argued that 'the only

---

[35] Ibid., *Part III*, p. 55.
[36] Ibid.
[37] Ibid., *Part III*, p. 58.
[38] Ibid., *Part III*, p. 59.
[39] Ibid.
[40] Ibid.
[41] Ibid.
[42] Ibid., *Part III*, p. 60.
[43] Ibid.

way to convey a little secular information to the people, is by introducing an occasional paper into periodicals . . . The *Amaethydd* (or Agriculturist), is not such an exception as will in any way affect the truth of my assertion, for that publication was given away, as a supplement to a newspaper, and even then it failed'.[44] Furthermore, the linguistic proficiency produced in the Sunday schools was oral, not written.[45]

Johnson's assessment, then, based on the plethora of reports which he had received from his assistants, was that the people of north Wales were 'far superior to the same class of Englishmen in being able to read the Bible in their own language, supplied with a variety of religious and poetical literature, and skilled in discussing with eloquence and subtilty [sic] abstruse points of polemic theology, they remain inferior in every branch of practical knowledge and skill . . . For secular subjects they have neither literature nor a language'.[46]

Even where attempts had been made to bridge the gap between Welsh-language usage and secular concerns they had foundered on a difficulty which was to dog the teaching of Welsh perennially, that is the discrepancy between literary and spoken Welsh. This discrepancy was apparent, of course, in the Welsh used for theological discourse, but it posed far fewer problems because the Bible had been the main, and often the sole, textbook by means of which the Welsh had learnt to read, with mastery consolidated in the Sunday school. Attempts in a Welsh periodical to provide 'practical letters' for farmers had failed,[47] according to Johnson, because 'the farmers complained that they were far too difficult for them to understand. The author assured me that the style and expressions employed were so homely that he had been ashamed to be known as the writer'.[48]

The utilitarian supremacy of English was taken as axiomatic. Farmers, tradespeople and sailors alike were castigated: their inability to read or write in English prevented them from fulfilling their potential. Johnson's emphasis on the occupational impediments of not learning English were wholly in line with informed Victorian opinion and, of course, echoed those of his fellow commissioners. This was not the insult. That arose from the commissioners' blind acceptance that intelligence, culture and morality also equated with mastery of English. A telling indicator of the way in which the commissioners thought is provided by Johnson's dismissal of the north Wales quarrymen. He referred to evidence of their 'literary character', and proceeded to reveal his total incomprehension of the nature of this claim: 'few of them have access to any information, except what is contained in the Welsh language. Some are able to write, and the best scholars among them can read a newspaper in English, but very

[44] Ibid.
[45] Ibid., *Part III*, p. 61.
[46] Ibid.
[47] Ibid., *Part III*, p. 62.
[48] Ibid.

few so as to derive information.' The result, over the whole of north Wales, was judged to produce 'imperfect results of civilization'.[49] Such sentiments were entirely at one with Lord Macaulay's view, in 1834, that 'one single shelf of a good European library was worth the whole native literature of India and Africa'.[50]

Whatever the shortcomings of the statistical evidence accumulated by the commission, the general pattern of school education in north Wales emerges clearly. In a Welsh-speaking society, secular education was in English. Johnson's criticisms implied that this civilizing mission was ineffectual, partly – and here was the irony – because the kind of total immersion in English which parents and teachers desired was itself ineffectual. Some kind of bilingual approach was essential to reach the promised land of an English-speaking Wales. Beyond this, Johnson's attitude is exactly what we would expect of a member of his class and nation. However impressive the ordinary Welsh person's grasp of theology might have been, the language of progress and civilization was English. Minority languages across the Empire were symbols of inferiority of intellect and culture.

★ ★ ★

Jelinger C. Symons was responsible for investigating education in the counties of Monmouth, Brecon, Cardigan and Radnor. He reported on the first of these separately, a reflection of the equivocal administrative position in which the county had been placed by the Acts of Union. The number of schools in this burgeoning county was given as 127, of which 120 were conducted wholly in the English language. Symons condemned the lack of 'civilization' among the population of this county in which the activities of the Scotch Cattle and the Chartists had so alarmed the government. Here was a very different society from that which had occupied Vaughan Johnson's attentions and this was reflected in the nature of the schools and the linguistic background of the pupils. Private venture schools were prevalent, and there were some works' schools. At the British Iron Company's school in Abersychan it was reported that 'the majority do not speak Welsh at home'.[51]

The report did not hold that this made much difference to command of English, which was 'singularly defective'. According to Symons' correspondents, English was spreading rapidly all over the county. The response of some of the solid Monmouthshire citizenry who were entrusted with providing Symons with information about the language are instructive since they confirm a meeting of minds among the 'respectable' Welsh and the English commissioners. Once more

[49] Ibid., Part III, p. 63.
[50] Quoted in the *Times Educational Supplement*, 4 August 1995.
[51] *Reports of the Commissioners of Inquiry into the State of Education in Wales, Part II. Brecknock, Cardigan, Radnor, and Monmouth* (PP 1847 (871) XXVII), p. 283.

we have a demonstration of the way in which the solid Welsh Victorian middle classes linked the language with wider social ills and endorsed the notion that only the English language had any claim to cultural value. For example, Edward Phillips, a Pontypool doctor, wished profoundly for the speedier spread of English since he believed it would lead to greater co-operation between Welsh and English speakers, increase the influence of the established Church and lead to:

> the general improvement of the people in due deference to their superiors and respect for the law of the land; for a long experience has convinced me of the more peaceful and submissive character of the lower orders who are *members of the Church of England* over those of other sects, and it would facilitate their access to religious and literary works, which would improve their morals and refine their taste, as there is no literature of any real value and utility in the Welsh language.[52]

Inevitably, the Anglican clergy who formed the bulk of Symons' respondents reiterated this theme of the impoverished nature of the Welsh language. The views of the Revd James Hughes of Llanhilleth are typical:

> As the Welsh language has not any valuable writings, either in prose or poetry, and as the Welsh people have not one single interest unconnected with the English, I consider the language to be a nuisance and an obstacle, both to the administration of the law, and to the cause of religion . . .[53]

It was left to the Revd Augustus Morgan, rector of Machen, to be more explicit. Adding to the general chorus of Anglican condemnation of all things Welsh, he believed:

> it has been proved, that the meetings which preceded, and which were held during the chartist outbreak and Rebecca conspiracy in Monmouthshire and South Wales, were carried on altogether in the Welsh language, solely with a view that the extent of their proceedings should not be discovered by the police, and other agents sent down by the Government for the discovery and counteraction of their revolutionary plot.[54]

Symons' bias in his investigations in Monmouthshire is as much revealed by his choice of informants as by his stated attitude of condemnation of the Welsh language and the way of life with which he believed it was associated. But he was not taken in by the protestations of the employers, so that his summing up of social ills in Monmouthshire was essentially paradoxical. There was a great moral disease which opposed educational development, but the attitude of the poor was

---

[52] Ibid., *Part II*, p. 295.
[53] Ibid., *Part II*, p. 298.
[54] Ibid., *Part II*, p. 302.

conditioned by that of their immediate superiors and 'to sympathy and kindness these benighted people are well nigh utter strangers'.[55]

The economic structure of the counties of Brecon, Cardigan and Radnor was radically different from that of Monmouthshire. These were substantially rural counties, with agriculture the basic industry in areas of large estates owned by a gentry élite. For the mass of the tenant-farming and labouring population there was grinding poverty to contend with. The Rebecca riots in west Wales had been underpinned by pressure on holdings and tenant poverty, and had revealed the extent of physical hardship in rural Wales. Compared with pockets in the industrializing counties the population was sparse, but the rural economy could not support its natural increase. The surplus was driven inexorably to the iron towns of Glamorgan and Monmouthshire, with their intermittently voracious appetite for labour. Without this safety valve a similar fate to that of Ireland might well have befallen the Welsh.

There was a marked linguistic divide in these three counties. Radnorshire was an almost wholly English-speaking county. In Symons' view, the most grammatical English was spoken in the area between Rhayader and Presteigne. The vast majority of the inhabitants of the two other counties were Welsh speakers.[56] His estimate was that in Radnorshire almost all the population spoke English habitually, while in Cardiganshire, whose population was three times larger, the opposite was the case. More surprisingly, English was the language of nearly half the population of Breconshire.

The more traditional economic base produced a very different school system from that in the industrial counties. There were 240 schools in the three counties, compared with 127 in Monmouthshire, and they were predominantly denominational rather than private venture or industrial. We would expect that in Radnorshire, a marcher county bordering England, the language of instruction would be English and, indeed, all 43 of the county's schools were conducted wholly in that language. Eight of the 96 schools in Breconshire were conducted in both Welsh and English, but none in Welsh alone. Cardiganshire was one of the most Welsh of counties in language, with a large monoglot Welsh population, yet here again the predominant language was English. English was the only medium of instruction in 75 of its 101 schools, with one alone being held only in Welsh. Symons commented that this situation would 'be a subject of the utmost satisfaction to every friend to Wales'.[57]

The second of the commissioners sang much the same song as the first. The usual method of learning was by rote, with children repeating the words in their various reading books. In 45 of the 72 schools in Welsh districts there was no attempt to develop understanding, and very few pupils 'were able to give the

[55] Ibid., *Part II*, p. 305.
[56] Ibid., *Part II*, p. 34.
[57] Ibid., *Part II*, p. 33.

Welsh for ordinary English words'.[58] But it is significant that Symons, like Vaughan Johnson, coupled his criticisms of teaching Welsh-speaking pupils in a foreign language with a blanket criticism of the quality of teaching. Symons highlighted the grave inadequacies of even the meagre teacher training which existed in Wales by recounting his visit with Lingen to Brecon Normal College. It was not so much the quality of instruction which was at fault but the poor quality of the students, which, given the status of teachers, was inevitable:

> No man of ability with a prospect of ordinary success in life will undergo an elaborate training for a calling which will scarcely supply him with bare necessities; those only who are bereft of better resources will start for so poor a goal. The best normal school that it were possible to institute would die of inanition if established in Wales without some concomitant means of remunerating the abilities it called forth.[59]

So it emerges again that the 'vilely ill taught' English of the schools was an added complication. The standard of teaching generally was equally abysmal in many parts of England. What has so often been highlighted as the core of the educational 'problem' in Wales was part of a far wider problem of teaching standards. This was epitomized in Symons' comments on the inability of pupils who habitually spoke English to comprehend it in school because of the discrepancy between the spoken and written forms, a problem traditionally associated with Welsh.[60] But the significance of such comments rests in the light they shed on the verdict of the Blue Books on Welsh speakers. Essentially, Symons and his class used a different kind of language from that of the working class of England. Over a century previously Symons found fluent child readers constantly ignorant of words such as 'observe', 'conclude', 'reflect', 'perceive', 'refresh', 'cultivate', 'contention', 'consideration', 'meditation'. He might have been hard pressed to find such words in general use in many classrooms today. 'No working-class child', commented Symons, 'is in the habit of saying "I *observed* my brother pass by" &c . . .'[61] The surrealist tinge to such observations puts into context the whole of the commissioners' analysis of the educational implications of the Welsh language. It does not condone, but it does serve to modify our perception of malice. We are dealing with the educational analysis of people living in a different world from either rural Wales or the slums of Manchester so familiar to Kay-Shuttleworth.

Symons' general attitude to the Welsh language was unequivocal and there is no reason to doubt that his record of the opinions of local clergy is accurate. The visitor to the one Welsh-language school near Newcastle Emlyn was the Revd

[58] Ibid., *Part II*, p. 25.
[59] Ibid., *Part II*, p. 33.
[60] Ibid., *Part II*, p. 34.
[61] Ibid.

H. L. Davies of Troed-yr-aur, who believed the school would be far better attended if it were held in English.[62] Symons himself judged that the 'poor' in Wales wished above all to learn English for economic reasons and that 'any day-school master . . . would starve, if he sought to live on his own independent efforts to maintain a school for exclusively teaching the Welsh language'.[63]

In Symons' area, too, English was appallingly taught. We are presented with the usual catalogue of inadequacies. The teachers had the most rudimentary command of the language, even when conversing on common subjects. There are numerous examples of incorrect pronunciations, inadequate comprehension of material in the English language, lack of knowledge and understanding of the Bible and bizarre teaching methods.[64] There is no doubting the strength of Symons' condemnation, but it is important to recognize its nature. Of course, underlying it was the middle-class Englishman's disdain for the Welsh language, but it is clear once more that his strictures on schooling would have been hardly less forceful had he been commenting on parts of England. Welsh might be a further hindrance, but only in a fundamentally flawed system. British schools, national schools and private adventure schools alike were criticized: 'The endowed schools are little more efficient than the private ones', and 'The schools under Mrs Bevan's charity are, if possible, less efficient.'[65]

Once more the Sunday schools, within their lights, were an exception, though Symons did not praise them uniformly. For example, he cited evidence that those in the Cardigan area were less effective than those in the north of the county. He instanced inadequate understanding among teachers, rote learning and, most tellingly, restricted aims. But he also presented a whole range of evidence in their favour, despite the fact that they were conducted substantially in Welsh.[66] Of the 440 Sunday schools in the three counties, 228 were held in Welsh and a further 109 employed both languages. Of the 103 schools held solely in English, 56 were Anglican schools in the counties of Brecon and Radnor.[67]

The testimony of Congregationalists and Calvinistic Methodists was cited extensively, along with that of their Anglican counterparts.[68] As with the evidence from the north Wales counties, it illustrated children's wide knowledge of the Bible, along with their deficiency in 'secular knowledge', which these schools imparted only accidentally. A Calvinistic Methodist minister from Aberaeron asserted that if 'in the day-schools any scriptural questions are answered, it is more owing to the Sunday-schools than the day-schools'. Numerous quotations testify to the superiority of Scriptural knowledge among the mass of the population in

[62] Ibid., *Part II*, p. 33.
[63] Ibid.
[64] Ibid., *Part II*, pp. 36–40.
[65] Ibid., *Part II*, pp. 46–7.
[66] Ibid., *Part II*, p. 63.
[67] Ibid., *Part II*, p. 55.
[68] Ibid., *Part II*, p. 53.

Wales compared with that among the working class in England as a result of the work of the Sunday schools. While this evidence is hearsay, it is significant that Symons was prepared to give it prominence. His attitude, therefore, seems to reflect that which was so prevalent in contemporary Wales. The Welsh language was an effective and successful medium for the transmission of scriptural knowledge, but was an impediment in the secular world.

While it may be possible to argue that the commissioners' attitudes towards the Welsh language were more rational than is traditionally believed, this must be restricted to their analysis of the education system. It is difficult to see it reflected in their opinions on morality. Symons' report gives extensive coverage to the views of 'respectable' opinion in Wales, which included Nonconformist as well as Anglican testimony. For example, it was a Nonconformist who accused the inhabitants of Brecon of gambling, drunkenness and adultery. However, the overall picture of a society which did not conform to the ideals of respectable middle-class Victorian visions, the picture which gave rise to national outrage among the Welsh, emerged mainly from the evidence of Anglicans and landowners. That Symons' own judgements were far more temperate than those of many of his witnesses is often ignored. But he did quote extensively the notorious views of the Revd John Price, rector of Bleddfa, who highlighted the 'prevailing vice of the country' as 'a disregard for chastity, a breach of which is considered neither a sin nor a crime'. He was most notorious for having identified a prime reason as 'the *bad habit of holding meetings* at dissenting chapels or farmhouses after night, where the youth of both sexes attend from a distance for the purpose of walking home together'.[69] Symons did at least emphasize that drunkenness was confined to the towns and adultery 'entirely confined to one or two places'.[70] There was no specific attempt to link alleged moral deficiencies to the Welsh language. This was not so with the accusation that branded the Welsh as liars, at least in the law courts. It is also difficult to avoid the impression that allegations such as those of the clerk to the Lampeter magistrates amounted as much to frustration with the inefficiencies inherent in the system as to malice against the Welsh language *per se*. He, and others, testified to perjury by witnesses, the inability of prisoners and jurors to understand English, and the consequent confusion in proceedings. Edward Crompton Lloyd Hall, a Cardiganshire barrister, ascribed the evasiveness implicit in Welsh to its origins as the language of slavery.[71]

Within the parameters of detailed evidence, Symons concluded his report with a diatribe against the Welsh language which reflected his own prejudices – unsurprising in one of his background – but one which also drew on the information and opinion supplied to him by a variety of sources within Wales.

[69] Ibid., *Part II*, p. 61.
[70] Ibid.
[71] Ibid.

The commissioner's opening to the section has attracted particular notoriety: 'The Welsh language is a vast drawback to Wales, and a manifold barrier to the moral progress and commercial prosperity of the people. It is not easy to over-estimate its evil effects.'[72] Part of the condemnatory technique, here as with native languages throughout the Empire, was to invest it with primitiveness: 'It is the language of the Cymri, and anterior to that of the ancient Britons.'[73] Welsh was, therefore, devoid of cultural achievement, and 'dissevers the people from intercourse which would greatly advance their civilisation, and bars the access of improving knowledge to their minds. As a proof of this, there is no Welsh literature worthy of the name'.[74] There was grudging acceptance that monthly magazines in Welsh had resulted in saving the population from 'perfect ignorance' and 'utter vacuity of thought', but such publications were polemical and sectarian.[75] The remedy for ignorance and the distortion of truth, fraud and perjury which were a product of the use of Welsh in the courts was the proper teaching of the English language in efficient schools.[76]

Of course, such sentiments provoked varying degrees of outrage in Wales. Yet they remain consistent with Symons' belief that the education system generally was failing the Welsh people and impeding the progress to which their natural talents entitled them. He quoted the dean of St David's: 'The natural capacity of the Welsh is great to a very wonderful degree . . . the Welsh have a great capacity for learning languages. They are very quick.'[77] The impediment was the inability to speak English, which blighted individual prospects in agricultural and industrial economies. Here was the theme, almost the abiding refrain, of the reports. The commissioners, along with numerous Welsh observers, believed in the native wit, the intelligence, the innate capacity of the Welsh to take their place in the ordained Victorian entrepreneurial scheme of things. They were chained by their native language to, at best, an other-worldly theology, at worst a predilection to immorality (the contradictions remained mysteriously unremarked upon). Mastery of the English language would provide economic liberation, moral uplift and admission to the imperial top table. The existing school system could not deliver this because of the abysmal textbooks, the underfunding of the system and, above all, the appalling standard of teaching. The implications of such condemnation were obvious – and were precisely those for which Kay-Shuttleworth would have been looking.

The prognosis for the English language was fascinating from such an informed outside observer at a time before Welsh economy and society were remoulded

[72] Ibid., *Part II*, p. 66.
[73] Ibid.
[74] Ibid.
[75] Ibid.
[76] Ibid.
[77] Ibid., *Part II*, p. 67.

once more by the explosion in demand for coal. Unlike Lingen, who provided a more accurate forecast of future linguistic patterns, Symons believed that the English language would not 'diffuse itself over the whole country for one or two centuries to come, unless better means are taken to expedite its progress. These means would be found in thoroughly good schools for the purpose. They are desired by the people: and no reasonable doubt is entertained that a sound secular and religious education would raise their physical condition, and eventually remove their moral debasement. If the Welsh people were well educated, and received the same attention and care which have been bestowed on others, they would in all probability assume a high rank among civilized communities'.[78]

★ ★ ★

Civilization was the last word commissioner Lingen would have applied to that most controversial area of Wales for which he was responsible. In the first place it was the least homogeneous of the commissioners' 'circuits'. Linguistically there were complexities in the three counties of Pembrokeshire, Carmarthenshire and Glamorgan. Lingen's categorization here was interesting. He described the inhabitants of the area 'south of the London mail road, i.e. the entire southern coast line and the depth of a few miles behind it, from Cardiff to the coast of the Irish sea, with the exception of the interval between Swansea and St. Clears, where the south-east corner of Carmarthenshire reaches down to the Bristol channel' as having English as their mother tongue.[79] Elsewhere, though increasing numbers understood some English, it was not properly comprehended, certainly not spoken. For the majority in these areas their only acquaintance with the English language was in the day schools. Here the situation was similar to that in the rest of Wales – effective communication was made impossible by English-language textbooks explained only by rote. Lingen's unequivocal assessment, unanimous among the commissioners, was that: 'It would be impossible to exaggerate the difficulties which this diversity between the language in which the school-books are written, and the mother-tongue of the children presents.'[80] In these three counties, as in the rest of Wales, teachers' facility in English was so limited that they were unable to cope. Three-quarters of the Sunday schools, on the other hand, were conducted either in Welsh or bilingually.

By 1846 the economy of Glamorgan had been transformed by the iron industry and the concomitant growth in population and its urbanization. We have seen that the social tensions which had been generated had erupted in uprisings which had occasioned alarm in government and led to previous inquiries into educational provision. In retrospect we know that after 1848 the situation in

---

[78] Ibid., *Part II*, p. 68.
[79] Ibid., *Part I*, p. 31.
[80] Ibid.

Wales, as in England, became much less threatening to the established social order, but in 1846 industrialized Glamorgan seemed to pose a threat, perhaps to the point of revolution. Carmarthenshire and eastern parts of Pembrokeshire seemed little better. In the face of increased population, scarcity of land, growing pauperization and often appalling housing conditions, the traditional rural society of south-west Wales had begun to unravel. The chief manifestation of this disintegration was the Rebecca Riots in which time-honoured rituals of community sanction were brought to bear on a society under novel strains. Few contemporaries understood what was happening, least of all a government made paranoid by spontaneous uprisings in many parts of England as well as Wales. In this situation, too, the lack of education was seen as undermining the moral fibre of the people, especially a people who communicated in an alien and subversive tongue.

More clearly than his contemporaries, Lingen also argued that the situation was not amenable to traditional remedy. Industrialization had fundamentally altered the old order, parish vestries and Poor Law administration had been fatally undermined, and with them numerous social sanctions. The parish school no longer provided an answer. It was Lingen's startling claim, in the context of the 1840s, that the works had replaced the parish. A new system of local government was needed. But there was a problem. Any new regime of local government depended on the existence of a middle class, but there was none, and 'the elimination of a middle class is rendered still more complete when, to the economical causes tending to produce it, is superadded the separation of language'.[81]

Lingen's ruthless analysis of his area should be viewed in this context, as well as in terms of the prejudices of one of his background and class. We have seen that it was he who had the clearest perception of the socio-economic impact of the Welsh language, a view shared by so many contemporary middle-class Welshmen:

> Whether in the country, or among the furnaces, the Welsh element is never found at the top of the social scale . . . in his new, as in his old, home, his language keeps him under the hatches, being one in which he can neither acquire nor communicate the necessary information. It is a language of old-fashioned agriculture, of theology, and of simple rustic life, while all the world about him is English.[82]

Lingen paints a vivid picture, as revealing about himself as the Welsh people, of an 'underworld', cut off from the modern world, impinging on the wider consciousness only in the context of a 'Revival, or a Rebecca or Chartist outbreak'.[83] As a result of the economic and social isolation imposed on the native Welsh by their language, their 'mental faculties' had developed only in the field of

---

[81] Ibid., *Part I*, p. 31.
[82] Ibid., *Part I*, p. 3.
[83] Ibid.

theology, but this had only led in directions which further differentiated them from the classes above them. It would appear, then, that Lingen ascribed the lack of cohesion in Welsh society to the language. His conception of social cohesion was one in which his own class – the middle class – was the dynamic behind individual and communal, even imperial, progress. The society on which Lingen reported was one in which, he argued, the twin influences of industrialization and language combined to ensure that no Welsh middle class could develop.

On the other hand, he shared his fellow commissioners' admiration for what the Welsh had achieved for themselves both in chapel building and in theological discourse. From an educational perspective, this was most manifest in the achievements of the Sunday schools, which represented:

> the efforts of the mass of a people, utterly unaided, to educate themselves . . . These schools have been almost the sole, they are still the main and most congenial, centres of education. Through their agency the younger portion of the adult labouring classes in Wales can generally read, or are in course of learning to read, the Scriptures in their mother tongue.[84]

He, too, was prepared to accept their considerable command of esoteric theology, though within a context which has coloured our view of the Blue Books ever since. He believed that informal Welsh-language education in theology had helped to induce 'poetical and enthusiastic warmth of religious feeling' and 'the comparative absence of crime'.[85] These virtues, according to Lingen's primitive sociology, were accompanied by 'a wide-spread disregard of temperance, whenever there are the means of excess, of chastity, of veracity, and of fair dealing'.[86]

We have seen that all the evidence from all sides of opinion in Wales favoured mass literacy in English. Lingen's summary was trenchant:

> On the manifold evils inseparable from an ignorance of English I found but one opinion expressed on all hands. They are too palpable, and too universally admitted, to need particularizing.

But he also added that the only motive was profit, and 'affection leans to Welsh'.[87] He noted the social tensions generated by parental perceptions of English being an instrument of social mobility when the child was born into a community in which 'preaching – prayer-meetings – Sunday-schools – clubs – biddings – funerals – the

[84] Ibid.
[85] Ibid., *Part I*, p. 6.
[86] Ibid.
[87] Ibid.

denominational magazine (his only press), all these exhibit themselves to him in Welsh as their natural exponent . . .'[88]

Lingen's analysis of the educational implications was by far the most incisive to appear in contemporary literature on bilingualism. As a result of the educating influence of the chapel and the Sunday school, the Welsh were 'naturally voluble, often eloquent', with 'a mastery over his own language far beyond that which the Englishman of the same degree possesses over his'.[89] In this there was unanimity among the commissioners. But from this point onwards, Lingen revealed far greater perceptiveness of the forces at work in Wales. Welsh society, especially chapel society, cherished its eloquence, so the acceptance of the inarticulacy which accompanied the use of English was doubly difficult. Lingen went on to argue that, in any case, learning English in a formal context, without it being the vehicle for discussion and the dissemination of ideas in the community, was arid:

> Nor can an old and cherished language be *taught down* in schools; for so long as the children are familiar with none other, they must be educated to a considerable extent through the medium of it, even though to supersede it be the most important part of their education. Still less, out of school, can the language of lessons make head against the language of life.[90]

Crucially, Lingen saw this context of 'life' changing all around him. The linguistic monopoly of chapel society was being eroded by the consequences of the railways and the in-migration of labourers to the iron and coal fields. Lingen, alone of the commissioners, therefore saw the economic and social context as an 'encouragement vigorously to press forward the cause of popular education in its most advanced form'.[91] His summary was clinically perceptive:

> Schools are not called upon to impart in a foreign, or engraft upon the ancient, tongue a factitious education conceived under another set of circumstances (in either of which cases the task would be as hopeless as the end unprofitable), but to convey in a language, which is already in process of becoming the mother-tongue of the country, such instruction as may put the people on a level with that position which is offered to them by the course of events.[92]

Furthermore, Lingen realized that in circumstances in which the culture of the new language contrasted with the ideas embodied in the old it was the former which would triumph in the new Wales.

[88] Ibid.
[89] Ibid., *Part I*, p. 7.
[90] Ibid.
[91] Ibid.
[92] Ibid.

It was apparent, too, that others were at least dimly aware of the complex context of this infant sociology of language. Indeed, it is clear that the simplistic view of the period whereby informed opinion is credited with endorsing Welsh as the language of religion and yielding up all secular matters, including education, to English – an impression reinforced on occasion in the Blue Books – is distorting. Lingen makes clear that many influential clergy, both Anglican and Nonconformist, wanted to see the position of Welsh safeguarded in the day schools, along with English. They argued that only by means of the Welsh language could religious truths be made generally acceptable, that Welsh literature was neither 'contaminated' nor 'infidel', and that a person who spoke two languages was better educated than someone who knew only one. Lingen, however, did not comment.

Schooling, in Glamorgan especially, was more varied than in other areas of Wales. In addition to the traditional denominational schools, and relatively large numbers of private venture schools, there were 24 works' schools in Lingen's area, which he defined as those which were financed partly by workers' subscriptions. A few were of the highest calibre, particularly the Guest school in Merthyr. But the essential pattern of inadequacy in the teaching of English was as characteristic of this area as of the rest of Wales. Such inadequacy was doubly unfortunate in that Lingen, like his fellow commissioners, judged that 'the children appeared . . . to possess considerable arithmetical powers, if there had been anyone to cultivate them properly'.[93] The message was as unequivocal as in the other commissioners' reports. Schooling was desperately inadequate.

This was one of the common themes in the Blue Books. The commissioners and the witnesses they chose to cite had much else in common. They agreed that teaching resources were wholly inadequate, that teaching standards were abysmal, that the discrepancy between the language of the hearth and the school exacerbated the problem, that the Sunday schools had achieved much but in ways irrelevant to mid-Victorian realities, that moral shortcomings, including a tendency to riot, were associated with inadequate education and that the Welsh deserved better, both for their own sake and for that of their neighbours. Already Welsh parents endorsed an English-language future and in the longer term it transpired that the people of Wales agreed with much else in the Report.

The immediate political and national repercussions of the analysis provided and recorded by the commissioners in the 1847 Report was rather different, and helped to determine the climate of opinion evident in the election of 1868 and beyond.[94] The commissioners' strictures on the morals, religion and language of the Welsh dominated reaction at the time and historiography ever since. The 1847 Report certainly avoided the classic deficiency of educational history – its

---

[93] Ibid., *Part I*, p. 27.
[94] Jones, ' "Brad y Llyfrau Gleision" and Welsh Politics', pp. 103–65.

isolation from the social and economic contexts. Paradoxically, an emphasis on the commissioners' religious and class affiliations, and consequent mid-Victorian prejudices, has served to divert attention from what may well have been the intended purpose, namely to provide evidence about the educational state of Wales, and in doing so, the necessity for a state system of education.

This context is central. It was not only in Wales that industrialization had swamped erstwhile parishes, that a demographic revolution was taking place, that traditional forms of local government had broken down, and that there had been social upheaval. We have seen that Kay-Shuttleworth was familiar with the kinds of problems confronting Wales. He was an indefatigable campaigner for state funding of education and teacher training at a time when the usual government reluctance to spend money was allied with denominational rivalries which impeded reform. Kay-Shuttleworth wished the government to be presented with overwhelming evidence of the shortcomings of the existing system. It was axiomatic at the time that there was a link between educational provision and the moral and social well-being of the populace, but it suited Kay-Shuttleworth's purpose that it should be presented in the most extreme terms. We know that at some stage such considerations found their way into the commissioners' terms of reference; we shall never know just how this was translated into their end product.

What was least controversial at the time was the overt statement in the terms of reference that the report should concern itself with the effective learning of English. Given contemporary national and imperial attitudes within the economic and social structure, this was inevitable. As we have seen, it was an attitude shared by the English and Welsh middle classes. In terms of the immediate development of education, it was uncontroversial. When Robert Lowe's 1862 Revised Code introduced a system of payment to schools on the basis of pupils' performance in prescribed subjects, it was never considered that Welsh should be one of those subjects. Decades elapsed before the resurgent Welsh cultural nationalism of the 1880s resulted in Welsh becoming an approved special and class subject in the context of a more sympathetic attitude to the language in official circles.

Nevertheless, the Report raised issues which were central to Wales and Welshness, both then and since. That it did so in such graphic terms even had its benefits. The immediate effect on Welsh educational provision was limited, though Hugh Owen's efforts to inject energy into the British Society and into teacher training in Wales bore fruit. Neither movement involved any commitment to the Welsh language. Wales, inexorably falling in with the rhythms of the British state, had to wait for the Forster Education Act of 1870 before a more comprehensive system of elementary education provided schooling for the great majority. Although the board schools which soon came into existence did not implement the kind of coercive policies against the use of Welsh which occurred in some private schools, they certainly did nothing to encourage it. Educational objectives across the educational spectrum in Wales were to be realized in English, and very few dissented from this. Even when official attitudes began to change from the 1880s onwards, public and parental opinion did not. English was the language of 'getting on'. Arguably, public opinion on this matter did not alter fundamentally until after the Second World War, but for the first time the centrality of the relationship between Welsh education and the British state had been articulated graphically by the 1847 Report.

16

The British State and Welsh-language Education 1850–1914

W. GARETH EVANS

UNTIL THE final decades of the nineteenth century the Welsh language was regarded by central government as a 'problem' or 'difficulty' and a major cause of low educational standards, ignorance and backwardness in Wales. The state had no conception of a meaningful 'bilingual policy' for schools and colleges. Indeed, every effort was made to suppress the use of the Welsh language in public-funded schools.[1] Although Sir James Kay-Shuttleworth, the first secretary of the Committee of Council on Education, and the Revd H. Longueville Jones HMI in the 1850s appreciated the existence of two languages in Wales and were more enlightened in their attitudes than most of their contemporaries, central government did not begin to support limited use of Welsh in elementary schools until the 1880s.[2] Nevertheless, prejudice and cynicism towards the use of the native language still occluded the dawn of the twentieth century.

Parliamentary Reports

Ever since its publication in 1847, the Report of the Commissioners of Inquiry into the State of Education in Wales has been regarded as the *locus classicus* of hostile and negative attitudes towards the Welsh language by the state in Victorian times.[3] The publication of the Blue Books aroused intense indignation throughout Wales, for the morality, literature, religion and education, as well as the native language, had been subjected to such severe strictures that it constituted 'the censure of a nation'. In the view of the commissioners, efficient education was synonymous with English-medium schooling. The Report was to epitomize official attitudes towards the Welsh language for much of the nineteenth century.

---

[1] W. Gareth Evans, 'The "Bilingual Difficulty": HMI and the Welsh Language in the Victorian Age', *WHR*, 16, no. 4 (1993), 494–513.
[2] Idem, 'O. M. Edwards's Enlightened Precursors: Nineteenth-century HMIs and the Welsh Language', *Planet*, 99 (1993), 69–77.
[3] *Reports of the Commissioners of Inquiry into the State of Education in Wales . . . in three parts* (London, 1847) (PP 1847 XXVII).

The most detailed official survey of education in Wales during the 1850s was conducted in 1859 when John Jenkins, assistant commissioner for the Newcastle Commission, investigated 'the State of Popular Education in the Welsh Specimen Districts in the Poor Law Unions of Corwen, Dolgellau, Bala, Ffestiniog, Neath and Merthyr Tydfil in North and South Wales'.[4] Jenkins had been a Unitarian minister and schoolmaster prior to qualifying as a barrister. There was widespread concern about the quality of elementary education in voluntary schools in receipt of financial support from the state. Although comparatively little attention was given in the Report to the Welsh language, the assistant commissioner noted that the Revd John Griffith, Aberdare, and others who had given evidence had shown no enthusiasm for the native language.[5] Echoing the view of his predecessors in 1847 by concluding that 'the Welsh language is the language of the past and not of the present', Jenkins believed that it was essential that English be the language of education so that Welshmen might 'enter on the competition of life, on anything like fair terms, or with anything like equal chances of success'.[6] He was surprised that the majority of pupils in the schools he had visited were unable to speak English and that the teachers were unable to speak Welsh.[7] He feared that the lack of books and periodicals in the native language deprived aspiring Welshmen of the opportunity of succeeding in various careers, even as 'mechanics', and he believed that 'the final extinction of the old language of the country' was desirable.[8] He saw no virtue in bilingualism: advocates of two languages, where only one was necessary, were, in his view, misguided, and simply provided evidence of the way 'national predilections' could adversely affect judgement.[9]

During the 1860s the education of the middle classes was a major issue in England and in 1864 a Royal Commission was appointed, under the chairmanship of Henry, Baron Taunton, 'to inquire into the education given in schools not comprised within the scope of the Newcastle and Clarendon Reports'.[10] The detailed Taunton Report was published in 1868. Endowed and non-endowed private boys' and girls' schools in Wales were visited by two assistant commissioners, H. M. Bompas and James Bryce. Although the Welsh language was not specifically mentioned in the terms of reference of the inquiry, both assistant commissioners passed comment on the native tongue. Welsh was taught in two endowed schools only; there were twelve pupils at Lampeter and fifty-eight at Llandovery College. The trust deed of Llandovery College made it clear

---

[4] *Report of the Commissioners on the State of Popular Education in England and Wales* (Newcastle Report) (PP 1861 (2794) XXI).
[5] Ibid., *Part II*, p. 621.
[6] Ibid., p. 449.
[7] Ibid., p. 450.
[8] Ibid., p. 453.
[9] Ibid.
[10] *Report of the Schools Inquiry Commission* (Taunton Report), Terms of Reference, December 1864 (PP 1867–8 (3966) XXVIII).

that the study and cultivation of the Welsh language were principal objectives of the institution, and during the years between 1848 and 1875 Welsh was taught in all classes for one hour a day. James Bryce concluded that this obligation was 'a clog to the success of the school'[11] and was generally regarded as 'irksome, if not a waste of time'.[12] He believed the teaching of Welsh had adverse consequences, including the restriction of most teaching posts to Welshmen and the failure to recruit boys from England and Anglicized parts of Wales.[13] Nevertheless, he recognized that the founder's command was explicit and also acknowledged the utility of the grammatical study of the Welsh language for future clergymen. 'Correct and dignified diction' was essential in the pulpit at a time when colloquial Welsh, particularly in south Wales, was 'very irregular and corrupt'.[14] Although he was aware that some people associated with Llandovery College desired 'to see peculiarities removed which hamper it in the struggle with other schools', it could not be denied that interest in the Welsh language was closely associated with the school's foundation. In these circumstances, rather than seek the abolition of the teaching of Welsh, Bryce advocated its restriction to native Welsh speakers.[15] His colleague Bompas, like the Welsh community at large, saw the Welsh language as a barrier to progress. In some districts it was regarded as unfashionable for girls to speak Welsh. Bompas believed that such attitudes would lead to the rapid demise of the language among the middle classes.[16]

The *Report on the Employment of Children, Young Persons and Women in Agriculture* (1870) expounded the same negative attitude towards the Welsh language. It revealed that educational opportunities available in Wales were extremely limited and that girls, as well as boys, were subject to the dictates of early employment. The signatories of the *Report on Wales* – H. S. Tremenheere and E. C. Tufnell – concluded that, with the exception of a few localities, elementary education in Wales seemed to be making only slow progress.[17] This was attributed to an insufficient number of schools, the short duration of schooling for many pupils (mainly caused by apathy and parental indifference), and the 'obstacle' of the Welsh language.[18] Like their predecessors in 1847, Tremenheere and Tufnell provided a highly disparaging portrait of Welsh womanhood. In their eyes, women in rural Wales were the most unrefined and poorly educated creatures, much afflicted by 'the obstacle to Welsh civilization' caused by the prevalence of the Welsh language.[19]

---

[11] Ibid., *Vol. XX. Monmouthshire and Wales*, p. 92.
[12] Ibid., p. 88.
[13] Ibid., p. 92.
[14] Ibid., p. 88.
[15] Ibid., p. 92.
[16] Ibid.
[17] *Reports of the Commission on the Employment of Children, Young Persons and Women in Agriculture* (PP 1870 (C. 70) XIII), p. 6.
[18] Ibid., p. 7.
[19] Ibid., p. 19.

On 25 August 1880 the Education Department appointed 'a Committee to inquire into the present condition of Intermediate and Higher Education in Wales'.[20] Its members were Lord Aberdare (Chairman), Viscount Emlyn, Henry Richard MP, Professor John Rhŷs, Lewis Morris and the Revd Prebendary H. G. Robinson. The publication of its Report in August 1881 has been regarded as a defining moment in the history of education in modern Wales. It recognized the need to establish undenominational and democratically managed intermediate schools financed from the rates and Treasury grants, as well as two 'provincial colleges' of higher education, financially supported by annual parliamentary grants. It was also stipulated that the new system of education should be directly related to 'the particular circumstances and characteristics of the country'.[21] The committee's ambit included no especial reference to the Welsh language. Nevertheless, the Report identified the language as one of the 'distinctive characteristics' of Wales. It epitomized Welsh nationality as well as being the prevailing language in many communities. On the basis of E. G. Ravenstein's calculations following the census of 1871, the committee accepted that, of a population of 1.4 million, at least 1,006,100 regularly spoke Welsh. It also noted the healthy state of publications in the Welsh language: there were twelve newspapers with a weekly circulation of 74,500, eighteen magazines with a circulation of 90,300, and two quarterly publications bought by 3,000 Welsh readers. According to one witness, as much as £100,000 was spent on Welsh publications of all kinds in 1875. The native language was also the habitual medium for worship for as many as 870,220 of the people of Wales.

The recommendations relating to intermediate and higher education included no constructive role for the Welsh language. Indeed, only peripheral attention was given to the native tongue. It was assumed that secondary and higher education in Wales, particularly in the classics and humanities, were afflicted by the 'bilingual difficulty'. Welsh students lacked command of the English language. This was the inevitable consequence of the regular use of Welsh as the language of the home and community. Since it was futile to expect the immediate demise of the language, it was judged likely that the disadvantages and difficulties experienced by Welshmen in the competitive world of education would persist for many years, though their impact was likely to be less than in the past. The Committee's main linguistic concern was related to the alleged educational disadvantages which bedevilled Wales because of the prevalence of the native language. Members of this Victorian committee continued to equate 'progress' with the advance of the English language, rather than with the promotion of bilingualism or the survival of a minority language. Written and oral evidence led

---

[20] *Report of the Committee appointed to Inquire into the Condition of Intermediate and Higher Education in Wales, with Minutes of Evidence and Appendix: Vol. I, Report* (Aberdare Report) (PP 1881 (C. 3047) XXXIII).

[21] Ibid., p. xlvi.

the Aberdare Committee to conclude that able Welsh students suffered because of their inadequate vocabulary and inaccurate use of the English language. As far as universities were concerned, it was claimed that Welsh students had comparatively less success in classics, for which a thorough knowledge of English was required, than in mathematics and science.

The examination of witnesses, and their replies, in different centres between October 1880 and February 1881, revealed at best a negative attitude towards the native language. On numerous occasions, it received scant attention. In Cardiganshire, Welsh was not mentioned at all in the examination of Principal T. Charles Edwards and Professor J. Mortimer Angus at Aberystwyth, nor in the resolutions conveyed from the Nonconformist conference, nor in the evidence submitted by Ystradmeurig school. No one sought the opinion of many of the leading witnesses, including Hugh Owen, about the Welsh language.

The tenor of the questioning followed the same format throughout the inquiry. Lord Aberdare asked the first witness to be examined, namely the Revd David Jones Davies, rector of North Benfleet, Essex, and a native of Llanwrda, Carmarthenshire: 'Do you think that their imperfect knowledge of English operates very much against them in competing with English children for exhibitions at schools or universities?'[22] Likewise, Professor Thomas McKenna Hughes, Woodwardian Professor of Geology at Cambridge and a native of Carmarthenshire, was asked whether Welsh hampered the academic progress of students.[23] Thomas Ellis of Cynlas, Cefnddwysarn, whose brilliant son, Tom Ellis, was then a student at New College, Oxford, was asked whether he had been 'kept back' by any deficiency in his command of English.[24] Likewise, Clement Davies, headmaster of Bala Grammar School, was asked by Lord Aberdare whether the prevalence of Welsh in the district had had an adverse effect on educational performance, including entrance to university.[25] In similar vein, Dr Lewis Edwards, Principal of the Calvinistic Theological College at Bala, was also asked by Lord Aberdare whether the prevalence of Welsh was an obstacle experienced by prospective ministers of religion in their academic studies.[26] Such questions exemplified the assumption of the Aberdare Committee that the 'bilingual difficulty' blighted the educational progress of Welsh students.

Although not every witness subscribed to this view of the role of the Welsh language, the majority regarded it as an impediment and a disadvantage. The Warden of Llandovery College, the Revd A. G. Edwards, a native Welsh speaker and a figure of considerable standing, was particularly vociferous in his claim that Welsh-speaking boys were placed at a considerable disadvantage in their quest for

---

[22] Ibid., *Vol. II. Minutes of Evidence and Appendices* (Aberdare Evidence), p. 4.
[23] Ibid., p. 64.
[24] Ibid., p. 255.
[25] Ibid., p. 232.
[26] Ibid., p. 270.

university scholarships and exhibitions in classics. He maintained that the performance of a Welsh-speaking child in classics was detrimentally affected by his Welshness, and he quoted detailed statistics of scholarships and exhibitions awarded over a period of twenty-five years to substantiate his argument that Welsh-speaking boys were handicapped when competing with pupils from English-speaking schools in the classics and in general essay-writing in English. Lack of command of the English language adversely affected their translation of classical authors into English or of an English author into Greek or Latin.[27]

Similarly, the Revd Henry T. Edwards, dean of Bangor, claimed that his period on the staff of Llandovery College had persuaded him that Welsh-speaking boys were at a disadvantage in competing with English boys for university scholarships.[28] Convinced that 'the existence of the Welsh language is really the most difficult element in the problem of higher education', Canon R. W. Edwards of St Asaph called for effective teaching of English through the medium of Welsh in elementary schools.[29] Dr Lewis Edwards, one of the most influential leaders of Welsh Nonconformity, acknowledged that the prevalence of the native language placed his students 'under a difficulty' because 'they have to learn English as if it were a foreign language',[30] while the Revd Thomas Lewis, a tutor at Bala Congregational College, acknowledged that his students' 'imperfect knowledge of English' was 'a very great obstacle' to their academic progress. Seen in that light, the Welsh language 'would always be a hindrance'.[31]

Prevailing ideas of 'progress' and the influence of social Darwinism in Victorian Britain were evident in the testimony of several witnesses. The Revd David Williams, rector of Llandyrnog, claimed that the Welsh boy was handicapped 'in the race of life'. English was the language of 'educated Britain' and it was essential that it became the language of 'educated Wales' as well.[32] Rees Williams, a foreman at an ironworks in Swansea, believed that the Welsh language had proved a barrier to progress and that it was tantamount to having 'the German Ocean . . . between Wales and England'.[33] Major Robert Owen Jones, formerly of Bryntegid, Bala, firmly believed that the early demise of the native language would be advantageous for the ordinary people of Wales.[34] When Owen Roberts, a London barrister and a native of Caernarfon, was asked how long he thought the Welsh language would survive, he expressed the hope that its continued use would be minimal because it was such a major drawback for his fellow

---

[27] Ibid., p. 478. See also W. Gareth Evans, 'A. G. Edwards a'r Iaith Gymraeg yng Ngholeg Llanymddyfri', *Barn*, 151 (August 1975), 6–7.
[28] *Aberdare Evidence*, p. 105.
[29] Ibid., p. 197.
[30] Ibid., p. 270.
[31] Ibid., pp. 259–60.
[32] Ibid., pp. 217–18.
[33] Ibid., p. 594.
[34] Ibid., p. 236.

countrymen to contend with.[35] He went on to explain, however, that the disadvantage was not so much knowledge of Welsh as ignorance of English. Similar views were voiced by the headmasters of most of the grammar schools of Wales and by opponents of provincial colleges and a degree-conferring university in Wales. Higher education in an English university was deemed preferable to 'the narrowing influence of merely provincial institutions'. The Revd William Morgan, Vice-Principal of Caernarfon Training College, also accepted that there was a linguistic difficulty and maintained that it would be 'impossible' to utilize the Welsh language as a medium of instruction in a Welsh university.[36] The headmasters of Denbigh, Grove Park, Wrexham, and other grammar schools, as well as a number of other schoolmasters who gave evidence, also equated fluency in Welsh with backwardness in English and pointed out the educational disadvantages which thwarted the progress of Welsh students at universities.

Not all witnesses, however, held such negative and pessimistic views. The Revd H. D. Harper, Jesus College, Oxford, believed that the difficulties associated with the Welsh language were much exaggerated. He had not found students at Jesus College hampered in their studies on account of their Welsh origins.[37] Professor Thomas McKenna Hughes of Cambridge maintained that Welsh-speaking students were on a par with other students in the formulating of ideas, though their lack of command of English sometimes affected their powers of expression and communication.[38] The Very Revd Joshua Hughes, bishop of St Asaph, did not believe that Welsh speakers were at a disadvantage in learning classics provided they had achieved a high standard of English at elementary and secondary school: 'I maintain that the language, instead of a hindrance, will be a benefit, because the knowledge of two languages rather sharpens and quickens the intellect.'[39] Principal F. J. Jayne of Lampeter believed that 'the linguistic difficulty' had no effect on the study of mathematics and that a bilingual student had an aptitude for learning other languages. But in translating Latin and Greek into English, he thought that Welsh students were at a disadvantage because of their inferior command of their second language.[40] A few other witnesses also acknowledged that a working knowledge of the vernacular would be of value to clergymen, doctors, lawyers and works managers in Wales.

HMI Reports

Further evidence of the negative and often hostile attitudes which prevailed towards the Welsh language is provided in the reports of Her Majesty's Inspectors.

[35] Ibid., p. 337.
[36] Ibid., p. 146.
[37] Ibid., p. 29.
[38] Ibid., p. 64.
[39] Ibid., p. 168.
[40] Ibid., p. 445.

For almost half a century following the commencement of their work in 1840, the Inspectorate regarded the native language either as a 'problem' or a 'difficulty' which needed to be surmounted in order to achieve educational improvement and progress in Wales. In short, this entailed promoting the English language.

The negative and hostile attitudes espoused in the nineteenth century by representatives of the British state towards the use of the Welsh language in schools and colleges may partly be explained in terms of internal colonialism. Wedded to the belief in progress and the superiority of English culture, the Victorian state perceived the Welsh language as a 'bilingual difficulty' and a major obstacle to the Welshman's social and economic advancement. Anglicization of the Celtic periphery was a *sine qua non* of the perception of Britain as an English national state. Uniform educational policies and practices were regarded as essential to the promotion of cultural and ideological uniformity. In such a 'colonial' model, the existence of peripheral vernaculars was an undesirable cultural difference.[41]

The establishment of the Inspectorate in December 1839 and the appointment in 1846 of the Parliamentary Commission of Inquiry into the State of Education in Wales had occurred during a period of significant social and political unrest in Wales. In the era of the Merthyr Rising, the Rebecca Riots and the Chartist disturbances, the Welsh language came to be regarded as a barrier to the effective acculturation, socialization and ideological control of the 'lower orders'. Some observers even believed that the Welsh language and Nonconformity possessed dangerous revolutionary potential.[42] In his first Report in 1840 – 'An Inquiry into the State of Elementary Education in the Mining Districts of South Wales' – H. S. Tremenheere HMI noted that only a limited amount of English was taught in the elementary schools in areas where there had been Chartist disturbances.[43] In his important speech in Parliament on 10 March 1846, William Williams MP quoted the evidence of H. S. Tremenheere HMI and also a report by the Revd H. W. Bellairs HMI highlighting the danger to society of 'an ill-educated and undisciplined population, like that existing amongst the mines in South Wales'. The inspector had maintained that it would be much cheaper to employ 'a band of efficient schoolmasters . . . than a body of police or soldiery'.[44] He attributed the 'very considerable difficulties' in the national schools of Monmouthshire to the prevalence of the native tongue – 'the Welsh language is still commonly spoken'.[45] At a time when the Blue Books provided a sweeping indictment of the

---

[41] See Michael Hechter, *Internal Colonialism: The Celtic Fringe in British National Development, 1536–1966* (London, 1975); D. Tecwyn Lloyd, *Drych o Genedl* (Abertawe, 1987).

[42] G. Williams and C. Roberts, 'Language and Social Structure in Welsh Education' in *World Yearbook of Education: Education of Minorities* (London, 1981), pp. 147–63; V. E. Durkacz, *The Decline of the Celtic Languages* (Edinburgh, 1983).

[43] *Minutes of the Committee of Council on Education*, 1839–40 (PP 1840 XL), pp. 155–71.

[44] Quoted in Daniel Evans, *Life and Work of William Williams M.P.* (Llandysul, 1940), p. 85.

[45] *Minutes of the Committee of Council on Education*, 1847–8 (PP 1847–8 L), p. 290.

Welsh language and national character, an effective English-medium system of elementary education was regarded as an essential instrument for inculcating deference and discipline into pupils, as well as teaching the basic skills of reading, writing and arithmetic. The ideal Victorian elementary school would teach the essential lingua franca of industrial Britain and be an agent of social control. Again, in 1854, the Revd H. W. Bellairs HMI emphasized the problems caused by the Welsh language in Monmouthshire: he believed it was an obstacle which prevented effective contact with the metropolis and other advanced areas of England.[46]

The failure to realize the potential of a 'bilingual' education policy until the final decades of the century led inevitably to the perception of the native language as a 'problem' and a 'difficulty'. Bilingualism was not associated with educational and social advancement. In 1849 the Revd Joseph Fletcher HMI voiced opposition to teachers who used any aids or apparatus which might facilitate the teaching of Welsh. He considered the language to be a major obstacle to 'the worldly promotion' of the people, and every generation was faced with 'the labour of emerging from it'.[47] A year later Fletcher described the Welsh language as 'the great stumbling block of the whole race' and bitterly criticized teachers for their lack of fluency in English. He had earlier highlighted 'the peculiar difficulties' which bedevilled the teaching of young, monoglot Welsh-speaking teachers in north-east Wales.[48] The Victorian school inspectors' hostile perception of the native language both epitomized and influenced the prevailing view of the educational establishment for most of the century.

A corollary of viewing the Welsh language as a 'problem' was the belief in the superiority of English culture and the association of educational 'improvement' and progress with the speedy acquisition of the English language in Wales. The classic exposition of the seminal importance of English education was voiced in Matthew Arnold's first report for the Inspectorate in 1852.[49] He argued that the educational condition of British schools in Wales highlighted the linguistic handicap faced by Welsh-speaking children. A romantic interest in the preservation of ancient languages, he argued, should not be allowed to impede the attainment of a unified English-speaking state. It would always be 'the desire of a Government to render its dominions as far as possible, homogeneous'. Eventually the linguistic difference between Wales and England would probably be obliterated, but that was to be welcomed for both social and political reasons.[50] Arnold regarded schools as vital agencies for 'the promotion of the use of English in Wales', and his prejudices were to be reiterated in his volume *On the Study of*

[46] Ibid., 1854–5 (PP 1854–5 XLII), p. 408.
[47] Ibid., 1848–9 (PP 1849 XLII), p. 294.
[48] Ibid., 1847–8, p. 281.
[49] Ibid., 1851–2 (PP 1852–3 LXXIX, LXX), pp. 1016–18.
[50] Ibid.

Celtic Literature (1867): 'The sooner the Welsh language disappears as an instrument of the practical political social life of Wales, the better, the better for England, the better for Wales itself.'[51] It was inevitable that views enunciated by such an eminent Victorian would influence public opinion and they certainly did incalculable harm to the Welsh language in the nineteenth century. The merits and demerits of the Welsh language were clearly being judged by the standards of middle-class, mid-Victorian England. Likewise the inspection of British schools in north Wales during the years 1858–64 convinced the Revd W. Scoltock HMI that the Welsh language was 'a great obstacle', particularly in rural areas where children spoke only Welsh. Efforts to promote English in school were undermined by 'the habitual language of the family'.[52] Similarly D. R. Fearon HMI, educated at Marlborough and Balliol College, Oxford, declared in his survey of British schools in 1867 that educational improvement and a positive attitude towards the English language went hand in hand. Knowledge of English was spreading among the working class and the lower middle class in Wales and they were most anxious to learn it.[53]

While it might be expected that such school inspectors would epitomize their English middle-class backgrounds, the Welsh-speaking Revd Shadrach Pryce HMI, who inspected schools in mid- and south-west Wales, proved to be even more hostile to the native language.[54] He believed it was 'deficient in all educational and technical terms', a serious drawback 'to the intellectual and commercial progress of the people', and 'not a mercantile language'.[55] Progress and improvement, he maintained, were synonymous with learning English and an English-medium education. It was essential, if possible, to exclude Welsh altogether from the elementary schools. He was firmly of the opinion that the hallmark of a good teacher was the ability to ensure that children abandoned Welsh and spoke only English at school.[56] From 1867 to 1894 this native of Dolgellau was unremitting in his hostility to the Welsh language. In 1869 he argued that Wales would benefit educationally from 'the disuse of Welsh as a spoken language. It was only spoken in a limited area whilst the condition of Welsh literature was backward'.

In order to promote fluency in the English language among Welsh children, it was believed essential that the native language should be proscribed in schools. Always equating educational improvement with the promotion of English and Anglicization, the Revd Shadrach Pryce welcomed the teaching of English in elementary schools, the influence of the railways, and the influx of English capitalists and labourers, for these were the developments which would 'slowly

---

[51] Matthew Arnold, *On the Study of Celtic Literature* (London, 1867), pp. xi–xiii.
[52] *Report of the Committee of Council on Education*, 1859–60 (PP 1860 LIV), p. 637.
[53] Ibid., 1868–9 (PP 1868–9 XX), pp. 165–6.
[54] W. Gareth Evans, '"Gelyn yr Iaith Gymraeg" – Y Parch Shadrach Pryce A.E.M. a Meddylfryd yr Arolygiaeth yn Oes Fictoria', *Y Traethodydd*, CXLIX (1994), 73–81.
[55] *Report of the Committee of Council on Education*, 1869–70 (PP 1870 XXII), p. 343.
[56] Ibid., 1882–3 (PP 1883 XXV), p. 420.

drive away Welsh even from its last retreat the hearth and altar'.[57] He insisted that 'there was no place for the native language in the modern world', however interesting the ancient language might be to philologists and linguists.

Until a more positive attitude towards the Welsh language and bilingualism emerged among Her Majesty's Inspectors in the late 1880s and 1890s, only the Revd H. Longueville Jones HMI, who inspected national schools from 1849 to 1864, evaluated the Welsh language on its own merits rather than according to the yardstick of 'progressives' and 'utilitarians' who equated a good education with English-medium teaching.[58] In 1849 Sir James Kay-Shuttleworth was persuaded by Sir Thomas Phillips, Principal Reed of Carmarthen and several Welsh clergymen of the need to provide efficient bilingual instruction in elementary schools in Wales. He encouraged the Revd Longueville Jones, a Welsh speaker and a newly appointed inspector, to associate himself with the bilingual experiment launched at the South Wales and Monmouthshire Training College, opened at Carmarthen in 1848. He was instructed to set a 'Welsh Paper' containing a passage to be translated from Welsh into English and another from English into Welsh, together with questions on the grammatical construction of the language in lieu of one subject in the college's annual examinations. Welsh examination papers were prepared for student teachers at Carmarthen between 1850 and 1861. By 1855, however, the Inspectorate showed no real enthusiasm for the use of the Welsh language in the training of teachers. R. R. W. Lingen, who had succeeded Kay-Shuttleworth as Secretary of the Committee of Council on Education in 1849, was less supportive of the Welsh language than his predecessor, and had already revealed his antagonism to bilingualism during the infamous inquiry and compilation of the Blue Books in 1846–7. After making enquiries among schoolmasters, local school managers and others, the Revd B. M. Cowie HMI concluded that it was a mistake to set a Welsh examination because the community at large saw no educational value in the teaching of Welsh. In 1861 he argued that it would be more beneficial for the few who were examined in the Welsh paper in the teachers' certificate examination at Carmarthen to spend their time learning arithmetic. The negative attitudes of R. R. W. Lingen and Her Majesty's Inspectors, as well as lack of public demand, ensured that one of the few modest concessions by the Victorian state to the Welsh language ended in failure.[59] The Welsh language did not reappear even on the periphery of the subjects examined in training colleges until the changed circumstances of the 1890s.

---

[57] Ibid., 1868–9, pp. 165–6.
[58] H. G. Williams, 'Longueville Jones and Welsh Education: The Neglected Case of a Victorian HMI', *WHR*, 15, no. 3 (1991), 416–42; W. Gareth Evans, 'John Rhŷs a Byd Arolygwr ei Mawrhydi yng Nghymru Oes Victoria', *LlC*, XVIII, no. 3 and 4 (1995), 340–58.
[59] W. Gareth Evans, 'The "Bilingual Difficulty": The Inspectorate and the Failure of a Welsh Language Teacher-Training Experiment in Victorian Wales', *NLWJ*, XXVIII, no. 3 (1994), 325–33.

Victorian inspectors of schools and commissioners of inquiry encountered little opposition to their predetermined view concerning the non-utility of the Welsh language. They soon discovered that their beliefs were in harmony with the desire of middle-class people in Wales for an English-medium education. There was no attempt to disabuse them or to emphasize the value of both languages. The inspectors did not question the higher premium placed by Welsh people on English rather than Welsh. They highlighted the considerable desire among Welsh farmers that their children should learn English in order to be able to converse, and to read and understand English newspapers and books.[60]

Evidence presented to the Newcastle Commission in 1859–61 and to the Aberdare Committee in 1880–1, together with responses by headteachers to a questionnaire organized by the Honourable Society of Cymmrodorion in 1884 concerning the introduction of Welsh into elementary schools, also highlighted the prevailing connection between improvement, progress and the dominance of the English language.[61] A witness who came before the Newcastle Commission in 1861 referred to the 'fear parents had that Welsh might be used as a medium of instruction'.[62] In his evidence, the dean of Llandaff stated that 'there is an idea prevailing that the knowledge of it [the Welsh language] is another name for ignorance and bigotry'.[63] English was regarded as the essential vehicle for material advancement. Teachers and parents in Victorian Wales were greatly influenced by the writings of the Revd J. R. Kilsby Jones and other leading Nonconformists in the 1850s and 1860s who saw little long-term future for the Welsh language. They viewed the imposition of the Welsh Not and the exclusion of the Welsh language from the classroom as essential for the effective promotion of the English language. In 1922 Sir Henry Jones recalled his schooldays in Llangernyw in 1864 when 'the speaking of Welsh was strictly forbidden both in school and in the playground'.[64] Parents opposed to the teaching of Welsh viewed it in 1884 as 'a doomed language' and since it was 'dying a natural death, why try to resuscitate it?' In Cardiganshire it was said that 'the chief and great desire of the people is for the spread of English'.[65]

Although the negative attitudes of the educational establishment towards the Welsh language were not enshrined in a proscriptive clause in the Education Act of 1870, the legislation gave no support to the native language, nor did it contain any special consideration for Wales. In 1870, during the deliberations on the

---

[60] *Report of the Committee of Council on Education*, 1882–3, p. 420.
[61] The Honourable Society of Cymmrodorion, *Report of the Committee appointed to inquire into the advisability of the introduction of the Welsh language into the course of elementary education in Wales* (London, 1885).
[62] *Newcastle Report, Part II*, p. 569.
[63] Ibid.
[64] Henry Jones, *Old Memories* (London, 1922), p. 32.
[65] *Report of the Committee appointed to inquire into the advisability of the introduction of the Welsh language into the course of elementary education in Wales*, Appendix, p. 9.

Elementary Education Bill, there was a demand in *Y Goleuad* for an 'Education Bill for Wales' and criticism was voiced of the Inspectorate for neglecting the Welsh language and for examining pupils in a foreign tongue: 'What would be thought if a Frenchman totally unfamiliar with the language of the English was appointed to examine English schools?' ('Pa beth a feddylid o benodi Ffrancwr hollol ddieithr i iaith y Saeson, i arholi ysgolion Saesonig?')[66] But such criticisms were the exception rather than the rule. There was no nationwide stand in Wales for special consideration in 1870. Indeed, Dr Lewis Edwards and other leading figures in Wales were resigned to the view that the demise of the Welsh language was inevitable.

Nevertheless, it could be argued that an instrument of greater significance for the Welsh language in the schools of Wales was already in force by 1870. The Revised Code exercised firm control over the elementary school curriculum and ushered in the age of 'payment by results'. It was introduced following the Report of the Newcastle Commission into the condition of elementary education in England and Wales. The implementation on 1 August 1863 of the Revised Code of Regulations for the Administration of Grants to Schools reinforced the prevailing negative attitudes towards the Welsh language.[67] A new utilitarianism was now to characterize the view of the state of elementary education: this entailed increased emphasis on basic linguistic, reading and arithmetical skills. Welsh disappeared from the syllabus of the Carmarthen and Caernarfon Training Colleges, and schools were henceforward subjected to even more rigorous inspection by Her Majesty's Inspectors. No consideration was given in the Revised Code to the linguistic situation in Wales, although the 1875 Code allowed a limited use of Welsh for the purpose of examining pupils. Although the Revised Code did not actually proscribe the Welsh language, it has been claimed that 'the idea of its permissibility did not dawn on teachers'.[68] The native language was not a grant-earning subject, and in the age of 'payment by results' a proportion of a teacher's salary was dependent on the performance of pupils in annual tests conducted through the medium of English. The Welsh language came to be viewed as an educational handicap by teachers and inspectors who had already shown much hostility to it. Inevitably, teachers were influenced by the attitude of the Inspectorate. The Revised Code led to the more widespread use of the Welsh Not by Welsh and non-Welsh-speaking headteachers and an increase in rote-learning in the English language as Her Majesty's Inspectors rigorously scrutinized its implementation. To a considerable degree, the elementary school became an alien institution for generations of pupils in Victorian Wales. O. M. Edwards's memoir in *Clych Atgof* of his childhood at Ysgol y Llan in Llanuwchllyn

---

[66] *Y Goleuad*, 18 February 1870.
[67] *Education (Revised Code) 1862: Code of Regulations for the Administration of Grants to Schools revised in the light of the Report of the Newcastle Commission. In operation 1 August 1863* (PP 1862 XLI).
[68] Durkacz, *The Decline of the Celtic Languages*, p. 170.

in the 1860s became the best-known account of the trials experienced by victims of the Welsh Not.[69]

Although attitudes towards the Welsh language in elementary schools had become more positive by the end of the century, in 1893 O. M. Edwards, who was at that time an Oxford don, identified fundamental problems which had contributed to the unsatisfactory position of Welsh in schools. These included a lack of books, lazy and unsuitable teachers, ignorant and foolish parents, and also unsympathetic, prejudiced and unsuitable inspectors. He claimed that since teachers' salaries depended on favourable reports by inspectors, their attitude to the native language in the era of the Revised Code could radically influence linguistic policies within schools.[70]

Changing Attitudes and Policies in the Late Nineteenth Century

Changing attitudes in the 1880s and 1890s focused in particular on the advocacy of the bilingual method of teaching in elementary schools. Of crucial importance was the presentation of evidence to the Cross Commission on Elementary Education in 1887 and the Report's recommendation in favour of using Welsh in elementary schools.[71]

Henry Richard MP, a member of the Commission, insisted that the Royal Commission on Education 'should be requested to take into consideration the bilingual situation of Wales', and from 1891 onwards Welsh was included in the Code as a grant-earning specific subject for older pupils. Bilingualism was now officially recognized in elementary education, though Welsh was still only an optional subject. Welsh was already being taught as a specific subject in some schools in accordance with the terms of an approved scheme. An account of the examination of pupils in the schools of the Gelli-gaer School Board by Dan Isaac Davies, sub-inspector for the area, was included as an appendix to the 1886 HMI Report on the 'Welsh Division'.[72] It was an optimistic account which deliberately highlighted the importance of bilingualism in industrial Glamorgan. Significantly, it was also stated that the English grammar of standards V, VI and VII, had been improved by the teaching of Welsh as a specific subject. Davies claimed that one powerful reason for teaching Welsh was that the demand for bilingual officials was increasing in all parts of Wales, especially in the populous mining districts of east Glamorgan, where there had been a significant increase in population, many of whom were Welsh. The 1893 and 1894 Codes allowed schools to make greater

---

[69] See E. G. Millward, *Cenedl o Bobl Ddewrion: Agweddau ar Lenyddiaeth Oes Victoria* (Llandysul, 1991).

[70] 'Cymraeg yn yr Ysgolion Dyddiol', *Cymru*, V, no. 26 (1893), 134.

[71] *Royal Commission on the working of the Elementary Education Acts (1886–88), Final Report, 49–50. Minutes of Evidence*, Vol. 2, 1887, Q. 42446 (PP 1887 XXIX).

[72] *Report of the Committee of Council on Education*, 1886–7 (PP 1887 XXVIII), pp. 365–6.

use of the Welsh language in the curriculum. Bilingual books could be used and in Welsh-speaking districts pupils were required to explain in Welsh the meaning of passages which they read. Given the prevailing mood of the time, the provision for Welsh in the Codes of the 1890s heralded a significant change of attitude. The Revised Instructions to Her Majesty's Inspectors in 1893 recognized the value of Welsh as a medium for promoting the understanding of English and also the need to encourage a bilingual education. It was acknowledged that in many cases in Welsh-speaking districts the use of Welsh in the school side by side with English would greatly facilitate an intelligent understanding of English.[73]

The Welsh language was also given more attention in the training colleges during the 1890s. In evidence presented to the Cross Commission in 1888, the principals of the Training Colleges in Wales revealed that Welsh was not taught in any of the colleges. In May 1893 H. E. Oakeley, HMI of training colleges, visited Carmarthen Training College in the company of Shadrach Pryce HMI. Oakeley believed that the new regulation which permitted students to take Welsh in their certificate examination would be an advantage there because 'several students think in Welsh and some English subjects must be very hard for them'.[74] Welsh was also available as an optional subject in the Queen's scholarship examinations which led to admission to training colleges.

The more enlightened attitude towards the Welsh language was also evident in the initial deliberations of the Central Welsh Board established in 1896. It revealed a far more positive attitude towards the native language than many historians have led us to believe. At the first meeting of the full Board on 11 and 12 December 1896, significant attention was given to a motion by Professor Thomas Powel, seconded by Principal John Rhŷs, advocating 'the great importance of introducing the Welsh Language as a subject of instruction into all schools in Welsh-speaking Districts'. It was carried unanimously. The neglect of the native language in elementary and intermediate schools in Welsh-speaking communities was strongly criticized, but it was still not thought appropriate for the Central Welsh Board to dictate to all the county governing bodies that Welsh should be taught in all schools. In the view of members of the Board, linguistic policies should be determined regionally.[75]

Several factors generated a more sympathetic attitude on the part of the state towards the Welsh language. The inclusion of Welsh in the 1891 Code as a grant-earning, optional specific subject for children above the 5th standard was an important turning point in official attitudes towards the native language in the elementary schools of Wales. To a very great extent this attested to the remarkable

[73] Ibid., 1892–3 (PP 1893–4 XXVI), pp. 331–2.
[74] Ibid., 1893–4 (PP 1894 XXIX), p. 144.
[75] *Report of Proceedings of First Meeting of Central Welsh Board held at Shire Hall, Shrewsbury, 11 & 12 December 1896* (Cardiff, 1897); W. Gareth Evans, *An Elected National Body for Wales: The Centenary of the Central Welsh Board* (Cardiff, 1997).

success of the Society for Utilizing the Welsh Language, also known as 'Cymdeithas yr Iaith Gymraeg', established in 1885, and especially to the influence of its leading advocates, Dan Isaac Davies and Beriah Gwynfe Evans.[76] The evidence presented to the Cross Commission in 1887 by Davies, Evans, H. Isambard Owen and T. Marchant Williams underlined the critical importance of utilizing Welsh as an effective means of learning English rather than teaching it for its own sake. English was given priority in their concept of bilingualism. It is possible that this was a deliberate strategy designed to secure a concession in favour of the Welsh language.[77] Significantly, William Williams HMI believed it was important to inform the Education Department that the Society did not intend 'to try to retard the spread of the English language or to interfere with the teaching of English in Welsh schools; on the contrary, one of the main objects is to make the teaching of English more intelligent and thorough'.[78]

This was also a time when a number of influential individuals – J. E. Lloyd, Thomas Powel, H. Isambard Owen, Ellis Jones Griffith, Tom Ellis, T. Francis Roberts, T. Marchant Williams and Robert Ambrose Jones (Emrys ap Iwan) – as well as leading members of the Honourable Society of Cymmrodorion, were demanding more attention for the Welsh language in the schools of Wales. In 1884 the Cymmrodorion Society prepared a questionnaire which was circulated to headteachers of elementary schools to ascertain their attitude to the inclusion of Welsh as a specific subject in elementary schools. In 1885 an analysis of the responses was published in the *Report of the Committee appointed to inquire into the advisability of the introduction of the Welsh language into the course of elementary education in Wales*. The Cymmrodorion Society and, in particular, two of its leading members – T. Marchant Williams and H. Isambard Owen – voiced strong support for bilingual education policies. In 1882 *Y Cymmrodor* – the Transactions of the Honourable Society of Cymmrodorion – included an article by the Revd D. J. Davies on 'The Necessity of Teaching English through the Medium of Welsh', which vented prevailing attitudes towards bilingualism.[79] Thomas Powel, editor of *Y Cymmrodor*, also published an article on 'What the Government is doing for the Teaching of Irish', in which he used Irish parallels to illustrate the importance of giving Welsh its rightful place in schools: 'The intellectual advantage of possessing an adequate knowledge and ready command of two languages is simply incalculable.'[80] In 1893 A. H. D. Acland MP, Vice-President of the Education Department 1892–4, accepted the 'Scheme of Instruction for Use in Elementary Schools' submitted by the Society for Utilizing the Welsh

---

[76] See J. Elwyn Hughes, *Arloeswr Dwyieithedd: Dan Isaac Davies 1839–1887* (Caerdydd, 1984).
[77] B. L. Davies, 'A Right to a Bilingual Education in Nineteenth Century Wales', *THSC* (1988), 147–9.
[78] *Report of the Committee of Council on Education*, 1885–6 (PP 1886 XXIV), p. 364.
[79] D. J. Davies, 'The Necessity of Teaching English through the Medium of Welsh', *Y Cymmrodor*, V (1882), 1–13.
[80] Thomas Powel, 'What the Government is doing for the Teaching of Irish', ibid., 14–38.

Language and also declared that the Education Department would endeavour 'to show the teachers and inspectors that in Welsh-speaking districts the subject of Welsh was not merely tolerated, but officially sanctioned and encouraged . . . Welsh would be removed from the ante-room to the full light of day'.[81]

Of crucial importance was the more favourable attitude of the Inspectorate towards the Welsh language in the 1880s and 1890s.[82] Dan Isaac Davies, a sub-inspector at Merthyr, was one of the founders of the Society for Utilizing the Welsh Language, which exerted a profound influence on the Cross Commission. William Edwards HMI, a native of Denbigh, who was educated at the Liverpool Institute and Queen's College, Oxford, served as one of Her Majesty's Inspectors for thirty-eight years in Glamorgan. He supported the Society for Utilizing the Welsh Language and agreed with Dan Isaac Davies's advocacy of Welsh as a grant-earning subject in the evidence he presented to the Cross Commission. His reasons for supporting the introduction of Welsh into the curriculum of elementary schools, included in an appendix to the official 1886 Report, constituted a fair and balanced analysis of the policies of the Society for Utilizing the Welsh Language. William Edwards maintained that Welsh was the native language of a very large proportion of the inhabitants of Wales, besides being the language of many newspapers and periodicals. It was thus expedient that it should be taught as long as it retained its position as the language of the majority. Furthermore, many children who passed through the elementary schools would, in later years, fill positions in which a satisfactory grammatical knowledge of Welsh was extremely desirable, if not absolutely indispensable. He also believed that bilingual instruction was useful in improving the faculties of thought and expression, since it facilitated the presentation of one idea in two different modes. It also made the acquisition of a third language easier. He did not believe that the spread of English would be retarded by the teaching of Welsh, for translations would be required not only from English into Welsh, but also from Welsh into English. Translation was both an aid and an exercise in composition. He was also aware that in Scotland, Ireland and various continental countries, the necessity of bilingual instruction was conceded, and the advantages which accrued from it were acknowledged to be considerable. Since Welsh was intended to be optional, there was no danger of it being introduced against the parents' wishes.[83] He also believed that the machinery for teaching Welsh already existed, although a little preparation might be required. He acknowledged that 'teachers of Welsh nationality' were already chosen in preference to English teachers for service in Welsh schools. If Welsh teaching was required in schools conducted by Englishmen, it would be easy to provide the special instruction 'without unsettling the staff'.[84]

[81] *Western Mail*, 13 March 1893.
[82] Evans, 'O. M. Edwards's Enlightened Precursors', 69–77.
[83] *Report of the Committee of Council on Education*, 1886–7, p. 365.
[84] Ibid.

William Edwards believed that the Welsh people themselves were responsible for allowing the native tongue to be neglected in the schools of Wales. Although he was in favour of including Welsh in the curriculum of elementary and intermediate schools, he did not believe that official recognition of the language would necessarily guarantee its survival. He claimed that when every Welshman spoke English as well as he spoke Welsh, and there was no 'nucleus of monoglots to act as a preservative', the weaker language would then rapidly die. But it would die an honourable death, 'instead of being strangled in disgrace'. In the Merthyr District, Edwards discovered in 1891 that 'Welsh as a specific subject does not gain favour'. Wherever it had been introduced, teachers found that little success had been achieved. But Edwards insisted that it was being introduced at too late a stage in the schooling of pupils. It was inopportune to commence the teaching of Welsh when the pupils were about to leave school. They needed to be acquainted much earlier with Welsh books and the written form of the language.[85] He therefore recommended that in all Welsh schools one of the reading books used should be 'wholly or partially in the vernacular'. In commenting on the attitudes of parents, he uttered one of the most enlightened statements by a Victorian HMI concerning the language. The fact that parents were not demanding change was not 'a proof of its inexpediency', for they were misguided in believing that learning Welsh involved 'the depreciation of English, the language of advancement and material progress'. He was convinced that through bilingual education a Welsh child would 'not lose in a material sense' and that he would also 'gain intellectually'.[86]

Again, in 1892, Edwards voiced significant observations on the utility of the Welsh language. Their importance was underlined by the Chief Inspector, William Williams HMI, who requested that they be given 'special attention'. Edwards emphasized the need for the introduction of Welsh in Welsh-speaking districts much earlier than the 5th standard, since this would lead to educational benefits. He maintained that a Welsh child would derive considerable intellectual advantage from reading and writing his own language, and that he should not be denied this experience because of the presence of a few English children.[87] Some of Edwards's colleagues shared his enlightened views. In 1896 Thomas Darlington, an Englishman, was appointed HMI and settled in Aberystwyth a year later. A classical scholar, he was highly supportive of the Welsh language and of the efforts of the Society for Utilizing the Welsh Language. He regarded the Welsh language as the essence of Welshness: 'the loss of the Welsh language involves the loss of all that is most characteristically Welsh . . .', and he was optimistic regarding its future role.[88] He believed that the Welsh language had 'acquired a

[85] Ibid., 1890–1 (PP 1890–1 XXVII), p. 409.
[86] Ibid.
[87] Ibid., 1892–3, p. 107.
[88] Ibid., pp. 282–6.

new interest and importance in the eyes of the world' and that 'anglicization is no longer preached as the social gospel for Wales'. His views were in stark contrast with those expressed by his forebears thirty years previously.

The Extent of Change by 1914

By the outbreak of the First World War, Welsh was still only an optional subject in the elementary schools and continued to be regarded by many as a medium which facilitated the more effective learning of English rather than as a language worth teaching for its own sake. In the well-established endowed grammar schools it still remained conspicuous by its absence. Even at Llandovery College, where the linguistic policies of Warden A. G. Edwards, 1875–85, and his successors had led to the demise of the native language in the curriculum, it was not until 1920 that the trustees were threatened with legal action by the Charity Commission for ignoring a key clause in the trust deed of the school.[89] The Welsh Intermediate and Technical Education Act of 1889 had given no especial attention to the Welsh language and in the newly-established intermediate schools Welsh was only allocated an optional, peripheral position.[90] In 1896–7, when opposition was voiced against the appointment of A. G. Legard as Chief Inspector in Wales because he did not speak Welsh, a protest conveyed to the Education Department was rejected in language which suggested that there had been little fundamental change in official attitudes since the 1860s and 1870s. It was claimed that critics were misinformed in assuming there was a significant difference between the conditions of elementary education in England and Wales, and that to demand a Welsh-speaking Chief Inspector was entirely unrealistic.[91] Legard served as HMI in Wales until 1907. In 1897 five of the six newly appointed Central Welsh Board inspectors of intermediate schools were also non-Welsh speakers.

Nevertheless, there is no question that by 1914 a significant change had occurred in the educational policies of the state concerning the Welsh language. When the Board of Education (Welsh Department) was established in 1907 and O. M. Edwards appointed Chief Inspector of Education for Wales, the Inspectorate became increasingly supportive of the Welsh language and impressed anew upon schools their linguistic obligations. But the first Reports of the Welsh Department showed that the elementary schools of Wales remained extremely Anglicized. In 1906 the Chief Inspector of the Central Welsh Board reported that '2,180 pupils in 53 intermediate schools received instruction in the Welsh language'. However,

---

[89] W. Gareth Evans, *A History of Llandovery College* (Llandovery, 1981).
[90] Idem (ed.), *Perspectives on a Century of Secondary Education in Wales 1889–1989* (Aberystwyth, 1990).
[91] 'The Chief Inspectorship of Schools in Wales', *Young Wales*, III (1897), 44.

at that time there were 10,143 pupils receiving education in 93 intermediate schools in Wales.[92]

In 1907 the first separate Code for Wales stipulated that the Board of Education desired that every teacher should 'realize the educational value of the Welsh language and of its literature'. The wealth of romance and lyrics in the Welsh language was believed to be most appropriate for the education of the young. The curriculum of elementary schools in Wales, therefore, 'should, as a rule, include the Welsh language'. Any of the subjects of the curriculum could be taught through the medium of Welsh. Furthermore, where Welsh was the mother tongue of the infants, it should be their medium of instruction in school.[93] Likewise, the regulations for secondary schools in Wales included provision for Welsh as the medium of instruction. In Welsh-speaking districts, Welsh should not only be a subject of instruction, together with English, but also a medium of instruction in any of the other subjects of the curriculum. Teachers' Training Colleges in Wales were also urged to offer an effective course in Welsh.

In 1908 O. M. Edwards acknowledged that the neglect of Welsh was the major weakness in the system of secondary education in Wales. He emphasized that it was taught in just over half the intermediate schools and it was often the alternative to Latin or Music or Scripture. He maintained that the neglect of Welsh constituted an unnatural break in the education of Welsh-speaking children since it led to a chasm between education in school and in the home. Neglect of the native language was also a disadvantage for future aspirants to the teaching profession.[94] Within the Board of Education O. M. Edwards urged strongly that secondary schools should provide more widespread provision for instruction in Welsh. He reminded officials that Welsh was now a compulsory subject in a large number of elementary schools in Wales. He had made enquiries at Aberystwyth Day Training Department, which revealed that none of the students leaving in 1908 were competent to teach Welsh.[95]

Visits to Cardiff elementary schools early in 1908 generated optimism regarding changing attitudes towards Welsh in the elementary schools of south Wales. There was now greater recognition by local education authorities both of 'the undoubted educational value of the secondary language' and also of 'the practical use of the language'. It was said that Swansea drapers and others would not employ apprentices and servants who did not speak Welsh. O. M. Edwards discovered middle-aged men learning Welsh at evening classes in Cardiff because they found it was necessary for their business. Having been introduced into Cardiff elementary schools in 1897, Welsh was already being taught in the lower

---

[92] *Central Welsh Board. Reports, Inspection and Examination of County Schools, 1907* (Oxford, 1907).
[93] *Board of Education, Code of Regulations for Public Elementary Schools in Wales, 1907* (PP 1907 (Cd. 3604) LXII).
[94] *Report of the Board of Education (Welsh Department) . . . for the year 1908* (PP 1909 XVIII), p. 8.
[95] PRO Ed. 91/13, Minute, E.H.P. to Mr Mayor, 4 May 1908.

standards in all schools by the direct method. The Chief Inspector was also conscious of an 'extreme Welsh party' and an 'anti-Welsh section' in Cardiff and the need for sensitive handling of the Welsh language in the elementary schools. Nevertheless, he emphasized that the key question was not whether Welsh should be taught at all but 'whether it was to be taught compulsorily from the Third Standard up'.[96]

There was much opposition in Cardiff to any attempt to make the teaching of Welsh compulsory in the elementary schools. Earlier, in 1906, R. L. Morant at the Board of Education had shown no support for the promotion of Welsh in Cardiff schools. He believed that educational and other interests were being 'recklessly subordinated' to the demands of the Welsh-language campaigners. He was informed that many parents were highly incensed that their children's education was being 'spoilt in the interests of an exaggerated propaganda of supposed Welsh nationalisms' in a city where the majority of secondary school pupils were non-Welsh speakers.[97]

Elsewhere, however, there was significant activity in favour of effective provision for the native language. David James (Defynnog), secretary of the Society for Utilizing the Welsh Language, was particularly active in the Rhondda, where he exerted much influence on fellow teachers. He also organized a series of successful summer schools held between 1903 and 1928 in locations such as Aberystwyth, Rhyl, Swansea, Llandrindod, Llangollen, Brecon, Pwllheli and Trefriw. Schemes for the teaching of Welsh were prepared and adopted by several local authorities, including those of Anglesey, Cardiganshire, Denbighshire and Carmarthen Borough. In 1907, at the time when Augustine Birrell's proposals for a National Council for Education in Wales were before Parliament, sixteen Welsh MPs, including W. Llewelyn Williams and Alfred Thomas, sent a letter to the minister of education informing him that the Welsh language had now been made a school subject by the majority of the education authorities in Wales (including Monmouthshire). They anticipated that within a few months every Welsh authority would have taken the same course. In their view, it was essential that all students from Wales in the training colleges of Wales should either pass a qualifying examination in Welsh or study Welsh as an obligatory subject. Welsh was not a dying language, but the mother tongue of large numbers of people. It was the language of the home, religion, intellectual culture and, to some extent, commercial life.[98] At the South Wales Training College, Carmarthen, too, attitudes were changing. In 1906 a Welsh tutor was appointed and twenty-nine students began studying Welsh. Similarly, more attention was given to the native language at Bangor Normal College. Throughout Wales, Central Wales Board

---

[96] PRO Ed. 91/13, Memo 23 August 1908: The Teaching of Welsh at Cardiff.
[97] PRO Ed. 91/13. Minute, R. L. Morant to W. N. Bruce, 22 November 1906.
[98] PRO Ed. 91/13. Letter to Rt Hon A. Birrell MP.

inspectors were supportive of Welsh in education. In 1899 the Chief Inspector claimed that since many pupils in the intermediate schools would remain in Wales, the study of Welsh grammar and literature would be at least as valuable 'an intellectual possession as a schoolboy knowledge of a dead or foreign language', but six years later it was emphasized 'there is still room for advance' regarding the teaching of the Welsh language and literature. In 1912 the Chief Inspector expressed pleasure with the 'distinct progress' made in the study of Welsh in the intermediate schools. Significantly, however, it was not pointed out that whereas a total of 4,100 pupils from ninety-four schools had taken examinations in French, only 1,943 pupils from seventy-one schools had been examined in Welsh.

The native language remained on the periphery of the work of the intermediate schools. Only thirty-nine of the ninety-five intermediate schools were teaching Welsh to examination level in 1904. Nor had there been any appreciable progress within the University of Wales – a situation bitterly criticized in 1904 by O. M. Edwards: 'It grieves me that the Welsh Colleges are sacrificing Welsh to everything' ('Drwg gennyf fod Colegau Cymru yn aberthu'r Gymraeg i bopeth').[99] In spite of the county's language scheme, Denbighshire elementary schools in 1907–9 gave little attention to Welsh. Strong opposition was voiced in 1912 to the teaching of Welsh in elementary schools in Newport: T. A. Evans, the Education Officer, claimed it was 'a useless subject' which should not be allowed 'to interfere with work likely to prove beneficial in later life'. It was 'merely an added burden with no utility at all'.[100]

Yet, in 1909, in the highly critical so-called 'Wooden Report' on the domination of the curriculum of the intermediate schools by external examinations of the Central Welsh Board, the Department of Education claimed that the position of the Welsh language had improved appreciably during the previous five years.[101] By November 1908 the language was taught in seventy-eight intermediate schools. But quite justifiably it also noted that there was an overemphasis on formal grammar teaching and that little attempt was made to promote interest in Welsh literature. It also noted that it was unacceptable that there should be such a high examination standard for Welsh compared to the comparatively low standard in French, the alternative to the native language in most schools. Inevitably, more pupils chose French than Welsh. At Honours level all candidates passed in spite of grammatical weaknesses, while only two-thirds were successful in their native language.[102] Following vigorous criticism by an

---

[99] Letter from O. M. Edwards to J. Glyn Davies, dated 7 October 1904, quoted in Gwilym Arthur Jones, 'Dysgu Cymraeg rhwng 1847 a 1927' (unpubl. University of Wales PhD thesis, 1978), p. 154.

[100] PRO Ed. 91/57. Letter from T. A. Evans, Education Officer, Newport.

[101] *Report of the Board of Education (Welsh Department) . . . for the year 1909* (PP 1910 XXII), pp. 11, 14; G. E. Jones, *Controls and Conflicts in Welsh Secondary Education 1889–1944* (Cardiff, 1982), pp. 21–4.

[102] Ibid., p. 15.

oversensitive Central Welsh Board of the overall tenor of the Report, its author, O. M. Edwards, prepared a detailed response. Reference was made to the teaching of Welsh in order to substantiate previous criticisms of overall teaching methods in intermediate schools. Although Welsh was taught in almost every intermediate school, he maintained that 'the teaching is often very poor'. He noted that at a Conference of Directors of Education of the Empire held in London in 1907, the Languages subcommittee had stated that the Empire would look to Wales for the solution of the chief problems of bilingual teaching.[103] However, if the Conference were to meet again, his report would be 'one that will be humiliating to make'. Wales had not yet given serious consideration to the problems of bilingual teaching and he was unaware of any school in Wales where language teaching was carried out on scientific principles. This situation was epitomized by the use of the English alphabet for the occasional teaching of Welsh to native Welsh speakers and the common practice of teaching Welsh through the medium of English.[104]

Again in 1910 Edwards unflinchingly condemned the method of teaching. Rather than focusing on teaching the pupil to speak the language, he complained, the emphasis was on loading the memory with grammatical rules. Consequently, 'the deadening of interest' rather than vivacity and the readiness to speak dominated Welsh classrooms. This was in contrast to 'the bright teaching of French on modern lines'.[105] Welsh was often taught as if it were already 'a dead language', and it was often taught through the medium of English even to Welsh-speaking children. Too much attention was given to the dictionary and grammar and too little to its 'fresh and living literature'. Half the intermediate schools had fewer than twenty Welsh books in their libraries, and it was disquieting to find that there were virtually no Welsh books in the libraries of schools in some of the most Welsh-speaking parts of Wales.[106]

With emotions running high in Welsh education circles and relations between the Central Wales Board and the Welsh Department at their nadir, O. M. Edwards enjoyed the full confidence of senior officials at the Board of Education. It was recognized that he spoke with undoubted authority on the educational problems of Wales, and his enthusiastic devotion to the promotion of education in Wales was unquestioned.[107] Lloyd George had described Edwards in 1907 as 'a man of fresh ideas and high national ideals'.[108] In 1912 Edwards reviewed six years of 'incessant work' and felt justified in claiming that the Welsh Department had 'placed our own ideals, especially in secondary education clearly before the

---

[103] PRO Ed. 24/588. Report by O. M. Edwards to the President, 14 November 1910.
[104] Ibid.
[105] *Report of the Board of Education (Welsh Department) . . . for the year 1910* (PP 1911 XVIII), p. 13.
[106] Ibid., pp. 16–17.
[107] PRO Ed. 24/588. Reply from H. C. Maurice to A. A. Sanderson, 12 November 1910.
[108] Quoted in Jones, 'Dysgu Cymraeg rhwng 1847 a 1927', p. 177.

country'. He was also sufficiently confident to prophesy that 'if anything happens to me my work will go on without any break'.[109]

As a result, the Welsh Department now viewed the Welsh language as a 'bilingual opportunity' rather than a 'bilingual difficulty' in the schools and colleges of Wales. O. M. Edwards epitomized the significant change which had occurred in the attitude of central authority towards the Welsh language by the early twentieth century. Intermediate schools which gave more attention to French than to Welsh were loudly criticized, and bilingualism was heralded as an economic, social and cultural advantage to every citizen of Wales. Addressing the Imperial Education Conference of 1911, Edwards declared: 'We do not regard the bilingualism of our country as a disadvantage in any way. We look upon it as an advantage.'[110] By 1914 central authority, as represented by the Welsh Department, was committed to a policy of bilingual education in the schools of Wales. Its policy, however, did not appeal to many Welsh headmasters, councillors and parents.

---

[109] PRO Ed. 23/145, 31 March 1912, quoted in Jones, 'Dysgu Cymraeg rhwng 1847 a 1927', p. 192.
[110] Jac L. Williams, *Owen Morgan Edwards: A Short Biography 1858–1920* (Aberystwyth, 1959), p. 53.

17

Elementary Education and the Welsh Language 1870–1902

ROBERT SMITH

In seventeen years Wales has built up a system of education second to none in the United Kingdom . . . it is a system founded upon a thoroughly democratic basis, so that higher education in Wales depends entirely for its success upon the effectiveness of the primary schools.[1]

The above words, written by J. Vyrnwy Morgan in the introduction to *Welsh Political and Educational Leaders in the Victorian Era* (1908), convey the feeling of celebration and pride in an education system which characterized the outlook of its founders. Morgan and others of his generation were convinced that the creation of the Welsh education system constituted the crowning achievement of Liberal and Nonconformist endeavour during the nineteenth century. This attainment united Nonconformist commitment to education, which had manifested itself most impressively in the Sunday school movement, with the Liberal principle that the provision of an educational ladder of opportunity was the solution to social problems. The system was regarded as intrinsically democratic in two ways. Firstly, its creation had been supported by a broad social coalition in Wales and the provision that was now available was considered to be educationally democratic. It served as a ladder from the elementary school to the university, an open system which was accessible to all on the basis of merit and free from the inherent élitism that was deemed to characterize its English equivalent. Secondly, education was the means by which the status of the Welsh nation would be elevated, for the newly established facilities and opportunities would enable Welsh children to contribute their talents to the wider world.

The immense pride with which the Liberal and Nonconformist leaders spoke of Welsh education is understandable in view of its impressive development over a relatively short period of time. As Gareth Elwyn Jones has demonstrated, the

---

[1] J. Vyrnwy Morgan (ed.), *Welsh Political and Educational Leaders in the Victorian Era* (London, 1908), pp. 22–3.

commissioners who inquired into Education in Wales in 1847 furthered the purposes of those who were anxious to institute a system of elementary schools by highlighting the flagrant deficiencies of the existing provision.[2] The reaction to the 1847 Report galvanized public opinion in Wales in a way which shaped the political views of Nonconformists for several generations and it certainly resulted in a polarization of opinion regarding the Welsh language. Yet, at the same time, it engendered a new determination to establish schools and it began the process which would overcome the traditional Nonconformist antipathy to government assistance for education.

The progress achieved between 1847 and 1870 should not be denigrated. Yet those attainments were by no means adequate, and they did not address the absence of basic educational provision within Wales, a fact clearly demonstrated by the returns of the inspectors in 1870. It was the 1870 Forster Education Act which provided the impetus by which Welsh communities were able to expedite matters in relation to the creation of elementary schools. The Act stipulated that where voluntary bodies such as the Anglican Church or the Nonconformist-led British and Foreign School Society had failed to provide a school, a School Board should be constituted and charged with the task of erecting a school funded by the local rates. When the School Boards were abolished in 1902, they provided for the schooling of 65 per cent of Welsh children and, even if full attendance was never achieved, it remained the case that each child had access to a place in an elementary school should he or she choose to take advantage of it. The elementary schools were crucial to the well-being of Welsh society. They provided the only instruction given to the vast majority of children aged between five and thirteen. In 1897, when the foundation of the greatly esteemed intermediate schools was nearing completion, those schools served only 6,427 children, an insignificant number compared to the 368,191 who were enrolled in elementary schools.[3]

The disparaging comments of the commissioners of 1847 were condemned by an array of commentators, both at the time of their publication and in later years.[4] However, the main thrust of each attempt to challenge the findings of the commissioners was directed to their comments upon the moral and religious condition of the Welsh people. Although their observations on the Welsh language were not ignored, these were not the main features of the response which the Report provoked. The Welsh language was of little significance to leaders of educational opinion in Wales at the time, a point affirmed by the fact that many years later the Welsh language was rarely mentioned during the heated

[2] Gareth Elwyn Jones, 'Llyfrau Gleision 1847' in Prys Morgan (ed.), *Brad y Llyfrau Gleision: Ysgrifau ar Hanes Cymru* (Llandysul, 1991), pp. 22–48.
[3] John Williams, *Digest of Welsh Historical Statistics* (2 vols., The Welsh Office, 1985), II, pp. 210–12.
[4] *Reports of the Commissioners of Inquiry into the State of Education in Wales . . . in three parts* (London, 1847) (PP 1847 XXVII).

arguments concerning the details of the 1870 Education Act. Indeed, the most noticeable features of that debate were the degree to which leaders of Nonconformist opinion emphasized the need to make common cause with their English counterparts, and the absence of any proposition that Wales should develop a distinctive education system. This is clearly a reflection of the fact that, despite the bitter sectarian divisions which affected the voluntary schools of Wales before the Forster Act, there was remarkable unity on the issue of language policy. The Nonconformist managers of British schools, such as the Rhondda colliery schools or the Tai-bach company schools, were as committed to the maintenance of Anglicized schools as were the Anglican managers of national schools at Llanystumdwy in Caernarfonshire or Llanuwchllyn in Merioneth.[5] This chapter will consider the gradual erosion of these attitudes and analyse both the means by which the Welsh language came to be recognized as a feature of Welsh education and the response of the community to the need to develop a system of school provision which recognized that, for a significant number of pupils, the language of instruction was an alien tongue.[6]

It is obvious that these considerations had a bearing on the functions of the schools. Children from monoglot Welsh homes were placed in an alien environment, an experience which often resulted in a dislike of learning. This perspective was conveyed by commentators such as O. M. Edwards, T. Gwynn Jones, Henry Jones and Watkin Hezekiah Williams (Watcyn Wyn), each of whom also condemned the elementary school system for introducing the Welsh Not as a means of proscribing Welsh from the school.[7] Edwards maintained that it created alarming social divisions and was a source of friction within Welsh-speaking communities.[8] It certainly formed a significant part of his testament, and he gained considerable credit for the eradication of the Welsh Not and the attitudes that fostered its imposition. The evidence offered by Edwards and others has generated a notion that the Welsh Not led many to make a conscious decision not to speak Welsh and that this was a major factor in the decline of the language in the late nineteenth century. But the existence of the Welsh Not was not the only explanation for the language change which occurred in Wales in this period. The evidence of school logbooks, such as those of the school at Trap near

---

[5] A. L. Evans, *The Story of Taibach and District* (Port Talbot, 1963), pp. 122–6; William George, *My Brother and I* (London, 1958), p. 40; W. J. Gruffydd, *Owen Morgan Edwards: Cofiant* (Aberystwyth, 1938), pp. 48–50.
[6] The Liberation Society under the Secretaryship of Henry Richard insisted that demands made by Welsh Nonconformist leaders should apply equally to Nonconformists in England.
[7] T. Gwynn Jones, 'Bilingualism in Schools' in *NUT Souvenir of Aberystwyth Conference* (London, 1911), p. 249; Henry Jones, *Old Memories* (London, 1922), p. 32; Watkin Hezekiah Williams, *Adgofion Watcyn Wyn* (Merthyr Tydvil & Caerdydd, 1907), pp. 14–18. Careful consideration to the Welsh Not is given by E. G. Millward, 'Yr Hen Gyfundrefn Felltigedig', *Barn*, 207–8 (April/May 1980), 93–5. Millward reveals that the Welsh Not was a feature of the era before the 1870 Act, rather than a product of the system created by Forster.
[8] O. M. Edwards, *Clych Atgof* (Wrecsam, 1921), p. 17; Gruffydd, *Owen Morgan Edwards*, pp. 71–3.

Llandeilo, suggest that although the Welsh Not was in existence it was used for a short period only and was certainly no part of a sustained or general effort on the part of teachers to eradicate Welsh from the classroom.[9] The evidence also suggests that its use was confined to the lowest age group, and that its main purpose was not to punish a child for speaking Welsh but rather to underline the fact that English was the language of the school.[10] In addition, it was believed to be essential to demonstrate the difference between home and school, a matter of great importance for teachers who faced the task of teaching children whose parents had no experience or understanding of a school. Moreover, both the logbooks and testimony, such as that revealed by Elizabeth Williams in her study of Anglesey[11] and that provided by Thomas H. Davies of Port Said, indicates that the Welsh Not was most common in the period before 1870.[12]

Despite the comparative absence of a formal Welsh Not in the period discussed in this chapter, there is ample evidence that the use of the Welsh language was not encouraged in schools, even in those areas where it was the language of the vast majority of the population. English was the language of education at Pencader in Carmarthenshire[13] and W. J. Gruffydd noted that the atmosphere of the school he attended at Bethel in Caernarfonshire was almost wholly English, even though the community was overwhelmingly Welsh speaking and noted for the wealth of its Welsh culture.[14] More recent studies of individual localities also point to the Anglicized nature of the elementary school. Margaret Evans notes that Welsh was not encouraged in the schools of Montgomeryshire in the period between 1850 and 1900[15] and Ernest Jones has revealed efforts to discourage the use of Welsh in the schools of Ffestiniog before 1880.[16] The Welsh Not may not have been a prevalent feature of Welsh schools, but the mentality which underpinned it was a continuing influence on teachers and educational leaders, and this ensured that the atmosphere of the school was one in which Welsh was little regarded and seldom encouraged. The consequences of schooling Welsh children in a foreign tongue were that these children had poor academic results and less than fond memories of their schooldays.

Yet there is no evidence to suggest that the Education Department was at any time officially committed to the use of the Welsh Not nor that it was part of a

---

[9] Logbook of Trap school (Carms.), recorded in October 1866 (Private Collection).
[10] T. I. Williams, 'Patriots and Citizens: Language, Identity and Education in a Liberal State – The Anglicisation of Pontypridd, 1818–1920' (unpubl. University of Wales PhD thesis, 1989), pp. 36–58.
[11] Elizabeth A. Williams, *Hanes Môn yn y Bedwaredd Ganrif ar Bymtheg* (Llangefni, 1927), p. 253.
[12] NLW, W. J. Gruffydd Papers, 224. Letter from T. H. Davies to W. J. Gruffydd, dated 9 January 1938.
[13] D. Derwenydd Morgan, *Trem yn Ôl neu Oes Gofion* (Llandysul, 1940), pp. 11–12.
[14] W. J. Gruffydd, *Hen Atgofion: Blynyddoedd y Locust* (Aberystwyth, 1936), pp. 118–20.
[15] Margaret J. Evans, 'Elementary Education in Montgomeryshire 1850–1900', *MC*, 63 (1973), 1–46, 119–66.
[16] Ernest Jones, *Stiniog* (Caernarfon, 1988), p. 65.

concerted campaign to eradicate the mother tongue. The Department's initial approach was to ignore the language; it did not encourage its use nor attempt to pursue any vigorous policy that would lead to its eradication. It is questionable whether the Education Department can be blamed for the decline of the use of the Welsh language in schools or for failing to recognize the desirability of bilingualism. In many ways, it had no need to exhibit animus against the Welsh language, for the Welsh themselves had long been conditioned to believe that Welsh should be subordinate to English in educational matters. The real disinclination to provide an equitable status for the Welsh language arose because of attitudes which prevailed within Welsh society, not least within Welsh-speaking communities.

The sentiments which denied the Welsh language a place in education reflected more general perceptions of the position of minority languages in Britain. R. V. Cromerford observes that, in common with Wales, the issue of language did not arise in debates concerning education in Ireland despite the fact that a quarter of its population continued to speak the language in 1831 and that nationalist sentiments were much more pronounced than in Wales. In both Ireland and Wales, English was considered the language of business and social progress.[17] English was the language of commerce and academic life; it was the medium of official business and the use of Welsh (like that of Irish) was widely regarded as a mark of inferiority among those who aspired to an elevated position in society. As a result, there was a body of influential opinion which regarded Welsh as an impediment to personal advancement and social progress. Within educational circles in Wales there were few people in 1870 who challenged the notion that it was essential that every child should acquire a sound knowledge of English, and it was this goal, together with ensuring that a child had an understanding of basic numeracy, which attracted both policy-makers and leaders of opinion in Wales. The effect of this was to make English the language of instruction as well as general communication in the schools, and to deny Welsh any place as a subject of study even at a subsidiary level.

Even so, the period under study saw some degree of change on the language issue for three important reasons. Firstly, a vociferous group began to advocate the introduction of Welsh in order to enable children to achieve a better understanding of English. Their argument constituted a rejection of the 'direct method' of teaching a new language; yet it did not necessarily imply an appreciation of the intrinsic value of Welsh. Secondly, there was an opinion which opposed the total Anglicization of education in Wales. Its advocates included those who urged that Welsh be adopted as an informal language, both in the playground and in the classroom, in those cases where the teacher considered

[17] R. V. Cromerford, 'The British State and the Education of Irish Catholics, 1850–1921' in J. Tomiak (ed.), *Schooling, Educational Policy and Ethnic Identity: Comparative Studies on Governments and Non-dominant Ethnic Groups* (New York, 1991), p. 14.

it desirable. A third group sought to establish a more permanent role for the Welsh language by ensuring its recognition by the Education Department as a subject to be studied in school as a subsidiary to the basic subjects. These views began to receive a more sympathetic hearing towards the end of the period discussed in this chapter. Although there was never a wholehearted commitment to the inclusion of Welsh in the school curriculum, let alone as a medium of instruction, a distinct softening of the hitherto prevailing hostility may be discerned among key figures in the debate.

The more sympathetic attitude towards Welsh in education, which was a gradual development, was clearly reflected in the viewpoint of the official agencies, notably the school inspectors. As a body the Inspectorate from 1847 to 1870 had remained loyal to the perverse view of the Welsh language espoused by the 1847 commissioners. Although there were some notable individuals who doubted the wisdom of the linguistic conclusions of the Report of 1847, an anti-Welsh language animus permeated the reports of school inspectors, and strongly influenced both the teaching profession and managers of voluntary schools.[18] The opinions of the inspectors had a particular relevance in that they determined whether a school should receive an annual grant from the Education Department, and the precise amount of that grant, thereby creating a situation in which it was financially expedient for both teachers and managers to maintain a compliant conformity. The school inspectors also had an influential role as advisers to the Education Department. Although they were never in a position to dictate policy, their observations were crucial in formulating the Department's directives on educational matters. The debate concerning the introduction of Welsh initially centred on the merits of the 'direct method', as opposed to using Welsh to teach English and, since the matter fell within the sphere of educational responsibility, the Inspectorate was able to exert greater influence than it might have had if the Welsh language had been considered solely as an administrative or political matter.

The initial attitude of the school inspectors was that Welsh hindered educational progress in the same way as did the regional dialects in England. Indeed, the Revd Herbert Smith, inspector for north-east Wales and Cheshire, considered that the Cheshire dialect was a greater obstacle to the promotion of grammatical English than the Welsh language. The views of inspectors such as Herbert Smith were somewhat tempered by comparison with the strictures of others, notably the Revd Shadrach Pryce. As inspector for the strongly Welsh-speaking area of Carmarthenshire, Pryce had first-hand experience of the difficulties facing both pupils and teachers in a school system conducted entirely through the medium of English. He admitted that he had once been an advocate

---

[18] W. Gareth Evans, 'The "Bilingual Difficulty": HMI and the Welsh Language in the Victorian Age', *WHR*, 16, no. 4 (1993), 494–513.

of the use of Welsh as a means of encouraging an understanding of English. However, he had undergone a total conversion to the merits of the direct method (whereby the new language was taught without recourse to any other language), a cause which he espoused with remarkable zeal.[19] His reports are littered with examples of the progress achieved in those schools where Welsh was prohibited and children denied the option of translating. He openly recommended the eradication of what he considered to be the problem posed by the Welsh language, and regarded the adoption of such a policy as a prerequisite of educational progress in Wales. Significantly, however, his views were not confined to the sphere of school provision. His reports celebrated the fact that English was increasingly the language of daily conversation not only in the playground but also in the street and on the hearth.[20] In his view (shared by other likeminded inspectors), Welsh should be eradicated from all spheres of life as well as excluded from schools. The fact that this never became the official policy of the Education Department does not detract from the influence which such views exerted both on civil servants within the Department and on managers and teachers who were charged with providing education in Wales.

Nevertheless, these views were challenged, notably by John Rhŷs, inspector for the counties of Flint and Denbigh.[21] John Rhŷs was an exceptional figure among nineteenth-century school inspectors, not least because he had actual experience of teaching. The two schools where he had taught – as pupil teacher at Pen-llwyn in Cardiganshire and teacher at Rhos-y-bol in Anglesey – were both areas where Welsh was dominant and, as a result, Rhŷs could speak authoritatively about the best methods by which children, often from monoglot Welsh homes, could be taught sufficient English to meet the requirements of the annual examination.[22] His thesis rested on the conviction that denying the use of Welsh placed an additional burden upon teachers whose work was already fraught with other unavoidable difficulties, and he also expressed concern that the time lost through insistence on the 'direct method' was a major reason for the failure of Welsh schools to attain standards achieved in England.[23]

His views appeared highly individualistic by comparison with the consensus of opinion among school inspectors in the 1870s. Yet, by the 1880s the views represented by Rhŷs were also being advocated by younger inspectors, notably William Edwards and Dan Isaac Davies. In comparison with their predecessors, many of whom owed their appointments to their experience as inspectors of Anglican schools in the period before the 1870 Act, officers such as Edwards and Davies had a better understanding of educational issues and were representative of

---

[19] *Report of the Committee of Council on Education*, 1878–9 (PP 1878–9 XXIII), pp. 669–78.
[20] Ibid., 1882–3 (PP 1883 XXV), pp. 416–29.
[21] Ibid., 1875–6 (PP 1876 XXIII), pp. 390–9.
[22] T. H. Parry-Williams, *John Rhŷs, 1840–1915* (Cardiff, 1954). See also *DWB*, s.v. John Rhŷs.
[23] *Report of the Committee of Council on Education*, 1875–6, pp. 390–9.

a new philosophy within the Education Department which emphasized the role of the inspector as an adviser to the teacher rather than an adversary.[24] William Edwards openly advocated reforming the education system in order to acknowledge the desirability of using Welsh in districts such as his locality in Merthyr Tydfil, where Welsh was the language habitually used outside the school. Furthermore, he concurred with the views of John Rhŷs that failure to utilize the Welsh language was contributing to the comparative decline in educational standards in Wales. His arguments were supported by Dan Isaac Davies, who urged curricular reforms which would allow Welsh to be taught as a subject in schools, both for its own sake and in order that children gain a better understanding of grammatical constructions.[25]

The development of a more benign attitude towards the Welsh language was facilitated by the sympathetic response elicited from William Williams, the chief inspector for the Welsh district. Williams was a representative of the older generation of inspectors, but he differed from the majority of his former colleagues in that he was a Nonconformist and had served as an inspector for British schools before the passing of the 1870 Act. Yet, despite the fact that his background was more akin to that of the Welsh community at large, his support was qualified to the extent that he advocated the introduction of Welsh only as a means of facilitating the teaching of English, and at no time did he declare that the language should be taught in order to promote its own status.[26] His attitude demonstrates that the hostility of inspectors to the introduction of Welsh into the school curriculum cannot be attributed to the fact that the majority were Anglicans, divorced from mainstream opinion in Wales. Rather, it indicates that the educational establishment in Wales saw no intrinsic value in the Welsh language. While many were converted to the use of Welsh, the overwhelming majority of inspectors remained committed to the goal of assimilating Wales to the English-speaking world rather than to the development of a bilingual nation.

The views of inspectors were regularly transmitted to the Education Department. Although such views were not particularly favourable to the Welsh language in the early part of the period under consideration, there is little evidence to suggest that the Education Department either sought to eradicate Welsh or was advised of the desirability of doing so. Wales did not witness anything resembling the determined efforts to eradicate lesser-used languages elsewhere, for instance, by the Norwegian government in relation to the Sami and Finnish languages, or by the French in relation to Breton and Gascon.[27] Both the

---

[24] Ibid., 1886–7 (PP 1887 XXVIII), pp. 364–6.
[25] Ibid.
[26] Ibid., 1888–9 (PP 1889 XXIX), pp. 335–70.
[27] This evidence accords with the argument of Gareth Elwyn Jones that forces within Wales were chiefly responsible for the decline of the language. Gareth Elwyn Jones, 'What are schools in Wales for? Wales and the Education Reform Act', *Contemporary Wales*, II (1988), 83–97. See also Williams, 'Patriots and Citizens', pp. 36–52.

Norwegian and the French governments embarked on a deliberate policy of promoting a popular appreciation of the benefits of a common language in administration and commerce and as a means of enhancing national cohesion,[28] something that was never openly attempted in Britain.[29] The relatively impartial attitude evolved by the Education Department broadly reflected the advice which it received from its own officials within Wales. That advice was sometimes hostile but, in the majority of cases, it was simply indifferent. Thus, the policy of the Education Department can be regarded as one of passive acquiescence in the process which led to the gradual assimilation of Welsh speakers with the English-speaking majority of the United Kingdom. Initially this process was interpreted in Wales as one which required Welsh speakers to abandon their own background and culture and adopt a British outlook. This view, which regarded cultural diversity as a problem, was later ameliorated by those who influenced education policy in Wales, not least because of the fact that Welsh children did not perform as well in examinations as did their English and Scottish counterparts, and also because of the dire problems associated with school attendance in Wales.

Yet at no time was there an active promotion of the Welsh language and, in the absence of a positive policy, the emphasis remained on the desirability that Welsh speakers should embrace the English-speaking culture. From this viewpoint, cultural differences were seen as problems which would be resolved over a period of time by the decline and eventual death of the language. By the late 1880s, as has been indicated already, there was some modification of these attitudes. The claims of Welsh were recognized by policy-makers such as William Hart-Dyke as an inescapable feature of Welsh education. Arthur Acland, another key figure in the development of education policy, adopted a highly positive approach to the language which reflected two significant developments. The first was educational, and was concerned with the needs created by the fact that children were disadvantaged by their inability to cope with instructions in a new language. The second acknowledged the intrinsic value of the Welsh language and culture as well as the practical advantages of the use of Welsh. These considerations had far-reaching implications in the elementary school, where education touched the interests of the greatest numbers.

Opinion within Wales was greatly influenced by perspectives adopted by religious and political groups. The views of the leaders of Nonconformist denominations were a crucial factor in the debate concerning the Welsh language in education, not least because they sought to articulate and influence the views of the majority of Welsh worshippers. Nonconformity had benefited immensely from the reaction against the Anglicized nature of the Anglican church in Wales,

---

[28] Knut Eriksen, 'Norwegian and Swedish Educational Policies vis-à-vis Non-dominant Ethnic Groups, 1850–1940' in Tomiak (ed.), *Schooling*, pp. 63–86.

[29] Vaughan Rogers, 'Brittany' in Michael Watson (ed.), *Contemporary Minority Nationalism* (London, 1990), pp. 67–85.

and part of its appeal was derived from the fact that their chapels provided religious services in the vernacular. Moreover, the Nonconformist denominations were the centres of a vibrant Welsh culture based on those chapels and the denominational press. Both the leaders of Welsh Nonconformity and the tribunes of the Liberal Party in Wales stressed linguistic considerations as they sought to convince the people of the need to end the domination of the landed gentry. Yet the leaders did not demonstrate a wholehearted commitment to the Welsh language either in their public pronouncements or as members of School Boards. Indeed, prominent figures such as the Revd J. R. Kilsby Jones were particularly averse to any attempts to bolster the Welsh language, and these attitudes were reflected in the Anglicized attitudes of many of the Nonconformist leaders of this generation, a matter of some poignancy given that, in the estimation of many, the Welsh of the pulpit constituted the ideal to be emulated.

Nonconformist leaders such as Henry Richard and Lewis Edwards were only gradually convinced of the desirability of broadening the domain of the language. Although both Edwards and Richard were converted to the principle of using Welsh as a means of teaching English, they believed that the essential function of a school was to ensure that all children gained fluency in the English language. Edwards, in particular, represented those within the denominations who did not regard the survival of the Welsh language as part of the mission of Nonconformity. Indeed, his growing advocacy of English-medium chapels and the holding of English services in Welsh-speaking chapels in order to accommodate English-speaking newcomers emphasize that it was the spiritual message of Nonconformity, rather than the language in which it was delivered, which was his primary consideration. Edwards was certainly lukewarm about the introduction of Welsh into the elementary schools. Yet it would be wrong to deduce from this that he and others of the same view had no regard for the well-being of the Welsh language. Rather, Edwards placed his faith in the ability of the Sunday school movement to ensure that children gained a grammatical knowledge of Welsh.[30] This demonstrates, firstly, the prevalence of the view that Welsh was believed to be a suitable medium for spiritual matters and for discourse in the home, but that English was the language of commerce and secular education, and, secondly, that many Nonconformists initially advocated establishing totally secular schools in which no form of religious instruction was taught. This was a reflection of the faith Nonconformists placed in the ability of the Sunday school to provide

---

[30] For a detailed assessment of the life of Lewis Edwards, see Thomas Charles Edwards, *Bywyd a Llythyrau y Diweddar Barch. Lewis Edwards* (Liverpool, 1901). For Henry Richard and elementary education, see Margaret V. George, 'An Assessment of the Contribution of Henry Richard to Education' (unpubl. University of Wales MEd thesis, 1975).

spiritual guidance for Welsh children; they certainly regarded the Sunday school as complementary rather than subsidiary to the day school.[31]

A new approach to Welsh in education was indicated by the position adopted by the following generation of Nonconformist leaders, a viewpoint best expressed in the comments of Principal Thomas Charles Edwards at a meeting in Aberystwyth in April 1889, when he advocated a greater appreciation of the value of Welsh in education. In his opinion it was fatuous to deny the educational merit of a language which was the medium of intellectual stimulation and religious observance in Wales.[32] His views represented an adjustment in the outlook of the Nonconformist leaders who were, by this time, influenced by the national revival which was under way in Wales. A vigorous promotion of the claims of Welsh in the schools was evident in the pronouncements of Michael D. Jones and Robert Ambrose Jones (Emrys ap Iwan), both of whom advocated that Welsh be accorded a proper place in the education system as part of their broader campaign to raise the status of the language in all spheres of life.[33] Their efforts were in harmony with many of the declarations of the Welsh Nonconformist press. The Congregational paper *Y Tyst* advocated the use of Welsh to teach English in 1886,[34] and the Methodist *Y Goleuad* went further, four years later, by urging the study of Welsh:

Wele ein hen iaith anwyl, ar ol cael ei throi allan gyda dirmyg, wedi cael ei gosod o'r newydd mewn safle o anrhydedd, o barch, ac o ddefnyddioldeb yn ein hysgolion. Na fydded bellach i neb esgeuluso y manteision enillwyd iddynt.[35]

(At last our dear language, after being rejected with contempt, is now being placed anew in a position of honour, of respect and of usefulness in our schools. Let no one henceforth neglect the benefits which have been gained for them.)

An equally forthright approach was taken by E. Pan Jones in his paper *Y Celt*. One of the most colourful characters of the Welsh pulpit, Pan Jones had wide experience of education, mainly through the Sunday school movement. His commitment to Nonconformity and the Welsh language was total, partly because of his experiences in Flintshire, where Anglicization caused by industrialization had resulted in a dramatic increase in the number of Roman Catholics in the county, an encroachment which he deplored. He strongly advocated measures to enhance the position of Welsh in the schools. In March 1891, during a campaign

---

[31] Both R. Tudur Jones, *Yr Undeb: Hanes Undeb yr Annibynwyr Cymraeg, 1872–1972* (Abertawe, 1975) and T. M. Bassett, *The Welsh Baptists* (Swansea, 1977) include valuable analyses of this interesting and important subject.
[32] *Cyfaill yr Aelwyd*, X, no. 1 (1890), 7–9.
[33] *Y Celt*, 23 September 1892.
[34] *Y Tyst*, 23 April 1886.
[35] *Y Goleuad*, 10 April 1890.

to convince the Nonconformist School Boards of the need to safeguard the language, he asserted that no Welsh scheme of education was possible unless an honourable position was granted to the language:

> Sonir llawer am gael cynllun addysg cenedlaethol ac arbenig i Gymru, ond pa fodd y mae hyny yn bosibl cyhyd ag y cauir allan yr iaith genedlaethol o'u sefydliadau – son am addysg genedlaethol, tra yn cadw allan yr arwedd gryfaf o genedl, sef ei hiaith . . .![36]

> (Much is said about a national scheme of education specially for Wales, but to what extent is this possible while the national language is shut out of its institutions – why talk of national education while keeping out the strongest badge of nationality, namely its language . . .!)

The more sympathetic attitude of the Nonconformist denominations was apparent in the declarations of their leaders, but their public attestations did not always reflect their personal conduct. J. Vyrnwy Morgan, who was deeply sceptical of the movement in favour of compulsory Welsh, noted that many of those who were most anxious to promote the language in education chose English as the principal language within their homes:

> It is a remarkable thing that the recent outcry for compulsory Welsh emanated chiefly from the middle-class Welsh that so sadly neglect it themselves. English is the language of their home and offspring, and all their social functions are carried on in English; only in cases of absolute necessity do they speak Welsh in ordinary conversation, and even then it is neither elegant nor intelligible. Yet, they cry for compulsory Welsh – of course, compulsory for others. Is it reasonable to expect headmasters to teach Welsh to children of Welsh parents that constantly speak English at home?[37]

Clearly, since Morgan was an Anglican, his sardonic observations were partly prompted by his distaste for his Nonconformist counterparts, but his comments also reveal that the first loyalty of Nonconformists was to their respective denominations rather than to their native language. As E. L. Ellis has illustrated, personalities such as Thomas Jones openly claimed that it was Nonconformity rather than any national aspirations which were the most potent influences on their early views. Jones recalled that he 'felt and knew myself to be a Methodist much more actively and intensely than I felt myself to be a Welshman', a standpoint which bears a close resemblance to that of Nonconformist leaders like Lewis Edwards a generation earlier.[38]

---

[36] *Y Celt*, 6 March 1891.
[37] Morgan (ed.), *Welsh Political and Educational Leaders*, p. 17.
[38] E. L. Ellis, *TJ: A Life of Dr Thomas Jones, C.H.* (Cardiff, 1992), p. 24.

Despite this dichotomy in the outlook of the leaders of Nonconformist and radical opinion, their increasingly sympathetic declarations regarding the need to use Welsh in schools were in tune with those of a new generation of social and educational thinkers in Wales. Their opinions had largely been shaped by research undertaken by educational campaigners such as J. E. Southall, one of the most effective tribunes of Welshness in the schools. An Englishman who had learnt Welsh, Southall was totally committed not only to maintaining the position of the Welsh language but also to reversing the tide of Anglicization which was in evidence in his adopted Monmouthshire. He avidly noted instances in which the children of English and Irish émigrés in south Wales had gained proficiency in Welsh and he confidently predicted that, given a positive attitude on the part of the education authorities in Wales, the country would become fully bilingual. Of equal significance were his pioneering efforts to gain official recognition for Welsh as a language of commerce and law.[39]

These views gained a substantial following among those Welsh exiles who demonstrated a renewed interest in their native country and exerted a growing influence on public discussion in Wales.[40] Their views were reflected by organizations such as the Cymmrodorion Society, which emerged as the focus for an intellectual élite that included both expatriates and a significant number of resident professionals.[41] These organizations sought to guide public opinion on a variety of subjects, among them the issue of elementary education. Thus, intellectual weight was given to the argument in favour of teaching Welsh (as opposed to using Welsh) through papers such as 'The Advisability of the Teaching of Welsh in Elementary Schools in Wales', read to the Cymmrodorion in London by Thomas Powel, Professor of Celtic at the University College of South Wales and Monmouthshire, in May 1884.[42] The influence exerted by those who held these views is evident in the initiatives of other members of the Cymmrodorion Society, notably H. Isambard Owen and T. Marchant Williams, who were instrumental in establishing the Society for Utilizing the Welsh Language in 1885. The English title adopted by the founders was a misnomer and the Welsh title, 'Cymdeithas yr Iaith Gymraeg' (the Welsh Language Society), although less specific, was a more suitable description since the Society was not concerned with the utilization of the language alone. It would be wrong, however, to overestimate its importance. The Society did not attract a significant membership in Wales and it should not be assumed on the basis of its voluminous contributions to news-papers and periodicals that it articulated the views of a large body of Welsh speakers. For the majority in Wales, the religious arguments between

---

[39] J. E. Southall, *Wales and her Language* (Newport, 1892), pp. 167–70.
[40] Jones, *NUT* (1911), p. 251.
[41] Southall, *Wales and her Language*, pp. 110–37.
[42] J. E. Lloyd, 'Cymdeithas yr Iaith Gymraeg: Trem ar Hanes y Mudiad', *Y Llenor*, X (1931), 207–14.

Anglicans and Nonconformists were still accorded greater priority than linguistic debates. The influence of the Society stemmed from its ability to attract support from those in a position to secure a change in the policy both of the Education Department and, to a lesser extent, the School Boards.[43]

During this period each child had access to a place in a school for the first time and, as a result, the influence of the school could penetrate every home in Wales. Practice in those schools was undoubtedly influenced by the Education Department and by school inspectors. Yet the education system also allowed a considerable amount of local autonomy. In national and church schools, the views of the clergy and trustees were a potent influence on the language policy adopted by the school. Likewise, the board schools were influenced by the views of elected members accountable to the electorate. Both the Anglican managers and the School Boards sought to articulate the educational aspirations of Wales and their perceptions of what the community desired was a major influence on the policy adopted by the schools in relation to the Welsh language.

Liberal–Nonconformist groups dominated School Boards throughout Wales and although no formal Liberal policy was imposed on these Boards the ideas which influenced the Liberal Party inevitably permeated the policies they pursued. The promotion of the Welsh language in education was therefore facilitated by the decision of the North Wales Liberal Federation to urge its constituent bodies to support the introduction of Welsh into education,[44] a decision which influenced the attitude of the leaders of several School Boards in Wales. Thus, School Boards in Bangor,[45] Caernarfon,[46] Llangar,[47] and Ffestiniog[48] not only ensured that Welsh was employed as an informal teaching medium in the school but that the language was also introduced into the school curriculum as a subject of study. A more debatable issue was whether candidates for teaching posts were required to be Welsh speakers. This condition was implemented by a growing number of Boards throughout the country, most notably by those in rural areas.[49] But it was a controversial proposal and there were many within Liberal and Nonconformist circles who doubted the wisdom of giving preference to candidates who, although Welsh speaking, did not possess qualifications equal to those of other candidates.[50]

[43] For a detailed assessment of the Society for Utilizing the Welsh Language, see J. Elwyn Hughes, *Arloeswr Dwyieithedd: Dan Isaac Davies, 1839–1887* (Caerdydd, 1984). For the career of Beriah Evans, see Juliana E. Edwards, 'Beriah Gwynfe Evans, ei Fywyd a'i Waith, ynghyd â Mynegai Dethol i *Cyfaill yr Aelwyd*' (unpubl. University of Wales PhD thesis, 1989).
[44] *Carnarvon and Denbigh Herald*, 21 December 1888.
[45] Ibid., 13 July 1888.
[46] Ibid., 9 March 1888.
[47] Gwynedd Archives, Dolgellau, Llangar School Board Papers, A 52.
[48] *Carnarvon and Denbigh Herald*, 20 December 1889.
[49] Ibid., 10 January 1890.
[50] Ibid., 28 July 1893. See also Williams, 'Patriots and Citizens', pp. 36–52. He notes that Boards and School Managers often failed to appoint Welsh speakers and that the presence of monoglot English teachers was an Anglicizing influence.

The fact that School Boards even considered that a knowledge of Welsh was a qualification for appointment was, however, an important development and it illustrated the extent to which ideas expressed by Shadrach Pryce in the 1870s had receded from the minds of policy-makers on education in Wales.

Insistence upon the appointment of Welsh speakers was a policy most relevant in the more strongly Welsh-speaking areas. Yet it was in the highly Anglicized areas of south-east Wales that the most spectacular evidence of a new attitude on the part of members of School Boards may be found. Several Boards in that area introduced Welsh into their schools not only as a subject for study by those conversant with the language, but also as a means of encouraging newcomers to learn the language. Originally Welsh was introduced on a trial basis, for instance in the schools in the Gelli-gaer district, and subsequently in those of the Mynyddislwyn and Bedwellte School Boards. In both Mynyddislwyn and Bedwellte Welsh was introduced after parents had been consulted by means of a referendum, which in both cases resulted in a clear majority in favour of the introduction of Welsh.[51] Significantly, both areas had witnessed considerable in-migration, and the results of the referenda suggest that the policy was not imposed by a Welsh Nonconformist élite on the School Board against the wishes of the community. These Boards were certainly committed to the teaching of the Welsh language and the subsequent failure to execute the policy efficiently occurred because of the dearth of Welsh-speaking staff and suitable teaching materials.[52] The extent to which the school authorities championed the interests of the Welsh language varied considerably, but it can hardly be claimed that the decline of the Welsh language in south-east Wales was attributable to the education system managed by the School Boards. Indeed, what is remarkable is the commitment which many such Boards demonstrated in comparison with their counterparts in areas where the language was in a much stronger position.[53] Yet it is also the case that this policy was adopted nearly twenty years after the passing of the Education Act. During the previous two decades it had been assumed that the language of education was English and this inevitably affected the daily life of communities in a period which witnessed the in-migration of large numbers of English speakers. The introduction of Welsh as a secondary subject, to be studied as an auxiliary to the central work of the school, i.e. reading, writing and counting in English, was not likely to overcome the powerful Anglicizing tide.

[51] For a detailed assessment of these cases, see Southall, *Wales and her Language*, p. 387. The result of the referendum at Mynyddislwyn, for instance, recorded 1,275 votes in favour of teaching Welsh, 146 against, and 117 abstentions. The teaching of Welsh in Glamorgan and Monmouthshire also attracted the interest of Tom Ellis, as testified by his correspondence with Southall. NLW, T. E. Ellis Papers, 1947.
[52] Ibid. and Merthyr Tydfil Public Library, Education Collection.
[53] Williams, 'Patriots and Citizens' also argues that in those areas the policy was implemented despite the presence of large numbers of English-speaking in-migrants who had a right to expect an education through their mother tongue.

The deliberations of the School Boards formed a major feature of public debate in Wales in the late nineteenth century, not least because they were democratically elected and publicly accountable bodies. Yet even at the height of their power in c.1900, board schools were only responsible for the education of 65.2 per cent of the children of Wales; the remainder were taught in voluntary establishments, 60 per cent of which were Anglican or national schools.[54] Those schools received a considerable part of their funding from the contributions of the Welsh landowning class. The number of children in voluntary schools was considerably higher in rural areas and as a result the attitudes of the clergy and the gentry dictated the language policy of the schools in predominantly Welsh-speaking areas. The Welsh upper class had largely been assimilated into English society and was widely perceived to have adopted English values, language and culture. While a number of landowners were able to engage in simple conversation in Welsh, their command of the language was limited.[55] The view that Welsh was the language of the lower classes remained, as did the impression that Welsh was an obstacle to the social and intellectual development of the nation. Many of the more politically-motivated landowners, such as Charles Fitzwilliams of Cilgwyn, Newcastle Emlyn, considered that Welsh was being exploited by radical political forces in an effort to undermine the position of the Anglican and landowning community.[56] The clergy, who were responsible for the management of the national and church schools, were also reputed to be distinctly unsympathetic towards the Welsh language. The evidence presented by the Anglican fraternity to the Cross Commission in 1888 certainly supports this view. The Revd Daniel Lewis, rector of Merthyr, warned the Commission not to countenance the introduction of Welsh into the elementary schools, for he believed that Welsh literature was second-rate material, most of which could be described as sectarian and political polemic wholly unsuitable for schoolchildren.[57] The fact that Lewis was supported by other prominent figures in the Anglican church, such as the Revd Thomas Briscoe of Bangor,[58] indicates that his views were representative of a significant body of opinion within the Anglican church in Wales.

Such comments were used by Liberal and Nonconformist leaders in the 1890s, most notably by those in the Cymru Fydd movement, as evidence of the fissure between the broader community in Wales and the established Church. Yet it is also clear that the national revival in Wales had an effect even within the ranks of the

---

[54] *Report of the Committee of Council on Education*, 1898–9 (PP 1900 XIX), p. 10.
[55] O. M. Edwards, 'The Welsh Not', reprinted in Meic Stephens, *A Book of Wales: An Anthology* (London, 1987), pp. 55–7.
[56] NLW, Dolaucothi Correspondence, L. 11765. Gentry attitudes are also discussed by H. M. Vaughan, *The South Wales Squires* (London, 1926), pp. 199–205, esp. pp. 202–4.
[57] *Royal Commission on the Working of the Elementary Education Acts* (1886–8), Minutes of Evidence, Vol. 3 (PP 1887 XXX), Qs. 42, 764–850.
[58] Ibid.; PRO ED 92/8. File on the introduction of the Welsh language into the elementary schools of Wales.

landowners and clergy. By the closing decades of the nineteenth century very few of them advocated the eradication of the language and, as Hywel Teifi Edwards has indicated, several landowners were promoters of the Eisteddfod at both local and national level.[59] The Cymmrodorion Society boasted of its association with the Welsh gentry and many of the proponents of Welsh in education, notably Dan Isaac Davies, urged the Welsh gentry to regain a sense of Welshness in order to reclaim the leadership of Welsh politics from the radical helmsmen whom he distrusted. The movement to promote Welsh within education gained some support from landowners. Lord Dynevor was an early supporter and the movement also attracted the sympathies of more controversial figures such as Lord Penrhyn and the Marquess of Bute.[60] The support elicited from Dynevor can be attributed to his practical experience as a school manager and as a member of the School Board in the Welsh-speaking area of Llandeilo Fawr, and his views illustrate his more general unprejudiced conduct in public life. In other cases, however, a more pronounced political motive can be detected. In an essay published in *Cymru Fydd* in 1889,[61] J. Arthur Price urged the Welsh gentry to strive to regain a sense of Welshness in order to rebuild their relations with the community. His argument concurred with that of Dan Isaac Davies and was based on the premise that, while it would be impossible to establish a consensus on issues such as the land question or disestablishment, the matter of the language was a cultural issue which could transcend political and religious divisions. Likewise, voices were raised within the Anglican church, notably by David Williams and John Griffiths, both of whom urged the church to develop a closer relationship with the Welsh-speaking community and thus overcome its image as an enemy of the Welsh language and culture.[62] These were powerful figures, but they failed to secure a major change in the outlook of an important influence on Welsh education. The fact that the local clergy retained responsibility for the day-to-day administration of church schools meant that a large group needed to be convinced of the merits of Welsh. The failure of the Welsh element within the church to influence the majority of the clergy bears witness to the ingrained Englishness of the Anglican church in Wales.

Hitherto, this chapter has considered the effect of Anglicizing influences on those who controlled education in Wales. But it is also necessary to consider the views of parents and teachers. Shadrach Pryce, the most vocal opponent of the use of Welsh in schools, constantly reminded the Education Department of the fact that the majority of parents were anxious that their children should learn English and that they displayed little sympathy with the demands of those who advocated

---

[59] Hywel Teifi Edwards, *Gŵyl Gwalia: Yr Eisteddfod Genedlaethol yn Oes Aur Victoria 1858–1868* (Llandysul, 1980), pp. 352–60.
[60] Cardiff Central Library, Evans Papers, D. I. Davies to B. G. Evans, n.d.; Southall, *Wales and her Language*, pp. 206–10.
[61] J. Arthur Price, 'Welsh Education and Welsh Public Life', *Cymru Fydd*, II, no. 11 (1889), 593–604.
[62] Southall, *Wales and her Language*, pp. 210–11.

the introduction of Welsh into the schools.[63] The evidence offered by Pryce must be tempered by an appreciation of his own rigid standpoint on the issue; yet it is worth noting his comment that those views were most pronounced among monoglot Welsh parents. This group was acutely aware of the disadvantages of being unable to speak English and its wholehearted commitment to the English language was prompted by lack of access to various forms of employment. The testimony offered by Pryce is supported by other inspectors, among them George Bancroft, inspector for north Pembrokeshire, who also noted that parents in his district were disinclined to support the introduction of Welsh.[64] Unlike Pryce, Bancroft did not harbour prejudice against the native tongue; indeed, he demonstrated considerable sympathy with those in his district who advocated the use of the Welsh language. Significantly, however, Bancroft noted that a greater awareness of the value of Welsh was emerging among parents in his district,[65] an inclination in tune with the evidence of parental support, noted by Southall, for the policy of introducing Welsh in Mynyddislwyn and Bedwellte. Clearly parents could be influenced by positive leadership on the part of teachers and education authorities and many were becoming convinced that an education system which excluded Welsh altogether was not appropriate in Wales. Nevertheless, the overwhelming bulk of the evidence indicates that most parents were unconvinced of the need to promote the cause of Welsh in the elementary school.

Teachers faced the difficult task of reconciling official policy, which maintained that the main purpose of a school was to ensure that pupils acquired a firm understanding of English, with the practical reality of a classroom dominated by monoglot Welsh-speaking pupils, many of whom attended school so irregularly that the most basic principles had to be retaught continually.[66] There can be no doubt that, in many cases, teachers preferred to act in accordance with their own opinions rather than implement a policy imposed upon them. Individual recollections, such as those of T. E. Nicholas at Hermon in the heart of Welsh-speaking Preselau, and T. Gwynn Jones or Henry Jones,[67] point to the total exclusion of Welsh from the school at the insistence of the schoolmaster. The National Union of Elementary Teachers (NUET) included a significant element which strongly objected to making any concession to the Welsh language. Among them were members of the Lampeter and Aberaeron branch, who remained convinced of the virtue of the direct method of teaching English even though they served in one of the most thoroughly Welsh-speaking areas in Wales.[68]

[63] *Report of the Committee of Council on Education*, 1882–3, pp. 416–29.
[64] Ibid., 1888–9, p. 366.
[65] Ibid.
[66] Tom Elias, 'The Problems of Teachers in the Rural Areas of Wales' in *NUT Conference: Aberystwyth Souvenir* (Aberystwyth, 1933), pp. 134–9.
[67] T. Gwynn Jones in *NUT Conference Handbook* (London, 1911), p. 249; Jones, *Old Memories*, p. 32; David W. Howell, *Nicholas of Glais: The People's Champion* (Clydach, 1991), p. 6.
[68] Cardiff Central Library, Evans Papers, Lampeter and Aberaeron NUET Branch to B. G. Evans, n.d. Williams, 'Patriots and Citizens' also notes a tendency to dismiss those who had genuine reservations concerning the teaching of English through the medium of Welsh as 'anti-Welsh'.

These attitudes were also underlined by the English ethos of the new intermediate schools, whose ambience reflected the powerful influence of the classical tradition of the characteristic English school. The fact that they failed to pursue at intermediate level an approach which was by then being advocated at the elementary level is arguably a greater blemish on their achievement than that incurred by the founders of the elementary schools in 1870.

Even so, it is not true to say that Welsh was excluded from all schools. Individual examples, such as that of the Ystumtuen schoolmistress who was reprimanded by a school inspector in 1878 for speaking Welsh to her pupils,[69] can be cited as evidence that some teachers were forced to risk official reprimand or public censure given they had no alternative but to use the Welsh language in school. In Caernarfonshire, E. T. Watts HMI noted that English was becoming a secondary language in some schools, a development which he deplored, even though he was a strong supporter of the practice of allowing a reasonable amount of Welsh to be spoken in school.[70] The importance of the issue was recognized by the NUET, who faced a concerted campaign on this issue from their members in Wales. Firstly, several NUET members were anxious that examination standards in Wales be reduced in order to take account of the difficulties which confronted the profession in Wales when faced by a community whose first language was Welsh. This was a particularly important issue at a time when teachers' salaries depended upon favourable examination results. Yet the NUET did not confine its activities to the promotion of a less rigorous form of examination. The union was the forum for a detailed discussion both of the use of Welsh when teaching English and the intrinsic value of the Welsh language. Again no clear pattern emerges from the pronouncements of individual branches. Yet it is clear that a number of prominent activists, including some from outside Wales, saw the merit of using and nurturing the vernacular.[71] Research conducted by the Cymmrodorion Society in 1885 indicated that the majority of teachers (rather than simply union members) were in favour of making Welsh a topic for study in school. More than half (53.9 per cent) responded positively to the question 'do you consider that advantage would result from the introduction of the Welsh language as a specific subject into the course of elementary education in Wales', with 40.9 per cent against and the remainder undecided. The sample accounted for approximately 6.8 per cent of the total number of teachers in Wales and there are grounds for doubting the scientific pedigree of the experiment.[72] Nevertheless, it

---

[69] Griffith G. Davies, 'Addysg Elfennol yn Sir Aberteifi, 1870–1902', *Ceredigion*, IV, pt. 4 (1963), 367.
[70] David Thomas, 'Reminiscences of a School Inspector', *NUT* (1933), pp. 146–57.
[71] *Llanelli Guardian*, 30 October 1884; *The Schoolmaster*, 9 February 1884; NLW, T. E. Ellis Papers, 2111.
[72] The 1891 census noted that there were 9,137 teachers of various descriptions in Wales.

remained the case that, even on the evidence presented by a body committed to the promotion of the language, the issue was one which divided opinion among the teachers of Wales.[73] The effectiveness of the teaching profession in making its case to the Education Department must also be questioned. The NUET was its only vehicle, yet it was not a fully developed trade union at this time and it did not represent the majority of teachers. Many of its branches confined their activities to holding lectures and social events. In addition, the fact that there was no common view on the Welsh language prevented the union from advocating either the exclusion or the promotion of Welsh in school. Moreover, a body that might have exerted a powerful influence on policy-makers was hampered by its own lack of clarity on the issue. A teacher's life in late nineteenth-century Wales was certainly not easy. As a group, teachers had an ill-defined social status and many were loath to contribute to controversial topics. The vast majority adopted the prudent policy of following the lead of prominent figures in the community. Furthermore, the teaching profession was in the invidious position of relying on the favourable reports of school inspectors for their salaries and, on occasion, for the retention of their posts. In such circumstances the views of the inspectors, especially those responsible for the individual district in which the teacher was employed, inevitably coloured the views of the teachers. Many teachers who pioneered the use of Welsh as an unofficial language did so surreptitiously, out of necessity rather than design.

By the end of the School Board era, the position of the Welsh language in elementary schools was certainly stronger than it was in 1870. A more sympathetic attitude had emerged from the Education Department as a result of the adoption of the recommendations of the Cross Commission, which had been appointed to investigate all aspects of the implementation of the 1870 Act in England and Wales and which had presented its final report in 1888.[74] Welsh had been accorded the status of a specific subject, and was thus recognized as an official part of the school curriculum and as a subject deemed by the Education Department to be worthy of study.[75] Yet despite the importance of official recognition, the extent to which Welsh was employed remained limited. Its inclusion as a specific and later as a class subject did not result in Welsh becoming an intrinsic part of the work of the school. This was a period in which schools concentrated almost exclusively on reading, writing and counting, and those activities continued to be conducted in English. The position of Welsh was subsidiary, akin to that of art, geography or history, part of the work that many

---

[73] *Report of the Commissioners appointed to Inquire into the Elementary Education Acts, England and Wales* (Cross Commission). Appendix of written evidence from the Society for Utilizing the Welsh Language (PP 1888 XXXV).
[74] *Report of the Commissioners appointed to Inquire into the Elementary Education Acts.*
[75] PRO ED 92/8. File on the introduction of the Welsh language into the elementary schools of Wales.

teachers considered to be educationally valuable and stimulating but of no primary importance. The Welsh curriculum contained some formal grammar, a translation from English to Welsh and from Welsh to English, a piece of dictation, the learning of a Welsh verse and an item of composition in Welsh. There was little scope to develop new vocabulary and children were certainly more aware of the great names of English history and literature than of their Welsh equivalents.

The Welsh language was not an issue which aroused the passions of the majority of the people of Wales and not many parents lamented their children's loss of Welsh. Many parents believed that the Welsh language had no place in a modern, progressive world which was being forged by industrialization and imperialism. Welsh was associated with the rural past rather than with the thrusting urban society that was being lauded by the Welsh press as offering exciting possibilities for the future.

Perceptions of the value of Welsh which existed at the end of the School Board era were different from those which had influenced both official attitudes and public opinion in 1870. Although Welsh was no longer considered an impediment, many people remained convinced that it possessed no great merit. After 1902 control of elementary education passed into the hands of the county councils, and as a result the domination of the Anglicized Anglican element over a substantial portion of Welsh elementary schools ended. Yet there would be little improvement in the status accorded to Welsh in schools. After the Morant regulations of 1905 had established the principle of curricular freedom within elementary schools, the role of the Education Department in schools became even more restricted. Welsh schools did not use this freedom to develop either a more prominent position for the Welsh language or to adapt the curriculum to suit specific Welsh needs. Welsh may have continued as the unofficial language of the playground and taught as a subsidiary subject, but English remained the language of elementary education, with few exceptions.

A powerful bias against the Welsh language and culture was thus generated in the minds of the rising generation. In a review of J. E. Southall's *Wales and Her Language*, Michael D. Jones claimed that by excluding Welsh and securing a limited knowledge of English only, the education system rendered children less articulate and therefore failed in its most important function.[76] Similar sentiments were expressed by Tom Elias, headmaster of Rhydlewis school. An early advocate of a more Welsh form of education (in terms of curriculum as well as language), Elias pointed to the pernicious psychological effects of an Anglicized system of education in which the denigration of the native language resulted in children abandoning Welsh in later years.[77] Schools created in the wake of the 1870 Act

---

[76] *Y Celt*, 23 September 1892.
[77] Elias, *NUT* (1933), pp. 136–7.

might not have destroyed the Welsh language, but many of them were responsible for fostering attitudes which persuaded a significant number of Welsh speakers to take a conscious decision not to pass on the language to the next generation.

18

The Welsh Language and Politics 1800–1880

IEUAN GWYNEDD JONES

BEFORE the Reform Act of 1832, the Welsh language was only marginally and adventitiously the language of politics in Wales. There were a number of reasons why this should have been so. First and foremost, Welsh was a dominated language,[1] and politics, both at local and parliamentary level, was a domain from which it was effectively excluded. English was the language of power: it was the language of constitutional usage, of law and government, of official returns, and of the bureaucratic activities of officials associated with elections and electioneering. Since Welsh was the language of politically subordinate and excluded classes, of the unenfranchised rather than the enfranchised, it had no place in such high and prestigious affairs as the return of Members of Parliament, or the election of local government representatives and officials. In these respects it was the language of the powerless.

This is not to say that Welsh was not a language of political discourse or that political discourse was not possible through the medium of the Welsh language. On the contrary, Welsh had always been the medium for the discussion of ideologies and the policies of government, especially in those areas of private and public life where policy infringed on religious rights as defined by the Toleration Act (1689) and subsequent legislation. In this respect Welsh Nonconformists shared a common culture with their English co-religionists. They were disadvantaged, however, by the fact that most of the key texts – philosophical, theological and legal – were not available in Welsh, and although there had always been Welsh scholars who endeavoured to ensure that important new works should quickly be made available in Welsh, their main interests were in theology,

---

[1] Michael J. Shapiro, *Language and Political Understanding: The Politics of Discursive Practices* (London, 1981), p. 191.

and philosophical and political works were neglected.[2] Over the years there had developed a wary and sceptical understanding of the processes of government, but there was no critical body of knowledge about the constitution and the nature of government. Throughout the eighteenth century Nonconformists were often called upon to defend their individual and corporate rights, and to resist persecution by all legal and constitutional means, but because of their unavoidable reliance upon their English friends, especially the Protestant Nonconformist Deputies,[3] much of this activity at the highest levels could take place only through the medium of English. At the level of the congregation, however, the common discourse was in Welsh.

The Welsh language itself, because of its lack of prestige and its exclusion from the domains of administration and government, could, in certain circumstances, provoke occasions for political action on the part of people who had reason to resent the social consequences of the status ascribed to it. Examples in the first half of the century included the abolition of the Courts of Great Sessions in 1830,[4] the proposal by the Church Commissioners in 1836 to unite the sees of Bangor and St Asaph in order to create a new see at Manchester,[5] and the publishing of the Report of the Commission of Inquiry into the State of Education in Wales ('Brad y Llyfrau Gleision') in 1847.[6] These were very diverse issues which affected different classes of people, ranging from gentry, Anglican clerics and ordinary middle-class and working-class persons and communities, but all shared a passionate concern for the integrity and importance of the Welsh language. Defenders of the Courts of Great Sessions emphasized their antiquity, and the fact that, over the years, their jurisdiction had come to be accepted by all manner of persons, and that in their administration of the law due recognition was given to the Welsh language. The gentry of west Wales were prominent in the campaign

---

[2] Meredydd Evans, 'Athronyddu yn Gymraeg: Braenaru'r Tir', *Efrydiau Athronyddol*, LVIII (1995), 68–85. See *Yr Adolygydd*, III (1850), 390, for the view that it was not strange that philosophy and logic were but little studied in Wales when all political and legal matters were carried on in English. *The Star of Gwent*, 1, 1859, was of the opinion that some English authorities despised the Welsh and treated them as if they were below the standard of civilization. Sir Thomas Phillips attributed to this policy the administrative incapacity of Welshmen. Sir Thomas Phillips, *Wales: The Language, Social Condition, Moral Character and Religious Opinions of the People Considered in their Relation to Education . . .* (London, 1849), p. 59.

[3] Bernard Lord Manning, *The Protestant Dissenting Deputies* (Cambridge, 1952).

[4] R. T. Jenkins, *Hanes Cymru yn y Bedwaredd Ganrif ar Bymtheg* (Caerdydd, 1933), pp. 98–100. The fullest account is in John Rhys and David Brynmor-Jones, *The Welsh People* (London, 1900), pp. 386–94. For the Act itself (An Act for the more effectual administration of Justice in England and Wales, 1 Will. 4, c.70), see Ivor Bowen (ed.), *The Statutes of Wales* (London, 1908), pp. 239–48. See also Hywel Moseley, 'Gweinyddiad y Gyfraith yng Nghymru', *THSC* (1973), 16–36.

[5] Roger L. Brown, *Lord Powis and the Extension of the Episcopate* (Tongwynlais, 1989); Owen Chadwick, *The Victorian Church* (2 vols., 2nd ed., London, 1970), I, pp. 229–30, 235.

[6] Prys Morgan (ed.), *Brad y Llyfrau Gleision: Ysgrifau ar Hanes Cymru* (Llandysul, 1991), passim, and Ieuan Gwynedd Jones, *Mid-Victorian Wales: The Observers and the Observed* (Cardiff, 1992), pp. 103–65.

to prevent their abolition, but ordinary persons were also involved. At the heart of the case against uniting the two north Wales sees, too, was their great antiquity, and that they were Welsh institutions in which the ancient language of Wales occupied a dominant place, and enjoyed a vigorous life. There is no doubt that the printing of the 1847 Report marked a turning point in the development of Welsh political feeling, and that young men like Henry Richard, who thereafter took up positions from which to attack the establishment in church and state, took their inspiration from the general reaction of the nation to it.

Nor was it merely or only a matter of discussion. The defence of constitutional rights also involved certain forms of political action, in particular the petitioning of Parliament. In essence, petitioning was a rudimentary political activity, but since it was the only constitutional way in which individuals and communities could make their views known to the legislature on specific measures, and the only way in which the pressure of public opinion could be brought to bear in debates, it became increasingly common, especially during the period of the French Revolution and the French Wars.[7] Petitioning was a favourite method of moderate radical agitation, much to be preferred to the rioting and popular clamour, which was the method of agitation deployed by the newly emerging working classes but which disturbed the peace and brought the soldiers in. Its relevance in relation to the use of the Welsh language for political purposes is that it necessarily involved organizing large numbers of people in support of, or in opposition to, particular policies, usually by means of public meetings and demonstrations. With very few exceptions, petitions were drawn up in English, but the discussions and debates on which they were based would have been in Welsh. Many of these meetings were reported in Welsh periodicals, such as *Seren Gomer*, which often printed model petitions which were thereupon copied, collected and given to a sympathetic Member of Parliament for presentation in the Commons, or to a peer in the Lords. Petitioning was thus an important element in the political education of the people.

Welsh petitioning was always strongest on the topic of religion, and it was in connection with religion that Welsh political life found a distinctive voice and learnt to use it to good effect.[8] The question of Catholic emancipation, for instance, which agitated the country from 1825 onwards, called forth many scores of petitions either for or against that measure. In 1828 over 150 petitions calling for the repeal of the Test and Corporation Acts, which debarred Nonconformists from political office, reached the Commons from Wales. They were sent from

---

[7] On petitioning, see O. S. Opp, *Wharton's Law Lexicon* (London, 1938), p. 760. Subject to certain limitations, the right of the subject to petition the sovereign or the two Houses of Parliament was embodied in the Bill of Rights. See also Elie Halévy, *A History of the English People in the Nineteenth Century, Vol. 1, England in 1815* (London, 1960), pp. 153, 159.
[8] See Ieuan Gwynedd Jones, 'Wales and Parliamentary Reform' in A. J. Roderick (ed.), *Wales Through the Ages* (2 vols., Llandybïe, 1960), II, pp. 134–5.

most of the Welsh counties, but mainly from south Wales, and from all the denominations, with the important exception of the Calvinistic Methodists, who were increasingly reluctant to permit their churches to identify themselves with any political activity of a radical kind. Five of the leading members, including Hugh Hughes the artist, of Capel Jewin, the largest and most prosperous Welsh Calvinistic Methodist church in London, were excommunicated for petitioning in favour of Catholic Emancipation in 1829, an action which was later confirmed by the General Assembly of the denomination.[9]

The repeal of the Test and Corporation Acts in 1828 was regarded by Nonconformists generally in England and Wales as their first great triumph: other grievances remained, such as church rates, tithes, the exclusion of Nonconformists from the universities of Oxford and Cambridge, and the scandal of the refusal of parish incumbents to allow Nonconformists to be buried in parish churchyards according to their own rites. The success of their agitation against the penal legislation was evidence that the area of Nonconformist political activity was now widening, but the lack of any well-organized denominational structures, and the consequent isolation of the chapels, did not augur well for the future success of similar campaigns against the remaining grievances.

In fact, even in these limited fields, they were being too sanguine, for on secular issues, including the all-important one of parliamentary reform, Wales was very backward. There is some slight evidence that early reform societies, such as the London Corresponding Society, founded in 1792, were intermittently active in some parts of Wales, and that some of their literature was translated into Welsh.[10] Reform movements were more active in the post-Napoleonic War period, when political Nonconformity of a more radical kind came to prominence in Merthyr Tydfil and the iron towns of south Wales, and in the vale of Glamorgan. The radical Nonconformist congregations, which were mainly though not exclusively Unitarian, were led by immigrant Welshmen belonging to the emerging middle and lower middle classes, well educated in 'modern' subjects, passionately democratic and patriotic. They supported friendly societies, some of which, like the 'Ancient Britons', were probably Welsh, were sympathetic to the incipient trade unionism, and keen supporters of the eisteddfod.[11] They were familiar, as befitted Nonconformists, with the arts of petitioning, but far less reluctant than orthodox Nonconformists to apply the same methods of agitation to contemporary political issues. They attempted to petition for

[9] For the *cause célèbre*, see Gomer M. Roberts, *Y Ddinas Gadarn: Hanes Eglwys Jewin, Llundain* (Llundain, 1974), pp. 62–8, and Peter Lord, *Hugh Hughes: Arlunydd Gwlad 1790–1863* (Llandysul, 1995), pp. 159–67.
[10] David Wager, 'Welsh Politics and Parliamentary Reform, 1780–1832', *WHR*, 7, no. 4 (1975), 427–49.
[11] For this early radicalism, see Gwyn A. Williams, *The Merthyr Rising* (London, 1978), passim and Sian Rhiannon Williams, *Oes y Byd i'r Iaith Gymraeg: Y Gymraeg yn Ardal Ddiwydiannol Sir Fynwy yn y Bedwaredd Ganrif ar Bymtheg* (Caerdydd, 1992), esp. chapter 3.

parliamentary reform in 1815,[12] but were prevented from doing so by the ironmaster William Crawshay. As post-war distress deepened, however, they were in the van of those who attributed the depression to misgovernment, and who renewed the agitation for the reform of Parliament. Judging by the increasing amount of space devoted to politics and the state of the country in the periodicals and newspapers of the time, an important stage in the politicization of the people had been reached, and the Welsh language was being increasingly used for political purposes.[13]

People at that time, and for many years afterwards, complained of the political apathy of Welsh people, and there is evidence that they were not mistaken. Its root cause may very well have been the geographical isolation of Wales, and the profound social and cultural differences between the Welsh people and their English neighbours. Compared with the industrial towns and the wealthy agricultural counties of England, Wales was an undeveloped country, possessing only the most rudimentary means of educating the people politically. Newspapers and periodicals, English as well as Welsh, were few in number and, for the most part, they existed on the edge of bankruptcy. Periodicals were especially dependent on the religious denominations for their readership.[14] Despite the growth in their numbers in the middle decades of the century, this was a recurring complaint in Welsh radical circles well into the second half of the century.[15] An increasing number of English tracts and speeches were translated into Welsh, but what circulation they achieved is problematical. Welsh Nonconformist radicals, with few exceptions, tended to regard people who sought to change the structure of government as dangerous fanatics and disturbers of the peace. Of the four hundred or so petitions presented to Parliament in 1817 calling for reform, only one emanated from Wales.[16] There were frequent disturbances, but they were caused by recurrent economic depressions, agricultural as well as industrial, rather than by the force of ideologies and pressure for political change. During upturns in the economy the reform movements died away, political discussion ceased, or

---

[12] Williams, *Oes y Byd*, p. 73.

[13] On the growth of the political press, see Thomas Evans, *The Background of Modern Welsh Politics 1789–1846* (Cardiff, 1936), Jenkins, *Hanes Cymru*, and Aled Gruffydd Jones, *Press, Politics and Society: A History of Journalism in Wales* (Cardiff, 1993).

[14] For the periodicals, see Huw Walters, *Llyfryddiaeth Cylchgronau Cymreig 1735–1850 / A Bibliography of Welsh Periodicals 1735–1850* (Aberystwyth, 1993), pp. xxv–xlv, and for newspapers Beti Jones, *Newsplan: Report of the Newsplan project in Wales. Adroddiad ar gynllun Newsplan yng Nghymru* (London/Aberystwyth, 1994), pp. 35–42.

[15] For example, the literary historian Thomas Stephens of Merthyr Tydfil, though he was glad that 'Cambrian literature' was being divorced from the tavern and entering into alliance with the chapels, deplored the fact that the nation was 'unable or unwilling to maintain its publications unless they are associated with religious denominations, but such is the case'. See Walters, *Bibliography*, p. xxvii.

[16] Wager, 'Welsh Politics', 434.

was carried on undemonstratively and quietly in private homes or in the back rooms of pubs.

Such conditions determined the scope and scale of political activities, and could easily be mistaken for apathy. The Welsh language itself was a major barrier to communication, and was thought to inhibit the communication of ideas from one country to the other. Some religious leaders, including Bishop William van Mildert of Llandaff, regarded this as a positive advantage in that it 'inoculated' Welshmen against the infections of infidelity, religious ignorance and atheism which were believed to be rampant in England.[17] Also, most of the Welsh religious leaders were moderate and prudent men, who deplored excess and violence, and who preferred the solid benefits which their reliance on Whig leaders had brought them in 1828 to the dangerous rhetoric and wild schemes of the extreme radicals.

Hence it was that parliamentary reform became a live issue in Wales only at a very late stage in the history of the reform movement as a whole – in 1830 – when the long Tory rule was ending in political confusion and social unrest in town and country. Even then, judging by the majority of the petitions sent to Parliament, the call from Wales was for a moderate measure of reform rather than for thoroughgoing reforms, including manhood suffrage, the ballot, and annual, or triennial, parliaments, which were being demanded by the radicals. The Welsh agitation, which accompanied the progress of the three bills through Parliament, was middle class in character, and the pressure which came from the classes below them, from ironworkers and colliers, skilled and unskilled labour, merely provided the clamour, which they were very ready to exploit, but which also added an element of fear and panic, as in Merthyr Tydfil, where the rioting turned into a 'rising'.[18] All the periodicals, especially *Seren Gomer*, which was the most politically alert and well-informed of the few that then existed, reported the debates on the succession of Reform bills, and rejoiced at the eventual passing of the 'Great Reform Bill' in June 1832.[19]

In general, the changes introduced by the Reform Act in the Welsh electoral system were greatly to the benefit of Wales. The total number of seats increased from twenty-seven to thirty-two, the counties gaining three new seats and the boroughs two, including the key industrial constituencies of Merthyr Tydfil and

---

[17] 'Happy, indeed, is it for the lowly and sequestered, in such times as these, if he hears little of what is stirring in the busier world. Enviable is his lot, if, secluded in his native mountains, and unacquainted with any but his own aboriginal language, the wretched effusions of impiety and sedition issuing from the presses of the metropolis are to him almost, if not altogether, inaccessible. In this respect, many parts of the Principality may have reason to rejoice in retaining their vernacular tongue.' William van Mildert, *A Charge delivered to the Clergy of Llandaff in 1821* (London, 1821), p. 16. By the middle of the century this was thought no longer to be the case. See *Y Diwygiwr*, XVI, no. 189 (1851).

[18] On this episode, see Williams, *The Merthyr Rising*.

[19] On the passing of the Reform Bill, see Michael Brock, *The Great Reform Act* (London, 1973), and Charles Seymour, *Electoral Reform in England and Wales, 1832–85* (Newton Abbot, 1970).

Swansea, the two largest towns in the country. More important was the enfranchisement of eighteen new boroughs as contributory boroughs, a change of great importance, for it increased enormously the potential for active participation of their voters in British politics.

Crucial to any such developments were the changes in the franchise introduced by the Reform Act, for any extension of the franchise would inevitably increase the numbers of Welsh-speaking persons with a stake in politics. From the beginning the changes introduced were quickly recognized to be less radical than even the sedate editors of Welsh periodicals had hoped for. They made little numerical difference in the counties, where the freeholder vote continued as before, but now with the addition of copyholders and certain classes of tenant farmers. Potentially, the addition of tenants, especially of tenants-at-will or small farmers on annual leases, to the lists of registered voters was of profound importance, for it secured the domination of the traditional families. Nothing seemed to have changed. In the boroughs a new uniform £10 householder franchise was introduced, and this significantly increased the numbers of voters in the boroughs, including the newly enfranchised ones. However, as with the county constituencies, so with the boroughs, the Act ensured that the representation would, with the passage of time, become less representative. The old freeman franchise by which, in some boroughs, virtually all males over the age of twenty-one had possessed the vote, was to die out with their possessors. In newly enfranchised boroughs, such as Merthyr Tydfil, where there were no freemen, the Act restricted the right to vote to persons of property. All but the upper reaches of the working classes, such as skilled and highly paid ironworkers, were effectively excluded, and the bulk of the five hundred men enfranchised in 1832 were middle-class, or lower middle-class shopkeepers and small traders. Thus the new franchise ensured that the constituencies would remain narrow, and all, or most of them, liable to control by the gentry in the counties and small rural boroughs, and by the ironmasters and copper smelters and the other manufacturers in the industrial boroughs. Out of a total population of just over 900,000 there were 37,000 county voters and 11,000 borough voters, a total of 48,000, or just over 5 per cent of the population.[20] It was resentment at the numerical restrictions, the social exclusiveness, and the prohibitions in the new system which lay behind the Chartist Movement, and the six points of the Charter, adopted by the National Charter Association at its formation in the summer of 1840, were intended to make good the deficiencies of the Reform

---

[20] On the nature and extent of the franchise as it operated in different boroughs and in the county constituencies, see Ieuan Gwynedd Jones, 'Franchise Reform and Glamorgan Politics in the Mid-Nineteenth Century', *Morgannwg*, II (1958), 47–64 and idem, 'The Elections of 1865 and 1868 in Wales with Special Reference to Cardiganshire and Merthyr Tydfil', *THSC* (1964), 41–68. See also I. W. R. David, 'Political and Electioneering Activity in South-east Wales, 1820–52' (unpubl. University of Wales MA thesis, 1959).

Act.[21] The Welsh delegate to the Manchester conference was David John, jnr., of Merthyr Tydfil, who, on his return, published *Udgorn Cymru*, the first of the Welsh unstamped newspapers.

At the level of constituency politics, the political classes consisted of two essential parts. At the top in the counties were the great parliamentary families who, ever since Wales had been given representation in the early sixteenth century, had competed for the honour of being returned to Parliament, and for the power and prestige in county affairs which Members of Parliament enjoyed.[22] Attached to them by ties of family or obligation or deference were the lesser gentry whose electoral support was a necessary condition of success. Below them were the properly registered voters. It is difficult to know to what extent Welsh was used by the gentry in their communications among themselves: probably very little, as the surviving collections of correspondence would seem to indicate, though in the most Welsh-speaking counties the lesser gentry would certainly have used Welsh. On some occasions, as in hotly contested elections, pamphlets and other election material in the Welsh language were distributed, and this would be the function of agents, usually lawyers, who were invariably Welsh speaking, except in the most Anglicized constituencies.

As for the electorate, its composition varied greatly from constituency to constituency. Borough constituencies tended to be more socially diverse: properly enfranchised burgesses and ratepayers might come from all social classes. In some of the old borough constituencies, like Llantrisant or the 'scot and lot' boroughs of Flintshire, virtually all adult males were enfranchised. Others were closed, like Beaumaris, their burgesses few and their numbers limited. County constituencies were much larger, and the freehold franchise, which did not necessarily have to be in land, produced a less socially differentiated electorate than was the case in the boroughs.

In both kinds of constituencies the gentry families held sway and determined the nature of politics within their respective spheres of influence. Almost all the parliamentary families were thoroughly Anglicized, and there seemed to be no justification in the structure of constituency political arrangements why electoral affairs should be conducted through the medium of Welsh. Most borough constituencies were under the influence of one or more such gentry families, and

---

[21] For Chartism, see D. J. V. Jones, *Chartism and the Chartists* (London, 1975); idem, *The Last Rising: The Newport Insurrection of 1839* (Oxford, 1985). See also Angela V. John, 'The Chartists of Industrial South Wales 1840–1868' (unpubl. University of Wales MA thesis, 1971). For the Six Points, see Appendix II, Aims and Rules of the National Charter Association in Jones, *Chartism*, p. 195.

[22] See David W. Howell, *Land and People in Nineteenth-Century Wales* (London, 1978); idem, *Patriarchs and Parasites: The Gentry of South-West Wales in the Eighteenth Century* (Cardiff, 1986), and David J. V. Jones, *Rebecca's Children: A Study of Rural Society, Crime, and Protest* (Oxford, 1989), esp. chapter 2. See also R. J. Colyer, 'The Gentry and the County in Nineteenth-century Cardiganshire', *WHR*, 10, no. 4 (1981), 512–35.

in that respect they differed hardly at all from the counties. County freeholders tended to vote in accordance with the wishes of their patrons or, in the case of tenants, with their landlords. The same was true of the boroughs, except that the contributory system made it more difficult for the various gentry families involved to agree among themselves on the representation, and easier for carpet-baggers to intrude, so that contests tended to be more frequent. The expense involved in electioneering in both counties and boroughs provided a sufficient reason for contests to be avoided, but to the extent that contests were a factor in the political education of the people, it follows that their avoidance deprived the people of the exercise of their rights. In effect, therefore, the electoral system discouraged the development of the Welsh language in the domain of politics. Yet, paradoxically, it was the Welsh language itself which was ultimately instrumental in bringing about fundamental changes which would give it a central role. Only the coming of democracy would bring about change, and that change could only come about through the medium of Welsh.

This fundamental transformation of the political world of Wales began not with parliamentary politics directly, but with reforms in local government. The Poor Law Amendment Act (1834), the Municipal Corporations Act (1835), and the Public Health Act (1848) significantly widened the local government franchise.[23] All of these major pieces of legislation provided for the election of governing bodies by plural voting of ratepayers graded according to the value of the property rated. To be registered, claimants had to be able to show that they had paid their rates and had not received any relief in the course of the year. When one considers that sudden changes in the trade cycle of particular industrial localities, or inclement weather in rural places, could plunge people on the lower scale of the franchise into unemployment, it can be seen that this was a system which favoured the middle rather than the working classes. To what extent such property qualifications were a hindrance or a help to the development of the Welsh language in the new domain of local politics can only be surmised, but the fact that the franchise now reached into social strata lower than those of the parliamentary franchise, even though the control of all these bodies was firmly in the hands of the traditional governing classes, strongly suggests that the reformed system of local government worked to the advantage of the use of Welsh in politics. Also, local government elections were held at regular intervals, so that there was at least the possibility that local issues would be more frequently a matter for discussion than were national issues. As weekly newspapers multiplied, and the space they gave to local affairs expanded, so opportunities for the use of Welsh grew significantly. Finally, local authorities, especially Boards of Health

---

[23] On this legislation, see K. B. Smellie, *A Hundred Years of English Government* (2nd edn., London, 1950), and esp. Bryan Keith-Lucas, *The English Local Government Franchise: A Short History* (London, 1952).

and of Guardians, found it increasingly necessary to publish information for the instruction or guidance of the communities for whom they were responsible to the central government, and central authorities themselves found it expedient from time to time to publish in Welsh changes in the law that they were required to administer. In all these ways, new avenues were opening in which the use of the Welsh language was essential.

Such gradual and slow changes, however, were incidental and structural rather than fundamental in the growth of democracy. They opened up possibilities for the growth of opinion, the conflict of ideologies, the participation of individuals in the affairs of government, the formation of pressure groups, and the regularities and formalities associated with them accustomed the people to the functions of representative bodies. Democracy could only develop in societies where there existed politically well-informed and mature social groups, of unenfranchised as well as enfranchised, people. Such conditions were slow to develop and could hardly be said to have existed anywhere in Wales until well into the second half of the century. In the 1860s it was still a common complaint in some of the leading Welsh periodicals and newspapers that ignorance was widespread and that apathy prevailed, especially in the rural parts of the country. Some commentators ascribed it to an excess of emphasis and concentration on religion and religious culture.[24] Such criticisms were typically made by supporters of the emerging political Nonconformity of the time, and may have reflected not the reality of the political configurations of the countryside but rather the frustrations of activists who were unable to accept the fact that Welshmen could not possibly be other than Liberals.[25]

The turning point came as a result of the activities of three political movements, namely the National Charter Association, the Anti-Corn Law League, and the Liberation Society.[26] These three movements had much in common. All originated in the years between 1839 and 1844, that is to say, in the aftermath of the Reform Act and the first legislative measures and economic policies of the reformed Parliament, especially the new Poor Law and the changes in local government. These were also the years of an ever deepening conviction that the agitation for reform of Parliament had been in vain. They had in common, too, the grand design of politicizing the working classes, with the objective of mobilizing them behind the particular programmes of radical reform which they

---

[24] For example, *BAC*, 1 January 1868, and 2 September 1868.

[25] Muriel Bowen Evans notes the survival of Toryism in some agricultural districts in Carmarthenshire, and stresses that Liberalism was a slow growth. Muriel Bowen Evans, 'The Community and Social Change in the Parish of Tre-lech a'r Betws during the Nineteenth Century' (unpubl. University of Wales MA thesis, 1980).

[26] For all three of these, see Ryland Wallace, *'Organise! Organise! Organise!' A Study of Reform Agitations in Wales, 1840–1886* (Cardiff, 1991). Also, Patricia Hollis, 'Pressure from without: an introduction' in eadem (ed.), *Pressure From Without in Early Victorian England* (London, 1974), pp. 1–26.

existed to bring about. In the case of the Anti-Corn Law League, this was 'the total and immediate repeal' of the corn duties, and of the Liberation Society, or the British Anti-State-Church Association as it was known when it was founded in 1844, the 'liberation of religion from all governmental or legislative interference', or the separation of Church and State. The aims of the Chartists, to democratize the electoral system especially by means of manhood suffrage, were therefore fundamental in the strategies developed by all three movements.

Chartism, the Anti-Corn Law League, and the Liberation Society were not all equally successful in Wales, but they contributed profoundly to the politicization of the nation and, therefore, to the extended use of the Welsh language in politics. To a large extent, they shared a common methodology regarding how to proceed in this enormous task. Early in their separate histories they all realized the importance of the Welsh language: without it, the people could not be reached. Press, platform and pulpit all required the Welsh language. The Chartists understood this even before the National Association as such had been formed, for they operated within a tradition and style of political action in which Welsh was a prerequisite. In Merthyr they had established two newspapers, the *Advocate and Merthyr Free Press* and *Udgorn Cymru* (March 1840 to October 1842). The combined circulation of the two sister-papers was reported to have reached 1,500, and it is not implausible that the Welsh readership may have been higher than the English. There was a distinct disadvantage in publishing in Welsh because, in the eyes of the authorities, sedition could lie concealed in the Welsh language. *Udgorn Cymru* lasted for only forty issues before it was hounded out of existence by the authorities.[27] What the actual readership of this first Welsh political newspaper for the working classes of Merthyr and district was cannot be known. Certainly, the actual readership would have been far higher than the circulation figures, for it was hawked around clubs and pubs and read out to the illiterate and, no doubt, translated for the benefit of English hearers. The same was true of the Chartist newspapers, tracts and pamphlets which circulated in the industrial districts. The *Northern Star*, which was the major organ of the Chartist movement, in addition to reports of speeches, conferences and such like, often carried news from the Welsh branches, and it was vital for their morale that they should be translated and disseminated among the membership.

The same was true with regard to the work of missionaries and lecturers sent from over the border to Wales. It was during these years that Welshmen began to develop that insatiable taste for lectures, for which they later became notorious, and the task of translating from the one language to the other must have been an enormous challenge for the leaders. In the 1850s, when 'moral force' Chartism was the norm, sympathetic ministers of religion would be expected to fulfil this

---

[27] On this, see Gwyn A. Williams, *When was Wales? A History of the Welsh* (London, 1985), pp. 189ff., Jones, *Chartism*, p. 99, and idem, *The Last Rising*, esp. chapters 1 and 2.

onerous duty, but in its earlier manifestations, especially of its 'physical force' side, only the Unitarians seem to have co-operated. *Udgorn Cymru* was established and edited by Morgan Williams and David John, jnr., both Unitarians, and it is certain that both were acutely aware of the crucial role of the Welsh language in industrial Wales, and the movement must have depended hugely upon their readiness to present the message in whatever language was appropriate. It was said of Dr William Price, Llantrisant, an early Chartist who was deeply involved in the planning of the Newport insurrection, that he had organized a group, known as 'Price's scholars', to study Welsh, but probably they concentrated on politics. No doubt, Price would not have differentiated between the two studies: in Chartist circles, to study Welsh was the same as to study history, and politics was contemporary history. This accords well with the importance of education in the Chartists' programme, and in their local round of activities in their branches. Literacy was supremely important to them, and it is possible that Price was teaching people who were not attached to the chapels.[28]

The attitude of organized religion was critical to the success of these reform movements, if only because of the practical dependence of their leaders on the co-operation of the chapels. We have already noted that 'physical force' Chartism was supported wholeheartedly only by some of the Unitarians in the Merthyr district. The other denominations admonished their members to avoid contact with them. How effective such admonitions were is not clear, and much would probably have depended to a large extent on the denominations of the particular chapels concerned. The South Wales Association of the Calvinistic Methodists agreed to excommunicate all known Chartists among its members.[29] But Ebenezer Congregational chapel, Sirhywi, was also reported to have excommunicated its Chartist members,[30] and *Seren Gomer* had not changed its old opinion that the Chartists were madmen, political antinomians to be avoided at all costs. It was because of this bitter hostility that some of the Chartists set about establishing their own churches. On the other hand, Aberdare Chartists attended a religious service on the eve of the march on Newport to hear a sermon by the Revd John Davies, which, while applauding the movement's struggle for constitutional rights, pleaded with his hearers to abandon physical force and to rely on the moral force of their opinions and their behaviour.[31] This long-sustained hostility on the part of the religious denominations, combined with the

---

[28] See Jones, *Last Rising*, and Ivor Wilks, *South Wales and the Rising of 1839* (London, 1984). For Price, see Brian Davies, 'Empire and Identity: The "Case" of Dr William Price' in David Smith (ed.), *A People and a Proletariat: Essays in the History of Wales 1780–1980* (London, 1980), p. 76. See also Angela John, 'The Chartist Endurance: Industrial South Wales 1840–68', *Morgannwg*, XV (1971), 23–49.
[29] See the report in *Y Gwladgarwr*, VII (1839), 253.
[30] *Llythyr yn rhoddi hanes yr ymraniad a gymerodd le yn ddiweddar yn eglwys yr Anymddibynwyr a arferai ymgynull yn Ebenezer, Sirhowy, o dan ofal y Parch. R. Jones* (Crickhowell, 1841).
[31] John Davies, *Y Ffordd Dda* (Aberdâr, 1840). See Jenkins, *Hanes Cymru*, pp. 161–2.

opposition of the press, both Welsh and English, were important factors in the decline of Chartism in Wales, but there can be no doubting the importance of its contribution to the growth of political opinion and of the political education of the common people. It had been a movement which had developed in the bilingual parts of the country: contemporaries noted that it had not succeeded to anything like the same degree in the overwhelmingly Welsh-speaking counties of west Wales,[32] but it was likewise observed that Welsh was the majority language in the mining and manufacturing districts most affected.[33]

Of the other societies agitating for the reform of Parliament, the extension of the franchise and the ballot, the Anti-Corn Law League and the Liberation Society had much in common. Both accepted the need to operate through the Welsh language, and both realized the necessity of gaining the support of the chapels. The Anti-Corn Law League was established in Manchester in September 1839 with the objective of 'total and immediate repeal' of the corn duties; Wales was brought within its organization in April 1840 when Walter Griffith was appointed lecturer.[34] Griffith soon came to understand two closely related facts about the people among whom he was working. First was their ignorance not only about the work of the League but also about politics in general, and second was the absolute need to publish tracts, flysheets and other material in the Welsh language. Above all, it was necessary to publish their own newspaper in order to counter the attacks, as he put it, of the Tories:

> The Tories have their 'Haul', 'Brytwn', and 'Protestant' etc, and every church clergyman takes a copy and sends it to their neighbours; but we have no publication, except what belongs to religious denominations, therefore they are not widely circulated . . . Therefore I think it would be very well to the League to assist the Welsh repealers to establish a publication, in order that they may gain the country before the Tories comes. It is the opinion of great many, that Lectures will do good, but they would be more if there was a publication published monthly to work with the lectures.[35]

This led to the founding of *Cylchgrawn Rhyddid* in the autumn of 1840, with Griffith as editor, succeeded in 1841 by the Revd William Williams (Caledfryn), Congregational minister at Caernarfon. The cost was borne entirely by the League, and it is probable that more copies were circulated gratis than there were of subscribers. But this was an expense that the League's leaders could accept as an effective means of spreading the message. *Cychgrawn Rhyddid* was arguably the first

---

[32] *Northern Star*, 6 July 1839.
[33] *Y Gwladgarwr*, VII (1839), 373–4.
[34] Wallace, *Organise*, pp. 12–34.
[35] Ieuan Gwynedd Jones, 'The Anti-Corn Law Letters of Walter Griffith', *BBCS*, XXVIII, pt. 1 (1978), 115.

modern political periodical in the Welsh language. It ceased publication in the spring of 1842, by which time the League's strategy had shifted from opinion-forming activities to political activities, such as organizing pressure groups in key localities, creating reliable and systematic statistical knowledge about the electorates in key constituencies, their political complexion and the nature of political control in each, who the political families were, the voting behaviour of their MPs in Parliament, the state of the electoral registers, and all other necessary preliminaries to successful electioneering. This information was made available to the League's supporters and published in the weekly and monthly press, so that, for the first time, a body of information, more or less reliable, regarding the political character of Wales existed and was widely disseminated throughout the country. In this way, Wales began to be educated politically in a more mature and sophisticated manner than had previously been the case, and although the practical results seemed negligible at the time, in perspective one can understand that this was a highly significant development.[36]

It was an education in Welsh because of the nature of the support which the League received in Wales. Nonconformist ministers were prominent from the beginning of the agitation until its termination in 1846 following the success of the parliamentary campaign. This support was of crucial importance because of the influence ministers could exert on their congregations, and because of their control of virtually the whole of the Welsh periodical press. As we have seen, the League established its own Welsh monthly, but its support for the existing Welsh periodicals grew over time. Its agents contributed articles and reviews, and ensured that news of current activities reached the editors. This by no means politicized the press: the column space given to political affairs, including reports of debates in Parliament, was still small in comparison with that given to religious affairs, but the League's religious rhetoric and its ever closer connection with the denominations ensured that its contribution to the growing discussion of politics was significant. In particular, it served to highlight the importance of themes other than religious ones, to take cognizance of secular forces in the shaping of events, and to encourage readers to widen their intellectual horizons. A systematic reading of these periodicals through to the 1880s shows to what extent their readers had become more sophisticated in their understanding of the political life of the country, both at the levels of central and local government, and of political thought and ideology. This development was hastened and strengthened by the founding of new periodicals, such as *Y Dysgedydd* (1840, previously *Y Dysgedydd Crefyddol* 1821), and especially *Y Traethodydd* (1845), which was a non-denominational literary and critical quarterly, and *Yr Adolygydd* (1850) which, though founded by Congregational ministers, was likewise designed to be a

---

[36] On this theme, see Wallace, *Organise*, pp. 22–5.

literary and critical quarterly, rather than a denominational magazine.[37] There is no doubt that it was the Anti-Corn Law League which, almost certainly unwittingly, laid the foundations for this great transformation.

Although the Anti-Corn Law League and the Liberation Society had much in common, including a realistic acceptance that propaganda needed to be through the medium of the Welsh language, and that the co-operation of religious leaders was vital to the realization of their aims, there were fundamental differences of emphasis and of understanding between the two. Religion became important in the propaganda of the League only after its leaders decided that repeal of the corn laws was best presented as a moral question rather than, or as well as, an economic question. But religion was of the very essence of the philosophy underlying the Liberationist argument. It was possible to argue convincingly that the separation of religion from the state was a necessary condition for the healthy development of all religious organizations, and that the religious establishment, as embodied in the established Church, was a positive hindrance to true religion. One needed to have a very sceptical turn of mind not to be influenced by such arguments, and the work of the Society came to be presented as a moral crusade rather than a political campaign. In fact, modelling itself on the Anti-Corn Law League, it became the most powerful political force, and the most successful pressure society ever to function in Victorian Wales.

This was not immediately apparent. Twenty years were to pass before the Society made much of an impact on Wales, despite the fact that Welshmen were prominent in its Council and some of its committees; the historian, Dr Thomas Rees, editor of *The Eclectic Review*, for example, was one of its first honorary secretaries, as was its long-serving secretary, John Carvell Williams.[38] In fact, the Welsh connection was a powerful one from the beginning; the Revd J. R. Kilsby Jones, a sparkling writer on political affairs, had been present at the Leicester conference at which the decision to establish the Anti-State-Church Association (as the society was originally called) had been taken, and the Council of 200 included thirty-eight Welsh representatives (excluding pastors of Welsh churches in London). Nor was this surprising. There already existed a strong tradition of radical Nonconformity in which disestablishment was a key objective, and a number of very gifted Welsh-speaking ministers, including the Congregationalists Samuel Roberts of Llanbryn-mair, William Rees (Gwilym Hiraethog), Caledfryn and David Rees of Llanelli, all of whom had been active in that older tradition, now engaged themselves fully in the work of the new society. All four were powerful advocates of disestablishment in the press, platform and the pulpit; indeed, they were among the most powerful, able and influential men of their time. All four were founder-editors of periodicals, David Rees of *Y Diwygiwr* in

---

[37] On *Yr Adolygydd*, see Huw Walters, *Yr Adolygydd a'r Beirniad: Eu Cynnwys a'u Cyfranwyr* (Aberystwyth, 1996).
[38] For Williams, see *DNB*.

1835, Samuel Roberts of *Y Cronicl* in 1843, and William Rees of *Yr Amserau*, also in 1843, published in Liverpool, where he had recently settled as a Congregational minister. *Yr Amserau* was the first Welsh newspaper, and William Rees remained its editor until it was taken over by Thomas Gee, the Denbigh publisher, and amalgamated with *Y Faner* in 1859. The influence of these two Welsh-language newspapers (as distinct from the periodicals) on Welsh political developments, both ideological and electoral, can hardly be exaggerated, and there is no doubt that the support of *Yr Amserau* and later of *Baner ac Amserau Cymru*, as it became in 1859, was crucial to the eventual success of the Liberation Society.[39]

The major difference between the Liberation Society, as it was renamed in 1853, and its predecessors was its realization from the beginning that electoral activity was the essence of its mission. This did not mean that its propaganda on the over-arching theme of the inherent evil nature of religious establishments was neglected. On the contrary, the publication policies of the Society dwarfed even those of the Anti-Corn Law League, on which it modelled itself. Tracts and pamphlets aimed at the public at large, or intended for chapel-goers, or for working-class supporters, were published by the hundreds of thousands, and distributed by agents, paid and unpaid, and its weekly newspaper, *The Liberator*, was sent gratis to every minister of religion. But it also published, under its own imprimatur, heavy works of history and politics, on the constitution and on political thought.[40] The intention was to create a well-informed and active public.

By the middle decades of the century the emphasis, especially by the late 1850s and early 1860s, was on the politics of electoral influence, the overriding necessity to persuade Parliament to abrogate all legislation antipathetic to the perceived needs of Nonconformists, and, finally, to bring about the separation of the church from the state. The establishment was, they believed, the *fons et origo* of the injustices from which Nonconformists suffered, and breaking it would be not only an act of justice but would also free the Anglican Church from the encumbrances of the state and its interference in its affairs. The only way this could be done was to bring pressure to bear directly on Parliament, not merely through petitioning but also by influencing elections in individual constituencies where there was sufficient support to be effective. Thus, when issues of importance to Nonconformists were being debated in the Commons, for example, the regular attempts to repeal the burial laws, to abolish church rates, or to allow Nonconformists to graduate in the universities of Oxford and Cambridge,

---

[39] For these and other periodicals of the time, see T. M. Jones (Gwenallt), *Llenyddiaeth fy Ngwlad: sef hanes y newyddiadur a'r cylchgrawn Cymreig yng Nghymru yn nghyd a'u dylanwad ar fywyd 'Cenedl y Cymry'* (Treffynnon, 1893), and Walters, *Bibliography*.

[40] The Society was instrumental in publishing works by Dr Robert Vaughan, Congregational minister and Professor of History at University College London on the Stuart and Commonwealth period.

nationwide campaigns would be organized with the aim of sending petitions of support to the legislature. Basically, this activity was no different from the age-old agitations of the eighteenth- and early nineteenth-century Nonconformists; only the scale and the efficiency of the way it was done were different. What was novel in the new policy was direct interference in constituency elections. In effect, the Society took over from where the Anti-Corn Law League had left off. Like the League, it initiated detailed profiles of every constituency, their economies, the size and character of their electorates, their electoral histories, the religious or denominational mix in their populations, the identification of political leaders in local affairs, the existence, or lack of, registration societies, the state of the electoral register, and so on. If necessary, it could send its agents to do this work, or encourage local sympathizers to do so. Ideally, it would put up its own candidates, and often threatened to do so if Liberal candidates refused to support measures advocated by the Society. The ideal state of preparation it aimed for was to be ready for contests wherever and whenever they might occur.

The greatest hindrance to the success of such policies was the restricted nature of the electorate. The numbers of registered voters had been growing slowly since 1832, in the Welsh boroughs by 50 per cent, but by only 15 per cent in the counties, the most substantial growth being in the industrializing counties – Monmouth, Glamorgan, Denbigh, Flint and Caernarfon – but the total electorate remained only marginally above that of 1832, being 4.9 per cent of the population in the counties, and 17.5 per cent in the boroughs. Unfortunately, from the point of view of the Society, concurrent changes in the nature and structure of the electorate were not everywhere to its advantage. To achieve its aims it was an absolute necessity that the electorate should expand substantially, and in particular that more of the respectable working class in the boroughs should be enfranchised. By 'working class' was meant not only men who worked for a wage, but also craftsmen who might employ others but who were dependent upon their work for their livelihood; in other words, the upper strata of the working class and the lower middle class. The proportions of the electorates which came under this definition varied greatly from borough to borough; it was above 25 per cent in only seven of the fifteen constituencies.[41] The Society's problems were different in the county constituencies. In these, it was the nature of the qualification which was crucial to success, in particular the balance between freehold voters and tenant voters, especially the numbers of tenants-at-will, who were the class most liable to be pressurized by their landlords. This latter category as a whole constituted just over a quarter of the total county electorates, though it was over a third in Merioneth and Montgomeryshire.[42] Equally important to the

---

[41] This is based on an analysis of 'Numbers of Working Class Voters; showing the percentage of such voters to all others; in each Borough or district' (PP 1866 (296) LVII).
[42] This is based on 'Return of Numbers of Electors in each County for 1864–65' (PP 1866 (418) L).

Society, therefore, was the imperative need to eliminate corrupt practices in elections.[43] Bribery and treating, undue influence and intimidation were rife in constituencies where contests were the norm. The Society, therefore, joined powerfully in the growing agitation for the ballot in the conviction that only secret voting could free voters from the influence of powerful and arrogant landed proprietors and ruthless industrial masters. To succeed, the Liberation Society had to reinvent itself as a reform society.

One of the insuperable difficulties faced by the Liberation Society in Wales, and by all other reform societies, was that elections were relatively rare events, with the result that opportunities for electioneering were infrequent. In the ten general elections between 1832 and 1865 there were consistently more uncontested than contested elections in both county and borough constituencies, rather more so in the counties than in the boroughs.[44] Of the 404 elections in Wales between 1832 and 1880, only 139 were contested. In this way, it was thought, voters were being deprived of an education in politics which contested elections were thought to provide. Some argued that this was no bad thing, given the disorderly behaviour, rioting and drunkenness endemic in elections in many places. But in Wales the almost unique way in which religion and politics had developed together, and the religious and moral rhetoric of Liberal and Liberationist candidates and their supporters, were thought to discourage such behaviour. The Merioneth election of 1859, the Cardiganshire elections of 1865 and 1868, and the Merthyr Tydfil election of 1868 were evidence that this might indeed be the case.[45] That is why, in the 1860s, the Society sought to strengthen its links with the chapels, with the dual purpose of encouraging their members to register their votes, to build up pressure locally for parliamentary reform, and to take advantage of the ability of the denominations to provide large captive audiences of people who could be expected to be sympathetically inclined to the aims of the Society. The bicentenary celebrations of the Puritan ejections of 1662, for example, which were held in Swansea and Neath and Denbigh in September 1862, were exploited so as to publicize its fundamentally religious and moral attitude to parliamentary reform.[46] These were followed by a series of lesser conferences in various centres which were extensively reported in the press.[47]

Throughout the 1860s the Society carried out an enormous amount of research into the electoral histories of the Welsh constituencies. It could produce

---

[43] See Cornelius O'Leary, *The Elimination of Corrupt Practices in British Elections 1868–1911* (Oxford, 1962), chapter 1.

[44] Cf. Neal Blewett, 'The Franchise in the United Kingdom, 1885–1918', *P&P*, 32 (1965), 27–56.

[45] For these elections, see Ieuan Gwynedd Jones, *Explorations and Explanations: Essays in the Social History of Victorian Wales* (Llandysul, 1981), chapters 3, 4 and 5, and idem, *Communities: Essays in the Social History of Victorian Wales* (Llandysul, 1987), chapter 12.

[46] For the speeches and resolutions, see *Coffadwriaeth Ddau Can Mlwyddol 1662–1862: Adroddiadau Cynhadleddau Castellnedd a Dinbych* (Llanelly, 1862).

[47] As, for example, in *BAC* in September, October and November 1866.

impressive profiles of constituencies whenever and wherever necessary. These could be published in pamphlet form, both in Welsh and English, presented as copy for newspapers and periodicals, and distributed by agents, sympathetic ministers and others. Its lecturers were thus armed to the teeth with hard facts regarding the composition of the Commons and the voting behaviour of Welsh members. These publications were invariably bilingual. John Jones's *Llyfr Etholiadaeth Cymru* (Caernarfon, 1867) was the first Welsh guide to electoral behaviour, and its publication marks an important point of transition in the development of Welsh politics in the modern period. Jones, a Baptist minister at Brymbo, was a vice-president of the Reform League and an ardent Liberationist who had served as an agent of the Society in north Wales. No doubt both societies provided him with the statistics and voting records which his book contained.[48]

It is impossible to tell what proportion of electioneering was in Welsh: newspapers, which are one of the main sources for the study of elections, rarely disclose such detail, and clearly much would depend on the linguistic mix of particular communities and the language of the newspapers reporting news of current affairs. But the reliance of the Society on the chapels and the press for the educational or ideological side of electioneering, especially the moral and religious tone of the rhetoric employed, inevitably increased the amount of Welsh used in elections. The general election of 1859 in Merioneth is an example of an election in which Welsh was virtually the exclusive language. The two candidates spoke Welsh, the local landowners were mainly Welsh speaking, and they communicated with their tenants in Welsh. In Bala, where the contest took place, all the political leaders were Welsh speakers: it would appear that only activists from among the gentry in the south of the county were English. Of the influential leaders in Bala, two stood out. Dr Lewis Edwards, principal of the Calvinistic Methodist College in Bala, was one of the country's leading theologians, and no one was better equipped than he to put the philosophical, moral and religious case in favour of voting for the Liberal candidate and for refusing to vote for the Tory.[49] When he wrote to the election committee, which included English landowners, it was in English, but his letter was immediately translated and published in the Welsh newspapers. The other outstanding leader was the Revd Michael D. Jones, Congregational minister and principal of the Congregational academy at Llanuwchllyn. He was a greater orator than Lewis Edwards, capable of the most biting sarcasm and invective, a passionate patriot and politically one of

---

[48] On the NRU and its Welsh connections, see Wallace, *Organise*, pp. 105–6.
[49] For Lewis Edwards, see Thomas Charles Edwards, *Bywyd a Llythyrau y Diweddar Barch. Lewis Edwards* (Liverpool, 1901) and Trebor Lloyd Evans, *Lewis Edwards: Ei Fywyd a'i Waith* (Abertawe, 1967). See Jones, *Explorations*, pp. 102–3 for quotations from his speech 25 March 1858, pp. 129–30 for quotations from one of his letters, and pp. 141–2 for a précis of a speech on 19 August after the ejection of certain tenants on the Rhiwlas estate.

the most radical and far-seeing men of his generation. Michael D. Jones was a fervent supporter of the Liberation Society, and no one could better expound the political aims of the Society within the moral context of the Welsh experience of social inferiority than he; indeed, few Victorian polemicists did more to define its nature and its causes or to resist the constant denigration of the value of the Welsh language which was becoming ever more fashionable; and there is no doubt that it was in Merioneth during these middle decades of the century that his ideal of a Welsh homeland overseas took shape.[50]

The extraordinary importance of this election in Welsh politics is precisely that the concerns raised and the issues treated were Welsh issues, and that, although the Tory candidate had been returned, it had been shown that where Welsh communities were led by their own élites rather than by local aristocrats, and were sufficiently convinced of the rightness of their principles, they could make a deep impression on the political character of their counties. The county's Welsh Nonconformist Liberals failed again in 1865, but it was their victory in 1868 which taught the nation that it was possible for ordinary people to resist the enormous powers of entrenched privilege, and even to overcome them. The election of 1859 in Merioneth thus marked the most significant turning point in the development of Welsh politics in the age of Victoria.

It was all the more remarkable because it had been fought under the old electoral system and in one of the least advanced counties in Wales. The 1868 general election in Merthyr Tydfil, however, differed in fundamental ways from the Merioneth example.[51] Firstly, it was sociologically at the opposite pole to rural Merioneth, the largest constituency in Wales as against the smallest. Secondly, the election was fought under the new electoral system introduced by the 1867 Reform Act. Under the Act, the right to vote in the boroughs was now to be given, with certain reservations, to all adult male householders qualified by two years' residence and personal payment of the rates. At a stroke, the number of electors grew from about 1,300 to over 14,000, all of whom, with the exception of about 1,500 who, for whatever reason, preferred to qualify under the old householder franchise, were working-class people. In other words, the new electorate was overwhelmingly working class. Thirdly, Merthyr was not homogeneous linguistically, nor had it ever been, and the proportion of English and Irish in the population was probably growing at an increasing pace. But though it

---

[50] For Michael D. Jones, see R. Tudur Jones, *Ffydd ac Argyfwng Cenedl: Cristnogaeth a Diwylliant yng Nghymru 1890–1940. Cyfrol 2, Dryswch a Diwygiad* (Abertawe, 1982), pp. 245–6; Evan Pan Jones, *Oes a Gwaith y prif athraw y Parch. Michael Daniel Jones* (Bala, 1903) and Glyn Williams, *The Desert and the Dream: A Study of Welsh Colonization in Chubut, 1865–1915* (Cardiff, 1994). See Jones, *Explorations*, pp. 151–3 for examples of his arguments, and for extracts from his speech at a Liberation Society conference in Bala, September 1866, see *Welsh Nonconformity and the Welsh Representation: Papers and speeches delivered at the Conferences held September and October 1866* (London, n.d.).

[51] For this election, see Jones, *Explorations*, pp. 193–214.

was culturally pluristic, it was overwhelmingly a Welsh town. The manufacturing periphery was dominated by Welsh people, and the cultural and linguistic mix was most pronounced in the core of the town ('the village'), which was the trading centre of the place. But here also the Welsh were still in a majority.[52] Finally, its religious structures closely resembled those of Merioneth. Nonconformity was its most prominent characteristic, with the main denominations between them making provision for over 70 per cent of the total population.[53] Thus, even though the two places were divided economically and sociologically, they were united by language and religion.

These latter points of similarity were crucial in bringing about the greatest Liberal victory of any constituency in Wales, and Henry Richard, the Welsh Nonconformist Liberal candidate, understood precisely how to exploit them to his advantage. It was not simply that he was a Welshman by birth and as fluent in Welsh as in English, though that was an important factor in a constituency still overwhelmingly Welsh in its popular structure and in which no alternative cultural identities had emerged to challenge the hegemony of the majority culture. More important was the fact that he was able to articulate a set of political ideas, and to put forward a political programme in a language, which could be either Welsh or English, or both, and which, because it appealed to ideals and experiences which they all had in common, was therefore immediately intelligible to the vast majority of the voters. They understood and responded positively to his rhetoric. His reliance on, and use of, the Welsh language in this wider, cultural sense of providing the vital unifying factor in a culture which was experiencing rapid and violent change, was crucial in his appeal to the electorate as a whole. Such solidarity as they now felt was at the very opposite pole to that which they had experienced in the 1830s. Then there had been violence, a calf ceremoniously killed and its blood used to dye a flag red, and armed men defying the power of the state, destroying some of its institutions and even driving its armed forces into retreat.[54] Now the cry was for peace and constitutional action, for achieving their social demands by means of political action, and for arbitration in disputes between men rather than confrontation.

So sure was Henry Richard of his audience and his message that he issued an Address to the Nonconformist electors of Wales generally (*At Etholwyr Anghydffurfiol Cymru*),[55] as if he were a party leader issuing a manifesto, enumerating the

---

[52] Harold Carter and Sandra Wheatley, *Merthyr Tydfil in 1851: A Study of the Spatial Structure of a Welsh Industrial Town* (Cardiff, 1982), esp. pp. 114–15. See also *Slater's Directory* for 1858–9.

[53] Jones, *Explorations*, p. 197.

[54] For all these exciting events, see Williams, *Merthyr Rising*, and Glanmor Williams (ed.), *Merthyr Politics: The Making of a Working Class Tradition* (Cardiff, 1966) for the essay by Gwyn A. Williams, 'The Merthyr of Dic Penderyn', pp. 9–27, and by Ieuan Gwynedd Jones, 'The Merthyr of Henry Richard', pp. 28–57.

[55] Printed as a pamphlet and as an election address in most of the Welsh newspapers, such as *BAC*, 28 Hydref 1868, and in English, or bilingually in some, such as *The Cardiff and Merthyr Guardian* and *The Merthyr Express*, where it appears in the columns of election addresses.

planks in the party programme, articulating the party cry, and calling for a disciplined, non-violent turnout at the elections. In a uniquely original and novel way Henry Richard was indeed a party leader, even though that party had yet to be brought into being. He could call into action a 'party' machine which was universally present throughout the country, a force in every constituency, and better integrated, potentially more disciplined, more informed with passion and drive than the ad hoc committees of the rival political parties. Nor was it impossible that the rival denominations could be brought to believe the same political things and be mobilized to achieve by constitutional means their common objectives. Pride in their language and nationality, love of country, belief in religious equality, constitutional and human rights, and the force of moral obligation between men and nations – these were the fundamentals in his understanding of the current aspirations of the Welsh people. He was able to present himself as the 'candidate for Wales' ('Yr Aelod Dros Gymru') because he believed that the Welsh people already believed, or could be persuaded to believe, the same political things. They already possessed a profound understanding of themselves in the context of their history, especially of their ancient and still vigorous literary tradition: and they believed that they had created the most wonderful religious organization that any country had ever known. They had done this in the face of aristocratic resistance and of a priestly caste which despised them, and they had learnt the values of democracy through their active participation in the life of the churches, and had suffered on its behalf.

Thus, the key to the new political life which Henry Richard and his fellow Nonconformists thought they were inaugurating was the Welsh language. For a short time, a generation in some rural constituencies, only a few years at best in the new industrial places, it would remain the key. The determining factors would be demographic – the ebb and flow of people and the moving frontier of language use – but everywhere, even in those places where English would become so dominant as to almost totally obliterate the Welsh, this legacy would remain.

More problematic was the extent to which political identity could or should be based upon language. Language on its own did not provide a secure or permanent foundation for political identity, since conflicting ideologies and class or group solidarities might prove more powerful than the tolerance upon which linguistically mixed communities depended. This was particularly the case in industrial and manufacturing places, where working-class interests were being channelled into trade unions which, by definition, existed to protect particular and sectional interests rather than the more nebulous and seemingly less relevant cultural aspects of political identity. Considerations such as these emerged in the course of the great colliers' strike in the Aberdare and Rhondda region in 1873–4, which coincided with the general election of that year, when Thomas Halliday, the leader of the Lancashire-based Amalgamated Association of Miners, stood as a

Liberal with the backing of his union and the Labour Representation League. In many ways Halliday was an ideal candidate in this Welsh working-class constituency. He was a collier, the son of a collier and of a Welsh mother, a Nonconformist (Wesleyan), and well-known in the colliery valleys of south Wales where he had been active on behalf of his union since 1867. In his policies he differed hardly at all from Henry Richard, whom he greatly admired, and he was in favour of conciliation and arbitration in industrial relations.[56] He lacked only one thing: the Welsh language, and that may have been his undoing. That his speeches were translated by a sympathetic Baptist minister, the minutes of his union's lodges kept in Welsh, and that he himself recognized and apologized for his deficiency would appear not to have been sufficient. But most of the newspapers, English as well as Welsh, were against him, and without the support of these 'shapers of opinion' his cause seemed hopeless.[57] Even so, Halliday polled nearly 5,000 votes[58] (25.2 per cent),[59] which would seem to suggest that language and nationality were not prime considerations for a large section of the workforce in that particular election. Moreover, his union was regarded as an unwelcome importation from England, and the majority of miners appear to have put their confidence in a union of their own making which was held to be more sensitive to their feelings and aspirations than the English one.[60]

Six years later, at the election of 1880,[61] the Welsh language was certainly not a contributory issue. All three candidates were fluent Welsh speakers.[62] Henry Richard gained 40.2 per cent of the votes, the lawyer, Charles Herbert James,[63] a native of Merthyr, polled 37.6 per cent, and W. T. Lewis, a native of Aberdare and one of the most powerful industrialists in south Wales, soon to be knighted

---

[56] See E. W. Evans, *The Miners of South Wales* (Cardiff, 1961); 'William Abraham' by John Saville in Joyce M. Bellamy and John Saville, *Dictionary of Labour Biography*, Vol. III (London, 1976), pp. 91–4.

[57] For accounts of this election, see Kenneth O. Morgan, 'The Merthyr of Keir Hardie' in Williams, *Merthyr Politics*, pp. 59–60, Wallace, *Organise*, pp. 221–9.

[58] Because of the absence of poll-books it is impossible to tell how many individuals this figure represented. This was because in two-member constituencies each voter could cast two votes, which could be given to one of the candidates – 'plumping', in the terminology of electioneering – and evidently there were many 'plumpers' in this election.

[59] Arnold J. James and John E. Thomas, *Wales at Westminster: A History of the Parliamentary Representation of Wales 1800–1879* (Llandysul, 1981), p. 74.

[60] See Aled Jones, 'Trade Unions and the Press: Journalism and the Red Dragon Revolt of 1874', *WHR*, 12, no. 2 (1984), 197–224.

[61] This most revealing election can be studied in the files of the newspapers circulating in Merthyr and Aberdare, esp. *Y Gwladgarwr, Amddiffynnwr y Gweithiwr, Seren Cymru, Cardiff and Merthyr Guardian* and the *Aberdare Times*.

[62] For the candidates and numbers of votes cast, see James and Thomas, *Wales at Westminster*, p. 76.

[63] For James, see Charles Wilkins, *The History of Merthyr Tydfil* (Merthyr Tydfil, 1908), pp. 451–2, and many scattered references in that curious but invaluable book. See also copious references in W. W. Price, *Biographical References*, in the NLW.

and, later, raised to the peerage as Baron Merthyr of Senghennydd,[64] polled 22.2 per cent of the votes, only slightly fewer than Halliday in 1874, and it also appears that, as in the case of Halliday, most of his votes were cast in Aberdare. More interesting is the fact that he obtained so large a share of the poll despite his Toryism. Most of his electioneering was taken up with protestations that he was a Liberal and in agreement with the other candidates on a number of issues, but few could have believed him. No doubt many would have voted for him because of his connections with Aberdare, his mining interests in the valley and in the Rhondda, and in the belief that one of the members for Merthyr should be an industrialist. But some, how many it is impossible to tell, would have voted Tory out of conviction, like the working-class Tories of Bethesda in north Wales. That town, as working class in its structure as any industrial town in the country, had a Cymdeithas Geidwadol y Gweithwyr (Conservative Working Men's Association), led by Dr Hamilton Roberts, and a Conservative newspaper, *Llais y Wlad*.[65] Even though there were no similar institutions in Merthyr and Aberdare, except briefly in this election and then only in the form of a registration society, there is no reason to believe that there were no Conservative voters in the constituency. But this was the election when only two of the thirty-two Welsh members returned were Tories, a majority of the Liberals being Nonconformists. When, at a great Welsh demonstration at the Crystal Palace to celebrate the victories attended by some four hundred persons, most of whom had arrived by excursion trains laid on for the occasion, Henry Richard spoke in Welsh, referring, in passing, to Sir Watkin Williams Wynn as a member of an almost extinct species, a Welsh Conservative Member of Parliament.[66]

Yet it was not in parliamentary politics that the crucial importance of the Welsh language manifested itself, but rather in trade unionism. In the course of the decade after the election of 1868, working-class activists became increasingly determined to take an active part in the running of their own affairs and to furthering their own sectional interests. This had been their most characteristic and powerful contribution to the election of 1868, when they had insisted on the inclusion of working-class objectives in the platforms of all the candidates, and had succeeded in organizing the defeat of H. A. Bruce.[67] That had been the achievement of miners and ironworkers together, both of which occupation groups had become organized in numerically powerful unions during the 1860s

---

[64] For Lewis, see Michael Lieven, *Senghennydd, the Universal Pit Village 1890–1930* (Llandysul, 1994), chapter 1 for a summary of his career; John Williams, 'The Coalowners' in idem, *Was Wales Industrialised? Essays in Modern Welsh History* (Llandysul, 1995), pp. 97–122; W. D. Rubinstein, *Men of Property: The Very Wealthy in Britain since the Industrial Revolution* (London, 1981), p. 77, describes him as 'a half millionaire'.

[65] Geraint Davies, 'Bethesda – The Growth and Development of a Slate Quarrying Town, 1820–90' (unpubl. University of Wales PhD thesis, 1984).

[66] Charles S. Miall, *Henry Richard, M.P.: A Biography* (London, 1889), pp. 313–14.

[67] For this election, see Jones, *Explorations*, pp. 193–214.

and early 1870s, when boom conditions in the two basic industries favoured a greater militancy than had been characteristic of the small district and pithead unions which had existed since the middle 1850s. The ironworkers were organized by John Kane's National Amalgamated Malleable Ironworkers Association of Great Britain, an English union with its base in Darlington.[68] During the boom the union recruited heavily, but came near to collapse during the slump of 1874, as was the case with the Halliday's AAM. The slump provided the conditions for the successful formation of a new, Welsh-led ironworkers' union in south Wales. There were a number of reasons for this, but high among them was the feeling that Kane's union was an alien import, and that Welsh workers should have their own union to protect their own interests, rather than having to pay union dues to support English leaders whose interests were not necessarily congruent with their own. Nationality and language were important ingredients in this striking event as, indeed, they had been ever since the union began to recruit Welsh ironworkers. In the event, the Welsh ironworkers withdrew from Kane's union and formed their own, Y Ddraig Goch/The Welsh Dragon, relying on the Welsh newspapers of the coalfield to report their activities rather than the English *Ironworkers' Journal*, which Kane edited.[69]

Concurrently, and as part of the same drive for independent Welsh unions, the tinplate workers, whose numbers were expanding enormously from the mid-1860s, also succeeded in remaining outside the ranks of the Amalgamated Ironworkers Union. The tinplate industry, like the slate-quarrying industry of north Wales,[70] was highly localized and concentrated in west Wales, mainly in Cydweli, Llanelli and Swansea and their valley hinterlands.[71] Many of the industrial villages which developed around the works were virtually monoglot Welsh communities, far more so even than Aberdare and the colliery villages in the hills of Glamorgan. Like the ironworkers and colliers of Merthyr and Aberdare, the west Wales tinworkers in effect chose to form their own union rather than join an existing English one which had been created for the benefit of English ironworkers rather than Welsh tinplate workers. The Independent Union of Tinplate Makers was formed in 1871, under the leadership of Jenkyn Thomas (president) and William Lewis (Lewys Afan) (secretary).[72] It grew out of a union formed in Ystalyfera about 1868, with James Williams, a rollerman at the Ystalyfera Iron Works, as secretary.

---

[68] On the NAMIA, see *Men of Steel, By One of Them* (London, 1951), pp. 32–56, and for Kane, see Bellamy and Saville, *Dictionary of Labour Biography*, vol. 3, p. 176.
[69] Jones, 'Trade Unions and the Press'.
[70] R. Merfyn Jones, *The North Wales Quarrymen 1874–1922* (Cardiff, 1981), p. 106.
[71] For the tinplate industry, see W. H. Minchinton, *The British Tinplate Industry: A History* (Oxford, 1957), and J. H. Jones, *The Tinplate Industry* (London, 1914). Also Paul Jenkins, *'Twenty by Fourteen': A History of the South Wales Tinplate Industry 1700–1961* (Llandysul, 1995).
[72] Jones, *Tinplate*, pp. 38–9, and Minchinton, *The British Tinplate Industry*, p. 115. See also Jones, 'Trade Unions and the Press', passim.

All these developments in industrial unionism possessed a cultural and political ethos in a society in which the Welsh language had a constitutive role, playing a central part in the workmen's apprehension and understanding of reality. It was an active force in society in so far as it protected and armed them against those who would control them.[73] Judged by the criteria of the market, they may not have been very effective *qua* unions. They tended to strike against a falling market, for example; but their Welshness marked them off from the English unions in more ways than one. They were intensely proud of their language and of its adaptability in times of rapid social change, and until the beginning of the twentieth century they nourished a complete confidence in its ability to protect them and their interests in the industrial field, even as in religion and culture generally it could express to perfection their innermost thoughts and longings. There was no question of conducting their affairs in English, therefore, because to do so would be to adopt an alien means of communication, one which could not adequately express their ideas and feelings, and which would consequently put them at a disadvantage. They kept the language for utilitarian reasons, therefore, but also in order to protect what was most precious in their private and public lives. Thus, they all supported Welsh institutions, such as the eisteddfod, and the Welsh friendly society, the Philanthropic Order of True Ivorites (Y Gwir Iforiaid), rather than English Orders, like the Oddfellows, which many considered to be anti-Welsh.[74] The Ivorites had more than 150 lodges in south and south-west Wales in 1878.[75] They supported the Welsh newspapers and periodicals of the region, which flourished as a consequence, and they helped to build and maintain the hundreds of chapels which were the most characteristic and precious emblems of their culture.

Above all, they differed from most of the English unions in respect of the philosophy which shaped their understanding of the nature of industrial society and, therefore, of their role as part of it. They were not generally militant, and they preferred conciliation to confrontation, except when they believed the employers to be arrogant and intransigent, or to be making unjust demands on their members. They preferred negotiation to strikes, and they put their confidence in, and remained loyal to, leaders such as William Abraham (Mabon), even after the initiative had passed into the hands of a new generation of leaders.[76]

---

[73] See, for example, Hywel Francis, 'Language, culture and learning: the experience of a valley community', *Llafur*, 6, no. 3 (1994), 85–96, esp. p. 89 where he writes of the 'impenetrable nature of Welsh nonconformity, in language, culture and essential democracy [providing] a counterpoint to the coalowner, a veritable religious and cultural citadel'.

[74] Elfyn Scourfield, 'Cymdeithasau cyfeillgar yn Ne Cymru yn ystod y bedwaredd ganrif ar bymtheg' (unpubl. University of Wales PhD thesis, 1984), p. 34.

[75] For fuller details, see *Report of Select Committee on Friendly Societies*, 'Orders of Welsh Origin or Designation, and all other Orders not included in the previous Parts' (PP 1889 LXXI – Part II (F)).

[76] For Mabon, see E. W. Evans, *Mabon: A Study in Trade Union Leadership* (Cardiff, 1959).

Thus, there had developed in the manufacturing and mining regions of Wales a political culture in which the Welsh language was not merely an alternative means of communication to English but was also, and primarily, the medium through which, and by which, the inherent democratic inclinations of the Welsh people were institutionalized. This culture was so creatively adaptive that it could survive the enormous social changes that were already taking place in Wales, in particular the linguistic changes which transformed the character of the nation. This political culture, however, contained within it characteristics which still persist, and while the Welsh language continues to survive so will whatever is distinctive in Welsh politics likewise survive.

19

The Languages of Patriotism in Wales 1840–1880

PAUL O'LEARY

IN 1864 R. J. Derfel, a Welsh poet who made his living as a travelling salesman in Manchester, published a collection of 'patriotic poems'. He prefaced the volume with a definition of patriotism:

> Gwladgarwch, medd y Geiriaduron, yw cariad at wlad: ac ar y dybiaeth yna, y ffurfiwyd y gair yn ein hiaith ni: ond mae y gair yn golygu cariad, hefyd, at y bobl, eu hiaith, eu defodau, a'u llwyddiant; a'r ystyr olaf i'r gair yw'r pwysicaf a'r mwyaf. Nid ydym yn caru y tir er ei fwyn ei hun – ond yr ydym yn gwneud hyny a'r cenedl . . . Felly ystyr benaf a phwysicaf y gair gwladgarwch, ydyw cariad at ein cenedl ac eiddigedd dros ei hiawnderau a'i gogoniant.[1]

> (Patriotism, say the Dictionaries, is love of one's country: and on that supposition was the word formed in our language: but the word also means love of the people, their language, their customs and their success, and this last meaning is the greatest and most important. We do not love the land for its own sake – but we do so with the nation . . . So the principal and most important meaning of the word patriotism is love of our nation and jealousy for its rights and glory.)

However, the meaning of patriotism for contemporaries was not to be found in dictionaries but in the values associated with it and in the language used to describe the country and its people. For Derfel, patriotism was a responsibility placed on the shoulders of all 'civilized nations'. More than that, it was a divinely-ordained responsibility: 'God made us a nation and gave us a language to keep us a nation.' Such heavy responsibilities entailed onerous duties, including the preservation of the Welsh language, despite pressures to adopt English as the sole language of social and political life. Derfel believed that true patriotism meant striving to ensure that 'the means of education and elevation' were brought within the reach of all classes of his compatriots.[2] His concerns derived from a

---

[1] R. J. Derfel, *Caneuon Gwladgarol Cymru* (Wrecsam, 1864), p. 3.
[2] Ibid., pp. 3–4.

democratic sensibility and embodied a desire for political and economic modernization.

Derfel's writings reveal that his patriotism consisted of a curious mixture of radical impulses and conservative concerns. In his poetry and prose he was a passionate and eloquent friend of the poor and oppressed in society, an indefatigable advocate of liberty and a tenacious opponent of slavery in all its forms. He made a powerful argument in favour of establishing a national university, a national library and museum, and a daily Welsh-language newspaper. Yet, at the same time, he could compose poems invoking God's blessing on the Prince and Princess of Wales on the occasion of their marriage, while the prince's emblem appeared like a talisman on the cover of his slim volume of patriotic poems. Loyalty to the state combined with a desire to establish Welsh national institutions was characteristic of Welsh patriotism in general in the mid-nineteenth century.

The origin of a patriotic rhetoric in Wales lies in the closing decades of the eighteenth century when expatriate Welsh societies in London breathed new life into the study of Welsh history and literature. Their legacy during the early nineteenth century was largely preserved by Anglican clerics and members of the gentry, such as Lady Llanover, who patronized cultural events in north-west Monmouthshire. Nearly all the first examples of Welsh words for 'nationalism', 'nationalist' and 'nationality' listed in the University of Wales Dictionary date from the late eighteenth or nineteenth centuries, and especially the 1850s and 1860s.[3] During the latter decades the discourse of patriotism began to cohere around specific institutions, especially the National Eisteddfod, which effectively dates from 1858, the press and the Nonconformist chapels. The country also acquired a national anthem when 'Hen Wlad Fy Nhadau' (Land of My Fathers), composed by Evan and James James of Pontypridd in 1856, achieved popularity after being sung during the National Eisteddfod at Chester in 1866.[4]

The contrast with radicalism earlier in the century is stark. In the 1830s Welsh radicalism entered its insurrectionary phase, with the Merthyr Rising of 1831 and the Chartist Rising at Newport in 1839. The language of politics in those years was couched in terms of a demand for universal political rights and democracy, as exemplified by the six points of the Charter, which set out a rudimentary programme of constitutional reform. As the early radical press demonstrates, the language of politics at this time was predominantly Welsh. In contrast to the development of mass politics in the Irish countryside in the early nineteenth century, which occurred through the medium of English, movements such as Chartism and the Anti-Corn Law League established Welsh-language newspapers,

---

[3] Glanmor Williams, *Religion, Language and Nationality in Wales* (Cardiff, 1979), p. 143.
[4] W. Rhys Nicholas, 'The Authors of "Hen Wlad Fy Nhadau": Evan James (1809–1878) and James James (1833–1902)' in P. F. Tobin and J. I. Davies (eds.), *The Bridge and the Song* (Bridgend, 1991), pp. 29–43. This article contains the text of the anthem and an English translation by Eben Fardd.

disseminated information in that language and clearly used Welsh extensively in political campaigns and meetings.[5]

From the 1840s, however, Nonconformity established a hegemony over Welsh public life based on a particular set of values and expressed through a vocabulary which increasingly determined the boundaries of political debate. As Ieuan Gwynedd Jones has written, the public face of mid-Victorian Wales was 'respectable, religious, [and] petty bourgeois in style and aspiration'.[6] Pride in their religiosity was a feature of social life which served to confirm a widely-held belief that the Welsh were an elect or chosen people descended directly from one of the tribes of Israel.[7] The Religious Census of 1851 demonstrated beyond all doubt that a larger proportion of people attended a place of worship in Wales than in England, and that the gulf between religious observance in town and country was much narrower than was the case over the border. For patriots this was a cause for rejoicing, especially as it was claimed that the peaceful character of the country and the loyalty of its inhabitants could be ascribed to it.[8] This self-image was shaped decisively during the furore surrounding the publication of the controversial government Education Report of 1847, which cast its long shadow over debates on all aspects of social and cultural life in subsequent decades. When the nationalist Michael D. Jones observed in 1849 that 'the hearts of hundreds are now enthusiastically boiling over with the language of patriotism' ('y mae calonnau cannoedd yn awr yn frwd berwi allan iaith gwladgarwch'), he had in mind the stimulus to activity provided by the Blue Books controversy.[9] Paradoxically, the Report provided a spur to the patriotic sensibilities it had mercilessly denigrated.[10]

The accusations of Welsh immorality, made by three English and Anglican commissioners who possessed no knowledge of Wales, its language or popular education, was widely interpreted as an attack on Nonconformity, which had made great strides in winning popular support during the first half of the century. By 1851 some four out of every five people who attended a place of worship were Nonconformists, and the fact that the commissioners had based their conclusions overwhelmingly on evidence provided by Anglican ministers allowed the charge of treachery to be levelled against fellow Welshmen. Following the publication of R. J. Derfel's satirical play *Brad y Llyfrau Gleision* (The Treachery of the Blue

---

[5] Ryland Wallace, *Organise! Organise! Organise! A Study of Reform Agitations in Wales, 1840–1886* (Cardiff, 1991), pp. 32–3, 42.
[6] Ieuan Gwynedd Jones, 'The Dynamics of Politics in Mid-Nineteenth-Century Wales' in idem, *Explorations and Explanations: Essays in the Social History of Victorian Wales* (Llandysul, 1981), p. 270.
[7] Williams, *Religion, Language and Nationality*, pp. 6–8.
[8] See, for example, 'Crefyddolder y Cymry', *Y Gwladgarwr*, 26 June 1858.
[9] Quoted in R. Tudur Jones, 'Michael D. Jones a Thynged y Genedl' in Geraint H. Jenkins (ed.), *Cof Cenedl: Ysgrifau ar Hanes Cymru* (Llandysul, 1986), p. 103.
[10] *Reports of the Commissioners of Inquiry into the State of Education in Wales . . . in three parts. Part II. Brecknock, Cardigan, Radnor, and Monmouth* (London, 1847) (PP 1847 (871) XXVII), p. 88.

Books) in 1854, the event was fixed in radical Nonconformist mythology as a wrong to be righted and a spur to political action.[11] Anglicans such as Sir Thomas Phillips and Jane Williams (Ysgafell) were among the first to launch into print with their denunciations of the Report,[12] but their protestations were soon drowned by the volume of Nonconformist indignation. Long after the precise details of the controversy had been forgotten, the accusation of treachery continued to resonate in political discourse and made a reasoned discussion of the episode difficult. The language of patriotism was mobilized to make sense of this event and organize the response to it. Paradoxically, by castigating the Welsh language as an inferior tongue the Report entrenched the mentality which accorded Welsh respect in cultural matters but perceived the acquisition of English as the key to material success. While the other slights of the commissioners were hotly denied by critics, their view of the Welsh language was increasingly accepted by the Welsh themselves, one consequence being that, as David Howell has pointed out, 'language as such did not constitute a vital element in Welsh ethnic mobilisation in the nineteenth century'.[13] Nevertheless, the Welsh-language press was a powerful propagator of patriotic discourse.

Benedict Anderson has claimed that nations are 'imagined communities' which must establish effective ways of communication among their members if they are to become reality. In order to do this they require a common language through which a shared identity can be created and expressed: this is the language of patriotism. During the mid-nineteenth century the emergence of this way of thinking about an individual's affiliation to the national community was conditioned by wider changes in society and politics.[14] That mid-Victorian Wales succeeded in cultivating such a powerful self-image is in part attributable to the

---

[11] Prys Morgan (ed.), *Brad y Llyfrau Gleision: Ysgrifau ar Hanes Cymru* (Llandysul, 1991); idem, 'From Long Knives to Blue Books' in R. R. Davies, Ralph A. Griffiths, Ieuan Gwynedd Jones and Kenneth O. Morgan (eds.), *Welsh Society and Nationhood: Historical Essays Presented to Glanmor Williams* (Cardiff, 1984), pp. 199–215; Ieuan Gwynedd Jones, *Mid-Victorian Wales: The Observers and the Observed* (Cardiff, 1992), chapter 5; Gwyneth Tyson Roberts, '"Under the Hatches": English Parliamentary Commissioners' Views of the People and Language of Mid-Nineteenth-Century Wales' in Bill Schwarz (ed.), *The Expansion of England: Race, Ethnicity and Cultural History* (London, 1996), pp. 171–97.

[12] [Jane Williams], *Artegall: or Remarks on the Reports of the Commissioners of Inquiry into the State of Education in Wales* (London, 1848); Sir Thomas Phillips, *Wales: The Language, Social Condition, Moral Character and Religious Opinions of the People Considered in their Relation to Education* (London, 1849).

[13] David Howell, 'A "Less Obtrusive and Exacting" Nationality: Welsh Ethnic Mobilisation in Rural Communities, 1850–1920' in idem (ed.) in collaboration with Gert von Pistohlkors and Ellen Wiegandt, *Roots of Rural Ethnic Mobilisation* (Aldershot and New York, 1993), p. 79. He adds: 'It is still legitimate, nevertheless, to argue that at the core of Welsh ethnic consciousness in the nineteenth century was the existence of the Welsh language.' Ibid., p. 81.

[14] Benedict Anderson, *Imagined Communities: Reflections on the Origin and Spread of Nationalism* (2nd ed., London, 1991). See also idem, *Language and Power: Exploring Political Cultures in Indonesia* (Ithaca and London, 1990).

fact that Welsh was already a print language. This enabled the creation of new ways of communicating between people, and it was this which allowed writers like R. J. Derfel, who lived in Manchester, to intervene in debates at home.[15] In this respect, the periodical and newspaper press was crucially important as a creator of communities of interest, both in terms of the content of publications and the ritual of reading a newspaper. The press was already a rooted aspect of public life by the 1840s despite the inhibiting effects of a variety of taxes which increased the costs of production. But the repeal of the Stamp Acts in 1855 and the abolition of the duty on paper in 1861 provided a fillip to its further growth.[16] More than any other institution, it was the press which created a vehicle for the dissemination of patriotic discourse, ensuring that it became part of the integument of civic life. Yet the prolific variety of the press in Wales, representing different communities of interest, ensured that that discourse would be contested.

★ ★ ★

In his study of the 'keywords' of cultural analysis, Raymond Williams has emphasized the need to see words not in isolation but in clusters; that is, the meaning of key concepts can be appreciated fully only by exploring their associations in a specific context and at a particular historical juncture.[17] This is true of the various words, or vocabulary, associated with patriotism. A useful starting point for an analysis of the vocabulary of patriotism in mid-nineteenth-century Wales is the weekly newspaper *Y Gwladgarwr* (The Patriot), published in Aberdare from May 1858. The political development of one of its founders, William Williams ('Carw Coch'), provides an insight into the processes of political change which radicalism underwent in the mid-nineteenth century. Williams was a Unitarian and member of a society of 'Free Enquirers' at Aberdare and had been a contributor to the Chartist organ *Udgorn Cymru*. His concern for the Welsh language and culture was demonstrated in the popular eisteddfod he established at his public house, the Stag Inn, at Trecynon.[18] *Y Gwladgarwr* demonstrates the nature of the ideological shift which had taken place by the late 1850s.

---

[15] In his autobiography in *Llais Llafur*, 4 November 1905, Derfel remarked of this period: 'I was an enthusiastic Welsh nationalist, as anyone who read my works, prose or poetry, will speedily see. I must have been drunk on patriotism, for I used to pray patriotism, talk patriotism, preach patriotism, and write patriotism. In fact, patriotism ringed all my thoughts and influenced all my work.' Quoted in Eddie Cass, 'Robert Jones Derfel: A Welsh Poet in the Cotton Factory Times', *Llafur*, 7, no. 1 (1996), 56.

[16] Aled Gruffydd Jones, *Press, Politics and Society: A History of Journalism in Wales* (Cardiff, 1993). When, in 1836, a reader of *Y Papyr Newydd Cymraeg* from Llansanffraid Glan Conwy complained that it was difficult to transport copies of the publication to outlying districts, the local postmaster agreed to deliver Welsh papers to the village for a ½d as a sign of his 'genuine patriotism'. Ibid., p. 99.

[17] Raymond Williams, *Keywords: A Vocabulary of Culture and Society* (London, 1983).

[18] *DWB*, s.v. Williams, William.

The paper was edited by John Roberts (Ieuan Gwyllt), who had previously edited *Yr Amserau*.[19] In the first issue the editor recognized with due gravitas 'that it was no small presumption to choose this name for our newspaper' ('nad beiddgarwch bychan ar ein rhan ydoedd dewis yr enw hwn ar ein newyddiadur'), and he proceeded to outline in greater detail his justification for adopting the title, in so doing elaborating on what he considered to be the principal components of Welsh patriotism. Firstly, he emphasized that patriotism was a virtue, despite the 'scorn of some unfeeling, narrow-minded and mean-spirited men – men without an ember of the fiery muse in their breasts' ('gwawd rhai dynion oerion eu teimladau, cul eu syniadau, crintachlyd eu hysbrydoedd, a chrebachlyd eu meddyliau – dynion heb dewyn o dan awenydd yn eu mynwesau') towards the attachment of the Welsh to their country, nation, institutions and language. Secondly, he emphasized the antiquity of patriotism and its scriptural lineage, a blatant act of historical invention, but one which would have been congenial to his readership. 'The most prominent men in the Bible were patriots', he wrote, 'and the Saviour of the World was a Patriot too' ('Yr oedd dynion amlycaf y Bibl yn wladgarwyr. Ac yr oedd Iachawdwr y Byd hefyd yn Wladgarwr'). As literacy in Welsh had been acquired in a religious context, the imagery and concepts of the Bible came easily to journalists and politicians alike. Consequently, the language of patriotism was deeply imbued with scriptural rhetoric.

After offering a staunch defence of the general principle of patriotism, the editorial was less clear about the character and content of its specifically Welsh variety. An element of defensiveness can be discerned in the determination to reassure readers that the Welsh need not fear a comparison of their dignity, courage, morality and religion with the best in humanity. This anxiety to prove the good character of the Welsh as a people vis-à-vis other nations was a prominent feature of the discourse of public life in Wales in the decades after 1847. Perhaps the paper's most succinct definition of patriotism can be found in the statement that it was determined to 'support lovers of civic and religious freedom at home and across the face of the whole earth, – to fight all violence and injustice, – to exalt literature, knowledge, art, science and virtue' ('gynal breichiau caredigion rhyddid gwladol a chrefyddol gartref a thros wyneb yr holl ddaear, – dyrnodio pob trais ac anghyfiawnder, – dyrchafu llenyddiaeth, gwybodaeth, celfyddyd, a gwyddoniaeth, a rhinwedd'). To this can be added the paper's prized 'independence'. In a bold statement it promised that it would not be a sectarian publication or that any individual would profit financially from it. It was claimed that this newspaper was public property: 'every other paper is personal property', the editorial stated, 'but this one belongs to the nation' ('eiddo personol yw pob

---

[19] J. E. Jones, *Ieuan Gwyllt, Ei Fywyd, Ei Lafur, Ei Athrylith, Ei Nodweddion a'i Ddylanwad ar Gymru* (Holywell, 1881), pp. 52–3, 125; Jones, *Press, Politics and Society*, pp. 42–3.

papyr arall, ond eiddo y genedl yw hwn'). As evidence of its loyalty to the state, the editorial appeared under a symbol of the feathers of the Prince of Wales.[20]

The kind of vocabulary used to discuss Welsh patriotism in this editorial is representative of a wider discourse in mid-nineteenth-century Wales. For the purposes of analysis it is possible to divide this into three principal categories, denoted by the following keywords: liberty, virtue and loyalty. Patriotism was presented in terms of consensual values intended to reaffirm the solidarity of the nation. However, it would be misleading to accept this at face value, since each of these words was keenly contested in the fierce debates about the moral condition of Welsh society and culture in the mid-nineteenth century, and to that extent made patriotism one of the key concepts in the contest over power and authority in society.

To begin with, liberty. It is impossible to discuss the language of patriotism in mid-nineteenth-century Wales without taking account of the centrality of 'liberty' in the discourse of politics. But what exactly did contemporaries mean by this? Following the decline of Chartism from the late 1840s the initiative moved away from those radicals who couched their analysis in terms of fundamental constitutional change towards those espousing a conception of liberty nurtured by Old Dissent since the seventeenth century. For them the aim of achieving religious equality (and franchise reform as a means to that end) was uppermost. The repeal of the Test and Corporation Acts in 1828 had created a public space in which Nonconformists could organize politically and affirm their claim to civil rights, and they took full advantage of the means at their disposal to create a new public opinion sympathetic to their demands in the localities.

At its most basic, liberty came to mean the freedom of the individual to live and worship without the arbitrary interference of the state. Attaining this meant organizing politically and agitating as a group to achieve common goals. This meaning can be discerned in the writings of the radical newspaper editor David Rees of Llanelli who wrote a report of the 'Anti-State-Church Conference', held in London in 1844, at which there was a strong Welsh representation. 'We are pleased to understand', he informed readers, 'that the friends of freedom in general in England, and many in Wales, have chosen to take part in this conference. The friends of religious and civil freedom are multiplying daily' ('Mae yn dda genym ddeall fod cyfeillion rhyddid yn gyffredinol yn Lloegr, a llawer yn Nghymru, wedi dewis cenadau i'w cynnrychioli yn y gynnadledd hon. Mae cyfeillion rhyddid crefyddol a gwladol, yn lluosogi beunydd').[21] The term 'religious and civil freedom' ('rhyddid gwladol a chrefyddol') would recur time after time in political debate in Wales in subsequent decades and it acquired a

---
[20] *Y Gwladgarwr*, 15 May 1858.
[21] *Y Diwygiwr*, IX, no. 106 (1844), 156. Reprinted under the title 'Crefydd a Gwleidyddiaeth' in Glanmor Williams (ed.), *David Rees, Llanelli: Detholion o'i Waith* (Caerdydd, 1950), pp. 10–11.

particular resonance in the debates about the disestablishment of the Church from the late 1860s onwards. This way of thinking of freedom also surfaced in the debates on popular education, when some Nonconformists declared that a state system of education was potentially as oppressive as a state church since it inevitably entailed the propagation of the doctrines of that Church. In January 1848, for example, David Rees argued forcefully that Wales should not 'yield to the calamity of accepting money from the state to teach herself' ('ildio i'r brofedigaeth o dderbyn arian y wlad i'w dysgu ei hun').[22] In practice the attraction of grant aid for education was too tempting a carrot to ignore, and the sterling efforts of Hugh Owen earlier in the decade to publicize state grants for education in Wales were particularly successful in mobilizing opinion. But suspicions of Church influence in the field of education persisted.

One organization above all others embodies the post-Chartist conception of civil and religious freedom in Wales, that is the Liberation Society – the name of the Anti-State-Church Association after 1853. Following its conference in Swansea in 1862 it redoubled its efforts in Wales, ensuring that the move towards organizing the people politically was combined with the demand for religious and civil freedom.[23] Tom Nairn's incisive comment that the new middle-class intelligentsia had to 'invite the masses into history' is apposite here; furthermore, as he pithily observed, 'the invitation-card had to be written in a language they understood'.[24] On one level this simply meant utilizing the vernacular for the purposes of propaganda as opposed to a higher status language (in this case, Welsh rather than English), but in a more general sense it also meant presenting a political message in an idiom comprehensible to the masses who remained outside the political system, reflecting their own concerns and values. In Wales in the 1860s it was the Liberation Society, in alliance with the Liberal Party, which issued the 'invitation card', and through the practical experience of landlord oppression in the elections in Merioneth in 1865 and more widely in the countryside in the aftermath of the general election of 1868 the masses achieved an understanding of Liberation politics in the light of personal experience.[25] As a result, the campaign for political reform in the 1860s had an undeniably religious flavour in Wales, a factor which helped to cement the relationship between a patriotic rhetoric informed by scriptural imagery and political allegiance to Liberalism.

A theme running through the discourse of patriotism was that of the need to defend quintessentially Protestant liberties. A common feeling among Protestants that they represented a bastion of freedom against the ambitions of Popery was a

[22] *Y Diwygiwr*, XIII, no. 150 (1848), 33. Reprinted under the title 'Adroddiad Addysgol, 1847' in Williams (ed.), *David Rees: Detholion*, pp. 32–6.
[23] Ieuan Gwynedd Jones, 'The Liberation Society and Welsh Politics, 1844 to 1868' in idem, *Explorations and Explanations*, pp. 236–68.
[24] Tom Nairn, *The Break Up of Britain* (London, 1977), p. 340.
[25] Ieuan Gwynedd Jones, 'Merioneth Politics in Mid-Nineteenth Century' in idem, *Explorations and Explanations*, pp. 83–164.

strong element in Welsh culture at the beginning of the nineteenth century, reinforced as it was by the propaganda of the Napoleonic Wars. At times of perceived crisis, such as the passing of Catholic Emancipation in 1829, the Maynooth controversy in 1845 and the so-called 'Papal Aggression' incident in 1850, public opinion was quick to assert Protestant freedoms and denounce the oppressive influence of the Papacy.[26] At such times anti-Catholic sentiments broke the surface to influence the course of political life. But anti-Catholicism also had a more pervasive and continuous daily presence in the Welsh press, so much so that it can be characterized as an attitude or a mentality as much as a doctrinal objection to a different religious persuasion. Sensationalist reporting in the press of events in Catholic countries reinforced the perceived threat to fundamental freedoms from priest, confessional, convents and monasteries. Catholicism was always associated with the oppressive regimes of continental Europe and thus represented the essential 'Other', the negation of all those characteristics held dear by 'free-born' Protestants.

Even though Catholicism enjoyed no more than a weak presence in Wales in the mid-nineteenth century, vigilance was considered the price of freedom. During the 1840s the Oxford movement within the Church of England was seen as an insidious half-way house to Popery, thereby fracturing a united Protestant front, or at least repositioning it in the form of the Evangelical Alliance which was formed in 1846. In the columns of the Welsh press, 'Puseyism' and 'Popery' were synonymous terms.[27] As Nonconformists gained confidence in the political sphere and began to challenge the privileged position of Anglicanism, attacks on the Church for harbouring a fifth column became more frequent. It is against this background that we must view the injection of anti-Catholic rhetoric into the debates on the Blue Books, which ostensibly had nothing whatsoever to do with the Catholic Church. Thus, when Evan Jones (Ieuan Gwynedd) cautioned his fellow Nonconformists in 1847 against the widening sectarian divisions in their ranks, he held out the prospect of Catholic triumphalism as the inevitable consequence. 'Catholicism takes advantage of the party spirit in our midst, and of our minor squabbles', he averred, 'it howls until the stones echo that Rome is united, while the Nonconformists bite and devour each other' ('Cymer Pabyddiaeth fantais ar yr ysbryd plaid sydd yn ein mysg, ac ar ein mân-ymrysonau . . . oernada nes adsain y creigiau fod Rhufain yn un, tra y cnoa ac y traflynca yr Ymneillduwyr eu gilydd').[28] He offered this counsel in the spirit of 'freedom and

---

[26] A. H. Williams has referred to the strong feeling of anti-Catholicism as a phenomenon which has not received the attention it deserves by historians. See his lecture, *Efengyliaeth yng Nghymru, c.1840–1875* ([Caerdydd], 1982), pp. 21–3.

[27] Ibid.; 'Maynooth', *Y Traethodydd* (1845); 'Yr Undeb Efengylaidd', ibid. (1846); 'Y Puseyaid Cymreig', ibid. (1852), collected in Lewis Edwards, *Traethodau Llenyddol* (Wrexham, n.d.), pp. 27–32, 422–35, 598–602.

[28] *Y Dysgedydd*, XXVI (September, 1847), 275. Reprinted in Brinley Rees (ed.), *Ieuan Gwynedd: Detholiad o'i Ryddiaith* (Caerdydd, 1957), pp. 43–4.

truth and the happiness of the whole nation' ('rhyddid, a gwirionedd, a dedwyddwch yr holl genedl').[29]

That Catholicism was a diehard opponent of freedom was an unquestioned verity for Protestants. In 1880, for example, one commentator expressed his opposition to Papal restrictions on the individual's freedom in staccato fashion: 'Always an indignant enemy of freedom. This fair angel [freedom] cannot live in the odour of its breath. Quickening the conscience with the rope of oppression – putting up the stake – waving the scourge – opening the dungeon – and lighting the bonfire is her delight' ('Gelyn digofus rhyddid erioed. Nis gall yr angeles deg [rhyddid] fyw yn sawyr ei hanadl hi. Cylymu cydwybod â rhaff gormes – codi yr ystanc – chwifio y fflangell – agor y daeardy – a chyneu y goelcerth yw ei phleserwaith hi').[30] The message was disseminated by itinerant 'No Popery' lecturers, preachers and journalists and a prolific pamphlet literature. Thus, when *Y Genedl Gymreig* defined the Welsh nation in 1877, it did so in terms of Protestant freedoms, stating that it would join heartily with anyone who fought against the superstition and oppression of Catholicism in whatever form it came to light.[31] Anti-Catholicism was one strand of the support given by some Welsh radicals for movements seeking self-determination on the Continent, most notably Mazzini's 'Young Italy'.

Central though it was to the thought of middle-class contemporaries, liberty was considered potentially dangerous in the wrong hands, especially if it was devoid of virtue, the second keyword in the vocabulary of patriotism. Despite the general condemnation of the infamous Blue Books in 1847, all critics accepted the central premise of the commissioners that the nation was a moral entity with a collective character which could be studied and thereby determined. The virulence of their indignation derived from the depiction of the Welsh as an immoral people, not because the commissioners had linked morality and nationality *per se*. That critics and commissioners alike shared the same underlying frame of reference is demonstrated by the writings of the Congregational minister Ieuan Gwynedd, the principal scourge of adverse reports on Nonconformists. He strove to disprove the assertions contained in the Report by carefully analysing the criminal statistics for Wales and comparing them with those for England. But beneath this scrupulous statistical analysis, which was published in English, lay a way of understanding the nature of morality and the causes of crime which would be influential in Nonconformist circles for the remainder of the century. In a revealing article written in Welsh in 1852 he warned that attempting to determine the moral character of any people was 'a rather difficult and dangerous' task, especially in the case of the Welsh who, he claimed, 'depended to a great extent

---

[29] *Y Dysgedydd*, XXVI (September, 1847), 276; Rees, *Ieuan Gwynedd: Detholiad*, p. 47.
[30] 'Y Babaeth a Rhyddid', *Y Diwygiwr*, XLV, no. 543 (1880), 377–9.
[31] 'Y Genedl', *Y Genedl Gymreig*, 8 February 1877.

on their character'. In spite of his own warning, he proceeded to emphasize the necessity of exposing the weaknesses of a variety of different nations to his readers, while carefully underlining the honesty of the Welsh by contrast.[32]

Since Ieuan Gwynedd was willing to reason within the same framework imposed by the commissioners, he used the same false logic as they had used to condemn the Welsh in order to apportion moral weaknesses to other nations. This was merely one of the first of a torrent of speeches, articles and books which over the next half century would reveal an obsession with moral character. The Education Report cast a long shadow over public debate in the mid-century, with prominent Nonconformists feeling the need to restate continually the virtue of the Welsh. Thus, in 1868 Wales was described as 'the most moral and religious glade in the United Kingdom' ('y lanerch fwyaf moesol a chrefyddol yn y Deyrnas Gyfunol').[33] By the end of the century the country had acquired an enviable reputation for the absence of recorded crime, rejoicing in the name of 'the Land of the White Gloves' ('Gwlad y Menig Gwynion').

In fact, some individuals were stung so deeply by the accusations contained in the Report of 1847 that they were unable to extricate themselves from the intellectual straitjacket the experience imposed upon them. This was shown most clearly in the response to the accusations that Welsh women were especially immoral. A concern with virtue and morality demanded that the pristine purity of Welsh womanhood be established and assiduously cultivated. The first women's periodical in Welsh, established in 1851, implicitly reflected these concerns in its title *Y Gymraes* (The Welshwoman). Edited by Ieuan Gwynedd, it was an organ with a mission to improve the moral condition of women. It chose to ignore the day-to-day realities of women's lives in heavy industry and their associational activities in chapel and friendly society, and presented instead a romanticized picture of domestic service and femininity.[34] This was womanhood as a symbolic cultural marker rather than as a reflection of a lived experience.

An awareness of, and concern for, gender distinctions informed the response to the Blue Books and the discourse of patriotism in general. Did not the title of the newly-minted national anthem, 'Land of my Fathers', make this point? In an essay titled 'The Patriotism of the Welsh', published in 1864, R. J. Derfel used the family as a metaphor for the nation in order to revile those Welshmen who boasted that they were 'something more than a Welshman'. Those who rejected Wales were, in his eyes, the equivalent of a man who neglected his family, a heinous crime for those who espoused respectability in mid-nineteenth-century

---

[32] 'Drwg a Da Cenedl y Cymry', *Y Gwron Cymreig*, 7 January 1852, reprinted in William Williams (ed.), *Gweithiau Barddonol a Rhyddieithol Ieuan Gwynedd* (Dolgellau, 1876), pp. 470–2.
[33] *Y Gwladgarwr*, 29 August 1868.
[34] Sian Rhiannon Williams, 'The True "Cymraes": Images of Women in Women's Nineteenth-Century Welsh Periodicals' in Angela V. John (ed.), *Our Mothers' Land: Chapters in Welsh Women's History, 1830–1939* (Cardiff, 1991), pp. 69–91.

Wales. A rejection of patriotism was equated with emasculation: being less than a Welshman meant being less than a man.[35] But it was the role of women which received closest attention. Dr Lewis Edwards was not untypical when he wrote that Christianity had freed women from slavery and enabled them to nurture 'the principles of liberty and civility in their husbands'. He invited Welsh women to ponder the position of Queen Victoria who, as a constitutional monarch, left the formal business of government to her ministers yet wielded considerable influence in private; her position, he asserted, was stronger as a result.[36] This view was consistent with the ideology of separate spheres for men and women, with the emphasis on the latter cultivating a domestic environment sufficiently warm and welcoming as to dissuade the husband from succumbing to the temptations of the public house.

The third keyword of patriotic discourse was loyalty. Loyalty to the state was conceived by Nonconformist radicals as an essential counterbalance to their demands for civic and religious freedom. Following the upheavals of the first half of the nineteenth century, radicals strove hard to distance themselves from the slightest whiff of seditious behaviour, so much so that the events of the 1830s and 1840s were relegated to the status of a minor diversion in the uplifting story of the progress of the Welsh people from Popish ignorance and superstition to their present state of Protestant enlightenment. To the extent that these events were acknowledged at all, they were attributed to the insidious work of outsiders.

As early as 1841 a treatise on the character of the Welsh people insisted that 'the many-headed beast called Chartism' ('yr anghenfil amlbenawg a elwir yn breinlenaeth') was not of Welsh origin: 'England gave birth to it' ('Lloegr a roes enedigaeth iddo'). Consequently, it was unfair to tar all Welsh people with the brush of sedition.[37] This cry was repeated with gusto by other figures in public life after 1847, and particularly in response to *The Times*'s splenetic comments about the Welsh in 1866. According to *Y Gwladgarwr*, Welsh loyalism could boast a greater longevity than that of the English themselves.[38] This belief was emphasized particularly strongly by two of the key ideologues of Nonconformist Wales, Henry Richard and Dr Thomas Rees, who acted as public moralists and helped to establish the parameters within which the language of patriotism operated. Influential publications by them in the 1860s constructed a picture of the Welsh as virtuous, Nonconformist and loyal. Henry Richard was effusive in his praise for Welsh loyalty:

---

[35] R. J. Derfel, 'Gwladgarwch y Cymry' in idem, *Traethodau ac Areithiau* (Bangor, 1864), pp. 217–19.
[36] Lewis Edwards, 'Merched Cymru' in idem, *Traethodau Llenyddol*, p. 338.
[37] William Jones, *Traethawd Gwobrwyol ar Nodweddiad y Cymry fel Cenedl yn yr Oes Hon* (Llundain, 1841), p. 74.
[38] *Y Gwladgarwr*, 22 September 1866.

I doubt whether there is a population on the face of the earth more enlightened and moral, more loyal to the throne, more obedient to the laws, more exemplary in all the relations of life, than the inhabitants of Wales.[39]

He, too, ascribed Chartism to an alien influence which had found a receptive audience in an Anglicized corner of Wales that, in his view, could no longer be considered intrinsically Welsh; by contrast, he claimed, 'the normal condition of the Principality is one of profound calm, rarely ruffled even by a breath of popular discontent'.[40] These views were supported by Thomas Rees, who felt that those Welsh workers who were 'undiluted' by foreign elements were 'as a class of people . . . remarkable for their loyalty and submission to their superiors'.[41] An essay by John Williams, published in 1869, made much the same points.[42] These tracts were published in English and were intended for the edification of an English audience – like a great deal of the pamphlet literature produced in the wake of the Blue Books – but Henry Richard's work was translated into Welsh for newspapers and provides a good example of how such controversial pamphlet literature, designed for an external audience, could feed back into the culture which produced it.[43] This fact suggests that the sentiments and arguments expressed in these publications were not uncongenial to a Welsh-speaking readership and that they hold a key to the emerging self-image of the Welsh.

One aspect of loyalty to the state was an attachment to monarchy, whose stock was particularly high in Wales in the 1860s. 'Albert Dda' (Albert the Good) was the subject of the bardic competition at the National Eisteddfod at Swansea in 1863. The organizers clearly expected all entries to be characterized by nothing less than fulsome praise of Victoria's consort; they were not disappointed.[44] The marriage of the Prince of Wales in 1863 was received with unbridled enthusiasm. The day of the marriage was a public holiday, with special events organized throughout the country, including processions, celebratory teas, bonfires and sports. That the prince and the land of his title were strangers to each other was ascribed not to his lack of interest in Wales but rather to the failure of the Welsh (especially the gentry) to win his attention and favours.[45] One of the boasts of the press was that the combined poetic, musical and artistic talents of the country had been pressed into the service of celebrating the wedding. Among R. J. Derfel's

---

[39] Henry Richard, *Letters and Essays on Wales* (2nd ed., London, 1884), p. 36.
[40] Ibid., pp. 81–2.
[41] Thomas Rees, *Miscellaneous Papers on Subjects Relating to Wales* (London, 1867), p. 14.
[42] John Williams, *A Defence of the Welsh People Against the Misrepresentations of their English Critics* (Caernarfon, 1869), p. 16.
[43] It appeared in three Welsh-language newspapers, including *Y Gwladgarwr*. See *Cymru Fydd*, February 1888. I am indebted to Neil Evans and Kate Sullivan for this reference.
[44] See John Jones (Talhaiarn), *Awdl Er Coffadwriaeth am y Diweddar Dywysog Cydweddog 'Albert Dda'* (Liverpool, 1863), and Gwalchmai, 'Albert Dda', *Y Traethodydd*, XX (1865), 171–94.
[45] *BAC*, 4, 18 March, 1 April 1863.

collection of patriotic poems, published in 1864, was an ode to the marriage of the Prince of Wales, which invoked divine protection for him and his bride, 'so that the crown never faces adversity' ('fel na bo'r goron byth yn groes'). Derfel was not the only patriotic Welsh poet to find inspiration in the event.[46] That same year, the heraldic arms of Queen Victoria and the Prince of Wales were displayed prominently on the backdrop to the stage at the National Eisteddfod.

Strenuous efforts were made to secure the Prince as the Eisteddfod's patron, but he failed to attend the festival until the London Eisteddfod of 1887.[47] A reluctance to grace the Eisteddfod with his presence seemed merely to increase the appetite for royal recognition, and it is possible that devotion to this distant (and it would seem, largely uninterested) figure maintained the monarchy's popularity in Wales at a time when republicanism was gaining ground in some circles in England. There is scant evidence of reciprocal devotion on the part of the sovereign. In a revealing comparison, John Davies has calculated that during her 64-year reign Queen Victoria spent a total of seven years in Scotland, seven weeks in Ireland and only seven nights in Wales.[48] Nevertheless, enthusiasm for the monarchy remained undimmed by this comparative neglect. Where criticism of the monarchy occurred, it tended to concentrate on the excessive cost to the public purse rather than on the institution itself.[49]

On the whole, the majority of Welsh patriots saw no conflict between their attachment to Wales and their loyalty to the British state. Those who did seek a political expression for a distinctive Welsh identity had little success in these decades, for the ideas of writers like Michael D. Jones had a greater impact on later generations than on his immediate contemporaries. In fact, a sense of Britishness was an integral part of Welsh patriotism, not an addition to it,[50] a fact reflected in the readiness to pursue national grievances in politics after 1868 through the Liberal Party rather than by the establishment of a separate political party on the lines of the Irish Home Rulers. This theme was made explicit in the titles and content of a number of publications. For example, *Y Brython* (The Briton), edited by the Anglican D. Silvan Evans, addressed its readership in the opening editorial in 1858 'not only as *Welshmen*, but also as *Britishers*, or *Britons*; that is, as members of the British State, and as members of the British [*sic*] Church' ('nid yn unig fel *Cymry*, ond hefyd fel *Prydeiniaid*, neu *Frythoniaid*; sef yw hyny, fel

---

[46] Ibid.; Derfel, *Caneuon Gwladgarol Cymru*, pp. 24–5; Gwilym Pennant, 'Priodas Tywysog Cymru', *BAC*, 8 April 1863.

[47] Hywel Teifi Edwards, *Gŵyl Gwalia: Yr Eisteddfod yn Oes Aur Victoria* (Llandysul, 1980), pp. 44, 54–6, 170.

[48] John Davies, 'Victoria and Victorian Wales' in G. H. Jenkins and J. B. Smith (eds.), *Politics and Society in Wales, 1840–1922: Essays in Honour of Ieuan Gwynedd Jones* (Cardiff, 1988), pp. 7–28.

[49] There are few echoes in Wales of the upswing in republicanism in Britain in the early 1870s, although there were republican clubs in Cardiff and Merthyr Tydfil in 1872–3. See Wallace, *Organise*, p. 144.

[50] This theme is examined extensively in Gwyn A. Williams, *When Was Wales? A History of the Welsh* (Harmondsworth, 1985).

aelodau o Deyrn-wladwriaeth Prydain Fawr, ac fel aelodau o Eglwys Prydain Fawr [sic]').[51] Similarly, in 1879 a new Welsh-language magazine for women was titled *Y Frythones* (The Female Briton) as a successor to *Y Gymraes* (The Welshwoman). Likewise, Nonconformists saw no contradiction between maintaining their distinctive cultural identity and membership of the larger polity, although they did seek reform such as disestablishment of the Church to establish their equality within the larger framework.

★   ★   ★

In distilling the principal components of patriotism by analysing the language used to articulate it, we must beware of imposing an ideological coherence it did not possess. It has been written about Britain in an earlier period that 'becoming a patriot was a political act, and often a multi-faceted and dynamic one'.[52] The same is true of the emergence of a heightened sense of patriotism in mid-nineteenth-century Wales. Virtue, freedom and loyalty can be seen as terms and values delimiting the linguistic boundaries within which patriotism was expressed, but different elements were emphasized at different times and in different contexts. Moreover, as has been seen, not everybody shared the same language of patriotism, with both Anglicans and Nonconformists contesting the exclusive right to speak for the nation by the 1860s.

Patriotic rhetoric was designed to establish the boundaries of the group. This inevitably produced heated debate about the nature of those boundaries and highlighted the question of where power resided in society. For landowners and employers, the simple answer was that property conferred privilege and power which were reinforced by institutions such as the established Church. The alienation of the majority of the people from that church and the allegiance of a significant proportion of them to Dissent meant that that nexus of Church–class–property was implicitly challenged. The effect of the Report of 1847 was to pitch the one against the other in a struggle over who possessed the moral right to speak for the whole community. The religious conflict was epitomized by the bitter exchanges over many decades between the Anglican newspaper editor David Owen (Brutus) in *Yr Haul* and David Rees ('The Agitator') in *Y Diwygiwr* during the years 1835–65.

Denominationalism featured strongly in the debate on nationality stemming from the controversy over the Education Report, for it had been an attack not only upon the Welsh nation but upon a specifically Nonconformist Welsh nation. Here the writings and speeches of Henry Richard require special attention. Above all others he embodied the attempt to marry the ideology of Nonconformist

[51] *Y Brython*, 25 June 1858.
[52] Linda Colley, *Britons: Forging the Nation, 1707–1837* (London, 1992), p. 372.

Wales with political action. Known as the 'Member for Wales' after his election to Parliament for Merthyr Tydfil in 1868, he had been a full-time employee of the Liberation Society and an influential propagandist for Nonconformist rights. Stung into action by an editorial in *The Times* in 1866 deprecating the Welsh, Henry Richard published a series of articles in the London press claiming to be 'in some humble measure an interpreter between Wales and England'. He provided a historical analysis which emphasized the utter failure of the established Church in Wales since the time of the Protestant Reformation. He used this platform to drive home the point that the grievances which Nonconformists perceived as stemming from the existence of the church were not of a temporary or superficial nature – and thus capable of piecemeal reform – but 'sprang largely from the very constitution and character of an establishment'. By contrast, the religious needs of the people had been supplied by voluntarism, the untiring efforts of the Nonconformist denominations. The combination of these factors had, in his view, undermined the rationale for established religion. It was the question of disestablishment, above all others, which transformed religious dissatisfaction into political action. As Richard insisted, 'you cannot vivify a nation's life with new and earnest religious convictions without influencing its character in other directions than those which are expressly religious'.[53]

Religion was the fault line in Welsh society along which political allegiances were determined. But this division was compounded by social distinctions. Richard believed that the majority of the Welsh were Liberals by sympathy and that the minority of the population which constituted the superior classes used their social position and influence to impose uncongenial political opinions on the majority. He identified those guilty of such behaviour as the gentry, the Anglican clergy, and the agents or stewards of the legal profession who acted as middlemen between the gentry and the people. These groups he characterized as Tories to a man. The remainder of society was comprised of a mythical homogeneous Welsh-speaking, Nonconformist, and Liberal *gwerin*, who strove valiantly against the odds for their rights.[54]

These views did not go uncontested. Addressing a meeting at Builth Wells in 1866, D. Noel, curate of Gelli-gaer, rejected the notion that the Welsh were an oppressed people and rejoiced in the fact that they enjoyed the same freedom and privileges under the law as the English. His attitude to the Welsh language was self-consciously utilitarian: it was not its ancient lineage which was of greatest importance, but rather the extent of its present-day practical utility. 'Who is the true patriot?', he asked:

---

[53] Richard, *Letters and Essays*, pp. v, 15, 90.
[54] On the myth of the *gwerin*, see Prys Morgan, 'The Gwerin of Wales: Myth and Reality' in I. Hume and W. T. R. Pryce (eds.), *The Welsh and Their Country* (Llandysul, 1986), pp. 134–52.

Ai yr hwn sydd yn cramio meddwl Cymro gwladaidd ag ystorfa draphlith ac annhrefnus o ddarlleniaeth cyfnodolion Cymreig, neu yr hwn mewn hynawsedd a ddyga i ymarferiad y iaith Seisonig a llenyddiaeth Seisonig i'w bentref cauedig ac anghysbell? Dywedaf yn benderfynol mai yr olaf, canys yr ydym yn byw mewn oes adenedigol – oes y mae pob peth yn newydd, neu wedi ei adferu, hyny yw, pob peth oddi eithr llenyddiaeth Gymreig, yr hon sydd wedi ei threulio allan o'i dywalltiadau aruchel ein beirdd hynafol . . .[55]

(Is it he who crams the mind of the Welsh countryman with a disorderly and chaotic store of reading from Welsh periodicals, or he who in kindness brings the use of the English language and English literature to his secluded and remote village? I tell you resolutely the latter, because we live in an age of rejuvenation – an age in which everything is new or has been restored, that is, everything except Welsh literature, which has been worn out by the majestic outpourings of our ancient bards . . .)

This was an attempt to appropriate the language of patriotism for utilitarian purposes, stressing the need to embrace the English language and literature if the Welsh were to succeed in the modern world. It was the duty of the patriotic Welshman to ensure that this occurred. Such sentiments were not confined to members of the established Church. In fact, this was an echo of debates within the National Eisteddfod itself during the 1860s, when those who set up the predominantly English-language 'Social Science Section' perceived the Welsh language as a romantic relic of former times with little practical utility for the modern age.

Paradoxically, according to this view, prominent Nonconformists such as Henry Richard were to be arraigned before the court of public opinion for their *lack* of patriotism. Richard's achievements were contrasted unfavourably with his constant appeal to patriotism. The new MP for Merthyr Tydfil was reprimanded for his carping correspondence in the press attacking the landowning class, while at the same time he was criticized for failing to display adequate support for the National Eisteddfod. Significantly, Richard's claim that Nonconformity had made Wales a less criminal society was attacked head on by his Anglican critics. It was claimed that fewer serious crimes were committed by the various Celtic peoples than by Teutons; thus, if variations in the incidence of criminal behaviour were to be attributed to racial characteristics, the claims of Nonconformists to have had a beneficial effect on the people's morals could not be sustained. Moreover, in a statement which resurrected the ghosts of 1847, it was claimed that in the areas dominated by Methodism 'the moral atmosphere . . . is full of a black fog, which gives rise to every accursed sin' ('Mae yr awyr foesol . . . yn llawn tawch dudew, yr hwn sydd yn rhoddi bodolaeth i bob pechod ysgymun').[56] Such swingeing

---

[55] D. Noel, 'Ein Gwlad a'n Cenedl', *Yr Haul*, X, no. 120 (1866), 356.
[56] Caron, 'Henry Richard a Moesoldeb Cymru', *Yr Haul*, XIII, no. 156 (1869), 363–5.

criticisms can be seen as part of a struggle for the high ground of Welsh politics which members of the established Church believed could still be won in the 1860s. The entrenchment of Liberalism in Wales over subsequent decades and the controlling influence of Nonconformity over its agenda and priorities rendered this an increasingly fruitless task, despite a revival in Anglican fortunes towards the end of the century.

Shortly before the general election of 1868 Richard wrote that 'it can be said in general terms that the Welsh are a nation of Nonconformists' ('Gellir dyweyd mewn termau cyffredinol fod y Cymry yn genedl o Anghydffurfwyr'), while in his election address at Merthyr Tydfil he presented himself as a suitable candidate to represent a constituency 'where close to the whole population are Nonconformists' ('bwrdeistref lle y mae yn agos at yr holl boblogaeth yn Anghydffurfwyr').[57] This was plainly an ideological statement directed at the pretensions of the Anglican establishment rather than an accurate description of the religious affiliation of the people, for despite the strong support for Dissent nowhere near a majority of the population of Wales (or Merthyr, for that matter) were Nonconformists.[58] Aware that statements of this kind could lead to a charge of sectarianism which might prejudice his chances of being elected as a representative of all voters, Richard claimed that his views were 'so far from being sectarian that they are, by contrast, anti-sectarian in the extreme; because your aim in choosing a Nonconformist as a candidate was to prevent one tyrannical sect [the Church of England] from keeping in its own hands the whole representation of Wales' ('mor bell o fod yn sectyddol, fel y mae, i'r gwrthwyneb, yn wrth sectyddol i'r eithaf; oblegid eich dyben wrth ddewis Anghydffurfiwr yn ymgeisydd, oedd lluddias un sect tra-arglwyddiaethus i gadw yn ei llaw ei hun holl gynrychiolaeth Cymry [sic] . . .').[59]

These sentiments were rooted in a vibrant democratic culture which challenged the power of landlordism and the religious establishment and the politics of deference upon which they depended. Increasingly Richard moved beyond a simple appeal to a Nonconformist constituency to defining the Welsh nation exclusively in terms of Nonconformity. This particular way of thinking about Wales shaped the dominant language of politics for decades afterwards. The full impact of this democratic (yet at the same time implicitly sectarian) ethos can be seen in a powerful speech to electors in 1868 when Richard eloquently fleshed out his view of the nation:

> The people who speak this language [Welsh], who read this literature, who own this history, who inherit these traditions, who venerate these marvellous religious organizations, the people forming three-fourths of the people of Wales – have they not

[57] *Y Gwladgarwr*, 13 June, 18 July 1868.
[58] John Davies, *A History of Wales* (London, 1993), pp. 423–7.
[59] *Y Gwladgarwr*, 13 June, 18 July 1868.

a right to say to this small propertied class . . . We are the Welsh people and not you? This country is ours and not yours, and therefore we claim to have our principles represented in the Commons' House of Parliament.[60]

This can be seen as an attempt to create a myth of an organic Welsh nation in the image of Nonconformity. According to this definition, the key institutions are the chapels, and the people who frequent them are defined against an Anglicized or English ruling class. The definition establishes a system of shared identifications, thereby charting boundaries between those who belong and those who do not. Thus, the 'nation' was not coterminous with the entire population of Wales.

The élite of this Nonconformist nation found their martyrs in the general election of 1868. The results of the election were a decisive affirmation of support for Liberalism. There were famous political upsets – such as those which occurred in industrial Merthyr Tydfil in the south and Denbighshire in the north – but the social character of the country's political representatives remained little changed. Of the twenty-three Liberals elected, the vast majority derived from the landed class, as did all ten Conservatives. The political order was shaken, but remained largely intact. The true significance of 1868 lies in the aftermath of the elections when numbers of tenants who had voted against the wishes of their landlords were evicted. The popular outrage against these actions can be gauged by the fact that a fund for the relief of homeless tenants raised the not inconsiderable sum of £20,000.[61] Against this background, the epigram *Trech gwlad nag arglwydd* (A land is mightier than a lord) acquired new, and immediate, shades of political meaning.

The events of 1868 mark a decisive point in the politicization of Welsh patriotism, even if the crucial watershed in parliamentary representation did not occur until the 1880s. If the language of Welsh patriotism was shaped by the Blue Books controversy, its grammar was codified in 1868. Whereas it had been possible for Anglicans to assert their Welshness before this, it now became increasingly problematic for them to do so. Moreover, as Anglicans were routinely coupled with Conservatism, they were hampered by developments in England in the 1870s where the language of patriotism underwent a shift to the right under the influence of Disraeli and the fragmentation of the radical patriotism of the Chartist era, and became associated more closely with a self-conscious Englishness. No such development occurred in Wales. While the language of tyranny no longer seemed appropriate to the liberalized British state of the 1870s, the language of oppression found new resonances in Wales in the battle against landlordism and the campaign for disestablishment. In such a context, the self-

[60] *Aberdare Times*, 14 November 1868. Quoted in Kenneth O. Morgan, *Wales in British Politics, 1868–1922* (3rd ed., Cardiff, 1980), p. v. The speech is analysed fully in Ieuan Gwynedd Jones, 'Henry Richard ac Iaith y Gwleidydd yn y Bedwaredd Ganrif ar Bymtheg' in Geraint H. Jenkins (ed.), *Cof Cenedl III: Ysgrifau ar Hanes Cymru* (Llandysul, 1988), pp. 117–49.
[61] Morgan, *Wales in British Politics*, pp. 25–7; Jones, *Explorations and Explanations*, chapters 3–5.

consciously English nationalism championed by Disraeli was poorly placed to make headway in Wales.[62]

This is demonstrated by the reaction of the Welsh press to Disraeli's speeches in Manchester and at the Crystal Palace in 1872, where he attempted to educate his party in the fundamental principles of Conservatism by emphasizing that the Liberals represented 'cosmopolitan' principles, whereas his own party embodied 'national' principles. This was clearly an attempt to appropriate the rhetoric of patriotism from the Liberals who had hitherto monopolized it.[63] The response of the Welsh press suggests that at the level of language as well as parliamentary representation this was a failure. One paper felt that Disraeli's audience would have been disappointed to hear nothing more than platitudes about the British constitution and national institutions, and asserted that on this evidence there was nothing to distinguish Tory statesmanship ('gwladlywiaeth') from that of Gladstone.[64] Other newspapers did not consider this aspect of his speech of sufficient importance to merit attention. *Y Tyst a'r Dydd* reported the Manchester speech almost entirely in terms of the implications of his comments for Nonconformity.[65] Reporting from a denominational perspective ensured that Disraeli's appeal for loyalty to national institutions was filtered through a mesh of cultural assumptions which neutered its political impact.

Symbolically, many Welsh-language newspapers failed to report Disraeli's speech at the Crystal Palace. But they did give extensive coverage to an event which occurred at the same venue shortly afterwards – the national Musical Competition, in which a choir from south Wales was triumphant. The success sent commentators into raptures of national pride:

Dyma oresgyniad Lloegr gan Gymry heddychlawn. Dyma orchest a wna iawn am gyfnod maith o wawd a dirmyg. Bu y Saeson yn chwerthin am ben ein gwlad, yn poeri ar ein defodau, yn cablu urddas y Cymry. Buont yn gosod yr Eisteddfod fel bwgan brain o flaen llygaid y cenhedloedd . . . a chyhuddent y genedl fwyaf ffyddlawn i'r awdurdodau o deyrn-fradwriaeth, am ei bod yn meiddio bod yn genedlgarol . . . Ond dyma droi y byrddau arnynt. Wele Eisteddfod Genedlaethol y Cymry, yn ngwaethaf y *Times* a'i ddynwaredwyr, wedi dyfod yn Eisteddfod Ymherodrol Prydain fawr . . .[66]

(Here is the conquest of England by peaceful Wales. Here is a feat which makes amends for a long period of scorn and contempt. The English laughed at our country, spat on our customs, blasphemed against the dignity of the Welsh. They placed the Eisteddfod before the eyes of the nations like a scarecrow . . . and they accused the most loyal of

---

[62] Hugh Cunningham, 'The Language of Patriotism, 1750–1914', *History Workshop Journal*, 12 (1981), 8–33; idem, 'The Conservative Party and Patriotism' in R. Colls and P. Dodds (eds.), *Englishness: Politics and Culture, 1880–1920* (London, 1986), pp. 238–307.

[63] Cunningham, 'The Language of Patriotism', 22.

[64] *BAC*, 10 April 1872.

[65] *Y Tyst a'r Dydd*, 12 April 1872.

[66] Ibid., 12 July 1872.

nations of being traitors, because they dared to be patriotic . . . But now the tables have been turned on them. And now the National Eisteddfod of the Welsh, despite the *Times* and its imitators, has become the Imperial Eisteddfod of Great Britain . . .)

The symbolic significance of the victory was enhanced by the fact that the choristers were drawn mainly from Henry Richard's own constituency, and in a reception in London to mark their success he warmly congratulated them for their part in projecting a more positive view of the Welsh among their English neighbours.

That this choir had an appeal far wider than the geographical origins of its local membership was emphasized long before the competition took place by the campaign to collect voluntary contributions to ease the financial burdens of the choristers who, as working men, incurred onerous costs not only because of train fares and subsistence but also through the loss of wages during their absence. Supporting an appeal for help at the beginning of June, the north-Wales-based *Baner ac Amserau Cymru* commented 'we are all by now beginning to look upon it in a kind of "national" light' ('yr ydym oll erbyn hyn yn dechreu edrych ar y peth mewn math o oleu "cenedlaethol" ').[67] The paper applauded the choir's victory as enthusiastically as did the press in south Wales.

Success in the first competition in 1872 raised hopes for a repeat of the achievement the following year. On this occasion no room was left to doubt that the 'South Wales Choir' represented the whole of Wales – even the Welsh in America presented it with a sum of money to help defray expenses. The Conservative *Western Mail* dispatched a special correspondent to accompany the choristers on the rail journey to London. He was left in no doubt that 'this musical contest affair is a national thing – not local, sectional, or peculiar to a class: it is an event which goes to the core of the people's heart'. On arriving in London he presented the choir with a cheque for £14 18s. 10d. on behalf of his paper's manager.[68] Given the tremendous popularity of the event, it made sound commercial sense for the paper to provide its readers with full reports of the competition, its patriotism reinforcing self-interest. However, more surprising was the newspaper's audacious attempt to capture the patriotic rhetoric of the time. In the edition reporting the choir's second success, the leader titled 'Cambria's Triumph' asserted that events in the Crystal Palace concluded an episode begun in the thirteenth century:

This morning we publish to the people of Wales the news that King Edward's massacre of the Welsh bards has at length been avenged. It will be observed that on this occasion we display – and surely on this occasion we have sufficient reason for doing so – the

[67] *BAC*, 5 June 1872.
[68] *Western Mail*, 8–9 July 1873. Messrs. Howell and Co. of Cardiff presented the choir with the national flag.

utmost contempt for Mr FREEMAN and the whole modern school of historical critics. We eagerly accept the legend upon which GRAY's ode is founded, for the purpose of pointing out that the designs of the 'ruthless King' have, after the lapse of centuries, been signally defeated. The spirit of Welsh song, which the PLANTAGENET conqueror fondly imagined could be crushed by the slaughter of the sweet singers – which sometimes under the ban of proscription, and never until now under the sunshine of aristocratic and princely favour, has haunted the valleys of Cambria – has at last burst from the narrow limits which could no longer restrain its ever-increasing vitality, and asserted itself as a power which commands the attention of the United Kingdom.[69]

For a Welsh Conservative paper, it made startling reading. Ironically, in one sense it is a tribute to the dominance of the ideology of Nonconformist Wales, for it uses the same underlying 'grammar' of patriotic discourse. Its approach to the competition in 1873 was clearly an attempt to appropriate this popular event from the Nonconformist Liberal press in general and from Henry Richard in particular. As in 1872, Henry Richard basked in the reflected glory of the choir's achievement when he presented its leader with the Silver Cup in the Crystal Palace. Welsh honour had been vindicated by retaining the prize on the second occasion, with the Welsh-language press describing the five hundred simply as 'the Welsh choir'.[70] However, the *Western Mail*'s arrangement to telegraph the results of the competition for display outside its offices throughout Wales as soon as they became available made it the country's most advanced purveyor of news.[71] The crowds which gathered outside its offices to hear the news could not fail to recognize that the Tory newspaper had stolen a march on its Liberal rivals.

The 1870s was a period of Conservative counter-attack. Conservatives were so incensed about the force and impact of Henry Richard's speeches and writings that the *Western Mail* went so far as to give its tacit support for Thomas Halliday's candidature as a direct representative of labour in the Merthyr Boroughs constituency in 1873.[72] The implication was obvious: Richard had been elected by a combination of the Nonconformist and miners' vote in 1868; by dividing that coalition, it was possible that he would lose his seat at the next election. In the event, Halliday polled strongly, but not sufficiently well to unseat the incumbent.

Liberal hubris after 1868 had been encouraged by the passing of the Secret Ballot Act in 1872, partly because of the testimony on Welsh evictions presented to Parliament by Henry Richard. However, although the Act held out the

---

[69] Ibid., 11 July 1873.
[70] *Y Tyst a'r Dydd*, 13 July 1873.
[71] *Western Mail*, 11 July 1873. It published a poem composed by Mr J. H. Hughes of Newport, 'Cambria's Five Hundred', based on Tennyson's 'Charge of the Light Brigade'.
[72] Ibid., 2 July 1873. It alluded in disparaging terms to Richard's patriotic rhetoric as 'his native instincts' which were 'constantly ventilated in the sickly sentimentalism of his speeches'.

prospect of the removal of intimidation from elections it did not have the immediate impact which had been anticipated. Many voters had an imperfect understanding of the new provisions, and the memory of landlord intimidation died hard. Furthermore, compared with 1868, the Conservatives found much to cheer them in the general election of 1874 when they won fourteen seats in Wales compared with the nineteen retained by the Liberals. Even these figures give an inflated picture of Liberal fortunes since three of their representatives were returned by the narrowest of margins.[73] Any comfort Conservatives derived from this would be curtailed from 1880 when Liberalism consolidated its electoral strength in Wales and extended its successes once again. From then until after the First World War (and beyond), the Conservatives would remain a minority party in Wales.

However, the 1870s also witnessed attempts to fashion a new patriotic ideology for the established Church in Wales which took account of the new religious and political realities. The example of Irish disestablishment, the tireless propaganda of the Liberation Society and the advocacy of Henry Richard in Parliament prompted some clerics to rethink their position in society.

A direct counter-attack on the Nonconformist conception of Welsh nationality was led by articulate and influential figures such as Henry T. Edwards, vicar of Caernarfon and subsequently dean of Bangor. Edwards believed that the underlying religious unity of Wales had been fractured by the Methodist secession from the Church in 1811 and the spirit of sectarian Dissent which resulted from that split. While he was willing to recognize that the fault lay in part with the practice of appointing English bishops unsympathetic to Welsh spirituality and the resulting closure of opportunities for Welsh churchmen, it is plain that he believed the Church to be the only institution with the ability to restore unity. His letter to William Gladstone in favour of the appointment of Welsh-speaking bishops to Welsh dioceses, published in 1870, offered an alternative interpretation of Welsh history from the standpoint of the Church in which he acknowledged the manifest reality that 70 per cent of the Welsh people had deserted established religion. Even this figure erred on the optimistic side. However, Edwards was of the opinion that this was not the result of opposition to the Church's dogma; he believed it was a 'protest . . . against the cold, alien, mechanical forms of thought, feeling and diction, in which these doctrines have been preached, and those Sacraments have been administered to the souls of an impassioned race'. In his view, the problem lay 'not in the spiritual treasures of the Church, but in the earthen vessels to which they have been committed'.[74] His analysis depended upon a racial contrast between the English as a more practical and 'energetic'

---

[73] Morgan, *Wales in British Politics*, pp. 37–9.
[74] Henry T. Edwards, *The Church of the Cymry: A Letter to the Right Hon. W. E. Gladstone, M.P.* (London, 1870), pp. 4–5.

people, and the spiritual Welsh. Edwards recognized the distinctive character of the Welsh people:

> Every respect has been studiously paid to the spirit of Scotch nationality. Is it fair that the equally ancient Cymric nationality, more strongly marked, as it is, by the retention of its national language, should be crushed out? True sentiment and true expediency alike declare, I believe, against a policy so ungenerous, so expressive of the worst attributes of the English national temper – attributes which, above all others, have had the effect of involving the empire in strife and perplexity . . . Surely every generous sentiment . . . dictates that this ancient, loyal, industrious and order-loving people should, within the obvious limits compatible with the imperial welfare of the entire British people, be permitted to cherish the traditions, and to develop the free impulses of their distinct national character. The truest utilitarianism will also be found in harmony with the dictates of this sentiment.[75]

'The obvious limits compatible with the imperial welfare of the entire British people' were not specified. While he declared his support for a national university and a Welsh (and Welsh-speaking) episcopate, Edwards was unwilling to welcome disestablishment.

Despite these limitations, a faint echo of Gladstonian principles as they were to evolve over the coming decades is discernible. For Edwards, Welsh nationality was not to be extinguished in favour of a centralist and monolithic 'Britishness'. As far as he was concerned, 'the distinct national character of the Cymry is an objective reality – one of the living forces in the imperial life of the British people'.[76] Establishing limits to this once Ireland had already been granted disestablishment on the grounds of circumstances deriving from a different nationality entailed walking a precarious tightrope. The position was exposed even further during the 1870s. Moreover, it is not clear how many other Anglicans subscribed to this analysis.

Edwards's lectures and publications during the 1870s represent a determined attempt to wrest the initiative from Nonconformity by fashioning an interpretation of the historic role and future destiny of the Church in Welsh life. This entailed recognizing the past failures of the Church and arguing in favour of reforms which fell short of disestablishment. By continually underlining the fact that he was actuated by a spirit of patriotism, his writings can be construed as an attempt to engage with the debate on nationality begun by Nonconformists in the 1860s rather than merely dismissing their claims out of hand. His views were sufficiently worrying for the Nonconformist press to attack him for failing to read the signs of the times.[77] Edwards confronted the claims of the Liberation Society

---

[75] Ibid., pp. 50–1.
[76] Ibid., p. 52.
[77] See, for example, *Y Tyst a'r Dydd*, 28 November 1873.

head on, partly by holding out the prospect that Catholicism ('that dangerous false theocracy') might occupy the place vacated by a disestablished Church. Taking as a cautionary example the separation of church and state in America, he claimed that the divided Protestant sects in that country had been unequal to the task of opposing the 'Catholic Peril'. The growth of the Catholic Church in America was so great that he foresaw it capturing the reins of government and electing a 'Popish President' by 1900.[78]

Edwards was happy to be labelled a 'political parson', and continued to attack Nonconformist ministers not for their participation in political life but for overstepping the legitimate bounds of their intervention by agitating against landlordism and the Church during the 1868 elections. While rejecting the dictum that 'requires every clergyman to sink the citizen in the Priest, and because he is a minister of religion, to forget that he ought to be a patriot', he was critical of the use of electioneering during chapel services and the substitution of a political harangue for the sermon.[79] 'Designing self-seeking agitators' who ruthlessly pressed their demands on the inexperienced multitude were to be deplored. In 1868 the effect of such agitators in many new constituencies ('being young and green, and somewhat warm in their affections') had been to reject 'the most solid, sensible, sober-minded suitors' in favour of 'landless adventurers'.[80] Consequently, he insisted that his opposition to disestablishment was grounded in Welsh patriotism and a desire to protect his native land.

Not all of Edwards's swingeing comments were directed at external opponents. His trenchant address at the Church Congress held at Swansea in 1879 could scarcely have endeared him to his fellow clergy. While he recognized the material progress made in recent decades in terms of the erection of places of worship, parsonages and schools, and the effort expended on restoring the cathedrals, he pointed out that this had not attracted people back to the pews. He also believed it was necessary to change popular perceptions of Anglicanism. The Church had to be treated as belonging to the Welsh people, rather than as a preserve of the English-speaking minority, and this entailed directing resources to the training of Welsh-speaking ministers who were fluent and powerful preachers in the

---

[78] Henry T. Edwards, *The Position and Resources of the National Church* (Cardiff, 1876), p. 7. Translated as *Sefyllfa ac Adnoddau yr Eglwys Genedlaethol* (Rhyl, 1876).

[79] Henry T. Edwards, *Politics in Wales: The Dangers of Pilatism* (Llangollen, 1872), pp. 1–3. Edwards adroitly alluded to the accusation that Nonconformist ministers had used the chapel 'screw', while stating that he had no definitive evidence to prove or disprove it. On this issue, see Matthew Cragoe, 'Conscience or Coercion? Clerical Influence at the General Election of 1868 in Wales', *P&P*, 149 (1995), 140–69.

[80] Edwards, *Politics in Wales*, pp. 14–19.

language.[81] Several members of the audience found the force and directness of his speech unpalatable, and the chairman, Lord Aberdare, was clearly discomfited.

Regarding the Welsh-language press, Edwards complained that 'although professedly religious organs', they were, with few exceptions, 'printed in the gall of sectarian bitterness, their overriding aim being to secure the disestablishment and disendowment of the Church'.[82] A sign of the determination of the Church to regain the initiative can be discerned in the heated discussion of the condition of the Welsh Church press and the steps necessary to reform it which took place at the Church Congress held at Swansea in 1879. An address delivered by David Williams, rector of Llandyrnog in Denbighshire, did not please his audience. Williams claimed that the Church's only weekly, *Y Dywysogaeth*, was 'in a moribund condition' and that the few papers 'given to teach Church principles and constitutional forms of government' were 'feebly conducted, indifferently circulated, and lead a most precarious existence'.[83] He spared his audience no blushes in attributing this state of affairs to bishops who sneered at the Welsh language – a statement which agitated and angered the elderly bishop of Llandaff, who was present. The outcome of this heated debate was productive in so far as it breathed new life into the Church press. Indeed, there occurred a revival in Anglican fortunes despite the heated controversy over the appointment of Welsh bishops and the increasingly sharp public exchanges between Nonconformists and Anglicans on the question of the disestablishment and disendowment of the Church of England in Wales. Nevertheless, the language of politics was increasingly determined by the Nonconformist conscience.

The dominant Welsh patriotism, expressed through an attachment to Liberalism, continued to be oppositional in the sense that it sought to reform the British state according to the principles of Protestant Nonconformity. But it sought a comparatively limited reform to achieve equality within Britain rather than a root and branch transformation. In some senses, patriotic discourse in the mid-nineteenth century can be seen in terms of a struggle for power over the values and agenda of political life. The Conservative Party, which was inextricably associated with Anglicanism and an Anglicized aristocracy, had little support in Wales, and failed to win a majority of Welsh seats in any election down to 1914. But Anglicans and Tories did not abandon the battleground without a fight. To this extent, the debates of the 1870s, when individuals within the Church

---

[81] *Report of the Nineteenth Annual Meeting of the Church Congress Held at Swansea, 1879* (London, 1880), pp. 354–8. This demand was made at a time when the Welsh Nonconformist denominations were increasingly preoccupied with the question of whether or not they should provide chapels for English in-migrants. The 'English causes' are discussed in Hywel Teifi Edwards, *Codi'r Hen Wlad yn Ei Hôl, 1850–1914* (Llandysul, 1989), chapter 5, and Frank Price Jones, *Radicaliaeth a'r Werin Gymreig yn y Bedwaredd Ganrif ar Bymtheg* (Caerdydd, 1977), chapter 6.

[82] Edwards, *The Church of the Cymry*, p. 39.

[83] *Report of the Nineteenth Annual Meeting of the Church Congress . . . 1879*, pp. 558–9.

attempted to wrest the initiative from Nonconformity, have been unduly neglected by historians. During this decade there was a sustained effort to challenge and undermine the assumptions which underpinned the ideology of the Nonconformist nation. That this challenge ended in failure is attributable in part to the enduring memory of the evictions of 1868 and the onset of the Tithe War in north-east Wales in 1886. These events were sufficient to reinforce the lesson assiduously taught by the Liberation Society that politics and religion were conjoined.

Although both Liberals and Nonconformists strove hard to appropriate the language of patriotism, it was not the property of one sector of Welsh society alone. Rather, it defined the contested territory between Nonconformists and Anglicans, and between Liberals and Conservatives. It was on this territory that the key cultural and political battles of the period were fought. This can be seen in the attempts by Anglicans to regain the initiative in Welsh life in the 1870s by addressing their own neglect of the Welsh language and the drive to create a vigorous Anglican Welsh-language press. This development suggests that, while the Welsh language was not at the heart of ethnic mobilization in nineteenth-century Wales, some groups whose patriotism was perceived to be in doubt were willing to emphasize language as a symbol of their patriotic credentials. By comparison, Nonconformists felt sufficiently secure in their Welshness not to make this an issue.

At the same time, other languages of patriotism began to emerge around a more self-conscious loyalty to empire and the monarchy. In this respect, the Welsh experience mirrors wider developments in the United Kingdom. However, there were equally significant differences. Whereas during the 1870s the language of patriotism in England was appropriated by Disraeli and the Conservative Party, in Wales Liberalism continued to dominate the political landscape and acted as the glue which locked the two countries together. Only rarely was the voice of a more assertive nationalism heard. R. Merfyn Jones has claimed that the slate-quarrying communities of north Wales possessed no more than 'limited, closed and essentially defensive ideas of nationality'.[84] This judgement is borne out by a more general study of the language of patriotism. But patriotism was more than an epiphenomenon to be dismissed as mere rhetoric. On the contrary, it shaped – and in turn was shaped by – the central debates in Welsh society.[85]

From the 1880s significant changes are discernible in the nature and expression of patriotism in Wales. Some politicians and intellectuals flirted with a more assertive political nationalism in the form of the Cymru Fydd ('Young Wales') movement, while the birth of the Society for Utilizing the Welsh Language in

---

[84] R. Merfyn Jones, *The North Wales Quarrymen, 1870–1922* (Cardiff, 1980), p. 71.
[85] As shown by the language used by journalists to report the 'Red Dragon Revolt' of Welsh trade unionists in 1874. See Aled Jones, 'Trade Unions and the Press: Journalism and the Red Dragon Revolt of 1874', *WHR*, 12, no. 2 (1984), 197–224.

1885 provided evidence of limited, but unprecedented, campaigning on behalf of the Welsh language in education. At the same time, the first stirrings of agitation for labour representation can be discerned in the election of William Abraham (Mabon) in the Rhondda in 1886. Yet, the terms in which patriotism had been expressed in the mid-century were not entirely cast aside in the face of changing political and cultural conditions. A concern for the good reputation of the Welsh people among outsiders would remain a prominent feature of public life as the Welsh frequently protested their loyalty to the Empire in the late Victorian and Edwardian periods. It was within and against these values, expressed through a language of patriotism, that the debates about cultural and linguistic change were conducted.

20

'Yn Llawn o Dân Cymreig'[1] (Full of Welsh Fire): The Language of Politics in Wales 1880–1914

NEIL EVANS and KATE SULLIVAN

IN THE LATE nineteenth century Welsh became a major language of politics, sharing this position with English.[2] Welsh was always more widely used in north and west Wales, where monoglot Welsh speakers were a substantial part of the population. In the counties of Anglesey, Caernarfon, Merioneth and Cardigan they formed around half the adult male population in 1901 and over a third in Carmarthenshire and a fifth in Denbighshire. In Radnorshire and Monmouthshire, however, the proportions of Welsh speakers were extremely low. In these circumstances, the emergence of Welsh as a political language was a substantial result of the widening of the franchise between the 1860s and the 1880s.

In 1862 people bemoaned the fact that Welsh was rarely heard in elections, and that this contributed to political apathy in Wales: 'They can scarcely be expected to throw their hearts into an occasion that excommunicates their mother tongue' ('Prin y gellir disgwyl iddynt daflu eu calon i amgylchiad sydd yn esgymuno iaith eu genau').[3] Within a decade Welsh was making some headway in politics. One Welsh MP, E. J. Sartoris, felt obliged to learn sufficient Welsh to enable him to communicate with his constituents at Pontarddulais.[4] Non-Welsh-speaking candidates were at a disadvantage in the largely Welsh-speaking electorate of Merthyr. In the 1874 election both the ironmaster Richard Fothergill and the trade union leader Thomas Halliday were obliged to use Welsh translators at their meetings.[5] The use of Welsh in elections increased considerably during

---

[1] A description of a speech by the Revd T. Evans at Trecastell, Breconshire, reported in *BAC*, 24 March 1880.
[2] We would like to thank Vincent Comerford, Ieuan Gwynedd Jones, Mark Ellis Jones, Rosemary Jones, David W. Howell, Marion Löffler, Jon Parry and Einion Thomas for their help and for references.
[3] *BAC*, 27 August 1862.
[4] *Seren Cymru*, 20 September 1872.
[5] Elizabeth Cunningham, 'Thomas Halliday and the Merthyr Election of 1874' (unpubl. University of Wales Diploma in General Studies dissertation, Coleg Harlech, 1996).

Gladstone's second government; Tom Ellis's campaign in Merioneth in 1886 was credited with bringing Welsh to the fore as a political language.[6]

This position might appear unremarkable, but it contrasted starkly with the limited role of the Irish language in politics. Daniel O'Connell brought mass politics to Ireland but, despite the fact that he was a fluent Irish speaker, he rarely used the language in political meetings. As a utilitarian, he saw the disappearance of Irish as a badge of modernization and hence as part of Ireland's claim for repeal of the legislative union. It was only in exceptional circumstances that he, and some of his supporters, used the vernacular, usually when there were pressing practical reasons for doing so. He may have been influenced by the approach of the Catholic Church, which tended to see Irish as a pagan survival, and by the fact that his major appeals were made outside areas where Irish was habitually spoken and at a time when the early strongholds of his political movement were cities like Dublin and Cork.[7] By the time mass voting arrived in Ireland, the native language was in a steep decline. In the course of the nineteenth century the proportion of monoglot Irish speakers fell from half the population to half of one per cent: in 1901 one in seven of the population understood Irish and only one in 200 did not understand English. Irish was adopted by the Gaelic League – as a symbol like harps and shamrocks – when it was losing ground in the real world. Cultural nationalism flourished after the collapse of the Home Rule movement in the wake of the fall of Parnell. The early publications of the Gaelic League were almost entirely in English and no role was envisaged for the Irish language in politics. Only between 1910 and 1920 did the League shift towards political involvement, though Irish did not become a language of politics. The general feeling seems to have been that voters would have felt insulted had they been addressed in Irish. It would have been a sign that they did not understand English.[8]

This contrast between Ireland and Wales impressed Michael Davitt when he embarked on his famous lecture tour of Wales in 1886. He was informed that a considerable proportion of his audience in Blaenau Ffestiniog were not fluent in English though they understood it, and some surprise was expressed that the quarrymen listened to him speak in English for almost an hour and showed by

---

[6] *South Wales Daily News*, 6 April 1899.
[7] Oliver MacDonagh, *The Hereditary Bondsman: Daniel O'Connell* (London, 1988), pp. 11–14; Fergus O'Ferrall, *Daniel O'Connell* (Dublin, 1981), pp. 138–9; idem, *Catholic Emancipation: Daniel O'Connell and the Birth of Irish Democracy, 1820–30* (Dublin, 1985), pp. 192, 194; K. Theodore Hoppen, *Ireland since 1800: Conflict and Conformity* (London, 1989), pp. 2, 19, 28, 131; David Dickson, 'Second City Syndrome: Reflections on Three Irish Cases', a paper presented to the British Academy / Central Community Relations Unit Conference on 'Integration and Diversity in the British Isles since 1550', University of Ulster, Coleraine, 1–3 April 1996.
[8] Georg Grote, *Torn between Politics and Culture: The Gaelic League, 1893–1993* (Münster / New York, 1994), pp. 44, 49, 51–2, 57, 59, 111–14; Hoppen, *Ireland since 1800*, pp. 2, 131.

their interjections that they had understood him.[9] Davitt himself felt that he was inhibited by not being able to address his audience in their native language:

> All the speeches except my own were delivered in Welsh, and the enthusiasm and native eloquence evoked made me wish that I could get at the hearts and intellects of the people through the medium of their tongue.[10]

In north Wales, at least, it was necessary to use Welsh in order to gain a full hold on the sympathies of the electorate. Tom Ellis was credited with advancing the use of Welsh in politics, and certainly his generation of new MPs showed a commitment to the language which had been lacking in the past. But the use of Welsh for political purposes was already well established before he arrived on the political scene. In 1880 election addresses had been delivered in Welsh at Dolgellau and Corwen in his native Merioneth.[11] Indeed, in that year Welsh was used in political meetings in places as far apart as Wrexham, Tregaron, Bethesda and Denbigh, all of which were situated in predominantly Welsh-speaking counties with large monoglot populations.[12] Elsewhere, too, Welsh was used more widely. In 1880 Henry Richard spoke in 'Cymraeg loyw' (polished Welsh) at Merthyr and at a huge demonstration at the Crystal Palace to celebrate the great Liberal election victories of that year. In later elections William Abraham (Mabon) spoke Welsh at Maesteg and Maerdy, and other speakers used the language in Swansea and at Hirwaun.[13] From 1885 to 1910 many speakers routinely spoke Welsh at political meetings: William Jones at Borth, Osmond Williams in Merioneth, Mabon in the Rhondda, Lloyd George at Carmarthen and at Conwy, and W. Llewelyn Williams added a rousing Welsh peroration to an English speech delivered at Carmarthen. Even in Anglicized Cardiff there was at least the tokenism of singing 'Hen Wlad fy Nhadau' (Land of my Fathers) at the end of a meeting. Similarly, J. Herbert Lewis's wife explained the reasons for her husband's absence in Welsh before turning to English to address political issues. Alfred Mond's wife was given an enthusiastic welcome when she spoke a few words in Welsh in Swansea at the start of a political meeting.[14]

Although Welsh speeches were still being delivered in the Rhondda in 1906, by 1910 there were complaints about the growing use of English in political meetings. A Welsh speech delivered by W. Llewelyn Williams was said to have been so magnificent that it ought to be repeated in all parts of Wales in order to

---

[9] *Cambrian News*, 19 February, 23 April 1886; NLW, William George Papers, Lloyd George Diary, 12 February 1886.
[10] Davitt to Bryant, *Cambrian News*, 23 April 1886.
[11] Ibid., 19 March 1880.
[12] Ibid.; *Carnarvon and Denbigh Herald*, 20 March 1880.
[13] *BAC*, 24 March 1880, 18 March 1885, 20 January 1892; *Cambrian News*, 8 January 1892; *Western Mail*, 11 January 1910; Charles S. Miall, *Henry Richard, M.P.: A Biography* (London, 1889), p. 314n.
[14] *Cambrian News*, 9, 23 October 1885; *Western Mail*, 4, 5 July 1892; *South Wales Daily News*, 23 December 1905, 4 January 1906, 10 January 1910; *BAC*, 5, 22, January 1910.

revive the practice of addressing audiences in Welsh.[15] In Monmouthshire 'Welsh is never heard at public meetings',[16] but the language was still being used in industrial Glamorgan. In 1910 bilingual meetings were held in many parts of south Wales – in Burry Port, East Carmarthen, Felindre, Pentre-bach, Blaen-y-pant and Dowlais. More surprising, perhaps, was the use of Welsh at political meetings at St Helens and Birkenhead. However, its use across the border was often fraught with difficulty. One Welsh woman who interjected in her native tongue when Lloyd George was speaking at Cannock was almost ejected on suspicion of being a suffragette![17]

It is not possible to be precise about the language of meetings or about the proportions of Welsh and English used, for often the press reports upon which we are largely dependent do not specify which language was employed. Sometimes reporters noted that certain speeches were delivered in Welsh, but it is evident that English-language newspapers frequently failed to record the fact that they were reporting Welsh speeches in English. Conservatives were often abused for their inability to speak the native language, but no indication was given that the Liberals were speaking Welsh. In many areas there was no need to comment on the fact that political meetings were conducted in Welsh: it was one of the fixed points in life and society. A slightly later example gives us some indication of the extensive use of Welsh as a political language in some parts of Wales. When, in 1922, the quarrymen's leader R. T. Jones won Caernarfon for Labour, the *Daily Herald* recorded, a little incredulously, that only one of the eighty-nine election addresses he had delivered in the month of November had been in English.[18]

Quantitative evidence of the language of Liberal politics is provided by the speakers' lists which the party issued towards the end of our period. The first annual report of the Welsh Liberal Council contained a substantial list. Sixty-one speakers were bilingual and, although they originated from various parts of Wales, a disproportionate number were natives of mid- and north Wales. Only five of the forty-seven whose speeches were in Welsh hailed from industrial south Wales, two of whom came from Llanelli. The forty-one English speakers were from south Wales. The implications of this are clear, though they do not mean that Welsh was excluded from meetings in south Wales, given the number of bilingual speakers available. In a list of 1910 there is a confusing categorization. Of the fifty-eight speakers, nine spoke English only, twenty-eight were bilingual and three spoke Welsh only. Eighteen remained unclassified. Another list issued at the same time had eleven bilingual speakers, eight Welsh speakers and seven English speakers.[19]

---

[15] *Tarian y Gweithiwr*, 6 January 1910.
[16] *South Wales Daily News*, 18 January 1910.
[17] Ibid., 1, 3, 5, 7 January 1910; *BAC*, 19 January 1910; *Y Brython*, 20 January 1910; *Western Mail*, 17 January 1910.
[18] Gwynedd Archives Service, North Wales Quarrymen's Union Collection, XNWQU 256. Scrapbook of R. T. Jones, cutting from *Daily Herald*, 26 February 1923.
[19] NLW, WPA, Welsh Liberal Council, Annual Report, 1898–9; List of Speakers, 1910.

The Liberals also provided considerable quantities of political literature in Welsh, a tradition which at least dated to the 1860s, when Henry Richard's *Letters on the Social and Political Condition of the Principality of Wales* had been translated into Welsh and appeared in at least three Welsh-language newspapers.[20] Portions of Gladstone's Midlothian speeches appeared in Welsh – 'Argraphedig at Wasanaeth Etholwyr Cymru yn Gyffredinol' (Printed for the Benefit of the Electors of Wales in General)[21] – as did his later speeches in the constituency in 1885.[22] The official party machinery began to translate leaflets into Welsh from the time of the creation of the North and South Wales Liberal Federations in 1886 and it was considered essential that the colporteur established in north Wales should have the ability to speak both languages. This ensured that articles on the Home Rule issue were translated into Welsh.[23] Most of the major pamphlets on Welsh politics in this period appeared in both languages; for instance, Henry Jones's *Wales and its Prospects*, the various writings of T. J. Hughes (Adfyfr) on the land question and other issues, Mrs Wynford Phillips's *Appeal to Welshwomen*, and a pamphlet by Tom Ellis on the Local Government Act of 1888.[24] A series of pamphlets published by the Cobden Club on free trade was also translated into Welsh, as was a satirical pamphlet, originating from Birmingham, *Llyfrau Benjamin*, lampooning Disraeli's government with the aid of biblical references. Despite all this effort, however, the bulk of the available political literature was in English. Welsh politicians could draw on the whole of the resources of England and seem to have done so freely. In 1887 the South Wales Liberal Federation listed its recommended political publications in both languages. The Welsh publications number eleven, the English thirty-eight.[25]

Election addresses were commonly printed in both languages, or separately in Welsh and English. The main exception to this pattern of bilingualism is to be found in south Wales at the end of this period. In 1910 one newspaper believed that candidates should issue their election addresses in Welsh in south Wales, given the strength of Welsh patriotism; the implication of this is that few were doing so. This defect was only partly remedied by *Tarian y Gweithiwr*, which published Edgar Jones's election address in Welsh.[26] Some quantitative basis for the language of election addresses can be given by counting the number of bilingual, English and Welsh addresses which survive. This may not be entirely representative, however, since the survival of election addresses is random. However, almost half of them were either in Welsh or bilingual, and only in the Edwardian period did they become overwhelmingly English.

[20] *Cymru Fydd*, February 1888.
[21] *Areithiau Mr Gladstone yn Ysgotland, Tachwedd, 1879* (Caernarfon, 1880).
[22] NLW, WPA, *Anerchiad Mr Gladstone at Etholwyr Midlothian* (1885).
[23] *Cymru Fydd*, January, March, April 1888.
[24] T. E. Ellis, *Cymru a Deddf Llywodraeth Leol* (Wrecsam & Caerdydd, 1888).
[25] NLW, WPA, XJN 1156–1160, Y Blaid Ryddfrydol, South Wales Liberal Federation Annual Report, 1887; T. J. Hughes, *Landlordiaeth yn [sic] Nghymru* (Caerdydd, n.d.).
[26] *South Wales Daily News*, 14 January 1910; *Tarian y Gweithiwr*, 13, 20 January 1910.

Table 1. The Language of Surviving Election Addresses

Year	Total	Bilingual	Welsh	English
Pre-1880	7	1	2	4
1880	7	1	4	2
1885	12	2	3	7
1886	7	3	2	2
1892	11	4	3	4
1895	7	4	1	2
1900	6	2	0	4
1906	25	4	2	★19
1910	23	3	1	19
Undated	21	2	★★14	5
TOTAL	**126**	**26**	**32**	**68**

Source: Surviving Election Addresses in NLW and the Gwynedd Archives Service (Caernarfon and Dolgellau)
Notes
★ Figures distorted by a large cache for the Merthyr election.
★★Figures distorted by many local government elections in Caernarfonshire.

The Liberal Party fashioned its command of the Welsh language into a political weapon. There were many bilingual political jokes which could be aimed at opponents. In one meeting it was pointed out that in Wales they were well acquainted with 'chwarae teg' (fair play) but that the Conservatives were trying to introduce them to 'tylwyth teg' (fairies).[27] In 1910 a Conservative speaker, arriving at a meeting in Carmarthenshire with a limited knowledge of 'the language of the people', asked frantically: 'Dim fi yn gwobod beth yw Tariff Reform yn Cimrag, fi lico gwobod beth yw e'?'(I don't know what Tariff Reform is in Welsh; I'd like to know what it is). 'Starvo!' (Starvation!) was the droll reply of 'an ancient looking rustic'.[28] It was alleged that the Conservative candidate for Carmarthen in 1906 could not pronounce 'Llanelly'.[29]

Language could also be used less light-heartedly. Frequently there were calls of 'Cymraeg!' in Conservative meetings and refusal to grant this could lead to uproar.[30] In Denbigh in 1892 a request that a Conservative speaker use English because one member of the audience could not understand him seems to have been genuine.[31] On another occasion a Conservative supporter who was able to

[27] *Cambrian News*, 9 October 1885.
[28] *South Wales Daily News*, 10 January 1910.
[29] Ibid., 5 January 1906.
[30] *Herald Cymraeg*, 17 March 1880; 4, 11 January 1910; *BAC*, 30 January 1892; 5 January 1910.
[31] *BAC*, 13 January 1892.

speak Welsh was denied a hearing because he spoke in English.[32] To some extent this was a tactical manoeuvre. Even when they used Welsh, Conservatives might be denied a hearing. In one case a Conservative candidate was still greeted with poor attendance at a meeting at Llangefni although he had brought two Welsh speakers with him. In 1910 *Tarian y Gweithiwr* claimed that a certain Conservative candidate was unable to speak the native tongue and that he could find no one to translate his speeches into Welsh. When another candidate used a translator, the Welsh version of his speech was greeted with stony silence.[33]

Conservatives recognized that they were at a disadvantage in this respect and they made some efforts to remedy the defect by seeking Welsh-speaking candidates, writers and public speakers. In 1880 the Hon. G. T. Kenyon was pleased to have gained the services of Lloyd Evans, who would bring a good deal of 'Cymric zeal' to campaigning. In 1892 Conservatives in Caernarfonshire were delighted to secure a 'noted and tried Welsh writer' who would work for them in the election.[34] In south Wales they could count on the services of R. J. Richards, an agent in the Rhondda and then in Merthyr who was 'an effective political speaker in both English and Welsh'.[35] Not all such efforts came to fruition. When Cardiganshire Conservatives secured the services of a 'good Welsh speaker' in the autumn of 1914, meetings had to be abandoned because of the outbreak of war. The previous year they had hoped to secure the services of 'a good Welsh speaker' at a major meeting at Aberystwyth.[36] Similar problems were witnessed in Anglesey where the Conservative Association required the services of two Welsh-speaking female canvassers to establish Ladies' Committees throughout the island.[37] There was also a dearth of suitable candidates. In Caernarfonshire in 1906 Arthur Hughes boasted that he had maintained his Welsh and could use both languages in public, but often the Conservatives lacked Welsh-speaking candidates.[38] It was ironic that its achievements included securing a Welsh-speaking candidate in South Glamorgan in 1892 and in Cardiff in 1910, arguably the Welsh constituencies where they were least likely to reap political dividends.[39]

Conservatives also attempted to distribute political literature in Welsh. A speech by J. H. Bottomley in Bangor was translated into Welsh and distributed as a pamphlet.[40] Church Defence leaflets were produced in both English and Welsh

---

[32] Ibid., 6 June 1892.
[33] *Carnarvon and Denbigh Herald*, 20 March 1880; *North Wales Chronicle*, 10 April 1880; 7, 14 January 1910; *Herald Cymraeg*, 25 January 1910; *Tarian y Gweithiwr*, 13 January 1910.
[34] Gwynedd Archives Service, Caernarfon, Vaynol Papers, 2404, N. P. Stewart to George Owen, 14 April 1892.
[35] F. J. Harries, *History of Conservatism in the Rhondda* (Pontypridd, 1912), p. 17.
[36] NLW, WPA, XJN 1140, The Conservative Party, 1876–1949. Annual Reports of the Cardiganshire Conservative and Unionist Association, 1913, 1914.
[37] Ibid., Report of the Anglesey Conservative Association 1911, p. 12; ibid., 1912, p. 10.
[38] *North Wales Chronicle*, 29 December 1905, 5 January 1906.
[39] *Western Mail*, 4 July 1892; *South Wales Daily News*, 3 January 1910.
[40] J. H. Bottomley, *Paham yr wyf yn Geidwadwr* (Caernarfon, n.d., c. 1880).

in 1906, and the Women's Unionist and Tariff Reform Association distributed large amounts of literature in both languages in 1913–14.[41] In south Wales in the same period Conservatives distributed a number of Welsh leaflets paid for by the South Wales Tariff Reform Association, while the West Carmarthenshire Unionist Association published an article on 'Small Ownership' in Welsh. A series of questions on the Insurance Act was also translated into Welsh and Pembrokeshire Conservatives published a bilingual leaflet, which included material on old age pensions, with quotations from Balfour and Asquith.[42]

The political advantage did not always lie with the Liberals in this way. Conservatives used Welsh more often than the Liberals liked to think. Meetings were conducted wholly or partly in Welsh whenever possible. Conservatives used Welsh at meetings in several towns, including Corwen, Tregaron, Caernarfon, Conwy and Cricieth.[43] Translators were also employed to render English into Welsh on many occasions and this often drew the fire of the crowds.[44] Some speakers invited antagonism by continuing to speak in English when there was a demand for Welsh.[45] Nor did all Liberal candidates speak Welsh. In 1892 the *Western Mail* claimed that a monoglot English Liberal candidate was making little headway with monoglot Welsh electors in Cardiganshire.[46] Excuses and tokenism were widely invoked; these included opening a meeting in Welsh and then using English for the substance of politics, or learning a few Welsh tags for use in an English speech. Despite this, the Liberals claimed a monopoly on the language of politics. Conservatives were not the sole victims of their attacks; many socialists, who were frequently less than able in the language of heaven whatever their advocacy of heaven on earth, were also fiercely criticized. Whenever Keir Hardie was attacked for his lack of knowledge of Welsh, he would reply that whatever his problems with Welsh might be, he did speak the language of the House of Commons. Liberals who emphasized the Welshness of his opponent, Edgar Jones, were acutely embarrassed when his election address appeared in ungrammatical Welsh![47]

Making available political reporting and the discussion of political ideas were vital functions of the Welsh press. This was clearly an area where the English language was predominant, simply because there were more English-language

[41] *Western Mail*, 4 January 1906; NLW, WPA, XJN 1140. 4th Annual Report of the Women's Unionist and Tariff Reform Association, Flintshire Branch, Year Ending 1 April 1914.
[42] NLW, WPA, XJN 1140. West Carmarthenshire Unionist Association, Annual Report, Year ending 25 March 1912; Pembrokeshire Conservative Association, Leaflet for Marley Samson, Prospective Conservative Candidate (n.d.).
[43] *Cambrian News*, 19, 20 March 1880; *North Wales Chronicle*, 3 April 1880; 3 April 1910.
[44] *Cambrian News*, 26 March 1880; Gwynedd Archives Service, Caernarfon, XD6 Gorddinog Papers. 197, Newspaper cuttings from Colonel Platt's Candidature as a Conservative in the Northern Division of Caernarfonshire 1885 elections.
[45] *BAC*, 17 March 1880, 30 January 1892.
[46] *Western Mail*, 2 July 1892.
[47] *Aberdare Leader*, 1, 8, 22, January 1910.

newspapers and no daily Welsh-language newspapers. This put the Welsh-language press at a disadvantage, though it was possible to translate material which came from daily English newspapers or from the new agencies. The press performed important functions, notably in providing comment and basic information in Welsh, and in printing translations of vital material into Welsh which was not available elsewhere. However, none of the Welsh newspapers could maintain a staff of reporters necessary for extensive political coverage.

English-language newspapers which sought to maintain a local coverage also faced this problem. In 1885 the *Cambrian News* complained about the cost of maintaining political reporting,[48] and twenty years later the *Carnarvon and Denbigh Herald* complained that other newspapers failed to employ reporters who had an adequate knowledge of Welsh.[49] The disparity in resources between Welsh and English newspapers is confirmed by Annie Ellis's description of the difficulties she encountered in tracing the Welsh-language speeches of her husband, Tom, for publication. Unlike his English speeches, Tom Ellis rarely wrote Welsh addresses in advance, and many of his extempore Welsh speeches were delivered in remote places unfrequented by newspaper reporters. This reflects the limited resources of the Welsh press.[50] By the end of this period the dearth of Welsh-language newspapers in south Wales was widely deplored and this hampered meaningful discussion about social reform in Welsh. Housing reformers complained before the First World War that they received much better support from the English-language press in Wales than from the Welsh-language press. The Welsh press was already distancing itself from the industrial areas of south Wales and consequently the Welsh vocabulary was failing to keep pace with the new social politics.[51]

So far we have discussed the medium. What was the message and was it affected by the medium? Henry Richard's classic speech at Merthyr in 1868 set the agenda for political discussion throughout late nineteenth-century Wales.[52] Richard emphasized the unity of the Welsh nation. The Welsh were a people who spoke a common language and shared a history and a literature. These were the people of the cottage rather than the mansion, and they had never been represented in Parliament. The clear implication of this was that the gentry – who were Anglicized – were not a part of the Welsh nation. The way to express Welshness in politics, therefore, was to vote for a Liberal and Nonconformist candidate. This was a persistent theme in late nineteenth-century Wales: 'Devotion to Liberalism is a Welsh national trait; it is inherent in the Welsh national character.'[53]

[48] *Cambrian News*, 2 October 1885.
[49] *Carnarvon and Denbigh Herald*, 26 January 1906.
[50] *Speeches and Addresses by the late Thomas E. Ellis, M.P.* (Wrexham, 1912), pp. v–vi.
[51] Welsh Housing and Development Association, *Llyfr Coch Cymru / The Red Book of Wales Part II: Housing and Social Conditions in Wales* (London, 1911), pp. 38–9.
[52] Ieuan Gwynedd Jones, 'Henry Richard ac Iaith y Gwleidydd yn y Bedwaredd Ganrif ar Bymtheg' in Geraint H. Jenkins (ed.), *Cof Cenedl III: Ysgrifau ar Hanes Cymru* (Llandysul, 1988), pp. 117–49.
[53] *South Wales Daily News*, 12 January 1906.

In Liberal eyes, casting a vote was not simply part of a struggle for power and the advancement of certain creeds; it was a moral responsibility and something which defined the whole of a person's manhood. A Welsh newspaper in 1880 succinctly summed up the attitude by claiming that a man should vote with the same seriousness as he prayed, and do so for the party of justice and peace.[54] The pressing need, according to *Y Faner*, was to break free from the grip of an ancient aristocracy, and the extension of the vote allowed people to achieve this.[55] In Europe aristocrats fomented war, but Wales was a deeply religious country and would not sanction murder and injustice on the Continent.[56] The Church of England, like the Catholic Church, took bread out of the mouths of women and children,[57] and brewers were just as greedy and oppressive.[58]

Liberalism offered a different approach from landlordism; it was a creed based upon talent. Liberals were people who had risen through work, while their opponents were members of the nobility. In the contest in Caernarfon in 1880 Nathan Williams was depicted as a pure Welshman, while his opponent, George Douglas-Pennant, was merely his father's son. Liberalism therefore portrayed itself as the creed of the fiercely independent and upright. Support for its opponents could be dismissed as self interest (for a few) and the cringing of the sycophant. The Conservatives of Anglesey were denounced as landlords, churchmen, idlers and drunkards. Quarrymen who supported Conservatives and landlords were called 'cynffonwyr' (blacklegs) and 'Jingoes'. Landlords might try to exert pressure on people to secure their votes, but doughty Liberals would resist them.[59]

By constantly emphasizing the unity of Wales in the face of the Conservatives, Liberals implied that the true Welsh person supported their cause only. This theme, so vividly depicted in Henry Richard's speech, was further developed in the 1880s when Home Rule and Scottish discontent rewrote the agenda of British politics. The idea that Britain was composed of four nations and that the Welsh were a constituent part of this complex was often advanced,[60] and reached its apogee with the Liberal landslide in 1906, when the Liberals captured 'Cymru Gyfan' (The Whole of Wales):

> the most stunning blow that the party of privilege and monopoly has ever had . . . the people have been aroused from a long political indifference, and have illustrated the old Welsh adage, 'Trech gwlad nag arglwydd' (A country is mightier than a lord), with a passionate vengeance . . . The unanimity of the Irish Nationalists is held up as an

---

[54] *Tarian y Gweithiwr*, 2 April 1880.
[55] *BAC*, 25 February 1885.
[56] *Cambrian News*, 19 March 1880.
[57] *BAC*, 9 January 1880.
[58] Ibid., 8 April 1885.
[59] Ibid., 17 March 1880; *Herald Cymraeg*, 17 March, 1880; *Carnarvon and Denbigh Herald*, 6 March 1880; *Cambrian News*, 26 March 1880.
[60] *Cymru Fydd*, 1888, passim.

illustration of unswerving fidelity to Home Rule. We claim that a clean Welsh sweep is equally significant of Welsh opinion on the Education Act and Welsh Disestablishment.[61]

These views, voiced in a Rhondda newspaper, were echoed by Lloyd George in an electrifying victory speech at Caernarfon: 'The old nation has risen from one end to the other. For the first time Wales has become one in the cause of freedom, like the Israelites of old, it has commenced its march out of the house of bondage without leaving a single tribe behind.'[62]

How did the Conservatives counter this political rhetoric? If Henry Richard supplied the classic Welsh Liberal speech, Benjamin Disraeli provided the classic Conservative riposte. It is not inappropriate that this should have come from an English politician. It was central to the Conservative position that Wales was a part of the Empire and only rarely did the party seek to develop a specifically Welsh position. Whereas the ground of Welsh national identity was largely conceded to the Liberals, the Conservatives chose to emphasize and protect British national identity. The problem was that British national identity was rarely distinguishable in any meaningful sense from English national identity. Colin Matthew has remarked that all subsequent Conservative election addresses were essentially variations on the speech delivered by Disraeli at the Crystal Palace in 1872. Playing the patriotic card, Disraeli accused the Liberals of seeking to break up the Empire. 'The Queen, the Church of England and the Empire: these were the three simple, telling cries of Tory rhetoric, with the odd nod to social reform when convenient.'[63] These themes were also widely rehearsed in Wales. In Anglesey in 1880 voters were enjoined to:

> vote for
> Captain Pritchard-Rayner
> and thus as Englishmen or as true Welshmen express their
> loyalty to the queen
> their love for their country
> their faith in conservatism, and
> their mistrust of all
> radicals and home rulers.[64]

Conservatives also offered themselves as practical men of affairs, thereby contrasting themselves with what they believed to be lack of solidity and

---

[61] *Rhondda Leader*, 3 February 1906.
[62] *Carnarvon and Denbigh Herald*, 26 January 1906.
[63] H. C. G. Matthew, 'Rhetoric and Politics in Great Britain, 1860–1950' in P. J. Waller (ed.), *Politics and Social Change in Modern Britain: Essays Presented to A. F. Thompson* (Brighton, 1987), p. 50.
[64] *North Wales Chronicle*, 3 April 1880.

practicality among Liberal candidates. Electors in Cardiff in 1880 were reminded that both the Marquess of Bute and the Conservative candidate, Arthur Guest, had provided many jobs. In 1906 they would be offered the practicality of Sir Fortescue Flannery in place of the allegedly ineffectual Ivor Guest. Nor did they accept that their use of the pressure of such power was unique, for were not the Liberals guilty of using the 'chapel screw' wherever possible? Where the Liberals lauded democracy, Tories often saw the licence of the mob. A 'Torrent of Radical Rowdyism is sweeping South Wales', they complained during the 1880 election. Thirty years later the radicals were believed to be conducting a 'Reign of Terror' in Caernarfon.[65]

The assault on Liberal attitudes towards Ireland began even before Home Rule became a central issue in politics in 1885–6. In 1880 Liberals were condemned as republicans and Home Rulers, men who cared not a button for the honour and safety of the country. This theme became more insistent from the mid-1880s. It was alleged that if the Liberals were elected they would neglect domestic issues and focus on Ireland. John Rolls informed the electors of Monmouthshire that Conservatives had given Ireland peace and freedom from murderers. Ireland offered a particular angle from which to view the union, the centrepiece of Tory rhetoric: Sir J. T. D. Llewelyn, speaking at the Albert Hall in Swansea in 1892, explained the actions of the Liberal Unionists: 'They left the Liberals because they felt that the cause of the union should not be trodden underfoot. Unity was his motto, Unity was strength . . .'[66] Tariff reform, a creed which had the happy consequence (from the Conservative point of view) of uniting Britons against foreigners, also fitted neatly into this framework of British patriotism. It also had the virtue of addressing some of the economic problems of the day. Quarrymen were urged to support tariff reform in order to keep their jobs.[67]

What is surprising about the Conservatives in Wales is the limited extent to which they tried to develop a specifically Welsh appeal. The point at which rhetoric was best developed was on the eve of the 1906 elections when the *Western Mail* made a powerful case for voting Conservative:

> Wales as a nation owes nearly all the advantages it possesses to Conservative Administrations . . . the single solitary statute squeezed out of the Radical Governments by the fighting band of M.P.'s has been the Welsh Sunday Closing Act . . . faddist Radical legislation which makes evils and multiplies them a thousand fold by presenting a quack remedy for imaginary ills. . . . For the rest the record of Radicalism in Wales has been one of attempted destruction – destruction of the Church and the destruction of education.

---

[65] *Western Mail*, 23 March 1880; December 1905; January 1906, passim.
[66] *North Wales Chronicle*, 3 April 1880; *Western Mail*, 2, 4 July 1892; *Cambrian*, 1 July 1892.
[67] *North Wales Chronicle*, 21 January 1910.

If Radicals destroyed Wales, the Conservatives were its most effective builders:

> To the Unionists Wales owes its Intermediate Education Act of 1889, which made the Principality the leader of the modern educational movement, envied and admired by all other nations in the union . . . By forming the Central Welsh Board the Unionists gave to Wales its first distinctively Welsh educational authority . . . Step by step the constructive work of Welsh nationalism has gone on, aided and encouraged by successive Conservative governments as it has never been aided and encouraged before . . . Still, with all this there was still something wanting. Wales was without its capital, the heart-centre and the intellectual centre of its national life. The King, acting on the advice of Conservative ministers, appointed the City of Cardiff to be the capital of Wales . . . More than that the Conservatives have given us our county councils and our light railways.[68]

Liberals and Conservatives fought their political battles in both English and Welsh, but to what extent did the language used shape the rhetoric of politics? Was the giving of a political speech in one language rather than the other simply a matter of literal translation? Were there particular difficulties attached to using Welsh? It has been suggested that Irish was too metaphorical to be a modern political language and too limited by the vocabulary of a rural society.[69] The frequent invocation of the stereotype of the impassioned Welsh speech might also suggest something of the same kind. It has also been suggested that the societies of the Celtic 'fringe' looked back to a primitive heroic era. Those who stood up to lairds – or *arglwyddi* (lords) – could be seen as being endowed with supernatural powers.[70] But could the mythic adapt to the modern world?

Those who did not understand Welsh frequently feared what was being said about them in that language. The creation of the North and South Wales Property Defence Leagues during the agrarian crises of the 1880s was partly a reflection of such fears regarding the Welsh language. The North Wales League was anxious to provide translations of parts of Welsh newspapers and generally fought a successful campaign to keep this potent enemy at bay. The same concerns were shown by H. Byron Reed MP, who regaled the House of Commons with horror stories of the wickedness contained in Welsh-language periodicals.[71] Suspicion that the Welsh radical press might have been the instigator

---

[68] *Western Mail*, 12 January 1906.
[69] Grote, *Torn between Politics and Culture*, pp. 29–30.
[70] Christopher Harvie, 'Gladstonianism, the Provinces and Popular Political Culture, 1860–1906' in Richard Bellamy (ed.), *Victorian Liberalism: Nineteenth-Century Political Thought and Practice* (London and New York, 1990), pp. 152–74.
[71] Gwynedd Archives Service, Gorddinog Papers, 169; Circular from the North Wales Property Defence League, 11 November 1887 and copies of translations from *Y Werin*, 15 October 1887 and *BAC*, 12 October, 2 November 1887. H. Byron Reed, *The Church in Wales* (London, 1889), pp. 16–20; for the context, see J. P. D. Dunbabin, *Rural Discontent in Nineteenth-Century Britain* (London, 1974), chapter XIII.

of the Tithe War ran through a parliamentary investigation of some of its conflicts. One witness dated it to the publication of a series of articles in *Y Faner* and the participation of the newspaper's staff in public meetings.[72] At the very least, it was constantly claimed, the Welsh were 'a highly rhetorical people'.[73]

Was there anything in particular to fear from the Welsh language? There were times when the bite and bile of invective expressed in Welsh seemed more powerful than that expressed in English. Whereas the Welsh language was heavily influenced by religion and the Bible, English rhetoric was often urbane. A Cardiff Liberal celebrated the defeat of local Conservatives in 1880 in the following manner:

> The Cardiff Conservatives are rapidly recovering from the[ir] recent attack of political rheumatism. From what I have seen during the past week the inquiries of friends and foes alike may be safely answered in the old fashioned manner, considered so suitable in particular cases. Many times in the past few weeks has the anxious question been asked 'How are they?' It is consoling now to be able to answer 'They are as well as can be expected.'[74]

Similar sentiments were expressed in *Tarian y Gweithiwr* in Aberdare:

> Y mae Toriad yng nghanol pangfeydd marwolaeth bron yn wrthrych tosturi. Y mae ei lewygfeydd, yn enwedig yn y *Telegraph* gwallgofus, yn ddigon i dori calon dyn cydymdeimladol. Y mae hysterics gwyllt wedi ymaflyd yn eu holl natur. Teimla ei bod yn ddiwedd byd arno. Y mae holl ffroth ei ymffrost wedi cael ei chwythu ymaith gyda'r gwynt. Ymddangos fel pe byddai ei goron arglwyddiaethol wedi syrthio i'r llaid. Nid oes neb efallai yn fwy truenus na Beaconsfield. Y mae amcanion wedi trengu, ei gynlluniau wedi cael eu dyrysu, a'i ddylanwad llywodraethol wedi myned ymaith fel gwlith boreol.[75]

> (A Tory in the pangs of death is almost a subject for pity. His swooning, especially in the insane *Telegraph*, is enough to break the heart of a sympathetic man. Wild hysterics have taken hold of his whole nature. He feels as if the end of the world is imminent. All the froth of his boast has been blown away by the wind. It appears as if his lordly crown has fallen into the mud. There is no one perhaps more pitiful than Beaconsfield. His aims have perished, his plans have been confused, and his governmental influence has evaporated like morning dew.)

The sentiments might be similar but there is a cruder bite to the Welsh. Similarly, it was the unbridled style of E. Pan Jones that landowners found so offensive,

---

[72] *Report of an Inquiry as to Disturbances connected with the levying of Tithe Rentcharge in Wales* (PP 1887 (C. 5195) XXXVIII), esp. Qs. 967–74; 982–9; 1034; 1191.
[73] John Griffith, *The Church in Wales* (Cardiff, 1872), p. 8.
[74] *Cardiff Times*, 24 April 1880.
[75] *Tarian y Gweithiwr*, 16 April 1880.

particularly his references to landlords, agents and clergy as 'a trinity of robbers'.[76] Yet English language rhetoric could also employ similar figures of speech. In Cardiff there was much comparison of the Butes with the Tsar and it was generally believed that an ogre dwelt in the Castle. Certainly the folk story of Liberalism was one of heroic struggle against tyranny. Yet there was a rather sharper edge and a different 'Other' in Welsh rhetoric. When Cardiff Liberals thought of Tsarist comparisons, they viewed themselves as the liberal intelligentsia. In Welsh-language sources the comparison could be with the serfs. Wales was believed to have been so heavily oppressed since 1282 that, by the mid-1880s, the condition of its people was no better than that of the serfs of Russia. Welshmen needed to learn self-respect and to cherish their language and their writers; if they did so, they would no longer be scorned.[77] Similar rhetoric could be used in English, but it was less common; the linguistic difference seems to have been perceived as something which greatly widened the social gulf and intensified the oppression of Wales.[78] An even stronger sense of oppression is detectable in the frequent comparison of Welsh people with slaves in the southern states of America and the Caribbean. It was found most brutally in the Merioneth election of 1865 when there were references to the Liberal voters as 'niggers'.[79] This was not an isolated reference; it persisted into the 1880s and the early 1890s: Adfyfr opined that Parliament might have liberated slaves, but that Nonconformists still lived in perpetual serfdom.[80]

Liberal rhetoric of this kind combined well with biblical language. The Old Testament is a story of an oppressed people moving out of slavery and the Welsh were not the only nineteenth-century European nation to think of this analogy. The House of Lords was a 'Goliath Philistaidd' (Philistine Goliath) and Lloyd George a 'prophet' bent on liberation.[81] But such language could also come from the New Testament, and Nonconformists who voted Conservative were called 'Judases'.[82] The Welsh press, too, was full of biblical allusions in its denunciations of the established Church.[83] A particularly striking example comes from the campaign over tithes: the visitation of a bailiff in Cardiganshire was satirically compared with a visitation by the archangel:

Tebyg fod perchnogion y 'crysiau gwynion' o'r plwyfi uchod wedi meddwl nad oedd eisau ond yn unig i'r 'angel teilwraidd' hwn ddangos ei hunan i'r amaethwyr cyn y

---

[76] Gorddinog Papers, 169; translation from *BAC*, 12 October 1887.
[77] *BAC*, 19, 30 December 1885; 13 February 1886.
[78] An English-language letter likened the farmers of Brecon to slaves. *BAC*, 10 March 1886.
[79] Gwynedd Archives Service, Dolgellau, ZM/59/6. An Election Song: 'The Squire and the Screw'.
[80] *BAC*, 31 March 1880; 30 January 1892; *Tarian y Gweithiwr*, 2 April 1880; T. J. Hughes, *Neglected Wales* (London, 1887), p. 17.
[81] *Y Brython*, 27 January 1910.
[82] *BAC*, 6 June 1892.
[83] See the passages quoted in translation in Reed, *Welsh Church*, pp. 16–20.

byddai iddynt blygu yn isel mewn gostyngeiddrwydd ac edifeirwch yn y llwch wrth ei draed cysegredig a thalu 'hur y weinidogaeth estronol' yn ufudd . . .[84]

(It is likely that the owners of 'white shirts' of the above parishes believed that once the 'tailored angel' revealed himself to the farmers they would bow low in humility and repentance in the dust at his sacred feet, and pay the wages of the 'foreign ministry' obediently.)

Much of the Conservative fear of Welsh was a fear of the unknown, and such rhetoric was not wholly absent in English. Yet there does seem to have been some substance in their fears about the insolent nature of Welsh political rhetoric. It reflected a distinct culture, as Adfyfr observed: 'The Welsh talking their own language and reading their own newspapers and magazines, have been living their own life.'[85] This line of argument, however, can be taken too far. English was far from immune to biblical rhetoric and much of the liberal rhetoric couched in the Welsh language was little different from its equivalents in English, though there were some variations.[86] Adfyfr's 'passionate rhetoric' was something of an embarrassment to the more urbane Stuart Rendel and he was capable of expressing the same ideas in both languages.[87] However, newspapers like *Y Werin*, which were the *bête noir* of Conservatives, were prepared to challenge property rights, and were perhaps able to use another language to say what would otherwise have been unsayable. If so, they were a valve which released pressure within rural Wales, much as the Royal Commission on Land did in the 1890s.

Welsh was naturally much in evidence in rural conflicts such as the Tithe War and it was sometimes used as a weapon in the dispute. At a sale at Glanteifi there were demands that the auctioneer speak Welsh, pleas which were not assuaged by his (admittedly strange!) plea that he was a 'Sais Tregaron' (a Tregaron Englishman). At Wentloog in Monmouthshire a hostile crowd insisted that an auction be conducted bilingually.[88] It is also clear that there were many complications in the policing of tithe disturbances because the crowds used Welsh and church officials and senior policemen did not understand it. Instructions given by magistrates, such as the reading of the riot act, had to be translated into Welsh.[89] Witnesses called to an inquiry into the disturbances either did not feel comfortable speaking English or wanted to make a political point by giving their evidence in Welsh and having Professor John Rhŷs interpret it for the other commissioners. There was certainly a problem of translation: as Howel Gee remarked, what the com-

[84] *BAC*, 13 January 1892.
[85] Hughes, *Neglected Wales*, p. 3.
[86] See *Rhondda Leader*, 20 January 1906, for instance, where Joseph Chamberlain is compared with Samson.
[87] NLW, J. Herbert Lewis Papers, Rendel to Lewis, 26 November 1906.
[88] *Cambrian News*, 20 January 1888; *Cardiff Times*, 4 February 1888.
[89] *Report of an Inquiry as to Disturbances connected with the levying of Tithe Rentcharge in Wales*, passim and esp. Qs. 489, 496, 1021, 1099, 2169.

missioners called 'The Tithe Defence League' was more accurately rendered by the Welsh as 'The League of Tithe Oppressed'.[90]

The coming of the trade unions to the mining industry in the mid-nineteenth century was also marked by the use of Welsh. Miners' meetings at Aberdare during the strike of 1850 were conducted in Welsh.[91] By the time of the 1871 strike both languages were actively used by the Amalgamated Association of Miners and complaints were made that masters issued their statements in English only. Welsh appears to have been the predominant language. It was a serious disadvantage to Thomas Halliday, the trade unionist who made a bid to be a Lib–Lab MP in Merthyr in 1874, that he was not Welsh, and it partly explains his failure.[92] The early trade unions sustained the newspaper *Tarian y Gweithiwr*, which reported the technicalities of disputes, safety and wage rates in the Welsh language, though it has been claimed that it was more interested in bardic disputes than such matters.[93] Miners' meetings were still conducted partly through the medium of the Welsh language as far east as the Rhymney Valley in the late 1890s.[94] When Jim Connell visited Maerdy to address a miners' meeting during the great lockout of 1898, at least one member in the audience thought he should speak Welsh and that, if he was unable to, he should learn it![95]

But there were already signs of linguistic conflict within union circles. The Miners' Federation of Great Britain established its roots in Anglicized Monmouthshire and among English hauliers rather than the Welsh-speaking colliers. It became known as the 'English Union', and Mabon denounced William Brace, its leader in south Wales, as an 'English influence'.[96] When 'Morien' tried to use Welsh at a union meeting in Pontypridd in the hauliers' strike of 1893, he was shouted down.[97] The same thing happened to David Watts Morgan when he tried to use Welsh at a union meeting at Caerphilly in 1905. Several men left the hall; Morgan protested at their rudeness but resumed speaking in English.[98]

A complex pattern of language use was the case thereafter. Aberdare was the stronghold of *Tarian y Gweithiwr* and of the Welsh language, and as late as 1912

---

[90] Ibid. Evidence of Abel Hughes, Edward Davies, Moses Williams and William Roberts; and Q. 2888.
[91] See accounts of the meetings in *Cardiff and Merthyr Guardian*.
[92] Alexander Dalziel, *The Colliers' Strike in South Wales: Its Cause, Progress & Settlement* (Cardiff, 1872), pp. 50–3, 85–6, 104, 148–51, 193, 195; Cunningham, 'Thomas Halliday and the Merthyr Election of 1874', passim.
[93] T. I. Williams, 'Patriots and Citizens: Language, Identity and Education in a Liberal State: The Anglicisation of Pontypridd, 1818–1920' (unpubl. University of Wales PhD thesis, 1989), p. 730.
[94] *Tarian y Gweithiwr*, 26 August 1897.
[95] *Labour Leader*, 2 July 1898.
[96] L. J. Williams, 'The New Unionism in South Wales, 1889–92', *WHR*, I, no. 4 (1963), 428 n. 2; R. Page Arnot, *South Wales Miners: Glowyr De Cymru: A History of the South Wales Miners' Association, 1898–1914* (London, 1967), pp. 30–1.
[97] Tim Williams, in a BBC Wales TV documentary in the series 'On the Move', September 1995.
[98] Michael Lieven, *Senghennydd, the Universal Pit Village, 1890–1930* (Llandysul, 1994), pp. 98–9.

Charles Stanton believed that the ability to speak two languages was a vital requirement for a miner's agent. But in some of the newer pits around Pontypridd from the 1880s, Welsh was rarely heard and many of the miners came from Lancashire, Yorkshire, and the west of England. There was no local equivalent to *Tarian y Gweithiwr*; nor was there any obvious need for one since less than 40 per cent of the population of Pontypridd spoke Welsh in 1901 and only 20 per cent in 1921. The last monoglot Welsh speaker in Pontypridd died in the course of the 1890s and English was 'the unifying language of the area'. By 1903 all miners' meetings around Pontypridd, with the exception of Cilfynydd, were held in English. Increasingly, meetings were conducted in English because of the cosmopolitan nature of the mining community. This was even true of the western part of the coalfield where Welsh-speaking miners were placed at a disadvantage. In some parts of the anthracite district, however, lodge meetings and even general meetings continued to be held in Welsh up to the 1950s.[99]

The knot of these complex strands was tied together in Maerdy where the minutes were kept bilingually in 1907–9; when a checkweigher was appointed in 1910, Welsh-speaking candidates were given ten minutes over and above the ten minutes in English which all others were given to make their case. However, a non-Welsh speaker, Arthur Horner, was appointed and he gave his reports in English, though they were immediately translated into Welsh. The last Welsh minutes of the Maerdy Lodge appeared in January 1914. What was true of Maerdy was true of the Rhondda in general. The Rhondda District of the Fed published its rules bilingually from 1901 and summarized every report in Welsh from 1901 to 1907. From 1908 to 1911 a synopsis of the minutes was given in Welsh, and from then until 1931 the agenda was published bilingually. A similar pluralism was heard in the language of the street action when 'wild threats in Welsh and English' were made at Tonypandy in November 1910 before 'the work of destruction' began.[100] Yet the bias towards English was unmistakable in a comment made at the monthly meeting of the Rhondda District in July 1909. Did anyone want the resolution in Welsh, enquired the chairman? 'Everyone here understands English' was the reply.[101] Welsh came to be seen by many as a conservative force. When the Fed was obliged to debate the proposals for its reform contained in *The Miners' Next Step* (1912), it broke with its usual practice

---

[99] *Llais Llafur*, August, 1911, passim; Bert L. Coombes, *These Poor Hands: The Autobiography of a Miner Working in South Wales* (London, 1939), pp. 88–9; Hywel Francis and David Smith, *The Fed: A History of the South Wales Miners in the Twentieth Century* (London, 1980), p. 299, n. 5; Williams, 'Patriots and Citizens', pp. 710, 732, 734, 749, 792, 795–6, 805.

[100] David Smith, 'The Future of Coalfield History in South Wales', *Morgannwg*, XIX (1975), 59; idem, 'Tonypandy 1910: Definitions of Community', *P&P*, 87 (1980), 180, citing the magistrate T. P. Jenkins.

[101] David Smith (ed.), *A People and a Proletariat: Essays in the History of Wales 1780–1980* (London, 1980), p. 12.

of simply printing agenda for meetings in English and printed them bilingually – though this was a general decision of principle. Following the conference a copy of the report was sent to each member and 10,000 of these were in Welsh.[102]

The difficulties faced by trade unions in respect of the language were nothing compared with those encountered by the early socialists. It was a commonplace to observe that the lack of Welsh-language orators delayed the spread of socialism into Wales:

> The movement towards independent Labour representation has been to some extent handicapped by the fact that the most strenuous advocates of the new method have failed to take national sentiment into account. The candidates put forward on behalf of the Labour Party have often been men who cannot speak the vernacular, and Welsh-speaking Liberal champions have been able to win the seats by playing on national feeling.[103]

It was an issue which socialists themselves recognized and to an extent tried to deal with. 'We must look for our Socialist leaders in Wales . . .', wrote E. Morgan Humphreys, 'we have suffered enough from alien bishops, alien judges, alien capitalists, and alien officials . . .'[104] H. M. Hyndman, visiting Llanberis during the quarrymen's strike of 1886, also perceived the problem:

> It would certainly be well to have our short literature translated into Welsh and distributed in the Principality. The people are much quicker to grasp revolutionary doctrines than our own rural population, and seem to turn naturally towards Socialism, though their language might interfere somewhat with the spread of our doctrines.[105]

But Hyndman could not avoid being patronizing and came away with the impression that the Welsh used their inability to speak English to distance themselves from people with whom they were politically unsympathetic. Using Welsh was simply a means of keeping the political outsider at a distance. Similarly, propagandists for the Socialist League noticed the strength of Welsh in the Rhondda and Cynon Valleys: 'The vitality of the Welsh language and the depth of national feeling is strikingly evident throughout these valleys, where one scarcely hears a word of English.'[106]

---

[102] David B. Smith, 'The Re-building of the South Wales Miners' Federation, 1927–1939' (unpubl. University of Wales PhD thesis, 1976), pp. 21–2. For the decision of principle, see University of Wales Swansea, South Wales Coalfield Archive, Minutes of the South Wales Miners' Federation, Annual Conference, 5–6 June 1913.
[103] 'Observer', 'The Mind of the Miner II', *The Welsh Outlook*, III (1916), 247.
[104] E. Morgan Humphreys, 'Socialism and Welsh Nationality', *Socialist Review* (1909), 118, 122.
[105] *Justice*, 23 January 1886.
[106] *Commonweal*, 3 September 1887.

The Social Democratic Federation, which was metropolitan and freethinking in origin, found Wales difficult territory, though it made some headway in the Anglicized ports and in the devastated tinplate industry in the 1890s.[107] During that decade, however, it confronted considerable difficulties in other parts of Wales.[108] In 1887 a Socialist League speaker found responsive audiences in the Barmouth area but admitted that, although his audiences could understand a fluent English speaker, very few of them were capable of reading English books. Another commentator with inside knowledge of the same area observed that, while English was understood, Welsh was the language of thought and speech.[109] In an attempt to shock workers out of their adherence to Liberalism, the SDF adopted an abrasive political tone which was not likely to win friends. In 1886 Hyndman was threatened with a libel action for comments he made about the quarry strike at Dinorwig. They included the condoning of violence against the quarryowners.[110] During the coal strike of 1898 the SDF was apoplectic: coalowners were described as 'Bethel-endowing tyrants' and a speech by Mabon – 'that jelly-fish Liberal Labour nonentity' – was reckoned 'unworthy of any save a poltroon'. At Pontypridd a Socialist League speaker aroused the opposition of one member of his audience for his 'outspoken way of calling thieves thieves'.[111]

Welsh-language expositions of the socialist creed were rare. Eventually, however, the Fabian Society published three translations of its pamphlets and one pamphlet in Welsh as the original language.[112] Three of these were concerned with the relationship between religion and socialism. These efforts were limited and there was a yawning gap which was only slowly filled as the period advanced. A key figure was R. J. Derfel. As the socialist newspaper, *Llais Llafur*, pointed out to its readers: 'Mr Derfel . . . holds the unique position of being the only Welshman who has devoted himself to these questions in the Welsh language.'[113] Derfel read a paper (in Welsh) on 'The Reconstruction of Society' to the Welsh National Society (of Manchester) in 1888 and this was subsequently issued as a pamphlet. This was followed by thirty letters in Welsh for the Liverpool newspaper *Y Cymro* and at the turn of the century by another series in *Llais Llafur*.[114] Yet, as Derfel himself admitted, his letters would have made a greater impact had they been published in book form. He stressed that socialism was the

[107] Jon Parry, 'Trade Unionists and Early Socialism in South Wales, 1890–1908', *Llafur*, 4, no. 3 (1986), 44–5.
[108] Social Democratic Federation, Annual Reports, 1893, 1897.
[109] *Commonweal*, 22 October 1887; Humphreys, 'Socialism and Welsh Nationality', *Socialist Review* (1909), 119.
[110] *Justice*, 6 February 1886. For the libel case, see ibid., 5 June, 17 July 1886.
[111] Ibid., 11 June, 3 September 1898; *Commonweal*, 27 August 1887.
[112] *Paham Mae y Lluaws yn Dlawd?*, Fabian Tract no. 38, n.d.; John Clifford, *Sosialaeth a Dysgeidiaeth Crist*, Fabian Tract no. 87, 1899; John Clifford, *Sosialaeth a'r Eglwysi*, Fabian Tract no. 139, 1908; J. R. Jones, *Sosialaeth yng Ngoleuni'r Beibl*, Fabian Tract no. 143 (London, 1909).
[113] NLW, MS 23449B, 'Brief Biography of R. J. Derfel' (cuttings from *Llais Llafur*, 5 August 1905).
[114] Ibid. and MS 23448B, 'Cymdeithasiaeth (Socialism)' gan R. J. Derfel.

only way to transform society and much of his message was couched in biblical language.

Not until the eve of the First World War were satisfactory accounts of the new socialist creed published in Welsh: David Thomas published his *Y Werin a'i Theyrnas*, which brought together a wide range of socialist and social reform thought for Welsh speakers, while the Revd D. Tudwal Evans provided a workmanlike history and anatomy of the creed.[115] Yet this did not entirely fill the gap; David Thomas's Welsh-language bibliography contained only six short pieces, while his English-language reading list ran to some eighty items, many of them substantial books.[116] When, in 1911, it was proposed to establish a Welsh Labour Party by fusing the existing branches of the ILP and reorganizing the national structure, it was still considered necessary to pass a resolution calling for more socialist literature in the Welsh language.[117] In no sense was the socialist attempt to produce political literature in Welsh as successful as that of the Liberals in the 1880s. Keir Hardie's classic exposition, *The Red Dragon and the Red Flag*, comprised thirteen printed pages in English and a Welsh synopsis of three pages.[118]

The appearance of *Llais Llafur* in 1898 indicated that things were beginning to stir in Welsh-language socialist politics. Yet in the period 1893 to 1906 no newspaper espoused by the Independent Labour Party appeared in the Welsh language. The Cardiff-based *Labour Pioneer* (1900–2) and the Swansea-based *South Wales Worker*, both of which could be loosely grouped as ILP productions, were English publications.[119] It would be 1912 before a Welsh-language socialist paper, *Y Dinesydd Cymreig*, appeared in north Wales and, predictably, it was the work of the indefatigable David Thomas. By that time, *Llais Llafur* had largely turned to English – one disgruntled observer believed it should be renamed 'Sais Llafur' (English Labour). By 1915 *Llais Llafur* had become *Labour Voice*.[120]

In the 1890s the Social Democratic Federation had recognized that its progress in Wales was being hindered by the lack of Welsh-speaking propagandists and the same point was made over a decade later in respect of socialism in general.[121] Eventually some progress was made in the provision of Welsh orators for the cause. David Thomas became a vigorous propagandist for socialism in the Welsh

---

[115] David Thomas, *Y Werin a'i Theyrnas* (Caernarfon, n.d., *c.* 1910); D. Tudwal Evans, *Sosialaeth* (Abermaw, 1911).

[116] For instance, there was a Welsh pamphlet on Liberalism in Wales by Keir Hardie. Gillian B. Woolven, *Publications of the Independent Labour Party 1893–1932* (Coventry, 1977) and a Welsh pamphlet outlining the aims and objects of the ILP. Humphreys, 'Socialism and Welsh Nationality', 119.

[117] *Llanelly and County Guardian*, 17 August 1911; *Llais Llafur*, 19 August 1911.

[118] J. Keir Hardie, *The Red Dragon and the Red Flag* (Merthyr Tydfil, 1912).

[119] Deian Rhys Hopkin, 'The Newspapers of the Independent Labour Party, 1893–1906' (unpubl. University of Wales PhD thesis, 1981), pp. 315–17.

[120] *Llais Llafur*, 22 November 1913.

[121] SDF Annual Report, 1897; Humphreys, 'Socialism and Welsh Nationality', 118–19.

language as did other emerging leaders like R. Silyn Roberts of Blaenau Ffestiniog and T. E. Nicholas (Niclas y Glais).[122]

The socialist cause was also aided by the development of a rhetoric which was more appropriate than that employed by the SDF. In his celebrated speech, 'The Red Dragon and the Red Flag', Keir Hardie claimed that socialism was an international movement in which the Red Dragon and the Red Flag could be combined. On another occasion, he emphasized that 'Jesus belonged to the working class and worked at the carpenter's bench':

> The Gospel of Jesus was self-sacrifice. In so far as society was based upon self-interest, it was anti-Christian, and it was up to every man and every woman who desired to see God's kingdom established on earth to do everything he or she possibly could to overthrow an order based upon injustice and introduce a new order based upon fraternity and justice to all alike.[123]

Socialists also used the rhetoric of slavery, recalling the earlier use of the trope by Liberals. David Thomas believed that the events of 1859 and 1868 revealed that farmers had been slaves, and that their descendants were still enslaved to 'landlords and wage-lords'.[124] When the *South Wales Worker* was launched in 1913, it proclaimed its belief that: 'The slave alone can struggle against the conditions which hold him in slavery . . .'[125] The parallel between some kinds of Liberal rhetoric and that of the socialists seems to have been the basis for the frequently expressed socialist conviction that the Welsh people were ripe for socialism if only they could be reached in their own language. The radical rhetoric on the land question was a basis for this.

If there was one area where the Welsh language was truly secure in the labour movement it was in the North Wales Quarrymen's Union. Welsh was the language of its activities and its minutes were recorded in Welsh throughout its existence.[126] But as the Union began to recruit leaders from its own ranks, they were expected to acquire and advertise their fluency in English. In a leaflet which formed part of his campaign to be elected treasurer in 1908, R. T. Jones stressed his fluency in both languages.[127] It was becoming increasingly necessary for union leaders to communicate with the non-Welsh-speaking world beyond the *caban* and beyond Gwynedd. During its annual May Day Festival the Quarrymen's

---

[122] David Thomas, *Silyn (Robert Silyn Roberts) 1871–1930* (Lerpwl, 1956), chapters 4, 6, 7; David W. Howell, *Nicholas of Glais: The People's Champion* (Clydach, 1991), pp. 13–14, 21.
[123] Hardie, *Red Dragon and Red Flag*; Emrys Hughes (ed.), *Keir Hardie's Speeches and Writings (From 1888 to 1915)* (4th ed., Glasgow, n.d.), pp. 151–3, quotation at p. 153.
[124] David Thomas, 'Socialism and Wales', *Socialist Review* (1912), 432–4. This article was originally published in Welsh in *Y Genedl Gymreig*, 17 January 1911.
[125] *South Wales Worker / Gweithwyr y De*, 24 April 1913.
[126] Gwynedd Archives Service, XNWQU; Minute Books 1912–21.
[127] Ibid., XNWQU, 255.

Union frequently invited not only a leading cultural figure to speak in Welsh but also a prominent, monoglot English-speaking figure from the British labour and radical movement. Since it was connected to the wider British labour movement, the Union was obliged to acknowledge and use the English language, and once the Union was amalgamated into the Transport and General Workers Union in 1922 its use of English must surely have accelerated.

In many ways the efforts of the women's suffrage movement to propagandize in Wales ran parallel with those of the socialist movement. It was seen very largely as an alien importation, though there was a rhetoric which stressed the essential equality between the sexes in Celtic society. Some efforts were made to provide translations into Welsh of key works. This was done both by the Bangor branch of the National Union of Women's Suffrage Societies and by the Revd Ivan Thomas Davies, who published his efforts in *Y Faner* and *Seren Cymru*.[128]

The use of Welsh as a political language in this period reflected the nature of politics. With the opening up of the franchise from the 1860s onwards, it became essential for politicians to use Welsh in order to reach the growing electorate. The number of voters who were either monoglot Welsh speakers or who had a very imperfect grasp of English was considerable; reaching them was a vital part of winning elections and power. It was also a key part of the Liberals' approach to politics in Wales. They publicized themselves as the party which expressed the new identity of Wales and their widespread use of Welsh served them well in struggles with both the Conservative and Labour parties, both of which had greater difficulty in procuring candidates and propagandists than did the Liberals. In the course of this struggle they made Welsh into a language which could be employed effectively with regard to the central issues of nineteenth-century politics — religion and the constitution.

Yet popular involvement in politics set limits to the development of Welsh as the language of politics. Throughout the period the ethnic composition of the Welsh population was changing rapidly. The period when migration had been a process which largely redistributed people within Wales, while adding an assimilable mixture of newcomers, gave way to one in which the non-Welsh came in increasing numbers and shifted the linguistic balance within diverse communities. By the eve of the First World War, particularly in the eastern part of the South Wales Coalfield, to reach 'the democracy' increasingly meant using English rather than Welsh. The change in the composition of the Welsh population strengthened the shift in political issues from rural, religious and governmental issues to the social concerns of the new coalfield society. Perhaps it

---

[128] Kay Cook and Neil Evans, '"The Petty Antics of the Bell-Ringing Boisterous Band"? The Women's Suffrage Movement in Wales, 1890–1918' in Angela V. John (ed.), *Our Mothers' Land: Chapters in Welsh Women's History, 1830–1939* (Cardiff, 1991), pp. 170–1; Peter Ellis Jones, 'The Women's Suffrage Movement in Caernarfonshire', *TCHS*, 48 (1987), 94; Angela V. John, '"Run Like Blazes": The Suffragettes and Welshness', *Llafur*, 6, no. 3 (1994), 36.

was harder for the Welsh language to adapt to these concerns. The groundwork of religious publishing had been laid in depth over several centuries and to develop a political language out of this was a simpler task than to do so out of the more sociological concerns of the late nineteenth century. Welsh lacked an equivalent word for 'housing'. This seems indicative of a wider problem.[129]

In some ways Liberals exaggerated their adherence to the Welsh language. They had an appreciable number of candidates who could not speak Welsh and were forced to find other reasons for supporting them. On at least one occasion – a Home Rule meeting in Cardiff – Lloyd George was greeted with cries of 'Cymraeg!' (Welsh!).[130] In north Wales, the rules and regulations of Liberal Federations were often bilingual, as were many annual reports of organizations, though English was frequently the first language to appear.[131] In south Wales there was no evidence of Welsh in the official printed reports of the Liberal organizations. Only one meeting of political activists in south Wales, held in Cardiff in 1888, was conducted in Welsh. We have no evidence that this experiment, which was hailed as a great success, was repeated.[132]

The surviving notices of Liberal Party meetings for activists are overwhelmingly in English, suggesting that it was assumed that the politically informed were conversant with English. When people were drawn in from a wide area the probability that there would be monoglot English speakers among them rose exponentially. To take an obvious example, the presence of just one man, Stuart Rendel, who spoke no Welsh, in the upper echelons of Welsh Liberalism in the 1880s and 1890s must have exerted enormous pressure to use English, even if there had been a previous commitment to using Welsh for political purposes. In private one suspects that politicians used English far more often than they did on the public political platform. The great bulk of surviving political correspondence of the period is in English. The letters of Lloyd George to his wife are almost entirely in English, though he did switch to Welsh whenever confidential matters arose. With the switch of language we can almost hear the tones of *sotto voce*. This seemed to say that while one language was suitable for the discussion of public matters, another could communicate intimate, secret or even dangerous thoughts. The vast bulk of J. Herbert Lewis's correspondents wrote to him in English and he used to reply in English. Yet he was regarded as a man who spoke good Welsh both in private and in public meetings.[133] Even Tom Ellis, whose commitment to the Welsh language was unequivocal, conducted most of his correspondence in English; the exceptions were more intimate friends from north Wales, and

---

[129] *Llyfr Coch Cymru*, pp. 38–9.
[130] NLW, William George Papers, Lloyd George to William George, 5 February 1890.
[131] NLW, WPA, XJN 1156–1160.
[132] *Cymru Fydd*, March, April 1888.
[133] NLW, J. Herbert Lewis Papers, John Owen to Lewis, 27 October 1903.

especially Merioneth, like D. R. Daniel and O. M. Edwards.[134] It is hard to tell which language politicians spoke to each other in private. We know that Lloyd George and Tom Ellis spoke Welsh to one another in the House of Commons, but little other evidence has survived.[135] Perhaps the correspondence reflects that the political élite placed a high premium on English but occasionally found it useful to speak Welsh to some of its audiences. For Liberals this had the advantage of limiting the political agenda to issues with which it was more comfortable; social issues were more frequently discussed in English than in Welsh.[136]

From the mid-nineteenth century onwards Welsh proved to be a suitable medium in which to attack the squirearchy and to foster the values and culture of the *gwerin*. It could be refashioned to deal with threats to the Liberal hegemony from the left as well; it was a versatile and durable political weapon. Both Conservatives and socialists recognized this and made considerable efforts to remedy the shortcomings of their own parties in this regard. However, the sharp fall in the monoglot Welsh columns in the censuses after 1891 sealed the fate of Welsh as a language of politics over much of the country. As a vigorous language of politics Welsh belonged only to the final quarter of the nineteenth century. Thereafter its days were numbered.

---

[134] Kenneth O. Morgan (ed.), *Lloyd George Family Letters* (Oxford and Cardiff, 1973), passim.
[135] *Western Mail*, 6 April 1899.
[136] Ieuan Gwynedd Jones, 'Language and Community in Nineteenth-Century Wales' in Smith (ed.), *A People and a Proletariat*, pp. 58–62.

21

'The Confusion of Babel'[1]?: The Welsh Language, Law Courts and Legislation in the Nineteenth Century

MARK ELLIS JONES

DURING the nineteenth century the administration of law in Wales was governed by the so-called 'language clause' of the Act of Union of 1536, which stated:

> That all Justices Commissioners Sheriffs Coroners Escheators Stewards and their Lieutenants, and all other Officers and the Ministers of the Law, shall proclaim and keep the Sessions Courts Hundreds Leets Sheriffs Courts, and all other Courts in the English Tongue.[2]

This was an unequivocal statement that English was the official medium of legal transactions in Wales. Nevertheless, it was inevitable that a great deal of Welsh would be heard in the law courts simply because the vast majority of the population were monoglot Welsh speakers.[3] The use of Welsh in the courtroom would have been made possible by the fact that most of the magistrates were Welsh speakers during the Tudor and Stuart period. The 'language clause' did not seek to exclude Welsh speakers from office, but insisted that they should have a mastery of English, which, according to Peter R. Roberts, was meant as 'an inducement to the Welsh to become bilingual'.[4] The status of English in the domain of the law was further reiterated by an Act in 1732–3,[5] which ensured that legislation of the previous year, which stipulated that English was the medium of law in England, was also applicable to Wales. Historians of the early modern period have claimed that it is difficult to say with authority how the Welsh

---

[1] The quotation derives from a letter which opposed the notion of the Welsh language as the medium of law. *Carnarvon and Denbigh Herald*, 18 December 1858.
[2] Ivor Bowen, *The Statutes of Wales* (London, 1908), p. 87. Initially the clauses of the Act of Union were unnumbered. In Owen Ruffhead's *Statutes at Large*, published in 1762–5, the 'language clause' was numbered clause 20. In a later edition of *Statutes at Large*, published in 1817–28, the same clause was numbered 17. Bowen used the earlier version.
[3] W. Ogwen Williams, 'The Survival of the Welsh Language after the Union of England and Wales: The First Phase, 1536–1642', *WHR*, 2, no. 1 (1964), 72.
[4] Peter R. Roberts, 'The Welsh Language, English Law and Tudor Legislation', *THSC* (1989), 28.
[5] 6 George 2, c. 14, ss. 3. See Bowen, *The Statutes of Wales*, pp. 204–6.

language was accommodated in the courts.[6] The historian of the nineteenth century, however, is more fortunate. The stenographers who reported on court cases for the prodigious number of Welsh newspapers during the nineteenth century provide a much fuller account, unlike the succinct court records. Furthermore, newspapers were increasingly sensitive to the question of nationality and were more likely to comment if the Welsh were unfairly treated in the law courts.

This chapter is chiefly concerned with the Welsh language in the Great Sessions, the Assizes, the Quarter Sessions, the Petty Sessions and the County Courts. No mention is made of the various manorial courts or ecclesiastical courts which, by the beginning of the nineteenth century, were largely defunct. It also deals with legislation which affected the Welsh language, although space does not permit discussion of legislation relating to the Welsh language and the established Church, such as the Pluralities Act of 1838. The first section discusses the treatment of the Welsh language in the courts in the early part of the nineteenth century, a time which witnessed the abolition of the Great Sessions in 1830 and the creation of the County Courts in 1846. The second section deals with the middle decades of the century. This was a time when there was a more general debate about the Welsh language, especially following the publication of the Blue Books in 1847. Thirdly, the debate concerning Welsh County Court judgeships is examined. This was an issue aired frequently in the latter part of the century, as was the question of the Welsh magistracy, which is the subject of the fourth section. Finally, the use of Welsh in the law courts at the close of the century is discussed. Nineteenth-century views on whether the Welsh language should or should not be used in the legal system are extensively used in this study in order to gauge contemporary attitudes towards the native tongue during a period of profound social, economic and political change.

★ ★ ★

This section is concerned with the administration of the law and the Welsh language in the first half of the nineteenth century. The prospect of the abolition of the court of Great Sessions, a judicature founded in 1543 and peculiar to Wales, provided an opportunity not only to articulate the perceived strengths and weaknesses of the court but also to examine the question of language. The Great Sessions were established to serve Wales (excluding Monmouthshire) and Cheshire, and consisted of four circuits, each with two judges, who presided twice a year. The court was unique in that it dealt with criminal, civil, and equity

---

[6] Bowen, *The Statutes of Wales*, p. xcviii; Roberts, 'The Welsh Language', 32–3; Ivor Bowen, 'Grand Juries, Justices of the Peace, and Quarter Sessions in Wales', *THSC* (1936), 69; J. Gwynfor Jones, *Law, Order and Government in Caernarfonshire 1558–1640: Justices of the Peace and the Gentry* (Cardiff, 1996), p. 68.

cases, and was apparently cherished because of its cheap method of recovering debts.[7] The overwhelming majority of judges were Englishmen. It has been calculated that only 30 of the 217 judges who served the Great Sessions during its lifespan were Welshmen, very few of whom were conversant with the Welsh language.[8] The fact that judges served the same circuits year after year shocked the sensibilities of early nineteenth-century legal reformers. The continuity of judges, however, was believed to be advantageous in some quarters, since it gave them ample opportunity to become accustomed to the 'peculiarities' of the Welsh. This opinion was offered by Lord Dynevor to a Select Committee in 1817, and by a prophetic commentator in 1829, who foresaw judges, 'normally acquainted with things in England [losing] patience with things in Wales' because of the time consumed interpreting the evidence of witnesses.[9] Court proceedings were therefore dependent on the use of the 'imperfect medium' of the interpreter, the quality of whose work was sharply criticized by two London-Welsh radicals, John Jones (Jac Glan-y-gors) and Thomas Roberts, Llwyn'rhudol, in the 1790s.[10] Although judges were not Welsh speakers, many court officials were. In a select committee in 1821 which investigated the Great Sessions, one witness stated that court officials regularly corrected the interpreter.[11] This presumably meant that the accuracy of the proceedings was not always dependent on untrained translators and that a safety net was sometimes available to avoid miscarriages of justice. Whatever linguistic injustices they might encounter, the court was nevertheless very popular with the lower orders of society. One explanation why the courtroom was not as daunting to the monoglot Welshman as one might expect was the fact that he knew that members of the jury would understand his evidence. In a sense, therefore, the interpreter was sworn in mainly for the benefit of the judge and counsel.

In February 1828 Lord Henry Brougham delivered his famous six-hour speech to the House of Commons in which he outlined his proposals for legal reform.[12]

---

[7] The best accounts of the Court of Great Sessions are by W. Llewelyn Williams, 'The Courts of Great Sessions, 1542–1830' in idem, *The Making of Modern Wales* (London, 1919), pp. 128–94, and Glyn Parry, *A Guide to the Records of Great Sessions* (Aberystwyth, 1995), esp. pp. iv–xl.

[8] W. R. Williams, *The History of the Great Sessions, 1542–1830* (Brecknock, 1899), p. 19; Mark Ellis Jones, '"An Invidious attempt to accelerate the extinction of our language": The abolition of the Court of Great Sessions and the Welsh Language', *WHR*, 19, no. 2 (1998), 226–64.

[9] *Report and Evidence from the Select Committee on the Administration of Justice in Wales* (PP 1817 V), p. 108; *The Cambrian Quarterly Magazine*, I (1829), 258. It is suggested in *Wellesley's Index* that this article was written by R. G. Temple, brother-in-law to A. J. Johnes, a littérateur and one of the first County Court judges in Wales.

[10] For Glan-y-gors, see his satirical poem, 'Hanes y Sessiwn yng Nghymru', reproduced in A. E. Jones, 'Jac Glan-y-gors, 1766–1821', *TDHS*, 16 (1967), 80–1; for Roberts, see his pamphlet, *Cwyn yn erbyn Gorthrymder* (London, 1798), p. 19.

[11] *Minutes of Evidence from the Select Committee on the Administration of Justice in Wales* (PP 1821 IV), p. 34.

[12] This speech is reproduced in *The Speeches of Henry, Lord Brougham* (4 vols., Edinburgh, 1838), II, pp. 287–315.

Among his recommendations was the abolition of the Great Sessions, a conclusion which was subsequently reached by the Royal Commission which his speech had instigated. An examination of the report of the Royal Commission leaves the reader in little doubt that the main reason for the abolition of the Great Sessions was that English legal reformers greatly envied the Welsh judicature, with its eight judges, at a time when overburdened central courts in London had only twelve.[13] It was perhaps inevitable that the commissioners, imbued with the spirit of utilitarianism, would view the Great Sessions as an anomaly.[14] This, however, was more than a matter of tidying up in the field of law; it was also a convenient opportunity to assimilate Wales more permanently into England. Why should Wales, 'because it happens to be termed a principality', have its own legal system, asked Brougham?[15] Although the Great Sessions were not abolished because of the existence of the Welsh language, an interesting insight into the *mentalité* of the commissioners is provided by the inclusion of one of the questions put to the witnesses:

> Do you think that the manners and habits of the people of Wales have in any material degree, and within a recent period, become more assimilated than formerly to those of England? . . . Do you think its further progress desirable, or likely to be increased by a union with the English judicature?

A number of the witnesses specifically referred to the Welsh language in answering this question and provided interesting statements about the perceived strength of the tongue. Sir William Owen, attorney-general on the Carmarthen circuit, and John Jones, MP for Carmarthenshire, suggested that the language had been rejuvenated of late. It is curious that witnesses failed to see how the abolition of the Great Sessions might dilute Welshness, which may suggest that the law was not necessarily seen as an agent of Anglicization. The attorney-general of the Chester circuit, John Hill, and Jonathan Raine of the King's Council, asserted that legal changes would make no difference to the court proceedings because of the 'marvellous tenacity' of the Welsh in using their language 'even when they can speak English very well'.[16]

Two subjects which came under the censure of the commissioners were the judges and the Welsh juries. We have already seen how the fact that judges served

---

[13] Williams, 'Courts of Great Sessions', p. 191.
[14] For contemporary criticism of the commissioners, see *Quarterly Review*, XLII (1830), 209.
[15] Brougham, *Speeches*, p. 347. A similar argument was presented by Lord Cawdor, a vociferous opponent of the Great Sessions, in *Letter to the Right Hon. John, Baron Lyndhurst, Lord High Chancellor of England, on the Administration of Justice in Wales* (London, 1828).
[16] *First Report and Supplement of His Majesty's Commission Appointed to Inquire into the Practice and Proceedings of the Superior Courts of Common Law*, Appendix E (PP 1829 IX), pp. 440, 442. For another example of the attachment of Welsh witnesses to their language, although conversant with English, see *Monmouthshire Merlin*, 29 August 1829; this was made in the context of the Monmouthshire Assizes.

the same circuits may have been advantageous to Welsh litigants, but there was also a fear that this obstructed impartiality. This was also believed to be the case with juries which, it was said, were summoned from too small an area to ensure objectivity. The intimacy of Welsh communities had prompted some English people to seek justice outside Wales, as had happened in the well-known case involving Augustus Brackenbury. Brackenbury's attempts to construct a mansion on Mynydd Bach, Cardiganshire, were opposed by local people, and in 1826 the building was destroyed by a mob of some six hundred people. In the case which followed, those who stood accused of the incident were acquitted, and it was claimed that this had been largely due to the prejudice of the Welsh-speaking jury.[17] As a result, Brackenbury sought a retrial in an English court. When Christopher Temple, barrister, was asked by the Select Committee of 1820 why plaintiffs took their cases to English courts, he replied that the search for impartial juries was the main incentive.[18] In order to achieve greater impartiality the commissioners recommended the creation of four new Welsh assize districts, and parts of the Welsh Marches were to be attached to English assize districts.[19] These were proposals which completely ignored traditional county borders, and indeed the border between England and Wales. The reaction to these proposed changes to the legal boundaries serves to reaffirm the central importance of trial by jury to the Welsh. According to John Lloyd (Einion Môn), a teacher and poet, writing to the *North Wales Chronicle*, the changes would deny the Welsh 'the dearest rights of Britons in a greater degree than they are at present', and would constitute an 'invidious attempt to accelerate the extinction of our language'.[20] It was recognized by Einion Môn and the London-Welsh societies that many Welshmen would be faced not only by a judge and counsel who did not understand Welsh but, more ominously, by an English jury. The London Welsh wanted the Welsh language to become the medium of legal transaction,[21] but at this juncture expediency led them to petition against the amalgamation of Welsh and English counties and the less radical demand of the appointment of better interpreters and a Welsh-language synopsis of English legislation.[22] This petition was presented to the House of Lords by Lord Dynevor on 14 June 1830. The petitions drawn up in the county meetings against the abolition of the Great Sessions did not dwell on

---

[17] *Carmarthen Journal*, 10 November 1826. See also D. J. V. Jones, *Before Rebecca: Popular Protests in Wales 1793–1835* (London, 1973), pp. 48–50; David Williams, 'Rhyfel y Sais Bach', *Ceredigion*, II, no. 1 (1952), 39–52; D. J. V. Jones, 'More Light on "Rhyfel y Sais Bach"', ibid., V, no. 1 (1964), 84–93.
[18] *Report – Evidence from the Select Committee on the Administration of Justice in Wales* (PP 1820 II), p. 51.
[19] For the proposals, see *First Report and Supplement of His Majesty's Commission Appointed to Inquire into the Practice and Proceedings of the Superior Courts of Common Law*, pp. 41–4.
[20] *North Wales Chronicle*, 3 June 1830.
[21] See, for example, the speech delivered by Isaac Simon, president of the London Cymreigyddion, on 9 January 1830, in *Lleuad yr Oes*, IV, no. 2 (1830), 61.
[22] For the petition, see *Seren Gomer*, XIII, no. 178 (1830), 219–20.

the matter of language, save that penned at Haverfordwest, which feared the changes would entail cases from the 'Englishry' of south Pembrokeshire being tried by Welsh-speaking jurors at Carmarthen.[23] In the House of Commons an objection to amalgamating counties was raised by English MPs, one of whom feared the consequences of having juries 'half English and half Welsh'.[24] Colonel Wood, the Conservative member for Breconshire, spoke of the 'prejudice' of the Welsh while giving evidence in their language, a 'prejudice that ought to be respected', and which made it imperative that juries should be composed of Welshmen.[25] Fears that Welshmen might be tried by English juries, however, were allayed when the bill was amended to ensure that the new assize districts followed county borders. Trial by jury may well have been one of the inalienable rights of the 'Freeborn Englishman', but to the monoglot Welshman it had even greater significance: since jurors were Welsh speakers, it was the only institution which could ensure something approaching a fair hearing. It is worth emphasizing, too, that acquittal rates in Wales were somewhat higher than in England.[26]

Besides losing a judicature which many deemed cheap and efficient, the most deeply-felt consequence of incorporation into the English system of Assizes was that the Welsh were now visited by judges who had never previously presided in Wales. When, in 1832, Lord Lyndhurst instructed non-English-speaking jurors at the Caernarfonshire Assizes to leave the jury box, a correspondent in *Seren Gomer* claimed it was tantamount to an attempt to exterminate the Welsh language.[27] Baron Gurney irritated many at the Cardiganshire Assizes in 1834 when he expressed his belief that the English language should be propagated in Wales and that there were 'difficulties, nay, indeed, impossibilities, to obtain the truth'.[28] The editor of the *Carmarthen Journal* replied that it would be easier for 'the Bench and Bar to learn Welsh than for a million people to learn English'.[29] The burgeoning Welsh newspapers and magazines of this period indicate that the treatment of Welshmen in law courts was widely debated. Although this was by no means a new grievance, there was now more cause for concern since judges

---

[23] This petition can be found in *The Cambrian Quarterly Magazine*, II (1830), 116. A similar objection was raised by J. Frankland Lewis, who maintained that he would not wish to see cases from Radnorshire tried by Welsh-speaking juries in Brecon. NLW, Harpton Court Papers, C/604, letter from Frankland Lewis, 24 April [1830].
[24] *Parliamentary Debates (*Hansard), 2nd series, vol. 25, col. 504 (18 June 1830).
[25] Ibid., vol. 24, col. 107 (27 April 1830).
[26] For a discussion of the significance of trial by jury for the English, see Douglas Hay, 'Property, Authority and the Criminal Law' in idem et al. (eds.), *Albion's Fatal Tree: Crime and Society in Eighteenth-Century England* (London, 1975), pp. 17–63. For the lower Welsh acquittal rate, see D. J. V. Jones, 'Life and Death in Eighteenth-Century Wales: A Note', *WHR*, 10, no. 4 (1981), 536–48.
[27] *Seren Gomer*, XV, no. 205 (1832), 301.
[28] *Carmarthen Journal*, 21 March 1834.
[29] Ibid., 28 March 1834.

were less tolerant and an increasing number of people were coming into contact with the legal system following the boom in criminal prosecutions.[30] An important factor in stimulating greater interest in the issue was the proliferation of cultural societies, notably the Cymreigyddion, whose *raison d'être* was the preservation of the Welsh language.[31] There is much evidence of their desire to see Welsh become the medium of law: it was often chosen as the subject for essay competitions, such as that organized by the Carmarthen Cymreigyddion in 1834,[32] and sometimes the subject of a lecture.[33] The motive for securing Welsh as the language of law was more than an attempt to obtain justice for the monoglot Welshman – it was part of a larger strategy to restore the national language.[34] By making Welsh the medium of law it was hoped that the upper echelons of society would acquire the language and that educational institutions would teach it. The London-Welsh societies set themselves the task of channelling the discontent over the treatment of the Welsh language into what they hoped would be a co-ordinated petitioning campaign.[35] In addition to the Cymreigyddion, great interest was shown by philanthropic friendly societies, particularly those affiliated to Wales, such as the Ivorites, and that remarkable group of individuals which centred around Lady Augusta Hall, the 'Llanover Circle'.[36] There is also evidence that local communities sought to address the matter themselves; for instance, a petition from Aberystwyth demanded that either English-medium education be instituted throughout Wales or that Welsh should be used in the law courts.[37]

The prospect of a new set of courts was expediently used by those who sought more equitable treatment for Welsh in the legal system. The County Courts were specifically concerned with the recovery of small debts which, since the abolition of the Great Sessions, had been made more difficult. From December 1843 the

---

[30] For an analysis of the crime figures, see David J. V. Jones, *Crime in Nineteenth-Century Wales* (Cardiff, 1992), chapter 2, and Clive Emsley, *Crime and Society in England 1750–1900* (2nd ed., London, 1996), chapter 2.

[31] Sian Rhiannon Williams, *Oes y Byd i'r Iaith Gymraeg: Y Gymraeg yn Ardal Ddiwydiannol Sir Fynwy yn y Bedwaredd Ganrif ar Bymtheg* (Caerdydd, 1992), chapter 3; R. T. Jenkins and Helen M. Ramage, *A History of the Honourable Society of Cymmrodorion and of the Gwyneddigion and Cymreigyddion Societies* (London, 1951).

[32] *Seren Gomer*, XVIII, no. 233 (1835).

[33] NLW, MS 22714B, 'Rhestr Gweithredawl, Cymmreigyddion Caerludd . . . yn dechrau gyda y vlwyddyn 1835', lecture given by Dewi Watkins on 9 January 1840.

[34] NLW, MS 2769C, 'Anerchiad at Genedl yr Hen Gymmry (oddiwrth Cymreigyddion Caerludd)', 22 August 1832.

[35] *Seren Gomer*, XV, no. 199 (1832), 107–9. Letter from the secretaries of the London Cymreigyddion.

[36] At one of the earliest meetings of the 'Llanover Circle' it was decided to petition Parliament for Welsh-speaking judges. See ibid., XVIII, no. 232 (1835), 24. A brief exploration of the 'Circle' is provided in Mair Elvet Thomas, *Afiaith yng Ngwent: Hanes Cymdeithas Cymreigyddion y Fenni, 1833–1854* (Caerdydd, 1978).

[37] *Y Gwladgarwr*, III, no. 33 (1835), 25.

secretaries of the London Cymreigyddion urged their fellow countrymen to send petitions to ensure that Welsh speakers were appointed to the judgeships created to serve the new courts.[38] Petitions were drawn up and presented to Parliament, such as those of March 1845, which were presented to the House of Commons by Charles Wynn and Sir Watkin Williams Wynn.[39] By the autumn of the following year it was claimed that some twenty thousand people had signed the petitions.[40] Almost from the outset the campaign for Welsh appointments was connected with Arthur James Johnes, author of a well-known tract which attributed the growth of Dissent to the neglect of the Welsh language by the established Church.[41] When Lord Dynevor asked the Lord Chancellor whether he intended to appoint Welshmen, Lord Cottenham replied that he would if suitable candidates could be found.[42] Three of the five judges appointed to serve the Welsh County Court circuits in 1847 were Welsh speakers, namely A. J. Johnes, John Johnes, and E. L. Richards. For those who wished to see Welsh given official status in law, these appointments represented a step in the right direction. There is evidence that Welsh was used by judges – much to the delight of litigants – and that entire cases were sometimes held in Welsh.[43] The desire for fairer treatment for the Welsh language had to some degree been met, but by the mid-nineteenth century there were increasing numbers who were determined to undermine these gains.

★ ★ ★

During the middle decades of the nineteenth century the fate of the Welsh language in the courts was widely debated, and an insight into the ideas of contemporaries can be gained from the myriad tracts, letters and articles which appeared in Welsh newspapers and periodicals. Contemporaries frequently referred to the problems encountered in the law courts to substantiate more general arguments about language. These, however, invariably reflected the thoughts of the more articulate section of the population rather than the 'silent majority' of monoglot Welsh labourers, tenant farmers, craftsmen and miners who were faced with the daunting ordeal of witnessing court proceedings in a medium unintelligible to them. It appears that some Welsh people with a grasp of English, but who refused to use anything other than their mother tongue, were prepared to stage a form of popular protest. It has already been seen how the Welsh were characterized as 'intransigent' in matters relating to their language, but in the less

[38] *Yr Amserau*, 27 December 1843.
[39] *North Wales Chronicle*, 25 March 1845.
[40] *Yr Amserau*, 8 October 1846.
[41] Marian Henry Jones, 'Judge A. J. Johnes, 1808–1871, Patriot and Reformer', *MC*, LVII, no. 1 (1963–4), 3–20.
[42] *Parliamentary Debates* (Hansard), 3rd series, vol. 88, col. 280 (3 August 1846).
[43] For example, see *Carnarvon and Denbigh Herald*, 29 May, 5 June, 12 June 1847.

tolerant circumstances following the abolition of the Great Sessions this was a perilous course of action. In a case of rape held at the Monmouthshire Assizes in 1852, in which the defendant was a Catholic priest, one of the witnesses declined to give her evidence in English, preferring to give it in the language with which she was better acquainted. In response the judge threatened to refuse to grant her expenses. The conduct of the judge was raised in the House of Lords by the Earl of Powis who, together with Lord Dynevor, defended the right of the Welsh to be examined in the language of their choice. The response of the Lord Chancellor was intriguing: he claimed that experience had taught him that the Welsh had a tendency to deny a knowledge of English, and 'in order to induce them to speak English, [they needed] to be told that they would not be allowed their expenses unless they did so'.[44] At the Flintshire Assizes in the following year a witness was sentenced to a month in gaol for contempt of court because he claimed he was unable properly to answer a question unless it was put to him in Welsh.[45] Such forms of protest were not a rejection of the legal system *in toto*, but rather a rejection of the linguistic injustice they encountered. Although the Welsh had their own traditions of obtaining justice outside the legal system, most notably the *ceffyl pren*, the legal system was of central importance to the lower orders. David Jones argues that attacks on magistrates who neglected their responsibilities in the late eighteenth and early nineteenth centuries show how important the efficient pursuit of justice was to the people.[46] The centrality of law to the lower orders is also indicated by their willingness to prosecute despite the costs involved. Presumably, therefore, people who believed in the efficacy of redress via the courts were more likely to resent linguistic injustices.

It might be expected that any incident of popular insurrection in this period would provide an opportunity to air linguistic grievances relating to law. The Rebecca disturbances of 1839–44 did not, however, include such a dimension. It may be that this was not deemed to be their domain, especially at a time when the issue of Welsh-speaking County Court judges was busily being pursued by the Cymreigyddion societies. Only the utterances of the most vocal Rebeccaites have been recorded for posterity, and since many of them were bilingual they were not necessarily likely to champion linguistic grievances. In his fine study of Rebecca, David Jones asserted that costs were far more pressing problems for the litigant than language, and there were indeed many occasions when such matters were raised, for instance, at the meetings held at Cynwyl Elfed, Allt Cunedda and Pen Tas Eithin.[47] In addition to costs, another area of concern in relation to law was

---

[44] *Parliamentary Debates* (Hansard), 3rd series, vol. 121, col. 1175 (27 May 1852).
[45] *Carnarvon and Denbigh Herald*, 9 April 1853. For a similar case, see *Merthyr Guardian*, 11 April 1835.
[46] Jones, *Before Rebecca*, p. 63.
[47] David J. V. Jones, *Rebecca's Children: A Study of Rural Society, Crime, and Protest* (Oxford, 1989), p. 157. For these meetings, see *The Welshman*, 23 August, 29 September, 3 November 1843.

the magistracy, who were acknowledged by many, including Thomas Campbell Foster, correspondent of *The Times*, as having played a large part in instigating the troubles. The want of confidence in the magistracy led protesters to press the case for stipendiary magistrates.[48] The demand for professionally trained JPs once more reveals the importance of law to the people, although it can only be assumed that they wanted Welshmen to fill the posts. According to the commissioners who investigated the causes of the disturbances, the appointment of stipendiary magistrates would be unwise since it would entail the arrival of 'strangers, unconnected with the usages and manners of the people'.[49] Foster suspected that linguistic differences accounted for the lack of confidence in the magistrates, but when this was put to a group of farmers they replied that magistrates fully understood what they had to say, but that they resented their demeanour. One farmer claimed that they were treated like 'beasts and not human beings'.[50] It is difficult to believe that the overwhelming majority of magistrates were competent Welsh speakers, and it was for this reason that the commissioners recommended that the magistrates' clerk should, as a rule, be fully conversant with the indigenous language.[51] But although the Rebecca Riots often witnessed complaints about the appointment of non-Welsh speakers to posts such as magistrates' clerks, land agents, and officials in the workhouse, during this period of hardship the treatment of the Welsh language in the courts was much less prominent. For instance, Thomas Emlyn Thomas, schoolmaster, radical and Unitarian minister, wrote of the need for Welsh-speaking judges in an article published in *Seren Gomer* in 1843, but said nothing of the matter in the Rebecca meetings which he attended.[52]

Perhaps the most important linguistic dimension to the Rebecca disturbances was that, together with the Chartist march on Newport in 1839, it provided contemporaries with evidence of the need to launch a comprehensive programme of English-medium education to 'civilize' the Welsh. In a speech which instigated the education commission of 1846–7, William Williams, MP for Coventry, spoke of the disturbances in this light, and noted the dire consequences which faced the Welsh in law courts. To illustrate his case, Williams raised the possibility of a Welshman being sentenced to death without having understood one word of the proceedings; of cases in which juries reached verdicts which flew in the face of the evidence, and which invariably meant acquittal; and of a case in which one of the jurors was required to translate evidence for the benefit of the other eleven

---

[48] This was also raised at meetings held at Cynwyl Elfed, Allt Cunedda and Pen Tas Eithin.
[49] *Report of the Commissioners of Inquiry for South Wales* (PP 1844 XVI), p. 34.
[50] *The Times*, 19 August 1843. The assertion that the magistrates spoke English only was rejected in a letter to *The Welshman*, 25 August 1843.
[51] *Report of the Commissioners of Inquiry for South Wales*, p. 32. See also the evidence of John Rees, Llannarth, p. 59.
[52] *Seren Gomer*, XXVI, no. 336 (1843), 266.

members of the jury.[53] In Williams's opinion, the Welsh people 'did not want us to translate the laws into, or to administer them in their language, but they ask and pray us to send English schoolmasters amongst them to teach them the language in which the laws are written, that they may understand and obey them'.[54] This was an unusual comment to make in view of the campaign which had managed to muster thousands of names in support of Welsh-speaking County Court judges. There is, however, evidence to suggest that there was a genuine desire among the lower orders to see their children acquire a knowledge of English. The Revd H. Longueville Jones, inspector of Church schools, who took the enlightened view of advocating bilingual methods of teaching, noted a desire to acquire English 'without yielding in one iota of respect or affection for the mother tongue of our beloved country'.[55] Those who condemned the findings of the Blue Books did not on the whole question the assumption that English held the key to the future, but they were enraged by the animus against the cherished ancient tongue and the critique of Welsh morality. The Welsh were portrayed as a people with a propensity to petty crime, sexual deviance and drunkenness. Also denounced was the behaviour of the Welsh in the law courts: 'The evil of the Welsh language', it was said, 'is obviously and fearfully great in the courts of justice.'[56] It was claimed that the language 'distorts the truth, favours fraud, and abets perjury', and, on the question of perjury, one of the witnesses, Edward Lloyd Hall, a barrister from Newcastle Emlyn, maintained that there were few cases in which perjury did not figure to some extent.[57] The belief that the Welsh were prone to perjury was by no means confined to the Blue Books; contemporary literature referred to it and it was sometimes lamented by Assize judges. The extent to which perjury occurred because of misunderstanding caused by linguistic differences is impossible to ascertain, and Welsh petty juries may have preferred acquittal for reasons best known to themselves.

As the belief that the English language held the key to the future made deeper inroads in mid-Victorian Wales, so the programme of the Cymreigyddion to elevate Welsh to officialdom became more difficult to sustain. The notion of Welsh-speaking judges began to smack of the notion of 'Wales for the Welsh' in the minds of those who celebrated political union with England. For some, the success in obtaining Welsh-speaking County Court judges was only a temporary measure. According to the editor of *The Welshman*: 'The education of the Welsh in the language of the laws they are compelled to obey must come, but in the mean time it is something to have judges who understand the evidence upon

---

[53] *Parliamentary Debates* (Hansard), 3rd series, vol. 84, col. 857–8 (10 March 1846).
[54] Ibid., col. 858.
[55] Quoted in H. G. Williams, 'Longueville Jones and Welsh Education: The Neglected Case of a Victorian H.M.I.', *WHR*, 15, no. 3 (1991), 432–3.
[56] *Reports of the Commissioners of Inquiry into the State of Education in Wales . . . in three parts. Part II. Brecknock, Cardigan, Radnor, and Monmouth* (PP 1847 (871) XXVII), p. 66.
[57] Ibid., p. 90.

which they must ground their decision.'[58] In the midst of the debate over language, an increasing number gave reasons why Welsh should not become the language of law. One anonymous correspondent stressed the costs which the translation and printing of legislation on the statute book in Welsh would entail; far cheaper, he claimed, would be the establishment of English-medium schools.[59] Another claimed – not without a hint of sarcasm – that only by founding a 'Welsh Lincoln's Inn . . . at Bala or elsewhere' could legal men be trained to operate such a system. Also mentioned was the problem of finding appropriate vocabulary to express legal terminology. One commentator insisted that the need constantly to refer to English legal texts and William Owen Pughe's much derided Welsh dictionary would 'bring the confusion of Babel into the Law Courts'.[60] While there was probably a kernel of truth in the claim that the Welsh language did not possess an extensive range of legal terms (partly because it had been proscribed from the courts since the sixteenth century), such assertions underestimated the ability of the language to coin new words and rapidly assimilate them within popular parlance, as had been the case in other domains such as politics, printing and science in the late eighteenth and early nineteenth centuries.[61]

Despite the pessimism of those who loudly sounded the death knell of the Welsh language and the almost universal desire to see English more widely understood, there were still some who were prepared to champion the cause of the national language during the decade or so after the publication of the Blue Books. Such people derived strength from what appeared to be the rejuvenation of the language:

> Y mae [yr iaith Gymraeg] yn adnewyddu ei hieuenctyd fel yr eryr – ei newyddiaduron, ei chyfnodolion, ei geiriaduron, a'i llyfrau o bob math, yn lluosogi yn gyflym; gan hynny, rhaid fod nifer ei darllenwyr a'i choleddwyr yn amlhau hefyd. Os dileu yr hen iaith oedd un o amcanion gwreiddiol y llywodraeth yn appwyntiad gweinyddiad y gyfraith yn yr iaith Seisoneg yn Nghymru, y mae yr amcan wedi llwyr fethu.[62]

(The Welsh language has renewed its strength like an eagle – her newspapers, periodicals, dictionaries, and books of all description, are multiplying rapidly; and so, therefore, must the number of readers and cherishers of the language. If the original intention of the state in administering the law in English was to eradicate the old language, the policy has failed utterly.)

The areas which witnessed this growth were, however, primarily divorced from the secular world. Self-congratulation regarding the strength of the national

---

[58] *The Welshman*, 23 April 1847.
[59] *Carnarvon and Denbigh Herald*, 26 June 1847.
[60] Ibid., 18 December 1858.
[61] Prys Morgan, 'Dyro Olau ar dy Eiriau', *Taliesin*, 70 (1990), 38–45.
[62] *Baner Cymru*, 27 January 1858. See also R. J. Derfel, 'Cadwraeth yr Iaith Gymraeg' in idem, *Traethodau ac Areithiau* (Bangor, 1864), p. 159.

language was not unjustified since this had been achieved despite the hostility of the state. In the words of Thomas Gee, editor of *Baner ac Amserau Cymru*: '[The Welsh language] was locked out of the law courts, and to an extent, from the churches in the hope that this would seal the fate of the tongue; but far from perishing, the old language has emptied the churches, and rendered the law courts superfluous' ('Cauwyd hi allan o'r llys barn, ac i raddau o'r eglwysydd, gan gredu y buasai farw yn union; ond yn lle marw, y mae yr hen iaith wedi gwaghau yr eglwysydd, ac wedi gwneyd llys barn yn ddianghenrhaid').[63] Those who questioned the virtue of confining the national tongue to certain functions such as religious instruction and worship were much fewer in number. Unlike Scotland, with its well-organized, although short-lived, National Association for the Vindication of Scottish Rights, founded in 1853, the Welsh did not possess a movement capable of airing its national grievances.[64] Even the eisteddfod did its utmost to avoid making statements which could be interpreted as encouraging the Welsh language.[65] The nearest thing to a national association was the Association of Welsh Clergy in the West Riding of the County of York, whose members met every St David's day to celebrate their nationality and debate issues which affected the well-being of their countrymen. There can be no doubt about the sincerity of the desire of these clergymen to see Welsh adopted as the language of law,[66] even though their endeavours for the most part have been written out of Welsh history largely because such an Anglican initiative is difficult to reconcile with the Nonconformist interpretation of the past.[67] The West Riding Association was seriously hamstrung by its affiliation to an institution which had been demonized following the 'treason' of its clerics in the Blue Books. The alienation of the churchmen from the new definition of Welshness was perhaps the most unfortunate consequence of the Blue Books controversy, but it was symptomatic of a much broader entrenchment of denominationalism within Wales: 'The ethos of denominationalism always transcends that of the national spirit' ('[Y] mae yr ysbryd enwadol bob amser yn gryfach na'r ysbryd cenedlaethol'), lamented the editor of *Baner Cymru*.[68] In such a climate there was little hope that R. J. Derfel's dream of establishing 'Cymdeithas Amddiffyn Cymru' (the Welsh Defence Association) to pursue issues such as the rights of Welshmen in courts of law

---

[63] *BAC*, 31 October 1860.

[64] For the Scottish Rights Association, see H. J. Hanham, 'The Mid-Century Scottish Nationalism: Romantic and Radical' in Robert Robson (ed.), *Ideas and Institutions of Victorian Britain* (London, 1967), pp. 164–71.

[65] The complicated relationship between the eisteddfod and the question of language is explored in Hywel Teifi Edwards, *Gŵyl Gwalia: Yr Eisteddfod Genedlaethol yn Oes Aur Victoria 1858–1868* (Llandysul, 1980), chapter 5.

[66] See, for example, *Report of the Proceedings of the Association of Welsh Clergy in the West Riding of the County of York, March 1st, 1856* (Caernarfon, 1856), pp. 44–7.

[67] But see R. Tudur Jones, 'Yr Eglwysi a'r Iaith yn Oes Victoria', *LlC*, 19 (1996), 152–5.

[68] *Baner Cymru*, 12 May 1858.

would come to fruition.[69] Patriotic littérateurs, such as Derfel himself, Michael D. Jones, the Revd R. W. Morgan, and William Rees (Gwilym Hiraethog), who called for fairer treatment for Welsh in the law courts, were isolated voices. But this is not to say that their ideas fell on deaf ears, for their views were widely published and presumably reflected a wider undercurrent of opinion. It remains to be seen to what extent the MPs elected after the extension of the franchise in 1867 vented this grievance.

★ ★ ★

Efforts made by the Liberation Society to politicize the Welsh came to fruition with the extension of the franchise in 1867.[70] Although the significance of the election of 1868 has often been exaggerated, Wales did at last have a cadre of politicians who could air her grievances with greater determination. All but ten of her thirty-three representatives were Liberals. In terms of the question of language, it must be borne in mind that MPs such as Henry Richard, George Osborne Morgan and Watkin Williams were not from the same school as the small-nation cultural nationalists of the late 1880s and 1890s, such as Tom Ellis, J. Herbert Lewis and David Lloyd George. As David Howell has pointed out, the election of 1868 was 'a victory for Nonconformist radicalism, not Welsh nationalism'.[71] According to Howell, linguistic grievances were set aside during the post-1868 campaign in favour of political and religious rights. It must also be remembered that many of the radical Nonconformist middle-class opinion-makers who had made the election result possible were ambivalent towards the Welsh language.[72] Nevertheless, during the first premiership of W. E. Gladstone the matter of language was addressed on two important occasions. Firstly, in 1870 Gladstone appointed a Welsh speaker, Joshua Hughes, to the episcopacy of St Asaph, the first Welsh-speaking bishop since 1715. Secondly, in October 1871 the appointment of Homersham Cox, a monoglot Englishman, to the judgeship of the mid-Wales County Court circuit prompted George Osborne Morgan, one of the county members for Denbighshire, to propose a motion in March 1872 to

---

[69] Derfel, 'Pethau wnawn pe gallwn' in idem, *Traethodau ac Areithiau*, p. 259.
[70] Ieuan Gwynedd Jones, 'The Liberation Society and Welsh Politics, 1844 to 1868' in idem, *Explorations and Explanations: Essays in the Social History of Victorian Wales* (Llandysul, 1981), pp. 236–68; Ryland Wallace, *Organise! Organise! Organise! A Study of Reform Agitations in Wales, 1840–1886* (Cardiff, 1991), chapter 8.
[71] David Howell, 'A "Less Obstructive and Exacting" Nationalism: Welsh Ethnic Mobilisation in Rural Communities, 1850–1920' in idem (ed.) in collaboration with Gert von Pistohlkors and Ellen Wiegandt, *Roots of Rural Ethnic Mobilisation* (Aldershot and New York, 1993), pp. 51–97.
[72] For the influence exerted by the Nonconformist middle-class, although in the context of politics, see Matthew Cragoe, 'Conscience or Coercion? Clerical Influence at the General Election of 1868 in Wales', *P&P*, 149 (1995), 140–69.

prevent similar appointments in the future.[73] Homersham Cox was appointed to succeed Tindal Atkinson, also a monoglot Englishman, who had served the circuit for a little less than a year. Atkinson's appointment had caused much resentment in some quarters; the editor of the *Carnarvon and Denbigh Herald* had written: 'We are justly indignant that a Government, the members of whom are conversant with the circumstances and requirements of Wales, should flagrantly set aside public convenience and the demands of justice.'[74] Shortly after Atkinson's arrival in Wales, Osborne Morgan made no reference to the recent appointment when he addressed his constituents to outline his political agenda.[75] One angry correspondent demanded to know why Welsh MPs had not opposed the appointment, and lamented that even under the Liberals the needs of Wales were neglected.[76] News that another Englishman had been chosen to serve the circuit added insult to injury. Following Cox's appointment, more attention was given to the issue when a letter written by J. J. Hughes (Alfardd) to the Lord Chancellor in September 1871 was published in the Welsh press.[77] Since Alfardd was the sub-editor of *Yr Herald Cymraeg*, a staunchly Liberal newspaper, it is not surprising that Osborne Morgan, and other Liberal MPs, vowed to pursue the matter. At a meeting held at Denbigh on 25 October, Morgan promised to draw the Lord Chancellor's attention to the discontent felt over the appointment,[78] and pledged to raise the matter in Parliament should his initiative prove unsuccessful.[79] Pressure 'from below' had clearly forced the hand of Morgan and his colleagues at Westminster on the question of Welsh County Court judges.

Osborne Morgan faced a novel challenge when he presented his motion to the House of Commons. This was one of the first occasions that a specifically Welsh grievance, unrelated to religion, had been heard in Parliament. It is interesting to note that the pursuit of Welsh issues, in this case County Court judgeships, had to be distanced from the demand for home rule since there was evidently a fear that it smacked of a demand of 'Wales for the Welsh'. Watkin Williams MP explained that the question was solely concerned with securing equality for the Welsh within the political union. In *The Times* Morgan claimed their actions were designed to secure justice for 'that half a million of their Majesty's subjects, who, from no fault of their own, have never been taught English'.[80] In the debate of

[73] *Parliamentary Debates* (Hansard), 3rd series, vol. 209, col. 1648ff. (8 March 1872). A discussion of the case involving Homersham Cox can be found in Hywel Teifi Edwards, *Codi'r Hen Wlad yn ei Hôl, 1850–1914* (Llandysul, 1989), pp. 173–86.
[74] *Carnarvon and Denbigh Herald*, 17 December 1870.
[75] Ibid., 7 January 1871.
[76] *BAC*, 18 October 1871.
[77] This letter was widely reproduced in the Welsh press; see ibid., 14 October 1871.
[78] This correspondence was subsequently reproduced in the form of a Parliamentary Paper; see PP 1874 LIV, 'Welsh County Court Judges'. Copy of correspondence dated November 1871, between [the Lord Chancellor] and George Osborne Morgan MP.
[79] *BAC*, 28 October 1871.
[80] *The Times*, 15 November 1871.

March 1872 much emphasis was placed on the belief that the County Courts demanded special linguistic provision. This point was presumably pressed to allay fears that the Welsh MPs wished to apply the principle throughout the legal system in Wales, as many in Wales had in fact hoped.[81] In Parliament Morgan told of how justice was 'of a rough and ready kind' in the County Courts, where the plaintiff and defendant were invariably undefended and the sentence passed solely by the judge, unlike the situation at the Assizes and Quarter Sessions, where the jurors often understood the evidence directly. This line of argument, however, meant that linguistic injustices in the higher courts were overlooked. As had been the case in the 1840s, the call for Welsh-speaking judges was underpinned by the presentation of petitions to Parliament. No longer, however, were the Welsh dependent on exiled countrymen in London. Most of the eighty-nine petitions presented by Osborne Morgan were drawn up following a meeting held at Porthaethwy, on the Menai Straits, a month earlier.[82] It was claimed at this gathering that a concerted effort was required to transcend all religious and political differences, and to that end W. C. Davies, editor of the Conservative newspaper, *Cronicl Cymru*, was appointed secretary. Individuals chosen to collect names from different regions included a large number of poets, including David Griffith (Clwydfardd), Richard Davies (Mynyddog) and John Ceiriog Hughes.[83] Osborne Morgan's motion regarding the desirability of Welsh-speaking appointees was accepted on behalf of the Liberal government by the Home Secretary, Henry Austin Bruce, who had been a stipendiary magistrate in Merthyr, and was not, therefore, unfamiliar with the problems encountered in the Welsh law courts. Osborne Morgan's motion had been amended following remarks made by Charles Hanbury-Tracy, Liberal MP for Montgomery. Although supportive of the general thrust of the motion, Hanbury-Tracy feared that there might be difficulties in finding suitable Welsh-speaking candidates since he believed that there were only eight suitable candidates at that time.[84] The motion, therefore, included the clause that the judge should be Welsh speaking 'as far as the limits of selection will allow', a principle, as we shall see, that was subsequently applied to further legislation which included the desirability of Welsh-speaking appointments.

News that the motion had been accepted by the government was warmly welcomed. The effort invested in returning Liberal MPs was now believed to be paying rich dividends. According to one newspaper editor, the 'traditional English

[81] *Baner Cymru*, 12 May 1858.
[82] For the proceedings of this meeting, see *BAC*, 7 February 1872.
[83] A list of the areas which provided the petitions presented by Osborne Morgan and other MPs is provided in *Carnarvon and Denbigh Herald*, 16 March 1872.
[84] *Parliamentary Debates* (Hansard), 3rd series, vol. 209, col. 1660 (8 March 1872). It is interesting to note that Hanbury-Tracy's father, Baron Sudeley, had supported the application of the Welsh speaker A. J. Johnes to the County Court judgeship of mid-Wales in 1846. See Marian Henry Jones, 'The Letters of Arthur James Johnes, 1809–71', *NLWJ*, X, no. 4 (1958), 336.

policy' which consisted of 'bigotry and arrogance, [and] which has striven for ages to confound natural and legitimate Welsh nationality with a cry for "Wales for the Welsh", and to bound our love for the language of our forefathers as a species of disloyalty to the British Crown' had been abandoned.[85] Before long, however, it became obvious that the motion was a dead letter. Despite a succession of vacancies in English circuits, Cox remained firm in his place. In July an exasperated Osborne Morgan asked the Attorney-General to take action,[86] but there was evidently a reluctance on the part of the English state to appoint Welsh speakers. In the correspondence between Osborne Morgan and the Lord Chancellor in November 1871, the latter expressed the view that Welsh judges would not win the trust of English litigants and that even if Welsh speakers were appointed the language of law would still have to be English.[87] Implicit in the Lord Chancellor's assumptions was the belief that the administration of law in Welsh would entail the loss of one of the incentives to acquire English. These sentiments were presumably widespread in the corridors of power.

Opposition to Cox became more deeply entrenched following several cases in which he showed scant regard for the Welsh language. In October 1873 Cox non-suited one Robert Jones from Llansannan because he would not comply with his demand that he use English. In December of the same year Cox was at loggerheads with a solicitor at Aberystwyth on the issue of language. The incident, involving Robert Jones, was cited by Osborne Morgan when he addressed Parliament in July 1874. During the debate Morgan gained the support of the Conservative MPs Sir Watkin Williams Wynn, Charles Wynn and Sir Eardley Wilmot, but even in the face of growing opposition to the judge the Conservatives proved mulishly stubborn. In fact, they flaunted public opinion by appointing Horatio Lloyd, who was not a fluent Welsh speaker, to succeed R. Vaughan Williams as the north Wales County Court judge.[88] But not until 1883 did Homersham Cox leave Wales for an English circuit, and he did so with cries of derision and anger ringing in his ears. Cox had provoked an outcry when he claimed at Llanidloes in September 1883 that the propensity of the Welsh to perjure 'made his blood boil'. In the wake of this 'national insult', many joined forces in the campaign to expel the judge and to renew demands for a Welsh speaker to replace him. In 1884 Osborne Morgan's motion finally bore fruit when Gwilym Williams was appointed to the circuit, before shortly moving to a circuit in south Wales. He was replaced by Judge Bishop, who appears to have had some knowledge of the Welsh language.[89]

---

[85] *Carnarvon and Denbigh Herald*, 16 March 1872.
[86] *Parliamentary Debates* (Hansard), 3rd series, vol. 212, col. 957 (11 July 1872).
[87] 'Welsh County Court Judges' (PP 1874 LIV).
[88] *Carnarvon and Denbigh Herald*, 19 and 26 September 1874.
[89] Ibid., 25 September 1891, letter from 'Anti-Humbug'; Abel Thomas MP stated: 'I have heard him many times [speaking Welsh], and he understands and speaks it', *Parliamentary Debates* (Hansard), 4th series, vol. 1, col. 844 (19 February 1892).

The question of the Welsh County Courts was brought to light once more in Parliament following the appointment of Cecil Beresford to the mid-Wales circuit in 1891. Beresford was the godson of the prime minister, Lord Salisbury.[90] It appears that he was aware of the sensitivity of the question of language; for instance, he granted William George's wish to retry a case which had previously been tried in English because the plaintiff had not understood the proceedings.[91] Nevertheless, a meeting of the Welsh Liberal MPs unanimously decided to table a motion in the House of Commons deploring an appointment which clearly contravened Osborne Morgan's motion.[92] The motion was tabled by David Lloyd George on 19 February 1892.[93] Once more it was deemed necessary to distance this issue from that of 'Wales for the Welsh', and D. A. Thomas unequivocally stated that this was not a programme to 'stimulate the Welsh language by artificial means'.[94] Lloyd George and William Abraham (Mabon) both stressed that this was not a partisan matter and asserted that many Conservatives agreed that Beresford's appointment was unjust, a claim proven when Lord Kenyon and the Welsh-born member for Devonport, John Puleston, supported the motion. In pointing out that the government would not be breaking new ground should it provide some latitude for the Welsh language, Tom Ellis reminded them of the clause of the Factory and Workshop Act of 1891, which legislated on the desirability of appointing Welsh-speaking inspectors. Unlike Osborne Morgan's motion of 1872, this motion failed, albeit by twenty-three votes only. The issue, however, was not laid to rest. When Gladstone returned to power for the fifth and final occasion in August 1892, the campaign to oust Beresford was given a new lease of life, and pressure was exerted on the Lord Chancellor.[95] By June 1893 the laborious campaign could claim victory when Beresford was replaced by David Lewis, the Welsh-speaking recorder of Swansea. When Lewis first presided on the circuit at Aberystwyth the benefit of a Welsh-speaking judge was immediately felt when he declared that witnesses should feel free to speak their mother tongue, although he made it abundantly clear that the proceedings should still be conducted in English, in accordance with the terms of the Act of Union.[96] A few months later, however, the judge proved to be more pragmatic when he permitted the entire proceedings to be heard through the medium of Welsh at the County Court at Blaenau Ffestiniog.[97]

[90] Ibid., col. 830, speech of D. A. Thomas; *Carnarvon and Denbigh Herald*, 23 October 1891.
[91] *Carnarvon and Denbigh Herald*, 20 November 1891.
[92] NLW, J. Herbert Lewis Papers C1, Minute book of meetings of the North Wales Liberal Foundation, February 1890 – May 1895.
[93] *Parliamentary Debates* (Hansard), 4th series, vol. 1, col. 827ff. (19 February 1892).
[94] Ibid., col. 830.
[95] NLW, J. Herbert Lewis Papers C1: meetings held at the National Liberal Club, London, 30 November 1892 and at 1 Carlton Gardens, 30 January 1893. See also J. Herbert Lewis to Lord Herschell, 13 December 1892 (NLW, J. Herbert Lewis Papers, A2/6).
[96] *Carnarvon and Denbigh Herald*, 28 July 1893.
[97] Ibid., 1 September 1893.

In matters affecting the Welsh language, Welsh Liberal MPs by no means confined their interests to County Court judges. Although still dwarfed by issues such as disestablishment and education, linguistic matters became more central as cultural nationalism took root from the late 1880s. In an article in *The Welsh Review* in 1892, W. Llewelyn Williams, at that time a young author and journalist, recognized that the nineteenth century was the age of nationalism and that the 'great wave' had finally reached Wales. With the extension of the franchise in 1884–5, he maintained that a political expression had been given to a 'national sentiment which hitherto found expression only in religion and its literature'.[98] The pursuit of linguistic injustices by the Liberals seemed to confirm the impression that they constituted the legitimate party of Wales. Welsh Liberal MPs ensured that legislation in the late nineteenth century, such as the Coal Mines Regulation Act of 1887, took into account the linguistic needs of Wales.[99] Parallels can be drawn between the debate over this Act and events involving Homersham Cox and Cecil Beresford. An amendment proposed by William Abraham, MP for Rhondda, sought to make Welsh a necessary qualification for the inspectorate which was to be established under the Act.[100] Opposition to the amendment was similar to that articulated in the debates about judges, such as the assertion that the number of Welsh speakers was in decline, a notion vigorously denied by Abraham and Sir Hussey Vivien MP, and that giving preference to the Welsh would prevent the free movement and promotion of candidates within the British Isles. As had been the case with Osborne Morgan's motion in 1872, the proposal was compromised. The Conservative Home Secretary, Henry Matthews, was prepared only to give preference to Welsh speakers 'among candidates equally qualified'.[101] This principle was also applied to other Acts, namely the Factory and Workshop Act of 1891, the Quarries Act of 1894, and the Factory Act of 1901.[102] In addition Liberal MPs urged the appointment of Welsh speakers in a number of roles which were not stipulated by law, such as post-masters, Poor Law officials, and the chief inspectorate of schools.

Liberals not only campaigned for legislation which made provision for the Welsh language but also did much to obtain Welsh translations of important legislation from the late 1880s onwards. To the delight of *Baner ac Amserau Cymru*, the question of the translation of legislation was raised at a meeting of the executive committee of the North Wales Liberal Federation in April 1888, and during a meeting in October a Welsh rendition of the newly passed Local Government Act was demanded.[103] The matter of the Local Government Act was taken up by

---

[98] W. Llewelyn Williams, 'Welsh Nationalism', *The Welsh Review*, April 1892, 591.
[99] Bowen, *The Statutes of Wales*, p. 271.
[100] *Parliamentary Debates* (Hansard), 3rd series, vol. 319, col. 569ff. (15 August 1887).
[101] Ibid., col. 584.
[102] Bowen, *The Statutes of Wales*, pp. 280–1. Bowen makes no reference to the Factory and Workshop Act of 1891.
[103] NLW, MS 21171D, Minute Book of the North Wales Liberal Federation 1886–91.

William Rathborne MP and A. J. Williams MP, but the Local Government Board maintained that the government could not undertake the task and that if there was a demand it would no doubt be undertaken by private enterprise.[104] When Osborne Morgan took up the issue in the House of Commons in November, he, too, was given short shrift.[105] In March 1889, however, a volte-face occurred, and the Conservative government sanctioned a translation.[106] This was the first time that a piece of legislation had been officially rendered into Welsh *in extenso*, even though it was prefaced by a proviso that it 'did not have any legal effect whatever'.[107] The task of translation was undertaken by John Morris-Jones, a young Welsh scholar.[108] Morris-Jones's tutor, Professor John Rhŷs, had been responsible for the translation of the findings of the Royal Commission into the working of the Welsh Sunday Closing Act of 1881, published in 1890 – the first parliamentary paper to be published in Welsh.[109] Once the Local Government Act had been translated, a precedent had been set which could be applied to future legislation. Tom Ellis urged J. Herbert Lewis to exert pressure on the Flintshire councillors to obtain copies of the Act so as to ensure that the Intermediate Education Act of 1889 would also be translated.[110] This was followed by the translation of the Local Government Act of 1894.[111] The Welsh language may not have been a central issue in the 1870s, but by the 1880s it was receiving unprecedented attention, much more so than is sometimes suggested.[112] Thanks largely to the efforts of Welsh Liberal MPs, a number of gains had been made on behalf of the native language. In his study of the treatment by the state of the Welsh language during the reign of Queen Victoria, Daniel Lleufer Thomas spoke of a new latitude to the language, quoting as examples the translation of legislation and the law in respect of the Welsh language in the established Church. Yet, he noted, one key domain remained in which the treatment of the Welsh language was lamentable, namely the law courts.[113]

★ ★ ★

In matters relating to the Welsh language within the legal system, the appointment of County Court judges was not the only contentious issue. In the latter part

[104] Ibid., meeting of 20 November 1888.
[105] *Parliamentary Debates* (Hansard), 3rd series, vol. 330, col. 1510 (19 November 1888).
[106] Ibid., vol. 337, col. 963, 4 March 1889.
[107] *Carnarvon and Denbigh Herald*, 7 June 1889.
[108] William George, *Cymru Fydd: Hanes y Mudiad Cenedlaethol Cyntaf* (Lerpwl, 1945), p. 65. I owe this reference to Lord Gwilym Prys-Davies.
[109] B. Ll. James, *Parliamentary Papers (Wales), 1801–1914* (unpubl. FLA thesis, 1973), p. 117.
[110] NLW, T. E. Ellis Papers, 2883, T. E. Ellis to J. Herbert Lewis, 24 July 1889. The translation was available by November 1889. See *Carnarvon and Denbigh Herald*, 1 November 1889.
[111] *Parliamentary Debates* (Hansard), 4th series, vol. 22, col. 1112 (2 April 1894).
[112] Kenneth O. Morgan, *Wales in British Politics 1868–1922* (3rd ed., Cardiff, 1980).
[113] D. Lleufer Thomas, 'The Laws and Enactments of the Queen's Reign in Reference to Wales', *Young Wales*, III, nos. 32–3 (August 1897), 156.

of the nineteenth century the Welsh magistracy was also widely discussed. The magistracy administered law in the Petty Sessions and Quarter Sessions, and in the latter tribunal they dominated local government until the creation of county councils by the Local Government Act of 1888. In the Quarter Sessions jurisdiction involved trial by jury, which provided monoglot Welsh litigants with the same advantages as those within the Assizes if the jurors were Welsh speakers.[114] The Petty Sessions was a more *ad hoc* affair, usually consisting of one or two magistrates, who dealt with cases of a less serious nature, either monthly or whenever required, at the magistrates' abode or in a tavern. The advantage of summary jurisdiction was the rapidity and cheapness of its proceedings and, as a result, during the course of the nineteenth century the powers of magistrates at the Petty Sessions were gradually increased by means of legislation such as the Criminal Justice Act of 1855 and the Summary Jurisdiction Act of 1879.[115] The fact that the majority of cases were dealt with summarily and that the Welshman no longer had the advantage of trial by his fellow countrymen made it imperative that magistrates, the vast majority of whom were drawn from the gentry class, were either Welsh speakers or sympathetic to the native tongue.[116]

In the 1880s and 1890s Liberal MPs raised the matter of the magistracy on several occasions, although the chief concern was the method by which they were appointed. It was intended to bring the JPs more closely into sympathy with the Welsh people, which meant securing more Liberals and Nonconformists on the bench. Dissatisfaction with the magistracy was by no means unprecedented. Nonconformists were resentful because the majority of JPs were Anglicans, and in the 1830s around a quarter of them were beneficed clergymen.[117] It has been suggested that clerical JPs were frequently more conscientious in performing their duties than their colleagues, which, of course, may also account for their unpopularity.[118] It was inevitable that beneficed clergymen were prominent among the Welsh magistracy since they were often among the few residents who possessed the necessary qualifications.[119] Assuming that the Pluralities Act of 1838, which legislated that clergymen were to be Welsh speakers in those areas where parishioners were 'imperfectly or not at all instructed in the English language', was

---

[114] For the procedure of the Quarter Sessions, see J. M. Beattie, *Crime and the Courts in England 1660–1800* (Oxford, 1986), chapters 6 and 7.

[115] David Philips, *Crime and Authority in Victorian England* (London, 1977), pp. 131–3; Jones, *Crime in Nineteenth-Century Wales*, pp. 18–19.

[116] For the predominance of the gentry on the bench, see Carl H. E. Zangerl, 'The Social Composition of the County Magistracy in England and Wales, 1831–1887', *Journal of British Studies*, XI, no. 1 (1971), 113–25.

[117] See, for example, *Y Dysgedydd*, XV, no. 170 (1836), 46–50. See also Eric J. Evans, 'Some Reasons for the Growth of English Rural Anti-Clericalism, *c.*1750–*c.*1830', *P&P*, 66 (1975), 84–109.

[118] Esther Moir, *The Justice of the Peace* (London, 1969), p. 107; Sidney and Beatrice Webb, *English Local Government from the Revolution to the Municipal Corporations Act* (London, 1906), pp. 350–6.

[119] On the problem of the dearth of resident JPs in rural Wales, see *Report of the Commissioners of Inquiry for South Wales*, p. 32; David Williams, *The Rebecca Riots* (Cardiff, 1955), p. 37.

obeyed, such magistrates would have had a command of Welsh.[120] It is difficult to say with authority how the magistrates accommodated the Welsh language. It would appear that there was no hard and fast rule, other than that English was the official medium, as was recognized by the fact that court records were kept in that language. It is harder to generalize about the oral aspects of the proceedings. When interpretation was required, it was usually undertaken by the magistrates' clerk or someone sworn in specifically for the task. The most important factor in determining the language used in the proceedings of the Quarter and Petty Sessions was the linguistic ability of the magistrates and their attitude towards the native language. It is difficult to believe that they resolutely implemented the 'language clause' of the Act of Union at the Petty Sessions held at the Talbot Inn, Tregaron, or the Black Lion Hotel, Lampeter, when the presiding magistrates were fluent Welsh speakers.

In the Quarter Sessions the chairman assumed the greatest importance. In 1858 *Baner Cymru* published an article on the chairmanship of the Welsh Quarter Sessions, in which it was claimed that five of them were fluent Welsh speakers, four were completely ignorant of the language, and the remainder had some knowledge of the tongue.[121] But the assumption that a Welsh-speaking chairman would necessarily be an improvement was not always reliable. For example, at the Anglesey Quarter Sessions in 1871, John Williams, Treffos, prevented counsel from addressing the primarily monoglot Welsh jury in Welsh in spite of the pleas of the foreman of the jury.[122] In the following year Williams explained that it was of no importance to him in which language proceedings were held; he claimed to have used both languages in the past, but of late he had invariably resorted to English for the benefit of his fellow magistrates.[123] Conversely, it should not be assumed that a non-Welsh-speaking chairman would prove hostile to Welsh: we have seen how the chairman of Montgomeryshire Quarter Sessions, the Earl of Powis, defended the right of the Welsh to give evidence in their mother tongue. Yet a Welsh-speaking chairman was undoubtedly beneficial because it was his responsibility to sum up the evidence and pronounce sentence, tasks which were undertaken in English at the Assizes. Much benefit accrued following the appointment of Thomas Hughes, Astrad, as chairman in Denbighshire. He was elected in 1855 partly on the strength of his knowledge of Welsh. His nominee stated:

> It [the Welsh language] was a qualification which public opinion had lately brought forward, and as of some consequence: for no appointment had recently been made by

[120] Bowen, *The Statutes of Wales*, pp. 252–3.
[121] *Baner Cymru*, 19 May 1858.
[122] *BAC*, 28 October and 1 November 1871.
[123] Ibid., 20 April 1872.

the Government in Wales without parties being acquainted with the Welsh language. The utility of such knowledge was witnessed in the County Court judges. He felt so full satisfied that a knowledge of the Welsh language was necessary that he expected the next step to be the appointment of a Welsh bishop (hear! hear!).[124]

Appointments such as these, warmly welcomed by Welsh patriots such as the West Riding clergymen, convinced the author of the article in *Baner Cymru* that a new mood of patriotism had been instilled among the upper echelons of society.[125] Such a mood was illustrated by the emphasis placed on the Welsh language by some magistrates when chief constables were appointed following the passing of the Counties and Boroughs Police Act of 1856. Committees of magistrates at Flintshire, Denbighshire, Caernarfonshire and Anglesey filled the vacancies with Welsh speakers.

Nevertheless, there were sufficient examples of Welshmen being poorly treated by magistrates to give credence to Henry Richard's well-known portrait in *Letters on the Social and Political Condition of the Principality of Wales* (1866). Richard believed that the yawning gulf which divided the Tory and Anglican governing classes from the Liberal and Nonconformist lower orders was accentuated by differences of language. Several instances bear out this claim. In 1882 magistrates refused to renew the licence of a publican in Llanarmon-yn-Iâl unless he made a request in English.[126] At St Asaph a witness was condemned by magistrates for attempting to use his mother tongue, a case which was taken up in the Police Committee by J. Herbert Lewis, chairman of Flintshire County Council and future MP for the county. Lewis accepted that no injustice had been done, but none the less he claimed it was an 'insult to the Welsh nation'.[127] A more serious case occurred at Abergele in 1897 when a plaintiff, having been offered the choice of which language to employ, opted for Welsh, and was fined an extra shilling to meet the costs of the interpreter. The additional fine was queried by one of the magistrates, but the chairman deemed it legitimate because the man had a knowledge of English and so 'the interpreter was not really necessary'.[128]

In a pamphlet entitled *The Welsh Magistracy* (1888), T. J. Hughes (Adfyfr) portrayed magistrates as being grossly out of sympathy with the 'Welsh people'. By his reckoning, only 10 to 20 per cent of JPs were Welsh speakers and, in a highly partial manner, he suggested that only Liberal JPs would champion the Welsh language:

The Liberal Nonconformist people of Wales are not prepared to tolerate further iron yoke of a prejudiced and interested Church, Tory and landed magistracy . . . Welsh

---

[124] *Carnarvon and Denbigh Herald*, 29 September 1855.
[125] *Baner Cymru*, 19 May 1858.
[126] *Y Celt*, 23 June 1882.
[127] *Carnarvon and Denbigh Herald*, 26 December 1890.
[128] Ibid., 9 April 1897.

Wales – Liberal Nonconformist Wales – requests that the Welshman and the Nonconformist shall have fair access to the magisterial position . . . How long would England tolerate aliens in language, politics, and religious profession as her sole arbitrators of magisterial justice?[129]

It is likely that the reference to the Welsh language was added in order to emphasize the gulf within society rather than as part of a concerted effort to enhance the status of the Welsh language. One method by which the Liberals might break into the 'rural House of Lords' was suggested by A. J. Williams MP in a debate over the Bill to establish county councils. Williams's motion sought to ensure that councillors had a voice in the nomination of county magistrates to the Lord Chancellor, rather than merely to the Lord Lieutenant of the county.[130] The motion failed, but the Local Government Act of 1888 is of further interest because it raised the question of the status of the Welsh language in the new councils. In the Merioneth County Council the Welsh nationalist Michael D. Jones enquired how the language was to be accommodated, and the matter was taken up by the chairman of the council, Samuel Pope QC, a monoglot Englishman, who wrote to the Attorney-General, Richard Webster, seeking his opinion. Webster was adamant that the proceedings should be in the English language in compliance with the 'language clause' of the Act of Union; he pointed out that this had been the case in the Quarter Sessions, where much of the business of the councils had been previously transacted.[131] The outcome of this query was brought to the attention of Parliament by Tom Ellis, who enquired whether the government was aware that the clause cited by the Attorney-General also stipulated that Welsh speakers should be barred from office.[132] This was, of course, a misreading of the Act; it had not been enacted that Welsh speakers should be expelled from office, but that they should have a mastery of English. Nevertheless, it is significant that there was a concerted effort to repeal the clause which stated that English was the official medium of the law. The debate was confused by the fact that it could be argued that the 'language clause' had already been repealed. The Statute Revision Act of 1887 repealed clause 20 of the Act of Union, which, in Ruffhead's edition of *Statutes at Large*, 1762–5, was the 'language clause'. In reality the Statute Revision Act referred to a later version of *Statutes at Large*, published in 1817–28, in which the 'language clause' was numbered clause 17. There was no doubt, however, in the mind of the First Lord of the Treasury, W. H. Smith, that the clause to which the Welsh Liberal MPs referred was still on the statute book.[133] Smith promised to draw the attention of

---

[129] T. J. Hughes (Adfyfr), *The Welsh Magistracy* (London, 1888), p. 9.
[130] *Cymru Fydd*, I, no. 8 (1888), 484; *BAC*, 25 July 1888.
[131] The correspondence, dated 14 and 17 February 1889, is reproduced in *BAC*, 6 March 1889.
[132] *Parliamentary Debates* (Hansard), 3rd series, vol. 333, col. 1155 (7 March 1889).
[133] Ibid., col. 1400 (11 March 1889).

the Statute Law Revision Commission to the matter, but the 'language clause' was not repealed until the passing of the Welsh Courts Act in 1942.[134]

Another means by which Liberals and Nonconformists might find a niche on the magisterial bench was included in a bill presented by Alfred Thomas in favour of home rule for Wales. Two clauses in the National Institutions (Wales) Bill in 1892 made reference to the matter: the first proposed that a secretary of state for Wales rather than the Lord Chancellor should be entrusted with the appointment and removal of magistrates on the commission; the second proposed that the county and borough councils should prepare lists of suitable candidates for the bench for the benefit of the secretary of state.[135] The creation of a Welsh Assembly was also seen as an opportunity to address the issue of the status of the Welsh language in the legal system; the Welsh secretary of state could 'order that the proceedings in Her Majesty's courts of justice in Wales should be wholly or partially conducted in the Welsh language whenever such a course should appear to him desirable and expedient'.[136] The bill was little more than a pipe dream and did not receive a reading in the House of Commons.[137] Yet the attempt to secure greater numbers of Welsh-speaking Nonconformist and Liberal magistrates continued to exercise the likes of J. Herbert Lewis and Samuel Smith, members for Flintshire, a county where the Lord Lieutenant was said to be determined to oust Liberal Nonconformists from the bench. Although there was often genuine concern among the Liberal MPs for the plight of the monoglot Welshman in the law courts, it is probably fair to say that in matters relating to the magistracy allusions to language were convenient additional criticisms by Liberal propagandists against the much-reviled upper classes of Welsh society. Yet the fact remains that the overwhelming majority of JPs at the end of the nineteenth century were not Welsh speakers, and the treatment of Welsh speakers at Petty and Quarter Sessions throughout the century depended largely on the predilections and whims of individual magistrates.

We have seen how Welsh parliamentarians debated the treatment of the Welsh language in the law courts in respect of the magistracy, and, more specifically, the County Court judgeships. There was, however, a problem involved in the championing of these causes; they could be interpreted as a programme to nurture the Welsh language, when in fact the overriding concern of many was to ensure that the 'poor monoglot Welshman', who had not yet learnt English, received justice. The concept of supplanting Welsh for English as the medium of law was anathema to the English state and would not have been universally popular with

---

[134] J. A. Andrews and L. G. Henshaw, *The Welsh Language in the Courts* (Aberystwyth, 1984), p. 12; D. Watcyn Powell, 'Y Llysoedd, yr Awdurdodau a'r Gymraeg: Y Ddeddf Uno a Deddf yr Iaith Gymraeg' in T. M. Charles-Edwards et al. (eds.), *Lawyers and Laymen* (Cardiff, 1986), pp. 297–9.
[135] Alfred Thomas, 'Welsh Home Rule', *The Welsh Review*, April 1892, 549.
[136] Ibid.
[137] The fate of the bill is discussed in J. Graham Jones, 'Alfred Thomas's National Institutions (Wales) Bills of 1891–2', *WHR*, 15, no. 2 (1990), 218–39.

the Welsh electorate. Yet Welsh MPs were determined to secure fair treatment for Welsh speakers in the courtroom. There were others, however, who were less ambiguous. Flinty Welsh radicals like Michael D. Jones believed that the rights of the national language in the law courts could only be achieved if people took matters into their own hands. Others called for the Welsh to refuse to give evidence in English in the law courts as part of the campaign for Welsh appointees.[138] This method was adopted by Robert Ambrose Jones (Emrys ap Iwan) in 1889 when he refused to speak English at the Petty Sessions in Ruthin. This standpoint was praised by the radical Welsh press, but reviled by *The Times*.[139] Although Emrys ap Iwan's stance was not universally applauded in Wales, the case attracted considerable public attention. The courtroom was filled to the brim, and it was alleged that preparations had been made to demonstrate outside should the defendant be prevented from using Welsh.[140] In the event the case was adjourned and Emrys ap Iwan's presence was not required when the case was retried. It was suggested by one correspondent in the radical newspaper *Y Celt* that a society should be formed in which members would vow not to use English in court.[141] The potential for such a society existed in the shape of the Society for Utilizing the Welsh Language, founded in 1885.[142] The principal aim of the Society was to gain a place for the teaching of Welsh in the education system, but there is sufficient evidence to show that some members were also concerned with the fate of the language more generally. At a meeting of the Society in 1889, the County Court judge, Gwilym Williams, urged the members to press for enhanced status for the language in the domain of law. He claimed to have held cases through the medium of Welsh, adding: '[I] was told after the event that it was an illegal proceeding on his part. Well, . . . if it was illegal that it was highly necessary that it should be legalized (hear! hear!).'[143] The matter of the law courts was vented once more at a meeting of the Society at Blaenau Ffestiniog, where it was claimed that too much attention was focused on education.[144]

Although not fuelled by the same motives as the likes of Michael D. Jones and Emrys ap Iwan, many Welsh witnesses were reluctant to give evidence in English in late nineteenth-century Wales. Some may have done so to avoid jury service, while others feared they might not do justice either to themselves or to the course of justice should they use their second language. Many English assize judges had

---

[138] Michael D. Jones, 'Gwaseidd-dra y Cymry', *Y Geninen*, XII, no. 4 (1894), 267–70; *Y Celt*, 22 May 1891.

[139] *BAC*, 19 October 1889; *The Times*, 15 October 1889. See also T. Gwynn Jones, *Emrys ap Iwan: Cofiant* (Caernarfon, 1912), pp. 179–80.

[140] *BAC*, 30 October 1889.

[141] *Y Celt*, 25 July 1890.

[142] J. Elwyn Hughes, *Arloeswr Dwyieithedd: Dan Isaac Davies 1839–1887* (Caerdydd, 1984); Robin Okey, 'The First Welsh Language Society', *Planet*, 58 (1986), 90–6.

[143] *Carnarvon and Denbigh Herald*, 6 September 1889.

[144] *BAC*, 4 June 1890.

difficulty in grasping this point.[145] In a sense, therefore, the Welsh person with a smattering of English was less well treated than the monoglot Welsh speaker. This is not to say that all Assize judges acted in this way, but it was not until the Welsh Courts Act of 1942 that legal sanction was given to the Welsh to give evidence in their mother tongue, and even then it was a right given only to those who felt that they 'would otherwise be at any disadvantage'.

When defending the right to give evidence in the Welsh language, there was a tacit assumption that English was the official language. This made it imperative that the services of interpreters were made available. It is widely acknowledged that translation in law courts is a task fraught with difficulties.[146] Unlike modern interpreters, those chosen – often indiscriminately – to carry out the task had no qualification other than that they were believed to have a mastery of English and Welsh. There was much discontent over the use of the magistrates' clerk at Petty Sessions and Quarter Sessions, the registrar at County Courts, or even bystanders sworn in at the Assizes. It was suggested that incompetent translators were the chief cause of alleged perjury, rather than mendacity on the part of the Welsh themselves. In 1875 Morgan Lloyd MP proposed that a select committee be set up to inquire into the benefits of creating official interpreters, financed by the state.[147] The proposal was not granted, and the question of the quality and payment of translators continued into the twentieth century. Some were prepared to put their faith in interpreters, and it was even suggested that all the proceedings should be translated from one language to the other.[148] Few were as patient as Judge Kennedy, who ensured that every sentence was translated into both languages for the benefit of everyone present at the Caernarfonshire Assizes in 1899.[149]

The only alternative to a system dependent on interpreters was to overhaul the entire legal machinery in Wales. This was acknowledged by Thomas A. Levi in a paper published in *Y Traethodydd* in January 1891. Levi believed that something rather more cerebral was required than a demand for 'Welsh judges for Wales', but he also recognized that Welsh-speaking judges were required, and that all officials needed a knowledge of the tongue.[150] In essence, Levi's programme involved dispensing with the Assizes and creating a 'Prif-Lys Cymreig' (a Welsh High Court), consisting of four judges. Below this court the Petty, Quarter and County Courts would deal with the bulk of the litigation. These changes were to be introduced by means of a 'Welsh Judicature Act'. One problem which was not fully addressed by Levi, and which had received a hearing in the debate over the County Court judges, was the issue of available candidates. This was addressed by

---

[145] See, for example, remarks made by Judge Darling at the Caernarfonshire Assizes, in *Carnarvon and Denbigh Herald*, 24 February 1899.
[146] Rachel Halliburton, 'Lost in the translation', *The Independent*, 8 May 1996.
[147] *Parliamentary Debates* (Hansard), 3rd series, vol. 222, col. 1394ff. (8 March 1875).
[148] *Carnarvon and Denbigh Herald*, 21 February 1896.
[149] Ibid., 14 July 1899.
[150] Thomas A. Levi, 'Cymru yn ei Pherthynas â'r Llysoedd Barn', *Y Traethodydd*, LV (1900), 31–2.

T. R. Roberts (Asaph), a solicitor's clerk and interpreter. In his proposed change for the legal system, published in *Young Wales* in 1900, a less radical programme than that of Levi was presented, which entailed securing Welsh-speaking barristers, County Court judges and stipendiary magistrates in every county. This plan alone would have required some twenty-five qualified barristers, which Roberts conceded were not presently available.[151] It was assumed, of course, that a new generation of native-bred lawyers would necessarily seek to improve the lot of the Welsh language, and this at a time when Michael D. Jones lamented the fact that many professional middle-class Welshmen, such as doctors, accountants, and lawyers, were doing their utmost to purge themselves of their nationality.[152] Daniel Lleufer Thomas pointed out that Wales needed a school of law.[153] Such a school arrived in 1901: a Department of Law was opened at the University College of Wales, Aberystwyth, and the first professor to be appointed was Thomas A. Levi.[154]

It is difficult to summarize the role of the Welsh language in the legal system during the nineteenth century. The lot of the Welsh speaker clearly depended on the whim of those who presided at the law courts. It is hard to agree with Osborne Morgan, who claimed that the 'language clause' of the Act of Union was a 'dead letter' during the parliamentary debate over the appointment of Homersham Cox in 1871. Although some evidence indicates a surprisingly benevolent treatment towards the language at times, on balance few who operated the legal system questioned the authority of the 'language clause'. Another difficult question to answer is the extent to which the law was an agent of Anglicization. In many ways, the Welsh language was maintained regardless of its treatment in the courts; indeed, the Welsh continued to use the courts to such a degree that they earned a reputation of being a litigious people. Nevertheless, the fact remains that the language was not an 'official' medium, and it became confined to restricted domains, such as the home, the place of worship and the Sunday school. The nailing of the national language to the mast of religion by those who liked to portray Wales as 'gwlad y menig gwynion' (the land of the white gloves), a nation apparently free from crime, ultimately proved perilous for the language at a time when the Welsh were becoming increasingly secularized. It is interesting to speculate whether the Welsh language would have fared better by the end of the nineteenth century had it gained a greater foothold in secular domains such as the law.

---

[151] T. R. Roberts, 'Welsh speaking Judges for Wales', *Young Wales*, VI (1900), 33.
[152] *Y Geninen*, XIII, no. 4 (1895), 275–7. This is almost certainly the work of Michael D. Jones.
[153] D. Lleufer Thomas, 'Y Sessiwn yng Nghymru', *Y Geninen*, X, no. 2 (1892), 22.
[154] J. A. Andrews, 'The Aberystwyth Law School, 1901–1976', *The Cambrian Law Review*, 7 (1976), 7–10.

Index

Ab Ithel see Williams, John (Ab Ithel)
Aberafan 72
Aberdare 382
Aberdare Report see *Report of the Committee appointed to Inquire into the Condition of Intermediate and Higher Education in Wales* (1881)
Aberffro 63, 438
Abergele 5, 43, 152–62
  compared with Aberystwyth 173–5
  entertainment 154–5
  language figures 156–9
  population figures 153–4
  religion 155–6
Abergwili 43
Aberystruth 42
Aberystwyth 43, 72, 162–72
  compared with Abergele 173–5
  entertainment 164–6
  language figures 167–70
  population figures 163–4
  religion 166–7
  tourist industry 170–2
  University College 26, 111, 313, 614
Abraham, William (Mabon) 28, 31, 93, 530, 560, 563, 577, 604, 605
academies
  Abergavenny 247, 248
  Llanfyllin 247
  Nonconformist 247–51
Acland, A. H. D. 474–5, 491
Act of Union (1536), language clause 33, 587, 604, 610–11
Adar ein Gwlad, John Ashton 429
Address to Lord Teignmouth . . . By a Country Clergyman, An, Thomas Sikes 232
Addresses, D. L. Moody 325
Addysg Chambers i'r Bobl 423
Addysgydd 352
Adfyfr see Hughes, T. J. (Adfyfr)
'Adgyfodiad, Yr', Eben Fardd 270
Adolygydd, Yr 353, 363–4, 376, 414, 416–17, 423, 518

Advocate and Merthyr Free Press 515
Aelwyd F'Ewythr Robert, William Rees 280, 397, 398
Agricultural Holdings Act 114, 127
agriculture 101–30
  education 106–14
  publications 112–14
  tenants 125–30
Alfardd see Hughes, J. J. (Alfardd)
Allor Deuluaidd, Yr 345
Allotment Act 113
Alltud Eifion see Jones, R. Isaac (Alltud Eifion)
Allwedd Llysieuaeth, Ellis Jones 429
Allwedd Myfyrdod neu Arweinydd i'r Meddwl Segur, Azariah Shadrach 279
Alun see Blackwell, John (Alun)
'Alun Mabon', Ceiriog 295
Amaethwr, Yr 114
Amaethydd, Yr 114, 358, 414, 443
'Amaethyddiaeth', Dewi Wyn o Eifion 267
Amalgamated Association of Miners 577
Amalgamated Ironworkers Union 529
Amddiffynydd y Gweithiwr / The Workman's Advocate 395
Amddiffynydd yr Eglwys 352
Amlwch 43
Amserau, Yr 11, 114, 280, 380, 383, 384, 398–9, 520, 538
  see also *Baner ac Amserau Cymru*
Ancient Airs of Gwent and Morganwg, Maria Jane Williams 302
Anderson, James 111
Anderson, Robert 122
Anglesey 54, 436, 438, 561
Angus, J. Mortimer 463
Anianydd Cristionogol, Yr, trans. Thomas Levi 419
Animals of the Farm 325
Anthropos see Rowlands, R. D. (Anthropos)
Anti-Corn Law League 128–9, 514, 515, 517–19, 534
Anti-State-Church Association 515, 519, 540
Appeal to Welshwomen, Nora Phillips 565

'Ar lan Iorddonen ddofn', Ieuan Glan Geirionydd 271
'Ardderchog Lu y Merthyri', Iolo Carnarvon 277
Arfonwyson see Thomas, John William (Arfonwyson)
Arweinydd i'r Anllythrenog i ddysgu darllain Cymraeg 252
Asaph see Roberts, T. R. (Asaph)
Association of English Causes in North Wales 256
Association of English Causes in South Wales and Monmouthshire 256
Association of Welsh Clergy in the West Riding of the County of York 226, 296, 599
At Etholwyr Anghydffurfiol Cymru, Henry Richard 525–6
Athan Fardd see Jones, John Athanasius (Athan Fardd)
Athenaeum, The 422
Athraw, Yr 376, 415–16, 429
Athraw i Blentyn, Yr 352, 376
Atkinson, Tindal 601
Aubrey, William, Llannerch-y-medd 361
'Awdl ar Hiraeth Cymro am ei Wlad mewn Bro Estronawl', Ieuan Glan Geirionydd 298
Awyriad Anneddau 414

Bala 382
  Calvinistic Methodist College 248–9
  Congregational College 249
Bancroft, George 500
Baner ac Amserau Cymru 22, 114, 369, 380, 388, 401, 520, 553, 599, 605
Baner y Groes 352
Bangor 43, 63, 382
  Normal College 479
Baptists 239, 255, 257–8, 351–2
Bardd a'r Cerddor, Y, Ceiriog 273
Bardd Alaw see Parry, John (Bardd Alaw)
Barddoniaeth, Islwyn 275
Barry 72
Bath Harmonic Society 297
Beddgelert 62
Bedyddiwr, Y 376
Beirniad, Y 354, 357, 363, 424
Bellairs, H. W. 466–7
Beresford, Cecil 33, 604, 605
Berllan, Y 410
Bethel 486
Bethell, Christopher, bishop of Bangor 219
Bethesda 15, 74
Bevan, Thomas (Caradawc) 300
Beynon, Thomas, archdeacon 229, 230, 296
Bibliotheca Celtica 320
Bird, William, Cardiff 334
Bishop, Judge 603
bishops 217–23
Blackwell, John (Alun) 223, 271–2, 290, 299, 350
Blaenau Ffestiniog 74

Blair, Hugh 242–4, 246–7
Blodau Ieuainc, Daniel Silvan Evans 271
Blodeugerdd Barddas o'r Bedwaredd Ganrif ar Bymtheg, R. M. Jones 266
Blodeugerdd o'r Bedwaredd Ganrif ar Bymtheg, Bedwyr Lewis Jones 266
Blue Books see Education Reports (1847)
Bompas, H. M. 460, 461
Bottomley, J. H. 567
Boughrood 66
Bowen, George, Llwyn-gwair 119
Brace, William 577
Brackenbury, Augustus 105, 591
Brad y Llyfrau Gleision, R. J. Derfel 535–6
Brecon 59, 318
  College 248, 433, 447
Breconshire 43, 59, 62, 66, 70, 446, 448
'Breuddwyd Pabydd wrth ei Ewyllys', Emrys ap Iwan 370
British and Foreign Bible Society 231–5
British Society 433, 456, 484
Brougham, Lord Henry, 589–90
Bruce, H. A. 295, 528, 602
Brud a Sylwydd: The Chronicle and Observer 358, 416, 429
Brutus see Owen, David (Brutus)
Bryce, James 460–1
Brymbo 439
Brython, Y 183, 272, 350, 355, 392, 416, 546
Builth Wells 66
Burgess, Thomas, bishop of St David's 218, 222, 224–5, 229–30, 236, 296
Burry Port 72
Bute, Marquess of 572
Bydoedd Uwchben, Y, Caradoc Mills 429

Caerfallwch see Edwards, Thomas (Caerfallwch)
Caernarfon 381–2
  Training College 471
Caernarfonshire 43, 49, 93, 436, 440, 561
Caledfryn see Williams, William (Caledfryn)
Calvinistic Methodists 90, 240, 258–60, 350–1, 385
Cambria Daily Leader 293
Cambrian 380
Cambrian Journal, The 350
Cambrian News 569
'Cambrian Olympiads' 297, 298
Cambrian Register, The 350
Cambrian societies 223, 296
Cambro-Briton, The 350, 354
Campbell, James Colquhoun, bishop of Bangor 217–18, 219
Caneuon, Watcyn Wyn 276
Caniadau, Eben Fardd 271
Caniadau, Islwyn 275
Capel Curig 62
Capel Newydd 42

Caradawc see Bevan, Thomas (Caradawc)
Cardiff 4, 84
Cardigan 43
Cardiganshire 54, 74, 106, 167, 446, 447–8, 561
Cardiganshire Landlord's Advice to his Tenants, A,
    Thomas Johnes 410
Carmarthen 43, 317
    Presbyterian College 248, 421
    Training College 433, 469, 471, 473, 479
Carmarthen Journal 334, 592
Carmarthenshire 43, 69, 72, 93, 451, 561
Carn Ingli see Hughes, Joseph (Carn Ingli)
Carnarvon and Denbigh Herald 569, 601
Carnhuanawc see Price, Thomas (Carnhuanawc)
Cartrefi Cymru, O. M. Edwards 287
'Carw Coch' see Williams, William ('Carw Coch')
Castell Caereinion 103
Catechism o'r Scrythur, Yn Nhrefn Gwyr y Gymanfa 239
Catecism byr i Blant, trans. Jenkin Evans 240
Catholicism 540–1, 557
ceffyl pren 595
Cefn-llys 66
Ceiriog see Hughes, John Ceiriog
Celt, Y 30, 367, 493, 612
'Celt, Y', Emrys ap Iwan 294
Celtic Britain, John Rhŷs 7
Cenarth 43
Central Welsh Board 473, 477–8, 479–81
'Cerdd Hela', Alun 271
Cerddor, Y 344
Cerddor Cymreig, Y 352
Cerddor y Cymry 352
Ceridwen Peris see Jones, Alice Gray (Ceridwen Peris)
Cerrigydrudion 39, 41
Charles o'r Bala 280, 361
Charles, Thomas 231–3, 279, 351
Chartism 6, 27, 90, 432, 444, 452, 466, 511–12, 515–17, 534, 539, 544, 596
Chatterjee, Chundermohun 302
Chester, printing 318
Chester Chronicle 272
Christian Philosopher, Thomas Dick 419
Christian Preacher, The, Edward Williams 243
Church of England Treatise Society 224
Church Union Society 224
churches 89, 215–37
    evidence from parish churches 37–44, 59–63, 65
Clarke, Isaac 322, 343
'Clasuron Cymreig, Y' 345
Cleaver, William, bishop of Bangor 217, 218
Clwydfardd see Griffith, David (Clwydfardd)
Clych Atgof, O. M. Edwards 471–2
Coffin Greenly, Lady 301
Cofiant Dai Hunan-dyb, Brutus 282
Cofiant Ieuan Gwynedd 345
Cofiant John Jones, Talsarn, Owen Thomas 282
Cofiant Siencyn Bach y Llwywr, Brutus 282

Cofiant Wil Bach o'r Pwll-dŵr, Brutus 282
Cofiant y Tri Brawd, E. Pan Jones 327
Coginiaeth a Threfniadaeth Deuluaidd cyfaddas i anghenion gwragedd gweithwyr Cymru, S. A. Edwards 412
Colby, Thomas, Pantyderi 101, 119
Coll Gwynfa, trans. William Owen Pughe 270
Collection of above three hundred receipts, A, Mary Kittelby 411
Colwyn Bay 72
'Comparative Merits of the Remains of Ancient Literature . . . , The', Carnhuanawc 304
Congregationalists 239, 255–7, 352
Conservatives 28, 517, 551–5, 566–8, 570–6
Constitution of Man, The, George Coombe 408–9
Cooke, Thomas Herbert 108
Corbet, Edward, Ynysymaengwyn 120
Corph y Gaingc, Dafydd Ddu Eryri 266–7, 268
Corris 74
Corvinius see Williams, John (Corvinius)
Counties and Boroughs Police Act (1856) 609
County Courts 588, 593–4, 600–6
Court of Great Sessions 33, 506–7, 588–94
Court of Quarter Sessions 588, 608
Cowie, B. M. 469
Cox, Homersham 32, 33, 600–1, 603, 605, 614
Cranogwen see Rees, Sarah Jane (Cranogwen)
Creuddynfab see Williams, William (Creuddynfab)
Crickhowell 66
Criminal Justice Act (1855) 607
'Crist yn Graig Ddisigl', Eben Fardd 270
Cronicl, Y 114, 364, 424, 520
Cronicl Cymru 311, 602
Cronicl y Cymdeithasau Crefyddol 352, 359, 376, 377
Cronicl yr Oes 380
Cross Commission on Elementary Education 315, 472–4, 498, 502
Culture and Anarchy, Matthew Arnold 309
Cwrs y Byd 30, 376
Cyfaill Eglwysig, Y 352
Cyfaill Meddygol, Y, John Davies 408
Cyfaill y Werin 184
Cyfaill yr Aelwyd 354, 371, 376
'Cyfres Boblogaidd yr Aelwyd' 345
'Cyfres Milwyr y Groes' 345
'Cyfres y Ceinion' 345
'Cyfres y Fil' 346–7
'Cyfres yr Ugeinfed Ganrif' 345
Cyfrinach y Bedyddwyr 352
Cyfrinach yr Aelwyd, William Rees 397
Cylchgrawn, Y 415, 442
Cylchgrawn Cymru 354, 372
Cylchgrawn Rhyddid 517–18
Cylchgrawn y Gymdeithas er Taenu Gwybodaeth Fuddiol 350, 354–5, 361
'Cymdeithas Gymroaidd Gwynedd' 223
    see also Cambrian societies
'Cymdeithas y Maen Chwyf' 300

'Cymeriadau ymhlith ein Cynulleidfaoedd', Daniel Owen 283
Cymmro, Neu Drysorfa Celfyddyd a Gwybodaeth, Y 358, 416
Cymmrodor, Y 474
Cymmrodorion 88, 95, 296, 350, 470, 474, 495, 499
Cymreigyddion 350, 593, 594, 597
  Aberdare 300
  Abergavenny 300–1
  Carmarthen 593
  eisteddfodau 296
  Merthyr Tydfil 300
  Pontypridd 300
Cymro, Y 265, 285, 397, 420, 580
Cymru (O. M. Edwards) 163, 269, 277, 287, 340, 346, 372, 373–4
'Cymru Fu: Cymru Fydd', John Morris-Jones 277, 278, 316
Cymru Fydd 29, 33, 129, 368, 372, 498–9, 559
Cymru Fydd 33, 372–3, 499
Cymru, yn Hanesyddol, Parthedegol a Bywgraphyddol, Owen Jones 282
Cymru'r Plant 372, 376
Cynghorion Meddygol a Meithriniad y Claf, D. G. Evans 407
Cynghorion priodor o Garedigion I ddeiliaid ei dyddynod, Thomas Johnes 113
Cynghorydd Meddygol Dwyieithawg, Y 358
'Cynnadledd y Cryddion', Samuel Evans 399
'Cywydd i'r aderyn bronfraith', Thomas Jones 268
'Cywydd Ymweliad â Llangybi, Eifionydd', Eben Fardd 270

Daearyddiaeth, Robert Roberts 419
Dafydd Ddu Eryri see Thomas, David (Dafydd Ddu Eryri)
Dafydd Ionawr see Richards, David (Dafydd Ionawr)
Daniel, D. R. 585
Daniel, John, Carmarthen 334
Darlington, Thomas 476–7
Darlith ar Seryddiaeth, Arfonwyson 413
Davies, Clement, headmaster of Bala Grammar School 463
Davies, D. P. 425
Davies, Dan Isaac 13–14, 25, 94, 95, 315, 339, 370, 472, 474, 475, 489, 490, 499
Davies, David, Llandinam 136, 146
Davies, David Jones, rector of North Benfleet 463
Davies, Griffith, mathematician 420
Davies, Revd H. L., Troed-yr-aur 447–8
Davies, Ivan Thomas 583
Davies, John (Siôn Gymro) 245
Davies, John, Cardiff 256, 364
Davies, John, Llandeilo 408
Davies, John, Nerquis 242
Davies, Joseph, Liverpool 358
Davies, Richard (Mynyddog) 272, 320, 602
Davies, Richard, rector, Llantrisant, Anglesey 225
Davies, Richard, Treborth 263
Davies, Samuel 245
Davies, T. Witton 249–50
Davies, W. C. 602
Davies, Walter (Gwallter Mechain) 118, 121, 223, 232–6, 350, 354
Davies, Dr William, Ffrwd-fâl 250
Davitt, Michael 562–3
Dawson, William, Otley 335
Ddraig Goch, Y 365
Ddraig Goch, Y / The Welsh Dragon (union) 529
Defence of the Reformed System of Welsh Orthography, A, John Jones 236
Defynnog see James, David (Defynnog)
'Deluge, 1939', Saunders Lewis 98
Denbigh 72, 75
Denbighshire 42, 59, 93, 442, 436, 561
'Deng Noswaith yn y Black Lion', trans. Daniel Owen 280, 361
Derfel, R. J. 22–3, 31, 305, 325–6, 327, 365, 533–4, 545–6, 580, 599, 600
Detholiad Magwriaeth a Rheolaeth y Da Byw mwyaf priodol i Dywysogaeth Cymru, John Owen 113
Dewi Brefi see Rowland, David (Dewi Brefi)
Dewi Môn see Rowlands, David (Dewi Môn)
Dewi o Ddyfed see James, David (Dewi o Ddyfed)
Dewi Silin see Richards, David (Dewi Silin)
Dewi Wyn o Eifion see Owen, David (Dewi Wyn o Eifion)
dialects 11, 13–14, 398–401
Dic Penderyn 93
Dictionarium Duplex, John Davies 410
'Dietetic Phrenology', Morgan Philip 409
Dillwyn, Lewis Weston 422
Dinas 62
Dinesydd, Y 31
Dinesydd Cymreig, Y 581
'Dinistr Jerusalem gan y Rhufeiniaid', Eben Fardd 270
Diwygiwr, Y 114, 352, 357, 360, 364, 376, 415, 519, 547
Dolanog 65
Dolwyddelan 74
Domestic Medicine, William Buchan 406
Douglas-Pennant, George 570
Dreflan, Y, Daniel Owen 285
Drych i'r Anllythrennog, Robert Jones 252
Drych yr Amseroedd, Robert Jones 279, 281
Drych Ysgrythyrol, George Lewis 252
Drysorfa, Y 265, 283, 351, 361, 376, 378, 397
Drysorfa Gynnulleidfaol, Y 371, 375, 376, 415
Drysorfa Ysbrydol, Y 279
Dryw, Y see Hughes, Edward (Y Dryw)
Duwinyddiaeth Naturiol neu Yr Amlygiadau o Dduw mewn Natur, trans. Hugh Jones 419
'Dwymyn Seisnig yng Nghymru, Y', Emrys ap Iwan 259
Dyfed see Rees, Evan (Dyfed)

Dysgedydd, Y 184–5, 245, 352, 355, 376, 397, 518
Dysgedydd Crefyddol, Y 518
Dywysogaeth, Y 387, 558

Eastern Origin of the Celtic Nations, James Cowles Prichard 303
Eben Fardd see Thomas, Ebenezer (Eben Fardd)
Eclectic Review, The 519
education 7–8, 16, 22, 23–7, 91, 95, 196, 216, 294, 363, 431–504
　adult 441–2
　elementary 433, 461, 466–8, 470–9, 483–504
　HMI reports 465–72, 488–91
　intermediate and higher 462–3, 480–2
　parliamentary reports 459–65
　teachers, language of 437–41
Education Reports (1847) 7–8, 10, 21, 22, 32, 34, 91, 96, 196, 215–16, 294–5, 361–3, 459–60, 506, 535–6
　evidence of H. V. Johnson 435–44
　evidence of J. C. Symons 444–51
　evidence of R. R. W. Lingen 451–5
Edwards, Alfred George, archbishop of Wales 221, 463–4, 477
Edwards, Charles 370
Edwards, Clem 31
Edwards, Henry T., dean of Bangor 23, 28, 217, 219, 221 464, 555–8
Edwards, John (Meiriadog) 314
Edwards, Lewis 19, 368–9, 471
　and Bala MC College 248–9
　and literature 270, 286, 325, 329, 351
　and politics 523
　and religion 364, 463, 464, 492, 544
　and sermons 248, 258–61
　and *Y Traethodydd* 359
Edwards, O. M. 585
　and education 24, 477–9, 480, 481–2, 485
　and literature 21, 269, 285, 286, 287–8, 324, 340, 345, 372, 377, 485
　as Chief Inspector of the Welsh Department 26, 105, 477–82
Edwards, Canon R. W., St Asaph 464
Edwards, Roger, Mold 283, 360, 378, 380, 397
Edwards, T. Charles 26, 463, 493
Edwards, Thomas (Caerfallwch) 354, 408, 414, 427
Edwards, Thomas (Twm o'r Nant) 267, 280, 290
Edwards, William, HMI 25, 475–6, 489–90
Efangylydd, Yr 352, 356, 362
Eglurhaad o Gatechism Byrraf y Gymanfa 240
Egluryn Phraethineb 354
Eglwysilan 61
Eglwysydd, Yr 352
Egwyddorion Gwrteithio, C. Bryner Jones 113, 429
Eiddil Ifor see Watkins, T. E. (Eiddil Ifor)
Eifionydd see Thomas, John (Eifionydd)
'Eifionydd', Eben Fardd 270

Einion Môn see Lloyd, John (Einion Môn)
'Eisteddfod, Yr' 306, 308–9, 311, 315
eisteddfodau
　Beaumaris (1832) 297
　Cardiff (1834) 301
　Carmarthen (1819) 223, 297
　Carmarthen (1823) 235
　Cymreigyddion of Abergavenny 22, 300, 302–4
　Denbigh (1819) 267
　Denbigh (1860) 306
　Denbigh Royal (1828) 297
　Dolgellau (1853) 421
　Eisteddfod y Cymry, Neath (1866) 311
　Liverpool Ordovices 314
　Llandudno (1864) 421
　Llangollen (1858) 305
　local 23
　London (1887) 546
　Powys (1824) 270
　provincial 22, 295–6, 297
　science 420
　Rhuddlan (1850) 270
　St Dogmaels 420–1
　Tremadog (1811) 267
　Welshpool 297, 299
　Wrexham (1820) 297
　see also National Eisteddfod
elections 512–13, 523
　1868 569, 600
　1880 527–8, 563, 570, 571–2
　Merioneth 522, 523–4
　Merthyr Tydfil 522, 524–5, 550–1
Elfed see Lewis, H. Elvet (Elfed)
Elfenau Rhifyddiaeth, J. W. Thomas 413–14, 429
Elias, David 249
Elias, John 18
Elias, Tom 111, 503
Ellis, Annie 569
Ellis, Thomas 463
Ellis, Tom 28, 33, 115, 474, 562, 563, 565, 569, 584, 585, 600, 604, 606, 610
'Elusengarwch', Dewi Wyn o Eifion 267
Emmanuel, Gwilym Hiraethog 329
Emrys ap Iwan see Jones, Robert Ambrose (Emrys ap Iwan)
Emyniadur yr Eglwys, Daniel Lewis Lloyd 222
Enoc Huws, Daniel Owen 278, 285
Enwogion Cymru, Isaac Foulkes 282
Esboniad ar Ddammegion Crist, Evan Evans 337
Esponiad ar y Testament Newydd, George Lewis 252
'Essay on the Celtic Languages . . . , An' 303
'Essay on the discovery of America in the 12th century by Prince Madoc ap Owen Gwynedd, An' 305
'Essay on the Influence of Welsh Tradition upon European Literature, An', John Dorney Harding 304
'Essay on the Influence of Welsh Tradition upon

the Literature of Germany, France and Scandinavia, An' 303, 304
essay on the physiognomy and physiology of the present Inhabitants of Britain, An, Thomas Price 423
Eurgrawn Wesleyaidd, Yr 351, 375, 376, 415
Evangelical Alliance 541
Evans, Adam, Machynlleth 321, 343
Evans, Beriah Gwynfe 12, 20, 354, 371, 398, 474
Evans, Christmas 18–19, 240–1
Evans, D. Tudwal 581
Evans, Dafydd, Ffynnonhenri 242
Evans, Daniel Silvan 271, 350, 354, 355, 390, 428, 546
Evans, Evan (Ieuan Fardd) 223
Evans, Evan (Ieuan Glan Geirionydd) 223, 268, 271, 298, 299, 350
Evans, Gwenlyn, compositor 333
Evans, Jane, Highmead 119
Evans, John (Ieuan ap Gruffydd) 300
Evans, John, Carmarthen 319, 361
Evans, P. M., Holywell 335
Evans, Samuel, Carmarthen 385, 390, 399
Evans, T. A., Education Officer 480
Evans, Theophilus 30

Fabian Society 580
Factory and Workshop Act (1891) 604, 605
Falcondale 122
Faner, Y 129, 259, 286, 294, 312, 339, 419, 424, 520, 570, 583
see also *Baner ac Amserau Cymru*
farmers and labourers 114–18
Fearon, D. R. 468
Fellten, Y 393
Fertilizers and Feeding Stuffs Act 113
'First Principles of Agriculture', Tanner 111–12
Fishguard 74, 75
Fitzwilliams, Charles, Cilgwyn 498
Fitzwilliams, E. C. L., Cilgwyn 108
Flannery, Sir Fortescue 572
Fletcher, Joseph 467
Flintshire 42, 59, 70, 72, 436, 438, 442
Foresters, Friendly Society 358
Forster Education Act (1870) 24, 456, 484–5, 502
Foster, Thomas Campbell 32, 596
Fothergill, Richard 561
Foulkes, Edward 354
Foulkes, Isaac 282–3, 285, 322, 345
French language, in Canada 95–6
Friendly Societies 358
Frythones, Y 180, 182, 185, 190–1, 201, 547
'Fy Nhad sydd wrth y llyw', Ieuan Glan Geirionydd 271
Fy Oriau Hamddenol, Glasynys 272

Garddwr Cymreig, Y, R. M. Williamson 411
Garddwr i'r Amaethwr a'r Bwthynwr, Charles Ewing 410
Garddwriaeth y Bwthyn . . . yr Ardd Lysiau, John Davies 411
Garthbeibio 65
Gee, Thomas 312, 315, 599
and *Baner Cymru* 22, 380, 520, 599
and printing 318, 321, 325, 328–9, 331, 334, 335–7, 339, 344–5
and railway workers 141
and the Tithe War 129
and *Y Traethodydd* 359
Geiniogwerth, Y 376
Geiriadur Bywgraffyddol 343
Geiriadur Ysgrythyrawl, Thomas Charles 20, 233, 252, 278, 279
Gemau Diwinyddol, Robert Jones 282
Genedl Gymreig, Y 114, 542
Geni a Magu, sef, Llawlyfr y Fydwraig a'r Fag-wraig, D. W. Williams 407
Geninen, Y 30, 31, 286, 315, 364, 367, 371, 376
gentry 118–25
George, David Lloyd 28, 143, 563, 564, 571, 584, 585, 600, 604
Glamorgan 3, 13, 43, 49, 54, 58, 61, 66, 67, 70, 72, 81, 83, 93, 451–2, 455, 472
Glan Alun see Jones, Thomas (Glan Alun)
Glanaman 102, 103
Glanffrwd see Thomas, William (Glanffrwd)
Glaslyn see Owen, Richard Jones (Glaslyn)
Glasynys see Jones, Owen Wyn (Glasynys)
Glynne, Sir Stephen, Hawarden 123
Goleuad, Y 369, 385, 386, 470–1, 493
Goleuad Cymru 351
Goleufryn see Jones, William Richard (Goleufryn)
Golud yr Oes 353, 371
Golwg ar y Byd 419
Golygydd, Y 376
Gomeraeg 353
'Gorsedd Gras', Elfed 276
Grawnsyppiau Canaan, Robert Jones 268
Greal, Y 350, 352, 416
Greal: Sev Cynulliad o Orchestion ein Hynaviaid a Llofion o Vân Govion yr Oesoedd . . . , Y 350
Greal y Bedyddwyr 352, 415
Greal y Corau 352
Griffith, David (Clwydfardd) 602
Griffith, Ellis Jones 474
Griffith, John, Aberdare 460
Griffith, John (Y Gohebydd) 20
Griffith, Walter 517
Griffiths, Ann 268–9
Griffiths, D., Holywell 428
Griffiths, David, Nevern 229
Griffiths, Evan, Swansea 353
Griffiths, John, rector 8, 14, 309, 311, 315
Ground Game Act 113
Gruffydd, W. J. 265
Guest, Arthur 572
Guest, Ivor 572

Guilsfield 44, 59
Gurney, Baron 592
Gwaith Goronwy Owen 345
Gwaith Islwyn 275
Gwallter Mechain see Davies, Walter (Gwallter Mechain)
'Gwarth y Cymro a gywilyddio arddel Iaith ei Wlad' 299
Gweithiwr, Y 93
'Gwêl uwchlaw cymylau amser', Islwyn 275
Gweledigaetheu y Bardd Cwsc, Ellis Wynne 252, 288
Gwen Tomos, Daniel Owen 285
Gwenllian Gwent 198
Gwenynen Gwent see Waddington, Augusta (Lady Llanover)
Gwenynydd, Y, H. P. Jones and Michael D. Jones 414
Gwerinwr, Y 353, 363
Gwersi mewn Llysieueg, George Rees 429
Gwilym a Benni Bach, W. Llewelyn Williams 346
Gwilym Cowlyd see Roberts, W. J. (Gwilym Cowlyd)
Gwilym Hiraethog see Rees, William (Gwilym Hiraethog)
Gwilym Tawe see Morris, William (Gwilym Tawe)
Gwir Fedyddiwr, Y 352
Gwir Iforydd, Y 358
Gwladgarwr, Y (1833–41) 354, 355
Gwladgarwr, Y (1836) 415
Gwladgarwr, Y (1851) 358
Gwladgarwr, Y (1858) 537–9, 544
Gwrgant see Jones, William (Gwrgant)
Gwron, Y 93, 384, 387, 399
Gwron Odyddol, Y 358
Gwyddoniadur Cymreig, Y 20, 278, 282, 289, 312, 337, 338, 344, 423
Gwyddonydd, Y 430
Gwydir, estate 124
Gwyliedydd, Y 224, 350, 354, 415, 420, 426, 427
'Gwyn ap Nudd', Elfed 276
Gwyneddigion 88, 296, 350
Gwynn, Eirwen 430
'Gymraeg, Y', William Thomas (Glanffrwd) 312
Gymraes, Y 180, 186, 201, 301, 364, 376, 543, 547

Hall, Augusta see Waddington, Augusta (Lady Llanover)
Hall, Sir Benjamin 230, 301, 302
Hall, Edward Crompton Lloyd 119, 449, 597
Hallam, Henry 304
Halliday, Thomas 526–7, 529, 554, 561, 577
Hanbury-Tracy, Charles 602
Hanes Bywyd Siencyn Penhydd, Edward Matthews 281
Hanes Cymru a Chenedl y Cymry, Thomas Price 223
Hanes Llenyddiaeth Gymraeg, Thomas Parry 266, 274–5

Hanes Plwyf Llandyssul, W. J. Davies 410
Hanes y Brytaniaid a'r Cymry, Gweirydd ap Rhys 282
Hanmer, estate 123
Hardie, Keir 568
Harper, H. D. 465
Harris, Howel 89, 350
Harris, Joseph 354, 357
Hart-Dyke, William 491
Hartley, Lewis, Manchester 313
Haul, Yr 265, 281–2, 352, 356, 362, 375, 376, 387, 392, 409, 414, 547
Haverfordwest 318
College 249–50
Hawarden 72
Heath, Charles, Monmouth 318
Heber, Reginald, bishop of Calcutta 299, 312
Heddyw 372, 376
Helyntion Bywyd Hen Deiliwr, William Rees 397
'Hen Wlad fy Nhadau' 534, 563
Herald Cymraeg, Yr 601
Herbert, David, Llansanffraid 229
Hill, John, attorney general of Chester circuit 590
HMI reports 465–72
Holl Gelfyddyd Cogyddiaeth 411
Holyhead 74
Holywell 383
Hopkin, Lewis, Llandyfodwg 87
Horner, Arthur 578
Howell, Revd D., vicar of Wrexham 23
Hughes, Charles, publisher 317, 322, 328, 331, 335, 336, 338, 339, 341, 342, 344
Hughes, Charles Tudor 323, 342, 345
Hughes, Edward (Y Dryw) 299, 312
Hughes, Hugh, artist 416, 508
Hughes, Hugh (Tegai) 428
Hughes, J. J. (Alfardd) 601
Hughes, Revd James, Llanhilleth 445
Hughes, John (1796–1860) 251
Hughes, John, Everton 329
Hughes, John, Pontrobert 268
Hughes, John Ceiriog 21, 104, 146–7, 148, 272–4, 295, 343, 602
Hughes, Joseph (Carn Ingli) 226, 228, 296
Hughes, Joshua, bishop of St Asaph 23, 218, 465, 600
Hughes, Ruth 268
Hughes, T. J. (Adfyfr) 565, 575
Hughes, Thomas, Astrad 608
Hughes, Thomas McKenna 463, 465
Humphreys, E. Morgan 346, 579
Humphreys, Revd Edward 245
Humphreys, Hugh, Caernarfon 333, 335, 371
Hunangofiant, Thomas Jones 281
Hwyr Ddifyrion, Watcyn Wyn 276
Hyfforddwr, Yr, Thomas Charles 240, 252, 253
'Hyfforddwr i'r Gwyddorau' 421
Hymnau, Eben Fardd 270

Hymnau &c. Ar Amryw Destunau ac Achosion, Edward Jones 269
Hymnau o fawl i Dduw a'r Oen 268
hymns 268–70, 276
Hyndman, H. M. 579

Iaith Gymraeg, 1785, 1885, 1985! Neu Tair Miliwn o Gymry Dwy-ieithawg mewn Can Mlynedd, D. Isaac Davies 94
Idris o Gybi see Roberts, Robert (Idris o Gybi)
Ieuan ap Gruffydd see Evans, John (Ieuan ap Gruffydd)
Ieuan Fardd see Evans, Evan (Ieuan Fardd)
Ieuan Glan Alarch see Mills, John (Ieuan Glan Alarch)
Ieuan Glan Geirionydd see Evans, Evan (Ieuan Glan Geirionydd)
Ieuan Gwyllt see Roberts, John (Ieuan Gwyllt)
Ieuan Gwynedd see Jones, Evan (Ieuan Gwynedd)
Ifor Ceri see Jenkins, John (Ifor Ceri)
Ifor Hael 358, 376
Iforydd, Yr 358
industrialization 81–99
Inner Wales 45, 54, 58–9, 63–5, 69, 74
'Inquiry into the State of Elementary Education in the Mining Districts of South Wales, An' 466
Intermediate Education Act (1889) 26
Ioan Pedr see Peter, John (Ioan Pedr)
Iolo Carnarvon see Roberts, J. J. (Iolo Carnarvon)
Iolo Morganwg 87, 223, 297, 300, 354, 426
Ireland 3, 58, 59, 85, 92, 97, 99, 474, 487, 562–3
Ironworkers' Journal 529
Islwyn see Thomas, William (Islwyn)

Jac Glan-y-gors see Jones, John (Jac Glan-y-gors)
James, Charles Herbert 527
James, David (Defynnog) 95, 479
James, David (Dewi o Ddyfed) 219, 220, 226, 296, 312
James, David Gwalchmai 416, 429
James, Evan and James, Pontypridd 534
James, J. B. R., St John's Training College Highbury 313
James, J. R., Cardigan 420
James, Thomas (Llallawg) 227
Jayne, F. J. 465
Jenkin, T. J. 108
Jenkins, John (Ifor Ceri) 222, 223, 225, 271, 296, 297–8, 350, 354
Jenkins, John, Commissioner 8, 460
Jenkins, John, Hengoed 353, 418
Jenkins, R. T. 323
Jenkinson, John Banks, bishop of St David's 218
Job, J. T. 294
John, David jnr. 512, 516
Johnes, Arthur James 594
Johnes, John 594
Johnes, Thomas, Hafod 110, 118, 122

Johnson, Henry Vaughan 294, 295, 434, 436–44
Jones, Alice Gray (Ceridwen Peris) 204
Jones, D. T., Professor of Welsh, St David's College, Lampeter 230
Jones, Canon David 236–7
Jones, David, Gwynfe 246
Jones, E. Pan 30, 327, 493–4, 574–5
Jones, Edgar 565, 568
Jones, Evan (Ieuan Gwynedd) 8, 186, 263, 301, 319, 323, 326, 327, 338, 342, 364, 416, 541–3
Jones, Griffith, Bala 322
Jones, Griffith, Llanddowror 87, 240, 433
Jones, Gwesyn, Rhayader 420
Jones, H. Longueville 459, 469, 597
Jones, Sir Henry 470, 485, 500
Jones, Dr Hugh 245
Jones, Hugh, Llangollen 353
Jones, Dr J. Harris 249
Jones, J. R. Kilsby 9, 19, 30, 250–1, 263, 326, 363, 369, 470, 492, 519
Jones, J. T. 418
Jones, J. T. and T. I. Jones, Aberdare 335, 343
Jones, John (Jac Glan-y-gors) 280, 589
Jones, John (Talhaiarn) 272, 274–5, 290, 296, 304, 305, 308
Jones, John (Tegid) 234, 235, 236, 354
Jones, John, archdeacon of Merioneth 225
Jones, John, MP, Carmarthenshire 590
Jones, John, Llanidloes 321
Jones, John, Llanrwst 331, 334
Jones, John, Tal-y-sarn 19, 241, 250, 328, 423
Jones, John, MP, Ystrad 119
Jones, John Athanasius (Athan Fardd) 341
Jones, John Puleston 370
Jones, Josiah Thomas 353, 358, 375, 384
Jones, Lewis, Almondbury 227
Jones, Michael D. 29–30, 33, 251, 261, 263, 365, 377, 614
  and Bala College 249
  and education 493, 503
  and the county councils 610
  and the law courts 600, 612
  and O. M. Edwards 372
  and politics 368, 523–4, 546
  and the Eisteddfod 294
  articles in *Y Celt* and *Y Geninen* 367–9
  his contributions to *Y Ddraig Goch* 365–6
Jones, Owen (Meudwy Môn) 353
Jones, Owen (Owain Myfyr) 223, 350, 353
Jones, Owen Wyn (Glasynys) 272
Jones, Peter (Pedr Fardd) 268, 269–70
Jones, R. Isaac (Alltud Eifion) 416
Jones, R. T., MP 564, 582
Jones, Richard, Aberangell 341
Jones, Richard, Llanhychan 226
Jones, Richard Mawddwy 365
Jones, Robert, Llanllyfni 248, 251
Jones, Robert, Rhos-lan 279

INDEX

Jones, Robert Ambrose (Emrys ap Iwan) 30, 33, 263, 377, 474
  and Abergele 156
  and education 493
  and English services 19, 259–60
  and literature 21, 265, 286–7
  and scientific words 425
  and the courts 612
  and the Eisteddfod 294
  and the periodical press 365
  and *Y Geninen* 368–9
Jones, T. Gwynn 278, 286, 485, 500
Jones, Thomas (Glan Alun) 415, 419
Jones, Thomas, CH 494
Jones, Thomas, Denbigh 268, 278, 351
Jones, Thomas, head of Penmorfa Board School, Penbryn 111
Jones, Thomas Lloyd 328
Jones, Thomas Tudno (Tudno) 276
Jones, W. Basil, bishop of St David's 221, 263
Jones, William (Gwrgant) 427
Jones, William Richard (Goleufryn) 415
journalism 379–403, 509

Kane, John 529
Kay-Shuttleworth, James 434–5, 447, 450, 456, 459, 469
Kennedy, Judge 613
Kennedy, Dr John 248
Kenyon, Lord 604
Kenyon, G. T. 567
Knight, William Bruce 235–6

labour movement 31, 580–3
Labour Pioneer 581
Labour Voice 581
Lampeter, St David's College 225, 229–31
Land League 129
Landsker 39, 61
law 31–2, 587–614
Lectures on Homiletics, Ebenezer Porter 247
Legard, A. G. 477
Letter to a Country Clergyman, occasioned by his Address to Lord Teignmouth 233
Letters on the Social and Political Condition of the Principality of Wales, Henry Richard 565, 609
Levesque, René 96
Levi, Thomas A. 376, 613–14
Lewellin, Llewelyn 230
Lewis, David, recorder 604
Lewis, H. Elvet (Elfed) 245–6, 276–7
Lewis, J. Herbert 584, 600, 606, 609, 611
Lewis, Lewis William (Llew Llwyfo) 20, 282, 384
Lewis, Richard, bishop of Llandaff 220, 221
Lewis, Thomas 464
Lewis, W. T., Baron Merthyr of Senghennydd 527–8
Lewis, William (Lewys Afan) 31, 529

Lewsyn yr Heliwr 93
Lewys Afan see Lewis, William (Lewys Afan)
Liber Landavensis (Book of Llandaff) 303
Liberation Society 514, 515, 517, 519–22, 524, 540, 559, 600
Liberator, The 520
Liberals 28, 525–31, 564–5, 568, 569–75, 584–5, 605–6
libraries 318, 421
Lingen, R. R. W. 215, 294, 295, 431, 435, 436, 451–5, 469
literature 265–91
Literature of the Kymry, The, Thomas Stephens 302–3
Llais Llafur 22, 31, 580, 581
Llais y Wlad 528
Llallawg see James, Thomas (Llallawg)
Llanbedrog 65
Llanbedrycennin 39
Llanbryn-mair 103
Llanddeiniolen 65
Llandderfel 440
Llan-ddew 59
Llandeilo Fawr 43
Llandenni 61
Llandingad 43
Llandovery College 460–1, 464, 477
Llandudno 41, 43
Llandybïe 43
Llandyrnog 439
Llandysilio (Anglesey) 65
Llanelen 61
Llanelli 69, 72
Llanerfyl 65
Llanfaelog 63
Llanfair Caereinion 59, 65, 103
Llanfair-is-gaer 438
Llanfair Nant-y-gof 61–2
Llanfair Pwllgwyngyll 65
Llanfechain 59, 102
Llanfihangel Abergwesyn 66
Llanfynydd, Flintshire 439
Llangadog 43
Llangathen 43
Llangollen 440
Llangorwen 62
Llangrannog 62
Llangwm 61
Llangynfelyn 24–5
Llanhilleth 42
Llanidloes 102
Llanllwchaearn 59
Llanmerewig 43–4
Llanover, Lady see Waddington, Augusta (Lady Llanover)
Llanover Circle 33, 593
Llanrhidian 66
Llan-rhos, church 43

Llanstinan 61–2
Llanwrtyd 66
Llanyblodwel 44
Llanychlwydog 62
Llanymawddwy 103
Llan-y-wern 59
Llechryd 62
Llenor, Y 372
'Llenyddiaeth Grefyddol y Cymry Gynt', Emrys ap Iwan 370
Llenyddiaeth y Cymry 345
Lleuad yr Oes 362
Lleucu Llwyd ynghyda Chaneuon eraill, Glasynys 272
Llew Llwyfo see Lewis, Lewis William (Llew Llwyfo)
Llewelyn, Sir J. T. D. 572
'Llinellau i'r Gog', Daniel Silvan Evans 271
Lloyd, Mr, Waunifor 120
Lloyd, Dr Charles 235
Lloyd, Daniel Lewis, bishop of Bangor 222
Lloyd, Evan, smith 342
Lloyd, Herbert, Carmarthen 122
Lloyd, Horatio 603
Lloyd, J. E. 474
Lloyd, John (Einion Môn) 591
Lloyd, Morgan, MP 23, 613
Llwyd, Morgan 370
Llwyd, Simon 418
Llyfr coginio a chadw ty, Thomas Thomas 412
Llyfr Etholiadaeth Cymru, John Jones 523
Llyfr Meddyginiaeth a Physygwriaeth . . . Thomas ab Robert Shiffery 411
Llyfrau Benjamin 565
'Llyn y Morynion', Elfed 276
Llysieuaeth Gymreig, Hugh Davies 422
Llysieulyfr Teuluaidd, Y 409–10
'Llythurau 'Rhen Ffarmwr' (Gwilym Hiraethog) 11, 114, 280, 398
Local Government Act 605–6, 607, 610
London Corresponding Society 508
London Review 312
Lyndhurst, Lord 592

Mabinogion 303
Mabon see Abraham, William (Mabon)
'Mae Robin yn swil', Ceiriog 274
'Maes Bosworth', Eben Fardd 305
magistracy 607–11
Manafon 103
Manual of English Composition and Rhetoric, A, Alexander Bain 247
Matthews, Edward, Ewenny 249, 281, 289, 361
Matthews, Henry, Home Secretary 605
Mawl i'r Oen, Titus Lewis 269
Mechanics' Institutes 421
Meddyg Teuluaidd, Y (1820s) 358
Meddyg Teuluaidd, Y (1827) 414
Meddyg Teuluaidd, Y, H. Ll. Williams 408

Meddyg Teuluaidd, Y, W. E. Hughes 407, 429
Meddyg y Fferm – Arweinydd i Drin a Gochel Clefydau mewn Anifeiliaid, James Law 410
medical books 406–9
Medical Guide, The, Richard Reece 406
Meiriadog see Edwards, John (Meiriadog)
Mêl Awen, Pedr Fardd 269
Merioneth 49, 51, 58, 436, 440, 561
Merthyr Telegraph 384, 394, 401
Merthyr Tydfil 4, 42, 84, 89, 508
  Merthyr Rising 466, 534
  newspapers 382, 383
  works' schools 433, 455
Meudwy Môn see Jones, Owen (Meudwy Môn)
Mills, John (Ieuan Glan Alarch) 352
Miners' Next Step, The 578–9
Mochdre 59
'Molawd Clynnog', Eben Fardd 270
monarchy 545–7
Monmouthshire 3, 43, 49, 54, 70, 72, 82–3, 89–90, 95, 444–5, 446, 467, 561
Montgomeryshire 42, 43, 54, 59, 65, 75, 103, 106, 436, 486
Morgan, Augustus 445
Morgan, David Watts 577
Morgan, Edward, Dyffryn Ardudwy 242, 328
Morgan, George Osborne 143, 308, 600, 601–2, 603, 604, 605, 606
Morgan, J. Vyrnwy 483, 494
Morgan, Jennette 328
Morgan, Owen (Morien) 354
Morgan, R. W. 28, 600
Morgan, Richard Humphreys 372
Morien see Morgan, Owen (Morien)
Morris, Lewis 462
Morris, Lewis, of Anglesey 349, 350, 373
Morris, Richard 350
Morris, William (Gwilym Tawe) 306
Morris-Jones, John 265, 277–8, 286, 288–9, 354, 370, 606
Moses, D. L. 415
Municipal Corporations Act (1835) 513
Murray, Alan 112
Murray, George, bishop of St David's 218
'Myfanwy Fychan o Gastell Dinas Bran', Ceiriog 295
'Myfyrdod ar Lan Afon', Eben Fardd 271
Mynyddog see Davies, Richard (Mynyddog)

Nanney, Hugh Ellis, Gwynfryn 119
'Nant y Mynydd', Ceiriog 274
Nanteos 122, 124
National Association for the Vindication of Scottish Rights 599
National Charter Association 514
National Eisteddfod 22, 94, 293–316, 534, 549
  Aberdare (1861) 293, 313
  Aberdare (1885) 315

Aberystwyth (1865) 146
Caernarfon (1886) 293–4
Caernarfon (1894) 315
Cardiff (1899) 304
Chester (1866) 309, 534
Conwy (1861) 332
Llandudno (1864) 314
Llanelli (1903) 294
London (1887) 312, 546
Merthyr Tydfil (1881) 293
Pontypridd (1893) 315
Ruthin (1868) 314
Swansea (1863) 312, 545–6
Swansea (1891) 293
Wrexham (1876) 23, 314
see also eisteddfodau
National Society 433
National Union of Elementary Teachers 500–2
National Union of Women's Suffrage 583
Natural Theology, William Paley 419
Neath 84
'Necessity of Teaching English through the Medium of Welsh', D. J. Davies 474
New Book of Cookery, The; or every Woman a perfect Cook 411
New Testament in Welsh and English, The 235
New View of Society, A, Robert Owen 91
Newcastle commission
  see *Report of the Commissioners on the State of Popular Education* (1861)
Newcastle Emlyn 43
newspapers 21–2, 280, 379–403, 509
Nicholas, T. E. 31, 500, 582
Nicholas, Thomas 9, 22, 313, 432, 433
Nofelydd, a Chydymaith y Teulu, Y 361
Nonconformity 17–18, 89–90, 93–5, 98, 120–1, 195, 239–63, 491–6, 548–51
North Wales Chronicle 591
North Wales Quarrymen's Union 582–3
Northern Star 515

O'Connell, Daniel 562
Oakeley, H. E. 473
Oddfellows, Friendly Society 358
Odlau'r Efengyl, Watcyn Wyn 276
Odydd Cymreig, Yr 358
Offrymau Neillduaeth, Daniel Owen 284
old literary clerics 222, 271, 354
Ollivant, Alfred, bishop of Llandaff 219
'On the advantages of preserving the language and dress of Wales', Lady Llanover 301
'On the Origin of the English Nation . . . ', John Beddoe 308
On the Study of Celtic Literature, Matthew Arnold 8–9, 309, 467–8
Orgraph yr Iaith Gymraeg 332
Oriau'r Bore, Ceiriog 343
Oriau'r Hwyr, Ceiriog 273

Origin of Species, Charles Darwin 423
Oswestry 44
Outer Wales 45, 54, 58–9, 69–70, 74
Owain Alaw see Owen, John
Owain Myfyr see Jones, Owen (Owain Myfyr)
Owen, Bob, Croesor 25
Owen, Daniel 21, 265, 278, 283–5, 289, 290, 319, 328, 345, 361, 397
Owen, David (Brutus) 242, 265, 281–2, 289, 352, 356–7, 375, 392, 547
Owen, David (Dewi Wyn o Eifion) 265, 266, 267
Owen, Goronwy 267, 269
Owen, H. Isambard 10, 474, 495
Owen, Hugh 9, 22, 26, 94, 314, 432, 456, 463, 540
Owen, Hugh, Orielton 119
Owen, Canon Hugh 225
Owen, John (Owain Alaw) 274
Owen, Dr John 242
Owen, John, Principal of St David's College, Lampeter 230
Owen, Owen Eilian 354
Owen, Richard Jones (Glaslyn) 340
Owen, Robert 91–2, 424
Owen, Thomas Ellis, rector of Llandyfrydog 225
Owen, Sir William 590

Parnell, Charles 562
Parry, Abel J. 251
Parry, David, 'Y Gloch Arian' 229
Parry, John (Bardd Alaw) 297
Parry, John, Chester 351
Parry, John Humffreys 353, 354
Parry, Robert (Robyn Ddu Eryri) 358
Parry, Thomas, agricultural lecturer 112
patriotism 533–60
'Patriotism of the Welsh' 543
Pedigree of the English People, Thomas Nicholas 308
Pedr Fardd see Jones, Peter (Pedr Fardd)
Pedrog see Williams, John Owen (Pedrog)
Pembrokeshire 39, 43, 61, 62, 66, 70, 74, 75, 451
Pencader 486
Pencerdd Gwalia see Thomas, John (Pencerdd Gwalia)
Penmachno 440
Penmaen-mawr 72
Penrhyn Quarry strike 15
periodicals 21, 349–78, 509
  denominational 93, 351–3
  for children 93, 352
  literary 353–5
  market 375–7
  philanthropic 358–9
  science 357–8
Perl y Plant 352
Perowne, J. J. S. 22
Peter, John (Ioan Pedr) 420
Pethau Newydd a Hen 352

petitioning 507–9
Petty Sessions 588
Phelp, W. E. 124
Philanthropic Order of True Ivorites 358, 530
Phillips, Sir Thomas 469, 536
Planu Coed a Phregethau Eraill 246
'Plicio Gwallt yr Hanner Cymry', Emrys ap Iwan 369–70
Pluralities Act (1838) 588, 607
poetry 266–78
politics 27–31
   1800–80 505–31
   1880–1914 561–85
   local 513–14
Pontrobert 65
Pontypool Baptists' College 248
Pontypridd 84
Poor Law Amendment Act (1834) 513
Pope, Samuel 610
population
   growth 2–3, 49
   migration 2–3, 15–16, 50–7, 92
Powel, Thomas, 95, 473, 474, 495
Powell, W. E., Nanteos 124
Powell, W. T. R., Nanteos 124
Powis, Earl of 595, 608
'Practical Phrenology', Morgan Philip 409
Prestatyn 72, 75
Price, John, Bleddfa 449
Price, Richard 88
Price, Thomas (Carnhuanawc) 223, 263, 299, 302, 303, 304, 350
Price, Dr William, Llantrisant 516
Primitive Physick, John Wesley 409
printing and publishing 19–20, 93, 317–47
   authors 325–9
   binding 337–8
   output 323–4
   print runs 336–7
   technological changes 329–36
   type 331–2
Profedigaethau Enoc Huws, Daniel Owen 278, 285
prose 278–91
Protestant, Y 415
Pryce, Shadrach, HMI 105, 468, 473, 488–9, 499–500
Pryse, John Hugh, Mathafarn 120
Pryse, Sir Pryse, Gogerddan 120
Pryse, Pryse Loveden 120
Pryse, Rhys 415
Public Health Act (1834) 513
publishing see printing and publishing
Pughe, John, Aberdyfi 407
Pughe, William Owen 223, 231–6, 246, 270, 288–9, 350, 353–4, 426, 598
Puleston, John 604
Punch Cymraeg, Y 24, 137, 360, 371
Pwyllwyddeg ac Mesmeriaeth, A. W. Jarvis 409

Radnorshire 42, 49, 51, 59, 66, 70, 72, 446, 448, 561
railways 4–6, 131–49
   attitude of the companies to the Welsh language 138–9
   influence on tourism 151–2
   poetry 137–8
   stationmasters 147–8
Raine, Jonathan 590
Randolph, John, bishop of Bangor 226
Rathbone, William 606
Ravenstein, E. G. 462
Reasons for declining to become a Subscriber to the British and Foreign Bible Society 233
Reasons for rejecting the Welsh Orthography 235
Rebecca riots 32, 90, 105, 119, 432, 452, 466, 595–6
Red Dragon and the Red Flag, The, Keir Hardie 581, 582
Reed, Principal of Carmarthen College 469
Reed, H. Byron 573
Rees, David, Llanelli 324, 353, 357, 360, 368, 377, 519, 539, 540, 547
Rees, Ebenezer, 31
Rees, Evan (Dyfed) 289
Rees, Evan, rector of Rhiw 226
Rees, Henry 242, 251
Rees, Rice 230
Rees, Sarah Jane (Cranogwen) 205
Rees, Dr Thomas 18, 19, 21, 256, 364, 519, 544, 545
Rees, W. J., Casgob 220, 222, 223, 229, 271
Rees, William (Gwilym Hiraethog) 19, 20, 242, 251
   and agriculture 115
   and courts of justice 600
   and journalism 265
   and literature 282, 361
   and *Y Faner* 419, 424
   and *Yr Amserau* 280, 380, 383, 384, 520
Reform Act (1832) 510–11
Reform Act (1867) 524
religion 17–18, 215–63
Religious Census (1851) 17, 89, 535
Remarks, Historical and Philological, on the Welsh Language 236
Rendel, Stuart 576
Report of the Commissioners on the State of Popular Education 8, 460, 461, 470
Report of the Committee appointed to Inquire into the Condition of Intermediate and Higher Education in Wales 322–3, 462
Report of the Schools Inquiry Commission 460
Report on the Employment of Children, Young Persons and Women in Agriculture 461
Report on the State of Popular Education in the 'Welsh Specimen Districts' 295
'Rhagorfraint y Gweithiwr', Elfed 276

Rheolau i ffurfiaw a threfnu yr Ysgolion Sabbothawl, Thomas Charles 252
Rhifyddiaeth yn rhwyddach, Evan Lewis 414
Rhiwlas 123
Rhodd Mam 253
Rhodd Tad 253
Rhondda 4, 13, 41–2, 92, 95
Rhondda Scheme for Teaching Welsh, The 95
Rhos-y-bol 65
Rhosllannerchrugog 14
Rhyl, newspapers 382
Rhys Lewis, Daniel Owen 285, 327
Rhŷs, John 314, 316, 370, 462, 473, 489, 490, 576, 606
Rhys, John, Penydarren 421
Rhys, Morgan John 88
Richard, Edward, Ystradmeurig 231
Richard, Henry 8, 28, 256, 396–7, 462, 472, 492, 507, 525–6, 527, 528, 544–5, 547–50, 563, 569, 600
Richards, David (Dafydd Ionawr) 290
Richards, David (Dewi Silin) 223
Richards, Judge E. L. 594
Richards, R. J. 567
Richards, Richard, Caerwys 225
Richards, Thomas, Llangynyw 223
Richards, Tom 31
Robert ap Gwilym Ddu see Williams, Robert (Robert ap Gwilym Ddu)
Roberts, Hamilton 528
Roberts, J. Bryn 142, 143
Roberts, J. J. (Iolo Carnarvon) 276, 277
Roberts, John (Ieuan Gwyllt) 352, 538
Roberts, John (Siôn Lleyn) 266
Roberts, John (J. R.) 26, 245, 352, 359, 364, 365
Roberts, John, Tremeirchion 231–2, 235, 350, 354, 372
Roberts, Joseph 344
Roberts, Kate 205
Roberts, O. E. 430
Roberts, R. D. 424
Roberts, R. Silyn 582
Roberts, Robert (Idris o Gybi) 419, 420
Roberts, Samuel, Llanbryn-mair 115, 352, 365, 424, 519, 520
Roberts, T. Francis 112, 474
Roberts, T. R. (Asaph) 614
Roberts, Thomas, Llwyn'rhudol 589
Roberts, W. J. (Gwilym Cowlyd) 341, 343
Robinson, Revd Prebendary H. G. 462
Robyn Ddu Eryri see Parry, Robert (Robyn Ddu Eryri)
Rolant, Dafydd 242
Rolls, John 572
Rowland, Daniel 350
Rowland, David (Dewi Brefi) 222, 223
Rowlands, David (Dewi Môn) 248
Rowlands, R. D. (Anthropos) 20

Royal Commission on Education (1886–7) 10
Ruba'iyat (Omar Khayyám), trans. John Morris-Jones 278

Saint Hilary 61
Salisbury, E. R. G. 294
'Salm i Famon', John Morris-Jones 278, 316
Sartoris, E. J. 561
Saunderson, Robert 318
schools
 British schools 437, 440, 448, 467, 485
 church schools 231
 intermediate schools 484, 501
 national schools 437, 439–40, 448, 485
 private schools 433, 448
 Sunday schools 18, 87, 251–4, 261, 434, 442, 448–9, 453–4, 492–3
 works' schools 433, 455
science 405–30
 agriculture 410–11
 cookery books 411–12
 eisteddfod 420–1
 gardening 411
 herbal books 409–10
 lectures 420
 mathematics 413–14
 medicine 406–8
 periodicals 414–17
 phrenology 408–9
 vocabulary 424–30
Scoltock, Revd W. 468
Scotch Cattle 444
Scotland 58, 59
Seren Cymru 93, 385, 390–4, 399–401, 583
Seren Gomer 114, 351, 354, 357, 362, 376, 380, 389, 390, 414, 420, 427, 507, 510, 516, 592, 596
Shadrach, Azariah 279
Shepherds, Friendly Society 358
Short, Thomas Vowler, bishop of St David's 218
Siôn Gymro see Davies, John (Siôn Gymro)
Siôn Lleyn see Roberts, John (Siôn Lleyn)
Slebech 122
Smith, Herbert 488
Smith, Samuel, MP 611
Smith, W. H., First Lord of the Treasury 610
Social Democratic Federation 580, 581
Society for Utilizing the Welsh Language 25, 315, 474, 475, 495–6, 559–60, 612
Solffaydd, Y 352
South Wales and Monmouthshire Training College 469
South Wales Daily News 22
South Wales Miners' Federation 31, 577–9
South Wales Worker 581, 582
Southall, J. E. 13, 21, 27, 34, 321, 495, 500
Spectator 312
Spurrell, William 321, 375

Stanley, H. M. 332
Stapledon, R. G. 130
Statute Revision Act (1887) 610
Stephens, Thomas 362, 375
'Storm, Y', Islwyn 275
Straeon y Pentan, Daniel Owen 285
Summary Jurisdiction Act (1879) 607
Sumner, Charles Richard, bishop of Llandaff 218
Swansea 4, 318
    College 433
Sweet, Henry 11
Symons, J. C. 294, 295, 434, 444–51

Tadau Methodistaidd, Y 290
Tagore, Dwarkanauth 302
Tagore, Rabindranath 302
'Tal ar Ben Bodran', Talhaiarn 275
Tal-y-llyn 65
Talhaiarn see Jones, John (Talhaiarn)
Taliesin 93
Taliesin Tradition: A Quest for the Welsh Identity, The, Emyr Humphreys 84–5
Tanner, Henry 111
Tarian y Gweithiwr 22, 565, 567, 574, 577–8
Taunton Report see *Report of the Schools Inquiry Commission*
Tegai see Hughes, Hugh (Tegai)
Tegid see Jones, John (Tegid)
Telyn Tudno 276
Telynegion, Daniel Silvan Evans 271
temperance 93, 204–5
Temple, Christopher 591
Ten Nights in a Bar Room and What I Saw There, Timothy Shay Arthur 280, 361
tenants 101, 125–30
Tenby 66
Test and Corporation Acts 507–8, 539
Testament yr Ysgol Sabbothol 290
Thirlwall, Connop, bishop of St David's 218, 219–20, 236, 302
Thomas, Abel 143
Thomas, Alfred 479, 611
Thomas, D. A. 604
Thomas, Daniel Lleufer 32, 606, 614
Thomas, David (Dafydd Ddu Eryri) 268
Thomas, Ebenezer (Eben Fardd) 201, 267, 270–1
Thomas, Jenkin (1746–1807) 281
Thomas, Jenkyn, unionist 529
Thomas, John (Eifionydd) 31, 370
Thomas, John (Pencerdd Gwalia) 274
Thomas, John William (Arfonwyson) 413, 414, 427
Thomas, Owen, Liverpool 19, 155, 240, 241, 242, 259
Thomas, Thomas Emlyn 596
Thomas, William (Glanffrwd) 14, 312
Thomas, William (Islwyn) 275
Times, The 32, 312, 402, 596, 602, 612

Tithe Defence League 577
Tithe Wars 559, 576
Tlysau yr Hen Oesoedd 349–50, 373
tourism 151–75
trade unionism 528–9, 577
Traethawd ar Iawn-lythreniad neu Lythyraeth yr Iaith Gymraeg, John Jones 236
Traethiadur Gwyddorawl, Y, Taliesin T. Jones 428
Traethodau Llenyddol, Lewis Edwards 337
Traethodydd, Y 114, 294, 353, 359, 363, 376, 518, 579
Trawsgoed 123
Trefdraeth (Anglesey) 24, 216
Trefeca College 249
Tregaron 105
Tregynon 44
Treherbert 14
Trelawnyd 41
Trem ar y Ganrif, sef Arolwg ar y Bedwaredd Ganrif ar Bymtheg, J. Morgan Jones 289–90
Tremenheere, H. S. 461, 466
Trevethin 61
'Tri Brawd a'u Teuluoedd, Y', Roger Edwards 283, 360, 397
Troed-yr-aur 62
Trudeau, Pierre 96
Trysorfa Efangylaidd 352
Trysorfa Grefyddol Gwent a Morgannwg 352
Trysorfa y Plant 93, 352, 376
Trysorfa Ysprydol, Thomas Charles 232, 351
Tudno see Jones, Thomas Tudno (Tudno)
Tufnell, E. C. 461
Turner, Sir Llywelyn 12
Twm o'r Nant see Edwards, Thomas (Twm o'r Nant)
Tyst, Y 493
Tyst a'r Dydd, Y 134
Tyst Apostolaidd, Y 376
Tywysog Cymru 413
Tywysydd, Y 352
Tywysydd yr Ieuainc 376

Udgorn Cymru 512, 515, 516, 537
Unitarians 352, 508, 516
Uzmaston 66

van Mildert, William, bishop of Llandaff 510
Vestiges of the Natural History of the Creation, Robert Chambers 423
Vindication of the British and Foreign Bible Society, An, William Dealtry 234
Vivian, Sir Hussey 313, 605

Waddington, Augusta (Lady Llanover) 33, 301, 311, 534, 593
Waddington, Frances 302
Wales and its Prospects, Henry Jones 565

INDEX

Wallace, Alfred Russel 422
Warren, John, dean of Bangor 225
Watcyn Wyn see Williams, Watkin Hezekiah (Watcyn Wyn)
Watkins, T. E. (Eiddil Ifor) 18
Watson, Richard, bishop of Llandaff 218
Watts, E. T. 501
Watts, Thomas, Keeper of the Department of Printed Books at the British Museum 377
Wawr: Sef Cylchgrawn Llenyddol a Chelfyddydol, Y 358, 363, 365, 375, 376, 417
Wawr-ddydd, Y 376
Webster, Richard, attorney-general 610
Welsh Books Centre 340
Welsh Botanology 422
Welsh Church and Welsh Nationality, The, David Jones 236–7
Welsh Courts Act 611, 613
Welsh Defence Association 599
Welsh in Education and Life 45
Welsh Intermediate and Technical Act (1889) 477
Welsh Land Commission 13, 112, 115, 122
Welsh Language Act (1967) 33
Welsh Magistracy, The, T. J. Hughes (Adfyfr) 609
Welsh MSS Society 303
Welsh Not 24, 25, 434, 438–9, 470, 472, 485–7
Welsh Review 605
Welsh Sunday Closing Act (1881) 93, 606
Welshman 597
Wenynen, Y 415, 419
Werin, Y 576
Werin a'i Theyrnas, Y, David Thomas 31, 581
Wesleyan Methodists 90, 254–5, 351
Western Mail 22, 554, 568
What is a Welshman? R. S. Thomas 97
'What the Government is doing for the Teaching of Irish', Thomas Powel 474
Wil Brydydd y Coed, Brutus 282, 397
Williams, A. J., MP 606, 610
Williams, David, Professor of Welsh, St David's College, Lampeter 230
Williams, David, Romsey 224
Williams, Eliezer, vicar of Lampeter 222, 231
Williams, Judge Gwilym 603, 612
Williams, J. Valant 409
Williams, James, Ystalyfera 529
Williams, Jane (Ysgafell) 303, 536
Williams, John, Archdeacon 230
Williams, John (Ab Ithel) 305, 350
Williams, John (Corvinius) 415, 427
Williams, John, 'Yr Hen Syr' 231
Williams, John, Newcastle Emlyn 250
Williams, John, Treffos (d. 1826) 225
Williams, John, Treffos 313, 608
Williams, John Carvell 519
Williams, John Owen (Pedrog) 276

Williams, Maria Jane 302, 311
Williams, Morgan 516
Williams, Nathan 570
Williams, Osmond 563
Williams, R. Vaughan 603
Williams, Robert (Robert ap Gwilym Ddu) 266, 267–8
Williams, Rowland, Ysgeifiog 223, 224, 354, 415
Williams, T. Marchant 10, 474, 495
Williams, Thomas, Merthyr Tydfil 256
Williams, W. Llewelyn 315, 479, 563–4, 605
Williams, Watkin, MP 600, 602
Williams, Watkin Hezekiah (Watcyn Wyn) 276, 324, 485
Williams, William (Caledfryn) 243–4, 298, 353, 517, 519
Williams, William ('Carw Coch') 537
Williams, William (Creuddynfab) 147, 408
Williams, William, HMI 474, 476, 490
Williams, William, MP, Coventry 91, 432, 466, 596–7
Williams, William, of Wern 251
Wilmot, Sir Eardley 603
Wilson, James, agricultural lecturer 112
Winllan, Y 352
women 16–17, 177–213
 and their neighbours 189–91
 calling day 210–11
 Clwb Te 207
 fairs and markets 188–9
 gossip 192–5, 212
 hearth 197–8, 209
 in public places 187–8
 in the workplace 189
 protest 203–4
 relationship with their children 185–6
 relationship with their husbands 184–5
 votes for 583
Women's Unionist and Tariff Reform Association 568
'Wooden Report' 480
Wrexham 42, 72, 318, 330
Wynn, Charles 594, 603
Wynn, Sir Watkin Williams 119, 528, 594, 603
Wynne, Ellis 370
Wynne, W. R. M., Peniarth 119
Wynne-Finch, Colonel, Voelas 123

Ymddiddan ar fwngloddfeydd, William Hopton 414
Ymofynydd, Yr 352, 376, 415
Youatt, William 113
Young Wales 614
Ysgafell see Williams, Jane (Ysgafell)
Ystorfa Weinidogaethol, Yr 352
Ystradmeurig, school 231, 463
Ystradyfodwg 92